HARLEY-DAVIDSON®

This book is a revised edition of the 1998 two volume book
"Ride Free Forever. The Legend of Harley-Davidson"
and is licensed by Harley-Davidson Motor Company.
All property rights of H-D are identified within the book.

© 2000 Könemann Verlagsgesellschaft mbH
Bonner Straße 126, D-50968 Cologne

Creative and Art Director: Peter Feierabend
Managing Editor: Kirsten E. Lehmann
Assistant: Britta Harting
Layout: Christian Maiwurm, Ralf Podratzky, Christina Berghoff,
Nik Kesten, Gerald Behrendt,
Photo Credits: Ursula Kollenbach
Picture Research: Dieter Rebmann, Oluf F. Zierl and Monika Bergmann
Production: Mark Voges
Reproduction: Omniascanners, Milan, (Litho)

© 2000 Könemann Verlagsgesellschaft mbH
Bonner Straße 126, D-50968 Cologne
For the English Edition:
Translation from German: Gavin Falconer, Stephen Hunter, Andrew Rylands,
Umsankar Sankarayya, Dereck Stockdale
English Language Editor: Philip De Ste. Croix (facts and style)
and Chris Murray (style)
Proofreaders: Timothy J. Gluckman and Luke Roskilly
Managing Editor: Bettina Kaufmann
Assistants: Lilian Bernhardt and Claudia Schmidt-Packmohr
DTP: Peter Hynes
Reproduction: Divis GmbH, Cologne, (Text)
Printing and Binding: Imprimerie Jean Lamour, Maxéville

Printed in France
ISBN 3-89508-297-X

10 9 8 7 6 5 4 3 2 1

Oluf F. Zierl

HARLEY-DAVIDSON®

The Legend

Photographer:
Dieter Rebmann

Creative and Art Directors:
Peter Feierabend, Christian Maiwurm

KÖNEMANN

9 Foreword

10 Introduction

12 History

14 The Workshop of the U.S.

16 The Wild Days of the Pioneers

18 The Unbelievable Challenge

20 De Dion–Bouton

21 Expansion

22 The Company

25 1005 Points

26 The Birth of an Immortal

28 Technology Goes Trendy

30 Racing and the Sidecar

31 The Debut of Exporting

32 Harley's Early Racing Successes

34 Baptism of Fire

36 The Superiority of the American Motorcycle Industry

37 The Failed Mission

38 The Largest Motorcycle Factory in the World

40 The Sport Twin

41 A Winner on All Fronts

42 The Harleyquins

43 The Exports

43 The Harley During Prohibition

44 Business as Usual

46 The Alternative to the Single–Cylinder Prince

48 The Dawn of the Big Twins

50 The Typical Family Response

51 The Stressful 1930s

52 Always on Call: the Servi–Car

53 American Arch Enemies

54 Knucklehead: A Feast for the Eyes

56 The Far East Adventure

57 Club Events

57 The Patriachs Retire

58 Harley Goes to War

62 The Speedy Brits Arrive

64 The Company Plays Host

65 The Outlaw Syndrome

66 The Dinosaurs Rear Their Heads

69 Revenge of the Intimidated

70 The Japanese Invasion

72 The Restless 1960s

74 An Unequal Union

76 Public Confidence Confused

77 The New Strategies

78 The End of the Minibike

80 Radical Cure

81 The New Masters

83 The Turnaround Year

86 The New Year's Eve Cliffhanger

87 The Road to the Stock Exchange

88 A Satisfying Balance Sheet

90 The Four Unions

90 Harley–Davidson Credit

91 The Davidson Dynasty

94 The Million Dollar Deal

97 The Production Plants

100 The Impressive Production Process I

103 The Imposing Production Process II

104 Good Vibrations

106 The Development Center

108 The Smooth Seduction

109 Well-Ordered Chaos

112 Talladega Test Facility

113 Powerful Production

114 Service Schools

115 The Abundent Archive

116 The Abundant Archive II

118 Harley–Davidson and a New Era

120 The New Generation

121 The Future

122 Models

124 The Mysterious Number One

126 Production Starts on the First Models

127 The Single–Cylinder in 1906 and 1907

128 The Single–Cylinder in 1908 and 1909

130 The Single–Cylinder from 1910 to 1913

132 You Never Forget Your First Love

133 The Single–Cylinder from 1913 to 1918

134 The Legendary Harley V–Twin

135 The V–Twin Operating Cycle

136 The Birth of a Legend - 1909: The First V–Twin - Model 5D

138 1911: The Second V–Twin – Model 7D

140 The Twin–Cylinder from 1912 to 1921

142 Superbikes of a Bygone Age: Harley's OHV Eight-Valve Machines

144 An Unsuccessful Outsider: the Sport Twin

146 The 61 cubic inch Big Twin Models from 1921 to 1929

148 The Model J Two Cam from 1928 to 1929

150 Single–Cylinder Motorcycles from 1926 to 1935

152 The 30 cubic inch Side–Valve Single–Cylinder Model C from 1929 to 1934

154 1929: the Dawn of the Forty–Five – the Model D

155 1932: the Second Edition of the Forty–Five

156 The 74 cubic inch, Side -Valve Big Twin

158 The 80 cubic inch Big Twin VLH and UH/ULH from 1935 to 1941

160 From 1937 to 1951: the Third Forty–Five – the W Series

162 The War Machine

164 The Military Model WLA/WLC from 1939 to 1946

166 A Military Type – the Model XA

168 The Forecar

170 The Servi–Car

172 The Great Breakthrough – the Knucklehead Engine

174 The Knucklehead E/EL from 1936 to 1947

176 The Knucklehead F/FL from 1941 to 1947

178 125 Model HS, ST 165 Super Ten, Hummer

180 The Panhead Engine – a Year of Change

182 Postwar Premiere: the Panhead

184 Increasing Comfort I – the Hydra Glide

186 Increasing Comfort II – the Duo Glide

188 The Electric Starter

190 The New Model K

192 The KR and KRTT

194 Pacer, Scat, Ranger, Bobcat

195 The 250 and 350 Sprint

196 Minibikes and Small Motorcycles

198 MSR 100, ML 125, 125 SS, 250 SX, Baja, Rapido and Others

200 Not So Trendy: the Topper Scooter

202 Harley's New Premium Engine – the Shovelhead

204 The FL and FLH Electra Glide

206 FLT Shovelhead Tour Glide

208 The FX Super Glide
210 The Smash Hit
211 The Fat Bob
212 Shadow of the Night
214 The Wild Boy's Bike
216 The Comfort Cruiser
217 Experiment in Free Form
218 New Kid on the Block
220 The XLH
222 The XLCH
224 The Model XR 750
226 The XLCR Cafe Racer
228 The Model XLX 61 Standard
229 The XLT/XLS
230 The XR 1000
232 Evolution
232 Development of the Evo Engines
233 Fuel Injection
234 Electras, Classics and Ultras
236 The FLTC and FLTCU
237 FLTR – a New Elegance
238 Niche Fillers: the Electra
240 Customized Bikes: Bowing to the Inevitable

241 Centerfold

In Minute Detail: the Microcosm of a Legend

242 Bewildering Variety – the Low Rider Series 1982-1983
244 The Low Rider Series: FXRT
245 The Low Rider Series: FXLR and FXRS–SP
246 The Low Rider Series: FXR
247 The Low Rider Series: FXRS and FXRS–CON
248 The Myth Lives On
249 The Springer Fork
250 The FX Softail
252 The FL Softail
253 The Heritage Softail Series: FLST, FLSTC
254 The Heritage Softail Series: FLSTS, FLSTN
255 The Heritage Softail Series: FLSTF
256 Modern Engineering and a New Dynamism
257 The Dyna Glide Series: FXDB, FXDWG, FXD, FXDS and FXDL

258 The Evo Sportster
260 The Sportster Series: XLH 883 Standard, XLH 883 Deluxe, and Hugger
262 The Sportster Series: XLH 1100 and 1200, XL 1200 Custom and Sport
264 Harley's New Superbike: the VR 1000
266 The Buell Series: the 1998 Models
268 A Magnificent Array – the 1998 and 1999 Ranges
270 1998 Motorcycle Colors
271 Cracking the Code

272 Special Editions

274 Special Editions
276 The Lost Generation
277 The Unfortunate Nova Era
278 The Third Wheel - the First Sidecars
280 The Goulding Story
282 Three's Company
284 Japan's Harley: Rikuo, the King of the Road
284 Spin–Offs
286 In the Service of Law and Order
289 Extras for Police Motorcycles
290 CHP and LAPD
291 The Fire Brigade and the Red Cross

292 Dealers

294 Oppressive Contracts
296 A Belated Appreciation
300 The Denver Affair
300 The Scherer–Budelier Episode
301 The Risden–Van Order Affair
302 Compulsory Get-Togethers
303 The Dealers' Rebellion
304 U.S.A.: Dealerships in the 70s
306 The Veteran of San Francisco
307 Once a Year – the Love Ride
308 A Creative Genius in Oakland, California
309 Dealer to the Stars
310 The Guardian Angel of Daytona
311 America's Oldest Harley Dealership in Ohio
311 The Man from Texas
312 U.S.A.: Dealerships Today

314 Dealers' T–Shirts
316 A Taste for the Non–Functional
317 An Old Man and the Company
318 Dealers' World I
320 Dealers' World II
322 The German Harley Legend

324 Races

326 The Meaning of Racing
328 Board Track Racing
330 The Wrecking Crew
332 The FAM, MATA and AMA
333 The AMA and Its Rules
334 Every Man's Racing Model
336 Hill Climb
338 Perpendicular Racers - Hill-Climbers
340 Speedway - Just Drifting Around
342 The Peashooter
343 A Period of Change
344 The W Series Side–Valve Racers
345 Harley–Davidson Race Models
346 Who, What, When?
348 Flat Track
350 It's Not Whether You Win or Lose ...
351 Racing Machines from Varese
352 Road Racing
355 America versus England and Japan
356 Battle of the Twins
358 The German Harley Cup
358 Entertainment and Professional Sports
359 The Sundance Team

362 Company

364 The Company Requests the Honor
367 Night of the Snappy Dressers
368 MDA: Let the World Know About It
368 Jerry's Kids
370 Everybody Is Welcome
371 Crowned Heads
372 Happy Birhtday To You
373 Welcome Home!
374 Harley Ages Gracefully

375 Facts About Faaker
376 A Family Chronicle
378 Helps You Know What's What
380 Ya Wanna Buy a Watch?
382 H.O.G. – One Big Happy Family
383 Fun and Games with New Friends
384 Being a H.O.G. Member
384 H.O.G. Germany
386 Women on the Road – The Famous "Ladies of Harley"

388 People

390 How to Spot a Harley Rider
394 Types of Harley–Davidson Riders
396 Belt Buckles
398 A German Specialty
399 A Sense of Having Arrived
400 The Diversity of Harley Riders
402 Confessions of an Incorrigible Man
404 The Sex Machine
406 Show–Offs
406 Obscenity as a Means of Rebellion Against a
     Prudish Society
407 A Different Way of Selling Ice Cream
408 The Biker
410 Turtle's Chopper
411 The Moment that Never Ended
412 True Bikers
414 Women in the Saddle
418 Real Women Ride Harleys
418 News from the U.S.A.
419 Babs and Her Panhead
420 The Motor Maids
422 Woman Racers
424 Harley Toys
426 Family Ties
428 Rug Rats on Harleys
429 Kid's Party
430 Animals
431 Harley VIP's I
432 Harley VIP's II

434 Clubs

436 A Sworn–In Community
438 An Organized Community
440 The Shadow of the Past
441 What Really Happened in 1947 in Hollister?
443 The Famous *Life* Report Dated July 21, 1947
444 The Rise of a New Biker Culture
445 In the Name of the Company
446 The Baptism
448 A Very Special Veterans' Association
449 Jesus is Lord
450 The Hell's Angels
452 The Origin of the Outlaw Motorcycle Clubs (C.P.)
454 Secret Signs
456 Lifetime Bikers
458 The Biker Scene in Germany – Harleys on the Other Side
     of the Ocean
458 German Biker Clubs and MCs
459 Typical Biker Clubs in Europe
460 Brothers in Mind
462 Harley Clubs Worldwide
464 Biker Weddings
465 Funerals – The Last Ride
466 ABATE – Dedicated to Freedom of the Road
467 ABATE Statement – Does History Repeat Itself?
468 The Unpopular Helmet

470 Events

472 Daytona Bike Week
477 On the Beach
479 Main Street
480 Welcome Bikers!
484 A Summer Storm in the Black Hills
484 Circus Maximus
485 Party 'Till You Drop
487 Sturgis Bike Week Facts and Figures
488 Rolling Thunder
492 Racing, Rumbles and Riotous Living
494 An Old-Style Festival
496 A Hot Party in the Deep South for Harley Riders
498 Traditional European Meetings
500 Free Wheels Party

501 Route 66
502 Ibiza Bike Week
502 German Bike Week
503 10th Annual Biker Union Rally
504 Will the Party Ever End?
506 Doing it for the Kids
507 Uniformed Benefactors
507 The Ancient Arabic Order
508 You Can't Beat a Good Party!
510 The Most Memorable Kind of Get–Togethers
512 The Biker's Favorite Food
514 Today's Gladiators
520 Sightseeing I
522 Sightseeing II

524 Customs

527 The Spoils of Madness (H.R.)
527 Harley Trailers for the Grand Tour
530 Choppers (H.R.)
533 Peter Meets His Great Love (O.Z.)
534 Full Dressers (H.R.)
536 The Custom Harley
537 (H.R. Taildraggers (H.R.)
538 Streamliner/Lead Sled and Harley Trikes
538 Classic Style/Indian Style
539 The Bike as a Work of Art (H.R.)
540 Red Dragon versus Yellow Beast
541 High Performance
544 Rat Bikes
545 Under It All, It's Just a Rat (O.Z.)
546 Designs I (H.R.)
552 Designs II
556 The Harley Aftermarket (H.R.)
559 Harley – Real or Imitation
560 The Big Cheese at the Rat's Hole
564 Show 'Em What You Can Do!
565 Whatever You Do, Don't Miss Kent!
568 Bike Shows in the U.S.
569 The Poetone, Chicago Bike Show in July 1996
570 It's a Small World After All
572 The Impossible Is Always Possible
576 Motorcycle Nostalgia

579 A Kind of Heaven

582 Swappin' Time

584 Sports

586 Hell On Wheels

588 The Need for Speed

588 Categories of Racing Organizations

590 Classes and Procedures

591 Ground Rules

592 Building Powerhouses

594 All About Dragsters

596 European Dragsters

598 European Dragster Racing

600 Heroes of the Scene

602 Dragster Racing for All Comers

604 Digging Away in the Sand

606 Vintage Races

607 To the Limits of the Imagination

608 Climbing the Walls

609 The World's Greatest Motorcycle Daredevil

610 Circus Acts on Two Wheels

612 Taking It to the Limit

615 An Italian on a Stallion

616 Have Harley, Will Travel

618 Touring in Europe

620 Goin' on a Roadtrip

622 On the Road Again

623 Dave Barr

624 Tags

626 Art & Culture

628 Tattoos

630 A Theme in Art

632 Biker Cartoons

634 Small Sculptures

635 Homespun Art

636 Art on a Bike

640 Harleys for the Kids

641 Dwarfs and Giants

642 Image Exploitation

643 Demolishing the Competition

644 A Ride Through Time

646 The Power of the Press

646 Harley Books

647 Easyriding from the Beginning

648 Imitating Life

650 Women in Biker Films

651 Videos and Books

652 A Live Concert in the Black Hills

653 German Oldies

654 Biker Music

655 Harley and Music (C.P.)

656 http://www.harley–davidson…

659 Appendix

660 Harley-Davidson Production Figures from 1903 to 1998

660 Models and Their Technical Data from 1903 to 1997

670 Associations and Clubs

670 Motorcycle Museums

671 Films featuring Harley-Davidsons

672 Abbreviations

672 Index

681 Photo Credits

682 Acknowledgements

Several texts within this volume have been contributed by the following authors: Chris Pfouts (C.P.); Horst Rösler (H.R.); OlufF. Zierl (Essays/O.Z.); These contributed texts are indicated in the table of contents.

Sportster 883

(1998)

The Harley-Davidson Rider's Garage

If you have entered the sacred territory of a Harley owner's garage, you have entered a space that can with respect be compared to a place of worship. The walls are decorated with Harley-Davidson posters, photographs of rides taken with pals and of new friends made at rallies, motorcycle parts (favorites with those pleasing shapes from past bikes) and countless, detailed images of the Harley-Davidson motorcycle on its kickstand, now in the middle of the room ready to ride. There will be an army surplus ammo box filled with cleaning and polishing agents and an orange crate from the 1960s crammed with lubricants and fluids. One's wife or husband or children are not allowed to mess around even with these and certainly not permitted to touch the bike at rest. Just about everything in this garage is hand-chosen. There's a table over there in the corner with motorcycle manuals, magazines and only the best books. This book belongs on that table. Oluf Zierl and Dieter Rebmann have created a work that captures the spirit of owning, riding and admiring Harley-Davidson motorcycles. I am proud to have this book in my garage. I enjoy the ritual of reading it and looking through it while my Harley-Davidson Softail Springer engine, cooling down after the day's ride, clicks and snaps pleasantly as if to punctuate my contemplative and respectful time with the book. This book should be on every Harley enthusiast's garage table. And it should be the one item in the garage that visitors are permitted to touch; in fact, it should be offered to all those who are fortunate enough to enter, for it presents an authentic and passionate rendering of Harley-Davidson history and culture.

Dr. Martin Jack Rosenblum

Historian of the Harley-Davidson Motor Company

Listed below are all of the Harley-Davidson trademarks at present and their proper markings:

	Harley Owners Group ®	Roadster ®	Wide Glide ®
	Harley-Davidson ®	Screamin' Eagle ®	Willie G. ®
	HD ®	Soft Glide ®	
	Heritage Softail ®	Softail ®	
	Heritage Springer ®	Sport Glide ®	
	H.O.G. ®	Sportster ®	
Biker Blues ®	Hog Tales ®	Springster ®	
Disc Glide ®	Hugger ®	Super Glide ®	
Dyna Glide ®	Ladies of Harley ®	The Enthusiast ®	
Eagle Iron ®	Low Riders ®	The Legend Rolls On ®	
Electra Glide ®	Motorclothes ®	Tour Glide ®	
Evolution ®	Night Train ™	Tour Park ®	
Fat Boy ®	Pre-Luxe ®	Twin Cam 88 ™	
H-D ®	Road Glide ®	Ultra Classic ®	
Harley ®	Road King ®	V^2 ®	

About this book

Perhaps it would be more apt to call this work an encyclopedia rather than merely a book. The world of Harley-Davidson is, after all, an extremely complex one. The company's history and its motorcycles are one aspect of this world – the people who built them and the people who ride them another. But there's more to Harley-Davidson than that. What about the businessmen? The dealers? The speed freaks and the custom enthusiasts? And then there are the shows and events and everything in between. The people who live for, with and indeed because of their Harleys. Young and old, rich and poor, famous and unknown the world over, with their parties, favorite bars and the countless other little things they share in common in addition to their passion for Harley-Davidson.

This second edition has changed in the sense of being an official licensed publication. With the coopreation of the Harley Davidson Motor Company there have been some changes and corrections to the text which the Company considered necessary. These corrections have been included according to the Company's editorial stipulations, without the involvement of the author.

Like no other motorcycle manufacturer in the world, Harley-Davidson can look back on a vivid history full of contradictions, some of them quite extreme. A history that catalogs the economic and human rules of behavior of the Milwaukee-based company through all its ups and downs. Were the considerations that determined the fascinating path of this company purely of a commercial nature, or more involved in the human aspects? The company's business policies have sometimes been very controversial, however, but Harley-Davidson has also shown quite a deal of personal affection in its concern and care for employees and dealers alike, demonstrating a quality that was virtually unique in the industrial world of the early 20th century.

An accurate account of the history of Harley-Davidson also has to cover the relationship between the Company and the AMA. Some people would say the Company exerted undue pressure on the AMA and its functionaries. In any event the company prospered. And of course, fortune and misfortune in equal parts also shaped the company's development, sometimes helping to keep its head above water, while sometimes plunging it into the depths of economic ruin and near-bankruptcy.

A Harley is far more than a motorcycle in the usual sense. While other motorcycles are regarded as little more than a means of transportation or a contraption used for sports and leisure, or even an embodiment of technological refinement, a Harley is a deeply emotional phenomenon. Born as a legend, it already reached the status of social symbol in its infancy. Nevertheless, it wasn't until after World War II that Harley ultimately became what it is today: a "Way of Life."

As of 1998, the year it celebrated its 95th anniversary, the company has produced some three million motorcycles since its was founded. Not really a spectacular number in comparison with production figures of other motorcycle companies, but they do not produce Harleys.

Some people might argue that the age of the internal combustion engine is drawing to an end. If this is a fact, there can be equally no doubt as to how wonderful, passionate and exciting that brief age has been. Many of the old (technical) traditions are being replaced by new technologies and a new awareness of our environment. Even from a technical and modern point of view, some would argue that Harley's original large volume V-Twin cannot survive. But the Harley still drives on, no matter its age and its technology.

The door to the industrial age which had flung open so wide at the beginning of this century is slowly but surely closing. Only a small gap now remains for the incorrigible nostalgics, dreamers and adherents of the past. Harley enthusiasts, and particularly the "genuine bikers," attempt to resist this encroaching threat to their world with all the powers at their disposal. But fifty or a hundred years from now (what are a few years more or less?), the legend in its current form may be a thing of the past.

Nowadays, Harley-Davidson has a different management, cultivates a different image and has modified its goals. In order to keep the myth alive as long as possible, Harley-Davidson has no choice but to diversify. After all, the very survival of Harley depends on the survival of the legend.

Where is Harley headed?

There was a time when technology determined the model policy of Harley-Davidson. Nowadays, it's chiefly the model policy that determines the technology. To date, the company has sold almost three million motorcycles the world over – motorcycles that, unlike much of the competition, don't simply end up on the junkyard after a few years. While this book attempts to shed light on many questions concerning the history of the company, the question of Harley's future is perhaps even more interesting. Will the tide of nostalgia continue to break on the shores of worldwide Harley fandom? Will new models bear the myth not only into the next century, but also into the ones that follow? Will the "Big Twin" – the original manifestation of this legend – survive, and if so, in what form?

Who are these people who are faithful to this marque, no matter what? Who not only stick to the bike but also identify themselves with the image and the philosophy a Harley stands for? A biker who chooses a legendary Harley as a companion is not just any old biker, but stands for an idea, a way of life. No other motorcycle offers its owner such a feeling of independence, liberty, superiority and machismo as the monstrous Milwaukee machines. Whoever denies these facts, has not understood what a Harley is all about. Harley-Davidson customers are diverse and numerous. They include the longtime Harley rider to the weekend enthusiast. The faces of Harley-Davidson riders look very different. The fans are young and old, male and female, and people of color. No matter the profession or the social status, the spirit of Harley unites them all. They are all united by a common spirit that is characterized by freedom and individuality but which defies a single interpretation. They cannot be lumped into a target market or focus group. This edition concentrates on these issues and tries to offer insight into the human-motorcycle mixture, which is characteristic of the scene. This edition also focuses not only on the commonalities but also on the differences among Harley fans. Whether this book has the answer to the question of what is so facinating and special about Harley, well, the reader can decide.

This book could be called an attempt, albeit a futile one, to render correlations and relationships universally apparent. But how can a truly comprehensive account of a subject of such monstrous diversity and volatility as Harley-Davidson be compressed into this volume? How many Harleys are there? Millions, yet we can only show the reader a few hundred. How many bikers are there? Again, millions. And again, we can only introduce the reader to a few hundred of them. How many clubs, dealers and extravagant custom Harleys are there? Everything we show within this book is merely an excerpt from the world of Harley-Davidson. However, this excerpt is extensive and stimulating enough to provide some insight as to the overall extent of the legend known as Harley- Davidson. Any claim to completeness would be pretentious, but such a claim was never planned. If it had been, then this book would already have drowned long ago in a sea of thousands of archived documents and photographs.

The words "myth" and "legend" occur repeatedly throughout this work, but that's alright. Granted, they have become established buzzwords frequently and readily used to denote just about anything involving the nebulous world of human emotions. But Harley-Davidson is something other. Everything to do with Harley really is of mythical or legendary proportions in one way or another, be it the motorcycles, the engines or the typical Harley sound. The only thing that matters is that it bears the name "Harley-Davidson." The Harley legend is venerated, nurtured, sometimes laughed at and, of course, sold without inhibition, not to mention marketed to the extreme.

Is this an emotional book? Of course! How can anyone ride or even look at a Harley without experiencing strong emotions? The myth and the legend have played a major role in shaping Harley-Davidson over the years, and will be of intrinsic value in the years to come.

And now reader, we hope you enjoy your "ride."

Oluf F. Zierl
Dieter Rebmann

History

The Workshop of the U.S.

A Breathtaking Leap in 150 Years

A land of breathtaking beauty, the State of Wisconsin with its famous town Milwaukee is situated in the north of America, nestled between Minnesota and Iowa to the west and Lake Michigan to the east. The name Wisconsin has its origins in the Amerindian tongue and means "the place at which the waters gather," which is an appropriate reference to the state's well-stocked fishing lakes. Wisconsin used to be home to numerous Native American tribes, such as the Winnebago, Ottawa, Potawatomi and Menominee. But then the white man arrived, shattering the idyllic calm overnight with far-reaching consequences. The United States eventually took the vast territory and its huge lakes into its political and economic guardianship. These events took place over a relatively short period lasting just 250 years...

So read the usual historical descriptions of the pioneering age of America – not necessarily worded exactly the same way, but more often than not sounding just as lackluster. In fact, the period was marked by countless breathtaking events, especially in the course of the last 150 years, and one story in particular is to be recounted here. But let us start at the beginning...

The west bank of Lake Michigan was initially home to three small settlements, established sometime around 1835 and named after their founders: Juneautown, Kilbourntown and Walkers Point on the banks of the Milwaukee and Menominee rivers. Bitter rivalry between these settlements was the order of the day until 1846, when all three towns and their 20,000 or so inhabitants were merged – not entirely of their own free will – to form the "City of Milwaukee." The first mayor of Milwaukee was Solomon Juneau, a former trapper and fur dealer who had settled in the area in 1818. By 1846, an unstoppable wave of energetic and success-seeking immigrants from economically impoverished and politically torn Europe had surged onto the land. These people were mainly Germans, as well as British, Poles, Mexicans and immigrants from Scandinavia. They were all industrious, full of ideas, and fired with enthusiasm for the adventure of carving out a new life in a new land.

The city soon came to be known as "America's workshop." Although an exemplary administrative system coupled with the attractiveness and sheer beauty of the city's location contributed to Milwaukee's success, it was based chiefly on the metalworking industries.

At the beginning of the 21st century, Milwaukee had a population of 630,000 (with the trend on the decline), over 2,500 variously sized production sites and factories and famous breweries such as Pabst, Miller and Schlitz. Added to this are numerous TV stations and radio stations, about 12 universities and colleges, as well as more than 100 carefully tended parks. At the turn of the 20th century, Milwaukee was just one of many industrial centers struggling to gain footing in America's Steel Belt. But for many years now this city has been established as the "center of the universe" for millions of people around the world.

Downtown Milwaukee: the imposing setting of a new-age industrial city. In contrast: a pre-industrial idyll on the bustling Milwaukee River.

© Harley-Davidson

15

The Wild Days of the Pioneers

Not Too Many Ideas but Loads of Enthusiasm

The history of Harley-Davidson began around the turn of the 20th century in the city of Milwaukee, an ideal birthplace which provided unique conditions for the growth of such an enterprise. Let us look at those conditions more closely: the entire country, particularly the industrially well-developed East, was literally seething with enterprise and inventiveness. As the 19th century drew to a close, America's emergence as an industrial power had already earned it a name it still bears today: "the land of opportunity." The United States of America was ready for one of the great inventions of civilized man, albeit one that was not noticed at first – the development of the internal combustion engine.

The age of the covered wagon was long gone. The railroads had already laid their tracks across the country. Now the nation was faced with the third and largest revolution in terms of domestic mobilization in its history: individual transportation had come knocking on the door of the new century, and that door was flung wide open. The dawn of the age of the internal combustion engine appeared quite modestly to begin with. A mere 4,000 self-propelled vehicles were registered in the U.S. at the turn of the 20th century. But what an opportunity there was, what a market! And then, a new toy was invented by a society thirsting for technology: the motorcycle. Granted, the first models looked more like motorized bicycles, but the most explosive innovation – in the truest sense of the word – was the engine.

Invented in Europe, it soon found its way across the Atlantic to a country whose enthusiasm for all things technical presented few obstacles to its unbridled expansionist urge. The first organized races were held around 1900: Some death-defying men (and women!) pitted their skill and fortune on a grand scale on fragile, thundering mounts to the delight of the enthusiastic and paying public: bigger, better, faster, the riders thundered around splintered wooden ovals and sandy horseracing tracks. Others successfully attempted to cross virtually impassable rough and pitted tracks, overcoming all obstacles over vast distances. Records were broken literally everyday, often going totally unnoticed at the time.

These bizarre vehicles were often just strengthened bicycles with an engine, fuel tank, ignition, toolbox, battery and other necessities of self-propelled locomotion simply attached somewhere – and somehow – to the frame. This period in the motorcycle's history was subsequently referred to as the "clip-on era." With no suspension whatsoever, it took a great deal of effort to get the machines rolling on virtually impassable roads; the speed, brakes and engine were barely controllable. Nevertheless, this did little to dampen the enthusiasm of their owners. Indeed, the speed junkies of old on their steel mounts paid little or no attention to human crowds and panic-stricken horses that foolishly attempted to bar their way. This attitude was no coincidence. The Americans shared at least one thing in common with Europeans: a deep-seated enthusiasm for bicycle riding. More than three million so-called "iron horses" already graced the roads and paths of the U.S. in 1895, and hundreds of bicycle clubs had sprung into existence. The first of many magazines dedicated to cycling was founded in 1877: *The Bicycle World*. In the fall of 1902, motorcycle riding had become so popular that the magazine changed its title to *The Bicycle World & Motorcycle Review*. The first pacer motorcycles with De Dion engines were used in bicycle races in New York's Madison Square Garden in 1898. In 1901, the Coliseum in Chicago hosted the first "Automobile and Motorcycle Show" in the Midwest – an event that proved to be a real sensation. Well-known European motorcycle manufacturers, such as Werner, exhibited their wares at the show in the hope of making a killing.

In the meantime, the Americans had taken the mobilization of their vast continent into their own hands. In 1899, one of the first ever motorized bicycles, an Orient Aster from Orient Cycles in Waltham, Massachusetts, could be seen – and doubtless heard – clattering along the roads of New England. This trend was followed in 1900 by the Marsh Cycle Company in Brockton, Massachusetts and by the long-successful bicycle company of Colonel Albert A. Pope in Hartford, Connecticut and Toledo, Ohio. Carl Oscar Hedstrom, who had already enjoyed great success building pacer motorcycles and was one of the most talented manufacturers in the field, unveiled the first road-going motorcycle in 1901. The machine was built by Hedstrom's company in Springfield, Massachusetts and belonged to a certain Mr. George M. Hendee, who christened it the Indian Motorcycle. Other motorcycles followed, such as the Mitchell that appeared in Racine, Wisconsin, the Columbia in Westfield, Ohio, and the Wagner in St. Paul, Minnesota – as well as numerous other machines which seldom made it into volume production.

Motorcycle factories – if they could realistically be called that – shot up like mushrooms in the period from 1902 to 1905: The Aurora Automatic Machinery Company integrated the engines designed and built by Hedstrom and Hendee in its Thor models. Audi-Bi was opened in Buffalo, New York, while Dyke set up business in St. Louis, Missouri. Curtiss & Erie was founded in Hammondsport, New York; Freyer & Miller in Cleveland, Ohio; Holley in Bradford, Pennsylvania; Geer in St. Louis, Missouri; Merkel in Milwaukee, Wisconsin; Rambler in Racine, Wisconsin; Reading Standard in Reading, Pennsylvania; Steffey in Philadelphia, Pennsylvania; and, last but not least, Harley-Davidson in Milwaukee, Wisconsin.

Horses were still used for transporting goods at this time, while engines were already being bolted onto common bicycles for personal transportation.

© Harley-Davidson

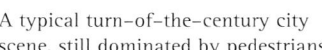

A typical turn-of-the-century city scene, still dominated by pedestrians.

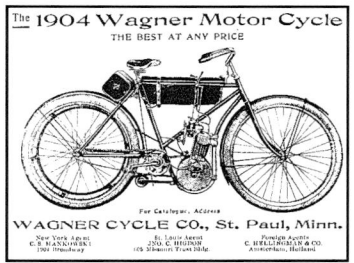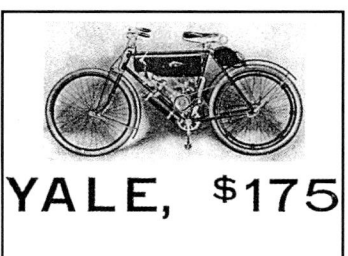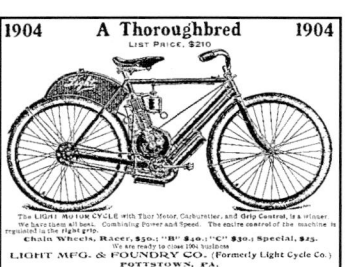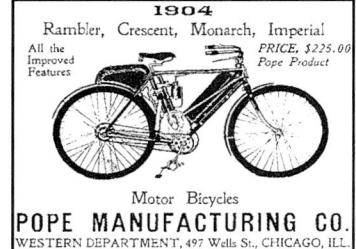

Competition: just some of the many motorcycle companies already in existence and against which Harley-Davidson had to prevail.

Numerous trade publications covered this latest trend with unbridled enthusiasm, titles such as the *Cycling Gazette* or the *Horseless Age*. These were joined in 1901 by the *Automobile and Cycle Trade Journal*, followed by *Motorcycle* and *Bicycle Illustrated* and, finally, *Motorcycling* and *The Motor-cyclist*.

More and more cycling clubs metamorphosed into motorcycling clubs, which by this time were even holding their own sporting events. On September 7, 1903, 92 members of the New York Bicycle Club and the Alpha Motorcycle Club in New York founded the Federation of American Motor-cyclists – FAM for short – a national organization that was the antecedent of the American Motorcycle Association (AMA).

Scores of canny bicycle dealers now recognized a golden opportunity to boost their turnover by establishing a lucrative sideline selling motorcycles. The demand was enormous. Unfortunately, the same cannot be said for peoples' knowledge of the newfangled technology in those days. Nevertheless, America was already home to 65 motorcycle manufacturers by the turn of the century.

However, the really "big business" was slow in coming. The technology was primitive and liable to failure. Neither informative technical literature nor an industry geared up to supply parts were available, and on the few occasions when gasoline could be found, it was generally of pretty poor quality. On top of that, there was simply a lack of capital, the driving force behind any successful production. New concepts were dreamed up all over the place, as much out of desperation as out of enthusiasm. Designs were redrafted, actually built on some occasions, tinkered with, and tested. Backyard toolsheds became workshops and some of those workshops actually became factories, although many were doomed to failure right from the start.

Wild and crazy years indeed. Although we can look back on them today with an amused chuckle, those very same years must have been alive with an indescribable feeling of creativity and industry. For the time being, however, let us return to that decisive year of 1900, to a small industrial town mentioned earlier on: Milwaukee…

The Unbelievable Challenge

The First Baby Travels 100,000 Miles Without a Breakdown

The worldwide legend known as Harley–Davidson began quite inconspicuously. The name stems from the friendship that developed between two young men growing up in the same neighborhood, both typical working children of European immigrants.

William S. Harley, born in 1880 and the son of an English immigrant from the industrial region around Liverpool, was already at a very early age a skilled handyman interested in all things technical. He had a particular talent for drawing and a great love of nature, boating and fishing and, above all, riding his bicycle. William's interests were shared in roughly equal measure by his friend Arthur Davidson, born in 1881, the youngest son of William C. Davidson. His father was an energetic and successful carpenter who had emigrated from Aberdeen, Scotland, directly to Milwaukee in 1872 and had already set up home on the corner of 38th and Highland Boulevard in a three-story house, which also had its own workshop. Arthur had two sisters, as well as two brothers, William and Walter. Together with various other relatives, they represented a typical Scottish family clan, constantly helping one another out and displaying an iron-willed family loyalty that allowed them to rise to the challenges of their new world.

The two young friends attended the same school. Bill Harley left school at the age of 15 to take up a job as a mechanic at a small bicycle factory in the north of Milwaukee where he stayed for three years. He then got a job as a draftsman at the Barth Manufacturing Company, a metalworking company in which his old buddy Arthur already worked as a pattern maker.

That was at the turn of the 20th century, which is when the astonishing story of Harley–Davidson truly starts. The main catalyst for what was later to become a legend was a since-forgotten German colleague who probably was called Kröger or Krüger. Whatever his name, he emigrated to America from France, where he had worked for the Aster corporation which manufactured De Dion–Bouton engines under license, bringing with him not only detailed technical knowledge, but also some extremely interesting blueprints, containing information of such an advanced technical nature that it was hitherto unheard of in America. The two friends — already very interested in the new engine technology — were fascinated by the possibilities hinted at by these blueprints. They exhaustively discussed the steps to be taken, acquired the relevant literature, insofar as it was available, and carefully observed the emerging motorcycle industry and its products. It can be assumed that they also visited that first famous major automobile and motorcycle show in nearby Chicago in 1901.

During this time, the uncertain ideas and notions of the two friends gradually coalesced until the great goal was defined — the manufacture of a reliable and sturdy motorcycle of world-class quality, to be built in as great a number as possible. It was little more than a vague dream to begin with, and both Bill and Arthur were luckily still unaware of the endless obstacles and problems that would start to litter their path from that day on. However, even such knowledge would have done little to prevent them from striving to achieve their goal, for this particular dream was just too

attractive, too big and too realistic to be given up so easily. And so it was that they resolutely went to work to make their dream come true, experimenting under extremely primitive conditions in the cellars of their parents' homes. Bill Harley drew up the first drafts while Arthur built the first molds in which the two entrepreneurs subsequently poured molten mixtures of gray cast iron. Over long nights of filing and sawing, hammering and drilling, the first crankshaft cases were produced, together with the first cylinders, connecting rods, pistons and valves. If something didn't work properly, it had to be rebuilt, or reinvented.

Except for their natural enthusiasm, Bill and Arthur had virtually nothing in those days: neither the requisite knowledge nor high-quality tools, not even when Arthur's brother William, himself a talented toolmaker, sometimes lent a helping hand or offered advice. But above all, they lacked money, which led to Arthur taking on part-time jobs in a desperate attempt to cover their rapidly exploding costs.

There were other explosions as well. The biggest problem at that time was the carburetor. Although they experimented with various systems, it wasn't until after mother Davidson's kitchen had been almost literally blown up on several occasions that a relatively simple and practical solution was discovered — a pitot-tube carburetor, initially cobbled together using an empty tomato can! This breakthrough was partly attributable to a third member of the team: a temporary partner who likewise went on to become famous: Ole Evinrude. He actually stayed with Bill and Arthur for

only a short time, before devoting his efforts entirely to the manufacture of his outboard boat engines.

Despite Ole Evinrude's departure, the two somehow managed it alone and the first test engines were soon up and running. The fuel needed for the engines was obtained in half-liter or one-liter bottles from nearby Laab's Drugstore on Vliet Street. Needless to say, Bill and Arthur quickly became regular customers. The small one-cylinder, four-stroke engine, had a 2.12 inch (54 mm) bore and a stroke of 2.87 inches (73 mm), displacing about 10.7 cubic inches (175 cc). Although promising, it was a veritable catastrophe when it came to practical use. It had virtually no power, peaking at roughly one-and-a-half horsepower, it leaked and tended towards unpredictable and uncontrollable functioning. Nevertheless, it worked!

The two partners built three examples of this early prototype and fitted them into various bicycle frames for testing. This proved to be an exercise in futility, as the frames were just not strong enough to bear the weight of the engines. They either fell apart, shook uncontrollably, or the bearings locked solid. The most reliable engine was subsequently fitted with a shaft and propeller and used to power a motorboat.

Inspired by his "successes," Arthur wrote many enthusiastic letters during this time to his older brother Walter, who had just taken on employment as a machinist at the Missouri, Kansas & Texas Rail Road in Parsons, Kansas, asking him more and more urgently to return home and

De Dion-Bouton
An Early General Purpose Engine

As early as 1882 the Comte de Dion was already busily working on self-propelled two- and three-wheelers in France with his two partners, Messieurs Bouton and Trepardoux, concentrating initially on steam-engine drive systems. However, when De Dion increasingly recognized the potential of fast internal combustion engines, Trepardoux — a firm advocate of the steam engine — dropped out of the partnership in 1894.

Together with the unpretentious mechanic Georges Bouton, De Dion developed a small, air-cooled 7.3 cubic inch (120 cc) single-cylinder four-stroke engine in 1894 with a 1.97 inch (50 mm) bore and a 2.36 inch (60 mm) stroke. The engine was fitted with a simple surface carburetor. An automatic suction valve (also known as a blow valve) served as the intake and the correct firing sequence was ensured by an adjustable ignition tube powered by a 4-volt/30 amp battery. The crankshaft case was made of aluminum and split longitudinally. These small but singularly reliable engines developed roughly one half of a horsepower at an astounding 1800 rpm.

De Dion soon developed into a major industrial company, able to offer an entire range of the most diverse fitted and clip-on engines. Numerous companies in America and abroad sought to become authorized dealers or to secure a manufacturing license. Furthermore, De Dion was extremely successful in selling not only complete engines, but also every accessory required for the manufacture of motorcycles or automobiles. However, there was no such thing as international patent protection in those days, and De Dion engines were soon being copied the world over. Messrs. Edmond was responsible for the sale of De Dion products in the U.S.

perform the first test drives with their amazing new vehicle. Although Arthur's enthusiasm possibly represented more idealistic illusion than hard reality, Walter was nonetheless very interested.

Upon returning to Milwaukee on April 29, 1903 for the wedding of his brother William, he soon realized — as an experienced engineer — that the new project still required a lot of work before he could carry out his first test ride. Already keen to try out the newfangled contraption and never being one to waste more time than necessary when it came to making a decision, Walter promptly handed in his notice in Kansas and took on a new job at the Chicago-Milwaukee Railroad, where he had worked previously, so that he could also contribute to the project.

The young entrepreneurs, who by then were getting to the end of their tether on account of the seemingly endless worries involved, were again blessed by a lucky turn of events when they were given permission to use the workshop of a mutual friend, complete with a lathe and a drill press, which was driven by a small gas engine.

It was in this workshop that a new, improved engine first saw the light of day in early 1903. This time, however, the engine was mounted in a specially designed and sturdier loop frame. The embryo already displayed many characteristics of a modern motorcycle. The engine had a bore of 3.0 inches (76 mm) and a stroke of 3.5 inches (89 mm), displacing just over 24.4 cubic inches (400 cc) and yielding about three horsepower. Thanks to its larger flywheel, the engine was now able to develop sufficient torque to handle inclines easily, and Walter was able to put the new vehicle through its paces to his heart's content. By this time, he was thoroughly convinced of the merit of the new concept.

Once an agreement had been reached as to the right wording of the company's name, with the outstanding role played by designer Bill Harley leaving little doubt as to whose name should come first, artistically talented Aunt Janet painted the classic Harley-Davidson logo for the first time ever on the motorcycle's "piano black" fuel tank using red letters with a gold border.

The life of this first Harley-Davidson which was produced for the series can be traced fairly accurately. It changed hands several times, having a total of five different owners, all of whom covered such long distances with the motorcycle that it ultimately clocked up an amazing 100,000 miles without a serious breakdown. There could have been no better proof of the reliability of Harley-Davidson motorcycles and the meticulousness with which they were built — a fact that was later to be trumpeted in a successful and much-acclaimed advertising campaign.

By the year 1904, the good reputation of Harley-Davidson had already spread throughout the local region, and there were soon plenty of customers, both enthusiastic and eager to try out this new mode of transportation. This meant that most of the subsequent models were already bought and paid for before they even left the modest workshop. The Chicago-based bicycle dealer C. H. Lang, whose unorthodox sales methods later made him one of America's most successful motorcycle dealers, sold the machines for 200 dollars a go — a price that obviously included a decent profit margin.

The modest workshop built for the newly created company by father Davidson in his backyard in 1903, measuring just 10 by 15 feet and with the immortal words "Harley Davidson Motor Co." painted in clumsy letters on its wooden door, soon proved to be far too small. It was expanded

A photo from 1907 showing the entire workforce, with Walter Davidson in the middle wearing the white jacket. © Harley-Davidson

to twice its original size and, now measuring 10 by 30 feet, became Harley-Davidson's first true production facility.

Another eight machines were built there in the year 1904, true to the company philosophy of producing the best motorcycles in the world. In his capacity as test rider, Walter missed no opportunity to enter the motorcycles in competitions and local races, and numerous trophies testify to his successes and victories in those early days.

In the meantime, the company was literally inundated with orders, and although several additional workers were employed, it soon became apparent that some fundamental and far-reaching decisions would have to be made regarding the future of the company. As quick off the mark as ever, Walter Davidson grasped fate by the hand and took the first step towards self-employment by resigning from his job at the railroad. By this time, Arthur was mainly responsible to take care of sales and marketing, but he was still too cautious to devote himself to the company on a full-time basis and continued to hold down part-time jobs, just in case. Bill Harley, the newly appointed chief engineer and technical director, took what was probably the most important step for the young company in 1903 by resigning from his well-paid job at Marsh and registering for a degree course in engineering at the University of Wisconsin in neighboring Madison. He had quickly realized that he needed to know more about the technology involved in building internal combustion engines. He earned his living by working as a waiter in the students' dining hall.

Meanwhile, the small factory had become a hive of activity. The bosses labored to the point of exhaustion, working on the motorcycles themselves when necessary, and rarely got to bed before midnight. They were even late home on Christmas Eve, not arriving for the family festivities until the last moment.

The number of enthusiastic articles appearing in the relevant magazines was growing, and on December 13, 1905, Arthur Davidson wrote the following words to a customer: "Following exhaustive study, we can honestly claim to manufacture what is currently the fastest single-cylinder engine. One of our records was set during a 15-mile race in Chicago on July 4, when we finished the course in just 19.02 minutes, which is ample proof of the reliability and good cooling of our engines."

Expansion

A Slow, Hard and Steep Path

Events progressed at a blinding pace in the years that followed: be it the procurement of materials, the expansion and outfitting of production facilities, tests and race competitions, design improvements or customer service and sales, everything had to be done virtually at the same time.

If they were not living with their parents, the Davidson brothers stayed in apartments close to their small workshop, where they often worked late into the night. They stashed their earnings in a medicine cabinet in their parents' house, considering this to be a safe place for the money. However, their mother – appalled at the dirt and oil her sons left behind them after their "experiments" – had hired a cleaner, who discovered the money jar in the cabinet. Although several of the cleaner's thefts eventually came to light, they had no immediate influence on the small company...

The Harley-Davidson catalog made its first appearance in 1906. The prerequisite for this milestone was the production and sale of 50 motorcycles. These were offered in piano black or Renault gray, the latter color being the origin of the name of the famous "Silent Grey Fellow" model. The original logo designed by Aunt Janet in gold-edged red letters was retained.

Despite his cautiousness, even Arthur now realized that he had to relinquish his job as a pattern maker at Barth, as the new company simply took up all his time and demanded all his energy. With the help of uncle James McLay's low-interest loans and skill as a broker, the young business partners purchased a larger allotment of land in the industrial area directly next to the Chicago-Milwaukee Railroad, on 37th and Chestnut Street. This was later to become Juneau Avenue, the historical base of today's headquarters.

In the fall of 1906, a two-story wooden building measuring 28 by 80 feet was erected on this site. However, when the framework was finished, the railroad surveyors determined that it was in the way of their railroad track. No time was wasted, and with the help of a dozen able-bodied men, the entire framework of the building was lifted and moved roughly one and a half feet to "safety," as Walter Davidson later recalled.

Shortly thereafter, the factory building was expanded to twice its original size, and better tools and a couple of other machines were purchased. It was now the turn of the oldest brother, William A. Davidson, to give up his job at the railroad. Attending various courses in Chicago, he became acquainted with the latest acetylene welding techniques, which he soon incorporated into the production process.

By this time, the company had 18 employees and it built and sold 150 motorcycles in 1907. These motorcycles were now fitted for the first time with the Sager-Cushion springer fork – a concept designed by Sager and purchased by Harley who refined it. In fact, this system was retained until 1949. Every cent they made, including the earnings of their very industrious sister Elizabeth, was plowed back into the business.

The factory was expanded again in 1907 in order to cater to the ever-growing demand for the Silent Grey Fellow in the coming year.

21

The Company

This Harley-Davidson Does the
Work of Three Horses

The rapidly rising demand, the excellent reputation of Harley-Davidson motorcycles, and their technological lead over aggressive, if not always serious, competition called for some fundamental decisions to be made. At the end of the day, ingenious ideas, skilled craftsmanship, organizational talent, and the ever-growing loans from a well-meaning uncle were simply not enough. The small team of aspiring manufacturers harbored no illusions: they knew they had to venture into new territory. They had to make the transition and develop into an industrial establishment of altogether different dimensions if they wanted to seize the moment of opportunity – and they had to do so quickly.

One day, after Walter Davidson had returned from yet another victorious competition, this time having won the two-day Endurance Run from Chicago to Kokomo, Indiana, the company was officially registered as a "corporation." It was on that day of September 17, 1907 that the founders' names were entered in the commercial register of the United States of America in meticulous calligraphy. Walter Davidson, now President and General Manager, subscribed 50 share certificates at 100 dollars, i.e. a total of 5,000 dollars, William A. Davidson, the new Vice President and Production Manager subscribed 4,000 dollars, Arthur Davidson, Secretary and Sales Manager 4,700 dollars and William S. Harley, Chief Engineer and Treasurer, 500 dollars.

In the tradition of true Scottish frugality, the four shareholders and newly appointed directors approved a sum of five dollars each as ample compensation for the meeting, and this was scrupulously recorded under article III, section 6 of the founding charter. The corporation now had 14,200 dollars at its disposal – a modest capital base, but adequate nonetheless,

particularly when it came to fulfilling the legislative provisions. And so the craftsmen became responsible executives. However, from this moment on, the success or failure of the company would also be influenced largely by banks and advertising agencies.

William Harley had by then finished his course of study at Madison University, graduating with honors, and he returned to Milwaukee as a fresh Bachelor of Engineering, eager to get to work and full of ideas. The young company now developed at a breathtaking pace. The small wooden factory was soon bursting at the seams once again and was expanded to occupy an impressive 4,760 square feet. Harley-Davidson now had a workforce of 36, which produced 450 motorcycles in 1908. These machines were sold as the Model 4, with 1904 being regarded as the "Model 0" year. The threefold increase in production was due in part to the highly acclaimed and publicized Endurance Run victory of the previous year. Now, Harley-Davidson was in a position to gain the confidence of the all-important banks, and the first major loans were guaranteed by the Milwaukee Marshall & Ilsley Bank (M&I) and the First Milwaukee National Bank. The cooperation between the banks and Harley-Davidson flourished from that point on and lasted until 1969, soon making the company one of the largest motorcycle manufacturers in the world. In all fairness, it must be said that Harley's success was due not only to bank loans, but also to a local advertising agency with which the company founders concluded a somewhat unusual agreement.

Walter Dunlap, the manager in charge of the recently founded advertising agency Klaus van Peterson & Dunlap, was prepared – to a certain extent – to finance all advertising campaigns and brochures up-front. Of course, in line with its corporate philosophy, Harley-Davidson could be

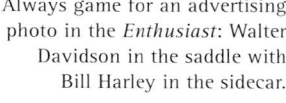

Always game for an advertising photo in the *Enthusiast*: Walter Davidson in the saddle with Bill Harley in the sidecar.

relied on to pay a correspondingly respectable fee afterwards. This cooperation proved to be extremely fruitful for all concerned and Klaus van Peterson & Dunlap's debut in the world of motorcycle advertising was characterized by enthusiasm and intelligent ideas, a recipe for success that lasted many decades. The serious and informative advertising strategy conceived by the agency broke with the traditions of the usual marketing clones, a welcome change indeed. One of the most successful slogans of Harley-Davidson's early years was a short sentence that went on to become famous: "This Harley-Davidson does the work of three horses." The company's links with the Milwaukee-based Pohlmann photographic studio, which took all the photographs that were needed for the brochures, was equally successful and long-lasting.

By now, Arthur Davidson was spreading the corporate image in his own way. In his capacity as new (and old) marketing director, he traveled the country tirelessly, signing up one new dealer after the other. But Arthur was choosy, and took a good, long look at his future representatives before concluding hitherto unheard-of franchise contracts, which basically integrated the dealers as subcontractors within the Harley-Davidson corporation. At the same time, he established training courses in Milwaukee for the new dealers and their mechanics, a tradition that is still worth its weight in gold today. By 1908, Harley-Davidson already had dealerships in New York, Chicago, Philadelphia, Atlanta and Newark, as well as Los Angeles, San Francisco and Seattle on the west coast. The first foreign ties were also established by this time.

Thanks to Arthur Davidson's skill at marketing, as well as the publication of the company's first brochure, albeit a rather modest and technical affair, the attention of large companies and government organizations was increasingly drawn to the robust motorcycle that looked ideal for use by field staff and outdoor workers.

And so it was that in 1908 the first police departments and mail services had already ordered their Harleys. Bell Telephone considered the new mode of transportation perfect for repair and maintenance work in rural areas. One decisive aspect in favor of this decision was the possibility of fitting the motorcycles with various kinds of sidecars. Boasting all manners of individual assemblies, these so-called "package trucks" were later, in 1915, promoted by Harley-Davidson as worthy alternatives to real vans or trucks. Attachments for mounting in front of the motorcycle were also manufactured. However, most of the company's extensive production of sidecars was soon outsourced to supplier firms because of lack of space. Factory space was once more at a premium at Harley-Davidson, so the plant was expanded yet again, this time becoming a multi-story brick building, emblazoned with the company logo in huge letters.

The single-cylinder Model 5, the famous Silent Grey Fellow, was enhanced by a number of improvements. The frame was further reinforced and the wheelbase extended by six inches. The engine was provided with a larger bore, measuring 3.35 inches (85 mm), and now had a displacement of 30.16 cubic inches (494 cc). The Silent Grey Fellow achieved an output of 4.3 horsepower and was available for purchase in numerous versions: the Model 5A sported magneto ignition, in which a precision Bosch magneto system was used for the first time. The standard model had battery ignition and 28-inch tires, while the Model 5C had 26-inch wheels and magneto ignition. Even the drive-belt drum could be ordered in different versions. This made the machine adaptable and possible to use in hilly regions or on flat terrain. A combined tank with separate reservoirs for gasoline and oil was another successful detail. And the Silent Grey Fellow certainly lived up to its name: the end of the muffler pipe was fitted with a cover which the motorcycle rider was expected to close — quite reasonably so — in urban areas. Of course, most riders were more than happy to put up with the unbridled roar of the engine once beyond the city limits.

The entire range of Model 5 Harleys was now designed and ready for the coming year 1909 — and that was the year in which the legend of Harley-Davidson was to be truly born...

A document from the incorporation of Harley-Davidson Motor Company on September 17, 1907.

Courtesy of: H.D. Archives

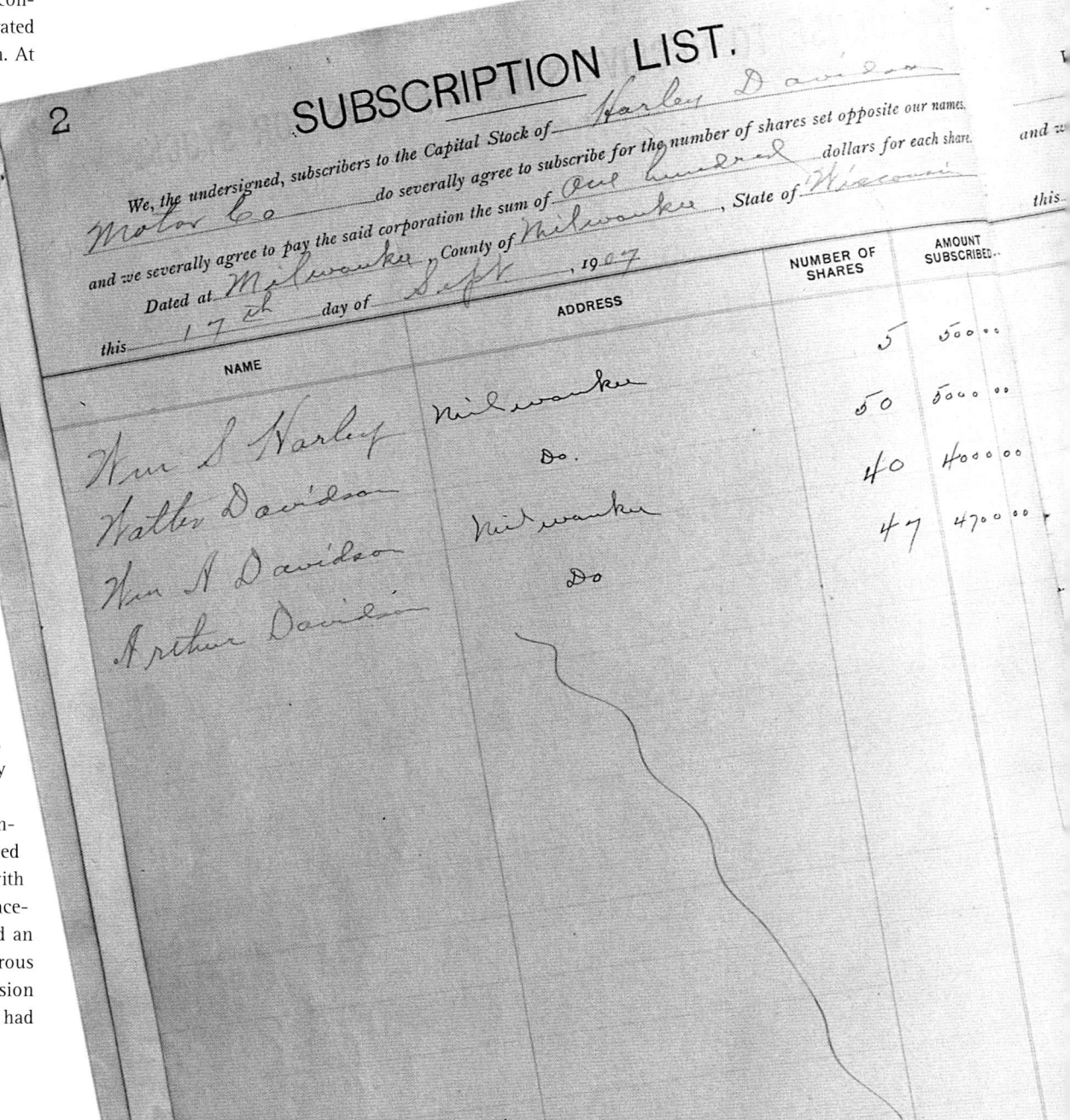

Silent Grey Fellow

(1908)

1005 Points

A Sensational Victory to Number One in the U.S.

The first President, Walter Davidson, with his factory-produced best-seller after winning the Endurance Run.

© Harley-Davidson

In 1908, the five-year-old Federation of American Motorcyclists, or FAM for short, once again held one of its major race competitions in the eastern United States: the New York State Great Endurance Run. The course began in Catskill on the Hudson River, headed towards Brooklyn and then looped around Long Island to the finish line. The two-day event was popularly regarded as a remorseless battle for "sorting out the men from the boys" in respect of both man and machine, which is why it was held in such high regard by many trade magazines and leading sports motorcyclists.

The 61 participants that began the race in the craggy Catskill Mountains on the morning of June 29 included a hitherto unknown contender from the Midwest, riding an equally unknown motorcycle, the only Harley-Davidson registered in the race. No real threat, the other motorcyclists must have thought. However, the unknown contender was none other than keen racing fan Walter Davidson, recently appointed general director and manager in charge of a small motorcycle factory with a mere 36 employees. He inconspicuously rode a stock single-cylinder model from the company's own modest product range. But after just the first few stages of this demanding course, the newcomer had become a real threat to several favorites. Despite difficult steep stretches, badly rutted passes and arduous cross-country tracks, he reached one checkpoint after the other, stage for stage, always within the time limit and as precisely as clockwork, achieving top speeds of up to 50 miles per hour on the way.

To the dismay of the other 46 participants still in the race and much to the astonishment of all the spectators, Walter repeated this outstanding performance the next day, completing the 180-mile Long Island circuit perfectly. Walter Davidson thus won this arduous race with the maximum score of 1,000 points, a score never previously achieved. In fact, the judges were so impressed that they even awarded Walter another five bonus points — which were not actually provided for in the rules — simply for achieving the most consistent performance.

But that was not enough for Walter: just one week later, he took part in the Economy Run, a competition decided on the basis of fuel consumption, using exactly the same motorcycle. The course stretched 50 miles through the rough countryside around Roslyn, Long Island and Walter achieved the unbelievable record of about 188 miles per gallon — the lowest fuel consumption figure recorded up to that day.

The press enthusiastically celebrated this sensational result and in one fell swoop Harley-Davidson became the No. 1 American motorcycle. One of the most successful advertising campaigns in the history of Harley-Davidson was later based on this triumph, and from that day on the company also enjoyed a very special relationship with the Federation of American Motorcyclists, and particularly with its successor organization, the AMA, or American Motorcycle Association.

The Birth of an Immortal

From the Marquis de Dion to Harley's V-Twin Motor

A first attempt but still far from perfection: the legendary original Model 5D from 1909.

Courtesy of: H.D. Archives

The highly respected magazine *Bicycling World & Motorcycle Review* presented a brand-new Harley-Davidson V-Twin in its issue dated April 25, 1908, describing the machine as the latest product on the motorcycle market. This machine was the Model 5D. The 5D featured essentially the same cylinder as the robust single-cylinder models but had twice as many: two gray cast iron "F heads," each made from one casting and with valves incorporated in steel pockets with springs — so-called "pocket valves." The inlet valves were still automatic, using the suction valve technique and were actually outdated by this time. Indeed, the technological features of this model appeared impressive: twin 3.0 inch (76 mm) bores and a stroke of 3.5 inches (89 mm) resulted in an engine displacement of 49.48 cubic inches (810.83 cc) which yielded about 7 horsepower.

A Model H Schebler carburetor was used in Harley's V-Twin, mounted between the two cylinders which were inclined at 45 degrees to one another, forming the "V" after which the V-Twin motorcycle was named. The machine had a listed top speed of 65 mph. So far, so good.

It was a pilot project, but time was running against the company. In the small motorcycle factory in Milwaukee, the demand for more powerful motorcycles had reached a point where it could no longer be ignored. A host of competing companies already had twin-cylinder models on the market, chalking up notable successes in the field of motorcycle racing, in particular. These twin models proved themselves extremely fast in the increasingly popular flat-track races. However, William Harley had begun working on the development of a twin-cylinder model years before, and after exhaustive pilot studies and trials the company rolled out its latest sensation in 1909.

Harley-Davidson had already built some twin-cylinder models for private customers in the years preceding the debut of the Model 5D and these had been successfully competed in various races, although racing was a sport the corporate management was determined not to become involved in. One of these customers was a certain Harvey Bernard, who won the Algonquin hillclimb race in Illinois in 1908 on a 1000 cc Harley V-Twin, which led to Harley-Davidson concentrating

Hillclimbing was one of the first motorcycle sport disciplines to become popular.

all the more on endurance competitions. In 1909, Walter Davidson led a team of (private) Harley riders that courageously won a 325-mile FAM Endurance Run from Cleveland, Ohio to Indianapolis and back again with the highest possible score.

The principle of the Model 5D was simple and certainly not new: the explosive force in the combustion chambers pushed down two pistons and the two connecting rods transmitted the force directly to the crankshaft via a common crankpin. William Harley was basically still attached to the old De Dion-Bouton concept, cautious and conservative as ever and more concerned about assured reliability than with venturing into new realms of engine technology which had already spelt the ruin of numerous competitor companies. Nevertheless, that is how the immortal Harley V-Twin engine was born. It went on to become the heart and soul of an entire engine generation and, modified and improved countless times, dearly loved and criticized as outdated in equal measure, remains fundamentally the same type of engine today.

But that isn't to say that the Model 5D was perfect. Although the engine was as reliable as expected, its unusual power yield was too much for the leather drive belt, which suffered continually from slippage problems. Customers complained, and eventually the company withdrew the troublesome model from the market. Bill Harley worked on developing a new transmission system.

In light of this development, most of the thousand or so motorcycles sold by Harley-Davidson in 1909 were the tried-and-tested, as well as very popular, single-cylinder models. The Pittsburgh police department was proud of the fact that its mounted officers no longer had to make do with the power of one horse, but could now perform their duties on the back of a motorized steed from Milwaukee.

Walter Davidson and Bill Harley also took the opportunity to demonstrate their motorcycles at a congress of the Rural Free Delivery mail service in Milwaukee. The delegates were impressed and from that day on, Harley-Davidson motorcycles represented the "preferred" form of transportation for rural mail deliveries.

A total of 3,168 motorcycles was produced in 1910. Acetylene lamps were now also available as optional extras for improving the rider's field of vision in the dark. William S. Harley submitted a patent application for a twin planetary gear that was incorporated in the rear-wheel hub — a design that did not actually reach the production stage in that form. But a new belt-drive system was introduced in 1912, and a "free-wheeling" clutch mechanism on the rear wheel characterized the state-of-the-art belt-driven power transmission. However, the problem with the slipping belt persisted, particularly in wet conditions.

By now, motorcycle racing had firmly established itself as the most popular sport in America, with the favorites being dirt-track racing and a wild form of competitive motorcycling in which the machines were raced around steeply banked wooden board-tracks. Once it was realized that the wooden eighth-of-a-mile or sixth-of-a-mile velodromes originally built for bicycle racing were too dangerous for the more powerful motorcycles (and particularly for the spectators), wooden-floored bowl-shaped arenas were erected, these circuits measuring a quarter-of-a-mile or a third-of-a-mile in length. They were called motodromes and became extremely popular, as did dirt-track racing on horseracing tracks. While the machines thundered around these

© Harley-Davidson

wooden arenas with flames blasting from their exhaust pipes, drifting and swerving from side to side and kicking up sand and dust, the enthusiastic crowds, loved the excitement. After all, where else could such exciting entertainment be experienced at such close hand? Radio was still unheard of and movie production was still in its infancy. Race tracks and motodromes thus sprang up all over the country and the loud, fast spectacle on the circular race courses soon became a nationwide hit. Regional championships were held throughout America, making the advertising potential of the highly publicized victors and their winning makes of motorcycle truly enormous.

However, the bosses at Harley-Davidson were less than enthusiastic about pure motorcycle racing, although they were not averse to exploiting such events for advertising purposes, as demonstrated by an advertisement in the September 1911 issue of the leading motorcycle periodical, *Motorcycle Illustrated*: "No, we don't believe in racing and we don't make a practice of it, but when Harley-Davidson owners win races with their own stock machines hundreds of miles from the factory, we can't help crowing about it." This was doubtless one of the company's more curious advertising statements. Harley-Davidson's honorable, but outdated, fixation with pure endurance and reliability was no longer in tune with the times, not to mention the extremely negative effect it had on the company's image and sales success.

Excelsior, Indian, Pope, Merkel, Reading-Standard and Thor were the big names at that time, proclaiming their superiority in motorcycle racing with blazing headlines. So what if Harley had once again scooped first, second and third place in the 225-mile endurance run from Harrisburg to Philadelphia and back with an eight-man team of privateers (without any support from the company whatsoever) beating the highly trained factory teams from Indian, Flying Merkel, Pope and Thor? Indian and Excelsior, then the largest motorcycle manufacturers in the world, were able to celebrate overwhelming success elsewhere, specifically on the race tracks, sometimes winning 90 percent of all motorcycle races held in the U.S. During the summer of 1911, Indian was also able to gloat about its triple victory at the Isle of Man TT. Up until the 1970s this event was the most famous and toughest motorcycle race in the world. This Indian victory ensured that the American marque would benefit from a large number of exports to Europe for many years to come. At that time, Indian was a true giant of the motorcycle industry, selling almost 20,000 motorcycles in 1912, with the figure reaching about 35,000 in 1913. More than 2,000 authorized Indian dealers throughout the world guaranteed an outstandingly organized sales network. The times were definitely changing, and by 1910 Harley-Davidson recognized the trend and designed its racing model: the 6E stock racer, the successor of the famous serial number 1 of 1903.

The Starting Ceremonies
Already Breathless

"Following thorough preparation and a final visual inspection of the vehicle, the rider checks that there is sufficient gasoline and oil, that the inlet taps are open and that all lubricating points have been properly greased." The instructions for starting a motorcycle must have read pretty much like this in the first decade of our glorious century of technology. Luckily, the strenuous days of having to push-start motorcycles, running alongside them as fast as possible until either the engine finally gasped into life or the prospective rider ran out of breath, were long gone. In those early days of motorcycling, that rider would have had to muster whatever energy he had left to jump into the saddle — more or less accurately — in an attempt to keep the jolting and sputtering beast running, while tinkering with various levers to regulate the fuel intake and ignition. Heaven forbid should he suddenly have to stop or be forced to manhandle the machine up a slope...

By this time, in contrast, the motorcycle was just rocked up onto its rear kickstand and the engine fired into life via a drive belt that simply required the rider to peddle like mad, at an even pace. Once the engine was running hot enough, the rider could release the clutch and ease the motorcycle down from its stand. Once actually in the saddle, all that was needed to keep the vehicle running was some skillful manipulation of clutch, fuel feed and ignition timing. The wonders of modern motorcycling.

Harleys were extremely popular among farmers.

Technology Goes Trendy

We No Longer Build Special Racing Machines But…

In the first brochures and manuals, Harley-Davidson extensively pointed out the latest technical features and innovations of its respective models.

Harley-Davidson's major breakthrough occurred in 1911. Looking back, 1911 can probably be called up to that point the most successful year in the early history of the company as far as technology was concerned. The factory premises were again proving too small and were doubled once more, now to 8,050 square feet. A workforce of 481 personnel built 5,625 motorcycles in that year. Long-term bank loans had to be taken out in order to finance the huge operating investments, and the equally long-term repayments would swallow virtually every cent of the company's profits for many years to come. For the meticulously correct owners of Harley-Davidson, imbued as they were with a typically Scottish spirit of parsimony, this must have seemed pretty much like playing with fire, which probably isn't such a bad analogy since ultimately, Harley-Davidson emerged from this period like a phoenix from the ashes…

The new V-Twin, which the company had worked on so feverishly the year before, was finally ready to face the competition. Together with Henry Melk, Bill Harley had developed an efficient rear-wheel clutch that could be operated via a hand lever or a foot pedal, solving the earlier problems with the belt tension. Also, it was now possible for the engine power to be transmitted via a chain, the use of which William Harley had doggedly opposed until the problem in finding a reliable clutch had been remedied. One thing was certain: the technical maxims to which the company was unconditionally dedicated – reliability, sturdiness and simplicity – had to be given priority, which turned out to be beneficial. The V-Twin engine still had a displacement of 50 cubic inches (810.83 cc), yielding just under 7 horsepower. High-

performance chrome vanadium steel was used for the connecting rod and the valves were made of nickel steel.

However, the most significant technical innovation was the inlet valve, now operated mechanically. This was achieved by means of a long tappet pushrod which opened the valve via a lever on top of the cylinder head, known as the rocker arm. Of course, this meant the inlet valve was exposed and required constant lubrication with an oil can. The exhaust valve was mounted below it in the "F-head" cylinder, and was opened directly by means of a lifter arm via the twin cams, which were likewise situated underneath on a shaft. This offset valve array–inlet above, outlet below – was characteristic of the "inlet over exhaust" F-head engines, also known as IOEs. This development heralded the demise of the old, weak, inefficient suction valve, which was automatically opened by reduced pressure in the cylinder sucking the valve in.

A more robust frame was also built for this new Harley-Davidson motorcycle, designated the Model 7D, and customers could choose between magneto or battery-powered ignition.

In 1912, just a few years after founding an unassuming workshop business, Harley-Davidson was booming, becoming a huge, dynamic enterprise: 9,500 motorcycles were manufactured that year, the company had 1,076 employees and a number of supplier firms were working at full capacity to provide the requisite components. The factory was expanded yet again. It was now housed in a multi-story brick building occupying 18,775 square feet, and numerous auxiliary buildings and warehouses had to be built. Shift work became necessary.

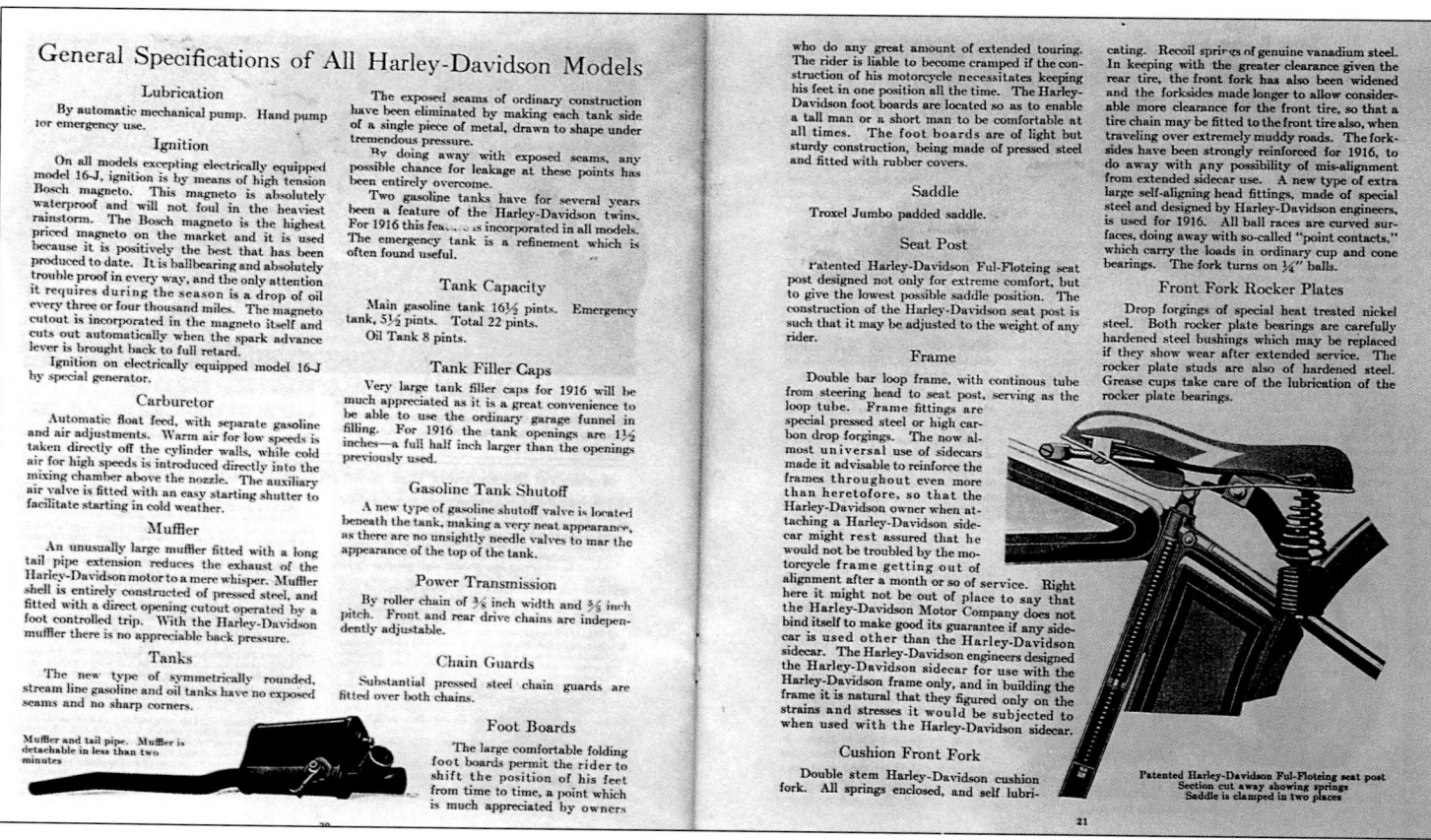

The company also launched a trade magazine called *The Harley-Davidson Dealer* as a new method of communication and to improve its corporate image. The magazine covered sales techniques and extolled the particular benefits of all Harley products in order to demonstrate the company's superiority over the competition. But above all, the magazine was aimed at unifying sales policy and methods.

This was an important factor as differences in marketing policy were already becoming apparent. The renewed victory of Harley V-Twins in the third annual Bakersfield, California Road Race and the San Jose, California Road Race (on December 8, 1912) was primarily due to the substantial financial support of local Harley dealers. At a distinct disadvantage with the competition, both riders and dealers criticized Harley-Davidson's official reluctance to become involved in racing, despite the fact that the company was quite willing to brag about such successes, much to the chagrin of those who had actually achieved them. In a full-page ad in an issue of the *Pacific Motorcyclist* dated September 1913, Harley reiterated its very arrogant and unfortunate position: "Don't blame us if a Harley-Davidson wins a race, because we're not interested in racing. We don't employ factory riders and we don't build special racing machines. Nevertheless, we believe the results speak for themselves." This statement triggered a wave of angry protest. However, Harley was quick to learn and had already decided to enter the arena of motorcycle racing with a vengeance.

While this debate was still raging, the new motorcycles were considerably improved: the V-Twin Model X8E was fitted with a robust drive chain in addition to the already widespread "free wheel control" clutch. The rider's comfort was enhanced by introducing the "ful-floteing" (sic) saddle, which rested on 14-inch spiral springs and could shift four inches up or down on a sprung seat post. In fact, this principle remained popular until the introduction of the Electra Glides in the 1960s!

The first perfectly functioning clutch mechanism, incorporated in the rear wheel, had finally eradicated the annoying shuddering of the engine when starting up. In addition, a new oil pump with a semi-automatic negative pressure system was installed in which the oil was precisely metered through a transparent glass container into the crankcase via a valve. In addition a hand pump was available for increasing power under extreme loads. With these features and the increased displacement of 60.32 cubic inches (988.55 cc), the engine was now competitive in all respects. The somewhat less powerful Model 8D with an engine displacement of 49.48 cubic inches (810.83 cc) was also still available.

In 1913 an improved single-cylinder Model 9 – also known as the "5-35" because of its power output of 5 horsepower from a 35 cubic inch engine – was built. This model was equipped with the mechanically controlled inlet valve already used in the twins, primary and secondary drive chains, a reliable twin-gear system with the familiar rear-wheel clutch and a Bosch high-voltage magneto, although this was later replaced with a similar American system from Remy or Dixie on account of the war. Its IOE engine displaced 34.47 cubic inches (565 cc), which marked the upper limit of modifications for this engine. However, the numerous improvements ultimately made the Silent Grey Fellow a sensational new product, celebrated and exalted accordingly both in test reports and in advertising. As for the color of the motorcycle, the company chose

Soon to become the most popular bike ever: the Silent Grey Fellow with its powerful V-Twin engine.

© *Harley-Davidson*

battleship gray, which had recently become fashionable, with only the design of the company emblem being varied.

1913, the year of the Model 9 series, was a successful year for the company, which had now manufactured almost 13,000 motorcycles. Harley-Davidson had become a major player in the motorcycle manufacturing industry, second only to Indian. By this time, however, the first signs of the coming recession could no longer be overlooked. Henry Ford had just installed the world's first assembly line for producing his famous Ford Model T automobile. A Harley-Davidson could be had for 200 to 300 dollars, plus another 75 dollars to upgrade it to a family or commercial vehicle by adding a robust sidecar. The Model T on the other hand, still cost 850 dollars. Over the years Ford's million-dollar machine was to become cheaper and cheaper. The people of America were quick to shift to the more comfortable automobile, sales figures of which in 1913 were already 30 percent up on the previous year. The motorcycle industry was threatened by this phenomenon and the first motorcycle manufacturers soon vanished from the market without a trace. Moreover, motorcycling outside the cities of North America was comparable with today's sport of motocross. A road network, such as was known in Europe, just did not exist, so there were limits to the enjoyment of motorcycling. After all, a car was much easier to control on those muddy tracks. Only Indian, Excelsior and Harley-Davidson were still able to record a growth in sales.

In 1908, the police of Detroit converted to Harleys. In 1909, the Cincinnati Police Department followed their example, at least as far as its summertime operations were concerned. It was a successful decision not only for the police but also for the company.

Racing and the Sidecar

Even in Britain Passion Becomes Respectable

The sturdy Harleys were used ever more frequently by companies for deliveries. This documentation is from the 1920s.

© Harley-Davidson

"The only motorcycle with a one-year guarantee!" was the slogan used by the London Harley import agent in 1915 to advertise the Silent Grey Fellow.

No matter what Harley–Davidson's original corporate philosophy was, racing was becoming ever more popular among the Milwaukee motorcycle scene – a fact that could no longer be ignored. Motorcycle magazines, local newspapers, advertising brochures and advertisements – all were filled to the brim with lively reports and sensational accounts of this spectacular sport. Admittedly, enthusiasm for some of the darker aspects of motorcycle racing was less marked, especially with regard to the wild events of the earliest races, but even these features greatly contributed to the success of one particular make of motorcycle. Fatal accidents and catastrophes were common in the extremely dangerous speedbowl races held in those wooden–paved "death bowls," and this exerted a peculiar hold over the fans, combining shock and morbid fascination. Harley–Davidson had long viewed such highly profitable popular entertainment as an unjustifiable alternative to conventional motorcycle racing and had rightly distanced itself from such sensationalism, despite the numerous private Harley riders involved in the sport. But with flat–track races on level, sandy, horseracing circuits

becoming more serious all the time and, above all, better organized, there was no denying the trend. The debate was long and heated, but the company executives ultimately decided to enter the attractive arena of motorcycle racing. However, they did this with their usual thoroughness and requisite technical expertise. To this end, William Harley lured Bill Ottaway, chief engineer of the Thor Motorcycle Division of the Aurora Automatic Machine Company, away from Aurora, Illinois and brought him to Milwaukee in the spring of 1912, appointing him Deputy Chief Engineer at Harley–Davidson. Bill Ottaway was a brilliant engineer whose moment of glory had finally come, under the patronage of Bill Harley. He immediately set to work with a vengeance, building up a perfect racing division with an equally perfect-ly drilled team. At the same time, he optimized the technology of the company's racing motorcycles, his expert eyes not missing the tiniest detail. However, it was mainly the tuned version of the 61 cubic inch (1000 cc) pocket–valve engine that later guaranteed the company's dazzling successes in the 11K racer of 1913 that provided testament to Ottaway's supremely inventive technical skills and the discipline of his racing team. The racing success of the Harley-Davidson Team, albeit not yet perfected, went on to earn worldwide acclaim in the year 1913. For Bill Ottaway, however, this "training year" was merely the beginning of a legendary career in motorcycle racing.

The standard road models also became more technically refined. The 1914 Model 10 boasted the first step-starter. This meant the rider could keep one foot on the ground when starting his machine, eliminating the need to raise the motorcycle up onto its kickstand. The engine was started by pushing a pedal forwards with the other foot. A well-designed system of pawls and cams prevented the machine from backfiring. Broad, fold-up footboards were attached to the motorcycle, so the rider could rest his feet when riding. The long-awaited brake and clutch foot pedals were also featured. Gears were shifted via a lever on the left of the fuel tank. A rod led to the rear wheel, the hub of which bore the integrated twin gearbox and clutch. The rear-wheel hub was also the location of the single brake, an effective combination for the period comprising a drum-shoe brake with an additional, tension-adjustable outer band. In view of this highly complicated technical solution, it is astonishing that nobody had come up with the easier alternative of a front-wheel brake system by this time.

With more and more families now able to afford the inexpensive luxury of a motorcycling adventure, sidecars soon became big business. The many firms that had long recognized the cost-saving combination as an ideal mode of transportation played more than a minor role in orchestrating this boom. Furthermore, the numerous styles of rig available made the motorcycle and sidecar or sidevan combination the perfect delivery vehicle for a host of applications. However, Harley-Davidson simply did not have the space to cater to the constantly growing demand, and was left with no choice but to outsource the greater part of its sidecar production to other companies.

Thus, a company that had been involved in making sidecars since 1910, Rogers of Chicago, received a commission for Harley sidecars. A first batch of 2,500 sidecars with reinforced chassis was delivered, but when another order for 5,000 sidecars was received in 1915, Rogers only managed to produce 3,000, also due to insufficient factory space. In the end, Harley sold 8,500 sidecars in the year 1915. The production of three-wheeled versions with front-mounted structures — so-called forecars or motorcycle trucks — were also quite successful. The four-wheeled cycle car, on the other hand, was more of a curiosity, and was never manufactured in large numbers.

Mr. Duncan Watson

The Debut of Exporting

After several exhaustive but necessary preparations, Arthur Davidson decided to try his hand at the export business. The first stop was in Great Britain, at a British importer called Duncan Watson, a shareholder of Robertson Motors in Great Portland Street in London. The first shipload of single-cylinder and twin-cylinder Harley-Davidsons from America arrived there in the spring of 1914. By this time, the country was already busily preparing for the approaching war and the entire British motorcycle industry had more or less halted civilian production. Knowing this, Watson expected the imported motorcycles to be a roaring success. The press was invited and encouraged to put the American motorcycles to the test: although not overly impressed by the rather "primitive" and robust single-cylinder models, they could barely contain themselves when it came to the 8 horsepower Big Twins. The test-riders from the press were loud in their praise of the handling and beauty of these machines. They were delighted with the smoothness of the clutch and some very non-British displays of emotion were encouraged by the comfortable riding position and the fold-up footboards. Only the twin-gears left some room for improvement when using a sidecar and the fuel inlet in the gas tank was considered a little too small. Otherwise, the unanimous verdict was that the motorcycle was incredible. Unfortunately, the war intervened and only 350 motorcycles reached Great Britain in time. Nevertheless, Duncan Watson remained dauntless and attempted to establish branch offices in Paris, Amsterdam, Brussels and Copenhagen — in vain as it turned out, since the military began running things in Europe.

Back from a hillclimb with the victor's trophy: a Harley sportsman in typical attire.

Harley's Early Racing Successes

Harry Ricardo Generates a Sensational 55 HP

The new three-speed transmission of the Model J was a major technical improvement.

Harley-Davidson made its official debut in the world of racing under the outstanding guidance of William "Bill" Ottaway. In the face of virtually overwhelming competition, primarily from Indian, Excelsior, Pope and Thor, Bill Ottaway was left with no choice but to employ a systematic approach to attaining his goal, with absolutely no compromise. He recruited the best motorcycle riders for his factory team, taught them, trained them and motivated them, with precise instructions concerning absolute loyalty to the company and disciplined behavior. Otto Walker, by then a legend in his own right, became team manager, with the team comprising Floyd Clymer, Harry Brant, Sam Corrento, Harry Crandall, Fred Ludlow, Paul Gott, Irving Jahnke, Ray Weishaar and Jim Davis, among others, as well as the superstar "Red" Parkhurst, who was renowned for his unswerving loyalty to Harley and his outstanding technical competence. This extraordinarily intense and, above all, harmonious cooperation on a personal level resulted not only in a seemingly unstoppable wave of victories and records, but also achieved precisely what Harley wanted: a flood of technical improvements to the product range and an enormous boost to the image of the company, together with an associated rise in sales figures.

In the first two years of Harley's racing participation, 1914 and 1915, hardly a race went by in which the Harley-Davidson factory team was not victorious, and usually by a substantial margin. Be it the overwhelming success in the 300-mile Dodge City Classic, the 300-mile race at Venice, California, the 200-mile race at Phoenix, Arizona or the 150-mile race at

Oklahoma City, Oklahoma, the team remorselessly steamrolled anyone and anything that stood between it and victory, a tendency which soon gave rise to its highly respectable nickname: "The Wrecking Crew." Bill Ottaway not only had the best motorcycle riders, but also the best motorcycles, fitted with a special racing engine.

During testing of the new high-performance eight-valve OHV engine which had been developed under Ottaway's guidance, one problem after another seemed to occur, mainly with the ignition. Overhead valves were indispensable in order to achieve higher performance. Performance could be increased further still if four, rather than two, valves were provided per cylinder, as was the case with the eight-valve racer.

Bill Ottaway had reached the limits of power yield with regard to the constantly improved pocket-valve twin-cylinder, and considerably more power was promised by the new principle, which had four overhead-controlled valves "suspended" in the combustion chamber (a principle Oscar Hedstrom had already employed in Indian engines in 1911). This principle was based on the momentous inventions of British motor engineer Harry Ricardo, who was considered a specialist in the field of combustion-chamber technology. When Bill Ottaway was finally lost for a solution, he asked Walter Davidson for permission to invite the amazing British engine specialist to America.

However, the latter was not really happy with this idea, particularly due to the high cost of Ricardo's sea passage and the unappetizing prospect of "foreign" involvement in his company. It wasn't until Bill Ottaway informed him that the 25,000 dollars already invested in development work would possibly be wasted that Walter Davidson gave in and authorized Ricardo's visit. The famous engineer soon arrived in Milwaukee and immediately set to work, with enormous success. The costly investment paid off quickly and the new Model 17 racer, with an eight-valve OHV engine, became an overnight sensation. In its first test runs, the 61 cubic inch (1000 cc) engine yielded an unbelievable 55 horsepower — even more amazing considering it was only 1915!

Whereas four years earlier Indian built the world's most powerful motorcycle engine delivering 35 horsepower, Harley-Davidson was now launching what was probably the most unbeatable racing engine of the day, albeit with one minor blemish. In contrast to other commercial racing motorcycles, such as Indian's racing model which cost "just" 350 dollars, Harley's new "Production Racer Sixty-One" was not for sale to just anyone, and when it could be purchased, the asking price was a hefty 1,500 dollars.

Harley-Davidson purposefully set the price so high in order to prevent publicity-seeking, inexperienced greenhorns getting hold of the deadly machine and possibly damaging the company's image with accidents. However, the Sixty-One virtually guaranteed victory for experienced racers, thus making it a sensible investment.

The highly productive cooperation between the two engine makers Bill Ottaway and Harry Ricardo was also extremely successful in terms of the normal motorcycle manufacturing sector. The year 1915 saw the debut of the Model J, which introduced a model range with continuously refined state-of-the art technology and the reliable 61 cubic inch (1000 cc) V-Twin engine — a model that was so successful that it remained in the company's product range until 1930. The most important modifications to this new model were a robust three-speed gearbox situated in the frame directly

Two famous racers and friends: Otto Walker and Dud Perkins.

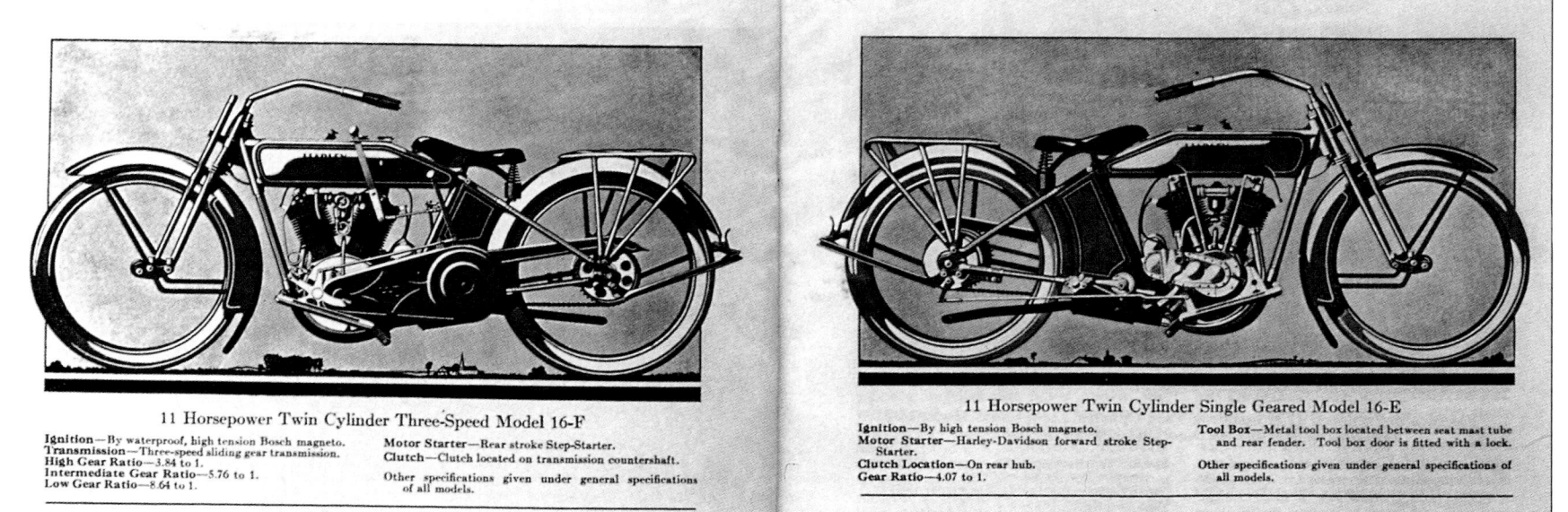

11 Horsepower Twin Cylinder Three-Speed Model 16-F

Ignition—By waterproof, high tension Bosch magneto.
Transmission—Three-speed sliding gear transmission.
High Gear Ratio—3.84 to 1.
Intermediate Gear Ratio—5.76 to 1.
Low Gear Ratio—8.64 to 1.

Motor Starter—Rear stroke Step-Starter.
Clutch—Clutch located on transmission countershaft.
Other specifications given under general specifications of all models.

11 Horsepower Twin Cylinder Single Geared Model 16-E

Ignition—By high tension Bosch magneto.
Motor Starter—Harley-Davidson forward stroke Step-Starter.
Clutch Location—On rear hub.
Gear Ratio—4.07 to 1.

Tool Box—Metal tool box located between seat mast tube and rear fender. Tool box door is fitted with a lock.
Other specifications given under general specifications of all models.

behind the engine and a multiple disk clutch. From then on, both of these features were representative of the characteristic shape of the primary chain case. The Model J was also equipped with a genuine kickstarter in 1916, replacing the old step-starter. In short, the Model J was the technically refined progenitor of all Harley-Davidson V-Twin generations to follow.

Harley's production figures once again reached fantastic levels: 16,427 motorcycles were built in 1914, 16,493 in 1915 and an amazing 19,924 in 1916. But the war began casting its first dark shadows over the

blossoming motorcycle industry. Imports of accessories ground to a halt, raw materials became scarce, the economy was hit by inflationary prices and the civilian market dwindled — the war had reached out and touched America with its blighting hand.

In the fall of 1916, a decision was reached by the FAM and motor-cycle manufacturers to halt all motorcycle races — military needs now had priority. So the first successful chapter in Harley-Davidson's racing history ended. The champions of the race circuits were now needed elsewhere...

Harley's technology profited enormously in the second decade of this century from the experience gained from racing. The photo shows the Models 16 E and F.

Ever victorious: the members of the famous Wrecking Crew. Shown here is the Venice Team with their mascot.

Baptism of Fire

Olive-Drab as a Symbol of Patriotism

Preparing for war: the light motorcycle cavalry practicing their shooting skills.

In April 1917 the U.S. entered the war. Up until then America had greatly supported its British and French allies with supplies of war material and in 1916 the motorcycle industry was also busy preparing for the expected military contracts. The olive–drab color scheme became symbolic of patriotic commitment and allied conviction. The management board of Indian, themselves not motorcycle riders, made the fatal mistake of giving government (i.e. military) manufacture priority over civilian orders and offered the U.S. Government the majority of Indian's enormous production capacity at ruinously low prices. Some 20,000 solo machines were to be sold to the Army at the rock–bottom price of just 187.50 dollars per motorcycle, with the matching sidecars costing just 49.50 dollars. Indian's huge dealer organization was left with virtually no stock whatsoever.

Harley-Davidson's senior management on the other hand, was more cautious, offering the government just 7,000 machines at a price that was still profitable to the company, with roughly 10,000 motorcycles still being allocated to the civilian market. It was not until mid–1917 that Harley-Davidson turned over 50 percent of its overall production capacity to the insatiable juggernaut of Uncle Sam's war machine.

All told, the defense procurement offices of the U.S. military — convinced of the varied military applications for motorcycles since the thwarted expedition to capture Pancho Villa — purchased 26,468 motorcycles from Harley-Davidson, 41,000 from Indian, 2,600 from Excelsior and some 200 lightweight two–stroke machines from Cleveland. Almost 20,000 of these motorcycles — mostly Harleys and Indians — were shipped overseas, although only 7,000 or so actually reached the battlefields of France. The majority were used in American military bases, by the pioneer corps or the supply and delivery services of field hospitals, as well as by the intelligence services. Several found their way to central America, to Cuba or Panama, as well as to the Philippines, with others being used (not necessarily for military purposes) by American military staffs in England. Even the Czarist military supposedly imported 65 Harley "motorcycle trucks" to Russia via the British exporter Robertson for transporting munitions.

One of the main problems following the introduction of the first motorcycles to military service was the lack of training facilities and servicing workshops. These were quickly established under the guidance of government appointee Thomas Calahan Butler, with a total of 3,000 or so mechanics and instructors being recruited to serve in these Training & Service Facilities. However, the majority of these facilities, which were mostly situated on the east coast, were not fully up and running by the time the war ended. Nevertheless, the idea proved its worth and the major motorcycle manufacturers built their own service schools immediately after the war, with Joseph Ryan being responsible for establishing Harley-Davidson's service school.

When hostilities came to an end, Harley had no great difficulty in resuming civilian production at full capacity: its civilian models were virtually identical to those for the military and the olive-drab color scheme remained very popular until the early 1930s. A sales network of more than 1,000 dealers ensured Harley the requisite turnover.

A military group photograph with a Harley.

All the photos on this double-page spread: © Harley-Davidson

The Motorized Infantry Units
Harley–Davidson versus Pancho Villa

To some extent, Harley–Davidson's baptism of fire, at least with regard to the military applications for its motorcycles, was provided by none other than Pancho Villa, the freedom fighter who took part in the 1910 Mexican revolution against the dictatorship of Porfirio Díaz. Angered by America's support of Mexico's ruling government, the "Bandito" general, backed by a strong force of followers, raided and plundered several townships along the border with New Mexico in 1916. During one attack on the town of Columbus, 19 people were killed, an action which almost brought the U.S. to the brink of war. Mexico's President Francisco I. Madero, whose deadbeat troops were unable to overpower Pancho Villa's Yaqui Indian strongholds, gave the American government permission to conduct military operations in his own country, in the hope of capturing the rebel leader and putting an end to this particular headache.

The U.S. Army dispatched a punitive expedition comprising 20,000 soldiers to the Rio Grande under the command of General J.J. "Black Jack" Pershing. This force was equipped with fast motorized units for rapid deployment in the otherwise impassable terrain and included roughly equal numbers of Indian and Harley–Davidson motorcycles, as well as a couple of Excelsiors. These comprised both solo motorcycles and motorcycle–sidecar combinations, some of which were heavily armored and fitted with machine guns and light cannons. These units were known as Mounted Infantry or Motor Mobile Infantry and were used wherever the heavier vehicles of the military force couldn't maneuver. But this was to no avail: not even these highly mobile units could capture Pancho Villa and his bandits. Villa was himself the proud owner of an Indian, so he was well acquainted with the way motorcycles might be used in warfare, as well as with the native mountains of his homeland.

Nevertheless, the ill–fated mission provided some useful lessons in tactics and logistics for the military, who were particularly impressed with the maneuverability and reliability of the motorcycle units and their steeds.

Ready for war: a sidecar combination in full military outfit.

35

The Superiority of the American Motorcycle Industry

When Harley-Davidson Was Simply the Best

Battalion of the Oregon Military Police with 12 Electrically Equipped Harley-Davidson Motorcycles and Sidecars
The Oregon military police protects the industries and wharves on the Portland water front. It also does forest protective work, ferrets out cases of disloyalty, and is ready for a call to any part of the state in case of emergency

The American motorcycle industry was the undisputed world-leader when the opening shots of World War I were fired. And there were several good reasons for this. First of all, the American products were designed to be extremely reliable and as comfortable as possible. The machines had to be powerful and reliable to cover huge distances under the poorest conditions imaginable, on virtually impassable roads in all weather. In other words, they needed a stable chassis, good front suspension (the existing rear suspension, as on the German NSU Army model, worsened the handling dramatically), as well as dependable and powerful engines. An electrical system that never malfunctioned was just as important in this context as thick tires and useful accessories. In sum, American motorcycles were practical in every respect.

Another reason was the American Standard System. America had gained plenty of experience regarding the logistics of military technology during the Civil War and that experience led to compatibility being viewed as an issue of utmost importance, i.e. the standardization of all technical parts, including tools and production machines. While European industry battled against a wave of ever more complicated patents with new designs being invented all the time, it had already been decades that all replacement parts in America were available, virtually unaltered, from every hardware store, and a potential buyer could rest assured that every screw or every spanner fit. This principle of compatibility was not only highly beneficial for the customers, but also for the manufacturers and dealers.

When World War I broke out, the European motorcycle industry was already caught up in a more-or-less destructive whirlpool of military production, while civilian and sporting requirements could still be catered to as before in the U.S. This was another reason why the American motorcycle industry had become an enormous force, dominating the entire world market. This success was partly attributable to the three largest companies, Indian, Excelsior and Pope, which were all adequately capitalized and had sufficient real estate and well-equipped manufacturing facilities right from the start.

Unlike European models, the most common American motorcycle models did not really differ from one another all that much in principle. The typical American motorcycle between 1914 and 1918 had a powerful, reliable engine, a simple three-speed gearbox, a chain and sprocket drive, an excellent front fork, a twist-grip for controlling the throttle and the ignition, a comfortable, broad, well-sprung saddle, convenient footrests and thick, oversized tires. The motorcycles were thus perfectly equipped for demanding journeys under the most extreme conditions, precisely this factor being decisive with regard to their military utility. This is where Harley-Davidson motorcycles once again entered into the equation; these were machines which had been developed and built consistently to cater to the needs of the customer and which had been marketed honestly and seriously. This quality soon catapulted Harley to the top of a gigantic motorcycle industry that was already populated by countless makes of motorcycle possessing roughly the same qualities: Flying Merkel, Henderson, Reading-Standard, Pierce, Yale, Thor, Dayton, Curtiss, Peerless, Militaire, Cyclone and Schickel, to name but a few of the more important ones. However, when it came to America's defense procurement offices and the huge purchasing power that they represented, only the very best was good enough and proof of adequate production capacity had to be furnished – a stipulation which literally opened the door wide to Harley-Davidson.

Recruiting officers were also under way in London to find new recruits.

The Failed Mission

In the Staff Headquarters of the Fifth Bavarian Division

In the wake of the patriotic celebration of the heroic experiences of Harley-Davidson riders during World War I, a famous and much-published photograph was taken that shows a motorcycle-sidecar combination next to a long military convoy of horse-drawn carriages obviously on the retreat. The handwritten note on the photograph read "The first Yank and Harley to enter Germany" and still bore the historic date of November 11, 1918 – the day on which hostilities drew to a close. The place and the name of the rider were then unknown.

It was not until 1944, when an elderly gentleman visited the editorial staff of the *The Enthusiast* with a request for some issues of the publication, that the identity of the unknown Harley rider was revealed. That very same gentleman turned out to be a businessman named Roy Holtz from Chippewa Falls in Wisconsin, formerly a U.S. Army dispatch rider with the rank of corporal who carried out his duties on a Harley-Davidson motorcycle-sidecar combination. Mr. Holtz went on to recount the following astonishing and highly amusing story to the editorial staff.

On the night of November 8, 1918, Corporal Holtz was ordered to chauffeur his lieutenant on a night mission. Their unit was positioned just short of the German lines at Spa in Belgium, and everyone expected the cease-fire to be declared at any moment. Nonetheless, they set off into the dark, rainy night, with the lieutenant riding in the sidecar. Unfortunately, it didn't take long for the dashing officer to lose his bearings completely in the dark. Corporal Holtz, familiar with the area from his dispatch duties, had no doubt whatsoever that they were heading straight for the enemy lines but was curtly told to keep his opinion to himself and obey his superior's orders. Some time later, they noticed a light in a farmhouse on top of a hill, and the corporal was ordered to go and ask where they were. Holtz knocked furiously on the door. However, when the door was opened, Holtz was not greeted as expected by a Belgian farmer, but by a group of dumbstruck German officers gathered around a card table. Unwittingly, Holtz and his lieutenant had stumbled across the headquarters of the Fifth Bavarian Division.

With a certain pleasure, Holtz called his "buddy" the lieutenant to join him and together the two entered what was truly to become an absurd period of captivity. Because Holtz – to the astonishment of all present – spoke remarkably good German, he was interrogated by a friendly Bava-

rian general, who served his captive a hellishly strong potato schnapps. The two unlucky prisoners of war were subsequently ordered to be escorted to the German headquarters in Spa. A German lieutenant had the embarrassing task of directing them to Spa from the hard and uncomfortable baggage rack of the Harley-Davidson motorcycle-sidecar combination, and eager for revenge, Corporal Holtz went out of his way on this frustrating journey to hit every single hole in the already badly damaged road.

Three days later, the war was over and Corporal Holtz and his lieutenant – both already posted as missing – were able to return to their unit. Alas, they were held up for an entire day in a small village on the Belgian border, where they were noisily celebrated as the first liberators. They then rattled along bumpy cobble roads past seemingly endless convoys transporting the defeated German army back to Germany. The famous photograph was most likely taken during Holtz's ride to the west, passing retreating Germans, to join the Allied advance.

An advertisement for the U.S. Army: the first motorcyclist riflemen honing their marksmanship.

The famous picture of Corporal Holtz.

© *Harley-Davidson*

The first Yank and Harley to enter Germany. 11/12/18

The Harley-Davidson Enthusiast

A motorized unit of the U.S. Army deploying in the first world war.

The Largest Motorcycle Factory in the World

Further Expansion – The Headquarters Become a Historical Monument

An uninterrupted flow of well-packed Harleys leave the factory in their shipping crates.

Praise be! The war was over, the Allies were victorious and those heroes who had survived the wholesale slaughter returned home with their heads held high and their chests swollen with pride. Everything was looking rosy.

Harley-Davidson had no great difficulty in returning to civilian production. After all, its civilian models were virtually identical to the military versions, and business was scarcely damaged by the fact that much of the military stock of Harley twins was now being sold off at bargain prices. Not so with Indian, which had geared just about all its production capacity to cater to military needs and now lacked the necessary stock for the all-important domestic market – a situation that threatened the livelihood of many Indian dealers. As canny and farsighted as ever, Arthur Davidson accomplished the amazing coup of winning over many of Indian's troubled dealers to his own company. He did this by offering them a rescuing hand in the form of exclusive – what else? – dealership agreements for selling Harley motorcycles. Harley-Davidson thus secured the largest dealer network in America.

Harley's huge sales network was organized along strict lines. The success and loyalty of the dealers was under constant scrutiny and the annually renewable franchise agreements were only guaranteed if the detailed reports of numerous district representatives were correspondingly positive. On the other hand, these district representatives assisted all dealers with technical and commercial problems, as well as advising them on financial matters and large-scale local operations.

The factory's PR office was generous in supplying its dealers with brochures, catalogs, user manuals and servicing instructions, as well as other literature aimed at promoting sales. Every customer was presented with an exhaustive Owners Manual and also received the company magazine – the *Enthusiast* – free of charge. By now, this had a monthly circulation of 50,000 copies. Exclusive accessories and fashionable Harley clothing could only be purchased from authorized dealers. Extensive advertising campaigns in magazines catering to popular science and hobbies supplemented this marketing strategy. In return, the dealers were expected to display unconditional loyalty to the company. The new and supremely important job of publicity manager was created and given to well-known motorcycling pioneer Julian C. "Hap" Scherer, whom Harley had headhunted from the Firestone tire factory.

In view of the highly promising and thoroughly optimistic forecasts, the four general directors abandoned their old and carefully maintained corporate policy of caution and thriftiness and took a leap forward of a previously unheard-of scale.

Armed with a huge line of credit from their bank Marshall & Ilsley (one mentioned the sum of three million dollars), an awesome L-shaped factory complex was erected in late fall of 1911 on Juneau Avenue and finished in 1914. The complex covered an overall area of 600,000 square feet and was up to six floors high in places. The factory still stands today – under national heritage protection – and serves as the corporate headquarters. The facility was designed according to the most modern principles of the day and was fitted with state-of-the-art automated machines. With a workforce of 2,400 blue-and white-collar workers, up to 35,000

Engine production in the factory, showing cylinders being inspected.

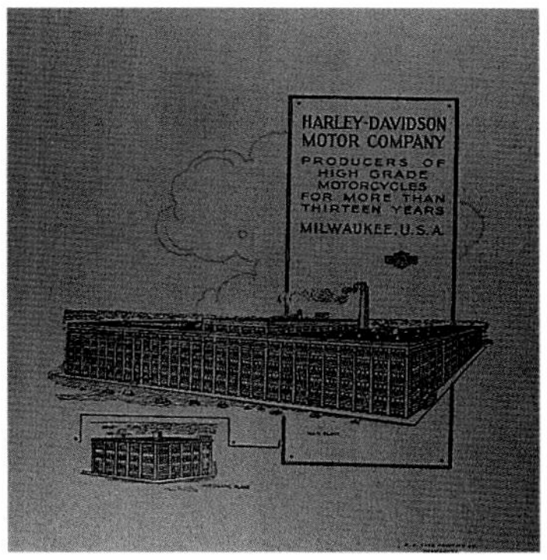

motorcycles could now be produced each year. Virtually overnight, Harley-Davidson became the largest motorcycle manufacturer in the world. The four unflagging company founders were finally able to congratulate each other – after just ten years – on having become the No. 1 in the motorcycle industry.

The strictly maintained principle of only manufacturing to the highest quality was refined to the point of perfection. Every innovation, large or small, was channeled into Harley's production as soon as it had proved itself in test and development. In this context, the company founders quickly terminated their previously happy relationship with a company called Remy, whose electrical products no longer met the required high standards. Instead they developed their own ignition systems and generators. When the new Harley electrical components were still proving trouble-some, the company secured the services of George Appel, an experienced electrical engineer who up until then had worked for Remy. Thanks to his know-how, the J-series models were improved. The J suffix signified the electric version, with battery ignition, lamps and a horn, while the F series continued to rely on magneto ignition. Harley's entire production capacity was focused initially on the 61 cubic inch (1000 cc) F-head V-Twins.

In 1919, the single cylinder was withdrawn from the market due to lack of demand and subsequently (until 1924) it was only supplied as the commercial CD model with a 21 cubic inch (350 cc) engine upon special request. More than 27,000 Harley-Davidson motorcycles were sold worldwide in 1920 – an unprecedented high point in the rising curve of the company's success story.

Harley-Davidson was keen to depict the enormous factory on as many company brochures and catalogs as possible, simply to provide an idea of its vast production capacities.

Great value was placed on meticulous inspection during the series production of individual parts.

The five-floor factory building on Juneau Avenue around 1910.

Manufacturing the frames.

The Sport Twin

Touring the Valley of Death

Hap Scherer on one of his PR rides.

© Harley-Davidson

In April 1919, Harley-Davidson unveiled a sensation. It rolled out a new, quite untypical — if not to say wholly exotic — all-purpose motorcycle into the booming marketplace: a motorcycle that caused both managers and designers alike to conclude that something fundamental had changed while they weren't looking.

Harley's new middleweight had a 35.64 cubic inch (600 cc) horizontally opposed flat-twin engine with an integrated three-speed gearbox and a multiple-disk wet clutch. The engine acted as a stress-bearing member within an open keystone frame. The chain and sprocket drive was totally enclosed within a chain case. The motorcycle weighed 265 pounds, yielded just over 6 horsepower and supposedly reach-ed top speeds of over 50 mph. Its excellent road-handling — a result of the low center of gravity of the boxer motor and the stiff frame – was further enhanced by a new Cushion trapezoidal fork. It was significantly named the Sport Twin and received the model designation WF (WJ with battery ignition).

To experts, it vaguely resembled the British Douglas, hitherto unknown in America, but it boasted such a wealth of technical innovations that the fleeting resemblance vanished upon closer inspection. Furthermore, the new flat-twin was a technical punch on the nose for the outdated opposed-twin Model O from Indian — a 3 horse-power lightweight machine based on the Douglas which had been pretty unsuccessful since its introduction in 1917.

Harley's new publicity manager Hap Scherer wasted no time in proving the reliability and speed of the new Sport Twin. He took advantage of the popular and highly-publicized long-distance record runs across America, events that generated a lot of publicity, particularly when the star of the scene, "Cannonball" Baker, was involved. On June 21, 1919, Hap Scherer rode a factory-prepared Sport Twin in the Three Flags Race which ran from the Canadian border to Mexico, setting a new record in this competition of 74 hours and 58 minutes to cover a distance of 1,689 miles. This victory gave rise to a stubborn rumor that Harley dealers throughout Southern California had reach-ed certain agreements with the otherwise strict highway police – who were renowned for mercilessly punishing every single speeding offense – whereby the police would look the other way in the case of Harley-Davidsons, so as not to hinder the sales-boosting victory...

With the help of the enthusiastic Harley dealer Walter W. Whiting, Hap Scherer struck again in spring 1920, covering the 1,224-mile run from Chicago to Denver, this time beating the existing record set by Floyd Clymer (on a Henderson Four) by sixteen-and-a-half hours.

However, the Sport Twin really shot to fame when outdoor pioneer Edwin Hogg decided to depart on a survey expedition of several weeks' duration in the hitherto unexplored Death Valley. He did not use the usual mule train, but instead relied on a single, lightweight motorcycle capable of handling extremely adverse terrain. Of course, the motorcycle he chose was none other than the new Sport Twin. On behalf of the Death Valley Railroad, the Tonopah & Tidewater Railroad and the Pacific Coast Borax Company, Hogg covered over 900 miles of tortuous desert, wearing out nothing more than a set of tires. After returning to civilization, he sent an exuberant and enthusiastic report of the fantastically reliable expedition vehicle to Lacy Crolins, then head of advertising for Harley-Davidson.

Yet for some reason, the Sport Twin was not the expected hit in its targeted market: young people, students, female motorcycle enthusiasts and sport-oriented tourists. In fact the ultramodern, avant-garde Sport Twin turned out to be a flop. Dealers and male motorcyclists still preferred the larger-capacity and more macho V-Twin. It almost seems as if the immortal myth of the powerful engine had worked its way a little too deeply into the hearts of bike enthusiasts. Ultimately, the highly celebrated Model W was withdrawn from Harley's program in the 1920s, despite the fact that export sales of the machine were wholly positive. But exports alone failed to justify the enormous technical effort and financial expenditure involved in its production.

Even the Postal Service made use of the reliable Sport Twins.

Cover of the *Harley-Davidson Enthusiast* from October 1920.

© Harley-Davidson

A Winner on All Fronts

23 Records in One Day at Daytona Beach

© Harley-Davidson

With an unusually generous annual budget of a quarter of a million dollars, the Harley-Davidson racing team evolved into a force of unprecedented power. Put on ice for the duration of the war, the legendary "Wrecking Crew" soon assembled again under the guidance of Bill Ottaway and his new team manager R. W. Enos and quickly got back to peak performance. With top riders such as Jim Davis, Ralph Hepburn, Walter Higley, Fred Ludlow, Otto Walker, Ray Weishaar and, of course, Leslie "Red" Parkhurst, they won one race after another, and were virtually unbeatable.

In addition to the tried-and-tested V-Twin racing motorcycle, the team now competed in ever more races with the new OHV eight-valve machine. Harley-Davidson motorcycles broke just about every existing record. However, it became apparent that this unsurpassed wave of victories was due less to the undeniably excellent technology and reliability of the factory racing machines than to the thorough and meticulously organized planning of Bill Ottaway before and during the races.

At the Ascot Park Race held in Los Angeles on January 4, 1920, Harley-Davidson not only won the race, but also secured second, third and fourth place, a real victory.

Fred Ludlow, Red Parkhurst and Otto Walker set a total of 23 new records at the opening of the race season at Daytona Beach on February 13 of that year, in the most abysmal weather conditions. The FAM had been disbanded in 1919 by the AMMA (American Motorcycle Manufacturers Association) on account of mismanagement and a new parent organization, the AMA (American Motorcycle Association), was founded, and these were their first officially recorded and confirmed results. These 23 records included the new top speed for a series production machine of 103 mph over one mile and 111 mph over seven miles with an eight-valve machine.

In the same year, Ray Weishaar won America's second most popular race after Dodge City on the excellently prepared five-mile circuit course at Marion in Indiana, with a four-minute lead. Spurred on by the cheering of the huge crowd, Weishaar relegated the previous favorite Indian to second place. William Harley and Arthur Davidson attended the race with all the other top executives and Indian's CEO Frank J. Weschler shook their hands with honest enthusiasm – a heartfelt gesture full of the sporting spirit of fair play.

On the occasion of this event, the local newspapers – for the first time – published rather modern-sounding cautionary notices: "To all race visitors! Beware of the highway police. Remember that functioning front and rear lamps are prescribed by law for all motorcycles, and that all sidecars also have to be fitted with a side lamp. Particular caution is recommended on the popular high-speed stretch of the Old National Trail, as the police set up speed traps along this stretch!"

The first high-speed races were held on wooden board tracks.

The Harleyquins

The Power of a Harley Can Make You Fly

Of the many military tales concerning Harley-Davidson motorcycles, one even dates from the Spanish Civil War. During the 1930s, Harley-Davidson sold its motorcycles via representatives in the cities Madrid, Barcelona and Seville to both the Fascist Franco regime (which was extremely embarrassing to the company and was supposed to be kept a secret) as well as to the constitutional government of the Spanish Republic.

During the siege of the fort at Toledo by the Fascists in 1936, the cadets defending the fortress removed the front and rear wheels from a VL model and used the engine to run a generator that maintained the fort's entire supply of electricity for several days. The engine was cooled using two normal household ventilator fans.

Another story mentions a flour mill that was also powered by one of the two Harleys in the fortress, thus providing the defenders with the flour needed for fresh bread each day.

Although never a subject of official interest for the company, certain ties nevertheless have existed between Harley-Davidson and the world of aviation.

When the British daily newspaper the *Daily Mail* announced in 1923 that it was holding a competition for light planes at Lympne Aerodrome in order to promote interest in low-cost aviation technology, the resultant wave of enthusiasm also swept across the Atlantic and reached the United States, where many unemployed military aviators from World War I were waiting for new adventures with bated breath. Once the engines had been limited to 750 cc displacement according to an announcement at the *Daily Mail* Air Show and the suitability of the engines used thus documented, Harvey Mummert, an aviation engineer at the factory of Curtiss-Wright Aviation in the United States, started work on a competitive ultra-light aircraft. Because Harvey was also an enthusiastic Harley rider, he decided to use a modified 61 cubic inch (1000 cc) J-series Harley twin engine for propulsion. Normally, such an unevenly firing type of engine was not suitable for powering aircraft, since it would literally shake the aircraft to pieces in the air. But not so in the case of Mummert's sport plane. He carefully balanced the crankshaft and discovered that the maximum propeller efficiency was achieved at a rate of just 1800 rpm. However, although Mummert's ultralight plane won several races and was otherwise a success at numerous air shows, it remained a one-off design.

The aviation pioneer Lester "Les" Long from Beaverton, Oregon, had more success with his light aircraft, which later became known as the Harleyquin Plane. Long modified an air-cooled opposed-twin-cylinder engine originally designed for propelling a boat, using Harley cylinders from the J series, as well as Harley pistons and other components. An elongated connecting rod gave his engine a displacement of 80 cubic inches (1311 cc) and he designed the crankshaft case himself. The entire engine weighed in at less than 90 pounds, yielded about 30 horsepower at 2750 rpm and cost – ready for installation – less than 100 dollars. In the early 1930s, Long tried to persuade Harley-Davidson to produce his Harleyquin, but to no avail – the company was not interested. Finally, Long produced several hundred engines on his own and the light Harleyquins soon earned a reputation for reliability throughout America. This was before Cessna claimed the lion's share of the business for itself.

Apparently, there were also other early experiments with Harley aircraft engines, such as the legendary three-cylinder radial engine. In the mid-1980s, Kris Kusto reported that an aircraft had been discovered that was fitted with a 1928 Harley-Davidson engine. Luckily, with the help of Harley expert Bruce Lindsay, the aircraft was rescued from a barn in almost pristine condition. In addition, issues of *Aviation Revue* dating from the 1920s and 1930s often contained reports of ultralight aircraft with Harley-Davidson engines.

To a certain extent, even the Red Army performed early aircraft trials with small aircraft powered by Harley engines. In a book written by Russian designer Alexander Yakovlev (known to Harley fans), he recounts how the former Chairman of the Revolutionary War Council and peoples' commissar Mikhail Frunse visited a Russian aviation training facility in the summer of 1925. Small, light planes were constructed at this establishment, being patched together from various spare parts. However, engines were in short supply, so the engines of motorcycles left over from World War I – mainly Italian Anzanis – were pressed into service and later fitted into aircraft manufactured by the famous designer Tupolev. Some of these engines included 13 horsepower Harley-Davidson models, obviously early twins. The test pilot W.P. Nevdatschin presented a light plane called the Burevestnik (Petrel) that was powered by one such Harley engine and made several demonstration passes over Moscow airport. Both pilot and machine survived in one piece.

Three-cylinder aircraft engine with
Harley IOE technology.

*Courtesy of: Dale Walksler/Wheels Through
Time Museum, Mount Vernon, Illinois*

The Exports

Sir Duncan Reigns at London's Harley Palace

The Harley During Prohibition

Standard Equipment of Bootleggers

© Harley-Davidson

The founders of Harley-Davidson were faced with a host of new problems in the early 1920s. The drastic drop in sales figures was taking a long time to rebound: 10,786 motorcycles were sold in 1922. Sales rebounded to 17,046 in 1923 and 17,648 in 1924, before dropping back again in 1925 to 15,731. The main cause was the conquest of the automotive market by Henry Ford's popular Model T car, which meant that the motorcycle was left, just as before World War I, as a vehicle for enthusiasts.

The expanded factory increasingly became a burden for Harley-Davidson: virtually the entire company's earnings were needed to pay off the interest on the loan. Major competitors, specifically Indian and Excelsior, had introduced successful new models onto an ever-shrinking market and the dealer network could no longer be maintained. Nevertheless, the shareholders reacted in their usual unshakable hands-on manner: they rolled up their sleeves and launched a series of aggressive advertising campaigns, including the publication of ads in major interregional daily newspapers for the first time.

The most significant factor in this context was export. Under the strict organization of Harley-Davidson's Traffic Manager Eric von Gumpert, who was actually responsible for the logistics side of shipping and sales, the old prewar contacts were reactivated and expanded around the world. The most important markets were Commonwealth countries, such as the Dutch colonies and the U.S. military bases in the Pacific, Canada, England, Australia, New Zealand, Burma, Malaya, Indonesia, the Philippines and South Africa. Business was also up and running in Europe by now, with Harleys being ordered from Ireland, Germany, the Netherlands, Belgium, Italy, Spain, Sweden and Denmark. Brochures, owners manuals, catalogs and servicing instructions were printed in seven different languages and 60,000 copies of the *Enthusiast* were ultimately distributed throughout 115 countries in 1925.

The energetic and wily importer Sir Duncan Watson, who had received a knighthood from King George V and was now Mayor of London opened a majestic sales emporium in Newman Street in London and devised plans for opening even newer outlets elsewhere. However, his activities and plans were dashed in spring, 1925 when Great Britain introduced a 33.5 percent import tax on all foreign motorcycles. Sir Duncan quit the services of Harley-Davidson.

In the meantime, Prohibition had swept over the U.S. like a tidal wave, leaving a trail of corruption and organized crime in its wake on a scale previously considered impossible. The black market flourished and hitherto incorruptible police officers degenerated into paid lackeys. The ban on alcohol brought about by the temperance movements, moralists, inhibited pietists, indignant feminist associations and eternal do-gooders plunged America and its people into sociopolitical disaster.

Today, we can look back on the Roaring Twenties with amusement but it can be argued that it was in that decade that America lost the moral innocence which had been so painstakingly striven for with the creation of the remarkable and unique Constitution.

Prohibition had devastating effects, particularly in Milwaukee, the largest beer-brewing city in the United States. Thousands of workers lost their jobs literally overnight and respectable brewers became disrespected and hunted bootleggers, as water and fruit juice alone could not quench the nation's insatiable thirst for alcohol.

Against this background, the moonshiners, engaged in a constant battle to evade the seemingly omnipresent law enforcement authorities, were anything but disappointed when Harley-Davidson launched its new, more powerful Big Twin Model JD onto the market in 1921, with a redesigned 74 cubic inch (1200 cc) F-head engine with an output of 18 horsepower, making it ideal for use with sidecars. The new Seventy-Four, even with a sidecar, easily managed speeds of 56 mph while a solo rider could count on 68 mph-plus. This factor, together with its maneuverability and off-road capability, soon made it a standard item with bootleggers. However, the true historic significance of this powerful motorcycle was that it went on to establish itself as the ancestor of all subsequent generations of Harley Big Twins.

Not only popular among bootleggers: the powerful Model JD.

Business as Usual

Meetings, Patents
and Boats for Two

The business world was offered all manner of motorcycle-sidecar combinations, such as the "Package Truck."

While the directors of Harley-Davidson were well aware of the predicament the motorcycle industry was in, the trade press — which ultimately survived from advertising — completely ignored the actual situation and continued to wallow in eulogies, naively optimistic forecasts, and equally pretentious and confusing reports of sales records. News of technological advances was put about with ever more original and falsified reports of success. One could describe this wishful thinking as a "journalist's wonderland."

When Norman G. Shidle, the publisher of the economic magazine *Automotive Industries*, produced his realistic market analysis in 1921 entitled "Where is the motorcycle going," a wave of (well-feigned) indignation was triggered — the industry was officially shocked and, above all, insulted. But even laymen recognized the writing on the wall as prices of Ford automobiles were dropping year after year and the public demand for used cars was increasing daily. Of course, the very same industry had already started to react to the situation unofficially. Although the bosses of Harley-Davidson maintained a reluctance of cooperating with the competition in any form whatsoever, they had in fact been meeting with other companies for a number of years, sometimes in New York, sometimes in Chicago, in order to facilitate a sound working relationship.

It was at one of these meetings that Walter Davidson promoted the idea that all authorized dealers, be they from Harley-Davidson or Indian, be encouraged to sell one brand of motorcycle. Indian's president Frank Weschler, well-acquainted with the problems of his own dealers, did not object to this view. As a result of this philosophy, many previously loyal dealers pursued other directions, albeit dealers that may have been generating significant profit for the company, which created some concern for the Harley-Davidson. However, despite the ramifications of this approach new business directions were often sought.

The fact that small motorcycle manufacturers were forced into bankruptcy was quite unfortunate but typical for tough competition and business.

In 1922, the most inexpensive Harley-Davidson motorcycle, the 61 cubic inch (1000 cc) model with magneto ignition, cost 335 dollars. The most expensive, the 74 cubic inch (1200 cc) JD with battery ignition, cost 390 dollars. These prices corresponded roughly to those for the equivalent models from the competitors Indian and Excelsior. At the beginning of the 1920s, a new Ford automobile could be bought for around 400 dollars.

In the meantime, sidecar production had also gained greater economic significance for Harley-Davidson. In 1921, the company commissioned its supplier firm Rogers to build wide-bottomed sidecars for two passengers. It is unlikely that these were used for transporting illicit alcohol as government agents would have had little trouble in catching such a ponderous vehicle. In general, however, the motorcycle-sidecar combination was soon regarded as the ideal solution for quickly solving transportation and supply problems. The Seaman Body Company (later to become Nash Motors) manufactured the most bizarre attachments and rigs for different firms to fit on sidecars, such as cameras, shoe stands, and the highly popular ice cream and candy stalls. This was not the case abroad though, where the three-wheeler became the lightweight transporter of choice. As reported by Jerry Hatfield, a Soviet government official named Karsov purchased 1,200 sidecars via the British Harley agent Charles Cartwright with a loan from a New York bank.

In 1924, Harley-Davidson was forced to produce its sidecars itself once more. Following the death of B.F. Rogers, the long-established metalworking company was sold and the new owner was more interested in manufacturing other, more profitable, products. On the whole, 1924 was a turbulent year for Harley-Davidson. Victor Bendix of the

A broad variety of specially manufactured sidecar models was available. Right: the catalog picture of a sidecar manufactured especially for the Fanny Farmer Inc. candy factory in Rochester, NY.

Eclipse Machine Company in Elmira, New York, sued Harley for infringing the patent of several details of his clutch design for the absolutely lethal sum of 1.1 million dollars, possibly in the hope of an inexpensive takeover if he succeeded. It was not until five years later, with a part payment of 18,000 dollars, that Harley-Davidson managed to extricate itself from this unpleasant affair that had hung over the company like the sword of Damocles. The clutch design was quickly changed and patent rights in general were now treated rather more carefully than they had been in the past.

In 1927, the motorcycle manufacturer Ace went bankrupt and was taken over by Indian, which led to the original Ace inline four–cylinder model becoming the Indian Four. Ace's former development engineer Everett O. DeLong got a temporary job at Harley, commissioned secretly to develop new prototypes in total isolation. DeLong initially designed a four–cylinder inline engine, but this was rejected on the grounds of excessively high manufacturing costs. A quite advanced V–four engine, with two J–model engines placed side–by–side on a joint crankcase, also failed to win the approval of William Davidson and all documents, including the models, were destroyed.

The thoughts of the bosses at Harley were increasingly shifting in a different direction. Impressed by the sales success and public response to the lightweight and middleweight motorcycles of Indian and Excelsior, they hoped to be able to open up additional markets, particularly overseas, by building similar models. William Harley and Walter Davidson visited Western Europe to study the situation, while sales manager Eric von Gumpert did the same in Southern Europe and Arthur Davidson departed on a long fact–finding journey to Australia and New Zealand, where flat–track speedway racing was extremely popular, especially with British single–cylinder machines.

A striking advertisement: a milk bottle as a transport container.

The Alternative to the Single-Cylinder Prince

At Last a Front-Wheel Brake for the Big Twins

No sooner had Harley-Davidson recovered some of its former strength in the mid-1920s than the research and development department was directed to design — as quickly as possible — an alternative to Indian's increasingly successful single-cylinder Prince, a 21.25 cubic inch (350 cc) lightweight side-valve single-cylinder motorcycle.

The result was the Twenty-One, which made its debut in Harley's product range in 1926 and was immediately and enthusiastically advertised as a lightweight motorcycle similar in design, but technologically superior, to the Prince. The Harley had a displacement of 21.10 cubic inches (345.73 cc). The economical side-valve model, which actually sold better and was popularly used by the postal service, rural delivery services and dispatch riders, cost 210 dollars in the basic version, with the racier and somewhat faster (up to 60 mph) OHV Models AA and BA costing 250 and 275 dollars respectively. Much like the Prince, both engines had removable cylinder heads and the combustion chambers had been designed according to Harry Ricardo's latest recommendations.

This design meant that the side-valve model, which initially tended to destroy the pistons at continuous high speeds, was easy to repair, although many experienced workshops replaced the susceptible gray cast iron pistons with superior models from Oldsmobile as a precautionary measure, or offered these pistons to skilled hobby mechanics as "optional extras" to install themselves. The more reliable OHV model was spared this problem because of its modern, high-performance aluminum pistons.

The Model AA subsequently gave rise to the famous flat-track and hillclimb racing motorcycle with the legendary name of Peashooter. The name derived from the characteristic dry staccato noise that came from its short exhaust pipe, which sounded like shots from the revolver of the same name.

At about the same time, the racing department was busily working on a considerable improvement to the 61 cubic inch F-head engines under the management of Arthur A. Constantine. Although the R & D department was neither willing nor able to make large investments at this time, the necessity of introducing technical innovations in the still-dominant IOE racing motorcycles was something that was generally acknowledged. In this vein, a twin-cam valve-control system had already been introduced in 1924 with four lifter arms — a system that was adopted as a twin-cam version in the Model J production range in 1928 following its successful racing trial.

The new 74 cubic inch JDH Two-Cam engine made its debut in 1928.

In the meantime, Arthur Constantine was working on a new and improved design for a small-capacity V-Twin engine. However, a dispute arose between himself and Harley's bosses concerning the project, so he took his skills to Excelsior, together with all his design documents, where he was welcomed with open arms by boss Ignaz Schwinn and his chief engineer Arthur Lemon. Not long after, the new 45 cubic inch (750 cc) Super-X V-Twin was launched onto the market, becoming a commercial hit virtually overnight.

For the time being, Harley was content with countless improvements to and new features for its well-established Model J series Big Twins. These were fitted with balloon tires, a more robust clutch, a streamlined teardrop tank with two lateral recesses for the top-mounted rockers, the revolutionary Alemite lubrication system (a dry-sump throttle-controlled oil pump), twin-fork suspension, an extremely low saddle, twin mufflers, a mileage counter and speedometer and, from 1928 onwards, an auxiliary brake on the front wheel for the first time ever — an addition that had previously been considered unnecessary, if not downright dangerous.

Also in that same year, the new twin-cam models, known as Two-Cammers were finally available for sale to the general public as the Model H: the two models were the 61 cubic inch (1000 cc) JH and the 74 cubic inch (1213 cc) JDH.

The bike that forced Harley to react: Indian's "Prince."

The two new 21.5 cubic inch single-cylinder models: the OHV Model BA and the SV Model A (far right).

Opposite: all photos are courtesy of Max Middelbosch, Zwolle, Netherlands.

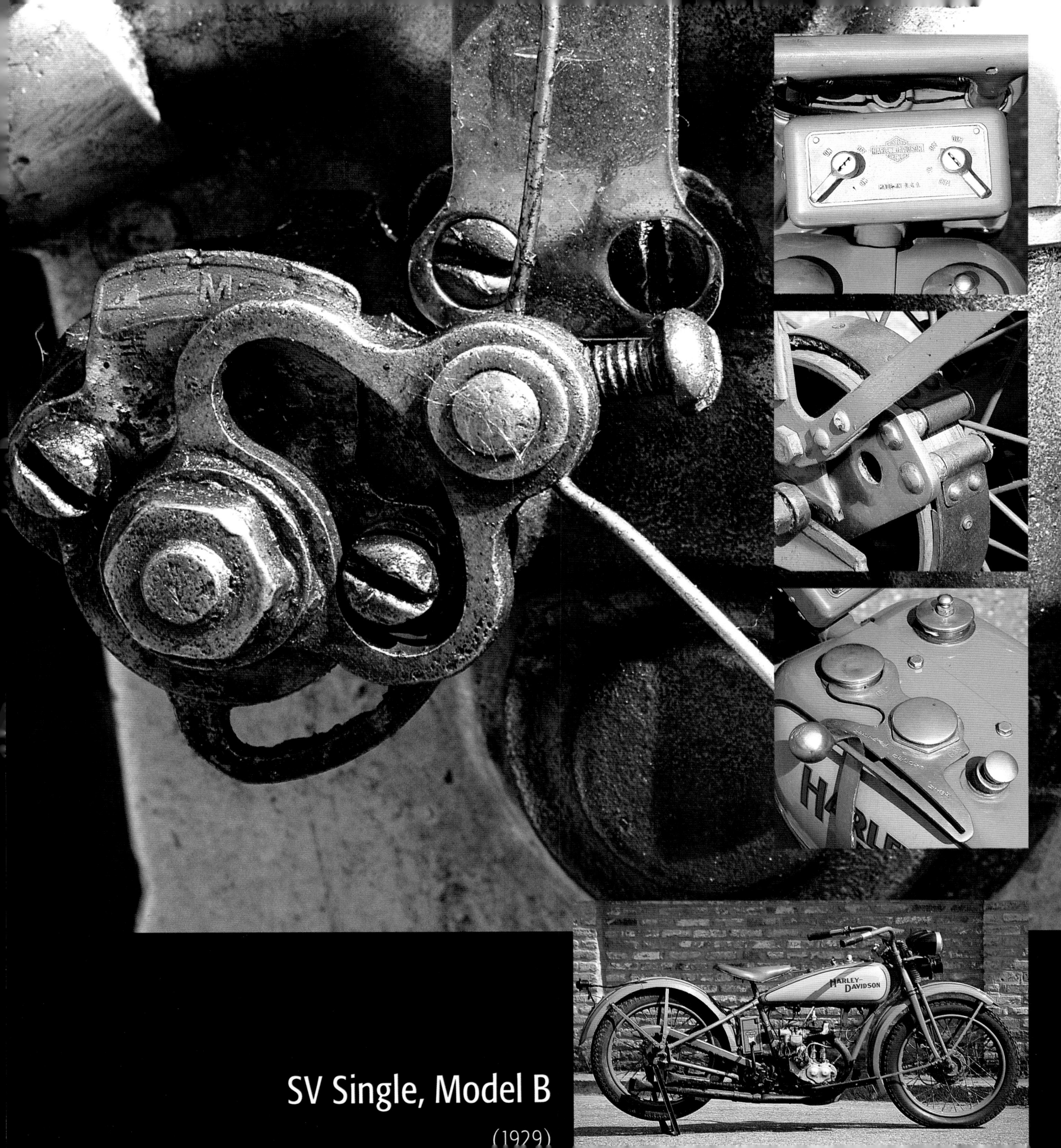

SV Single, Model B

(1929)

The Dawn of the Big Twins

The Timeless Stars of the Past Are Today's Classics

It seems somewhat peculiar that Harley-Davidson toyed with the idea of introducing an inline four-cylinder engine in 1928 of all years — a year in which the signs of an impending economic crisis were already more than obvious. Perhaps it was merely because Harley was now in a position to purchase the Cleveland Motorcycle Manufacturing Company which had already been building high-quality inline four-cylinder models for quite some time but was now experiencing financial difficulties and was up for sale. However, the management eventually abandoned the idea (probably because Harley had already developed its own blueprints along similar lines) and concentrated fully on a new project that justifiably gave rise to great expectations. In 1929, Harley-Davidson released what was probably the most successful motorcycle of the period up to and including World War II: the Model Forty-Five, with a newly developed 45 cubic inch (750 cc) side-valve engine. This was produced in huge numbers as an unflagging workhorse and continued to be used in Servi-Cars until 1973.

The main reason for Harley-Davidson changing from the old F-head engines to the new, but not necessarily modern, side-valve engines, instead of the more advanced OHV models, was probably the enormous success and widespread popularity of the Indian 45 cubic inch (750 cc) Scouts and the 61 and 74 cubic inch (1000 and 1200 cc) Chiefs, all of which were side-valve models and much loved by the American public.

Indian's side-valve motorcycles were also often superior to the otherwise highly praised OHV machines in racing competition. And when it came to the rough business of everyday working life and having to cover long distances, motorcycle riders much preferred the considerably calmer, quieter running, and more robust side-valve models. Furthermore, there was definitely some concern of what might happen if one of the overhead valves in an OHV engine actually dropped into the combustion chamber in the event of engine damage — not a pleasant thought, particularly when miles away from the destination or civilization.

Things looked promising to start with — the Forty-Five, as it popularly became known, was available in three versions (all with electric systems and the typical twin headlamps): the Model D, with a lower compression ratio of 4.3:1, was sturdy and reliable, if somewhat less powerful due to its mere 14 horsepower, while the Model DS was suitable for pulling a sidecar and had a shorter transmission. Finally, there was the Model DL which, with a higher compression ratio of 5:1, could be called the racer version of the three. The compression ratio of this latter model was later

A modern outfit with twin lamps, teardrop fuel tank and lowered saddle: the side-valve V model 74 from 1930.

increased to 6:1 in the DLD version. In general, however, all models were fitted with the rather modest 45.32 cubic inch (746.63 cc) V–Twin side–valve engine, which was nevertheless technologically superior to its main competitor, the less powerful Indian 101 Scout, and power was in vogue with the speed–freaks in those days.

The dilemma faced by Harley-Davidson was that the company wanted to cater to everyone's tastes and simultaneously launched an improved version of the Twenty-One onto the market, the Model C. This had a robust 30.1 cubic inch (500 cc) side–valve engine, yielding 12 horsepower, a three-speed gearbox and it soon became known as the Baby Harley or the Thirty-Fifty.

Although sensible in theory, Harley's plans to design both single-cylinder and V–Twin machines that were almost identical except for their engines, thus making almost all parts compatible between models, proved anything but easy to implement in practice. The robust chassis was too heavy for the 30 inch single-cylinder and slowed it down way too much, while the well-designed gears and clutch from that model were not up to the task in the Forty-Five.

Dealers throughout the country inundated the Harley factory with complaints of constant technical difficulties and exasperated customers. As if that wasn't enough, attempts to link the new twin to a sidecar proved to be catastrophic. Even when fitted with an ultralight sidecar, the machine was unable to cope with the slightest incline with an extra passenger on board. Luckily, this soon changed in 1929 when Harley unveiled its first Big Twin — the heavy 74 cubic inch (1200 cc) side–valve Model VL. With an impressive 26 to 28 horsepower and weighing in at around 550 pounds, the VL was truly worthy of membership in the heavyweight class of motorcycling. Indian's Chief, the hitherto uncontested market leader in this class, had finally met its match! Even to this day, the VL styled by William Harley and Bill Ottaway is still considered one of the most beautiful Harley classics ever built.

And despite the fact that the VL (3.44 in/88 mm bore, 4.0 in/102 mm stroke, 73.71 cubic inches/1208.19 cc displacement) was plagued by numerous teething troubles, it nevertheless heralded the breakthrough into a new era. However, this new era began with a development that nobody had expected: on Black Friday in October 1929, the bankruptcy declaration of the American national bank plunged the entire U.S. economy into its greatest catastrophe ever — the Great Depression, which in turn ushered in an economic crisis of global proportions.

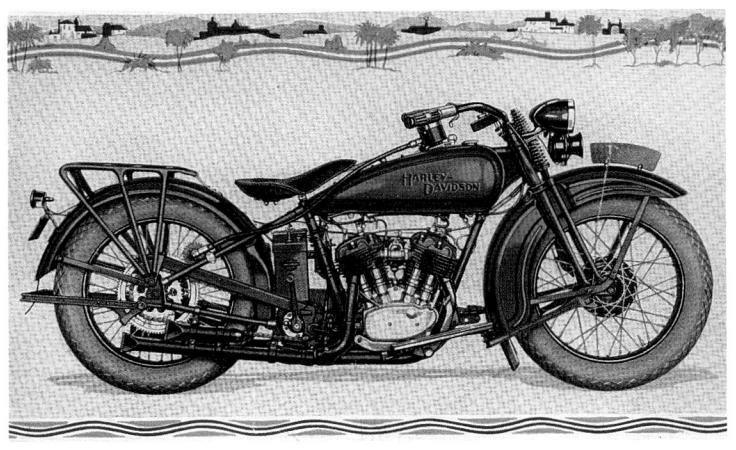

SWOOP LIKE AN EAGLE!

Split the wind, with the keen air fanning your face, and the red blood zipping through your veins!

In all the sports, there's no thrill like motorcycling—astride a 1931 Harley-Davidson. Here is speed that just melts the miles—power that laughs at hills — getaway that nearly takes your breath away.

Let your nearest Harley-Davidson Dealer show you the amazing new Twins, and the thrifty Single. Ride one or all of them—see how easy they are to handle—get the thrill of their performance. See him soon.

Mail the Coupon for Illustrated Literature showing the new 1931 Motorcycles and Sidecars.

Ride a **HARLEY-DAVIDSON**

HARLEY-DAVIDSON MOTOR COMPANY
Dept. P., Milwaukee, Wis.
Interested in your motorcycles. Send literature.

Name

Address

My age is ☐ 16-19 years, ☐ 20-30 years, ☐ 31 years and up, ☐ under 16 years.
Check your age group.

The Typical Family Response

Gypsy Tours and the Demise of the Olive-Drab Color

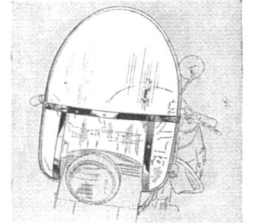

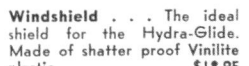

Windshield . . . The ideal shield for the Hydra-Glide. Made of shatter proof Vinilite plastic $18.95

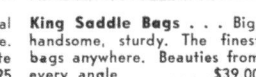

King Saddle Bags . . . Big, handsome, sturdy. The finest bags anywhere. Beauties from every angle $39.00

HARLEY-DAVIDSON
JACK PINE WINNERS

1. Oscar Lenz, winner in 1923, '25, '26, '27, tied in '32, and top man again in '35 and '36. 2. Ted Konecny, now a Sergeant in Italy, won the coveted cowbell in 1938 and again in 1940. 3. Introducing another ace Jack Pine competitor — Dan Raymond of Muskegon, the champion in '28 and '29, '31, tied in '32, and high scorer in 1933. 4. In 1930, the cowbell left Michigan for the first time when William H. Davidson, now president of the Harley-Davidson Motor Co., emerged the winner. 5. In 1941, Don Loucks of Grand Rapids, Mich., rolled up the best score. 6. Presenting a Saginaw, Mich., rider, William Muehlenbeck, Jr., who won in 1937 and again in 1939. 7. The second and only other time the cowbell left Michigan was in 1934 when Wisconsin's outstanding rider, Ray Tursky of Madison, beat the field. These, indeed, are heroes of the Jack Pine Trail!

For the first time ever, the future President William H. Davidson won the famous "cowbell" trophy in the 1930 Jack Pine competition.

The women of the Buckeyes Girls Club proudly pose in their award-winning outfits.

The initial reaction of the motorcycle industry, or what was left of it, was to act as if nothing had happened. Indeed, Harley-Davidson advertised its new products with greater energy than ever before. In 1930, William Herbert Davidson, the son of William A. Davidson, won the Jack Pine Enduro competition against Oskar Lenz who came in second, also on a 45 cubic inch (750 cc) machine. Joe Petrali, now also employed at Harley-Davidson, confidently rode to victory in one hillclimb or flat-track race after another, soon making him the darling of the public.

At the start of the 1930s, America was home to some 300 motorcycle clubs, most of which were dedicated either to Harley-Davidson or Indian, and both companies tried as best they could to motivate their dealers to become involved with these clubs and organize so-called Gypsy Tours — joint visits to races and other motorcycling events.

With a highly diversified roster of various accessories that were only available for purchase from authorized dealers and at discounts far exceeding those granted on motorcycle sales themselves, Harley-Davidson attempted to reinforce the brand loyalty of its existing customers, while winning over sufficient new customers to safeguard the livelihood of its dealers. New catalogs were printed all the time, depicting ever more colorful and more or less useful Harley accessories aimed at enticing customers and encouraging riders of other motorcycles to switch sides and experience the thrill of a Harley-Davidson.

However, Harley chiefly owed its survival in those days to numerous large orders from the police, mail delivery services and other official organizations, who were delighted with their representative large-caliber Harleys, fitted with a host of special equipment and bought at special terms. The company also made a good profit on the highly popular Servi-Car, a multipurpose cargo three-wheeler fitted with the economical 45 inch (750 cc) side-valve twin. Nevertheless, widespread unemployment and the acute market crisis ultimately eroded even Harley's sales figures: whereas 10,407 machines were built in 1931, only 7,218 left the factory in 1932, with the figure plummeting in 1933 — the worst year of all — to a mere 3,703 of the total of 8,000 motorcycles produced in the U.S. that year.

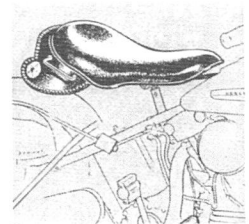

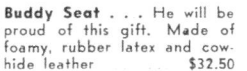

Buddy Seat . . . He will be proud of this gift. Made of foamy, rubber latex and cowhide leather $32.50

Cyclette Cap . . . A beautiful asset to her riding outfit. Choice of many stunning colors $3.50

Goggles . . . Protect the eyes from sun glare, wind and dust. A must for every motorcyclist $9.95

© Harley-Davidson

Ignaz Schwinn of Excelsior had already closed its doors in 1930 and Henderson had also shut down its factory. Only the four–cylinder models continued to be popular with the police. Of America's motorcycle manufacturers, only Harley-Davidson and Indian were left, and both fought desperately to survive. Harley-Davidson introduced short hours in order to avoid massive layoffs. With the factory now only running at a fraction of its full capacity, some workers reported for work just two or three times a week. But at least they had work to go to, and they remained loyal to the company.

During this time, Harley was untiring in its search for new sources of income. One such source came in the form of license fees paid by Richard A. Child for the manufacture of Harley copies in Japan. The fees brought in up to 10,000 dollars a year and more than 32,000 dollars for machinery no longer needed in Milwaukee.

By now, the leading paint manufacturer and giant of the chemical industry, E. Paul DuPont, a long–time motorcycling enthusiast and Indian fan, had taken over the Wigwam, as the Indian factory in Springfield was known. The first result of this takeover became noticeable when Indian's product range was suddenly enhanced by splendid new richly–colored finishes. Harley immediately accepted the challenge and by the year 1932, all models were available in an entire range of different and vibrant colors. The Brewster green so reminiscent of its military origins had finally had its day. What's more, special paint finishes in the most tempting color combinations could be ordered for a small added charge (around 20 dollars). Various combinations of standard finishes in vermilion red or azure blue, adorned with stripes in gold, black, silver or copper, provided potential customers with a new impetus. Even cadmium–rimmed wheels were now available instead of the usual painted ones.

Following a two–year market absence, an improved version of the 21 cubic inch (350 cc) Model B was available in 1932 at the giveaway price of 195 dollars. At the same time, the manufacture of industrial engines was halted. The main reason for this step was the cancellation of all orders from Sears-Roebuck, who wanted larger, more powerful engines for its tractors.

William H. Davidson posing on his Flathead in front of the factory.

During the Depression Harley-Davidson tried to attract customers with price reductions.

The Stressful 1930s
Living With and From the Economic Crisis

With the euphoric tide of expansion having receded and the newly built factory running at only ten percent capacity in 1931, the first major test of Harley-Davidson's stamina quickly returned the company to the hard world of economic reality.

However, Harley-Davidson had long been too big to simply perish like so many of its competitors. Its founders were also thankfully blessed with sufficient stubbornness, frugality and prudence to press on in the face of adversity. In fact, they had very little choice in the matter. Although the financial well-being of every family member was adequately safeguarded by the ownership of real estate, equity and holdings, the banks still persistently demanded their interest payments and for Harley's thoroughly correct founders, concerned as ever for their good reputation, this represented an imperative obligation to keep the company going. The sale of their empire, built up painstakingly over the years, was as a matter of principle simply not a subject for discussion for the owners of Harley-Davidson. They were determined to remain on their original course without compromise.

Furthermore, the prospects for the future were anyway not that bad. With the exception of Indian, the competition had been virtually eradicated and the export business was getting off to a good start, despite a few fluctuations and problems caused by wars and import regulations. The Japanese branch managed by Richard A. Child continuously passed on contributory payments and license fees and still ordered many engines and motorcycles. More and more police departments and other public services were equipping their motorcycle pools with Harleys. The company still kept a tight rein on its dealers, who ensured that the best possible sales figures were achieved, while intensive advertising and a rich array of Harley accessories and stylish clothing strengthened the bond between the company and its customers. Brand image and brand exclusiveness were the catchwords of the day.

On the other hand, threatening clouds were gathering on the politico-economic horizon. The Great Depression had inflicted incalculable damage, the unions grew powerful and were now able to enforce their demands more frequently. A frustrated director summed up this predicament by saying: "On the one hand, we can't raise our prices — on the other hand, we can't cut our costs!" Harley was in a Catch 22: the cost of mater-

ials was going up while the sales price was going down. As if this wasn't enough, the motorcycle market had developed its own set of laws. The customers had changed, and their demands had changed with them. The dealers were not only faced with problems, but also caused problems themselves. The general interest in motorcycle racing either declined or refocused on other types of sports. The fratricidal war with Indian was a drain on strength and on the loyal employees and ultimately damaged not only Harley-Davidson, but the entire motorcycle industry as well.

Today, it seems an easy matter to pass judgment on the sense or absurdity, the right or wrong of Harley-Davidson's corporate policy and business decisions back then. But regarded historically, those policies and decisions proved successful in the final analysis. It was a merciless strategy aimed at nothing less than sheer survival. Granted, it had its price, but it also had its rewards.

Despite this bitter struggle, or perhaps precisely because of it, Harley-Davidson truly shined in the 1930s, making, in the eyes of Harley enthusiasts, the most splendid and reliable motorcycles in the world. Only Brough Superior and Vincent-HRD in Great Britain and BMW and Zündapp in Germany built to the same standards, although friends of the Indian marque saw things a little differently!

Always on Call: the Servi-Car

More Than Just an Annoyance to Parking Offenders

Owning a Servi-Car promised lucrative business opportunities. Of course, the appropriate livery was also obligatory. The robust steed was virtually unequaled for delivery and tow services.

© Harley-Davidson

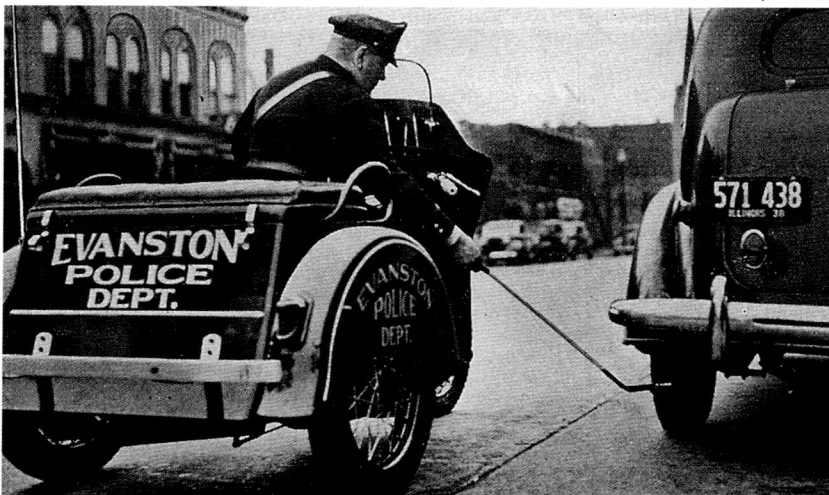

The number of parking offences in Evanston dropped once Servi-Cars were used to mark the tires of parked vehicles.

The global economic crisis had reached its peak in 1933 by which time President Roosevelt had declared his New Deal. Harley-Davidson produced a mere 5,690 motorcycles, of which only 3,700 were actually sold. The entire company was locked in a desperate struggle for survival. Export orders from South America, Japan, Spain, Germany, the Netherlands, and Scandinavia provided some glimmer of hope, but Harley was still forced to cut the salaries of all office workers earning more than 100 dollars a month by 10 percent. In a truly exemplary show of cost-cutting solidarity, the four founding members also cut their own salaries by half.

The 45 cubic inch (750 cc) V-Twin D series made room for the improved Model R series: the high-compression RL (5.1:1) and RLD Sport (6:1), as well as the standard R and lower-geared RS for use with a sidecar. However, the faithful workhorse among Harley-Davidson engines was now tasked with yet another role — one which it would fulfill until 1974.

In the year 1932, Harley-Davidson launched its latest model in the G series — the Servi-Car: a sturdy, easily handled three-wheeler with chain drive and a differential, fitted with a roomy cargo compartment and powered by the hard-wearing, low-compression 45 cubic inch V-Twin side-valve engine, which was proverbially everlasting. The demand for an inexpensive, reliable and simple mode of all-weather transportation was greater than ever at this time and the Servi-Car ingeniously fulfilled these prerequisites perfectly. The Servi-Car was initially envisaged more for use by municipal traffic authorities than by anybody else. The traffic departments had long been on the lookout for a slow vehicle from which traffic cops could mark parked automobiles while driving past so that they could be identified for fining later on. Armed with their chalk marker sticks, these particular cops soon became the scourge of all parking offenders, who parked their cars longer than allowed, while the many female parking-meter attendants retained their popularity as attractive meter maids.

The commercial use of the Servi-Car soon developed into a booming success. Although it initially aroused little enthusiasm among dealers, it was quickly accepted by a broad array of traders and craftsmen. Just like its predecessor, Indian's Dispatch Tow, the Servi-Car was also fitted with a tow-bar with which the automobiles of the day, susceptible as they were to technical faults, could be towed home. A telephone call was all it took — one mechanic could handle everything.

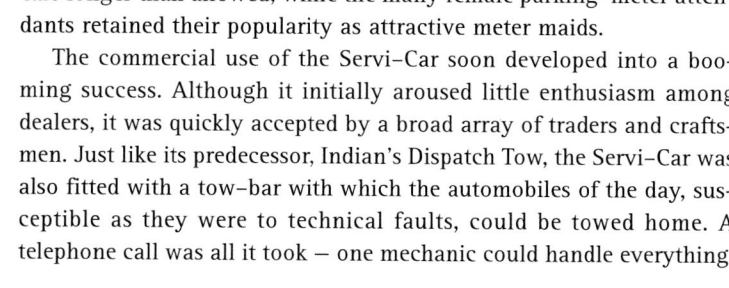

Knucklehead F/ FL

(1941 – 1947)

The Far East Adventure
Emperor of Japan to Disappointed Homecomer

Harley-Davidson service in Tokyo! Here we see the sales and service force of the Harley-Davidson Sales Co., Tokyo, Japan. This famous establishment is renowned for its service which covers the whole of Japan. Sixth from the left (sitting) is Mr. A. R. Child, business manager. On his right, is Mr. Fukui, director.

U.S. Navy Admiral Harry Jarnell is escorted to his departure from Shanghai in 1939 by a Chinese motorcade.

Rich Child leaves Yokohama in 1936 on board the "Empress of Britannia," together with his new sidecar combination.

Unequivically, no other outsider played as significant and dramatic role in the export business of Harley-Davidson's early history than Alfred Rich Child, an avid Harley rider, adventurer, self-made man, sales genius and globetrotter.

An unconventional man indeed, Child's path through life was certainly no less unconventional. Born the son of a naval officer in England and meticulously brought up in a cadet academy, Child ran away from home in 1907 and subsequently arrived in New York without as much as a dime to his name. After stints working as a butler and as a salesman of small hardware goods and bicycle accessories, Child applied for work at Harley-Davidson and was appointed regional representative for the Southern States.

He first proved his undoubted sales talent in 1921 on a trip to Africa, where he wasted no time rehabilitating the South African dealerships before traversing the continent all the way to Cairo, selling Harleys to missionaries, native tribal leaders and war chiefs on the way. The impressed bosses of Harley-Davidson then sent him to Japan in 1922, where Baron Okura's mysterious import company Nippon Jidoshe was engaged in some rather shady business deals in Japan, Korea and Manchuria. Rich Child provided order, fired the scheming businessman Charles Cable from San Francisco, broke away from the arrogant Baron Okura, and, together with the Japanese pharmaceutical combine Sankyo, founded a new, exclusive Harley-Davidson sales company for the Far East, becoming its Managing Director in the process. From that day on, all sales deals were conducted honestly and business went splendidly.

Thanks largely to Sankyo's widespread contacts, virtually the entire Japanese military was soon equipped with Harleys, particularly the Japanese navy and the police. When the dollar's value against the yen plummeted by almost half during the worldwide economic crisis in 1929 and the company's lucrative business ties threatened to vanish almost overnight, Rich Child managed to convince the bosses of Harley of the merit of independent, licensed manufacture in Japan. Thanks to the financial support of the Sankyo combine and the help of Harley's sales manager Harry Divine, as well as several competent factory workers,

Child built Japan's first motorcycle factory in Shinagawa. Blueprints, machine tools and parts lists from Milwaukee allowed the branch factory to start full production of the 45 and 74 cubic inch side-valve models under the management of chief engineer Fred Barr from 1935. However, Child's relationship with Sankyo came to an end in a dispute concerning the license conditions for manufacturing the still imperfect Knucklehead, after which he was authorized to establish his own Harley sales company – Nichiman Harley-Davidson Sales in Tokyo. Sankyo continued to manufacture the side-valve Harley-Davidsons in the Shinagawa factory under the name Rikuo (King of the Road).

When the warmongering military government came to power in 1937, Child was paid off on the spot and ordered to leave the country. The Rikuo continued to be built in Shinagawa as a military motorcycle until 1946, and a three-wheeled goods transporter rather like the Servi-Car was developed. The factory also manufactured torpedoes and other weapons for use against the Americans in the war.

By this time, Rich Child had served Harley-Davidson loyally for more than 16 years and he expected to be offered employment at the company upon his return to the U.S. But this was not to be the case and, frustrated as he was, Child went to North China as sales manager for Bendix before opening an agency for BSA motorcycles in New York. After the war, Child's son Richard founded the Balcolm Company in Takanawa, Tokyo and became sole importer of Harley motorcycles and BMW automobiles, thus laying the cornerstone for Harley fandom among the new generation of Japanese motorcyclists.

In the end, the factory in Shinagawa also manufactured Panhead copies, but only about 1,500 a year, and those mainly for the police. The Rikuo factory was closed in 1959. One other factory – the Kurogane Company in Hiroshima – manufactured precise copies of the 74 cubic inch (1200 cc) VL Harleys from 1937 onwards, but this factory was destroyed in 1945 by the atomic bomb.

Club Events

Fashion and Chrome–Plated Harley Parades

© Harley-Davidson

Harley-Davidson toyed with the idea of building a new high-performance 45 cubic inch (750 cc) OHV V–Twin engine, primarily because the old Forty–Five still tended to overheat under extreme racing conditions but also perhaps to counter the appeal of the still successful and very fast Indian Sport Scout. However, despite having already reached the prototype stage, the project was scrapped because it was too expensive.

Instead, the specification of the model range was improved: the machines were now fitted with new streamlined, teardrop–shaped, airplane–style speedometer dials, and the old, unshapely 18 mm sparkplugs were replaced with models with a 10 or 14 mm thread. For those owners who wanted a little extra something, a vast range of

accessories was available that allowed them to customize their Harleys to the point that some of them resembled highly decorated Christmas trees, which gave them a fair chance at winning the coveted "Best Equipped" trophy.

As this increased in popularity, more and more club events became dazzling chrome–plated festivals for a Harley–riding society geared to custom–jobs and glamour. The members clad themselves in stylish pants, police–style caps, and shiny black high–leg boots, and the *Enthusiast* regularly announced winners of the "Best Dressed" group. These "uniforms" were fashionable among motorcyclists, but once the war started, they exchanged their motorcycle duds for a uniform of a different kind — courtesy of the U.S. of A.

The Patriarchs Retire
Farewell to the Founders' Generation

On April 21, 1937 William A. 'Bill' Davidson, who had not been in good health, died after two days of difficult negotiations with the trade unions about policies concerning production and staff. He had been suffering from diabetes and before his death doctors had amputated both his legs. Big Bill was responsible for the very soul of the factory, and for the high standard of manufacturing. Although he had never ridden a motorcycle himself, Bill knew his way around the material and technology like no other, and the welfare of his workers had always been a matter close to his heart. Following his death, William Ottaway initially took care of production management, until he was later replaced by Bill's son, William H. Davidson, who became the new Vice President in the family hierarchy. In 1937 and 1938, the board of directors welcomed William J. Harley, Robert P. Nortmann and Gordon Davidson as new members.

On February 7, 1942, Walter Davidson, the company's President and the oldest of the three brothers, succumbed to stress and liver failure. The charismatic Scottish–born entrepreneur was a giant of industry and his patriarchal personality was admired and respected just as much as it was feared, and sometimes even hated. It was Walter Davidson who had established the family's policy and although his uncompromising decisions were sometimes contrary to the desires of dealers and their customers, they unfailingly served the interests and well-being of the company. The acceptance of his own personal style of leadership was

Harley Goes to War

After Victory, Enough Spare Parts to Make 30,000 Motorcycles

reflected in the greatness of Harley-Davidson. He was succeeded by his nephew, William H. Davidson, who served as the new President into the 1970s. His sons Walter C. and Gordon were later responsible for the sales department and production management.

On September 18, 1943 at the age of just 63, the third founding member William S. Harley died of a sudden heart attack. The brilliant engineer and designer had been the creative heart of the legend known as Harley-Davidson. A quiet and artistically talented man, he had many artistic ambitions and his skill in this field was reflected in his excellent drawings and photographs. He loved the beauty of nature – a passion he frequently shared with like-minded friends on trips into America's countryside. After his death, his work was initially continued by his son William J. Harley, Bill Ottaway, Arthur Constantine and Joe Petrali.

When Bill Ottaway entered retirement in 1945, William J. Harley, who had inherited his father's skills, took over the design and development department. A host of new and trailblazing projects were developed under his guidance: the Panhead, the K and Sportster model series, the Servi-Car with an XA opposed-twin engine, the Topper Scooter, the DKW-inspired 125 Model S and numerous prototypes, such as parallel twins and the Model KL, and finally, a 750 OHV twin with two overhead camshafts, a design that never got further than the drawing board.

Arthur Davidson was the sole survivor of the founding generation, but he now withdrew more and more from the forefront of management tasks. On account of his popularity and the great many friendships he had forged during his countless journeys throughout the United States, he was elected President of the AMA in 1944.

On December 30, 1950, the fourth and probably most active of the company founders, Arthur Davidson, died in a fatal automobile accident together with his wife. His successor was George D. Gilbert, who had come to Harley from the Baldwin-Duckworth chain factory.

USA-4

PHOTOS BY U. S. ARMY SIGNAL CORPS   *U. S. Armored Regiment*   © CURT TEICH & CO., INC.

America was already convinced in 1939 – two years before Pearl Harbor – that it would be drawn into the conflict Hitler had ignited in Europe. In fact, even before actively joining the war, America had delivered 5,000 Indian motorcycle-sidecar combinations to France and 5,080 solo Harley motorcycles to England, following the destruction of the Triumph factory in Coventry by the German Luftwaffe. Uncle Sam's immense war machine overlooked no one – the American armaments industry was insatiable and running at full steam.

The whole country flourished. Everyone had work, high wages were paid and overtime was typical. Harley-Davidson wasted no time expanding its production facilities and began manufacturing motorcycles at a furious rate. The company took on 500 new workers and shifts worked around the clock. Harley-Davidson became a defense contractor vital to America's war effort, complete with all the disadvantages and advantages which it entailed. However, those advantages were not to be sneezed at.

In 1939, exhaustive testing of military suitability of motorcycles and three-wheelers from Indian, Harley-Davidson and Delco began in various army training camps – the strategists had certain ideas of what such suitability might involve. Harley-Davidson even maintained its own test grounds at Fort Knox and in Louisiana, where the bosses and their technicians sought to cater to the wishes of the men in uniform.

The test motorcycles were subjected to merciless endurance and fatigue tests, and improvements and criteria for their use in the war were evaluated. Finally, Harley-Davidson presented the military experts with the ultimate two-wheeled war machine: the WLA (A for Army).

The WLA was the good-old 45 cubic inch (750 cc) side-valve twin, a reliable machine whose compression ratio had been lowered somewhat and which had been militarized by fitting aluminum cylinder heads to prevent overheating, giving better power transmission at lower speeds and a special large air-filter for the Linkert carburetor. Harley's new war horse also had crash bars to protect against severe bumps, a protective steel plate beneath the frame and various attachments for all kinds of weaponry. The standard equipment package also included a broad, pressed-steel baggage rack and an attractive leather scabbard for securing rifles or submachine guns.

All told, Harley-Davidson supplied the army with 88,000 such motorcycles, plus 20,000 WLC models for the Canadian armed forces (the C stood for Canada). In contrast to the WLA, the WLC had the clutch lever and brake pedal on the left and the foot change on the right and was also fitted with a so-called auxiliary box on the front fender. Some time later, a sidecar version – the WSR – was also manufactured for Russia, with indeterminate numbers being shipped via convoy to Murmansk as part of the lend-lease aid pact between the

Advertising and reality: patriotic postcards and displays of combat readiness vie to win recruits as WLA-mounted dispatch riders.

Disembarking from British troop transports was no easy task.

Allies and Stalin (some sources report 30,000 units being shipped, but such a high figure seems extremely unlikely). A considerable number of these doubtless found a watery grave on the ocean floor.

As far as domestic supply was concerned, Harley delivered a few thousand motorcycles to the U.S. Navy military police, painted gray and unmistakably adorned with the letters SP for Shore Patrol. Procurement offices also ordered several 74 inch UA side–valve models and a few 61 inch E and ELC OHV models for military staff use.

In 1941, amidst hectic preparations for the war, Harley–Davidson launched its new 74 cubic inch (1200 cc) OHV motorcycle: the 74 F and FL Knucklehead which, with a top speed of 100 mph, was one of the fastest and heaviest motorcycles of the day. However, the extremely high performance was also reflected in the equally high price of 465 dollars, making the F and FL Knucklehead an exclusive jewel in Harley's product range — a jewel that continued to be fashioned until 1947.

During the final years of the war, civilian production had given way almost totally to military needs. Anyone wanting to buy a motorcycle for private use had to obtain an official permit from one of the 37 responsible government agencies which were extremely tightfisted when it came to issuing such items. In fact, permits were almost only issued in exceptional cases, mostly for civil defense purposes. Accordingly, all civilian machines were of the same color — a uniform gray.

59

Too Heavy, Too Expensive, Too Late

Doubtless impressed by the victories of the German general Erwin Rommel in North Africa, the American military decided it needed a motorcycle for the war in the desert that was just as successful as the German BMW R 75. Thus, in the fall of 1942, it commissioned both Harley-Davidson and Indian to develop a sand-resistant motorcycle, i.e. a shaft-drive model. The Harley management managed to acquire a BMW R 12 from the Netherlands and immediately built a copy under enormous time pressure. Due to a lack of space in their own factory, this 45 cubic inch (750 cc) side-valve opposed-twin BMW replica, known as the XA, was built at General Motors. However, after about 1,000 units had been manufactured, the army canceled its order. If the horrendously high development costs are included in the calculation, the unit price was somewhere around the 1,000 dollar mark. As it was, not one single XA found its way to the battlefields. It was simply too late, as the Jeep had since proven to be the ideal means of transportation over difficult terrain. The remaining stocks of XAs were later sold at low prices on the civilian market.

This put the dealers in a desperate position. People now had enough money and the demand was huge, but they simply couldn't deliver. Slogans such as "the war comes first, enjoyment comes second" may have been stirring, but they did little for the livelihood of the dealers.

At the end of the war, several thousand unused WLAs were still left over, together with enough spare parts to build 30,000 more. Most of these motorcycles were sold on the civilian market at rock bottom prices up until 1956, complete with the original military equipment and sporting full war paint.

At a prestigious military ceremony in 1943, Harley-Davidson was awarded the coveted Army-Navy "E" (for excellence) Award for its exceptional service to America's wartime production.

Sensing the imminent victory, the army canceled 11,331 orders for motorcycles even before the war came to an end. Harley-Davidson had to dismiss 500 workers and by the summer of 1945, the working week had returned to 40 hours. Harley slowly shifted its attention back to production for the neglected, but extremely promising, civilian market. After all, the war had been won.

Man and machine are made ready for military service in combat maneuvers (Camp Oglethorpe/GA, top) and on difficult terrain.

Opposite: courtesy of Mark Jonas, Milwaukee, Wisconsin

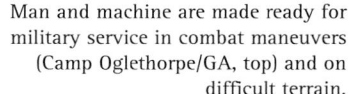

WLA Model

(1939–1946)

The Speedy Brits Arrive

Leather Jackets on Beefy Panheads Hold Their Own Against Them

Presented in the fall of 1947, the new OHV Panhead was the showpiece of Harley–Davidson.

The 61 or 74 cubic inch engine was cradled in a wishbone frame up until 1955. However, the old springer fork was already replaced by a telescopic fork in 1949.

The production range of the Big Twins in 1948, with the SV Flathead and new OHV Panhead.

The economic industrial situation in postwar America was characterized by persistent shortages of raw materials. Even the only two remaining motorcycle manufacturers, Harley–Davidson and Indian, had initial difficulties in converting to peacetime production. Nevertheless, the demand for motorcycles, barely catered to during the war, increased all the time. New jobs meant more money and the population's buying power rose accordingly. The backlog demand was enormous, but one fundamental aspect had changed: the customers now wanted something different.

Small motorcycles were suddenly in demand – lightweight or middle-weight bikes for fun and pleasure, corresponding more and more to the new smart lifestyle of an aspiring (and above all young) affluent society, intent on harvesting luxury and comfort as the spoils of victory in a world war that had deprived them of so much.

At first, Harley–Davidson could only cater to this new trend with its old prewar product range, limited production of which was decided on in 1946. This range was headed by the refined 61 and 74 cubic inch (1000 cc and 1200 cc) OHV Knuckleheads, followed by the sturdy but ponderous 74 and 80 cubic inch (1200 cc and 1340 cc) side-valve U models and, last but not least, the good old 45 cubic inch (750 cc) side-valve WL, slow as it was but a war veteran, the engine of which continued to serve valiantly in the Servi-Car. However, the military contracts were still running and an official permit was still required in order to buy a motorcycle for private use...

In the meantime, the European Recovery Program devised by former U.S. Army chief of staff, George C. Marshall had taken effect. Among other things, the Marshall Plan led to U.S. import tariffs being dropped to eight percent, while export duty remained at 35 to 50 percent. Having been almost totally annihilated in the war, the British motorcycle industry was now up and running at full capacity, producing the most modern motorcycles of the day. Needless to say, the British jumped at this opportunity and launched their advanced 250 to 500 cc singles and twins on the new and receptive U.S. market and they were frantically consumed in large numbers by America's sales-hungry dealerships. The racy new toys from overseas that went by such names as Norton, BSA, Triumph, Ariel and Royal Enfield were associated with high profit margins for the dealers and scarcely any limitations or restrictions, strings or competitive regulations were demanded by the European manufacturers.

The domestic industry had nothing with which to counter this deluge of imports, except perhaps for the rather entertaining single-cylinder Cushman Scooter from Lincoln, Nebraska, which although a bargain at just under 150 dollars, was not a real motorcycle. The management of Harley–Davidson only tolerated its sale through Harley dealerships because it enticed new, younger customers into the showrooms. However, this situation changed abruptly in 1947. The good-looking, modern and maneuverable British motorcycles were easy to control thanks to their foot-operated gearshift and hand-operated clutch and they were also becoming increasingly successful in motorcycle racing. In short, they posed an ever greater threat to the heavy-weight Harleys and the alarm bells were soon ringing in Milwaukee.

Once again, it was the shareholding family members, and this time more interested in profit than investments, who had to cough up the funds needed to help Harley–Davidson out of this predicament. This they accepted, albeit extremely reluctantly. The first step involved expanding the company's production capacity by purchasing the A.O. Smith Propeller Factory in Milwaukee's Wauwatosa suburb for 1.5 million dollars. Engines and gear-boxes were manufactured one year later in the new production facility on today's Capitol Drive.

The management harbored no doubts that Harley's dealers, neglected so much during the war and frustrated by the current import situation, had to be reactivated and, above all, remotivated. To this end, Harley hatched a classic carrot-and-stick plan.

In November 1947, Harley–Davidson held the largest dealers convention ever in the Schroeder Hotel in Milwaukee. The preprogrammed mood was highly patriotic and the slogan of the day was "Buy American." All dealers were expressly cautioned about British imports: "Don't touch the Limeys" – as the British motorcycles were disparagingly called – "or you'll discuss your franchise again!" Harley–Davidson also told the dealers that the same ban applied to the sale of absolutely any Cushman products with

Large numbers of new 125 cc two-strokes were produced from 1947 onwards. This photo shows final assembly at the Butler Plant.

The first two-stroke Harley is unveiled in 1948, with a 125 cc engine. Gordon Davidson, William Harley jr., Arthur Davidson and William H. Davidson pose for an advertising photo.

immediate effect. The urgently voiced question of what Harley-Davidson had up its sleeve in response to the growing demand for lightweight and middleweight motorcycles remained unanswered. However, chief engineer William J. Harley then ceremoniously unveiled Harley's latest weapon in the battle for the new customer classes, powered by a 7.6 cubic inch (125 cc) two-stroke engine. This was the 125 S, a copy of the German DKW, the patent of which was considered one of the spoils of war.

This model was later to be publicized as the Hummer and just like BSA had done with their copy, the Bantam, and nearly a dozen other manufacturers worldwide similarly, Harley-Davidson was able to build it quickly and relatively inexpensively. The sale price of 325 dollars for the lightweight motorcycle that was anything but typical of Harley-Davidson machines was just about acceptable, although the dealer's discounts in comparison with Cushman were ridiculously small. Nevertheless, the reliable and sturdy two-stroke model (also available with a 10 cubic inch/165 cc engine from 1953) sold well, almost certainly because it was far superior technically speaking to comparable British models from James, Villiers, Excelsior and Francis-Barnett.

The ensuing commotion in the Schroeder Hotel caused by the new star on Harley's horizon almost distracted everyone's attention from the premiere of a new OHV twin which was to replace the previous Knucklehead as of 1948: the modern EL and FL (in 61 and 74 inch form) highway steamer soon to be known as the Panhead – one of the most beautifully styled and trendsetting heavyweights of the postwar period.

In order to provide their dealers with a bit of a helping hand against the ever more aggressive competition, Harley launched a tremendous advertising campaign for its accessories. Never before had ads been so attractive and never before had the thick new catalogs been so extensive and diverse. And, for the first time ever, their pages were significantly adorned with the increasingly stigmatized black leather jacket.

Full-dresser mania was elevated to cult status, although its prime had actually come and gone. Many years were to go by before the cult was resurrected in the independent accessory stores of the custom scene.

The Company Plays Host

Spotlight on the 125 cc Two–Stroke Model S

Also a major social event: a dealers convention in Milwaukee's Schroeder Hotel, first published in *The Enthusiast*, 1948.

In its January 1948 edition, the corporate magazine *The Enthusiast* described in detail the famous postwar dealers convention of November 24 and 25, 1947, in Milwaukee's elegant Schroeder Hotel, attended by domestic and overseas dealers from 47 states and countries. The lobby in front of the conference hall – known as the Crystal Ballroom – was graced by a police Servi-Car sporting the latest technological achievement, a two-way Motorola radio.

The spare parts and accessories department had put its treasures on display next door in the Pere Marquette hall: "The world's largest display of motorcycles accessories." In his capacity as chairman of the proceedings, J.G. Kilbert first greeted the well-disposed participants before presenting Arthur Davidson to the high-caliber audience, all of whom most probably knew him personally. Once Arthur had delivered his (less than optimistic) assessment of the situation, the moment everyone had been waiting for with bated breath arrived: chief engineer William J. Harley unveiled the best-kept secret of the last two years with the ceremony of a professional showmaster. House lights out – spots on! The two black sheets to the left and right of the podium were dropped to the accompaniment of a general gasp of surprise from the audience, revealing two dazzling examples of Harley's Little Fellow. There it was in all its glory, the small 125 cc two-stroke Model S – the machine that was intended to open up a whole new market for Harley-Davidson.

After numerous other expert presentations and speeches, E.C. Smith, Secretary General of the AMA (well known to be fully under Harley's control), presented Arthur Davidson with a trophy in recognition of the company's generous support. Walter Davidson explained the new racing program and announced the launch of the company's future racing model, the popular WR.

A further surprise was in store to round things off: the participants were driven through a raging snowstorm in 14 buses to a secret destination in the suburb of Wauwatosa outside Milwaukee. Here a festive reception was to be held in Harley's new factory – an ultramodern and well-equipped production facility. The dealers were remarkably impressed, as Harley had intended all along. The glamorous convention closed with honors and awards being bestowed upon successful Harley-Davidson dealers, as well as with an opulent buffet of course.

• A real family reunion. The grand banquet scene in the beautiful Crystal Ballroom of the Schroeder Hotel on the closing evening of the Harley-Davidson National Dealers' Sales Conference.

PRINTED IN U.S.A.

The Outlaw Syndrome

Marlon Brando and the Harleys

While dealers and manufacturers contended with the threat posed by imports, a whole new form of motorcycle scene had developed almost unnoticed until the 1960s. These groups had nothing to do with the company but adopted the Harley as a symbol of their own. Although a few wild motorcycle gangs had been around before World War II, it was not until the return of scores of motorcycle-obsessed GIs from a gruesome, bloody and dehumanizing war that a sworn subsociety emerged that simply would not conform with – in their eyes – the hypocritical morality of a petty bourgeois populace. Stubbornly radical motorcycle clubs, or MCs, were formed, going by such provocative and offensive names as Boozefighters, Satan's Sinners or Winoes. These clubs loathed law and order as manifestations of the deadbeat, mendacious and corrupt mentality of a money-grabbing society. They were sworn to regard the police as their natural enemies, particularly the traffic cops. Their philosophy, if they had one at all, was rebellion against everything that represented a proper, neat and tidy middle class way of life and its moral constraints. Consequently, they called themselves rebels.

America's obviously shocked society called them outlaws – a title they wore with pride. Many dressed intentionally to inspire fear, their conduct was aggressive and characterized by machobrutality, and the motorcycles they rode were powerful, loud and as unconventional as possible. Wherever these outlaws appeared, their image sent a shudder of repulsion through every decent citizen, while secretly elevating them to status of idols in the eyes of a younger generation thirsting for freedom. Hollywood later embellished their image significantly with numerous films involving motorcycle gangs, thus making a major contribution to the birth of a new movement that soon established itself as the "Biker Lifestyle." This phenomenon was most widespread in Southern California. However, an event was soon to occur that would give rise to a new motorcycle movement, one with some very negative consequences for which bikers throughout the world must still atone today.

In 1947, the garlic-growing town of Hollister was the venue for the AMA Independence Day racing event, held every year on the 4th of July. Unsurprisingly, downtown Hollister was also the venue for numerous raucous brawls between more or less drunken and rowdy bikers. Nothing special considering the circumstances, and after several fights, the police quickly had everything under control again. The real misfortune was the reporting of the event by the powerful *Life* magazine which, supported by a sensation-seeking media, boosted the topic to the status of a national problem, triggering a witchhunt.

Civilian militias popped up overnight to protect upright citizens from these marauding hordes of bikers that were apparently terrorizing the whole of America, leaving a devastating trail of rape and pillage in their wake. The call for lynch justice once again reared its head, and heaven forbid the unfortunate biker who dared to show his face. A statement by the AMA claiming that "99% of all motorcyclists are well-behaved riders" also fanned the flames of this problem. Publicly stigmatized and branded as national enemies, a cry of outrage resounded throughout the rebel biker world that can still be heard today. Biker symbolism, such as the feared "1%" symbol, became the embodiment of an anti-establishment biker movement, albeit a movement that has since been marketed rather well.

CYCLIST'S HOLIDAY

He and friends terrorize a town

On the Fourth of July weekend 4,000 members of a motorcycle club roared into Hollister, Calif. for a three-day convention. They quickly tired of ordinary motorcycle thrills and turned to more exciting stunts. Racing their vehicles down the main street and through traffic lights, they rammed into restaurants and bars, breaking furniture and mirrors. Some rested awhile by the curb (*above*). Others hardly paused. Police arrested many for drunkenness and indecent exposure but could not restore order. Finally, after two days, the cyclists left with a brazen explanation. "We like to show off. It's just a lot of fun." But Hollister's police chief took a different view. Wailed he, "It's just one hell of a mess."

Initially, all this had little to do with Harley-Davidson as a company. However, the fact that the heavyweight from Milwaukee – exhaustively customized, of course – became more and more the preferred status symbol of the wild biker hordes, placed the company in an extremely difficult position. The painstakingly avoided "bad boy" image that was cultivated became a nightmare for the company, totally incompatible with the meticulously promoted and serious image of its high-class motorcycles. This attitude effectively blocked Harley's access to the booming accessories market for decades.

Stanley Kramer had just produced his 1954 film based on the events of Hollister. Brilliantly filmed by director Laslo Benedek, "The Wild One" had hardly been released to movie theaters throughout the country before the nation's rebellious youth elevated it to cult status. The AMA, in its self-appointed role of representative of the offended "good guys" called for the film to be boycotted and indignant club members gathered in front of many movie theaters.

Although the main character played by Marlon Brando rides a Triumph Speed Twin in the rebel legend, this fact was readily overlooked by America's adolescent outlaws: it was a question of symbolism and Harley-Davidson was "the" heavyweight cult symbol. Since then, the new rebel movement spread from California throughout the rest of the country like an epidemic. The prewar "boppers" became "choppers," and lovely Harleys were mercilessly stripped, customized to the point of no return and their engines tuned to the absolute limits – the wilder, the better. No other motorcycle could be modified as wonderfully as a Harley-Davidson, and every biker true to his name just had to have such a fabulous steed.

The Dinosaurs Rear Their Heads

Harley-Davidson Against the Rest of the World

The second and third generations: President William H. Davidson and his two sons, John and William G.

Contrary to expectations, the Model S sold exceptionally well and by 1949, 10,000 had already passed into the ownership of schoolboys throughout America, which isn't to imply that none were sold to school-girls. In fact, the lightweight motorcycle became an increasingly popular form of practical, simple transportation for women, particularly for hopping between home, school and the ice cream parlor.

Once established in the business of producing nimble two-stroke engines, Harley-Davidson diversified in the early 1960s into other machines that truly had very little in common with motorcycles: golf-carts and snowmobiles (1971-75).

In 1954, the ailing Model K was modified to a displacement of 55 cubic inches (900 cc) and became a popular motorcycle for sporting events. Rock 'n' roll idol Elvis Presley even posed atop a Model KH on the front cover of *The Enthusiast* in May, 1956. A more powerful 10 cubic inch (165 cc) two-stroke machine bearing the model designa-tion ST and STU entered into the lightweight scene, while in 1955, the 125 cc Hummer became Harley's most successful small motorcycle — a status it held until 1957. The rather strangely proportioned Topper scooter appeared in 1960, with its 10 cubic inch (165 cc) engine yielding

almost 3 horsepower. The larger two-stroke models subsequently metamorphosed into ever newer model types, such as the Scat, Pacer, Ranger and, in a more modern design in 1966, the Bobcat.

On the other hand, the new OHV EL and FL Panheads were still ex-periencing teething troubles, particularly regarding the hydraulic valve lifters and overheating at high speed. But it took just one year for a de-cisive improvement to be made to the riding comfort of these motorcycles: the Panhead's old springer forks were replaced in 1949 with modern oil-damped telescopic front forks, giving rise to the famous name, "Hydra Glide."

Still, dealers from many areas were angry about Harley's poor and, in their opinion, unfair allocation rates and complained of the exces-sively restrictive ties to the company's products, while their independent colleagues made a fat and easy profit on British imports, especially on the larger and more powerful 650 twins that BSA and Triumph were ma-king available in ever greater numbers alongside the smaller capacity models. Although these were still considered more or less the preserve of motorcyclists who could tinker with the engines themselves, the motorcycle press lovingly embraced the imports, praising their technical

An as-yet relatively unknown Elvis Presley astride his new 1956 Model KH.

superiority with the same enthusiasm with which they accused American motorcycles (i.e. Harley-Davidson in particular) of being totally outdated and overweight dinosaurs.

Under the guidance of its President Ralph B. Rogers, Indian tried a final gambit to turn their ailing ship around and conclusively decided in favor of the production of promising lightweight motorcycles. However, this soon proved to be the wrong decision and Harley-Davidson's long-time competitor finally threw in the towel and ceased production in 1953.

Even without the demise of Indian, most of the American motorcycle market had long been firmly in the control of British manufacturers. The only market for Harleys by this time was made up of police departments and loyal clubs. Therefore, in 1950, Harley-Davidson asked the U.S. Tariff Commission to increase the protective tariffs imposed on foreign motorcycles to 50 percent. However, the Commission rejected the request a year later, forcing the company to deal with the existing situation.

Finally, the long-awaited 45 cubic inch (750 cc) Model K was unveiled at the annual dealer convention at the end of 1951, this time in the Milwaukee City Hall. The Model K was Harley's newest and greatest hope to take on ever stronger British competition. The newly designed, more powerful side-valve engine was intended to satisfy the dealers' increasingly urgent demands for a competitive motorcycle in the middleweight class.

Although the racy design of the engine was light and, on account of its integrated gearbox, operated via a hand clutch and foot lever which made it correspondingly easier to service and repair than the old WL Model, the Model K proved to be something of a catastrophe in practice. It was not until its engine capacity was increased to 55 cubic inches (900 cc) that it could keep pace with the maneuverable and fast Nortons or BSAs. Harley-Davidson had again effectively denied itself access to the highly lucrative market sector of middleweight motorcycles. On the other hand, the more thoughtfully designed KR and KRTT racers turned out to be an astonishing success on American race tracks.

By this time, the 330-plus shareholders of the Harley and Davidson families were no longer prepared to invest any more money in the company. Indeed, they secretly believed that the increasingly aging

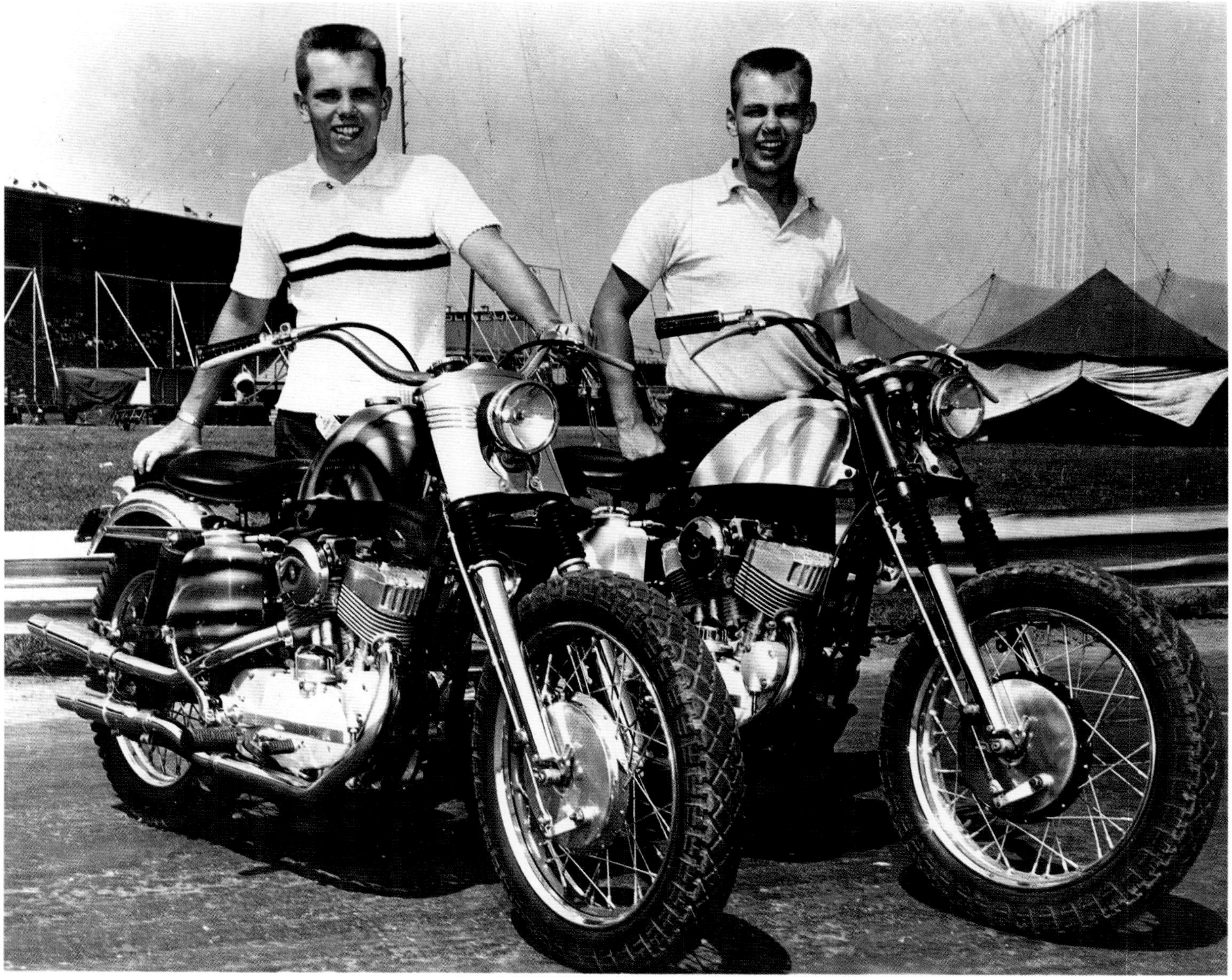

The young members of the family: the third generation, John and William G. Davidson with the latest K models.

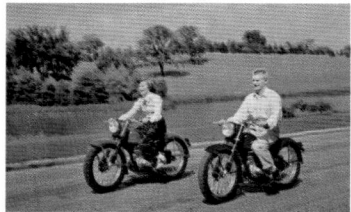

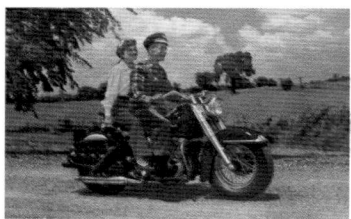

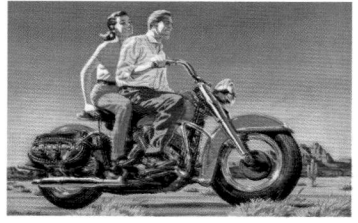

Life was enjoyable, most of all with someone you love: Harley motorcycles provided plenty of fun and also brought couples "closer together."

company had little or no chance of survival and preferred to place their money in more profitable investments.

A 45 cubic inch (750 cc) ohc prototype designated the KL which had a powerful 60 degree V-Twin engine was not built, allegedly because the patent lay in the hands of a British company called Vincent.

Sales dropped by 20 percent in 1953, the year in which the company celebrated its 50th anniversary. America's enthusiasm for technology was concentrating increasingly on more comfortable automobiles, which had developed into plush monsters of chrome, steel and plastic. Furthermore, the value of the British pound had dropped considerably, making British motorcycles even cheaper than before, while Harley-Davidson's costs continued to rise. At a price in excess of one thousand dollars, the Panheads just could not be sold at a profit any longer.

One after the other, the heavily pressed dealers also rebelled against the intolerant, dictatorial corporate policy that did anything but extend a helping hand in these difficult times, with the smaller dealerships suffering worst of all. Heated disputes arose until the point was reached at which Harley was finally forced to intervene. Although this intervention occasionally led to some shocking consequences, the company nevertheless permitted several particularly profitable dealerships also to sell products from other companies – a concession that contravened the sacred and much quoted principle that "a Harley dealer only sells Harley products."

At about the same time, a deafeningly loud and high-tech motorcycle sport was emerging in America – one that had already been pursued in England for quite some time under the name "sprinting." They were veritable speed orgies over a quarter of a mile from a standing start. In America, these races became known as drags and they were soon made tremendously popular by early dragster pilots, such as Mike Tucker, Joe Smith or Bob George, who thundered along the drag strips on their souped-up Harleys.

Both Harley-Davidson and the AMA, which broadly shared the same opinion as the company, totally ignored the sport of drag racing, despite its huge potential for the future. However, crafty dealers had long realized the enormous advertising effectiveness of these popular speed duels and many soon took the step of graduating from being a well-behaved Harley dealership to an innovative small industrial operation, building up not only highly respected racing teams, but also vast numbers of new customers in the process.

Revenge of the Intimidated

Management Is Dealt a Blow when Protectionist Tariffs are Not Received

Harley's second generation proudly presents the new Model K: Chief Engineer and Treasurer William Harley jr., Secretary Walter Davidson jr., Gordon Davidson and President William H. Davidson.

When the point had been reached at which the increasingly aggressive marketing of British motorcycles had created an economic situation that represented a genuine threat to the survival of Harley-Davidson, the company commissioned its export manager Eric von Gumpert to submit an official request to the U.S. Tariff Commission for a 40 percent increase in the import tariff imposed on foreign motorcycles. The British Motorcycle Dealers Association, by now a powerful organization, immediately took up the challenge and readied itself for a counteroffensive under the leadership of its President, Triumph dealer Denis McCormack. When it was time for each party to present its evidence as requested in a public hall on the second floor of the Senate Office Building in Washington D.C., where seats were already overflowing with the members of the press and countless interested motorcyclists and dealers all anxiously waiting, Harley-Davidson's finest specimen almost missed its cue: the large full-dresser motorcycle barely squeezed in the elevator!

During a hearing lasting the better part of July 1951, numerous former friends and employees of the company who had been rejected and duped on frequent occasions in the past (but who were all well established by now in the lucrative business of importing British motorcycles) grasped the opportunity to avenge themselves on Harley-Davidson, particularly Alfred Rich Child, Floyd Clymer and the former factory rider Hap Alzina. This they did by exposing the arrogant and customer-hostile practices of the company in a merciless and deeply polemical manner, denouncing Harley as un-American, anti-democratic and a capitalist monopoly.

The appalled managers of Harley-Davidson, and especially William H. Davidson, kept silent — and that was that. The import tariff request was promptly rejected. And although the seditious "reputation killers" later offered William H. Davidson some rather shabby and formal apologies, the damage had been done: the good image of Harley-Davidson had been overshadowed.

The star of the 1950s: a customized Duo Glide

The Japanese Invasion

A Nightmare from the Fully Unprotected U.S. Flank

While the small runarounds from Honda were becoming ever more popular in America, the same was also true of Harleys in Japan. 22-year-old pilot Kikuko Matsumoto on her Harley.

After 1959, Harley-Davidson was faced with a new and – this time – far more serious threat. Following intensive, scientifically based marketing studies, the newly awakened Japanese motorcycle industry had decided to conquer the American market and the chances of them succeeding were very good indeed. The first shots in this new war were fired by Honda with its 50 cc four-stroke mopeds (with electric ignition!), followed by the futuristic 250 cc Dream and 350 cc Super Hawk models. It soon became apparent that the Japanese had targeted a segment of the American market that had been left wide open to attack by domestic manufacturers. Suzuki and Yamaha were quick to follow Honda's example.

At first, nobody took the high-tech products from the Far East seriously, regarding them as cute little run-arounds, totally ignoring the fact that they were not only powerful, but above all, inexpensive. Except the motorcycle press once again bent over backwards in its praise and enthusiasm, particularly Floyd Clymer's *Cycle* magazine, which this time accurately recognized the trend of the times. The initial reaction to Honda's advertising slogan "You meet the nicest people on a Honda" was amused derision. But that slogan was soon to become yet another nightmare for Harley-Davidson, all the more so because it this time characterized a segment of the motorcycle scene that Harley considered to be firmly in its grasp. The first wave of radically new Japanese mopeds and lightweight motorcycles to be launched in America landed like a bomb on the criminally neglected market and neither the British nor Harley-Davidson had the technology or the strategies to counter the Japanese invasion.

'59 HARLEY-DAVIDSON DUO-GLIDES

finest for you...
comfort for two

© Harley-Davidson

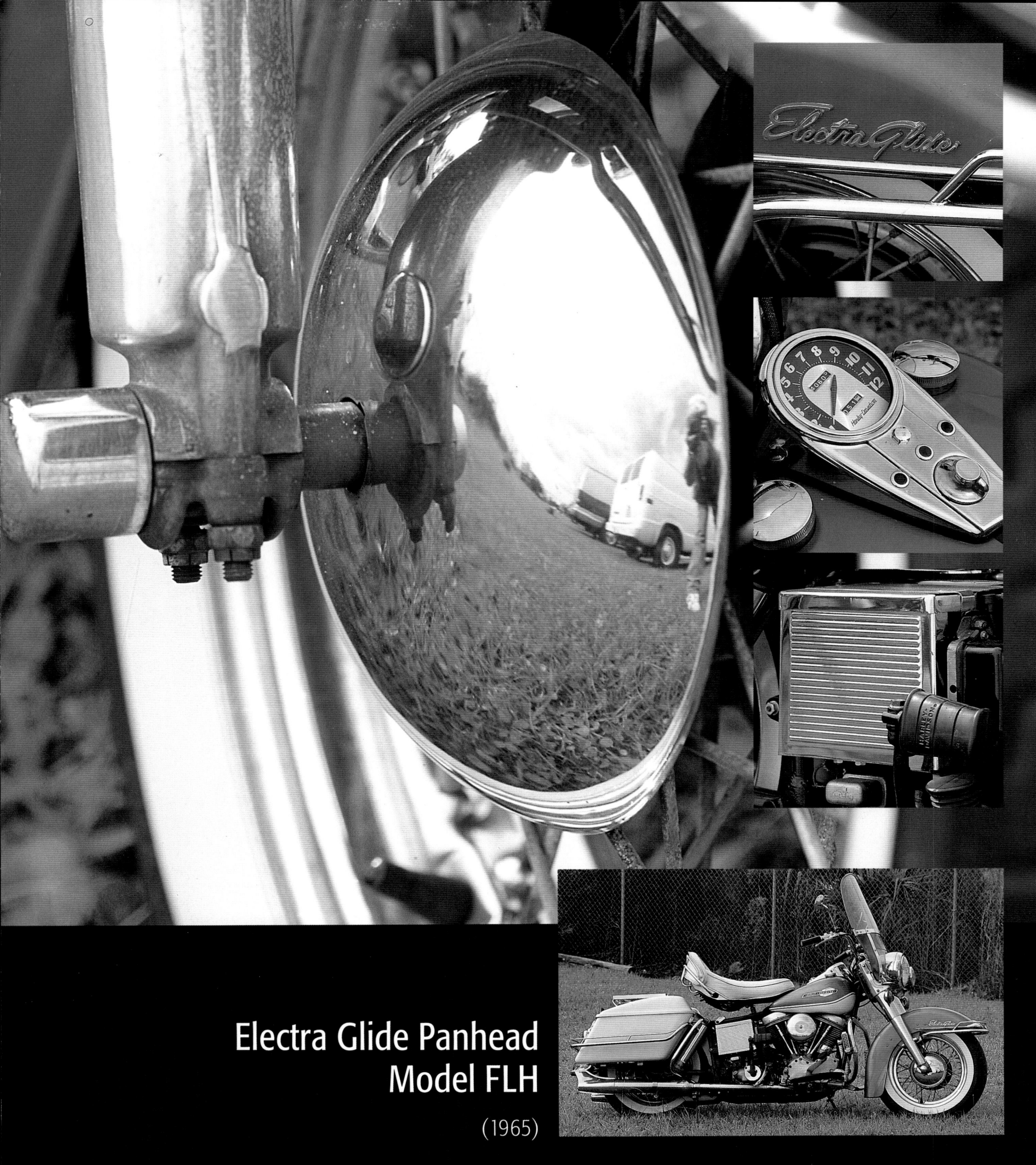

Electra Glide Panhead
Model FLH

(1965)

The Restless 1960s

Easy Rider

Although Harley now had a complete range of motorcycles spanning all classes, the Electra Glide continued to be the company's flagship.

In 1960, Harley-Davidson purchased 50 percent of the troubled Italian company Aermacchi, whose medium and lightweight motorcycles were henceforth sold bearing the double-barreled name from Milwaukee. They enhanced Harley's product range initially with the 250 cc four-stroke Sprint models, followed by the small 50 and 65 cc mopeds of the later called Leggero series and subsequently some additional two-stroke models — not necessarily to the joy of Harley's dealers and hardly a real alternative to the ever more abundant and aggressively marketed Japanese models. Harley-Davidson's own lightweight 10.7 cubic inch (175 cc) two-stroke BT, BTU and BTH models were upgraded to become the Bobcat, Pacer and Scat, which were joined between 1960 and 1964 by the rather stout but enthusiastically advertised Topper scooter with a 10 cubic inch (165 cc) two-stroke engine and automatic gearshift. But regardless of the enthusiasm, the Topper yielded a mere 3 horsepower and was generally considered too heavy, too slow and too expensive (600 dollars in 1960).

William J. Harley became President of Aermacchi-Harley-Davidson. From then on, John A. Davidson was responsible in Milwaukee for dealing with the dissatisfied dealers and Willie G. Davidson took charge of the design department in 1963, simultaneously beginning a slow metamorphosis from smart, smooth-shaven and snappily dressed executive to an even smarter, top-management biker sporting a full beard.

In the meantime, Harley had bought 60 percent of the Tomahawk boat factory in Tomahawk, Wisconsin in 1962, where it then produced all plastic and fiberglass components for its motorcycles, as well as for its golfcarts.

A new technically oriented motorcycle magazine also made its debut in 1962 — *Cycle World*, which was not afraid to openly criticize the practices of the AMA, and thus also Harley-Davidson, although its publisher Joe Parkhurst fervently denied doing this. Harley-Davidson punished Parkhurst by cutting its advertising volume in the magazine down to the bare minimum.

By this time, the company's financial situation was very gloomy. In order to acquire new liquid funds, 1965 saw Harley hazard its first step onto the public financial markets, commissioning reliable Wall Street brokers with the issue of a new share certificate. The members of the Harley and Davidson families cautiously retained the share majority of 53 percent. Nevertheless, the Bangor Punta financial group, renowned for its hostile takeovers, secretly attempted to acquire as many shares in Harley-Davidson as possible. Mere speculation or a genuine bid? Harley's management was deeply concerned.

In the same year, Harley launched a major counteroffensive against the competition, presenting the ultimate heavyweight motorcycle — the Electra Glide. The legendary luxury machine that was to become known as the King of the Highway now had a 12-volt power supply, an electric starter (which older Harley freaks consider to be rather superfluous) and, once again, a host of technical problems. These problems were finally solved, resulting in a thoroughly new engine being introduced in 1966: the Shovelhead.

The FL was optionally available with hand- or foot-operated gearshift, a displacement of 74 cubic inches (1200 cc) and the designation Electra Glide or Electra Glide Super Sport, but was still fitted with the old Panhead engine substructure with the front-mounted generator — also referred to by experts as the "Early Shovel" — until 1969.

Although it was regarded with suspicion and still treated with absolute ignorance by Harley-Davidson, the custom market exploded and underwent massive expansion. More and more dealers embraced this lucrative new business and numerous companies established themselves with products that simply were not available from Harley-Davidson, but which thousands of Harley-owners in search of that little something special were extremely keen on buying.

Dennis Hopper and Peter Fonda starred in "Easy Rider" in 1969.

The Jammer Company built springer forks and belt drives and the front cover of its extensive catalog was already adorned with a typical airbrush painting by Dave Mann. W & S Engineering offered conversion kits for Sportsters, Tom Sifton advertised his high–performance products in the trendy motor-cycling magazine *Easyriders*, Little John Ltd in Denver, Colorado offered the first ever five–speed gearbox and STD had decided to improve the engine housing. In other words, the business in aftermarket parts and components for Harleys was booming and customizing became fashionable.

But the company had other problems. The spare parts and accessories department was taken over in 1967/68 by John Harley – Gordon Davidson died on March 6, 1968. In the same year, Harley–Davidson sold 26,600 motorcycles, only little more than 15,000 of which were produced in America. The entire board of directors openly admitted the danger of going bankrupt and desperately sought a new partner, or rather, a powerful buyer prepared to rescue the American motorcycle institution from downfall. Bangor Punta once again attempted a takeover. In desperation, William H. Davidson turned to his old friend and long–time Harley enthusiast Rodney C. Gott, director and President of the AMF conglomerate, which was also interested in a takeover, and formally asked for help. Rodney C. Gott enthusiastically plunged himself and the American Machine & Foundry Company into the new two–wheeled adventure, and Harley–Davidson was finally taken over by AMF in 1969. It was a complicated and doubtless humiliating affair, but in the end, Harley–Davidson had been saved.

Coincidence or omen? Albeit heavily censored, a film appeared in the very same year involving drugs, motorcycles and hippies that conveyed a message that was extremely critical of America's society: "Easy Rider." In a single triumphant blow, this film catapulted Harley–Davidson to the status of cult symbol the world over, because Harleys were used for stunts.

An Unequal Union

Harley-Davidson and Aermacchi

The "Italian Adventure" began with the takeover and expansion of the small motorcycle factory in Varese, Italy, and introduced a new generation of racy, middle-class motorcycles to the roads and dirt-tracks of America.

In the end, Harley's attempt to dress up in foreign clothes fell flat, even though the small, sporty, two-and four-stroke machines from Italy are an integral part of Harley-Davidson's history.

The American motorcycle market could not be compared to markets in European countries, particularly that in Italy, although this was not so clearly recognized at the end of the 1950s. Shocked by the amazing successes of lively Japanese lightweights, Harley started to look for ways to extend their elderly range to include some of these apparently very profitable, sporty "fun bikes."

After William H. Davidson had spent nearly two years (1958–1959) traveling around Europe gathering information, the Italian firm Aeronautica Macchi, known as Aermacchi for short, seemed like a gift from heaven. The company, which was first based in Milan, then in Varese, had previously been an aircraft manufacturer. It had expanded on the strength of Mussolini's armaments orders, then, after World War II, had been forced to take a step down and become a motorcycle manufacturer, albeit with a series of fast and sporty, two- and four-stroke machines up to 250 cc, which enjoyed great success in Italy.

Aermacchi was acquired cheaply because it had just made considerable losses through speculation on the Indian motorcycle market, and had already been written off by its creditor banks as a loss-maker. So Harley-Davidson was regarded as its savior and, through the mediation of a Swiss bank in Lugano, was able to obtain a 50 percent holding for just a quarter of a million dollars. William J. Harley became the President of the new company, Aermacchi Harley-Davidson. To optimize production, the factory was moved from Varese to nearby Schiranna.

By the end of 1960, the first motorcycles for the new market had been built and shipped to the U.S. From the Aermacchi range of 250 cc four-stroke models with the famous, horizontal, single cylinder (Ala Bianca, Ala Azzurra, Ala Rossa, and the racing version Ala D'Oro), the managers in

Milwaukee decided on the street version Ala Verde, although this was a name which Americans could neither understand nor pronounce. So it was given the honorary title "Wisconsin." However, this was soon discarded as it was not considered attractive enough, and the new "child" was renamed the "Sprint," although it was often called the Baby Sportster.

From 1961 the Sprint appeared in Harley catalogs as the street version C, and later as the sports model H, which then, from 1964, led to the off-road machine R, a Scrambler without lights or fenders. Originally a Scrambler was a motocross bike that was unsuitable for use on the road. From the 1960s onwards, it was turned into something that looked like a suitable off-road version of a tourer.

However, since such lightweights were regarded as little more than toys in America at that time, the management in Milwaukee decided on a stronger version of the Sprint, upgraded to 350 cc, with a longer piston stroke. It was sold in various versions, designated the SS 350 and SX (Scrambler) in the U.S., known in England as the Sprint and in Italy as GT and GTS. However, 75 percent of production went to America. But the model that superseded the 250 Sprint in 1967 did not sell well and, in 1974, AMF ceased production of four-stroke machines in Italy.

Other toys were on the way in: youngsters were switching more and more to sporty little Japanese machines, so the Varese/Schiranna works now started producing mopeds: first, in 1965, the 50 cc two-stroke M–50 Leggero (the name arose in 1968 or 1969), which was upgraded to M–50S, M–65 and M–65S forms, and marketed extensively. For a while it was quite a good seller.

This was followed, in 1968, by the 125 cc, two-stroke lightweight Rapido, in TX, SX and SXT versions, and in 1970 by the 100 cc SR and MSR Baja. These did not sell very well. They were ignored by genuine Harley enthusiasts, while new customers changed their allegiances faster than expected, switching to the far superior and more powerful Japanese two-strokes. AMF, the sole owner of Aermacchi since 1972, tried to copy the Japanese and

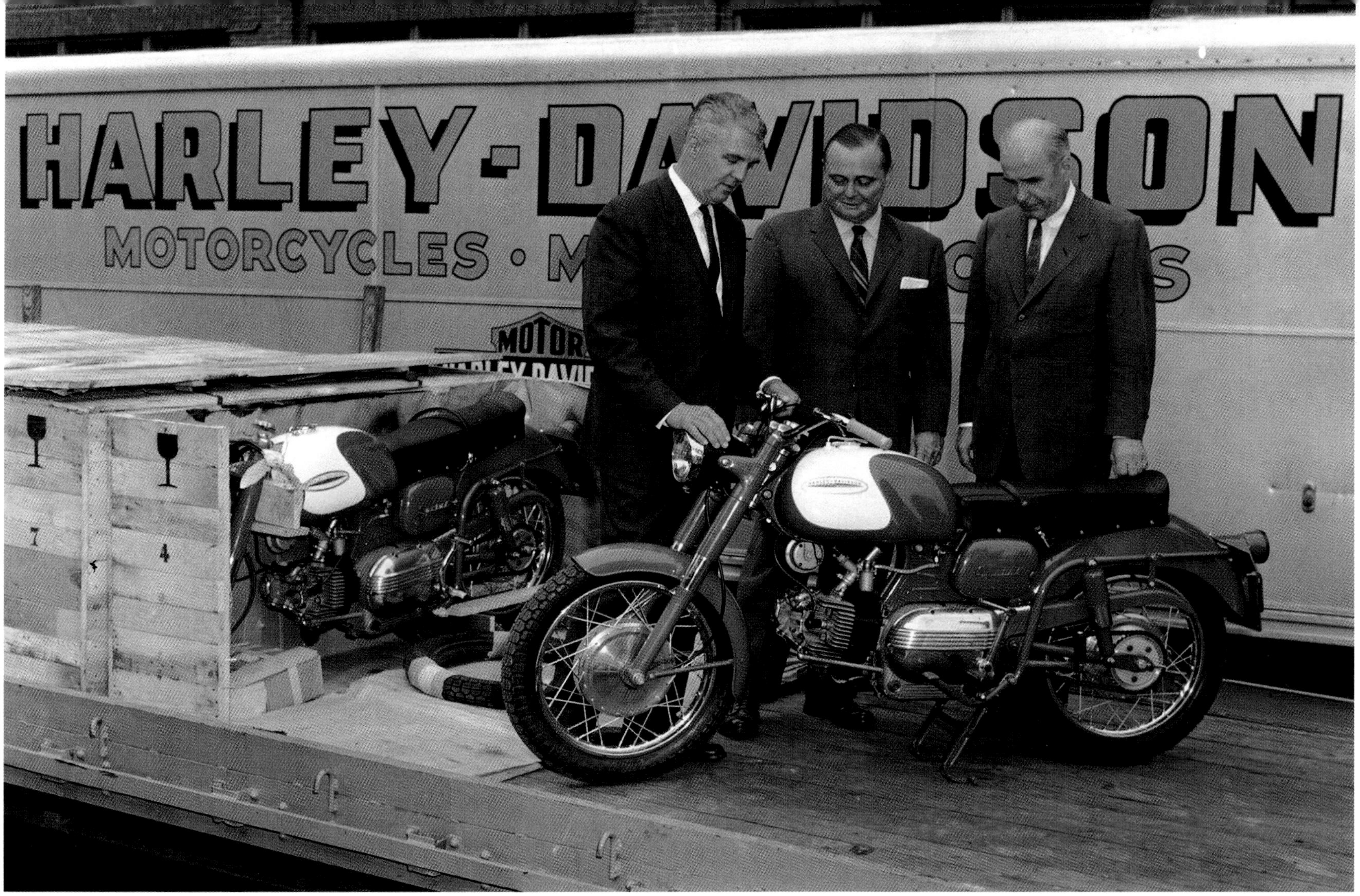

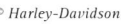

Wisconsin 250 cc.
130 Km./h

started to produce more powerful, two-stroke, single-cylinder machines in Italy, which were marketed as 175 cc motorcycles from 1974, with the 250 street machine SS and Enduro SX being added in 1975. It was all in vain, however: despite the three world championships of the Harley–Italia racing team star Walter Villa in the 250 class, AMF was forced to abandon the Italian adventure and it sold the Varese/Schiranna factory in 1978 to the Castiglioni brothers, who then successfully marketed their Caviga range.

The first four-stroke model from Italy: the owners of (by now) two companies proudly regard the "peculiar" product. The first Sprint models were called "Wisconsins" and displayed typically Italian design features.

Public Confidence Confused

Harley–Davidson Struggles Against an Explosively Bad Media Image

© Harley-Davidson

© Harley-Davidson

AMF Scenario:
A Quick Change

During the 12 years (1969 to 1981) of American Machine & Foundry rule, the once-so-stable boardroom chairs of Harley-Davidson's President, Vice President, and Chief Executive Officer became veritable ejection seats. All told, six Presidents tried their hand, not always in the way AMF's board of directors wished.

Against this background, Walter Davidson jr. felt demoted to a mere puppet and angrily resigned his position as Sales Director and Vice President in 1970.

The President in those days was William Herbert Davidson (the father of Willie G.), who had held the office of CEO since 1942. On September 30, 1971, he withdrew from that very same office. His successor was John H. O´Brian, who held onto the title for somewhat longer before being replaced by a former AMF manager E. Gus Davis. Vice President Vaughn L. Beals, who had successfully restructured the development department in his capacity as Chief Engineer, became the Senior Executive at Harley-Davidson in 1977. The last President under AMF rule entered office in 1980 – Charles K. Thompson, who had already held the Vice Presidency and headed the spare parts and accessories department at Harley since 1979. Thompson died suddenly of a heart attack in 1988.

A fresh wind was now blowing along the corridors of AMF. The managing executives of AMF were no longer interested in cautiously reserved family policies, the sense of security fostered by the authority of a patriarchal reign and certainly not in brand legends. The front-line of the dealers were no longer taken into account and the still-loyal customers were no longer listened to.

On the other hand, Harley-Davidson had little choice but to subordinate itself to the new management. Still, the chasm between the traditionalist Harley-Davidson board of directors in Milwaukee and the AMF directors in distant New York now gaped wider than ever before.

Harley's entire motorcycle production was outdated, both in terms of the model policy the company adhered to and the technical aspects. Production capacities were exhausted and in no way equipped for the major business promised by the impending – and already clearly recognizable – motorcycle boom. The financial means available had shrunk so drastically that far-reaching decisions on upgrading production were impossible to make. The entire company was effectively blocked by its own principles. In short, the motorcycle market had taken on dimensions that a family business with its typical structures could no longer cope with.

AMF's dictate for its new child was blunt: produce motorcycles, regardless of the cost, numbers are all that matter. As a result of this, over 60,000 motorcycles were sold in 1972 – an impressive sales figure, admittedly, but one that was soon to rebound on the company. After all, a Harley was never intended to be a mass-produced article.

In this context, the necessary logistics system for distributing accessories and spare parts, one of the single most important aspects for the company's survival, was neglected to an extent that can only be called criminal and consequently ground to a virtual halt.

Harley-Davidson, robbed of all but a bare minimum of independence, had to look on while its renowned know-how was remorselessly dragged into the economically down-to-earth machine of a modern, market-oriented conglomerate. Because manufacturing capacities at its factory in York, Pennsylvania were currently underutilized, AMF decided not to build a new factory in Milwaukee, but instead erected new manufacturing lines in the generously dimensioned production facilities of AMF-York.

Production started there in February 1973 and whatever was needed from Milwaukee in the way of components, such as engines and gearboxes, was transported almost 750 miles overland via truck. Needless to say, the first global oil crisis in 1974 promptly sent the gasoline bills rocketing.

The corporate policy of AMF naturally suffered from the obligation (or obsession?) of turning Harley-Davidson into a profitable asset and it was thus left with no choice but to pump further millions into motorcycle production. However, contrary to the goals of AMF President Rodney C. Gott who was ultimately responsible for Harley-Davidson, the as yet unmodernized headquarters in Milwaukee could not fulfill the demand from York. Bad feelings and seemingly endless problems concerning logistics and personnel arose between the two production sites, separated as they were by such a vast distance. Nevertheless, production was stepped up another notch – a step that resulted in total chaos. While workers at the York factory desperately waited on deliveries from Milwaukee, plan after plan was repeatedly dashed by the harsh facts of reality. The executives of the Motorcycle Group, as it was called, were replaced in ever faster succession – to no avail. An astonishing number of managerial positions at Harley-Davidson were filled with AMF staff members not in the least familiar with the world of motorcycles and motorcycling.

The demands and needs of the workers were largely ignored. Personnel were transferred back and forth on a seemingly whimsical basis and massive shift restructuring and a rigorous dismissals policy soon caused morale to plummet to its lowest point ever. Unions were no longer negotiated with at all. The hitherto loyal workforce was unmotivated – a sorry fact that opened the door to shoddy workmanship, and even extended to sabotage on some occasions. The 101-day strike of 1974 was a dangerous warning sign. Damage was severe, but the consequences were virtually nonexistent. Hundreds of rejected Harleys occasionally had to be stockpiled in York, awaiting improvement because of a renewed shortage of specific components on the production lines. The consequences when one of these unfinished machines ended up in a dealer's showroom or was prematurely sold to a customer are easy to imagine, but the thought of a motorcycle magazine tester getting hold of one of them was even worse. The damage to Harley's image and guiding principle of "highest quality" was literally devastating.

But that was only one side of the coin of AMF rule. That coin also had a more positive flipside in the form of a new, market-oriented management structure that was up to the challenge of a new era. The strategy makers of old had to rethink their plans. On September 30, 1971, William H. Davidson withdrew from his position as President of Harley-Davidson and handed over the wheel (only with AMF's approval, of course) to innovative and energetic John H. O´Brian. New paths and opportunities suddenly appeared on the horizon. In light of the facts, it can probably be stated that had it not been for AMF, Harley-Davidson would soon have ceased to exist.

The New Strategies

The Harley Heartbeat and Total Freedom

© Harley-Davidson

The market situation had undergone a major transformation. The motorcycle had changed from being a mode of transportation and sporting machine to an accessory on which to have fun and enjoy your leisure time. New customers wanted a pleasant, uncomplicated (and of course inexpensive) toy — and they wanted it right away. This desire was backed up by significant purchasing power — the sign of a new, hitherto unknown affluence in America's society; virtually anything could be sold, and new products would be literally swallowed up overnight if only they could be thrown onto the market quickly and efficiently enough.

Following exhaustive market analyses, the giant Japanese motorcycle industry, particularly Honda, took advantage of this boom and launched a product offensive, the furious economic, technical and commercial intensity of which had never before been seen. AMF reacted as best it could: ever larger sums of money were invested in making the Harleys a worthy contender to counter the invasion from the Far East. Some 45 million dollars were invested in machines and tools for the manufacture of new gearboxes alone — a highly dangerous adventure from an economic viewpoint, as the Boston Consulting Group anxiously pointed out. And that was only the start: under the brilliant management of Jeffrey L. Bleustein, a highly talented chief engineer at AMF who had been appointed by Harley-Davidson's new boss Ray Tritten (AMF) to be manager in charge of the development department as part of his general restructures, a modern generation of the legendary V-Twin engine was now also planned and ultimately built: the Evolution.

Unfortunately, the Evolution failed to make it to the production line during AMF's reign. Nevertheless, design director Willie G. Davidson injected some radical new ideas into the moth-eaten and conservative model policy. Initially regarded with distrust and even actively blocked on occasion, the custom models such as the Super Glide, Fat Bob, Low Rider,

Sturgis and — above all — Wide Glide, was met with a hugely enthusiastic response from the public.

The extent to which thought was given to the future under the AMF regime became evident at the debut of Project Nova, which was subsequently regarded with horror. Granted, the V-four engine developed at Porsche was totally atypical of Harley engines, but it would certainly have been an effective response to the aggressive and successful attack by Honda on Harley's hitherto unchallenged big bike monopoly. But once Project Nova had finally been scrapped (and justifiably so, as it turned out!), Harley had to relinquish a hefty segment of the heavyweight market to the quiet-running and extremely comfortable highway cruisers of Honda — the Gold Wing GL 1000 and GL 1100.

The earlier mentioned heralded not only a change in the corporate image, but also in the image of Harley riders in general. The rebels and outlaws were now respectable bikers; beards and tattoos, black leather jackets and tuned-up macho machines were suddenly no longer the terror of every god-fearing citizen, but rather an expression of the motorcycle-riding American Way of Life. Windswept hair and unbridled freedom on two (Harley) wheels became the cornerstone of a new philosophy. In contrast, the feature-laden cruisers of the highways were now considered to be "out" and were regarded more and more as the domain of the older generation, at best still good for shows, parades and family trips across the country. Willie G.'s new model range admittedly also included its fair share of flops, such as the midnight black Cafe Racer which embodied more of a typically European styling element which failed to impress the public. In terms of performance, price and handling, it could not compete with the exemplary Italian cafe racers. For the sports rider who wanted to stand out from the crowd, which had been Harley's target market, Ducati, Moto Guzzi and Laverda set the trend.

While initial attempts at a more racy design with the Cafe Racer were destined to failure, Harley managed to convince AMF's CEO Rodney Gott of the potential of the new 1200 cc engines at the Butler Plant in Milwaukee.

The End of the Minibike

Think Big and Let the Eagle Fly

Motorcycle dreams on a warm summer night: this typical picture from Harley-Davidson's brochure is guaranteed to trigger longing in the heart of any biker.

In another step aimed at injecting vitality into the new motorcycle division of AMF, the conglomerate's director Ray Tritten appointed the skilled engine technician Vaughn L. Beals to the position of Technical Director of the engineering department. As of 1976, Beals set to work with a vengeance to rid Harley-Davidson's top management of the apathy that had afflicted it for so long.

In 1978, Harley-enthusiast and AMF director Rodney C. Gott entered retirement. Although some poor decisions can be attributed to Gott, it was ultimately thanks to his larger-than-life personality and enthusiasm for Harley-Davidson motorcycles, although his enthusiasm did wane over the years, that the company actually survived at all.

His designated successor Tom York, on the other hand, had little interest in Harley-Davidsons and indeed little interest in motorcycles whatsoever. To a great extent, he left Harley's corporate policy pretty much to Vaughn Beals and the respective CEOs. Of course, such policy still had to

be approved beforehand by the AMF board, which increasingly led to tension and disagreements between Milwaukee, York and the AMF headquarters in New York. In the meantime, Vaughn Beals had initiated an effective program of quality and production control going by the impressive sounding motto of "I make the Eagle fly" and gave the neglected workers renewed motivation and, perhaps most importantly, responsibility.

As early as in the 1970s, the U.S. finance authorities investigated the dumping price practices of Japanese motorcycle manufacturers at the request of Harley-Davidson's President John A. Davidson. By now, the Japanese had established themselves in America with their own domestic manufacturing facilities and flooded the market with wave after wave of surplus products at rock bottom prices. If a verdict went against the Japanese (which was what Harley-Davidson hoped for), the result would be a corresponding rise in the import tariffs. The independent International Trade Commission (ITC) which carried out the market

The men in charge: Rodney C. Gott/AMF (far right) and Vaughn Beals/Harley-Davidson Division.

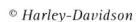

© Harley-Davidson

analysis, requested evidence from all parties involved. This, however, proved to have a boomerang effect for Harley. During the hearing, several unhappy dealers had their revenge on Harley by bluntly informing the commission that the unpopular lightweight motorcycles under consideration, which came from Harley's Italian Aermacchi production line and which the company forced them to sell, simply did not fulfill their expectations regarding demand, design and reliability or service. By comparison with the Japanese technology, they were hopelessly outdated. The ITC ruled against Harley, but simultaneously charged the Japanese manufacturers because of their dumping price practices.

However, the ITC ruling — as devastating as it was for Harley-Davidson — did have its positive aspects: the Japanese had to stop selling its surplus stock at such ridiculously low prices and Harley made the thoroughly correct decision of terminating its Italian adventure as quickly as possible. The lightweight Aermacchi machines still filling Harley's parking lots nevertheless had to be sold — at well below the list price — so the company did precisely what the Japanese had been doing up until then. But the age of the two-stroke motorcycle and minibike was finally over, and Harley-Davidson never again became involved in that particular market. "Think big" was the new motto, as well as "Do, and improve, what you do best."

Vaughn Beals, in particular, doggedly supported this newly revived corporate policy — a policy that ultimately proved to be the right strategy despite all the obstacles placed in its path. But for the time being, things were still very much in the balance. While Harley-Davidson still controlled the market for heavyweight motorcycles above 45 cubic inches (750 cc) in 1973 with a 77.5 percent share, this figure had dwindled to 30.8 percent by 1980 — a near fatal situation for a manufacturer that only built bikes of this class. Things looked even worse for AMF: although originally intended to be a profitable subdivision, the 17 percent turnover share provided by Harley-Davidson only yielded a profit share of about 1 percent. For safety's sake, Tom York started looking for more profitable holdings — in short, AMF wanted to rid itself of the trouble-plagued company from as soon as possible — and more than one vulture hoped for easy pickings from yet another exhausted family business. But this was not to be. As the driving force behind Harley, Vaughn Beals had better ideas and, in the final analysis, better arguments...

AMF Scenario:
Ups and Downs – The 1970s

1969 - The AMF shareholders' meeting decides to take over Harley-Davidson and, to the tune of 21 million dollars, purchases the majority stock of the company, which is valued at 40 million dollars. Rodney C. Gott is appointed.

1970 - A new racing model is unveiled: the XR 750.

1971 - The new AMF Harley-Davidson logo appears on all Harley-Davidson products. Production is started at the former AMF factory in York. The corporate complex on Juneau Avenue is converted into a warehouse and administrative headquarters and was more than a mere a production location. A business deal is concluded with Evel Knievel. The FX Super Glide designed by Willie G. makes its debut as the first official custom Harley.

1974 - The union organizes a strike that lasts 101 days. The Super Glide is now available in the FXE version with electric starter. The partnership with Evel Knievel is terminated.

1976 - The XLH/XLCH, FLH and FX/FXE models receive special Liberty Edition tank decals on the occasion of the 200th anniversary of America's independence.

1977 - The company opened a museum in this year in York which was named the Rodney C. Gott Museum.
A new custom model from Willie G.'s design workshop is included in the Sportster series – the XLCR Cafe Racer.

1978 - Harley-Davidson celebrates its 75th anniversary. The company's holding in Aermacchi is terminated and sold. A new Sportster model – the XLT 1000 – is unveiled, as well as the first 80 cubic inch (1340 cc) Shovelhead engine in the FLH 80.

1979 - The Nova project is scrapped and during the AMF's reign Porsche was commissioned to produce the EVO engine. The Super Glide model range is expanded to include a new custom bike: the FXEF Fat Bob, available with a 74 cubic inch (1200 cc) or 80 cubic inch (1340 cc) Shovel engine. The Classic line makes its debut in the FLH series.

1980 - The XLS 1000 Roadster model is added to the Sportster series. Custom versions of the Super Glide series are unveiled: the FXWG Wide Glide and FXB Sturgis, both sporting the 80 cubic inch (1340 cc) Shovel engine.

1981 - With a frame designed by Erik Buell, Harley presents the FLT Tour Glide with an 80 cubic inch (1340 cc) engine and five gears. Under the management of Vaughn Beals, Harley-Davidson buys itself back from AMF.

Radical Cure
Buyback and New Ideas

© Harley-Davidson

A historic moment as the documents for buying back Harley-Davidson are signed in June 1981: Ralph Swenson, Charles K. Thompson, AMF President Ray Tritten (seated) and Vaughn Beals (from left to right).

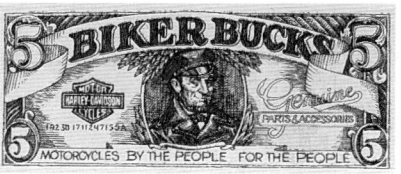

Under the most difficult conditions and often in an icy atmosphere, the initiator of the buyback scheme, Vaughn Beals, worked for months on the deal with – or rather against – his own boss Merlin Nelson (AMF). Jack Reilly from Citicorp Bank gave powerful support to the LBO (Leveraged Buyout), and finally, at the beginning of 1981, Beals invited 13 selected Harley directors and department heads to a memorable meeting in Stamford, Connecticut. At this meeting he put forward the possibility of their purchasing the Harley-Davidson Company, which had been put up for sale by AMF, themselves. It was one, final, desperate attempt to save the company. But the idea of purchasing a capital-consuming factory, which seemed to be fighting a losing battle for survival in the motorcycle market, and having to invest around ten million dollars to do so, was laughable, just too absurd.

The great savior in this crisis was the Citicorp Industrial Credit Bank, which put up the approximately 80 million dollar purchasing price asked by AMF, although with outrageous conditions attached. Just to be able to pay the 16 percent interest charge, Harley-Davidson would virtually have to double its profits, even though the economic outlook was pretty dismal at that time.

However, Citicorp kept its commitment. John A. Davidson got cold feet about this mad adventure and pulled out. His brother Willie G. remained fearlessly with the others, now apparently nothing more than a bunch of highly motivated, but personally liable, gamblers committed to victory or destruction. They included President Charlie Thompson, Vaughn Beals, Dr. Jeffrey Bleustein, Willie G. Davidson,

Kurt Woerpel, Dave Lickerman, Chris Sartalis, John Hamilton, James Paterson, Timothy Hoelter, David Caruso, Ralph Swenson, and Peter Profumo.

Finally the deal was completed and Harley-Davidson again belonged to its own people, although not entirely so, as both they personally and the company itself were liable to their creditor Citicorp for all their assets. On June 16, 1981, in a publicity parade led by Willie G. and the directors, they celebrated the much-acclaimed Homecoming Ride from York to Milwaukee, where it had all started 78 years earlier. The right propaganda slogan was also found: "The Eagle Soars Alone," although at first this sounded more like a desperate attempt at encouragement. Vaughn Beals' optimism was both limitless and crucial.

The company motto was more direct: "Motorcycles by the people, for the people." The philosophy – already conceived under the AMF regime and now supported wholeheartedly by Citicorp – was both revolutionary and convincing. The main problem was clearly quality control. A new method "imported" from Japan, Employee Involvement (EI), was adopted: all employees are involved personally in direct quality control, in other words directives do not come from remote office-bound managers and engineers but from the people who actually take part in the work process. This brought with it a further important innovation: the Material As Needed (MAN) system. This meant goodbye to stock being held in large, often excessive, quantities, kept for years on shelves and other hiding places, rotting, aging, or being damaged in some other way. Instead, refined, computer-controlled logistics ensured delivery of parts exactly when and where they were needed. This now-common practice has since become known as Just In Time (JIT). Finally, perhaps most important element of the new production methods, Statistical Operator Control (SOC). All the employees checked their own work against carefully formulated monitoring and inspection processes. Experience has shown that they are the ones who can best recognize and correct mistakes and most effectively formulate improvements. When all three elements are put together, we can see what has made the great miracle of "Motorcycles by the people, for the people" – MOTIVATION. Ron Hutchinson took over Planning and Implementation, and soon a whole crowd of expensive bureaucrats, engineers and inspectors became surplus to requirements.

That was exactly how Vaughn Beals intended to slim down the operation. He had meanwhile taken some hard management decisions: jobs disappeared, manual and office workers were made redundant, top managers' salaries were frozen, bonuses and social payments cancelled, health care was cut – there were economies everywhere. In the fall of 1981 200 staff and 1,600 manual workers were made redundant, including the young John Harley, the last member of the Harley family. In 1982, when these economies had bitten just about as deep as they could, production increased to 31,000 and the factories were again working to 50 percent capacity.

The New Masters
A Fresh Start in the 1980's

When the deal for buying back Harley-Davidson from AMF was finally concluded in mid-1981, new managers took over the decision-making positions in the newly independent company. The most important of the people involved are listed below:

Vaughn L. Beals

Regarded as the architect of and the brain behind the buy-back. His family originated in Nova Scotia and he studied aeronautics at the Massachusetts Institute of Technology (MIT), specializing in rocket systems ballistics. After holding a management job at Cummins Diesel, he was appointed Vice President of the Motorcycle Group of AMF Harley-Davidson, mainly due to his brilliant management skills. Up until his 45th birthday, Vaughn L. Beals had never even sat on a motorcycle. Nevertheless, he displayed an astounding talent for controlling Harley's powerful bikes and soon became a keen Tour Glide rider. Renowned for taking care of every last detail, Beals was once summed up by these words: "If anybody can get something done, then it's Vaughn Beals!"

Charles K. Thompson

President and CEO of Harley-Davidson, Thompson was friendly with John Davidson from childhood. After initially working as a school teacher and football coach, he was in charge of Harley-Davidson of Louisville from 1966 to 1969. Thompson had loved motorcycling since his youth and soon became the proud owner of an FLT, on which he undertook many a long-distance tour in his ultimate capacity as Harley's President. In 1969, Charlie Thompson was appointed Sales Manager and later Vice President to Harley's President John Davidson. During the AMF era, he became General Manager of the Parts & Accessories Division in 1976 and finally President of Harley-Davidson in 1980. He died in 1988 from a heart attack. Charlie Thompson was an extremely popular and jovial man who was always involved in the world of motorcycling and the biker scene.

William (Willie) G. Davidson

Willie G. had studied at the Art Center College of Design in Los Angeles and had visited numerous motorcycle and biker gatherings, shows and parties during that time. He loved being surrounded by kindred spirits and became intimately familiar with the biker lifestyle, which greatly influenced his subsequent work as Chief Designer at Harley-Davidson. After having spent five years working for Brook Stevens (Excalibur Sports Car), the Continental Division of Ford Motor Company, his father William H. Davidson, then President of the company, appointed Willie G. to the position of Styling Director on February 18, 1963. His response to this appointment went down in the annals of company history: "I'll bring my crayons and be right down..."

Willie G. after winning an Endurance Run in 1952.

Almost certainly with mixed feelings, the new owners of Harley-Davidson pose for an official group photo after the buy-back. From left to right are: John Hamilton, Dr. Jeffrey Bleustein, Kurt Woerpel, Chris Sartalis and William G.Davidson (standing), James Paterson, Timothy Hoelter, David Lickermann, Peter Profumo, David Caruso, Ralph Swenson, Charles Thompson and Vaughn Beals (seated).

© Harley-Davidson

Jeffrey L. Bleustein

Bleustein was a native New Yorker and received his Ph.D. in engineering from the University of Columbia. He was posted to England by NATO and also worked as a technical instructor at Yale University. In 1971, Bleustein was appointed Director of the Research & Engineering Department at AMF, and later became Chief Engineer of AMF Harley-Davidson's Engineering Department in 1975. The main problem he had to solve there was compliance with the stringent Noise & Emission Regulations imposed by the Federal Environmental Protection Agency (EPA), which Harley-Davidson regarded as the greatest challenge to its future survival.

Timothy K. Hoelter

Hoelter was an attorney from Milwaukee and corporate counsel for the company, although not actually employed by either AMF or Harley-Davidson. He counseled the company in financial matters while associated the Milwaukee-based law firm Whyte & Hirchboek S.C. He had earned his law degree at Harvard Law School. Tim Hoelter's task was to take care of the legal and copyright interests of the company and to distance Harley-Davidson from any association with negative images such as drugs, deadheads and Nazi emblems, etc – a task he attempted to fulfill in personal meetings more than via court rulings. He also advised Harley-Davidson on how to treat its dealers.

David Caruso

Caruso was born in Chicago, studied technology at the Illinois Benedictine College and received a Master's Degree from Purdue University. After spending some time at the Cummins Engine factory and a short term as General Sales Manager for Golf Carts, Caruso was appointed Director of the newly structured Parts & Accessories Department in 1973 by John Davidson, succeeding John Harley who died in 1974. David Caruso developed the Parts & Accessories Department into an independently managed unit and was primarily involved in matters concerning licensing rights. David Caruso became Vice President under President Charlie Thompson and General Manager responsible for all of Harley-Davidson's marketing activities (advertising, public relations, displays, trade shows and dealer relations).

Chris Sartalis

Sartalis began his career as Manager and Auditor of AMF's Lawn & Garden Recreational Group in 1966 before becoming Accounting Supervisor of the Motorcycle Group. Afterwards, he ascended the corporate ladder in his capacity as a loyal and talented auditor for Harley-Davidson and became Vice President.

Peter L. Profumo

Profumo was born in New Jersey and graduated as an auditor at Fordham University in New York City. In 1968, after a short period of service with the U.S. Army, he became Internal Auditor at AMF. As Vice President of the Motorcycle Division, Profumo was responsible for all prototypes and pilot projects and for ensuring that the proper marketing activities were implemented. His responsibilities also included determining when a product was ready for the market and when the market was ready to receive a new product. Peter Profumo is an avid Harley enthusiast and a sworn solo rider.

James Paterson

Paterson came from Connecticut, where he graduated from the local university. After a job with Kraft Food in Chicago, he went to AMF in 1971 where he was later responsible for budget analyses and bank connections. Together with Vaughn Beals, he masterminded the financial framework of the buy-back from AMF. James Paterson is a keen sailor who also loves the distinctive sound of a Harley-Davidson.

Ralph Swenson

Swenson was born in Brooklyn in 1920 and was thus the oldest of the new Harley management. He earned his degree at a college of technology, took a four-year apprenticeship as machinist and toolmaker, worked for the U.S. Navy and joined AMF in 1947 where he remained in the Brooklyn plant until it was closed in 1968. After a short spell at AMF's Des Moines plant, he was tasked with installing the assembly equipment for the Harley production line in York in 1972. Together with three other AMF employees from York (Art Donofrio/industrial design, Art Jenkings/planning and Curt Tucker/computation), he attended the Harley-Davidson Service School in order to learn more about the assembly of motorcycles. He subsequently organized the construction of the Sportster assembly line in just six months, allowing the first Sportster models to roll off the line in 1973. Ralph Swenson was President of Harley-Davidson York until 1982.

David R. Lickerman

Like Caruso, Lickerman also came from Chicago. He joined AMF in Mexico where he had worked in his father's engineering company and became Vice President of AMF Mexico in 1962. In 1975, he was appointed Chairman of the International Bowling Equipment Department of AMF. As President of Harley-Davidson International, he remained at Harley's export headquarters in Stamford, Connecticut (which Harley had taken over from AMF) better to manage the company's overseas markets. Responsible for all overseas exports, Lickerman primarily had to deal with the safety regulations of the various countries to which Harley exported. Every Harley-Davidson shipped abroad had to be modified to comply with the local safety regulations. David R. Lickerman is a keen Harley rider and the proud owner of an FLH Classic.

The Turnaround Year

State of the Art Technology and Newfangled Spin Doctors

1983, the year of the turnround. The first modest profits. The hard measures taken by the company management seemed to be effective; quality control, SOC, and the JIT system had quickly reduced the huge mountains of rejects, and the company, now slimmed down to a healthy size, slowly started to recover. Aggressive advertising and marketing campaigns were starting to have an effect; most dealers were prepared to keep to the carefully conceived requirements, and to brighten up their shops.

There was also a technical revolution: the new Evolution engine was now finally able to satisfy the environmental regulations on noise and exhaust emissions, which had been in force for some time. A maintenance-free electronic ignition system, the Magnavox Control Module, had replaced the old contact breaker, and new models were getting unmistakable names: the XLX 61 Sportster, the FXDG 80 Disc Glide – a Wide Glide with a disc rear wheel – and the Super Glide II and II De Luxe. Still rather inexperienced in the new customer motivation strategy, various formulas were tried to discover and concentrate on what Harley buyers actually wanted. Somehow they managed to perform the trick of transforming the old, well-loved legend of the large-capacity 45-degree air-cooled V-Twin engine, which technical experts had long ago consigned to the scrapheap of motorcycle history, into a frontrunner, ensuring its continued success for the foreseeable future. The worldwide Harley community breathed a sigh of relief and scraped their savings together, and even well-to-do enthusiasts suddenly found it really chic to show up on the prestigious model from Milwaukee. The customized models sold like hot cakes, but particularly those with the nostalgic retro look...

But the most important event of this year was probably the formation of the Harley Owners Group, or H.O.G. for short. Harley-Davidson had long recognized that motivation is a key factor in purchasing a motorcycle, and H.O.G. symbolized this corporate policy perfectly. This almost family-like relationship, as managed by the company, is quite unique in the world. It is difficult to imagine a Japanese boss shaking oil-smeared hands, and drinking a can of beer with rough but good-hearted guys at earthy biker parties. But Harley bosses do it and the Harley-Davidson management now regularly attends all the big H.O.G. events.

The frequent Chapter Runs and parties supported by local dealers were particularly well regarded by the general public

Jointly responsible for improved production technology and increased quality standards: Manager Dave Gurka and Engineer Tom Gelb.

and the media, mainly because of their charitable nature, which led to a complete reversal of the previous slightly unsavory biker image.

H.O.G. and Harley-Davidson pushed on vigorously: frequent new special models, lots of accessories, spectacular rallies and advertising campaigns, presentations (in Daytona or Sturgis even), factory visits, sales promotions (demo rides), and bosses whom you could touch, guaranteed high emotions and even higher sales figures. The club's own magazine *HOG Tales*, published in various versions, promoted an "ideal world" family atmosphere and concentrated on attracting new members. New Harley owners were automatically given a year's free membership of H.O.G.

What had really happened? Harley was actually beginning to market its image. A casual, but nonetheless telling, remark was made by Germany's general importer Klaus Zobel: "We sell dreams, Harleys provide them free of charge." Nicely put, but indicative of a hard and effective sales strategy.

New, attractive models appeared, such as the FXST Softail, which gave the illusion of being a rigid-frame hardtail machine, such as were still much-loved by genuine bikers. Willie G. had discovered the innovative rear end, with two shock absorbers hidden below the transmission in the frame. Another sensation was the XR 1000, the street version of a genuine racing machine, although unfortunately only a few were ever built. The beautifully styled, powerful sports motorcycle is now a valuable collectors' item. Additional income was provided by a further government order for practice bombs for the U.S. Navy and the production of cabling systems for the computer control of small jets.

However, the small Tri Hawk three-wheeler, which was produced in very limited quantities (11 per month) in an unpretentious factory in Dana Point, California, bought by Harley in 1984, was not a success. On the other hand, new perspectives were opened up by the German designer Hans A. Muth, and at the same time, a gifted young designer in America, already closely connected with Harley-Davidson, was making moves in the same direction. His name: Erik Buell.

Harley-Davidson's first attempt at launching a genuine racing machine onto the market for private customers: the new XR 1000. However, its success didn't live up to expectations.

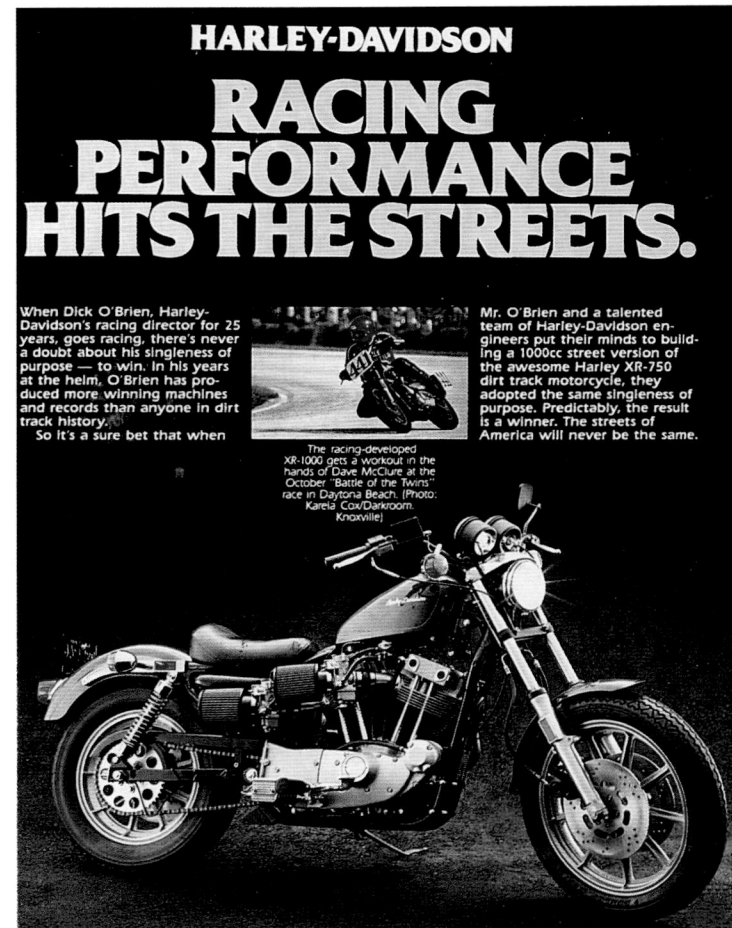

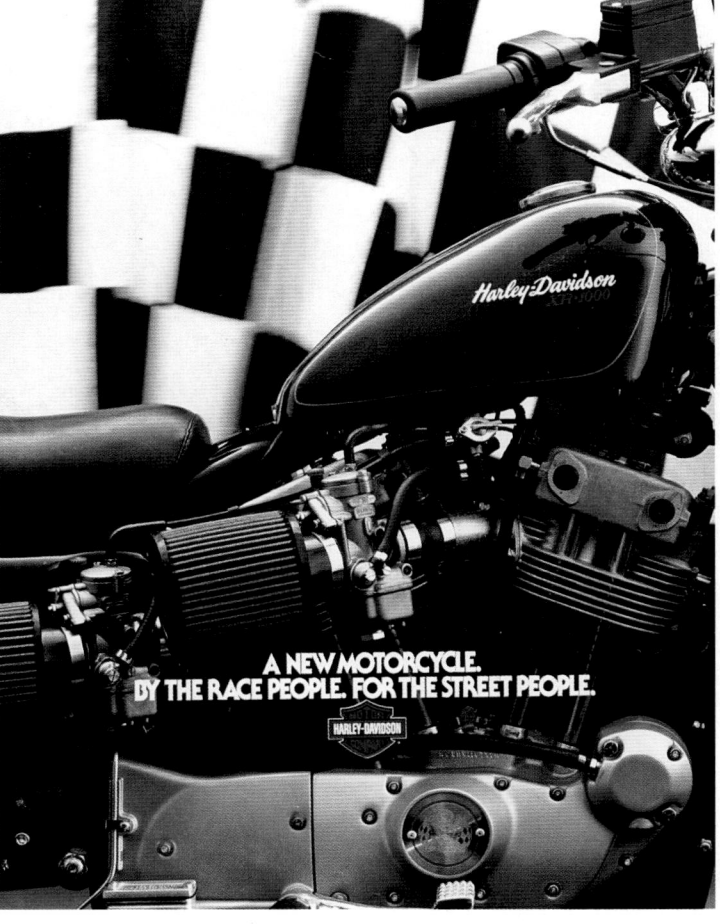

XLCH Sportster

(1970)

The New Year's Eve Cliffhanger

Saving Signatures Just before Midnight

All's well: a happy Rich Teerlink a few years after that fateful New Year's Eve.

In 1984 it looked as if Harley had finally made it. The annual balance sheets made good reading and the new company strategy was clearly on course for success. But now a new storm was brewing over the company, and a more threatening one than any previously experienced. The origin of the potential catastrophe was the change of loan officer at Citicorp.

Jack Reilly, who had always been well disposed towards Harley, was replaced by Todd Slotkin who had spoken out against the Harley credit arrangement from the start. He believed an economic forecast suggesting that Harley would be particularly badly hit by the coming recession, and, on top of that, he had a poor relationship with Vaughn Beals — in short, Citicorp wanted to get rid of a now suspect debtor as quickly as possible. "Look around for someone else," was Slotkin's disdainful comment. And he made the recommendation: no more overdraft facilities! That was the death sentence — Harley was again threatened with liquidation. However, finance director Rich Teerlink and CEO Vaughn Beals entered into urgent negotiations with Citicorp and obtained a short stay of execution in 1985, limited to six months, but Citicorp was resolute; the sentence would be carried out on January 1, 1986. The only way out was to pay back the whole loan in that period, but even though Citicorp cut the payback amount by about ten million U.S. dollars, it was a hopeless situation. The lethal bullet, which would bring the soaring eagle down from its high altitude flight, was already in the breech and the trigger was cocked...

But there was a tiny ray of hope. On the recommendation of Steve Deli, the manager of the Chicago office of the finance company Dean Witter Reynolds, Norm Blake, the boss of the Heller finance company, also based in Chicago, started to look seriously at the possibility of taking over the loan. However, the Citicorp "discount" worked against the deal, for what bank would voluntarily lose 10 million dollars just to get rid of a customer. There must be something seriously wrong! There were frustrating meetings and tough negotiations. Bankers are interested in certainties, not myths and legends.

On December 23, 1984, 11 days before the final deadline, disaster struck. For whatever reason, Norm Blake withdrew his offer. Rich Teerlink, Vaughn Beals, and Vice President Tom Gelb, who received the bad news together in the Heller office, went deathly pale. But they did not give up. With the help of Steve Deli, they managed to persuade Norm Blake to return to the negotiating table. Finally an emergency agreement was reached: with a three-month period of notice, Heller Financing agreed to provide the necessary capital, but with horrifying conditions attached. Harley managers had no choice but to sign,

but there was no relief, time was running out fast. The dramatic moments on the last day before the final deadline are described by Peter C. Reid in his book Well Made in America, as follows:

"It was like a cliffhanger novel that left the reader in suspense at the most gripping moment." According to Thomas Rave, Vice President of the First Wisconsin National Bank of Milwaukee, Rich Teerlink appeared in his office Tuesday morning on December 31, dressed casually in jeans and a flannel shirt and promptly sat down to make sure that the money being made available from various money-lenders actually made its way to Citibank, in order to pay off Citicorp Industrial Credit.

As this was the last working day of the year, Citibank was determined to close its own telegraph room at exactly midday, balance the accounts and close the business books for the current year. In the meantime, Citicorp informed Rave and Teerlink that the entire loan would be called in at the end of the day if the payment was not received on time. In this case, Harley would either have to apply for protection pursuant to Chapter 11 of the American Trading Act or be faced with the liquidation of its business.

On that very same Tuesday morning, Walter Einhorn, who represented Mellon Bank East in Philadelphia in the transaction and who had also signed the loan agreement on behalf of his bank, was unable to find anybody with the appropriate authority to order the requisite telegraphic transfers that were indispensable for finalizing Harley's new financing package.

Teerlink was still seated in Tom Rave's office when he received a call from Heller Financing, informing him that the entire affair could not be concluded on time as nobody was available at the Mellon Bank who could sign the documents needed to authorize the telegraphic transfer. The fact that everyone was looking forward to that evening's New Year celebrations also meant that Heller would be closing shop earlier than usual.

Teerlink succeeded in persuading Heller to postpone closing business a little longer and called Einhorn to tell him how desperate the situation had become. As Rave put it, "He didn't let up until he finally received the necessary signatures. The money was transferred literally seconds before the deadline ran out."

When Teerlink recalled that day for us, he sighed deeply and said "It was damned close. But we managed to get the deal through after all, and that saved us from financial ruin."

The Road to the Stock Exchange

The President Pays a Visit to the Company

The first company to ever hold a parade to Wall Street on the occasion of going public.

Success and triumph: Ronald Reagan congratulates Vaughn Beals on May 6, 1987, in York.

© Harley-Davidson

The financial breathing space, with the threat of bankruptcy as ever looming in the background, demanded new thought processes. "How would it be," said Steve Deli, the financial ideas man, "if you were to be listed on the stock exchange?" It was called "going public." Harley-Davidson as a proper corporation? To publish all balance sheets, income and expenditure information, with no internal secret strategies to counter ever–hostile competitors? And what would the giants of Wall Street make of such a pint–sized newcomer?

In the summer of 1987 Harley-Davidson was listed on the NYSE (New York Stock Exchange). Instead of the usual inaugural dinner, the top management organized a highly emotional, patriotic motorcycle parade from 59th Street, via Fifth Avenue, to Wall Street, where they were given a warm welcome by the President of the NYSE himself on the steps of the Stock Exchange building. It was the first such acceptance ceremony in the history of the New York Stock Exchange, and a very effectively organized PR stunt.

The new shares were offered for sale at 11 dollars each, but doubled in value soon after commencement of trading. Many Harley employees, who had become shareholders out of a sense of loyalty to the company, were therefore rewarded with useful extra income. At the end of 1986, Harley had an unexpected cash surplus of 50 million dollars and were looking for a profitable way of using this money. Again it was Steve Deli who advised Harley of the Holiday Rambler Corporation in Indiana, which was up for sale. The purchase price was around 150 million dollars, however, and the deadline for the deal was tight. Harley finally accepted the tough terms and now boasted the most luxurious range of campers in its portfolio. Vaughn Beals could see a product connection: "making big toys for big boys." The Rambler RVs (Recreational Vehicles) produced healthy profits, but the business was sold ten years later.

At the beginning of 1987 Harley-Davidson declared that they could now do without the protection of the customs tariff imposed in 1983. In any case this was scheduled to run out in 1988. The truth was that the constant rise in exports made the protectionism offered by the U.S. government morally indefensible. But at the same time Harley showed the whole world that they no longer needed any help from the government. The glittering high point of their politically coordinated, promotional activities was the visit of President Reagan to the assembly works in York in May 1987.

In 1988 – the year of the Company's 85th anniversary – Harley-Davidson was proud to present its balance sheets: every Harley built was sold, the turnover reached 757.4 million dollars, with net income of 27.2 million dollars, not including the profits from selling Holiday Rambler, and those from a further U.S. Navy order for bomb casings. It was gratifying too that the ground lost, mainly to Kawasaki with respect to supplying the police, was regained – the CHP (California Highway Patrol) placed a large order with Harley. Exports, particularly to Japan, also showed a marked increase.

The two–year–old 67 cubic inch (1100 cc) Sportster was now finally replaced by the big 74 cubic inch (1200 cc) XLH, a sports motorcycle to match any in the heavyweight class, and as a consequence Harley-Davidson was able to increase its market share in this class from 23.3 percent (1983) to 46.5 percent. The old enemy Honda, the market leader in 1983, with 44.3 percent of the heavyweight class, were now put in their place, with their share reduced to 24.1 percent, figures which brought joy to Harley hearts.

So it was not surprising that the festivities to mark Harley's 85th birthday in Milwaukee, with over 40,000 participants, were the dazzling climax of a much celebrated event. Emotions and expressions of motivation followed one another in quick succession. At the same time, more than half a million dollars was collected for the muscular dystrophy charity program "For Jerry's Kids," run by Jerry Lewis, which was now sponsored by Harley-Davidson.

Technical perfection of the Sportster range: the 1200 cc XLH Sportster was launched in 1988.

The new Harley-Davidson shares quickly increased in value and boosted confidence.

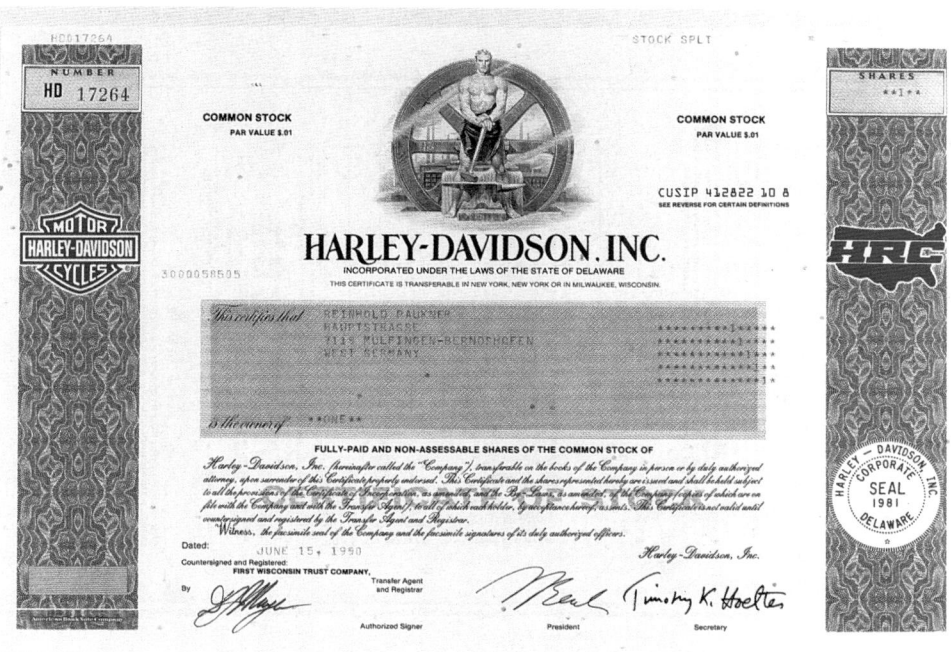

A Satisfying Balance Sheet

Every Other Motorcycle in the U.S. Seems to Be a Harley

From its 95th year, Harley-Davidson has had a proud image as an impressive, coherently structured, efficiently managed, and globally active industrial corporation. Indeed, the annual balance sheet reveals some very interesting facts. In 1996, Harley-Davidson recorded a turnover of some 1.5 billion dollars, with an operating profit of 228 million dollars. A total of 118,771 motorcycles were produced, as well as 2,800 Buell models. Harley's Genuine Motor Parts & Accessories operation recorded 210.2 million dollars in turnover, of which 90.7 million dollars were attributable to clothing alone. A worldwide dealer network of more than 1,000 franchised dealers provided for constant growth in sales. The company employed some 5,000 personnel directly, and spent 179 million dollars solely on the expansion of production plants and investments.

The breakdown of national and international activities for 1996/97 yielded the following picture:

America: 77 percent of all motorcycles produced by Harley-Davidson remain in the U.S. There are 593 Harley dealers in America, 76 in Canada, and 14 in Latin America and Mexico.

Europe: 15 percent of all Harley-Davidson motorcycles are exported to Europe. At the end of the 1990s, there are more than 250 Harley dealers in Europe, overseen by a central headquarters based in London. Independent Harley-Davidson branches are also located in Germany, France, The Netherlands, and Great Britain. Several independent suppliers also cater to other countries, and direct dealerships can be found in the Middle East as well as South Africa.

Asia and the Pacific Rim: eight percent of all Harley-Davidson motorcycles produced each year are shipped to the Asian/Pacific Rim, where 40 Harley dealers are overseen by a Harley-Davidson headquarters in Japan. Three independent importers supply 64 dealers in Australia and New Zealand, and dealerships are also located in Korea, Malaysia, Singapore, Taiwan and Thailand.

Spurred on by favorable market forecasts, an unabated rise in sales figures and the global success of the activities of the Harley Owners Group (H.O.G.), Harley-Davidson has undertaken major efforts in recent years to modernize the entire corporation, switch to larger capacities, and to ensure as great a degree of financial security as possible. The extent to which Harley-Davidson is currently expanding and simultaneously consolidating becomes evident when the new corporate structure is examined in greater detail.

A proud team: Jeff Bleustein, Willie G., Bill Davidson and Rich Teerlink (from left to right).

Another guarantee for success: Chief Designer Willie G. in 1993.

1996: H.D. market shares for motorcycles in the 650 cc class upwards:

America (USA and Canada):

Harley-Davidson	47.6 %
Honda	18.6 %
Kawasaki	12.3 %
Suzuki	9.1 %
Yamaha	6.4 %
BMW	2.8 %
Other	3.2 %

Europe:

Honda	20.7 %
Yamaha	20.7 %
Suzuki	17.4 %
BMW	13.6 %
Kawasaki	11.6 %
Harley-Davidson	6.8 %
Other	9.2 %

Asian / Pacific Rim, (Japan and Australia):

Kawasaki	22.9 %
Harley-Davidson	21.9 %
Yamaha	18.5 %
Honda	13.3 %
Suzuki	8.8 %
BMW	5.4 %
Other	9.2 %

(Source: Harley-Davidson 1996 Annual Report)

The registered office, the central administrative headquarters and the extensive corporate archives of Harley-Davidson are still located at their original, historical address on West Juneau Avenue, which now enjoys national heritage protection.

Harley-Davidson, Inc.
3700 West Juneau Avenue
Milwaukee, Wisconsin 53208

Powertrain Operations, i.e. the engine and transmission plant, also known as the Butler Plant, is located in Wauwatosa, a suburb of Milwaukee, Wisconsin.

Harley-Davidson
Powertrain Operations
11700 West Capitol Drive
Wauwatosa, Wisconsin 53222

The Product Development Center (PDC) which was opened in July 1997 is located virtually next-door.

Willie G. Davidson
Product Development Center
11800 West Capitol Drive
P.O. Box 25527
Wauwatosa, Wisconsin 53225

The Pilgrim Road Facilities - a new plant in which the FL/FX (1340 cc) engines and transmission are to be manufactured – was only recently part-purchased/part-leased from Messrs. Briggs & Stratton (Vanguard plant) and is situated somewhat more to the north in Menomonee Falls. Production started in spring 1998.

Harley-Davidson
Powertrain Operations
Pilgrim Road West 156
North 9000 Pilgrim Road
Menomonee Falls,
Wisconsin 53051

The Franklin Distribution Center is Harley's newly built Parts and Accessories (P & A) distribution center, encompassing more than 250,000 square feet.

Buell Motors, the current production plant for all Buell motorcycles, is located to the west of Milwaukee. The engines are supplied from the Capitol Drive Powerplant.

Buell Motors
2815 Buell Drive
East Troy, Wisconsin 53120

The Harley-Davidson Assembly Plant York is the former AMF plant in Pennsylvania in which all Harley-Davidson 1340 cc and 1450 cc Sportster and FL models are currently assembled. This plant also houses the new paint shop.

Harley-Davidson York
1425 Eden Road
York, Pennsylvania 17402

The Tomahawk Fiberglass Plant is where all the plastic components for Harley-Davidson motorcycles are produced and is located in the north of Wisconsin. The plant was recently expanded by more than 5,000 square feet.

Harley-Davidson Tomahawk
426 East Somo Avenue
Tomahawk, Wisconsin 54487

The Talladega Test Facility is where Harley-Davidson maintains its own testing and proving grounds in Alabama, directly next to the Talladega Superspeedway.

Harley-Davidson
Talladega Test Facility
144 Division Street
Lincoln, Alabama 35096

Harley-Davidson Kansas City is the Sportster production plant and was completed in 1998. The factory, which covers more than 300,000 square feet and has a workforce of some 300 personnel.

Harley-Davidson Kansas City
1225 Bedford
North Kansas City,
Missouri 64116

Harley-Davidson Credit now has a new Operations Center in Carson City. Harley-Davidson's own credit and insurance company, Eaglemark Financial Services, also has branch offices in Chicago, Illinois and Plano, Texas.

Harley-Davidson Credit
Carson City, Nevada

Corporate branch offices and headquarters abroad:

Harley-Davidson Europe
32 Frances Road
Windsor, Berkshire
England, SL43AA

Harley-Davidson European
Distribution
Center Cleton & Co BV
Schrijnwerkerstraat 2
2984 BC Ridderkerk
Rotterdam Port Area
The Netherlands

Harley-Davidson Japan
Isuzu Shiba Building
4/2/3 Shiba, Minato-Ku
Tokyo, Japan 108

Harley-Davidson Singapore
Representitive Office
111 North Bridge Road
11-04/06 Peninsula Plaza
Singapore, Malaysia

© Harley-Davidson

© Harley-Davidson

The Four Unions
Worker Participation After Decades of the Patriarchs

In the age of patriarchal company structures, "Old Bill" (William A. Davidson) looked after his factory workers and employees like a father-figure. He was always responsible and ready to help out, and proved this with the consistent level of employment that the company maintained during the Great Depression of the 1930s. But times changed, and under the modern management of Vaughn Beals the advantages of close cooperation with the unions were realized. In 1988 the two sides signed a cooperation agreement laying out future common goals. Eighty experts sat down with company managers and union representatives in order to clear away the remaining problems and areas of difficulty. It was to prove a worthwhile course of action, and since then Harley-Davidson has received several awards from the four unions concerned, which is a source of great pride: the first-ever Union Label Award was presented by the AIW (Allied Industrial Workers) Local 209 to the Capitol Drive factory in Milwaukee; and later awards were given by AIW Local 460 to the plant in Tomahawk; by the IAM (Machinist and Aerospace Workers) Lodge 175 to the plant in York; and by the IAM Lodge 78 to the toolmaking factory in Milwaukee. Today no large-scale project is undertaken without detailed consultations with the unions.

The proud creditor and his equally proud debtor: Jim Ryan of Harley-Davidson Motor Credit (left) and Texan Harley dealer Sherman Barnett.

© Harley-Davidson (Photo: Barnett)

Harley-Davidson Credit
The Company's Own Bank

Clever financial managers have long known that the best security and guarantee for the continuous and predictable sales of their products is a serious financing system with proper terms and conditions that relieves dealers and customers alike of the worry of exorbitant third-party loans. At Harley-Davidson, this knowledge was turned into a long-overdue corporate strategy of vital importance to the company's survival.

The strict business principle of only delivering goods that were paid for upon receipt (COD – short for Cash On Delivery) led to many dealers being unable to purchase their stocks of Harleys without third-party financing, particularly in the critical 1980s. Because their customers didn't pay until after a sale was completed, the dealers faced little choice but to accept the often scandalous terms and conditions demanded by local banks or financing companies, which placed Harley dealers throughout America in an absurd situation. The latest models often spent several weeks in the warehouse of a money lender as security for a loan, instead of being on display in the dealer's showroom, as should have been the case. Because of this, some customers were frequently offered a discount if they agreed to leave their motorcycle on display in the dealer's showroom a while longer. Dealers even joined forces and formed pools to be able to supply their motorcycles more effectively. Unfortunately, this approach failed to save many dealers from bankruptcy.

The remorseless and ever more urgent complaints from its dealers were not the only reason for the birth of Harley's financing program. Harley-Davidson itself had long realized that in-house financing was the best way to help dealers and customers alike to purchase its products. To this end, Harley-Davidson founded its own financing empire which provides customers and dealers with guarantees and security. In the event that something should go wrong with a deal, the stock returns to Harley's ownership and not into the hands of greedy liquidators.

Of course, making sure that such an independent financial empire is truly crisis-proof calls for financial resources in such magnitude that not even huge international corporations can pull it out of a hat. Nevertheless, Harley-Davidson managed to surmount even this obstacle and did so quite admirably.

Harley-Davidson Credit functions much like any other bank. The subsidiary Eagle Mark Financial Services (EMF) provides dealers with moderately-termed financing for motorcycles, stock, insurance, real estate and end-user financing packages. EMF (a 100 percent holding of Harley-Davidson) takes care of the holders of all Harley-Davidson credit cards. This used to be handled in cooperation with American Express, but is now done with Visa, whose latest attraction is the HD Chrome Visa Card. The end-users can submit their loan applications directly via the dealer and the EMF representative then visits the dealer personally. These representatives have at their disposal a whole armory of financing and insurance plans aimed at catering to any customer wish imaginable. The headquarters of Harley Financial Services in Chicago continuously provides information concerning the Advisor program and the Harley Credit Report, as well as how to use the various options available through these financing programs as effectively and profitably as possible. Today, the danger of the eagle dropping out of the sky no longer exists, as Harley-Davidson Credit is the wind beneath its wings.

The Davidson Dynasty

From a Family Firm to a Global Family Affair

The Davidson clan today:
Amy D., Carrie D.-Wood, Michael D.,
Willie "G." D., Nancy D., Karen D.,
Bill D., Carlie and John D.

There is no doubt that its four founding fathers saw Harley-Davidson as a family firm. The name itself is evidence of this unspoken understanding between them. Consequently, members of both families were always willingly integrated into the company but this policy did not always succeed, since new generations often have different ideas and interests. Nevertheless, in 1930 for example, 17 Davidsons and three Harleys were working in more or less important posts, all of whom had begun their careers at the bottom of the ladder. A large proportion of family members became co-owners of the firm by virtue of buying stock, which in most cases guaranteed them a carefree existence. The participation was, however, kept strictly secret, since the family wished to prevent any possible and unfortunately all too common media revelations which might damage the business. Even today it is almost impossible to unravel the complicated and intertwined structures of family ownership.

Furthermore, Harley-Davidson had long since grown too large and too powerful, to continue to function as a private family concern. But the end of the road was to come long after the death of the four patriarchs, when AMF replaced the increasingly powerless, family management in 1969. For the remaining scions of the family it was a bitter experience that a privately managed company could no longer assert itself at that level in the modern world's economic and industrial order. This is not the place for idle speculation of the "what

if" variety, but it is worthy of note that in the continuation of the family dynasty, of all people it was the two brilliant, company founders, William S. Harley and Arthur Davidson, who played the smallest role. Today the Harleys have completely disappeared from the day-to-day running of the company, but in the case of the Davidsons, the third and fourth generations of William A. "Bill" Davidson's progeny have once again woven themselves into the fabric of the family myth, with all the myriad associations you would expect, through the outstanding personality of grandson Willie G. together with his children, particularly Bill and Karen Davidson.

And so a unique legend of the motorcycle world has come full circle, and today Harley-Davidson is once more, albeit in a greater and figurative sense, a family affair.

The four company founders demonstrate solidarity in 1910.

© *Harley-Davidson*

The Father

William S. Harley

Born December 29, 1880 in Milwaukee. A schoolfriend of Arthur Davidson. At the age of 15 he worked in a bicycle factory and together with Arthur Davidson designed the first Harley–Davidson motorcycle. In 1903 he studied engineering at the University of Wisconsin in Madison. William was a talented draftsman, a lover of nature, and had an excellent technical mind. He loved riding his motorcycle and took part successfully in numerous enduro competitions. With the founding of the company he became Chief Engineer and Treasurer of Harley-Davidson. In both World Wars he had sole responsibility for contacts and relationships with the armaments offices of the U.S. War Department. For 24 years William Harley was a leading figure in the competition committee of the AMA. He enjoyed playing handball and was a member of the local Businessmen's Sketch Club of Milwaukee, a respectable organization of amateur artists. William S. Harley died of a heart attack on September 18, 1943.

The Sons/ Second Generation

William J. Harley

This engineering graduate, born in 1912, received no special privileges. From the age of 19 he worked his way up, starting out as a draftsman in the production department. After Bill Ottaway's retirement, he took over the design and development department. His time there saw the creation of, among others, the Model S 125, the K models and the first Shovelheads. William J. Harley passed away in 1971.

John Harley

The second son of William S. Harley was an assistant and later manager in the Parts Department at the beginning of the 1940s. For a time John Harley was Chairman of the AMA board and also became its Treasurer.

The Grandchildren/ Third Generation

John Harley jr.

Nothing is written about him in the company annals, and that is the way it should stay.

The Father

Arthur Davidson

Born on February 11, 1881 in Milwaukee, Arthur was the dynamo of ideas and far-sighted visionary behind the new firm he had created with schoolfriend William Harley shortly after the turn of the century. He immediately concerned himself with sales, building up a large and efficient dealer network at home and abroad and developing new marketing strategies. From the beginning he was Vice President, Secretary and Sales Manager of the company. In 1923 Arthur Davidson became President of the Kilburn Finance Corporation for a time. His commitment as President of the M&ATA later led to his Presidency of the AMA, which he held for six years until his death. Although he retained a strong feeling of loyalty towards the firm, he declined the Presidency of Harley-Davidson in his later years. Arthur Davidson was an enthusiastic farmer in his leisuretime and bred Guernsey cattle. He died along with his wife in an automobile accident on December 30, 1950.

The Son/ Second Generation

James Davidson

James Davidson makes no appearance in the company chronicles either. It is known, however, that James too, lost his life in an automobile accident, together with his wife, in 1965.

The Father

Walter Davidson

A railroad engineer by trade, Walter Davidson was a pioneer as a materials and tool specialist and developed quickly from being an accomplished builder of motorcycles and competitive rider in endurance and reliability contests to his role as the persnickety and patriarchal President of the company. He held this post until his death on February 7, 1942, having made a selfless personal contribution to the firm. Walter Davidson was considered the head of the company, and his large personality and charisma taken with his personal modesty, his humor, and "quick–witted craftiness" (as author Wolfgang Wiesner has it) made him an industrialist respected and feared in equal measure. Walter Davidson used his power consistently and without compromise (some would say mercilessly) for the good of Harley-Davidson. He was an incorruptible perfectionist and someone who grasped the wider picture and thought in the long term. History has proved him right. As the most influential personality in the American motorcycle industry, he had an important function in the AMA and was, among other things, on the board of directors of the Northwestern Mutual Life Insurance Company and the Milwaukee Gas Light Company. Walter Davidson was married to Emma and had two sisters – Janet and Elisabeth, later Davidson-Marx.

The Sons/ Second Generation

Walter C. Davidson jr.

Walter C. Davidson jr. joined the company in 1936 and initially worked as an assistant to his uncle Arthur, then head of sales. In 1943 he became a director, in 1951 Secretary and Vice President. As head of sales and Treasurer he was a gifted purchaser and organizer, and demonstrated this above all during World War II. At the same time he was faced with rebellious dealers, since the company, which had switched completely to war production, was unable to deliver enough motorcycles for the home market. When AMF took over Harley-Davidson at the end of the 1960s, Walter C. Davidson resigned from his post in frustration and went into retirement. Duck shooting and horseriding numbered among his hobbies. His wife, Née Briggs, owned a considerable number of Cushman shares.

Gordon M. Davidson

As a teenager Gordon took part in the well-known publicity ride from Milwaukee to Los Angeles. Later he became Vice President and for a time head of production. A popular and humorous man, Gordon Davidson died of lung cancer in 1967.

Robert Davidson

There is no particular mention made of Robert Davidson in the company history.

The Father

William A. Davidson

William A. Davidson, eldest of the three Davidson brothers – born in Scotland on October 14, 1870 – came to the firm as an experienced toolmaker and a man well-versed man in material and machines. He gave up a remunerative job on the railroad to become the final co-owner of Harley-Davidson. Although he never rode a motorcycle himself, as works manager and head of personnel he concerned himself with all the production processes, technical developments, plant and machinery, and purchasing in an extraordinarily successful and effective manner. More than anything he was the mentor of his workers and employees, with whom he enjoyed an almost paternal relationship. He was always ready to help, be it with good advice or with loans of money (which in many cases he never got back). "Old Bill," as he was lovingly called, was the heart of the company. He died from diabetes on April 21, 1937 – two days after he was forced to sign a long-fought-over agreement admitting the unions to his factory.

The Sons/ Second Generation

William H. Davidson jr.

William Herbert Davidson was born in 1905, graduated with honors from his business studies course at the University of Wisconsin and joined the company in 1928, initially as a worker. He was highly talented and so was able to work his way up from foreman through being manager of various sections to leading positions. Through his father William A. Davidson's large stock holding, he achieved an influential position in the company. In 1942 William H. Davidson became President of Harley-Davidson and remained in this post within the AMF Motorcycle Division. Conflict with AMF's strategy and the chaotic market situation led to his resignation in 1973. William H. Davidson jr. died in 1992.

Allan Davidson

Like his nephew Gordon, Allan Davidson took part in the 1929 publicity ride set up by Harley-Davidson to introduce its 45 cubic inch side-valve model, but remained with the company for only a short time thereafter.

The Grandchildren/Third Generation

John A. Davidson

John A. Davidson learned to ride a Harley motorcycle at the early age of 13 under the tutelage of his father William H. Davidson jr., and as a teenager he took part in numerous cross-country events with his equally enthusiastic brother Bill. After his graduation in 1957 as an economist from Lawrence University in Appleton, Wisconsin, followed by a two-year management course and employment at the Milwaukee motor producers Allis Chalmers, he joined Harley-Davidson in 1961, initially as head of the Dealer Relations Department. John A. Davidson occupied numerous positions in the company and as sales manager became Vice President in 1969. In 1971 he was head of the marketing department and Executive Vice President, and in 1973 finally became President of Harley-Davidson. In the same year he was elected President of the AMA. He supported the buy-back of the company, but in 1981 withdrew from all his company posts.

William G. Davidson

Having grown up with motorcycles, Willie G. graduated in graphic art from the University of Wisconsin and then went to the Art Center College of Design in Pasadena, California, where he encountered the biker and custom motorcycle scene. After his education in California he worked initially in the design department at Ford in Detroit, and thereafter for five years at Brook Stevens ("Excalibur"), where he was already designing his own custom motorcycles and choppers. In 1963 his father William H. Davidson jr. summoned him to the company and asked him to take over the design department. Often tagged as a non-conformist, Willie G. calmly began to develop new and revolutionary stylistic directions, at first in the face of the reservations and resistance of the company management. He created completely new model series, beginning with the famous FX Super Glide – Willie G. had recognized the spirit of the age only too well at the many biker meetings he had attended.
Today Willie G. is Vice President and Director of Styling. Along with his wife Nancy, he is a tireless, ever-friendly and always accessible representative at innumerable Harley events, some large, some small, and he has long been a legendary symbol of the family and firm.

Great-grandchildren/ Fourth Generation

Bill Davidson

Bill Davidson began his motorcycle career at the age of seven on an M-50. Later larger Harleys were added. Since 1984 he has worked for Harley-Davidson, recently as manager of the Harley Owners Group, a job which took him to H.O.G. events around the world. Today he is director of the Motorcycle Product Development Department and can be seen, now as then, at most Harley events. He is a long-time supporter of the MDA-Kids charity.

Karen Davidson

Karen is director of the Motor-Clothes department at Harley-Davidson. Like the rest of the family, she loves riding her motorcycle.

Michael Davidson

Michael (see the Davidson family picture on page 91) also works as an artist in New York and is a consultant to the Harley-Davidson Store Design department.

The Million Dollar Deal

New Horizons with Erik Buell at 150 mph

Erik Buell (above) and his racing machine that belonged to Willie G.

At first Erik Buell wanted to be a rock musician, but then he got into motor sport. He rode just about anything that was good, fast and expensive: Kawasaki, Velocette, Yamaha, Honda, and finally the Harley-Davidson XR 1000. But something in him remained unfulfilled, and finally, he decided to build his own ultimate racing machine, making use of his degree in mechanical engineering.

Buell worked successfully in this capacity in the Development and Construction Division of Harley-Davidson from 1978 to 1984 on the improvement of frames (the Tour Glide frame is an innovation of his, for example). During this period he purchased the rights to a two-stroke, square-four engine, which was made by Barton Engineering, and constructed his own highly specialized frame. With this first racing machine, which he dubbed the RW 750, he intended to play a major part in the AMA's elite class, Formula 1, and on it he reached a top speed of 178 mph at the Talladega Speedway.

But just as he was about to really get started at his new "Pittsburgh Performance Products" workshop, the AMA declared that 1985 would be the last year of the Formula 1 Class and that a new top class was to be created: the Superbike category. It looked as if Erik Buell was finished. However, he managed, using his charm and calling in some favors at the company, to persuade Harley-Davidson to let him have 50 left-over XR 1000 engines. These supersportsters (constructed from 1983 to 1984) though ridden with some success by Gene Church and David McClure in the BOTT ("Battle of the Twins") Class, had been a sales flop.

Buell hoped to construct a better competition motorcycle for this class around them. The experiment was a success, and from 1985 to 1988 50 of these 90-100 horsepower RR 1000 Battletwins were built, using particularly effective aerodynamics. Eventually a road version was also made in order to satisfy the homologation regulations. When the XR 1000 engines ran out, Erik Buell fitted the new four-speed Evo Sport-

The factory in East Troy; next to it, the engine warehouse and assembly line. Assembly was still performed by hand.

ster 1200 cc engine into the frames. By 1989 a total of 65 examples of this new 1200 Battletwin had been created.

In the same year, the RS 1200 Westwind was developed from this. 102 of these were built by 1991 as road–going sport bikes for a new clientele who up to then had used Japan production models. In 1991 the improved RSS 1200 Westwind, with a five–speed transmission and six–piston, front brake caliper, evolved from this. A total of 325 of them had been built by 1993.

In 1993 Harley–Davidson brought a 49 percent shareholding in Buell for around a million dollars, and so became a partner in the new Buell Motorcycle Company, which, with its works based southwest of Milwaukee in East Troy, now became a division of the Harley–Davidson Motor Company. This allowed Harley–Davidson to finally break into the domain of the supersports bikes. The first joint models were the S2 Thunderbolt and the S2T Thunderbolt, a two–seat sport touring version, of

which an edition of 1,500 was produced, and a further 429 in 1995. In 1996 the S1 Lightning appeared, with a production run of 1,407. Then in 1997 two more sensational sports motorcycles arrived, the updated S3 Thunderbolt, with its touring stablemate equipped with saddle bags, the S3T Thunderbolt, and also the M2 Cyclone, which immediately received rave reviews from all test riders.

With these half–racing, half–sports motorbikes Harley–Davidson attracted those who prefer superfast, muscle bikes. A wide range of equipment and accessories are now available for all Buell models, from matching clothing to special spark plugs, plus a lot of tuning parts not sold by Harley. Anyone who would like to try out one of these projectiles for themselves can do so on one of the many demo rides on offered at any of the major events where Harley itself is also represented.

Rick Kuchenbecker, a police officer in East Troy, with what was probably the only – unofficial – Police White Lightning: a special edition manufactured by Buell.

Assembly, final testing and packaging at the Buell works. By now, Buell had become a fully–owned subsidiary of Harley–Davidson. Although Jerry Wilke was CEO, Erik Buell was still Technical Director.

Flathead Big-Twin
Model VL

(1930 – 1936)

The Production Plants

50 Years Without an Assembly Line

This Immense Plant is Devoted Exclusively to the Manufacture of Harley-Davidson Motorcycles

Dealers from all over the world like to advertise the scope of Harley-Davidson products available in imaginative brochures, such as the one in the above photo from Walter Andrews in Toronto.

Opposite: courtesy of Franz Simmerlein, Germany

Three years after the first motorcycle was sold, the small 10 x 15-foot shed, which William sr. had provided for his motorbike-mad sons in the garden of the family home on Highland Avenue, was bursting at the seams. The orders for Harley-Davidson motorcycles were increasing daily, and the four young entrepreneurs needed some kind of production plant for themselves and their six regular employees.

When, in 1905, they acquired a large plot in a western suburb of Milwaukee, with the help of a substantial loan from their uncle, James McLay (Honey Uncle), who was always on the lookout for investments, they could never have imagined that in just 20 years they would own the largest motorcycle factory in the world!

In 1906 the Davidsons and Bill Harley, together with a few friends, used some of the ample land at the crossing of 37th and Chestnut Street (later Juneau Avenue) to construct a 30 x 80 foot two-story wooden building, which at first stood in the way of a railroad track. In 1907 there were already 18 employees working in the small factory. One year later the number had increased to 35 and a 28 x 80 foot brick extension was erected.

By 1910 the working area was again too small and cramped, so the three-year old corporation took out a hefty loan with its new house bank Marshal & Ilsley in order to construct its first purpose-built manufacturing facility. Now there were 9,250 square feet available.

In 1911, one counted 418 employees! Again the premises were too small. The next building had to have more floors. In 1912 (1,076 employees!) another five-story production building was added; this was the red brick building which still serves as the company headquarters: 3700 West Juneau Ave. In total, the production area of all the plants was now 187,000 square feet. In 1914 another floor was added, the sixth, so that the total floor space was now 300,000 square feet. It was a mighty plant, good to look at and to show off to visitors, and contributing greatly to the pride of Milwaukee industry. 16,427 Harleys were produced there in that year, and a further 2,500 sidecars were ordered from Rogers.

Meanwhile, the most modern machine tools and production machines had been installed in the still cramped workshops. Huge transmission systems with numerous leather belts kept them in constant motion.

Government and U.S. postal service orders brought a new impetus to production. Output was now almost 30,000 units, but the motorcycles were only assembled on receipt of orders and then delivered as quickly as possible. The ever-changing models and color combinations placed ever greater demands on space for storing the large numbers of prefabricated parts required. So in 1918 the company borrowed a further three million dollars from its house bank, bought more land and built a new, five-story factory at right angles to the main works. Now there were 542,258 square feet available and, in 1920, when the whole site was complete, Harley-Davidson became the largest motorcycle factory in the world.

The Harley-Davidson factory c. 1911.

© Harley-Davidson

The early factory with its famous water tower on Juneau Avenue.

Changing shifts at the front office exit. The Department of War (later to become the Department of Defense) awarded Harley the flag for excellent performance.

The company proudly announced this superlative achievement in glossy brochures and lavishly illustrated press announcements as well as advertisements. The new plant now employed 2,400 manual and office workers, and sales rose in this year to record levels.

The company soon paid the price for this huge increase in size. In the year 1921 the factory was forced to close from mid–March to mid–April because of insufficient incoming orders; World War I was over and the economic recession was casting dark shadows over the industry. In 1925 the company opened its own factory solely for side-car production.

The official production figures for the 1920s, which are virtually identical to the sales figures, give a good insight into the problems faced by Harley–Davidson with its huge plant:

1920: 27,040 units	1923: 17,046 units	1926: 22,275 units
1921: 11,460 units	1924: 17,648 units	1927: 18,546 units
1922: 10,786 units	1925: 15,371 units	1928: 20,684 units

In 1929 of all years, the year of "Black Friday" which marked the beginning of the world economic crisis, the company returned its third best production figures ever recorded: 23,989 motorcycles. But after that, things did not look so cheerful:

1930: 18,036 units	1931: 10,407 units	1932: 7,218 units

Foreman and factory chief in Milwaukee during the first world war (far left): J. P. Ryan, head of the HD Service School for many years.

Then, in 1933, the almost fatal low point of just 3,703 units. This was a difficult time for the company as they made serious losses, and the plant operated at only one-tenth capacity.

At this time exports played a significant role. In 1932 a contract was signed with the Japanese agent Alfred Rich Child, representing the Sankyo organization, for the supply of blueprints, machines and tools which were surplus to requirements. This arrangement brought some money into the hard-pressed coffers. Other income was mainly from sales to government authorities.

After large orders from the U.S. Army during World War II and the virtual shutdown of civil production, 1944 saw another reverse – the U.S. Government canceled an order for 11,331 military machines. Over 500 workers were made redundant and in October 1945 the work-force went out on strike for two weeks.

In 1946 the order situation improved; production increased to 16,222 machines, in 1947 to 20,115 and in 1948 it increased yet again, to a new high of 29,612. In the same year, the company had purchased a further single-story production building in the western suburb of Butler/Wauwatosa from the former machine-building factory A.O. Smith for 1.5 million dollars. This had been used during the war for producing propellers for combat aircraft.

In a surprise move, the Butler Plant (later known as Capitol Drive) was presented to dealers attending the Dealer Convention in 1947. The workshops, with floor space of over one million square feet, were mainly filled with machine tools, gear production equipment, turning, milling and grinding machines. In 1954 came a further extension – at the northeastern end of the Butler Plant another single-story factory building was erected, containing the heat-treating and plating department, which would overcome the tiresome task of transport to and from Juneau Avenue. In 1962 Harley bought a boat factory in Tomahawk, Wisconsin, 180 miles to the north, where all the plastic components used on their motorcycles were laminated and lacquered.

During the AMF era the Butler Plant on Capitol Drive mainly produced engines and gearboxes. Owing to lack of space, final assembly, frame and Sportster production were switched to the former AMF armaments and sports goods plant in York, Pennsylvania. In the early 1970s, against the wishes of the conservative Harley board, AMF was finally able to introduce conveyor-belt production and assembly, over half a century after Henry Ford had first "invented" this automated method of production.

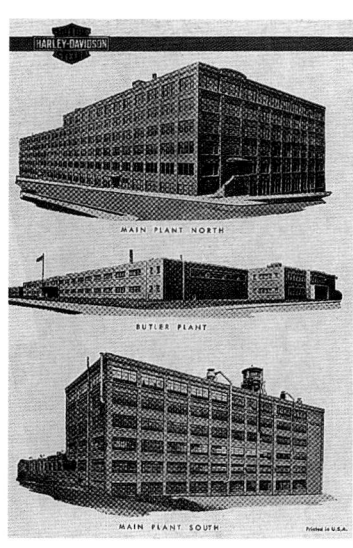

A Harley-Davidson brochure shows the plant facilities from the 1950s.

99

The Impressive Production Process I

A Tour of the Company Around 1939

In 1939, in a three-part series in the Harley magazine *The Enthusiast*, Howard E. Jameson, writing under his pseudonym Hap Hayes, gave a detailed insight into Harley-Davidson's extensive production processes, including the countless departments and the individual production areas found within the factory complex on Juneau Avenue, at that time covering over 430,500 square feet. The following is an abridged summary:

The Display Room, a spacious hall where models under current production as well as some of the company's historic motorcycles are proudly displayed.

The Engineering Department, Planning Department, Experimental Department and the Drafting Boards: that is the whole planning center, research and development and design offices, all with a large "No admittance" sign on their doors.

The Tool Department: this houses the many machine tools, chucking devices, die-casting machines for models, and machine parts which are supplied to the whole factory on a self-sufficiency basis. Then there are all kinds of bar steel in stock, in various colors to identify the intended application and material quality required. Particularly impressive: the high-speed thread-cutting machines for screws and bolts in all sizes; 130 automatic machines looking like a battery of guns. Here all the blanks for gears, ball bearings and small parts are cut from the long steel bars, milled, turned and bored.

The Automatic Screw Machine Department uses around 1,500 gallons of cooling oil per month while processing about 80 tons of steel into screws.

The Punch Press Department houses the gigantic, two-stories-high, 100-ton steel press which is used to produce all the moldings required for production, from half tanks to fenders, all from sheet steel. Its muffled pounding makes the whole building vibrate. Other presses in this department are used for processing thinner sheets. Next to them are the punches, which are just as powerful. Bakelite parts for the electrics are also pressed here.

A small section from the ground floor of the Butler Plant.

© *Harley-Davidson*

In just a few years, primitive workshops like this one from the turn of the century developed into gigantic, fully mechanized manufacturing plants.

Maintaining huge stocks requires a corresponding logistics system.

The welding, soldering and annealing of frames was a hellish job.

The Gear Cutting Department produces the gears; three types mainly helical, bevel and spur gears, in about 30 different sizes. A whole battery of gear shapers, precision cutters which are also called enveloping gear generators, work to a precision of half a ten-thousandth of an inch. Not for nothing are Harley gearboxes famous for their quiet operation and easy gear changes. But the greatest technical marvels are the Bullard Multi-Matics machines which, using 15 cutting tools simultaneously, finish all the round parts in five operations: crankshafts, rear wheel gear rims, dynamo bodies, brake drums, connecting rods, and smaller parts all get their finishing touches here.

The Lathe and Drill Press Department mainly prefabricates smaller parts; long rows of automatic lathes and milling machines see to that.

The Plating Department, together with the Heat Treating Control Department, is where copper, nickel, and chromium plating is carried out, where parts requiring special hardening are prepared in precisely, temperature-controlled furnaces and oilpans. Next to these heat-producing departments is the Brace Department where, for example, the frame bushings are hard-soldered. Moving from production to assembly, you would encounter the following departments and processes:

The Small Assembly Department is the place in which small parts are carefully assembled by hand. In this part of the factory there are a number of other final processing departments: the Enameling Department, the Grinding Department, the Milling Department, and many special sections of the General Assembly Department. Incidentally, the enameling department uses 10,000 gallons of paint, glazing and thinners per year. In a furnace kept at precisely 325 degrees Fahrenheit, the layer of paint is stoved twice and smoothed with the finest sandpaper between the two operations. Tanks get an extra glazing. Ornamental lines are applied individually by a steady hand with a paint brush — as it is still done today.

In the Generator and Ignition Department everything required for electrics and ignition is produced, including spark plugs and ignition coils which other companies buy in from outside suppliers.

All the finished components then go on to perhaps the most important department, the General Inspection Department where everything is tested to its minimum tolerances, mainly by women with a particularly sensitive touch. Modern precision measuring tools are used, for example Johansson Gage Blocks, metal blocks which are

Crystal Haydel – The First Biker Lady

In the opening chapter of his book *Harley-Davidson 1930–1941* Robert Wagner gave a very impressive description of who could be found where at the factory at the beginning of the 1930s. Here, a few extracts are presented in summary form.

In Reception was the switchboard operator, Stella Forge. In the Company Secretary's Office there was Arthur Davidson, the Sales and Advertising Director, with his secretary Francis Miller. The Sales Office contained T.A. Miller, Hermann Schulke and the Export Manager Eric von Gumpert. Then the Company President's Office – Walter

101

Davidson was in residence here, with his secretary, a certain Miss Crystal Haydel, who was responsible for the accounts, personnel and stock transfers. It is believed, that she was also the first woman in Wisconsin to officially ride a motorcycle. The Finance and Accounting office was the domain of Joe Kilbert and Jack Balsom. In the Parts & Accessories Department, Harry Devine was the boss, and in the Service Department Joe Ryan, the grumbling Irish giant with the amazing memory.

The Factory Service School & Training Department was the responsibility of Orin Lamb, and in the Racing Department Hank Syvertsen was in charge.

In the Editorial Department, known as the "Fountain Pen," were *The Enthusiast* staff, Walter Kleimenhagen and Howard E. Jameson who, as "Hap" Hayes, gave technical advice in the "Uncle Frank says..." column. Whatever had to be recorded was transcribed by the shorthand typist Nellie Newkirk. "Big Bill," the Vice President, and Factory Manager William A. Davidson, sat in the presidential office, when he was not hunting or fishing. Then his Plant Superintendent George Nortmann took over. He was often called the fifth Davidson: since 1907 he had devoted his whole life to the company. In the Company Treasurer's office were Chief Engineer William S. Harley and his personal secretary Joe Geiger, who handled all the plans, design documents, drawings and thousands of other papers, as well as dealing with Bill Harley's correspondence. When he retired in 1982, Joe was the longest-serving Harley-Davidson employee, with 63 years to his credit. The Head of the Engineering and Development Department was William Ottaway who had been responsible for the Racing Department since 1913. He now worked closely with his foreman Rudy Moberg. Passing through the factory and assembly sheds, it was amazing how often you would hear German spoken.

Assembly in the old plant on Juneau Avenue was time-consuming and awkward. The various models were pushed from one assembly point to the next on carts (top).

accurate to one millionth of an inch. Every single component is checked carefully at each production stage and, after final inspection, receives a fully initialed inspection card. This meticulous quality control guarantees Harley a product to be proud of.

The components then go on to the Motorcycle Assembly Department, where the machines are assembled in the desired combinations to meet incoming orders. Lastly, to the Final Inspection Department. Here, everything is checked once more by inspectors, and all the parts are finally greased and oiled.

Naturally, each motorcycle is function-tested individually in the Testing Department, then it is partly disassembled and goes to the Crating Department. Here the joiners are at work, and large quantities of boards and battens, already cut to size, are waiting to be used to crate up the brand new Harleys.

In the Shipping Department, the crated motorcycles are prepared for shipping and loading. But in the huge warehouse is the mighty Parts and Accessory Department. Parts ready for assemblage into the final product are stacked here in endless rows of shelving, right up to the roof. This storage takes up 33,000 square feet. Tanks, roll bars, motors, fenders, wheels, seats, lamps, gearboxes, mufflers, handlebars, small parts, all in long rows, precisely labeled and neatly packed. Around eight million parts go through this department every year.

Now just a brief look at the top floor, the sixth, where sidecars and Servi-Cars are assembled. This tour of the factory ends in a plain, bare room in which the whole history of the company, year by year from 1904, is laid out in order: the Historical Display shows all the types ever produced, an impressive parade to make the heart of any Harley enthusiast beat a little faster.

The Imposing Production Process II
Technological Advances – Touring the Company in 1998

At the end of 1946, Harley-Davidson purchased the former propeller factory of A.O. Smith – by then standing empty – because of the urgent need to expand production capacity. The spacious factory halls now known as Powertrain Operations are situated in Wauwatosa, roughly 10 miles to the west of Milwaukee at 11700 West Capitol Drive. The factory used to be known simply as the Butler Plant.

Initially, the 860,000 square foot production plant was a machine shop, until the production of engines and transmissions was also moved there in 1973. Today, the Harley-Davidson Engine and Transmission Plant casts, processes, assembles, hardens and powder-coats clutches, drive units and numerous small components. Some 1,200 employees carefully and expertly operate the countless milling machines, lathes and grinders according to the MAN/JIT procedure (Material As Needed/Just In Time), working in specially installed Machine Cells, each responsible for his or her own respective stage in the production process.

Numerous robot tools are installed in the preprocessing hall. A Cell Robot, for example, produces the teeth for belt-drive sprockets, while a computer-controlled Transmission Sound Test robot tests all transmissions for any annoying noises. Automatic cylinder and cylinder-head processing machines ensure compliance with the extremely tight manufacturing tolerances. Six computer-controlled multi-spindle machine modules, each of which can be fitted with up to 80 different tools, process the Sportster

housing. All the tools needed for this are manufactured in Harley's own tool center. Manual and computer-monitored manufacturing checks guarantee a hitherto unheard of standard of quality.

One particular attraction enjoyed by thousands of Harley fans each year is the factory tour that takes place three times each working day (9 am, 10:30 am and 12:30 pm). As is also the case at the York and Tomahawk plants, visitors here have the pleasure of experiencing the production process up close – a tradition that ranks as one of the more effective of the company's advertising measures.

Engine manufacture at the Power Train Plant on Capitol Drive. It goes without saying that the employees also rode Harleys, which they proudly parked in their own parking lot in front of the main entrance.

103

Good Vibrations

The Road Trip of a Lifetime to West Juneau Avenue

At least once in his life every real Harley freak must fulfill the dream of their biker existence by making a pilgrimage to the source of their precious legend. In the state of Wisconsin, about 75 miles north of O'Hare Airport, on the western side of the famous brewing city of Milwaukee on Lake Michigan, you will find the legendary headquarters of the Harley-Davidson Motor Company.

One's heart may start pounding as the turn is made from 35th Street onto Juneau Avenue, and the old-fashioned, redbrick buildings get ever closer. Up above is the characteristic water tower, a conspicuous symbol which has been etched permanently into one's memory through repeated sightings in many old pictures. Partly hidden by trees, are various stores and other buildings marked with the famous emblem, and there, on the right, just past a small shopping plaza, is the huge, six-story factory building, the headquarters, proudly flying the American flag, with the company flag underneath. At the time of this visit, there is a building site which turns out to be a suitable place to take a photograph of Harley's headquarters as a memento of the trip.

But when one finally arrives and touches the good old brick walls themselves, there is a feeling of being overwhelmed by the magic of the fascinating history emanating from such a down-to-earth building. Because surely no one can be so coldblooded as to be immune to the "good vibrations" which are almost palpable as you stand before the simple, black and white, house number plate with the number 3700 on it, knowing that this was once the old Chestnut Street address, where the first production plants were built over 90 years ago. They almost encroached on the nearby railroad lines, and behind was a large scrap yard for disposal of all the reject parts, much to the pleasure of many rascals who squirmed through a hole in the wire fence to uncover supplies of cheap spares.

It is still all there, almost the same as in the beginning and, happily, the whole site is protected as a historical monument. This is the achievement

A much admired exhibit behind glass: Serial Number One in the reception hall at Harley-Davidson's headquarters.

A much-photographed symbol: the Bar and Shield emblem that can be seen in front of all Harley-owned buildings.

of Marty Rosenblum, the highly committed company historian, who has finally managed to realize a lifelong goal.

There is only an unobtrusive, narrow entrance door to the heart of the company, which is approached by means of a plain set of stairs to one side. Then one is immediately in a small reception area. One could almost believe that one is in the office of a small, provincial firm — no swank or pomp, no glass or chrome, as you might expect in a place like this, just a simple room with unremarkable seating, a reception desk, everything quite unassuming and sedate. If there are more than ten people present at the same time, it's a bit cramped.

In one corner, almost as if pushed to one side, there is a glass case containing the most prized piece of company history, a strange hybrid of bicycle and motorcycle, the famous first single-cylinder model, the ancestor of everything that followed. Opposite that, a few precious trophies and photographs of the four founders. A friendly security man ensures that no

unauthorized persons pass through the swing door leading to the company's complicated nerve center. Until 1973, this building housed the production areas as well as administrative offices. On the various floors, working from orders received, the motorcycles were carefully assembled to very tight schedules. Both the required individual components and the finished machines themselves had to be transported by freight elevators, a system which often resulted in jams and holdups. Huge, continuous transmission systems, driven by steam engines, supplied the power to the machine tools. There must have been a real din here in earlier days...

A Mecca for all Harley fans: the current building on Juneau Avenue, with the original steps leading up to the headquarters, is under national heritage protection. The small shed in which it all began was lovingly maintained inside the vast manufacturing facility — until it was accidentally crushed.

The Development Center
Thorough Testing – Even in the Rain

Since 1997, the ultramodern Willie G. Davidson Product Development Center (PDC) – named after Harley's legendary Styling Director Willie G. Davidson – has been located right next door to the Powertrain Operations facility on West Capitol Drive. Harley-Davidson spent 25 million dollars on this development center – an investment that will prove vital to the future survival of the company.

The ground floor of the two-story state-of-the-art building houses nine development and testing laboratories equipped with the latest analysis and testing facilities, including the Noise, Vibrations & Harshness laboratory (NVH) that tests and monitors the acoustic properties so important to Harley in two sound-proof test chambers. If necessary, the good sound of a Harley engine can be adjusted here to comply with specific regulations.

One of the most advanced vehicle simulators in the world, the so-called Structures Laboratory, generates every conceivable test of wear and tear that a Harley-Davidson can be expected to encounter over its service life (as well as quite a few that no Harley is ever likely to encounter), ranging from poor road surfaces to faulty maintenance. The Electronic High-Frequency System Laboratory tests the reliability and compatibility of all electronic components. The laboratory also has a water chamber in which 24 hours of continuous rainfall can be simulated. The ground floor is completed by the test bed for measuring exhaust gas emission values, the Materials Testing Laboratory and a laboratory for testing prototypes.

In the future, Harley-Davidson engines will mainly be developed in the company's plant in Milwaukee.

The first floor of the development center houses an exhibition room not open to the public, in which all design studies and future models are displayed, as well as offices, a Documentation Department, Styling Department and the Development Office for the entire accessory range, all equipped with the latest in communications technology. Indeed, functionality and communication are the prime principles that govern the entire PDC building. Of course, one major advantage is the fact that the manufacturing plant in which the PDC's designs are put into production is only a few yards away.

Willie G. Davidson in his office.

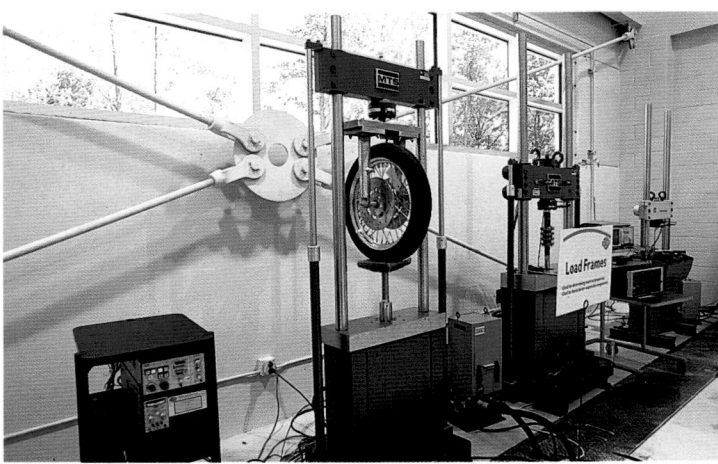

The new Product Development Center with its modern technical facilities was established on the grounds behind the Capitol Drive Plant.

The Testing Department's "wet cell" is able to simulate tropical rainfall.

The generous storage capacities are designed for expansion.

All engine and transmission functions are tested and measured in the sound-proofed Engine Test Room.

The Smooth Seduction

At Harley–Davidson, Even Plastic Becomes a Cult Object

The aesthetic value of plastics is a debatable issue, but one thing cannot be denied: plastic components are certainly useful. They don't rust, they don't dent, they're easy to repair and they last almost indefinitely. Plastic components also don't require heavy-duty embossing and molding presses, since they are processed with more delicate techniques, which is why Harley's plastic components are today still the result of intricate manual work, albeit with a little mechanical help...

The letter T on Harley's plastic components is an indicator of their origin in the Tomahawk Plant some 200 miles to the north of Milwaukee. The Tomahawk Division was founded in 1962, when Harley-Davidson purchased a former boat factory. This division of Harley specialized in the processing of artificial resin in order to meet the demand for plastic and fiberglass, initially for the bodywork of golf carts and Harley's commercial Utility-Cars, then for sidecar bodies, and nowadays primarily for saddlebags (so-called Tour-Packs) and any other parts made of plastic.

Anyone who ever visits the resin processing plant in Tomahawk cannot fail to be impressed by the extremely high standard of quality on display. The superior finish and superb fit of all parts combined with the perfectly matched color tones and seductively smooth surfaces are features that can only be achieved at the hands of experienced experts. It's not only Harley enthusiasts that think that the aesthetic value of plastic is proved by the components that leave the Tomahawk Plant. Indeed, plastic components have long become a cult symbol for Harley-Davidson motorcycles. Once manufactured, the parts are shipped by truck directly to the York plant in Pennsylvania for assembly.

Be it the drilling of holes, final painting, deburring or the finishing of sidecars, the manufacture of all plastic components here in a special production hall is pure craftsmanship.

Well–Ordered Chaos

How a Legend Is Born

The author once visited the factory and recalls: We took a tour of Harley–Davidson's enormous, two million square foot assembly plant in York, Pennsylvania, 830 miles from Milwaukee. This plant once belonged to the American Machine & Foundry Corporation (AMF), who used it to manufacture military and bowling equipment. Since 1973, all Harley–Davidson V-Twin motorcycles have been assembled in the York Plant, which currently employs 2,400 personnel. Visitors are welcome to tour the factory and look over the shoulders of the people working here.

The flat, sprawling white assembly plant resembles a giant spaceship the way it shimmers amongst the surrounding trees and meadows. The visitors parking lot was full to overflowing, with every U.S. state represented somewhere among the array of license plates.

The cool air in the shop floor reception area came as a welcome relief from the oppressive heat outdoors. This hall serves as a holding area where visitors wait to embark on their factory tour. Visitors can also purchase some of the numerous Harley–Davidson souvenirs for sale here, or simply browse and enjoy a cool drink from the Coke machine while watching the factory itself on the huge video wall of the Visitor Center. But first, visitors have to register at the registration desk, as the line for the next tour is probably already long.

With a polite 'Don't miss it!' we were assigned to Tour Number 26, which started at 2:25 pm. Our group was called right on time and indeed, we got the impression that the staff here is used to dealing with large numbers of visitors each day. Our tour guide was Janet, a friendly lady of retirement age. But before she was allowed to introduce us to the mysteries of the production process, which runs at full steam, we were all familiarized with the inevitable and compulsory safety regulations of the security service: cameras and bags were relinquished for the duration of the tour, safety glasses were donned, we all had to fit plastic safety caps to our shoes and everybody was issued with a tiny radio receiver that fits snugly into the ear, so that we could always hear what Janet was saying – after all, the noise from the production lines is deafening. The heat did not go unnoticed either. We carefully made our way into the vast assembly hall. 'Please do not cross the white lines!' resounded from the radio receiver. As if we would! The white lines could be seen all over the place, marking danger zones and preventing excessively inquisitive visitors from being crushed or seriously injured by the machines on the assembly lines.

This is where the various components are assembled to create the motorcycles, but somehow it seemed as if we've started the tour at the wrong place. What in reality is a highly complex and ingenious system that

An overview of the production lines of the York factory, showing the individual work cells that are continuously supplied with fresh material by the JIT Department.

109

The engine storage warehouse. The engines were delivered directly from Milwaukee on these pallets.

has been planned down to the tiniest detail appears to be total chaos to the unsuspecting visitor. Industrial load carriers trundle along pathways everywhere the eye can see, countless forklifts rotate to-and-fro, heaving pallets full of engines, transmissions and other familiar components onto the racks of the individual assembly stations, where men and women install them in their final position with visible enjoyment and practiced skill.

Semi-finished Harleys glide past these assembly stations suspended from slowly advancing cradles, undergoing a subtle transformation from the initial framework to a finished motorcycle. This procession of half-assembled motorcycles includes Electra Glides, Dynas, Super Glides, Softails, Tour Glides and special models. It gradually becomes apparent that all these motorcycles are fitted with the large 80 cubic inch (1340 cc) engine, and virtually all sport a different color. The motorcycles are given their colorful finish in Harley's new paint shop, which is the most modern of its kind in the world. Indeed, Harley-Davidson paid 24 million dollars to install the electronically controlled and monitored priming and electro-coating marvel from Dürr, Parker-Amchem and PPG Industries. Up until 1991, the old paint shop was still the sore point in the entire manufacturing process — today, the new paint shop is the pride and joy of the whole factory. Only the beautifully flowing decorative pinstripes are still applied by hand with a brush.

But back to the endless monorail conveyor. Every part has to be on hand as needed at the various assembly stations. The logistics of the Just In Time (JIT) process are subject to their own set of laws, determined by the time cycle and speed of manufacture. If a green light starts flashing somewhere on the line and a certain signal is sounded, the supply personnel know that more parts are needed. A yellow light and a different signal indicate that a specialist is required to provide assistance. A red flashing light and a siren bring the entire line to a stop whenever a serious problem arises somewhere in production. The latter always represents a critical situation — stopping the assembly line can quickly cost a large sum of money and thwart even the best-calculated plans. However, thanks to constant monitoring via the SOC (Statistical Operator Control) and EI (Employee Involvement) systems, such total stoppages hardly ever occur.

The Sportster models are assembled in an altogether different manner. They don't take as long to put together, so Harley removed the Sportsters from the FL and FX assembly line and installed a special Sportster line in order to prevent downtimes. All XL/XLH models with the 54 cubic inch (883 cc) and 74 cubic inch (1200 cc) engines are accompanied by three builders who serve as midwives performing at all assembly stages, all the way from the naked frame to the finished model. The baby — suspended from its carrier — passes through 15 stations and a total of 45 different manufacturing stages accompanied by its three builders. At each station, Operators 1, 2 and 3 have precisely three minutes to install the respective component. A warning signal and hazard lamp warn the operators that time is running out before the monorail line continues its incessant journey to the next station. Once having passed through Station 15, the Sportster is ready for the road and is conveyed to the test bed. If the Cosmetic Inspector gives the thumbs up, the new motorcycle is taken to the Shipping Department. If not, the possible cause of the error is discussed in detail and the sick child sent to the refinishing department. The assembly team then returns to Station 1 and starts over on a new motorcycle. Each team thus assembles seven Sportsters each day, five days each week, 237 days a year.

Craftsmanship is once again an important element of the production processes at the York factory.

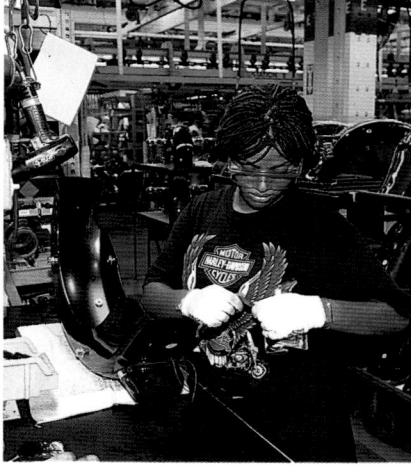

The assembly hall is bustling with industrious workers supplying the individual assembly stations with the requisite parts. One particularly impressive aspect is the manual spoking of the wheels, which takes from three to five minutes per wheel. Compared with modern automotive production, which is usually only performed on fully automated robotic production lines, the sheer amount of work performed by hand in this plant becomes all the more fascinating and impressive — a fact that reflects positively on the legend of Harley-Davidson. Automation in the pre-production phase is thoroughly normal, but final assembly is performed by hand, as no robot can yet replace the advantages of a keen human eye and a feel for the motorcycle being built — which is good to know and even better to experience up close.

Those components that need a particularly shiny finish are polished on polishing machines, while the rest of the components come from the fully automated electroplating plant. The frames, which mark the first stage in the assembly line, are shaped and welded in the flexible frame machine. This machine can handle any frame desired for the Dyna, Softail, Sportster and FL models, turning out up to 400 units a day. Fuel tanks and fenders are pressed, punched and hammered to ensure an accurate fit. Brake disks, primary housings and hundreds of different aluminum components from special individual departments are received for measuring. The numerous deliveries from outside companies are also promptly incorporated in the assembly process: tires, cast wheels, telescopic forks, shock absorbers, electronic components and countless other small parts. When taking a long, good look at the process here in the assembly hall, the impression of hugely satisfied workers assembling a fascinating puzzle of which they are tremendously proud simply cannot be ignored.

As we finally made our way back to the parking lot, still somewhat overwhelmed by everything we had seen, a huge 48-wheel truck in Harley's black-and-orange fleet sounded its horn and the driver waved at us. He was on his way to the container port, fully laden with brand-new Harleys for the overseas markets. A similar truck is pulling in on the other side of the road, this one delivering another load of engines and transmissions from Milwaukee.

Talladega Test Facility

Where All Harleys Are Put to the Test

While Harley-Davidson has since 1997 mainly conducted its simulated tests in the new Product Development Center, the company still puts its motorcycles through practical tests year in and year out, at the Talladega Test Facility under the mostly blazing sun of America's deep South. Since 1981, Harley-Davidson has had its own proving grounds and test facility virtually next door to the famous Talladega Superspeedway in Alabama. Of course, engine and brake test beds are also available, as well as facilities for the precise measurement of noise and emissions. The ever-more-stringent regulations and ordinances, of which California has the strictest in the world, represent an ever greater obstacle for the somewhat old-fashioned, air-cooled, long-stroke machines with their large displacements. Nevertheless, priority is given to the nostalgic wishes of the customers when it comes to technical developments. After all, a Harley is supposed to be a Harley, something the company simply can't afford to change.

Harley tests its motorcycles at Talladega like no other motorcycle manufacturer in the world. The engineers are frequently faced with seemingly insurmountable problems. When putting the latest models for future product ranges through their paces on high-speed and endurance runs, concern as to whether the fine balance between what the customer wants and what the law prescribes can actually be achieved is always a factor. All Harley motorcycles are inspected at Talladega for final approval with regard to technical and official specifications, both for the domestic and for the international market. But in the end, the system works and the test personnel in Alabama have no doubt that Harley-Davidson will stay on the road.

Lateral displacement is clearly visible in a wind tunnel. An engine and exhaust-gas test bed. (None of the photos on this page are from Talladega.)

Powerful Production

20 Acres of Technology, Training and Storage

In 1998 another production facility was added in the greater Milwaukee area: of the 890,000 square feet of empty floorspace in the engine plant of long–time associates Briggs and Stratton, partly rented, partly purchased outright in October 1996, 400,000 square feet are intended as a new production facility for FL engines and gearboxes, including powder–coating and tempering. 100,000 square feet are reserved for future expansion as it becomes necessary, and a further 390,000 square feet are to be used as warehouse and training facilities.

The new Pilgrim Road production facilities in Milwaukee.

Service Schools

From Handyman to Fully Qualified Mechanic

In 1947/48, the first Panhead was unveiled on the factory parking lot on Juneau Avenue. The occasion was attended by Arthur, William and Gordon Davidson, and John Harley, as well as numerous district managers and dealers.

Technical training was always meticulous.

Courtesy of: H.D. Archives

According to an official account found in the Harley-Davidson archives, in its edition of September 16, 1917, *The Motor Cycle* included a report on the first class of students of the Harley-Davidson School of Instruction. Next to a picture of this class, the account reported that the company was also systematically instructing army officers, police officers and postal workers in the skills of maintenance and repair of Harley motorcycles.

This program of instruction, as initiated by the Service Department in 1917, has grown into a venerable institution with university status, and all authorized dealers and their mechanics, military and civil instructors may attend. In the 1950s, 3,500 students enrolled in this motorcycle university and passed their examinations with flying colors. The term factory-trained is an honorary title for the most highly-qualified Harley mechanics. More readily available is the private Motorcycle Mechanics Institute (MMI), which provides training towards a mechanics diploma (Factory-trained and PHD Certification) at its two training centers in Orlando, Florida and Phoenix, Arizona. In addition, for the last ten years or so, it has been possible to train there as a recognized Harley specialist, through a program authorized by Harley-Davidson and run in close collaboration with the company. For some years MMI has also offered specialist courses for older Harley motorcyclists, such as the Early Model Program (1936–1969: Panhead, Knucklehead and Flathead restoration and repair) and the Late Model Program (from 1970 to the present, that is Shovelheads and Evos). There is also the Performance Program one may attend to learn special engine tuning.

Just like Harley-Davidson, MMI offers several tours of its workshops daily. For anyone interested, MMI's addresses and are listed below:

Motorcycle Mechanics Institute
2844 W. Deer Valley Road
Phoenix, Arizona 85027

Motorcycle Mechanics Institute
4065 L.B. McLeod Road, Suite A
Orlando, Florida 32811

© *Harley-Davidson*

The Abundant Archive

Marty Rosenblum, the Guardian of Secret Treasures

Sometimes one has that rare piece of luck when the normally locked doors to the treasure house of history are flung wide open, allowing a remarkable look back into another world usually hidden from view, which can be an experience breathtaking in its immediacy. This was what happened to the author and the photographer during their research when they got to know Marty Rosenblum, Harley-Davidson's Historian and guardian of the company's treasures.

At the time we met, the archives were stored in an inconspicuous outbuilding near the administrative center, but in reality it was a high security annex protected by a host of technological measures, a windowless bunker to which only three trusted individuals knew the open-sesame password: the historian Marty Rosenblum in the role of academic high priest, his assistant Susan Fariss, and the Chief Restorer Ray Schlee, who close friends get to call Chicago Ray. Marty pressed a couple of mysterious buttons and hidden switches, and suddenly we found ourselves in the holy of holies.

So help me God, there were things lying around there that nobody else gets to see: prototypes, design models, experimental motors, ancient relics, and the whole spectrum of motorcycle history from good times and bad. The two-wheeled treasures were ranged together in silent expectation, a little dusty perhaps, but it was the venerable dust of a truly glorious history. At some point the plan is for them to rise again in all their splendor, and they will too, in order to present the long history of the Harley-Davidson marque to a fascinated audience of millions. An expensive and labor-intensive project which will take years to achieve, but Marty and his restorer are optimistic. Ray was engaged in a particularly tricky task: screened off from the outside world in the solitude of a tiny neon-lit room, on an old

assembly table he was piecing something together which the legendary founders of the company had created 95 years earlier as their first model, the famed Number One.

Every detail, no matter how small, was precisely described, photographed, cataloged and carefully retained. Whatever part had to leave the bunker to be reworked on the machines, something which Ray was unable to do in the heart of the archive, went through countless checks and counterchecks and was watched over and accompanied by a squad of security guards. A vast quantity of documents, company papers, blueprints, old magazines and publications, photos and correspondence was tucked away in the filing cabinets around us, some of them as yet unopened. We were astonished by the mass of irreplaceable material. Wherever Marty pulled out a drawer or opened a cabinet door, destinies, decisions, successes and failures, facts and data were there to be seen and those long-buried episodes were returned to the light of day once more...

In 1997, the entire archive moved into newly vacant rooms in the company headquarters opposite. The bunker itself is now history.

A treasure trove is opened.

Marty Rosenblum displays an early device for testing the hardness of metal.

Now already history: the factory collection, stored in bunkers.
Courtesy of: H.D. Archives

The Abundant Archive II

A Time Machine on 18 Wheels

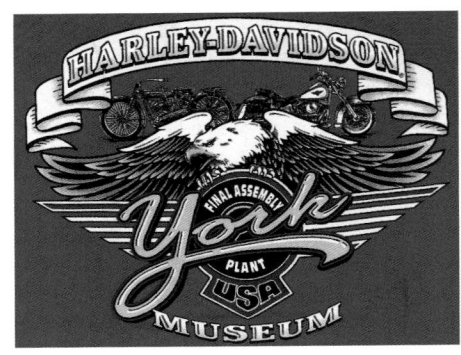

The Museum truck on an exhibition tour.

For a long time people may have got the impression that the company's glorious past and the history of its individual models were little more than burdensome relics from a time considered better forgotten. Archives, documents, prototypes and motorcycles were coldly moved in and out of storage and where possible forgotten. As early as the 1920s, how-ever, a company museum had been established in which models of motorcycles built by Harley – together with some of the prototypes – were exhibited. In addition, unusual items were constantly being bought from dealers and private individuals. This collection was later to form the basis of the museum in York, opened in June 1977 on behalf of AMF President John Davidson in honor of their Harley-mad director Rodney C. Gott as a frontage to the York assembly plant and as a permanent attraction for all visitors.

The York Harley-Davidson Museum, in which naturally only a fraction of the treasures stored in the company collection can be shown at any one time, consists of six themed sections. First the visitor enters the Trophy Room, in which all the prizes, trophies and certificates from 1906 onwards are exhibited. Then there follows the Historic Collection which contains the most important models from the company's entire lifetime. A separate section is dedicated to Organizations and Public Service, in which police and military machines are on view. The

Engineering section displays technological developments and models. Proud owners have the opportunity to introduce their rarest and most beautiful Harleys in another section. The most successful, sporting and racing models, and awe-inspiring pictures of their triumphs and their riders form the finale in the Heritage of Winning section.

Since 1988 parts of the museum have been transferred outside and temporarily have gone on the road: a converted Peterbilt semi-trailer brings a variety of exhibits to the big Harley events. The black and orange monster is transformed into a shrine calling itself the Traveling Museum.

It was initially sponsored by ITT, one of Harley-Davidson's financial partners. Six specially-trained drivers from the Harley-Davidson Transportation Division are responsible for the 66 foot-long air-conditioned rolling museum furnished by the Harley-Davidson archive. This unique attraction is absolutely free for every visitor, but donations for the Muscular Dystrophy Foundation are gladly accepted...

One of the alternating exhibitions also displayed famous racing machines. The photos show a track racer and Joe Petrali's record Knucklehead (right).

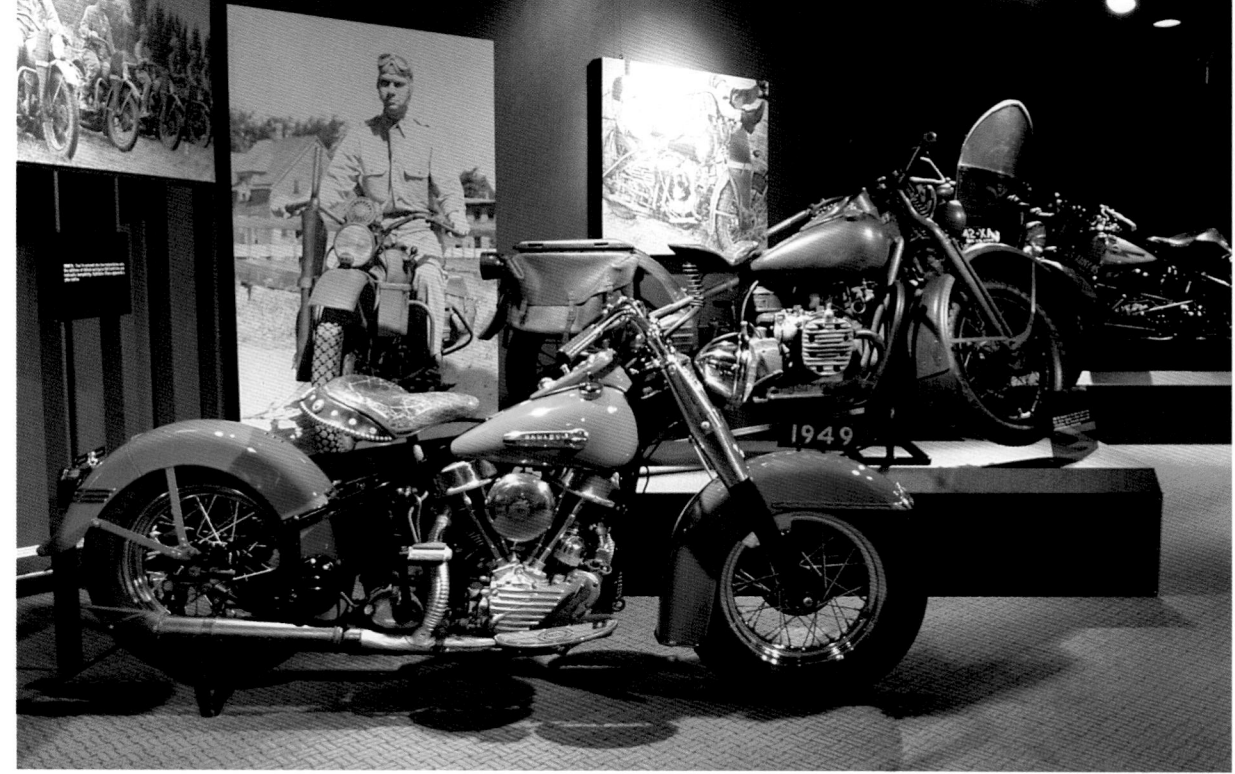

The company museum in York provides a look back through the history of the company and production, carefully sorted into thematic categories.
Above: A display of the 1920s.
Left: A sample from World War II.

Harley–Davidson and a New Era

Into the Future with a Proven Partner

What do Porsche and Harley-Davidson have in common? Most people's spontaneous reply would be: nothing. However the longer the question is left in the air, the more parallels become clear. After all, both marques hold tradition dear and arouse strong emotions. After mature consideration, the common ground becomes obvious: both employ an air-cooled engine, which defines the character of the vehicle. Harley-Davidson and Porsche build the last, air-cooled dinosaurs.

While a Harley is meant for cruising, and the Porsche is intended more as a sports vehicle, the engines at the heart of each machine have made a telling contribution to the legend of each manufacturer. Since 1909 Harley-Davidson has been building the legendary, long-stroke engine with two cylinders arranged in a "V" formation (at 45 degrees inclination), the connecting rods of which share a single crank pin. This simultaneous ignition in the cylinders means that there is virtually no balancing of masses and that the engines can always be identified by their characteristic vibration. Indeed, they delight in this unforgettable sound, which is similar to the human heartbeat:

b'dum, b'dum. Even those competitors who have stretched the cubic capacity over six cylinders have contributed to the singular character of Harley-Davidson motorcycles.

Since 1963 the number six has been sacrosanct to Porsche as well, as the number of cylinders, in opposed cylinder (Boxer) configuration, in their 911 sports car of the century, according to a survey of 15, internationally renowned, motoring journalists carried out by the French magazine *Sport Auto*. Another important feature is that Porsche has an air-cooled engine identified by an incomparable booming noise. The sound of these vehicles is so characteristic that both a Harley-Davidson and a Porsche 911 will be recognized immediately by their sound alone by anyone who has just a little gasoline in their blood, even children. And that trend is a characteristic both manufacturers intend to continue into the future.

Even the controversial subject of catalytic converters is no longer foreign territory for Harley-Davidson. Motorcycles for the Swiss market, for example, already have an unregulated catalytic converter.

It is positioned before the end pot. The injection system which is also required to reduce exhaust emissions is now available in Germany as well, for all Electra Glide models at an extra cost of 1,500 German Marks. It improves cold starting and optimizes torque development.

Harley-Davidson and Porsche have entered into a joint venture, the object of which is to produce components for Harley-Davidson motorcycle models. According to the sports car manufacturer, production will take place at one of Harley´s factories in America. The capital outlay for each party will provisionally be just ten million dollars.

Development and construction of prototypes will carried out in close cooperation between the companies. Porsche and Harley-Davidson will work closely together until this production gets off the ground. Both companies are very pleased about their relationship and confident of its future success.

Specific production decisions will be made as the relationship moves forward. The Company has ever-expanding opportunities. In 1998

Harley-Davidson opened a new 333,00 square-foot assembly plant in Kansas City, Missouri. The first Sportster motorcycle rolled off the line in Kansas City in January 1998, and now, all Sportster final assembly production takes place there. Also in 1998 Buell completed a new 43,000 square-foot Research and Development Center.

The opening by Harley-Davidson of its own Product Development Center, or PDC for short, in Milwaukee on July 8, 1997, is a clear indication of its confidence in the marque for the future. The traditional manufacturer thus has the most modern measuring and test equipment available, and it makes it very clear that the equipment is always kept up-to-date. Harley has big plans.

Since spring 1997, the two companies have also been linked in another way: the first Porsche/Harley-Davidson Club. Harley fever has gripped the Porsche workers who founded this club. The chairperson of the club, Franz Steinbeck, chairs the main works committee. So there is nothing to stop interesting meetings taking place on factory premises.

The New Generation

The Twin Cam 88 cubic inch Engine

Harley-Davidson has succeeded once again in outwitting the new and ever-more-stringent official restrictions to safeguard the survival of the popular air-cooled 45 degrees V-Twin engine for yet another round.

The new Twin Cam 88 engine now displaces 88 cubic inches (1449 cc) with a bore of 3.75 inches (95.3 mm) and a stroke of 4.0 inches (101.6 mm), has a compression ratio of 8.8:1 and develops roughly 50 kW at 5,400 rpm. The Milwaukee-developed engine sports a new design both inside and out: its cylinders and cylinder heads are more prominently ribbed, the valve covers are new, two separated cam shafts are now located in the engine block and the integrated tappet housing has been displaced inwards, as has the new, reinforced oil pump. The engine is provided with a new carburetor and electronic ignition and fuel injection system (the ESPFI Electronic Sequential Port Fuel Injection System), the latter yielding somewhat more power than before.

The following models of the 1999 series will be fitted with this engine: FXDX Dyna Super Glide Sport, FXD Dyna Super Glide, FXDWG Dyna Wide Glide, FXDL Dyna Glide Low Rider, FLTRT Road Glide Injection (ESPFI), FLHRCI Electra Glide Road King Classic (ESPFI), FLHR Electra Glide Road King and FLHT Electra Glide Standard.

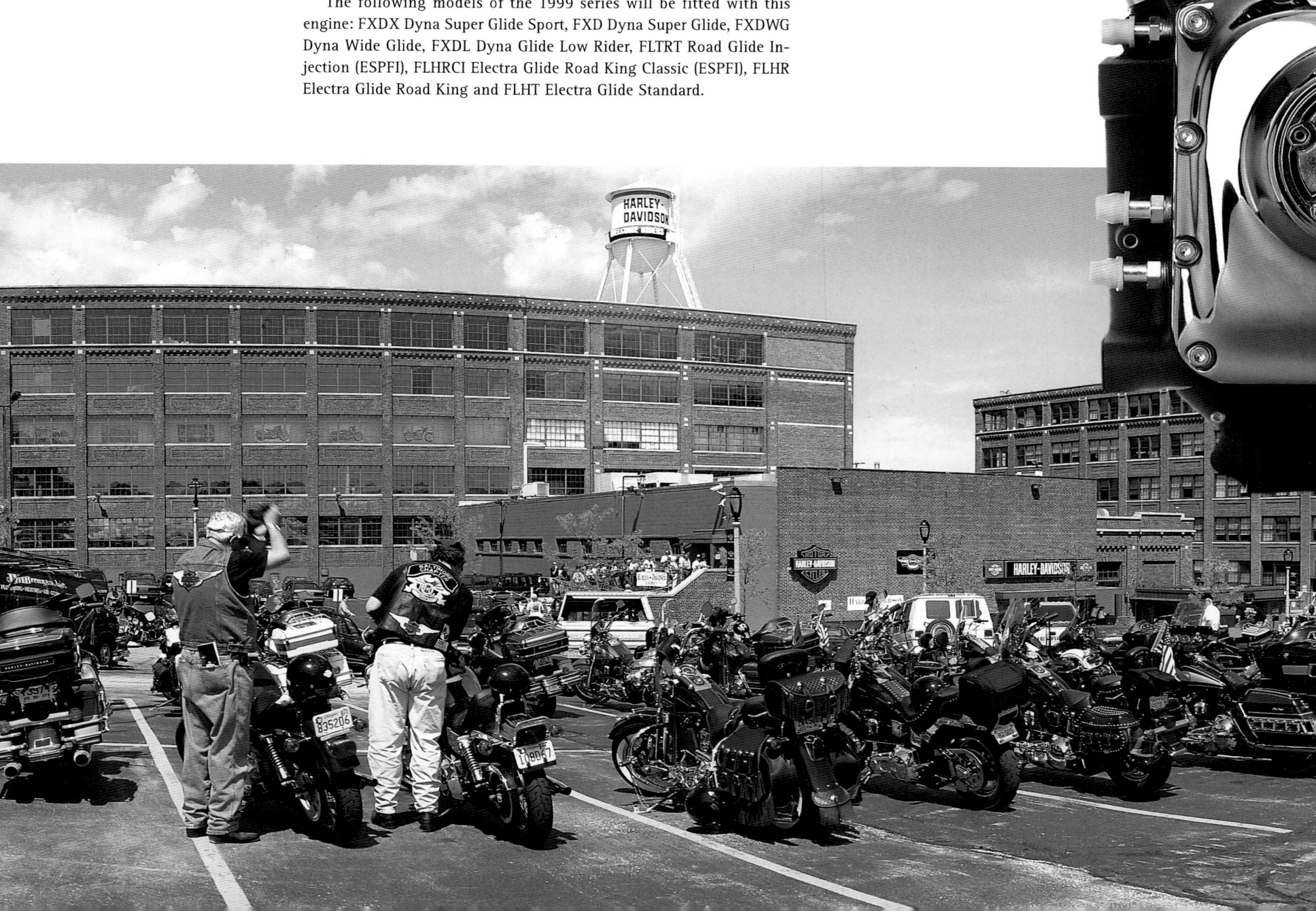

The Future

A Challenge

The future: it goes without saying that this chapter has to be constantly rewritten, and since we cannot see into the future, it is a continuous source of excitement. But industry managers who have to develop a product today which is intended to sell, successfully, years from now, have to be accomplished futurologists, because a decision to pursue the wrong product, which may hit the wrong market at the wrong time, is inevitably fatal. This is even more true for a motorcycle which is dependent like no other marque on its own legendary reputation.

Harley's strengths are its renowned popularity and unchanged classic design. Its weaknesses are the technical specifications which forever have to be measured against state-of-the-art technology and ever more rigorous, environmental regulations. Harley cannot afford to go in for many experiments, but its successful stakeholding in Buell has shown that there are a large number of new buyers who do not purchase a Harley simply for its nostalgic highway-cruiser look. Will Harley's customers stay loyal to the brand? Will they learn to love new technology? The investments of the last few years leave Harley no choice because the company must expand. Will the myth be strong enough to adapt to changed economic and market structures, and so be able to keep the legend alive? One just has to wait and see...

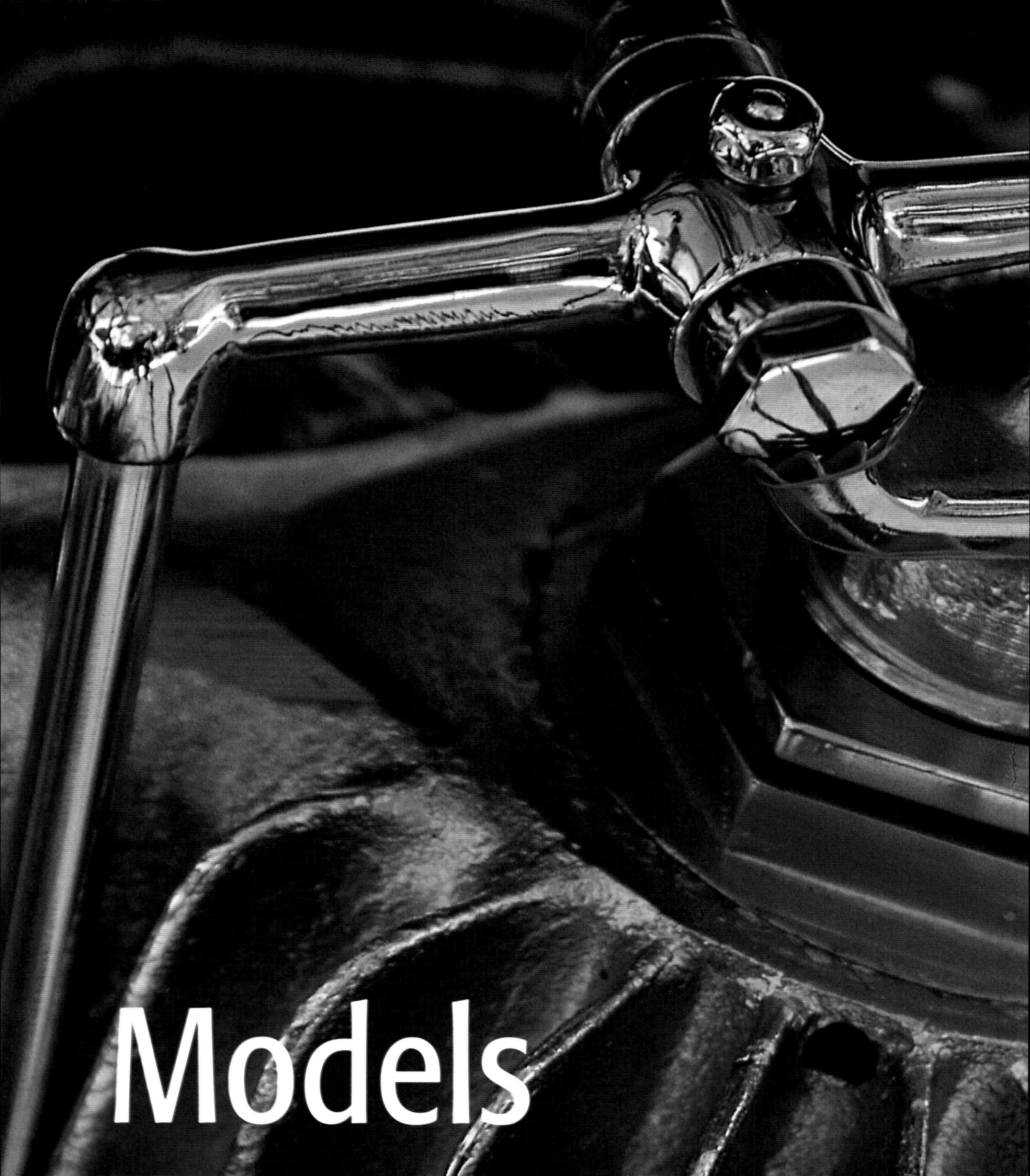

Models

The Mysterious Number One

"Number One" led a relatively inconspicuous life for a long time, occasionally being dusted off and displayed symbolically and being shipped from one place to another before finally entering a 20-year slumber in a glass showcase in the corner of the reception area of Harley's headquarters on Juneau Avenue. The machine bore a kind of license plate on the front fender with the equivocal dates 1903–1904, which seemed to imply that it was indeed the oldest model from the legendary years of the company's foundation. But nobody knew for sure. No one was able to fully trace or recall its history. The unsolved mystery of the motorcycle's origins nagged away at Harley's historian Marty Rosenblum and prevented him from getting any peace whatsoever. And although he burrowed through reams of company files, many already yellowed with age, the whole affair only became even more mysterious.

Almost all clues led to false trails or dead ends. One machine, which was built by the Harley and Davidson brothers for their own use and not for serial production could be the famous Number One. Alternatively, it could also be a motorcycle of a certain Mr. Meyer which changed hands several times and clocked up some 10,000 miles before finally being returned to the company.

However, when Marty Rosenblum and his restorer "Chicago Ray" Schlee examined the motorcycle a little more closely, more questions were raised. The paintwork could not have been original, as decorative stripes and logos were first introduced in 1908. What's more, the frame had certainly not been produced in 1903, and they found that the tires, which were constantly flat, did not even have inner tubes. With the agreement of the Harley management,

the decision was reached that only by completely dismantling the mystery-enshrouded motorcycle could its secrets be finally brought to light. Thus Ray Schlee began on what almost everyone expected to be a dream job, but that in fact almost turned into a nightmare of frustration.

Nevertheless, some astounding and very surprising discoveries were made. The author had the great fortune of being one of the privileged few allowed to witness the moment when Chicago Ray inspected the dismantled motorcycle in the innermost "top secret" area of the hermetically sealed "Bunker" (where the Harley-Davidson Corporate Archive was located at the time). Marty referred to the inspection as the "reincarnation of a spirit," and everyone present was deeply moved. For some reason, one got the feeling that the ghosts of Bill Harley and the three Davidson brothers were actually watching over Ray's shoulder, they themselves inspecting that very same engine they had once assembled with so much hope all those years ago.

It was indeed the first production engine ever manufactured by Harley-Davidson. The number "one" visible on the crankshaft was unequivocal proof. Who punched that historic number onto the engine so many years ago and what thoughts went through his head? Still, the engine did not belong to either of the two other motorcycles destined for sale that year. It was a prototype with a larger displacement than the retail models, obviously built as a competition racing machine for the company and which had always been in the company's possession. According to the latest information, it was indeed modified several times in its early years, and the current frame at least is a combination of the 1905 and 1906 models. The earliest record of

The legendary Number One — back in its original condition after extensive restoration.

The first Harley logo only adorned the left side of the piano-black fuel tank.

All photos on this double-page-spread are courtesy of: H.D. Archives

The moment of truth: Number One reveals
its secrets.

Ray Schlee giving the fully-restored
Number One a final check.

the first Harley dates back to 1915: on the occasion of the Panama-Pacific
Exhibition held in San Francisco that year, the good old Number One was
needed to supplement the display of Harley's model range and was apparently
quickly "civilized" at the last minute, as Marty Rosenblum refers to it. It was
fitted with fenders and all kinds of additional parts to replace those that were
probably missing.

Why such an old motorcycle should have been dressed up for an exhibition of new models remains a puzzle even today. Perhaps the company simply
needed to display a "historical" model, and no others were available at the time.
Harley-Davidson had already built 3,000 single-cylinder machines in 1914,
most of which sported a chain-and-sprocket drive and an advanced F-head
engine. Nevertheless, Harley-Davidson decided to lay the cornerstone for
what is today a unique and unrivaled historical collection. Number One was
evidently repaired and restored, albeit none too professionally, during the
reign of AMF and initially exhibited in the York Museum before being
relocated to Harley's headquarters in Milwaukee. Today, thanks to the
historical research and painstaking effort of Ray Schlee and the specialist
for historic paintwork, John Rank, Harley-Davidson's Number One is once
again back to its original condition and in its rightful place.

Production Starts on the First Models
The Single–Cylinder from 1903 to 1905

Harley's first series-production model sported the new, improved type of engine, instead of the small De Dion replica designed in 1901 (with a displacement of 10.2 cubic inches, 167 cc and a bore and stroke of 2.125 inches x 2.87 inches, 54 x 73 mm). The new engine type displaced 24.74 cubic inches (405 cc) (with a bore and stroke of 3 inches x 3.5 inches, 76 x 89 mm) and its flywheel was twice as large, with a diameter of 9.8 inches (24.9 cm). Bill Harley also designed a new, sturdier loop frame for this considerably more powerful engine. The front fork in this case was also a reinforced bicycle fork. The only sprung parts were the saddle and the tires. The speed was regulated by means of a linkage system fitted between the handlebars, frame, and carburetor. The carburetor was developed by the young entrepreneurs themselves and could be adjusted by the rider. The oil supply was part of a "total-loss" lubrication system, with the oil tank located on the central frame tube above the fuel tank. The direct belt drive system was such that the belt could be tightened if needed. The ignition

interrupter was situated on the outer camshaft (for operating the exhaust valve) on the outside right-side of the large, sturdy crankcase. As was customary for bicycles, the battery was housed in a small, triangular container stowed beneath the saddle in the upper part of the rear frame.

Three of these motorcycles were built in 1903, two of which were genuine production models. The number rose to four in 1903/1904, all of which were probably sold. The history of one of these 1904 models can even be traced today. A certain Mr. Meyor (or Meyer) sold it to George Lyon after having covered almost 6,000 miles himself. Mr. Lyon then bumped up the mileage to about 21,000 before reselling it to a Dr. Webster. The 1903/1904 Harley then changed ownership again, being sold to Mr. Louis Fluke before changing hands a final time. Apparently, its final owner, George Sparrow, rode the early model Harley so long that it clocked up an astounding 100,000 miles before he put it to a well-earned rest. A truly amazing performance and one the company gladly used for advertising purposes.

Type:	**F–Head Single**
Model:	**Single–cylinder**
Years of manufacture:	1903–1905
Engine:	Air–cooled four–stroke IOE single automatic (suction) inlet valve
Displacement:	24.74 cu in (405.20 cc)
Bore x stroke:	3 x 3.5 in (76.20 x 88.90 mm)
Power output:	3 hp
Carburetor:	H–D 22 mm ø
Transmission:	None
Primary drive:	Direct drive
Final drive:	Leather belt
Battery:	6 volt (non–rechargeable)
Ignition:	Battery–coil
Frame:	Loop, tubular steel
Front brake:	None
Rear brake:	Coaster
Suspension:	None (cushioned saddle)
Wheelbase:	51 in
Weight:	178 lb
Fuel capacity:	1.5 gal
Oil capacity:	2 qts
Tires:	2.5 x 28
Top speed:	35 mph
Price:	$200
Model versions:	Piano black

© Harley–David.

The first photograph advertising the 1903–1905 model range

The Single-Cylinder in 1906 and 1907

The engine volume was increased to 26.8 cubic inches (440 cc) by means of a larger 3.125 inch (79.4 mm) bore, which yielded one horsepower more. The engine was now also secured to the above frame by means of a four-point attachment. The carburetor control had been replaced by a more efficient twist-grip chain linkage system. The Springer front fork, recently bought from Sager by William Harley, made its debut in 1907 and the design remained in service for the next 46 years.

When not riding in built up areas, a flap on the muffler could be opened that also increased the performance a bit. The paintwork for the 1906 model (the first brochures did not appear until 1907) came in the respectable shade of Renault gray or black and soon earned the single-cylinder Harley a legendary nickname that was quickly adopted for Harley's clever advertising campaigns: "The Silent Grey Fellow." A total of 50 of these models were built in 1906, followed by 152 in 1907, all of which were sold without difficulty.

Type:	F–Head Single Silent Grey Fellow
Model:	**1908: 4**
Years of manufacture:	1906–1908
Engine:	Air-cooled four-stroke single-cylinder IOE with automatic (suction) inlet valve
Displacement:	26.8 cu in (439.9 cc)
Bore x Stroke:	3.125 x 3.5 in (79.4 x 88.9 mm)
Power output:	4 hp
Carburetor:	Schebler
Transmission:	None
Primary drive:	Direct drive
Final drive:	Leather belt
Battery:	6 volt dry-cell
Ignition:	Coil
Frame:	Looped tubular steel
Front brake:	None
Rear brake:	Coaster
Front suspension:	Springer fork with twin springs
Rear suspension:	None
Wheelbase:	5 in
Weight:	225 lb
Fuel capacity:	1.5 gal
Oil capacity:	2 qts
Tires:	2.5 x 28
Top speed:	40 mph
Price:	$210
Model versions:	In black or Renault gray.

A jewel behind glass: one of the first models in the lobby of Harley-Davidson's headquarters on Juneau Avenue.

Courtesy of: H.D. Archives

Traveling in style in a wickerwork sidecar.

© *Harley–Davidson*

The Single-Cylinder in 1908 and 1909

The successor to the 26.8 cubic inch (440 cc) Model 4, of which 450 units were built in 1908, was the new Model 5 introduced in 1909, which had a larger engine, now displacing 30.16 cubic inches (494 cc), a reinforced springer fork, extended wheelbase and either a battery-coil ignition or the new magneto system. Harley customers were now once again able to choose between 28-inch wheels or 26-inch wheels.

This model was so reliable and sold so well (Walter Davidson won the Catskill Mountain Endurance run in 1908 on a Model 4) that the now-legendary Silent Grey Fellow soon became immensely popular throughout America. One fact that obviously assisted in the sales of this model was that the price for the standard battery-ignition model was kept at a steady 210 dollars. A potential customer wishing to purchase a model with magneto ignition, on the other hand, had to fork out an additional 40 dollars.

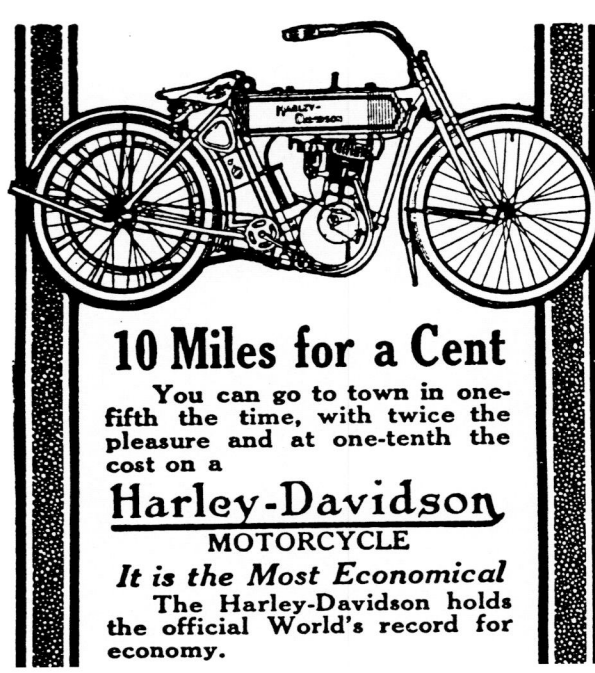

The battery-powered single-cylinder in Renault gray with the logo designed by Aunt Jane adorning the fuel tank.

Type:	**F-Head Single**
	Silent Grey Fellow
Model:	**5 and 6**
Years of manufacture:	1909–1910
Engine:	Air-cooled four-stroke IOE single
	with automatic (suction) inlet valve
Displacement:	30.17 cu in (494.05 cc)
Bore x stroke:	3.3125 x 3.5 in (84.14 x 88.90 mm)
Power output:	4.3 hp
Carburetor:	Schebler
Transmission:	None
Primary drive:	Direct drive
Final drive:	Leather belt
Battery:	6 volt dry-cell
Ignition:	Battery or magneto
Frame:	Loop, tubular-steel
Front brake:	None
Rear brake:	Coaster
Front suspension:	Springer fork with twin springs
Rear suspension:	None
Wheelbase:	56.5 in
Weight:	235 lb
Fuel capacity:	1.5 gal
Oil capacity:	2 qts
Tires:	2.5 x 28 (5B/5C: 2.5 x 26)
Top speed:	45 mph
Price:	$210 battery ignition,
	$250 magneto ignition
Model versions:	5/6: Battery ignition, 28-inch wheels
	5A/6A: Magneto ignition, 28-inch wheels
	5B/6B: Battery ignition, 26-inch wheels
	5C/6C: Magneto ignition, 26-inch wheels
	6E: Series-production racing
	model with 30 cubic inches ($275)

The fuel feed was regulated via a thumb-operated lever on the right-side handgrip. The remaining tank-mounted controls operated a flap in the exhaust pipe and the ignition timing. The new Sager–Cushion spring fork was introduced in 1907.

Production Figures for 1909

Model 5	(battery ignition, 28-inch wheels)	864 units
Model 5A	(magneto ignition, 28-inch wheels)	54 units
Model 5B	(battery ignition, 26-inch wheels)	168 units
Model 5C	(magneto ignition, 26-inch wheels)	36 units

The old Harley carburetor still in use.

All photos on this double page-spread are courtesy of: H.D. Archives

129

The Single-Cylinder from 1910 to 1913

The models available for the years 1910 (Model 6) and 1911 (Model 7) were virtually identical, both motorcycles being fitted with a 30.16 cubic inch (494 cc) engine and automatic suction valve. It was not until 1912 that Harley-Davidson introduced a considerable improvement in the form of the new Model 8.

The engine displacement was enlarged to 31.85 cubic inches (522 cc) and also was provided with a hand-operated oil pump. However, the most important of the new features was the extraordinarily effective clutch, ingeniously designed by William Harley and Henry Melk and integrated in the rear wheel hub. "Free Wheel Control" was the name given to this clutch, which was operated via a lever mounted on the left of the fuel tank. An "X"

in the model designation (X8) indicated that this new Harley invention was fitted. The new "Ful Floteing Seat" (sic), anchored to the tubular steel frame with an internal 14-inch spring, was also a major improvement on the primitive saddles of earlier models and proved so successful that the design was left virtually unaltered until well into the 1970s.

All models were available with either battery or magneto ignition and 26-inch or 28-inch wheels. The customer could also choose between belt or chain drive. The box which contained the battery was now located in the frame beneath the seat. From 1912 onwards, the only color available for all models was gray.

The single-cylinder models were also fitted with magneto ignition from 1909.

This unique Harley was spotted at a swap-meet in Syracuse, New York in the early 1990s. Retail price: over U.S.$100,000.

The constantly slipping belt was tightened by means of a newly patented adjustable hand lever.

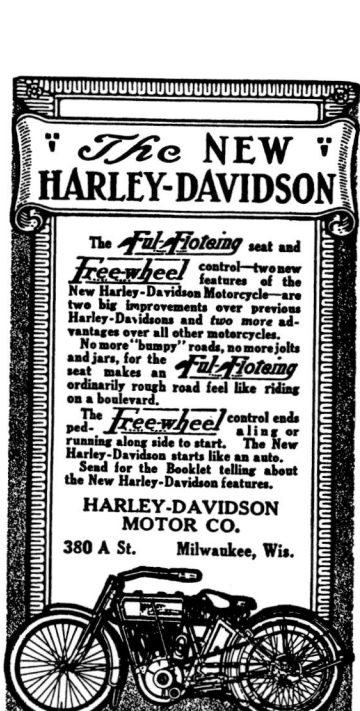

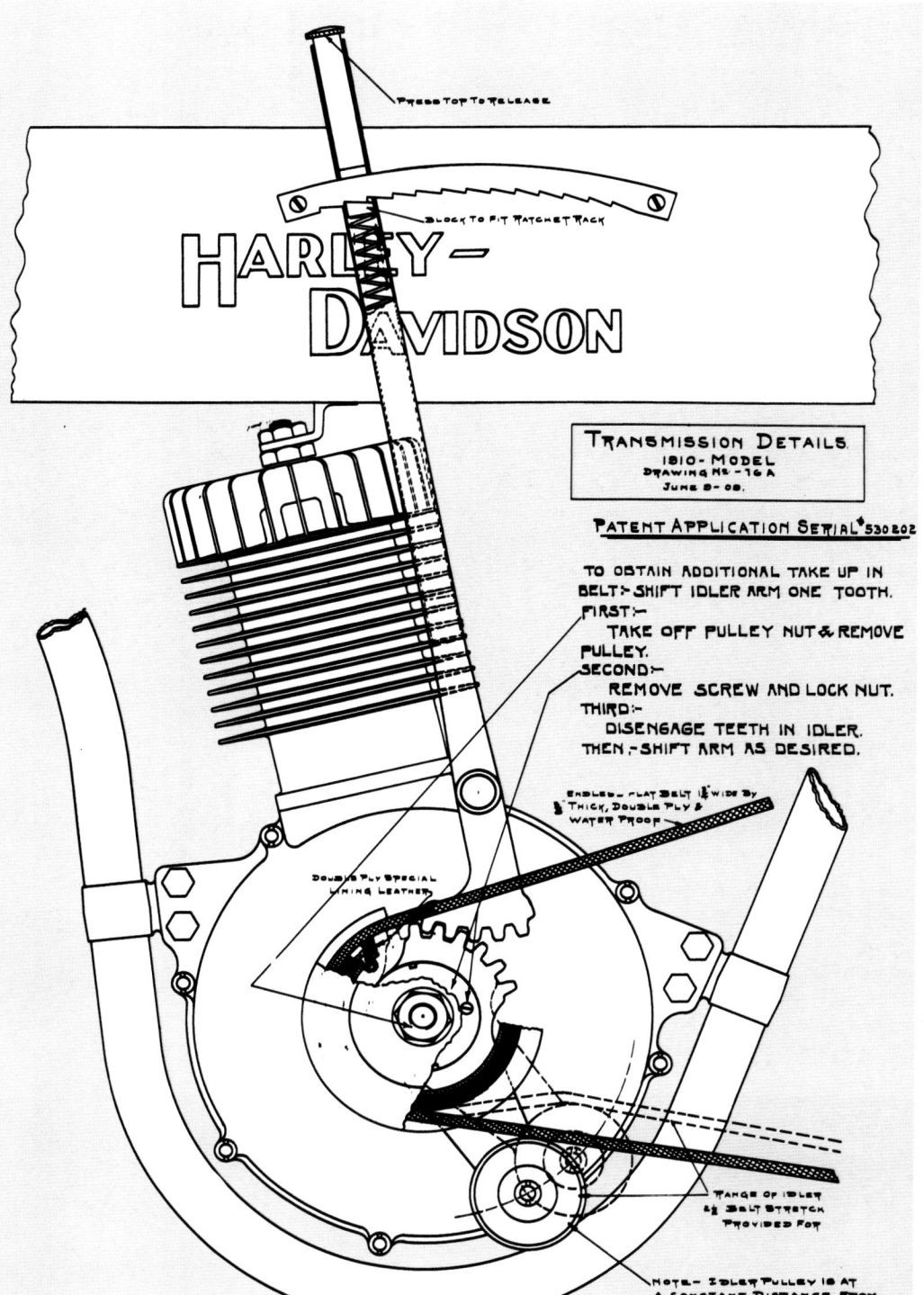

HARLEY-DAVIDSON

PRESS TOP TO RELEASE

BLOCK TO FIT RATCHET RACK

TRANSMISSION DETAILS
1910-MODEL
DRAWING No - 7 & A
JUNE 9 - 09.

PATENT APPLICATION SERIAL 530 202

TO OBTAIN ADDITIONAL TAKE UP IN
BELT:- SHIFT IDLER ARM ONE TOOTH.
FIRST:-
    TAKE OFF PULLEY NUT & REMOVE
    PULLEY.
SECOND:-
    REMOVE SCREW AND LOCK NUT.
THIRD:-
    DISENGAGE TEETH IN IDLER.
    THEN:- SHIFT ARM AS DESIRED.

ENDLESS FLAT BELT 1⅜ WIDE BY ⅜ THICK, DOUBLE PLY & WATER PROOF

DOUBLE PLY SPECIAL LINING LEATHER

RANGE OF IDLER 1½ BELT STRETCH PROVIDED FOR

NOTE - IDLER PULLEY IS AT A CONSTANT DISTANCE FROM DRIVING PULLEY CENTER AT ALL TIMES.

© Harley-Davidson

29620
N.Y. 1917

Type:	**F-Head Single Silent Grey Fellow**
Model:	**X 8 A**
Year of manufacture:	1912
Engine:	Air-cooled four-stroke IOE single with automatic (suction) inlet valve
Displacement:	31.85 cu in (552 cc)
Bore x stroke:	3.5 x 3.3125 in (89 x 84 mm)
Power output:	4.3 hp
Carburetor:	Schebler
Transmission:	Free wheel control
Primary drive:	Direct drive
Final drive:	Belt or chain
Ignition:	Bosch magneto
Frame:	Loop, tubular steel
Front brake:	None
Rear brake:	Coaster
Front suspension:	Springer fork with twin springs
Rear suspension:	None
Wheelbase:	56.5 in
Weight:	245 lb
Fuel capacity:	2.5 gal
Oil capacity:	4 qts
Tires:	2.5 x 28
Top speed:	50 mph
Price:	$225

Model versions, prices and production figures:

1910

Model 6 (battery ignition, 28-inch wheels)	$210	2,302 units
Model 6A (magneto ignition, 28-inch wheels)	$250	334 units
Model 6B (battery ignition, 26-inch wheels)	$210	443 units
Model 6C (magneto ignition, 26-inch wheels)	$250	88 units

1911

Model 7 (battery ignition, 28-inch wheels)	$225	2,302 units
Model 7A (magneto ignition, 28-inch wheels)	$250	334 units
Model 7B (battery ignition, 26-inch wheels)	$225	443 units
Model 7C (magneto ignition, 26-inch wheels)	$250	88 units

1912

Model 8 (battery ignition)	$200
Model X8 (battery ignition and rear-wheel hub clutch)	$210
Model 8A (magneto ignition)	$225
Model X8A (magneto ignition and rear-wheel hub clutch)	$235

You Never Forget Your First Love

A Harley in Its 82nd Year

"What on Earth is that?" is the common reaction to the unusual looking contraption. The author recalls his first encounter: It was rattling and spluttering towards me, its rider leaning forward as his mount jolts over holes in the road, putting his foot heavily on the pedal whenever the road slopes just a little bit. A bicycle with an engine? Doesn't really sound like one. The weird-looking machine finally stops next to me or rather it shudders to a gasping halt just short of my feet. The man sitting astride it turns his dust-caked face my way, grins in a jovial manner and says "Hello."

This is Jeff, or more precisely "Indian Jeff" – good ol' Jeff McGeary, motorcycle restorer and universal genius. He's taken four days to travel from Seattle to the biker gathering here in Sturgis, South Dakota. This is the 21st time he's made the journey, once again on his trusty old Silent Grey Fellow.

At first, I can't believe my eyes. This is a genuine Harley single from 1912, something that belongs locked up behind armored glass in a museum somewhere. "No," says Jeff, "this is where it belongs – on the road! That's what it was built for in Milwaukee 82 years ago!"

At this point, I must add that this particular model was once involved in a serious accident, which cost the life of its first owner, and the scars of that crash are still visible today. The victim's mother didn't want to set eyes on the motorcycle again after that day and initially hid it before finally agreeing to sell it. Somebody also used the engine for an altogether unintended purpose at some stage, powering a chain saw with it. Jeff purchased the machine from a good friend, plastered in oil and sawdust. Now it's back on the road again, after a hiatus that began in 1950. All that Jeff needed to fully restore the historic machine were new piston rings and a contact breaker.

I ask him what he's carrying on the luggage rack (which he shamefacedly admits to removing time and again because it did not originally belong to this motorcycle). His answer is enlightening: the standard equipment for motorcycle tours, i.e. a sleeping bag and toothbrush. Of course, Jeff isn't alone when he's on the road. Numerous friends accompany him, particularly when it comes to longer distances. After all, it might not be all that wise for Jeff to be left alone with this antique in the middle of nowhere. "Nonsense," retorts Jeff. "This Harley is as sturdy and reliable as ever." Its modest 4.34 horsepower nevertheless yields a top speed of 80 miles per hour, when the road's reasonably flat and straight (or perhaps when going downhill?). Jeff sometimes even sleeps in roadside ditches next to his historic steel comrade when there's not enough money to rent a room for the night. In all other respects though, it is an inexpensive and above all, adventurous form of travel: Jeff's Silent Grey Fellow runs on any grade of gasoline and does an amazing 80 miles to the gallon! The 32-inch (522 cc) engine achieves 1800 rpm at top speed – a figure the Bosch magneto (U.S. production from New York) just about manages to keep up with. However, the magneto isn't powerful enough to cope with the lamps, so Jeff relies on his good-old acetylene headlamp. In fact, all Jeff has to worry about is the oil, which just spurts out all the time – total-loss lubrication is the term for it.

Jeff covers one thousand to one-and-a-half thousand miles on his Harley single each year. And so far, it's always managed to get him home again at the end of a journey. Or so he claims. Breakdowns? "Yes," he says, "I had a flat tire once – nasty business, a flat tire..."

The Single-Cylinder from 1913 to 1918

Three years after the development of the V-Twin engine, the 1913 single-cylinder model (Model 9) with the designation "5-35" (5 horsepower from 35 cubic inches) also received the F-head engine with mechanical inlet valves. In the same year, magneto ignition became standard for the large-capacity, long-stroke (4-inch stroke) model. The color was still the familiar Renault gray and the model was available with chain or belt drive, as well as 28-inch or 26-inch wheels.

The Model 10 of 1914 was enhanced with a whole array of further improvements: a "step-starter" system, clutch and brake pedals and, above all, a two-speed transmission. In 1915, the two-speed transmission was replaced by a three-speed version and the step-starter, which was kicked forward to start the motorcycle, was finally replaced by a genuine kickstarter. From 1916 onwards, all models were designated according to the year in which they were built. All models also sported a military-looking olive drab finish from 1917 and, as of 1918, the last single-cylinder models were fitted with high-performance, high-tension magnetos.

Model versions

Year	Model	Price	Units
1913	Model 9A (belt)	$290	1,510 units
	Model 9B (chain)	$290	4,601 units
1914	Model 10A (belt)	$200	316 units
	Model 10B (chain)	$210	2,034 units
	Model 10C (chain and two-speed transmission)	$245	877 units
1915	Model 11B	$200	670 units
	Model 11C (two-speed transmission)	$230	545 units
1916	Model 16B	$215	292 units
	Model 16C (three-speed transmission)	$230	862 units
1917	Model 17B	$215	124 units
	Model 17C (three-speed transmission)	$240	605 units
1918	Model 18B	$235	19 units
	Model 18C (three-speed transmission)	$260	251 units

Type:	**F-Head Single**
	Silent Grey Fellow
Model:	**9A/B "5-35" (5 PS/35 cu in)**
Years of manufacture:	1913–1918
Engine:	Air-cooled four-stroke IOE single with mechanical inlet valve
Displacement:	34.47 cu in (565 cc)
Bore x stroke:	3.3125 x 4.0 in (84.14 x 101.6 mm)
Power output:	4.5 hp
Carburetor:	Schebler
Transmission:	From 1914 – two-speed; From 1916 – three-speed
Primary drive:	Direct drive
Final drive:	Belt (9A), chain (9B)
Ignition:	Bosch magneto
Frame:	Loop, tubular steel
Front brake:	None
Rear brake:	Coaster
Front suspension:	Springer fork with twin springs
Rear suspension:	None
Wheelbase:	56.5 in
Weight:	316 lb
Fuel capacity:	1.5 gal
Oil capacity:	3.5 qts
Tires:	2.75 x 28 or 2.75 x 26 (US Empire or Goodyear)
Top speed:	50 mph
Price:	$290

© Harley-Davidson

6 Horsepower Single Cylinder Single Geared Model 16-B

Two early models in original condition: the 16B of 1916 (far left) and the 11B of 1915 above with its first license plate.

133

The Legendary Harley V-Twin

The word "legend" conjures up something mysterious. But can there be a mystery attached to something purely technical? In this case one could say "yes" – in a way. For there is something that defies explanation about this big, powerful V-Twin engine, with its two in-line cylinders inclined at 45 degrees. One needs to spend time looking at it, listening to it and above all feeling it. Some say that its combustion cycle is on the same frequency as the human heartbeat. This is hardly something that the firm's founders, and later generations of engineers, will have thought about; they were interested in building a robust, reliable motorcycle, not creating a legend. But that's what happens when people tinker around with these things over the years: a whole philosophy and a mystical V-Twin, of a kind that no other V-Twin manufacturer has been able to endear to its owners in quite the same way.

This pounding, adrenaline-pumping power unit is essentially a one-cylinder design that has simply been upgraded to deliver twice the power: two big pistons moving up and down in phase, firing in each cylinder in turn, their explosive hammer blows converted into the rotary movement of a mighty crankshaft, between whose two massive steel disks – the crank webs – the two connecting rods are mounted on a common crankpin. The sheer mass of the crank webs is sufficient to deliver more than enough torque even at low revolutions – the famous "bottom-end boom" – making the whole engine shake and tremble with that delicious sustained vibration that enthusiasts refer to as a "whole body massage." Then there's the deep, thunderous beat of the exhaust, the bass boom sounding fuller and deeper the longer the mufflers are, even though environmental legislation is firmly opposed to such sonic pleasures. As a precautionary measure, Harley-Davidson has actually copyrighted its engine note...

One could go on and on about the mystique of the marque, the Harley as status symbol, etc, but the fact is, even the most hard-bitten biker has his sensitive sides and one of them is related to the Harley V-Twin engine. It's not a matter for debate and argument: you either "get it" – in which case there's no need for explanations – or you don't – in which case all explanations are pointless. So let's leave it at that. The fact is, the legend lives: long live the legend!

The IOE type V-Twin engine: a dismantled 1920 version and a 74 cubic inch (1200 cc) JD version from a 1924 Harley brochure (center).

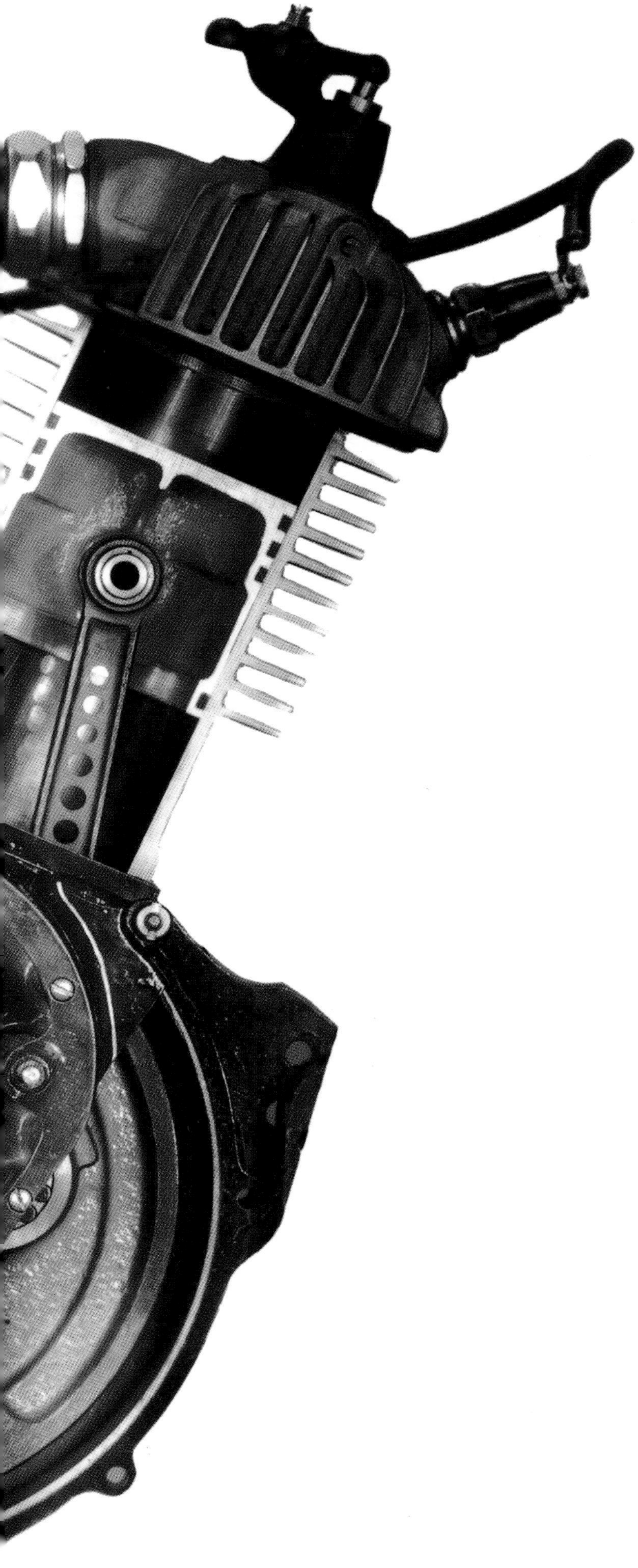

The V-Twin Operating Cycle
for OHV types

Position of the pistons during ignition

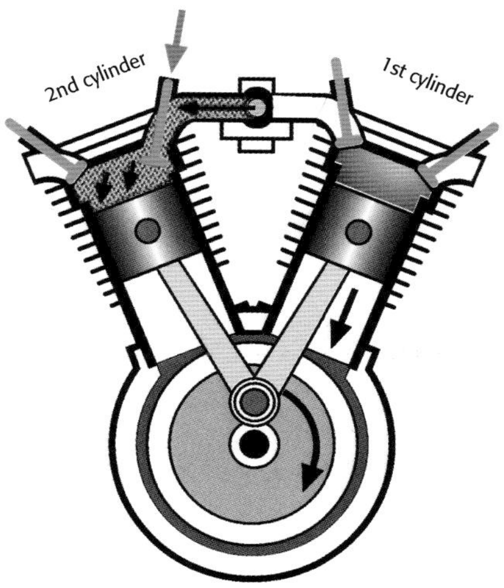

After ignition, both pistons are raised:

2nd cylinder: Inlet valve opens
                   Induction cycle

1st cylinder: Both valves closed
                   Operating cycle

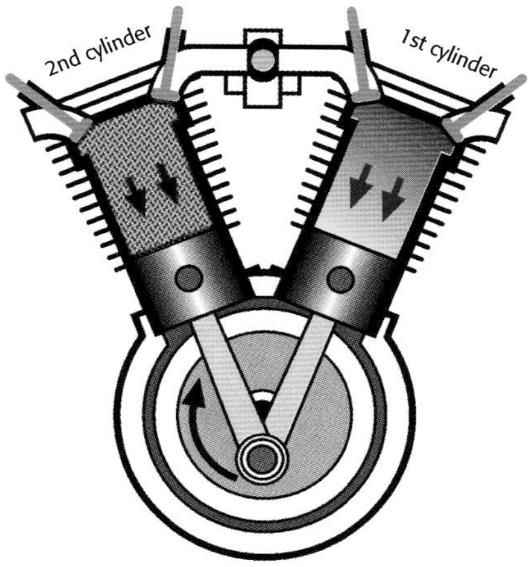

Both pistons are lowered:

2nd cylinder: Both valves closed
                   (compression)

1st cylinder: Both valves closed
                   Operating cycle (combustion)

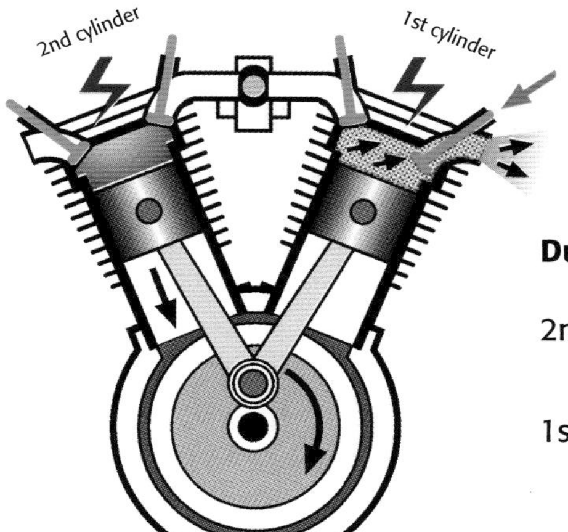

During ignition, both pistons are raised:

2nd cylinder: Both valves closed
                   Operating cycle (ignition)

1st cylinder: Outlet valve open
                   Exhaust cycle (idle ignition)

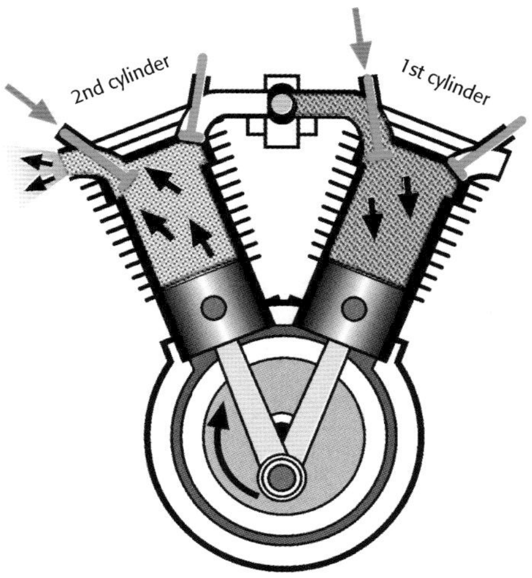

Both pistons are lowered:

2nd cylinder: Outlet valve opens
                   Exhaust cycle

1st cylinder: Inlet valve open
                   Induction cycle

The Birth of a Legend
1909: The First V–Twin – Model 5D

Long-expected and announced beforehand as a major innovation, Harley-Davidson first attempted to launch a competitive twin-cylinder model onto the market in 1909. This was the classic V-Twin, with two connecting rods on a single crankpin. For the most part, it still comprised components from the successful single-cylinder models.

Although the crankcase and its bearing were strengthened, the cylinder heads still retained the automatic inlet (suction) valve known as the blow valve, which no longer functioned properly due to the different pressure/negative pressure ratios of the larger crankcase. The 49.46 cubic inch (811 cc) engine was a poor starter and it did not run smoothly. In addition, much to the annoyance of every rider, the belt often slipped on account of the excessively weak power transmission. Once 27 units had been built, Harley-Davidson halted production, in order to search for a solution to the V-Twin's teething troubles.

The powerful but far-from-perfected horizontally ribbed twin-cylinder engine of the Model 5D which had a displacement of 49.46 cubic inches (810.42 cc).

The early Model H Schebler carburetor (far left) and the famous exhaust pipe flap.

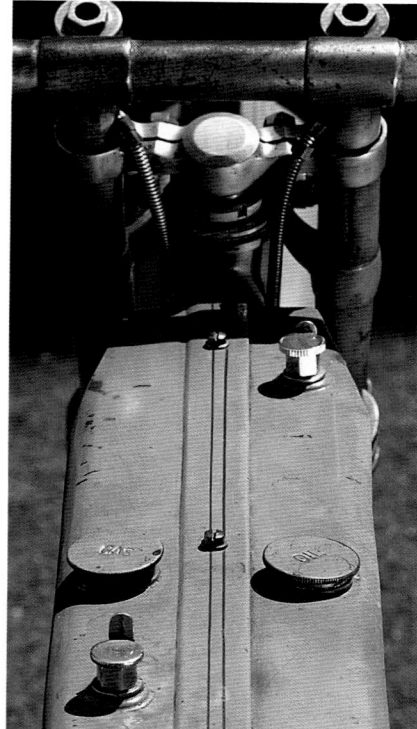

The new company logo on the steering head.

The left half of the tank was for oil, the right half for gasoline. The mechanism for the auxiliary hand-operated oil pump can be seen to the top right.

Type:	**F-Head V-Twin First Twin**
Model:	**5D (Double Cylinder)**
Year of manufacture:	1909
Engine:	Air-cooled four-stroke IOE 45° V-Twin with automatic inlet valve and horizontally ribbed cylinders
Displacement:	49.46 cu in (810.42 cc)
Bore x stroke:	3.0 x 3.5 in (76.20 x 88.9 mm)
Power output:	7 hp
Carburetor:	Schebler, Model H
Transmission:	None
Primary drive:	Direct drive
Final drive:	Belt
Ignition:	Bosch magneto
Frame:	Loop, tubular steel with two horizontal tubes for the split fuel tank
Front brake:	None
Rear brake:	Coaster
Front suspension:	Springer fork with twin springs
Rear suspension:	None
Wheelbase:	56.5 in
Fuel capacity:	1.5 gal
Oil capacity:	2 qts
Tires:	2.5 x 28
Top speed:	45 mph
Price:	$325
Model versions:	In black or Renault gray. Only 27 units were built and recalled from sale in 1909.

The large belt rim was secured next to the actual wheel with mounting brackets.

Although the powerful engine had a broad drive belt, there was no belt-tensioning device.

All photos on this double page-spread courtesy of: H.D. Archives

1911: The Second V-Twin – Model 7D

Harley's second attempt with an overall much-improved twin-cylinder model was a far greater success than the first version. The newly developed IOE (inlet over exhaust) F-head engine now had a top-mounted inlet valve mechanically controlled by a cam. The engine still had a displacement of 49.8 cubic inches (810 cc), yielding 6.5 horsepower. An improved belt-tensioning device prevented the annoying problem of the belt constantly slipping and a reinforced frame provided for greater stability. However, just how many of the units produced (known annual production figure for 1911 is 5,625 units) comprised the new twin-cylinder models can no longer be determined for sure. All the relevant documents were destroyed by water damage.

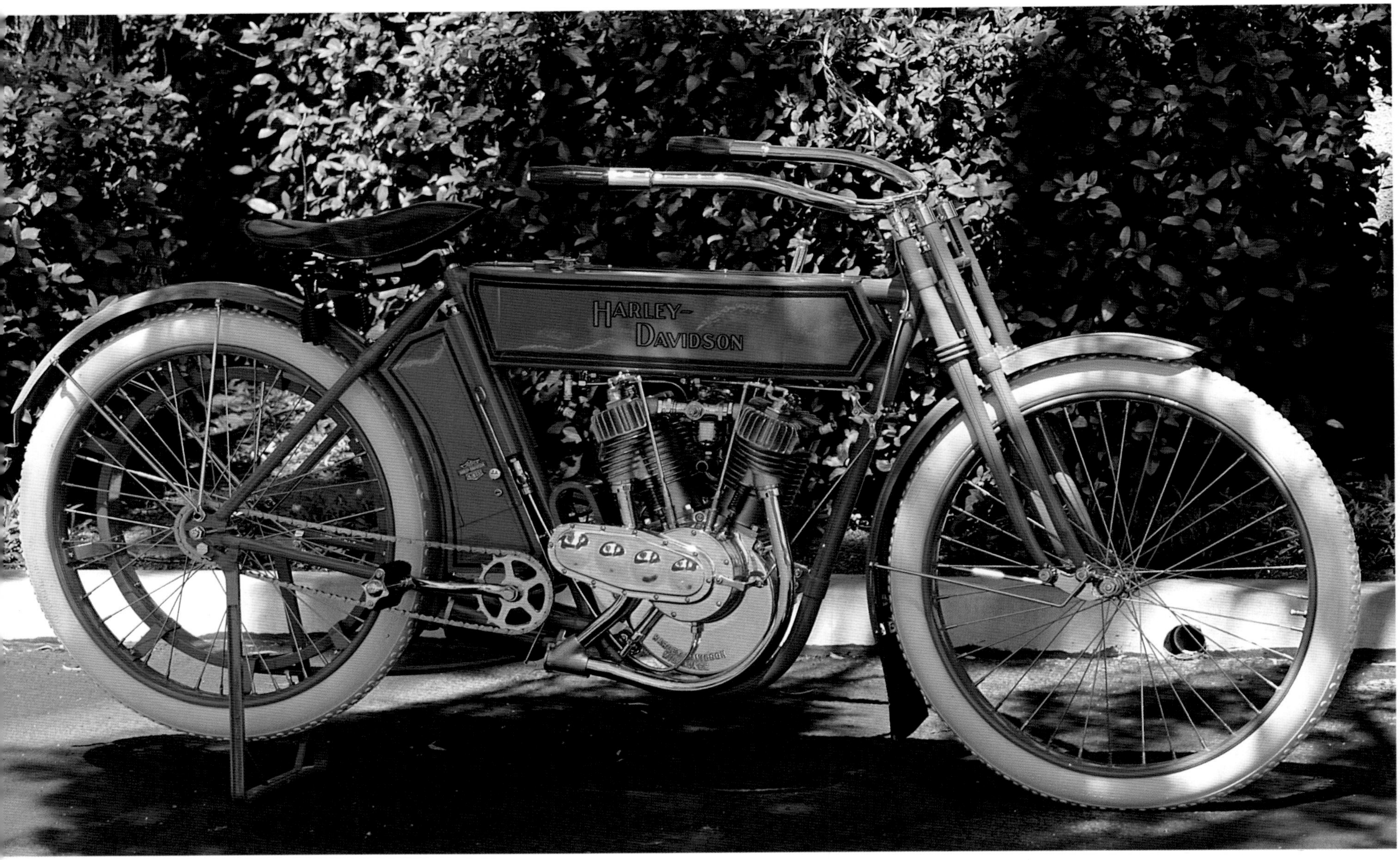

All photos on this double page-spread courtesy of:
Otis Chandler/Vintage Museum of Transportation, Oxnard, California

New: the reinforced nickel-plated chain for starting and braking.

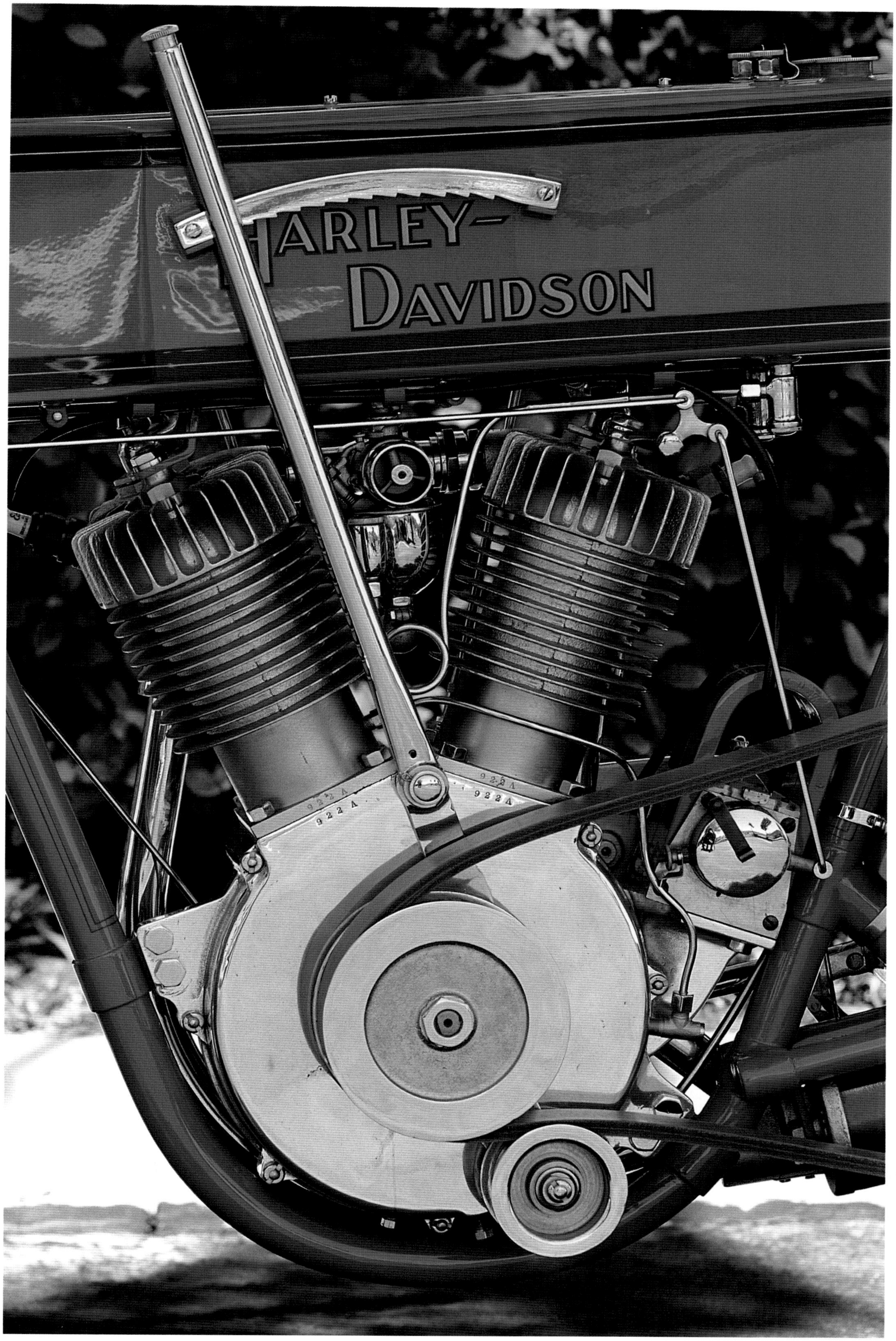

Type:	**F-Head V-Twin**
	Early Twin
	Silent Grey Fellow
Model:	**7D**
Year of manufacture:	1911
Engine:	Air-cooled four-stroke IOE 45° V-Twin with mechanically controlled inlet valve and vertically ribbed cylinders
Displacement:	49.46 cu in (810.42 cc)
Bore x stroke:	3 x 3.5 in (76.20 x 88.9 mm)
Power output:	6.5 hp
Carburetor:	Schebler
Transmission:	None
Primary drive:	Direct drive
Final drive:	Leather belt with tensioning device
Ignition:	Bosch magneto
Frame:	Loop, tubular steel
Front brake:	None
Rear brake:	Coaster
Front suspension:	Springer fork
Rear suspension:	None
Wheelbase:	56.5 in
Fuel capacity:	2.5 gal
Oil capacity:	4 qts
Tires:	2.5 x 28
Top speed:	60 mph
Price:	$300
Model versions:	Broad decorative stripes in red or gray

The new F-head engine with its vertical cooling ribs and an adjustable device for tensioning the drive belt. The twin decorative stripes on the Silent Grey Fellow have been restored to their original design, as has the logo.

The first use of mechanical control of the fuel inlet valve. Here, the rocker arm can be seen on one of the cylinder heads.

The Twin-Cylinder from 1912 to 1921

The manufactured series of F-head 61 cubic inch twin-cylinder motorcycles displayed differences in details between 1912 and 1921, as well as a growing number of improvements, some of which were fitted as standard while others were available as optional extras. The technicians changed the bore-to-stroke ratio several times, in order to optimize the relatively new engine.

In this context, the Model 8 and Model 9 (1912 and 1913) each displaced 63.7 cubic inches (1044 cc) and achieved 8 horsepower. Further new features were an additional hand-operated oil pump, the recently patented "ful floteing" (sic) saddle and, available as optional extras, an acetylene lighting system and a newly developed two-speed transmission in the rear wheel hub, although the latter feature was initially only intended for commercial models.

The type designation "X" for the model referred to the extremely advanced "free wheel control" clutch in the rear wheel hub. The designation "E" could be found in all models that sported a chain as the final drive system.

In 1914 two types of engines were on the market: the 49.5 cubic inches and the stronger 60.3 cubic inches engine. New features included a step-starter that had to be kicked forwards, brake and clutch pedals, fold-up footboards and an improved HD-Band-Brake on the rear wheel. The large array of accessories included sidecars, speedometers and the Prest-O-Lite gas lighting system.

From 1915 onwards, the twin-cylinder models again displaced 60.3 cubic inches (988 cc) and boasted an automatic oil pump with glass inspection port. For the first time, a two-unit lighting system known as the Remy Model 15 was made available, comprising a headlamp, a removable rear light and a horn.

As of 1916, all models were named according to the respective year of manufacture. A new standardization system was introduced that meant all model types were fitted with the same frame, footboards and brakes. The new kickstart system was introduced, whereby the pedal was kicked backwards as opposed to forwards in the case of the step-starter and the last relics of the motorcycle's bicycle ancestry (the pedals) were finally removed from the three-speed models. All standard models were finished in olive-drab as of 1917.

A broad array of special accessories available as countless options allowed the most diverse upgrades and modifications. These included sidecars in all conceivable designs for one or two passengers, special paint finishes, emblems and decorative stripes, different tires and wheel sizes, broader fenders, more comfortable saddles, larger fuel tanks, hand- or foot-operated clutches and brakes and a variety of specially manufactured technical components intended primarily for the ever more popular sport of motorcycle racing. The standard range of commercially available motorcycles was supplemented by an extraordinarily broad range of sports and racing machines.

A 1914 V-Twin model with acetylene lamps and hand-operated klaxon horn, in original condition and not restored.

Courtesy of: Dale Walksler/Wheels Through Time Museum, Mount Vernon, Illinois

The cast cylinder used in the F-head made it difficult to install internal components.

Model versions, prices and production figures:

1912
Model 8D	(magneto ignition and belt drive)		$275
Model X8D	(magneto ignition, belt drive and rear wheel hub clutch)		$285
Model X8E	(magneto ignition, rear wheel hub clutch and final chain drive)		$285

1913
Model 9E	(with chain drive)	$350	6,732 units

1914
Model 10E	(with chain drive)	$250	5,055 units
Model 10F	(with chain drive and two-speed transmission)	$285	7,956 units

1915
Model 11E	(direct drive)	$240	1,275 units
Model 11F	(with three-speed transmission)	$275	9,855 units
Model 11H	(direct drive with electrical lighting system)	$275	40 units
Model 11J	(with three-speed transmission and electrical lighting system)	$310	3,719 units

The model designations FS and JS refer to sidecar versions

Price and production figures for the V–Twin–Series: 1916 to 1921

	Model E (direct drive)		Model F (three-speed transmission)		Model J (three-speed transmission with electrical lighting system)	
1916	$240	252 units	$265	9,496 units	$295	5,898 units
1917	$255	68 units	$275	8,527 units	$310	9,180 units
1918	$275	n.a	$290	11,746 units	$320	6,571 units
1919	–	–	$350	5,064 units	$370	9,941 units
1920	–	–	$370	7,579 units	$395	14,192 units
1921	–	–	$450	2,413 units	$485	4,526 units

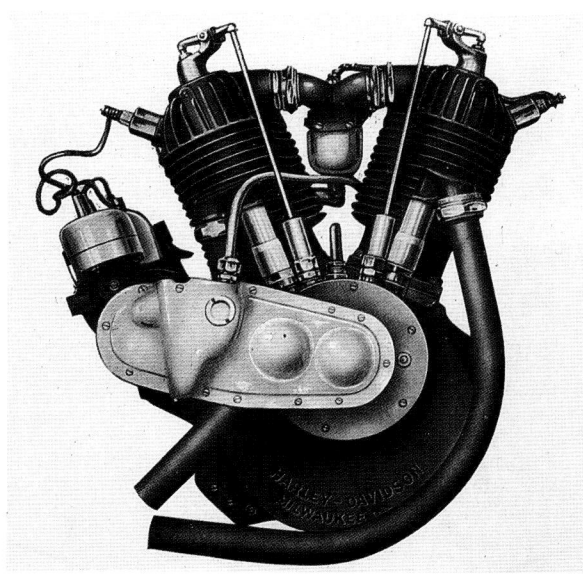

Harley-Davidson 7-9 h.p. engine dismantled. Note unique cam gear

IOE F-Head V-Twin engines (solenoid and battery ignition) with open and closed timing case covers.

Type:	**F–Head V–Twin** **Early Twin** **Silent Grey Fellow**
Model:	**16J**
Years of manufacture:	1916–1920 (model designation according to year as of 1916)
Engine:	Air-cooled four-stroke IOE 45° V–Twin
Displacement:	60.33 cu in (988 cc)
Bore x stroke:	3.3125 x 3.5 in (84 x 89 mm)
Power output:	11 hp (16 as of 1917)
Carburetor:	Schebler (DeLuxe from 1917 onwards)
Transmission:	Three-speed with kickstarter
Primary drive:	Chain
Final drive:	Chain
Battery:	6 volt
Ignition:	Battery-coil
Frame:	Loop, tubular steel
Front brake:	None
Rear brake:	Drum
Front suspension:	Springer fork
Rear suspension:	None
Wheelbase:	59.5 in
Weight:	325 lb
Fuel capacity:	2.75 gal
Oil capacity:	2.5 qts
Tires:	3.00 x 28
Top speed:	60 mph (65 mph as of 1918)
Price:	$295
Model versions:	16E
	16F
	16R Road Racer
	16T Track Racer
	1916: HD gray, in olive-drab from 1917. Production from 1917–1920 concentrated mainly on military models.

Type:	**F–Head V–Twin** **Early Twin** **Silent Grey Fellow**
Model:	**11J**
Year of manufacture:	1915
Engine:	Air-cooled four-stroke IOE 45° V–Twin "High-Duty Twin-Cylinder Engine"
Displacement:	60.30 cu in (988.10 cc)
Bore x stroke:	3.3125 x 3.5 in (84.14 x 88.90 mm)
Power output:	11 hp
Carburetor:	Schebler
Transmission:	Three-speed with step-starter
Primary drive:	Chain
Final drive:	Chain
Battery:	6 volt
Ignition:	Battery-coil
Frame:	Loop, tubular steel
Front brake:	None
Rear brake:	Drum
Front suspension:	Springer fork
Rear suspension:	None
Wheelbase:	59.5 in
Weight:	325 lb
Fuel capacity:	2.75 gal
Oil capacity:	2.5 qts
Tires:	3.00 x 28
Top speed:	60 mph
Price:	$310

Superbikes of a Bygone Age: Harley's OHV Eight-Valve Machines

In 1912, Indian, who had been having ever greater success in motorcycle racing, brought out a lightning fast, eight-valve, overhead-valve, V-Twin, racing machine. Selling at 350 dollars, it was only slightly more expensive than the stock street model. As sales of this machine grew in the wake of its success on the racetrack, Harley-Davidson realized that something would have to be done.

The company's answer was the eight-valve, V-Twin, R (R for racing) model, which was sent into battle for the first time in 1915 after a certain amount of initial teething trouble. This was after William Harley had finally, in 1913, managed to convince his partners Walter and Arthur Davidson, both previously opposed to the formation of a factory racing division, of the promotional effectiveness of high-profile success on the racetrack.

This then led to the hiring of the development engineer William Ottaway, who had been enticed away from Thor, to form a Harley-Davidson racing team. The unusual eight-valve machine was developed under his leadership, with the assistance of the English combustion chamber expert Harry Ricardo, who had made significant improvements to the aviation engine principle of using a spherical combustion chamber with four overhead valves.

The FAM's competition regulations of the time prescribed a maximum displacement of 61 cubic inches (1000 cc), and the models also had to be freely available to the public. However, the price tag of 1,500 dollars put the motorcycle beyond the reach of the private rider, as did the purchase price of 1,400 dollars for a similarly constructed 500 cc OHV four-valve single-cylinder machine. In fact not one of these eight-valve OHV racing machines was sold to a private rider. Indeed, the total production figure for this machine is unknown, with estimates varying between 20 and 60 motorcycles. Some 10 to 15 of these were used in races in the U.S., while the rest were sent to the various works teams abroad — mainly those in England, Australia and New Zealand.

At 50 horsepower, Harley's new racer was sensationally powerful by the standards of 1916. The aggressive-looking, eight-valve, production racer was produced in a variety of different designs. There were versions with varying rockers, with one or two camshafts, with or without an exhaust pipe, with hand or mechanically operated, oil pump, with Harley or Flying Merkel forks, and with compressions ranging from 6 to 9.5:1, ratios suggesting the use of alcohol mixes. The compression (normally 8:1) was so high that the motorbikes had to be towed by a car in order to start them. Kickstarts and a ridiculously feeble rear band brake were not added until later on — the standard version had no brakes at all! Power transmission was by one primary and one final drive-chain with no gears, and just a double pinion gear in between. The power train was eccentrically positioned so that both chains could be tensioned by moving it. The engine was screwed to the single-tube, steel frame with two steel plates forming the load-bearing elements.

All eight-valve, production racers had a single Schebler carburetor fitted between the two cylinders. However, Freddy Dixon, an Englishman who successfully raced the machine at Brooklands, added a second carburetor. This racing machine was most frequently used on oval, steep-banked tracks or flat tracks for high-speed races and record-breaking attempts. In 1921 Otto Walker achieved a new and long-standing record speed of 107.78 mph (173.4 kph) on the steep bends of the Fresno Oval in California. Floyd Clymer was one of the first, successful, works riders entrusted by Harley with the task of racing this fast but sensitive machine.

Race team boss Bill Ottaway always employed an unusual strategy when racing the eight-valve motorbikes: right from the start he would race them hard, using their incredible speed to force the competition to strain their engines to the limit in the effort to keep up. The result was engine damage for the majority of the machines. However, the unreliable eight-valve Harley was also likely to suffer some damage, so the more reliable Harley F-head racers, which up to that point had been raced at less than full power, would then take up the running and generally win the race. This tactic was usually successful. The eight-valve bike just had to last until the competing bikes broke down — as they nearly always did, since Harley had the better machines, more skillful maintenance teams and the best riders.

This legendary Harley-Davidson "Wrecking Crew" scored its greatest successes using this more or less unbeatable race strategy. In 1922 the Harley racing team was disbanded most likely because sales failed to meet expectations despite the incredible run of racing success, and the majority of the eight-valve machines were summarily consigned to the scrapheap.

Exquisite racing technology —
Harley's Eight-Valve Production racer.

All the photos on this double-page spread are courtesy of: Otis Chantler/Vintage Museum of Transportation, Oxnard, California

Type:	**Eight–Valve Racer**
Model:	**I6 R**
Years of manufacture:	1915–1921
Engine:	Air-cooled four-stroke overhead-valve V-Twin OHV with four valves per cylinder
Displacement:	61 cu in (986 cc)
Bore x stroke:	3.31 x 3.5 in (84 x 89 mm)
Compression ratio:	8 : 1
Power output:	c. 50 hp at 4000 rpm
Carburetor:	Schebler 27 mm ø
Transmission:	None/dry multiplate clutch
Primary drive:	Chain
Final drive:	Chain
Battery:	None
Ignition:	Bosch magneto
Frame:	Steel tube
Front brake:	None
Rear brake:	None
Front suspension:	Springer forks
Rear suspension:	None
Wheelbase:	51.5 in
Weight:	265 lb
Fuel capacity:	1.43 gal
Oil capacity:	2.5 qts
Tires:	3.0 x 28
Top speed:	Up to 112 mph
Price:	$1,500

Model versions:
A converted, 500 cc, OHV, four–valve, single–cylinder version without a rear cylinder was available at a cost of $1,400.

The ultimate in racing technology: once the decision was made to participate in racing, Harley–Davidson invested enormous efforts in taking the latest advances in engine design into account.

An Unsuccesful Outsider: the Sport Twin

After World War I came to an end, the motorcycle enjoyed a flourishing career as a fun and leisure-time vehicle, forcing Harley-Davidson to take a whole new approach to motorcycle design. The Model W Sport Twin, designed as a lightweight sport machine with a side-valve 35.64 cubic inch (584 cc) horizontally opposed engine, represented quite a risk for the company, venturing into territory that was hitherto unexplored from both a technical and a commercial vantage point.

Nevertheless, the Sport Twin proved to be an improvement on the design of the British Douglas model with a horizontally opposed engine – one of the most popular motorcycles in Europe. However, it unfortunately turned out to be ahead of its time.

The side-valve boxer engine, which acted as a stressed member in the frame, may only have produced a modest 6 horsepower, but the Sport Twin still managed to reach a top speed of 50 mph thanks to its low overall weight of just 265 pounds. A whole battery of technical refinements indicated beyond any doubt the direction motorcycle design would be taking in future: all four valves were controlled by a single camshaft, the intake manifold coupled with the exhaust manifold used the heat of the exhaust gas to improve combustion, the fully enclosed chain was protected against dust and dirt and the specially sprung Merkel fork provided for a high degree of comfort, even over rough terrain. Simple maintenance was ensured because all parts were easy to get at. The Sport Twin was also available with an electrical lighting system as of 1920.

Although the model sold well abroad and clocked up numerous spectacular successes in long-distance and endurance runs at home, it did not prove popular with buyers. Americans have always preferred the V-Twin. Harley-Davidson realized that the time of the Sport Twin had not yet come and removed it from its model range in 1923.

All photos on this double page-spread are courtesy of: Otis Chandler/Vintage Museum of Transportation, Oxnard, California

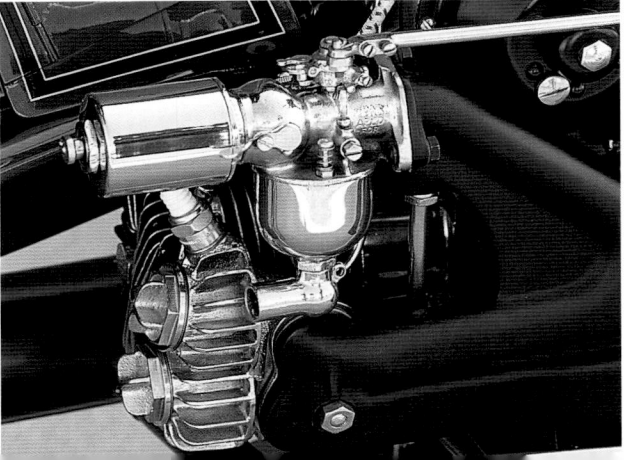

The special dust-protected standard Schebler carburetor with the long manifold for the top-mounted connecting pipe that provided both cylinders with the correct fuel mixture.

The 4 h.p. unit combining engine, gear box clutch and spiral drive from engine to gear box

Type:	**Flathead Opposite–Twin**
Model:	**W Sport Twin**
Years of manufacture:	1919–1923
Engine:	Air-cooled four–stroke horizontally opposed side–valve twin
Displacement:	35.64 cu in (584.03 cc)
Bore x stroke:	2.75 x 3.0 in (69.85 x 76.20 mm)
Power output:	6 hp
Carburetor:	Schebler
Transmission:	Three–speed
Primary drive:	Helical gear wheel
Final drive:	Chain
Battery:	6 volt
Ignition:	Magneto
Frame:	Loop, tubular steel
Front brake:	None
Rear brake:	Outer band
Front suspension:	Trailing link springer fork
Rear suspension:	None
Wheelbase:	57 in
Weight:	265 lb
Fuel capacity:	2.75 gal
Oil capacity:	2 qts
Tires:	3.00 x 26
Top speed:	50 mph
Price:	$335
Model versions:	WF: magneto ignition
	WJ: with electrical lighting system

Model versions, prices and production figures:

1919

WF (magneto ignition)	$335	753 units

1920

WF (magneto ignition)	$335	4,459 units
WJ (with electrical lighting system)	(n.a.)	810 units

1921

WF (magneto ignition)	$415	1,100 units
WJ (with electrical lighting system)	$445	823 units

1922

WF (magneto ignition)	$310	388 units
WJ (with electrical lighting system)	$340	455 units

1923

WF (magneto ignition)	$275	614 units
WJ (with electrical lighting system)	$295	481 units

The complete engine unit from an original brochure. The inlet and exhaust pipes, mounted adjacently, can be clearly seen.

The left–hand side of the longitudinal twin engine with its large, round dust cover for the kickstarter pinion gear.

The 61 cubic inch Big Twin Models from 1921 to 1929

The general trend towards large-volume, powerful and reliable motorcycles caused Harley-Davidson to introduce a new displacement class in 1921, in addition to its 61 cubic inch (1000 cc) models: the new 74 cubic inch (1200 cc) D series, comprising the basic models FD (magneto ignition) and JD (battery ignition with electrical lighting system). With motorcycle-sidecar combinations becoming ever more popular (indicated by the letter S in the model designation), Harley also produced engines with special compression plates and sidecar transmissions.

A whole range of commercial and private sidecars were now available in Harley's product range, with numerous engines and a wealth of optional extras. The standard paintwork changed in the year 1922 to the darker Brewster green color.

From 1923 onwards, Harley also offered numerous engines with cast iron pistons (A type and C type) or iron/aluminum alloys. Harley-Davidson also once again improved the 74 cubic inch model in 1925, providing it with a new, lower-slung frame complete with engine mounting plate, a lower saddle with a spring in the central tube that was increased in length from nine inches to 14 inches optimizing the seating position and wider 26-inch balloon tires. The new features also included a single-pipe speedster muffler. This model went on to become widely praised as the "most comfortable motorcycle in the world."

A vast range of conversion options was available for all models, as well as an enormous number of parts and accessories, such as speedometers from Corbin Brown and Jahns-Manville, ammeters, luggage racks, heel-operated brakes, Zenith carburetors, tandem seats from Mesinger, Firestone "Non-Skid" tires, the Jiffy stand (1928) and a fuel-tank-mounted toolbox. The familiar olive-drab was standard with certain color options available in the years to come.

Courtesy of: Max Middelbosch, Zwolle, Netherlands

The electric horn and toolbox beneath the raised lamp.

Courtesy of: Max Middelbosch, Zwolle, Netherlands

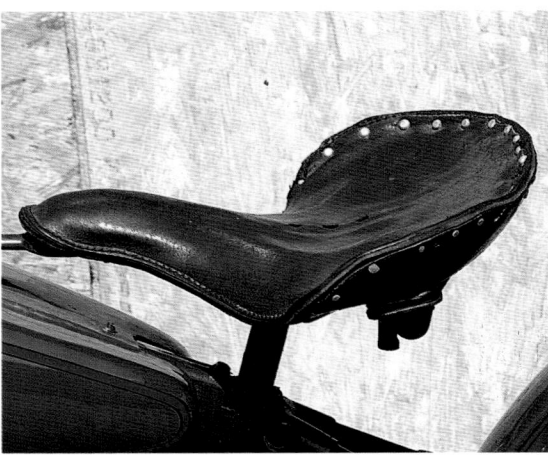

The classic "Ful-Floteing" (sic) solo seat.

Courtesy of: Max Middelbosch, Zwolle, Netherlands

Available as an optional extra: the stop display for the electric rear lamp.

Courtesy of: Otis Chandler/Vintage Museum of Transportation, Oxnard, California

Announcing The New World's Champion

A New "61" Twin at A New Low Price

We built *more* value, *more* riding comfort, and *more* mechanical conveniences into this Harley-Davidson "61" Twin, and then *we* reduced the price. This 1923 low-priced, popular twin model includes all the new improvements from the new spring fork to the "Staylit" shock-absorbing tail lamp. Note these 1923 *reduced* prices:

61F magneto twin $285
61J electric twin $305
F. O. B. Milwaukee

Here's Value that Interests You

The new, improved 1923 Harley-Davidson Royal Tourist Sidecar is *increased* in value and *reduced* in price! An improved sidecar hub keeps out all dust and dirt. Wider and stronger braces add strength to the mudguard supports. Get a Royal Tourist Sidecar at this low price. *Double* your motorcycling pleasures and pocket the saving at this new, *reduced* price:

Harley-Davidson $98
Royal Tourist Sidecar
Two Passenger Sidecar Reduced to $125
All Prices F. O. B. Milwaukee

The 1923 "74" Twin —more value for less

Here is the thoroughbred among motorcycles. Its abundance of sure, silent and eager power has made it the choice of sidecar motorcyclists. The new improvements, made possible by a year's engineering concentration, emphasize the outstanding value of this super-powered 1923 Harley-Davidson "74" Twin at these *reduced* prices:

74FD magneto twin $310
74JD electric twin $330
F. O. B. Milwaukee

1923 HARLEY-DAVIDSON MOTORCYCLES and SIDECARS

Original 1923 brochure portraying the new 61-inch and 74-inch V-Twins.

Typical characteristic of the J model: recesses in the right-half of the fuel tank to accommodate the rocker arm controlling the fuel inlet valve.

Courtesy of: Max Middelbosch, Zwolle, Netherlands

Type:	**F–Head Big Twin**
Model:	**21 JD**
Years of manufacture:	1921–1924
Engine:	Air–cooled four–stroke IOE 45° V–Twin
Displacement:	74.21 cu in (1215.96 cc)
Bore x stroke:	3.43 x 4.0 in (87.31 x 101.6 mm)
Power output:	18 hp
Carburetor:	Schebler 32 mm ø
Transmission:	Three-speed
Primary drive:	Chain
Final drive:	Chain
Battery:	6 volt
Ignition:	Battery-coil
Frame:	Loop, tubular steel
Front brake:	None
Rear brake:	Drum
Front suspension:	Springer fork
Rear suspension:	None
Wheelbase:	59.5 in
Weight:	365 lb
Fuel capacity:	2.75 gal
Oil capacity:	2 qts
Tires:	3.00 x 28
Top speed:	70 mph
Price:	$485
Model versions:	21 JD Solo 21 JDS Sidecar 1921 in olive-drab; in Brewster green from 1922.

Type:	**F–Head Big Twin**
Model:	**25 JD**
Years of manufacture:	1925–1929
Engine:	Air–cooled four–stroke 45° V–Twin IOE
Displacement:	73.7 cu in (1207 cc)
Bore x stroke:	3.4 x 4.02 in (87 x 102 mm)
Power output:	24 hp
Carburetor:	Schebler 32 mm ø
Transmission:	Three-speed
Primary Drive:	Chain
Final Drive:	Chain
Battery:	6 volt
Ignition:	Battery-coil
Frame:	Looped tubular steel
Front brake:	None
Rear brake:	Drum
Front suspension:	Springer fork
Rear suspension:	None
Wheelbase:	59.5 in
Weight:	493 lb
Fuel capacity:	4 gal
Oil capacity:	2.5 qts
Tires:	3.85 x 27
Top speed:	97 mph
Price:	$335
Model versions:	25 FE, 25 JE, 25 FDCB, 25 JDCB, 25 FES, 25 JES 25 FDCBS, 25 JDCBS

Control lever on the left of the fuel tank.
Courtesy of: Max Middelbosch, Zwolle, Netherlands

Available as an optional extra: an electrically illuminated speedometer.

Courtesy of: Otis Chandler/Vintage Museum of Transportation, Oxnard, California

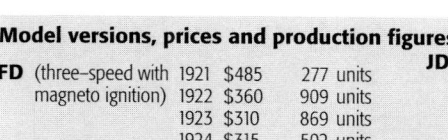

Model versions, prices and production figures

FD (three–speed with magneto ignition)			JD (three–speed with battery ignition and electrical lighting)		
	1921	$485	277 units	1921	$520	2,321 units
	1922	$360	909 units	1922	$390	3,988 units
	1923	$310	869 units	1923	$330	7,458 units
	1924	$315	502 units	1924	$335	2,955 units
(1925 also as **FDCB**)	1925	$315	433 units	(1925 also as **JDCB**) 1925	$335	9,506 units
	1926	$315	232 units	1926	$335	9,544 units
				1927	$320	9,691 units
				1928	$320	11,007 units
				1929	$320	10,182 units

For use with sidecars: **FDS** (1921–1925)
FDCBS (1925)

For use with sidecars: **JDS** (1921–1929)
JDCBS (1925), **JS** (1929)

Special models:

A engine/cast iron pistons (from 1923): **FDA, FDCA, JDA, JDCA**
Alloy pistons, lighter connecting-rod (from 1924): **FDSCA, JDCA, JDSCA**

The Model J Two Cam from 1928 to 1929

Announced in 1927, Harley's best, most powerful and ultimately last F–head V–Twin motorcycle, available with either 61 or 74 cubic inch (1000 or 1200 cc) high-performance engines, appeared at the end of 1928. The valve control system was now operated by two camshafts (hence the name Two Cam), as had been used in racing models for several years already, albeit by means of tappets this time instead of roller arms. Twin inlet valves allowed higher engine speeds and thus more power. Pronounced ribbing on the cylinder heads provided for improved cooling. The pistons were made of a particularly durable magnesium alloy known as Dow metal. The oil pump, now controlled by the throttle, improved the overall lubrication characteristics. However, the extremely quiet two-stage muffler, with four end tubes referred to as the Pipes-O'Pan, was not all that popular. After all, such a powerful engine should be heard.

The Two Cam model (also referred to as the Two Cammer) was available as the 61 inch (1000 cc) JH and the 74 inch (1200 cc) JDH (price in 1929: 370 dollars). With a small 4.75-gallon fuel tank, Two-Bullet twin headlamps used only in 1929 and 1930 and 18-inch wheels with balloon tires, it looked impressive, to say the least. The front-wheel brake finally provided for acceptable braking performance. The low-slung, extra-wide Solo "ful-floteing" (sic) saddle could be replaced with the popular twin Buddy Seat. This latter seat squeezed the two occupants close together when two people were mounted on the motorcycle, but it allowed for relaxed riding for a solo rider thanks to the various positions available. The standard color was still olive-drab, although a rich array of two-tone finishes were available as optional extras, such as azure blue, police blue, coach green, maroon, fawn gray, cream or orange.

Instruments, gate-type gearshift, oil and gasoline filler caps on the left side of the fuel tank.

All photos on this double page-spread are courtesy of H.D. Archives

Type:	**Two Cam IOE**
Model:	**28 JHD**
Years of manufacture:	1928–1929
Engine:	Air-cooled four-stroke IOE 45° V-Twin
Displacement:	74.21 cu in (1215.96 cc)
Bore x stroke:	3.43 x 4.0 in (87.31 x 101.6 mm)
Compression ratio:	6.5 : 1
Power output:	29 hp
Carburetor:	Schebler
Transmission:	Three-speed
Primary drive:	Chain
Final drive:	Chain
Battery:	6 volt
Ignition:	Battery–coil
Frame:	Loop, tubular steel
Front brakes:	Drum
Rear brakes:	Drum
Front suspension:	Springer fork with two springs
Rear suspension:	None
Wheelbase:	59.5 in
Weight:	408 lb
Fuel capacity:	4.75 gal
Oil capacity:	2 qts
Tires:	3.85 x 18
Top speed:	85 mph
Price:	$370
Model versions:	JDH: 74 cu in (1200 cc) Two Cam
	JH: 61 cu in (1000 cc) Two Cam

Although written off as an outdated design by most leading manufacturers, the Two Cam developed by Bill Harley and Bill Ottaway was a highlight of American motorcycle manufacture.

Single–Cylinder Motorcycles from 1926 to 1935

Harley-Davidson's immediate reaction in 1926 to Indian's single-cylinder Prince was to introduce two new 21 cubic inch (350 cc) singles: the side-valve Solo model as Type A with magneto ignition and Type B with battery ignition and lights, both with roughly 8 horsepower and at the highly competitive prices of 210 dollars and 235 dollars respectively.

For the more demanding customer, Harley launched the Sport Solo model, with the more complicated and powerful overhead-valve engine which yielded about 12 horsepower. This model was available as Type AA with magneto ignition and Type BA with battery ignition and lights for 250 and 275 dollars respectively. Furthermore, the OHV racing model S (with Sager fork and 27-inch wheels) could be had for 300 dollars. This model became popularly known as the Peashooter.

Harley's new models were particularly easy to repair, had fully removable cylinder heads with combustion chambers designed by Harry Ricardo, a three-speed transmission, the streamlined teardrop fuel tank which allowed an even lower seating position on the "ful floteing" saddle, fold-up footboards, a rear-wheel stand, a kickstarter (of course), 26-inch balloon tires and (in the case of the Model B and Model BA) a black klaxon horn. In 1927, the Harleys were fitted with reinforced frames, stronger clutch springs and improved mufflers. The standard tool package included an Alemite grease-gun, an air-pump and an adjustable wrench.

The Model B received alloy pistons in 1928 and a lighter camshaft. In the same year, all models were fitted with an air-filter, a throttle-controlled oil pump (Alemite system), and front-wheel brakes.

From 1929 onwards, only Models B and BA were available with the complete electrical system, optionally with a novel Pipes-O'Pan four-tube muffler system. Harley-Davidson continued to build all models in small quantities upon request up until 1935.

In true Harley tradition, a wealth of special options was also available for these single-cylinder models, including air-filters, Mesinger tandem seats, various handlebars (solo or speedster), cadmium-rimmed wheels, a high-performance conversion kit, the Jiffy stand, a speedometer and special balloon tires.

Side-valve Model A with acetylene lamps.

Courtesy of: Suck, Hamburg, Germany

The competing model from Indian: the 21 cubic inch (350 cc) side-valve single-cylinder Prince (far left).

The Harley-Davidson 21-inch OHV Model BA.

The Model B with a full array
of electrical components.

Courtesy of: Fritz Simmerlein,
Nuremberg, Germany

The "Baby Harley" Model B
boasted large lamps with twin
bulbs, a solid speedometer
drive with two pinion gears
and a snap–up stand.

The ease with which the
side–valve cylinder head
could be disassembled is
demonstrated in a Harley
brochure.

Type:	**Flathead Twenty–One**
Model:	**26 A**
Years of manufacture:	1926–1928
Engine:	Air–cooled single–cylinder SV
Displacement:	21.09 cu in (345.6 cc)
Bore x stroke:	2.875 x 3.25 in (73.03 x 82.55 mm)
Power output:	8 hp
Carburetor:	Schebler DeLuxe
Transmission:	Three–speed
Primary drive:	Chain
Secondary drive:	Chain
Battery:	6 volt
Ignition:	Magneto
Frame:	Looped tubular steel
Front brake:	None
Rear brake:	Outer band
Front suspension:	Springer fork
Rear suspension:	None
Wheelbase:	56.5 in
Weight:	305 lb
Fuel capacity:	3 gal
Oil capacity:	4 qts
Tires:	3.30 x 26
Top speed:	56 mph
Price:	$210
Model versions:	B: With electrical system

Type:	**Sport–Solo Twenty–One**
Model:	**26 BA**
Year of manufacture:	1926
Engine:	Air–cooled four–stroke single–cylinder OHV
Displacement:	21.09 cu in (345.6 cc)
Bore x stroke:	2.875 x 3.125 in (73.03 x 82.55 mm)
Power output:	12 hp
Carburetor:	Schebler
Transmission:	Three–speed transmission
Primary drive:	Chain
Secondary drive:	Chain
Battery:	6 volt
Ignition:	Battery–coil
Frame:	Looped tubular steel
Front brake:	None
Rear brake:	Outer band
Front suspension:	Springer fork
Rear suspension:	None
Wheelbase:	56.5 in
Weight:	262 lb
Fuel capacity:	3 gal
Oil capacity:	4 qts
Tires:	3.30 x 26
Top speed:	60 mph
Price:	$275
Model versions:	AA: Magneto ignition
	BA: Battery ignition
	S: Racing model

Model versions, prices and production figures

Model A	1926	$210	1,128 units
(sv engine)	1927	$210	444 units
Magneto ignition	1928	$ n.a.	519 units
	1929	$ n.a.	197 units
	1930	$ n.a.	4 units
Model B	1926	$235	5,979 units
(sv engine)	1927	$235	3,711 units
Battery ignition,	1928	$235	3,483 units
electrical system	1929	$235	1,592 units
	1930	$235	577 units
Model AA	1926	$250	61 units
(OHV engine)	1927	$250	32 units
Magneto ignition	1928	$ n.a.	65 units
	1929	$ n.a.	21 units
	1930	$ n.a.	1 units
Model BA	1926	$275	515 units
(OHV engine)	1927	$275	481 units
Battery ignition,	1928	$255	943 units
electrical system	1929	$255	191 units
	1930	$ n.a.	9 units

The Model AAE and Model AAB were also built for export from 1926 to 1929.

The 30 cubic inch Side-Valve Single-Cylinder Model C from 1929 to 1934

The sturdy and reliable single with the 30 cubic inch (500 cc) side-valve engine had a reinforced frame like that used in the new Forty-Five motorcycle (750 cc side-valve twin), before the frame from the 350 cc Twenty-One model was adopted. The Model C sported the usual three-speed transmission and the engine essentially comprised the complete sub-structure of the Twenty-One with rebored cylinders and specially adapted cylinder heads. Its frame was reinforced once again in 1932 and the motorcycle was provided with an improved springer fork.

The 6 volt electrical system initially comprised a klaxon horn and Two-Bullet twin headlamps. These were replaced in 1930 with a so-called sunburst-face horn and a seven-inch John Brown headlamp with a flatter, diffused glass lens. The four-tube muffler was replaced with a twin-pipe muffler and the toolbox was now mounted on the fork. Several different handlebar designs were available. The color scheme was olive-drab, and by 1933 the new art-deco design of the emblem on the fuel tank depicted an eagle symbol. This model could also be modified and upgraded with a host of special accessories.

In addition to the Types CM, CR, CH, CC and CS (for export to Japan), a speedway racer with OHV engine intended primarily for export to England, Australia and New Zealand, was also available as the Type CAC.

The Model C — also known as the "Baby Harley" — did not sell all that well at home in America, but proved to be a very successful export model. It was still produced in the years 1933 and 1934 as the Model CB and was the last single-cylinder motorcycle to be built by Harley-Davidson until the 125 cc two-stroke Model S which appeared in 1948.

No longer in original condition but still roadworthy: a rare Model C from Switzerland.

NEW LOW PRICE
$235
at factory

THE IMPROVED 30.50 SINGLE FOR 1932

The Harley-Davidson "30.50" Single

FOR anyone who desires a lighter weight motorcycle that is just as sturdily built but even easier to handle than the "74" and "45" Twins, the new "30.50" Single is an ideal mount.

Designed exclusively for solo riding, this zippy new Single has a big, rugged motor that easily turns up better than mile-a-minute speed, and develops power enough for the toughest going. The motor has moderate high compression which means long motor life and exceptional operating economy. The light Dow metal piston minimizes vibration and gives quick acceleration.

The "30.50" motor is remarkably simple and accessible. Its genuine Ricardo cylinder head is easily removable and gives quick access to the valves and piston head. Carbon can be scraped and valves ground in twenty minutes. Anyone can do the job and no special tools are required.

Except for the motor, all parts of the "30.50" Single for 1930 are interchangeable with the "45" Twin. The new 1930 features of the "45," such as the double strength frame, drop forged forks, bigger tires, drop-center rims, wider and shorter tanks, theft-proof lock, improved clutch and enlarged front brake are standard equipment on the "30.50."

On the "30.50" Single, as on all the 1930 models, Harley-Davidson again sets the pace in electrical equipment with the new generator that automatically increases its output for night riding. When the rider switches on the headlights, the output of current from the generator is automatically increased to take care of the added consumption of current.

On pages 8 to 11 you will find complete details of design, construction and equipment of all the new 1930 models. ◆

The 30.50 cubic inch Single, Model 30C, fitted with a Dow metal piston, is intended for solo use only.

Type:	**Flathead Thirty–Fifty**
Model:	**C**
Year of manufacture:	1930
Engine:	Air-cooled side-valve single
Displacement:	30.05 cu in (492.48 cc)
Bore x stroke:	3.09 x 4.0 in (78.58 x 101.6 mm)
Power output:	10.5 hp
Carburetor:	Schebler DeLuxe
Transmission:	Three-speed
Primary drive:	Duplex chain
Final drive:	Chain
Battery:	6 volt
Ignition:	Battery-coil
Frame:	Loop, tubular steel
Front brake:	Drum
Rear brake:	Outer band
Front suspension:	Springer fork
Rear suspension:	None
Wheelbase:	57.5 in
Weight:	340 lb
Fuel capacity:	3.75 gal
Oil capacity:	3.75 qts
Tires:	4.00 x 18
Top speed:	60 mph
Price:	$260
Model versions:	C, CM, CR

Prices and production figures

Year	Model	Price	Units
1929	C	$255	1,570 units
1930	C	$260	1,483 units
1931	C	$260	874 units
1932	C	$235	213 units
1933	C	$225	112 units
1934	C	$220	220 units
	CB	$197.50	310 units

Illus. 2
Compression Release Lever Single Model
1—Lever in running position; 2—Move lever to this position to release compression.

Technical details from the Rider's Handbook: the compression release lever for easier starting of the engine (left) and the precise arrangement of the markings of the gearwheels for correct ignition timing.

The control side of the 30 cubic inch (500 cc) side-valve engine.

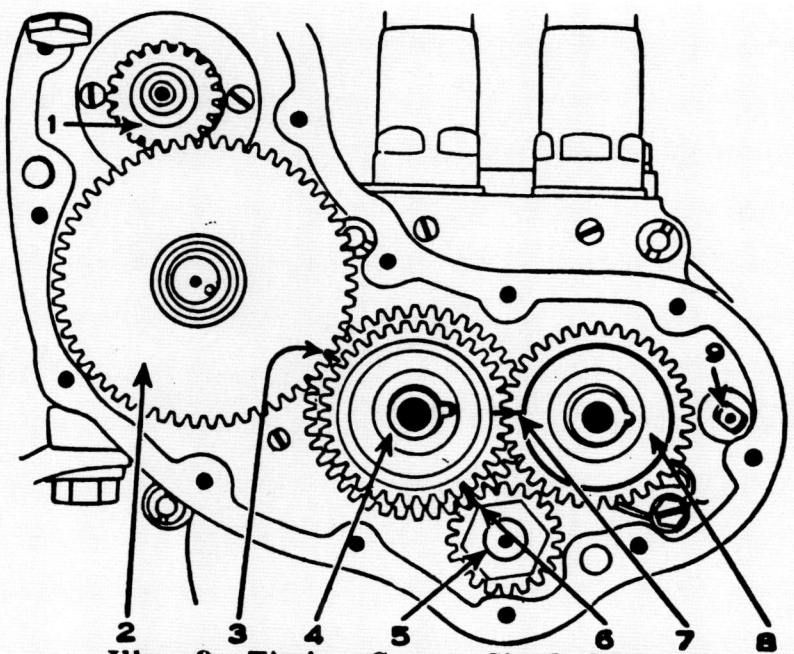

Illus. 9—Timing Gears—Single Model
1—Generator gear; 2—Intermediate gear; 3—This mark on gear 4 does not register with any other mark; 4—Inlet cam gear; 5—Pinion gear; 6—Marks on pinion gear and inlet cam gear correctly aligned; 7—Marks on inlet and exhaust cam gears correctly aligned; 8—Exhaust cam gear; 9—Compression release lever stud.

1929: the Dawn of the Forty-Five – the Model D

The new D model Harley introduced was an all-around motorcycle for everyday use and was a trail-blazing design that laid the foundations for Harley's future model ranges. The side-valve 45 cubic inch (750 cc) V-Twin flathead engine was available in a low-compression version for normal use (Model D and Model DS) and in a high-compression version for more demanding applications (Model DL and Model DLD). It was fitted with pistons made of Dow metal, a battery and coil ignition, the new 14-spring dry clutch, a kickstarter and the extremely quiet Pipes-O'Pan four-tube muffler. The initial equipment range included the twin headlamp, in use until 1930, a klaxon horn located beneath the headlamp and a rather puny front-wheel brake.

In 1930, the Model D was fitted with a stronger frame, which allowed an even lower seated position and improved ground clearance, a large bullet-shaped fuel tank and an anti-theft device. The round tool container was now secured to the fork beneath the headlamp and the exhaust system returned to a twin-pipe muffler design. The engine was further improved by use of double ignition coils instead of one, as well as an automatic chain lubrication system. Even more modifications were performed in 1931: the Schebler DeLuxe carburetor was added, as were a sunburst-face horn, the new seven-inch John Brown Motolamp headlight with matte reflector glass, a fish-tail-type muffler, Sifton frame reinforcing elements and, available as optional extras, standard or speedster handle-bars. Various small parts were chrome-plated.

The standard color of all Model D Harleys was the familiar olive-drab, although alternatives were available. The entire range of accessories and conversion kits was likewise available for the Model D.

A somewhat over-restored 1930 Model D: mirrors were not yet in use and the exhaust pipes were originally matt-black.

1932: the Second Edition of the Forty–Five – the Model R

From 1932 onwards a variety of major changes contributed to the further development of the Model D and its tried and tested 45 cubic inch (750 cc) side–valve engine.

The flathead engine was given stronger valve springs, a larger and more solid crankshaft, a new crankcase, aluminum pistons, an improved oil pump, and a new horizontally mounted generator. The carburetor was fitted with the characteristic swept–back, chrome–plated air filter. The sporting Model RLD now had an M–11

or M–16 Linkert carburetor, and its earthy sounding 2.5 inch fishtail muffler found favor with Harley followers, while the strengthened forks meant greater stability and driving safety.

In 1934 a new oil pump and a new High–Flo muffler also were added. The clutch, reduced to 12 springs, was now much easier to maintain, and streamlined fenders, an Airflow rear light, and a bucket, solo saddle made for a new look.

The Model D (here, a 1930 model) had extensive instruments and characteristic twin headlamps.

Courtesy of: Martin Unger

Model R (1932–1936) versions, prices and production figures

Year	Model	Price	Units
1932	R	$295	410 units
	RL	$295	628 units
	RLD	$310	98 units
1933	R	$280	162 units
	RL	$280	264 units
	RLD	$290	68 units
1934	R	$280	450 units
	RL	$280	743 units
	RLD	$290	240 units
1935	R	$295	543 units
	RL	$295	819 units
	RLD	$305	177 units
1936	R	$295	539 units
	RL	$295	355 units
	RLD	$295	540 units

Type:	**Flathead Fourty–Five**
Model:	**DL**
Years of manufacture:	1929–1931
Engine:	Air–cooled four–stroke side–valve 45° V–Twin
Displacement:	45.26 cu in (741.80 cc)
Bore x stroke:	2.75 x 3.8125 in (69.85 x 96.84 mm)
Power output:	18.5 hp
Carburetor:	Schebler
Transmission:	Three–speed
Primary drive:	Duplex chain
Final drive:	Chain
Battery:	6 volt
Ignition:	Coil
Frame:	Loop, tubular steel
Front brake:	Drum
Rear brake:	Contracting band
Front suspension:	Springer fork
Rear suspension:	None
Wheelbase:	57.5 in
Weight:	390 lb
Fuel capacity:	3.75 gal
Oil capacity:	3.75 qts
Tires:	4.00 x 18
Top speed:	70 mph
Price:	$290
Model versions:	D: Low–compression
	DL: High–compression (Sport)
	DS: Sidecar
	DLD: High–compression (Special Sport)

Type:	**Flathead Fourty–Five**
Model:	**RL**
Years of manufacture:	1932–1936
Engine:	Air–cooled four–stroke side–valve 45° V–Twin
Displacement:	45.26 cu in (741.80 cc)
Bore x stroke:	2.75 x 3.8125 in (69.85 x 96.84 mm)
Compression ratio:	Varies according to model version
Power output:	18.5 hp
Carburetor:	Linkert/Schebler
Transmission:	Three–speed
Primary drive:	Chain
Final drive:	Chain
Battery:	6 volt
Ignition:	Battery–coil
Frame:	Tubular steel cradle (single tube)
Front brake:	Drum
Rear brake:	Outer band
Front suspension:	Springer forks
Rear suspension:	None
Wheelbase:	57.5 in
Weight:	390 lb
Fuel capacity:	3.75 gal
Oil capacity:	4 qts
Tires:	4.00 x 18
Top speed:	70 mph
Price:	$295
Model versions:	R: low–compression
	RL: high–compression
	RS: low–compression (sidecar)
	RLD: fitted with Linkert M–16 carburetor
From 1936:	RLDR: competition racer

Model D (1929–1931): versions, prices and production figures

Year	Model	Price	Units
1929	D	$290	4,531 units
	DL	$290	2,343 units
1930	D	$310	2,000 units
	DL	$310	3,191 units
	DLD	$325	206 units
1931	D	$310	715 units
	DL	$310	1,306 units
	DLD	$325	241 units

The 74 cubic inch, Side-Valve Big Twins
V/VL from 1930 to 1936 and U/UL from 1937 to 1948

In 1930 the 74 cubic inch (1200 cc), side-valve V Series replaced the IOE Twin Cam J and JD Big Twins. The motor with its Harry Ricardo designed combustion chamber came in versions with different size pistons, and thus with different compressions.

The version with the lower compression was called V, or VS in the sidecar configuration with a reverse gear. The high-compression VL sports version was fitted with easily removable cylinder heads (as were the other models) and magnesium alloy pistons (and also, from 1934, as the model VFD, nickel-iron alloy). Each of its valves was controlled by its own cam. Initially the engine still ran with a total-loss lubrication system. There was also a special model, the VLM, which was fitted with a magneto.

The frame had been strengthened, making it around 25 percent heavier than that of the JD. The footrests could be folded away, and the ignition system was equipped with two independent coils. The 1930 design included Two-bullet headlights, a black klaxon horn, a twin-tube muffler, and a toolbox mounted on the forks. After 1932 the Big Twins were fitted with a Schebler DeLuxe carburetor, a chrome-plated sunburst-face horn, cadmium-plated pedals and the seven-inch John Brown headlight with a flat lens, later replaced by a convex one. From 1937 onwards the model became known as the U, and all Big Twins conformed with the modern E/EL Knucklehead as regards styling and design.

BLACK AND MANDARIN RED

THE 1933 HARLEY-DAVIDSON 74 BIG TWIN MODEL

The standard color scheme was still olive-drab, as can be seen on these two VLS models from 1930 and 1932. However, special and very striking art-deco finishes were also available at this time, one of which is portrayed on this brochure from 1933.

A UL from 1936.

Courtesy of: Max Middelbosch, Zwolle, Netherlands

156

The wealth of controls sported by the Big Twins was exhaustively explained in the accompanying handbooks.

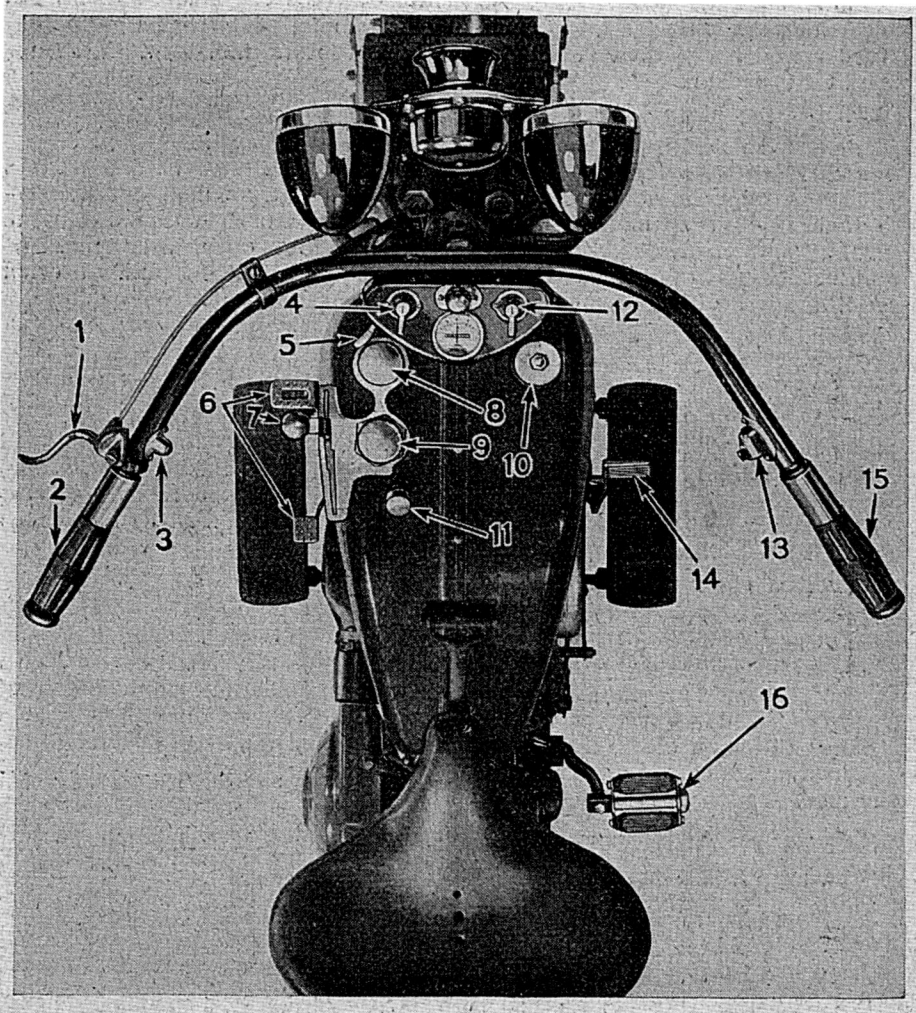

Figur 1, Bedienungsorgane

1. Handhebel der Vorderrad-Bremse; 2. Griff für Zündung (einwärts gedreht ist Früh-zündung, auswärts gedreht ist Spätzündung); 3. Signal-Druckknopf; 4. Zündungsschalter (man führe den Schlüssel ein und drehe gemäß Zeichen auf Schaltbrett); 5. Steuerungs-dämpfer [Sonder-Ausrüstung], (Drehen nach rechts stellt die Steuerung fester, nach links loser), 6 Kupplungspedal (Drücken nach hinten löst die Kupplung aus, Drücken nach vorne kuppelt ein); 7. Gangschalthebel; 8. Stopfen zum Öltank (Fassungsvermögen des Öl-tanks 3,8 Liter); 9. Stopfen zum Reservebrennstoff-Tank (dessen Fassungsvermögen ist

7

The DeLuxe carburetor with fan air-filter was available as an optional extra.

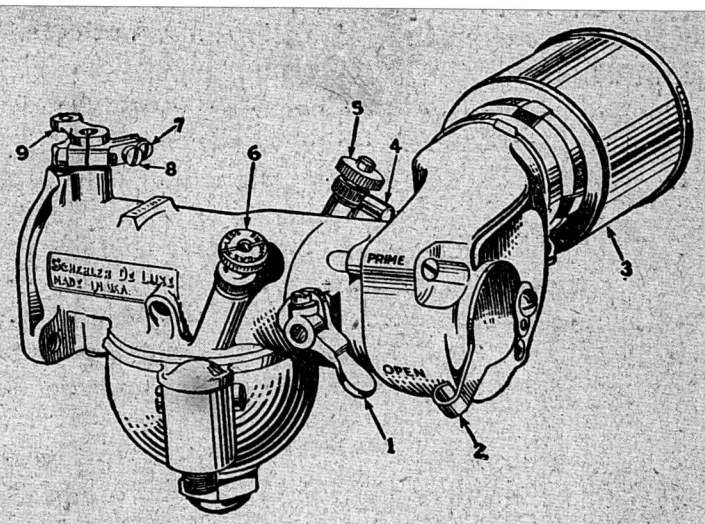

Figur 7. De Luxe-Vergaser.

1. Drosselhebel in Stellung OPEN (ganz herunter), der normalen Fahrstellung, 2. Luftzusatzklappe, nur bei hohen Geschwindigkeiten zu öffnen, 3. Luftreiniger, 4. Langsamlauf-Hebelnadel, 5. Langsamlauf-Stellnadel, 6. Schnellauf-Stellnadel, 7. Sicherungsmutter, 8. Dros-selanschlag-Schraube, mit der die Geschwindigkeit des Motors bei geschlossener Drossel reguliert wird. 9. Drosselhebel.

Type:	**Flathead Big Twin**
Model:	**VL**
Years of manufacture:	1930–1936
Engine:	Air-cooled four-stroke side-valve 45° V-Twin
Displacement:	74.21 cu in (1215.96 cc)
Bore x stroke:	3.4375 x 4.0 in (87.31 x 101.6 mm)
Compression ratio:	4.5 : 1
Power output:	30 hp
Carburetor:	Schebler 32 mm ø
Transmission:	Three-speed
Primary drive:	Duplex chain
Final drive:	Chain
Battery:	6 volt/22 amp
Ignition:	Battery-coil
Frame:	Tubular steel cradle (single tube)
Front brake:	Drum
Rear brake:	Drum
Front suspension:	Double-T springer forks
Rear suspension:	None
Wheelbase:	60 in
Weight:	528 lb
Fuel capacity:	4 gal
Oil capacity:	4 qts
Tires:	4.00 x 18
Top speed:	80 mph
Price:	$340
Model versions:	V: medium-compression (28 hp)
	VL: high-compression
	VS: sidecar
	VC: commercial (nickel-iron piston)
	VM: medium-compression + magneto
	VLM: high-compression + magneto
From 1933:	VLD: Special Sport Solo
From 1937:	U, UL, US

Model versions, prices and production figures

	V (Solo)		VL (Sport Solo)	
1930	$340	1,960 units	$340	3,246 units
1931	$340	825 units	$340	3,477 units
1932	$320	478 units	$430	2,684 units
1933	$310	233 units	$310	866 units

	VD (Solo)		VLD (Special Sport Solo)	
1933	n.a.	780 units		
1934	$310	644 units	$310	4,527 units
1935	$320	585 units	$320	3,963 units
1936	$320	176 units	$320	1,577 units

	U (Solo)		UL (Sport Solo)	
1937	$395	612 units	$395	2,861 units
1938	$395	504 units	$395	1,099 units
1939	$395	421 units	$395	902 units
1940	$385	260 units	$385	822 units
1941	$385	884 units	$385	715 units
1942	$385	421 units	$385	405 units
1943	$385	493 units	$385	11 units
1944	$385	580 units	$385	366 units
1945	$427.25	513 units	$427.25	555 units
1946	$427.25	670 units	$427.25	1,800 units
1947	$545	422 units	$545	1,243 units
1948	$590	401 units	$590	970 units

The 80 cubic inch Big Twin VLH and UH/ULH from 1935 to 1941

When Harley introduced the heavyweight 80 cubic inch (1311 cc) models in 1935, the company not only laid claim to the motorcycle with the largest displacement (next to Indian's Big Chief), but also the most comfortable in terms of typical American dimensions. The H-type motorcycles with their powerful side-valve V-Twins represented the first models of this series. With the exception of the somewhat larger and more powerful engines, the 80 cubic inch flatheads were identical to the 74 cubic inch (1200 cc) models. The Eighty was initially available with a lower compression ratio for the Solo models. This was increased to a medium compression ratio for the UH and UHS models, with the latter being intended for use with sidecars. The high-compression models were designated ULH.

Robust and solidly built: the handlebars and the cat's eye fuel-tank console.

Also typical of future models: the half-moon-shaped elastic-rubber running boards.

Highest riding comfort: the broad solo seat with central suspension.

Courtesy of: Mark Jonas, Milwaukee, Wisconsin

Type:	**Flathead Big Twin**
Model:	**VLH**
Year of manufacture:	1936
Engine:	Air–cooled four–stroke
	45° V–Twin SV
Displacement:	78.84 cu in (1292.6 cc)
Bore x stroke:	3.438 x 4.25 in (87 x 109 mm)
Power output:	34 hp
Compression ratio:	5.5 : 1
Carburetor:	Linkert 32 mm ø
Transmission:	Three–speed
Primary drive:	Duplex chain
Final drive:	Chain
Battery:	6 volt
Ignition:	Battery–coil
Frame:	Double–looped tubular steel
Front brake:	Drum
Rear brake:	Drum
Front suspension:	Springer fork
Rear suspension:	None
Wheelbase:	60 in
Weight:	662 lb
Fuel capacity:	3 gal
Oil capacity:	4 qts
Tires:	4.00 x 18 (or 4.00 x 19)
Top speed:	90 mph
Price:	$340
Model versions:	VFH: With nickel–iron pistons
	VFHS: With sidecar, three–speed
	transmission plus one reverse gear
As of 1937:	UH
	ULH
	UHS (sidecar combination)

Model versions, prices and production figures

1935

VLDD (Sport Solo)	$347	179 units

1936

VLH (3–speed)	$340	2,046 units

1937

UH (medium compression, four-speed)	$415	185 units
ULH (high compression, four-speed)	$415	579 units

1938

UH	$415	108 units
ULH	$415	579 units

1939

UH	$415	92 units
ULH	$415	384 units

1940

UH	$410	187 units
ULH	$410	672 units

1941

UH	$410	126 units
ULH	$410	420 units

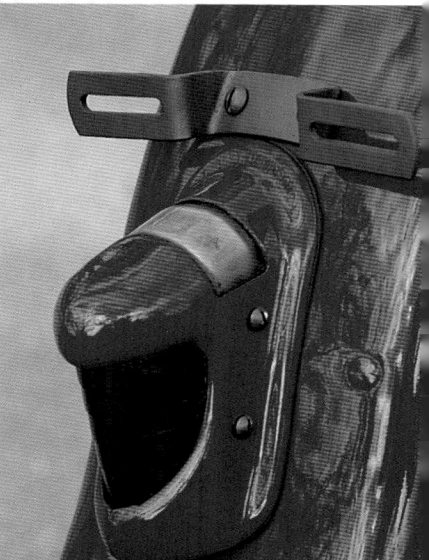

From 1937 to 1951: the Third Forty-Five – the W Series

The designation of the 45 cubic inch models was changed in 1937. The basic Models W and WS (S for sidecar) low-compression Solo and WL high-compression Sport Solo, as well as the production racer Model WLDR Competition Special (available for 380 dollars) made the newly designated W machines the most numerous of all series motorcycles. An export model was also introduced especially for Japan – the WSR.

The constantly improved 45 cubic inch (746 cc) flathead engine was now designed with horizontal ribs on the crankshaft case, a new lubrication system and an oil pump fitted on the transmission housing. The overall styling of the motorcycle thus resembled that of the modern 61-inch OHV Model E Knucklehead. The fuel tank was split – the left-half for gasoline and the right-half for oil. The newly designed instrument panel on the fuel tank (the so-called "white face" produced by Stewart Warner), with speedometer, tripmeter, ammeter and ignition switch unit, now was like that of the Big Twins.

Further improvements were made to the engine, transmission and chassis in 1938. A four-speed transmission was now available and the design adopted many details from the Big Twin series. Light gray became the standard color in 1941 and the WLRD racing model went on to yield a roadgoing version. The production racers, intended primarily for the AMA Class C, were redesignated WR (for track racing) or WRTT (for road racing and hillclimbing), fitted with high-compression engines with polished inlet ports and combustion chambers and were supplied without lamps or front fenders. While the old WL models were still fitted with gray cast iron cylinder heads, the WLDR models now boasted the sturdier aluminum cylinder heads, reinforced crankpins and valve springs and a larger carburetor capacity. These models were able to yield roughly 35 horsepower.

Other design modifications included the cat-eye instrument panel, the boattail taillight, the leather solo saddle, initially in brown but later replaced by black,

and further improvements to the engine and transmission.

The first WL prototypes were delivered to the U.S. Army in 1940, fitted with M 64 Linkert carburetors and sporting various conversions. The entire W model range was modified several times during the course of World War II, mainly to cater to the demands of the military. Civilians could not purchase the motorcycles during this time. It was not until 1947 that the WL model reappeared in the form of a modified 45-inch flathead V-Twin. This model, fitted with a three-speed or four-speed transmission, sported the new "tombstone" taillight, a black leather saddle, double-lamp instrument panel and a gleaming two-tone finish in either black, Riviera blue or ruby red. The Forty-Five was fitted with airflow fenders, new, striking fuel-tank emblems, a chrome-plated muffler or a straight-pipe racing exhaust. A gate-type gearshift on the left (or right) side of the fuel-tank and a clutch pedal likewise situated on the left-hand side remained obligatory right up to the end.

Popular and indestructible: the legendary pre-war 45 cubic inch WLD model.

All photos on this double page-spread showing a blue motorcycle are courtesy of: Mark Jones, Milwaukee, Wisconsin

W Model Series (1937–1951):
Versions, prices and production figures

Year	Model	Price	Units
1937	W	$355	509 units
	WL	$355	560 units
	WLD	$355	581 units
1938	W	$355	302 units
	WL	$355	309 units
	WLD	$355	402 units
1939	W	$355	260 units
	WL	$355	212 units
	WLD	$355	326 units
1940	W	$350	439 units
	WL	$350	569 units
	WLD	$365	567 units

Primarily military production from 1941 to 1946

Year	Model	Price	Units
1941	W 45	$350	4,095 units
	WL	$350	4,277 units
	WLD	$365	455 units
1942	WL	$350	142 units
	WLD	$365	133 units
1945	WL	$395.97	1,357 units
1946	WL	$395.97	4,410 units
	WL Special	$402.97	
1947	WL	$490	3,338 units
1948	WL	$535	2,124 units
1949	WL	$590	2,289 units
1950	WL	$590	1,108 units
1951	WL	$730	1,044 units

Type:	**Flathead**
Model:	**WL/WLD**
Year of manufacture:	1947
Engine:	Four-stroke side-valve 45° V-Twin
Displacement:	45.26 cu in (741.80 cc)
Bore/Stroke:	2.75 x 3.813 in (69.85 x 96.84 mm)
Compression ratio:	5 : 1
Power output:	24 hp
Carburetor:	Linkert
Transmission:	Three-speed
Primary drive:	Duplex chain
Final drive:	Chain
Battery:	6 volt
Ignition:	Coil
Frame:	Looped tubular steel
Front brake:	Drum, 28 mm ø
Rear brake:	Drum, 36 mm ø
Front suspension:	Springer fork
Rear suspension:	None
Wheelbase:	57.5 in
Weight:	670 lb
Fuel capacity:	3.5 gal
Oil capacity:	3.8 qts
Tires:	4.00 x 18
Top speed:	68 mph
Price:	$490

Almost a custom bike: a 45 cubic inch Flathead with two-tone paintwork and elegant white leather trimming is exhibited at the Daytona Bike Show complete with original tool set.

Tank instrument panel and its "good side" – the original design of a WLD from 1941.

The classic front view with high-mounted headlight, horn and crash bar, the somewhat complicated back view and the typical rear lamp lighting the license plate from below.

The War Machine

The first military model produced by Harley-Davidson was the 61-inch (1000 cc) Model IOE F-head V-Twin, delivered in solo or sidecar versions. These motorcycles had several applications in World War I, being used as courier bikes, for conveying personnel and general transportation, as well as for use by field hospitals. Armored add-ons were produced for combat, as well as various weapon mounts. During World War II, it was primarily the countless versions and vast quantities of 45 cubic inch (750 cc) side-valve WLA models manufactured that served the U.S. Army.

In 1942, 1,000 "all terrain" XA models were built, with a 45 cubic inch side-valve horizontally-opposed engine and shaft drive. However, this model never saw combat, as the North African battlefield for which the XA had been designed was firmly in the hands of the Allies by the time it was ready for service.

The WLC and ELC (with the C standing for Canada) models built in 1941 within the framework of the Lend and Lease Agreement, as well as several 74 cubic inch (1200 cc) side-valve Big Twins (Models UA and US), with or without sidecar, were delivered to the Commonwealth nations involved in the war via the British Supply Council. These models were not only used by the Canadian armed forces, but also by Britain, South Africa, Australia and New Zealand, being converted to British military standards before shipping.

The stock of motorcycles in the U.S. Army's arsenals diminished noticeably after 1945, although a few were kept on for use by the Military Police and Coast-guard. Some 418 Sportsters were supplied for Shore Patrol (SP) duties in the late 1950s and early 1960s. In 1967, the U.S. Army ordered another batch of XLA and FL (FLH) Solos for military service, primarily for escort duties and Military Police use at European U.S. bases in Belgium and the Netherlands. The military prototype XLA offered by Harley-Davidson originally due to be launched in the 1970s, was only produced in small numbers.

It was not until the oil shortage which took place during the years 1976 and 1977 that the military once again gave thoughtto the economically practical use of motorcycles in the service. Lightweight all-terrain motorcycles with low fuel-consumption were primarily in demand by them, but Harley's product range simply did not include such models at this time. However, several 250 cc two-stroke Enduros built by the Canadian snowmobile manufacturer Bombardier were converted for military use, fitted with Austrian Rotax engines and were entered into service as courier bikes in the U.S. Army and Navy in 1982.

On account of an impending large order for military motorcycles from the U.S. Government, Harley-Davidson purchased all manufacturing and design rights for the military Model MT 500 from the British manufacturer Armstrong Military Division on October 10, 1987. Only Harley-Davidson and Gilera/Cagiva were able to fulfill the specifications of the U.S. Government, easily beating the rather half-hearted competition presented by Yamaha and Kawasaki. The order volume this time around amounted to 5,000 motorcycles, for which Harley had earmarked the MT 500 – a lightweight enduro machine fitted with the 4-valve Rotax single-cylinder four-stroke engine manufactured in Austria.

Unfortunately, the negotiations were drawn out so long that the order was finally frozen, albeit temporarily. Harley-Davidson nevertheless received an order in 1993 from the British Ministry of Defense for 1,570 Model MT 35 military motorcycles, which were likewise fitted with the Rotax engine. These machines were intended for use by the "interarmed forces" of NATO and two motorcycles were built each day for four years in York.

An original U.S. Army 61 cubic inch V-Twin from 1917.

Courtesy of: Dale Walksler/Wheels Through Time Museum, Mount Vernon, Illinois

A 1943 XA with sidecar and additional telescopic shock absorbers on the front fork, as well as a hand-operated clutch and foot-operated gearshift.

A draft by Harley-Davidson for the standard vehicle of the U.S. Army: a "general purpose Servi-Car." However, the model delivered in 1940 for testing was not accepted by the Army, who instead decided in favor of the more effective and versatile Jeep.

An experimental armored motorcycle–sidecar combination that never entered military service.

One of the extremely rare 74 cubic inch OHV Servi-Car models with shaft drive which survived its military service. The wooden box was fitted later.

Courtesy of: D.W./Wheels Through Time Museum

Additional 418 Sportsters – such as this 1964 Model XLA – were delivered to the U.S. Army and Military Police in the late–1950s and early–1960s.

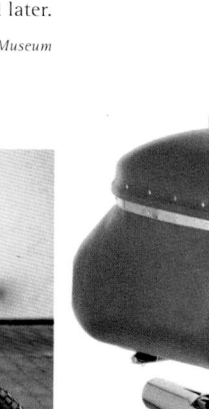

The Armstrong MT 500 was built for Harley-Davidson under license. The model shown sports a NATO finish.

The Military Model WLA/WLC from 1939 to 1946

As early as the beginning of 1939 Harley-Davidson sent two olive-drab painted civilian machines as test motorcycles to the Mechanized Cavalry Board's military test site in Fort Knox, Kentucky. These were 45 cubic inch (750 cc) WL side-valve machines with white rubber handlebar grips, unvalanced fenders and an additional skid plate. Here they were subjected chiefly to low-speed tests on rugged ground to test their military suitability: the heat of the engines, under strain from the continual low-speed running, was tested by hand. Unsurprisingly, technical objections were raised and the military insisted on comprehensive refitting. Most importantly, the hand throttle had to be moved to the left-hand side, as on the Indian, to make possible right-handed shooting, handing over of documents and saluting while riding. On the other hand, the motorcycle's off-road stability came in for particular praise and after endless negotiations Harley-Davidson received a lucrative government contract. The Russians also ordered WLA solo machines and the specially prepared "sidecar Russia" WSRs under the lend-lease agreement.

In 1940 the U.S. Army placed its first order for 745 WLAs, plus a further order of 185 military motorcycles (both WLAs and 74 cubic inch flatheads). By the end of the war a total of 88,000 WLA and WLC machines had been ordered, plus spare parts for a further 30,000, making the WL the best-selling Harley-Davidson ever. The new military machine involved a number of changes: the jet arrangement on the Linkert M 88 carburetor was altered by Harley to counteract coking in the combustion chamber. Further additions included a solid luggage rack which could hold up to 250 pounds of gear such as radio equipment and also the modern springer forks from the EL Knucklehead and the familiar half-moon footboards. All chrome-plated and nickel-plated parts were replaced with matt ones, having initially being camouflaged with stick-on strips.

In 1941 the dustproof oil-bath air filter with the characteristic large air filter cover and the horizontal connector pipe to the carburetor became compulsory. The headlight (fitted with a blackout cover) was fitted lower on the motorcycle, and sharply projecting crash bars provided accident protection. The civilian beehive rear light was replaced by the "stop & blackout" rear light. Due to the shortage of rubber, from 1943 all WLAs were fitted with plastic grips, an iron kickstart pedal and ribbed metal footrests. The seat was mounted further forward. The standard color was military olive-drab and all company logos and lettering was forbidden by the Army. The normal 6:1 compression ratio of the civilian machines was at first reduced to 4.3:1, though later brought back up to 5:1.

The WLC models produced for the Canadian and British armed forces had an additional front-mounted auxiliary rack, a British-style passenger seat with handles and a special right-hand-side hand-operated clutch instead of the foot clutch. As with the Big Twins the front and rear wheels were identical. The typically American scabbard for the Thompson sub-machine gun was absent from the WLCs. Numerous alterations to the instrument panel, headlights, rear lights, gearshift and various instruments, in line with British standards, were also carried out. There was also different engine paintwork.

The version delivered to the Red Army included the Goulding sidecar. Additionally, as with the WLA models, there was a wide range of special accessories such as ammunition and bandage boxes, machine-gun scabbard and radio equipment. However, continual refitting, re-equipping and repairs led to countless new variants which are far too numerous to list.

Sidecars with armor plating were developed for the deployment of medium and heavy military equipment in battle, generally in tandem with 74 or 80 cubic inch side-valve Big Twins.

A typical WLA with basic military equipment.

Courtesy of: Franz Simmerlein, Nuremberg, Germany

WLC models for the Canadian Army in standard British military configuration and winter camouflage. The first-aid box on the front fender was a typical feature of this model.

Courtesy of: Max Middelbosch, Zwolle, Netherlands

Type:	**Flathead**
Model:	**WLA/WLC**
Years of manufacture:	1941–45
Engine:	Air-cooled four-stroke side-valve 45° V-Twin
Displacement:	45.26 cu in (741.63 cc)
Bore x stroke:	2.75 x 3.813 in (69.85 x 96.84 mm)
Compression ratio:	5 : 1
Power output:	23.5 hp
Carburetor:	Linkert
Transmission:	Three-speed
Primary drive:	Duplex chain
Final drive:	Chain
Battery:	6 volt
Ignition:	Battery–coil
Frame:	Tubular steel cradle (single tube)
Front brake:	Drum
Rear brake:	Drum
Front suspension:	Springer forks
Rear suspension:	None
Wheelbase:	57.5 in
Weight:	550 lb
Fuel capacity:	3.375 gal
Oil capacity:	4 qts
Tires:	4.00 x 18
Top speed:	65 mph
Price:	$380
Model versions:	The WLC for the Canadian Army, equipped according to British standards.

A special WLA design in battleship gray for the U.S. Navy.

A special "winterizing kit" was supplied with the motorcycles in order to prevent the oil from freezing at extremely low temperatures.

Standard military versions and production figures

WLA	45 cubic inch side-valve for the U.S. Army	
	1940	n.a.
	1941	2,282 units
	1942	13,460 units
	1943	24,717 units
	1944	11,531 units
	1945	8,317 units
WLC	45 cubic inch side-valve for the Canadian Army	
	1942	9,825 units
	1943	2,647 units
	1944	5,356 units
UA/USA	74 cubic inch side-valve (S with sidecar) for the U.S. Army	
	1941	n.a.
	1942	426 units
ELA	61 cubic inch OHV Knucklehead for the U.S. Army	
	1942	8 units
ELC	61 cubic inch OHV Knucklehead for the Canadian Army	
	1942	45 units
WSR	45 cubic inch SV with sidecar for the Russian Army ("Sidecar Russia")	
	1945	n.a.
XA	45 cubic inch side-valve with sidecar for the Russian Army (the Sidecar Russia)	
	1942	1,011 units
Model G	Model G (Servi-Car) with 45 cubic inch side-valve engine	

«HARLEY-DAVIDSON WLA-42» ветеран второй мировой войны

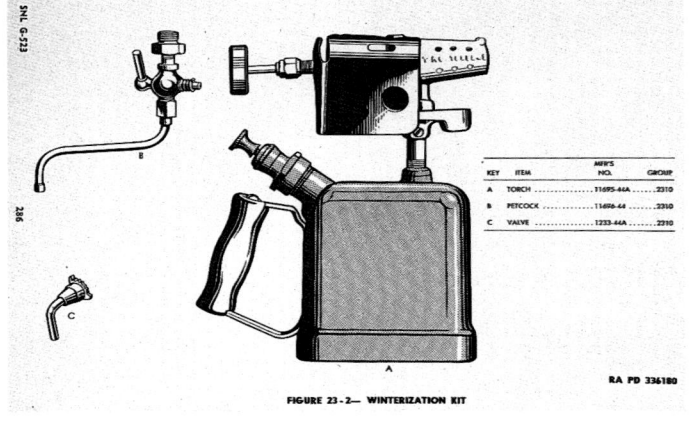

FIGURE 23-2— WINTERIZATION KIT

RA PD 336180

The WLA in original "Russian" garb for the Red Army, taken from the Russian motorcycling magazine *MOTO*.

The military prescribed darkened rear lights for the WLA.

Courtesy of: Franz Simmerlein, Nuremberg, Germany

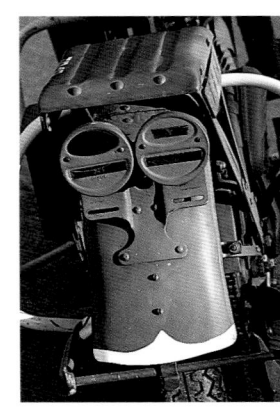

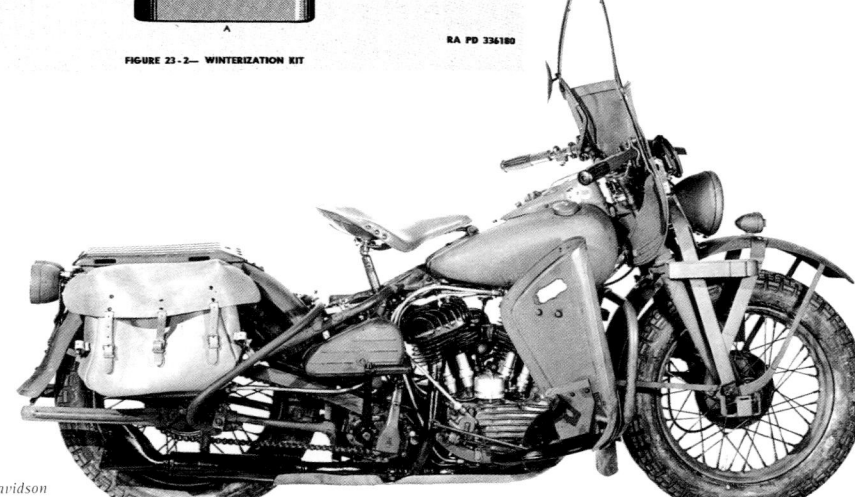

© Harley-Davidson

A Military Type – the Model XA

Impressed by the victories of German Field Marshal Erwin Rommel in the North Africa campaign, in which motorcycles played a significant role, high-ranking U.S. Army officers believed that the chain drives of American motorcycles were not suitable for use in desert conditions and commissioned Indian, Harley-Davidson and Delco with the development of a new shaft-drive model. William Harley "organized" an acquisition of a BMW R 12 via the Netherlands (a newer R 75 was actually wanted more than anything) and promptly had it copied, for lack of time rather than any other reason. Because Harley's own factory was fully tied up with defense contracts, the XA, as it was designated, was manufactured at General Motors.

The prototype was unveiled in 1941 and 1,000 units were supposedly to have been delivered by July 1942 at a price of 870 dollars and 35 cents each. The new hybrid was a peculiar mixture of a German BMW engine and frame and an American-designed fuel-tank, saddle and fork. The first trials were conducted at Camp Holabird from December 1941 to February 1942, along with Indian's shaft-drive Model 841, but they failed to prove particularly satisfactory.

The XA – an accurate copy of the side-valve BMW R 12 (1935–1938) – was fitted with a horizontally-opposed engine, which provided smooth running and virtually no vibrations. Operation of the valves was by means of a camshaft located on the crankcase, with the oil supply being ensured by a dry-sump lubrication system. Two carburetors ensured the correct mix. The kickstarter was almost concealed, needing to be kicked down to the side to start the engine. Instead of relying on the German telescopic fork, Harley used the tried-and-tested springer fork used in the Knucklehead. The fuel-tank, instruments and lighting system likewise derived from Harley's production lines.

Various items had to be modified and offered as options in order to comply with the standards required by the U.S. military. These included stays, equipment mounts, lamps, luggage racks and various small parts from the WLA production run that did not quite match the XA. The unit production cost for an XA from a run of just 1,000 units probably amounted to roughly 1,000 dollars each. As it was, the XA never even reached a battlefield. Just as production started, the battle for North Africa had already been won. In July of 1943, the U.S. Defense Department decided to halt all further production of the XA and canceled all orders it had already placed for the motorcycles.

Harley-Davidson subsequently drew up plans together with Allis Chalmers to continue using the horizontally opposed engines to power snowmobiles or stationary generators. However, their plans never reached fruition and when World War II was over, the U.S. government sold its remaining stocks of XAs on the civilian market at the bargain price of 500 dollars apiece.

One of the extremely rare XA models in original condition.

Courtesy of: Otis Chandler /
Vintage Museum of Transportation, Oxnard, California

Opposite: courtesy of: Mark Jonas,
Milwaukee, Wisconsin

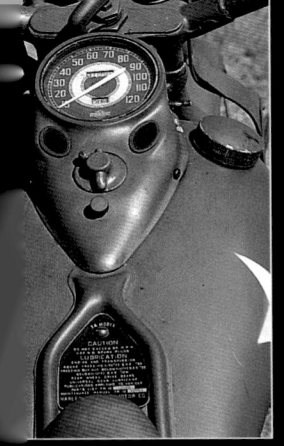

In addition to its unusual flathead engine, the XA also displays numerous military extras, such as fully-cast wheels, additional shock absorbers on the front wheel and heat-transmission plates on the cylinders.

Type:	**Flathead Boxer**
Model:	**XA**
Years of manufacture:	1942–1943
Engine:	Air-cooled four-stroke flat twin
Displacement:	45 cu in (738 cc)
Bore x stroke:	3.07 x 3.07 (78 x 78 mm)
Compression ratio:	5.7 : 1
Power output:	23 hp
Carburetor:	Linkert
Transmission:	Four-speed with hand clutch
Primary drive:	Gearwheel
Final drive:	Cardan
Battery:	6 volt
Ignition:	Battery–coil
Frame:	Double–looped tubular steel
Front brake:	Drum
Rear brake:	Drum
Front suspension:	Springer fork
Rear suspension:	Straight tracking
Wheelbase:	5.9 in
Weight:	653.7 lb
Fuel capacity:	4.1 gal
Oil capacity:	2 qts
Tires:	4.00 x 18
Top speed:	65 mph
Price:	$879.35
Model versions:	Prototype sidecar combination with sidecar drive

Left: ready for fitting – an XA engine, a strikingly similar copy of the pre-war BMW R12.

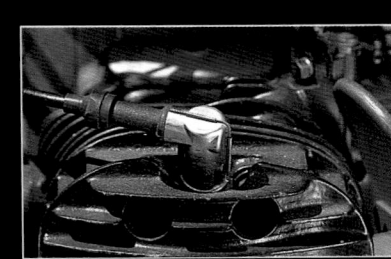

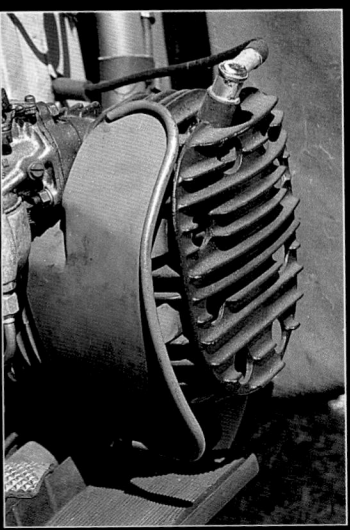

The Forecar – or Harley's Cargo Rickshaw

Without a doubt, one of the most peculiar vehicles Harley-Davidson ever built was the three-wheeled delivery wagon manufactured from 1913 to 1915. Intended purely for commercial use, including the conveyance of passengers, it fully reflected the new mobility of traveling salesmen and the general trend towards economical small-scale transportation. The load-carrying boxes mounted in front of the contraption were huge, ugly and often overloaded, but apparently fulfilled their purpose.

In 1913, the Model 9G made its debut. This was known as the Forecar Delivery Van and was powered by the 61 cubic inch (1000 cc) F-head V-Twin engine and had a front-mounted superstructure referred to by Harley as the "delivery box," available in a host of different designs. The van was provided with a two-speed transmission in the rear wheel hub in 1914, and a three-speed transmission in 1915. Numerous commercial sidecar models began to nudge the unwieldy and slow three-wheeler out of business from

1915 onwards. Package Trucks were considerably cheaper to produce and could be used for a variety of purposes. Today, original Forecars are among the rarest relics dating back to the earliest years of Harley-Davidson.

Production figures for the Forecar:

1913	Model 9G	63 units
1914	Model 10G	171 units
1915	Model G	98 units

© Harley-Davidson

Originally used extensively, no known commercial Forecars survive today. Only rare historic photographs document their existence. The Package Trucks in 1915 were an evolution of this vehicle and were succesfully marketed and adapted.

The first major order for
Forecars came from the
U.S. Postal Service (top).

The Forecars were
particularly popular
with street vendors.

© Harley-Davidson

169

The Servi-Car – Harley's Longest-Produced Model

Harley-Davidson's first three-wheeler was introduced in 1932, though it was first presented on November 9, 1931. It was called the Servi-Car and sold for 450 dollars. It came with the new low-compression 45 cubic inch (750 cc) side-valve engine from the D Series, with three forward gears and a reverse one and developing around 18 horsepower.

The Servi-Car was immediately met with enormous success and garages, the police and a variety of delivery and postal companies quickly began placing large orders. It enabled broken-down automobiles to be attended to rapidly and efficiently and finally gave the police the easily-serviced mobile vehicle they wanted to deal with parking offenses and supervise city traffic.

Incidentally, at this time Boxcars, which were similar to Servi-Cars, were being manufactured in Japan under the guidance of Alfred Rich Child. The Boxcars were fitted with the considerably more powerful 74 cubic inch (1200 cc) Big Twin engine. To what extent this very successful delivery vehicle influenced the Servi-Car remains unknown.

By the years 1933 and 1934, there were four variants of this G Series: with a larger or smaller rear box, with or without a trailer coupling and with space for an automobile's spare tire. In 1935 the Servi-Car got a new transmission, a strengthened rear axle and a foldaway tow bar allowing mechanics to use the Servi-Car to tow cars in for inspection or repair. The model variants available at that time bore the reference letters G, GA, GDT, GD and GE.

In 1937 the company brought out a new design with more modern styling and two years later Harley-Davidson built a test Servi-Car for the U.S. Army, fitted with the 61-inch (1000 cc) Knucklehead OHV engine and shaft drive. However, the 16 military trikes failed the Camp Holabird endurance test and it was not until 1940 that a second prototype was accepted by the Army. However, the success of the Willy's Jeep meant that the Servi-Car remained surplus to requirements with the U.S. armed forces and the company contented itself with the introduction of various improvements to civilian models.

In the years between 1940 and 1942, a strengthened axle housing was fitted to the model as well as an improved chain guide mechanism, a cast iron rear brake drum, a stronger clutch and the front wheel from the Big Twin series. The compression ratio was increased from 4.5:1 to 4.75:1. However, due to shortages of raw materials during the war, very few of these were ever made.

Shortly after the war Harley experimented with a K prototype incorporating the boxer engine from the XA and shaft drive. However, this project was quickly shelved. When the WL side-valve series was finally discontinued in 1953, its indestructible 45 cubic inch V-Twin engine was to remain in production for 20 more long years as the power unit for the Servi-Car.

Hydraulic brakes were first introduced in 1951 and the Hydra Glide's hydraulically damped telescopic forks were introduced in 1958. In 1964, one year before the first Electra Glide, the Servi-Car was fitted with a 12 volt battery and electric starter and became known as the GE. The old generator was replaced with a larger and more powerful one which was mounted on the front tube of the frame. From 1966 to 1967 the rear box was made of fiberglass. Harley finally ceased production of the Servi-Car in 1973/74, after more than 41 years of manufacture. However, the immortal Harley trike lives on today in the form of a multitude of customized machines.

One of the first Servi-Cars: a 1932 G Model in original finish.

Courtesy of: Bob Studer, Milwaukee, Wisconsin

Servi-Car models, prices and production figures

Year	G Price ($)	G Number	GA Price ($)	GA Number	GD Price ($)	GD Number	GDT Price ($)	GDT Number	GE Price ($)	GE Number
1932	450	(219*)					n.a.	36	n.a.	5
1933	450	80	n.a.	12	n.a.	60	n.a.	18	n.a.	12
1934	430	317	415	40	430	104	445	58	485	27
1935	440	323	425	64	440	91	455	72	495	17
1936	440	382	425	55	440	96	455	85	495	30
1937	515	491	500	55	515	112	530	136	570	22
1938	515	259	500	83	515	81	530	102		
1939	515	320	500	126	515	90	530	114		
1940	515	468	500	156	515	158	530	126		
1941	515	607	500	221	515	195	530	136		
1942	525	138	510	261						
1943	n.a.	22	n.a.	113						
1944	n.a.	6	n.a.	51						
1945	580	26	568	60						
1946	593.93	766	582.07	678						
1947	710	1.307	695	870						
1948	755	1050	740	728						
1949	860	494	845	545						
1950	860	520	845	483						
1951	1,095	778	1,080	632						
1952	1,175	515	1,160	532						
1953	1,190	(1,146*)	1,175	n.a.						
1954	1,240	(1,397*)	1,225	n.a.						
1955	1,240	394	1,225	647						
1956	1,240	467	1,225	736						
1957	1,367	518	1,352	674						
1958	1,465	283	1,450	643						
1959	1,500	288	1,470	524						
1960	1,530	(707*)	1,500	n.a.						
1961	1,555	(628*)	1,525	n.a.						
1962	1,555	(703*)	1,525	n.a.						
1963	1,590	n.a.	1,550	n.a.						
as GE-TYPE										
1964	1,628	725								
1965	n.a.	625								
1966	n.a.	625								
1967	1,930	600								
1968	1,930	600								
1969	2,065	475								
1970	n.a.	494								
1971	n.a.	500								
1972	n.a.	400								
1973	n.a.	425								

* G and GA together

Type:	**Flathead Servi-Car**
Model:	**G (with Towbar)**
Year of manufacture:	1932
Engine:	Air-cooled four-stroke side-valve 45° V-Twin
Displacement:	45.26 cu in (741.80 cc)
Bore x stroke:	2.75 x 3.8125 in (69.85 x 96.84 mm)
Compression ratio:	4.75 : 1
Power output:	18 hp
Carburetor:	Schebler
Transmission:	Three forward gears, one reverse
Primary drive:	Duplex chain
Final drive:	Chain/differential
Battery:	6 volt
Ignition:	Battery-coil
Frame:	Tubular steel cradle (single tube)
Front brake:	Drum
Rear brake:	Drum and parking
Front suspension:	Springer forks
Rear suspension:	Coil springs
Wheelbase:	61 in
Weight:	1360 lb
Fuel capacity:	3.7 gal
Oil capacity:	4 qts
Tires:	4.00 x 16
Top speed:	50 mph
Price:	$450
Model variants:	GA: without towbar
	GD: large commercial body
	GDT: large commercial body and airtank

Type:	**Flathead Servi-Car**
Model:	**GA**
Year of manufacture:	1941
Engine:	Air-cooled four-stroke side-valve 45° V-Twin
Displacement:	45.26 cu in (741.80 cc)
Bore x stroke:	2.75 x 3.8125 in (69.85 x 96.84 mm)
Compression ratio:	4.75 : 1
Power output:	22 hp
Carburetor:	Linkert M 25.4 mm ø
Transmission:	Three forward gears, one reverse
Primary drive:	Chain
Final drive:	Chain/differential
Battery:	6 volt
Ignition:	Battery-coil
Frame:	Tubular steel cradle (single tube)
Front brake:	Drum
Rear brake:	Drum and parking
Front suspension:	Springer forks
Rear suspension:	Coil springs
Wheelbase:	61 in/track 42 in
Weight:	1360 lb
Fuel capacity:	3.4 gal
Oil capacity:	3.5 qts
Tires:	5.00 x 16
Top speed:	50 mph
Price:	$510
Model versions:	G: with towbar
GD:	large commercial body
GDT:	large commercial body and towbar

Dispensing with the cargo box reveals the enclosed drive chain with differential and rigid axle, both screw and leaf-spring suspension, twin rear brakes, and a large muffler. The workmanship of the Servi-Car was very impressive.

The mechanic drove his Servi-Car to the customer's home, hooked it onto the back of the automobile in need of servicing, and drove the automobile back to the workshop together with the Servi-Car.

The Great Breakthrough – the Knucklehead Engine

In difficult economic conditions, Harley unveiled its first 61 cubic inch (1000 cc) OHV engine in 1936 with the Model E (compression ratio 6:1) and Model EL (compression ratio 7:1). This engine became known as the "Knucklehead" on account of the characteristic rocker covers on its cylinder heads. The Knucklehead yielded 40 horsepower at 4800 rpm – 10 horsepower more than the flathead Big Twins produced during that same period. Plagued by oil and lubrication problems during the first year of production, these were rectified in 1937. However, the Knucklehead proved itself a fast but sensitive engine. Its most important technical innovations were a centrifugal oil–pump, a speed–dependant "check valve" that closed automatically at high speeds, and a single central camshaft with four radial cams. Three steel and three fiberglass plates, as well as a pressure plate, gave the clutch 65 percent more contact area, facilitating its operation and gear shifting. In addition to its improved cooling and sturdiness, the Knucklehead was a fast engine. Indeed, it was even planned to break the world speed record in 1937, with a speed of 150 mph being the goal. Although Joe Petrali only actually achieved a speed of 136.183 mph at Daytona Beach, this was still enough to set a new world record. The first 74 cubic inch (1200 cc) Model FL was launched in 1941, but the war prevented the Knucklehead from being produced in large numbers. The last Knucklehead engine left the production line in 1947.

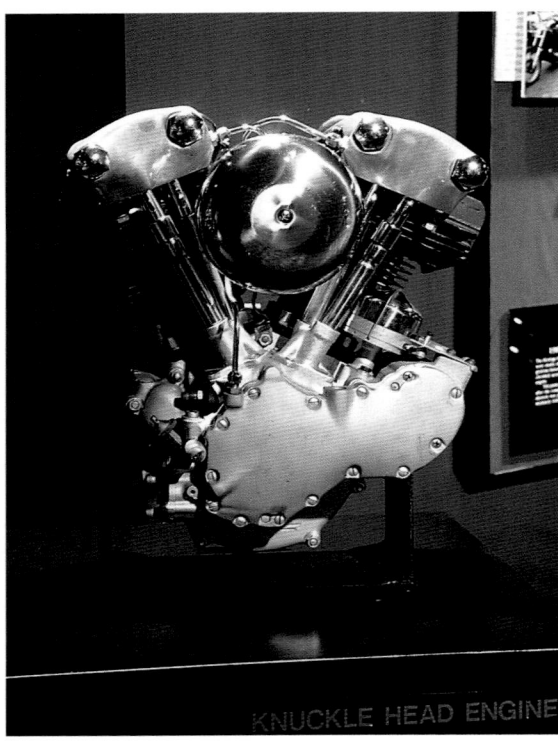

This 1939 61 cubic inch Model EL is on display in the company museum in York, Pennsylvania.

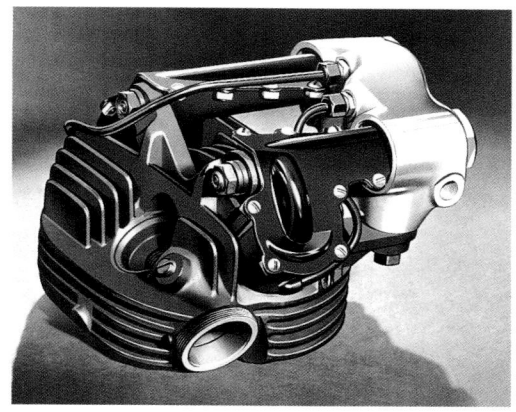

The cylinder head of the 61-inch OHV engine from 1938. The large rocker boxes gave rise to the name Knucklehead.

Oil circuit plan and exterior view of the 61 E/EL engine with original oil filter.

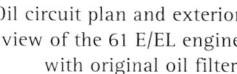

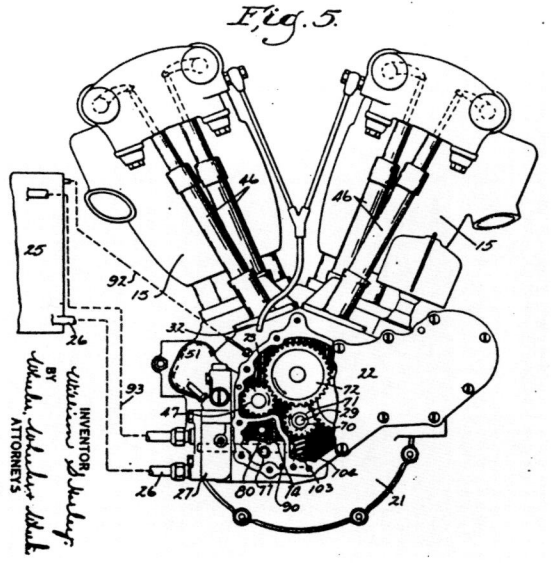

© Harley-Davidson

© Harley-Davidson

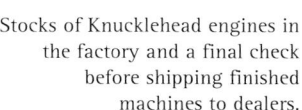

© Harley-Davidson

Stocks of Knucklehead engines in the factory and a final check before shipping finished machines to dealers.

Original brochure picture of the OHV 61 cubic inch (1000 cc) model from 1939.

© Harley-Davidson

173

The Knucklehead E/EL from 1936 to 1947

It must have taken a lot of courage and nerves of steel to design a radically new motorcycle during one of the worst periods of the Great Depression and particularly to invest the money required for new machines and manufacturing facilities instead of simply backing out while the option was still available and closing shop. However, the bosses at Harley-Davidson had no doubt that something had to be done in order to inject new life in the stagnant sales situation.

Harley was already busily working away at designing a completely new generation of overhead-valve V-Twin engines in 1931/32, with the (by this time) normal international displacement of 61 cubic inches (1000 c). This engine entered production in 1935 — somewhat too early in the opinion of Joe Petrali, who had been involved in its development and would have preferred to postpone the start of production another year, in order to iron out the last problems and get rid of the pesky oil leaks.

Nevertheless, dealers and customers alike were enthusiastic about the attractive racy design and the sheer power of the new Model E (medium-compression) and EL (high-compression) engines, which yielded almost 10 horsepower more than the stout 74 inch (1200 cc) side-valve twin. All told, more than 100 technical modifications had to be undertaken in the first year in order to rid the Sixty-One, as it was officially christened, or "the Knucklehead" as it became fondly known on the biking scene, of its teething troubles. The name Knucklehead, by the way, refers to the knuckle-like covers on the rocker-boxes.

This new OHV model marked a major coup for Harley-Davidson. The Knucklehead was pure technology, and its beauty and elegance convinced even the most ardent of its adversaries. Even today, the Knucklehead is still generally regarded as the most beautiful motorcycle Harley-Davidson ever built. The Sixty-One was fitted with a specially designed frame with a reinforced springer fork, made this time of chromium molybdenum steel. An easy-to-operate four-speed transmission was fitted as standard and the disk clutch with considerably enlarged contact surfaces provided for easier shifting and smooth riding. The front and rear brakes were redesigned, enlarged and their braking force improved. The fishtail muffler perfectly accentuated the popular sound of the engine.

In addition to a dry-sump lubrication system, the OHV engine also had an improved, throttle-controlled oil pump that provided for greater pressure at low speeds. Control of the overhead valves was by means of four individual cams on a central camshaft working via tappet pushrods and rocker arms. The modern yet somewhat complex engine had to be treated with love and affection and a skilled hand was needed for maintenance. If not correctly inspected, the engine tended to leak oil, particularly around the valve ports in the cylinder heads.

A 1936 EL61 restored to original condition, with offset air cleaner cover.

All photos on this double page-spread are courtesy of: Mark Jonas, Milwaukee, Wisconsin

The 1937 Model EL with special fuel-tank-mounted instrument panel.

Type:	**Knucklehead**
Model:	**EL**
Year of manufacture:	1936
Engine:	Air-cooled four-stroke
	45° V-Twin OHV
Displacement:	60.29 cu in (988.1 cc)
Bore x stroke:	3.313 x 3.5 in (84.14 x 88.9 mm)
Compression ratio:	7 : 1 (Model E 6.5 : 1)
Power output:	40 hp (Model E: 37 hp)
Carburetor:	Linkert 32 mm ø
Transmission:	Four-speed
Primary drive:	Duplex chain
Secondary drive:	Chain
Battery:	6 volt
Ignition:	Battery-coil
Frame:	Double-looped tubular steel
Front brake:	Drum
Rear brake:	Drum
Front suspension:	Springer fork with oval tubes
Rear suspension:	None
Wheelbase:	59.5 in
Weight:	686 lb
Fuel capacity:	3.7 gal
Oil capacity:	4 qts
Tires:	4.50 x 18
Top speed:	95 mph
Price:	$385
Model versions:	E: Medium compression
	EL: High compression
	ES: (Sidecar) Low
	compression: 5.5:1/6.5:1

The 61 cubic inch (1000 cc) Knucklehead: Prices and production figures

Year	Model	Price	Units
1936	E	$380	152 units
	EL	$380	1,526 units
1937	E	$435	126 units
	EL	$435	1,829 units
1938	EL	$435	2,289 units
1939	EL	$435	2,695 units
1940	EL	$430	3,893 units
1941	EL	$425	2,280 units
1942	E / EL	$425	620 units
1943	E / EL	$425	53 units
1944	E / EL	$425	116 units
1945	E / EL	$463.67	398 units
1946	E / EL	$463.67	2,098 units
1947	E / EL	$590	4,117 units

In 1938, the ammeter and oil pressure display were replaced by two warning lamps. A small lever was located beneath the ignition switch on 1937 and 1938 models for illuminating the speedometer.

The Beehire taillight of the Knucklehead models was adopted from the side-valve Big Twins.

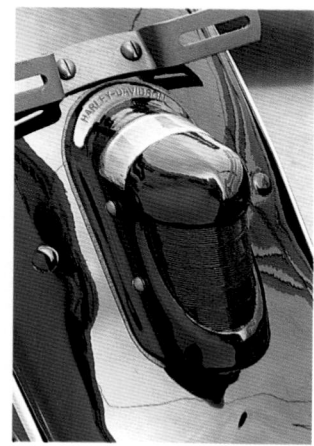

Front brakes, fender lamp, aircraft-style cat's-eye instrument panel on the fuel tank, and the new taillight of the 1935 Model EL.

Likewise a Model EL from 1939: the typical fishtail muffler and left-hand foot-operated clutch peddle, also known as the "suicide clutch."

175

The Knucklehead F/FL from 1941 to 1947

In response to countless customer demands, particularly those of the police for a faster duty motorcycle, Harley introduced the 74 cubic inch (1200 cc) Knucklehead in 1941 – a machine that yielded a very impressive 48 horsepower. Harley enthusiasts were finally able to overtake the competition from the Wigwam in Springfield with a mocking smile on their lips – Indian no longer had a model that could match the new OHV Big Twins. The engine received numerous improvements, including a reinforced crankcase, larger bearings, a new oil pump, improved brake and clutch, and a redesigned air intake. Initially neutral was found until 1939 between second and third gear, and it was only later that this was moved to between first and second gear. Both models were fitted with "airplane style" speedometers with black face and white numbers and needles, as well as the streamlined taillight. After the war, both models were upgraded with numerous chrome-plated extras, which actually increased the similarity in appearance of the two machines tono end. The first version of a new, hydraulically damped telescopic fork was tested on the Knucklehead in 1946, but never got past the prototype stage. Soon afterwards, however, the motorcycle was deemed outdated. It was replaced by the Panhead in 1948.

The 74 cubic inch (1200 cc) Knucklehead: Prices and production figures			
1941	F/FL	$465	2,452 units
1942	F/FL	$465	799 units
1943	F/FL	$465	33 units
1944	F/FL	$465	172 units
1945	F/FL	$465	619 units
1946	F/FL	$465	3,986 units
1947	F/FL	$605	6,893 units

A low-compression model designated S was also available for use with sidecars

The last Knucklehead to be built: the 74 cubic inch (1200 cc) Model FL from 1947.

All photos on this double page-spread courtesy of: Roger A. Kramer, Chesterland, Ohio

Type:	**Knucklehead**
Model:	**FL**
Year of manufacture:	1941
Engine:	Air–cooled four–stroke 45° V–Twin OHV
Displacement:	73.7 cu in (1208 cc)
Bore x stroke:	3.4 x 4 in (87 x 102 mm)
Compression ratio:	7 : 1 (Model F 6.6 : 1)
Power output:	48 hp
Carburetor:	Linkert 33 mm ø
Transmission:	Four–speed
Primary drive:	Duplex chain
Secondary drive:	Chain
Battery:	6 volt
Ignition:	Battery–coil
Frame:	Double–looped tubular steel
Front brake:	Drum
Rear brake:	Drum
Front suspension:	Springer fork
Rear Suspension:	Flat spiral springs
Wheelbase:	59.5 in
Weight:	699 lb
Fuel capacity:	3.7 gal
Oil capacity:	4 qts
Tires:	5.00 x 16
Top speed:	95 mph
Price:	$465
Model versions:	F: Medium compression
	FL: High compression
	FS: (Sidecar) Low
	+ medium compression

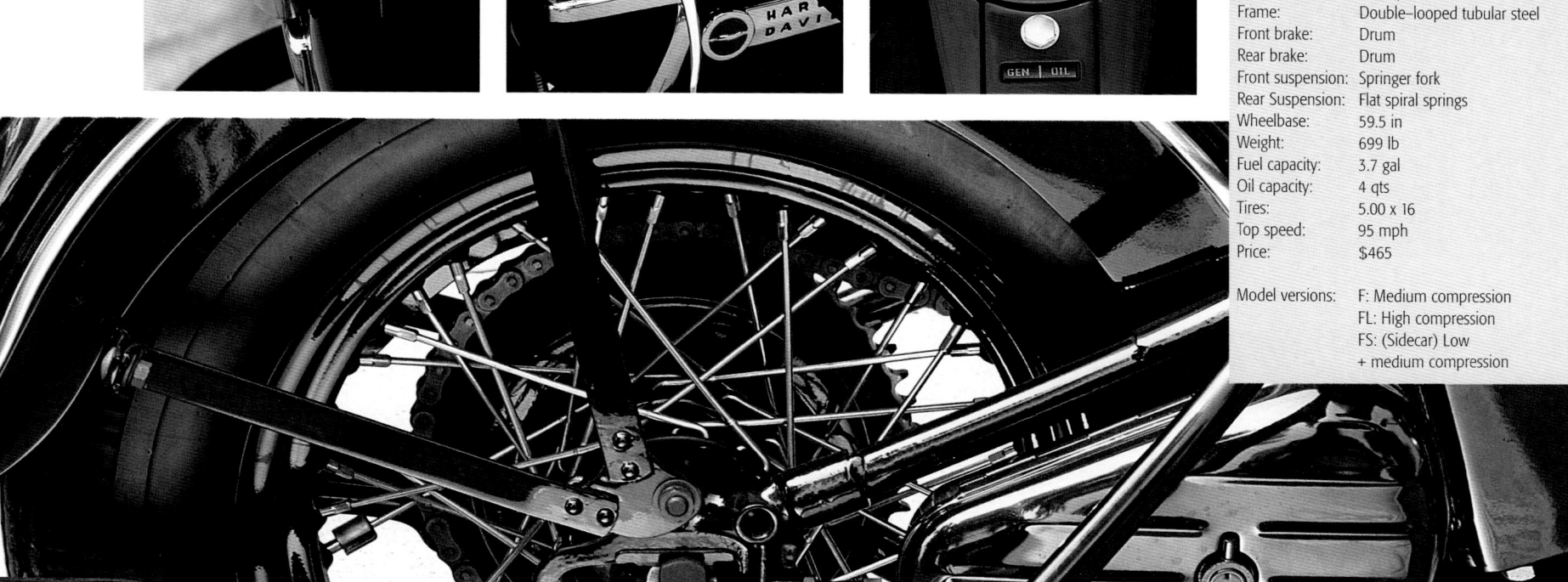

Details of the 1947 FL Knucklehead: gate shift, brake lever, and speedometer (top), short fishtail muffler and tool box (center), suicide clutch, brake pedal and taillight with rear–wheel stand (bottom).

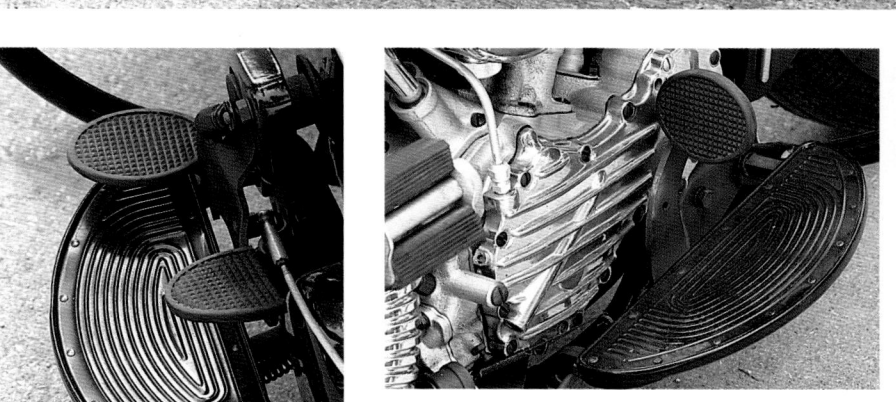

125 Model HS, ST 165 Super Ten, Hummer – the Lightweight Era

Immediately after World War II Harley-Davidson followed the new trend and adapted to the different market situation. Now, all of a sudden, the demand was for lightweight machines – a two-stroke species that the management of Harley-Davidson had never previously considered worthy of attention.

However, being from one of the war's victorious nations, Harley-Davidson grasped the opportunity of the moment. With the exception of the peanut fuel-tank which later became the hallmark of the Sportster, the 125 Model S unveiled by Harley amidst a huge advertising spectacle at the famous dealer convention in Milwaukee in November, The model was actually a copy of the German DKW RT 125. This machine had been built since 1939 and its patent rights became one of the spoils of war taken advantage of by numerous countries, namely Great Britain in the form of the BSA Bantam, Poland with the WSK and the Soviet Union with the Komet. Later on, Japan also

© Harley-Davidson

chose to copy it with the Yamaha YA 1. The sturdy, lightweight machine was intended to replace the four-stroke Cushman Scooter (which only cost half the price of the 125!), and was aimed primarily at America's youth. The technical features of this model were quite basic: a rigid frame, rubber-cushioned girder fork (replaced in 1951 by the Teleglide telescopic fork) and a 3 horsepower engine that produced anything but a typical Harley sound.

Yet despite its technical shortcomings, the sale of more than 10,000 units in the first half-year of production was a success that not even the most skeptical of dealers could ignore. A larger version of the S 125 was introduced in the early 1950s – the ST 165, also known as the Super Ten (on account of the engine displacement of 10 cubic inches). The 125 was converted into the Hummer in 1958 – a modernized lightweight motorcycle that once again conquered the market with the support of a vast and aggressive advertising campaign.

The lightweight 125 Model S – later also known as the Hummer – from 1948, with girder fork, windshield and saddlebags.

Courtesy of: Mark Jonas, Milwaukee, Wisconsin

An export Hummer model with girder fork from 1948.

Courtesy of: Christian von Alvensleben, Hamburg, Germany

Type:	**ST 165 Super Ten**
Years of manufacture:	1952–1957
Engine:	Two-stroke single–cylinder
Displacement:	10.1 cu in (164 cc)
Bore x stroke:	2.38 x 2.28 in (60 x 58 mm)
Compression ratio:	6.6 : 1
Power output:	6 hp
Transmission:	Three–speed foot–operated
Tires:	3.50 x 19
Fuel capacity:	1.75 gal
Price:	$445
Special versions:	Also available with 18-inch wheels

Type:	**HS125** (1948–1954)
	125 Hummer (1958–60)
Engine:	Two–stroke single–cylinder
Displacement:	7.6 cu in (123 cc)
Bore x stroke:	2.06 x 2.28 in (52 x 58 mm)
Compression ratio:	6.6 : 1
Power output:	3 hp
Transmission:	Three–speed foot–operated
Tires:	3.25 x 19
Fuel capacity:	1.75 gal
Price:	$375
Special versions:	With Teleglide telescopic fork as of 1951

Ad of the 165 Super Ten (S10), shown here with special raised handlebars.

Courtesy of: Dale Walksler/
Wheels Through Time Museum, Oxnard, California

Ad and original picture of the S 125 Tele–Glide from 1949.

The Panhead Engine – a Year of Change

In 1948, Harley-Davidson proudly advertised its new baby as the "Standard of the World." Only the best, latest and most reliable components were used to build this engine. And by this time, America was indeed the world's leading nation when it came to engine design. World War II had come to an end, and it was now time to refocus efforts on the civilian market, marked as it was by a tremendous demand for modern motorcycles.

Harley's new "super engine" had an ingenious aluminum cylinder head, the overhead valves were lubricated more efficiently, hydraulic valve lifters were placed on top of the pushrods, the engine cooling system was improved, and the old 18 mm sparkplugs replaced with newer models (the short 14 mm thread). The hydraulic valve lifters, the last feature to be taken from the automotive industry, were shifted to the bottom end of the pushrod in 1953, and as of that same year, only the powerful 74 cubic inch (1200 cc) models were available. Finally, in 1956, the crankshaft was fitted with new tapered roller bearings, in place of the old roller bearings. After its release, the Panhead represented the state-of-the-art in top performance engines for a long time to come. Even today, many fans of Harley-Davidson motorcyles still regard it as the ultimate engine.

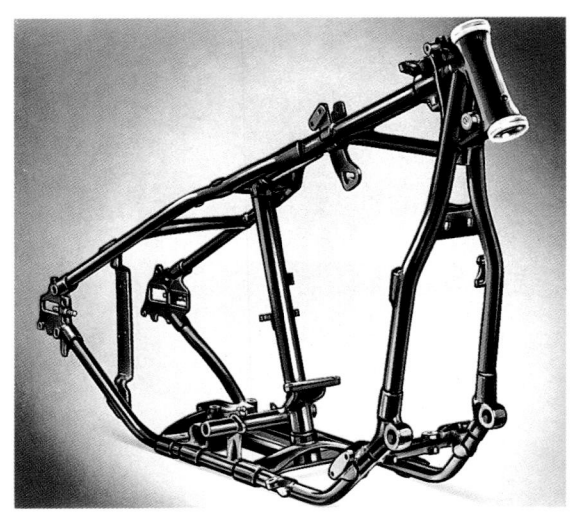

The first FL Panhead engine from 1948 on display in Harley-Davidson's York Museum.

Still in demand today: the wishbone frame from the 1948–1955 models.

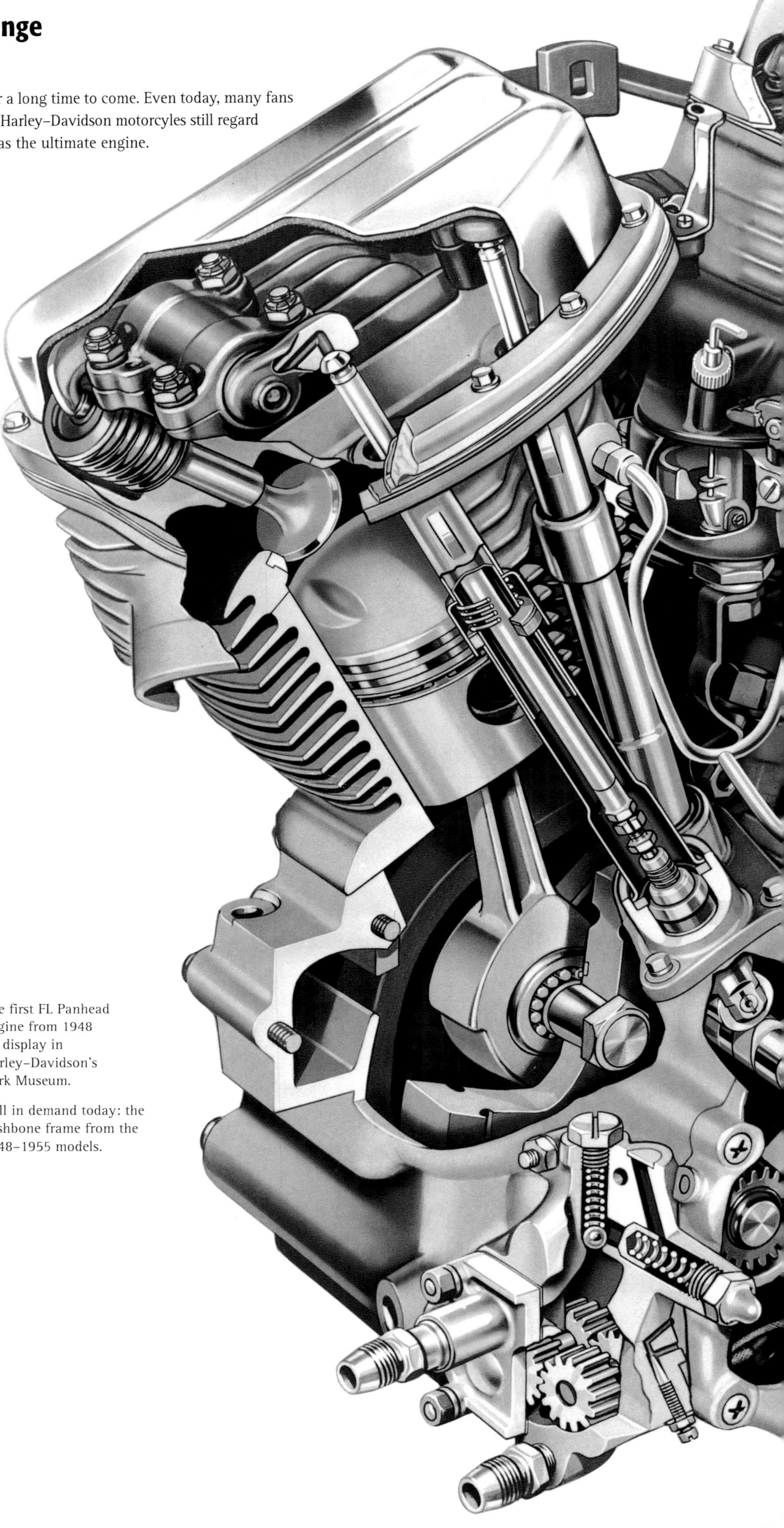

CYLINDERS, ROCKER ARMS, VALVES AND GASKETS 1965 & EARLIER (REAR SHOWN)

© Harley–Davidson

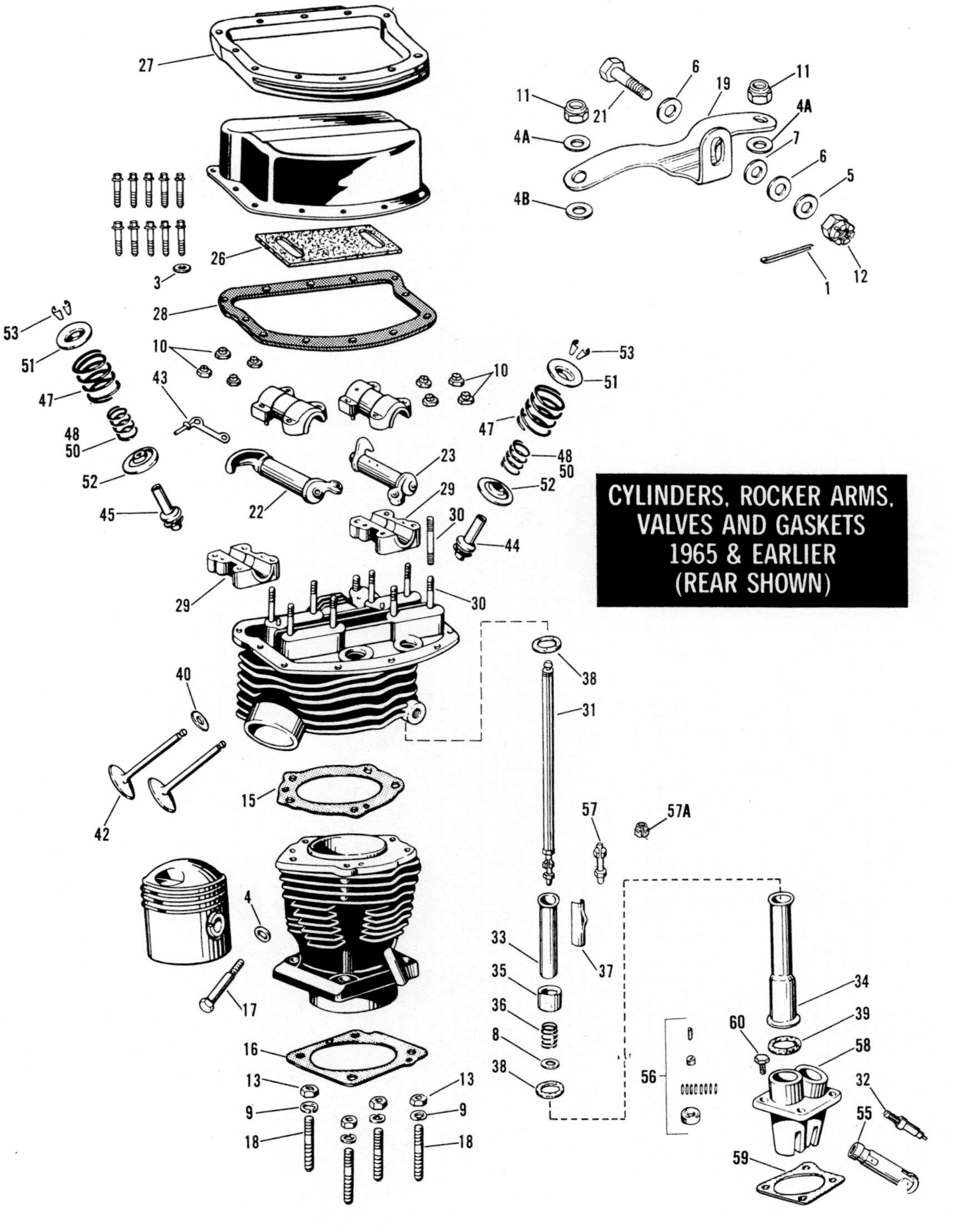

© Harley–Davidson

Exploded view of the Panhead engine

10. Locking nuts
15. Cylinder head gasket
16. Cylinder foot gasket
18. Cylinder foot bolts
22. Rocker arm
23. Rocker arm
26. Anti-drumming insert
27. Cylinder head cover and reinforcing base
28. Cylinder head cover cork gasket
29. Rocker arm bearing brackets
30. Cylinder head with fastening bolts
31. Tappet pushrod
32. Hydraulic tappet

33. Upper tappet cover
34. Lower tappet cover
37. Tappet lock
42. Valve
43. Oil inlet
44./45. Valve guide
47./48./50. Inner and outer valve springs
51. Upper valve stem retaining washer
52. Valve bush retaining washer
53. Key
55. Hydraulic tappet unit with roller
58. Tappet guide
59. Tappet guide gasket

181

Postwar Premiere: the Panhead

After World War II the time was once more ripe for improvement. There had been enormous technological developments and Harley-Davidson could no longer expect to excite the public's interest with the old-fashioned-looking prewar Knucklehead. A new engine had to be developed: one that was better, nicer-looking, more powerful. This was to lead to the development of a whole new motorbike.

In 1948, the company presented the new 61 cubic inch (1000 cc) E/EL as well as the 74 cubic inch (1200 cc) F/FL with a modified overhead-valve engine which, thanks to its characteristic pan-like rocker covers, was immediately dubbed the Panhead. Essentially, the lower end of the engine was constructed from the old knucklehead to which a new top end, with aluminum head, overhead hydraulic valve lifters and improved valve seats, had been fitted. Additional improvements included lubrication channels in the engine so that the external oil lines could be dispensed with, a more powerful oil pump and a modified camshaft.

Both models also had a new rigid frame which soon became known, due to its shape, as the wishbone frame. This was fitted with a mounting plate to which a one-piece crash bar could be fastened. The general styling was also modernized, though the tried and tested springer forks were retained, albeit only for one more year. The first Panhead perhaps hit the market a little too soon, since the Milwaukee designers and engineers had already moved on significantly...

The first 74-inch (1200 cc) FL Panhead was launched in 1948. During the first year of production it was fitted with the old springer fork. This was changed in the next model to a Hydra Glide fork. Shown here is an original 1948 model, albeit with chrome-plated parts fitted later. The actual standard version can be seen in the small picture from the Harley-Davidson brochure.

Courtesy of: Joseph M. Gardella, Redford, Michigan

Type:	**Panhead**
Model:	**74 FL**
Year of manufacture:	1948
Engine:	Air-cooled four-stroke overhead-valve 45° V-Twin
Displacement:	73.63 cu in (1206.39 cc)
Bore x stroke:	3.4375 x 3.968 in (87.31 x 100.8 mm)
Compression ratio:	7 : 1
Power output:	50 hp
Carburetor:	Linkert M 38 mm ø
Transmission:	Four-speed
Primary drive:	Duplex chain
Final drive:	Chain
Battery:	6 volt
Ignition:	Battery-coil
Frame:	Tubular steel cradle (double tube)
Front brake:	Drum
Rear brake:	Drum
Front suspension:	Springer forks
Rear suspension:	None
Wheelbase:	59.5 in
Weight:	565 lb
Fuel capacity:	3.75 gal
Oil capacity:	4 qts
Tires:	5.00 x 16
Top speed:	100 mph
Price:	$650
Model verions:	61 cu in (1000 cc) Model E The additional reference letter L designates the higher compression version of both models.

1948 — The first Panheads:

E **Sport Solo**
61 cubic inches (1,000 cc), medium compression

EL **Special Sport Solo**
61 cubic inches (1,000 cc), high compression

F **Sport Solo**
74 cubic inches (1,210 cc), medium compression

FL **Special Sport Solo**
74 cubic inches (1,210 cc), high compression

Increasing Comfort I – the Hydra Glide

The second version of the Panhead appeared the following year: in 1949 the old, tried and trusted springer fork disappeared and made way for a modern telescopic fork. The Hydra Glide fork was born. Once, the rear-wheel suspension was added, the model became known under the name Duo Glide.

The new Hydra Glide kept its old, rigid wishbone frame for another nine years, while it was styled in the extrovert fashion of the time, with long, downward sweeping fenders, baroque curving bars and mufflers, and lavish amounts of chrome-plating and stylish trim. A wide range of full-dress accessories were also available. A few details needed improving in the engine, too, particularly the hydraulic valve lifters, which caused frequent and expensive problems while the bikes were still under guarantee. The difficulty was finally solved in 1952 by shifting the bottom end of the pushrods into the crankcase.

From the year 1952 a foot-operated gearshift (reference letters FLF, FLHF) became available on all models as an optional extra. A comical leverage booster device, known affectionately as "the mousetrap," helped the operation of the hand clutch. The 61 cubic inch (1000 cc) E/EL models – which could no longer be distinguished externally from the 74 cubic inch (1212 cc) version – were taken out of production. In 1955 the reference letters for the high compression models changed: the FL now became the FLH.

With plenty of chrome and special accessories, this 1954 Hydra Glide embodies an affluent lifestyle and American luxury.

Courtesy of: Pistor Harley-Davidson, Stuttgart, Germany

Left side of the 1954 Hydra Glide.

Type:	**74 FL Panhead**
Model:	**Hydra Glide**
Years of manufacture:	1949–1955
Engine:	Air-cooled four-stroke overhead-valve 45° V-Twin
Displacement:	73.63 cu in (1206.39 cc)
Bore x stroke:	3.438 x 3.968 in (87.31 x 100.8 mm)
Compression ratio:	7 : 1
Power output:	60 hp
Carburetor:	Linkert "M" 38 mm ø
Transmission:	Four-speed
Primary drive:	Duplex chain
Final drive:	Chain
Battery:	6 volt
Ignition:	Battery-coil
Frame:	Tubular steel cradle (double downtube)
Front brake:	Drum
Rear brake:	Drum
Front suspension:	Telescopic forks
Rear suspension:	None
Wheelbase:	59.5 in
Weight:	590 lb
Fuel capacity:	3.75 gal
Oil capacity:	4 qts
Tires:	5.00 x 16
Top speed:	100 mph
Price:	$900 (in 1951)
Model versions:	ES, EP, FS and FP with special transmission (three forwards and one reverse gear in sidecar version).

1949–1957: The Hydra Glide Models

E   **Hydra Glide Solo**
61 cubic inches (1000 cc)
medium compression (until 1952)

EL **Hydra Glide Sport Solo**
61 cubic inches (1000 cc)
high compression (until 1952)

F   **Hydra Glide Solo**
74 cubic inches (1212 cc)
medium compression (until 1952)

FL **Hydra Glide Sport Solo**
74 cubic inches (1212 cc)
high compression

FLH **Hydra Glide Super Sport**
74 cubic inches (1212 cc)

Almost a real show bike: this Hydra Glide complete with chrome-barred buddy seat, fishtail exhaust, white-wall tires, and laden down with special accessories, shows the typical bombastic style of the late fifties.

Protruding decorative rails and a wealth of chrome-plated extras were typical characteristics of the 1950s.

Increasing Comfort II – the Duo Glide

In 1958 a further 74 cubic inch (1210 cc) FL/FLH model was introduced. It had a new frame with swingarm rear suspension with twin shock absorbers and it was duly dubbed the Duo Glide (the name again a protected trademark). Thus the old rigid frame had come to the end of the road. The engine had also been improved, with a strengthened crank mechanism and larger bearings and the high compression (H) version boasted a compression ratio of 8:1 and developed an impressive 60 horsepower. Additionally, the cylinder heads were strengthened and given bigger fins to allow better heat dispersal – the "pan" had become massive. The Duo Glide also had a much more effective hydraulic rear wheel brake, while the brake fluid container was mounted right next to the brake lever. Lavishly fitted with all manner of accessories, it was the most comfortable, but also most colossal, motorbike in the world. If it sometimes seemed like too much of a good thing, this extravagance nevertheless struck a chord with American tastes in the era of monstrously overblown giant-finned luxury automobiles.

1958–1964: The Duo Glide	
FL	**Duo Glide Sport Solo** 74 cubic inches (1212 cc)
FLH	**Duo Glide Super Sport** 74 cubic inches (1212 cc) high compression

Courtesy of: Axel Daibenzeiher, Aalen, Germany

3-point Suspension

hydraulically smooth front and rear

Front . . . back . . . mid-way . . . the *miracle ride* DUO-GLIDE gives you cushioned suspension where you need it! In the rear, the husky, hydraulic shock absorbers control the amazing swinging arm — giving you a level ride at all times. Hydraulically damped, Hydra-Glide® front fork swings into action on all surfaces — takes the ripples out of rough roads . . . makes smooth roads even *smoother*. And the spring-loaded seat post offers an *extra measure* of comfort.

DUO-GLIDE "3-point suspension" puts motorcycling in a new dimension! Take a ride . . . a DUO-GLIDE ride . . . *today!*

instant action hydraulic rear brake

187

The Electric Starter

By the beginning of the 1960s, the inroads made into motorcycle sales by foreign imports could no longer be ignored by American manufacturers. The public gets what the public wants, and the Japanese were showing everyone the way, with the press–button starter as the last word in luxury equipment.

In 1965 Harley–Davidson introduced its highway flagship, the FL/FLH with a 12–volt electric start mechanism and baptized it with the immortal and legendary name "Electra Glide" (a registered trademark). A new age had dawned and Milwaukee's advertising strategists enthusiastically dubbed it "The Modern Age of American Motorcycling." However the company's latest creation was initially a problem child. The untested 12–volt starter system proved to be unexpectedly susceptible to moisture and humidity and it was only in collaboration with the Homelight Corporation that the engineers finally managed to make the whole electrical system rainproof and watertight. However, in order to

achieve this, they had to add 76 pounds to the machine's weight in the form of a larger battery, an altered frame and (a new) starter unit.

This increase in weight set off a chain reaction: first, the brakes, which had not been changed for years, were now short on stopping power and had to be strengthened. Then the engine needed more power. This was achieved via higher compression and a modified camshaft, but this led to unacceptably high levels of vibration. This in turn placed too great a strain on the crankshaft, which required new, larger bearings. The brutal power of the machine was borne in full by the chain, which also proved too weak to stand the strain and had to be replaced with a heavier duty one. But this meant that the steering geometry was no longer right and the front wheel started to wobble alarmingly at high speed. This was remedied by stiffening the frame. However, Harley–Davidson managers were soon sick of the continual complaints and ordered their

constructors and engineers to sort things out once and for all before the image of the new Electra Glide was irreparably damaged.

The first Electra Glide from 1965 — still similar to Panhead design with a large battery and solo seat, but without any accessories whatsoever.

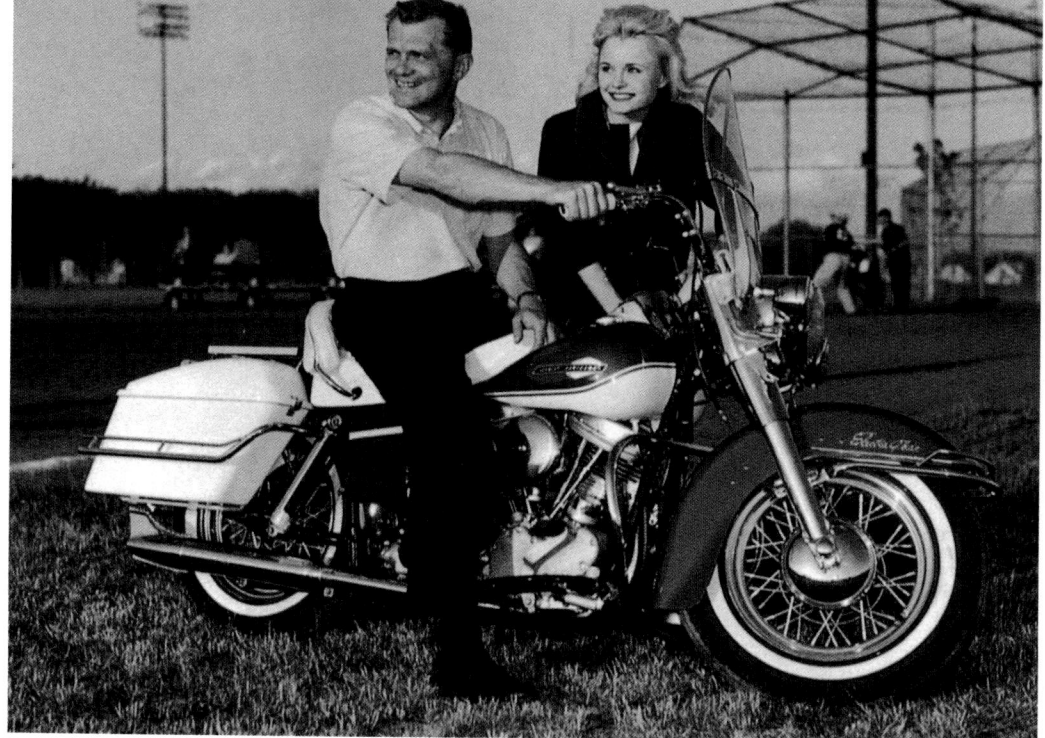

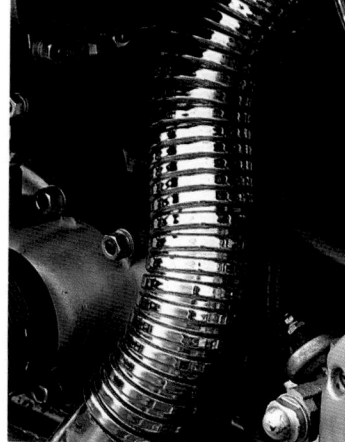

© Harley-Davidson

The famous photograph for the company's brochure: the new touring model Electra Glide with windshield, custom buddy seat and fiberglass saddlebags.

Courtesy of: Max Middelbosch, Zwolle, Netherlands

Type:	**74 FL Panhead**
Model:	**Electra Glide**
Year of manufacture:	1965
Engine:	Air-cooled four-stroke overhead-valve 45° V-Twin
Displacement:	73.63 cu in (1206.39 cc)
Bore x stroke:	3.438 x 3.969 in (87.31 x 100.8 mm)
Compression ratio:	8 : 1
Power output:	60 hp
Carburetor:	Linkert 38 mm ø
Transmission:	Four-speed
Primary drive:	Duplex chain
Final drive:	Chain
Battery:	12 volt
Ignition:	Battery–coil
Frame:	Tubular steel cradle (double downtube)
Front brake:	Drum
Rear brake:	Drum
Front suspension:	Telescopic forks
Rear suspension:	Twin-shock-absorber swingarm
Wheelbase:	60 in
Weight:	781 lb
Fuel capacity:	5 gal
Oil capacity:	4 qts
Tires:	5.00 x 16 in
Top speed:	100 mph
Price:	$1,595

MOTOR
HARLEY-DAVIDSON
CYCLES
MADE IN U.S.A.
66007-84

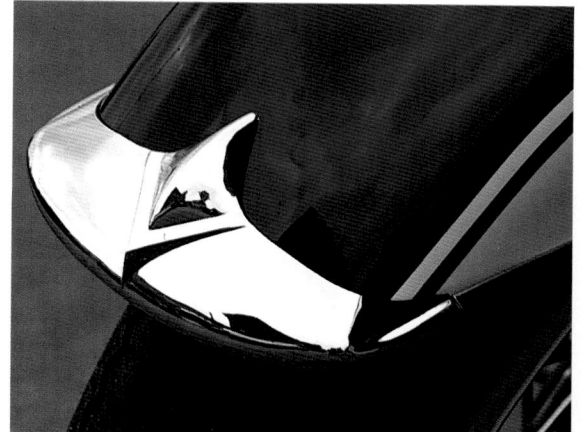

Typical chrome-plated cover on the front fender and – for the first time – the heavy-duty 12 volt battery.

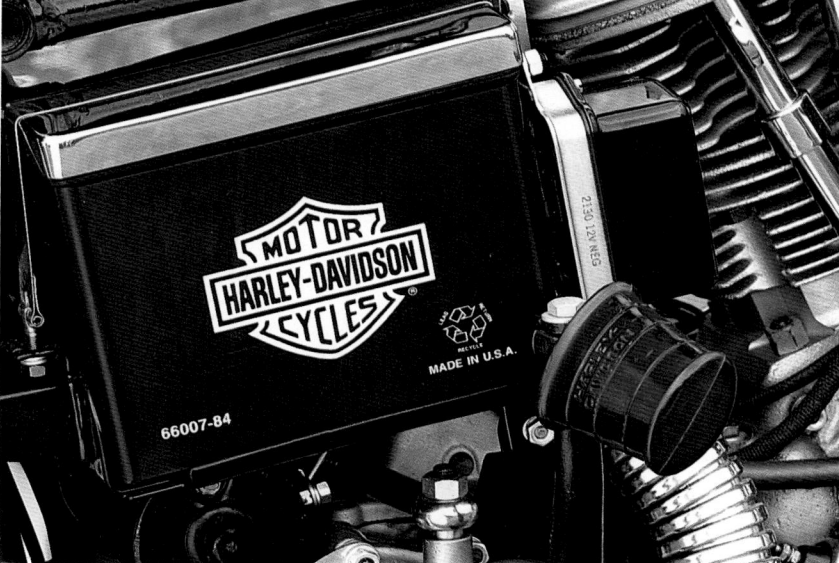

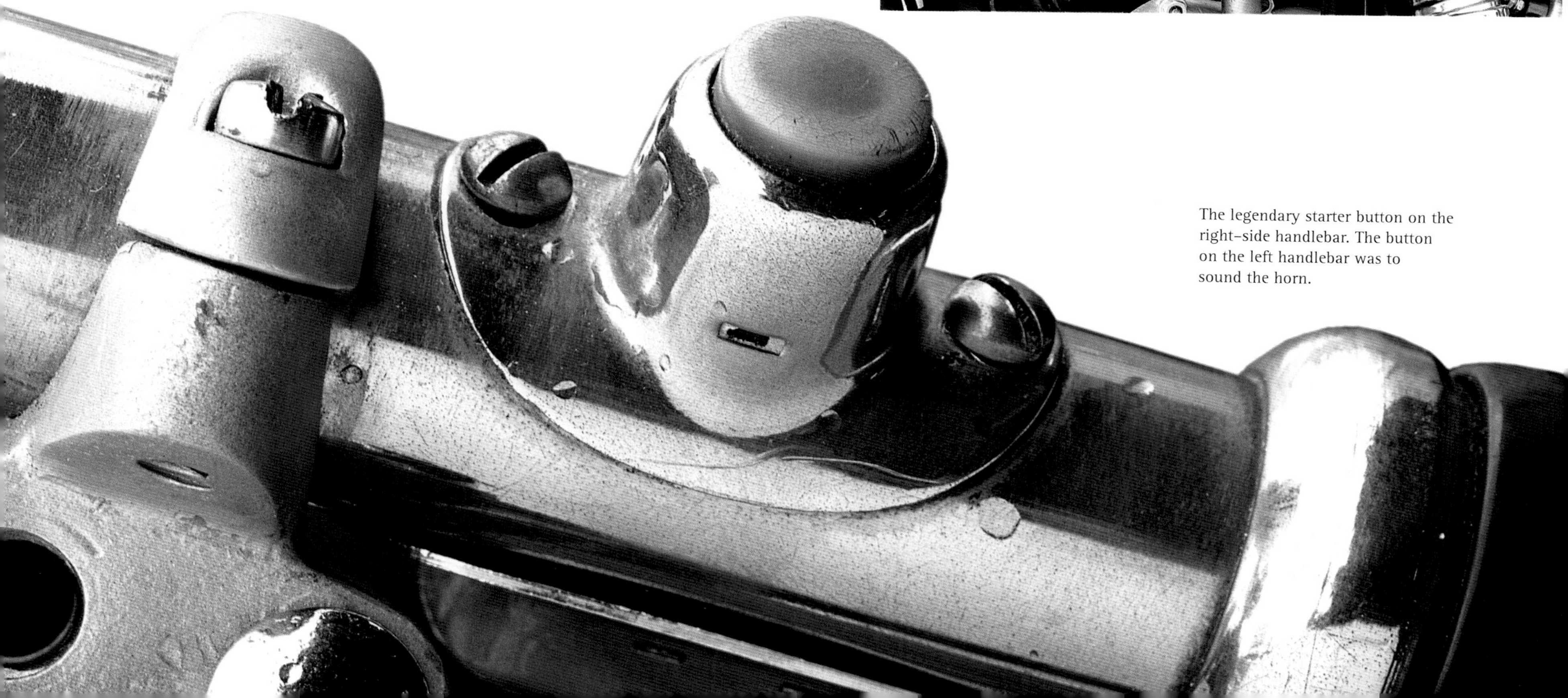

The legendary starter button on the right-side handlebar. The button on the left handlebar was to sound the horn.

The New Model K

It was beautiful, it was sporty and it looked like compact power. In 1952 Harley-Davidson reacted to the threatening invasion of mean British machines from Norton, BSA, Triumph and associates, which were tempting away many of America's power-hungry youth, with the introduction of the K model.

The K Sport Solo was a completely new model and the 45 cubic inch (747 cc) side-valve engine was about the only thing it had in common with the old W model. The engine and gearbox now formed a single unit, the foot gearshift and the chain were on the right, and the hand clutch was on the left-hand side of the handlebars. The sporty K was the first Harley with telescopic forks and rear suspension in the form of a swing-arm with two hydraulic shock absorbers, albeit fairly firm ones.

However, initial real-life experiences from illegal nighttime street races were sobering: the much-fêted K proved to be no match for its English rivals and the company realized it would have to pack considerably more horsepower into the newly designed flathead engine. Thus the KH 55 appeared in 1954 with a 54 cubic inch (883 cc) power unit and compression was raised from 6:1 to 6.8:1, leading to an increase in power output from 30 to 38 horsepower. In 1956 Harley again

tried to improve the situation, bringing out the KHK. It was all in vain: the British still had their noses in front.

A few customers turned their K models into sporty tourers by adding all manner of accessories, such as saddlebags, windshields and an incredibly ugly "buddy seat." However, this did not match the bike's original purpose and the trend did not catch on in a big way. Unfortunately, Harley's Development Department dropped the promising KL project for a 60 degree ohc V-Twin engine and instead backed the X project involving four cams mounted lower down.

The K Sports models had far better performance than the rather modest road version. In their highly-tuned racing versions the KK, KR, and the track racer KRTT were extremely successful for Harley for many more years. And often, for the more courageous Harley rider, a KK lived up to the promise suggested by the KH or KHK as hot-rods for everyday use...

The new Model K from 1952, shown here with buddy seat, modified taillight, shock absorbers, and additional bellows on the fork. The standard version is shown on the right in a picture from Harley's brochure.

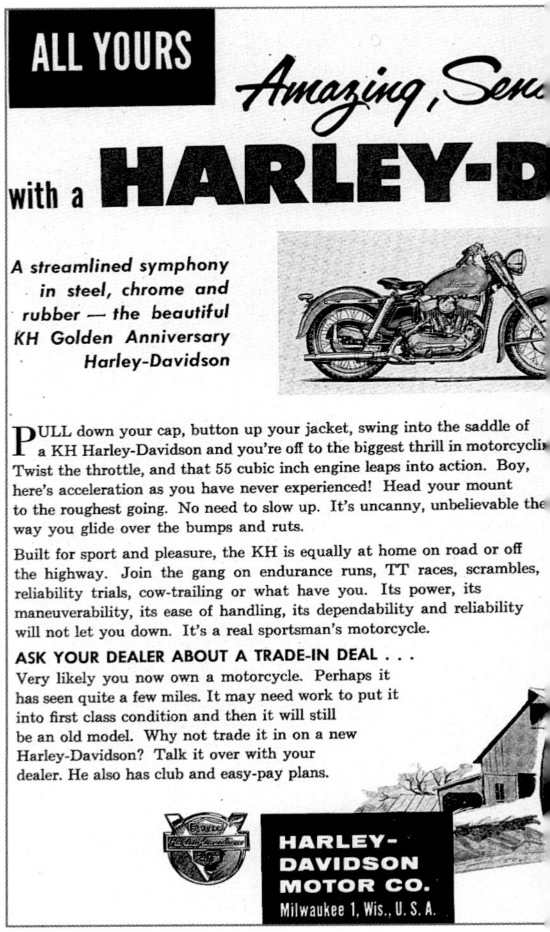

Courtesy of: Glenn Bator/Vintage Museum of Transportation, Oxnard, California

Performance
...IDSON
KH

With the great acceleration and power of the KH go brakes that are positive and highly effective. Front and rear brakes at your instant command — fully enclosed.

Swinging arm rear suspension deserves much of the credit for the great riding comfort of the KH. Helical springs are controlled by automotive-type shock absorbers.

© Harley-Davidson

The 1952 K model with standard solo seat (left) and touring accessories, such as windshield and saddlebags (below).

Courtesy of: Ernst Michl, Arkansas

Type:	**K 45**
Model:	**Flathead Sportster**
Year of manufacture:	1952
Engine:	Air-cooled four-stroke side-valve 45° V-Twin
Displacement:	45.26 cu in (741.80 cc)
Bore x stroke:	2.75 x 3.813 in (69.85 x 96.84 mm)
Compression ratio:	6 : 1
Power output:	30 hp
Carburetor:	Linkert "M" 38 mm ø
Transmission:	Integrated four-speed gearbox
Primary drive:	Triplex chain
Final drive:	Chain
Battery:	6 volt
Ignition:	Battery-coil
Frame:	Tubular steel cradle (single downtube)
Front brake:	Drum
Rear brake:	Drum
Front suspension:	Telescopic shock absorber
Rear suspension:	Twin-shock-absorber swingarm
Wheelbase:	56.5 in
Weight:	398 lb
Fuel capacity:	4.5 gal
Oil capacity:	3 qts
Tires:	3.25 x 19
Top speed:	80 mph
Price:	$865 (in 1952)

Model versions:
1954 the KH with 45 cubic inch engine and 6.8:1 compression and 38 hp;
1956 the KHK with racing camshaft, 4.00 x 18 rear tires as optional extra with 3.50 x 18 or 3.25 x 19 front tires.
Wide range of accessories for conversion into a Tourer.

1952–1956: The Model K	
1952/53:	K Sport/Sport Solo 45 cubic inch (750cc) side-valve flathead
1954/55:	KH "Roadster" Sport Solo 55 cubic inch (883 cc) side-valve flathead
1956:	KHK Sport 55 cubic inch (883 cc) side-valve flathead with racing cams

LEFT SIDE

© Harley-Davidson

191

The KR and KRTT – Powerful Side-Valve Models

In the summer of 1952, Harley-Davidson introduced the all new K model. The KR racing version was first available for the 1953 season, however, and at first it suffered from persistent teething troubles. Despite this, early trials were promising and Harley hoped to be able finally to beat the hated competition of the 500cc OHV Norton, BSA and Triumph bikes.

The KR still had a side-valve engine, but the heads, pistons and cylinders were made of alloy and the 750 cc V-Twin now had the transmission incorporated with the crankcase as well as a foot gearshift, a lightweight cradle frame, rear wheel suspension, and telescopic forks for the road-version KRTT, and a rigid frame for the KR, which was designed chiefly with American oval dirt tracks in mind.

After a number of frustrating failures, a series of victories began in 1953 when Paul Goldsmith beat all English competition to win the Daytona 200 at an average speed of 94.43 mph. Joe Leonard got a further winning streak underway riding a KR which had been upgraded by the talented tuner Tom Sifton of San José, among other things through reworked cylinder ports,

double-coil elliptical valve springs, sodium-cooled valves, chrome-plated piston rings and strengthened connecting rod bearings. This delivered 50 hp to the rear wheel which was an incredible performance for a side-valve machine.

In 1955 the rookie Brad Andres won the Number One White Plate while riding one of these machines. When pressure from the non-Harley teams forced the AMA in 1954 to raise the permitted compression ratio from 8:1 to 9:1, this mainly benefited the high-compression BSAs, Nortons, and Triumphs, since side-valve machines had now reached their absolute limit. Despite this, the Harley tuners worked wonders with the K engine, described disparagingly by the international press as the "anachronism of the twentieth century."

Another version of the K racing bike was the off-road KRM, mainly used in enduro and desert races. It was unsuccessful, however, mainly because it was too heavy for this type of event.

After the defeat by Triumph in 1967, the 1968–1969 KR, under race team leader Dick O'Brien, was once again reworked and developed, with a low-slung 'Lowboy'

frame, wind-tunnel tested cladding, Tillotson dual throat carburetor, hotter cams and altered exhaust valve timing. This achieved a power output of 60 hp at 7000 rpm. In the Daytona 200 Roger Reiman used it to achieve a new record average speed of 148 mph.

In 1968, only eight more KR 750 works racing bikes were built, all equipped with the best available components, such as Ceriani forks, Fontana drum brakes on the front wheel and disc brakes on the rear wheel. However, when in 1969 the AMA bowed to ever-increasing pressure, especially from the English participants, and lifted the restrictions on this class, the end had finally come for side-valve racing engines. Nevertheless, the super-robust KR continued to be used successfully for years on the oval dirt tracks.

A 1950s Flat Tracker – a KR Factory Racer from 1956.

Courtesy of: Otis Chandler/Vintage Museum of Transportation, Oxnard, California

Type:	**Racer**
Model:	**KR / KRTT**
Years of manufacture:	1953–1970
Engine:	Four–stroke side-valve 45º V–Twin
Displacement:	45 cu in (741 cc)
Bore x stroke:	2.747 x 3.812 in (70 x 97 mm)
Compression ratio:	9 : 1
Power output:	48 hp at 6600 rpm
Carburetor:	Linkert 33 mm ø
Transmission:	Four–speed
Drive:	Dual ignition
Frame:	Steel tube, lightweight cradle frame with swingarm and shock absorbers, (KR: rigid frame)
Front suspension:	Telescopic fork
Rear suspension:	Special hydraulic racing shock absorbers.
Weight:	335 lb
Fuel capacity:	2.25 or 3.25 gal; 6 gal
Oil capacity:	3 or 6 qts
Wheels:	18 in or 19 in with aluminum or steel rim
Tires:	KR: Goodyear Grasshopper 3.50 x 19/4.00 x 18
Top speed:	145 mph
Price:	KR: $1,295
	KRTT: $1,425

Special versions:
KRTT (Production Racer)
KRM (Enduro)

Successful riders:
Caroll Resweber, Joe Leonard, Bart Markel, Roger Reiman, Everett Brashear, Paul Goldsmith, Brad Andres, Mert Lawwill, Troy Lee.

Standard Flat Tracker – the 1956 Model KR.

A private road–racer – the 1959 KHRM from Kosma.

The KRTT Factory Racer for road–racing.

Pacer, Scat, Ranger, Bobcat – the Second Generation of Two-Strokes

Under pressure from the ever-more successful British competition, Harley-Davidson launched a new series of lightweight two-stroke motorcycles in the 1960s: the 175 cc Pacer and Scat models; the Ranger, designed as a pure trial bike; and in 1966, the Bobcat, a road bike whose fiberglass monocoque gave it a modern look that was indicative of the models Aermacchi would soon start to build in Italy.

Telescopic forks, drum brakes, and three-speed transmission were fitted as standard on these two-stroke models. The swingarm rear suspension that replaced the old, rigid frame in all models bar the

Ranger in 1963 was a particularly remarkable feature: the suspension unit was located beneath the engine, much like the Softail system introduced in 1984.

The entire production of American-built lightweight Harleys was halted in 1967. In 1966, it was decided to import all lightweight models from Italy, where the wishes of ever more demanding customers with regard to these smaller bikes could be better catered for. Once AMF gained a stake in Harley, they continued with this strategy.

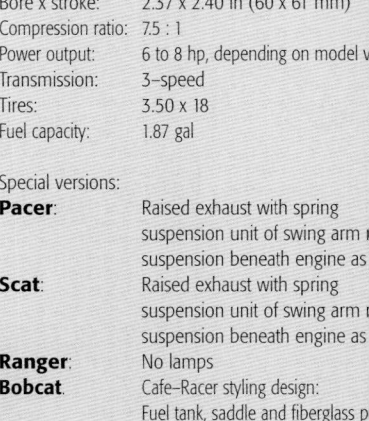

Type:	**Pacer** (Road model) 1960–1963
	Scat (Off-road model) 1960–1965
	Ranger (Trial bike) 1962
	Bobcat (Model BTH) 1966
Engine:	Two-stroke single-cylinder
Displacement:	10.7 cu in (175 cc)
Bore x stroke:	2.37 x 2.40 in (60 x 61 mm)
Compression ratio:	7.5 : 1
Power output:	6 to 8 hp, depending on model v
Transmission:	3-speed
Tires:	3.50 x 18
Fuel capacity:	1.87 gal

Special versions:
Pacer:	Raised exhaust with spring suspension unit of swing arm ▸ suspension beneath engine as
Scat:	Raised exhaust with spring suspension unit of swing arm ▸ suspension beneath engine as
Ranger:	No lamps
Bobcat:	Cafe-Racer styling design: Fuel tank, saddle and fiberglass p

The Bobcat, produced only in 1966, with an ultramodern rear–wheel cantilever swingarm.

Courtesy of: H.D. Archives

Still with a rigid frame: the pre–1963 175 (far left) and the Pacer.

The 250 and 350 Sprint – Lively Italian Four-Strokes

After Harley-Davidson had acquired an interest in the Italian company Aeronautica Macchi (Aermacchi) in 1960, the first horizontal single-cylinder four-stroke machine in the 15 cubic inch (250 cc) bracket appeared on the American market in 1961. This was developed from the Italian 250 cc model the Ala Verde and was initially called the Wisconsin, before receiving the somewhat snappier name Sprint and getting the model designation letter C.

Several racing versions with sporting trim were developed from this basic model over the following years. The most common of these was the somewhat higher compression Model H (H for hot) in enduro/scrambler design (2.6 gallon tank, 18-inch wheels, high-mounted exhaust) developing 25 rather than 18 horsepower. Additionally, pure competition racers could be ordered, such as the R Type (R for racing), with no lights and with open megaphones pipes and, from 1967, the

Sprint SS, a stripped version of the Italian CRS model. The typically spartan Italian design was strongly Americanized for the Sprint, with high handlebars, a tear-drop gas tank, etc., and it was available in a variety of versions. Basically the Sprint was an out-and-out sports motorcycle, making it very popular at the younger end of the market.

In 1969, after Harley-Davidson was taken over by the AMF Corporation, the 250 cc Sprint was replaced by the more powerful 21 cubic inch (350 cc) Sprint which was launched in 1969. However, the heavily-marketed Sprints still could not compete with the considerably less complicated, faster and above all cheaper two-stroke Japanese machines, and so in 1974 AMF Harley-Davidson (which now owned Aermacchi 100 percent) finally decided, despite considerable racing success in America and Europe, to end production of the Sprint four-stroke for import.

© Harley-Davidson

© Harley-Davidson

The 1971 350 cc Aermacchi SS "Sprint" in typical U.S. road-going outfit and a SX-350 model scrambler (right).

Type:	**250 Sprint C**
Years of manufacture:	1961–1967
Engine:	Horizontal overhead-valve four-stroke single-cylinder
Displacement:	15 cu in (246 cc)
Bore x stroke:	2.60 x 2.84 in (66 x 72 mm)
Compression ratio:	8.5 : 1
Power output:	18 hp at 7500 rpm
Carburetor:	Dell'Orto 24 mm ø
Transmission:	Four-speed gearbox, right-hand gear change
Primary drive:	Gear wheel
Final drive :	Chain
Ignition:	Battery-coil
Frame:	Tubular steel tube (double downtube)
Front brake:	Drum
Rear brake:	Drum
Front suspension:	Telescopic fork
Rear suspension:	Twin-shock-absorber swingarm
Wheelbase:	52 in
Weight:	275 lb
Fuel capacity:	4 gal
Oil capacity:	2 qts
Tires:	3.00 x 17
Top speed:	75 mph
Price:	$690
Production:	Approx. 40,000

Special versions:
Model H   25 hp (from 1962), with 9.4 : 1 compression, 2.6 gallon fuel-tank and 18-inch wheels;
Model R/CR   production racer type specially designed as a short-track racer.
Model CRS/SS (1967) with aluminum cylinder, also the road racer CRTT with full fairing.

Type:	**350er Sprint 350 Sprint SS (Street Scrambler)**
Years of manufacture:	1969–1974
Engine:	Horizontal four-stroke single-cylinder OHV
Displacement:	21 cubic inches (342 cc)
Bore x stroke:	3 x 3.2 in (74 x 80 mm)
Compression ratio:	9 : 1
Power output:	25 hp at 7,000 rpm
Carburetor:	Dell'Orto 27 mm ø
Transmission:	5-speed, left-hand operated
Primary drive:	Gearwheel
Final drive:	Chain
Starter:	Initially kick-starter, replaced later by electronic starter
Ignition:	12 volt battery coil ignition
Frame:	Double-looped tubular steel (from 1973)
Front brake:	Drum
Rear brake:	Drum
Front suspension:	Telescopic fork
Rear suspension:	Arm with telescopic struts
Wheelbase:	56 in
Height of saddle:	35.5 in
Weight:	415 lb
Fuel capacity:	3.5 gal
Oil capacity:	2 qts
Front tire:	3.25 x 19
Rear tire:	3.50 x 18
Top speed:	90 mph
Price:	$795
Production:	Approx. 40,000

Model versions:
Sprint SX: (road version from 1973 with electronic starter) as all-around enduro
Sprint ERS: as dirt-bike with 4-speed transmission and solenoid ignition
CRS und CRTT: racing versions 4,575 of the SS 350 models were sold in the first year of manufacture (1969).

Minibikes and Small Motorcycles

Alarmed by the increasing success of the sweetly purring Japanese-produced minibikes and mopeds, particularly the Hondas, Harley-Davidson realized that its market position in its own country, which was already threatened, was in serious danger. Its stake in Aermacchi gave the company the chance to enter the field of light-weight motorcycles — a strategic alliance that in the end totally backfired for Harley.

Initially, though, Harley made use of the Italian connection, in 1965 launching 3 cubic inch (50 cc) small bikes: the M 50, with its rather demure "ladies look" styling and the somewhat more masculine M 50 S (Sport).

In 1967 these were replaced by the more attractive and more powerful 4 cubic inch (65 cc) M 65 and M 65 S mopeds, later marketed under the exotic-sounding name "Leggero." However, sales were miserable and by the end virtually half the total production was being stockpiled and the small bikes were being sold at giveaway prices.

The dealers soon realized what the customers really wanted and clamored for a change in company model policies: the demand was for sporting leisure bikes which could also be used off-road. The first effort to meet this demand led to two peculiar hybrid models which stood in stark contrast to the Harley mystique. These were the

1972 Shortster — almost a real motorbike, but because of its size it was depicted in the ads being ridden over extreme terrain by fun-loving young people, and the X 90 (and the offroad version the TX), a strange-looking minibike which ironically became the most popular means of transport around the pit lane and motorhomes at race tracks. These two machines disappeared after two years and no one shed too many tears over their demise.

The X 90 became one of Harley-Davidson's most popular minibikes.

M 50, 1965–1966

M 50 S, 1965–1966

M 65 (Leggero), 1970–1971

M 65 (Leggero), 1972

All photos of this model series on this double page-spread are © Harley–Davidson

R 100 (Baja), 1973

X 90 (Minibike)

Z 90, 1973

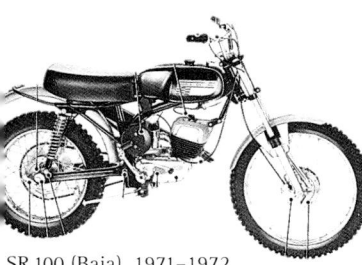

SR 100 (Baja), 1971–1972

MC 65 (Minibike), 1972

go beyond 3-D with H-D

Model:	**M 50**
Years of manufacture:	1965–1966
Engine:	Single–cylinder two–stroke
Displacement:	3.03 cu in (49.66 cc)
Bore x stroke:	1.53 x 1.65 in (38.8 x 42 mm)
Compression ratio:	10 : 1
Power output:	0.9 hp
Transmission:	Three–speed
Fuel capacity:	1.6 gal
Price:	$225

Model:	**M 65**
Years of manufacture:	1967–1970
Engine:	Single–cylinder two–stroke
Displacement:	3.89 cu in (63.86 cc)
Bore x stroke:	1.73 x 1.65 in (44 x 42 mm)
Compression ratio:	9 : 1
Power output:	1.4 hp
Transmission:	Three–speed
Fuel capacity:	1.6 gal
Price:	$230

Special versions:
Both models were available in an S (sports) version, which was slightly lighter and had a larger tank and a covered frame. A total of only 9,000 were made.

Discover new dimensions on live-action lightweights from Harley-Davidson. Like this hot, new M-65. And Harley-Davidson has real depth, from 65cc all the way up to 1200cc . . . all at prices that let you make the move. Check the Yellow Pages for your H-D dealer and add a new dimension to your life. It's time to move up to H-D!

HARLEY DAVIDSON

© Harley–Davidson

The Harley minibikes with 50 cc and 65 cc engines were available in open design and as closed sports models (left).

Courtesy of: Harley-Davidson Museum, York, Pennsylvania

MSR 100, ML 125, 125 SS, 250 SX, Baja, Rapido and Others

The long era of the Harley-Davidson two-stroke began in 1948 with the DKW copy called the 125 Model S and the association with Aermacchi gave new impetus to the production of small motorbikes. However, work was totally relocated to Varese in Italy from the mid-1960s onwards. After a fairly unhappy introduction to the minibike sector, Aermacchi Harley-Davidson now launched a whole range of lightweight two-stroke machines which, it was hoped, would make inroads, above all into the sales of the incredibly successful Yamaha DT 1. They did not achieve this goal, however.

The range was too varied, too confused and changed too often. All the 125, 175 and 250 cc models were available in numerous roadgoing versions (SS) and offroad versions (SX, TX, MX) for trial, endurance and motocross, while the somewhat careless use of the letters S, M and R — sometimes signifying "street," sometimes "sport" — inevitably led to a certain amount of confusion. Basically, however, most of the two-stroke models were intended for off-road rather than everyday use. When Aermacchi was sold in 1978, production of two-strokes by Harley-Davidson came to an end.

The sports version of the 125 cc was characterized by a longer fork, higher handlebars, a raised exhaust and cleat-profiled tires.

125 SS, 1975–1976

125 SX, 1975–1976

TX 125, 1973

MLS 125 Rapido

Life begins at 125...

The hard-sell for the all-around two-strokes, intended above all as sporty runarounds for young people. A 125 MLS, here in its civilian street form.

Courtesy of: Willi's Motorcycle World, Daytona Beach, Florida

Type:	**MSR 100 Baja**
Years of manufacture:	1970–1974
Engine:	Single–cylinder two–stroke
Displacement:	5.98 cu in (98 cc)
Bore x stroke:	1.97 x 1.97 in (50 x 50 mm)
Compression ratio:	9.5 : 1
Power output:	11 hp
Transmission:	Five-speed
Front tire:	3.00 x 21
Rear tire:	3.50 x 18
Fuel capacity:	2.5 gal
Price:	$670

Type:	**ML 125 Rapido**
Years of manufacture:	1968–1972
Engine:	Single–cylinder two–stroke
Displacement:	7.53 cu in (124 cc)
Bore x stroke:	2.21 x 1.97 in (56 x 50 mm)
Compression ratio:	7.65 : 1
Power output:	13 hp
Transmission:	Four-speed
Front tire:	3.00 x 18
Rear tire:	3.50 x 18
Fuel capacity:	2.5 gal
Price:	$395

Special versions:
Also as standard, street (S) and trial models

Type:	**125 SS**
Years of manufacture:	1973–1975
Engine:	Single–cylinder two–stroke
Displacement:	7.53 cu in (124 cc)
Bore x stroke:	2.21 x 1.97 in (56 x 50 mm)
Compression ratio:	10.8 : 1
Power output:	13 hp
Transmission:	Five-speed
Front tire:	3.00 x 19
Rear tire:	3.50 x 18
Fuel capacity:	2.8 gal
Price:	N/A (c. $800)

Special versions: Also as TX, SXT (Enduro

Type:	**250 SS/SX**
Years of manufacture:	1973–1975
Engine:	Single–cylinder two–stroke
Displacement:	14.8 cu in (243 cc)
Bore x stroke:	2.84 x 2.35 in (72 x 59.6 mm)
Compression ratio:	10.3 : 1
Power output:	16 hp
Transmission:	Five-speed
Front tire:	3.00 x 21
Rear tire:	400 x 18
Fuel capacity:	2.8 gal
Price:	$1,130

Special versions:
Also as SX 175 (1974), MX (Motocross) 1977/78: SX/SST 350 model with increased cubic capacity with 80 mm bore and 68 mm piston stroke as Enduro and road machines with 26 hp power output.

MLS 125 Rapido

MLS 125 Rapido

ML 125 Rapido, 1970–72 (road version)

All photos of this G: model series on this double page-spread © Harley-Davidson

Not So Trendy: the Topper Scooter

Not very fast, not particularly good-looking and not exactly cheap, the only scooter ever built by Harley did not enjoy a great deal of success. The machine, with a 10 cubic inch (165 cc) two-stroke engine generating a meager 9 horsepower and driven by an automatic belt drive, was no match for the popular scooters made by Cushman, Vespa or Lambretta. The much-fêted Topper scooter did not fit in either with the spirit of the times or with Harley's usual marketing philosophy. Between 1960 and 1965 a mere 3,000 of them were manufactured – far too few to cover the development and production costs.

Large numbers of Toppers waiting to be delivered.

The standard model of the Topper scooter.

© Harley-Davidson

Harley placed great value on marketing the Topper as an all-arounder by means of special brochures. Shown here is a sidecar combination suitable both for deliveries and for passenger transportation.

TOPPER H MOTOR SCOOTER AND "UTILITY BOX"
Build your profits . . . cut delivery operating costs with a Harley-Davidson TOPPER H and Utility Box. This compact toter has more than 5 cubic feet of cargo space capable of handling 200 lbs. of payload. It offers widespread application to all types of industry, delivery, courier, messenger and service work. Low initial cost and gasoline mileage of up to 100 M.P.G. will save you money on every job. Best of all, it's easy to ride, easy to park and glides through traffic. Call your Harley-Davidson dealer for a free demonstration.

TOPPER H MOTOR SCOOTER AND "SIDECAR"
Every member of your family will find the TOPPER H with a Harley-Davidson Sidecar the "greatest"! It's swell for commuting, errands and outings. You can take along a passenger in padded comfort or use it to carry groceries and packages on shopping trips. This handy combination will hold golf clubs, fishing and hunting gear, or any fun equipment. Get fun transportation with a practical side! Get TOPPER H with Sidecar! It's the economical way to get to work, school, the store, wherever you want to go.

The engine was started from the seat console by pulling on the cable control.

The speedometer was mounted forwards and integrated in the front paneling

Type:	**Topper Scooter**
Model:	AU/AH (1960 only: Model A)
Years of manufacture:	1960–1965
Engine:	Air–cooled single–cylinder two–stroke
Displacement:	10 cu in (165 cc)
Bore x stroke:	2.375 x 2.281 in (60 x 58 mm)
Compression ratio:	6.6 : 1 (Model AH: 8 : 1)
Power output:	6 hp (AU), 9 hp (AH)
Transmission:	Scootaway Drive Variomatik
Primary drive:	Graduated automatic
Final drive:	Chain
Battery:	6 volt
Ignition:	Battery–coil
Frame:	Steel frame with fiberglass bodywork
Front brake:	Drum
Rear brake:	Drum
Front suspension:	Shock absorber swingarm
Rear suspension:	Swingarm
Fuel capacity:	1.7 gal
Tires:	4.00 x 12
Price:	$430–$600 (from 1960–1965)
Model versions:	The Topper had a special sidecar either to carry a person or for use as a "utility box."

Harley's New Premium Engine – the Shovelhead

From 1966 onwards, the (initially unchanged) lower section of the Panhead engine was equipped with new cylinder-heads which bore a certain resemblance to those already fitted in the XL Sportster model built in 1957. The 74 cubic inch (1200 cc) engine yielded 54 horsepower in the FL model and 60 horsepower in the higher-compression FLH model – 5 horsepower more than the previous Panhead engine. The Shovelhead was also subject to less vibration and accelerated better. This was partly due to the Tillotson carburetor, which was equipped with a choke for improving cold starts. Other new features were a new oil pump and corresponding oil–pressure warning lamp. The generator and ignition system were integrated in a new crankcase in 1968. The Shovelhead also became available in an 80 cubic inch (1340) version in 1978 as the FLH. It was fitted with electronic V–Fire ignition in 1980 for the Tour Glide, and with the V–Fire II ignition in 1981. The only major problem back then was unleaded gasoline. The Shovelhead was replaced by the new generation of engine Evolution in 1984.

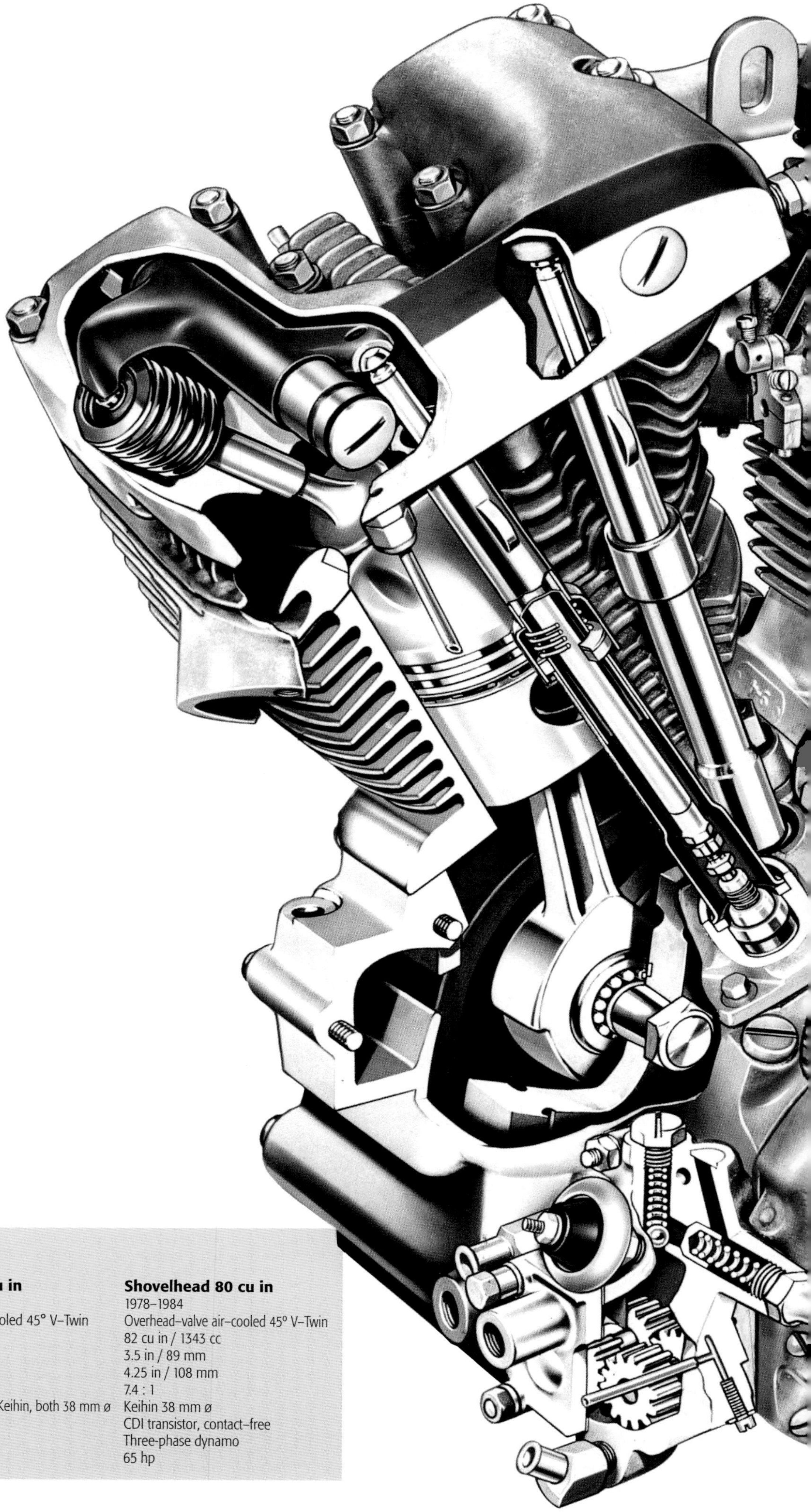

The Shovelhead Engine

	Early Shovel 1200 cc	Shovelhead 74 cu in	Shovelhead 80 cu in
Years of manufacture:	1966–1969	1970–1980	1978–1984
Engine:	Overhead–valve air–cooled 45° V–Twin	Overhead–valve air–cooled 45° V–Twin	Overhead–valve air–cooled 45° V–Twin
Displacement:	73,66 cu in / 1212 cc	73,66 cu in / 1212 cc	82 cu in / 1343 cc
Bore:	3.425 in / 87 mm	3.425 in / 87 mm	3.5 in / 89 mm
Stroke:	4.02 in / 102 mm	4.02 in / 102 mm	4.25 in / 108 mm
Compression ratio:	FL 7,25 : 1 / FLH 8 : 1	8 : 1	7.4 : 1
Carburetor:	Tillotson 38 mm ø	Bendix, then from 1976 Keihin, both 38 mm ø	Keihin 38 mm ø
Ignition:	Battery–coil	Battery–coil	CDI transistor, contact–free
Generation of current:	D.C.electric generator	Alternator	Three-phase dynamo
Power output:	60 hp (FL: 58)	66 hp	65 hp

1968
OIL
PUMP
KEY
PRESSURE OIL
LOW PRESSURE
OIL AND VAPOR

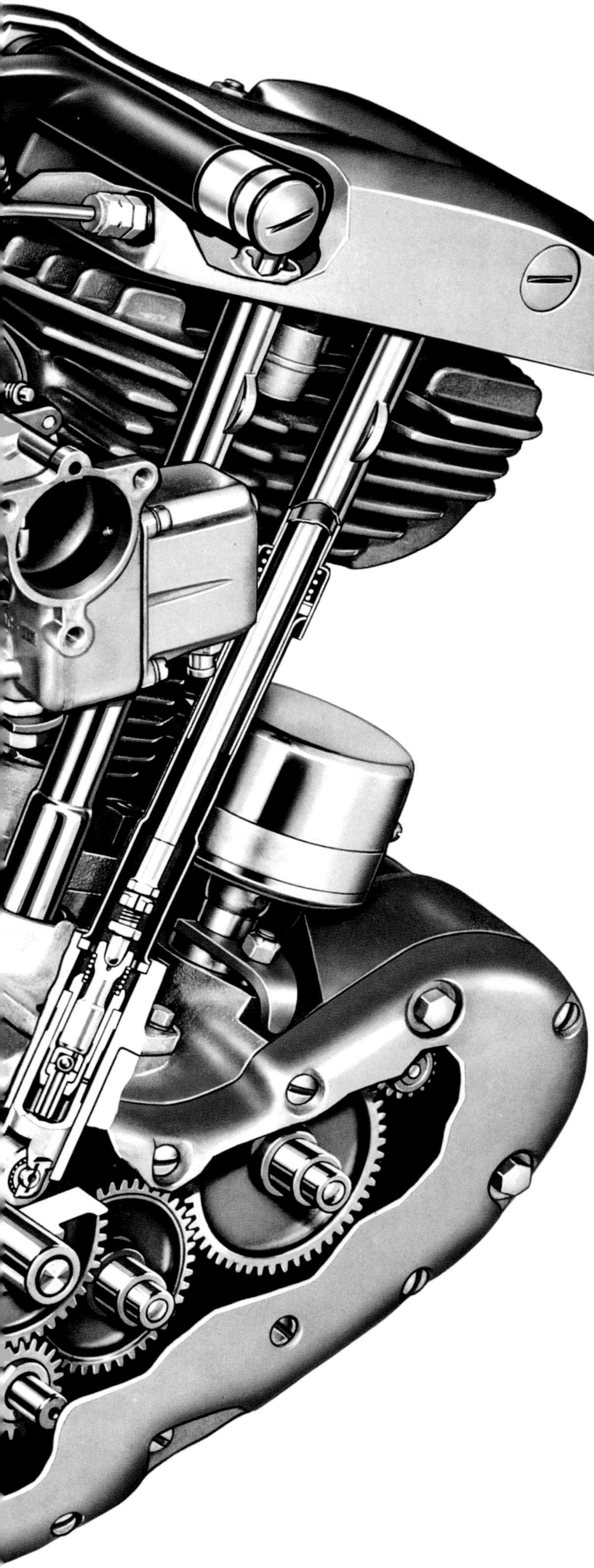

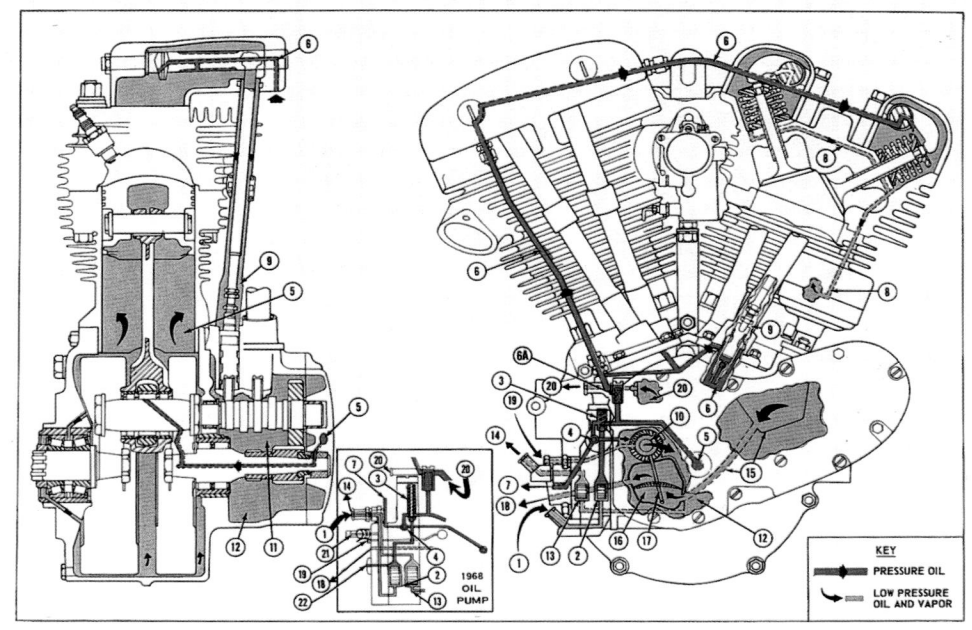

Figure 3A-3. Electra-Glide Lubrication System

© Harley-Davidson

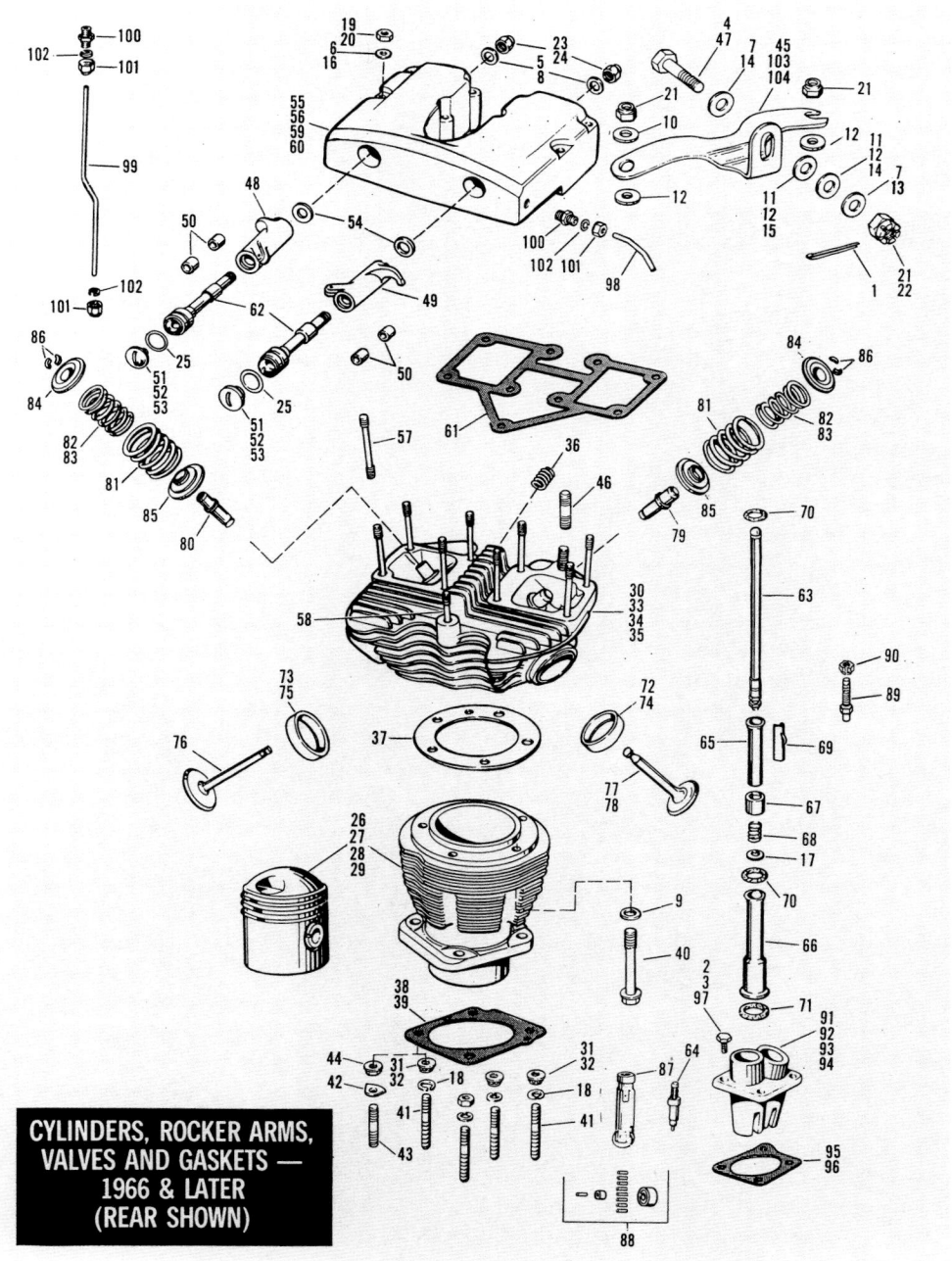

CYLINDERS, ROCKER ARMS,
VALVES AND GASKETS —
1966 & LATER
(REAR SHOWN)

© Harley-Davidson

The FL and FLH Electra Glide – the Shovelhead

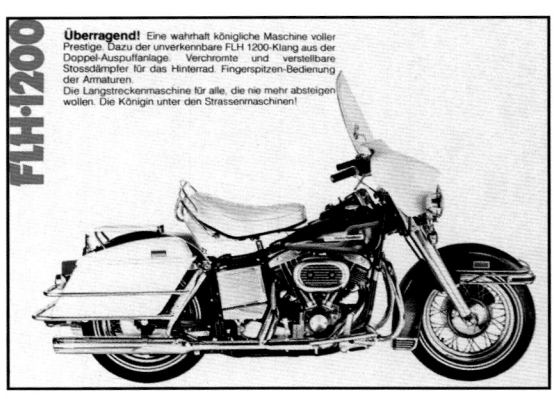

After the Electra Glide had gotten heavier due to its conversion to 12 volt electrics, it finally got a long-overdue new and more powerful engine in 1966. However, chiefly for reasons of cost, the significant improvements initially were confined to the top end. The roughly 10 percent improvement in performance was achieved by newly designed aluminum cylinder heads with reworked fins, higher compression pistons and a different camshaft with longer breathing times. Since the characteristic shape of the cylinder head rocker boxes, which had been copied from the XL Sportster, was spade-like in appearance, Harley fans soon dubbed the engine the Shovelhead.

At first, the lower end remained unchanged from the old Panhead engine, with the generator on the front and the distributor on the crankcase, and this series is called the Early Shovel by experts. It was not until the year 1970 that the engine was wholly changed with the introduction of a new lower end in which the distributor was replaced by a modern alternator, fitted inside the primary case. The voltage regulator remained, given its function, on the outside. The ignition system with the contact breaker and capacitor were also moved to the right-hand side directly over the crankshaft. The first models equipped with the new Shovelhead engine were the Electra Glide FL Super Solo and the Electra Glide FLH Super Sport with an additional B used to designate a hand-operated gear change and FB to indicate foot-operated gear change.

The standard FL at first generated 54, and later 57 horsepower, while the FLH with its slightly higher compression generated first 60, then later 62 horsepower. Both models were initially equipped with a Linkert DC carburetor and later with Tillotson, then Bendix and finally with the Japanese Keihin carburetor.

A wide range of accessories was available for both models, mostly grouped into two ranges: the Chrome Finish range with chrome-plated parts, covers and bars, and the King of the Highway range, along with special luxury extras such as the Buddy Seat, crash bars, chrome covers, fiberglass saddlebags, turn signals and panniers, and also Plexiglas windshields with lower halves tinted blue, green or red. On top of all this, one could, thanks to the many parts and accessories available as "optimal custom features," turn the Electra Glide into a Dresser or Full Dresser. It was not until the 1970s that Harley-Davidson itself moved in this direction with the introduction of the Classic, though even this ultimate tourer still left room for plenty of additional accessories.

A serious problem at the time, however, were the many production faults which cropped up particularly in the early 1970s under the new AMF regime and threatened Harley-Davidson's previous reputation for good quality control and reliability.

In 1978, the more powerful 80 cubic inch (1340 cc) version of the Shovelhead was introduced in the Electra Glide Classic, as an alternative to the 74 inch (1200 cc) engine. The engine, with a compression ratio of 8:1, generated 65 horsepower and had an electronic, contact-free ignition system. Although it was actually only 1311 cc in capacity, it was marketed internationally as a 1340 cc machine. In 1983, the FLHC 80 Electra Glide Classic was developed from the FLH 80 and in 1983, the final year before the introduction of the Evolution engine, the FLHT Electra Glide 80 and the FLHTC Electra Glide Classic appeared.

The Shovelhead Electra Glide Family

Years	Model	
1966–1969	**FL/FLH**	"Early Shovel" Electra Glide
1970–1980	**FL/FLH**	Electra Glide
1979–1981	**FLHS**	Electra Glide Sport (U.S. only)
1979–1982	**FLH 80**	Electra Glide
1978–1982	**FLH 80/FLHC 80**	Electra Glide Classic
1983–1984	**FLH 80**	Electra Glide
1983	**FLHT 80**	Electra Glide
1983	**FLHTC 80**	Electra Glide Classic
1984	**FLHX 80**	Special Edition

Typical of the early Shovelhead FLH was the timing cover in front of the generator.

The new fuel-tank console, aluminum lamp housing and handlebar attachment are typical design features of the early FLH model.

Type:	**FL/FLH Early Shovel**
Model:	**Electra Glide**
Years of manufacture:	1966–1969
Engine:	Air-cooled four-stroke overhead-valve 45° V–Twin
Displacement:	73.63 cu in (1206.39 cc)
Bore x stroke:	3.438 x 3.969 in (87.31 x 100.8 mm)
Compression ratio:	8 : 1 (FL 7.5 : 1)
Power output:	60 hp (FL: 58)
Carburetor:	Tillotson 38 mm ø
Transmission:	Four-speed
Primary drive:	Duplex chain
Final drive:	Chain
Battery:	12 volt
Ignition:	Battery–coil
Frame:	Tubular steel cradle (double downtube)
Front brake:	Drum
Rear brake:	Drum
Front suspension:	Telescopic fork
Rear suspension:	Twin-shock–absorber swingarm
Wheelbase:	60 in
Weight:	781 lb (standard)
Fuel capacity:	5 gal
Oil capacity:	4 qts
Front tire:	5.00 x 16
Rear tire:	5.00 x 16
Top speed:	100 mph
Price:	1966: $1,610; 1969: $1,900
Model versions:	FL Electra Glide Super Solo, also as police version with special "Police Groups and Equipment" accessories.

Type:	**FLH Shovelhead**
Model:	**Electra Glide**
Years of manufacture:	1970–1980
Engine:	Air-cooled four-stroke overhead-valve 45° V–Twin
Displacement:	73.63 cu in (1206.39 cc)
Bore x stroke:	3.438 x 3.969 in (87.31 x 100.8 mm)
Compression ratio:	8 : 1
Power output:	66 hp
Carburetor:	Bendix, then from 1976 Keihin, both 38 mm ø
Transmission:	Four-speed
Primary drive:	Duplex chain
Final drive:	Chain
Battery:	12 volt
Ignition:	Battery–coil
Frame:	Tubular steel cradle (single downtube)
Front brake:	Disc from 1972
Rear brake:	Drum
Front suspension:	Telescopic fork
Rear suspension:	Twin-shock–absorber swingarm
Wheelbase:	61.5 in
Weight:	781 lb (standard)
Fuel capacity:	5 gal
Oil capacity:	4 qts
Front tire:	5.00 x 16
Rear tire:	5.00 x 16
Top speed:	100 mph
Price:	$2,500
Model versions:	See box/appendix For the sidecar version the gearbox had three forward gears and a reverse gear.

205

FLT Shovelhead Tour Glide

In the year 1980 Harley-Davidson introduced a completely new re-engineered tourer to its heavyweight class: the FLT 80 Tour Glide. The bulky fairing and uncharacteristic double headlights gave it a somewhat front-heavy appearance.

However, appearances can be deceptive and in fact it was marvelously easy to steer: due to its innovative geometry the Erik Buell-designed frame handled significantly better. The steering head was set at an extreme 65 degree angle, while the telescopic forks were offset by three degrees from the steering head at an angle of 62 degrees. This daring design lived up to expectations, being easy to steer and at the same time offering good directional stability.

The frame-mounted fairing provided additional stability, while the powerful, rubber-mounted 80 cubic inch (1340 cc) Shovelhead kept its vibrations to itself — the familiar shaking and rattling and that tingling sensation in the soles of the feet as they rested on the wide footrests all belonged to the past.

Another new development was the gearbox, with an overdrive fifth gear which meant that the engine barely exceeded 3000 rpm even during high-speed cruising. The fully-enclosed drive chain purred smoothly in its oil bath.

Although the Tour Glide's engineering pointed the way to the future development of Harley-Davidson motorcycles, many fans of classic Harley design rejected the FLT due to its atypical and somewhat out-of-proportion overall appearance. On both sides of the Atlantic it proved difficult to shift from the showrooms.

A number of the improvements which were incorporated were also added to the various Electra Glide models in 1983. The T stood for "Touring" in the FLHT and FLHTC of that year, which were the last machines to use the 80 cubic inch Shovelhead engine.

© Harley–Davidson

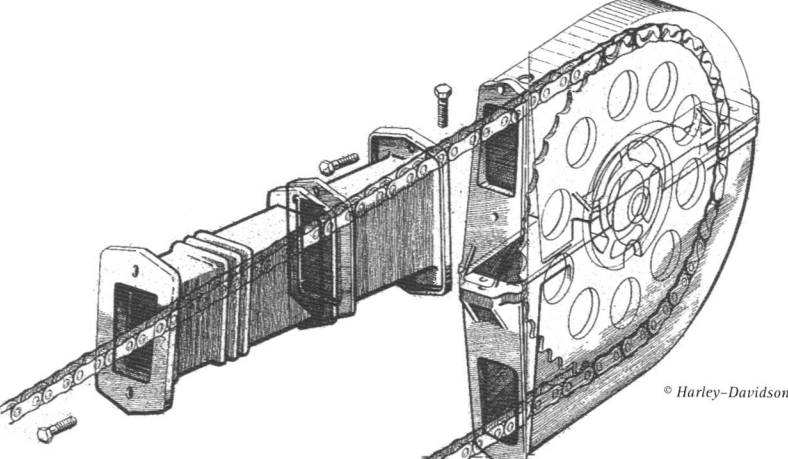

The FLTC with the 80 cubic inch (1340 cc) engine and a rather large cockpit with twin headlights from 1983. The chain was enclosed to protect it from dust and oil, as shown in the drawing on the left.

© Harley-Davidson

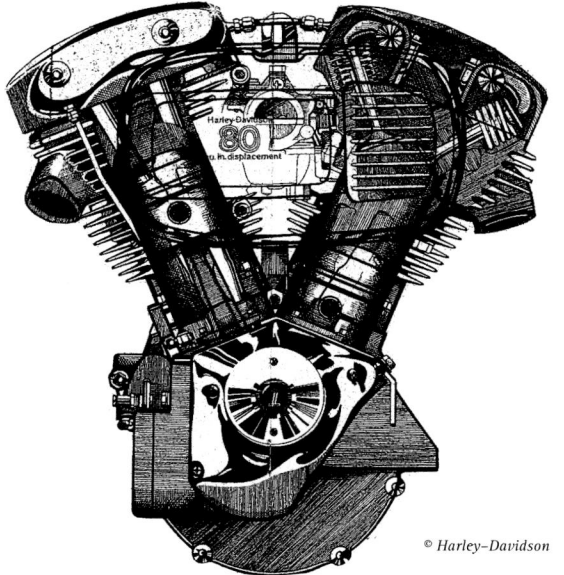

© Harley–Davidson

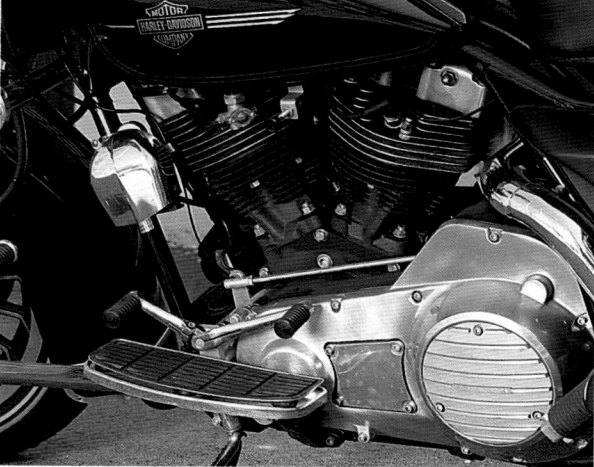

Presented purely as a detail: the new frame design with the forward–displaced steering head of the FLT provided for particularly stable road handling.

© Harley–Davidson

Type:	**FLT Shovelhead**
Model:	**Tour Glide**
Years of manufacture:	1980–83
Engine:	Overhead-valve air-cooled four-stroke 45° V–Twin
Cubic capacity:	82 cu in (1343 cc)
Bore x stroke:	3.5 x 4.25 in (89 x 108 mm)
Compression ratio:	7.4 : 1
Power output:	65 hp
Carburetor:	Keihin 38 mm Ø
Transmission:	Five–speed gearbox
Primary drive:	Duplex chain
Final drive:	Chain
Battery:	12 volt
Ignition:	CDI transistor, contact–free
Frame:	Single tube tubular steel cradle
Front brake:	Double disc
Rear brake:	Disc
Front suspension:	Telescopic fork
Rear suspension:	Twin shock absorber swingarm
Wheelbase:	62.5 in
Weight:	780 lbs (standard)
Fuel capacity:	5 gal
Oil capacity:	4 qts
Front tire:	5.00 x 16
Rear tire:	5.00 x 16
Top Speed:	95 mph
Cost:	$6,961
Model variants:	Also available with special equipment as FLTC Tour Glide Classic.

The Shovelhead Tour Glide Family

1980-1983	**FLT 80** Tour-Glide
1980-1983	**FLTC 80** Tour-Glide Classic

Working in conjunction with the elastomer mounts are two aircraft-type balljoint sta... on the same ... allowing th... absorb roa... while main... alignment.

... torque ... damp ...

... ener isolati ... and r ... and s ... dema

FLT TOUR GLIDE.

FLT TOUR-GLIDE CHASSIS CONFIGURATION

2½ sq. x 1.25

1⅛ x .095

25° rake

ADJUST TOP STABILIZER SO WHEELS ARE 90° TO GROUND WITHIN ±1° WITH FRONT WHEEL IN STRAIGHT AHEAD POSITION

FLT CHASSIS – FRONT VIEW ELASTOMER MOUNT LOCATION

ENGINE MOUNT

ELASTOMER TRI-MOUNT SYSTEM SWING ARM ASSEMBLY

Stabilizer
bilizer to Frame

ELASTOMER HOUSING

TRIANGULATED SWINGARM AXLE SUPPORT

SLOT

"FLT" FRAME

REAR SWING ARM — EXPLODED VIEW

1. Swing arm
2. Washer
3. Plastic ring
4. Clevebloc assy.
5. Tolerance ring
6. Nylon washer
7. Rubber mount
8. Pivot shaft
9. Washer - right side
10. Nut
11. Washer - left side

The classic design of the Tour Glide (FLTC) which is provided with additional round instrument dials on the left and right of the cockpit paneling (left).

Courtesy of: H.D. Archives

FLTC-Tour Glide Classic

© Harley–Davidson

The FX Super Glide – Harley's First Custom Bike

At the end of the 1960s America was in an extraordinary state of social and political turmoil. The Vietnam war was at its height and at home a generation of rebellious students and others made for troubled times. Woodstock became the symbol of the peaceful protests of the Hippie movement, and the film "Easy Rider" was emblematic of young people thirsting for freedom. Naturally the motorbikes ridden by the two charismatic heroes of the film were Harleys, but they were wild, extreme choppers rather than original factory machines.

Finally the Harley bosses in Milwaukee caught on to the spirit of the times. The outdated and conservative mindset which dictated that any motorbike rider on a custom bike was to be demonized as a dangerous outlaw was swept away by the new AMF management, and the company listened to customer wishes for the first time. Chief Designer Willie G. Davidson had a pretty good idea what the public wanted, having attended numerous biker parties and motorbike rallies in order to familiarize himself with the new trends, particularly in California.

Thus in 1971 Harley-Davidson brought out its first custom bike, designed by Willie G., an imposing cruiser called the Super Glide, bristling with "Easy Rider" mystique and patriotic symbolism. The red, white and blue color scheme and the language used to describe it betrayed much about the new mentality: the advertising proclaimed it the "All American Freedom Machine," while bikers gave it romantic names such as "Midnight Express" or "Night Train."

The marketing strategy was slick and well-thought-out and fitted in well with the existing Harley program. The new FX 1200 Super Glide was a successful combination of the narrow Sportster front end with a 19-inch, and later 21-inch, front wheel joined to the solid Electra Glide frame and a wide 16-inch rear wheel, driven by Harley's most powerful 74 cubic inch (1200 cc) Shovelhead engine. At 3.5 gallons the gas tank was also restyled and the bike was fitted with a kickstarter, obviating the need for a heavy battery. The extravagant fiberglass "boat tail" elongated seat was not popular and was replaced the following year by an elegant fender and standard seat. The tank was also replaced by a slimmer, more stylish one in 1973 and the FX then became a smash hit. In 1974 it was fitted with an electric starter and from then on the designation for this version was FXE.

The Super Glide was the first of a whole range of new custom models which, despite initial misgivings on the part of the company management, turned out to be the most successful Harley-Davidsons ever. Willie G. had been right all along...

Pure patriotism: the deep-blue "darkened" version of Willie G's first Super Glide — Night Train.

Courtesy of: Max Middelbosch, Zwolle, Netherlands

The first custom model designed by Willie G. was the 1200 cc FX with the characteristic boat-tail.

© Harley-Davidson

The stylistically more fortunate version of the FXE Super Glide in 1975.

© Harley-Davidson

Type:	**FX/FXE Shovelhead**
Model:	**Super Glide**
Years of manufacture:	1971–1980
Engine:	Air-cooled four-stroke overhead-valve 45° V-Twin
Displacement:	73.63 cu in (1206.39 cc)
Bore x stroke:	3.438 x 3.969 in (87.31 x 100.8 mm)
Compression ratio:	8 : 1
Power output:	58/65 hp
Carburetor:	Bendix, from 1976 Keihin, both 38 mm ∅
Transmission:	Four-speed (FX kickstart only)
Primary drive:	Duplex chain
Final drive:	Chain
Battery:	12 volt
Ignition:	Battery-coil
Frame:	Tubular steel cradle (double downtube)
Front brake:	Drum, from 1972 disc (later dual disc)
Rear brake:	Drum, from 1972 disc
Front suspension:	Telescopic fork
Rear suspension:	Twin-shock-absorber swingarm
Wheelbase:	62 in
Weight:	559 lb
Fuel capacity:	3.5 gal
Oil capacity:	4 qts
Front tire:	3.50 x 19
Rear tire:	5.00 x 16
Top speed:	110 mph
Price:	$2,500
Model versions:	See box and appendix

The Shovelhead FX Super Glide Family

1971–1980	**FX/FXE 1200**	Super Glide
1981–1983	**FXE 80**	Super Glide
1977–1979	**FXS 1200**	Low Rider
1980–1982	**FXS 80**	Low Rider
1979	**FXEF**	1200 Fat Bob
1980–1982	**FXEF 80**	Fat Bob
1980–1982	**FXB 80**	Sturgis
1983	**FXSB 80**	Low Rider Belt
1980–1983	**FXWG 80**	Wide Glide
1983	**FXDC 80**	"Disc Glide" Wide Glide
1982–1983	**FXR 80 / FXRS 80**	Super Glide II/De Luxe
1983	**FXRT 80**	Sport Glide

The typical fiberglass boat-tail of the first FX, shown here is an "All American Freedom Machine" finished in red, white and blue, cannot conceal its origins at the former boat factory in Tomahawk.

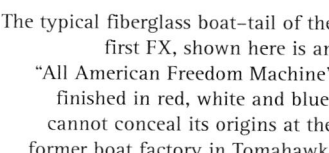

Almost an original: the 1976 FX Super Glide, with the only modification being a baggage rack from the parts and accessories range.

The Smash Hit

The FXS Low Rider was the second attempt by Willie G. Davidson and his crew to meet the enormous public demand for custom bikes. Although made using many standard Harley parts, the Low Rider came across as a unified whole – a genuine highway cruiser with the modern, universally popular, soft-chopper look. It had the typical very low 27-inch seat position which, for the rider at least, was extremely comfortable: leaning back slightly with his feet stretched forward and supported by the extra foot rests – "highway pegs" – and with a secure grip on the angled handlebars. From this position you could enjoy the ride in true "Easy Rider" fashion, with your face in the wind rather than over the gas tank. A powerful engine was added to this, at first the tried and trusted 74 cubic inch (1200 cc) Shovelhead, and later the 80 cubic inch (1340 cc) version, which curiously has always been marketed in cubic inches. Add to this the plump Fat Bob gas tank, the somewhat flatter Showa forks and the massive two-in-one exhaust and you had a successful overall package.

Opinions were sharply divided about the cast alloy wheels, but at least they were practical. The combination of electric starter and old-style kickstarter, on the other hand, was regarded as ideal. The double disc brakes on the front wheel were well up to the task of briskly stopping the 574-pound monster. In its first year on the market 3,742 Low Riders were sold, the following year the figure rose to 9,787 and by 1980, when the larger and more powerful 80 cubic inch engine was introduced, factory customs made up almost half of Harley's total sales. Their huge success had broken all records and not surprisingly meant that Willie G. Davidson and his design team got the green light for any future custom ideas. Of course a huge range of accessories were also available for this model. The Low Rider (a trademarked name) became the new symbol of the Harley customizing scene and Harley's suspicion of the custom "outlaws" was finally laid to rest.

Type:	**FXS Shovelhead**
Model:	**Low Rider**
Years of manufacture:	1977–1982
Engine:	Air-cooled four-stroke overhead-valve 45° V-Twin
Displacement:	73.63 cu in (1206.39 cc) (from 81.65 cu in, 1338 cc)
Bore x stroke:	3.438 x 3.969 in (87.31 x 100.8 mm) (from 1980 3.5 x 4.25 in, 89 x 108)
Compression ratio:	8 : 1 (from 1980 7.4 : 1)
Power output:	58 hp
Carburetor:	Keihin 38 mm ø
Transmission:	Four-speed
Primary drive:	Duplex chain
Final drive:	Chain
Battery:	12 volt
Ignition:	Battery-coil (from 1980 contactless electronic starter)
Frame:	Tubular steel cradle (double down...)
Front brake:	Dual disc
Rear brake:	Disc
Front suspension:	Telescopic fork
Rear suspension:	Twin-shock-absorber swingarm
Wheelbase:	63.5 in
Weight:	574 lb
Fuel capacity:	3.5 gal/4 gal
Oil capacity:	4 qts
Front tire:	3.25 x 19
Rear tire:	5.00 x 16
Top speed:	102 mph
Price:	$3,475
Model versions:	In 1984, still with the 80 cubic i... Shovelhead engine, the FXSB w... final belt drive.

The successful FXS Low Rider used a secondary drivechain until 1982. Also available in 1983 and 1984 – before the introduction of the Evo models – as the FXSB Low Rider, sporting the new toothed belt drive system.

The Fat Bob

The third Harley-Davidson custom to appear on the market was the FXEF Fat Bob. Though very similar to the FXE, it was indeed the burly member of the family, with a wider gas tank, high buckhorn handlebars, deep seats and an engine oozing torque.

The Fat Bob met the almost indecent demand of some riders to feel as close as possible to the heavy engine, with all the positive and negative associations that has – a machine for rough, tough, macho types, of whom there turned out to be an astonishing number. Despite an annual production of around 5,000, the Fat Bobs always sold like hot cakes.

In 1979, their first year, the 74 cubic inch (1200 cc) engine was available as an option, but thereafter it only came with the 80 cubic inch (1340 cc) Shovelhead. Like the Low Rider, the Fat Bob had the characteristic two-in-one exhaust (which later underwent slight modification). The nine-spoke alloy front wheel, compulsory in the U.S., could be exchanged for an original wheel with wire spokes. The kickstarter had been wholly superseded by an electric starter, which was now apparently totally reliable. Like the Low Rider, the Fat Bob's owners often fitted the bike with front-mounted footrests obtained from accessories retailers (so-called "highway pegs") – an option which Harley itself quickly added to its range of extras. The laid-back highway feeling was in...

Type:	**FXEF Shovelhead**
Model:	**Fat Bob**
Years of manufacture:	1979–1982
Engine:	Air-cooled four-stroke overhead-valve 45° V-Twin
Displacement:	81.65 cu in* (1338 cc)
Bore x stroke:	3.5 x 4.25 in (89 x 108 mm)
Compression ratio:	7.4 : 1
Power output:	58 hp
Carburetor:	Keihin 38 mm ø
Transmission:	Four-speed
Primary drive:	Duplex chain
Final drive:	Chain
Battery:	12 volt
Ignition:	Contactless electronic
Frame:	Tubular steel cradle (double downtube)
Front brake:	Dual disc
Rear brake:	Disc
Front suspension:	Telescopic fork
Rear suspension:	Twin-shock-absorber swingarm
Wheelbase:	62.6 in (63.5 in)
Weight:	638 lb
Fuel capacity:	4 gal
Oil capacity:	4 qts
Front tire:	3.50 x 19
Rear tire:	5.00 x 16
Top speed:	102 mph
Price:	$4,260 (in 1979)

*The indicated figure has never been published before.

The FXEF Fat Bob, with both primary and secondary chain drive, was supplied with a seat in brown, manmade leather. A typical characteristic is the two-into-one exhaust system, which loops around the ignition cover and extends into an exhaust muffler.

Courtesy of: Jürgen Ritter, Düsseldorf, Germany

211

Shadow of the Night

The idea for the Sturgis model is said to have come to Willie G. Davidson while he was returning from the famous biker gathering in the Black Hills of South Dakota whereupon, legend has it, somewhere out on the road he sketched the idea on a crumpled-up paper bag fished out of a garbage can. Later in Milwaukee he made his vision reality.

The basis of the FXB (the "B" stands for belt) was the Low Rider with its 80 cubic inch (1340 cc) Shovelhead engine, with both the primary and the final drive now fitted with a toothed belt made of Aramid nylon (Polychain) from the Gates Rubber Company. This was a courageous and also forward-looking

combination which, at first anyway, was very much on trial technically speaking. Despite the quiet ride and the belt's supposed durability, the public remained skeptical. After all, a broken belt on the road could be a very serious problem.

A new and longer transmission for the reworked four-speed gearbox did not do much for the acceleration, but did give a very smooth ride. Many parts (though not the engine) were rubber-mounted to absorb vibration, the handlebars were borrowed from the dragster scene, and to the approval of all true bikers, the Sturgis was fitted with a kickstarter as well as an electric one. The two-in-one exhaust was taken

from the Fat Bob, the nine-spoke wheels were new and extra front-mounted footrests (highway pegs) made for a relaxed ride position during long-distance cruising. Apart from this the Sturgis was all black right down to its cylinder ribs — a real night bird and a thoroughly elegant motorcycle. Despite all this, the FXB was never a best seller: in 1980, its first year, 1,470 were sold, the following year 3,543 and in 1982, its final year, just 1,883. Today, however, the Sturgis is much sought after by collectors.

All in black: the Sturgis with Shovelhead engine, dragster handlebars, Fat Bob instruments and two-in-one exhaust system.

While the secondary toothed drive belt proved ever more popular, it still remained a one–off experiment as the primary drive unit on the first Sturgis. The matt–black engine, on the other hand, did not regain popularity until the 1990s.

All photos on this double page-spread are courtesy of H.D. Archives

Type:	**FXB Shovelhead**
Model:	**Sturgis**
Years of manufacture:	1980–1982
Engine:	Air–cooled four–stroke overhead–valve 45º V–Twin
Displacement:	81.65 cu in (1338 cc)
Bore x stroke:	3.5 x 4.25 in (89 x 108 mm)
Compression ratio:	7.4 : 1
Power output:	65 hp
Carburetor:	Keihin 38 mm ø
Transmission:	Four-speed
Primary drive:	Toothed belt
Final drive:	Toothed belt
Battery:	12 volt
Ignition:	Contactless electronic
Frame:	Tubular steel cradle (double downtube)
Front brake:	Dual disc
Rear brake:	Disc
Front suspension:	Telescopic fork
Rear suspension:	Twin–shock–absorber swingarm
Wheelbase:	64.7 in
Weight:	629 lb
Fuel capacity:	4 gal
Oil capacity:	4 qts
Front tire:	3.50 x 19
Rear tire:	5.00 x 16
Top speed:	105 mph
Price:	$5,698

Model versions:
In 1983 the FXSB Low Rider Belt appeared, also fitted with the new twin–belt drive system for both primary and final drive.

The Wild Boy's Bike

Opinions were divided: some bikers said it had to come, others said it was a miracle that it happened at all. The FXWG Wide Glide, up to then the most radical custom creation to emanate from the design department, was an uncompromising acknowledgment of the importance of the once-demonized outlaw scene, now rebadged as the heavily courted and much-fêted "biker lifestyle" clientele.

However, some company hard-liners were highly suspicious of the Wide Glide (a trademarked name), regarding it as too evocative of the "bad boy" image. Due to this, they managed to block its production for a year and a half. However, when it finally appeared on the market, its thrilling embodiment of so many secret obsessions and yearnings of the customers made it one of Harley-Davidson's most successful models.

The Wide Glide's appearance, with its slimmed-down but wider-set FLH forks, its slim 21-inch wheels, the small high-mounted headlight, its extremely low-mounted seat with built-in sissy bar, its bulky five-gallon tank and the front-mounted footrests, brakes and gearshift, unmistakably signaled the breaking of an industry-wide taboo of advanced motorcycle engineering: it was no longer technological progress that was the decisive element but the philosophy, the Harley mystique. Despite all the differences, production-related concessions such as the additional electronic starter and other high-technology components in the frame, engine and equipment ensured that the Wide Glide was a genuine Harley through and through.

The most popular model on the biker scene was the FXWG Wide Glide with the wide, exposed Electra Glide fork, broad fuel-tank and classic Electra Glide instrument panel. The photograph shows the equally famous/infamous Wide Glide Flame edition.

Type:	**FXWG Shovelhead**
Model:	**Wide Glide**
Years of manufacture:	1980–1983
Engine:	Air–cooled four–stroke overhead–valve 45° V–Twin
Displacement:	81.65 cu in* (1338 cc)
Bore x stroke:	3.5 x 4.25 in (89 x 108 mm)
Compression ratio:	7.4 : 1
Power output:	68 hp
Carburetor:	Keihin 38 mm ø
Transmission:	Four–speed
Primary drive:	Duplex chain
Final drive:	Chain
Battery:	12 volt
Ignition:	Contactless electronic
Frame:	Tubular steel cradle (double downtube)
Front brake:	Dual disc
Rear brake:	Disc
Front suspension:	Electra–Glide elongated telescopic fork
Rear suspension:	Twin–shock–absorber swingarm
Wheelbase:	63.8 in
Weight:	585 lb
Fuel capacity:	5 gal
Oil capacity:	4 qts
Front tire:	M 90 x 21
Rear tire:	M 90 x 16
Top speed:	102 mph
Price:	$6,900
Model versions:	The Wide Glide Flame (1982) with special paintwork and flame tank, and the FXDG Disc Glide special edition of 1983.

The indicated figure has never been published before.

All photos on this double page–spread are courtesy of H.D. Archives

The Comfort Cruiser

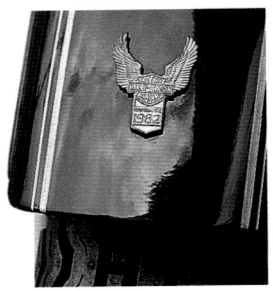

It's 1982 — "The eagle soars alone." Harley-Davidson was once again its own master and the second generation of Super Glides was due to be unveiled in the form of the FXR, the R standing for "rubber," a reference to the fact that the 80 cubic inch (1340 cc) Shovelhead engine was mounted on three "tri-point elastomeric" rubber components. The internal company term for the model was the Rubber Glide, making clear that all FXR models were slimmed-down versions of the FLT Tour Glide.

Due to the fact that the steering head was visible, the frame developed by Erik Buell for the FXRs was somewhat shortened, but the extremely stable, torsion-resistant new frame, stiffened by a variety of steel components, gave the motorcycle a smooth ride and nimble steering. The five-speed gearbox was used

for the FXR, while the rest of the motorbike was largely adopted from the new Super Glide series. All models had instruments, including a new electronic speedometer, mounted on the handlebars and the gas gauge and gas tank cap sat together on a slender console in the middle of the tank.

The very comfortable seat soaked up the last traces of vibration and the rubber footrests were set at an angle to prevent them grounding when the bike was leaned into corners. The FXRS model was equipped with more extras, including front-mounted highway pegs for relaxed cruising.

Both models were available with either spoked or cast wheels. The company, once again wholly independent, was particularly proud of the new Harley-Davidson tank logo now without the addition of the letters "AMF"!

With the third version of this model, the FXRT Sport Glide (a trademarked name), the T standing for Touring, Harley-Davidson almost returned to the old FLT Tour Glide concept — but not quite. The fairing still gave it

a somewhat front-heavy appearance, despite it having been aerodynamically developed in the wind tunnel, the rounded fiberglass saddlebags were considerably smaller (with the tour pack available as an optional extra), the fully-enclosed final drive chain ran with minimal wear in an oil bath and the bike was fitted with tubeless Dunlop Touring Elite tires. The forks used Erik Buell's anti-dive air suspension system. The FXRT, with an 80 cubic inch (1340 cc) Shovelhead engine, was only produced in 1983 in an edition of 1,458 machines, while the Shovelhead FXR (3,065 and 1,069 machines respectively) and the FXRS (3,190 and 1,413) were produced from 1982 to 1983 and they were often supplied from the factory in specially-ordered custom editions.

The standard design of the Super Glide II, which was produced in numerous versions.

Courtesy of: H.D. Archives

Experiment in Free Form

In 1983 Harley-Davidson brought out yet another interesting special custom edition, the Special Edition Twin Belt Wide Glide, with the reference letters FXDG, the DG standing for "Disc Glide" (a trademarked name). Willie G. Davidson called it the "ultimate Wide Glide" and indeed it did offer some highly unconventional combinations and incorporated some ideas that were not taken up again until years later. The Wide Glide, with its FLH fork elongated by 3.5 inches, was fitted with a wide, compact rear wheel contrasting with the slender 21-inch spoked front wheel. It also had the twin belt system, first road-tested on the FXB Sturgis, with toothed belt primary and final drive.

The exclusive package included 3-inch-longer apehanger handlebars, a solo seat with an added passenger seat with padded sissy bar, a high, swept-back, bobbed rear fender and a kickstarter as well as the electronic one which used the tried and trusted V-Fire II ignition

system. A 1919 company logo was emblazoned on the tank and the tool bag and fenders were decorated with medallions.

What stood out most, however, was the contrast between the special black paintwork on the engine, the Super Glide exhaust and the transmission, and the chrome plating of the external parts and trim. Only 810 examples of this remarkable special edition were produced, which sadly was soon forgotten as rapid technological developments left it behind.

© Harley-Davidson

Type:	**FXR Shovelhead**
Model:	**Super Glide II**
Years of manufacture:	1982–1983
Engine:	Air-cooled four-stroke overhead-valve 45° V-Twin
Displacement:	81.65 cu in (1338 cc)
Bore x stroke:	3.5 x 4.25 in (89 x 108 mm)
Compression ratio:	7.4 : 1
Power output:	65 hp
Carburetor:	Keihin 38 mm ø
Transmission:	Five-speed
Primary drive:	Duplex chain
Final drive:	Chain
Battery:	12 volt
Ignition:	Contactless electronic
Frame:	Tubular steel cradle (double downtube)
Front brake:	Dual disc
Rear brake:	Disc
Front suspension:	Telescopic fork
Rear suspension:	Twin-shock-absorber swingarm
Wheelbase:	64.7 in
Weight:	610 lb
Fuel capacity:	3.5 gal
Oil capacity:	4 qts
Front tire:	3.50 x 19
Rear tire:	5.00 x 16
Top speed:	108 mph
Price:	$6,690 (FXRS)
Model versions:	All FXR and FXRS models could be ordered with either metal spoked or cast alloy wheels. The FXRS was available slightly customized with multicolored paintwork, padded sissy bar and extra highway pegs. The FXRT was available with fairing, panniers, and anti-dive fork suspension, as well as fully dressed.

*The indicated figure has never been published before

© Harley-Davidson

The FXRT Sport Glide boasted a cockpit fairing and fiberglass saddlebags.

New Kid on the Block

In the mid–1950s, the general clamor for a new, powerful, two-wheeled plaything had become deafening: young people, whipped up to a frenzy by the newly fashionable V8 hot rods from Ford, Chevrolet and Chrysler, demanded something similar from the sports motorbike sector, and they wanted it now. Milwaukee was on fire again and Harley needed to find something better to set against the racy English twins than the KH Sportster, recently boosted to 54 cubic inches, whose long-stroke side-valve engine had finally reached the end of the road.

Since they had neither time nor money enough to develop a totally new product, Harley-Davidson decided to leave the lower part of the KH engine with its integrated four-speed gearbox essentially unaltered and to concentrate their efforts on a new top end. The cylinder bore was increased from 2.75 inches to 3 inches and the stroke reduced from 4.56 inches to 3.81 inches. Thus the cubic capacity remained at 54 cubic inches (883 cc), but the higher rpm meant an increase in horsepower.

The most important and probably revolutionary innovation, however, was the overhead–valve cylinder head whose enlarged valves now hung down in the semicircular combustion chamber and were each lifted by their own cam. This was known as the four-cam principle. However, the engineers retained the robust, tried and trusted, gray cast iron cylinder heads, which made the XL heavy, but on the other hand highly reliable. The bad experience of the many repairs under warranty needed by the aluminum heads of the first Panheads in 1948 was still fresh in the minds of the Harley engineers. Thus the new XL 55 Sportster (though it was actually only 54 cubic inches in capacity) appeared in the showroom windows in 1957 and America's youth greeted it with enthusiasm.

In reality, however, the XL looked more like a little sister of the bulky Electra Glide and was not as aggressive or powerful as had been hoped. The large gas tank, the bulky light on top of the wide fork shroud, long swept-back fenders, rigid or rubber-mounted buckhorn handlebars and a positively demure two-in-one exhaust did not exactly have the radical burnout sprinters beating a path to Harley's door.

Incidentally, the XL's foot gearshift was now on the right and the brake lever on the left, as was usual on the hated English rivals. The XL was now at least a few cc larger than the English bikes, not that this was a great deal of use given that, at 40 horsepower, the XL was 10-15 percent less powerful than the Nortons, BSAs and Triumphs.

Essentially the XL Sportster, with its 7.5:1 compression ratio, was the low compression version, but it remained the standard model until 1959. However, in 1958 Harley-Davidson introduced new, more powerful versions onto the power-hungry market, the XLH (H standing for "high compression") and also the pure sports machine the XLCH (C standing for "competition").

In 1959 just 42 of the old standard XL model were built and in total Harley-Davidson manufactured only 2,604 of them in its three-year existence. Nevertheless, it remained the forerunner of all future generations of Sportsters.

Courtesy of: Pat Keane, Crystal Lake, Illinois

© Harley-Davidson

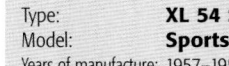

Type:	**XL 54 Shovelhead**
Model:	**Sportster 55**
Years of manufacture:	1957–1959
Engine:	Air-cooled four-stroke overhead-valve 45° V–Twin
Displacement:	53.87 cu in (882.8 cc)
Bore x stroke:	3.0 x 3.813 in (76.2 x 96.84 mm)
Compression ratio:	7.5 : 1
Power output:	40 hp at 5500 rpm
Carburetor:	DC 38 mm ø
Transmission:	Integral four-speed gearbox
Primary drive:	Triplex chain
Final drive:	Chain
Battery:	6 volt
Ignition:	Battery–coil
Frame:	Tubular steel cradle (single downtube)
Front brake:	Drum
Rear brake:	Drum
Front suspension:	Telescopic fork
Rear suspension:	Twin-shock-absorber swingarm
Wheelbase:	57 in
Weight:	495 lb
Fuel capacity:	4.4 gal
Oil capacity:	3 qts
Tires:	3.50 x 18
Top speed:	95 mph
Price:	$1,103

The OHV Sportster XL model built in the first year of production had a powerful light with integrated warning lamps and a protruding instrument panel cover.

The narrow inside brake shoe was quite modest.

The engine was primarily based on the new design of cylinder and heads with OHV drive.

© Harley-Davidson

© Harley-Davidson

Nostalgic elements from the Hydra Glide series: trumpet horn and upper fork cover with the powerful headlight.

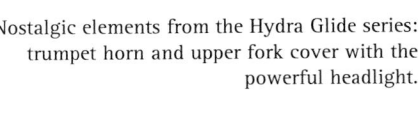

The XLH – Base Model of the New Sportster Generation

The XLH was introduced in 1958 as the successor to the XL and was conceived with a slightly calmer, less hot-headed rider in mind, being fitted with a wide range of comfortable extras for both street riding and touring. At first it had a somewhat lower compression ratio than its aggressive sister bike, the XLCH, and also battery coil and points ignition making it easier to kickstart. From 1961 the pillion seat came as standard equipment as was the new 3.7-gallon tank. From 1963 onwards the XLH was fitted with shorty dual pipes, which were also used on the XLCH. A wide range of accessories were also available, including a buddy seat, crash bars, saddlebags and numerous items of chrome-plated trim.

In 1965 a 12 volt electrical system was introduced (now with two series-connected 6 volt accumulators) and ignition timing was handled automatically instead of by a manual ignition timer on the throttle. This 12 volt system (with a larger accumulator) finally made possible the electric starter, which completely replaced the kick-starter from 1968, much to the disgust of purists.

In 1972 the cast iron OHV Sportster engine in both the XLH and the XLCH was bored out from 3.0 inches (76.2 mm) to 3.188 inches (80.9 mm), while the stroke remained the same at 3.8125 inches (96.8 mm), increasing the compression ratio to 9:1. With the new Bendix carburetor the new 61 cubic inch (1000 cc) engine developed 61 horsepower, or one "pony per cubic inch" as the slogan went and achieved an impressive top speed of over 110 mph. Other improvements included a wet clutch and an improved shifter drum. The assertive styling included an active breathing dual exhaust and from 1973, a front disc brake.

Due to new U.S. traffic regulations, the foot gearshift was situated on the left and the brake lever on the right. This was initially achieved via a mechanical rearrangement and from 1977 through a modified selector shaft.

On account of the continual improvements which were applied to both the XLH and the more sporty XLCH, by the mid-1970s the two models were becoming increasingly similar and finally in 1980 the XLCH was discontinued. In the year 1979 all Sportsters were fitted with the Cafe Racer (XLCR) frame, longer forks, flatter handlebars, a wide 16-inch rear wheel, and the renowned two-in-one-in-two "Siamese" exhaust. In 1982 the frame was again altered significantly and the cast iron junctions were dispensed with. This same year a much more drastic measure did serious harm to the image of the Sportster: due to the reduced octane of American gasoline, the compression ratio had to be significantly reduced and the XLH, which now in its street Sportster version weighed 495 pounds, was limited to a frustrating 99 mph. As a result sales were predictably poor and by 1983 the time was once again ripe for a radical change.

The classic Sportster: a 1972 XLH 1000 with the famous peanut fuel-tank.

XL 55, 1960

© *Harley–Davidson*

XLS 1000 Roadster, 1975 (fitted with Cafe Racer exhaust system) © *Harley–Davidson*

XLH, 1965 (in touring outfit)

XLH 1000 Sportster

© *Harley–Davidson*

XLH, 1970 (in touring outfit with twin mufflers)

XLH 1000, 1982

© *Harley–Davidson*

XLH 1000, 1975

© *Harley–Davidson*

XLH Sportster, 1983 (with FX fuel-tank)

© *Harley–Davidson*

Type:	**XLH**
Model:	**Sportster**
Years of manufacture:	1972–1985
Engine:	Air-cooled four stroke overhead–valve 45º V–Twin
Displacement:	60.81 cu in (996.54 cc)
Bore x stroke:	3.188 x 3.813 in (80.96 x 96.84 mm)
Compression ratio:	9 : 1
Power output:	61 hp
Carburetor:	Bendix 38 mm ø, from 1976 Keihin 38 mm ø
Transmission:	Four-speed
Primary drive:	Triplex chain
Final drive:	Chain
Battery:	12 volt
Ignition:	Battery–coil, from 1980 contactless electronic
Frame:	Tubular steel cradle (double tube)
Front brake:	Drum (disc from 1973)
Rear brake:	Drum
Front suspension:	Telescopic fork
Rear suspension:	Twin–shock-absorber swingarm
Wheelbase:	58.5 in
Weight:	528 lb
Fuel capacity:	3.7/3.3/2.2 gal depending on tank type
Oil capacity:	3 qts/4 qts
Front tire:	3.75 x 19, from 1980 MJ 90–19
Rear tire:	4.25 x 18 (4.25 x 16), MT 90–16
Top speed:	110 mph
Price:	$2,120

The Shovelhead Sportster XL Family

1957–1959	**XL 55** Sportster (883 cc)
1957	**XLA** (883 cc) (military model)
1958–1978	**XLH** (Street, from 1967 with electric starter)
1958–1971	**XLCH** Sportster (883 cc) **XLC** Scrambler
1972–1985	**XLH 1000** Sportster
1972–1978	**XLCH 1000** Sportster
1977–1978	**XLT 1000** Sportster
1983–1985	**XLX 61** Sportster (1000 cc) Standard
1978–1982 **1984–1985**	**XLS 1000** Roadster
1983	**XLS** Roadster (1000 cc) Custom Sport
1983–1984	**XR 1000** (Sport Version)

The XLCH – Harley's Hot Rod

It was designed right from the start as a venomous beast for purists and the macho hardcore, initially making its market debut in 1958 as a pure, offroad scrambler fitted according to the prevailing Californian taste. In this context, the in-house designation CH stood for "Competition Hot." The high compression, OHV engine yielded 55 horsepower and sported enlarged valves and high-domed, piston heads.

Indeed, the CH was rigged out for intensive sports use in just about every other respect too, with its minimal fenders, a 19 inch aluminum front wheel with off-road tires, a small, 2.25 gallon peanut fuel-tank, the design of which served as a model for all genuine, Sportster fuel tanks to follow, a solo seat mounted on two short springs and even a dynamo, despite the fact that no lights were fitted. Magneto ignition made starting the beast a battle

of strength, and the kick-starter was infamous for maliciously "kicking back" at the rider. Nietzsche might have described the brakes as "Beyond Good and Evil." The frame was an adventure all by itself and the engine noise was enough to instill fear in the hardest of men.

Nevertheless, the model XLCH was an American alternative to the racy British twins in terms of performance, and not least in terms of its sound. However, Harley decided to make the XLCH somewhat more amenable in 1959, and converted it into a "street legal" bike with a so-called eyebrow headlamp, a taillight, horn and speedometer. The DC electrical system was also replaced by an AC system. On the other hand, the raised two-in-one exhaust, intended to accentuate the bike's racy flair, was less well received and soon vanished.

In 1965, the XLCH was also fitted with a 12 volt system, and in 1966 with sharper cams and a Tillotson

carburetor, thus achieving a noteworthy 60 horsepower. The popular age of the open exhaust pipe officially came to an end in 1969: mufflers were now officially required and the era of legislative control began. But it did become easier to start the motorcycle: the magneto ignition of the XLCH was replaced with an automatically adjustable battery coil ignition.

In 1972, both the XLCH and the XLH were fitted with the new, more powerful, 61 cubic inch (1000 cc) engine with a compression ratio of 9:1. The engine's 61 horsepower yielded a top speed of 112 mph. However, neither the new engine nor the cosmetic improvements were able to make this Sportster competitive enough to stand up to the racy Japanese models. Some 10,825 XLHs were sold in 1973. In 1979, this particular model was finally deleted from the company's product range.

Two Sportster generations: the XLH from 1960 (right) and the XLH from 1979.

Courtesy of: Gale McFarland, Largo, Florida

© Harley-Davidson

The 1968 XLCH sported an instrument panel and a small headlight with a cover containing both the warning lights and a full hub–brake for the front wheel.

Type:	**XLCH**
Model:	**Sportster**
Years of manufacture:	1958–1979
Engine:	Air–cooled four–stroke 45° V–Twin OHV
Displacement:	54 cu in (883 cc)
Bore x stroke:	3 x 3.8 in (76 x 97 mm)
Compression ratio:	9 : 1
Power output:	45 hp
Carburetor:	DC 38 mm ø; as of 1966, MD 32 mm ø
Transmission:	Four–speed
Primary drive:	Triplex chain
Final drive:	Chain
Battery:	6 volt
Ignition:	Battery–coil
Frame:	Looped tubular steel
Front brake:	Drum
Rear brake:	Drum
Front suspension:	Telescopic fork
Rear suspension:	Arm with telescopic struts
Wheelbase:	57 in
Weight:	584 lb
Fuel capacity:	2 gal
Oil capacity:	3 qts
Front tire:	3.50 x 19
Rear tire:	4.00 x 18
Top speed:	155 mph
Price:	$1,155
Model versions:	Available from 1958 in a Sport and Off–road version with solenoid ignition and open exhausts

Type:	**XLH**
Model:	**Sportster**
Years of manufacture:	1958–1974
Engine:	Air–cooled four–stroke 45° V–Twin OHV
Cubic capacity:	53.87 cu in (882.8 cc)
Bore x stroke:	3 x 3.813 in (76.2 x 96.84 mm)
Compression:	9 : 1
Power output:	45 hp
Carburetor:	DC 38 mm ø
Transmission:	Four–speed gearbox
Primary drive:	Triplex chain
Final drive:	Chain
Battery:	6 volt
Ignition:	Magneto, later battery–coil
Frame:	Single tube tubular steel cradle
Front brake:	Drum
Rear brake:	Drum
Front suspension:	Telescopic forks
Rear suspension:	Shock absorber swingarm
Wheelbase:	57 in
Weight:	480 lbs
Fuel capacity:	2 gal
Oil capacity:	3 qts
Front tire:	3.50 x 19
Rear tire:	4.00 x 18
Maximum speed:	112 mph
Price:	$1,155
Model versions:	1958: Sport and offroad versions with magneto ignition and flared–exhaust

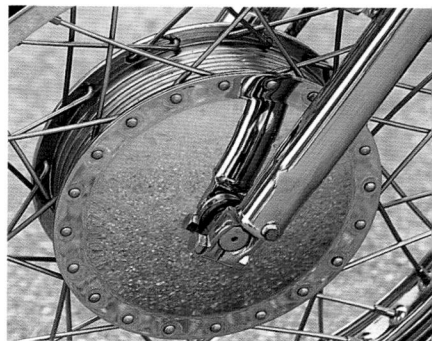

The Model XR 750 – Queen of the Oval Track

The XR 750 was presented by race team leader Dick O'Brien at the Texas Motorbike show in February 1970 as the latest AMF/Harley-Davidson, secret weapon to take on the ever-stronger English and Japanese competition. It was constructed in only four months to the specifications of the Dutch engineer Pieter Zylstra, and was intended to build on the success of the old KR 750. Basically a tuned version of the XLR Sportster engine mounted in the old KR frame, in its first road race at Daytona in 1970 the new XR 750 proved to be a complete disaster. The iron-barrelled engine experienced continual problems and breakdowns due to overheating. In the winter of 1970–1971 it was reworked. The main features were new, alloy cylinder heads fixed with continuous bolts, improved combustion chambers, and a better one-piece crankshaft. In the following season however, the transmission caused a lot of trouble.

The XR 750 was mainly used on the oval dirt-tracks where it was an undisputed favorite. The new aluminium engine was unveiled there for the first time in 1971, and was then used secretly in a road race in Ontario in October 1971. However, it had a hard time competing against the new Japanese two-stroke bikes, as well as the Triumph and BSA three-cylinder four-stroke machines in the now open AMA class. The first major victory was achieved by Cal Rayborn still on the old XR machine in the British-American Match Races in England. However, the XR 750 continued to enjoy greatest successes on the American half-mile and one-mile short-track oval courses.

Fitted as standard in all Flat Trackers: the powerful XR 750 two single-carburetor engine.

The XR 750 Flat Track racer. Shown here is a 1980 model.

Courtesy of: Otis Chandler / Vintage Museum of Transportation, Oxnard, California

The 750 Flat Tracker was a popular machine among racing teams, who liked nothing better than to tune it and match it to the respective conditions of the different oval tracks. Depicted are some typical examples from the pits.

Type:	**Racer**
Model:	**XR 750**
Years of manufacture:	1970–1980
Engine:	Side–valve four–stroke OHV 45º V–Twin
Displacement:	45 cu in (750 cc)
Bore x stroke:	3.125 x 2.983 in (80 x 76 mm)
Compression ratio:	10.5 : 1
Power output:	90 hp
Carburetor:	2 x Mikuni 36 mm ø
Transmission:	Four-speed
Primary drive:	Triplex chain
Final drive:	Chain
Ignition:	Magneto
Frame:	Lightweight duplex cradle tubular steel
Rear Brake:	Disc
Front suspension:	Telescopic fork
Rear suspension:	Swingarm, hydraulic shock absorbers
Wheelbase:	57 in
Weight:	320 lb
Fuel capacity:	2.5 gal
Oil capacity:	3 qts
Top speed:	130 mph
Production:	540
Price:	$4,000

Special versions:
XRTT (1971–1972) U.S. TT version
XR–RR (1972–1973) tuned in Varese

Successful riders:
Cal Rayborn, Mark Brelsford, Gary Scott, Mert Lawwill, Renzo Pasolini, Dave Sehl

The XLCR Cafe Racer – An American Dream of the Future

When it was first introduced in March 1977 at Daytona Bike Week, the XLCR Cafe Racer, was met with an enthusiastic reception. It was the most uncompromising piece of work produced by Willie G. Davidson, head designer at AMF-owned Harley-Davidson and it was a masterpiece. He had developed the machine virtually in secret, away from all company influences, working with his assistant Lou Netz in Jim Haubert's workshop.

The all-black machine resembled the English cafe racers in look, with its long, fastback rear end with the low-mounted rear light and license plate combination. Other features were an elongated, angular tank, bikini cockpit fairing, and completely redesigned instruments and controls, as well as cast alloy wheels and a Kelsey-Hayes double disc brake on the front wheel, and a single disc brake at the rear. The 61 cubic inch (1000 cc) Sportster engine was mounted in the frame which was used in the successful XR 750 racer. The matt black, performance boosting, Siamese, two-in-two exhaust was both unusual and striking. In short, this machine represented a promising new direction that was way ahead of its time in both styling and engineering.

Unfortunately, the courageous experiment came to nothing. Conservative American Harley fans preferred the old tried and trusted Sportster design, and the Cafe Racer only remained in production for two years. In 1977, 1,923 of them were produced, in 1978 the number lowered to 1,201 which was then followed by a final nine in 1979. Many of them languished unsold with dealers for years afterwards. Today the XLCR is a very rare and valuable collector's item in its original state, large numbers having undergone conversion and customizing.

In keeping with the British cafe racer tradition: the XLCR with its small fairing, boat-tail rear end and cast spoked wheels.

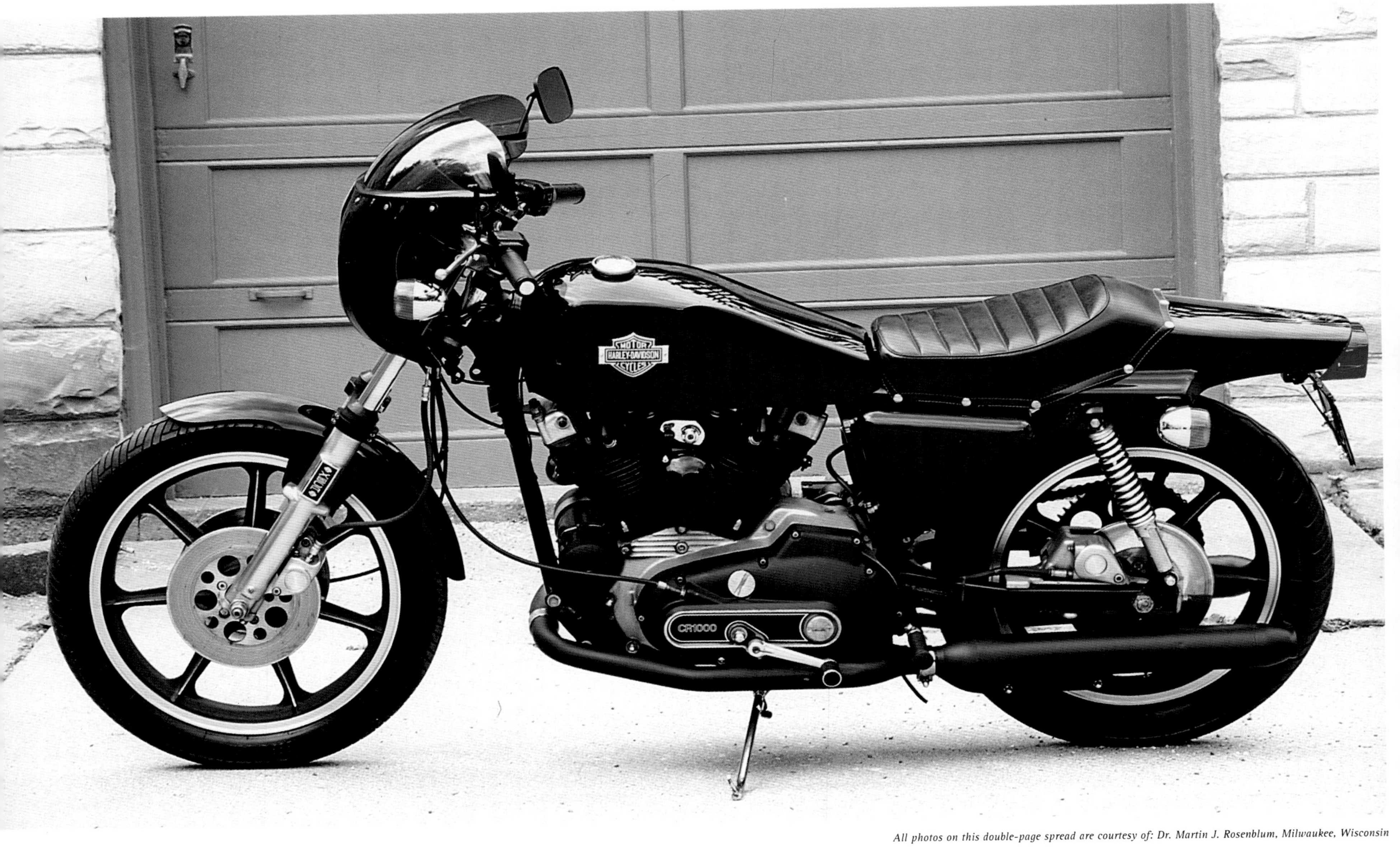

The typical fairing with integrated cockpit.

Type:	**XLCR**
Model:	**Cafe Racer**
Years of manufacture:	1977–1978
Engine:	Air-cooled four-stroke 45° V–Twin OHV
Cubic capacity:	60.81 cu in (996.54 cc)
Bore x stroke:	3.188 x 3.813 in (80.96 x 96.84 mm)
Compression:	9 : 1
Power output:	61 hp
Carburetor:	Keihin 38 mm ø
Transmission:	Four-speed gearbox
Primary drive:	Triplex chain
Final drive:	Chain
Battery:	12 volt
Ignition:	Battery-coil
Frame:	Double tube tubular steel cradle
Front brake:	Double disc
Rear brake:	Disc
Front suspension:	Telescopic forks
Rear suspension:	Shock absorber swingarm
Wheelbase:	58.5 in
Weight:	515 lbs
Fuel capacity:	4 gal
Oil capacity:	4 qts
Front tire:	3.75 x 19 or MT 90–19
Rear tire:	4.25 x 18 or MJ 90–16
Maximum speed:	110 mph
Price:	$3,623

The peculiar two-in-two exhaust system helped improve combustion.

The Model XLX 61 Standard – the Quintessential Sportster

The steady fall in the Sportster's sales and increasing concern over ever stronger competition from Japan prompted Harley-Davidson in 1983 to take emergency measures: a new XL Sportster was introduced on the market, and to entice the customers back, it was offered at the heavily publicized introductory price of just 3,995 dollars.

The XLX was the most basic Sportster ever put on the market. It was stripped down to the bare essentials: a peanut gas tank; a solo saddle; a minimum of instruments; a speedometer; short, straight handlebars; nine spoke, silver cast alloy wheels; and a matte black, dual exhaust system that went well with the motorcycle's attractive all-black paintwork. It was fitted with the latest version of the 61 cubic inch (1000 cc)

engine, incorporating a range of improvements such as electronic, vacuum, advance-ignition timing. However, the export models, particularly those destined for Europe, required a number of modifications. For example, there was a version limited to 49 horsepower by baffle plates in the muffler, and also incorporating an enlarged air filter and a double disc brake on the front wheel. This meant a considerable increase in the motorcycle's cost but did reduce the price of insurance. By 1985, the model's final year of production, it sold for 4,695 dollars in the U.S. With this machine the Shovelhead engine reached the end of the road.

Type:	**XLX–61**
Model:	**Sportster Standard**
Years of manufacture:	1983–1985
Engine:	Air–cooled four–stroke 45° V–Twin OHV
Cubic capacity:	60.81 cu in (996.54 cc)
Bore x stroke:	3.188 x 3.8123 in (80.96 x 96.84 mm)
Compression:	8.8 : 1
Power output:	61 hp (export version restricted to 49 hp)
Carburetor:	Keihin 38 mm ø with dashpot pump
Transmission:	Four–speed gearbox
Primary drive:	Triplex chain
Final drive:	Chain
Battery:	12 volt
Ignition:	Electronic contactless V–Fire III
Frame:	Double tube tubular steel cradle
Front brake:	Disc
Rear brake:	Disc
Front suspension:	Telescopic forks
Rear suspension:	Shock absorber swingarm
Wheelbase:	60 in
Weight:	486 lbs
Fuel capacity:	2.25 gal
Oil capacity:	3 qts
Front tire:	MJ 90–19
Rear tire:	MT 90–16
Maximum speed:	104 mph
Price:	$3,623

The export version was also available with a double disc brake on the front wheel

New minimalist design: the only instrument is the speedometer.

Powerful and compact: the Sportster engine.

The XLT/XLS – the Touring and Custom Models of the Sportster

In 1977, during its first year, and for one year only, a genuine touring version of the XLH was brought out. This was the XLT (T for Touring) fitted with Electra Glide saddlebags, a windshield and the Super Glide's 3.5 gallon gas tank. This aside, the narrow-wheeled XLT was just the good old Sporty beneath the surface.

From 1979 to 1982 this became a genuine Sportster. The first XLS (S for Special) Roadster took some design cues from the Low Rider, and was particularly note-worthy for the X shaped, "Siamese," two-in-two exhaust, which it adopted from the Cafe Racer. It was still fitted with the usual, small peanut fuel-tank which gave it a very limited range, straight dragbars mounted on a curved riser, just two instruments (the speedometer and rev counter) and a wide 16-inch rear wheel. However, in 1980 it was fitted with a larger tank, shorty dual exhausts and buckhorn handlebars as an optional extra.

From 1983 the XLS Custom Sport was converted into a genuine tourer with a large, 3.8 gallon Fat Bob tank with the tachometer mounted on it, the speedometer now being the only instrument fitted above the light on the handlebar. The wide solo saddle was particularly comfortable, while the pillion seat behind it was extremely uncomfortable. The XLS was available with either nine spoke, cast alloy wheels or with classic, wire spoke wheels. Any other extras desired had to come from the accessories catalogs.

This 1982 Harley-Davidson brochure shows the last old-style XLS Roadster.   © Harley-Davidson

Type:	**XLS**
Model:	**Roadster**
Years of manufacture:	1983–1985
Engine:	Air-cooled four-stroke 45° V-Twin OHV
Cubic capacity:	H61 cu in (999 cc)
Bore x stroke:	3.189 x 3.812 in (81 x 96.8mm)
Compression:	8.8 : 1
Carburetor:	Keihin 38 mm ø with dashpot pump
Power output:	61 hp
Transmission:	Four-speed gearbox
Primary drive:	Triplex chain
Final drive:	Chain
Battery:	12 volt
Ignition:	Electronic contactless V-Fire III
Frame:	Double tube tubular steel cradle
Front brake:	Disc/double disc
Rear brake:	Disc
Front suspension:	Telescopic forks
Rear suspension:	Shock absorber swingarm
Wheelbase:	60 in
Weight:	548 lbs
Fuel capacity:	3 gal
Oil capacity:	3 qts
Front tire:	MJ 90–19
Rear tire:	MT 90–16
Maximum speed:	104 mph
Price:	$4,995
Model variants:	Initially in XLT Touring version. The frequently altered XLS Roadster version came later.

© Harley-Davidson

An XLS Roadster (1983) with two-tone color scheme and elegant touring equipment: large fuel-tank, integrated instrument panel and filler caps and speedometer.

The XR 1000 – a Street Rocket

The impressive long-term racing successes of the legendary XR 750, the lord of the dirt track, led to ever louder calls for a street version of the XR. Finally, Harley-Davidson decided to produce a limited edition (originally planned at 1,100 motorcycles) for an exclusive clientele. The XR 1000 was presented at Daytona Bike Week in 1983. As luck would have it, Jay Springsteen, who was riding the XR 1000, won the opening race of the season, the Daytona Battle of the Twins, the first victory there since Cal Rayborn's great success in 1973. With a top speed of 166 mph it easily blew away the competition from Ducati, BMW, Triumph, BSA and the other twins.

The XR Sport 1000, based on the XR 750 racer, had newly-designed alloy cylinder heads tuned by Jerry Branch which were fastened to the engine housing by stay bolts. A short crankshaft, light connecting rods and two powerful 36 mm Dell'Orto slide carburetors developed an impressive 70 horsepower. The high matte black mufflers, a solo seat, the small peanut tank and a big double disc brake on the nine-spoke cast aluminum front wheel meant that it also looked like a genuine racer. Only the separate speedometer and rev counter on the handlebars gave something of a street look to the machine.

During 1983 and 1984 around 1,500 XR 1000s were sold – greater success was stymied by the countless conditions that had to be met and technical alterations made in most countries in order to obtain permission to ride the machines on public roads. The high price of around 7,000 dollars was an additional factor, so the XR 1000 remained an exotic curiosity.

For incorrigible power freaks there was a 100 horsepower conversion kit with a special camshaft, 10:1 compression ratio and a racing exhaust, making it a bullet that could only be mastered by expert riders.

The XR 1000 had a specially-designed cover for the ignition. The twin exhaust system routed high on the left-hand side in matte-black was copied from racing models.

Courtesy of: Otis Chandler/Vintage Museum of Transportation, Oxnard, California

Type:	**XR 1000**
Model:	**Sportster**
Years of manufacture:	1983–1984
Engine:	Air-cooled four-stroke overhead-valve 45° V–Twin
Displacement:	60.81 cu in (996.54 cc)
Bore x stroke:	3.188 x 3.813 in (80.96 x 96.84 mm)
Compression ratio:	9 : 1
Power output:	70 hp (90 with hp conversion kit)
Carburetor:	Twin Dell'Orto 36 mm ø
Transmission:	Four-speed
Primary drive:	Triplex chain
Final drive:	Chain
Battery:	12 volt
Ignition:	Contactless electronic V–Fire III
Frame:	Tubular steel cradle (double tube)
Front brake:	Double disc
Rear brake:	Disc
Front suspension:	Telescopic fork
Rear suspension:	Twin-shock-absorber swingarm
Wheelbase:	60 in
Weight:	485 lb
Fuel capacity:	2.2 gal
Oil capacity:	3 qts
Front tire:	100/90 x 19 V
Rear tire:	130/90 x 16 V Dunlop Sport Elite
Top speed:	115 mph
Price:	$6,995

The standard version of the XR 1000 engine had two independent Dell'Orto carburetors with large air filters, both on the right-hand side. The air filters were sometimes removed for racing.

231

Evolution — a Technical Program

In April 1976, Chairman Vaughn Beals called together a group of leading Harley-Davidson managers for a policy meeting in Pinehurst, North Carolina in order to lay out the strategy for both the company and the models to be produced for the next ten years. Out of it came the recognition that the Japanese invasion had to be countered by a technologically advanced product of the highest quality, including a guaranteed fulfillment of the increasingly strict limits on noise and exhaust fumes. With the almost inexhaustible financial reserves of AMF behind them, parallel to the priority development of a new V–Twin motor, the alternative project NOVA was initiated, later to be quietly laid to rest after unsatisfactory test runs. Another factor was the company's now overriding concern to satisfy the wishes of the customers, still demanding the classic design, and so in the motor project later to be known as "evolution" the nostalgic look of the typical V–Twin was maintained. After seven years' development the motor went into production in 1983, having gone through various prototypes and rigorous testing. In 1984 Harley-Davidson introduced five models fitted with the EVO motor. A new age had begun.

Although the old principal of the air–cooled 45 degree V–Twin motor (the Harley-Davidson legend!) was kept, the evolution motor is a completely new machine. Its basic concept is to get as much horsepower as possible out of the same cubic capacity (80 inches) at every rpm reading, to make the motor lighter, better cooled, and above all to eliminate oil spill. It is interesting to note that Harley had already worked for some time on larger–volume engines, all of which were however less efficient than their forerunner, the 1340 cc motor. So it was left at a 3.5 inch bore and 4.25 inch stroke, the compression being raised a little to 8.5. The new element in the EVO motor was more than anything else the material itself. The two (replaceable) cylinders and the head are made of a special light alloy, and the special flat Mahle pistons are fashioned from an SAE 42 aluminum alloy with 12 percent silicon. The play between the cylinder and the bore is only fourteen thousands of an inch (4/100 mm).

The innovative design of the cylinder heads, manufactured by a precise, complicated three–and–a–half million dollar machine, has particularly aerodynamic side–squish combustion chambers. The valves have a larger stroke and remain open longer. The steering times are values gained from experience in the development section of the racing department. The oil lubrication has been equipped with a more efficient system of return travel. All this means economic oil consumption and better cooling. The rocker box divided into three parts, from whose form the motor got its nickname "Blockhead," allows the simple installation and removal of the motor, although it sits snugly under the upper tubes of the frame. Massive steel bolts going all the way through keep the cylinder and head on the crankshaft housing. Naturally there are a host of other minor technical improvements which vary from year to year so that the already high quality is constantly honed further. To sum up: a mature, high–class engine, competitive on the modern motorcycle market, and despite all doom–laden prophesies it was a successful groundbreaker for the future of the Harley legend.

Development of the Evo Engines — the New Generation

Harley-Davidson motorcycles have always had the typical "enthusiast image." One of the greatest parts of that image is the Harley sound.

However, at times, that famed sound has posed challenges in Europe. Harley-Davidson met those challenges in part by working with Porsche. From its famous development center in Weissach, Porsche provided major support to Harley in revising its motorcycles to meet Europe's 80-decibel noise limits.

Nevertheless, while Harley-Davidson certainly worked with Porsche on these European noise issues, that was only a small part of the overall engine development, for which Harley employees are responsible and are to be credited. One of the prequisites, indeed almost a threat, was that the character of the engine should not change significantly. So, for example, a crank pin would be retained for both cylinders.

But at the same time Harley engineers were looking for ways to tame the engine and make it more stable. They were also hoping to stop the heavy oiling problem.

The new engine, considerably modified in some details vibrated less with the addition of balance weights, and it was also suspended in the frame on rubber mountings.

Dedicated Harley-Davidson motorcycle fans at first disapproved of this, but soon the new engine, with all its advantages, was generally accepted.

Contact with the Weissach development center has been maintained for certain purposes. Porsche's involvement with Harley-Davidson in certain capacities has continued. Harley-Davidson certainly appreciates the capabilities of the Porsche engineers with regard to reducing noise levels for the European market.

The generation of engine that was modified again for the still current 1995 model year surprised people with its relatively quiet-running engine, and was characterized by better traction with rather more horsepower. The typical noise was only slightly reduced, but the sound remained the same. The riders can still hear the twin throbbing, and they can still feel its vibration in their feet, hands and backside. Harley worked hard to ensure that its heritage and the overall look, feel and sound of its bikes would be maintained throughout any engine redesigns. After all, that heritage is what built its loyal following.

Despite all the trouble they have taken, since the introduction of this model variant Harley-Davidson has had to contend with increasing prejudice. "You think you're sitting on the wrong bike," is a remark often heard in the local bar. It is true that riding a Harley no longer means just making a loud noise. However, what is decisive is the subjective experience of the rider, who insists on traditional experience of the Milwaukee jackhammer, and a test drive will demonstrate that this has not been lost.

Fuel Injection – an Electronic Challenge

Since 1995, Harley–Davidson motorcycles have been available fitted with carburetor manufacturer Weber's Electronic Sequential Port Fuel Injection system (ESPFI). This guarantees improved fuel consumption, more reliable cold starting, less engine noise and also, particularly at low revs, up to 10 percent more torque. It also reduces exhaust emission levels, making the engine not only more economical but also more environmentally friendly.

The injection system with its two separate inlet ducts has replaced the carburetor. Injection nozzles, pressure regulator, manual throttle position sensors, air intake and temperature sensors, and many other components, all work together to ensure that the cylinders receive the optimum mix of fuel and air under all conditions. The electronic control module (ECM) hidden under a side cover processes all the data and converts them into the correct injection and ignition commands. The gas pump is fitted directly into the gas tank. The reserve tap has been discarded, and a red light comes on when gas is running short.

The new fuel injection system was first installed in 1995 in the special anniversary edition FLHTCUI Ultra Classic Electra Glide produced to celebrate the thirtieth anniversary of the Electra Glide and from 1996 it was available as an optional extra on the FLHRI Road King, the Electra Glide Classic and the Ultra Classic Electra Glide. ESPFI is now standard equipment on the FLTUI Tour Glide Classic. However, if the on-board electronics fail, you have an expensive problem. Only official Harley-Davidson dealers equipped with the necessary electronic diagnosis system can assist you. Nevertheless, Harley remains confident – in the future, the only elements of nostalgia incorporated into its beloved dinosaur will relate to its external appearance alone.

© *Harley–Davidson*

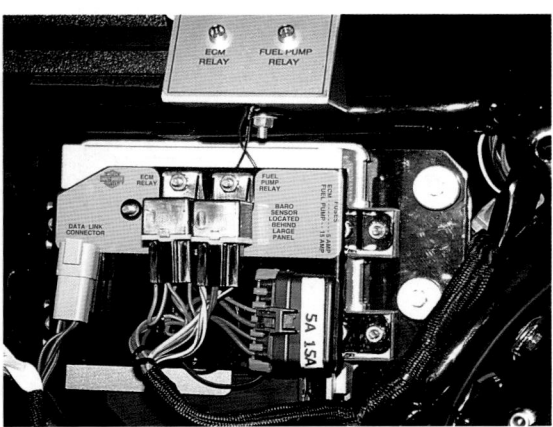

The electronic fuel injection system: the carburetor has been replaced by the injection element (right); the fuel pump (far right) is located in the fuel-tank, and the control electronics are behind the right-side panel (top right).

Electras, Classics and Ultras – The Latest Supertourers

Since 1995 the basic model of the hefty Electra Glide has borne the designation FLHT (not to be confused with the FLT Tour Glide models). Apart from the new 80 cubic inch (1340 cc) Evolution engine, this model incorporates a number of other novelties, though the five-speed transmission with final belt drive and also the classic fork-mounted fairing remained. In comparison with the Classic and Ultra Classic models, the FLHT has relatively little chrome, lacks the Tour-Pak luggage box and is painted in a single color. New features include the anti-slip diaphragm-spring clutch, the telescopic air-adjustable anti-dive forks and the rear suspension shocks, both contributing to a significant improvement in ride comfort.

The FLHTC Classic Electra Glide is even better equipped than the FLHT and correspondingly more expensive. Multicolor paintwork and lots of chrome-plating are the features that stand out most. Among the many other features are AM/FM radiocassette, engine guard, saddlebag bars, a standard Tour-Pak and passenger footrests. The Classic is, so to speak, the Full Dresser variant of the Electra Glide.

The FLHTCU Ultra Classic Electra Glide offers just about everything any rider could want. On top of the above features, there is ornamental trim, bulky pillow-soft seats, an 80 watt voice-operated stereo radiocassette system, CB radio in the helmet, cigarette lighter, a dual antenna, adjustable footboards, additional luggage space, additional lights, metal logos, etc.

Since 1995, when it was introduced on the occasion of the 30th anniversary of the Electra Glide, the FLHTCU has also offered electric fuel injection as an option, leading to yet another letter of designation, I, to the alphabet soup designation FLHTCUI. In this guise it easily reaches its maximum permissible weight of 1,250 pounds fully-loaded with two passengers. In fact the FLHTU practically comes across as a luxury car. The countless lamps and running lights offered in the accessory catalogs are powered by an superpowerful generator producing 445 watts even at low revs, and by a 20 amp/h 12-volt car battery. The luxury fittings of this mobile home are rounded off by cruise control for those wishing to rest their throttle hand and a stop sensor which cuts the engine if the mighty machine should ever topple over.

With a list price of 12,995 dollars, the 1995 Ultra Classic was around 1,000 dollars more expensive than the standard FLHT. Particularly in the U.S., a special edition fitted with the new ESPFI fuel injection system is available for the customer who wants that extra bit.

Standard version of a 1996 FLHT

As a factory Full Dresser, this FLHTCUI special edition for the company's 95th anniversary in 1998 had everything available in the way of original accessories for ultra–classic models: trims on the lamps and for pure luxury, a radio cassette, CB and intercom, and blow–up seat cushions with integrated speaker system.

The FLH Electra Glide Evolution Family

Year	Model	Description
1986	**FLHT**	Electra Glide
1987	**FLHT**	Electra Glide Sport
1985	**FLHTC**	Electra Glide Classic
1996	**FLHTCI**	Electra Glide Classic Injection
1989	**FLHTCU**	Ultra Classic Electra Glide
1995	**FLHTCUI**	Ultra Classic Electra Glide Injection
1988–1993	**FLHS**	Electra Glide Sport
1995	**FLHR**	Electra Glide Road King
1996	**FLHRI**	Electra Glide Road King Injection

Special Editions:
FLHTP Police Edition
FLHTC Shriner Edition

Price Increases

How the price of the FLHTC Electra Glide Classic has changed over time (in U.S. dollars):

Year	Price	Year	Price
1984	$8,199	1991	$11,745
1985	$8,999	1992	$12,250
1986	$9,974	1993	$12,949
1987	$10,045	1994	$13,285
1988	$10,145	1995	$13,875
1989	$10,799	1996	$14,410
1990	$11,300	1997	$14,745
		1998	$14,975

(Source: Harley–Davidson Sales Lists)

Type:	**FLHTC Evolution**
Model:	**Electra Glide Classic**
Year of manufacture:	1985
Engine:	Rubber-mounted air-cooled four-stroke overhead-valve 45° V-Twin
Displacement:	81.65 cu in (1340 cc)
Bore x stroke:	3.5 x 4.25 in (89 x 108 mm)
Compression ratio:	8.5 : 1
Power output:	60 hp
Carburetor:	Keihin 38 mm ø from 1990 Keihin CV 40 mm ø
Transmission:	Five-speed
Primary drive:	Duplex chain
Final drive:	Gates Polychain belt
Battery:	12 volt
Ignition:	Electronic, V-Fire III CDI Transistor
Frame:	Tubular steel cradle (double tube)
Front brake:	Double disc
Rear brake:	Disc
Front suspension:	Telescopic fork with air-assisted anti-dive system
Rear suspension:	Air-assisted anti-dive shock-absorber swingarm
Wheelbase:	62.7 in
Weight:	759 lb
Fuel capacity:	5 gal
Oil capacity:	4 qts
Front tire:	5.00 x 16
Rear tire:	5.00 x 16
Top speed:	90 mph
Price:	$9,199 (1985)

Model versions:
FLHT as standard Electra Glide model from 1986 to 1987 and 1995.
FLHTU as Ultra Classic Electra Glide from 1989 to 1995.
FLHTCU from 1995 to 1996. With fuel injection FLHTCUI 1995–1996 and FLHTCI 1996.

Special models:
1986: Special Anniversary Edition (536 produced)
    Electra Glide Liberty Edition (810 produced)
1987: Special Anniversary Edition (800 produced)
1988: 85th Anniversary Edition (715 produced)
1993: 90th Anniversary Edition
1995: 30th Electra Glide Anniversary
    FLHTU Ultra Classic Electra Glide:
1993: 90th Anniversary Edition
  1995: 30th Electra Glide Anniversary (FLHTCUI)

From 1994/95 the reference letter code was separated into the type: FLT and the model: FLHTC Electra Glide Classic

The FLTC and FLTCU – Long-Range Bombers

The late–1990s Tour Glide series shows that Harley-Davidson is taking one more step forward. It represents the ultimate touring machine, fitted with all imaginable equipment for riding in comfort, incorporating the latest high–tech motorcycle engineering. It differs from the FLHT Tour Glide in having a new stiffened Tour Glide frame with the steering head moved forward and a rubber–mounted 80 cubic inch (1340 cc) Evolution engine with a five–speed gearbox. The external appearance of the Tour Glide Classic and Ultra Classic is dominated by the fairing and the double headlight attached to the frame. The instrument panel is fitted with a range of instrumentation comparable to an automobile, plus pretty much all the features a rider could want, including a voice–activated intercom and music system. A newly–shaped gas tank, an extra–large topcase and special paintwork make the FLTC, from 1989 the FLTCU, the most luxurious touring bikes Harley-Davidson has ever produced. From 1996 onwards all Ultra Classic Tour Glide models were fitted with electronic fuel injection. The model was discontinued after 1997.

A nice looking Ultra Tour Glide FLTCU from 1989.

© Harley–Davidson

© Harley–Davidson

Type:	FLTC–Evo
Model:	**Tour Glide Classic**
Years of manufacture:	1984–1994
Engine:	Air–cooled four–stroke overhead–valve 45° V–Twin
Displacement:	81.65 cu in (1338 cc)
Bore x stroke:	3.5 x 4.25 in (89 x 108 mm)
Compression ratio:	8.5 : 1
Power output:	64 hp
Carburetor:	Keihin 38 mm ø from 1990 Keihin CV 40 mm ø
Transmission:	Five–speed
Primary drive:	Duplex chain
Final drive:	Toothed belt
Battery:	12 volt
Ignition:	Contactless transistor (CDI)
Frame:	Tubular steel cradle (double downtube)
Front brake:	Dual disc
Rear brake:	Disc
Front suspension:	Tubular steel cradle (double downtube)
Rear suspension:	Twin–shock–absorber swingarm
Wheelbase:	63.1 in
Weight:	779 lb
Fuel capacity:	5 gal
Oil capacity:	4 qts
Front tire:	MT 90 x 16
Rear tire:	MT 90 x 16
Top speed:	95 mph
Price:	$13,695 (1990)

Special Editions:

1986	FLTC	Liberty Edition
1986	FLTC	Special Anniversary
1987	FLTC	Special Anniversary
1988	FLTC	85th Anniversary Edition
1993	FLTCU	90th Anniversary Edition

The FLT Tour Glide Evo Family

1984–1994	**FLTC** Classic Tour Glide
1989	**FLTCU** Ultra Classic Tour Glide
1996	**FLTCUI** Ultra Classic Tour Glide Injection
1998	**FLTR/FLTRI** Road Glide Injection

FLTR – a New Elegance

A new edition of the Tour Glide launched on the American market in 1998 is the FLTR Road Glide (a trademarked name), with its low, tinted windshield and a new "twin oval reflector optic" double headlight fitted onto the fairing. A smooth, streamlined combined solo saddle and passenger seat, and new rounded instruments gives the somewhat overblown outfit a certain elegance and a hint of nostalgia. Out of sight, an improved nine–disk gearbox mounted in an oil bath makes for smooth gear shifting. Electronic fuel injection is available on the Road Glide as an option, as are your choice of wire–spoked or cast wheels. A limited 95th Anniversary Edition was also available during 1998.

Niche Fillers: the Electra Glide Sport and Road King

By bringing out the stripped-down FLHS Electra Glide Sport (a trademarked name), company designers finally took a leaf out of the book of Harley riders who regarded the Electra Glide as a well-proportioned machine, but one overloaded with equipment.

Harley called this its "back to basics" Tourer and indeed the new FLHS was a somewhat slimmed-down version of the FLHT Electra Glide, with an easily-removed clear windshield, no fairing, and the topcase replaced by a luggage rack and saddlebags, both of which were also easily removable. In 1988, the year it was introduced, 1,677 were sold, and it continued to be manufactured until 1993, when 2,500 were sold. Its price rose from 8,545 dollars in its first year to 11,700 dollars in 1993.

In 1994, the standard model FLHT, which was then discontinued, was changed to become the FLHTC Electra Glide Classic and its name was also changed, to the FLHR

Road King (a trademarked name). The windshield, saddlebags and passenger pillion seat were all easily removed, leaving you with a genuine solo Electra Glide. The hefty headlight and the shrouded upper forks remained, as did the 16-inch ten-spoke cast wheels. The electronic digital speedometer (from the Electra Glide Classic) was new (back to basics?).

In 1996, the FLHR Road King cost a handsome 14,035 dollars and the fuel-injected FLHRI version, the newest variant of the good old Electra Glide Sport Solo, available from 1996 onwards, was more expensive still.

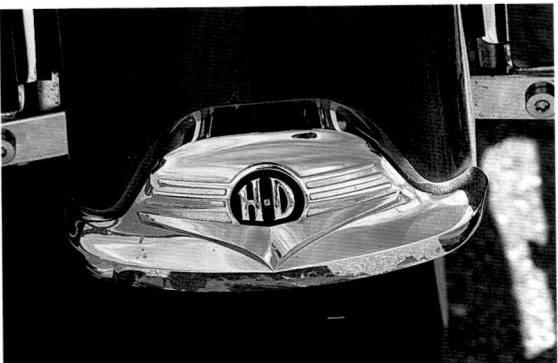

Road King FLHR, 1998.

The latest touring version of a leaner Electra Glide was issued in 1993 as the FLHS Electra Glide Sport. Particularly noticeable are the motor, kept matt, and the fiberglass oil–tank and battery covers.

Customized Bikes: Bowing to the Inevitable

The introduction of the Super Glide in 1971 was a long-overdue survival strategy that was crucial to attracting huge numbers of hitherto, badly neglected Harley fans into the fold. In addition, the introduction of the new Evolution engine in 1983 brought immediate success to the company as well. Its highly popular retro look, evoking all the mystique the name Harley-Davidson had taken on over the years, was extremely popular, but at the same time the Japanese, with their economically priced, reliable and luxurious high-tech machines, had bitten deep into the American big bike market. Harley-Davidson's production figures were slow to improve (1984: 38,825; 1985: 34,632; 1986: 39,116).

Moreover, in 1983 the company came up with a brilliant new marketing strategy: the Harley Owners Group (H.O.G.), which meant that all new Harley buyers suddenly found themselves part of a big Harley "family." The company was still strategizing over what kind of motorbikes their clientele wanted, and how far it could go in the direction of technological innovation.

In 1980 came the popular FXWG Wide Glide, also with a four-speed gearbox, the low seat, the wide Electra Glide forks, and a narrow, 21-inch, wire, front wheel fitted with a single disc brake: the ultimate radical chopper. Production of this very popular bike ran to 4,171 in 1985, and 1,200 in 1986. (Incidentally, a small number of motorcycles had been produced in 1984 with the old Shovelhead engine.)

In 1985, in the middle of this phase of radical transition, various new editions and improved custom models from Willie G.'s ever-creative design studio hit the showrooms. First there was the FXSB Low Rider, still fitted with the old four-speed gearbox and the conservative, not particularly attractive, but economical 19-inch, nine-spoke, cast alloy front wheel which evoked the now familiar outlaw look.

However, the third model in this range was a novelty: the FXEF Fat Bob, 2,324 of which were produced during its only year of manufacture. An attractive-looking, classical chopper had been developed from the old Shovelhead version, sporting a narrow 19-inch, wire-spoked front wheel, buckhorn handlebars, low 26-inch seat, and a hefty, 4.2 gallon gas tank on which a long, black, instrument panel was mounted.

All three models had the engine firmly screwed to the frame, so that the rider experienced the bike's "good vibrations" in full measure. However, a fundamental innovation was the final belt drive, which was viewed with suspicion by Harley fans before finally gaining acceptance. All three models only briefly survived in this form, and today, at the beginning of the 21st century, they are, in their original condition, much sought-after rarities from the beginnings of the Evolution era.

The FX Super Glide (Belt) Family	
1985	FXSB Low Rider (Belt) four-speed gearbox, 1985
1985–1986	FXWG Wide Glide (Belt) four-speed gearbox, 1985
1985	FXEF Fat Bob (Belt) four--speed gearbox, 1985

Standard version of the FXWG Wide Glide Belt from 1985.

A classic: the Electra Glide instrument panel of the FX Wide Glide.

Modest as ever: the single disc-brake in the 21-inch front wheel.

By now tried-and-tested and fully reliable: the Wide Glide's Gates Poly Chain toothed drivebelt (below).

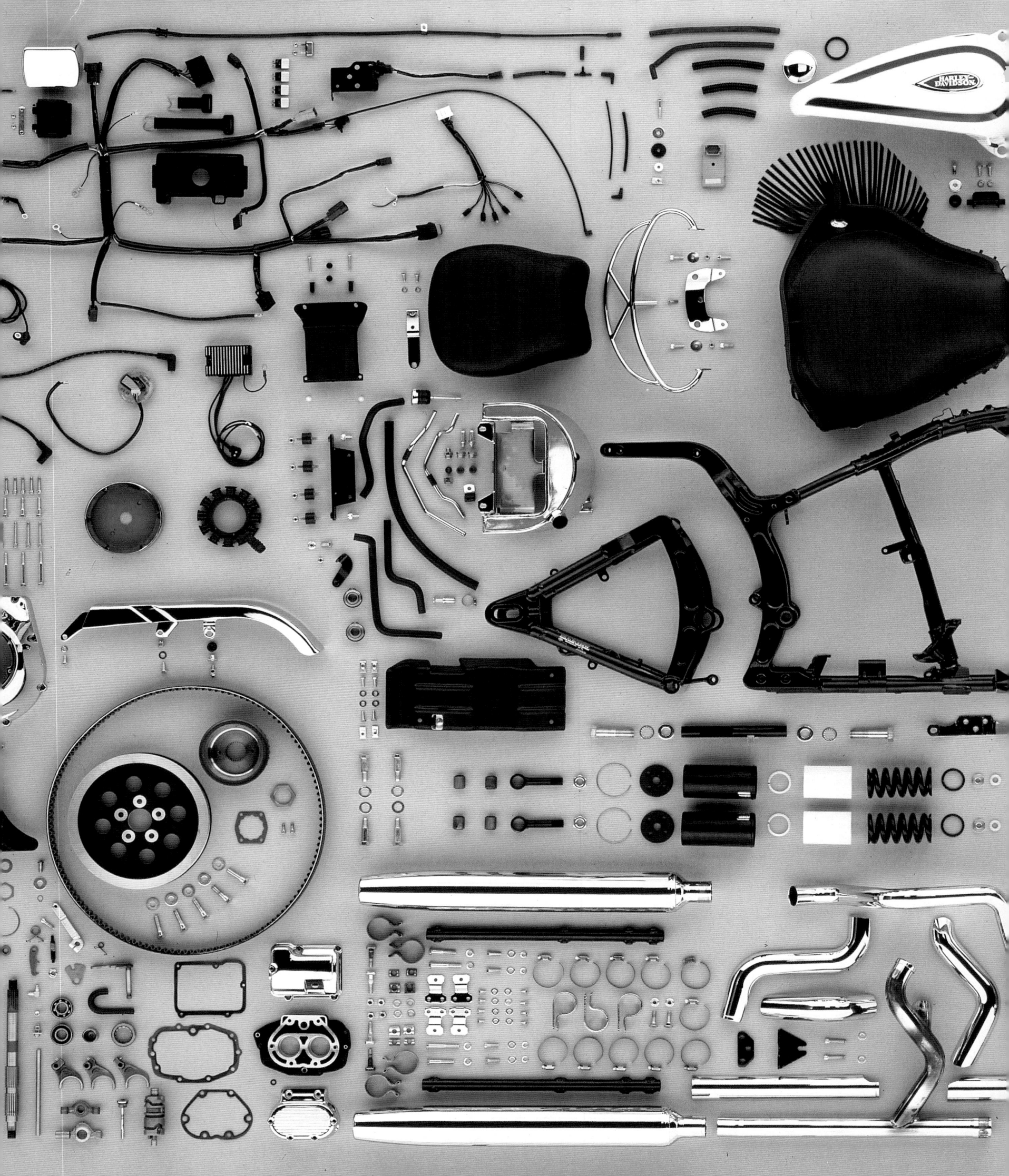

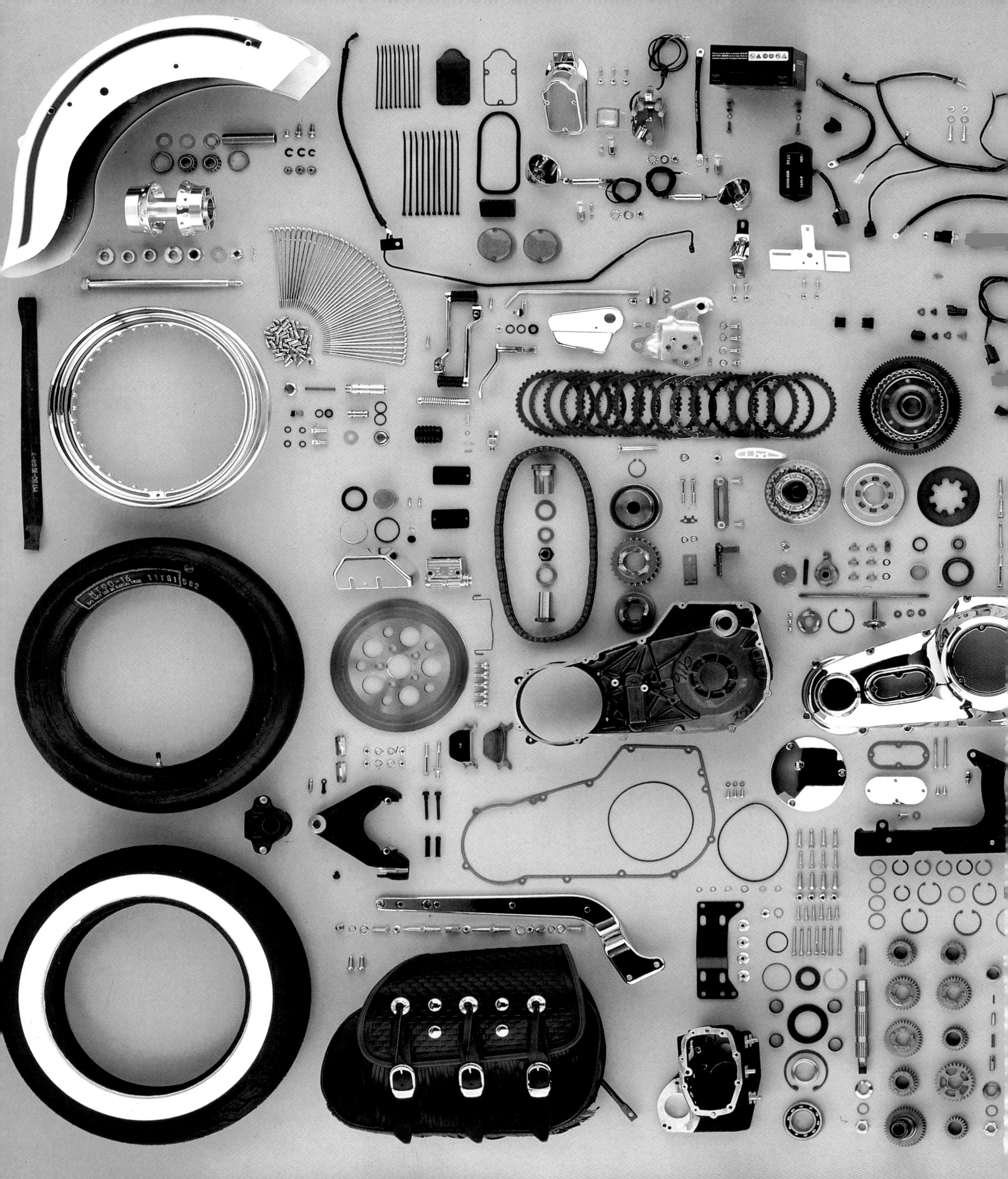

Imagine taking a modern Harley apart completely, that is, down to the smallest component. The only exceptions are those bits which are riveted or welded together. Then you must lay them all out neatly, and take a photograph of them in a single group. The photo will be 28 feet long and 8.5 feet wide, exposed with the utmost care on a fine-grained sheet of transparency film using an 8 x 10 inch special camera: this is the only way of being sure that even the tiniest part – a spring inside the automatic lifter which measures a mere 0.08 inches and is extremely delicate – can be recognized when reduced to a twentieth of its actual size. That's a real challenge! Finally you are able to see each of the production elements in all its glory, and display the innards of the legendary Harley just as you would on a dissection table. But it is no easy task to take to pieces all those parts which skillful hands and complex machinery have assembled: it demands the utmost concentration. After all, the owner will want their treasured Harley to run properly after it has been put together again. Then there are the logistics connected with displaying all the parts: no component, however small, none of the screws, nuts, split washers or shims, for example, can be lost. Are all the spokes and their nipples there? Just how many parts make up a modern Harley? Well, why not have a guess. Or count them...

To put it mildly, it's an expensive and time-consuming business to do this. A great deal of thought was put into as to whether there would be a cheaper way of producing this enormous photograph. Perhaps in separate sections, for example, which could then be manipulated on a computer and reassembled digitally. Each attempt at this was a complete and utter failure. It couldn't be done. So it was back to the original idea – one photograph, one flat surface, do it as a single take.

But this method demanded considerably more time and money than originally planned, due to the fact that it turned out to involve several operations, The parts, carefully dismantled and sorted, had to be arranged and the layout that was planned proved to be unsatisfactory the first time around. The arrangement and the height of the camera (19.7 feet) were just not right, even though (or perhaps because) a wide-angle lens was used: it resulted in totally unacceptable distortions in the photograph and the layout of all the parts got out of hand. The cost of this first (three-day) experiment amounted to 30,000 German marks (around 16,500 dollars).

Everything was collected up again and it was started anew. Six dedicated, highly motivated individuals labored away for another four days and nights around the clock, bent over, sliding around on their knees, moving the parts into their correct positions – working from the center concentrically outwards – in their stockinged feet or half crawling, half lying on mats in order to fix each part precisely where it had to be, sometimes even using plasticine to do this.

The photographer Dieter Rebmann was in command – and this is meant quite literally – from 50 feet up in the air where the camera was high enough to see everything; Harley specialist and master mechanic Reinhold Paukner and his wife, Karin, as well as Dieter Rebmann's wife, Gaby, oversaw the ground logistics of the operation. The first Polaroid photograph served as the guide to work from.

The advantage of this trial run was that the precise size and area occupied by the picture could be worked out, determined by the format of the centerfold, which made it easy to calculate the necessary height of the studio. It had to be 50 feet high, if there was to be just one single photograph. This was something to be really proud of. Just how many test photographs had to be taken is impossible to say — and each of them was on Polaroid sheet film measuring 20 x 25.5 (each costing 30 German marks, or about 16 dollars and 50 cents) which had to be developed on the spot. For the final photograph, fine-grained Velvia (50 ASA) sheet film was selected.

A gigantic studio was hired, one normally used for advertising takes and owned by the Rieker company in Stuttgart, for five action-packed days between Christmas and New Year — at a special price of 3,000 German marks (about 1,650 dollars) per day, including the laboratory (and the kitchen). The time just flew, during which the costs had started to exceed the planned budget many times over and in our times the project was developing an awe-inspiring will of its own. Sometimes a joke was made of it all, sometimes the turn of events was horrific.

But somehow or other it was finished, and with an explosion of flash bulbs from the enormous bank of lights, the final photograph was shot. A special vacuum plate holder contained the horizontal film sheet. The result is certainly impressive, isn't it? And, of course, packed with information. Afterwards, everything was collected together carefully and packed up. Over the next few months, it was the task of the master mechanic, Pauki, to watch over the reassembly of all the components to make a roadworthy 1997 Harley-Davidson FLSTS Heritage Springer again. Any more questions? Now, as they say, you know the whole story.

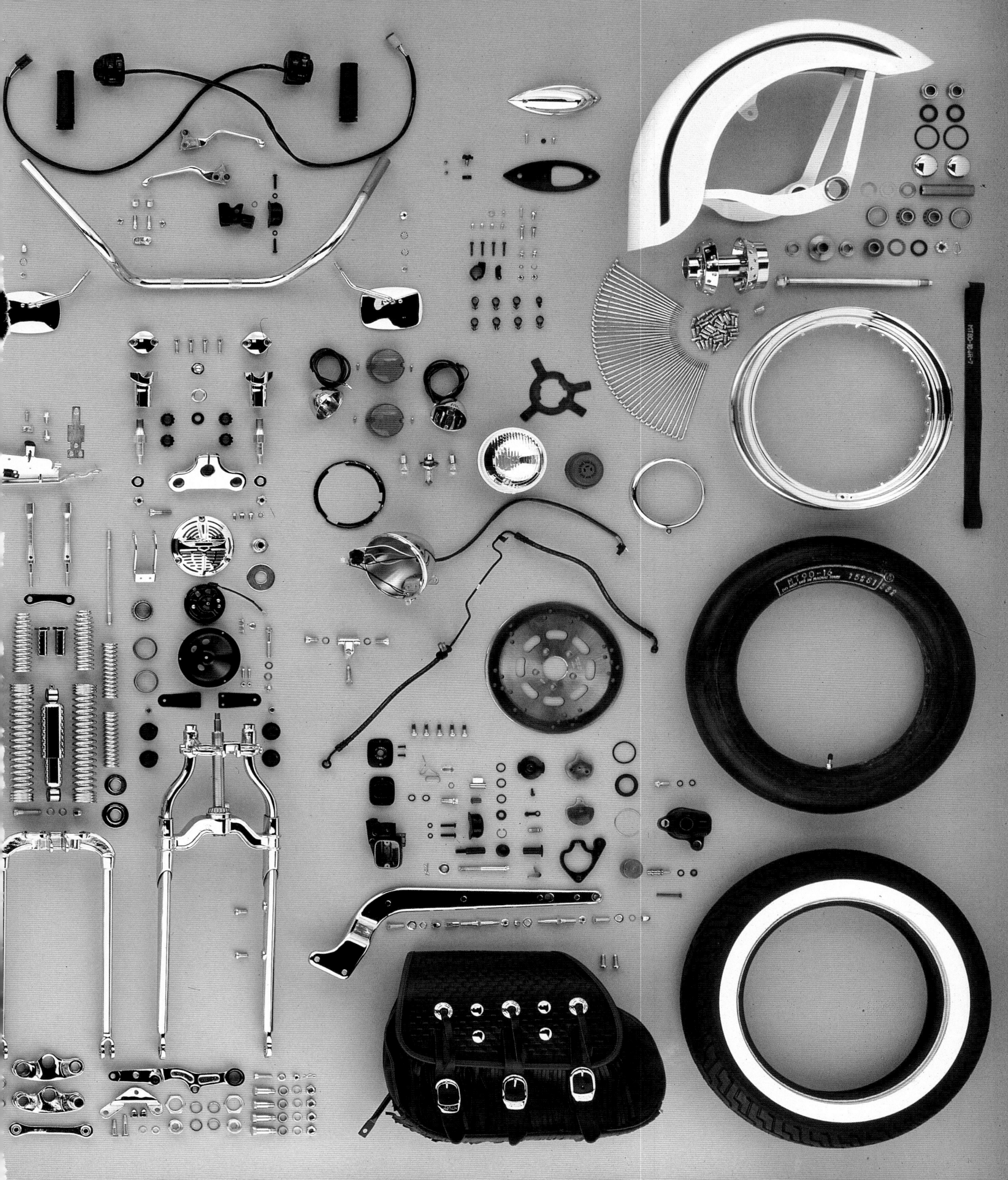

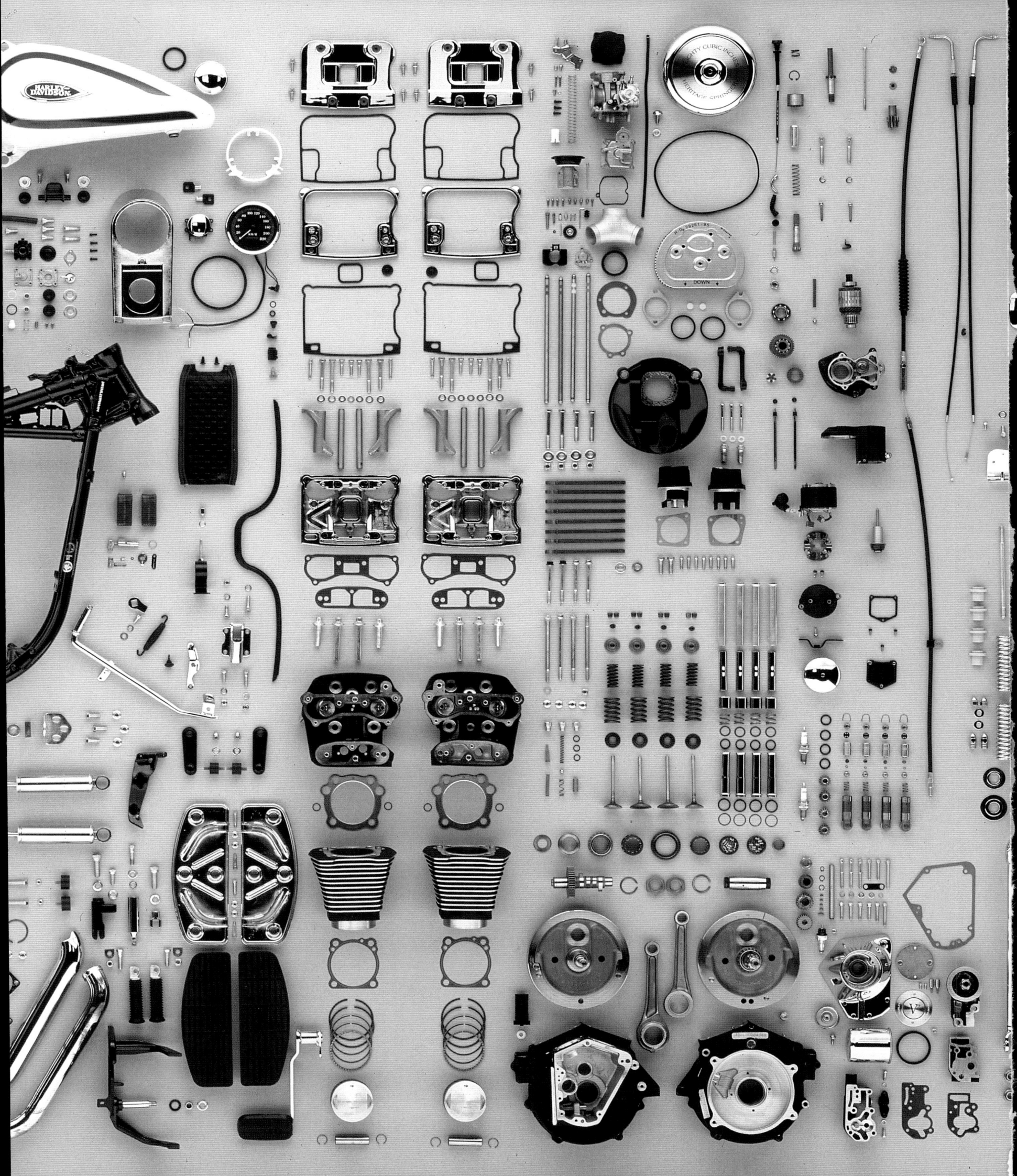

Bewildering Variety – the Low Rider Series 1982–1983

Harley called it the Low Rider series. However, that is not entirely accurate since Low Riders exist in other forms too. More accurate would be the designation the FXR series, though this is clearly not the most ecovative description. In this abbreviation, R is the reference letter for "rubber isolated drivetrain" i.e. the rubber mounted, V-Twin engine.

The first of these rubber-mounted FXRs appeared in 1982, one of five Harley models to be fitted during this year with the new Shovelhead engine. These were the FXRS Low Glide, the FXRT Sport Glide, and the FXRDG Disc Glide with the unusual, aluminum disc, rear wheel. Later a wide selection of custom combinations appeared in this range, such as the FXRC Low Glide Custom (1985), a new edition of the Super Glide, the FXR (1986), the FXRD Sport Glide Grand Touring and the FXRS, the second edition of the Low Rider (1990).

Two models do not fit into this reference letter scheme, in that they are designated with the suffix "LR" rather than "R," the LR standing for Low Rider. These were the FXLR Low Rider Custom (1987) and its sister bike the FXRS-Convertible Low Rider (1989), which was also sold as the FXRS-CON. This was a Sport/Touring combination on which the windshield and saddlebags could be easily detached or remounted as required.

In the year 1994 this FXR series was discontinued though the basic type still remained part of the Harley-Davidson program.

Some of the features of the Low Rider Series are as follows: the basic model was the FXRS Low Glide, renamed the FXRS Low Rider in 1990. This replaced the Super Glide II. Some of these were sold in 1982-83 with the old Shovelhead engine, though they already then had the new five-speed gearbox, final belt drive, and a three-disc brake system.

The FXRT Sport Glide was also first produced in 1983 with the old Shovelhead engine, leading in 1986 to the FXRD Sport Glide - Grand Touring Edition. A variant of this in the U.S. was a police version, the FXRP Sport Glide Police.

In 1985 a variant of the FXRS, the FXRC Low Glide Custom, appeared for a single year as a limited edition with wire wheels, and plenty of chrome.

In 1987 the FXLR Low Rider Custom was developed from the 1984 FXRDG Disc Glide. The motorcycle kept the Disc Glide's aluminum disc rear wheel and had a gauge-free fuel-tank – the speedometer mounted in front of the handle-bar being the only instrument. Another unusual feature of this model was the narrow 21-inch wire front wheel.

A feature of this whole model range was that, year after year, countless technical modifications were made and stylistic novelties introduced, making classification harder than ever. New tank logos, modified, stronger forks with increased travel and a variety of steering head angles, muffler systems, seats, highway pegs, multifarious instrument panel designs, sometimes belt and sometimes chain drive, all conspired to make it impossible to identify a clear model line. Harley was fully committed to this muddling policy, launching supposedly "new" models onto the market every year with a fanfare of publicity, although they were technically virtually identical. Essentially, what they did was to shuffle around the different basic components of frame, forks, handlebars, wheels, fuel-tanks, and accessories, always retaining the same engine and transmission, and entice the fans with a new combinations of letters and maybe a snappy new, trademarked name. The FXR range is a typical example of this policy.

The FXRDG Disc Glide (1984) took it name from the compact cast disc rear wheel.

The standard version FXRS Low Glide with hamcan air filter.

The Evolution FXR Low Rider Family:

1984–1987	FXRS (I) Low Glide
1984–1992	FXRT Sport Glide
1984	FXRP Sport Glide Police (U.S. only)
1984	FXRDG Disc Glide Limited Edition
1985	FXRC Low Glide Gustom Limited Edition
1986–1994	FXR Super Glide
1986	FXRT Sport Glide Grand Touring
1987–1993	FXRS–SP Low Rider Sport Edition
1987–1994	FXLR Low Rider Custom
1989–1993	FXLR–CON/FXRS–CON Low Rider Convertible
1987–1991	FXRS (II) Low Rider

The FXRC Low Glide Custom Limited Edition with seat upholstered in brown manmade leather.

Rear wheels: FXRS 1985 Low Glide, FXRDG Disc Glide with chain drive, and the FXRC Low Glide Custom Belt (right, from top to bottom).

The Low Rider Series: FXRT

Courtesy of: H.D. Archives

Type:	**FXRT**
Model:	**Sport Glide**
Years of manufacture:	1984–1992
Engine:	Air-cooled four-stroke overhead-v rubber-mounted Evolution 45° V-1
Cubic capacity:	81.65 cu in (1338 cc)
Bore x stroke:	3.5 x 4.25 in (89 x 108 mm)
Compression ratio:	8.5 : 1
Power output:	61 hp
Carburetor:	38 mm ø with accelerator pump
Transmission:	Five-speed
Primary drive:	Duplex chain
Final drive:	Gates Kevlar Poly Chain belt
Battery:	12 volt/19 ah
Ignition:	Electronic V-Fire III, breakerless
Frame:	Tubular steel cradle (double downtube)
Front brake:	Double disc
Rear brake:	Single disc
Front suspension:	Telescopic forks
Rear suspension:	Shock absorber swingarm
Wheelbase:	64.7 in
Weight:	683 lb
Fuel capacity:	4.2 gal
Oil capacity:	3 qts
Front tire:	MJ 90 x 19
Rear tire:	MT 90 x 16
Top speed:	96 mph
Price:	$9,156 (1987)

Standard version of the FXRT from 1984.

The Low Rider Series: FXLR and FXRS–SP

FXRS–SP Low Rider
Sport Edition, 1987

FXLR Low Rider Custom, 1987

Fuel–tank–mounted instrument panel
of the FXRS–SP, with integrated
filler caps, fuel gauge and twin
instruments displaced forwards.

Dragster handlebars on the FXLR with
a single instrument.

The Low Rider Series: FXR

Type:	**FXR**
Model:	**Super Glide**
Years of manufacture:	1986–1994
Engine:	Air-cooled four-stroke overhead-rubber-mounted Evolution 45° V
Cubic capacity:	81.65 cu in (1338 cc)
Bore x stroke:	3.5 x 4.25 in (89 x 108 mm)
Compression ratio:	8.5 : 1
Power output:	61 hp
Carburetor:	38 mm ø with accelerator pum
Transmission:	Five-speed
Primary drive:	Duplex chain
Final drive:	Gates Kevlar Poly Chain belt
Battery:	12 volt/19 ah
Ignition:	Electronic V–Fire III, breakerles
Frame:	Tubular steel cradle (double downtube)
Front brake:	Disc
Rear brake:	Disc
Front suspension:	Telescopic forks
Rear suspension:	Shock absorber swingarm
Wheelbase:	63.1 in
Weight:	594 lb
Fuel capacity:	4.2 gal
Oil capacity:	3 qts
Front tire:	MJ 90 x 19
Rear tire:	MT 90 x 16
Top speed:	93 mph
Price:	$7,920 (1987)

© Harley-Davidson

The indicator lamps of the FXR are integrated in the lamp cover.

Front view of the 1986 FXR Super Glide

The fuel–tank console of the FXR Super Glide houses the speedometer and fuel–tank filler cap.

The Low Rider Series: FXRS and FXRS–CONV

Type:	**FXRS**
Model:	**Low Rider**
Years of manufacture:	1987–1991
Engine:	Air–cooled four stroke overhead–valve rubber–mounted Evolution 45º V–Twin
Cubic capacity:	81.65 cu in (1338 cc)
Bore x stroke:	3.5 x 4.25 in (89 x 108 mm)
Compression ratio:	8.5 : 1
Power output:	55 hp
Carburetor:	38 mm ø with accelerator pump
Transmission:	Five–speed
Primary drive:	Duplex chain
Final drive:	Gates Kevlar Poly Chain
Battery:	12 volt/19 ah
Ignition:	Electronic V–Fire III, breakerless
Frame:	Tubular steel cradle (double downtube)
Front brake:	Disc
Rear brake:	Disc
Front suspension:	Telescopic forks
Rear suspension:	Shock absorber swingarm
Wheelbase:	63.1 in
Weight:	580 lb
Fuel capacity:	4.5 gal
Oil capacity:	3 qts
Front tire:	MJ 90 x 19
Rear tire:	MT 90 x 16
Top speed:	110 mph
Price:	$8,499 (1987)

Model versions:
Also available as the FXRS–CON Low Rider Convertible with detachable windshield and saddlebags.

Quickly removable front windshield and leather saddlebags: the 1993 FXRS Convertible.

The Myth Lives On – Nostalgia and the Softails

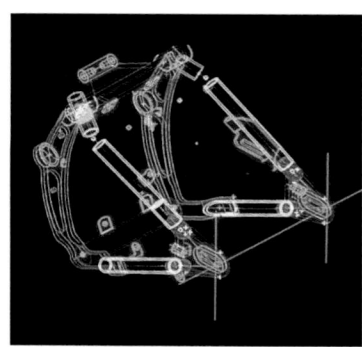

© Harley-Davidson

The Softail's rear swingarm suspension system is the invention of the St. Louis motorcycle designer Bill Davis, whose small company Road Work was already producing this brilliantly conceived mobile frame component which visually resembles a rigid, hardtail frame, before Harley-Davidson purchased the patent license from him.

With Willie G. Davidson's assistance a new Harley model was developed from this which bore an extraordinary visual similarity to the old rigid frame machines from the 1950s, but which, in fact, possessed a highly effective shock absorber, hence the name Softail. Its secret lies in the two gas-pressure shock absorbers which damp the rear swingarm from an invisible site under the transmission, which is firmly bolted to the frame. Actually, this technique is not entirely new: the small, two-stroke machines from the early 1960s, the Scat and the Bobcat, employed a similar suspension system, though only using a single strut, and the British company Vincent employed a similar technique way back in the 1930s. However, for Harley the Softail, which was introduced in 1984 along with the Evolution engine, was the definitive chopper.

There are two basic variants of the Softail: the FX model with the narrow, 21-inch, wire-spoke front wheel, and the FL model, fitted both front and rear with the wide, 16-inch, wire wheel of the early Electra Glide design. Both variants are also available in Classic and Custom versions with various extras, and special editions of each type are brought out, either fitted with the old springer forks for the nostalgia market, or in a couple of special custom models: the Fat Boy and the Bad Boy.

The Evolution FX Softail Family

1984	FXST Softail (with four-speed gearbox)
1985–1990	FXST Softail (with five-speed gearbox)
1986 onwards	FXSTC Softail Custom
1988 onwards	FXSTS Softail Springer
1995–1997	FXSTSB Bad Boy

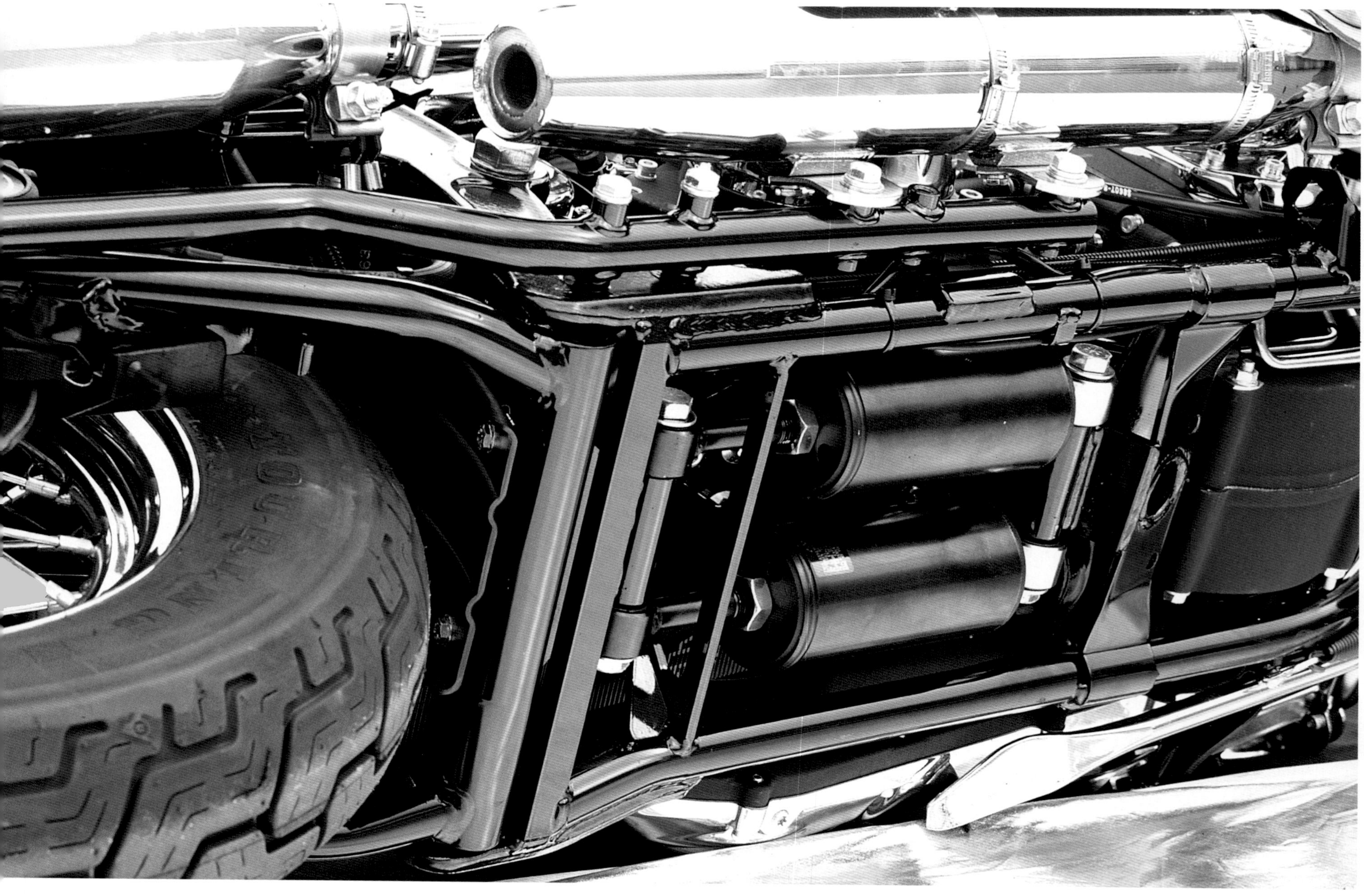

Only visible from below: the two shock absorber units of the rear-wheel swingarm beneath the transmission.

The Springer Fork

The reintroduction of the old springer front forks was both technically and stylistically a master stroke, but it was not altogether a simple matter. It enabled Harley to demonstrate clearly that a classic appearance and modern engineering demands could be reconciled.

Among the features of the new Softail Springer, which had double the spring travel of the 1948 version, were Teflon bearings, computer-aided engineering, and a powerful disc brake to replace the inefficient drum brake of the original. When introduced, customers complained about the high-mounted front fenders which resembled those of a dirt bike, so Harley, wanting to satisfy the wishes of the customers, used some clever engineering to make it possible to fit these closer to the narrow tires. Customers were pleased with the new look.

The "old" springer fork with additional shock absorber and custom minilamp in the chrome-plated standard design.

The front fender — initially raised — was soon lowered in line with customer wishes.

U.S. Patent 4,775,163 Patented Springer

The U.S. Patent Office granted a patent covering the "Springer." This excludes others from "making, using or selling this invention throughout the United States of America for the term of seventeen years from the date of this patent, subject to the payment of fees as provided by law."
Harley-Davidson engineers Tom McGowen and Steve Wentworth are listed on the patent as the inventors with Harley-Davidson as the assignee.   From: *The Enthusiast*, 1989

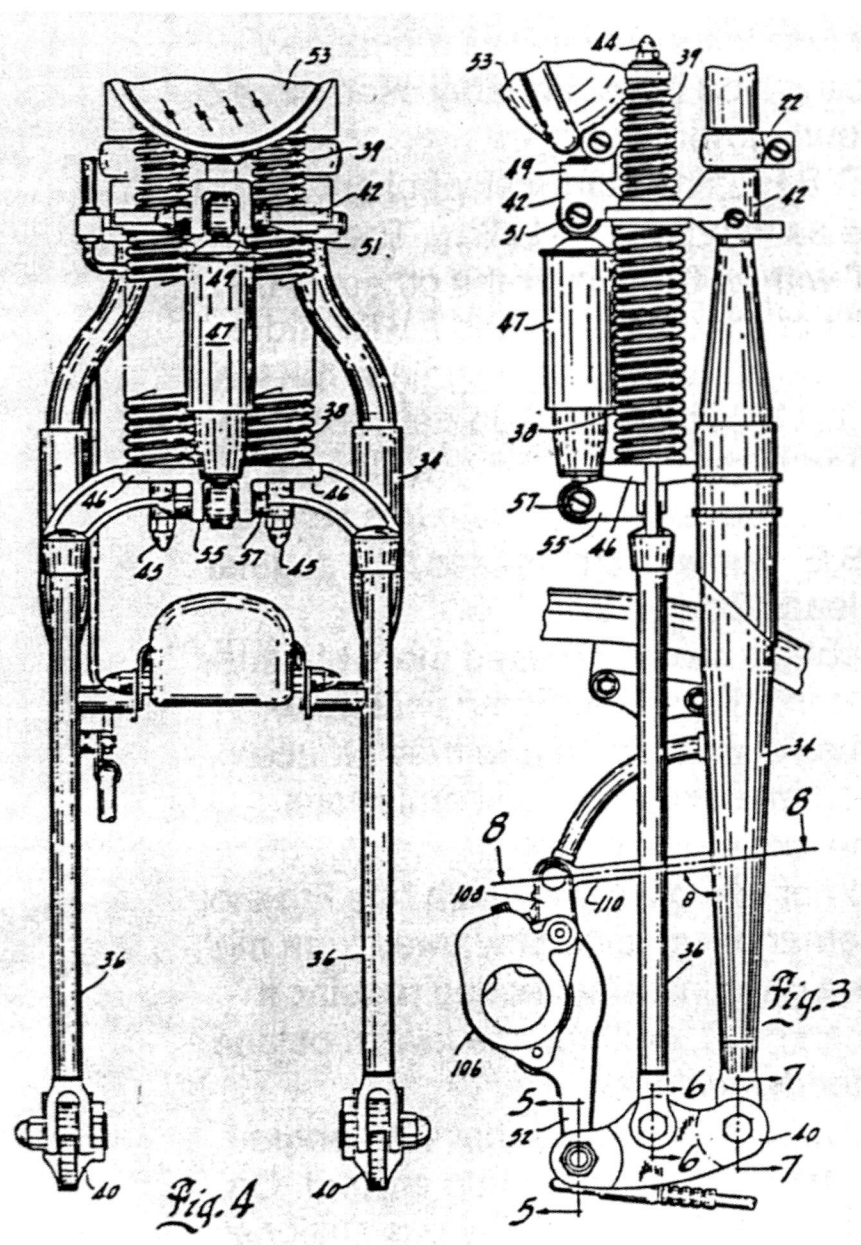

© Harley-Davidson

The FX Softail

The basic model was the FXST, a laid-back chopper with a low saddle position, the characteristic large, narrow front wheel, the long slanted forks, the staggered dual exhaust fitted on the right-hand side, and, of course, the new five-speed gearbox and final belt drive. The bulky gas tank with a classic instrument panel, the horseshoe oil tank, the small lights and the typical custom "bobbed" rear fender rounded off the 1950s look. This was even more pronounced in the heavily-styled FXSTC, the Softail Custom, which was dominated by solid aluminum rear wheels, still higher buckhorn handlebars, an extra sissy bar, and any amount of glistening chrome-plated trim. The Softail Custom was immediately a huge success, 3,782 being sold in 1986, its first year of production, a further 5,264 in 1987, 6,621 in 1988, and so it went on.

In 1988, the FXSTS, the first Softail with the reintroduced springer forks, appeared, initially as a special edition to mark the firm's 85th anniversary.

In 1995, yet another Custom model was brought out, the FXSTSB Bad Boy. This could not have been more radical. With its black springer forks, 21-inch front wheel, floating disc brakes, and the obligatory, slotted disc 16-inch rear wheel plus plenty of gleaming chrome, the Bad Boy was a mean machine even with a tinted windshield fitted.

Another classic: the fuel-tank console with speedometer, odometer, daily mileage counter, reset button and choke, as well as indicator lamps and ignition switch. The two fuel-tank filler caps are intended for filling the two separate tank halves, although both halves are connected by a fuel-level compensation hose.

© Harley-Davidson

From the Softail series: FXSTB Bad Boy 1996 (above), and FXST Softail 1989 (right).

FXSTS Softail Springer 1989 (above), and FXST Softail Custom 1998 (left).

Type:	**FXST**
Model:	**Softail**
Years of manufacture:	1985–1990
Engine:	Air–cooled four–stroke overhead–valve Evolution 45º V–Twin
Cubic capacity:	81.65 cu in (1338 cc)
Bore x stroke:	3.5 x 4.25 in (89 x 108 mm)
Compression ratio:	8.5 : 1
Power output:	65 hp
Carburetor:	38 mm ø with accelerator pump
Transmission:	Five–speed
Primary drive:	Duplex chain
Final drive:	Gates Kevlar Poly Chain belt
Battery:	12 volt/19 ah
Ignition:	Electronic V–Fire III, breakerless
Frame:	Tubular steel cradle (double downtube) with triangular swingarm
Front brake:	Disc
Rear brake:	Disc
Front suspension:	Telescopic forks
Rear suspension:	Softail swingarm with two, gas–pressure shock absorbers
Wheelbase:	66.3 in
Weight:	628 lb
Fuel capacity:	5.2 gal
Oil capacity:	3 qts
Front tire:	MJ 90 x 21
Rear tire:	MT 90 x 16
Top speed:	108 mph
Price:	$8,949 (1987)
Model versions:	FXSTC Softail Custom

Type:	**FXSTS**
Model:	**Softail Springer**
Years of manufacture:	1988 onwards
Engine:	Air–cooled four–stroke overhead–valve Evolution 45º V–Twin
Cubic capacity:	81.65 cu in (1338 cc)
Bore x stroke:	3.5 x 4.25 in (89 x 108 mm)
Compression ratio:	8.5 : 1
Power output:	61 hp
Carburetor:	Keihin 40 mm ø constant velocity
Transmission:	Five–speed
Primary drive:	Duplex chain
Final drive:	Gates Kevlar Poly Chain belt
Battery:	12 volt/19 ah
Ignition:	Electronic V–Fire III, breakerless
Frame:	Tubular steel cradle (double downtube) with triangular swingarm
Front brake:	Disc
Rear brake:	Disc
Front suspension:	New springer, 32º angle
Rear suspension:	Softail swingarm with two gas–pressure shock absorbers
Wheelbase:	64.4 in
Weight:	445 lb
Fuel capacity:	4.2 gal
Oil capacity:	3 qts
Front tire:	MJ 90 x 21
Rear tire:	MT 90 x 16
Top speed:	90 mph
Price:	$10,695 (1988)
Model versions:	1988 Softail Springer Anniversary

The new outfit of the old Springer fork: the old Techno logo of the first Springer fork serves as a reminder of its origins on the central shock–absorber of this FXST Softail Springer.

The FL Softail

Its main distinguishing feature was the wide, 16-inch front wheel from the earlier Electra Glide; up to a point this was a slimmed-down version of the massive highway cruiser, with the FX exhaust to one side, no fairing, but with the characteristic front end: the big headlights, the wide, shrouded front forks, and the large, front fenders.

The basic model was the FLST Heritage Softail, introduced in 1986, to which the FLSTC with the "studs and conchos" look was added a year later, with studded leather saddlebags and plenty of chrome-plated accessories. Once again this harked back to the highly popular 1950s look, as did the fishtail muffler (which was banned on the German version however), and the two extra headlights on either side.

Willie G.'s vision of the future, with the harmless-sounding designation FLSTF Fat Boy, appeared in 1990 like a bolt from the blue. This was an extremely futuristic design, both radical and at the same time vaguely reminiscent of the spacecraft of the Flash Gordon era, but all in all the absolute antithesis of the previous Softail policy. With its silver metallic paint and solid front and rear wheels, the uncompromisingly styled Fat Boy looked more like a space cruiser on two wheels than

a nostalgic Harley. The first 4,440 to be produced were snapped up at once, and today the highly popular Fat Boy remains an outsider among the largely nostalgically styled, classic, Harley model range.

In 1993 the FLSTN Nostalgia appeared in a limited edition. Colored off-white and black, it was nicknamed "Cow Glide" – a reference to the original leather cowhide inserts in the seat, which unfortunately tended to molt somewhat. Its distinguishing characteristics were the narrow leather saddlebags, the 16-inch wire wheels, and the swept-back rear fender. Although it kept the reference letters FLSTN after 1994, its name changed to the Heritage Softail Special, the cowhide seat disappeared, and the colors were changed.

In 1997 Harley brought out yet another model to add to the nostalgia range. This was the Heritage Springer, this time with springer front forks, and the old attachments used for the wide Hydra Glide fenders. The leather braided and tasseled saddlebags, whitewall tires, and wide 16-inch wheels front and rear meant that the Heritage looked almost like a 1948 Harley. Since, more than any other, this model embodies the charisma of the Harley-Davidson motorcycle, it has been chosen as the subject of the centerfold poster within this book,

thereby capturing the mystique and, in a manner of speaking, separating it into its component parts. Once reassembled, it reminds one of those marvelous old-style Western saloons in the movies, where any unpleasant reminders of the modern world are swept discreetly under the carpet.

The Evolution FL Softail Family

1987–1990	FLST	Heritage Softail
1988 onwards	FLSTC	Heritage Softail Classic
1990 onwards	FLSTF	Fat Boy
1993	FLSTN	Heritage Softail Nostalgia
1994 onwards	FLSTN	Heritage Softail Special
1997 onwards	FLSTS	Heritage Springer

The FLST Heritage Softail available from 1987 – a stripped-down version of the Electra Glide.

The Heritage Softail Series: FLST, FLSTC

Type:	**FLST**
Model:	**Heritage Softail**
Years of manufacture:	1987–1990
Engine:	Air-cooled four-stroke overhead-valve Evolution 45° V-Twin
Cubic capacity:	81.65 cu in (1338 cc)
Bore x stroke:	3.5 x 4.25 in (89 x 108 mm)
Compression ratio:	8.5 : 1
Power output:	65 hp
Carburetor:	38 mm ø with accelerator pump
Transmission:	Five-speed
Primary drive:	Duplex chain
Final drive:	Gates Kevlar Poly Chain belt
Battery:	12 volt/19 ah
Ignition:	Electronic V-Fire III, breakerless
Frame:	Tubular steel cradle (double downtube) with triangular swingarm
Front brake:	Disc
Rear brake:	Disc
Front suspension:	Telescopic forks
Rear suspension:	Softail swingarm with two gas-pressure shock absorbers
Wheelbase:	62.5 in
Weight:	628 lb
Fuel capacity:	4.2 gal
Oil capacity:	3 qts
Front tire:	MJ 90 x 16
Rear tire:	MT 90 x 16
Top speed:	103 mph
Price:	$9,329 (1989)
Model versions:	FLSTC Softail Classic
	FLSTN Heritage Softail Special

In the Classic version FLSTC, the Softail Heritage is also fitted with a windshield, as well as studded and fringed leather saddlebags.

The Heritage Softail-Series: FLSTS, FLSTN

FLSTS Heritage Softail Springer, 95th Anniversary Edition.

The 1993 FLSTN Nostalgia sporting its famous cowhide seat (Cow Glide).

The Heritage Softail Series: FLSTF

Type:	**FLSTF**
Model:	**Fat Boy**
Years of manufacture:	1990 onwards
Engine:	Air-cooled four-stroke overhead-valve Evolution 45° V-Twin
Cubic capacity:	81.65 cu in (1338 cc)
Bore x stroke:	3.5 x 4.25 in (89 x 108 mm)
Compression ratio:	8.5 : 1
Power output:	56 hp
Carburetor:	Keihin 40 mm ø constant velocity
Transmission:	Five-speed
Primary drive:	Duplex chain
Final drive:	Gates Kevlar Poly Chain belt
Battery:	12 volt/19 ah
Ignition:	Electronic V-Fire III, breakerless
Frame:	Tubular steel cradle (double downtube) with triangular swingarm
Front brake:	Disc
Rear brake:	Disc
Front suspension:	Telescopic forks
Rear suspension:	Softail swingarm with two gas-pressure shock absorbers
Wheelbase:	63.9 in
Weight:	657 lb
Fuel capacity:	4.2 gal
Oil capacity:	3 qts
Front tire:	MJ 90 x 16
Rear tire:	MT 90 x 16
Top speed:	90 mph
Price:	$10,995 (1990)
Model versions:	Also in various color combinations 95th Anniversary Edition 1998

The distinguishing feature of the futuristic-looking Fat Boy finished completely in silver is the yellow central cover on the cylinder heads.

© Harley-Davidson

Two fully-cast disc wheels and finished completely in silver: the FLSTF Fat Boy. A particularly noticeable characteristic is the yellow central element of the cylinder heads.

© Harley-Davidson

© Harley-Davidson

Modern Engineering and a New Dynamism

In 1991 a new generation of Harleys incorporating more advanced engineering appeared: the Dyna Glides, with their sophisticated frame benefiting from CAD (computer-aided design) techniques. The engine, which was inclined 4 degrees aft and moved slightly forward, was mounted in the steel frame by means of two rather than four vibration-damping, rubber components. The frame itself, the continuous backbone of which consisted of a solid, square-section tube, had extra bracing at the steering head. The oil tank was now situated under the transmission and the easy-open cap had a built-in oil dipstick. The crossover pipe of the low-mounted, FX exhaust system was hidden away, and the belt drive could now at last be replaced without first having to dismantle the rear wheel swingarm. The tank-mounted instrument panel was redesigned, and a forgery-proof manufacturer's identification plate was developed in collaboration with Wisconsin Forensic Laboratory. Incidentally, Trev Deeley played a major part in the development of the Dyna Glides; details can be found in his *Motorcycle Millionaire*.

The first Dyna Glide model was the all-black FXDB Sturgis, the second bike to bear this name. Like all Dyna Glides apart from the Dyna Wide Glide it had a 19-inch,

nine-spoke, cast alloy front wheel with a single brake disc. In 1992, the model's second year, two similar Dyna Glide models appeared in limited editions of 1,700: the FXDB Daytona in celebration of the 50th anniversary of Daytona race week, and the metallic silver and black FXDC Dyna Glide Custom with a powder-coated frame. In both models, the cast alloy front wheel was fitted with a double disc brake. On the European market a wire-spoke front wheel was available as an option.

In 1993 the third Dyna Glide appeared in the form of the FXDL Dyna Low Rider, again with the 19-inch alloy or wire-spoke front wheel with double disc brakes and "pull-back" handlebars: almost a conservative custom design in fact. New features included the electronic speedometer, now fitted on all Dyna Glides.

The FXDWG Dyna Wide Glide, which also debuted in 1993, was an entirely different combination. It was fitted with a big, 21-inch, wire front wheel with a single disc brake fitted in Wide Glide forks, which were slanted forwards at an angle of 35 degrees, Ape Hanger handlebars, forward-mounted highway pegs, the bobbed rear fender with the license plate fitted low, and the old Electra Glide instrument panel with a large speedometer on the gas tank. Otherwise it stuck to the Dyna Glide

format. In 1993, precisely 1,993 Dyna Wide Glides were produced to mark the 90th anniversary of Harley-Davidson's founding.

In 1994 the "sporty" FXDS-CON Low Rider Convertible was brought out, a model which could rapidly be changed from a normal Dyna Low Rider into either a Tourer or a Sport model, superficially at least. In reality, mounting or dismounting the windshield and leather saddlebags was little more than a visual gimmick.

In 1995 the stripped-down base model of the Dyna Glide series, the FXR Dyna Super Glide, finally appeared in its original form shorn of any fancy paraphernalia, and also with an alloy (wire-spoke was also available in Europe) front wheel fitted with just a single disc brake. In 1994 it was available in a single color as the most reasonably-priced Big Twin, costing 9,995 dollars.

The second Dyna Glide model was launched in 1992 – the Daytona.

The Dyna Glide Series: FXDB, FXDWG, FXD, FXDS and FXDL

© Harley-Davidson

FXDS-CON Dyna Low Rider Convertible (top).
FXDWG Dyna Wide Glide, 1995 (above).
FXD Super Glide, 1995 (right).
FXDL Dyna Low Rider, 1998 (below).

FXDB Dyna Glide Sturgis, 1991.

Type:	**FXDB**
Model:	**Dyna Glide Sturgis**
Year of manufacture:	1991
Engine:	Air-cooled four-stroke overhead-valve Evolution 45° V-Twin two-point rubber mounting
Cubic capacity:	81.65 cu in (1338 cc)
Bore x stroke:	3.5 x 4.25 in (89 x 108 mm)
Compression ratio:	8.5 : 1
Power output:	55 hp
Carburetor:	Keihin 40 mm ø constant velocity
Transmission:	Five-speed
Primary drive:	Duplex chain
Final drive:	Gates Kevlar Poly Chain belt
Battery:	12 volt/19 ah
Ignition:	Electronic V-Fire III, breakerless
Frame:	CAD tubular steel cradle (double downtube)
Front brake:	Disc
Rear brake:	Disc
Front suspension:	Telescopic fork wide-glide 35°
Rear suspension:	Swingarm/shock absorbers
Wheelbase:	65.5 in
Weight:	617 lb
Fuel capacity:	5 gal with fuel gauge
Oil capacity:	3 qts
Front tire:	MJ 90 x 19
Rear tire:	MT 90 x 16
Top speed:	99 mph
Price:	$12,120

Type:	**FXDWG**
Model:	**Dyna Wide Glide**
Years of manufacture:	1993 onwards
Engine:	Air-cooled four-stroke overhead-valve Evolution 45° V-Twin two-point rubber mounting
Cubic capacity:	81.65 cu in (1338 cc)
Bore x stroke:	3.5 x 4.25 in (89 x 108 mm)
Compression ratio:	8.5 : 1
Power output:	56 hp
Carburetor:	Keihin 40 mm ø constant velocity
Transmission:	Five-speed
Primary drive:	Duplex chain
Final drive:	Belt drive
Battery:	12 volt/19 ah
Ignition:	Electronic breakerless
Frame:	CAD tubular steel cradle (double downtube)
Front brake:	Disc
Rear brake:	Disc
Front suspension:	Telescopic fork wide-glide 35°
Rear suspension:	Swingarm/shock absorber
Wheelbase:	66 in
Weight:	650 lb
Fuel capacity:	5 gal
Oil capacity:	3 qts
Front tire:	MJ 90 x 21
Rear tire:	MT 90 x 16
Top speed:	99 mph
Price:	$12,550 (90th Anniversary Edition)

The FX Dyna Evolution Family

1991	FXDB Dyna Glide Sturgis
1992	FXDB Dyna Glide Daytona
1992	FXDC Dyna Glide Custom
1993 onwards	FXDL Dyna Low Rider
1993 onwards	FXDWG Dyna Wide Glide
1994 onwards	FXDS-CON Dyna Low Rider Convertible
1995 onwards	FXD Dyna Super Glide

The Evo Sportster

After the introduction of the Evolution engine in 1984, it was to be a further two years before the modern high-tech power unit was ready for the Sportster range. The new Evolution Sportster models were introduced into the market in 1986, replacing the old 61 cubic inch (1000 cc) XLH, XLS and XLX Shovelhead machines.

The development of the integrated transmission was not a simple matter, but Harley now had the most state-of-the-art production methods at its disposal: a rigorous quality control system, and computer-monitored and controlled production robots, which guaranteed the observance of minimum tolerances. This is necessary between the cylinder wall and the piston, and also at various other moving surfaces that are in direct contact in order to allow for variable expansion of metal components.

Harley-Davidson caused general surprise by opting for the displacement of the original 1957 overhead-valve XL Sportster: 55 cubic inches (in reality 53.9), or 883 cc, with an identical bore and stroke. But what a difference from that rather tame original in all other respects! The beautifully designed, new machine delivered 45 horsepower to the fat, rear tire, and that was just the end of the story. The Evo Sportster's alloy cylinders resembled those of its big brothers in the 80 cubic inch (1340 cc) range, and the old parallel Shovelhead valve covers had been replaced by integrated valve covers fitted underneath the cylinder head. The rocker boxes were only slightly altered and retained the typical layered construction allowing the cylinder heads to be removed without having to take the entire engine out of the frame.

However, the real advances had been made inside the engine. Apart from the alloy cylinders with iron liners and the entirely redesigned cylinder heads, new hemispherical combustion chamber and flat-topped pistons (now manufactured in the U.S.), the Evolution Sportster was also fitted with hydraulic valve lifters, a redesigned camshaft drive, a new crankshaft and crankcase, and featured improved oil circulation.

All these measures were designed to make the machine lighter, sharply reduce mechanical noise and improve engine cooling, thus significantly improving

A cut-away model of the new EVO Sportster engine.

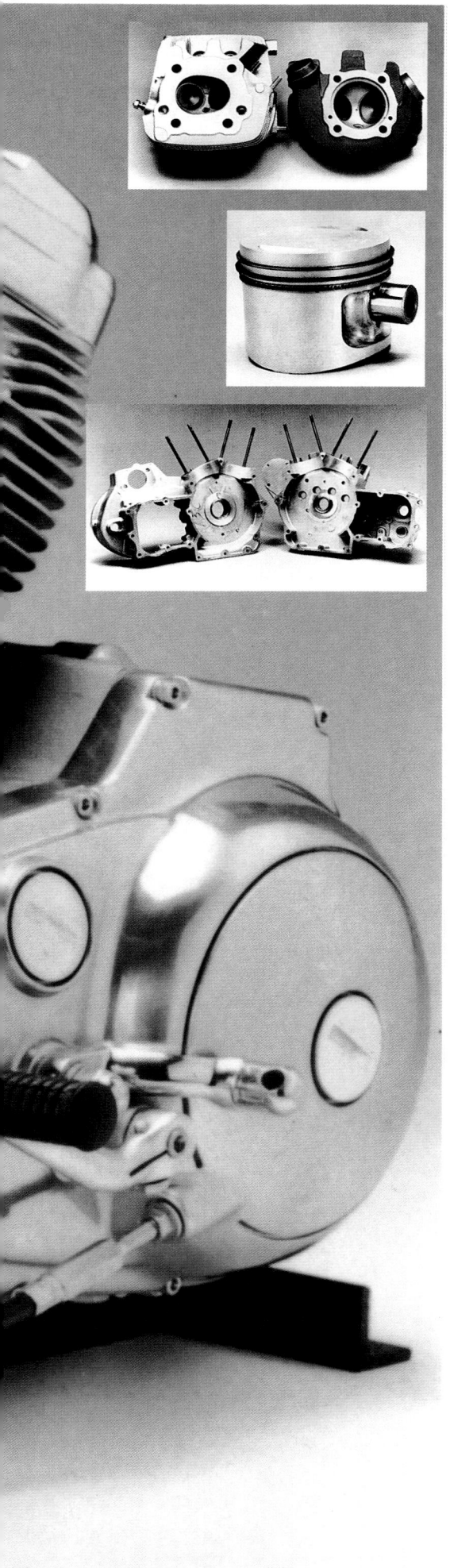

© Harley-Davidson

its life expectancy, this improvement being reflected in the fact that the interval between services was increased from 2,500 to 5,000 miles. Of the engine's total of 426 parts (the old one had 450), 206 were newly designed. One in particular stands out on closer inspection: the alternator was now in the primary case, and the oil filter was fitted in its old, easily accessible position where the generator had been previously.

In 1985, the Evolution Sportster 883 was presented to the press, and then went on sale in 1986, as did the almost identically constructed but somewhat more lavishly equipped XLH 1100 with the engine bored out to 67 cubic inches (1100 cc).

However, what more than anything else initially made the XLH 883 stand out was its sensationally low price. At 3,398 dollars it was 800 dollars cheaper than the previously most economical model in the Harley range: the 61-inch (1000 cc) Shovelhead Sportster, now quickly showing its age. This attractive price tag of less than 4,000 dollars was, despite all the high-sounding publicity, a telling blow against the hated cheaper imports from Japan. However, the company had cut the price to the bone and it could not be maintained for long, especially since not all dealers were prepared to go along with it. Nevertheless, the modern, extremely well-designed basic 883 cc model, developing a respectable 46 horsepower, and fitted with cast alloy wheels (in Europe spoked wheels were also available) and a solo seat, lacking turn signals, fitted with a single front disc brake, and only available in black or red, represented a brilliant marketing strategy at this aggressive price. Likewise the special offer, only briefly available, whereby the purchaser would be credited the full price of an XLH 883 Sportster when trading up to one of the big Harleys. In short, sales of the XLH 883 Sportster were excellent. In the first years over 10,000 were sold, and in the course of the next few years it became the best-selling model on the U.S. market. For the more demanding, there was a DeLuxe version with a double seat, rear footpegs, various chrome-plated parts, metallic paintwork, and a powder-coated frame.

In 1988 the single-seater Hugger 883 XLH appeared, which, with its extra-low ride position, immediately became a special favorite with women, though Harley had not particularly marketed

The XL Sportster Evolution Family

1986 onwards	XLH	Sportster	883
1986/1987	XLH	Sportster	1100
1988–1995	XLH	Sportster	883 DeLuxe
1988 onwards	XLH	Sportster	883 Hugger
1988 onwards	XLH	Sportster	1200
1996 onwards	XL 1200 C	Sportster	1200 Custom
1996 onwards	XL 1200 S	Sportster	1200 Sport

it as such. Although women have long ridden Harley models from right across the range, the Hugger was their favorite starter model. That same year the 1100 was replaced by the new XLH 1200. The powerful 74 cubic inch (1200 cc) engine developed 59 horsepower, but visually was barely distinguishable from the 883 series. With its new smaller valves, 40 millimeter constant velocity carburetor, and improved suspension, it produced 12 percent more power than its predecessor, the XLH 1100, and was the most powerful Sportster yet.

In 1991 all Sportsters got a new, five-speed gearbox which significantly improved their handling. In 1996 two new variants were added to the 1200 cc Sportster series: the XL 1200C Sportster 1200 Custom, and the XL 1200S Sportster 1200 Sport, so that the sporting class of rider might also succumb to the endless range of custom combinations. We can await the future offerings in this category from Willie G.'s creative Design Center with eagerness.

The main characteristics of the modified oil circuit are explaned in the *Service Manual*.

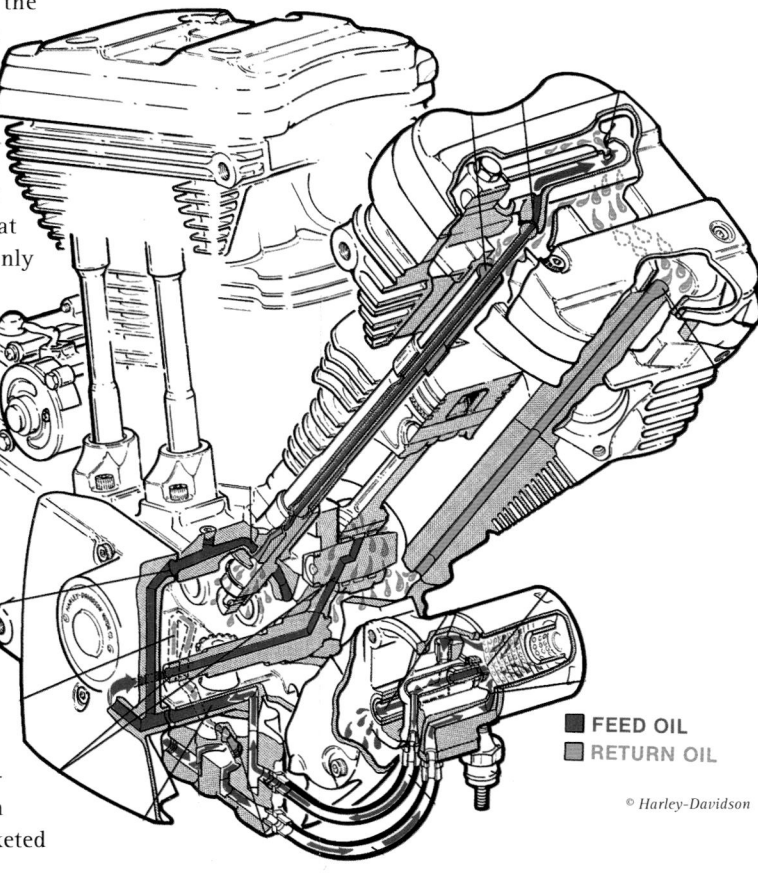

FEED OIL
RETURN OIL

© Harley-Davidson

The Sportster Series: the XLH 883 Standard, XLH 883 DeLuxe and Hugger

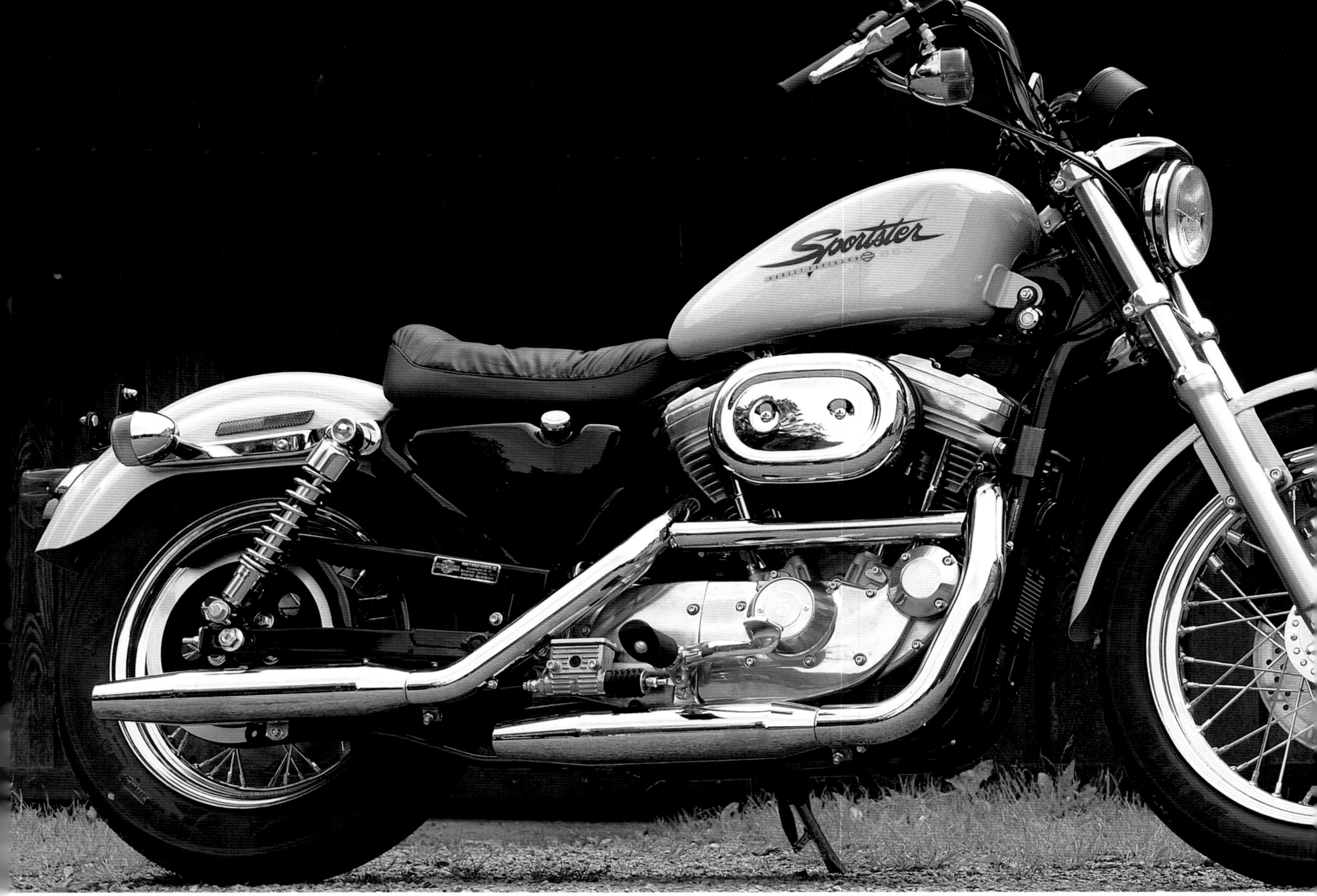

The XLH 883 Hugger – often preferred by women bikers – has a slightly lower seat than the standard XLH 883 and a sturdy buckhorn handlebar.

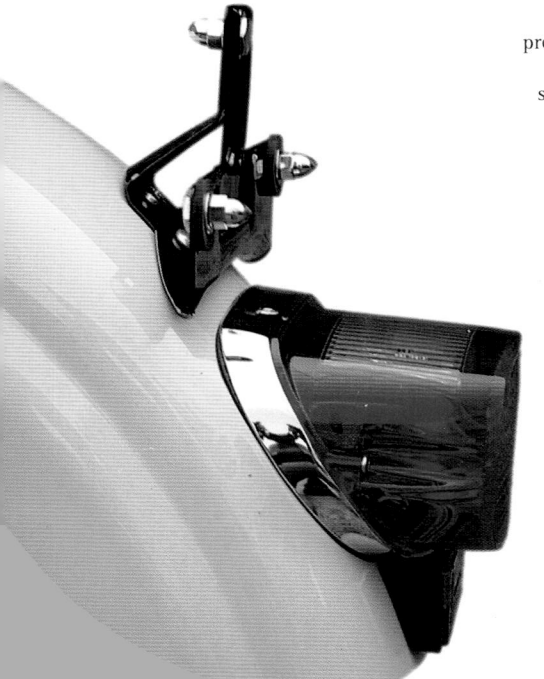

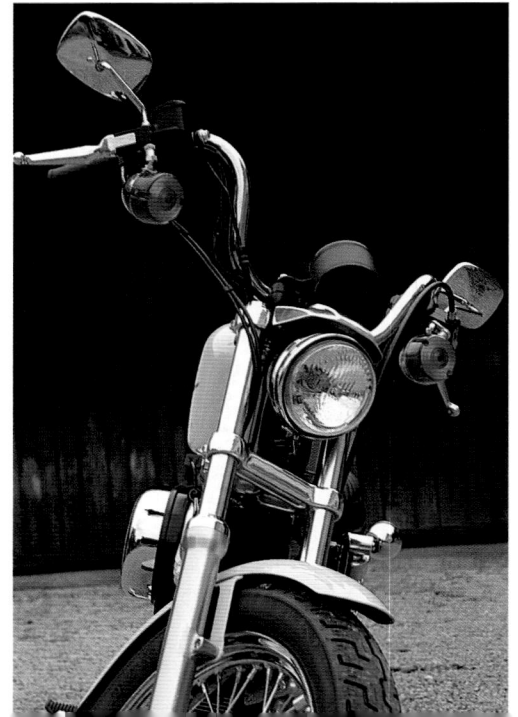

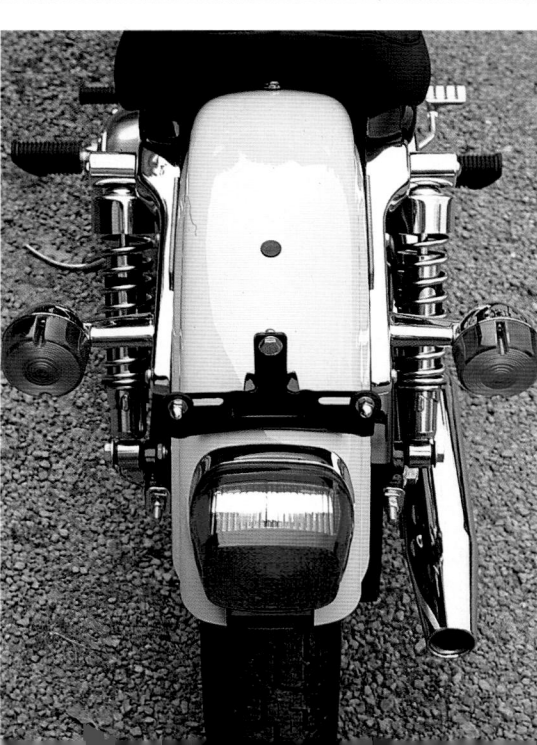

Standard edition XLH Sportster 883, built in 1993.

Type:	**XLH (XL/2)**
Model:	**Sportster 883 Standard**
Years of manufacture:	1986 onwards
Engine:	Air-cooled four-stroke overhead-valve Evolution 45° V-Twin
Displacement:	53.87 cu in (882.8 cc)
Bore x stroke:	3 x 3.8125 in (76.2 x 96.8 mm)
Compression ratio:	9.0 : 1
Power output:	46 hp (later 49 hp)
Carburetor:	Keihin 40 mm ø constant velocity
Transmission:	Four-speed (from 1991 five-speed)
Primary drive:	Triplex chain
Final drive:	Chain (later belt)
Battery:	12 volt/19 ah
Ignition:	Electronic V-Fire III, breakerless
Frame:	Tubular steel cradle (double downtube)
Front brake:	Disc
Rear brake:	Disc
Front suspension:	Telescopic forks
Rear suspension:	Swingarm/dual shock absorbers
Wheelbase:	60 in
Weight:	507 lb
Fuel capacity:	2.25 gal (later 3.3 gal)
Oil capacity:	3 qts
Front tire:	MJ 90 x 19
Rear tire:	MT 90 x 16
Top speed:	97 mph
Price:	$3,995 (1995 $4,995)
Model versions:	Sportster 883 DeLuxe
	Sportster 883 Hugger

The XLH 883 Standard — with secondary chain (above left) in 1985 and secondary toothed belt (above right) in 1996. Also available as the DeLuxe edition with double seat (left).

The Sportster Series: XLH 1100 and 1200, XL 1200 Custom and Sport

The XLH Sportster was only available with the 67 cubic inch (1100 cc) engine for two years.

Special edition built in 1987 to celebrate the 30th anniversary of the XL Sportster (below).

From 1988, the XLH Sportster boasted a 74-inch (1200 cc) engine. The photo shows the standard model from that year.

All photos on this page are courtesy of: H.D. Archives

Type:	**XLH (XL/2)**
Model:	**Sportster 1200**
Years of manufacture:	1988 onwards
Engine:	Air–cooled four–stroke overhead–valve Evolution 45° V–Twin
Displacement:	73.32 cu in (1201.59 cc)
Bore x stroke:	3.5 x 3.8125 in (88.9 x 96.8 mm)
Compression ratio:	9.0 : 1
Power output:	75 hp
Carburetor:	Keihin 40 mm ø constant velocity
Transmission:	Four–speed (later five–speed)
Primary drive:	Triplex chain
Final drive:	Chain or belt
Battery:	12 volt/19 ah
Ignition:	Electronic V–Fire III, breakerless
Frame:	Tubular steel cradle (double downtube)
Front brake:	Disc
Rear brake:	Disc
Front suspension:	Telescopic forks
Rear suspension:	Swingarm/dual shock absorbers
Wheelbase:	60 in
Weight:	520 lb
Fuel capacity:	3.25 gal (from 1995)
Oil capacity:	3 qts
Front tire:	MJ 90 x 19
Rear tire:	MT 90 x 16
Top speed:	109 mph
Price:	$7,200 (1995)
Model versions:	XL 1200C Sportster 1200 Custom with 21-inch laced front wheel and belt drive XL 1200S Sportster 1200 Sport with 19-inch 13-spoke cast front wheel and belt drive

Two special editions of the XLH 1200 Sportster were launched in 1998: shown here are the XL 1200 S Sport, with special instrumentation, twin ignition and — for the first time ever — a Vance Custom exhaust system.

263

Harley's New Superbike: the VR 1000

In 1994 the Harley-Davidson Racing Department introduced the VR 1000, a newly-developed motorcycle that is fundamentally different from the old V-Twins. It has a 60 degree cylinder angle, liquid cooling, twin overhead camshafts, and an extremely short stroke. All of these were completely new features which had little in common with traditional concepts of Harley-Davidson engineering. A new generation of V-Twin racing motorcycles was to bring Harley back up to speed with its rivals.

The engine, which was the product of five years of development work, has horizontally divided housing, with a one-piece top half and cylinders. The frame and the swingarm are made of light "Milwaukee alloy," and the bodywork is made of carbon fiber. Another noteworthy feature is the powerful Indy-car type disc brakes from Wilwood.

At the Daytona 200 in 1994, VP engineer Mark Tuttle gave the orange and black painted racer its inaugural race, with Miguel Duhamel, winner of the 1991 Daytona 200, in the saddle. To comply with the AMA race regulations, 15 VR 1000s first had to be built. (A street version had been planned, but this did not come to fruition because of excessively high production costs.) With the VR 1000 Harley-Davidson has experienced a successful comeback to Superbike and BoTT (Battle of the Twins) racing.

The VR 1000 enjoyed its most spectacular triumphs at the Daytona 200.

The mounted and unmounted VR 1000 motors clearly show the completely new concept behind the 60 degree watercooled V–Twin.

Type:	**Racer**
Model:	**VR 1000**
Year of manufacture:	1994
Engine:	Liquid–cooled eight–valve DOHC 60° V–Twin
Displacement:	60.78 cu in (996 cc)
Bore x stroke:	3.858 x 2.6 in ((98 x 66 mm)
Compression ratio:	11.6 : 1
Power output:	Between 135 ph and 149 ph, depending on tuning and atmospheric conditions
Carburetor:	Weber–Marelli EFI fuel injection
Transmission:	Five–speed gearbox
Primary drive:	Gear
Final drive:	O–ring chain
Ignition:	Electronic
Frame:	Aluminum section two–spar perimeter with engine forming a load–bearing component
Front brake:	2 x 320 mm Wilwood disc with six–piston aluminum calipers
Rear brake:	210 mm Wilwood disc with two–piston caliper
Front suspension:	Inverted forks with 46 mm tubes
Rear suspension:	Central strut with lever system
Wheelbase:	55.5 in
Weight:	390 lb
Fuel capacity:	4.5 gal
Oil capacity:	3 qts
Front tire:	3.50 x 17
Rear tire:	6.00 x 17
Top speed:	165 mph

The VR 1000 was first presented to the public in 1994, here at the H.O.G. Rally in Munich.

The Buell Series: the 1998 Models

These high-performance sport motorcycles were the brainchild of Erik Buell and with them the company started to attract a completely new type of customer: the middle-class sports fan with a relatively high income who still felt young at heart.

It was for this reason that Harley-Davidson acquired a 49 percent interest in the newly structured Buell Motorcycle Company in 1993: Jerry Wilke became President and Chief Operating Officer. Production is based completely in East Troy, Wisconsin where Buell motorcycles are hand-built with the greatest possible attention to detail. The intention is that in a few years time the motorcycles should go into high-volume series production in the new Sportster works in Kansas City, Missouri. In 1997 some 4,000 motorcycles were manufactured and marketed in East Troy.

Since 1998, five models have been available: the M2 Cyclone and the S1 Lightning are the sport and the super-sport versions and the solo machine is the ultra-sport S1 White Lightning using the Thunderstorm series engine boosted up to 101 horsepower. The S3 Thunderbolt is designed as the touring machine with partial fairing and a more comfortable seat, while the S3T Thunderbolt has additional saddlebags and fairing lowers as it is designed as a real sport-tourer.

The S3T Thunderbolt touring bike from Buell (1998).

The most extreme sports bike made by Buell – the S1 White Lightning.

Model:	**S1 White Lightning:**
	With the 101 hp Thunderstorm engine
Color:	Ice white pearl
Price:	$10,595
	S1 Lightning:
	With the 86 hp engine
Total weight:	425 lb
Colors:	Carbon black, Spark red, Billet metallic,
	Molten orange (frame and hubs in Nuclear blue)
Price:	$9,999
	M2 Cyclone:
	Two-seater with the 86 hp engine
Total weight:	434 lb
Colors:	Carbon black, Red snap, Blue streak
Price:	$8,995
	S3 Thunderbolt:
	With the 101 hp Thunderstorm engine
	(only available in the U.S.), fairing, flat touring handlebars,
	clock and ignition lock
Colors:	Black magic, Spark red, Amazon green, Billet metallic
Price:	$11,999
	S3T Thunderbolt:
	With the 101 hp Thunderstorm engine
	(available only in the U.S.), fairing, instrument console
	with clock and ignition lock, saddlebags with a capacity
	of 31.31 l, raised touring handlebars, Aegis tank protection
	and fairing lowers
Total dry weight:	465 lb, Load
capacity:	443 lb
Colors:	Black magic, Spark red, Amazon green, Billet metallic
Price:	$12,799

Extras and accessories:

For all of the Buell models there are conversion and tuning kits suitable for each model. The "Pro series" includes, for example, billet aluminum footrests, competition handlebars designed for racing, Twintail double seat or a single seat, a racing kit (manifold, exhaust, high-flow air filter, ignition module) – but these are not permitted for public highway usage. In addition there are racing fairings, the Cyclone-tachometer kit, Thunderstorm cylinder heads, aluminum fork bridges, a range of bags, tank bags, painted fairing lowers and the Aegis tank mask. In addition there are all kinds of clothing and helmets in the Buell range.

Type:	**Buell**
Model:	**S / M**
Year of manufacture:	1998
Engine:	Air-cooled four-stroke 45° V-Twin OHV
Displacement:	73.2 cu in (1203 cc)
Bore x stroke:	3.5 x 3.8 in (89 x 96.5 mm)
Compression ratio:	10 : 1
Power output:	86/93 hp
	(Thunderstorm engine: 101)
Carburetor:	Keihin 40 mm ø CV with a
	Helmholtz air cleaner
Exhaust:	Two-in-one, stainless steel
Transmission:	Five-speed
Primary drive:	Triplex chain to wet clutch
Final drive:	Kevlar belt
Battery:	12 volt
Instruments:	Speedometer with odometer and tripmeter, rev-counter, warning lamps for oil pressure, main beam, turn signals and neutral
Frame:	Tubular perimeter chrome-molybdenum steel frame, Uniplanar drive suspension
Front brake:	340 mm single disc, floating rotor with six-piston caliper
Rear brake:	240 mm single disc, with two-piston caliper
Front suspension :	White-Power inverted fork, with adjustable compression and rebound damping
Rear suspension :	Rectangular, chrome-molybdenum steel tubing swingarm, White-Power shock absorber
Wheelbase:	55 in
Weight:	434–465 lb
Fuel capacity:	4/5.5 gal
	(premium, grade unleaded)
Oil capacity:	2 qts
Front tire:	120/70 ZR 17 TL
Rear tire:	170/60 ZR 17 TL
Front wheel:	3.5 x 17 in 3-spoke cast aluminum
Rear wheel:	5.0 x 17 in 3-spoke cast aluminum
Top speed:	Over 120 mph

The S1 White Lightning and its characteristic details: the displaced instrument panel beneath the mini-paneling and the typical spring shock-absorber element under the frame.

A Magnificent Array

The 1999 model range pictured here differs in a number of significant details from the previous anniversary year: all the models in the Touring family (FLH) and the Dyna family (FXD) have been fitted with the new 88-inch (1449 cc) twin-cam engine. This all-new 68 horsepower (50 kW/ 5,400 rpm) power unit, developed in Milwaukee, is Harley's response to the demand for ever higher cubic capacities in the V-Twins, with corresponding powerful torque producing that mighty "rumble from the basement." The most important features distinguishing it from the previous Evolution 1338 cc engine are the double camshaft, improved oil circulation and a new bore/stroke ratio (101.6 x 95.3 mm). Apart from this, two new types have been added to the 1999 range of models: the FXDX Dyna Super Glide Sport and the FXST Softail Standard. The 1998 FXSTB "Night Train," initially only homologated for Europe, has been fully integrated into the 1999 range. Harley-Davidson's new worldwide commercial prospects are also based on an event that excited immediate speculation: at its Daytona Bike Week '99 presentation, Harley-Davidson announced a "Power Partnership" with Ford Motor Company, initially limited to a five-year period. This company partnership, dubbed a "strategic alliance," is intended to pave the way for new technological developments and marketing concepts. However, the main priority is probably sponsorship for Harley's Superbike program. An additional consideration is that these two classic US motor vehicle firms want to celebrate their centenaries jointly, both having been founded in 1903.

Touring-Family

FLHR
Road King

FLHRCI
Road King Classic

FLHT
Electra Glide Standard

FLHTC
Electra Glide Classic

FLHTCI
Electra Glide Classic

FLHTCUI
Electra Glide Ultra Classic

Softail-Family

FXSTC
Softail Custom

FXSTS
Springer Softail

FLSTF
Fat Boy

FLSTC
Heritage Softail Classic

FLSTS
Heritage Springer

Touring-Family FLTR
Road Glide
(no picture)

Dyna-Family

FXD
Dyna Super Glide

FXDL
Dyna Low Rider

FXDS-CON
Dyna Convertible

FXDWG
Dyna Wide Glide

95th Anniversary
Export Models in 1998

FXSTB Softail
Night Train

XL 53 C
Custom 53 Sportster

Sportster-Family

XLH
Sportster 883

XL 1200 C
Sportster 1200 Custom

95th Anniversary/
Special Models
in 1998

FLHTCUI
Ultra Electra Glide
Classic (EFI)

XLH
Sportster 883 Hugger

FXDWG
Dyna Wide Glide

FLHRCI
Road King Classic
(EFI)

XLH
Sportster 1200

FLSTF
Fat Boy

XL 1200S
Sportster 1200 Sport

FLSTS
Heritage Springer

XL 1200C
Sportster 1200 Custom

FLHTCI
Electra Glide Classic
(EFI)

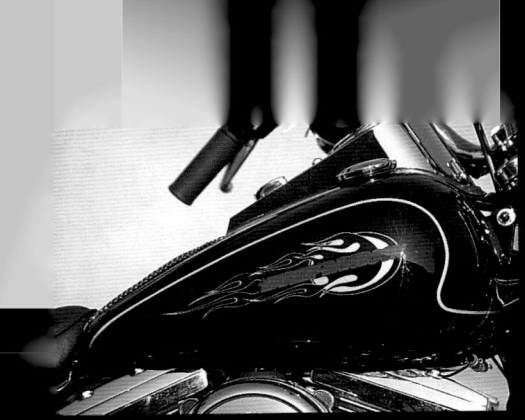

Vivid Black

Violet Pearl

Lazer Red Pearl

Sinister Blue Pearl

Mystique Green & Black

Lazer Red & Black

Sinister Blue Pearl & Platinum Silver

Midnight Red & Champagne Pearl

Custompaint Atomic Red & Grey

Special paint finishes (above left and center) are in celebration of the company's 95th anniversary. The above right is an example of a custom paint finish

What the hell is an FXST–FLSTN? It's simple: a 1998 Heritage Softail Special. Perhaps it is not as simple as that. Admittedly, Harley-Davidson's alphabet soup has not exactly got easier to understand over the past 30 years. However, here are a few simple rules that should help to cast light on this murky world of symbols and encourage a better understanding of the basic system. However, Harley themselves often had trouble with this over the years.

First comes the type designation: the initial reference letter F indicates all models with the big V–Twin engine (74 or 80 cu in, 1200 or 1340 cc) and separate transmission, or from 1984 onwards the 80 cubic inch (1340 cc) Evolution engine.

The initial combination FL indicates all Electra Glide models with 16–inch wheels and the wide 5.00/MT 90 tires both front and rear. The subsequent letters H and T stand for Highway and Touring respectively, while all FLT models are fitted with the newly–designed frame. This later led to the combination FLHT.

The initial combination FX designates all Super Glide models fitted with the wide 16–inch rear wheel but the narrow 19– or 21–inch wheel at the front (a blend of the Electra–Glide and the Sportster. The reference letter X stands for all models fitted with a 54, 61, 67 or 74 cubic inch (883, 1000, 1100 or 1200 cc) V–Twin engine with integrated transmission, i.e. the Sportster range.

Until 1984 an additional reference letter E (e.g. FXE) was used to designate an electric starter, but then this became redundant since all models were fitted with one.

In the case of the final reference letter the situation becomes rather more complicated since some letters came to take on multiple meanings over the years. For, example during the 1980s the final reference letters WG stand for Wide Glide, LR for Low Rider, F for Fat Bob or later for Fat Boy, and later the single letter L for Low Rider. Then a new type was added: the FXR Low Rider series, where the R stood for rubber isolated drivetrain, i.e. a rubber–mounted engine. Further types includes the ST series, with ST standing for Softail, and the D series, where D designates the new Dyna frame.

Here then, is a brief list to assist in deciphering the final reference letters:

B:	Belt	FXD:	Dyna Super Glide
C:	Classic or Custom	FXDX:	Dyna Super Glide Sport
CH:	Competition High Compression	FXDL:	Dyna Low Rider
	(in Sportster models)	FXDS-CONV:	Dyna Convertible
CON:	Convertible	FXDWG:	Dyne Wide Glide
F:	Fat Boy or Fat Bob model	FXST:	Softail Standard
E:	Electric Starter	FXSTB:	Night Train
G:	Glide	FXSTC:	Softail Custom
H:	Highway	FSXSTS	Springer Softail
I:	Fuel Injection	FLSTF:	Fat Boy
N:	Nostalgia	FLSTXC	Heritage Softail Classic
P:	Police	FLSTS:	Heritage Springer
R:	Rubber Mounted (or Isolated)	FLHT:	Electra Glide Standard
S:	Sport	FLHTC/FLHTCI:	Electra Glide Classic
SP:	Sport Edition or Special Police	FLHTCUI ULTRA:	Classic Electra Glide
T:	Touring	FLHR	Road King
U:	Ultra model	FLHRCI	Road King Classic
W:	Wide (WG: Wide Glide model)	FLTR/FLTRI	Road Glide
		XLH	Sportster 883
		XLH	Sportster 883 Hugger
		XL	883 C Sportster/883 Custom
		XLH	Sportster 1200
		XL 1200S	Sportster 1200 Sport
		XL 1200C	Sportster 1200 Custom

However, the confusion reached its peak in 1995, when an attempt was made to impose some order on the ever more muddling, reference letter chaos, by separating type and model designations. Unfortunately though, the company's efforts had precisely the opposite effect, and they soon put the matter aside. For the sake of completeness we are including this one-year wonder, though whether this will help to reduce the confusion surrounding the coding of new model combinations remains doubtful.

The following words and terms are trademarks of Harley-Davidson, many of which are registered:

Special Editions

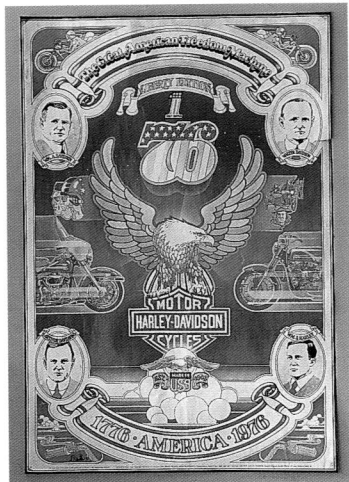

Special Editions

Limited Models for Special Occasions

Chronology of Special Editions

1976 – The first genuine special edition appeared: the Liberty Edition marking the U.S. Bicentennial. The models in this edition, which are listed below, were distinguished by a large decal on the gas tank in red, white, and blue, and also by the black metal flake paintwork.
XLH Sportster Super H
XLCH Sportster Super CH
FLH 1200 Electra Glide
FX 1200 Super Glide
FXE 1200 Super Glide

1978 – Harley brought out two machines for the 75th Anniversary Edition, painted 'midnight black' with gold stripes. These were the:
XLH Sportster
FLH 1200 Electra Glide

1981 – A special edition was produced painted in the old orange and green colors of the 1930s. This was the:
FLH Heritage Edition

1982 – Two limited editions were produced to mark the 25th anniversary of the 1957 XL Sportster. These were the:
XLSA Roadster (778 were units)
XLHA Sportster (932 units)
Each bike came with documents personally signed by the Chairman Vaughn Beals, the President Charlie Thompson and the Vice President Willie G. Davidson.

1984 – An all-black Limited Edition came out with a production run of just 499. It was the:
FLHS Electra Glide Sport

1986 – To celebrate the 100th anniversary of the Statue of Liberty on Ellis Island, and to help raise funds for its restoration, Harley–Davidson launched a major PR campaign. This involved the Los Angeles to New York "Statue of Liberty Run" by two separate cavalcades, the first one led through the south by Willie G. Davidson and the second taking a northern route and led by Vaughn Beals. Both ended at the Festival in Liberty State Park, where a check for over 250,000 dollars was handed over to the Statue of Liberty Foundation, to the cheers of thousands assembled riders. Harley– Davidson contributed 100 dollars to the statue fund for each Liberty Edition motorcycle sold.
FLTC Tour Glide Classic
FXRS Low Rider
FXRT Sport Glide
XLH 1100 Sportster
FLHTC Electra Glide Classic

Since the 1970s the tradition has grown for Harley–Davidson to produce ever increasing numbers of special editions. These may be to mark a company anniversary, in commemoration of outstanding classic motorcycles, or to celebrate national holidays. They are produced in relatively small numbers (normally between 1,000 and 2,000 machines), fitted with specially designed insignia, badges or logos, special paintwork, and other decorative trim. These limited editions serve not only to underpin the company's image as the custodian of a historic heritage, but they are also in many cases associated with smart public relations campaigns designed to attract people's attention and stimulate the interest of new customer target groups. These editions are often linked with successful marketing strategies involving associated demo rides and campaigns to raise funds for good causes.

Limited editions, special and anniversary models are not designed to be customized. Their paintwork and decals, logos and emblems are often the only signs of their special identity and should be carefully preserved: the better their condition the greater the historical and financial value of the machine. Limited editions are collectors' items and should remain so. Here is a brief overview of the subject.

The first motorcycles which could be described as special editions were the ones with the famous V fender badge, to commemorate the company's 50th anniversary in 1953. However, these first appeared on the following year's models and were not produced as limited editions.

Special model for the 30th anniversary of the Sportster in 1987.

One of the two Harley Softtails which led the parade of Super Bowl editions in Miami in 1989.

FXDB Dyna Glide Daytona 1992 for the 50th anniversary of Daytona Race Week.

The FXDWG Anniversary Edition for the 90th anniversary of the company, 1993.

Emblems and decals of the "Liberty Rides" for the 100th anniversary of the Statue of Liberty (opposite).

© Harley-Davidson

To these can be added the following Special Anniversary Editions:
FLTC
FXRS
FLHTC

1987 – Harley-Davidson brought out two 10 Years of Low Riders' special edition bikes:
FXLR Low Rider Custom
FXLR Low Rider
plus a Limited Edition with a golden emblem and battery cover, and complete with documents signed by Rich Teerlink and Willie G. Davidson, to celebrate the 30th anniversary of the XL Sportster:
XLH 1100 Sportster

1988 – A whole series of special models was made available in the 85th Anniversary Edition:
FXRS Low Rider
FLTC Tour Glide Classic
FLHTC Electra Glide Classic
FXSTC Springer Softail Custom

1989 – An exclusive special edition of just 106 motorbikes came out on the occasion of Super Bowl XXIII in January 1989 in Joe Robie Stadium, Miami:
FXSTC Springer Softail

1991 – The first special edition Dyna model was produced to celebrate the tenth anniversary of the first Sturgis model. This was the
FXDB Dyna Glide Sturgis

1992 – A run of 1,084 of the same custom model was produced to celebrate the 50th anniversary of Daytona race week:
FXDB Dyna Glide Daytona

1993 – No less than seven special editions were produced to mark Harley-Davidson's 90th anniversary, the 90th Anniversary Editions', in more or less limited quantities. These were the:
XLH 1200 Sportster
FXLR Low Rider Custom
FXDWG Dyna Wide Glide
FLSTN Softail Nostalgia
FLHTC Electra Glide Classic
FLHTC Ultra Classic Electra Glide
FLTC Ultra Classic Tour Glide

1995 – There was a single special edition to commemorate the 30th anniversary of the Electra Glide:
FLHTCU Electra Glide Classic Ultra

1998 – A further seven limited 95th Anniversary Editions were produced with special paintwork, special designs and badges:
XL 1200 C Sportster 1200 Custom
FXDWG Dyna Wide Glide
FLSTS Fat Boy (in "Heritage-Grey")
FLSTS Heritage Springer
FLHTCI Electra Glide Classic (EFI)
FLHTCUI Ultra Electra Glide Classic (EFI)
FLHRCI Road King Classic (EFI)
(EFI = Electronic Fuel Injection)

German Harley-Davidson dealers have brought out a number of their own special editions. These include the following:
1996 – XL 883 "Blackster"
1997 – FLST "Ten Year Heritage"

The Lost Generation

Models That Didn't Make It

The X 1000 – a beautiful model, but not typical for Harley, was unfortunately to be dropped.

The remains of the abandoned OHC KL motor.

For every motorcycle to hit the showrooms there is at least one, and probably several, prototypes. Those which make it to the mass production stage and are marketed at great expense soon become familiar and sought-after items, while the rejected models usually disappear without trace, the victims of company policy decisions. At Harley the situation is the same as in any other development facility. Originally conceived, constructed and refined by the best brains at the company with pioneering spirit, enthusiasm and cutting-edge technical knowledge, and at great expense of money and resources, almost all prototypes suffer the same undignified and often unjust fate. The secretly-developed machines, originally intended to strike fear into the hearts of competitors and secure the company's survival, become a taboo subject, and all documentation and hardware are mercilessly destroyed, their creators bound to secrecy (though not always successfully so), so that very few prototypes ever survive in any shape or form. Often all that is left are some fragments, photos, sketches or old reports in the trade press. At Harley-Davidson, prototypes are among the most closely-guarded company secrets, and tracking them down is one of the most exciting challenges for any chronicler of the company's history.

Here are some examples. In 1925 Harley-Davidson contracted the engineer Everett M. DeLong, formerly of Henderson, to develop a straight-four engine for the company. Accordingly DeLong designed an innovative four-cylinder engine fitted in the chassis of the J model.

Although the management was delighted with the model, Big Bill Davidson consigned the project to the scrap heap after coolly calculating the costs and taking into account the complicated production techniques that would be required.

In 1940 work on a new, 45 cubic inch (750 cc), overhead-valve twin engine had been going on for three years, only to be suddenly discontinued, again on grounds of cost and technical difficulty. Instead Harley concentrated on the development of a new, more saleable, 74 inch (1200 cc) OHV model.

After the war dealers were particularly keen to see rapid development of a competitor to challenge the evermore popular British singles and twins, and modernization of the old, 30.5 cubic inch (500 cc), OHV, single-cylinder engine was considered. Then-President William H. Davidson had already contracted a team of technicians, engineers, and designers to develop something new. However, when this team, led by John R. Bond, presented the results of their work, the shareholders of the company decided that the planned production was too costly, and all work on the project was discontinued. Thus William J. Harley and his team in the development department once again had to try to make something of the old prewar model, resulting in a massive loss of market share for which Harley suffered.

The KL Model

While the side-valve K series was still in production, a sensational, newly designed, 45-degree V-Twin, aluminium engine with an overhead chain-driven camshaft was being constructed. Even during the first test rides, the 45 cubic inch (750 cc) version of the engine proved to be significantly more powerful than the side-valve KH engine, which had been enlarged to 55 cubic inches (900 cc). This KL model had been developed to the point where it was ready to go into production, but nevertheless manufacture of it was repeatedly postponed and when, in 1957, the highly successful, overhead-valve, XL Sportster appeared, the KL was scrapped once and for all. Today a few fragments are all that remains of the brilliantly designed KL engine.

The X 1000

In 1966, long before the first Super Glide appeared on the market in 1971, Harley-Davidson presented a newly developed ultramodern tourer/sportster prototype which departed radically from the usual design of such machines, and, as it turned out, unfortunately nothing about it had the mystique of a "true" Harley. In appearance, the X 1000, with its transversely mounted, 1000 cc, four-cylinder engine, bore more resemblance to an MV Agusta. It was an elegant machine, and decidedly more attractive than the Honda CB 750 Four which was to take the market by storm a year later. However, it just was not a proper Harley. Dealers and Harley fanatics raised a storm of protest against this "Japanese American" hybrid as soon as the first publicity photographs appeared, making Harley drop the whole project like a hot potato.

The Unfortunate Nova Era

A Timely Change

Harley - always imitated, but never duplicated

There have always been a number of dubious motorbikes around claiming some connection with Harley, some with and some without the approval of the company. For example, after World War I Harley's general agent in Rome asked for permission to use a variant of the Harley name for a small, two-stroke, general purpose motorcycle produced by the Austrian company Puch, designed with a streamlined tank and painted khaki and red. It is unknown whether the company approved or not, but the Puch "Harlette" duly appeared in 1926-1927, with either a 123 or 173 cc two-stroke engine. In France it went on sale as the "Harlette Geco." In the 1960s a diminutive copy of the Electra Glide called the "Florida," with a 50 cc two-stroke engine, was produced in Italy by a company trading under the name HRD, whatever that was supposed to stand for: it had nothing to do with the English company HRD-Vincent. Small numbers of this motorbike were also exported to the U.S. Another strange machine is described by David K. Wright in his Official Eighty-Year History of Harley-Davidson: a narrow, gas turbine, moped prototype. A true custom Harley was produced single-handed by Buddy Stubbs, one-time stuntman and associate of Evel Knievel, and now a Harley dealer in Arizona. He developed his curious

machine from an 883 cc Sportster by removing the rear cylinder, an act of amputation which turned the V-Twin into a single-cylinder machine without having to make all that many changes. This was actually an old trick, first used by early racers in the 1920s in order to get a solid and well-constructed, large, single-cylinder machine.

This photo of an apparent Nova model was introduced by Harley-Davidson. It dosen't correspond with the actual shown on the top photo.

The problem is persistent, despite being a longstanding one. Air-cooled engines started causing headaches as early as the 1970s. They were simply too loud. But this throbbing sound was one of the characteristics which distinguished a Harley-Davidson. The street legends were threatened with extinction. It was not just Harley who had to face this problem. Porsche, who wanted to replace the revered Nine-Eleven with the water-cooled, eight-cylinder Porsche 928, were in a similar position. So Harley-Davidson asked Porsche for advice. This was quite understandable. In the first place Porsche had to overcome the same problems with their own vehicles, and the Weissach based, sports car manufacturer also had a world-renowned development center, which carried out subcontract work in its Engineering Services Department. One only has to look at patent statistics to realize that particularly creative engineers, who know much more than just Porsche technology, are employed in this small town in southern Germany. In the field of internal combustion engines alone, Porsche holds around half the patents filed.

The Harley four-cylinder engines which were developed in 1981, but never officially disclosed to the public, were technically very impressive. Engineers reported that engines purred more quietly than the Honda VF 750 S, which was used as a benchmark for testing.

This kind of quiet running was achieved by the Porsche engineers using subtle technology. A shaft between the cylinders drove the four overhead camshafts via two gear rims and chains. The 34 mm (inlet) and 32 mm (exhaust) valves, two per combustion chamber, were

operated via a cup tappet. A water jacket around the cylinders ensured that the engine stayed cool, while at the same time reducing noise levels. With such extensive modifications, the new V engine series stood outside the typical Harley displacement range. Also, perhaps more importantly, the new engines had two cylinders too many for dedicated Harley fans, i.e. four.

Here too there are parallels with Porsche cars, which are useful for comparison purposes. Experience to date has shown that a successful Porsche must have at least six cylinders; all attempts at using just four cylinders (924, 944, and later 968) failed, at least in terms of the cars' image. Sales actually held up quite well, as another target group was developed for these models. But Harley-Davidson was never meant to be a mass-market product and therefore did not need to follow trends set by Japanese motorcycle manufacturers. This fact was recognized in the 1980s, in time to halt the Harley-Davidson 800 V-four project. It stayed faithful to the huge air-cooled twins, which continued to vibrate and thump.

But it is not only because of the misconceived engines and the target group for which they were developed that the so-called Nova project still comes as a surprise to anyone investigating the Harley history from the 1980s. The overall appearance of the machine would have broken away from the Harley-Davidson tradition. Even the design studies looked ugly to the Harley faithful, and they are still kept under lock and key to this day.

The Third Wheel – the First Sidecars

One of the innumerable constructions made by the various firms under contract to Harley–Davidson to produce their "Commercial Package Trucks."

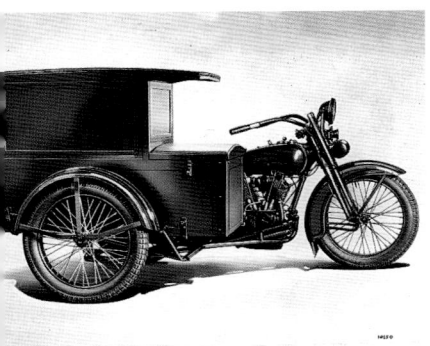

At first a sidecar–motorcycle combination was an extremely unstable contraption. The weird–looking vehicle had the irritating habit of breaking away in the opposite direction; it would wobble, shake to and fro in the most bizarre fashion and might even tend to tip over quickly. Designers, it seemed, had not quite mastered the complicated geometry demanded by the suspension – but it was possible, on the other hand, to transport a vast amount and assortment of things. Moreover, when left standing, the motorcycle neither fell over, nor did it have to be heaved onto its stand. In addition, it proved to be an ideal means of transport during the winter months on an icy surface.

As far as is known, Harley–Davidson is one of the oldest sidecar manufacturers to attach an extra container – a kind of trunk – to a motorcycle. The three–wheel combination proved to be a huge success and became popular overnight. It seems quite likely that the first side-

cars, built under contract by the Seaman company, were already around in 1912 and 1913. They were fixed to the more powerful V–Twin models. Previously two–wheeled carts and motorcycles had been joined together into forecars which served as motorcycle trucks for rural free delivery and as tradesmen's delivery vans. From 1914 on it was realized that sidecars were simpler and more practical solution. They could carry additional loads of up to 630 pounds which together with the weight of the driver amounted to a total weight of around 1,250 pounds, quite a load for a modest 6 horsepower engine. That's where quality counts.

The first genuine sidecar was built in 1914 on a very strong steel chassis with solid struts as a substructure. The third wheel had no brake of its own, making it a quick and simple matter to attach and detach the sidecar. The heavy-duty equipment had to be balanced

An original Harley–Davidson sidecar from 1920 with trapdoor and rain cover.

A delivery combination fit for winter weather, perhaps envisaged as a cash transport.

278

1915	L/L-L	solo sidecar for left or right position
	M	standard production sidecar
1916	XT	double-bar chassis with "suit box" top and motorcycle
	L/LC/LCL	solo sidecar for left or right position
	RFD	commercial sidecar with rural free delivery box
	P	double-bar chassis with closed box
	U	double-bar chassis with open box
	V	double-bar chassis with double covered box
	GC	military model with mount for gun/machine gun
	AC	model for ammunition transport
1917	N	standard rural free delivery box
1918	Q	wide sidecar chassis (56 inches) for two passengers
	QA	wide standard closed commercial van (56 inches)
	QB	same, with open box
	QD	two-compartment parcel car, closed
	QL	wide sidecar (56 inches) for two passengers, right-hand mounting
	QC3	wide three-stake platform Parcel Car
	QC4	wide four-stake platform Parcel Car
1919	LUS	solo sidecar, right-hand mounting, for U.S. government
1920	LR/L-LR	solo Roadster sidecar, right- or left-hand mounting
	LX	solo Speedster sidecar, right-hand mounting
	WD	two-tier, double compartment Parcel Car (56 inches)
	PC	wide chassis (56 inches) with double bar
1921	QL	two-passenger sidecar, right-hand mounting
1922	QT	two-passenger Tourist sidecar, right-hand mounting
	LT	solo Tourist sidecar, left- or right-hand mounting
1924	LT	solo Royal Tourist sidecar, right-hand mounting
	LX	solo Racer sidecar, right-hand mounting
	QT	two-passenger Family Delight sidecar, right-hand mounting
1926	MO	commercial Side Van, right-hand mounting, with open body
1928	MWX	commercial Express Van with screens, extra wide
	MW	commercial Side Van
	MWXP	commercial Express Van with panels, extra wide
	MX	standard Commercial Express Van
	MXP	same, with panels

Most of the models were available for right- or left-hand mounting.

correctly though, and set up carefully, otherwise it would pitch and roll just like a boat. These sidecars were given nicknames such as "gondola" or "Dutch shoe."

From 1915 on a side van became available and it was from this van that the Parcel Car and then the Package Truck with a narrow chassis (45 inches) or an extra wide chassis (56 inches) were developed. There were countless special bodies: flatbed trucks, tankers, ice cream containers and special transporters which could accommodate a variety of goods; but, above all, there were the most suitable combinations for each model. Just to run the rural mail delivery service, there were more than 5,300 motorcycle trucks in service in 1915!

The single- or the wider two-person sidecars had more than enough space (sometimes even for an entire family) and even had a small entry door and a running board. There was sometimes all-weather

protection, as was the case with a horse-drawn coach — all these versions sold incredibly well. In 1919 alone Harley manufactured 16,400 sidecars. Complete with wheel, the simple, solo version cost 85 dollars. A quarter of all the Harleys sold were equipped with one. Many of the contracts were passed through to specialist firms (Seaman, Rogers or Goulding, for example), because there was insufficient capacity in Harley's own factories to manufacture them. For example, in 1914 2,500 sidecars were ordered from Rogers and it was not until 1925 that Harley set up its own plant for producing sidecars.

An early combination from 1919 with an original Harley-Davidson sidecar and a JV-Twin model.

Courtesy of: John W. Parham, Anamosa, Iowa

The Goulding Story
Sidecars Made in Australia

Dot Robinson and her daughter in the 1940s on her famous Harley with the chrome Goulding Bomb at an early Motor Maids meeting in Laconia.

The history of the Goulding sidecar begins in 1910 in Australia where the motorcycle aficionado and Harley enthusiast James "Jim" Goulding built his first sidecars as a means of transport suitable for the notoriously bad roads in that part of the world. The springs were so good and the light but strong construction so practical that they sold really well. As a result Goulding was in a position to open a proper workshop for building sidecars in 1915. In the meantime his first daughter, Dot, had been born in 1912 (very nearly in the sidecar in which her father was carrying her mother) and this event was later to become a crucial part of the legend. In 1915 his wife gave birth to their son, Claude and he was soon to be followed by a second daughter, Edna, in 1917. In that same year Goulding's small factory in Melbourne produced around 100 sidecars a month and a patent was granted to Goulding for his sidecar design. Goulding became the leading sidecar manufacturer in Australia and New Zealand — above all for the Harley-Davidson motorcycles which were being imported in considerable numbers at that time.

In 1920 James Goulding undertook an adventurous six-month 12,000-mile trip together with his wife through the U.S. on a well-equipped Harley combination in order to discover new markets and find new business partners. In San Francisco he struck up a friendship with Harley dealer Dudley Perkins. In 1921, on a second trip to the land of opportunity, he finalized a contract with the Hastings Company in Goshen, Indiana, which now started to manufacture and distribute Goulding sidecars as National Sidecars in the U.S. A shortly afterwards he left Australia with his family to live in the United States, the country which he had grown to love so much, and settled first in

Milwaukee so that he could work more closely with Harley-Davidson. Later he was to develop a particularly practical sidecar model for the light Forty-Five motorcycle.

Jim Goulding set up a small factory on 4th Street where he was enthusiastically supported by Hy Haskell, a hard-working salesman and by Abresh, a local company which distributed the Lite Car. This move was the outcome of the disastrous business relationship with the Hastings Company, which had led to differences concerning patents, whereby the ever-trusting Goulding was well and truly duped. In 1926 Jim Goulding moved his business to Saginaw, Michigan, where he opened a small factory on Water Street. In 1928 he opened his official Harley dealership there. During this time (from 1920 through 1930) he received license fees from the A.G. Healing Company who were continuing to manufacture and distribute his sidecars in Australia — that was a deal which had been sealed with a handshake.

In 1931 his daughter, Dot, married the son of a local farmer, Earl Robinson, a genuine Harley fan. Two years later the young man took over the Harley-Davidson dealership with the assistance of Arthur Davidson. In 1936 Earl Robinson moved his Harley dealership from Saginaw to Detroit. By now Dot Robinson and Claude Goulding had become well-known in motorcycling circles. Supported by their father, they won (frequently in spite of questionable AMA objections) countless enduros, reliability trials, and Gypsy Tour competitions, all on Harleys with a Goulding sidecar.

In 1956 James Goulding stopped production of his sidecars due to a drop in sales and in 1967, he sold his firm to Crompton & Knowles in Wooster, Massachusetts.

Goulding Sidecars: Technical Details

The Goulding sidecar was built with a special suspension system which gave the sidecar wheel extra damping. At the front, below the sidecar body there were two coil springs and at the rear two leaf springs mounted one above the other. The sidecar body was secured on a solid tubular frame and the wheel axle fixed to a longitudinal swinging arm. There were only three points on the motorcycle at which it was connected to the sidecar. The body (which was also called a 'Dutch shoe' or a 'gondola' because of its shape) had all its components sprung against one another. The design really proved its worth on rough roads and tracks. Goulding manufactured ten different basic models, including:

The light body for the 45 cubic inch Harley Lite Car (1929–1945).

The Rocket model throughout the 1950s, also given the name 'Cruiser' or 'Zep' (because of its bulbous round front, which looked like a Zeppelin).

The Gould Car, a prototype trike with a Knucklehead motor which did not sell very well.

The luxury or top–of–the–line model was the Goulding sidecar in the so–called Superior design with the Wonder Chassis for the Big Twin models.

Massive and sprung in all directions: the legendary Goulding sidecar of the "Zep" type from the 1940s, this one with a slightly more modern Hydra Glide as workhorse.

Three's Company

A Harley with a Sidecar

Harley–Davidson's Sidecar: Models TLE and RLE

Sidecar Specifications

Body: Lightweight fiberglass with vinyl seat and cushioned sidecar step. Integrated footboard. Luggage storage behind seat.

Suspension: Semi–rigid sidecar connection with spring–mounted body.

Weather Protection: Contoured windshield.

Cover: Reinforced vinyl tonneau.

Sidecar Wheel:16–inch light cast metal with tubeless tire.

Mounting System: Quick disconnection design. Three different models (RLE, TLE, TLF) were available for the following types of motorcycle:

RLE: suitable for the Low Rider Sport Edition, Low Rider Convertible and Sport Glide, not available since 1994.

TLE and TLF: suitable for the FLHT and the FLT models.

Colors: Different for each of the models of motorcycles.

There is nothing to equal the experience of driving a motorcycle combination. One will still be riding the motorcycle as close as can possibly be to nature, exposed to all kinds of weather with the wind blowing in one's face, but steering it in a completely different way — at first, due to lack of experience, it probably will seem unnatural to use the handlebars to steer instead of shifting the weight of one's body. But with enough practice — and in this respect the Harley sidecar manual provides exactly the right kind of advice whenever things appear to be getting difficult — one will soon be full of enthusiasm for the immense maneuverability of the rig. But great care is needed when negotiating bends. Sidehacks have their own laws of gravity. Once one has learned how to use the brakes, gears and throttle correctly, then perhaps one will be in a better position to perform real stunts as a rider. The

experienced rider frequently takes great pleasure in terrifying a newcomer seated alongside in the sidecar. But apart from the typical sidecar stunts, a hack is an ideal way of getting about — not just for longer trips but also for crossing seemingly impassable terrain and, above all, for journeys over snow and ice in winter, a time of the year which is normally off–season for a motorcyclist. A combination is also an alternative method of family transport and children love traveling in the comfortable sidecar as much as riding pillion.

During the 1930s and 1940s Harley maintained their extensive range of sidecars, from solo rigs to load–carrying units for commerce and industry, more or less without introducing any changes. The Package Truck (the basic model M) continued to be available until 1957 and it was obtainable as a special body for some time after that. From 1959 there was the standard

An original 1948 74 cubic inch UL Big Twin with a replica of a 1945 sidecar. An exact replica from Krafft Harley–Davidson Germany, an LE sidecar from the 90s, and one of the many custom versions.

Many world-famous car manufacturers specializing in sidecars quite naturally decided to adapt the powerful Harley-Davidson touring motorcycles to make them suitable for use with sidecars – indeed, many replaced the telescopic fork with a sprung arm as just one of many innovations aimed at attaining the best possible on-road performance.

Here are just some examples:

Armec (Switzerland) builds a wide body on the Harley-Davidson leaf-spring chassis which is particularly suitable for families.

California Sidecar/Escapade Trailer (U.S.A.) offers the luxury Compagnon GT, and Friendship I–III models as well as the Escapade trailer.

EML (The Netherlands) produces a highly stable body which was developed on the basis of experience gained in motocross.

Liberty (U.S.A.) offers a classic remake of the 1936 model with rubber suspension, hydraulic third-wheel braking, polished and chromed leaf springs and a highly stable four-point connection.

Mobec (Germany) manufactures a spacious body with extra luggage space and extremely comfortable seating.

Sauer (Germany) constructs special and one-off models with an entry door and a lot of interior space. They also rebuild all Harleys to the highest specifications, including the Ultra Classic models and the Softails. One of their typical models is the Kondor sidecar.

Walter (Germany) concentrates on the construction of sidecars reminiscent of the "good old days." Their Side Glide and Freeway King models have an entry door and well-upholstered seats.

Of course there are an enormous number of highly skilled enthusiasts whose hobby it is to construct a sidecar just as they would like it, packed with their very own ideas. Nostalgic, vintage, classic or even bizarre – there will always be modern designs for motorcycle bodies of all kinds.

model, Type LE Sport Sidecar, from which Harley was later to develop the two basic models, the RLE (for all FXR series with a 300-pound additional load, third wheel brake, tonneau top, windshield and whitewall tire) and the TLE (with the same extras) for all FLHT and FLT motorcycles. The last of these was also available as the Ultra model which really had absolutely everything. In 1967 the manufacture of the fiberglass bodies was moved to the Tomahawk works and for all the combinations changes were made to the springs, shocks and steering geometry.

Although there are countless photographs of military combinations, Harley did not, in fact, supply the U.S. Army with any sidecars. The WLA had failed to meet the required standards; the Lite Car, constructed expressly for that purpose, was not awarded a government contract, much to the annoyance of

Jim Goulding, who was convinced of the suitability of his sidecar. No details survive of the few motorcycle combinations which were supplied to the U.S.S.R. The U.S. Navy took delivery of a mere 136 Type Us with the 74 cubic inch side-valve engine – all of them finished in battleship gray.

Harley-Davidson has included a luxury sidecar (TLE or TLF) in its range since the early 1990s which has been designed to satisfy every whim of the motorcyclist who enjoys riding around for the sheer fun of it, or who travels the globe in search of new adventures. It has been built for mounting to the big touring models in the F series. But it doesn't come cheap: with a price tag of about 6,800 dollars for the TLE and 8,000 dollars for the even more luxurious TLF, it is more expensive than a second hand medium-sized car. But that seems to make it all the more enjoyable.

One of the great number of humorous sidecar creations: as bottle (top), as special transporter (above) and Swedish shark bomb (right).

Japan's Harley:

Rikuo, the King of the Road

Spin-Offs

More Products Using the Harley Logo

The Harley-Davidson Motor Company has repeatedly turned its attention to equipment which has very little to do with motorcycles. The explanation for the company's taking an active interest in other companies is to be found in the fact that their own works were not always utilized to their full capacity and that they were always searching for additional ways of making a profit. In the end, the company came to realize that it was most important to limit themselves to the basics and to concentrate on what had made the legendary name world-famous: large-capacity motorcycles with a unique engine and design style. All the other products tended to be diversions. But nevertheless, the famous logo is still part of them.

As the 1920s gave way to the 1930s, the economic recession in Japan lead to a disastrous drop in the value of the yen and, as a result, American imports quadrupled in price. As a consequence Harley-Davidson launched their first joint venture under the guidance of Rich A. Child. Japan was now permitted to produce Harley motorcycles independently – albeit a single model only under the strict condition that this was solely for the home market and was under no circumstances to be exported.

After lengthy negotiations the Japanese factory launched into full production in Shinagawa, a Tokyo suburb, with the help of the pharmaceutical company Sankyo Seiyaku. Production started in 1935 with the 45 cubic inch (750 cc)

side-valve model, which two years later was given the name Rikuo (King of the Road) when the factory became 100 percent Japanese-owned. From 1936 to 1945 1,479 of these machines were built, mainly for the police and the Japanese armed forces.

Shortly before the outbreak of World War II Chief Engineer Sakurai developed the Model 97 which was to become the official Japanese military motorcycle, particularly in occupied Manchuria, in combination with the hard-wearing sidecar designed by Sakurai himself. In 1937, after the outbreak of the Sino-Japanese War, the works in Shinagawa was completely overwhelmed by the enormous size of the contract for supplying the military so it transferred part of the manufacturing to Jidosha and Mazda. During World War II Rikuo produced more than 18,000 of the 97 Model, which later saw service in the Chinese and subsequently the Pacific Rim.

After the war, in 1947, the Shinagawa works managed to sell 326 Rikuos and it was by then the largest motorcycle manufacturer in Japan. But the competition caught up very

quickly. In 1953 the popular, but nevertheless technically outdated, Rikuo (a 750 cc side-valve producing 15 horsepower!) was improved by the addition of a telescopic fork. Then a new RQ model was developed with aluminum cylinder heads with higher compression, which did at least raise the power to 22 horsepower. In all, 1,983 of these machines were sold. In 1954 Rikuo took a further step along the road to modernization with the introduction of the RT model which now had a 27 horsepower engine constructed entirely of aluminum. The RT now had, at last, been provided with dry-sump lubrication; but this innovation did not help significantly. The RX – which was an unlicensed copy of the 74 inch (1200 cc) OHV Panhead with rear-wheel suspension and aluminum hubs – managed to sell a mere 520 Rikuo machines in 1958. In the face of the modern parallel twins produced by Japanese competitors, the King of the Road had really no chance at all and the works in Shinagawa finally closed its gates for the very last time in the year 1960. With that Harley-Davidson's Japanese adventure had come to an end.

Bicycles (1917–1923)

For the six years between 1917 and 1923 Harley-Davidson also sold bicycles. They were manufactured by the Davis Sewing Machine Company, but the sales of the bike through the Harley-Davidson dealership network were not encouraging.

The dealers, used to big and heavy motorcycles, were far more concerned with the lucrative side of their business of selling the new Harley motorcycles then to take any real interest in selling bicycles or even to promote them.

It was Walter Davidson who quickly realized that bicyclists and motorcyclists have completely different interests and needs. Having come to this conclusion, he took a decision, which meant that the bicycle business ceased production.

The remaining bicycles were

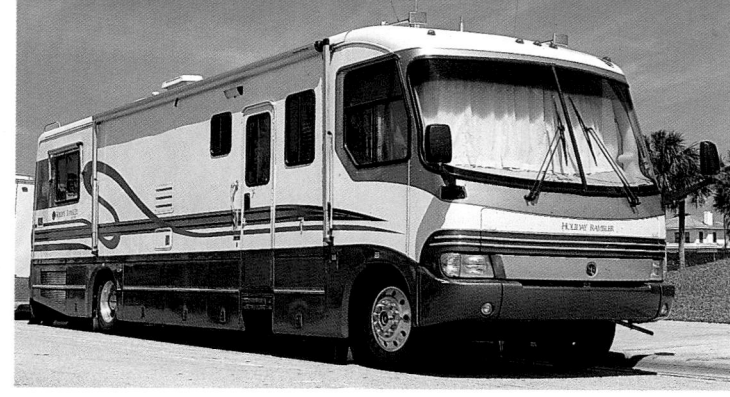

Modern version of the golf cart, the luxurious Holiday Rambler Motor Home, a stationary engine being used as a plow, one of the famous practice bombs made for the U.S. Army, an excellent snowmobile from another time and the modern snowmobile, mainly used in the northern U.S. and Canada.

Courtesy of: John W.Parham, Anamosa, Iowa

taken over by the Davis Sewing Machine Company which continued to supply Harley dealers with spares until 1924.

In 1996 Harley-Davidson granted a license for the manufacture of a Harley GT bicycle to a cycle factory in Santa Ana, California. The new custom bicycle was to have seven gears, an imitation gas tank and a thick saddle. Production was limited to 1,000 units.

Stationary engines

From its earliest days Harley-Davidson has from time to time manufactured various types of single- and twin-cylinder stationary engines to power various kinds of vehicles and equipment: engines for boats, saws, tractors, plows, lawnmowers and generators – to be used for civil, agricultural or military purposes. These engines came in various configurations: V-Twins, F-heads, Flat-twins and singles. The most popular models were, amongst others, the four-stroke single-cyliner model of 21 cubic inch (350 cc) capacity and the 23 cubic inch (400 cc) Model G. But, compared to the enormous home competition, they did not sell well even at the best of times and were never a financial success.

Snowmobiles (1971–1975)

In the early days snowmobiles were home-built contraptions – caterpillar-tracked V-Twins with a lengthened steering-column and really unpredictable handling. There was quite clearly a demand for proper factory-built machines in the American Snow Belt. So, in 1971, Harley-Davidson presented its dealers in the north, where there was no shortage of snow, with a new range of vehicles: the

Golf Carts (1963 onwards)

Here was something completely different: golf cart production rose to almost 20 percent of the entire production in the mid-1960s. Golf carts were available either with a gasoline-driven engine or with an electric motor; the former used the Dynastart system (a kick-down of the gas pedal – a dynastarter is usually a dynamo which can also function as a starter) and had disc brakes as well as an automatic parking brake.

These golf cars were assembled in Milwaukee, but their bodies came from the Tomahawk plant and were constructed from fiberglass. For heavier loads there was the Utilicar, a kind of universal mini-pickup.

snowmobiles. They were manufactured in the Capitol Drive factory in two basic versions, the Y-398 (24.29 cubic inches/398 cc) and the Y-440 (26.42 cubic inches/440 cc). The nifty snowmobiles with their two-stroke Harley engines were available as either with manual or electric start. They had chain drive, automatic transmission, power output of around 30 horsepower and naturally, skis.

Holiday Rambler (1986–1996)

An interesting venture outside the realm of motorcycles was the acquisition of the Holiday Rambler Corporation, a general merchandising company which had established itself 33 years previously in Wakarusa, Indiana. It had concentrated its business on quality recreational vehicles, camping equipment, motor homes and pickup trucks. The purchase price, totaling 155 million dollars, was financed partly by equity capital and partly by loans. The luxury mobile homes including the Imperial, the Presidential, the Alumalite, the Monitor and the Trailseeker were priced at between 10,000 and 180,000 dollars and yielded Harley a healthy profit.

Even though the company management never grew weary of explaining how well the Holiday Rambler program slotted into their own (since the target customer group was more or less the same and there was no foreign competition), Harley-Davidson divested itself of the luxury mobile homes ten years later. The Holiday Rambler Recreational Vehicle Division was sold to the Monaco Coach Corporation in Coburg, Oregon so that Harley-Davidson could devote its entire efforts to the business of manufacturing and selling motorcycles.

Bombcases

There was, though, one particularly lucrative business which Harley did not want to lose on any account. The Army Munitions and Chemical Command awarded a contract for practice bombshells. The company produces the bombshells in York and as result of improved quality and a cost reduction of 25 percent, was the winner of the CQCP (Contractor Quality Certification Program), a prize which is awarded by the Army.

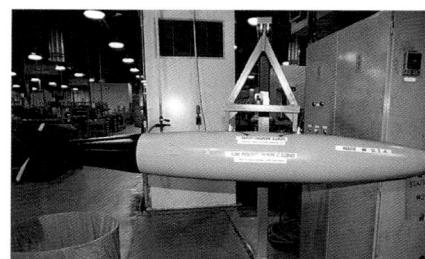

Contracting Out

As a result of company developments over a number of years in specific high-tech areas, Harley never ceases to win small contracts from companies which are outside the motorcycle industry. For instance, Harley has completed contracts with Acustar, Briggs & Stratton and with Kohler to manufacture parts and equipment, as well as computer wiring systems for the aircraft industry.

Trihawk (1984 and 1985)

Harley-Davidson's venture into the trike business ended in failure. The Trihawk sports two-seater was virtually unequaled by its competitors with its 1300 cc air-cooled front-mounted Citroën engine. The company had bought this vehicle from Robert McKee and Lou Richards in 1984, but it was not suitable for running on the Harley V-Twin engine. The small factory in Dana Point, California assembled between 10 and 15 of them a month. This mistaken investment was soon disposed of.

In the Service of Law and Order

Harley-Riding Officers

A typical action photo of a police unit during a risky operation.

Cover of the police special edition of the *Enthusiast* from February 1935.

It's official – according to the latest information from the Harley–Davidson Motor Company, the first policemen to use Harleys were located in Detroit, not, as previously believed, in Pittsburgh. The year was 1908. This is significant, as Detroit was America's automobile capital, so the earliest motorized rulers of the city would have been Ford and General Motors cars rather than Harley bikes. But the maneuverable, economical two–wheeled Motorbikes from Milwaukee had their advantages and increasingly replaced the police mounted on horseback. In 1911 San Francisco and Los Angeles followed suit, then Cincinnati in 1913, North Carolina in 1919, and by 1925 over 2,500 City and County Police Departments were using Harley-Davidsons. By the year 1930 this had risen to more than 3,000 departments.

This was the start of the remarkable history of a department set up specifically to deal with the demands of law–enforcement agencies. The manufacture and equipping of police motorcycles is still one of the most carefully organized departments in the Harley empire. But it was not until the 1930s that Harley provided any special accessories.

Police riders are subject to extreme risks, especially in high–speed chases, and they cannot be compared with normal motorcyclists. Both they and their machines have to meet special requirements and the riders need special qualifications. Just as in motorcycle racing, the police had to learn to deal with borderline situations and to be able to control their heavy machines in all kinds of circumstances. No wonder then that their rigorous training sessions led to a host of drill teams appearing in shows in which the police riders performed acrobatic feats. Motorcycle police had to pursue traffic offenders as well as criminals and needed to

catch them red–handed whenever the situation demanded it. They could choose neither the time of day nor the route, as that luxury was left to the person being pursued. If they decided to use gravel roads and sandy tracks, which is what most country roads amounted to before World War II, they had a better chance of escape. And even though motorcycle cops had a hard life, for many of them a chase could end in death.

The first motorcycle officers were real gentlemen. They gave out their tickets following an extremely polite ritual, a little schoolmasterly in manner perhaps, but respectful nevertheless. Long–winded lectures made the good citizens aware of their dangerous behavior. Speeders, drunks, noisy vehicles, drivers with faulty brakes, or no brakes at all, nothing and no one escaped their trained, watchful eye. And, unlike present–day double patrols, they always operated on their own and had, at the most, a pitiful 7 to 12 horsepower available. It was a hard life which was also badly paid.

Harley-Davidson has always given its "police fellows" good publicity and propaganda. In nearly every issue the company magazine the *Enthusiast* reports proudly on Harley–riding police, their successes, shows and parades, and is particularly pleased to highlight the precisely organized ranks of police motorcycles. Police matters have often appeared on the title page, and in 1935 a complete issue entitled "Police Special" was devoted to the uniformed guardians of the law.

But above all, the company never tired of pressing for improved safety on the roads ("...Servi–Cars solve the parking problem...") and declared war on the daily "traffic slaughter" caused by reckless (mostly drunken) drivers.

One of the first Harley police units in 1909.

City police in the 1930s on the trail of traffic pests.

The police service in winter, also from the 1930s.

An elite unit of the California Highway Patrol at the beginning of the 1930s.

In addition, Law Enforcement customers received special service and generous special conditions. At the beginning of the 1930s Walter Davidson, concerned by the decline in police orders (caused by the introduction of new, faulty VL models) mounted a special sales campaign. The price for police bikes was reduced to 195 dollars, which hardly covered production costs, and they were sold through specially trained agents, instead of through local distributors as before. Naturally, those dealers who were still interested in promoting trade and good relations with their police authorities took exception to this. But Harleys were not the only bikes used in police work. Indian and Excelsior machines were just as popular, especially the more expensive, but exceedingly comfortable, four-cylinder models. As times became harder and the competition ever more intense, Harley-Davidson had to try anything to encourage the procurement offices in public services to buy Harley motorcycles. The sales department developed specific strategies — for example local dealers were supposed to know how to deal with corrupt politicians who could influence these decisions. In the end, apart from a few foreign competitors, Harley-Davidson was left as the only possible supplier still in the business.

Along with a few other city administrations, the New York City Police Department had remained faithful to Indian motorcycles. When the company folded in 1953, the small Tete Flex Company took over building Indian Fours for the NYCPD, all finished in the classical Indian red, as specified by the police. But Harley was tendering for future orders with their own models, conforming to all the specifications laid down, and of course also painted in the obligatory Indian red. This aroused unanimous indignation amongst those police who were confirmed Indian supporters, and Tete Flex complained that the imitation was a patent infringement. Little good it did them — by the late 1950s all the Indians had been taken out of service and replaced by new Harley FL models, naturally still in the regulation Indian red.

Other Indian territories were not so easy to crack. For example, the warm personal and political relations existing between Indian dealer George Gonzales and the Governor of Louisiana, Huey P. Long, meant that New Orleans was a very difficult territory to conquer, even long after Indian had gone out of business.

The Praetorian Guard

Whenever any motorcycle enthusiast applied to join an elite group of men such as the Highway Patrol back in the 1920s, he would be entrusted with a Harley-Davidson, a book of rules and

regulations and an enormous revolver. In addition, all he needed was the martial outfit he donned and inextinguishable self-confidence. Even today most of the motorcycle cops (which is a name they don't really care for, the correct mode of address always being "Officer") do their best to cultivate an image that instills fear into the general public: dark glasses, lots of gold and silver on their black leather jackets, tight-fitting breeches tucked carefully into highly polished knee boots, these are as much a part of this image as is an immaculately kept motorcycle with all the accessories. Their word is law with a capital "L" and their omnipotence seems almost superhuman, even sacred. As with all officers, it's best not to get into an argument with one of them. It also seems that to be an American motorcycle officer astride a heavy Harley is one of the greatest ambitions of many bikers the world over. The heavyweight American police bike has just the same magnetism as always for the macho male, although there are also female motorcycle cops. Altogether they form a special kind of elite group, in a unique way, an incorruptible Law and Order caste. The same thought is expressed in the name of their closed motorcycle club, Blue Knights MC, which was founded in 1974 in Bangor, Maine as a private club. Sometimes sheriffs and policemen are held up to ridicule or depicted as corrupt criminals in uniform, but a highway policeman on a motorcycle still remains an unimpeachable symbol of the integrity of law and order.

The peaked police cap had to be secured with a tight band. Today the open police helmet is a necessary saftey measure for both male and female officers.

Extras for Police Motorcycles

Riding and Gunning

In the early years motorcycle officers had to order and even pay for their extras themselves; it was only in the late-1930s that the police departments took over this responsibility.

The regulation rigid police caps were a real pet peeve. They were always threatening to blow away in the wind, and had to be secured with all kinds of tapes and straps. The Helmet Law introduced after the war was a positive relief for motorcycle police.

Another problem was the kickstart. By the time the patrolman had managed to start his machine, the traffic offender was often long gone. There were angry reports of up to 40 attempts to get bikes started! So the introduction of the electric starter in 1965 was one of the most important measures ever taken to ensure effective pursuit of criminals by motorcycle.

There was also the constant demand issued by police authorities to have the throttle fitted on the left-hand side. How else could a right-handed policeman draw his gun and fire during pursuit?

Harley-Davidson Police Model, left side view, showing the DeLuxe Police Accessory Group. The DeLuxe Group includes the most neccessary accessories for Police Motorcycle service

The Arms Race

1930 – More powerful front and rear brakes, a specially calibrated and lit tachometer, accurate up to 100 mph.

1931 – A front wheel siren, a first-aid box, and the Pyrene fire extinguisher.

1934 – Roll bars, two types of pursuit lamps to choose from: Little King and Little Beauty.

1935 – The Jiffy side stand, a rear wheel siren, steering dampers, a robust luggage carrier, red and white flashlights, stoplight and windshield, one-way radio receiver and special finish in safety silver for better visibility in the dark.

1938 – Improved radio receivers from RCA operating in the AM band.

1948 – The first two-way radio, a powerful Motorola radio operating in the FM band, 152 kilohertz.

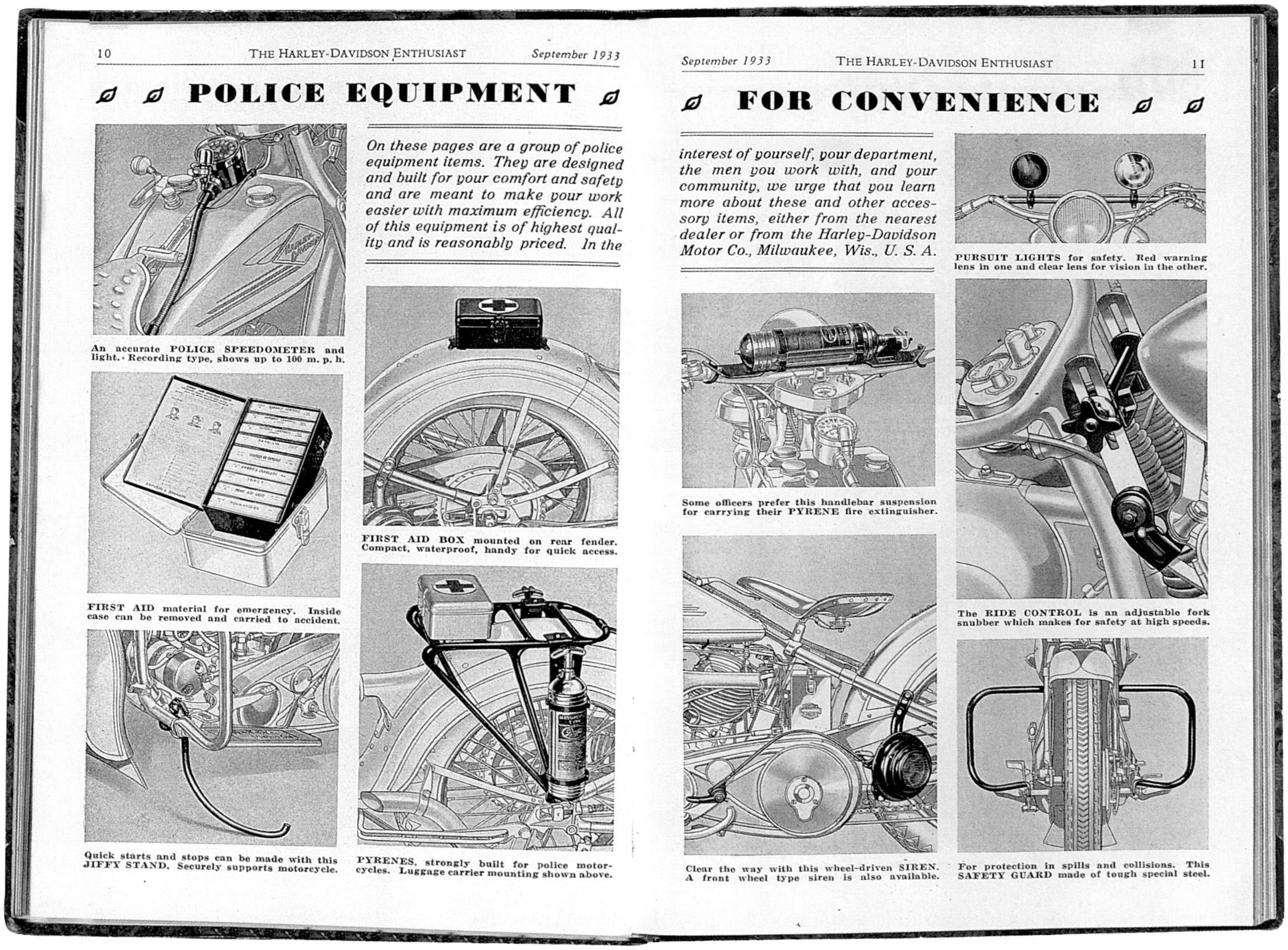

---

10 THE HARLEY-DAVIDSON ENTHUSIAST September 1933

POLICE EQUIPMENT

On these pages are a group of police equipment items. They are designed and built for your comfort and safety and are meant to make your work easier with maximum efficiency. All of this equipment is of highest quality and is reasonably priced. In the

An accurate POLICE SPEEDOMETER and light.- Recording type, shows up to 100 m. p. h.

FIRST AID material for emergency. Inside case can be removed and carried to accident.

Quick starts and stops can be made with this JIFFY STAND. Securely supports motorcycle.

FIRST AID BOX mounted on rear fender. Compact, waterproof, handy for quick access.

PYRENES, strongly built for police motorcycles. Luggage carrier mounting shown above.

September 1933 THE HARLEY-DAVIDSON ENTHUSIAST 11

FOR CONVENIENCE

interest of yourself, your department, the men you work with, and your community, we urge that you learn more about these and other accessory items, either from the nearest dealer or from the Harley-Davidson Motor Co., Milwaukee, Wis., U. S. A.

Some officers prefer this handlebar suspension for carrying their PYRENE fire extinguisher.

Clear the way with this wheel-driven SIREN. A front wheel type siren is also available.

PURSUIT LIGHTS for safety. Red warning lens in one and clear lens for vision in the other.

The RIDE CONTROL is an adjustable fork snubber which makes for safety at high speeds.

For protection in spills and collisions. This SAFETY GUARD made of tough special steel.

...Control to Patrolman...

In the era when there was no CB or two-way police radio, that is before 1948, contacting motorcycle patrolmen by radio was quite an adventure. While the officer was riding along the highway, the receiver would emit a long beep, an unmistakable call to stop immediately, put the motorcycle on its stand, and switch off the engine. If, by chance, his timing was right, the officer would then turn the loudspeaker volume up and attempt to listen to a crackly voice giving him his next assignment. The message would be more or less intelligible, depending on whether there was a powerful enough transmitter nearby, which was often not the case in rural areas. This message would be repeated three times, at intervals of 15 minutes. The patrolman was unable to confirm receipt of the message, so the dispatcher in the control room just had to hope that it been received by the motorized arm of the law.

CHP and LAPD

Harleys in a Trial of Strength

A traffic officer in Puerto Rico.

The Exported Symbol of Authority

The beefy status symbols are popular not just with American law enforcement agencies. Police departments all over the world, especially those in areas of immediate American influence, such as Central and South America, ride the heavyweights from Milwaukee. They are particularly popular for grand parades and prestigious escort duties.

As early as in the 1930s, the Montreal harbor police, the Shanghai French Municipal Council in China, police escorts in Rotterdam, Holland, the motorcycle corps and customs authorities of Cœcuta in Colombia, and the traffic police in Cape Town, South Africa, all had Harley police machines. Today there are police Harleys in over 20 countries; the Mexico City Police have the most, followed by the South Korean National Police, with around 1,500 Harleys.

In North America over 900 police authorities are Harley-Davidson customers. New York City Police are the biggest purchasers, followed by Florida, with over 90 police departments, then Texas and California. A well-organized maintenance and buyback system makes it easier for public services to decide in Harley's favor. The police machines from Milwaukee have long complied with all the requisite standards. A contributory factor in this respect was the work of the Police Advisory Council. Set up in 1992, it works in close collaboration with the Traffic Institute at Northwestern University to take note of all the suggestions and problems of police riders. The motorcycle officers receive ongoing instruction and training in the form of various rider and mechanics courses. Harley-Davidson also issues its own magazine especially for this important customer group and anyone interested in them: *The Mounted Officer*, a type of *The Enthusiast* for police riders.

It was called the Great White Fleet, and its captains were known as the hardest men in America – the motorcycle police of the California Highway Patrol, CHP for short. It was founded on August 14, 1929 and by 1933 had 550 officers, including administrative staff. They wore green uniforms, black boots, and black leather jackets. They packed a Smith & Wesson 38 caliber Police Special or a Colt, and the officers were highly trained in jujitsu.

The CHP fleet consisted of 402 solo motorcycles and two combinations, more Harleys than Indians, and all finished in white. It was not until later that this scheme changed to black and white, a color combination which no other vehicle in California was allowed to adopt. The motorcycles were fitted with various extras, such as a tachometer calibrated up to 100 mph, two more headlamps, one of them red, a fire extinguisher, a first-aid box, and of course the mechanical siren. On average these bikes were ridden about 15,000 miles per year.

The CHP was famous for having the highest standards and the strictest procurement regulations in the world. In the 1970s the CHP also tested Hondas and Moto Guzzis, but eventually decided on 130 Kawasakis, a tender for which Harley could not compete either in terms of price or quality.

Although Harley tried everything, the LAPD (Los Angeles Police Department) also soon stopped testing with Harleys and issued a sobering statement that the rival Kawasakis were ahead of them in respect of compliance with the required environmental standards. Not until 1983 was the LAPD prepared to test Harleys again. The result was a heap of criticisms: the curvature of the handlebars was unwieldy; the

clutch lever required too much force; the gearshift lever and the foot-brake lever were hard to reach; the sidestand was difficult to find; the windshield did not keep the wind out; riding stability was generally poor and the engine vibrations too strong; when cornering at an angle of 45 degrees the frame and footboard touched ground finally; 92 mph top speed was was not enough. Conclusion: failed!

It was not until 1985, with the new Evolution FXRP Pursuit, which was specially adapted to meet police requirements, that Harley-Davidson overcame these objections, and the testers reported in enthusiastic terms. The CHP and LAPD, two police departments in the U.S. predominantly equipped with motorcycles, both decided to order from Harley again. The political campaign urging people to "Buy American," which was gaining strength at that time, may have helped a little. The FXRP, and the FLHTP police models built from 1993 onwards, had returned to California, despite the endless repeats of the famous TV police series "CHiPs," featuring Erik Estrada forever astride a Kawasaki.

A typical police station of the California Highway Patrol in the 1930s (top).

The Fire Brigade and the Red Cross

Ready to Help at Any Time

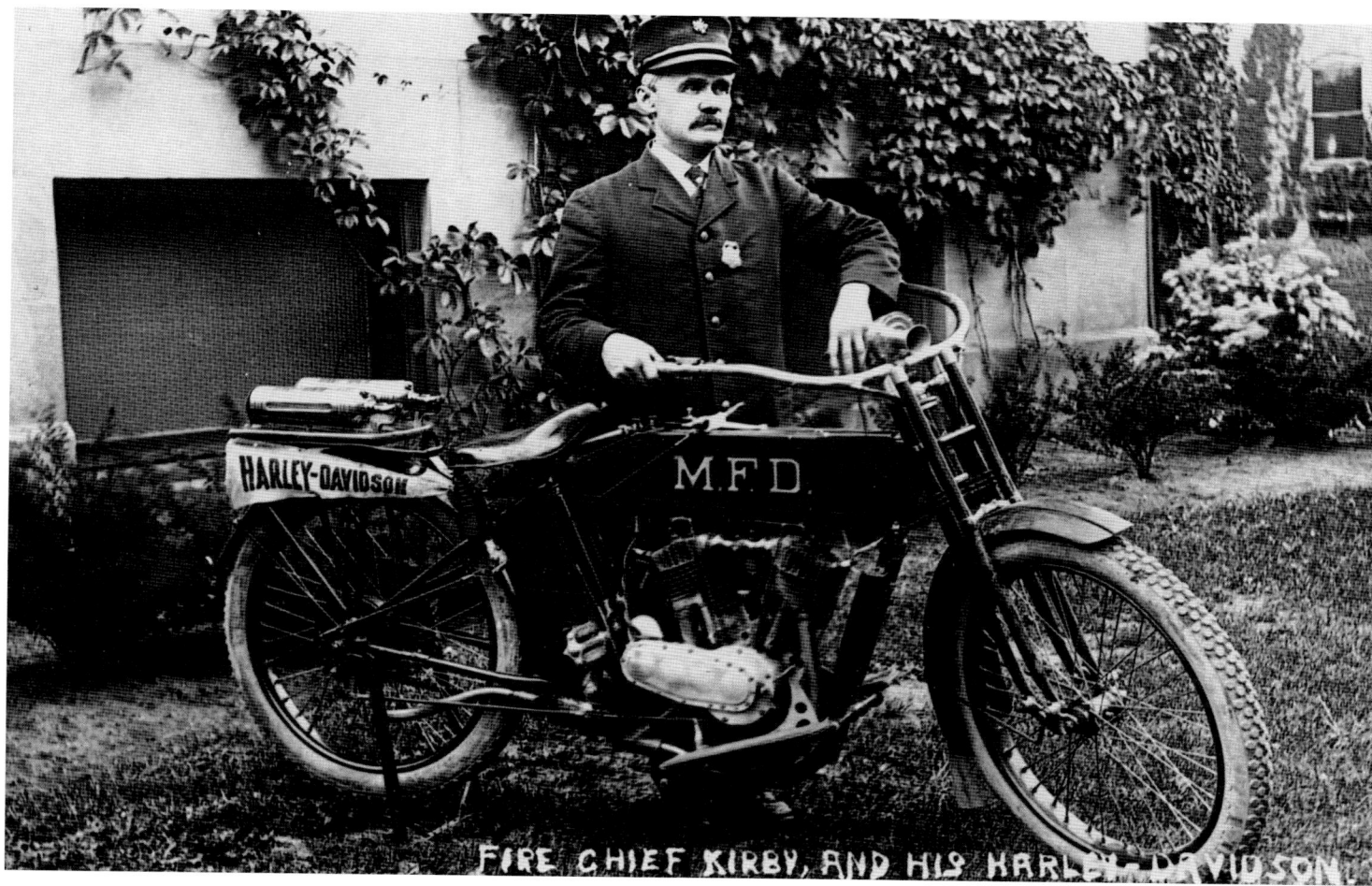

© Harley-Davidson

His responsibility is obvious and the machine on which he races to the scene is particularly speedy: Milwaukees's fire chief Kirby.

The *Enthusiast* No. 83 from 1925 reported the creative invention from Texan Andrew Morales with his private express ambulance (right).

Not only in wartime, but also in the course of normal, everyday life, Harleys have proved faithful and efficient aids to the work of official and communal organizations. Emergency transport, providing assistance at natural disasters, observation and inspection, these are all tasks which have often been better served by motorcycles than cars.

Here are a few examples. In Florida a fire chief loved his Harley so much that he made it his official vehicle. He had it painted the customary red and fitted with the necessary extras: siren, red lamps and fire extinguisher. From then on, he rode it out in front to all the fires in the district as an official vehicle. Today it is a museum piece, which is proudly displayed in parades.

During World War II, Harley-Davidson motorcycles and sidecars were often used for medical duties and transporting the wounded. But even after the war there were motorcycle units in the British Red Cross known as The Red Cross Flying Squad, which specialized in "flying" assignments, such as patrols, sports events and speedway racing.

In a press statement in 1985 Harley announced that its German subsidiary at Flörsheim–Wicker was donating two California Highway Patrol FXRP motorcycles to the German Red Cross. They were deployed, along with two local BMW machines, on a popular, tourist–filled highway, the A8 between Munich and Salzburg, as a test for that particular application.

Equipped with radios and emergency medical supplies, they could squeeze through miles of stationary traffic and were able to reach accident sites far quicker than any car. Ridden by qualified paramedics with specialized skills, they were commonly called out to deal with patients experiencing sudden feelings of weakness, heart attacks and even emergency births.

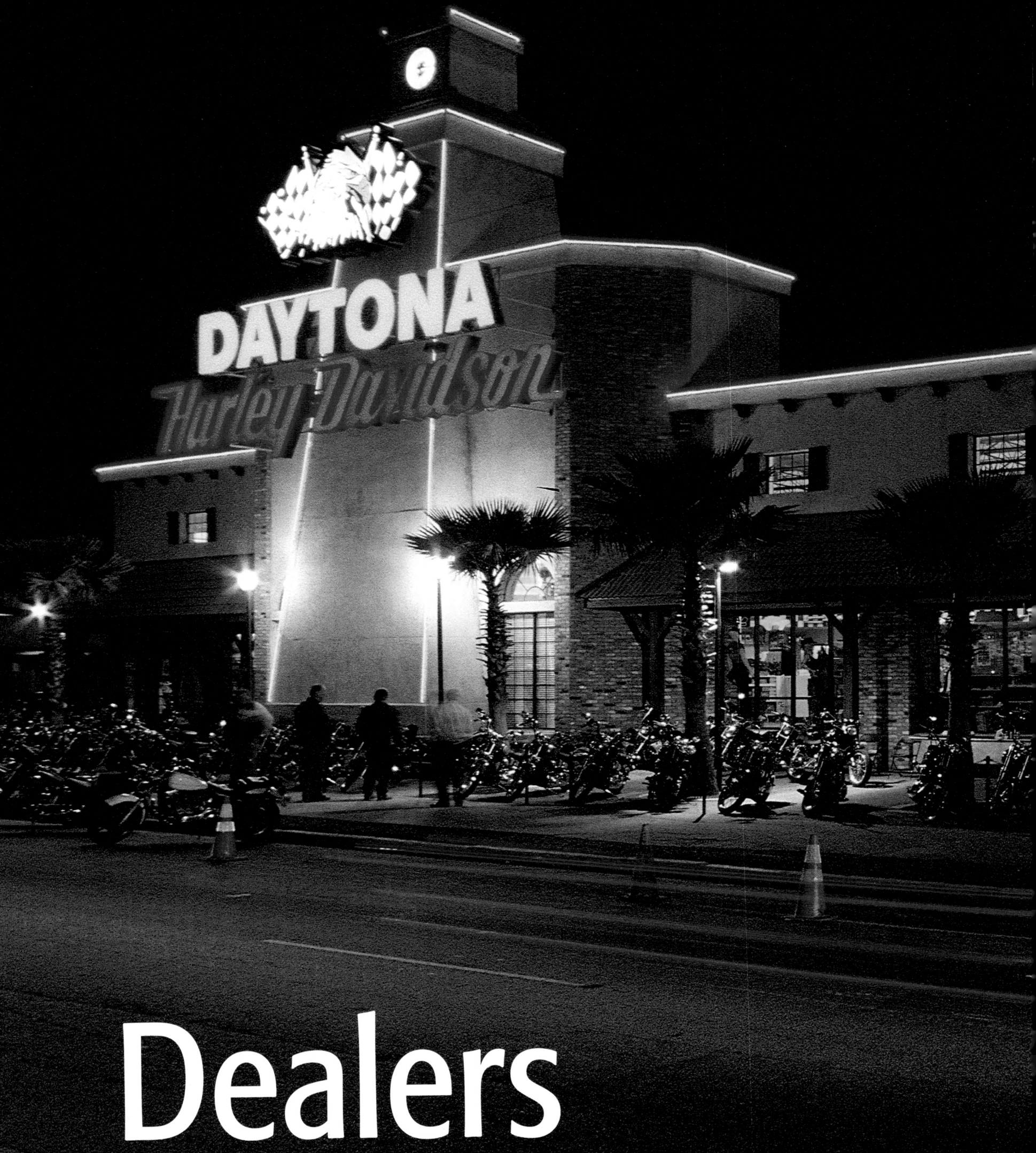

Dealers

Oppressive Contracts

Unfaithfulness Ruled Out and Payment Before Sale

Realizing that a well-developed and efficient dealer network was essential to secure sales and guarantee commercial success, Arthur Davidson went on the road in 1907, immediately after the company was officially founded, traveling all around the U.S. He started in New England and headed south from there, then out to the far west, building his future empire as he went.

As he embarked on his legendary recruitment campaign he had a quality product to sell – a product with a big future and plenty of profit potential: the new "Silent Grey Fellow," the universal motorcycle of its day. True to the business principle of brand loyalty to which he held unswervingly – loyalty to one supplier in return for guaranteed payments and benefits – Arthur sought out his new front-line troops with care. Most of them were already in a similar line of business – cycle or car dealers, mechanics and fitters – but there were also some complete newcomers among them, men who wanted to embark on a new career. He examined each candidate's personal and moral credentials, tested them at length on their technical understanding and ability, checked into their financial situations as well as their reputations in the community. In order to avoid future problems, he made a point of not hiring dealers who had already worked for other manufacturers.

The franchise agreements that he signed were masterpieces of legal drafting, carefully crafted down to the last detail – the refined instruments of a brilliant grand design: tough, businesslike and uncompromising in their financial conditions and loyalty clauses. This would cause the company a lot of trouble in later years. But while the standards were very demanding, there were exceptions. Dealerships were divided into four categories according to population density and in remote rural areas the company was always prepared to make more concessions. Special privileges, sometimes rather curious ones, were

Outside, in front of the showroom in fine weather, inside in poor weather – early dealers proudly presented their Harleys in as great a variety as possible, arranged in perfect formation, demonstrating both their commercial strength and their competence.

© Harley-Davidson

also given to very successful dealers. Others who didn't get along with Arthur were often rigorously excluded from the family circle. One fundamental rule was that dealers had to pay on delivery for the stock they ordered. Late payers were and are the bane of Harley-Davidson's financial management. Profit margins, particularly on sales of motorcycles, were kept pretty low – mainly as a hedge against fluctuating market fortunes, it must be said.

Successful dealers received an end-of-year bonus – another arrangement that would later prove controversial. In other respects dealers were left in the lurch financially by the company on whom they very soon became almost totally dependent. For example, they were charged interest at the rate of 1.5 percent a month on all unsold Harleys, which quickly ate up any profits they might have made. And the company kept a close watch on its dealers to make sure they didn't sell any competitor's products, whether motorcycles, spares or accessories. If the company management caught a dealer doing this, it normally terminated his franchise agreement which had to be renewed annually. As a general rule, anyone who had dealings with the competition (especially the arch-enemy Indian) was fired by Harley.

At the same time Harley-Davidson worked hard to ensure that its dealers were not forced to supplement their earnings in this way. From the early 1920s onwards – and particularly during the hard times of the 1930s – the company conducted an extensive and aggressive advertising campaign aimed at stimulating much-needed demand, at the same time supplying its dealers with all kinds of sales aids. Dealers received service bulletins, motorcycle manuals, engine repair manuals, blueprints of engines and gearboxes, instructions and guidance in various forms, including the company's "Standards of Practice," and a uniquely comprehensive range of spare parts and accessories. No

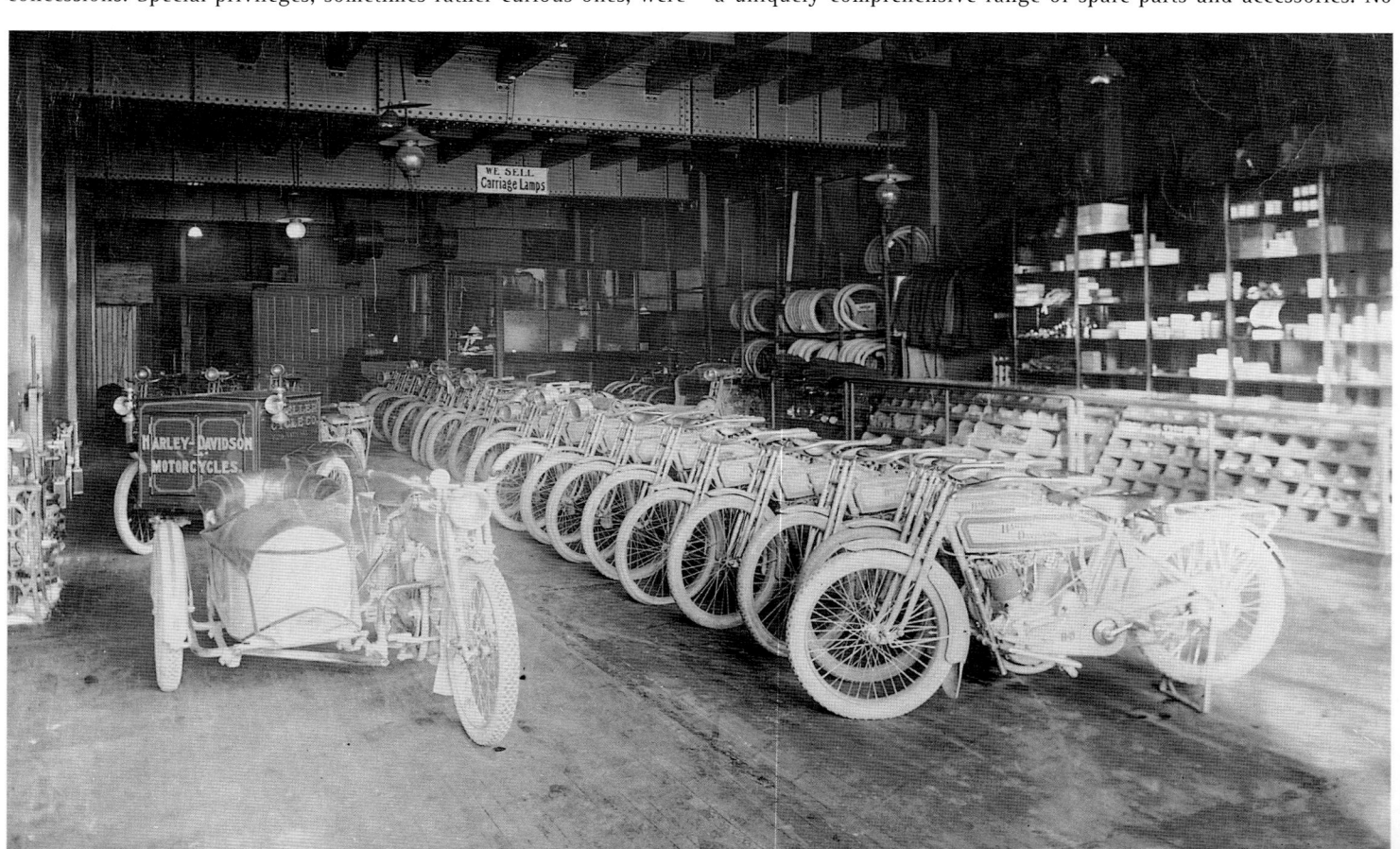

These Harleys have been lined-up in a long row in front of the dealer's showroom as if ready for a run. Notice the gasoline pump in the background.

A typical example of a presentation arrangement, photographed at the Hobbie Auto Co. in Hampton, Iowa.

other motorcycle manufacturer could match Harley-Davidson in this respect, which offered everything from a complete range of clothing to pencils and cigarette lighters embossed with the company logo. Such items helped generate a ferocious loyalty to the marque and an insatiable appetite for memorabilia among all Harley freaks. In addition, Harley dealers and their successes, including their local activities on the club and sports circuit, were profiled at length in various company publications. Up until 1919 that meant they were profiled in *The Harley Dealer*, which was superseded in 1916 by a monthly magazine known as *The Harley-Davidson Enthusiast*.

It soon became clear that Harley dealers were not just the submissive recipients of orders handed down from company headquarters in Milwaukee, but were characters in their own right, flamboyant businessmen, often pioneers of motorcycling and motorcycle culture, and with a good sprinkling of rebellious individualists. So it was only a matter of time before they came into conflict with company policy as well as with the wishes of their local customers. At sporting events, which were usually sponsored by the local dealership, these conflicts took on a sharper note. There were Harley dealers who remained completely loyal, of course.

In order to get a better grip on his dealer network, Arthur divided the U.S. into a series of large districts and regions, and then appointed District Managers to advise dealers within their district in business matters and to assist them with any problems. Their duties also included keeping an eye on the activities of the dealers and report back to company headquarters in Milwaukee. The district managers found themselves in the position of go-betweens or mediators, often acting as negotiators between the parties in times of crisis.

A difficult period for both sides, whose fortunes were linked for better or for worse, was undoubtedly the 1980s. Dealers in those years had to invest approximately 30,000 dollars of their own capital and pass demanding aptitude tests in order to secure a dealership for a limited period. Interest rates were very high, the foreign competition

was flourishing, but it was tough to share in their competitors' success. Many dealers had to give up their dealership or desert to the competition. The situation became critical. In the wake of AMF directives, production capacity had been determined by the Retail Sale & Warranty Registration (RSWR). Introduced in 1978, this stock monitoring system showed month by month what dealers had sold and what they still had in stock. Production levels were adjusted in the light of this information.

Naturally the company did everything possible to keep its dealers informed. Annual dealer conventions, always held in August, featured presentations of the latest products and strategies held in festive surroundings, accompanied by splendid banquets. These occasions were obligatory, but they didn't always address the concerns and wishes of dealers as they would have liked. Harley-Davidson had introduced internal training courses for mechanics and workshop staff at the time of World War I. In time these were expanded into a full-scale program of in-house technical training leading to a diploma.

In conclusion, it is fair to say that the relationship between Harley-Davidson and its dealers has always been a vivid one, with the typical up and downs. But both sides have learned to live together, in the sober knowledge that the only way they can coexist and make a profit is to respect each other's needs.

In the following pages you'll be introduced to a small sample of this huge, global dealer network, selected without prejudice to represent all their colleagues around the world – so far as that is possible within the confines of this book.

295

A Belated Appreciation

Price Negotiations

A typical Harley shop from the 1930s: Kenny's Harley–Davidson in Kansas City.

Young aggressive management

WALTER C. DAVIDSON
Vice President — Sales

As an authorized Harley-Davidson dealer, you will become an important member of a successful business organization.

Harley-Davidson has the experience gained from the past but is directed by a young, aggressive management team. The sons of the founders have grown up with the Company and are now directing the continued growth of the Company in a progressive manner.

Representatives of the major departments meet regularly to review Company operating policies, initiate searching market studies and to plan now — for your tomorrow. As a direct result of this team work, the Company is alerted to every opportunity which might improve its competitive position and make your dealership even more valuable and more profitable.

The Company is continuing to expand its line of motor-cycles and a whole new market is being opened up with the development of a line of motor scooters. Many new luxury features are being perfected and will be added on a regular basis to keep Harley-Davidson at the TOP in product quality and performance.

This young-minded man-agement team meets reg-ularly to plan now ... for your tomorrow. The suc-cess of Harley-Davidson Motor Co. is based di-rectly on the success of each dealer.

Harley dealers were a special group of people. From the very begin-ning they were a hard–to–manage bunch of colorful characters and individualists, with many a non–conformist among them — and quite a few rebels.

Especially in California, where motorcycling was big business, they frequently switched between different marques and activities, suppor-ting at first this sporting event, then that one; making a lot of money — and sometimes going bust; falling out with the company, the AMA or the FAM; sponsoring sportsmen, tuning and tweaking racing machines, founding and supporting motorcycle clubs or associations.

They also weren't always won over to the idea of absolute loyalty to Harley, much to the annoyance of company President Walter Davidson, who strictly forbade all contact with the competition, even on a purely personal level. Brother Arthur, who had seen the problems of dealers first hand and understood them better, frequently had to act as mediator.

In the fall of 1916 Arthur Davidson announced that the U.S. dealer network he had organized would be divided up into a number of geographical districts in order to strengthen the ties with company headquarters. The new arrangement also gave him tighter control over his dealers and their activities.

All district managers had to compile detailed dossiers on all the dealers within their territory and submit them to the scrutiny of the company management. Subsequent decisions about the renewal of a dealer's franchise were then made on the basis of this information.

Almost as if in a pharmacy: the presentation and sales room of a Harley dealer in Milwaukee.

© Harley-Davidson

Unlike their colleagues at Indian or Excelsior, Harley dealers were never able to buy direct from the factory. All purchasing was done through the district representative. The only exceptions were those made for local dealers in Milwaukee. However, in order to save on the transport costs, dealers could opt to collect their motorcycles in person from the Milwaukee plant. Those who did so were always offered a full guided tour of the factory.

Another directive the company management issued was a series of internal directives to Harley dealers instructing them to keep their showrooms and workshops clean and tidy and to make the decor bright and attractive to customers. The underlying message was clear: present the product in the right setting!

Although officially he refused to countenance any contact with other motorcycle manufacturers, Walter Davidson participated in meetings, some of which he had actually convened himself. As the representative of the biggest motorcycle manufacturer in the U.S., he was in a strong position, which he exploited ruthlessly against competitors such as Indian, Excelsior, Cleveland, Reading–Standard and others.

One of the most controversial ideas on which he sought to secure Harley-Davidsons survival was his insistence on total brand loyalty, a principle long since established within his own company. The idea was that all motorcycle dealers should be required to trade exclusively

in the products of a single manufacturer. Indian's president Frank J. Weschler agreed to this severe restriction with reluctance, knowing full well that his dealers were having a hard time.

But even Walter Davidson had to recognize that in the fierce competition that was clearly coming, this arrangement at least meant that the largest firms were likely to stay in business. Even though some dealers saw things differently at the time, the fact is that the simple and hard–headed business principle to which Walter Davidson adhered throughout — that being that his job was to look after the survival of his own comapny and not that of Indian, Excelsior or anyone else — finally won out.

Looking back today at what has become of all the great names in American motorcycle manufacturing, one can only marvel at Walter Davidson's single–minded resolve, so often dismissed as pig–headed and unfair.

One of the first Harley dealerships in New England. A whole row of Silent Grey Fellows is still waiting to be unpacked.

© Harley-Davidson

297

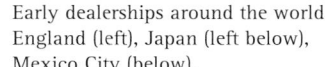

The company sought new dealers via large ads like this one from shortly before World War II (right).

Early dealerships around the world: England (left), Japan (left below), Mexico City (below).

BOY_ AM I GLAD I TRADED AND GOT THIS SWELL NEW HARLEY-DAVIDSON!

WHY NOT TRADE IN YOUR OLD JOB, TOO?

"Say, I made the deal of a lifetime when I traded in and got this sparkling 1938 Harley-Davidson. Sure, I was fond of the old bus that took me over so many miles, but she was getting old—a little repair here and a little fixing there. Now I am riding right up with the bunch all the time. Funny, too. I thought the payments on this new model would hit me rather hard, but say, with all the savings on repair and upkeep costs, I don't feel them at all. And is there a kick to riding this new 1938—smooth as silk, and how she responds to the throttle! Take it from me, see your Harley-Davidson dealer and trade in now, while you can still get a good allowance. Then you, too, will be in for a lot of swell times."

HARLEY-DAVIDSON MOTOR CO., Milwaukee, Wisconsin, U. S. A.

HARLEY-DAVIDSON

Dates and Facts

1913 — the first Harley dealership in Canada opened.

1920 — Harley-Davidson established a separate department to look after its South African dealers.

1921 — By this year Harley had authorized dealers in 67 countries.

1922 — the company was printing brochures for the export market in Danish, Italian, French, Spanish, Dutch, Swedish and German.

Issue No. 27 of Harley's magazine *The Harley-Davidson Enthusiast* from 1920 reports on numerous visits from overseas Harley dealers who toured the plant in Milwaukee and learned about production methods, repair techniques and sales strategies.

The visitors in 1919 included Mr. Mario Landucci and Mr. Amleto Orlandi from Lucca, Italy, as well as Mr. Gulliver, a representative of Bartle & Co. of Johannesburg, South Africa, who stayed for two months. Mr. W.W. Haak, from the same company's Pretoria branch had also made the long journey to Milwaukee. Other visitors to the plant included a Mr. L. Van Beckhoven from Holland and Mr. Frank R. Jones, a Harley-Davidson importer from Christchurch, New Zealand.

In 1924 the company announced a new dealership program aimed at providing better service to customers in small towns and rural communities: so-called part time dealers who were not directly employed in the motorcycle industry could sell Harley motorcycles on weekends or after-hours in the evenings. The main idea behind this curious initiative was to take business away from the smaller motorcycle companies.

In 1927 Arther Davidson came up with a new concept aimed at reinforcing customer loyalty. His appointed dealers were to organize trips and tours to sporting events for the customers, thereby encouraging them to participate in activities directly associated with the Harley marque. The name of the concept was "Pay as you ride."

As sales continued to fall in the 1930s, it became commonplace for dealers to strip down fully-equipped models so that they could sell off the parts they had removed as high-priced accessories. They

HARLEY-DAVIDSON NEWS PICTORIAL

Above are just a few of the big turnout of 200 riders and guests who attended the Atlanta, Georgia, Dealer Marion Roberts' Fish Fry at Allatoona Lake. They are shown in front of Dealer Roberts' attractive establishment. Robertson Photo.

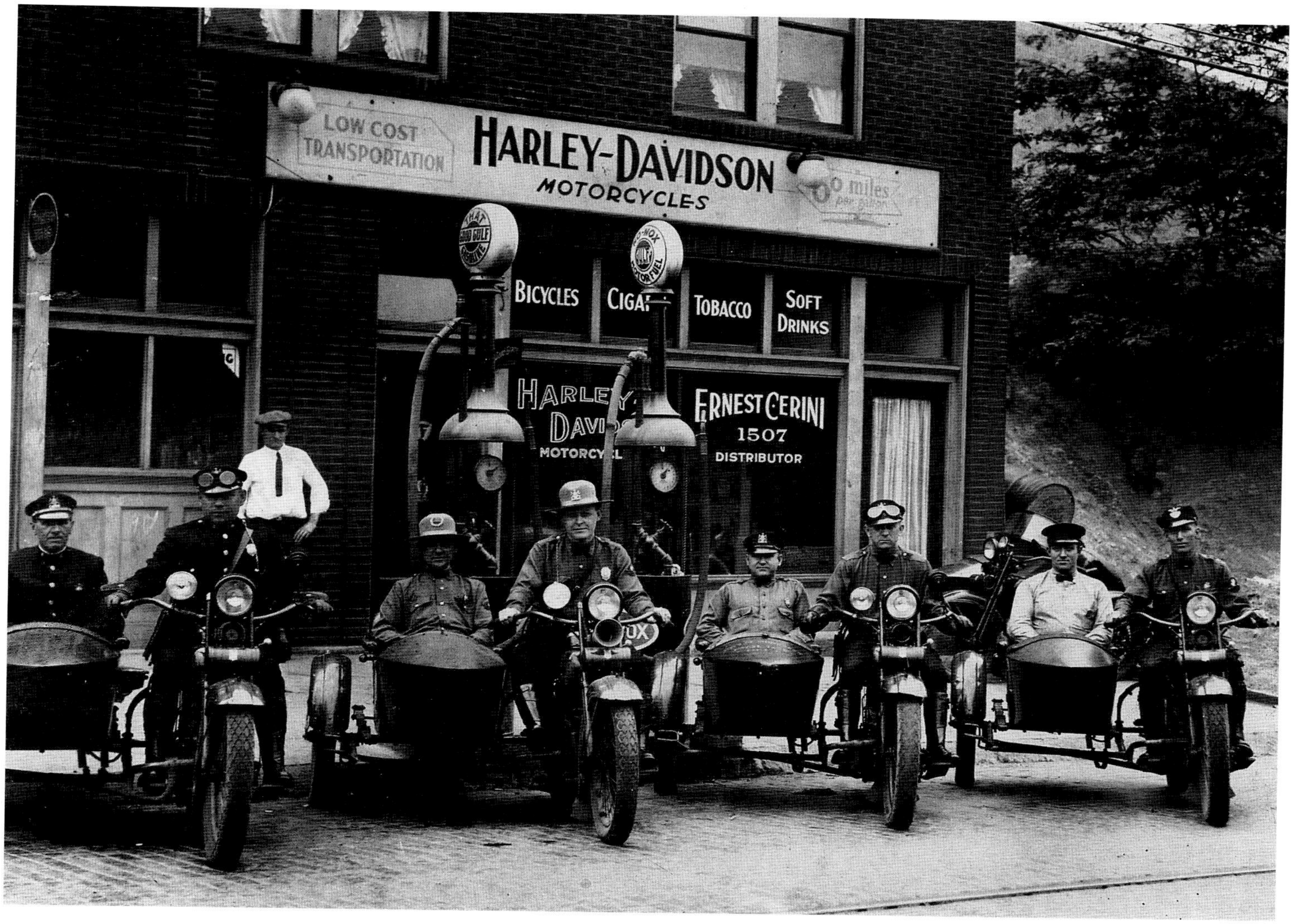

A truly versatile dealer: bicycles, tobacco products, soft drinks and a gasoline station — and above all, Harley–Davidson motorcycles. A typical picture from the 1920s with local law enforcement.

normally only offered the bare basic model with solo saddle, no windshield, no extra driving lights and no saddlebags. The trend was fueled by the heavily promoted club competitions of the day in which trophies were awarded for the Best Equipped Bike. A veritable orgy of accessorizing ensued and Full Dressers were all the rage: many a prize–winning Harley looked more like an over–decorated Christmas tree than anything else. But it was a clever marketing strategy, which enabled dealers to weather the worst of the Depression by making a little extra profit on the side.

In 1931 company President Walter Davidson announced that all police motorcycles would henceforth be sold to law enforcement agencies directly from the factory — an internal measure designed to run down old stocks more quickly (and more cheaply). This immediately

provoked furious protests from dealers who up until then had not only sold police motorcycles at a healthy profit, but had also maintained and repaired them on very favorable terms. They lost not only their local influence, but also their commission, which could amount to as much as 25 percent.

How hard life was during the Depression years of the early 1930s is recalled by Tom Sifton, a dealer from San Francisco, whose reminiscences are contained in a documentary account by historian Jerry Hatfield. It was normal to work a seven–day week and to work most days late into the night. It was very difficult to find buyers for motorcycles when hardly anybody had any money.

Meanwhile Tom Sifton was called out more and more often on repairs and breakdown recoveries, frequently traveling more than 200 miles to collect motorcycles of every kind to tow them back to his workshop. Weekdays or Sundays, day or night — it didn't make any difference. Most Sundays he also had to put in a lot of time on club activities, which were an important part of his responsibilities, which meant that his wife had to work just as hard as he did. He had to support both his business and his family on an average monthly income of around 50 dollars.

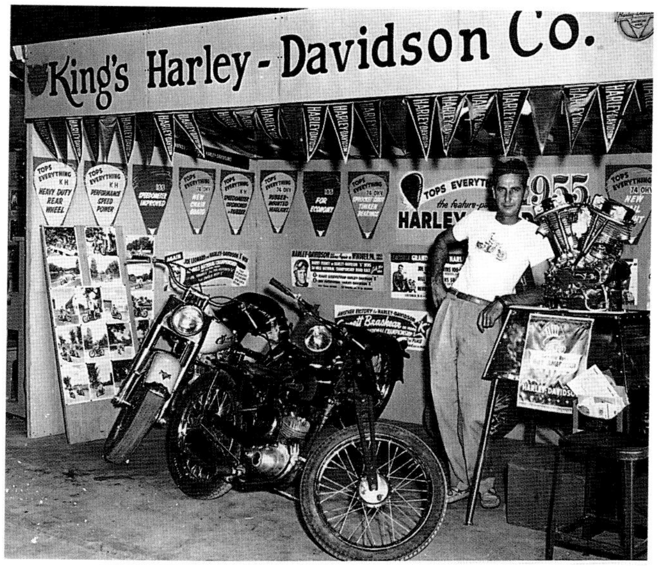

Shortly after World War II: Harley dealer King from Jonesboro, Arkansas, at the Craighead County Fair.

Harley-Davidson Sales and Service

The dealerships have always been a popular meeting place for Harley riders.

The Denver Affair
A Committed Biker Scene Falls Apart

The Scherer–Budelier Episod
Friendships Can Affect Your Work

He was the youngest car dealer and one of the most successful. Floyd Clymer, the energetic "boy car salesman" from Colorado also knew his way around motorcycles. In 1915 he won the Dodge City 200 mile race for Harley-Davidson. He also sold Indian and Excelsior motorcycles on the side, rode these marques to win many hillclimbs and endurance events, and was a real jack of all trades from childhood onwards. As a successful and enthusiastic bike racer he became closely involved with the AMA and its new subdivision, the M&ATA* — and of course with Harley-Davidson. In addition to all this he was a talented motoring journalist; although in 1930 he was given a 15-month jail sentence for blatant infringements of copyright.

In 1916 he acquired the Harley dealership in Denver, but two years later his franchise was withdrawn after contractual disputes and was transferred to the respected motorcycling pioneer Walter W. Whiting. Clymer stayed in the business and took over the local Indian dealership. But he got into so much trouble, particularly over his "hole in the windshield" auto spotlight, that he had to give up his Indian dealership too — this time to another motorcycle enthusiast, Leslie D. Richards. Now Richards and Whiting were good friends of long standing who jointly sponsored local motorcycling events and threw themselves into the club scene, which soon developed into an active and tight-knit motorcycling community. These goings-on were a source of enormous irritation to company President Walter Davidson, who let it be known to his Denver dealer Whiting that his associations — particularly with Indian – were deeply unwelcome. After some argument an embittered Whiting relinquished his franchise. Sensing his chance, Floyd Clymer moved quickly to take over the vacant Harley dealership again.

Meanwhile he still had a large stock of Indian spares, which he now tried to sell off cheaply. It seemed like a good idea, but the deal went bad — and Clymer went bust. The entire motorcycling community, particularly the (mixed) clubs, was thrown into a state of chaos and frustration by this affair, which gave rise to all manner of hostilities and intrigues, eventually drawing in the AMA, the M&ATA, and some Californian dealers. More than 250 motorcycle owners angrily returned their AMA membership books and the once-flourishing motorcycle scene fell apart in unseemly squabbling.

In 1920 the former sales director of the Firestone tire works, Julian C. "Hap" Scherer, who had successfully completed the Three Flags long-distance event on a Harley Sport Twin, was appointed as publicity manager at Harley-Davidson. As a thoroughly liberal, open-minded and far-sighted motorcycling enthusiast, Hap Scherer was universally popular among his fellow sportsmen and had many friends in the motorcycle industry. Like them, he was quite concerned about the deteriorating economic situation, in particular about the increasing number of bankruptcies in the automobile and motorcycle industry. He had no inhibitions about talking to the competition, and in the course of a number of internal secret meetings (involving Harley, Indian, Excelsior, Reading–Standard and other manufacturers) he spoke freely of his concerns. In the course of these discussions he became friends with the journalist and recently appointed head of PR at Indian, Leslie "Dick" Richards, as well as the engineer Norman G. Shidle, who had founded the trade journal *Automotive Industries* in 1919. Following publication of the latter's devastating but well-intentioned article "Where is the Motorcycle Going?" (1921), Hap Scherer was fired as PR manager by Walter Davidson, to whom any open contact with the competition was anathema.

To further complicate a story that was already a confused tangle of personalities and historical events, a second affair that was unfolding elsewhere now became entwined with it. Far-removed from the inhospitable climate of the American Midwest, the Californian motorcycling scene had emerged as a key factor for the U.S. motorcycle industry, primarily because of the constant warm weather enjoyed on the West Coast. However, the

---

* The Motorcycle & Allied Trades Association (M&ATA) was set up by a group of representatives for some of the leading motorcycle manufacturers as a more active alternative within the trade to the FAM, which had become bureaucratic and ineffectual.

The Risden–Van Order Affair
The Laws of Chance Revealed in a Burning Garage

position of Harley-Davidson in this market was being steadily undermined by the lackluster performance of dealers in the Los Angeles and San Diego areas. It was only when the then district-manager, Vern Guthrie, made the acquaintance of Rich Budelier and offered this tall, brilliant and charismatic motorcycle enthusiast the San Diego dealership, that sales of the motorcycles began to pick up.

Los Angeles, meanwhile, remained a great source of concern to the company. On an inspection tour, Arthur Davidson was appalled by the down-at-heel state of his local branch which was located on a seedy street lined with "dubious" motorcycle stores, which were always attracting the attention of the police. Vern Guthrie duly persuaded his boss to put Rich Budelier, the successful dealer from San Diego, in charge of the Los Angeles operation. Rich Budelier accepted the offer, entrusted his flourishing San Diego dealership to two experienced Harley hands and racetrack veterans, Roy Artley and William J. Ruhle, and opened a large and attractive new showroom in Los Angeles on the corner of Main and Adams, far away from the city's notorious "Motorcycle Row." It's at this point that the ever-popular Hap Scherer enters the picture again, having been fired by Harley in the meantime. Rich Budelier immediately offered his old friend Hap the job of sales manager. Walter Davidson was so furious that he wanted to tear up Rich Budelier's contract then and there, but brother Arthur finally persuaded him that Hap Scherer's popularity was an asset to the Harley-Davidson cause. So Budelier kept his job, as did his new sales manager. And very successful they were, too — despite the simmering resentment of their senior bosses...

Although Rich Budelier worked hard to recover the neglected territory of Los Angeles for Harley-Davidson, he lost the first few rounds to his local opponent and rival, the successful Indian dealer C. Will Risden, who snatched away a number of lucrative contracts with the police department from under his nose. In the meantime company President Walter Davidson had issued an internal directive warning all Harley dealers not to do business with Will Risden. But in 1925, when Risden was on the point of retiring, a curious incident occurred relating to the sale of his dealership. Instead of the business going as planned to an Indian man of impeccable credentials, one Thomas Callahan Butler, it was sold to a certain A.F. Van Order, founder of the motor racing association Trail Blazers and a close friend of Rich Budelier, who outbid Butler by a large margin. A few weeks after it had changed hands, the Indian dealership went up in flames under suspicious circumstances, and the rumor that Van Order and Budelier were behind it refused to go away, even though nothing was ever proved against them. For the next three years Los Angeles was without an Indian dealership – until Albert C. Crocker arrived from Kansas City in 1928 to rebuild the business. In the meantime Verne Guthrie, the Californian representative for Harley, had also resigned after falling out with Walter Davidson. He went on to run a car dealership in Monterey for Essex and Hudson. When this business failed in 1930, he became a freelance motoring journalist.

Both affairs caused feelings to run high among California's motorcycle dealer fraternity for a number of years, and many long-standing friendships were destroyed as a result.

The picture in the background shows a group photo of the "Northern California Harley-Davidson Dealers Association" at a conference in the 1920s. The first side-valve Single model delivered to California can be seen in the foreground.

Compulsory Get–Togethers

Success Began at the Bar

After 1930 the regular regional dealer meetings came to play an increasingly important role. These gatherings normally took place each year in the fall and sometimes in the spring to mark the opening of the new season; here the models for the coming year would be presented to the assembled sales force.

The press was not invited. But all the top people from the factory and company headquarters were there each year, led by Walter and Arthur Davidson, along with component suppliers, engineers and designers, plus family members and friends invited along as guests. All dealers were expected to attend and their attendance was effectively a condition of their franchise renewal.

As one can read in the account of the historian Harry W. Sucher who was present at a number of these gatherings, it was customary for President Walter Davidson to give a bombastic opening speech, in which he portentously extolled company policy and achievements, held up the family's conservative management methods as an example, and always took pleasure and pride in reminding his audience that the company had not yet fallen into the clutches of money-grabbing bankers. This was followed by various presentations on new model strategy, technical innovations, new accessories, new products (which were generally on display in the foyer) and sales tactics, as well as company policy in general.

There was little or no discussion with the dealers, who listened with a mixture of boredom and reverence. By common consent the best part of these meetings was the socializing that took place in the neighboring bar, where people got to know each other on a personal level, compared notes and discussed – or even solved – many of the problems they shared.

The official reports of these dealer conventions appeared in the company magazine, *The Enthusiast*. The tone was predictably tendentious, painting the kind of picture the company bosses wanted the public to see.

Constant training was one of the maxims of Harley-Davidson. This is the graduation photo of a class in the 1930s, with Walter Davidson fourth from left in the back row.

The Dealers' Rebellion

The Wrong Tone Creates Friction

The franchise conditions were, for the most part, extremely strict; and every year, in far-away Milwaukee, usually on the basis of meticulously compiled area representative reports, a decision was made as to whether the concession would be extended for a further year. But the dealers were always aware of their power – they are Harley-Davidson, at least as far as their customers are concerned. So there were always revolts, to a greater or lesser extent and, depending on the reputation and turnover of a rebellious dealer, the company either came down very hard on them or held back somewhat, but without sparing the warnings and threats. In order to ensure effective communication with their sales organization, even from the early days Harley-Davidson issued its own information sheet, the *Dealer News*, and later established an advisory group for dealers, the Harley-Davidson Dealers Advisory Council (DAC). The complaint often voiced that this committee was a company-owned puppet organization is certainly not true, but sometimes it seemed as if the management took decisions without adequately considering the wishes and problems of its front-line troops.

Matters came to a head in 1983 when, shortly after the buyback from AMF, Harley's CEO Vaughn Beals, steeled by the ruthless climate at board level, and forced to draw in the reins generally in order to give Harley a chance of surviving in a changed market, presented some hard facts to a dealers' meeting. With his typically direct approach, Beals emphasized that the way forward would be difficult and presented a new program of measures to be strictly observed with immediate effect: a customer oriented, attractive, showroom ambience (Designer Store) with uniform standards to be met, thus promoting the company's image, or Corporate Identity (CI) in business jargon. These new stores, the first point of contact with the company, would be extremely customer-friendly, clean, with good displays and not messy dumps in shady neighborhoods. Anyone entering the shop would be made to feel welcome; derisive remarks about "Japanese garbage," or other such offensive comments, were banned and, most important: "The customer is king, and is always right." Not a new concept, but for Harley quite a change of attitude!

The dealers listened with astonishment, and mixed feelings. But what infuriated them was Beals' proposal to reduce their margins (on Big Twin sales) from 25 percent to 20 percent. To compensate for this he offered them a bonus of 5 percent which they could earn as an extra if they accepted the new rules and conditions, and agreed to take part in training sessions. The closing statement sounded very dictatorial: "This is the way things are now, people, and that's that!"

For Harley-Davidson this was certainly the right way to go and, in the long run, it would also prove to be a successful policy for the dealers, but in terms of tone and presentation Beals got it all wrong.

The "Bonus Bucks" program brought a serious revolt. Many misled dealers who, for the most part, had remained loyal to the company for decades despite all adversities, joined a new organization, the National Harley-Davidson Dealers Alliance, which spoke out aggressively against the management and caused a lot of trouble, partly with false accusations. For almost two years the two sides remained irreconcilable. Vaughn Beals, who had to implement the board's decisions for better or for worse, had no choice but to remain immovable, so the dealers felt betrayed again, left alone to cope with all their cares and problems. Only with the passage of time was the Marketing Development Manager, Jim Marcolina, able to break down this barrier and convince the dealers that Harley-Davidson was really behind them.

When in 1949 Harley-Davidson strictly forbade its dealers from selling the Cushman scooters that had proved so popular with customers and so profitable for them, in order not to compete with sales of Harley's own lightweight motorcycles, the dealers were shocked and annoyed, but they gritted their teeth and observed the ban. But it wasn't long before one or two rebels stepped out of line – and with other products apart from the Cushman. One of them was the universally popular and highly successful and respected Harley dealer Arthur "Skip" Fordyce from Riverside, California. Arguing that Harley-Davidson had no equivalent mid-range model to offer, he took over a dealership for Ariel and Triumph, whose motorcycles (he felt) filled in the gaps in the Harley model range. Harley offered a straight choice between lightweight machines and big heavyweights, but there was now a steadily growing demand for 350 cc and 500 cc singles and twins.

Despite threats and warnings that he would lose his franchise, Fordyce stuck to his guns. A heated dispute ensued, in the course of which he was violently abused by the district manager, A.S. Goodwin, and Skip Fordyce became increasingly frustrated by what he saw as the company's dictatorial policy. Meanwhile he received hundreds of letters and telegrams of support from other Harley dealers and in the end he held on to his Harley concession. Another dealer was not so lucky. When the owner of Carl's Cycle Service in Minneapolis took on a sales agency for BSA and Zündapp, Harley-Davidson decided to make an example of him and withdrew his status as an authorized Harley dealer.

Meanwhile Skip Fordyce has remained true to the principle of coexistence. From his Riverside showroom he sells both Harley-Davidsons and motorcycles made by Harley's competitor, Honda. At publication, the sky hasn't yet fallen in.

A typical dealership from the 1970s: Harley-Davidson of Santa Fe, New Mexico.

U.S.A.: Dealerships in the 1970s

A few of the company's strongpoints are licensed Harley dealers. From the top: Petersen Harley-Davidson, Key West, FL, Harley-Davidson of Beaumont, TX, Sports Ltd. Harley-Davidson Hattiesburg, MS with dealer Andy Moore, Jim's Harley-Davidson in Yuma, CA.

NEXT EXIT SOUTH
HARLEY-DAVIDSON
Ocean Springs
ON CAMPBELL ROAD

New friends and always plenty to see – Harley dealerships in the 1970s acted as magnets for the diminishing but loyal Harley scene. Shown here are Robbie Robertson from Ocean Springs, MS (large photo), Mr. C's (Cutrera) of Harley-Davidson of Morgan City, LA (below) and Harley-Davidson of Colusa, CA (right).

The Veteran of San Francisco

Racing and Stunts as Bike Marketing

The most famous name of all in the roll-call of Harley dealers is surely Dudley Perkins. Born in Kern near Bakersfield, California in 1893, Dudley Perkins was obsessed with motorcycles and motorcycle racing from a very early age. He rode in cross-country races at every opportunity and during his school vacations he worked first in the Jerome Garage — a job that he got through the racing motorcyclist Hap Alzina who rode Indians — and later as a mechanic for the well-known Indian dealer Gus Shelane in San Francisco. By the age of 14 he was completely familiar with the motorcycles made by Reading-Standard, Excelsior, DeLuxe, Jefferson and Harley-Davidson, and in 1911 he won his first race, the One-Miler in Stockton. In 1914 he gave up dirt-track racing for the sake of his bride — "too dangerous" — and in 1915 he was competing enthusiastically and successfully in hillclimbs. Dudley Perkins was a life member of the AMA Competition Congress and carried the AMA membership number 12. For ten years he was the reigning West Coast National Hillclimb Champion. When it came to performing crazy (and therefore dangerous) stunts, he was always first in line. In 1914, acting initially in partnership with San Francisco motorcycle dealer Al Maggini, he opened his famous "exclusive Harley-Davidson dealership" at 626 Market Street — Harley-Davidson Dudley Perkins Co., San Francisco, which can now claim to be the oldest dealership still in business.

Shortly after the business opened he became America's biggest dealer for Package Trucks — sidecars built by Harley-Davidson for commercial users. In World Wars I and II he also did a roaring trade in Army surplus motorcycles, which he bought up cheap in large quantities, resprayed and sold. When the California Highway Patrol (CHP) was established, he supplied the force with Harleys and acted as technical instructor to its motorcycle officers. A successful racing motorcyclist himself, Dudley Perkins was quick to recognize the value of a racing pedigree for the marketing of a motorcycle marque and even in his later years he continued to devote himself passionately to the sport he had always loved. He sponsored a whole succession of racers, including Mert Lawwill and Mark Brelsford.

Dudley Perkins has had to enlarge and extend his premises several times over the years and today he owns two large showrooms packed with historic documents, photographs and motorcycles. In 1968 his son Dudley Jr. took over the dealership. For a number of years he also ran another branch in Oakland. A visit to the legendary family business is an absolute must for every true Harley enthusiast who goes to San Francisco — even if it's only to say with pride afterwards: "I've been to Dudley Perkins!"

The original shop belonging to Dudley Perkins, photographed here in the 1950s.

The interior of the new premises on Page Street (below) and an outside shot (left). The third photo (below, center) shows the storage room of the old dealership.

Dudley Perkins was one of the best-known hillclimb champions of his time.

Once a Year – the Love Ride

Oliver, Pamela and 30,000 Bikers

Prominent guests at the Love Ride: Peter Fonda (above) and Larry Hagman (right).

Founded in 1976, Harley–Davidson of Glendale is now one of the largest dealerships in the U.S., boasting an impressive collection of historic and contemporary Harleys in its lavishly appointed Art Deco showrooms.

The dealership also stocks a vast range of clothing, parts and accessories, together with the very best in aftermarket products — including custom parts. But Oliver Shokouh's main claim to fame is his annual Love Ride, a world–renowned charity event which raises money for the Muscular Dystrophy Association. The first Love Ride took place in 1984 and on that occasion the riders rode together in convoy for some 50 miles to reach their appointed destination, where a barbecue, live concerts with top bands, a huge trade show, and a big line–up of celebrities were there to greet them — including Jay Leno, Peter Fonda, Larry Hagman, Willie G. Davidson, Lorenzo Lamas, Jackson Browne, ZZ–Top and many others. The idea has since been taken up by the Swiss, who organize their own version of the event.

Since then the Love Ride has grown to become the world's biggest motorbike fundraising event, attracting between 20,000 and 30,000 motorcyclists from all over and raising over a million dollars for children suffering from muscular dystrophy.

Throughout the year Harley–Davidson of Glendale organizes a whole series of special events that have become extremely popular with local residents. These include the Easter Egg Hunt, a big fashion show featuring summer fashions and beach wear, a Weenie Bite Ride, the Midnight Madness Sale, the annual Halloween party and various Holiday Open House parties.

Initiator and Harley dealer Oliver Shokouh.

Other famous personalities at Love Ride II: Brett Michaels and Pamela Anderson.

307

A Creative Genius in Oakland, California

Bob Dron's Harley Empire

It started out more modestly, as shown in a photo from the 1970s: Bob Dron (2nd from left) with custom fans and Arlen Ness (far left).

The new Harley empire of Bob Dron in Oakland: a veritable palace with vast showrooms and an office in which the boss visibly feels comfortable.

Bob Dron is widely regarded as one of the most imaginative and far-out Californian custom designers, tuners and stylists, renowned for both his hot-rod cars and his Harley-Davidson conversions. In 1970 he founded his specialist firm American Chopper Enterprises in Concord, California. From his workshop emerged some of the most radical and extravagant creations in motorcycling history; machines that caused a stir and won prizes at many international shows and exhibitions — machines such as the famed Heritage Royale of 1990, which was selected for inclusion in the exhibition "The Art of the Harley" at London's Barbican Art Gallery in 1998.

Over the years after many unsuccessful applications, Bob Dron finally acquired the Harley-Davidson franchise for Oakland, California in 1981. In 1993, he opened the vast new company premises there which is now thought to be the biggest Harley-Davidson dealership in the world. The showroom alone, with its elegant Art Deco styling throughout, offers 32,500 square feet of floor space. In Bob Dron's new custom and hot-rod emporium, the latest Harley models rub shoulders with weird and wonderful custom bikes and cars that span the gamut from "mild to wild." Bob Dron has been awarded the company's coveted Bar & Shield Circle of Excellence no less than six times — a special award given for outstanding achievement and consistent performance.

In 1994, he and his wife Tracey were named as the country's top motorcycle dealer by the leading U.S. motorcycle trade journal *Dealer News*. In 1992, he was the winner of the Grand National Oakland Roadster Show. Every year Bob Dron organizes the well-known charity event known as the B.I.G. Run, in which large quantities of groceries are collected for distribution to needy citizens.

Dealer to the Stars

Bartels' Harley–Davidson in L.A.

"Come in and see!" reads the invitation outside the stylishly appointed Harley designer store owned by Bill Bartels in Marina Del Rey. As invitations go, this one is hard to refuse. The exterior is impressive enough – a palatial glass building that once housed an automobile display salon. But the fun really starts inside, with "Los Angeles' largest selection of officially licensed Harley-Davidson T-shirts, MotorClothes and accessories." It's a truly breathtaking display, even for customers who are used to the exotic sights and sounds of nearby Venice Beach. Naturally Bartels' Harley–Davidson also carries an extensive range of Harleys, both stock models and "super-custom" bikes, incorporating a host of wild design ideas. But that's not all. The name Bartels is also synonymous with the customized creations of specialist Gene Thomason, who builds specially modified Harleys for movie and video productions, not to mention stunt shows. Hollywood, after all, is just around the corner. Sometimes they get through as many as ten Harleys on a film shoot – each one hand–built to an exact specification.

At the same time Bartels runs one of America's most famous Harley-Davidson racing teams, sponsoring such renowned Harley champions as Jay Springsteen, Mike Hale, and Shawn Higbee. Workshop manager Will Pfizenmaier is the technical genius behind the Bartels racing department and the many victory trophies adorning Bill Bartels' showroom belong to him as much as anyone.

One of the most talented experts for Harley engines at work in Bartels Harley–Davidson in Marina Del Rey (far left, bottom): Will Pfizenmaier and his empire (below).

The Guardian Angel of Daytona

Robison Keeps Harley's Promises

The legendary Harley center in Daytona: the sales premises and workshop of Joe Robison (above, behind the counter). An early picture from his family album showing Joe with his son and daughter on a 1952 Model K in Ohio (below).

The author recalls: I met Joe Robison on my first visit to the Daytona Bike Week in 1975 — and it turned out to be a meeting that would change my life. As a Harley dealer, Joe stocked the machine of my dreams in many different versions. A year later he sold me one of them: a magnificent FX Super Glide costing 2,500 dollars, which in those days was a small fortune for a tourist of limited means from Germany. Joe looked out for us right from the start, making sure my friends and I had everything we needed. He gave us countless helpful tips, little extras to help us on our way, plus tickets to races and other events. In short, we soon became good friends and Joe Robison's magical showroom on Volusia Avenue (right behind the railroad-crossing gates) was always our first and most important port of call before we plunged into the hectic activity of the Daytona Bike Week.

Unfortunately my dream machine proved to be a disaster from the word go: rusty nuts and bolts came standard, and on the very first day the contact breaker spring broke. But the imperturbable Joe Robison soon had everything fixed as good as new ("no problem" — and no charge, of course), whereupon my girlfriend Claudia rode the beast the length and breadth of America without a major breakdown, covering 12,500 miles in the process. When we returned to our point of departure, I was able to say categorically that if it hadn't been for Joe Robison, my opinion of Harley-Davidson would probably have been very different.

In the early-1990s Joe Robison sold the Daytona Harley franchise for personal reasons (his daughter had become seriously ill). However, he retained the right to carry on running his business, i.e. the workshop and the racing team he had built up over the years (in his youth Joe had raced Harleys himself on a regular basis) for as long as he could continue to do it. However long that turns out to be, his name will forever be associated with the Daytona races and Bike Week.

America's Oldest Harley Dealership in Ohio

A Faithful Harley Supporter

Alfred D. Farrow (1889–1927), who opened A.D. Farrow Harley–Davidson in Nelsonville, Ohio at the age of 23, was one of that first group of 200 dealers whom Arthur Davidson took on in 1912 in the course of his legendary recruitment campaign for the company.

He remained fiercely loyal to the marque thereafter. Following his marriage to Lillian Matheny, he continued to run the business in partnership with his wife until 1924, when he had the opportunity to take over the Harley–Davidson dealership for Columbus, Ohio. The Farrows were fanatical devotees of motorcycles in general and Harley–Davidsons in particular – they didn't even own a car – and together they founded the famous Buckeye Motorcycle Club. When A.D. Farrow died unexpectedly on October 11, 1927 he left three children – Jane, Donald and Robert; his wife Lillian, who continued to manage the business expertly, thus became the first-ever female Harley dealer.

In 1939 the elder son died in a motorcycle accident. On January 21, 1948 Donald Farrow married his girlfriend Dorothy and took over the dealership which had been held in trust by their friend H.B. Kinnel. Among other things, Dorothy now took care of the bookkeeping. The Farrows opened a number of branch dealerships, including one in Newark, Ohio and one on Parsons Avenue in Langley, which was run by Jane Farrow. Jane also became an active member of the Motor Maids as well as a friend of the club's President, Dot Robinson.

In the 1960s the Farrows were heavily involved in dragster racing and the building of custom bikes. Increased sales of Harley–Davidson golf carts made 1963 a particularly profitable year for the Farrows. By now daughter Donna had become a fanatical Harley enthusiast, representing the family as the youngest active member of the Motor Maids at parades and similar public events. In 1970 Bobby Farrow (the son of Don and Dorothy) took over the family concern. In 1983 the business was sold to Al Doerman and his wife Pat, long-standing friends of the Farrow family. The new owners are particularly keen supporters of H.O.G. activities and in 1997 they threw a huge party to celebrate the 85th anniversary of the company that is privileged to call itself "the oldest continuously operated Harley–Davidson dealership in America."

The Man from Texas

Barnett Supplies Harleys

When Sherman Barnett opened his Harley dealership in El Paso in 1977 – back then it was still at 9501 Montana Avenue – few people could have guessed what a powerhouse of innovation the tall, dynamic Texan would become. But in no time at all "Sherm" Barnett had established a worldwide reputation through his international trade in used Harleys. In the early 1990s, there were virtually no Harley–Davidson motorcycles to be had in the U.S. so prices for the motorcycle skyrocketed. The only dealer who could deliver to order was Barnett. The price was high – high enough to scare off any middlemen looking to make a profit – but he was able to supply just about anything the customer wanted.

In 1995 Sherman Barnett opened a new dealership known as the Super Store at the junction of Interstate 10 and Gateway East. The grand opening was celebrated with a two-day party for the local community. More than 15,000 people turned up, six bands played to the crowd and everything – not just the new 55,000 square foot showroom – was on a truly Texan scale. It is a vast spare parts store stocked with new and used spares and accessories – it has everything a customer could possibly need.

In order to fund this operation Barnett took out the largest company loan ever approved by Harley–Davidson Motor Credit – 1.3 million dollars, borrowed for 30 days. That's roughly equivalent to two-thirds of his monthly turnover. But this Texan businessman is not shy when it comes to money.

One of his latest ventures, thoroughly crazy but immensely popular, is the Million Dollar Duck Race launched (so to speak) in 1997. 30,000 numbered plastic ducks, entered in the race at 5 dollars apiece, are dropped into the Rio Grande, the river that runs through El Paso and forms the border between the United States and Mexico. A mile or so downstream the ducks are caught in a giant funnel, like the balls in a lottery drum. The net proceeds go to a good cause, of course – in this case the YMCA Youth Center. Another popular event staged by Barnett is the Low Rider Show, which always attracts large numbers of entries.

Sherm Barnett and his new dealership in El Paso, Texas.

Distinguished visitors at Farrows: Willie G. and Nancy Davidson with current owners Pat and Al Doerman (far left).

U.S.A.:
Dealerships Today

Harley dealers today: Harley–Davidson of Santa Barbara, CA (above), Wisconsin Harley–Davidson in Oconomowok, WI (right), Phil Petersen, Harley–Davidson of Miami, FL (far right, top) and Harley–Davidson in Bettendorf, IA (far right).

Dale's Harley–Davidson in Mt. Vernon, ILL (above), Dick Farmer's Harley–Davidson, Orlando, FL (above, far right), Harley–Davidson, of Stuart, FL (right) and Hutchins Harley–Davidson, Yucca Valley, CA (far right).

Brunswick Harley-Davidson in Troy, NY (top), Harley-Davidson in Berwyn, IL (above left), Harley-Davidson in Bangor, ME (above) and White's Harley-Davidson in Lebanon, PA (left).

Dealers' T–Shirts

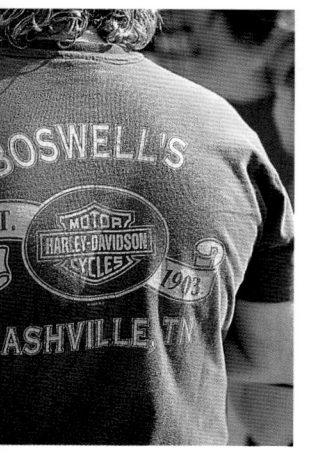

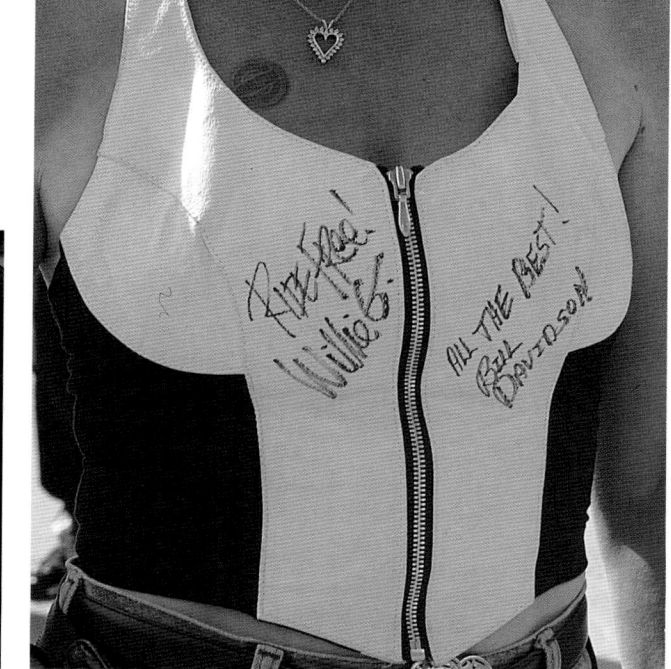

Which Harley fan can resist visiting a Harley–Davidson dealer without buying one of the popular T–shirts? Indeed, buying T–shirts as souvenirs is one of the most pronounced collecting activities of all Harley fans, and the dealers have a correspondingly attractive variety on offer.

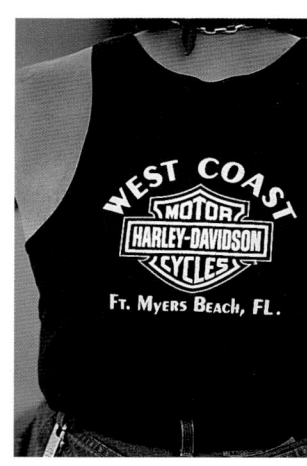

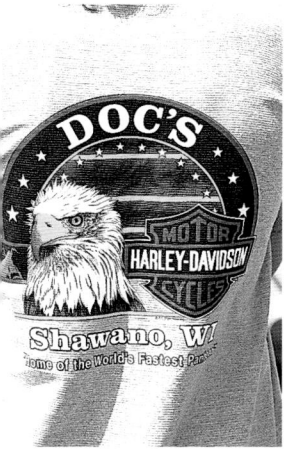

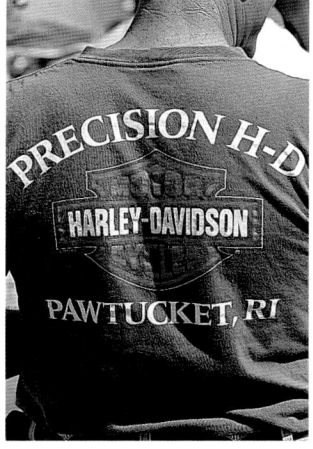

A Taste for the Non-Functional

From Harley Underwear to Bandanas

The new generation — some typical Harley designer and art deco stores, glamorous and classy, inside and out: Gerold Vogel AG in Weinfelden, Switzerland (above), Harley-Davidson of Chicago, IL (above center and top far right), Bartels Harley-Davidson in Marina Del Rey, CA (center below), Pauki's in Berndshofen, Germany (far right bottom), and Bob Dron in Oakland, CA (below).

The Harley shop seems like a paradise. In the old days one would only dare enter such a place with reverence and in awe. It smelled strongly of oil, gasoline and various lubricants, and in the background the mechanic would be clanking about with metal bits and pieces. Hog Heaven! The elitist center of a legendary motorcycle world. One could be sure that if what was wanted wasn't immediately found, one would hear: "Come back when you know what you want, you're just wasting my time, and tell your snot-nosed kids to keep their dirty fingers off the bikes...!" – or something very similar.

In those days one had to work hard to gain access to the illustrious, select circle. Even brochures were passed hesitantly out from under the counter. These were exclusive times, when not any old would-be freak could buy a Harley, just because he was trying to supposedly be "in" (and he had enough money).

But elitist behavior kept the market small. After all, who would want to buy a Harley if he first had to pass a critical test to gain acceptance, or even a face check? So, unfortunately, the sales numbers left a lot to be desired; even the old Harley freaks were quite wary about buying a new bike. However, times have changed. Nowadays Harley shops, or stores as they are now called, are often sparkling-chrome, neon-flashing palaces, packed with all kinds of treasures which are in some way connected with the Harley legend.

Harley stores should be a good advertisement for the company and, adapting to the new market situation after regaining its independence in 1982 and 1983, Harley required their dealers to conform to the CI (Corporate Identity) program. The "designer store" program was used as a basis for the new Harley store, a well-organized, highly polished shopping center designed to be bright, airy and friendly, a supermarket with various departments, where there is something for everyone, whether they want to buy a Harley or not.

The fashion boutique, for example, officially called "Harley-Davidson MotorClothes" where one can get all the original Harley garb – from Harley boxer shorts to the stylish fringed leather jacket, including countless fashion accessories from the obligatory sunglasses to that indispensable item of headgear, the bandana. Add to this gold and silver items and everything that Harley riders might need in their

daily lives: cologne, lotions, tableware, wristwatches, air fresheners and the like, up to billiard tables and Wurlitzer organs. All original Harley-Davidson products, of course!

In the coffee shop there is always the smell of freshly brewed Harley coffee and, if it is a particularly attentive dealer, there will also be a plentiful supply of donuts, so the customers can help themselves. Near to comfortable seating there should also be an "Infotheque," a place where brochures, catalogs or calendars of events and various magazines are provided free of charge and, most important, there should be a bulletin board overflowing with information, buying and selling notices, news and visitors cards. Anyone looking through them all should then be almost totally up-to-date with what's happening on the local Harley scene.

Another interesting feature within the stores are the collectors corners which hold a huge and frighteningly expensive collection of splendid odds and ends, which bring tears to the eyes of avid collectors, particularly if a diamond-studded silver model has a "not for sale" sign next to it. It may belong to the exclusive "Dealers Collection," a kind of shop-museum displaying historical photographs and other classical exhibits. All the walls and shelves are full of sparkling chrome "Genuine Harley-Davidson Parts & Accessories," with which Harleys can be equipped individually, to bring them up to the glittering "Full Dresser" status.

Naturally anyone can sit on the latest models, and for the children there are even Kids Corners, where they cannot do too much damage. In short, it is a pleasure to visit and root around a modern Harley Designer Store, and you always find something you want. But in the end, it is the personal and friendly atmosphere which makes the greatest impression on the customers, and so both enhances the reputation of dealers and Harley-Davidson's image.

An Old Man and the Company

Corporate Identity and Sentimentality Don't Mix

Harry Molenar in his old Harley shop received a plaque of honor from the company for his loyal service. When he retired, his shop was replaced by a new Harley-Davidson franchise.

Dealers' World I

The Battle of Britain

The U.K. – Harley's Most Difficult Market

Having entered World War I as a cavalry trooper, a young soldier named Frederick Warr returned home from France as a trained motorcycle mechanic. He became an official Harley dealer in 1924. In the 1920s and 1930s, Harleys already had a small but loyal following. However, the competition from England was not only strong, but also less expensive, and the large-capacity American bikes had a major problem competing against such venerable names as Triumph, BSA, Royal Enfield, Rudge, Velocette and Brough Superior.

Robert Warr, London's third-generation Harley dealer.

In 1939, Germany once again knocked on the door of its European neighbors, initially contenting itself with conquering the continental mainland in 1939 before stepping up its aggression against England in August and September 1940 during the Battle of Britain. However, neither the German bombers nor Hitler's secret V-weapons managed to hit the business premises at 611 Kings Road in London's Chelsea district. Once America entered the war, a veritable avalanche of material came for the second time this century from the U.S. to Britain. Once again, it was the V-Twins from Milwaukee that constituted a large share of the two-wheeled American support. The

WLAs were used as liaison, courier and transport vehicles by all arms of the Allied forces, albeit almost always far behind the front. After World War II, Harley enthusiasts in the U.K. had to wait a long time for new models from Milwaukee: England's ban on motorcycle imports protected its own manufacturers against competition until well into the 1950s. It was F.H. Warr, among others, who petitioned the British and American governments to lift the import ban. The actual petition submitted to Congress in March 1957, which marked the return of Harley-Davidson motorcycles to the U.K., is now framed and adorns the wall of F.H. Warr's premises in London. Having made do with the servicing and maintenance of "demilitarized" WLAs up to this time, Fred Warr was now Harley's official importer for England. However, the competition from British manufacturers, and subsequently also from Japanese firms, was still strong, and nobody could really speak of a genuine Harley boom, not even in the 1980s and 1990s. Nevertheless, in a country renowned for its strong ties with traditions, it hardly comes as a surprise that a hard core of Harley enthusiasts remained loyal to the V-Twins from Milwaukee.

A Recognized Authority
A Canadian with the Best Feeling for Bikers' Needs

He drove thousands of miles across the U.S. in his beat-up car, towing his flat-track WR Harley racer behind, just to be able to take part in the Daytona Beach races. As a good Canadian, he also sold British and German motorcycles alongside the Harley-Davidsons that were his real love. Despite warnings and opposition, he brought the first Japanese motorcycles into Canada, becoming the first importer for Honda – and later for Yamaha – in the English-speaking world. At the same time he was, and remained, distributor for Harley-Davidson in Canada. In 1985, at the age of 65, he was appointed to serve on the board of directors of Harley-Davidson for five years – the first non-U.S. citizen to enter the top ranks of the company management. It was due to his influence and opposition that the controversial NOVA project (for the development of a water-cooled four-cylinder Harley engine) was axed. He put many new models through a punishing test program, insisting on the application of even tougher standards. His suggestions were invariably accepted and his recommendations followed – such as the installation of a new automated paint shop at a cost of 23 million dollars. As a successful racing motorcyclist and track racer he continues to manage racing teams in Canada and the U.S. up until the writing of this book. He trained the Vancouver police drill team – and promptly donated 1,000 dollars when the Canadian biker rights organization BCCOM (British Columbia Coalition of Motorcyclists) was set up in alliance with the Hell's Angels to fight against police intimidation and coercion by the government and state. Trev Deely was duly enrolled with membership number one. His famous annual "Customer Appreciation Day" party was attended by more Hell's Angels of his acquaintance than by any other group of customers. He displayed an unerringly reliable instinct for what the market needed and what the motorcycling scene wanted, making him an absolute authority – and a millionaire – in the bargain. Trev Deeley – the third generation of a dealership dynasty that has dominated the market for cycles, cars and motorcycles: a racing motorcyclist, biker and manager, a man who has lived and breathed motorcycles almost from the day he was born. At the tender age of seven he was riding an Indian Scout – even if he couldn't make the thing stop! But his successes and victories never came easy. They were often overshadowed by set-

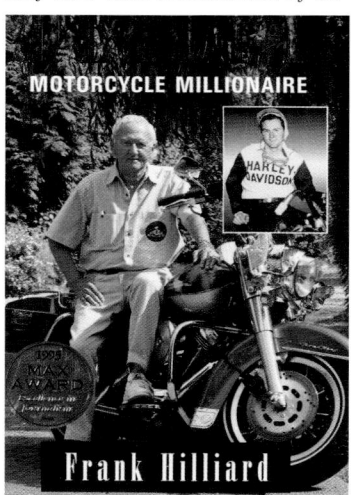

backs, defeats and personal tragedies. The journalist Frank Hilliard has written a fascinating biography documenting his varied and exciting life. In 1993 Fred Deeley Imports Ltd. opened a museum in Richmond, near Vancouver Airport, devoted to motorcycles – Harley-Davidsons in particular. Called the Trev Deely Motorcycle Museum, it is probably the finest establishment of its kind in the world – and admission is free.

319

Dealers' World II

Despite all similarities, every Harley shop around the world has its own character: Harley–Davidson, Prague, Czech Republic (above), Harley–Davidson of the United Arab Emirates in Dubai (above right), Harley–Davidson of Marseilles, France (below), Harley–Davidson Turin, Italy (bottom) and Harley–Davidson of Sao Paulo, Brazil (right).

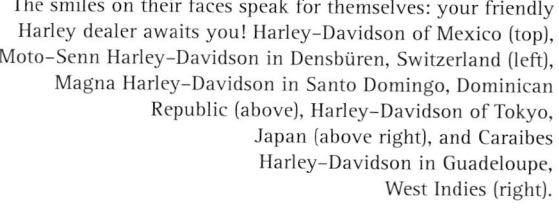

The smiles on their faces speak for themselves: your friendly Harley dealer awaits you! Harley–Davidson of Mexico (top), Moto–Senn Harley–Davidson in Densbüren, Switzerland (left), Magna Harley–Davidson in Santo Domingo, Dominican Republic (above), Harley–Davidson of Tokyo, Japan (above right), and Caraibes Harley–Davidson in Guadeloupe, West Indies (right).

The German Harley Legend

A Piece of Motorcycle History at Suck's in Hamburg

Georg Suck and his family on a ride in the countryside and in front of his shop in Hamburg.

Harley motorcycles ready to go – new or used – it was that simple then. Apart from the question of money, that is, because even the most beat–up of V-Twins were hardly among the cheapest bikes.

Even as a small boy, Georg Suck (born 1890) was interested in anything that had an engine. As a young man he repaired all sorts of vehicles, both two-wheeled and four-wheeled, that came into the nearby international port at Hamburg. In 1910 he started a business on his own, founding "Georg Suck," the only repair shop in that part of the world that knew its way around Harleys. Before long, most Harley owners who had crossed the Atlantic with their bikes began to gravitate naturally towards the little workshop in Hamburg. After World War I, times were not great and Georg Suck found himself struggling to survive. Eventually Harley-Davidson took note of him and appointed him as its German sales representative and in 1924 Georg Suck became an authorized Harley dealer and importer for Germany.

Between 1934 and 1956 a ban was imposed on the importation of Harleys to Germany and Georg Suck had to keep his business afloat by selling other marques, including Borgward, BMW Isetta and the NSU Janus. But he always had a couple of Harleys parked in his showroom and the company supported him with shipments of spares labeled as "gifts" to circumvent the ban. After the ban in 1956, Georg Suck became the first (and only) Harley-Davidson main dealer and general importer for Germany. When Georg Suck died in 1961, his son Ewald and his wife Waltraud continued to run Europe's oldest Harley dealership. And although Georg Suck started stocking Laverda and Honda in 1969, the family firm remained loyal to Harley-Davidson throughout, despite the 1971 ultimatum when Harley-Davidson imposed conditions on the renewal of the franchise that it was unable, and probably unwilling to meet – a 500 percent increase in turnover, plus payment for all stock on delivery.

The famous premises close to Hamburg's Deichtorhallen where the trains thunder past on the overhead tracks at regular intervals, is a place of legendary renown among Harley buffs, packed with the most amazing documents and relics from the earliest days of the company's history. Georg Suck – a German motorcycling legend that has added a new chapter to the history of Harley-Davidson...

Georg Suck's company was one of the most traditional Harley dealerships in the world. Georg Suck on his motorcycle–sidecar combination in the 1930s.

The company today, with son Ewald and his wife, and the shop beneath the railway lines at Dammtor railway station.

Races

The Meaning of Racing

Harleys Make It to the Finish

Bill Harley proudly presents the front page of the Dodge City Daily Globe showing Jim Davis's victory in the 200-mile run.

Racing Calendar:

The First 30 Years

1910-1911 – Various private riders achieve spectacular wins on Harley-Davidson motorcycles.

1912 – As they enter the racing arena, the four company founders sign up the genial engineer William (Bill) Ottaway, previously the engine tuner at the Thor factory.

1913 – Harley-Davidson announces the formation of its own Racing Department.

1914 – Bill Ottaway gradually builds up the racing team, and ensures that only first-rate components go into his machines.

1915-1918 – Harley-Davidson wins all the major National races, the most impressive being Otto Walker's triumph in the prestigious Dodge City Race at an average speed of 76.2 mph. The legendary Wrecking Crew – a name coined by a journalist – starts to enjoy success.

At the opening of the massive wooden Maywood Board Speedway near Chicago in September 1915, the Harley team rode the side-valve racing machines tuned by Bill Ottaway, beating almost everything that came before them. The legend of the Chicago Harleys was born in the 100-mile run with an average speed and new world record of 89.11 mph. On the left the riders encampment can be seen in the infield.

There is an old saying in boxing which goes as follows: "If one doesn't take training at home seriously, one won't make it in the ring." In the early years of the company, the Harley bosses had no inclination to enter the sporting arena in a big way as there was a lot of homework to be done first.

During the first ten years of the company's history, that is until 1913, it was understandable that they should ignore the somewhat questionable glory of the track and pay greater attention to real problems. If their motorcycles were to survive in the harsh world of bad roads, awful winters and poor servicing, they needed above all to be reliable and sturdy. Their frames, wheels, tires and forks were the critical elements, not those souped-up short-track racing machines. Consequently it was at reliability trials and economy runs that Harleys were to be seen: their success was astounding, as it soon became clear.

The fact that there were a lot of amateur riders with their own machines taking part in motorcycle races was something that did not really please the four men at the head of the company. They seemed to have taken leave of their senses when, in 1913, they issued a rather arrogant statement dismissing such race victories as a needless desire to impress and as something which is not necessary for a serious manufacturer of motorcycles.

In actual fact Harley-Davidson had already made up its mind to participate in motorcycle racing as a sport and had surreptitiously persuaded William "Bill" Ottaway to join the company from rival Thor and had given him the task of setting up a racing division. As good

businessmen they had rapidly recognized the enormous advertising pull of successful racing. Now they could make full use of the excellent and reliable raw material at their disposal so that they could climb into the ring undaunted.

An old racing maxim states that one has to finish a race to win it. Harley racing machines were sturdy enough to reach the finishing line in most cases and to survive the merciless punishment dished out during the tough events which put all the machines through a supreme test of their quality and durability. While other racebikes would often disintegrate into bits or break up completely, the Harleys would make it to the finish. All that was left was to get there first. This was the second element on which the company was to concentrate its attention.

In deference to the company principle that only the very best would do, Harley-Davidson pursued a deliberate policy for decades of recruiting the most talented riders, training them and encouraging them in every way. In later years, when outstanding talent and top-class material were no longer a guarantee of victory, Harley was no longer in a powerful enough position to have much influence on the rules. Considering that motorcycle racing was a second-class sport in the opinion of most Americans, Harley-Davidson's influence should not be underestimated. It is chiefly because of this deliberate company policy that two-wheeled and three-wheeled sport survived in the U.S. What's more to the point, the company itself made a healthy profit from it...

Line up of riders at the Beverly Hills Board Track in 1927 (top).

The most famous racer of them all, the incomparable Joe Petrali, who secured innumerable victories for Harley–Davidson and played a decisive role in building of the engines (above).

A photograph of the Harley–Davidson racing team with their pit crew after World War I (left).

Board Track Racing

Once Upon a Time in the West

Racing Calendar continued

1919 – After the interruption of World War I, Bill Ottaway, R.W. Enos, and C.C. Wilborn reorganize the company's racing team and the old/new Wrecking Crew celebrate one victory after another. Hap Scherer sets a new record of 31 hours and 24 minutes for the 1,012 mile run from New York to Chicago on an opposed-twin W Sport model.

1920 – Five National Championships. Fred Ludlow wins the 20-mile National in Syracuse. Hap Scherer establishes a new record for the long-distance race from Denver to Chicago.

1921 – Harley-Davidson wins all eight National Championships. Walter Davidson announces that, owing to financial difficulties, the company is to disband the Racing Department.

1923 – Freddie Dixon wins the 1000 cc world championship at Brooklands (England) on a Harley eight-valve.

1922–1925 – To improve Harley's chances in the increasingly important export markets, new 350 cc and 500 cc, single-cylinder, ohv engines are developed, under the direction of Bill Ottaway, Arthur Constantine, and Hank Syverston, especially for speedway racing which is popular in England, Australia, New Zealand, and South Africa. The legendary Wrecking Crew is finally wound up.

Parkhurst and Ludlow (in the sidecar) set various recognized world records at Daytona Beach in February 1920. The sidecar reached a speed of 83.9 mph over five miles. In the background on the left is one of the timers, R. Enos, manager of the Harley-Davidson racing team along with Hap Scherer, long-serving editor of *The Enthusiast*.

The nightly, infernal spectacle would be almost unimaginable today. In the flicker of crackling arc lights, a frenzied pack of bizarre racing machines sped around over the black oil- and lye-soaked boards of a huge, hot, wooden bowl; there was a powerful smell of burnt oil and all kinds of gasoline additives, blue flames exploded in staccato bursts from short, sawn-off exhausts, and from time to time both a rider and his machine were thrown on to the boards somewhere in the wide oval. Of course there were also races in the daytime, but they were nowhere near as spectacular. Those murderous board tracks were called such names as "Thunderdome," or "Speed Bowl" or a particular favorite name was "Arena of Death."

At speeds which would have been considered crazy in those days, on slopes banked at up to 60 degrees, one world record after another was broken (43 in 1912 alone), and 90 mph became commonplace. The fearless riders were the darlings of the public, the stars and idols of a whole nation.

The most successful motorcycle marques, such as Indian, Harley-Davidson, Excelsior, Thor and Cyclone, experienced a boom. Harley's riders included some of the most famous names: Ray Weishaar, Fred Ludlow, Red Parkhurst and Otto Walker, all members of the legendary Wrecking Crew. As they thundered along the slippery wooden track, the spectators urging them on wildly, half-blinded by oil and acid spray, blocking and jostling one another, always riding at the limit, their enthusiasm knew no bounds. Their crazy machines could only be ridden at full throttle and had no gearboxes or brakes. They could only be slowed down by using a short-circuit button. But if the rider pressed it for too long, the greasy plugs would soon give out, and the race would be over for him. It was better for the rider to press his boots, studded with nails, against the splintering wood until his oppo-

nent was forced to give way. The rigid tubular frames, which were similar to bicycles and therefore quite fragile, supported oversized, mostly two-cylinder engines which sprayed copious amounts of oil onto the wooden boards through the 'vent holes' drilled in the bottoms of the cylinders. This then had to be removed, or neutralized by using an acid and lye solution. Both Indian and Harley-Davidson developed special eight-valve OHV engines for these board track races, which led to unbelievable speeds. The Harley eight-valve production racer developed by Bill Ottaway had just one drawback, its price; 1,500 dollars was out of the question for unskilled beginners – in those days you could buy a house for that price.

The champions of this racing circus, traveling all over America, were well paid though. Salaries of 300 dollars per week were not uncommon, and those riders who were willing and able to travel the great distances involved could earn up to 20,000 dollars a year, at a time when normal, production racers cost about 350 dollars. That is, assuming the riders managed to survive for a year.

Although the operators or owners of the Speed Bowls generally had their own rules, they often tried to get their events sanctioned by the FAM. Spectators and competitors didn't really care; they just went wherever there was fame and money to be won. Board track racing was the most typically American motorcycle sport in the 1920s – powerful, raw, brutal, noisy, dangerous, very risky and extremely profitable.

At the beginning of the century, when dirt track racing on the dusty horseracing courses became impractical for riders and spectators alike, large, wooden arenas, like the ones already used now and then for cycle races, started to spring up everywhere.

The English-born, cycle racing champion Jack Prince recognized the opportunity and started to build professionally designed Speed

Ray Weishaar, winner of the International 200 Mile Championship.

Bowls in all the major cities in the U.S.; their bloody spectaculars attracted bigger and bigger crouds. In 1909 he opened the first of these Motordromes, specially created for motorcycle racing, in Los Angeles, followed by others in Atlanta, Chicago, Kansas City, Denver, Springfield, Beverly Hills, Fresno and many other cities.

The quickly rotting, wooden boards had become more and more dangerous and it was only after a growing number of gruesome accidents had shocked and outraged the public that any effort was made to come up with an alternative. The end of wooden track racing was hastened by the catastrophe in the Newark Motordrome, New Jersey, on September 8, 1912, in which eight people were killed, including four young spectators who were decapitated by a machine which flew spinning over the railings.

However, it was not until 1928 that the last Speed Bowl race took place – at the Rockingham Bowl Arena in New Hampshire. M.K. Frederik, riding a 1000 cc twin, achieved a record speed of 120.2 mph; then the oval was torn down and sold as building land.

The cover of *The Enthusiast* has a particularly moving detail: Otto Walker's wife assists in making his world-record machine roadworthy.

The beaming victor: Otto Walker with a pocket-valve production run-around at a board track facility.

The Wrecking Crew

Going After the Trophy with Discipline and Determination

Three famous members of the Wrecking Crew at Ascot Racetrack, 1919: Fred Ludlow, Ralph Hepburn and Otto Walker (with helmet).

Racing Calendar continued

1928-1929 – Harley-Davidson doesn't have any factory race bikes, but continues to support a few successful riders.

1929-1930 – AMA Secretary E.C. Smith, on a goodwill tour to promote his efforts to revive motorcycle sport under the authority of the AMA, gains the support of various Harley dealers, particularly in the west. They include W.J. Ruhle in San Diego, Rich Budelier in Los Angeles, Dudley Perkins and Claude Salmon in San Francisco, and Nelson Bettencourt in Vallejo.

1930 – William H. Davidson wins the 20th anniversary Jack Pine Endurance Race on a 30 DLD Harley.

1930-1931 – Bill Ottaway works on the new side-valve models, which are to replace the outdated two-cam J engines, even though these are still preferred by most racers. Harley-Davidson uses its influence with the AMA to establish the new side-valve class.

1931-1932 – Harley-Davidson wins the Daytona Grand National Championship. Joe Petrali wins the 5-mile and 10-mile races at Hamilton Speedway in new record times.

1933-1936 – Joe Petrali wins nearly all the races which he starts, including the National Hillclimb Championship, the 200-mile Expert Championship, the Miniature TT Championship, the 200-mile Speedway Championship, all 13 National Dirt-Track Championships and the 3, 10, 15 and 25 mile Championships, at Syracuse, New York. In the course of the three years he sets four new AMA records and in 1935 is crowned as dirt-track champion.

Three famous members of the Wrecking Crew at Ascot Racetrack, 1919: Fred Ludlow, Ralph Hepburn and Otto Walker (with helmet).

The factory's first excursion into the major league of racing was at Dodge City, Kansas, in 1914. It was the first running of the 300 mile dirt track event, which was destined to be christened the "Indianapolis of motorcycling." Five Harley-Davidsons were entered in the race, all of them special, brand-new, type 11K machines, and all were prepared personally by William Ottaway. There was strong competition, including eight-valve Indians, Excelsiors with oversize valves, and Merkel, Thor and Pope machines.

Harley's best rider was Walter Cunningham, a factory rider who ran in a very promising position until just over halfway through the race, when he was sidelined with chain and spark-plug problems. All the Harleys finished, and most people regarded that as a good first effort. But the factory was not at all pleased.

The next year was better, but the real breakthrough did not come until 1916. William Ottaway brought together a team of outstanding riding talents, soon to be known as the Wrecking Crew, who dominated American motorcycle racing completely from 1916 to 1921. The names changed slightly from year to year, but the hardcore remained: Jim Davis, Ralph Hepburn, Fred Ludlow, Otto Walker, Maldwyn Jones and Ray Weishaar.

The Wrecking Crew did not only have the best riders; they also had the logistic support and pit crews that no other team could match. The crew for the 1916 Dodge City 300 included team boss Otto Walker, Ray Weishaar, Floyd Clymer, Hary Brant, Irving Jahnke, Harry Crandall, Sam Corrento and Paul Gott. Rumor had it that William Ottaway and his assistant, E.E. Welborn, put the team through a near military

training regime, including tactics and precision, pit stop drills, and practice with the team's special flag signaling system. Ottaway also insisted on a hard training schedule for his team, including a strict diet and plenty of rest before a race.

The lineup for the 1916 season was led by Harley-Davidson's new eight-valve machines, but four-valve and F-head racers also competed. Only about half a dozen eight-valves were ever built. Dodge City was America's most important motor race, and the new eight-valves passed their baptism of fire against similar machines from Indian.

Young Floyd Clymer took the lead on the second lap and held it, alternating with teammate Irving Jahnke, for nearly the whole of the race. Just a few miles from the checkered flag, Clymer was forced to retire with a flat tire, leaving Jahnke to cross the line as the winner.

The Wrecking Crew was on its way. That way included 15 national championships during 1916. Team spirit was everything. In the longer races the factory's strategy was to storm away at the front with the eight-valves leading, then move the F-heads up for the victory, since these were considered more reliable. At the end of the 1916 season, because of the increasing preparations for war, motorcycle racing was stopped, and did not resume until after World War I in 1919.

After the war, the Wrecking Crew, with a slightly different lineup, was ready to go. The merciless hunt for trophies began again. Red Parkhurst was now in a Harley factory saddle and won the year's most important road race, in Marion, Indiana. Teammates Ralph Hepburn and Otto Walker took second and third places. Triumph followed on triumph, win upon win. A major factor again was the discipline of the pit crew, now headed by Dudley Perkins from San Francisco. Sources quote one example in which a rider was refueled, given oil, and had a rear tire change, all in 38 seconds. At the end of the year the Harley–Davidson team collected 552 miles of National titles, while Indian could only manage 67 miles. The powerful Excelsior team was left without a single Championship.

In 1920 the factory sent Red Parkhurst and a support crew headed by Bill Ottaway to Daytona. Parkhurst established several short-distance records, and used an eight-valve to set a new combination record. The Dodge City 300 was run for the first time since 1916. Maldwyn Jones set two new records for Harley–Davidson, and Jim Davis took the winner's trophy.

In the summer of 1997 Jim Davis was still making public appearances at the age of 101. He was alert and healthy, and inclined to say things like, "It doesn't hurt to fall off going fast. When you hit something, that hurts." He told a reporter with some pride, "I still hold the 300 mile record on a pocket-valve." That record was set at Dodge City in 1920. "The next year," Davis said, "Hepburn went a little faster on an eight-valve."

1921 was the really outstanding year for the Wrecking Crew, and Harley–Davidson's finest hour in racing. The Crew for 1921 included Jim Davis, Ralph Hepburn, Walter Higley, Fred Ludlow, Otto Walker and Ray Weishaar. The Crew did not just dominate, they reigned supreme. They won absolutely everything at national level, including the 1, 5, 10, 25, 50, 100, 200 and 300 mile championship titles. Otto Walker had a huge success in a smaller event in Fresno, California, setting the all-time 50 mile record on a board track, at 29 minutes, 34.8 seconds. It was also the first motorcycle race ever won at an average speed of more than 100 mph. Ralph Hepburn won in Dodge City on an eight-valve racer.

After 1921, Harley gave up its racing activities, leaving the field open to Indian and Harley private riders. Ray Weishaar died while racing at Ascot in 1924; Eddie Brinck was killed on a Harley during

a race in Springfield, Massachusetts in 1927; Ralph Hepburn continued to race until 1948, when he was killed in a car at Indianapolis Motor Speedway. Otto Walker retired from racing to a boat rental business.

A group photo from the most successful days of the famous racing team, probably 1917.
From the left: team manager Hank Syvertsen, beside him among others Ray Weishaar, Maldwyn Jones, Ralph Hepburn, probably Shrimp Burns, Otto Walker, and on the far right Bill Ottaway, head of the racing department.

Always a promising motif: the legendary Wrecking Crew at a press conference.

© Harley-Davidson

The FAM, MATA and AMA

How American Motorcycle Sports Were Handled Until World War II

Racing Calendar continued

1936 – At Harley-Davidson's request, the AMA Competition Committee bans all F-head J (IOE two-cam) models from their competitions to give the new side-valve machines a better chance.

1937 – After a year of secret preparations, Joe Petrali pilots an EL Knucklehead, which was originally streamlined, to a new world record speed of 136,183 mph at Daytona Beach.

1938 – Harley-Davidson gets Joe Petrali to do secret tests on one of the feared rival Crocker machines, but finds no grounds to claim patent infringements. Petrali leaves Harley-Davidson after his request for a pay rise is turned down.

1938-1940 – More victories for Harley-Davidson: Ben Campanale wins the Daytona 200-mile Expert Race, Sam Arena the 200-mile National Speedway Championship in Oakland, where Armando Magri is second. Babe Tancrede wins the 200-mile Classic Expert Race. Most riders use the WLDR model.

Late 1941 – The AMA halts all race meetings. America enters World War II.

At the beginning of the 20th century about 60 manufacturers in the U.S. produced up to 75,000 motorcycles per year in a kind of technological gold rush, with a number of jumbled aims: progress, profits, sport, speed and a little practicality. The growth of sporting activities and the safety measures required for them necessitated the immediate establishment of an executive authority to set the rules.

In 1903, 44 upright representatives of the Alpha Motorcycle Club and the New York Bicycle Club (based in Philadelphia), and several other interested parties and enthusiasts, got together at the Kings County Wheelman's Club, in Brooklyn, New York, to form the national Federation of American Motorcyclists (FAM). From then on, races and other sporting events took place according to their rules, insofar as there were any rules at all: there was no limit on power output, cylinder displacement was limited to a maximum of 50 cubic inches (819 cc) and the rider had to weigh at least 120 pounds.

Motorcycle manufacturers had quickly recognized the advantages of such organized activities, and launched into the racing scene with a lot of money and commitment, engaging well-known racers and building increasingly special competition motorcycles. But the necessary professionalization of referees and officials did not go so well. Despite special training courses for referees and timers, there were constant complaints and inconsistencies.

On the other hand, the early years from 1910 to 1916, often referred to as the Golden Age of the Motorcycle, was a wonderful time for promoting successful motorcycle marques, and the still young industry joined in vigorously. There were races everywhere, endurance runs, cross-country competitions, reliability runs, hillclimbs, and the unspeakable speed bowl, board track races. At country shows and fairs, dirt track races on the obligatory horseracing circuits were an extraordinary spectator attraction, which everyone wanted to put on. Countless clubs formed into active racing associations, and the FAM together with local motorcycle dealers organized picnics, rallies and runs for them.

In 1913 the FAM had 8,567 members, each paying an annual subscription of 2 dollars, with additional revenue coming from entry fees and

industrial support. But soon the FAM, struggling to administer its widespread territory, was no longer able to cope with the evermore complicated and expensive task of organizing sporting events. Members were frustrated, and there was talk of a crisis – by 1916 there were only about 2,000 members left and all of 340 dollars in the coffers. Because they didn't want to continue in penury and in organizational chaos, the West Coast members, who were active throughout the whole year, broke away from the FAM and formed their own racing organization, the Western Federation of Motorcyclists, with its headquarters in Los Angeles.

In order to save what was left, the FAM turned to the American Motorcycle Manufacturing Association (AMMA) and asked for (financial) help. So, in 1918, the Motorcycles & Allied Trades Association (M&ATA, or simply MATA) was formed to look after the concerns of racing. The first change involved new subscription rates: every motorcycle manufacturer, as an A member had to pay 100 dollars per year, while accessories companies and equipment suppliers had to pay 50 dollars as B members.

Then new rules were drawn up for board track, road racing, hillclimbing, and regular club events, and, to go with the unlimited Class A, a modified Class B was introduced which would offer less prosperous companies more chance of participating in racing. But this sporting organization, itself created by the motorcycle industry, did not last long – the manufacturers were so badly hit by the recession of the early 1920s that companies could no longer afford to keep their racing stables. While Indian at first carried on and brought many good riders into its camp, in 1921 Harley-Davidson announced that it was to disband its Racing Department.

Meanwhile discussions had been held with the FICM (Fédération Internationale de Compétition Motocyclette) in Geneva, to see if any common ground could be found, but without success. Today the FIM (Fédération Internationale Motocyclette) is still motorsport's highest authority. So great were the technical differences (Europe preferred the 500 cc class, America the 1000 cc twins), so great was the Americans' fear of foreign racing imports, that American motorcycle racing remained isolated from the rest of the world for the next 40 years.

In 1924 motor sports enthusiasts, clubs and corporate members of the MATA, together with the remainder of the FAM, which was still muddling along in the background, decided to make a serious attempt to get together and organize things properly. A Riders Division, founded in 1920, developed into the American Motorcycle Association (AMA), and appointed George T. Briggs of the Schebler carburetor factory as its first president. He was followed in 1928 by James A. Wright, Head of Purchasing at Indian, and from 1944 by Arthur Davidson. Although all three of them worked hard for the AMA, the real power of the new organization was vested in its executive secretaries: firstly A.B. Coffmann, then the tireless E.C. Smith, followed by Lin Kuchler.

Of course the AMA was also an industry-oriented organization – sometimes it was Indian, but mostly Harley which made its influence felt. But while most motorcycle manufacturers and accessories companies were quite reluctant even to fulfill their bare obligations, Harley-Davidson made large payments without which the AMA would soon have failed. Activities increased quickly. In dirt track racing, flexible sidecars were permitted but in 1925 they were banned again because of the large number of accidents. The clubs were increasingly courted; numerous "Gypsy

The present-day headquarters of the AMA: 5030 N. High Street, Columbus/Ohio.

The AMA and Its Rules

How to Deal with Foreign Competition

Tours" were meant to promote shared trips to race meetings and stimulate spectator interest in the new 350 cc and 500 cc single-cylinder classes which were becoming more and more popular, mostly in local events, in short-track, and other dusty track races. Then the 5-, 10-, 15-, and 20-mile road races came into fashion and, although Harley-Davidson was no longer represented by its own factory team, the company gave powerful support to successful private riders. But there were soon problems again at the AMA: in 1928 it had only 4,200 paying members and 64 affiliated clubs. Secretary Smith went on a relaunch tour, and in 1930 was proud to count 5,800 members and 93 clubs affiliated with the AMA.

Under the pressure of the worldwide economic crisis in the early-1930s, the AMA took its most significant step: in 1934 it introduced Class C participation in practically all racing events could take place with standard street machines ("strictly stock"), to which only very minor modifications could be made for racing: lamps, saddlebags, and fenders could be removed, but only standard engines were allowed, using standard pump fuel, and bikes had to be ridden personally to the racetrack not brought on a trailer. This made motor sport accessible to almost anyone, and its popularity increased accordingly. For the next 40 years Class C was the most popular competitive class — the way in to serious racing for the amateur.

Consequently, in 1937 the A class of professional racing teams was discontinued as it was no longer economically viable, first of all in the 350 cc single-cylinder class in which there was now little interest. The AMA came down hard on any race events which it had not sanctioned. Anyone caught taking part in these "outlaw" races could count on a year's ban from all AMA races. The effect of the introduction of Class C can be judged by the AMA membership figures: in 1938 it had 19,356 members and 687 clubs under its wing.

And of course Harley-Davidson was again well-represented, particularly by its legendary race rider and engineer Joe Petrali who, up to the outbreak of World War II, seemed to win almost everything he entered in any class. Another new trend emerged towards the end of the 1930s: sex appeal. Not only in the drivers' camp had beautiful women become popular mascots — they were also now seen as "Beauty Queens" on the winner's podium, often more decorated than the winner himself, and there were lots of kisses and pin-up photos, as well as the customary showers of champagne.

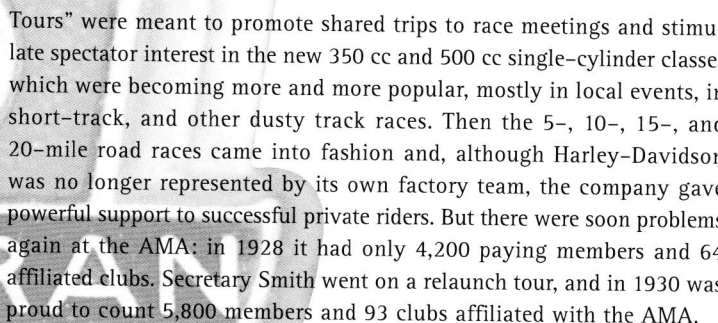

By far the most important development in the history of AMA racing rules was the creation of Class C in 1934. Racing had become an exclusive playground for manufacturers and a handful of wealthy dealers. Class C was meant to make motorcycle racing financially possible for the average rider, and the AMA hoped that a wider spectrum of participants would engender increased interest on the part of fans. It succeeded beyond their wildest dreams.

The time was ripe for such a venture because interest in motorcycles generally was very low. The Great Depression meant that motorcycle sales across the U.S. had fallen badly, and political maneuvering overseas had all but extinguished Harley-Davison's lucrative Australian market.

The big events which had really drawn the crowds were a thing of the past — the last board track in the U.S. was in Rockingham, New Hampshire, and it was demolished in 1929. In addition, the huge number of collisions and other accidents had brought calls for lower speeds to increase safety.

Class A racing, i.e. all the national and major events, was subject to rules which essentially made it accessible only to factory-sponsored riders. After the introduction of Class C, Class A began to lapse in 1935 into a kind of suspended animation — it could be reanimated again at any time if Class C did not prove successful. But that was not the case; Class C racing became very popular, and by 1938 it had virtually taken over. The last Class A championship was held in fall 1938 in Syracuse, New York.

Class C rules primarily applied to flat track and road races, and set a displacement limit of 750 cc for side-valves. Almost as an afterthought, OHV engines up to 500 cc, were also included. However, in 1933 this 500 cc inclusion

was not really significant, since there were very few imported 500 cc machines in the U.S., and only one dealer worth mentioning, Reggie Pink of New York. The rules on permitted engine modifications in Class C were very strict. The original wording stipulated that motorcycles had to be ridden to the event, and only standard pump fuel was allowed.

To prevent factory involvement, the motorcycles had to be standard road-going machines, with a minimum of 25 units built by the factory. All the riders also had to own the bikes they raced. For dirttrack racing the displacement limit was 750 cc and brakes had to be disconnected. The TT events had classes for both 750 cc and 1200 cc. During the course of time these lofty principles were watered down by Harley, and the highly modified, factory racers eventually sent out to do battle bore little resemblance to the corresponding street models.

Nevertheless, Class C remained dominant. The far-reaching effects of the Class C rules were felt most strongly in the postwar years, when it became clear that the 750 cc side-valve twins were not the last word in racing motorcycles. British machines, in particular, started flexing their muscles in all kinds of events. This resulted in some manipulation of the rules by Harley and Indian, with the support of the AMA bosses. In fact the first signs of the strength of British racing appeared before the war, when Norton machines won the 1939 Langhorne 100 and the 1941 Daytona 200.

The weapon turned against the foreign invaders was compression ratios. Since the American side-valve machines rarely ran at anything over 6:1, and the OHV engines were at their best running at a ratio of 9:1 or higher, specifying a lower compression would seriously handicap the more highly developed European machines. So, from the beginning, compression ratios were limited to 7.5:1. This was high enough to ensure that the imports were not completely emasculated, but also that they achieved well short of their best performance.

The compression ratio rule was challenged long and loud by British manufacturers and dealers in the motorcycle press. There were even greater protests in 1946 when the public became aware of an even tighter rule to reduce the maximum permitted compression ratio to 6.5:1. This would really have reduced overseas competition to toothless tigers and the action was regarded by almost everyone as extremely unsporting and as proof that American bikes stood no chance in a fair competition. In the face of such massive public protests, the compression limit was very quickly restored to 7.5:1.

In 1949 a Norton again won the Daytona 200, and the AMA, still very sensitive to accusations that they were unfairly protecting Harley and Indian, raised the maximum permitted compression ratio for OHV engines from 7.5:1 to 8:1. The limit would be raised again in 1955 after Indian had folded, and Harley had introduced its new KR model.

Every Man's Racing Model

The F-Head for Victory

Successful in Germany too: an intake-over-exhaust F-Head Racer, 1925.

For a long time prior to Harley-Davidson's official entry into racing, there were race riders who had great success with the new "pocket-valve" F-head V-Twin. Most riders tuned or converted their two-cylinder motorbikes themselves. When Bill Ottaway and Harry Ricardo then set up the Racing Department, it was the many F-head J/JD racers which attracted the greatest attention.

In contrast to the exclusive and deliberately overpriced eight-valve OHV racing machines, anyone could buy one of the IOE twins (there was also a single-cylinder model with the rear cylinder removed) at costs of between 260 dollars and 320 dollars. The F-head J model racing machines were highly popular, and prized for their reliability and toughness. They proved themselves under a wide range of racing conditions, from hillclimbing and oval-circuit to track- and long-distance races.

From 1915 onwards the range included six twin-cylinder racing models alongside the two IOE single-cylinder machines. The K models were supplied as stripped stock racers without accessories in the standard model. The engines of these series were given the reference letter M:

K: F-head V-Twin with magneto
KH: F-head V-Twin with battery
KT: F-head V-Twin track racer
KR: F-head V-Twin roadster with magneto
KRH: F-head V-Twin roadster with battery
KTH: Track racer with battery

The IOE Two Pocket Valve Racer was available with 61, 65 and 74 cubic inch (1000, 1065, and 1200 cc) engines. From 1919 they were fitted with two camshafts and came to be called the "banjo two-cam racer" because of the banjo-shaped timing cover, in which both the magneto drive and the cam control gears, which had previously been separate, were housed. Ignition was via a German Bosch magneto. The stock version had a direct chain drive with an adjustable pinion gear in between.

Later on a three-speed gearbox became available as an extra. The improved lubrication system could be fitted with either a hand pump or a mechanical pump. The combustion chamber had a high compression ratio, usually 8:1. None of the racing models had any starter system and had to be push-started: the pedals were there only to serve as footrests. The loop steel frame could be fitted either with a "Harley-Davidson original" frame or a special racing frame. The following were among the special models available:

FHAC: Two-cam racer, with a 61 cubic inch capacity
       and magneto ignition
FHAD: Hillclimber with 10:1 compression ratio
JHD: Basic two-cam model
SMA: With multigear transmission
JK: Special 61 cubic inch solo version plus alternator

Unlike the eight-valve OHV racing motorcycles, the pocket-valve racers were produced in large quantities and defined the racing scene until the mid-1930s.

However, from 1937 onwards they were banned by the AMA (at the insistence of Harley-Davidson). This was because their continuing success on the racetrack no longer fitted in with the range of motorcycles being marketed by Harley-Davidson, which since 1930 had consisted purely of side-valve machines, to which the new overhead-valve Knucklehead model was to be added from 1936. The Harley racing team, the notorious "Wrecking Crew," had had their greatest triumphs on these IOE twin-cylinder motorbikes.

The best-known among them were national heroes such as Hepburn, Parkhurst, Davis and Weishaar, to name but a few. The racing machines, which could reach speeds of 100 mph were also exported to Australia, New Zealand, England and other various European countries, where they also competed with great success, until being increasingly superseded, from the beginning of the 1930s onwards, by the D, R and W range of side-valve machines.

The 1926 FHAC two-cam factory racer.

Courtesy of: Otis Chandler/Vintage Museum of Transporation, Oxnard, California

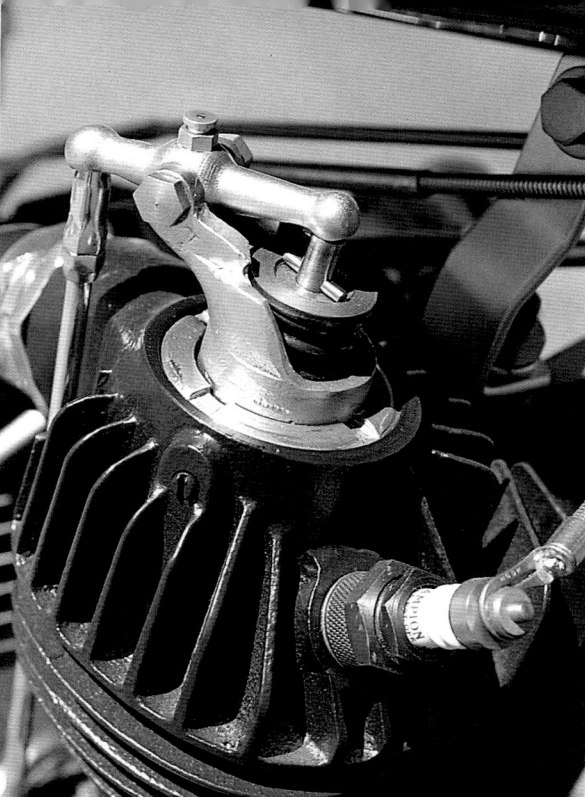

Intake valve of the 1926
FHAC board-tracker.

Rocker-arm connection of the FHAC's
springer front shafts.

Drive-side of 1926 FHAC two-cam
factory racer with magnet-
strengthened frame base.

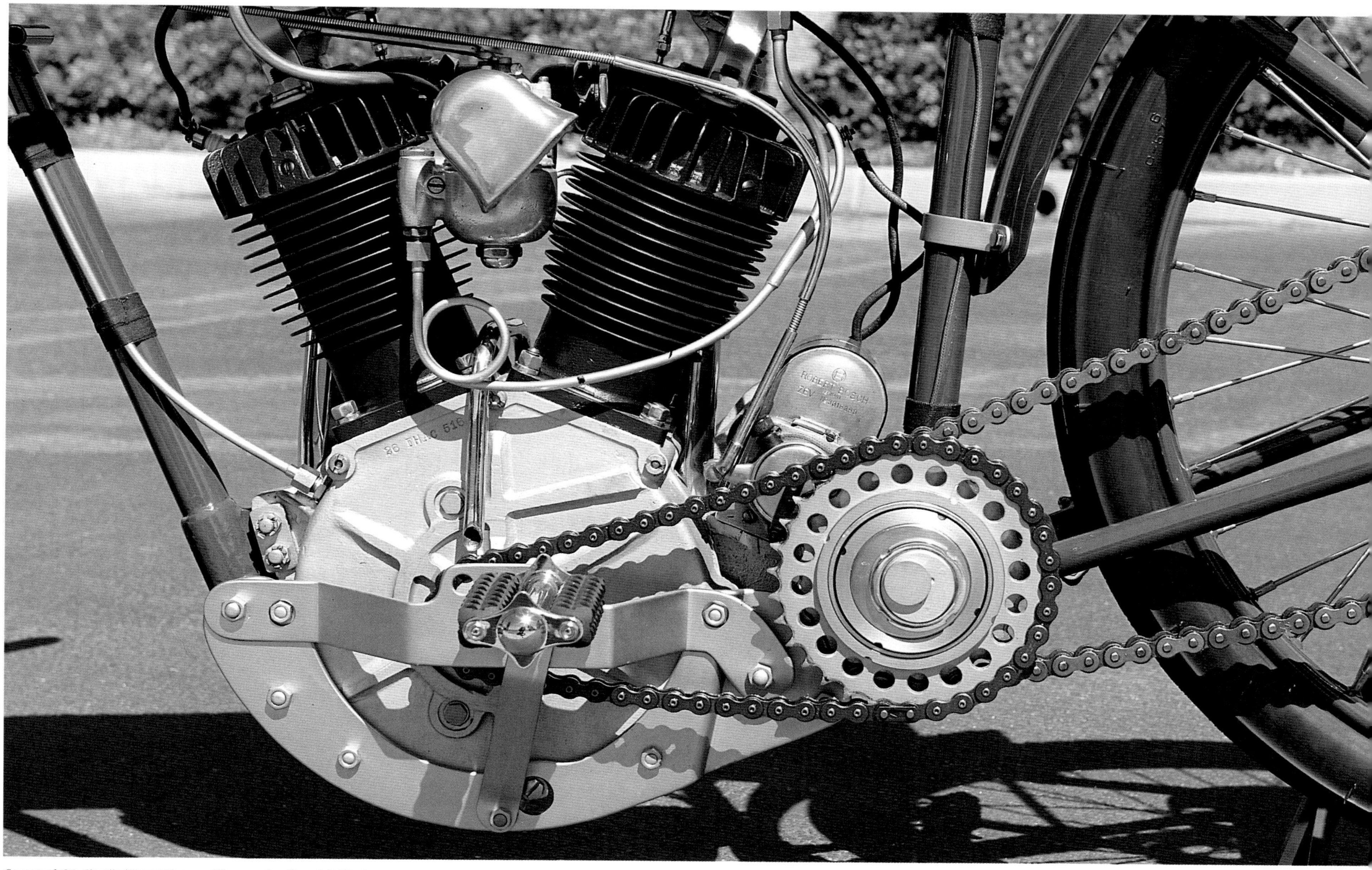

Hillclimb

There Ain't No Mountain High Enough

The cover of one of the many editions of *The Enthusiast*, this one from September 1937.

When one AMA historian was asked for his thoughts on Harley-Davidson and hillclimbing he immediately answered: "Joe Petrali." And not without reason: this multi-talented racing man was undisputedly a central figure, dominating the world of hillclimb racing on Harley-Davidson machines throughout the 1930s. In fact "Smokey" Joe was part of a fascinating era in motor sport which had begun long before he came to the fore.

From the beginning of the 1920s, hillclimbs were a highly popular form of motorcycle racing. The idea originated in Europe, where since the earliest days hillclimbs had provided a test of the endurance and power of the machines involved. However, these were really just a form of road race on paved or at least hard-packed surfaces demanding driver skill, continual gear changes and refined cornering technique. Naturally that was not exciting enough for the unsubtle Americans — they demanded a thrill a minute, danger and brutal engine power.

Thus the American hillclimb came into being as more or less a drag race up the steepest and toughest of mountainsides — slopes which at first sight appeared impossible for motorcycles to conquer. The American motorcycle men took on this challenge, built special bikes and roared up the most extreme of hills in a series of erratic jumps — slopes of up to 45 degrees were commonplace. They learned from experience, working out how to juggle the right combinations of gravity, centrifugal force and engine power to conquer the scree and loose rocks with breathtaking displays of motorcycle aerobatics apparently defying the laws of nature.

Whether the races were AMA-sponsored or outlaw meets, local and regional hillclimbs were ideal events for motorcycle clubs. All one needed was a suitable tract of land and a stop watch. The crowds came by the hundreds. A photograph from the earliest days at Hornell shows the entire hillside and the valley below packed with spectators. The spectacle they witnessed was one of an infernal roaring of engines as riders and machines shot up the hillside in crazy, zigzag courses leaving trails of dust and dirt spraying up behind them as they went. There was great excitement when a rider lost control of

his machine, which often somersaulted into the air and went tumbling with its rider back down the hillside, or even flew into the onlooking crowd. And then there was the thrill of seeing the victorious rider roaring over the crown of the hill to disappear from view as "King of the Hill."

The drama of hillclimb events was so great that both Fox and Movietone newsreels regularly showed action from races, with special emphasis on the wildest scenes and most spectacular accidents. That was hillclimb then, raw power and torque, and the large capacity V-Twin engines were ideal for generating power and torque.

Harley-Davidson was at the forefront in this discipline, but faced serious competition — both Excelsior and Indian were equally successful. All three manufacturers produced machines of similar quality, and Joe Petrali, the most famous exponent of the art, was also successful with other makes: during the 1920s, he was a regular winner on an Excelsior Super X. During the latter part of his career, with Harley-Davidson, Joe Petrali rode practically every machine competed by the company, but his special talent was for hillclimbing.

Of course Harley-Davidson also had other talented performers in this area: C.W. Hemmis, Joe Herb and above all Windy Lindstrom. Although Joe Petrali is the first name to spring to most people's lips, Windy Lindstrom was his equal, winning over 300 hillclimbs between 1925 and 1950. He preferred the normal factory-built hillclimber and scorned such technical alterations as stretched frames. He said his particular technique was to press the kill button whenever the front of the machine started to go up into the air. The racer Sam Arena, sponsored by Harley dealer Tom Sifton, also won many victories for Harley-Davidson.

Hillclimb motorbikes, whether built by privateers or by works racing divisions, are highly specialized machines. The early models bore no resemblance to the bikes which roar up the slopes these days. During the 1920s and 1930s it was believed that a short bike was best.

The bikes built specially for hillclimbing by Harley-Davidson were designated with an X for experimental, and had short forks with minimal travel which were sometimes fitted with an additional

There are a large number of spectacular hillclimb photos. This one (right) shows Windy Lindstrom who was one of the hillclimbing elite, winning numerous 45 and 61 cubic inch championships. A 45 cubic inch OHV hillclimb machine shortly before going head-over-heels (far right).

Shots of riders as here in the twenties, whether posed (above) or real (left) were always sought-after sports photos.

reinforcement similar to those used by wall-of-death riders. Some X frames had further reinforcement behind the seat in order to make them even sturdier and more resistant to torsion. These later came to be known as "keystone" frames. The factory hillclimbers also featured a small, strong-walled, gas tank which was not fitted to any other kind of racing model. Sometimes the seat was mounted directly on the tank so that the rider could readily transfer his weight forwards in order to prevent the bike from flipping over, a common occurrence, especially at the top of the course where the slope was usually steepest. The footpegs were fitted at a sharp downward angle so that the rider could more easily stand up and lean forwards when the front of the bike started to aviate into the air.

Harley-Davidson used only the best available engine components: usually OHV units running on methanol, with gearboxes reduced to two or even a single gear. When the AMA introduced Class C for amateurs, most events were reduced to 45 cubic inch engines, partly because they were more affordable for everyday riders, and also because their top speeds were much lower than those of the much more powerful 61 and 74 cubic inch machines, and thus were safer for beginners. An exception to this general rule was made in the case of hillclimbs,

because the raw power of the larger engines was an important factor in attracting the crowds.

Hillclimbs are not as popular today as they once were, but there are still many devoted fans eager to attend races, and crowds of 4,000 or more are not uncommon. The Harley-Davidsons running today in the 850 cc plus class use nitromethane and have greatly elongated swingarms and special knobbly tires, often with added chains for extra grip. The rear drive sprockets are about the size of a large pizza. Along with various tuning techniques, this allows the huge power of the engine to be transmitted to the steep scree slopes. These Harleys often compete against super-equipped Japanese machines, and normally they come out on top, as Kings of the Hill.

Sprouts Elder, seen here in Capistrano in 1925, was one of the best Hillclimb racers (below).

Perpendicular Racers – Hillclimbers
Special Machines for Climbing Fans

A typical hillclimb outfit with small, specially designed tank, forward slung saddle, traction chains on the back wheel and a particularly powerful V-Twin OHV motor, in most cases fueled with alcohol.

Harley-Davidson hillclimb motorcycles have a long tradition of seeking out and conquering the steepest of hills. A typically American form of motorsport, hillclimb was once among the most popular in the U.S., with renowned racing aces such as Harley-Davidson's Joe Petrali and Dudley Perkins parading their great skills and acts of daring before an enthusiastic public.

Hillclimb used both small 350 cc and 500 cc single-cylinder side-valve OHV machines, such as the legendary Peashooter; and also the big 750 cc, 1000 cc, 1200 cc and 1340 cc V-Twins, during the 1930s with IOE F-head engines and later with a wide variety of different OHV designs. High-compression engines running on alcohol were also popular, as were any number of homemade and customized machines. Today, supercharged Sportster power units are generally used.

A particular construction feature of hillclimber machines were the long, tough frames which became longer and longer, or rather their rear swingarms did, in order to prevent the machines tipping over. Originally chains were wrapped around the tires to give better grip; nowadays tires come covered with large studs. Some of the best-known models are illustrated here.

Hillclimbs are not as popular nowadays as they once were, but there are still many hardcore fans eager to attend races, and crowds of 4,000 or more are not uncommon. The Harley-Davidsons running today in the 850 cc plus class use nitromethane and have greatly elongated swingarms and special knobbly tires, often with added chains for extra grip. The rear drive sprockets are about the size of a large pizza. Along with various tuning techniques, this allows the huge power of the engine to be transmitted to the steep scree slopes. These Harleys often compete against super-equipped Japanese machines, and normally they come out on top, as Kings of the Hill. "No mountain too high" is today's motto for Harley's most successful offroad hillclimbers.

This refers to the AMA 800 cc National Hillclimb Championship Series, which covers more than a dozen professionally organized events in the U.S. The underlying principle is relatively simple to explain: people take the steepest hill they can find, and send a handful of crazy bikers up it.

Whoever makes it the furthest up the hill is the winner. Virtually no design restrictions are placed on the motorcycles in this context. The riders are free to improve their hillclimbing steeds as they see fit, with more powerful engines and longer wheelbases being the most popular – and effective – modifications.

The most outstanding winners of recent times in this spectacular discipline have been the Gerencers: a father and son combination from Middlebury, Indiana, who together have so far won five championships on their factory sponsored, XL Harleys.

Even today, hillclimb competitions have lost none of their attraction, as can be seen here in Sturgis, and it is still the monster Harleys which earn the most applause.
The hillclimb racers in use today have extremely long back–wheel rocker arms intended to prevent somer-saulting.

Speedway – Just Drifting Around

Short-Distance Races in the Commonwealth

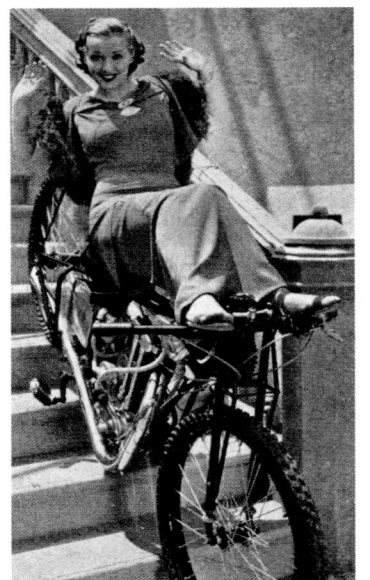

This peculiar pose, termed "beauty and steel" by one magazine, shows RKO star Dorothy Granger on a CAC short-track model.

The origins of speedway racing as a sport are to be found in the early American speed trials which took place at the beginning of this century on loose sand or cinder tracks which had originally been intended for horseracing. While this type of sport was soon to take a different direction in the U.S., it quickly grew in popularity in Australia and in England.

At first these short-track races, as they were called, became very popular particularly in New South Wales. Then, after a large-scale event held in Epping Forest near London in 1928, interest also grew rapidly in England. Speedway races soon became a mass sport in England. This should not come as a surprise, since the state subsidized the noisy entertainment heavily, naturally taking a sizable share of the proceeds itself in the process. It was by no means unusual to draw more than 30,000 spectators to one of these events!

In the spring of 1929 the Australian Lloyd B. "Sprouts" Elder brought his speedway racing team to California and set up his Flat-Track Shows in Los Angeles, Fresno, Emeryville and Oakland. In the early-1930s speedway racing over a distance of a quarter mile – which were also called short-track races – became one of the most popular sporting events in motorcycling.

The competing machines were mostly British 500 cc single-cylinder OHV machines – Rudges or JAPs (J.A. Prestwich & Co. Ltd.) – or the twin-cylinder high compression Douglas using alcohol as its fuel. The first American manufacturer to turned his attention in a serious way to speedway motorcycles was Albert G. Crocker, an Indian dealer from Los Angeles. Starting in 1931 he built very successful OHV and ohc single-cylinder racing machines. The designation OHC (overhead camshaft) describes machines with a camshaft across the cylinder heads operating the valves.

Speedway demands quite a specific riding technique. The machines themselves are relatively light and are slid around the bends drifting at top speed. (Dirttrack motorcycles do not have any brakes.) During the race the rider presses his steel skid boot as hard as he can into the surface of the track as a counterbalance when cornering. Four riders take part in each heat competing against each other and they are awarded points using the 4-3-2-1 system. A string of eliminating heats determines the overall winner with the highest number of points.

The organizers of speedway events were independent operators with their own sets of rules, officials and judges. There were, of course, some general AMA rules applicable to the sport and a modest fee for permission to stage the races was also paid into the Association's account in Columbus, but the size of prize money varied from event

A typical public-relations photo from the 1930s with a speedway model and elegant racing outfit together with an extremely fashionably dressed female fan (right).

The earliest track races were pure speed competitions and still took place on equine race tracks (far right).

The lineup for a circuit race
on the Ascot Speedway,
1919 (above).

to event and the profits went into the pockets of the independent owners. The first officially sanctioned AMA National Speedway Championship in Class A open to all comers took place in July 1934 in the Los Angeles Olympic Stadium. The only machines participating were 500 cc single–cylinder machines running on alcohol.

It was only in 1933, thanks above all to Joe Petrali that Harley-Davidson started to construct their own speedway machine, the 30.50 cubic inch (500 cc) OHV Model CAC. The official company history states that in 1933 and 1934 only nine of these machines were built and they did not prove successful. Just as before, British bikes, above all specifically the almost unbeatable JAPs, were continuing to dominate. After a few hectic years America's flirtation with the minority sport of speedway racing cooled again and was replaced by the traditional oval-track races over greater distances. There are even today a few short-distance speedway races in America, but the popularity which this sport enjoys today is far less than it was during the golden age of the 1930s.

The standard version of the CAC speedway machine was strikingly similar to the English JAP (above).

Courtesy of: Harley-Davidson, San Diego, CA

Special protections for the intake against the aggressive, omnipresent dust had to be designed (left).

Courtesy of: Harley-Davidson, San Diego, CA

© Harley-Davidson

The Peashooter

The Peashooter
The Bike with the Napolean Complex

Drive side of the Peashooter.

In 1925 Indian, Harley's great rival, brought out its latest lightweight model, the Prince, fitted with a 21 cubic inch (350 cc) side-valve engine (also available in a limited edition in an overhead-valve variant), at the cut-throat price of 185 dollars.

Harley-Davidson decided that it was high time they did something about it and so the company also brought out two new 350 cc motorbikes. These were the side-valve A and B types, both of which cost 250 dollars; and also, in smaller numbers, the OHV AA (with magneto ignition) and BA (with battery ignition and electrical system), both costing 275 dollars. However, these small single-cylinder motorcycles were chiefly aimed at the export market in the United Kingdom and Scandinavia, since American customers and dealers, as they always would, favored the Big Twins.

By now a new variety of motorsport had become hugely popular, especially in Australia, New Zealand and England. This was speedway, in which the small single-cylinder machines race on tight oval tracks. In the U.S. Big Twins were generally used in this type of racing.

The tuned-up and slimmed-down OHV AA model with magneto ignition (weighing 215 pounds) now quickly became one of the standard machines. In its competition version it was capable of a good 80 mph. It was chiefly used in the U.S., where it quickly became very popular for both track and hillclimb racing. Eddie Brink and Joe Petrali were the almost unbeatable star riders of these machines, often leaving the considerably more powerful 500 cc single-cylinder OHV machines standing.

In 1926 Harley-Davidson won 14 international titles, and in 1927 took three out of nine national races plus all the titles in the 350 cc class.

The motorcycle got the name "Peashooter" because of the characteristic dry popping noise produced by its extremely short exhaust.

There were three basic versions of the Peashooter. The prototype had an altered frame and a special gas tank, a one-port head and exhaust, and a Schebler DeLuxe carburetor. It had no gearbox, just a countershaft with two different sprocket wheels. Additionally there were flat-track racing versions with standard three-speed gearboxes, and, from 1927 onwards, a modified frame and gas tank and a manual oil pump. Other new features were the underslung handlebars and a new Wheeler-Schebler AX 4 carburetor.

The 1928/29 models had a twin-port head and also two exhaust pipes, a Schebler "Indianapolis barrel" carburetor, and also stronger connecting rods and piston pins. The export TT and roadracer was generally fitted with a three-speed gearbox and twin-port head. For special racing use, the A class Peashooter in particular had its compression ratio forced up to 12:1 and was run on alcohol. This model, intended for short-track races, had an extremely rigid frame and steep forks with virtually no suspension, and had to be push-started.

The Peashooter had its greatest successes in Sweden and New Zealand in grass track races (known as "cinder races" in Scandinavia), and also in hillclimbs and enduro races. Its run of success came to an end at the beginning of the 1930s, when it became unable to compete with the increasingly successful English 500 cc JAP engines, which were used by a variety of different manufacturers.

The racing version of the 350-cc OHV AA model with the typical short exhaust supports of a production racing machine.

Good for exports: President Walter Davidson poses on a CAC speedway machine together with William H. Davidson (opposite).

A Period of Change

New Rules for Race Competitions

In 1930 the entire motorcycle-racing scene in the U.S. was in a rather pitiable state. Races were getting to be more and more expensive, companies more and more cautious and the riders more and more frustrated. The sport was divided into three main categories:

Hillclimb In this category licensed Class A professionals were permitted to use machines only up to 750 cc. Most organizers of such events preferred to organize outlaw races instead, because the attraction of a good show put on by the public's daredevil favorites was important, as they were the only ones who could draw the enormous number of paying spectators.

Track Racing These competitions were staged either as short or long oval races, popular both as dirttrack and as speedway events and the machines used were mostly single-cylinder specials.

TT Racing Named after the famous Tourist Trophy races held on the Isle of Man, in America these were a combination of motocross and track racing. The rules for this type of sport, for which it was not necessary to build any special arenas, stated that almost all types of motorcycle could be entered, and prescribed at least one jump as well as several turns to the right.

Meanwhile, the United States had been divided into several separate AMA regions. Class B was no longer proving to be such an attraction for spectators, so the 45 and 80 cubic inch F-head engines were reserved exclusively for professional riders.

The management decided to devote more of its efforts to the sport and so hired the most outstanding rider of that time: Joseph "Joe" Petrali, who had ridden for Harley before but who had moved to Excelsior after his great victory in 1925.

He was paid 40 dollars a week. Trusty "Smokey Joe" was unbelievably successful for Harley time and time again. In 1933 Class A, in which only professional works teams participated and Class B, also for professional riders, were eliminated as they could not survive without major financial sponsorship. The time was ripe for AMA Secretary E.C. Smith to introduce a completely new AMA classification system. In 1934 Class C, which was open to all comers, was announced. Regulations now permitted more or less stock road machines to be entered for competitive events. Class C encompassed all racing categories – hillclimb, flat-rack, TT and road races – and was probably the main reason why motorcycle racing as a sport under the control of the AMA was able to survive at all. However, both Harley and Indian frequently circumvented the stock Class C regulations and would enter machines which had been specially tuned. The AMA took no notice whatsoever and feelings about this quite often ran high.

It was during this period that the Sifton affair occurred. The talented Californian racing engine tuner and technician Tom Sifton invented a special oil supply system for the Harley 45 side-valve racing engine and immediately incurred the displeasure of the Harley-Davidson racing division, which was trying to build its own racing machine under the leadership of Bill Ottaway. Attempts to discover the secret behind Tom Sifton's conspicuous success were fruitless. He did not reveal it and as a consequence lost his Harley franchise in San Jose.

There are other equally bizarre episodes connected with the politics of motorcycle racing. For reasons not explained in any detail, the AMA suddenly permitted the use in races of the 500 cc OHV single-cylinder engines as well as 750 cc side-valve twins, provided that their compression ratio was no higher than 7:1. For Harley this was a reluctant concession to riders of single-cylinder English machines which were competing more and more frequently and which were mostly superior to the awkward twin-cylinder side-valve machines. There was only one problem: the singles ran at a higher compression. This rule relating to compression, which was later suitably rectified, was the cause of bitter disputes in the AMA governing council.

In 1933 Harley-Davidson concentrated major development efforts on the Class A flat-track races and produced a new OHV single-cylinder 500 cc

machine – the CAC – which was a successful copy of the JAP and had been developed by Joe Petrali, amongst others, to challenge the well-nigh unbeatable JAP and Rudge speedway machines. They were successful mainly in Australia, South Africa and England.

Public relations were, by contrast, less successful. It was probably because they were thinking of the competition that the AMA, which was more or less in the grip of Harley, had failed to inform the press adequately about what was going on in racing. Consequently it was mostly only accidents that made the headlines, whereas the races themselves were reduced more and more to events of purely local interest.

Nevertheless, new crowd-pulling events were still staged. In 1935 the first 200 mile National long-distance race on a fast circular track was held at Camp Foster, close to Jacksonville, Florida – the first long-distance track event since 1920. It was at the same time a good opportunity to test the capabilities of the Class C street machines. It is worth noting that the official referee of this spectacular race was none other than Joe Petrali and that "Canonball" Baker was the judge. After the race the Harley President, Walter Davidson, became extremely irritated about the participation of the new Norton International and demanded that it should be excluded forthwith from Class C. But Norton had taken care to obey every one of the regulations to the letter and, under the direction of the head of Indian, James Wright, Walter Davidson was finally outvoted. This overreaction cast Harley in a bad light. Whether or not what happened next was revenge is not clear. In the fall of 1936 Harley persuaded the AMA that

the old – and indeed very popular and highly tuned – F-head J models should no longer be licensed for hillclimb races. After all, Harley wanted to sell their new VL, UL and 6l E machines and watch them win in Class B. Some older two-cam riders, such as Hap Jones and Fred Toscani, who swore by their JH machines and also had a vast store of spares as well, switched to Indian out of sheer annoyance. As well as the successful F-head Harley racers, another victim of the new regulations was the equally successful Super X motorcycle: its valve system and rear brakes were no longer acceptable.

The W Series Side-Valve Racers

Competitors Once Again

The 45 cubic inch Side-valve Racing Motorcycles: From 1927 to 1951

WLDR – Originally intended as a street machine which could be raced in open Class C, using a tuned engine which developed about seven horsepower more than the standard model WLD.

WLDD – An improved model that turned the WLDR into a pure racing machine by means of a 109 dollar conversion kit consisting of cylinders, heads, cam, valve lifters and air intake.

WR – Standard Production Racer. A particularly powerful magneto, vertically mounted ("three-cylinder Harley"), initially by Edison-Splitdorf, and from 1947 by Wico. Separate fuel and oil tanks. The WR's engine included larger, polished inlet ports, altered combustion chambers (a system partly adopted from Tom Sifton), and stronger valve springs. The WRs were supplied with either 18- or 19-inch wheels and 3.25- or 4.0-inch tires. In its flat-track version the racer was supplied with a strengthened chrome-molybdenum steel frame and was without brakes.

WRTT – A special version for road and TT racing. The WRTT did not have an electric light system. It had cut-down fenders, the standard WL frame, and clutch and brake pedals.

A rather fantastically designed WLDR flat-track racing machine from 1939 (above right) and a WR from 1938 (below).

Courtesy of: Otis Chandler/Vintage Museum of Transporation, Oxnard, California

Courtesy of: Symbolic Cars, La Jolla, California

When the AMA introduced Class C in 1933 – a class which was open to all amateurs, and in which both 500 cc OHV single-cylinder machines and also 750 cc side-valve twins were permitted – Harley-Davidson had at first to rely on the high-compression DL and DLD sports versions of the 45 cubic inch (750 cc) D series. Slimmed-down and tuned versions of these machines were employed in all types of racing: hillclimb, flat-track, TT, road, and track.

To compete with the successful arch-rival machine from Indian, the 750 cc Super Scout, William Harley wanted to produce a 750 cc V-Twin, but Walter Davidson considered the development and production costs to be too high, and the project was soon shelved. However, a few special machines such as the 750 cc OHV factory DAH hillclimber were built in the late-1920s, though Indian also produced similar machines.

In 1937 the new W Series of 750 cc side-valve motorbikes appeared, and the WLDR soon became the most popular of all racing motorcycles, winning the second Daytona 200 mile race in 1938, and many other races besides.

By now Class C had become the most important class in motorcycle racing. To comply with the regulations, machines also had to be suitable for street use, and Harley-Davidson made sure the WLDR was. It was given a higher compression ratio, larger valves, and aluminum cylinder heads with enlarged inlet ports. For racing purposes you just had to remove the lights, the fenders, the brakes and other superfluous "civilian" accessories.

One of the most famous tuners of the WL models was the Harley dealer Tom Sifton from San José, whose protegé Sam Arena was to win countless races. Later on Harley adopted for its own production racers many of the tuning ideas developed by Tom Sifton.

In 1942 the Harley-Davidson Racing Department, under the leadership of Hank Syvertson, developed a new production racer: the WR, marketed as the "standard 45 cubic inch racer." This was not too soon, as the Indian Sport Scout was still winning more races than any other motorcycle, especially with champion rider Ed Kretz in the saddle.

During this period the season's inaugural event, the Daytona 200, a race half on sand and half on a paved road running parallel to the beach, became ever more important, and it was here that the WR scored the first victories in what was to become a run of success lasting for many years.

Harley–Davidson Race Models

A Chronology of Harley–Davidson Racing Models up to 1972

1914 – The first racing models were offered. The identification numbers of the race engines begin with the letter M.

1915 – Eight racing models (type K) are listed: two, 35 cubic inch (500 cc), single-cylinder, track racer and roadster machines, and six, IOE, F-head V-Twins. A few hundred of these are produced. The roadster types (with a "fast engine") are available both with magneto ignition and battery ignition, and electrical system.

1916 – Harley presents its four-valve, single-cylinder, OHV machine at a price of 1,400 dollars; and an OHV, eight-valve, V-Twin at a price of 1,500 dollars. The AMA's race regulations require the machines to be available to anyone, but the high price ensures that Harley will retain control of the few machines produced.

1917 – For the tuned "fast engines" (engine nos. 500–999), new reworked cylinders and intake ports, sealed intake valves, improved valves, valve guides and springs, and pushrod guides are all standard, along with a number of other details.

1919 – For the V-Twin racing machine a two-cam timing gear is introduced and retained until 1929.

1921 – The V-Twin IOE racing engine is given the reference letter E.

1922 – The 74 cubic inch, (1200 cc) DCA engine is fitted with aluminum pistons and a lighter, connecting rod.

1923 – The two-cam, racing machine engines receive a new, peanut-shaped, timing case cover.

1924 – The two-cam, racing machine engines are further improved.

1928 – Four single-cylinder OHV 350 cc racing motorcycles are added to the range: the S Racer with magneto ignition, the SA Special racer (also magneto ignition), the SM racer (with transmission and magneto ignition), and the SMA (ditto). Additionally, there are several V-Twin, IOE big twins: the T-racer with magneto ignition and the 61 cubic inch (1000 cc) FHAD with magneto ignition in the U.S. version; and the FHAC as the export model. For special races and hillclimbing events, special engines with a high compression ratio of 10:1 and cylinder heads with Ricardo patented combustion chambers are used.

1932 – The DAC 750 cc OHV model is the most popular, hillclimb machine.

1935 – The introduction of the AMA Class C and the associated transition from professional to amateur racing, the racing version of the RLDR, 750 cc, side-valve V-Twin becomes the most popular Harley-Davidson all-around racing machine.

1938 – The new 750 cc, 27 horsepower side-valve WLDR model replaces the previous DR model and becomes the new standard racing machine of its time. The engine is given a higher compression ratio and larger valves.

1939 – After Harley adopts numerous refinements introduced by Tom Sifton's tuning shop, the WLDR is fitted with aluminum heads and larger intake ports, stronger crank pins, more rigid valve springs, better cams and a larger diameter carburetor. The combined effect of these changes is to increase the engine's output to 35 horsepower.

1941 – Production of the WLDR is discontinued. The WR Special 45 cubic inch (750 cc) takes its place as the Class C standard model. The WR variant is used for long-distance racing, and the WRTT for mountain and street races. The WR is Harley's most successful production racer of the postwar era.

1953 – The WR racer is replaced by the completely redesigned K models. The DR racer and the KRTT track racer are the racing versions of the side-valve, 45 cubic inch (750 cc) engine, equipped with magneto ignition, integral transmission, increased compression, and significantly more horsepower. A year later comes the KHRM racer, with its cubic capacity bored out to 55 cubic inches (883 cc).

1955 – Harley offers a range of five K racing models: the 883 cc, KHK Super Sport Solo, the 883 cc KHRM for scrambling and enduro events, the 883 cc KHRTT Tourist Trophy racer, the 750 cc KR track racer, and the 750 cc KRTT, a smaller Tourist Trophy racer.

1958 – The new Sportster Type X 55 cubic inch (883 cc) Tourist OHV version of the KRTT is introduced.

1970 – The new XR 750 OHV racer, which was based on the Sportster model, replaces the side-valve K models.

1972 – An all new XR 2750 OHV racer is introduced featuring an alloy engine. It is still the dominant dirt track racer today.

The 350 cc OHV production racer, Model G from 1926.

Single-cylinder racing model S for quarter-and-half-mile circuits from 1922. The intake-over-exhaust cylinder is the front half of a V-Twin motor, the rear opening simply having been closed. The air-filter could be closed for better starting and the keystone frame is identical to that of the two-cylinder racing model.

Who, What, When?

Harley's International Racing Successes

A winner for Harley: Mr. Takashima from Hiroshima, Japan (above).

The Harley–Davidson racing team of the 1930s, seen here in Italy (right).

An unknown, but happy, Harley-Davidson winner in prewar Germany (below).

The Harley-Davidson corporate magazine *The Enthusiast* is an inexhaustible source for tracing the venues of competitive duels between Harley3-Davidsons and other motorcycles worldwide. Since 1916, the journal has reported on every sporting event of relevance to the Milwaukee machines.

Indeed, since the earliest days of motorcycle racing, the name Harley-Davidson has cropped up time and again in old editions of motorcycle magazines from all around the world, marking important races in numerous cities, countries, and continents, and, above all, immortalizing the names of motorcycle riders that can be regarded as true Harley pioneers. In the modern motorcycle racing era of the 1990s, Harley is represented on virtually every circuit in the world. But what about in the past? Here are some examples of Harley-Davidson's pre-World War II successes:

Australia – Harley-Davidson rode to success down-under in 1929: C.H. Datson, E. Dennison, H.K. Knight. and W.A. Thomas won the 5-mile handicap races in Queensland and Clifford.

Austria – Rupert Kramer from Vienna was one of Austria's most successful riders atop a Harley in the 1920s.

Brazil – Domingos Lopez won the motorcycle–sidecar combination championship in 1920 at a new record speed of 80.77 mph.

England – In 1921, Douglas Davidson set a new record on the Brooklands race track with a speed of 100.76 mph.
Freddie Dixon won the 1000 cc championship in 1923 on an eight-valve Harley.

France – Lucien Vulliamy won the French championship in 1923 in the tourist

category of the 1000 cc motorcycle-sidecar combination class *The Enthusiast*.

Robert Tinoco won the 24-hour Bol d'Or race at Montlhéry in 1938 on an overhead-valve 61 inch model.

Germany – On his 750 cc Harley, Paul Weyres (Aachen) reaped numerous victories in both the solo and sidecar combination classes, including the Siebengebirge Golden Wreath in 1926, the Opel Circuit Prize in 1928, the German sidecar championship in 1930, and the Hannover-Eilenriede in 1932. He also came in second place in 1937 in the final of the German sidecar combination championship at Hockenheim in the class up to 1000 cc. In the year 1931, Weyres was already the four-time German champion in the category of up to 1000 cc. He received his international racing license from the German Motor Racing Union

(*Deutsche Motorsport Gemeinschaft/DMS*), which changed its name to the Supreme Motorsport Authority (*Oberste Motorsport Behoerde/OMB*) in 1928. Other successes for Harley-Davidson in Germany were achieved by P. Ruettchen from Erkelenz (first place at the Nuerburgring circuit in 1931), Peter Visé from Aachen (1927 European Grand Prix), Robby Jecker Jr. (Aachen), and Harley riders Mahlenbrey (Stuttgart), Stolberg (Hannover), Köhler, and Franz Heck (Berlin) (*Motor Und Sport*).

Italy – In 1925, Orlandi and Gantarini also reaped success on their Harleys. During the 1930s, a Harley racing team was formed in Italy comprising motorcyclists called Faraglia, Malvisi, Rogai, Ruggeri, Visioli and Winkler.

The Netherlands – Hans Herkuleijns achieved racing success with his Harley-Davidson motorcycle-sidecar combination in the late-1920s.

Russia – In 1916, Makovsky (Leningrad) set the all-Russian speed record of 68.35

mph in the class up to 750 cc on his Harley-Davidson. In 1924, Dimitriev (Moscow) won the first U.S.S.R. championship in the over-1000 cc class on his Harley. Zakresky set a new record of 106.88 mph in 1936 on a 1000 cc Harley (MOTO).

Scandinavia – In 1930, Olle Virgin won the Sweden/Denmark Dirt Track Series at a record speed of 111.75 mph on a 45 cubic inch OHV model.

Switzerland – Claude Ceresole became Swiss champion in the 1000 cc class in 1924, 1925, 1927 and 1929, initially riding an eight-valve racer before changing to the IOE Two-Cam.

Weyres and Stoll won the sidecar combination class of the Swiss Grand Prix of 1934 on Harley-Davidson motorcycles. In the year 1935, Borsetti rode to victory at the Solo Grand Prix on a Harley-Davidson motorcycle. Carmine and Laeser, riders from Switzerland, also rode Harley-Davidsons in the sidecar combination class.

Paul Weyres from Aachen, Germany secured innumerable German victories on his Harley-Davidson combination (above).

The Swiss Harley-Davidson rider Claude Cereole taking part in a hillclimb competition (left).

Flat Track

Start of the well-known 200 mile street run on the two-mile circuit at Marion, Indiana in 1920. Owing to the high compression, the racing machines were pushed on their way by helpers.

John Harley congratulates the famous motorcycle policeman "Babe" Tancrede, who won the 1941 Number One Plate as short-track champion. Here they are celebrating a flat-track meeting of the same year in Laconia.

Racing on oval tracks has a long tradition in the U.S., stretching back to the early years of the 20th century, when motorbike racing was in its infancy. Along with the endurance and hillclimbing events held in the open, track races on wooden boardtracks also enjoyed great popularity. These were gripping contests; collisions and fallers were the order of the day, and the stadium atmosphere generated its own excitement. Spectators could always see exactly what was happening throughout the whole race. The primeval V-Twin engines of Harley, Indian, and many other (long-lost) marques were housed in chassis which still very much resembled bicycles. Narrow tires and no brakes.

But in time, building and maintaining such tracks eventually proved too expensive, so, in the 1920s, resourceful Americans began to switch to alternative surfaces. Around the country there were numerous horseracing courses, and they were now monopolized by the race organizers (often local, motorcycle dealers). Racing counterclockwise to the left and sliding all the way, that's how it was in the early days of dirt track racing. Races were held in very primitive conditions and with varying regulations, or none at all.

Many riders arrived on the bike they were to race, hoping that everything would remain intact. Afterwards they would disappear with, at best, 20 dollars prize money and a new tire. "A hard and dangerous job," as Harley and Indian veteran Freddie Ludlow often remarked somberly: "In those days it was often so dusty that all you could do was follow the blue exhaust smoke of the man in front. After one race we found a poor fellow who had flown way over the fence and broken his neck. Even the spectators hadn't noticed this accident." Many races simply lasted until the local champion was finally in the lead.

A notable year for Harley-Davidson was 1935 when Joe Petrali, on the single-cylinder Peashooter, won all 13 races in his class, a unique record. There were races of diverse distances, in different classes, on tracks of various length: the half-mile oval and the mile. Sometimes the surface would be soft and sandy, other times very hard, as at the old Ascot miler in Los Angeles, where top speeds were almost as fast as on asphalt. There were also the so-called TT steeplechases, an adaptation of dirt track racing, similar to motocross, with bends and small jumps. Generally, the same bikes were used as on the track, but with the front brake disconnected.

In 1946 the American Motorcycle Association (AMA) began to award a national championship title: the coveted 'Number One Plate'. The champion was decided in a single race, the Springfield Mile in Illinois. This became pretty much the high point of the season, and in good years over 30,000 spectators assembled to admire their heroes. By 1953 six wins had been achieved by various Harley-Davidson riders at Springfield.

1954 signaled the start of what could be termed modern times in motorcycle racing. The AMA introduced a points system similar to the one used for Grand Prix racing, which compelled the riders to contest all the races counting towards the Grand National Championship. Of the five milers, six half-milers, five road races and two TT races, Harley rider Joe Leonard had to win eight races in order to secure the number one position.

Later, a fifth discipline was introduced, short track, on quarter-mile courses. Leonard certainly had a good machine under him: the side-valve KR model introduced just two years earlier was now seen to have matured. "Smokey Joe" was successful for another two years (1956 and 1957) before he switched to motorcar racing — he also collected national titles in that discipline. In the following years this series, not least because of its varied requirements, brought many excellent riders into prominence. And usually the Company's factory riders were at the forefront. Carroll Resweber won the Number One Plate from 1958 to 1961, four times in succession, a record which was not equaled until 30 years later. Between 1962 and 1972 Bart Markel (three times), Roger Reiman, Mert Lawwill and Mark Brelsford won the title.

Opponents in the drift, but good friends privately: the racing rider and later Harley dealer Robbie Robertson, his typical riding style here seen in action in the 1960s (left) and "Smokey" Joe Leonard (below).

Right from the start, the company magazine *The Enthusiast*, which since first appearing in 1916, has been a faithful recorder of all Harley activities, wanted to report as many sporting successes as possible. So, in the 20th edition in 1919, the countless American victories took up over 23 pages. Masses of victories and records from all over the world were squeezed in between:

Australia

Kalamunda – H.M. Smith wins the Lesmurdi Hillclimb in a new best time.

New South Wales – In the Newcastle Economy Test Run, Billy Thomas takes first place in the solo class on a Harley single, with a fuel consumption of 139.13 miles per gallon.

Perth – H.M. Smith wins the most points in the reliability competition.

Canada

Orilla, Ontario – Three out of six races are won by Harleys.

Denmark

Copenhagen – Walter Schmidt wins the solo race on a Harley. The sidecar class is won by F. Mortland, also riding a Harley.

Germany

Koblenz – Harley-Davidson takes first and second place in the solo class, and second place in the combination race.

Japan

Narua – Nageta Seigiro wins the 25 mile, and 50 mile races on a Harley-Davidson.

South Africa

Durban – Bobby Blackburn wins the 15 mile championship. The 10 mile handicap, heavyweight race also goes to Harley, and the 5 mile race against an aircraft!

Johannesburg – In the Johannesburg-Durban marathon, Bobbie Blackburn is victorous, achieving a record time on a 1917 stock Harley-Davidson.

Spain

Madrid – 28 riders take part in the 12 hour race at the Quadrama course – 11 Harleys finish.

Uruguay

Montevideo – Villaveiran wins the open sidecar race on a Harley-Davidson.

In the early 1970s American motorcycle racing was at a high point. In some seasons the AMA registered over 2,000 licensees, and with the modified XR 750 Harley-Davidson had absolutely the best machine for the track. The XR 750 had a short-stroke, V-Twin engine with two valves per cylinder; weighed 330 pounds; power, depending on the degree of tuning (according to the track length), 70 to 90 bhp. On the long straights of a mile oval (at least 500 yards), that was sufficient to produce top speeds of over 125 mph. A disc brake on the rear wheel had also become established as the last resort in case of an emergency.

The top riders were able to make dirt track racing profitable. From 1974 over a period of ten years, the tobacco company R.J. Reynolds pumped large amounts of sponsorship money into the series. The Grand National Championship therefore became simply the Camel or Winston Pro Series, named after the cigarette brand names.

As conventional as dirttrack machines appear to be, tuning them perfectly requires great knowledge and experience. This starts with the engine, and encompasses selection of tires and the transmission ratio. The motor tuner has a vital role, since the Harley riders all use the same basic material. One of the best at his craft is the Harley specialist Bill Werner, who has been in the job for more than 20 years. In July 1995, at the Oklahoma City Half Mile, he achieved a unique milestone: the hundredth victory by one of his riders!

But what is the use of having the best tuner if the rider cannot turn all his hard work into success? One rider who succeeded spectacularly was, and is, Jay Springsteen – a living legend and surely the most popular race rider the U.S. has ever known. "Springer" first stepped into the limelight in 1975, immediately finishing third in the championship and winning the "Rookie of the Year" award.

As HD factory rider he reigned supreme for the next three years, winning three successive championships, and looking likely to match Resweber until he was struck down by a lengthy stomach disorder. After that, the ever modest and down-to-earth, fair-haired

Springsteen was still successful, but could not compete again for the number one spot. So his comeback, in 1995, was quite amazing – Jay, now 38 years old, won the Pomona half-miler, to end a ten year dry spell with a real bolt from the blue!

The state of Michigan seems to be a special breeding ground for Harley dirttrack riders. Like his famous compatriots Bart Markel and Jay Springsteen, daredevil Scott Parker, from Flint (Michigan), matured from his early years into a series winner and is now regarded as the most successful racer of all time. In 1992 he just missed to on a fifth title in succession after four Number One Plates.

But Scotty and tuner Bill Werner can still do it, as they were victorious in 1994, 1995 and 1996, even against pretty good opposition. In 1995 were there as many as 11 different winners in the 19 races.

As regards the current situation, road races have for a long time been separated from the Grand National, and only a few TTs and short-tracks now remain in the program for the "experts." So in 1993 the AMA, with the support of the company, introduced an inexpensive marque cup for slightly modified 883 Sportster machines, aimed at old gentlemen like Springsteen and part-time racers who shy away from excessive technical expenditure. This was called the Pro National Dirt Track Series; in its first year it comprised 11 races.

It's Not Whether You Win or Lose...

Offroad and Enduro

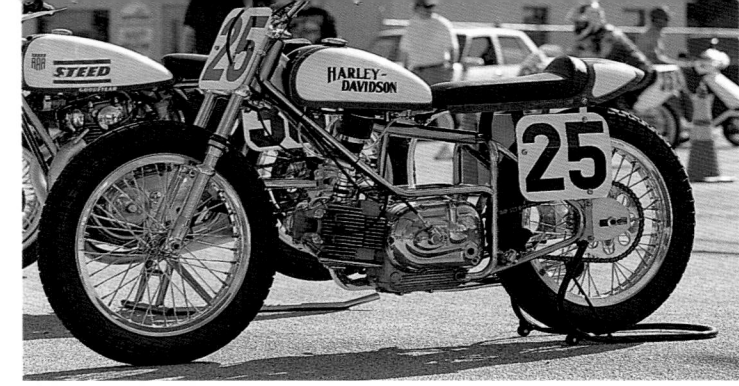

Courtesy of: Dale Walkster/Wheels Through Time Museum, Mount Vernon, Illinois

Offroad on a Harley V–Twin? By today's enduro and motocross standards, not a good idea! But in earlier times there just weren't any lightweight offroad bikes, the heavy iron machines went plowing down the tracks, and the terrain was just as evil. As early as 1908 no less a man than Walter Davidson himself stormed to victory in a Federation of American Motorcyclists endurance run. The trails, heavy offroad courses on which most of the race was run, were very tough and demanded everything from both man and machine.

At the beginning of the 1920s the Jack Pine Endurance Run, America's oldest and hardest, endurance race for motorcycles, was inaugurated. A total of 500 miles had to be covered in two days, and the course in northern Michigan included every conceivable type of terrain, including railroad lines and hazardous wooden bridges.

In its heyday (in the mid–1950s), up to 400 riders on more than two dozen different marques arrived from all over North America. In those days there were no proper spring dampers, offroad modifications were limited mainly to fitting knobbly tires and wide handlebars ... In three different solo, and two combination classes, the hunt was on for victory and placings; the winner received a magnificent cup and the rider with most points overall won the coveted Jack Pine cowbell.

Over the years Harley riders were tremendously successful, outstandingly so in the early years of the legendary Oscar Lenz, who won the trophy seven times between 1923 and 1936. In 1930 a certain William

H. Davidson entered the winners' lists, and this was also the first time that a successful Harley rider did not come from the state of Michigan. Many Jack Pines were so hard that only a handful of riders completed the course. In 1940, for example, only seven of the 51 starters actually made it to the finishing line. Of these seven, five were on Harley–Davidson machines – if that wasn't a proof of quality...

After the small Aermacchi models bearing the Harley logo appeared on the market in the 1960s as offroad scramblers, there was a movement away from the heavy V–Twins, even in the U.S. offroad scene. So–called desert races, the precursors of current world–famous battles in the sand such as the Paris–Dakar or the Atlas Rally, quickly became very popular. In the Mexican 1000 (first run in 1967), exactly 832 miles had to be covered, from the Mexican peninsula of Ensenada to La Paz.

Anything and everything with wheels was at the start, and the best of the motorcycle teams, with two riders in each team, completed the course in less than 24 hours. In 1971, Terry Clark and Dean Goldsmith, on a two–stroke Harley Baja 21, battled through sand, dust, and scree to win their class in a time of 21 hours, 9 minutes, and 47 seconds.

A CR track racer from 1969 (top right), and at the international rally in the "Great American Race," an apparently civilian side–valve Big Twin equipped with an experimental Harley motor (above and right).

Courtesy of: Dale Walkster/Wheels Through Time Museum, Mount Vernon, Illinois

Racing Machines from Varese

The Variety of Aermacchi

Here are a range of Aermacchi's motorcycles listed which date from AMF Harley-Davidson Era:

1966–1974 — The CRTT 350 was developed from the Ala D'Oro as a bored-out version of the Sprint, the CRTT 250, sold in the U.S. as the 350 SS or the CRS, was one of the fastest OHV single-cylinder motorcycles in production at that time. Renzo Pasolini rode it to third place in the 1966 world championship.

1971 — The RR 250, a two-stroke twin street racer, had a short-stroke, vertical twin engine with a bore of 2.21 inches (56 mm) and a stroke of 1.96 inches (50 mm), a six-speed gearbox, and a power output of 50 horse-power at 10,000 rpm. After conversion to water cooling the power output was improved to 58 horsepower. Walter Villa rode this motorcycle in the 250 cc world championships in 1974, 1975 and 1976, and in 1976 also won the 350 cc world title with a larger version of the same machine. Gary Scott and the Trev Deely team enjoyed championship success in the U.S. with this motorcycle.

1975 — A liquid-cooled two-stroke twin equipped with a 34 mm Dell'Orto carburetor also enjoyed success in the 500 cc class. This machine, running at a compression ratio of 12:1, was only produced in very small numbers (a total of just 25 machines) and was later brought into conformity with U.S. racing regulations. Its first rider was Jack Findlay.

1977–1978 — The 250 cc MX motocross motorcycle was developed from the 250 cc SX by the addition of a more powerful engine. A total of around 100 of these were produced.

1977 — In collaboration with BIMOTA, Aermacchi Harley-Davidson developed a new Grand Prix motorcycle with a piston- (later rotary disk valve-) controlled three-cylinder, two-stroke engine developing 76 horsepower at 12,000 rpm, some 10 horsepower more than Walter Villa's 1976 world championship machine. One characteristic feature was the differing dimensions of the three cylinders: the two outer ones were 125 cc each, while the inner cylinder was just 100 cc in displacement.

The 250 cc CRTT Ala D'Oro with her typical racing clothing (above) and the 250 cc Factory Racer RR from 1975 (bottom left).

All photos on this page are courtesy of: Otis Chandler/Vintage Museum of Transportation, Oxnard, California

Victories Given Away in Europe:
Pasolini, Villa, and the Aermacchi Team

Racing successes are gladly exploited as pegs on which to hang sales promotions, but in the 1970s the old recipe took on new dimensions. However, the question of just how much the many victories in faraway Europe under a foreign, unknown racing team, influenced American buyers and encouraged the sale of Aermacchi-Harleys, must be left unanswered.

But Harley had to do something to counter their Japanese competitors who were becoming ever more dominant, even on the racing scene. In 1971, at the request of Harley-Davidson, William Soncini, an engineer working at Aermacchi, developed a new racing twin with the main aim of competing with the fast Yamaha two-strokes in the 250 cc class.

This production racer, which was also used, bored out by 10 mm, in the 350 cc class, had the best components available at that time: Danzi ignition, twin Dell'Orto 30 carburetors, a Bimota chrome-molybdenum frame, Ceriani forks, a double drum brake at the front, a Fontana unit at the rear, and later a thermosyphon cooling system for the engine. In addition the bike was light and very stable — in short, the machine had every chance of success with a talented rider on board. In 1972 the only Aermacchi factory rider, Renzo Pasolini, won in Spain, Yugoslavia and at home in Italy, but he was unfortunately then killed in a pileup at Monza in 1973.

In 1974 Walter Villa was engaged as the Aermacchi Harley-Davidson factory rider for the newly created racing team Harley Italia. In addition to the production racer types RR 250 and RR 350,

from 1975 a second two-stroke machine was ready for the top class of the Grand Prix series: it was a 350 cc, two-stroke twin, which was remarkable for its four mighty Mikuni 34 carburetors. But Harley could not provide sufficient sponsorship to keep this racer at the top. Walter Villa got his revenge by winning a total of four world championships in the 250 and 350 classes. In all, Aermacchi-Harley-Davidson (from 1974 operating as AMF Harley-Davidson) amassed 28 Grand Prix victories, but with little effect on sales. The dealers, who in general had to sell a rather different range of motorcycles, kept complaining about unsaleable stocks, poor quality and an increasingly disinterested public. At the high point of its racing success, AMF broke up its Harley Italia racing stable in 1977, and a year later Aermacchi was sold.

Road-Racing

The European Tradition Conquers America

Harley's new racing machine, the VR 1000 at the 1997 Daytona Race (right).

Racing legend Roger Reimann with his father, one day before his fatal accident at Daytona's 1997 Battle of the Legends race (below).

Although the first competitions were fought out on the narrow, country roads of the Isle of Man in 1907, road racing in accordance with the classical European model was not introduced into the U.S. until comparatively late – the Americans were and still are too infatuated with their oval, nicely open, flat tracks. The first Daytona 200-mile race took place in 1937 on a three-and-a-quarter mile track, laid out more or less on the beach, where up to 70 riders were sent off on their journey at five-second intervals. Indian rider Ed Kretz won the first race at an excellent average speed of 72.7 mph. Although run on a sandy course, the 200-mile classic goes down in the annals, even now, as a road race.

In 1961 the race moved to the recently completed Daytona International Speedway, but first, as stipulated by the AMA, the riders had to declare themselves satisfied with the two-mile short course in the infield. It was not until three years later that they were finally allowed to emulate the cars and race on the famous, or infamous, steep banking. The most successful Daytona 200 competitor in this era was Roger Reiman, from Kewanee, Illinois, who won in 1961, 1964, and 1965 on the Harley KR 750 side-valve machine.

Reiman, who had the strongest possible support from his father Hank, and not only from a technical viewpoint, wanted to make it a three-in-a-row hat trick in 1966. At that time no one had ever won Daytona four times, but it was not to be. Victory was claimed by Buddy Elmore on his 500 cc Triumph twin, at a tremendous average speed of 95.7 mph. It was a tragic irony of fate that, long after finishing his active career, Roger should die during the Daytona Speed Week. In the 1997 BMW Battle of the Legends, a popular event for former U.S. race idols, he crashed and died shortly after arriving at the hospital.

After taking over the Italian company Aermacchi at the beginning of 1960, Harley-Davidson was suddenly represented in the smaller

engine classes. The frail 250 cc four-stroke with the pushrod-controlled, horizontal, single cylinder (model name CRTT 250 Sprint) was just about ideal for first-time racers and was soon enjoying growing popularity. There were already a few asphalt tracks and the AMA even started its own 250 cc championship. In 1963 Harley-Davidson rider Dick Hammer won the Daytona 250 cc race at an average speed of 70.8 mph from Jess Thomas (Honda) and the Ducati rider Jim Hayes.

By the mid-1960s KR side-valve engines outside the special authority of the AMA were no longer competitive at international level (OHV engines were limited to 500 cc both for racing and on the road). One thing which Harley-Davidson had gone along with for a long time was the regulation concerning compression ratio. It took more than two decades to raise the limit from 7.5 to 9:1 – for a side-valve engine the lower figure can physically scarcely be exceeded.

However, racing boss Dick O'Brien and his men did everything in their power to delay the end for KRs. There were new 'Lowboy' frames with 18-inch wheels, modified fairings, extensive engine modifications, with new cylinder heads and twin carburetors. And they were successful: in the 1968 Daytona Reiman reached a top speed of 149 mph. An output of 70 horsepower was not beyond reach.

But victory went elsewhere; road-racing specialist Calvin (Cal) Rayborn had finally propelled himself into the limelight with a brilliant exhibition. On a KR sponsored by the dealer Leonard Andres he lapped all but the second- and third-place riders Yvon Duhamel and Art Baumann (both on 350 cc two-stroke Yamahas), and was the first rider to win the race at an average speed of more than 100 mph. Rayborn, from California's Spring Valley ("hotter than a Florida sun and smoother than Southern Comfort"), first attracted the public's attention by winning a Championship race in Carlsbad two years

A racing scene from the 1997 Daytona BoTT street race, and with the VR 1000 racing team at the starting lineup.

earlier. In the year of his first Daytona success, the former motorbike courier also won three of the four road races in the U.S. Championship, thus confirming his reputation as the top man on tarmac.

In terms of production bikes, the side-valve engine had been forced to give way to the more modern OHV Sportster engine in 1957. With a displacement of 883 cc its power output compared well with the English parallel twins, so it attracted some attention on racetracks on that side of the Atlantic. The Californian Lance Weil came to prominence in England in 1967 riding a specially modified XLR Sportster with Lowboy chassis, and achieved some good results there in the 1000 cc class. To show the crowds exactly what he was riding, Weil dispensed with the usual full fairings and just fitted a thin half-fairing.

At the beginning of the 1970 season AMA changed the rule, and now specified a uniform displacement limit of 750 cc. Harley wasted no time in constructing a new racing engine based on the Sportster. But the XR 750 as it was called, designed by Pieter Zylstra, was anything but the final word, and experienced all sorts of problems with overheating of the cast iron cylinders and cylinder heads — it soon acquired the nickname "Iron Head." But the super-talented Rayborn was at the peak of his career and, when the iron head lasted the course, he was still a match for the best Grand Prix riders as in the Trans-Atlantic Match Race Series at Easter 1972, for example. With six match races counting towards the final result, against high-class opposition, including Phil Read, Ray Pickrell and others, and despite the British having home advantage, Cal scored three wins and three second places. Reason enough to give him a hero's welcome when he returned to the States.

The Racing Department soon reacted to the problems, and a reworked XR 750 with a short-stroke aluminum engine was ready in time for the 1972 season. Increasing the cooling fin surface area solved

1930 – An extremely unusual export model was the 45 cubic inch (750 cc) V-Twin street racer fitted with the OHV engine often used in hillclimb. The tank, saddle, and double-sided racing exhaust are typical features of a European set-up. The worldwide recession of the 1930s put a stop to production.

1930 – Another motorcycle produced in small numbers was the CAF 30, which was the street-racing version of a single-cylinder model chiefly intended for export to Europe.

1947 – The Midget Race Car, fitted with special side-valve V-Twin engines from Harley or Indian, was hugely popular. These midget racers with a 750 cc flathead Harley engine, for use in the Midget Micro 1000 Class, was produced in France.

1965 – This Harley liquid-cooled, twin-cylinder, two-stroke track racer with a

compression ratio of 12.8:1, and developing 53 horsepower at 11,200 rpm, competed successfully against its Japanese rivals. Gary Scott was among the champion riders to use this machine.

1983 – The Harley-Davidson 500 R dirt tracker had a 494 cc Rotax OHV four-valve single-cylinder engine with a bore of 3.5 inches (89 mm) and a stroke of 3.1 inches (79 mm), a Mikuni 38 mm carburetor, a five-speed gearbox and Marzocchi telescopic forks. The whole machine weighed a scant 249 pounds. The frame was built by Ron Woods. Springsteen, Parker and Goss were the most successful men to race this powerful motocross bike, which was also available in a bored-out 600 cc version produced by Chris Carr. The first series of this machine ran to just 25 motorcycles.

1983 – With minimal alteration the XR 1000 could also be used as a racing machine, both by private racers and company teams.

The Harley engine for the Model Midget Micro 1000 has been imported from France

Normally a restricted area: the Harley–Davidson racing team box with the VR 1000 in the Daytona Speedway Stadium in 1997 (above).

the overheating problem, and both the exhaust pipes now exited on the left side, to take advantage of the cooling airstream. But the Milwaukee V-Twin had for a long time faced powerful opposition. The Triumph/BSA triples, the Honda CB 750 and especially the water-cooled, 750 cc, three-cylinder two-strokes of Kawasaki and Suzuki had permanently improved. Rayborn, still wearing his typical half-helmet, did win the races at Indianapolis and Laguna Seca because, with relatively low fuel consumption, he did not have to stop for refueling.

In order to reinforce Harley's racing presence in Europe, and in view of the forthcoming Formula 750 world championships, the Italian star rider Renzo Pasolini got an XR 750 in the middle of the year. Although he had only been used to the Aermacchi 250/350 two-strokes, Renzo adapted well to the big "donna Americana" and, in Ontario (California), came third overall over two 125-mile races. For the spring 1973 meetings at Daytona and Imola, Italy, Pasolini was struck down by an infection. After that he wanted to concentrate on the Grand Prix season, racing against his great rival Jarno Saarinen. All went well until the fourth race in Monza when both died in a horrific crash.

Not a happy year for Harley-Davidson – the XR 750 had hardly made an impact on the road-racing scene before it was consigned to the scrapheap. Cal Rayborn had a run of bad luck with technical problems and injuries, and left the factory team at the end of 1973. Even worse news for all his fans was that Cal, of all people, suffered a fatal accident in his first race on a two-stroke Suzuki 500 in New Zealand in 1973-1974. The company then achieved world championship honors, one might say via the back door. The Aermacchi engineers, along with rider Walter Villa, followed in the footsteps of the great Pasolini, winning successive 250 cc world championships in 1974 to 1976. The

victorious machine was a water-cooled, two-stroke twin which had nothing in common with classic Harley technology, but in large letters on the tank and fairings you could see "AMF Harley-Davidson."

After that Harley withdrew from road racing for a few years to concentrate on the Battle of the Twins. But, at the beginning of the 1990s, all the talk was of a high-class, new, water-cooled, four-valve racing engine. Then in March 1994 it came to fruition: the debut of the "All American Superbike" VR 1000 at Daytona. With the experienced Superbike rider Miguel Duhamel in the saddle, the brand-new machine qualified straight away, although it dropped out of the race with engine trouble after 20 laps.

The small factory team under chief technician Steve Scheibe still had a lot of work to do, and found that the laurels on the National Superbike scene are not easily grasped, to say nothing of the world championship. The VR is a good motorcycle with excellent chassis qualities, but it lacks both engine power and sheer manpower: the Harley budget is not even half of what American Honda, for example, spends each year on Superbike racing. Riders Thomas Wilson and Chris Carr have so far not achieved any notable successes, and in the 1996 U.S. Championship they only finished ninth and twelfth.

At the end of the 1990s the VR 1000 is not currently fulfilling world championship ambitions, nor its originally planned role as a street version. In any case, there are currently no plans to build any more than the small series of 50 machines, which have been sold to private teams and collectors around the world. The Harley-Davidson management now sees racing – not forgetting also the feedback from proud owners – as a means of research and trials for future developments. If, one day, a new Harley Superbike were to emerge, it would probably be under the Buell name.

America versus England and Japan

Daytona 200 – The Opening Race of the Season

In 1937, the venue of the first, major, 200 mile race was changed from Savannah and Jacksonville to the renowned, high-speed course of Daytona Beach. This was in response to an offer made by the city fathers; half the course was on sand, the other half on the paved road running parallel to the beach. The season's opening race was to become an event that measured the relative success of America's last two, remaining, motorcycle marques. However, despite all attempts by the AMA to ward off the relentless wave of foreign competition (ploys such as the "compression rule"), it soon became apparent that the superior single- and twin-cylinder British motorcycles were relentlessly beating the WRs and Scouts to the flag.

In 1953, Harley's new K model managed to break this trend and regain pole position for the company's racers. As of 1961, the 200 mile race was finally moved inland to the NASCAR Speedway Stadium newly built by Bill France Sen. Shortly thereafter, the overwhelming Japanese put an end to the dream of American racing being dominated by American racers. Harley-Davidson finally bade farewell to its racing successes in 1971, and it was very rare indeed for a Harley racer to rank even among the top twenty in the years that followed. This hiatus was finally broken by the XR Sportster models – after some teething trouble – and victory was again secured for Harley, albeit predominantly on dirt tracks, where the XR 750 was considered virtually unbeatable. Today, at the end of the 20th century, the VR 1000 is the machine that is intended to reassert Harley-Davidson's dominance on the oval track.

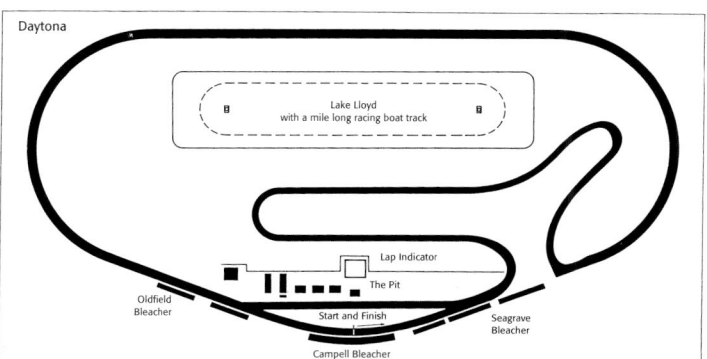

Daytona

The Daytona 200 Races

1937–1960 Speedway on the Beach
1961–1971 Daytona Int. Speedway Stadium

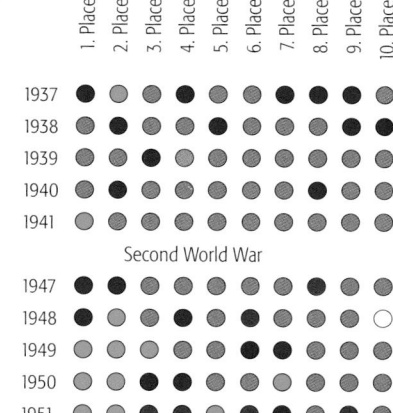

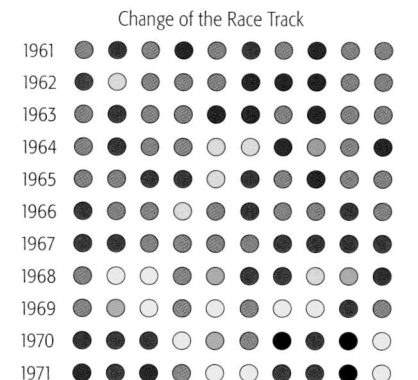

Legend:
- Harley-Davidson
- Ariel
- BSA
- BMW
- Honda
- Indian
- Kawasaki
- Matchless
- Norton
- Suzuki
- Triumph
- Vincent
- Yamaha

Battle of the Twins

Lucifers Hammer on the Track

In 1984: Gene Church on "Lucifer's Hammer."

Towards the end of the 1970s, when the popular U.S. Superbike class was firmly in the hands of the Japanese four-cylinder mob, a new idea took hold of fans of large-capacity two-cylinder engines: "Let's have our own races just for twins. We'll see off these irritating Japanese imports and then we'll be able to compete with our own!" No sooner said than done – Bill France, boss of the Daytona racing circuit, Norton specialist Dwayne Williams, and Harley tuner Jesse O'Brien did most of the administrative groundwork. Much to the displeasure of the AMA, who had no space left in their calendar for an extra class.

In the spring of 1981, right at the start of the new season, competition got under way. The first race of the appropriately named "Battle of the Twins" took place at the Daytona Speed Week. 88 riders showed up, and the list of starters read like a who's who of the most famous names in bike racing. BMW, Ducati, Harley-Davidson, Moto Guzzi, Norton, Laverda, Triumph, Vincent, and the Japanese twins Kawasaki Z 750 and Yamaha XS 650 – everyone was there!

To give a fair chance to all, there were four categories: stock production, modified production (both for first-timers and experienced teams) and Grand Prix; the displacement limit was set at 1000 cc. Victory in the Grand Prix class, in which the most liberal regulations were applied, went to Jimmy Adamo on a Königswellen-Ducati tuned by the Italian-American Reno Leoni. Other race organizers soon came to accept the thunderous twins, so that in the first year an eight-race championship was held. The Leoni/Adamo combination was dominant in the event, and the title went to this team in each of the first three years.

After a rather half-hearted effort in the form of the XLCR Cafe Racer which only sported a few style modifications, in 1983 the company made another attempt to adapt a racing bike into a street machine: this was the phenomenal XR 1000. Just at the time when the Japanese were starting to produce toned-down versions of the chopper, a Harley appeared which could not have been more genuine.

A pure driving machine, with only the most essential accessories, almost as if it had emerged straight from the dirttrack garage. To make this a public relations success, the racing department was asked to construct a racing machine based on this design which would be capable of winning the BoTT series. In just a few months racing boss Dick O'Brien and his team built a Hammer, based on a ten-year-old XR 750 frame and it made a sensational impact on its first outing at Daytona in spring 1983.

With dirttrack star Jay Springsteen in the saddle, the 104 bhp "Lucifer's Hammer" achieved a convincing victory, 24 seconds ahead of the rider in second place. Just a decade after the last factory rider had appeared in a road race in the States (Gary Scott at Laguna Seca in 1974), this represented a wonderful comeback to the track for Harley. "Springer" contested another three races with Lucifer in that season, but then his dirttrack obligations took precedence.

In the season's finale at Daytona the young Gene Church took over the mount for the first time and landed a victory, ahead of two Ducatis – Lucifer's Hammer had struck again!

Then the Harley Owners Group (H.O.G.) took over as sponsors, and Harley dealer Don Tilley together with rider Gene Church, concentrated on technical preparation of the bike. When the two of them were not somewhere around the course, they were working in Don's shop in Statesville, North Carolina. Church came originally from Turnersburg, North Carolina, and began his career on minibikes. Then he

It is 1986 — two beaming Harley victors: Gene Church (center) and Will Roeder (right).

had a try at 250 cc two-strokes and on flat tracks, before he began totally to dominate the American BoTT scene.

In 1984 Gene Church won the championship with three victories and three second places. The year after was even better; the title was won with five victories! In 1986 he suffered his first springtime defeat at Daytona at the hands of the former 500 cc world champion Marco Lucchinelli (Ducati) and Paul Lewis (Quantel Cosworth), but he finished up winning the championship yet again. But the factory would never get rich on the prize money! A victory in a BoTT race earned a Harley rider 1,000 dollars, and winning the championship brought in an extra 4,000 dollars.

In 1984 two Harley engineers with the Spread Eagle Racing Team, Steve Wentworth and Bob Crane, introduced the first Buell engine to the racetrack — the time seemed right to allow Lucifer I to enjoy a well-earned retirement.

The new Don Tilley machine also had a Buell frame, but a few teething problems with Lucifer II had first to be ironed out. Typical of the moderate 1987 season was Gene Church's crash right at the start of the season at Daytona; also new, stronger competitors emerged, such as the four-valve Ducatis and the Dr. John-Guzzi, which swept the board in 1987. 1988 and 1989 were both the high point and the end of technical development of the 1000 cc twin.

Jay Springsteen again had the opportunity of riding a new test bike, but he did not have much luck with it. A very compact ladder-frame chassis, developed for the factory by former dirt-tracker Mert Lawwill, concealed an XR 1000 engine tuned by Don Tilley, developing 111 bhp at the crankshaft. Unlike the Buell frame, and taking the Bimota as a model, a very small space was left between the swingarm bearing and the chain pinion, which had the effect both of countering a short wheelbase (in this case only 53.5 inches), and reducing the influence of the driving forces on the suspension.

However, the actual problem area was not the chassis but the mechanically highly-developed drive train. With an extremely high compression ratio of over 13:1 and a lot of painstaking precision work on the cylinder heads, Tilley finally squeezed an impressive 118 bhp out of Lucifer II at 8000 rpm, but the aging subframe could not keep pace. In addition, certain important assemblies were gradually breaking down; apparently, in 1989, only one five-speed racing gearbox was available.

Be that as it may, with an impressive top speed of 167 mph thanks to its refined aerodynamics, this projectile — when it was running — was one of the fastest twins that had ever had the hallowed Daytona track under its wheels. The chapter entitled "Battle of the Twins" (or Pro Twins, as they became known) was a relatively short one for Harley-Davidson, but all the more glorious for that reason. The future had begun, and the VR 1000 project was gradually taking shape.

The German Harley Cup

The Fine Line between Racing Entertainment and Professional Sports

Racing photographs and start of the short-lived "German Harley Cup," ridden exclusively by slightly modified 883 Sportsters.

In 1989, in oder to revive interest in racing and increase the number of competitors, the AMA, in collaboration with Harley-Davidson initiated a marque cup called the AMA H-D 883 Twin Sports, using basically series production Sportster machines. It went well, a carefully worded technical regulation kept the tuning (and therefore costs) to a reasonable level and made for exciting racing – the equality of the machines in terms of performance meant that riders' abilities were paramount. Racing-mad Harley dealers sponsored talented local lads, and from time to time established stars such as Roger Reiman and Jay Springsteen joined the colorful collection of Cup riders. In short, the concept seemed to work so it soon spread to other countries: England, France, Australia, Japan and finally Germany.

The first running of the German Harley Cup, as it was described for the national B license, took place in 1995 at the Fassberg airfield on Lüneburg Heath. "How can you race with such heaps of iron?" Such comments, from long-time fans, were good-humored and harmless. But they quickly discovered that competition was going well, as did many others. Naturally, with power outputs around 65 horsepower and a starting weight of over 400 pounds, lap records were not expected to be broken regularly, but that didn't seem to bother the riders! On the contrary, according to one of them: "This iron horse wants to be mastered. You're not only competing against the others, but against your own machine as well, and it doesn't forgive any mistakes ..."

The Harley team and their supporters distinct from the rest of the crowd, at least brought new splashes of bright colors to the otherwise rather dull, German racing-circuit scene. Long manes of hair, beards, chains, rings, tattoos, rider vests and particularly the black and orange Harley racing jackets were much loved accessories. All visitors were welcome in the Harley tent, which became a meeting point where live music and snacks satisfied their various appetites, and the hostilities enacted on the course were all forgotten in the evening over a few beers.

One year later, the cards were shuffled again, and even the organizers now formally supported the cup races. The most prominent rider was Michael Stöcker, who had finished 11th in the 883 Twin Sports at Daytona in March, the second-best placed foreigner behind an Australian rider, an achievement which had already brought him to the public's attention. Stöcker finally won the title, ahead of Windhager and Paul Maria Listl, Nevertheless, the bosses at Harley-Davidson Germany then decided to abandon the cup.

Disputes were obviously the result of troubles behind the scenes, with teams accusing one another of prohibited technical modifications (which had led to protests in the first year) and complaining about ineffective controls. Marketing boss Manfred Kozlowsky emphasized that, "our main concern is the events calendar, and the cup has drifted too much into tough race riding," but one can also see the riders' point of view: "This isn't a genteel game we're playing here. When I go racing, I want to win," is a commonly stated attitude. The cost of stricter enforcement of the rules (using a mobile test rig) was beyond the means of the Harley Mörfeld head office. Despite this, Manfred Kozlowsky, press spokesman for Harley Deutschland, did point out that the competition might well start up again, perhaps even using Buell machines, which would be more suitable.

The Sundance Team

One of the Best Racers Was Sent by Japan

Crazy about twins! This certainly applies to the Harley freaks around the Japanese dealer and tuner Takehiko Shibazaki. At his Sundance Custom Works in Tokyo he has the workforce and financial backing needed to assemble fantastic creations based on Harley-Davidson motorcycles. One of these is the racing machine "Daytona Weapon," based on a 1200 Sportster, but which now has very little in common with the original product.

A huge amount of development work has gone into the modified XR 1000 cylinder heads, the side intakes being radically altered. They are now placed at an angle of 45 degrees and are supplied with fuel mixture by two 41 Keihin FCR carburetors. The 1199 cc engine (bore x stroke 88.8 x 96.8 mm) has a compression ratio of 12:1 and provides a good 110 bhp at 6500 rpm. All the engine components have been made lighter or replaced by new ones made from better material, resulting in a better reliability.

Following the example of Buell, the V-Twin is suspended flexibly by rubber mountings and articulated heads in an aluminum frame supplied by the Japanese manufacturer Over. The result: no problems with vibration. The wheelbase is 57 inches, and weighs approx. 364 pounds dry. Wherever the Daytona Weapon appears, it draws admiring glances and rightly so because it is the sharpest Harley racer in the world.

Japanese Technicians Yutaka Teshima and "racer" Yoshiyuki Sugai (far right) photographed at the Daytona 200 Race in 1997.

With carefully honed technology and masterful construction of vehicle and frame, the Japanese firm "Sundance Custom Works" in Tokyo is attempting to lead a promising XR-based Harley competition machine to worldwide success.

One of the most famous racers ever and several times national champion: factory rider Jay Springsteen, shown here at a track race in the 1970s and at the Battle of the Legends in 1997.

The most prominent Harley champion of the 1980s was Scott Parker, shown here with his "Number One" plate at a dirt-track race.

FOR A JOB.... WELL DONE!

Harley-Davidson
The Great American Freedom Machines

Honoring the factory riders from the 1970s: (from left to right) Dick O'Brien, Renzo Pasolini, Mert Lawwill, Dave Sehl, William H. Davidson, John A. Davidson, Cal Rayborn, Scott Brelsford and Mark Brelsford.

In starting position for the 883 Finals, Daytona International Speedway, 1997.

Art Gompper, H.D. Racing Department.

Frantic preparations for the start.

Craig Fillmer, H.D. Racing Team.

Company

The Company Requests the Honor…

Harley-Davidson's Official Activities

On the road across the globe: the famous Harley trucks transport everything the company needs for its presentations.

Once, the market was smaller and tougher and the customer had become more choosy. Times were hard; there was not as much money around as there used to be, and trends change almost from week to week.

It is not enough any more just to manufacture good motorcycles, to protect and patent a legendary name, to be able to point to successes on the race track, or to be enveloped in an aura of mystery. In the long run, nothing sells itself, however good or fashionable it may be.

Of course, there is a highly efficient sales organization, thousands of energetic dealers, excellent advertising, logos and trademarks, hundreds of thousands of faithful H.O.G. members and maybe even a few friendly journalists. But that may not be enough.

What about the sales figures? Well, that's another story, as Harley-Davidson has found out from bitter experience. The worldwide Harley-Davidson phenomenon stands in stark contrast to the production figures, when measured against the motorcycle market as a whole. Buying as a form of investment? That too has also gone down the drain. Nevertheless buyers often have to shell out more for a 30-year-old Harley than for a new one.

What about the immortal and much-loved, large capacity, V-twin engine? One might wonder whether it has long since become out of date, superseded, environmentally unfriendly, a technological dinosaur, and totally outdated. The answer is — far from it. That old dinosaur has proven itself to be very durable.

Unlike other motorcycle manufacturers, Harley-Davidson cannot simply launch brand new concepts, engines, and products onto the market. Harley is unique, and that fact is at one and the same time not only a selling point but also a millstone round its neck. And it also imposes a duty. Irrespective of its popular image, it is significant that the company is seeking contact with the general public more than ever before.

Indeed, one could say that the customer does not so much come to Harley, as Harley reaches out to the customer. This is an important part of the company's new policy, but it is an incredibly expensive and difficult business.

Opposite: A Harley parade in Amsterdam, Netherlands, organized by H.O.G.

Usually the local dealer or H.O.G. chapter organizes the traveling motorbike circus, but sometimes the company also has a direct involvement, as evidenced by the presence of its trademark black, yellow, and red, 48-wheeler trucks (scaled-down versions of which are available as toys) parked in rows outside the headquarters.

Traditionally, Daytona Bike Week is a favorite venue for any Harley fan, and here Harley-Davidson's presence is unmissable at two locations in particular: the giant Ocean Center on Atlantic Avenue and at "Harley Heaven" on the southwest bend of the International Speedway Stadium. The company presents the same program of activities as at other major events, such as the Sturgis Bike Week and various international H.O.G. rallies. Let's take a look at what Harley-Davidson has to offer visitors, friends and customers:

An Exhibition, with some unusual displays, skillfully lit and presented in a nice atmosphere on quality carpeting.

Demo Rides, where anyone with the necessary driver's license can personally test ride the whole Harley-Davidson range.

A **Dresser Light Show**, a nightly parade of Full Dressers — heavily accessorized and flashing bikes.

A **Fashion Show**, where you can check out the latest Harley fashions from MotorClothes in order to find out what Harley men and women will be wearing next season.

Harley Heaven, the legendary meet to view the race-offs of the 200-mile Superbike Classic Races.

The **Harley-Davidson Museum**, a 48 foot long truck packed full of legendary history.

The **Tattoo Contest**, who would have thought that bikers' skin art would ever become an accepted part of the official Harley program. The company has plenty of prize money to offer for the winners of the "Show us your tats" contest!

The **MDA Poker Run**, free to H.O.G. members, while other entrants make a 5 dollar donation for children suffering from Muscular Dystrophy. Naturally there are prizes to win here as well.

Meet the Racers, an autograph session and a chance to meet and touch some legends of bike racing

Annual MDA Auctions, where rare Harley-Davidson souvenirs and motorcycles go on the auction block, with the proceeds going to the Muscular Dystrophy Association.

The **Ride-In Show**, a one or two day long custom bike show on a spacious outdoor site with plenty of different classes represented and excellent prizes to be won.

A **Parade**, held at the Speedway Stadium on Sunday. The mighty parade can sometimes be up to 15 or 20 miles long, and it is an unforgettable experience for all those taking part.

There are **Service Seminars** to demonstrate how to maintain and look after a Harley properly. The big first prize is once again the newest special model (personally signed by Willie G.). The price of a five dollar ticket gives everyone who joins in a chance of winning. Again, proceeds go to the Muscular Dystrophy Association.

There are also **H.O.G. Activities** for members and prospective members, and naturally all the Harley top management are there for everyone to rub shoulders with. Who could possibly resist?

The grand finale of a Harley fashion show at the launch of the 1998 motorcycle range in the Milwaukee Brewery with Willie G. and Nancy, Bill and Karen Davidson.

Endless columns of motorcycles
on the interstate heading
for Sturgis (top).

Ladies have their own Harley style:
Women and Harley (above).

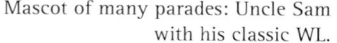

Mascot of many parades: Uncle Sam
with his classic WL.

Night of the Snappy Dressers

Daytona Beach, 8 p.m. Friday evening, and the sultry Florida night has fallen. In Parking Lot North behind the Civic Center the lights go out and darkness shrouds the many thousands of expectant onlookers. There is a drum roll, then blue flashing lights, police sirens — there is a rumbling in the wings, the excitement mounts, and then finally they arrive, to a chorus of "oohs" and "aahs" and generous applause. About 30 multicolored Harley Full Dressers with all their lights flashing make themselves seen, a truly impressive and fascinating display. Now it's plain for all to see what all the countless lamps, lightstrips and outsized lights are used for. The lighting accessories industry celebrates an illuminated triumph, and machines that merely provoked a few smiles by day show their true colors by night, when they become light shows on wheels! By comparison, the concluding firework display is an ephemeral spectacle — it lasts only a few minutes, but the Dressers shine on through the long night.

Early-morning exercises: the gathering begins at 5 a.m. for the parade through Milwaukee for the 95th anniversary of the company.

MDA: Let the World Know About It

Harley–Davidson and the Muscular Dystrophy Association

Jerry's Kids – VIP's in Wheelchairs

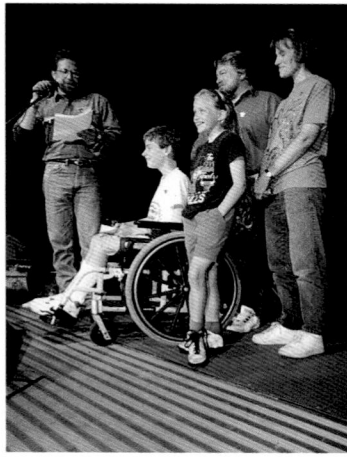

Money helps, but it does not necessarily make you happy. Presence counts more than anything else, so the bikers on their two-wheelers look after the small children in their wheelchairs. In no other country in the world are disabled children paid so much attention and shown so much warmth as in the United States, and Harley riders are in the forefront here. Children suffering from Muscular Dystrophy are the center of attention at all big MDA runs, rallies and parties: the children lead the parades, whether in the luxury limousine of a top guest or in the sidecar of a prominent Harley driver; they are presented on stage like movie stars and spoiled by everyone — unforgettable moments for the kids, whose life may not otherwise be so happy. The bikers give them the incomparable feeling that they do not always have to miss out on the good things in life.

MDA – 'Poster kids' at the grand end-of-celebration show for disabled children during the festivities for the 90th anniversary in Milwaukee. Above, far left: Bill Davidson is the emcee.

Willie G. insists on personally taking one of the MDA kids out for a ride in his sidecar. At the Farrow dealers' party, 1997 (right).

In 1980 Harley-Davidson initiated a charitable partnership as one of 16 corporate sponsors of the Muscular Dystrophy Association (MDA). By doing this, the company became an important fund raiser for children suffering from this terrible disease. The MDA is a private charity which, since the beginning of the 1950s, has been involved not only in fighting and researching the causes of this devastating illness, but also in caring for its victims, especially the younger ones.

The comedic actor Jerry Lewis took over the role of coordinating sponsorship for children suffering from muscular dystrophy in 1976, and since then they have been known as "Jerry's Kids." For Harley-Davidson the "Ride for Jerry's Kids" campaign has been a unique success story. At all major events and H.O.G. rallies, and almost all dealer's parties, collections are made and pledges raised for Jerry's Kids. In 1984, Harley's dealer in Glendale, California, Oliver Shokouh, started his first "Love Ride," and he raised 91,000 dollars in only his second year. Then he was outdone by the Denver dealer Ken Allen, who collected the incredible sum of 108,000 dollars for MDA. In 1991 the seventh Love Ride raised 825,000 dollars, up from 550,000 dollars the year before. In the meantime Oliver Shokouh's brainchild has spread to Switzerland, where the fifth Love Ride was held in 1997.

On the occasion of its 90th anniversary Harley-Davidson was proud to announce that, during its 13-year partnership with the MDA, the company had raised almost 13 million dollars for the organization.

These sober statistics reveal a characteristic element of the biker lifestyle: the desire to assist those in need of help, sick children in particular. This is in harmony with the American tradition which remains as strong today as it was in pioneer times. Instead of demanding or needing a safety net from the state, Americans prefer to offer their own, direct form of help, as an expression of thankfulness for the fact that they are healthy and free, and able to ride motorcycles, of course.

In no way should this, as is often insinuated, be seen as a way of pacifying a guilty conscience for a different lifestyle of boozing and revelry. Whether rich or poor, to be a biker in America involves a responsibility to help the disabled and needy, especially children, and the MDA is a worthy candidate. The idea has now taken hold all around the world.

Pledges for Sturgis Bike Week 1997 at Harley headquarters in Rapid City (above).

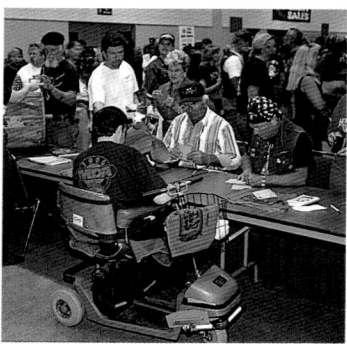

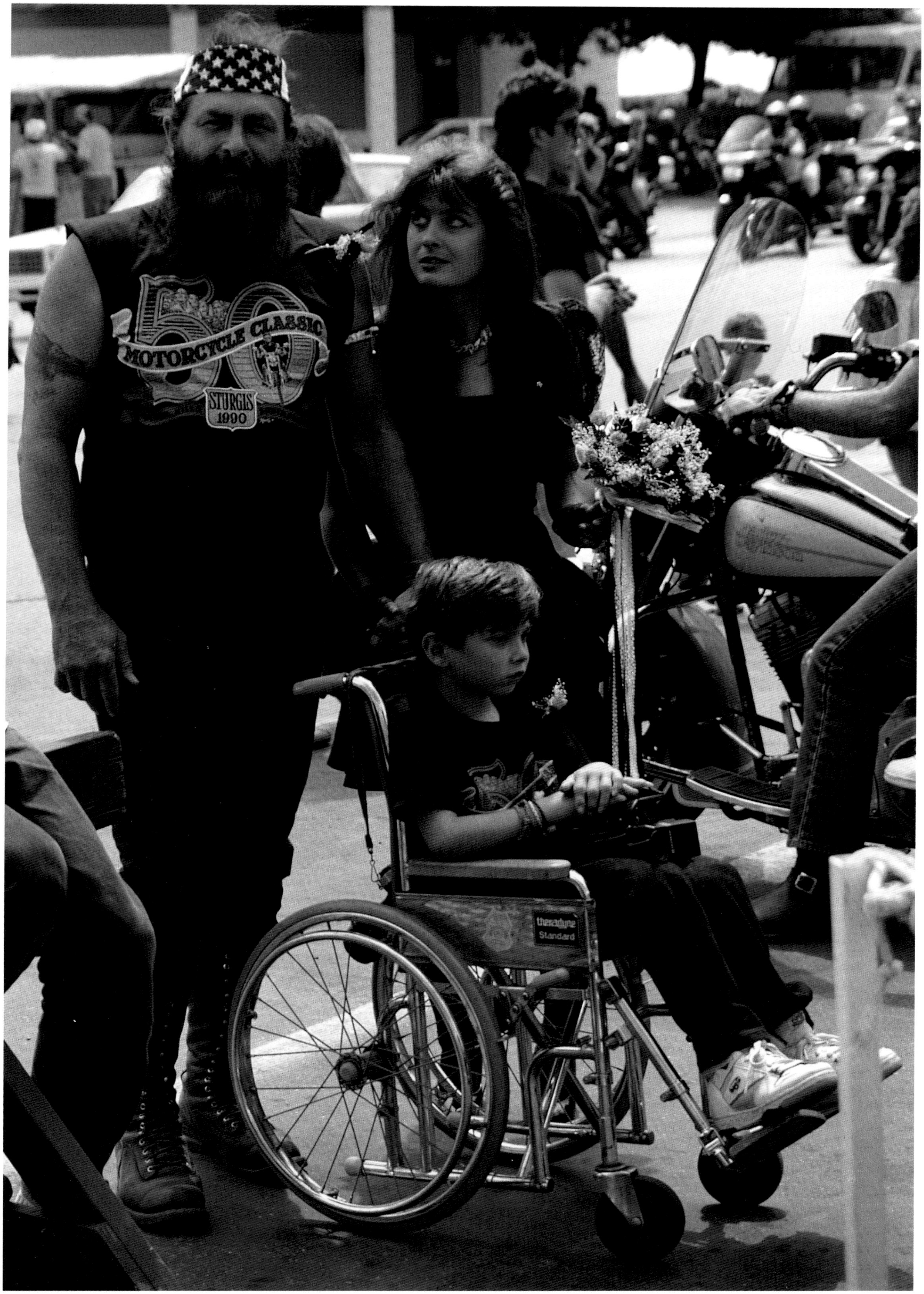

Always in the limelight and actively taking part: disabled children are the darlings of the biker community, as seen here in Sturgis in 1990 (left).

Everybody Is Welcome

Dealer Parties

A cut above: sometimes Harley are flown in to the dealer parties by air–freight.

Every Harley dealer organizes glitzy banquets or parties every year as part of his dealer convention work. This custom is useful above all for maintaining the spirit of cooperation necessary to the business, and as a social event it is reserved mainly for the invited guests.

Harley–Davidson usually leaves it to its dealers to organize parties, whatever size the dealer might be. It is at these events that the vital relationship between manufacturer and customer comes alive. Naturally such events are commercially oriented – that's the idea – but in reality there's a lot more to them than just attracting people and winning them over.

Dealer parties are internal roll calls of achievement. There are Harley motorcycles to touch and sit on, plenty of interesting people to talk to and invariably high-class service. It should go without saying that there is no obligation to buy anything.

Dealer parties were always an ideal medium to encourage loyalty to the firm and its products, and the feeling of belonging to one big family. Of course the company bosses and marketing strategists know this too. In the case of Harley–Davidson, this is part of company policy, since at every Harley party at least one high ranking company repre-

sentative is present. This additional attraction pays for itself through increased sales. The party also helps guests, potential customers, to overcome their bashfulness at quietly looking around to see how the allegedly elitist, Harley community actually lives.

There are other special reasons for dealer parties. Sometimes it's the opening of a new branch, sometimes a local fair or other large–scale event. Sporting events too, races or rallies, make a special day worthwhile for most dealers. Sometimes it's enough to show up at Christmas, New Year or on the boss's birthday. Some dealers throw parties monthly, making them into regular events – often linked to modest swap meets and an open house for a look around the business.

A dealer who fails to organize parties soon loses the interest of clients old and new. You shouldn't pass up the opportunity to visit one. They're always full of surprises, and those who don't (yet) ride a Harley themselves are always very welcome.

No cream cake, no Harley: Farrow's dealership celebrates its 85th anniversary.

It's worthwhile to wait the food is always delicous.

Congressmen, the Mayor and the Sheriff of Columbus, Ohio send off the parade to mark Farrow's anniversary (below, large photo).

Crowned Heads

Once upon a time, nobody could get by without female allure in the advertising world of beautiful people, so it was no surprise that Harley had its own official beauty queens. Their main task was to be decorative and ever available for the gangs of press photographers lying continually in wait. Thus they were contractually obliged to pose with tireless smiles in pretty but exhausting postures next to new motorcycle models and beaming race winners, and also posed for memento photographs on the side. Of course all the girls could ride a Harley, and tell a Sportster from a Dresser.

How was she chosen as a Harley Queen? Well, she had to be over 18, good looking, slim, but not too thin, possess a driver's license valid in the U.S. and Canada, and fill in a few application forms. She had to write an "essay" of a maximum of 50 words entitled, "Why I want to be Miss Harley-Davidson." She also had to submit a few photos, including a full-length one showing herself wearing a bathing suit. Candidates who made the short list (at the end it's narrowed down to just three) had to answer a few questions before a jury about their résumé and way of life. It was usual in such competitions, that the jury's decision was final. When she was crowned queen, she had to attend at least 25 weekend events and make herself available for all photo sessions. A dream job in fact. Nowadays, there are no queens any more, times and advertising concepts have changed.

Having just celebrated his 101st birthday, racing legend Jim Davis (center) is flanked by the current owners of Farrow Harley-Davidson, Pat and Al Dorman (above).

Famous and not-so-famous guests – Willie G. (second from left) expressing his congratulations, behind him Peter Fonda and on the right Biker Billy (left).

Happy Birthday To You – Harley's Anniversaries

Half a century passed before Harley-Davidson succumbed to the age-old tradition of celebrating a birthday. In celebration of its Golden Anniversary in 1953, Harley published a proud article in the special September issue of *The Enthusiast*. This article described the typical American success story and was lavish with self-praise. Concurrently, Harley presented its special anniversary models for 1954 – the KH Sports model, the 74-inch OHV FL Panhead and the ST 165 two-stroke, as well as the Servi-Car, all of which bore a commemorative Golden Anniversary medallion.

The Diamond Anniversary in celebration of Harley's 75th birthday took place in 1978 under "other" management, as Harley-Davidson was at that time firmly in the grip of AMF. An impressive party was thrown at the Daytona Beach Hilton on the occasion of Bike Week, complete with a special indoor show in which custom bikes, racers, dragsters and some old-timers were displayed for the first time ever.

In contrast, Harley's 80th anniversary in 1983 was hardly celebrated at all. Back under its own control, Harley was struggling to survive and celebrations were not a priority. However, all activities connected with the 1983 Daytona Bike Week at the Hilton were organized in line with the anniversary: an antique bike show, an MDA poker run, the choosing of Miss Harley-Davidson, a ride-in show, a kickstart competition and the by-now familiar Sunday closing parade to Harley Heaven, this time managed by the newly founded Harley Owners Group (H.O.G.). In 1988 the optimistic and success-oriented management took up the challenge of an attractive 85th anniversary celebration and launched a rally starting from all four corners of the U.S. and finishing in Milwaukee. The first of these Cross Country Rides became known as the Homecoming Run. A host of other activities running at the same time now included all Harley riders. The idea enjoyed even greater success than the events at Daytona, which almost dwindled to insignificance amidst the general excitement.

THE **ENTHUSIAST**

FROM HARLEY-DAVIDSON® SINCE 1916

SUMMER 1993

Good Vibrations Rock Milwaukee

© *Harley-Davidson*

Welcome Home!

Harley's 90th Anniversary

The older Harley-Davidson gets, the bigger its anniversary celebrations become. They now take place every five years, and are planned on a huge scale, with the participation of hundreds of thousands of Harley riders. At the 90th anniversary Homecoming in 1993, for example, ever-growing rows of Harleys rolled toward Milwaukee for days on end from the farthest corners of the U.S.A. and Canada. Each row was led by a company chief executive officer, all of them naturally riding the firm's own two-wheeled products.

From Vancouver, Canada – came Chairman Vaughn Beals' column, taking ten days to reach Milwaukee.

From Edmonton, Canada – Scott Miller, Head of Product Development, taking nine days.

From San Francisco, California – Rich Teerlink, General Director and Clyde Fessler, Vice President Department Director, taking ten days.

From Los Angeles, California – Willie G. Davidson, Vice President of Design, taking nine days.

From San Antonio, Texas – Tim Hoelter, Legal Department and Lou Boltik, Commercial Development, taking seven days.

From Orlando, Florida – Jeff Bleustein, President, taking eight days.

From Kittyhawk, North Carolina – Jim Ziemer, Financial Director, taking seven days.

From Washington D.C. – Mark Tuttle, VP of Engineering, taking seven days.

From Augusta, Maine – Ron Hutchinson, Director of Customer Services, taking eight days.

From Montreal, Canada – Darrel Fink, Sales Director taking seven days.

Every row was accompanied by other senior employees and directors and their families, all riding new 90th anniversary special edition Harleys, and acting as road captains along the way. The rows, some of which swelled in size to more than 6,000 participants, were backed up by service cars and first aid units. The company had booked large hotel complexes as meeting points and parties were celebrated at these night after night.

On Sunday, June 13 the monster event came to its climax as the whole of Milwaukee celebrated. Even for the U.S., it was a unique occurrence: the whole of the city's interstate highway system was closed for several hours. By early morning onlookers were already gathering on bridges and embankments, equipped with folding chairs and picnics. Children were hawking pennants and celebrating crowds thronged every single street.

Then the Harleys came rolling in. The crowd waved and applauded as vast columns roared by in the greatest demonstration of rolling thunder in history.

In and around the city they had gathered on stand-by sites and waited patiently until their turn came to be ushered into the endless procession. The cavalcade took almost five hours to pass down Wisconsin Avenue to Henry W. Maier Summerfest Park on Lake Michigan, which for the day had been turned into Harley Heaven. At the front were the bosses and their families on their 1993 Special Editions, ZZ Top with their night-blue HogZZillas and CadZZillas, then the Miss Harleys, attendants and escorts, the MDA poster kids.

Harleys forever powerful, loud and classically beautiful. The tolerance problem that the authorities grapple with constantly in other parts of the world, i.e. how to deal with the black sheep, the troublemakers who bring all other motorcycle riders into disrepute, was not an issue here. Noise is in, especially when emanating from the sonorous pipes of Harley-Davidson motorcycles. And though helmets were strongly recommended, everyone was free to let the wind blow freely through hair and beards. God bless America!

The police officers had everything under control: rangers on horseback surrounded by a sea of Harleys directed the enormous stream of motorcycles and special Harley-mounted units gathered together from far and wide acted as parking attendants. The city had set a limit of 60,000 entrance tickets to Summerfest Park, but in the end, many more people than that were present.

There was no standing on ceremony at this great gathering of the brotherhood: the company heads mingled freely and amicably with the festive crowd, swapping greetings and small talk. There were moving moments and thousands of commemorative photos taken, which will no doubt take on the status of holy relics. More than a few tears were shed at the Harleylujah farewell ceremony that evening, complete with fireworks and a magical stage show. The money collected for the children of the MDA came to a grand total of over 750,000 dollars. In sum, it was a superlative anniversary and just a small sampling of the 95th!

Through the honor guard for hours: the people of Milwaukee show their appreciation on Harley's 90th anniversary.

Harley Ages Gracefully

The 95th Anniversary of Harley-Davidson

Harley-Davidson celebrated its 95th anniversary in 1998 with two worldwide "Mega Events." These were held in Milwaukee, Wisconsin, from June 8 to 14, and at Faaker-See in Carinthia, Austria, from June 17 to 21. The Harley Owners Group also entered its 15th year in 1998.

Facts About Milwaukee

The 95th Anniversary Ride and MDA Fund Raiser

Five official Company rides, each headed by the top management, finished on June 9 at the Harley dealerships in Milwaukee.

Festival Venues

Miller Brewing Company, Milwaukee County Stadium, Wisconsin State Fair Park (H.O.G. Rally Site), Convention Center (Harley-Davidson Display), Rider's Ranch (Waukesha Expo Center Campground), Veterans Park (Festival Site) and Henry W. Maier Festival Park (Reunion Site).

H.O.G. Rally

Wisconsin State Fair Park Activities Grandstand/Infield, Chapter's Parade, Battle of the Champions race, drill team display, ride-in parties, Budweiser Pavilion (live concerts), Fat Boy Park (live concerts), Global Living Room (displays and Dave Barr seminars), Heritage Theatre (history and shows), H.O.G. Road House (historic exhibitions with Marty Rosenblum), Miller Genuine Draft Pavilion (live concerts), Soft Tail Coliseum (rodeo), Sportster Stage (live concerts), State Fair Park Pavilion (live concerts), State Fair Park Grounds.

Harley-Davidson Factory Tours

Daily from 9 a.m. to 4 p.m., Capitol Drive Power Train Facilities; daily from 10 a.m. to 5 p.m., Pilgrims Road Power Train Facilities

and Harley-Davidson Headquarters, 3700 Juneau Ave.; 1 p.m. to 3 p.m., Buell Motorcycle Co. in East Troy and Buell Battletrax. The Harley-Davidson Corporate Display is open daily from 12 noon to 8 p.m. at the Convention Center.

Parade

The parade began forming up in the staging area near the County Stadium at 5 a.m., with endless traffic jams and queues. At 8 a.m., the four-hour parade departed along Interstate 94 – blocked to all other traffic – to the festival sites of Henry Maier Summer Park and Lakefront Veterans Park. More than 100,000 "born to be mild" Harley riders were cheered on by over 120,000 emotional, patriotic and flag-waving spectators from bridges and the roadside. "Ride Proud, Ride Loud!" was the motto, and the rumbling of so many Harleys triggered automobile alarms miles away. The whole city shook to the roar of the typical Harley "sound." No accidents, and just four arrests.

Reunion

Veterans Lakefront Park (admission free of charge) 9 a.m. to 11 p.m.

Displays, shows, stands, fashion show, drill teams, *Asphalt Angels* magazine, travelling, museum, stars and concerts.

Summerfest Park from 9 a.m. to 11 p.m. (admission fee: 35 dollars, children free): Sold out and, with about 86,000 tickets, heavily overbooked. Non-stop shows and

events, live concerts, souvenir stands.

Marginalia

Targeted donation for MDA: 1.5 million dollars. "The times are a changing": wild outfits, tattoos, chains, studs, fur caps with animal heads, heavy silver jewelry. Free spirits: Harley "aficionados." Girls Bike Wash at Jimbo's Gin Mill: 10 dollars for MDA. Jesus is Lord – Christian missions and evangelical services in the CMA Headquarters. Jim Kobe: "I'm getting old, and want to give Harley something back." He donated his Pan Head, bought in 1948 for 950 dollars, to the Company. Police report: two motorcycle accidents ended in death.

Six Harleys reported as stolen. The "heavy beer drinkers (are) back to the brewing city." Large numbers of "welcome bikers" souvenir signs stolen. Harley Special Sales: Heritage Softail telephone for 69 dollars; Harley radio and cassette player for 79 dollars and 95 cents. Official Harley-Davidson 95th Anniversary Web Site: www.harley-davidson.com. Harley managers express their thanks in whole-page ads: "It takes a lot of faith to give 100,000 bikers the keys to a city." "Thanks Milwaukee, you opened your arms, your hearts, your streets and helped make the 95th Reunion unforgettable."

"Harleylujah": The three days in Milwaukee were the highlight for any biker.

Facts About Faaker

Reunion Ride of the H.O.G. Chapter and Harley riders from all over Europe to the festival grounds around the Faaker-See. 95 hours of non-stop action. Special events, with admission costing around 50 to 80 dollars.

Harley Village at Faak market place. Open from 9 a.m. Party, competitions and prizes, paper chase, fashion shows, historic company museum, factory sales, wall-of-death artistes (on Indian Scouts), Harley and Buell demo rides, live music, barbecue, Miller beer, VIP tent.

Evolution Tent of the Carinthian Harley Club in Egg: shows and live concerts, poker-run, "jailhouse" party, charity tours of the Vienna H.O.G. Chapter, lady's workshop.

Finkenstein Castle Arena: live concerts, ruin-biker clubbing.

Action Park on Arnitz camping site: kindergarten.

Concert Area in Ledenitzen: "Shakes & Beer" biker party, L'Oreal show, barbecue and live concerts; Saturday from 1 p.m. to 2:50 a.m.: "More Than A Sound" concert, also with a special appearance by John Bon Jovi.

"Alter Sportplatz" in Faak: live concerts and party.

Chez Fuzz in Unteraichwald: live concerts and party.

Drobollach: Host's festival, folklore show.

Messrs. Spedition Montau in Fürnitz: safety training, Ladies of Harley courses, workshop, Harley–Davidson Services: repairs and spare parts.

Harley Parade: Saturday, a parade forms up at 7 a.m. and begins at 10 a.m. Some 10,000 participants ride about 43 miles through the Rosental Valley and along the Wörthersee, led by the local delegation.

A Family Chronicle

The Enthusiast

 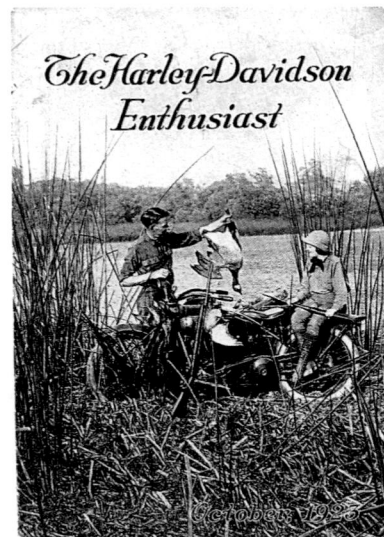 

One of *The Enthusiast's* greatest success stories was undoubtedly the invention of "Uncle Frank," alias Hap Hayes. Behind this pseudonym stood the veteran journalist and motorcycle expert Howard E. "Hap" Jameson, who had been employed by Harley-Davidson since 1912. During World War I he was the chief instructor at the first service school and also wrote most of the early service bulletins.

In "Frank's Mail Box" he answered reader's letters to *The Enthusiast*, giving technical advice and tips and in the regular column "Uncle Frank Says" he explained production methods. Particularly popular and smiled over were his insider stories about everyday life among the editorial staff and in the company, under the title "Steno." "Steno" was the penname of the editorial secretary and stenographer Nellie Newkirk, who faithfully recorded on paper whatever occurred to "Uncle Frank."

At first there was only a modest information sheet which kept dealers up to date – *The Harley Dealer* was introduced in 1913, when it was really nothing more than a sparsely illustrated circular full of bombastic statements. After continual requests and pressure from many Harley riders, this was then superseded by *The Harley-Davidson Enthusiast*, though *The Harley Dealer* continued to exist until 1926.

So the oldest official motorcycle magazine still in existence today came into being – a thorough and informative forum for all customers. Long before the company motto "for the people by the people" was born, the monthly *Enthusiast* bore the slogan "for the rider by the rider" on its editorial banner.

By 1923 its circulation had risen to over 50,000 and there was already a Spanish edition, *Los Entusiastas Latinos*, aimed chiefly at the Mexican and Central American market.

The subject matter of the magazine was varied, though largely consisting of dressed-up company advertising. It included information on new models and products, accessories and equipment, recommended tour and excursion routes all over the world, sporting events (provided they were AMA-approved), and of course, Harley race successes. It would also include articles about club life (but would not mention the hoodlums) and features on law enforcement (our friends and helpers...). The magazine would also cover internal matters from Milwaukee (we are the biggest factory...).

In the 1920s and 1930s *The Enthusiast* dealt chiefly with sidecar-related matters. In those days sidecar outfits sometimes sold in greater quantities than solo machines and were considered all-around vehicles and as the automobile of the man on the street. Female motorcyclists also received extensive coverage, generally accompanied by photographs of them in saucy poses with their motorcycle and plenty of frivolous text. In short, the motorcycle scene was presented as an ideal world full of Harleys.

To this day nothing has changed significantly. Problems, criticism and motorcycle sales figures were completely taboo subjects. A typical feature reflected a mood of continual, somewhat exaggerated, optimism which became even more enthusiastic when the company was going through tough times. Despite this, *The Enthusiast* remains the most comprehensive and reliable source of information about the company history of Harley-Davidson.

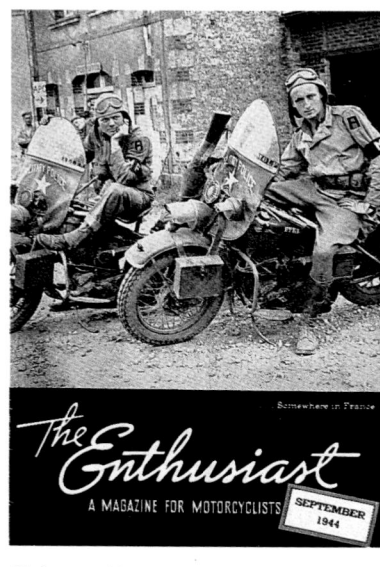   

All photos on this page are © Harley-Davidson

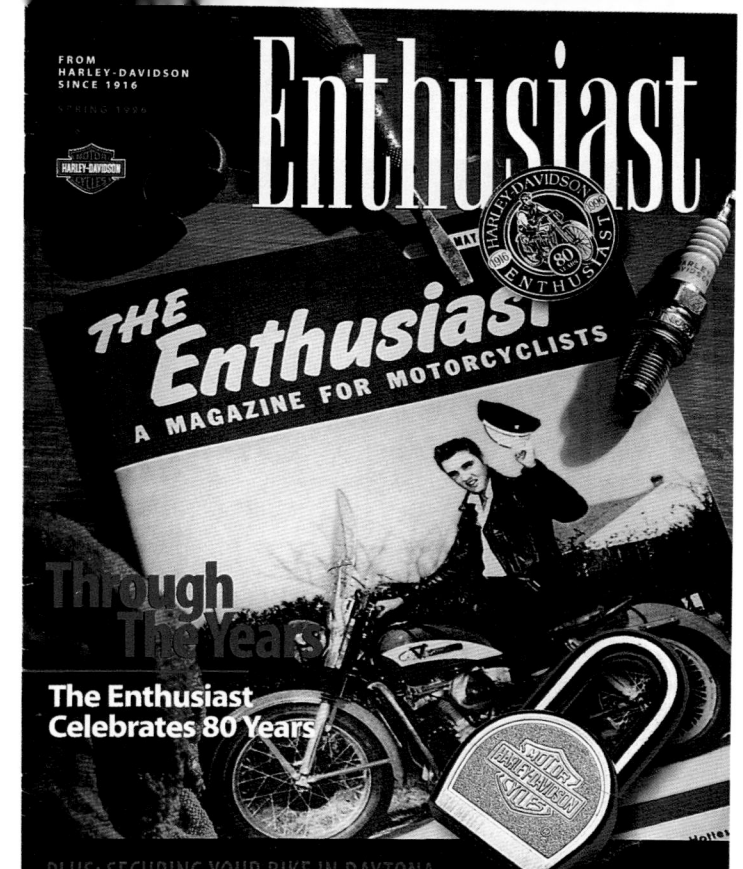

The title of the magazine changed several times, reflecting its varied 85 year–plus history. In 1916 it was founded as *The Harley–Davidson Enthusiast*, in the 1930s it became *Harley–Davidson Enthusiast,* then from 1938 *The Enthusiast – A Magazine for Motorcyclists*. At the beginning of the 1970s it was called simply *Enthusiast*, then from the 1980s once again *The Enthusiast*. In between it briefly came out under the title *The Motorcycle ENTHUSIAST in Action*, chiefly filled with advertisements for snowmobiles and the racing scene. Its scope and format were also changed many times.

At the beginning of the 1970s, subscriptions were increasing steadily but the budget allowed by the company's publicity department remained constant so money became scarce, and the magazine went from being a monthly to a bimonthly publication. Then in 1977 it became a quarterly, and from the beginning of the 1980s onwards it appeared just three times a year, in spring, summer and fall. On the other hand, the cover now appeared in a range of colors corresponding to the colors of the current range of motorcycles.

However, it was not until the end of the 1980s that the whole magazine increasingly came to be produced in color. Today it appears in full color and has a circulation of over half a million and is now once again a quarterly publication. *Dealer News* has now been revived as an information sheet in an economical format. Press information sheets are also put out regularly by the company. For all H.O.G. members there is the fortnightly *Hog Tales* which also appears in various foreign language editions.

With the lapse of copyright after 40 years, copied editions of *The Enthusiast* have been printed by various companies, though not by Harley itself. Original copies from the early days up to the 1930s change hands for several hundred dollars, while copies of the *Enthusiast* from the 1950s, which could be obtained only a few years ago for two or three dollars, now cannot be had for less than 15 to 20 dollars. So pick up a copy! These days they can be obtained free of charge at any Harley–Davidson dealer.

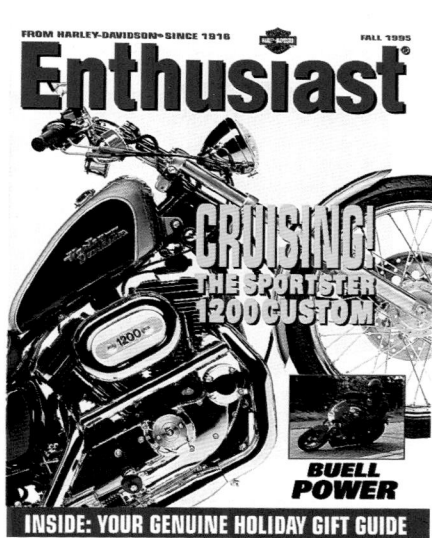

Helps You Know What's What

Harley Manuals

For true Harley freaks *The Enthusiast* is at best alternative, bedside reading. The real interest of any reader lies in intensive study of the almost scientifically–prepared *Service Manual*, in biker circles also known as "The Bible."

This details the entire engineering specification of a model or series down to the last washer or gasket, along with diagrams and data set out in long tables of precise measurements. The service manual brings every last secret from Milwaukee right out into the open, explaining all the hidden details of a Harley. For a long time these hefty handbooks and also the supplementary *Parts Catalogs*, were treated like highly sensitive official secrets, and were only available to official dealers and licensed garages. Hopeful DIY mechanics were not too popular with the factory.

For customers there were the *Riders' Handbooks*, later also known as *Owners' Manuals*, which contained the most useful information and tips for maintenance, running and servicing, but nothing on how to take apart and reassemble a gearbox, or how to get at the generator. Learning the "Bible" by heart was a condition of membership of many early hard–core biker clubs, and the time candidates took to strip down and reassemble an engine – the record is said to stand at 28 minutes, probably for an old Flathead – determined their status at the club. This old tradition, today almost forgotten, had its origins in the early days – until around the middle of the 1930s – when the ownership of a service manual was almost as important as the motorcycle itself. In those days the full name was the somewhat clumsy, if accurate, *Operation Maintenance & Specification: Instructions for the Operation and Care of Harley–Davidson Motorcycles*, which later became the *Manual and Instruction Book*.

All of these publications were carefully translated into the world's most important languages, which sometimes led to a certain amount of terminological confusion due to technical misinterpretations. Because of this the original American edition remains the basis for all technical knowledge, and all around the world a basic knowledge of English can be assumed of true bikers.

Unfortunately, this fine tradition of technical competence has become superfluous today due to improved standards of manufacture and year–long guarantees, and so has slowly fallen into disuse among regular Harley riders. The blessing or curse of modern times – after all, who wants to get their hands dirty nowadays, and what are tow–away and return services and letters of guarantee for?

Copious quantities of accessories and spare parts were available for technical improvement, as this 1929 catalog shows.

Easy Riding Mesinger Tandems

With a tandem seat on your bus you can give your pal or girl friend a lot of pleasure and have more fun yourself.

The famous Mesinger Tandems, shown at right, are well known for their easy riding comfort and can be readily attached in a few minutes.

The most popular tandem on the market is the Standard Mesinger Tandem. It has a very comfortable bucket type seat of finely grained leather mounted on two adjustable tension springs. A handle grip and convenient foot rests are also provided.

Standard Mesinger Tandem

The Mesinger Social Seat is by far the most comfortable tandem obtainable. The form-fitting saddle is fitted to a pair of long enclosed, adjustable cushion springs, to eliminate all road shocks. The handles are adjustable and the foot rests are amply large.

Standard Tandems

11237-25—For 1925 to 1929 big twins .... *$16.00 bebuy
11237-26—For 1926 to 1929 singles and 45" twins......... * 16.00 bebwa
11237-30—For 1930 74" twins..* 16.00 becaf
11237-30A—For 1930 singles and 45" twins............. * 16.00 becdi

Social Seats

11238-28—For 1925 to 1929 all models .... * 20.00 bebyc
11238-30—For 1930 74" twins.* 20.00 beefm
11238-30A—For 1930 singles and 45" twins.............* 20.00 beegn

Mesinger Social Seat

Fork Stabilizers

The fork stabilizer is made to slip over the spring fork ends and eliminate all vibration of the fork ends. Easily attached, and adds to the appearance of your machine.

Code

11525-22—For 1922 to 1929 big twins only .... *$1.50 bieiw
11525-26—For 1926 to 1929 singles and 45" twins.................. * 1.50 biemy
11525-30—For all 1930 models......* 1.50 biete

Harley-Davidson
Spark Plugs

Genuine Harley-Davidson Spark Plugs, built in our factory, were designed by our own engineers because no other manufacturer could build a spark plug that would continue to function satisfactorily in our present high efficiency motors. These plugs, since their introduction, have given satisfactory service the world over, under the most trying conditions. Built and guaranteed by Harley-Davidson.

		Code
36-11—⅞" for models prior to 1926	*$1.00	adcaf
37-09—Metric, for 1926 and later models	* 1.00	adcah
38-09A—Porcelain for Harley-Davidson Spark Plug	* .75	byijo
38-09B—Top Gasket for Harley-Davidson Spark Plug	* .05	byiou
38-09C—Bottom Gasket for Harley-Davidson Spark Plug	* .05	byity
38-09D—Spring Washer for Harley-Davidson Spark Plug	* .10	byiuz

Lodge Spark Plugs

The Lodge Spark Plug is specially designed and constructed for use in racing motorcycles. There is none better.

This plug should NOT be used in a stock model.

		Code
36-24—⅞" S.A.E.	.$3.00	byiva
37-24—Metric	3.00	byjag

Spark Plug Shield

Keeps the water from running down over the plug and shorting it.

		Code
43-09	*$0.10	byjio

1929 and 1930 Lenses

Standard equipment in the two bullet type headlights of the 1929 and 1930 models. These lenses spread a powerful, diffused beam of light to both sides of the road and far ahead. Legal in all states.

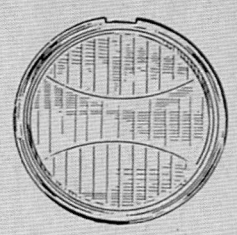

		Code
4906-29 —4⅛ inch diffusing lens	*$0.50	avmub
4906-29A—4⅛ inch plain lens.*	.50	ayjho

Monogram Lens

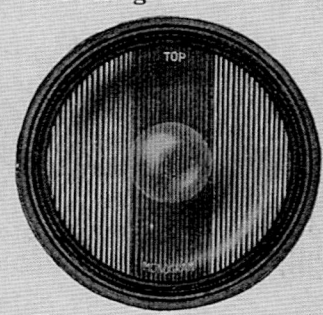

The Monogram is a diffusing lens that distributes the light over the full width of the road and still does not blind the approaching motorist. It transmits the full candlepower of the light and does not absorb it. This is the same lens used as standard equipment on 1928 and earlier model Harley-Davidsons. It is legal in all states.

		Code
11425-21—6⅛ inch	*$1.00	beuby

Standard Lens

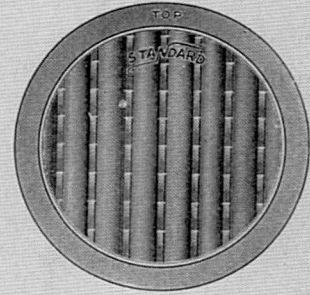

A reasonably priced lens that diffuses the light and takes away the glare. Legal in most states.

		Code
11426-21—6⅛ inch	*$0.30	beuda

All photos on this page are © Harley-Davidson

An early accessories catalog.

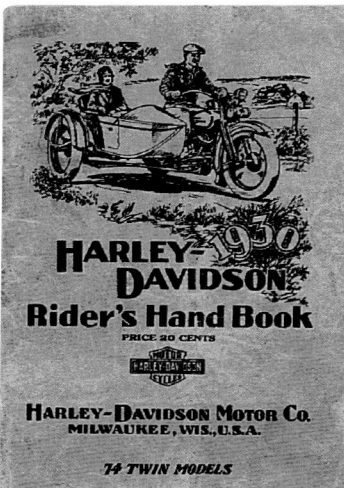

The unavoidable instruction manual.

Spare parts catalog.

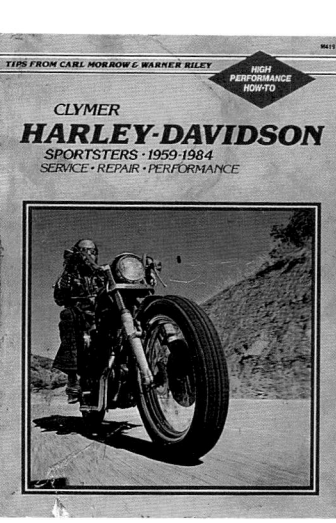

Service manual from the Clymer Press.

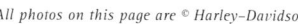

Potato…Potato…

Ya Wanna Buy a Watch?

Rights, Logos and Licenses

From Harley-Davidson's *Licensing Program Guidelines* for franchisees 1/98 (right).

THE HARLEY-DAVIDSON® SOUND

ENG-005

The sound which has been called the "most familiar rumble in all of motorcycling" is also available to our licensees on digital audio tape. The DAT cassette features the distinctive idle and acceleration sounds of a Harley-Davidson® V-Twin common crankpin motorcycle engine. The H-D® sound has been successfully incorporated into a variety of licensed products including motorcycle and engine replicas, telephones, and children's toys. If you believe that your product would be enhanced by the H-D sound, please speak to your General Merchandise representative to discuss how to add this unique feature to your merchandise.

HARLEY-DAVIDSON LICENSING PROGRAM GUIDELINES   DEVELOPING PRODUCTS 1/98
Please consult with your General Merchandise Representative before using any imagery shown in these guidelines and for appropriate use of trademark registration symbols.

Harley Truths

Harley-Davidson is exclusive.
It is not for everyone.
Harley-Davidson is mystical.
(If I had to explain, you
wouldn't understand.)
There is an intense obsession and
commitment to the sport.
Our design philosophy is unique.
(Clean, connected, evolutionary.)
Harley riders share a passion
for a unique sound, feel and
factory custom styling.
Harley-Davidson offers a complete
fulfillment of the experience.
(Fun, reasons to ride, H.O.G.
and much more.)

One of the most widely publicized offshoots of Harley-Davidson's trademark efforts has been the trademark registration it is seeking on the Harley sound. No matter what some might think, the decision makes sense. To the ears of a Harley lover, the Harley sound isn't a "noise," but a "sound," even though some environmentalists and regulators have at times tried to mute beautiful sounds like this. That applies particularly to the wildly popular, sonorous boom that can only be generated by a Harley. Just as Metro-Goldwyn-Meyer registered the famous roar of its lion mascot — featured on television and in film — Harley-Davidson has applied for a trademark registration of its "acoustic logo."

Anyone who is a true Harley fan is a fan of that famous rumble, an integral part of the Harley experience. But the sound is forbidden in many areas when it is too loud. Many people can live with 86 phons (a technical unit of sound), but many others obviously can't, especially not the members of the European Commission who sometimes seem like they want to eliminate exhaust sound completely.

How did Harley's chief executive Jeff Bleustein put it? "The typical Harley thunder is unique and a strong purchasing incentive for our customers." Let's hope that it stays that way, with or without a trademark registration.

After Harley-Davidson had spent decades utterly ignoring the multi-million dollar market for every conceivable manner of Harley accessory, in a manner that some may describe as elitist and tremendously arrogant, the new managers in the early 1980s attempted to make good the almost incalculable loss of revenue by means of an aggressive licensing policy; a policy they were prepared to enforce, if necessary, through the courts. However, this approach initially achieved very little: "Harley-Davidson" quickly became "American Made" or "V-twin," and police raids to seize non-licensed products, like the one at the start of the Daytona Bike Week in 1986.

At least the practices of certain slick entrepreneurs, who had been free for decades to adorn just about anything they could sell on the biker scene with the name "Harley-Davidson" and Harley logos and emblems, could no longer be conducted with the same degree of indifference. Nevertheless, the aftermarket was still huge and fully beyond the control of Harley-Davidson. The major accessory companies had become too well established with their cheap products, usually made in Taiwan or Hong-Kong. Moreover, the demand of their Harley-crazed clientele for modification and custom kits that Harley-Davidson itself was unable to deliver was too great to be ignored.

To tackle this problem, Harley's legal counsel and Vice President, Tim Hoelter, established three large new departments within the company. The Trademark Enforcement Department was initially tasked with exclusively safeguarding all Harley products as far as possible by making them "Trademarked" (™) and "Registered" (®). This included countless names, terms and products that were now protected by patent law when it came to their marketing and commercialization.

Under the management of the Marketing Vice President, David Caruso, the company secured a large chunk of an extensive line of high-quality accessories produced in the Far East. These accessories were then sold exclusively by licensed Harley representatives (Eagle Iron, Screamin' Eagle), but at a lower price than by Harley's Genuine Parts & Accessories.

The third department took care of the issuing of licenses for using brand names and logos to serious companies not directly involved in the motorcycle business, but who wished to adorn their own products with the prestigious Harley emblem and were now allowed to do so. These products included beer, cigarettes, perfume, toiletries, office and stationery goods, toys, bicycles and watches — all in all, it was an extremely lucrative business for both parties. Recently, Harley-Davidson has offered FRX 2 and FXR3, production bikes available fully accessorized from the factory and created by designers and engineers well-known on the custom scene.

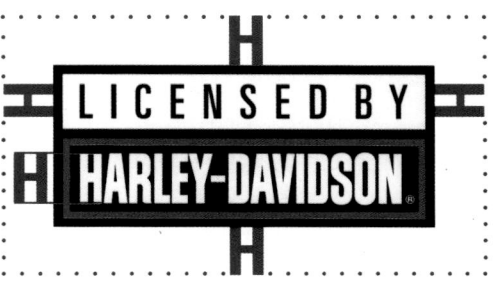

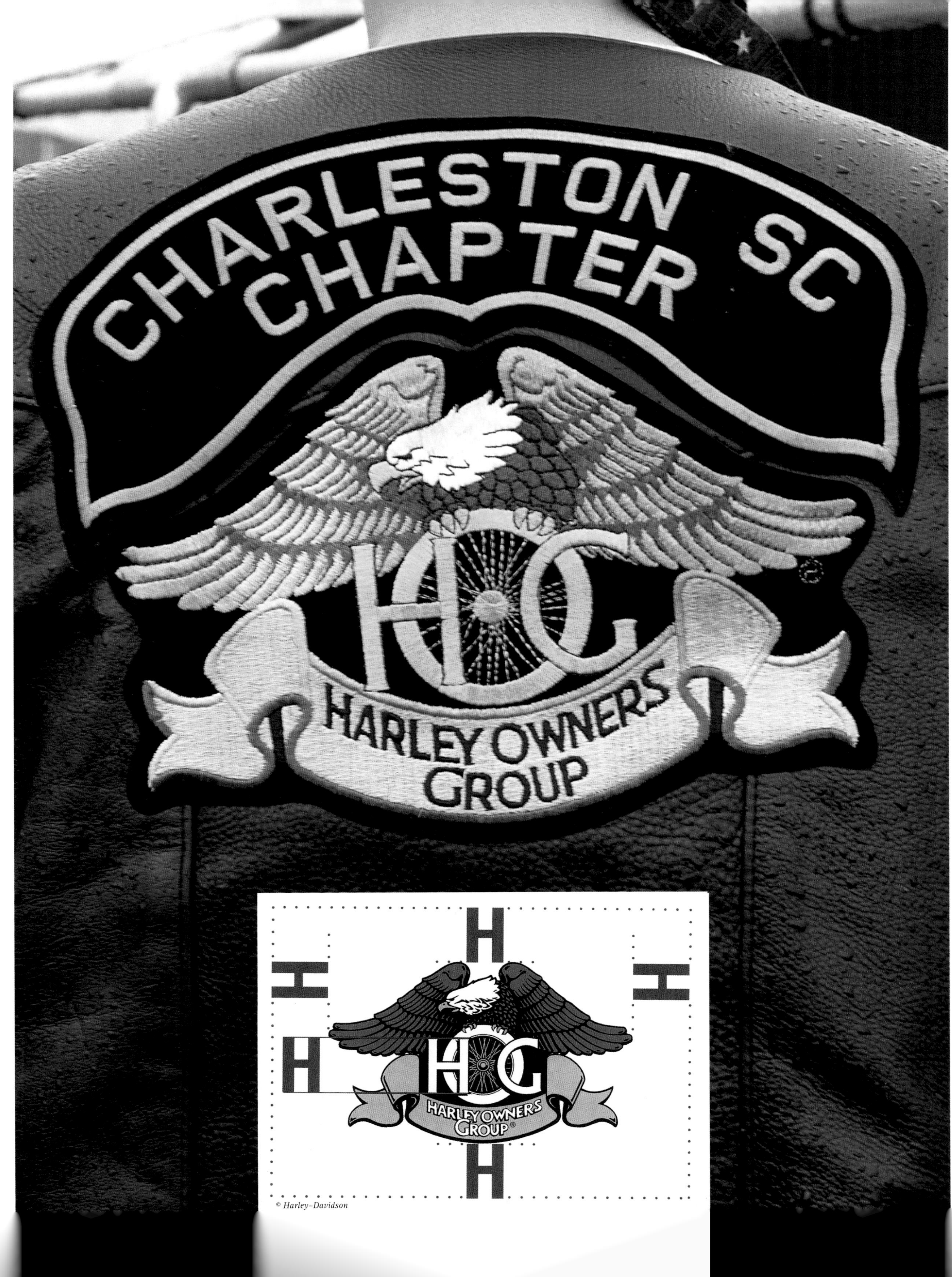

CHARLESTON SC
CHAPTER

HOG

HARLEY OWNERS
GROUP

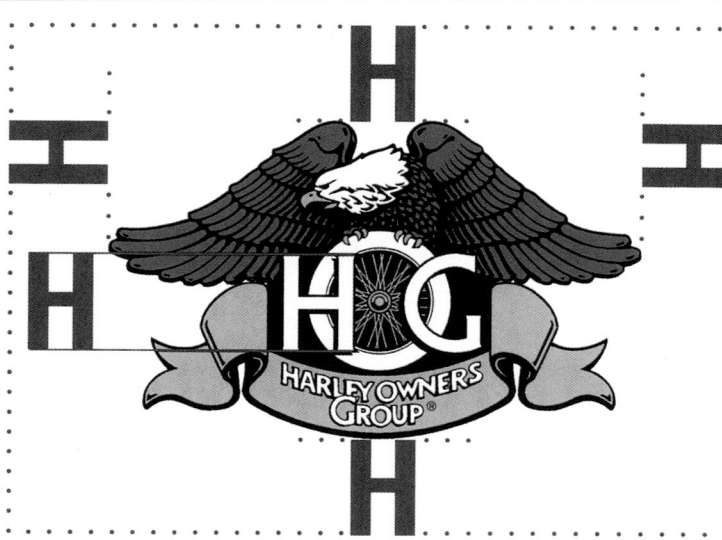

H.O.G. – One Big Happy Family

The Harley Owners Group

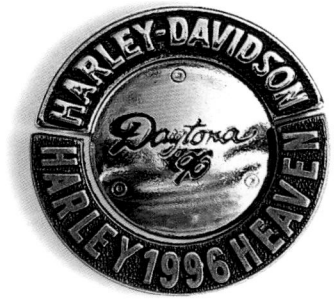

It's a family affair: H.O.G. members watch the Daytona 200 finals in their reserved seats at the south curve after the big parade (right).

Some H.O.G. Members wear art rather than their jackets over their shoulders.

The Harley Owners Group (H.O.G.) is an association fully supported, promoted and sponsored by the Harley-Davidson company and is open to every Harley owner. Behind this general statement lies the new company philosophy of management involvement: the aim is to be in direct touch with the customer.

Harley's VP of Communications, Kathleen Demitros, summed it up neatly: "H.O.G. is our long-term link with our customers." But making it a reality wasn't easy. H.O.G. was founded in 1983, during one of the company's worst periods. Harley-Davidson was facing low sales figures, pressing debts, the burden of outside control, a burden which had only recently been cast off and extremely aggressive competition from foreign manufacturers. As so often before, Harley-Davidson was struggling for its very existence.

At the time of the first public presentation of H.O.G. at Daytona Bike Week in March 1983, nobody knew whether the experiment would succeed or not. At the elegant Hilton Beach there was the poorly attended Ride-in Bike Show and an unforgettable cocktail party.

In that same year, H.O.G. also organized with unbelievable enthusiasm and at great promotional expense around 50 more get-togethers at race meetings. From the Ascot TT in Southern California to the Aspencade in New York State and from the Sacramento Mile to the Caribou Trail Rally in Vancouver, Canada, H.O.G. members came across as a united and easily identified body of people with their own headquarters and distinctive emblem. Other clubs were often left behind, due in part to the fact that membership was not so readily open to all-comers and the application process often became frustrating due to administrative problems.

After these joint outings unexpectedly proved to be so popular, H.O.G. began a complete program of events in 1984, with its own rallies: the national H.O.G. events. These first National H.O.G. Rallies were to bring together members from all parts of the U.S. Two big

meets were fixed: in Reno, Nevada and in Nashville, Tennessee. As a precaution, the number of participants was limited to 3,000. This figure proved to be way off: by 1985 there were already 63,000 members organized into 34 chapters; countless runs, rallies and parties were organized, as well as the Love Rides in aid of the Muscular Dystrophy Association, something close to the heart of H.O.G. members.

Since then the "Ladies of Harley" has also been founded and a fortnightly magazine published, *H.O.G. Tales*, which provides exhaustive coverage of chapters and rallies and a full calendar of events. In short, the H.O.G. concept hit the bull's-eye. The basic idea of bringing management and customers together in a family atmosphere and the joint leisure time activities such as motorbike rides, parties and individual games, took on undreamed-of forms at national and before long international, Harley events.

Whenever and wherever a national H.O.G. rally was taking place, the bosses and their families were always present – at weekends, on Sundays, or during public holidays – and they often covered up to a thousand miles on their own Harleys, mixing in and talking to anybody, eating hot dogs, drinking coke from the can. This experience, of all being part of one big family, was just great.

But this was only one side of the H.O.G. phenomenon. The other side shows even more clearly how the H.O.G. experience determines and influences everyday life for its members. Where once people had often been isolated with their newly acquired Harley, now they are immediately welcomed with open arms into a highly active community. Almost every week the local H.O.G. chapter organizes a joint excursion, with picnics, parties and small competitions, or weekday dinners in a local downtown joint.

In 1987 the annual fee was raised from 30 to 35 dollars. In 1988 Mark Cunningham became the Manager of H.O.G. and the Blue Ridge Parkway Rally to Ashville became an unforgettable experience. In

1989 the Love Ride in November was from Glendale to Malibu, California, just two out of many events, both large and small. Particularly active riders received the Mileage Merit Award. By now the number of H.O.G. members had grown to 90,000 and was still rising fast.

In 1990 the Black Hills Classic Bike Week in Sturgis grew in importance – the small western town was bursting at the seams – and Harley–Davidson avoided the crush by setting up in the Civic Center in nearby Rapid City so as to be able to attend fully to all H.O.G. members and friends.

In 1991 Bill Davidson, son of Willie G., became the new Director of H.O.G. In June of that year H.O.G. went overseas for the first time, when the founding of H.O.G. Europe was announced at a small press conference at the spa assembly rooms in Wiesbaden, Germany. Afterwards the Harley top management rode their Harleys to Paris to bring the same message to the French. From there they proceeded to the first big H.O.G. European International Festival over the English Channel in Cheltenham, England.

In 1992 the first joint European H.O.G. Rally followed, in Mulhouse, Alsace, France. There it was proudly announced that H.O.G. now had 180,000 members worldwide, organized into 7,000 chapters, 3,000 of them in Europe alone.

In 1997 the provisional figures show the pull of this vast "extended family:" 300,000 members, 36,000 of them in Europe, 10,500 in Germany alone.

Fun and Games with New Friends
H.O.G. Events

H.O.G. events are always big family occasions. These happenings quickly established themselves worldwide as central, communal occasions taking place in every area where Harley riders are to be found.

Members only stay in the best hotels at the location. Generally the banquets, lectures, seminars, exhibitions and indoor shows also take place in the luxurious hotels or other beautiful venues. All these events work out to be not too expensive, particularly when taking place in the U.S.

In the early days of H.O.G. major racing events were on the rally program. In the inaugural year of 1983, for example, these included the following:

May 7: First race in the Camel Pro Series Half Mile at Ascot Raceway in Long Beach, California.

May 14: Visit to the Springfield Mile Race in Springfield, Illinois.

May 18–22: Participation in the Aspencade Motorcycle Rally in Lake George, New York State.

May 22: Mid-Ohio Classic Motorcycle Road Race/Battle of the Twins (BOTT) at the Sportscar Course in Lexington, Ohio.

May 27: Texas Hill Country Tour in Austin, Texas.

June 4: Louisville Downs Half-Mile Race

June 5: BOTT Race at Road America at Elkhart Lake, Wisconsin (Road America Race Track)

June 17: BOTT Race at the Laconia Bike Week in New Hampshire.

July 2–3: Indy Mile Weekend Package: participation in Indianapolis Independence Day Indy Mile Motorcycle Race.

July 10: Caribou Trail Race in Vancouver, British Columbia.

July 16: Hagerstown Half Mile Race in Hagerstown, Maryland.

July 30: DuQuoin Mile Race in DuQuoin, Illinois.

This is just a small sampling of the events. H.O.G. has its own "H.O.G. Heaven" area at almost all the events where members can get an especially good view of the race action for a reasonable price.

To get even closer to the race action and to get to know the Harley race stars personally, the visitor or Harley rider can become a supporting member of the Harley race team for 15 to 20 dollars a year. The "H.O.G. Racing Support Group"offers privileges unavailable to a normal racegoer and your name is recorded permanently on the Honor Roll Plaque. "Keep the seventy-year tradition alive" is its motto.

Two out of a thousand: H.O.G. chapter colors.

In 1984 the first H.O.G. chapters met for picnics together. Here's a Mississippi chapter with Harley dealer Andy Moore from Hattiesburg (fifth from left).

Being a H.O.G. Member

Group Membership

A stylish outfit is a must for most H.O.G. members.

H.O.G. Germany

Most American Harley fans might not be aware of their fellow fans in Europe. Here described are the advantages of being a member of H.O.G. Germany. As with H.O.G. all over the world, the only condition of membership is ownership of a Harley. Once a member, there are lots of services offered:

The *Fly & Ride Program* allows rental of a Harley at favorable rates all over the world.

The magazines *HOG Tales* and *The Enthusiast*, plus the national newsletters keep members informed about what's new.

The *touring handbooks* (of worldwide destinations) lists all Harley-Davidson dealer addresses and has road maps.

Membership card, *yearly patch* and *pin*.

"H.O.G. Assistance" is H.O.G.'s Europe-wide breakdown assistance service. For about 43 dollars you get guaranteed assistance in the event of flats, accidents, running out of gas or loss of keys.

Rider programs such as the mileage program, ABCs of Touring and Safe Rider Skills are also offered.

The Harley Owners Group also supports regional organizations, known as 'chapters,' in order to promote motorcycling and to help build a close relationship between riders, the company and the authorized dealers. The chapter concept is intended to bring together H.O.G. members with joint interests at local events and activities. In Europe there are now 173 chapters, 42 of them in Germany. The only condition for joining a chapter is H.O.G. membership.

The Harley Owners Group is not just any motorcycle club. H.O.G. is a family as well as a way of life on two wheels. For various annual fees — the first year being free to each new purchaser of a Harley — one receives an attractive service package which becomes more valuable the more it is used.

H.O.G. is not for homebodies or posers. H.O.G. keeps its members in the saddle; H.O.G. today is a worldwide super-agency organized with the military precision which is essential for the smooth running of countless major events. These events offer many thousands of participants not only family harmony and togetherness but also food, drink, overnight stays, games and test rides, seminars and banquets, parades, shows and open air concerts, excursions and sightseeing tours — all of which is experienced en masse and each one perfectly planned and carefully timed.

Generally the local community is involved in the events, which can confidently be described as festivals. Local bigwigs and politicians from the community are in attendance and are eager to make use of the photo opportunities the events provide. This is a complete turn-around from when Harley riders were condemned as "hoodlums" terrorizing the nation.

Programs of events and conditions for membership are available at all Harley dealers. These events all over the world have a lot in common, but also individual regional characteristics. Here are some events that were offered in 1997 to H.O.G. members in Germany:

Whether in the lonely villages of the Pyrenees in Europe as in the case of the 1994 H.O.G. Rally (left) or to the isolated beaches of the Gulf of Mexico (below) as here with the 'World's End Run' in 1996, touring is always on the agenda.

A State Rally
Northern California (1997)

A principle of all major national events is that they are carefully organized in line with H.O.G. rules. Unlike biker parties, which are generally just about having fun, H.O.G. lays great emphasis on the cultural setting and plenty of local color.

As a typical example let's take the Northern California State Rally, which took place from Friday, June 6 to Sunday, June 8 at Auburn Fairground. Auburn is about 30 miles northeast of Sacramento in the goldrush area on Folsom Lake. For a participation fee of 25 dollars one got the H.O.G. Package which included vouchers, participation entitlements and reduced admission, plus a free barbecue dinner on Friday and of course the Run Pin – one more trophy for the denim jacket.

The program: registration took place on Friday from noon to 6 p.m. at headquarters in the Holiday Inn, the free barbecue was from 2 p.m. to 5 p.m., from 6 p.m. to 8 p.m. there was a bike show, and from 6:30 p.m. to 11 p.m. you could watch the Fast Friday Motorcycle Races.

On Saturday everything happened on the broad acres of the County Fairground. It kicked off at 7 a.m. with the compulsory breakfast. Whoever wanted to could join in the poker-run, which started at 9 a.m. and went on until late afternoon. If you drew the right cards at the control points, there were attractive prizes to be won. Local attractions included the Old Town Street Fair (from 9 in the morning to 6 in the evening) and the watery pleasures of the Waterslide Park. Of course if you wanted to check out the old days of the goldrush, you could book an Empire Mine Tour and experience the world of the forty-niners. Plus there were biker games going on all day and plenty for the kids to do. Finally there was the traditional, prize-giving ceremony.

After the evening barbecue dinner (6 to 8 p.m.) a live band played until midnight, the time of the big ceremonial tattoo to close the rally. Then on Sunday everybody went home as and when they pleased – what a weekend! Just one of many in the course of the year. And by the way: a total of 18 Northern California Harley dealers supported and participated in this rally.

Fun without Frontiers –
H.O.G. International

Alongside the H.O.G. scene in the U.S., Europe in particular embraces the new trend towards global motorbike family meetings. The powerful engines now available have encouraged a completely new type of biker: the "Cruiser," who crosses countries in style on a very big motorbike. This is very much in the spirit of Harley-Davidson, whose company policy has led to encouraging rises in export sales. Harleylujah fever is everywhere!

The Europeans in particular flock to H.O.G. events in great numbers and with unbridled enthusiasm. The big international Eurorallies have made it possible for members to visit their neighbors in their Harley outfits, all the way from the North Pole to Gibraltar and when the time comes, the big bikes pour out onto the freeways and highways to form rumbling row of Harley-Davidsons, their chrome glistening in the summer sun. At their destination the entire population forms an honor guard and that alone makes the often long and arduous journey worthwhile. If the nations of Europe are now riding off together into the setting sun of the twentieth century, the European H.O.G. rallies are playing their part in the process of growing together.

Where to Go from July to November
H.O.G. Activities Over a Six Month Period

Let's see what H.O.G. U.S.A. had to offer during the second half of 1997. For starters, the big State Rallies are always good for a few thousand participants. There were seven of them in July: Indiana (Indianapolis), West Virginia (Snowshoe Resort), Idaho (Blackfoot), New York State (Long Island), North Carolina (Wilkesboro), Montana (Great Falls) and Pennsylvania (University Park).

In the hot summer month of August, there were six more, necessarily somewhat further to the north. In October the State Rallies shifted back down towards the western and southern states, where the climate again becomes bearable at this time of year: Oklahoma (Eufaula), Nevada (Las Vegas), South Carolina (Myrtle Beach). All other states hold their rallies in the spring. All 50 U.S. states have at least one H.O.G. State Rally each year, some of them two.

In the second half of 1997 H.O.G. U.S.A. also put on, for lovers of big overland tours, a once in a lifetime convoy experience: the ten day "Posse Ride" through the northern states right along the Canadian border from Maine to Oregon, adapting the legendary Oregon trail to Route 2.

From July to September a further 150 (!) local H.O.G. chapter events took place throughout the U.S. – poker-runs, MDA fundraising runs, mystery runs, picnics, rallies, shows, benefit rides and so on. Whatever takes your fancy, nothing and nobody is left out. Naturally, H.O.G. also attends races where Harleys are competing: as ever the old AMA tradition is carefully kept up. Still in the second half of 1997, H.O.G. was virtually everywhere. Here are a number of places where events happened around the world: England; Quebec, British Columbia, Ontario and Newfoundland in Canada; the Vosges Mountains and Champagne, France; the Black Forest and Verden, Germany; Cadiz, Spain; the North Pole Tour in Norway; Mexico; New South Wales, Australia; Christchurch, New Zealand. In November and December came the big South Africa Tour from Cape Town to Johannesburg. Those mentioned are just the largest meets. Not included are the huge numbers of smaller local Harley Owners Group events all over the world.

Women on the Road

The Famous "Ladies of Harley"

The Ladies of Harley (LOH) was founded in 1986 by female riders and pillion passengers from among H.O.G. members. It was conceived as an independent organization, not just attractive window dressing within H.O.G., but intended to be active on its own account — girl power with the company's blessing. Indeed women have for a long time been welcome, not just as an ever-expanding target group for the marketing department (the 833 Hugger Sportster was designed as a women's Harley), but as full members of the family. LOH members also have their own individual events: special LOH ride-in shows, fashion displays and their own headquarters at all H.O.G. events, the breakfast get-together, "turn a wrench" technical and repair courses and their own excursions, runs and rallies.

The first President was Linda Zorzi, the personal secretary of the Harely-Davidson CEO of that period, Company President Vaughan Beals. She formulated the chief goals of the LOH: to support all women motorcyclists and help them with specific needs and problems, and to provide specially prepared, woman-oriented information and topics in their own communications and to develop woman-related motorcycling activities. The Ladies of Harley should not be confused with *Harley Women*, which is an independently run magazine for woman Harley riders which has been published since 1985 by Asphalt Angels Publications.

Just like the Harley Owners Group, membership to the Ladies of Harley is spreading all over the world. Possibly women need a little more courage to get on and ride a motorcycle for the first time, all the more so when it's a Harley-Davidson - a big machine with a traditionally macho image. But at Ladies of Harley, beginners are also warmly welcomed. Expect this club's membership to increase and for it to become more and more popular as the number of women riders increases.

Coffee mornings, Harley-style: the
LOH's German Chapter during one of
their many excursions.

Full-grown women on powerful
machines: the Ladies of Harley
have long since taken hold of
the handlebars.

People

How to Spot a Harley Rider

Lifestyle

Freedom on the road.

How can you recognize a Harley rider? Easy! By their Harley, of course, which is certainly a legitimate answer. But what if they're not astride their high performance alter egos? Well, even without their motorcycles, Harley riders can usually be identified by several distinguishing characteristics.

A sure giveaway is the outfit. Visitors attending one of the larger Harley events will generally be surprised at the sheer variety of styles on display and could be forgiven for thinking they've wandered into the middle of a bizarre mixture of circus show and carnival, scout camp, open air concert and flea-market. Nevertheless, such hedonistic exhibitions are relatively harmless and are in line with the somewhat modest motto: "We just want to have fun."

But that's just one aspect; others become clear when encountering a Harley fan in a more common, everyday setting involving straightforward human contact, for example on the road, in a bar, at the traffic lights, stuck in traffic in town or on the highway, at home, in the garage, the club, the dealer's showroom, at the workshop, a bike show, or far from home, cruising along some lonely highway. The possibilities for such contact are inexhaustible. Wherever Harley riders meet, certain visual, acoustic and philosophical characteristics always provide an obvious clue to their true identity. This is the so-called "Harley-Davidson lifestyle" ("Ride to live, live to ride"), that forges a bond between the most disparate of people and indeed even the most disparate of machines.

However, even this feeling of kinship is subject to certain limitations. A hard-core biker is extremely unlikely to be encountered in the company of a Rubby (Rich Urban Biker), and a grumpy weekend rocker is just as unlikely to strike up a friendship with his sworn enemy, the R & F (Rich & Famous) yuppie biker. So does this mean there are class differences within the apparently so brotherly Harley family? The honest answer to this question is yes and no. Distinct differences certainly exist in terms of outfit – from an almost militaristic, leather look to the most exaggerated and bizarre of costumes – and also in terms of the technical design of the motorcycles, both inside and out.

However, the author's experience has always been that the various categories of Harley rider understand one another perfectly. There may be introverted extremes, such as the hardcore MCs (Motorcycle Clubs), who, like some secret brotherhood, reject anyone who acts or dresses differently, but they are on the whole peripheral figures on the Harley-Davidson scene. Nor is the "scene" necessarily identical to the "lifestyle." Ultimately, however, the common denominator is the Harley-Davidson legend known as the V-Twin, and the Harley lifestyle is just as diverse and multifaceted as the people on this planet.

This Harley lifestyle is a daily battle with the elements: heat and cold, storm and rain, mosquitoes and oil, defective sparkplugs and arrogant policemen. The Harley lifestyle is also the family, the workshop, the motorcycle club and the local bar where fellow Harley owners gather to drink together.

People-watching: a new sport.

Riding is a pleasure, a relax-ation in your free time.

We're the girls!

Countryside charity run(below).

Most of the MCs have replaced the almost military uniformity of former days with sew-on club insignia and patches (the so-called club colors) and welcomed new, different thinking members into the fold of Harley & Co. These new members are generally young, dynamic and carefree. They occasionally dress in gaudy leathers and are regarded half-mockingly, half-respectfully as high-speed, high-tech freaks. Their credo is to show imports precisely what "American Iron" is still good for. Harleyluja at the extreme, but already an established part of the new lifestyle.

Another biker group is represented by those "original" bikers of old who haven't cut their hair since Hollister, and who invest just as much effort in maintaining their easy-rider lifestyle as they do in maintaining their seemingly tireless flatheads. These bikers regard themselves as keepers of the faith and have no time for the hysterical do-gooders of this world with their electronic ignitions and noise-pollution laws.

At the very least, the Harley lifestyle is an attempt to break free of the oppressiveness of a regulated, humdrum and materialistic society – albeit for just a moment. It embodies a craving for freedom, self-esteem, adventure and excitement. Big words that actually refer to the most basic things in the world: feeling the wind in your face and experiencing those famous "good vibrations." In short, there's simply no cure for those who've been bitten by that fascinating bug known as Harley-Davidson.

Charles Sprouse, Orlando, FL, Tattoo
Artist, '80 FLH

Maura Corey, Cloquet, MN, Artist, '72
Shovel 92 cubic inch Custom

Rob Jordan, Culver City, L.A., CA,
Photographer, Heritage Softail

David A. Brown jr., Newport News, VA,
Warehouse Manager, '69 FLH 1200

Gary "Bear" Spicer, Sturgis, SD,
Machinist, '80 FLT

Günter Jacoby, Pousthomy, France,
Restauranteur, Roadking Police Special

Cliff Pease, Virginia beach, VA, retired
Navy Pilot, '22 JD

Tineke Hartmann, Rotterdam, netherlands,
Traffic Manager, '93 Sportster Hugger 883

Philippe Chapelle, Charleroi, Belgium,
Mechanic, FXR '85

Robert Verniers, Saint-Niklaas, Belgium,
chef, '95 Softail Heritage

Chris Warler, Grandville, PA, Supervisor,
'86 Softail custom

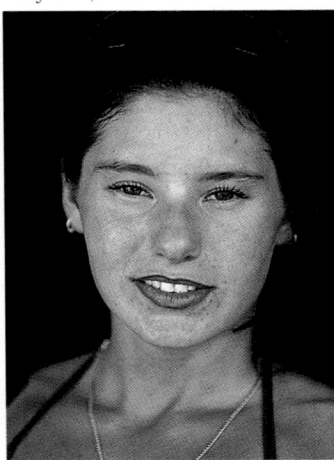

Melanie Dandurans, Quebec, Canada,
student, Heritage Softail '94

Jasper Orlando, Budlake, NJ,
Construction Inspector, '89 FXR

Darius Wolf, Sosnowiec, Poland,
Engineer, '96 Heritage

Michael Preuß, Berlin, Germany,
Scaffolder, HD '91 Softail

Manon Provost, Quebec, Canada, Barmaid,
'92 Sportster

Corallo Giancarco, La Spezia, Italy,
Leather Designer, Electra Glide '85

Hans Krah, Passau, Germany,
Physiotherapist, Softail custom

Jeny Franz, Luzern, Switzerland,
Mason, Softail '86

Max Middelbosch, Zwolle, Netherlands,
Antique Dealer, ID '28

392

Alisandra Bakor, Beverly Hills, CA, '95 Fat Boy

John Richeson, Louisville, KY, Vietnam Veteran, '69 Electra Glide

Douglas Lawry, Flint, MI, Motorcycle Dealer, '83 FHT

Michie Cohen, Daytona Beach, FL, Distributor, '90 Ultra Classic

Albert C. Humphrey, Los Aangeles, CA, Artist, '97 Heritage

Fred Riches, NSW, Australia, Engineer, '90 FXST Softail

Danny Spires Hertfordshire, UK, Building Contractor, Dyna Wide Glide '94 FXDWG

Monique Du Tar, Pretoria, South Africa, Fashion Designer, '96 FXD Super Glide

Heinz Schied, Dreieich, Germany, Businessman, '93 HD

Bill Tequila, York, PA, Printer, '49 Shovel Trike

John "Speed" Finlay, Cottageville, SC, Farmer, '51 Rat

Lori Signs, Hyx Valley Vista, CA, Musis Road Manager, 94 FXR 4 Streched

Jim Tsinois, Sydney, Australia, Bike Designer, 883 Sportster

Kazuyoshi "Janta" Ueda, Tokyo, Japan, Journalist, 1980 Wide Glide

Salvo Dell'Arte, Turin, Italy, Lawyer, '91 FXSTS

David Lainsamputty, Rijnwarde, Netherlands, Finance Officer, '79 FXE 1200

Dolores Karavides, Chicago, Insurance Manager, '96 Softail/Heritage

Leonidas Dimopoulus, Athens, Greece, Jeweler, 1944 WL

Monique Perverlli, Breda, Netherlands, '94 Sportster Hugger

Uwe Gänsch, Friesland, Germany, Stonemason, '85 FXER

Types of Harley–Davidson Riders

A Little Guide Through the Biker Scene

Although it may appear absurd to try to categorize the many Harley riders throughout the world, they created the differences themselves. On the one hand one has to remember that behind even the most bizarre and intimidating biker outfit is just another person like the rest of us; and that even the most eccentrically modified and transformed Harley-Davidson is built around the same legend from Milwaukee. On the other hand one also has to remember that the paradoxical uniformity of certain biking groups may disguise the fact that a desire for true individuality is the driving force behind the very varied Harley scene — and that classifications can turn into a superficial attempt to explain various relationships. Nevertheless, as Harley riders have always possessed a healthy share of critical self-awareness, a mildly humorous, slightly ironic approach to this topic has been taken here, though with all due respect to all the bikers, of course.

The Hard–Core Biker: The 1%ers

The hard-core biker is the most extreme and often the most terrifying example of an elite and uncompromising motorcycling species. More than anything else, he insists that his way of life is respected and wants to be left in peace. His practical outfit comprises a studded, greasy leather jacket worn beneath a cut-off denim jacket adorned with badges and patches; large old boots; and the obligatory dark sunglasses — worn even in the deepest night. Wild hair and striking tattoos are accompanied by a vocabulary in which every second word seems to begin with "f...." The image he projects is that of the rebel outlaw of the Wild West. Some people may wonder if these bikers are simply aggressive, macho posers. However, a word of caution: these guys are the genuine article, and are not to be messed with. His Harley is usually about as uncomfortable as they come — a brutal, powerful custom job, loud and aggressive and often illegal in more ways than one. This type of biker doesn't necessarily love the company but he is totally devoted to Harley's products, particularly when they fulfill his needs and expectations. One thing is certain: the hard-core biker will be around for a long time.

The Cult Biker

This category of biker is similar to the hard-core biker in some respects, but is generally considered to be a more sociable character and is not at all publicity shy. His clothing code (leather and jeans) is typified by the maxim: "Any color goes, as long as it's black!" His preferred accessories include heavy silver jewelry, exquisite dead heads and obscene tattoos. And although he likes to indulge in a certain degree of sexual license, he is often also a caring family man and hard worker — believing these qualities are incompatible is definitely a mistake. The cult biker's motorcycle is "modified," which may mean a thousand and one things. His bike may just bear the obligatory gold and chrome "Live to ride, ride to live" engine cover, but it has to be a Harley all the same — anything else is "worthless." Please don't get the wrong impression if you encounter one of these cult bikers who's usually to be seen with a can of beer in his hand. He is generally an affable, perpetually happy enthusiast always game for a laugh. You can talk to him about anything under the sun. Just don't mention the purpose of motorcycle helmets! This category of biker is also here to stay.

The Rubby (Rich Urban Biker)

This particular breed of Harley biker can be found at the other end of the scale: always well-groomed, up-to-date and the center of whatever's happening. These bikers are recruited from among the ranks of high salary earners, and perhaps more important to this upper-middle class biker than his motorcycle is his credit card (hence the rather derogatory designation "CC Riders"). His motorcycle is, therefore, almost always new, and it has not been bought for reasons of self-realization. He rides it simply for pleasure and relaxation. He enjoys the company of like-minded peers, and even regards a motorcycle tour (known as a "cruise") as a kind of oversized round of golf. Perhaps surprisingly, this class of biker is ready to acknowledge the emancipated female members, who hold the same status as their male counterparts.

A well-heeled person from Harley-Davidson's executive levels once admitted that when he sits on his Harley, he feels like a different person! Perhaps a better person, because once on the road, he's a biker just like everyone else.

The R&F (Rich & Famous) Biker

This biker is the most exaggerated aberration of the Rubby category and can generally be found at trendy, star frequented establishments, international jet set boulevards and the VIP corner of Harley events. The true Harley R&F biker is not really famous, just imitating his idols. This understandably leads to a somewhat strange appearance, particularly with regard to his outfit. He projects an eccentric lifestyle with the most unusual Harley Motor-Clothes and decidedly outrageous accessories, both for his motorcycle and for himself. As a Harley riding fashion slave, this biker considers no detail too small or absurd to be passed off to the rest of the world as the latest in biker philosophy. The company is particularly fond of this category of biker and invests ever more money in its exclusive range of MotorClothes. After all, somebody has to buy the drop-dead gorgeous Harley ties! Nevertheless, even this biker is as cool as any other Harley rider when astride his steed and cruising along the highway.

And All the Rest: The Normal Harley Family

The Harley-Davidson scene is completed by the vast remainder of Harley riders, in other words Ma, Pa, Grandma, Grandpa, the neighbor from down the street, Johnny from the gas station, and everyone else. For all these "normal" people, the Harley motorcycle (which doesn't have to be new) is an indispensable part of their way of life. They share a common philosophy which is characterized by the credo: "We can decide what's good for us and what isn't." Millions of individuals (yes, there really are millions) who flatly reject any form of uniformity or standardization. Loyal Harley people to the bone and completely faithful to their brand. These people are a pleaure to meet.

Belt Buckles

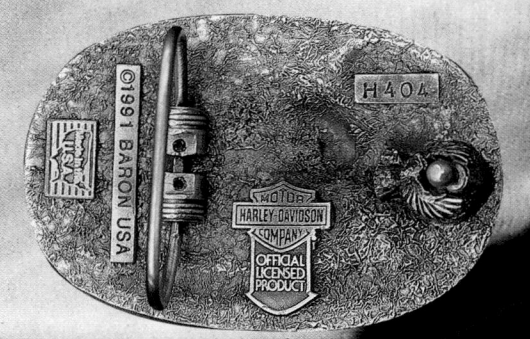

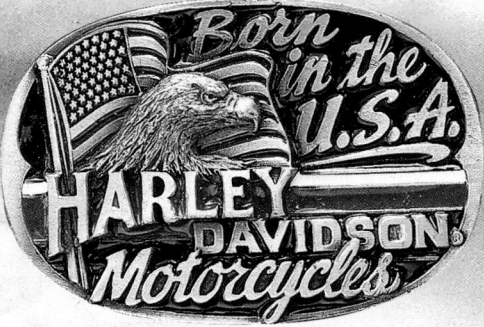

A German Specialty

The Sheriff of Bavaria

The "famous" German biker can usually be found in the parking lot of the Kloster-Andechs beer garden with a beer in his hand; or at the entrance to a biker party, providing a humorous running commentary on the visitors' comings and goings. Long since elevated to the status of a cult figure, the self-proclaimed Sheriff of Bavaria and roguish biker philosopher can undermine even the most deep-rooted views of life, as demonstrated by the following story, one of many about him. One day, having just bought a brand-new Low Rider, he did something that surely no other Harley fan would ever dream of doing. On arriving home with his new bike, he heated a barrel of tar and – using a rough paintbrush – coated the entire custom machine from top to bottom with the sticky, pungent tar. Chrome-plating, paint, seats, wheels, speedometer, lamp lenses – nothing was spared.

With his machine disfigured in this way, he promptly rode to the nearest smart Harley meeting place, where the rich and beautiful self-consciously pose next to their exquisite status symbols. The tar-smeared Low Rider landed in the midst of the elitist gathering of lovingly tended vanity machines like a bomb. With cries of disgust, the shocked Harley owners flocked to the vile blemish on their image and asked such predictable questions as: "How on earth can anyone do such a thing?" (which was by far the mildest question). Of course, the Sheriff of Bavaria had smart answers ready: "So that idiots like you can ask such dumb questions!" or "It's art! You just don't understand, stupid!" The Sheriff could be quite coarse if he wanted to be, and very direct in his response as well. But his antagonists soon began giving thought to his provocative statements and in the end, things turned out as expected: the Sheriff's "black dungheap" was the most photographed motorcycle on the scene, and the cool, matte-black "anti-glamor" trend was born. Indeed, the Sheriff's "paintwork" (suddenly catapulted to the height of fashion) is almost certainly destined to grace one venerable museum or another in the future.

A Sense of Having Arrived

A German Man's Experience

The well-to-do German company director had just fulfilled the unutterable dream of his admittedly, somewhat childish, second youth. This high-flown dream went by the name FXSTC – a Softail Custom, weighing in at six hundred pounds, that could only be described as "incredibly sexy."

All in all, it had cost more than 20,000 dollars. A trifling sum for one such as the Director, who spared no expense when it came to adorning his new toy with all manner of gleaming but completely superfluous extras. Much to the Director's delight, his fellow regulars at the local bar had given a fine display of slack-jawed astonishment. But what was he to do with the unwieldy status symbol once the initial novelty had worn off? He had bought a brand new plaything, only to discover that there was nobody else to play with. A frustrating situation, obviously – until the day his otherwise placid hometown hosted a H.O.G. rally. Having been automatically granted membership upon buying his Softail, the Director was of course invited; indeed, given his status, he was obliged to go.

And so it was on that fateful Saturday that the Director rode out to the familiar horseracing track where the rally was being held, finely groomed and clad in Harley's finest riding gear, complete with matching crash-helmet and stylish fringes. The horses had been replaced this day by bikers from throughout Europe, shamelessly plowing up the carefully tended grass. "What a bunch of clowns," the Director thought.

A corridor of these drunken, loud-mouthed bikers had formed up on the inside of the gate, leaving new arrivals just a narrow space to ride through.

The wilder the behavior of the arriving Harley-Davidson riders, the more outrageous the noise produced by their highly illegal exhaust pipes, the louder the roar of "Harleylujah!" that went up from the welcoming crowd. The worst offenders were greeted with the loudest roar and received frenetic applause, not to mention a celebratory shower of beer.

But not the Director. His overpriced steed and magnificent outfit generated no more than a spate of bored yawning among the few onlookers who actually noticed him at all. The crowd's attention had already been drawn to an outrageous and unkempt rocker, whose open pipes were making a noise like thunder.

All this riled the Director. So much so, in fact, that he regarded the spectacle quite some time, and then finally settled on an appropriate course of action. He tore the smart Harley tie from his throat, wrapped a genuine Mexican bandana around his graying temples, and concealed his well-fed and prestigious belly beneath an ankle-length Australian shepherd's coat, all of which actually did make him look rather scary and even dangerous.

Finally, he removed – though with some difficulty – the two tube-shaped chrome pipes from the exhaust. He then thundered back out of the rally grounds amid a staccato of explosions, in order to venture once again into the prestige parade of the horsepower gladiators, who would be differently disposed this time around.

He briefly stopped for a very glamorous girl in a miniskirt who hoped to enter the Harley Heaven free of charge in just this way, deposited her on the saddle behind him, and opened up the throttle for his second attempt.

The success of this carefully calculated strategy became immediately apparent as the Director was greeted with a deafening roar, showered with beer, and immortalized by countless cameras. What a triumph! Never before had he been so happy, and even his otherwise cold capitalist heart, that usually beat in time with the stock-market tickers, became warm with joy.

Outside, the police, armed with all manner of electronic gadgetry, were waiting in vans with blacked-out windows to apprehend traffic rowdies.

When the Director was asked what he'd do if they confiscated his beloved new toy, the answer he gave, in his newly acquired biker slang, was characteristic of the battle-scarred manager:

"I'll take my mobile out of the saddle bags, call my attorney, and tell him to haul his ass over here in the helicopter, 'cause the cops don't like my open shorties'..."

The Diversity of Harley Riders

Integration and the Harley Community

Proud owner of an Electra Glide built up with a great deal of gold, David A. Brown jr., Newport News, Virginia.

Emancipation has never been a problem with Harley-Davidson.

Members of the military police were known Harley enthusiasts.

What color skin does a Harley-Davidson have? As ludicrous as it may at first appear, some people are quick to offer an answer. As if it were that easy. Nevertheless, the question isn't without point. Although the company has rigorously avoided this subject, a Harley was long considered the classic and patriotic sporting and leisure vehicle of the "white male," despite the fact that there have always been plenty of Harley riders of different skin color and sex, particularly outside the U.S. The famous American rider Bessie B. Stringfield immediately springs to mind. In the early 1920s Richard A. Child made a marketing tour through Africa, successfully selling the two-wheeled vehicles from Milwaukee to African tribal chiefs (as well as white missionaries).

It wasn't until their widespread use by the police and the military that Harleys lost their pseudo-racist image, albeit very slowly to begin with, as can readily be seen from the military police picture dating back to the 1940s. It thus comes as no surprise that many non-white bikers seem to prefer Japanese products, though many others plainly ignore the negative associations and choose to ride a Harley anyway. Nevertheless, both individuals and clubs alike still have a difficult time becoming integrated in the Harley community – insofar as they even want to become integrated. Still,

anybody who pays a visit to Second Avenue during Daytona Bike Week could be in for a surprise. A relaxed lifestyle is the order of the day, and the author personally has rarely experienced such carefree happiness as that of the "Brothers of the Hood," as one refers to riders who meet on Second Avenue.

The African-American Harley community – which was not even allowed to participate in the gasoline-drenched excesses of Daytona Bike Week in 1949 – has found its own focus here on Second Avenue. The partying is loud, but well-mannered: sex and obscenities are taboo. Children play in the street, while the savory smells of cooking from every corner mingle with the fumes from exhaust pipes. And just like Main Street, Second Avenue can boast a host of fantastic Harley custom jobs. No trace is to be found here of the negative image such violent films as "Black Angels" or "Angels Hard As They Come" sought to attach to the African-American bikers. On one occasion, a president of a motorcycle club from the Deep South told why all bikers, regardless of their skin color, were allowed to take part in a typical Rebel Flag party. "Hell," he said, smiling; "That's easy. If a guy's okay, we couldn't care less 'bout the color of his skin. And if a guy's not okay, the same goes for that, too...." The simple facts of life.

A visit to Second Street: whether you're a member of H.O.G.
or G.A. Bad Boys MC, everyone is welcome here.

Confessions of an Incorrigible Man

The Transformation of a Domestic Hog into a Wild Boar

When I got my first Harley, nothing could be too flamboyant or showy for me. I loaded the motorcycle down with anything that would go on it: full fairing, lamps, saddlebags, tourpacks, crash bars and ornamental bars, seats with footboards and backrests, visors and grilles, instruments and electronics, pompoms and tassels – it just became a bazaar on wheels overloaded with trendy nonsense and polished trash, an accessories showcase almost like a rolling mini-IFMA.

One day someone asked me as he stared in astonishment at the chrome-plated monster: "... but where exactly is the engine?" Suddenly I realized just how ridiculously overblown my highway galleon had become. What had become of my beloved Harley if I could no longer see the mighty heart of this wonderful (though admittedly aging) machine under a pile of steel, chrome and plastic frippery?

I began to strip things down. First from my view of the world of two wheels, then from my Harley. Now I could

understand why some of my American Harley brothers rip everything superfluous off their Harleys and ride the hog in its pure form: a fairing is good for absolutely nothing. All it does is mask the wonderful smell of the country and nature, keeps the wind off your face (and the rain and cold, admittedly) and it adds to the engine noise. A fairing only protects the rider up to a point (the right clothing does the job much better), and anyway, anyone who has to stay dry at all costs should go buy themselves a car. Fitting a fairing for streamlining is another piece of idiocy. If you want to go racing then you should go to a race-track. In any case, Harleys aren't meant for record speeds and if you really want to shift, you don't need a flimsy wind-shield fluttering in front of you.

Neither is it true that it protects against dirt and rusting. The dirt and muck collect under the metal or plastic cladding and because you can't see it, you don't do anything about it. That putting a fairing on a bike helps it look good is not a matter of taste but a pure

advertiser's lie. What looks good on a motorcycle is the functioning engineering, the engine, the visible union of power generation, power transmission and engineering design working in harmony.

Now my Harley has to be free of adornment and accessories: everything must be easily accessible, with all superfluous items removed: everything visible, reachable, observable, easy to maintain. Classic simplicity. Understandable and trustworthy.

Who knows what bad engineering may be hidden under a colorfully gleaming shell – looks can be deceptive. Fairing and trim present a false façade, a dishonest and boastful display. A light should be just a light, not some fancy saucepan; a battery should not be a chrome-plated icebox, nor should an oil tank look like an espresso machine. Instead of having a plug-ugly air filter the size of a washbasin totally obscuring the mighty engine and revealing your vanity rather than actually filtering air, the whole power plant can become

visible again and show its true fiery face: it's a wide-open throat down which you can look deep into the fiery heart of the dragon (with an added abrasive effect because of the not-exactly dust-free surroundings thrown in for good measure).

Those cheap, slanting plastic panniers which are supposed to be aerodynamic but which are just a pain, having the stupidest fastening system I've ever seen: get rid of them! The tools come in a small leather bag which can be fitted under the light on the steering head. Honestly, it doesn't change the steering characteristics! Other luggage can be hung more easily and simply on the rear fenders in leather saddlebags than in that awkward and hare-brained plastic contraption.

It's nonsense to say that the primary chaincase has to be enclosed. Fenders and mini-chainguards are perhaps the last word in misguided styling. The apparent danger if you have flapping trouser legs is an illusion – and most bikers wear hefty boots in any case. I

have long since exchanged the monstrous soft double seat, a cumbersome couch which gives the motorbike an unproportioned look, for a spartan solo saddle fitted directly to the frame. Its extremely low ride position means that the mighty Harley is safe for my diminutive girlfriend, who can now support the quarter-tonner in any position without worrying that the monster will tip over and crush her.

While riding, you have direct contact with the roaring, vibrating engine and can feel any harshness or irregularity if you push it too hard. But when it's running smoothly and evenly, you feel a sense of peace and contentment.

Kickstart. A Harley without a kickstarter has always seemed to me like a drayhorse on rollerskates. Anyway, it's simply a cornerstone of the biker's macho world view that you bring your mighty steed to life with a powerful kick. "Anyone who can't start their engine using their own strength ought to be riding a moped" and "If you keep your engine in shape, it'll start OK." These

words of Harley wisdom ring true in my ears. Softies shouldn't be riding a Harley-Davidson anyway.

As my girlfriend has always put it: "A real man kickstarts his engine — only weaklings and little girls push a button!" Her forthright view is that "if I can't kickstart my Harley, I'm not worthy to ride it." She always hits the nail on the head, my little cutie pie.

In one other matter too I absolutely will not compromise and remain unmoved by any abuse, insults or fines. That is the deep heavy thundering sound from the long open pipes, which are of course banned — along with just about everything else which is enjoyable.

The powerful heartbeat from the two heavy cylinders is better than any rock music as it merges with the rider's own heartbeat to form a penetrating and insistent pulse.

This indescribable feeling, which fills you with strength and satisfaction, is simply not up for discussion. Either you get it or you don't. A true Harley rider does not need a radio: his favorite music

comes from the two open pipes as thick as your arm.

Then there are all the useless bits and pieces that make a Harley ugly. Instruments, for example, such as the pointless speedometer. You just ride as fast as you feel comfortable with or as the traffic situation allows. Nobody pays any attention to speed limits anyway and considerate road use is a question of character, not the speedometer.

The rev counter is also totally superfluous - you ride a motorbike by the sound and feel of the thing, and if you can't do that, continually glancing at the revs isn't going to help you.

What's the use — except to satisfy the traffic authorities — of all those extra lights and reflectors, which turn your Harley into some sort of Christmas tree? Anyone relying on a vibrating rearview mirror and brake lights cannot blame anyone, while anyone who counts on turn signals is already as good as dead. Ever been to Baghdad, Cairo, Istanbul or Mexico City? Good luck to you if you do, because turn signals are not as

important to the driving population in those cities.

Apart from that, if your Harley looks a little scruffy, remember that a few rust spots and oil stains don't do any harm. After all, as an old Harley saying goes: "It's not the chrome that gets you home." So my Harley reverted to being a true motorcycle.

Take care of yourself, as they say in the good old U.S.A., riding without helmet or speed limits. Legalized safety is deceptive - learn to trust only yourself. A proper radical Harley is a true survival machine, whatever the damn road traffic regulators have to say about it.

The Sex Machine

No one can deny the eroticism that a motorcycle symbolizes. Countless movies, T.V. shows, books, magazines, posters and even calanders have played on that fact. Millions of men won't deny that seeing a woman on top of a big, powerful motorcycle is a titillating experience. Indeed, many women will also attest that there is also something exciting about a man on a motorcycle – it fulfills the fantasy of a reckless, aloof, macho man with an aura of danger, the "bad boy." And while all motorcycles are erotic, for some reason, no other motorcycle embodies pure sexuality like a Harley-Davidson.

The masculine macho-sexism typical of enthusiasts in the past, now has to contend with the macho-feminism that has become well-established on the motorcycle scene since more and more woman are enjoying the fun, power and convenience of a motorcycle. The liberated female biker is fearless, and isn't averse to retaliating to male provocation with her own scathing brand of "below the belt" remarks.

The fact is, the liberation one can feel riding a motorcycle is not just limited to the sensation of having the wind blowing through your hair and the open road in front of you; it also can include sexual liberation, and the sexually liberated woman is, although not to everyone's liking, a part of the motorcycle-riding lifestyle. It is a feeling of freedom, and this kind of macho-feminism can only be achieved atop a Harley-Davidson. This sensation of power a woman can feel commanding a thundering, roaring, large-caliber V-Twin is unique – it would be totally absurd to compare it to a BMW or a Yamaha.

The commercial use of Harley eroticism and sexuality is an admittedly extremely effective advertising tool. A Harley is associated with the seductive portrayal of women more than any other vehicle in the world. The sexually emphasized combination of women and V-Twin fetishism seems to be decisive for the sales of print media as well as making audiences of public shows ecstatic. This reaction is not necessarily to the delight of the company, which has endeavoured to maintain and promote a decent public image through the years.

Nevertheless, in the realms of literature, there have been endless stories, articles and editorials acknowledging Harley eroticism and the sexual stimulation provided by Harley-Davidson's "whole-body massage." Known for breaking taboos, Franz J. Schermer, motorcycle tester and editor in chief of the motorcycling magazine *MO* wrote an editorial which tells of a couple who is not satisfied with their sex life:

"An old friend of mine, Axel, is a businessman, complete with the usual suit, tie, laptop and cellular phone. He's good at his job and leads his employees well, fulfilling his social responsibilities perfectly. His Harley is just over 20 years old but he only rides it occasionally nowadays, mainly due to the fact that he has a wife and three children today. Her mother lives in the apartment above them, and his wife seems to be trapped ever deeper in the quagmire known as "family life."

His wife's name is Conny, and she has changed a lot over the years. When Axel first started dating the pretty young graphic designer, she was far more easy-going, readily accepting Axel's invitations to take a ride on his Harley, and wore a leather jacket, jeans and some old boots. She enjoyed these rides, feeling the vibrations of the twin 108 mm piston strokes (...).

She literally flourished atop Axel's Harley: her skin cleared and the corners of her mouth crept up to form a smile. She was happy. When Axel would stop to tighten a nut or bolt on one of the myriad of parts and accessories (exhaust, carburetor, ignition coil, handlebars, headlamp, rear lamp, fuel-tank, seat, luggage rack, manual lever, forward-mounted pegs and sometimes even one of the axles of the front or rear wheel) he had fitted to the bike himself, Conny would sit on the curbside grass, gaze dreamily at the sky, and hum the melody to 'Je t'aime.'(...)

Since having the children, she regards motorcycling as stupid. This is due to Axel's "short trips around the block, just to see if it still runs." But instead being gone for an hour as promised, Axel usually doesn't return home until the next day, or the day after, generally muttering something like "I had to tinker with the engine to get things working properly," before promptly falling into bed, laying there – snoring – for 24 hours. Conny ends up on the couch in her mother's livingroom, with tears in her eyes, and not the remotest chance of sleeping. She frowns, knowing that something is fundamentally wrong in her life. But what? Everthing's alright, isn't it? The children are healthy and the best well-dressed on the block, since Conny goes into town every Thursday to buy things on sale at Benetton.

When she finally manages to fall asleep sometime in the early morning hours, she clutches the old cushion from earlier days to herself and dreams of riding on Axel's Harley once again, and of how they once stopped seven times between Cologne and Wuppertal to tighten the exhaust mounting bolts, to secure the carburetor and rear lamp and handlebars and..."

Rico Remburg wrote in his book *Sex on Wheels* (*Sex auf Rädern*, Stuttgart, 1970) of the entire range of erotic experiences and sexual emotions with and on motorcycles in the highly suggestive chapter, "An Engine Between your Legs":

"The automobile may well excite its driver sexually, but a motorcycle can do it far more intensely. Nevertheless, this presupposes both the right motorcycle and the right person – two conditions that are, however, relatively easy to fulfill today. The motorcycle promotes high sexual spirits not only through its symbolism of adventure, masculinity and latent power, but also in an extremely direct and mechanical manner, no matter whether the driver is a man or a woman (...)."

For some women, the sensations experienced astride a fast, heavy Harley-Davidson even seem to be more intense and lasting than for a man – the symbolism of the pistons moving up and down beneath them, the most primeval of all movements – can hardly be overlooked."

In his novel *Blaze of Embers* (London, 1960s, filmed with Marianne Faithful under the title "Naked under Leather"), the author and former French Cultural Affairs Minister André Pieyre de Mandiargues describes with poetic enthusiasm the sexual experience of his "Harley heroine" Rebecca in a particularly intense manner. The character of his book went on to claim a lasting place in the world of literature.

"The engine worked with all the strength of its two mighty pistons between her legs, spread apart as they were by the fuel-tank. Such a vital, vibrant and violent thing whose power still triggered the same enthusiasm within her as on that very first day. What a wild and unbridled creature!"

As so often in the classical literature since Shakespeare, Rebecca's sensuous journey ends tragically. At the moment of her ecstasy, she loses control of her motorcycle and crashes.

Although such books and articles in magazines depicting the motorcycle as a sex machine will probably never cease to appear, Harley-Davidson does not approve of and even actively discourages any sexual connotations their motorcycles might have. The women's motorcycle organization Women on Wheels takes a similar attitude towards this topic, strenuously rejecting every sexual connotation, even awarding "Golden Trashcans" for numerous offenses, particularly the combination of sex appeal and Harleys. Although there are groups who feel strongly against the sometimes pornographic innuendos, photographs and stories a Harley can provoke, it is, alas, inevitable, as the Harley motorcycle is a powerfully erotic and exciting machine, and riding on one truly is, in fact, an exciting experience.

No Pornos Please...

Although Harleys are often affectionately referred to as "hogs," the company attaches great value to its serious image, and has no desire to mar this identity with pornographic associations, not even when dealt with beneath the counter. When a pornographic video that included Harley-Davidson motorcycles appeared in the U.S., the company immediately sued for injunction and demanded that the producers relinquish their customer list, so that Harley – with police assistance – could recover those films that had already been distributed and sold.

Satisfied but not saddle–sore
cowboy chaps don't come
between a woman and her
thundering V-Twin.

Show-Offs

Obscenity as a Means of Rebellion
Against a Prudish Society

There's more to the world of Harley-Davidson than a motorcycling legend. The world of Harley-Davidson is also an elaborate show – a technical, artistic, and above all a human show. Perhaps a little too human, on occasion.

But what would the world be without show-offs especially the deafening world of the Harley macho exhibitionist. Show-offs are specialists when it comes to seeing and being seen, concealing their plain normality behind a garish and ostentatious exterior.

Generally loners, show-offs are laughed at, ridiculed, written off as amusing oddities – though often photographed. But it's unfair to dismiss them too quickly. It takes a lot of positive self-regard to perform these one-man shows, to play the harmless exhibitionist or court jester for a large and very mixed audience, each act having to be a perfect performance. Of course one won't find show-offs just anywhere. Like any good actor, the Harley show-off needs a stage and a receptive audience. Biker parties and major biking events are the preferred venue, where the aim is just to have a great time.

Isn't it wonderful that motorcycling (and riding Harleys in particular) doesn't have to be taken seriously all the time? In reality, these show-offs are just big kids who love masquerades and hammy play-acting – theatrical displays at which they themselves laugh most of all. If you ever get the chance to talk to one of these Harley entertainers behind the stage, or whatever is currently serving as a stage, you'll find he's almost certainly a "normal," agreeable, fun-loving person.

A crazy costume, an extraordinary outfit or almost naked – as long as one can show off everything is in and the show's perfect. Things that look good together belong together, a typical show-off combination.

A Different Way of Selling Ice Cream

He calls himself "The Ice Cream Man From Hell," a typical American idiom dating back to the 1950s. The vivid flames decorating his Servi-Car are his trademark, and he's even had the name patented. His product, on the other hand, has little to do with flames. "The Ice Cream Man From Hell" serves ice cream from the refrigerated trunk of his cherished 1971 Servi-Car, a service he particularly enjoys performing for the big-hearted women at shows and wet T-shirt contests. His performance always goes down well among the paying public and he's welcome at all major biker events. "The Ice Cream Man From Hell's" real name is Jim Trotta, born in Queens, New York and happily married now for 19 years. In addition to selling ice cream, he also peddles various souvenirs, quite happily and without the least inhibition. He occasionally runs into trouble on account of the red and white design of his Servi-Car, as this color scheme is reminiscent of a certain outlaw club. But Jimmy isn't an outlaw, and the decorations on his vehicle are simply an old American tradition. If things get too hot, he cools things down again with a generous portion of ice cream. Being his own promoter, he obviously has to make the most of every opportunity!

Be seen at all costs: show-offs are a sometimes bizarre, sometimes obscene, but usually lighthearted element at all Harley events, the fantasy and outfit of neither men nor women being subject to artistic or moral limits.

407

The Biker

A Secret Brotherhood

A great deal is written about bikers: sometimes it's well-informed, sometimes it's just trash. As soon as the subject is motorcycles, bikers will become the topic of conversation, and advertisers frequently delight in misusing them. Bikers are often confused with other types, usually rockers. Are bikers "rockers?" Or is it the other way round? Most people think they know exactly what rockers are: they are nasty guys on heavy, noisy motorcycles; crude, sometimes warm and friendly, mostly not averse to using violence; they are identifiable by their beards, their leather jackets and pants covered with metal studs, and the chains; they are always chasing women. Such clichés are deeply engrained in the minds of those who don't pause to think. In fact the rocker movement was a European phenomenon that developed in England during the 1950s.

So what are bikers? Basically, we are talking about a way of life; being a biker is in essence about the way in which you live your life and ride your bike. A biker is a typical product of the American lifestyle; a product of the unique social and political situation that exists in the U.S. What has arisen on the biking scene is a highly distinctive approach to life, and now an estimated 15 percent of all American motorcyclists could be described as bikers, provided it is not forgetten that there are clear distinctions to be made among them.

Nevertheless, it's by no means easy to define what you have to own or do to be considered a genuine biker. But, among other things, it has to do with an unmuffled, 45-degree, V-Twin engine making as much noise as possible with its explosive engine cycle; it has also to do with the "good vibrations" that this kind of engine produces. What is meant are the "vibrations" produced by a Harley-Davidson engine, something which, strangely enough, can't be produced at all by any other engine.

The term "biker" covers a wide range of people, and so it is important to correct a number of misconceptions. Unfortunately, a biker is frequently confused with a "cyclist" (somebody who rides a bicycle) a mistake that's unforgivable. Next, a great many people are convinced that anyone sitting on just about any motorcycle – nowadays casually designated a "chopper" – and clad in a leather jacket and jeans must be a biker.

Then people ask stupid questions that are best left unasked: why do these guys wearing those weird denim vests covered with emblems and medallions always cut off the sleeves? Why is their hair so untidy, why have they got beards and earrings, but no helmets, as they should have? Why don't they take a bath now and then? Why are their motorcycles not the genuine article but rather fire spitting, deafening, haphazardly assembled, and ugly-looking monsters, totally unroadworthy and disgustingly uncomfortable? What do all the letters and numbers that they have stitched on their clothes actually mean, and why are bikers always covered in so many tattoos? All these stupid questions all at once!

Well, here are the answers to some of the questions just to avoid any kind of unpleasantness arising from a misunderstanding. Bikers in the U.S. are outsiders in a society that they hate and despise, and this is exactly what they want. They have created their own social group with its own rules and code of morality, though it is by no means the case that sex and crime play the major role in this code, as outsiders tend to think. They are staunch patriots, a few are terrible racists; they have a healthy, though somewhat reluctant respect for state authority, but also demand that others respect them just as much within their own community. As far as the author ist concerned, they are the last heroes of the Wild West – a world of good guys and bad guys – in the best American tradition, a tradition that of course was not, in fact, always an admirable one. And, just like their machines, they have remained in a time warp.

There is nothing bikers detest more than the insensitivity of inquisitive outsiders attempting to penetrate their private world. But if someone does manage to get to know them better, it will soon emerge that, beneath that hard, outer shell, they are really wonderful human beings. There is nearly always something very special that helps to link them together, making communication possible: a Harley, that outrageous, unwieldy and powerful form of transport favored by so many of the bikers. In the U.S. bikers stand for "a lifestyle under pressure," applying above all to the ten percent or so of those bikers who have joined together to form MCs (of which only a small proportion can be considered hard-core bikers). This especially is a closed community to which no outsider will be casually admitted no matter how they may be dressed and no matter what type of souped-up machine they may be riding.

In addition, there are a few other criteria to be met. To describe somebody as a true biker does not automatically classify that individual as good or evil, clever or stupid, better or worse, rich or poor, nor indeed as male or female. Nor is a Harley rider necessarily a true biker either; and a true biker, come to that, might not even ride a Harley. Nevertheless, let's stay with the bikers who ride Harleys, since they form the majority. What really counts is the freedom in your soul, and the best piece of heavy metal that ever left Milwaukee, a 1000 cc or so engine and two enormous pipes. Well, okay – 750 cc would do in an emergency.

There's nothing that can separate a true Harley enthusiast from their trusty iron horse from Milwaukee. There is no technical advance, no matter how close to perfection, that would convince them. The enthusi-

asts remain stubbornly faithful to their antiquated machine in a spirit of true devotion that shuns the seductive charms of modern technology and progress. Neither racing success nor marketing strategy can shake their conviction that their Harley is the only genuine motorcycle that exists.

Though a biker is by nature coolness personified, a person who considers any form of emotional display or hysteria nauseating, there are some things they really do detest passionately: helmets and cops are two of these; others are the rules and regulations that restrict their freedom; and the never ending solicitude of those people who think they know everything and who want to decide for the bikers the way they should ride, the accessories they should use, and every detail of their biking life.

Germany is the second most important market for Harley-Davidson. But Harley enthusiasts hardly regard Germany as the land of freedom, for they are seldom allowed to ride their motorcycles in the way they want. In fact, the situation for Harley bikers in California is no better. It has to be acknowledged that for Harley bikers in many places, conflict with the authorities is becoming more and more likely.

Generally, bikers are purists who won't compromise. Independence and freedom are more important than anything else as far as they are concerned, and so their relationship with state control, or in fact with any form of officialdom, is far from cordial. A carefully cultivated external appearance, a tie, white shirt and perfectly creased pants are definitely not what counts; a close shave and stylishly cut hair are no guarantee of morality, honesty or sincerity. Of course a biker washes as often as anyone else, but the work they do is frequently much dirtier, at least outwardly. But anyone daring to call bikers simply ordinary members of the working class is doing them an injustice.

True bikers are not often found in the upper middle class, nor are they often comfortably ensconced in a boardroom, though the exception proves the rule. Mostly bikers are members of the hard-working stratum of society and have blisters on their hands, hands that are used to hard physical work; bikers are certainly quite at ease when working with heavy equipment.

We've come full circle: the much-loved Harley a real biker remains faithful to all his life, no matter what the company may demand of them. The bike must be exactly in keeping with their ideals, their ambitions, and their passions: strong, loud, powerful, heavy.

For a long time bikers have been a familiar sight all over the world; at least in those places where the Harley has found a home. No other motorcycle has achieved what has been achieved in Milwaukee: with its sturdy V–Twin engine, the Harley has been able to create its own unique and unmistakable community of kindred spirits even beyond the shores of the U.S.

Bikers are an integral part of this community. Freedom on the road is what they value most of all (not forgetting that the word "road" means "wherever a Harley can be ridden"). It's this philosophy that makes life worth living as far as they are concerned; and the Harley is part and parcel of this freedom. It's the very air they need to breathe, even though that air might be thin at times and difficult to inhale!

Turtle's Chopper –

Or, Surviving Between Heaven and Hell

Individual Fate

As I'd like to make it even clearer to the reader, what life means to a biker, I've selected two personal stories which, short though they are, deal with something that plays a dominant role in a biker's world: life with their beloved Harley – and death, which is never far away. Both stories describe events experienced by close friends of mine.

Turtle's Chopper was born during brief respites from the feverish hallucinations he experienced as he lay in an army field hospital somewhere in the jungles of Vietnam. At this time, Turtle, an 18-year-old sergeant, was fighting what seemed a hopeless battle against both the disease threatening to devour his body, and the powerful drugs the doctors were giving him in an attempt to save his life. At first, it was little more than the phantom image of a chopper that kept Turtle alive, a phantom that ultimately crystallized into a perfectly detailed image branded forever in his mind – the slender lines of the frame, the stretched and forward displaced, Springer fork, the 21-inch front wheel with its chrome-plated spokes, the pillion and sissy bar. Most of all, it was the powerful 74 inch (1200 cc) Panhead engine with its half gallon, teardrop shaped, fuel-tank that Turtle's mind's eye focused most often. There was nothing extra or superfluous on this machine: Turtle's chopper was pure motorcycle with only the nuts and bolts needed for riding it. In his pain-ridden dreams, Turtle did ride it. He rode it into a better world – a world of sunshine and freedom, a world without snipers lurking in treetops, without mines, without children who are blown into the air with you just because you let your guard down for a moment and offered them a bar of chocolate...

This imaginary motorcycle accompanied Turtle through countless hospitals and, when the doctors discharged him from their care, he set about turning his dream into reality. Turtle's home was somewhere in the woods of the Mississippi delta, where his uncle owned and ran a gas station, workshop, and recovery service. Because he'd become used to blood and death, Turtle agreed to recover the wrecked automobiles of drunk drivers who'd crashed in their alcoholic stupor and met a violent end.

However, the time came when Turtle finally had enough money saved to leave the restricting confines of his birthplace. By then, Turtle's chopper had become irresistible reality of sleek black and gleaming chrome. Another reason to go was Jennifer, a 19-year-old runaway from some East Coast city or another. A quiet, loving companion lacking a visible past. She could handle the motorcycle almost as well as Turtle but that wasn't what attracted him to her. It was the independence and freedom she granted him, though she was always there when he needed her. Although he loved their long, wild motorcycle runs together, Turtle sometimes felt that he was in hell. Because that was when the pain threatened to engulf him fully; the pain he picked up so many years ago in that war, and which no amount of tablets seemed capable of relieving. Other times, though, he imagined he was in heaven. That was when the powerful engine swept him and

his beloved down the highway, the cool air messing his hair and Jennifer cuddling up close from her pillion seat behind him. At those times, they pulled over somewhere, and if they were lucky they found friends who offered them safety and a sense of coming home. That was when Turtle could relax and drink a bit, until the alcohol kicked in and he was released from the agonies inflicted upon him so many years ago.

The next day, they hit the road once again, and slowly but surely his damaged soul begins to mend itself. For Turtle, the realization that there was something worth surviving for is the greatest pleasure he can experience in an otherwise despicable world. He survived for his chopper: the simple motorcycle of a Vietnam veteran and his lady. I should know, for Turtle was my brother biker and accompanied me on the lonely roads of the American Deep South for many years.

The Moment that Never Ended

For Frosty

This is in honor of Frosty — a biker whose real name was Erich Hufnagel. Frosty's dead. His misfortune — and I intentionally avoid using the word accident (though that's what it ultimately was, of course) — occurred like a bolt of lightning out of a clear blue sky. The picture I saw with horror in my rearview mirror will remain branded in my mind for the rest of my life: the huge reindeer ponderously crossing the road without a care in the world, and Frosty slamming into it without braking and careening over the embankment in an explosion of flesh and metal, hide and leather, animal and man. The rest was a bad dream, from which there was to be no awakening ...

I know, at this point, some of you may be thinking, "Well, it happens. And anyway, no matter how tragic this story sounds, what have I got to do with any of it?" But his story deserves to be told. One quiet moment, Frosty, 48 years old, told me that he'd always been a nonconformist — a maverick who loved nature above all else, and especially nature up in the North, where life is still simple and hard. Indeed he rode up to this northern paradise countless times, always alone and always full of joy. A year later, it was two good friends who rode north; two friends who were both fascinated by the challenge of the Arctic Circle. Frosty was the first German member of the originally American–only Wheels of Steel Club. He'd actually always been a loner, and not, as he claimed, a nonconformist, and he was anything but ice cold, as I once ironically called him on account of his love of the cool northern climes. He was an extremely warm–hearted and sensitive person, who simply knew how to hide it well. But anyone who got to know him was readily welcomed into his big heart.

All he owned was his Harley and this bike was always fully laden with the things needed to survive in the wilderness. But Frosty's wilderness wasn't just the Arctic Circle: it was also his apartment in Munich, Germany, his parties, his tours, and indeed the entire surroundings. He always had everything with him. In his bike club, which was his real home anyway from home, he was appointed to the rank of Road Captain.

When touring with friends, Frosty was always quick to point out some of nature's hidden wonders: places and people that we usually don't notice, or which we ride past without so much as a second glance. This made it all the more difficult for Frosty to talk about himself; of his time in the French Foreign Legion from which he deserted, or his victory over the bottle, and his job as a truck driver, or his repeated attempts to integrate himself into the corrupt, exploitative, remorseless, and pitiless society in which he had no choice but to live. His dream was to live like the Native Americans, somewhere in the unblemished solitude of nature. Damn it Frosty! Why couldn't you have been more committed to your dream and fulfilled it after all? It may seem futile to talk about it now but perhaps there's a little bit of Frosty in all of us. While we sat in a motel room in Rovaniemi, for two torturously long days, staring in despair at the intense blue sky, Frosty was alone on the intensive care ward, at that point in danger of dying (the doctors assured us), but still connected to numerous pieces of equipment and sprouting monitoring cables and various tubes. Lying there pale under the neon lights, he in fact never regained consciousness, never understood what had happened. The well–known biker clichés aimed at brushing off such tragedy with cool indifference kept coming back to me: "Live to ride, ride to live," and "Ride free, die hard." When the telephone rang at midnight, on August 7, I already knew what the call was about: Frosty was dead. He unfortunately didn't get to die a biker's death, with his boots on and cruising happily down the road, where he preferred to be most of all.

True Bikers

Leather–Covered Hearts of Gold

Women in the Saddle

Facts, Names and Dates

From the beginning, a fashionable outfit went without saying for emancipated female Harley riders, even if it was less than practical or sexy.

The Enthusiast also often showed Harley-riding beauties such as Senorita Aida Valenzuela from Guatemala, who in 1934 became Miss Central America.

Clara Wagner, who had already been involved in advertising the motorcycles built by her father, became a member of the American motorsport organization the FAM (Federation of American Motorcyclists) at the tender age of 17. However, her courageous victory in a 365-mile Endurance race from Chicago to Indianapolis in October 1910 was immediately declared "unofficial" and Clara was denied the trophy — the loss of face would have been too much for most of the male participants to bear.

On Independence Day, 1916, the Van Buren sisters, Adeline and Augusta (relatives of President Martin Van Buren), set off from New York on a journey that would take them to California and Mexico. They were riding Indian motorcycles. One of the most striking achievements of this tour was the successful climb, along an extremely difficult mountain track, to the summit of Pike's Peak, some 14,110 feet above sea level. However, the police arrested the intrepid duo on numerous occasions because of their "masculine uniforms."

The year before 1915, a mother and daughter crossed the United States from New York to San Francisco on a Harley-Davidson, motorcycle-sidecar combination. The two women were

Avis Hotchkiss and her daughter Effie. Effie had purchased a Harley when she was younger and attached a sidecar so that she could take her mother with her on her Pan-American (female) Odyssey.

Early issues of The Enthusiast were always careful to make respectful mention whenever a daring woman swung her leg over the saddle of a motorcycle. As a result of this positive reporting, increasing numbers of women Harley riders came to the fore and reported with enthusiasm their love of motorcycling, describing it as one of the most exciting experiences of their lives. While the AMA still harbored serious reservations regarding this development, Harley-Davidson welcomed the female motorcyclists warmly. One of them, a young lady named

Vivian Bales, wrote such nice letters to Harley that she was sponsored by the company, and went on to make her debut as the first "Enthusiast Girl" on the cover page of the November 1929 issue of the magazine. The Enthusiast of the 1920s and 1930s were brimming with pictures of women riding Harleys.

And as in other walks of life commonly regarded as "masculine," motorcycling had its own share of outstanding female personalities. Dot Robinson was to the world of motorcycling — and Harley-Davidson in particular — what Amelia Earhart was to the world of aviation. Practically born on the back of a motorcycle, Dot had been involved in the motorcycle business for as long as she could remember, being the daughter of sidecar manufacturer Jim Goulding. He owned a Harley dealership in Saginaw, Michigan, in which red-haired Dorothy worked. Her specialty was participating in endurance and arduous cross-country competitions, which she usually won in the class for

© Harley-Davidson

This photo is courtesy of: Milwaukee County Historical Society, Milwaukee, Wisconsin

Famous women of the Harley scene: Miss Ethel Bruce from Wooster, Ohio with her mother in the sidecar of the combination in which they had just contested an endurance race (right).

© Harley-Davidson

After her trans-American journey, Miss Effie Hotchkins christens her successful combination at the edge of the Pacific Ocean with Atlantic water she had brought with her. In the sidecar is her mother, in the background is the Cliff House and Seal Rocks (above).

Dot and Earl Robinson at a Harley dealers' convention in Milwaukee in 1952 with a Panhead motor model (top left).

Two unknown ladies posing in front of the company's Milwaukee factory building on a new machine in the 1920s, (left).

motorcycle-sidecar combinations. Dorothy was too small to reach the ground safely on difficult cross-country courses, which was why she specialized in riding the sidecar combinations, which she even painted in a provocative pink. Dot overcame the resistance of AMA Secretary E.C. Smith with a remarkable degree of commitment. Her daughter Betty — likewise encouraged to ride Harleys from a young age — was soon just as well-known as her outstanding mother. Dot vigorously advocated her philosophy of "ladylike" motorcycling, and the lipstick holder mounted on her Harley became a symbol of her conviction. She founded the Motor Maids at the end of the 1930s together with Linda Dugeau, and became the organization's first president in 1940, an office she held for 25 years. In 1991, at the age of 79, she still tirelessly rode her pink Full Dresser to all major events, where she was celebrated without exception as the "First Lady of Motorcycling." In her lifetime, she had clocked up more than one-and-a-half million miles on no less than 35 Harleys.

Another remarkable personality was Bessie B. Stringfield, who acquired a 1928 model Indian Scout at the age of 16, and indulged in her favorite sport by taking part in stunt shows and wall-of-death exhibitions whenever the opportunity arose. She purchased her first Harley in 1930, and immediately set off on a tour of America. She traveled alone on a journey that was to last six months, overcoming all imaginable obstacles placed in her way with astonishing courage and tremendous independence. Not only was Bessie short, she was also black, which meant the obstacles she faced were anything but minor irritations. She endured not only the ups and downs of biker life, but also extreme racial prejudice, and it wasn't until she was much older that she received the highest recognition and was inundated with honors. Unfortunately, her biography has yet to be written. But should pen ever reach paper to recount the story of Bessie Stringfield, it would most likely prove to be the most exciting and remarkable chronicle of a biker's life ever written.

© Harley-Davidson

The Silent Grey Fellow (opposite) was apparently a favorite of the ladies — the mudguard to protect the long skirts indicates that the lady actually rode her machine.

In Germany, women were happy to pose on new Harley machines, as here at Suck in Hamburg (top and above); the ladies of the Orange County Club of Santa Ana, California, have no weather to contend with and prefer lighter clothing (right).

© Harley-Davidson

417

Harley Women

Real women ride Harleys: this claim was true right from the start. Early motorcycling magazines, above all *The Enthusiast*, were full of pictures of women riding motorcycles. Their articles described adventures in which the mostly young and emancipated women had to come to terms with the pitfalls of technology, the harshness of the weather, the poor condition of the unpaved roads, and the occasionally uncomprehending intolerance of men.

Decently attired in flowing dresses, these motorcyclists simply didn't reflect the conventional motorcycle rider image (rowdy, rough and unkempt) nor, come to that, the ideal of that time period of a devoted housewife (modest, home-loving, and submissive). Nevertheless, ride motorcycles they did, having a whole heap of fun in the process. And not just in America; around the world women have ranked among the pioneers of the motorcycling age. The stylish leather outfits introduced in 1920s were also just the ticket for the new generation of motorized women. After all, the sexual revolution was already progressing at full throttle, even though accompanied by a raucous outcry of moral indignation. Still, America was a free country – albeit with some restrictions – with free citizens, and those citizens included women.

At first women were largely banned from participating in the AMA's sporting events: Dot Robinson put an end to this unacceptable situation in the 1930s. Nevertheless, female AMA racing licenses continued to be the exception to the rule. It wasn't until shortly before World War II that the Motor Maids managed to fully integrate women motorcyclists in the "Great American Society," finally making them socially acceptable.

Today, at the beggining of the 21st century, the image of a woman astride a motorcycle is taken for granted – at least in most countries of the world – even if many men still doubt the females' ability to handle a contraption as heavy as a Harley–Davidson. As if it has anything to do with strength! When a woman makes that small move forwards from the pillion to the driver's seat to grasp the handlebars, she undergoes a fundamental transformation, mutating from being a mere biker's "buddy" to being an individual free of sexual and gender cliches. In other words, it's no longer a "woman" riding the motorcycle, but a "person."

Today in biking, the differences between the sexes are totally irrelevant, even though these differences are still frequently alluded to by some men in a manner that is half-scorn, half-acknowledgment. As a consequence of this liberation, the Harley scene, which traditionally regarded itself as "masculine," and proudly bragged of its "macho" biker lifestyle, has had to face a dilemma, particularly as women's sexual allure is constantly flaunted for questionable marketing purposes in the media and in advertising. However, all this was less of a problem for Harley–Davidson. It had paid the greatest attention and respect to women right from the start, shrewdly acknowledging them as an important target group. "Sexual correctness" was regarded as a matter of course, and women today (those who ride Harleys, of course) have shed their special status as fabulous animals to be gazed upon in unbelieving wonder, and have acquired equal rights in all company positions, all the way up to that of Vice President. The chauvinistic and macho attitude – understandably enough – vigorously denied by Harley actually applies far more on the "hard-core" biker scene, which has developed its own set of rules.

It would be going too far to attempt to do justice to even a fraction of the thousands of outstanding women Harley riders throughout the world. So forgive the author please when, on behalf of all the others, just the few that immediately spring to mind or whose paths have been crossed over the years are mentioned. A handful of photos are often the sole keepsake of such encounters. Perhaps the best thing would be to go out and meet some of the countless women and girls of Harley in real life. After all, you can bump into them everywhere – that is, everywhere where Harleys are to be found!

Babs and Her Panhead

Harley Women or True Bikers?

There it is in the rain with a flooded engine. It stinks of leaded gas. A tempting brew as it were. A damn cool chopper in the Hydra Glide style, heavily modified however. Full of Panhead power, an oldie monster bike, mucho macho brutalo. And the guy riding it? Ain't a guy at all, it's a little girl, smirk.

Still the most pressing concern at the moment: starting problems – damn carburetor! The bike's killing itself in the process, coughing up its lungs – off with the jacket.

"Can you hold my lid?" (The helmet comes off.) But it looks good – there's no lack of spectators and supposedly sound advice. Then finally: it coughs into life! The sound of the motor starting.

At least you think that's what it is. Silence. Let's talk shop first. The little one's called Babs. She knows something about choppers. Does everything herself too. Then the ritual again: ignition off – four or five dry runs, left leg propped up at the back, right leg in kickstart position, look for OT, ignition on, deep breaths, jump up and ... again nothing. Enthusiastic applause from all quarters. But

Babs is a hardened karate kickstarter. She succeeds with her fifth attempt – the carburetor hesitates a bit, backfiring a couple of awkward farts before the motor from hell shakes itself warm. She fumbles with the choke – and VROOM! Those onlookers who don't ride Harleys step back in awe.

Finally in the saddle – better unsprung, low in the frame, pure vibrations. The clutch pedal is on the left at the very front: a hopeless proposition without biker boots. The suicide clutch: activated by means of a lever at the back pushed down forcefully – click, clack – the gear's selected.

You have to be able to do that. The two fat tires start to roll. Wide Glide forks and behind them three hundred pounds of air-cooled brute force.

The mud goes flying past the rider's ears. The beast pounds its way through the countryside. A blond mane trails in the wind behind (damn helmet!) – who's talking about dumb feminists now?

Whoever rides a Panhead like that can call himself brother without being contradicted, even if she is a girl. I just think we need to talk about exhaust pipes some time, Babs, don't you agree?

One huge organization: the Ladies of Harley (LOH), here shown in Germany.

419

The Motor Maids

Ambassadors for Equal Rights, Tolerance and Attractive Motorcycle Riders

Co-founder and long-serving President of the Motor Maids, Dot Robinson.

© Harley-Davidson

Group photo of the Motor Maids at their meet in Washington D.C. in May 1954.

Linda Allen Dugeau co-founded the Motor Maids in 1940.

For whatever reasons, the image of the motorcyclist worsened significantly during the 1930s. Motorcyclists had never enjoyed very high status among middle America, which considered them at best to be a wild bunch: scruffy, oil-stained, foul-mouthed hooligans all-too easily regarded as the scum of the earth.

Of course this was a prejudiced view which was far from the truth, but it became more and more widespread, to the consternation of serious riders and of course the AMA, which saw itself as the representative of the regular motorcycle rider. However, perhaps it was the AMA's sporting events (in themselves fair) which promoted this unflattering public image. Wild macho men, but what about the women motorcyclists? After all, there were enough women, and in the rough world of male bikers they demanded a certain chivalry, in other circumstances a very scarce commodity. However, manners were becoming noticeably worse, and so E.C. Smith, the General Secretary of the AMA, a man always concerned with questions of public image, was delighted when a certain Linda Dugeau got in touch with him one day....

Linda Allen Dugeau, a personal secretary and mother of four from Providence, Rhode Island, was a keen motorcyclist. She had owned an old 45 Flathead since 1931 which her husband had bought for 12 dollars in dismantled form and then rebuilt. Linda was worried about the increasingly poor reputation of motorcyclists and had the idea that women in particular could change it – women like herself.

In the summer of 1938 she began a remarkable mail campaign, sending every possible dealer, acquaintance and organization a famous circular which heralded the birth of one of the most extraordinary motorbike clubs in the world: the Motor Maids of America, or Motor Maids for short. In her own words:

"I am convinced that one way to help the sport of motorcycling remove the silly prejudice which so many hold against it, because of the actions of certain thoughtless members of our fraternity, is to persuade more and more girls to own and ride machines. No one condemns a girl because she flies an airplane and pretty soon I hope that no one will believe that because a girl rides a motorcycle, she must necessarily be tough, immoral and, in general, not fit for decent people's society."

The letter closed with her personal history and a call to all interested parties to reply with a photo and a short personal résumé. 51 women wrote back, and in 1940 Linda founded the Motor Maids of America with them. However, first she contacted the best-known and most respected female motorcyclist of her era, who had for a long time been regarded as an ambassador for women motorcyclists, Dorothy "Dot" Robinson, of Detroit, Michigan. Dot gave Linda's idea her enthusiastic support and naturally enough came to be President of the Motor Maids, a post which she went on to occupy for 25 years. The AMA gave the movement its full support, and in 1941 the Motor Maids became AMA Charter Club Number 509.

Several other well-known "lady riders" were members of the club's first board: Lou Rigsby of Chattanooga, Tennessee became Vice President, Helen Kiss of Pottstown, Pennsylvania was the Treasurer, Hazel Duckworth of Valley Falls, Rhode Island was a Secretary, and Linda herself became the first Secretary. There were four other important posts: Publicity Director, Advisory Editor, Supply Officer and Historian. The goal laid down in the Club Rules was to unify all women motorcyclists, to support motorsport in general and, above all, to use their presence to improve the image of motorcyclists. But the most important condition of membership was that every Motor Maid owned her own motorbike and generally rode it wherever she went.

The Motor Maids' outfit was suitably smart and striking: to the present day their uniform consists of a dark blue shirt, gray trousers, white gloves and white ankle-length leather boots – a complete contrast to the clothing hitherto worn by motorcyclists. Most of the Motor Maids rode large bikes, predominantly Harleys, with the aim of demonstrating thereby that the "gentler" sex could also handle heavy machines often weighing more than five times as much as they did, and ride long distances without having to have dirty fingernails and oil-stained clothing.

When they paraded in 1941 at Newsies Race, they were given the nickname "ladies of the white gloves," which they adopted with pride. Their provocative cream-and-pink painted bikes, for example the Indian ridden by Helen Kiss, also became notorious, and the term "Pink Lady" soon became a well-known synonym for a female motorcycle club.

Since 1944 the Motor Maids have held their national conventions in 25 U.S. states, and also in Canada. The 1944 meeting was attended by just 14 members, the main reason being the wartime rationing of gasoline. A number of Motor Maids served in the U.S. armed forces, for example Nellie Jo Gill, Marion Trow, and Arlene Sonnefeldt. After the war the club was reorganized by Vera Griffin and her friend Ruth

Fordyce, with the able assistance of Dot Robinson. It now had over 500 members, and their national convention in Nashville, Indiana was attended by 43 of them.

The State Director system had by now been introduced and the range of activities increased: club meetings, participation in Gypsy Tours, AMA motorsport events, parades and rallies. Road Runs were particularly popular, where the particpants' times were recorded at a succession of checkpoints.

Anyone taking part in two national conventions was entitled to become a life member. 25 years of membership qualified you for "Silver Life Membership," and any member attending at least ten national conventions and remaining an active member for 50 years achieved the ultimate accolade: Golden Life Membership. Quite a few of these have been awarded.

Dot Robinson stepped down from the Presidency of the Motor Maids in 1965 and entered an active retirement. She hardly ever missed a major event. Her successor was Dorine Hamilton from Wichita, Kansas, and the third President was Mary Cutright of Chillicothe, Ohio. They were followed by Kathleen Anderson and Jeanne Deak of Chardon, Ohio. The sixth and current President of the Motor Maids is Jane Barrett of Englewood, Florida.

In 1966 the first national convention was held in Sturgis, South Dakota on the occasion of the Sturgis Bike Week Black Hills Motor Classic, organized by Kathy Anderson and her daughter Pat Crosby. 89 members attended. Since the 50th anniversary of the Black Hills Motor Classic a voluntary yearly breakfast has been held at Mama Hoel's, the widow of the founder of this rally. Of course, the Motor Maids have now to some extent become an "Old Ladies Club," but there are also plenty of younger members who are keen to maintain the good old traditions. Motor Maids of America, Inc. has 420 members in the U.S.A. and Canada and a representative in Israel and Australia.

To celebrate their 50th anniversary, the Motor Maids posed in front of the AMA headquarters in Ohio (above) and paraded at almost all the larger events, as here at Sturgis Bike Week in Speedway Stadium.

Woman Racers

The dragster rider Annemarie Datzer from Germany (above).

The fifteen-year-old Joyce Holley (below).

It's hard to tell whether a racer is a woman; one often has to wait until they take off their helmets, which is a measure of just how well they ride. In what is, superficially at least, a man's sport, especially at the heavyweight end of things where Harleys are to be found, women were for decades barred by the AMA from holding a race license. In the view of the AMA, this was to spare them from the unseemly strenuousness of motorcycle racing. However, in modern motorcycle racing women are no rarity, even on heavyweight Harleys.

In the early years of motorsport on two wheels a lot of women competed, performing miracles on their bucking, difficult machines, particularly on enduro and long-distance courses, track, and mountain races, and also tough motocross trials. Granted, some forms of motorsport require enormous physical strength and plenty of guts. Among them are road-racing and dirt-track racing, and also speedway, hillclimb, and American TT — a test of toughness from which all the champion U.S. racers emerged. And here, too, a number of women racers have come right to the fore.

Among the best known are Diane Cox and Tammy Kirk, the "racing lady" from Dalton, Ohio. During the 1980s they raced in the AMA Camel Pro Series national dirttrack races on their XR 750 racers and dirt trackers, and became members of the exclusive 100 Miles Club. Tammy left a lot of male racers in her wake, and often got into hard-fought duels with Jay Springsteen. In 1984 she received the National Plate No. 57. Since 1987 Nancy Delgado has been racing a variety of different makes of motorcycle, among them an 883 cc Sportster, and was not deterred from carrying on after being involved in a serious accident when another contestant rode into her. Another

female rider Lynn Wilson was an important member of the Harley-Davidson enduro team.

However, women have always excelled at one category of motorsport in particular: Harley dragster racing. Handling these roaring, fire-breathing, V-twin monsters of horsepower excess requires less in the way of brute force, and more in the way of finesse and fast reactions. On top of this, dragster racing more than any other type is a family affair, and many of the women riders are daughters of dragster racers, or the wives or girlfriends of motorcycle engineers, Harley mechanics, or dragster freaks. They have long since received recognition and equal rights, and just as the men have their "King of the Hill" title, the women race for the title "Queen of the Hill."

One of the earliest Harley dragster racers during the 1970s was Bonnie Truett, famous for a number of spectacular starts. Cathy "Cat Lou" West was the first women to race at the AMRA Drags on a powerful Top Gas Harley. As early as the beginning of the 1970s, Mary Baisley from Portland, Oregon, raced a high-performance Sportster, constructed by her husband, in the AHRA Nationals. Debbie Bearup, a mother of two, rode her Low Rider dragster in the Pro Street Class at IDBA, AMRA and in drag bike races in the mid-1980s, resplendent in pink race leathers. She had been riding Harley-Davidsons since the age of 13.

Linda Jackson of Columbia, Missouri, was crowned Queen of the Hill by *Harley Woman* magazine in 1991 and she had been riding a 74 cubic inch Sportster in the Super Stock XL Class since 1988. However, she suffered a serious accident in 1992 when her frame broke while racing at almost 120 mph. She is the proud bearer of the Number One plate for her class.

Kristine Becker was the first women to win a Nitro (Top Fuel) Class race. Pam Cummings, a police inspector from Waukegan, Illinois, was another to race one of these nitro monsters on the dragstrip, and was in fact the first woman to race a Top Fueler. Her ex-husband was a mechanic, and her team was appositely named the Hellraisers. In 1993 her engine exploded during a race – a piston was fired 70 feet into the air, and she was thoroughly drenched in oil and nitro, but she survived the ordeal, suffering nothing worse than a couple of broken ribs.

Undoubtedly the most famous woman Top Fuel racer is Doris Wiggins, an outgoing, redhead hairdresser from Clayton, North Carolina. "Baby Doris" started out as an asphalt track racer before entering the HDRA race on a modified big twin in 1986. In 1992 she became the fastest woman in her class when she achieved a time of 7.9 seconds and a speed of 172 mph on her 113 cubic inch (1850 cc), 300 horsepower Nitro Super Pro Fueler. At one point a serious accident left her unconscious for five days but she was soon back in the saddle.

Equally well-known is Lori Volmert-Francis of St. Louis, Missouri, a.k.a. "Lady Thunder." She came out of the motocross scene and started racing dirt bikes in flat-track races when still a child. At the age of 23 she first rode in the Pro Stock Class on her tuned-up Sporty, becoming the second fastest woman in the U.S. in 1995 with a speed of 158.4 mph. Sharon Garrison of Alabama achieved eight national records on her Sportster in the Super Modified XL Class, and is another to hold the Number One plate in her class.

In Europe, too, increasing numbers of woman racers are competing, especially in the popular street and pro street classes, and also in the "run what you brung" class, often also called "public races." Once the woman racers have had their first taste of blood they often move up to the Pro classes, as did Gabi Weigand of Eichendorf, Germany, who reached a speed of 82.24 mph on her Sportster over the Street Class one-eighth mile. Another well-known name is Annemarie Datzer of Vilsbiburg, Germany, who raced the 1995 season. She began with tenth place on her 1450 cc, 90 horsepower Street Harley, finally achieving second place. Gerlind "Linda" Osthues of Berlin, Germany is another professional, drag racer who went to Frank Hawley's Drag Racing School in the U.S. After starting out in enduro in 1986 at the age of 30, she switched in 1992 to the faster Modified Class, racing an 883 cc Sportster, and later moved on to the Top Fuel Class, winning races at every level, to become established as the fastest woman racer in Europe.

And the next generation are also coming through, as two extraordinary young women demonstrate, both daughters of successful dragster racers, engineers, and Harley dealers.

First there is Joyce Holley, who has been riding cross-country Harleys in motocross and enduro competitions since she was a small child. Then her father, "Campi" Anson, a well-known, Top Fuel Harley dragster constructor from New Orleans, built her a genuine Pro Gas Dragster as a Café Racer replica, with which she raced some wild quarter-mile sprints at local IDBA events while still 15 years old. Then there is Kersten Hopkins of Shawano, Wisconsin, who got started at an even earlier age. When she was just 13 she rode her father "Doc" Hopkins', powerful Top Fuel Panhead dragster for the first time. This monster had an 1850 cc engine putting over 300 horsepower onto the tarmac. At the age of 15, she became the youngest licensed Top Fuel woman racer in the world in the blue ribbon, AHDRA Pro Dragster Class. Harley woman racers are clearly here to stay.

The well-known racing rider from the Robison team, Tammy Kirk (top), and the fifteen-year-old Kerstin Hopkins on her Top-Fuel dragster at the burnout (right).

Harley Toys

Never Too Old...
Harleys for the Kids

It roars, it peeps, it whistles, it has turn signals, and it takes pride of place in many kids' bedrooms. Dad brought it home a while back from K-Mart, or maybe from the dime store on the corner, and the battery has to be changed now and then. Occasionally a plastic policeman rides on it, and more recently the immortal Barbie and her arch rival Steffie Love, their long golden hair flowing down over their leather outfits. Their mount is a 12 inch high Electra Glide made of the finest plastic. Whatever would Barbie's boyfriend Ken say?

The ultimate Harley toy is available in sizes from a tiny matchbox model to a child's bicycle. The earliest toy Harleys, made of cast iron, were produced in 1928 by the Hubley Company, a toy maker based in Lancaster, Pennsylvania, later taken over by the CBS group. These Harley miniatures were robust, and could whiz around over the floor in a pretty impressive fashion.

Apart from countless motorcycle models and miniatures in all shapes and sizes, you can also find rocking horse Harleys, electric racetracks for miniature Harleys, Harley board and card games, including Harley Monopoly, and of course plenty of soft toys.

Many department stores provide electrical models for kids to ride on, while in amusement arcades there are electronic Harley replicas for young would-be racers. At fairgrounds, Harley carousels whirl round and round, the riders feeling like Betty Boop, the cartoon character who, with her ageless Harley, has become a sort of kiddy's vamp symbol.

When this generation of children finally grows up, their playthings will be genuine Harley-Davidson motorcycles.

Minature, 1980s

A metal toy replica
France, 1990s

Champion Hardware, 1930s

3 Cylinder Nomura, TN
Autocycle 1960s

A Die-cast Harley Hack

Racer, 1930s

Cast iron, 1930s Police,
Side Hack

Civilist, 1930s

Police, Champion hardware, 1930s

Hillclimber, Hubley, 1930s

Parcel Post, Hubly, 1928

Die-cast Harley Rider

Champion Hardware, 1930s

Steffi Love, 1990s

Metal toy replica

Police Auburn Company,
1950s

Police Servi-Car,
Nomura (Japan), 1960s

Side Hack, 1930s

Sexy Plastic Doll, 1980s

The Harley Barbie Doll, Mattel, 1998

Biker Plastic Doll, 1990s

Betty Boop KEYCHAIN

WARNING: choking hazard - small parts
Not for children under 3 years

A Statement of the Company:
The toys depicted here are not
all official licensed Harley-
Davidson products.

A "rocking" Harley (above and below).
Left, from top to bottom: a kiddie
Electra Glide with an electronic
motor, and a children's bicycle.
Last but not least, a "Sportster" bicycle.

A Betty Boop
Key–Holder

Family Ties

The Baby's Name is Harley

Whether they're with Mom in the sidecar or still in nappies, Harley kids are always there and no biker, no matter how hard, neglects their needs.

There has been a tradition of motorcycling families for a long time, particularly in the U.S. They came into being during the "Roaring Twenties" in rural areas, where the motorcycle–sidecar combination was the first inexpensive mode of transportation to offer the entire family a degree of mobility that allowed both travel and adventure. Although this role was soon taken over by the Model T Ford, a true biker still preferred to attach a sidecar to their Harley. And so it was that the sidecar became an important program at Harley-Davidson, with marketing concentrated on the family applications. A motorcycle–sidecar combination was the "automobile of the modest man," and if his family grew, a few solo machines could be expected to join the family gang.

True motorcycling families can be regarded as a sworn brotherhood. The motorcycle – and especially the faithful Harley – plays a central role in their family life, and is assigned the role as the family's mechanical pet, complete with its own character and need for care.

"Families who stay together, ride together." And that refers to all family members, young and old. The grandparents can travel in the sidecar, while the babies could be fitted into extra saddlebags, or strapped to mother riding the pillion... which wouldn't be a safe way to travel with your children. Whatever the solution, one has to be found, as a genuine biker family wouldn't be seen in an automobile.

However, being a biker family also means far more than just owning and riding a motorcycle. The motorcycle, particularly Harleys represent their philosophy of life, and forge a bond between like-minded families who help each other out when-ever and wherever possible. They not only play together, they also organize neighborhood help, ranging from babysitting and assistance in times of need, all the way to planning joint activities on any scale imaginable. The number of such "biker communities" that can be found both in rural and suburban America is astonishing. It would seem to be just as apt to say "Families who ride together, stay together."

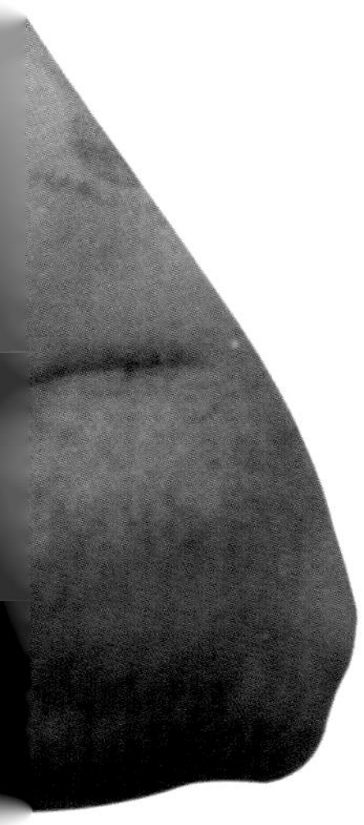

Motorcycle excursions were no problem for large families. There were outsized Harley sidecars for that, even if they were a little overloaded at times.

Rug Rats on Harleys

Kids in a Bikers World

The first tentative steps and ride: for kids there is nothing more exciting than climbing up on a Harley.

Rule number one applies here: Harley kids are something special! While they are still in diapers they become inseparably a part of the Harley myth — in Harley cots, which look deceptively like an FLH, with Harley pillows and Harley comforters. Naturally they come along on every excursion, depending on their age and temperament either up front riding on the gas tank (forbidden...), or placed between Mom and Pop (the sandwich method), or strapped on at the back, complete with H.O.G. teddy bear and mini-police helmet or, if there's no other way, in the sidecar (the safest way to travel).

The company has now realized the importance of the booming kids' market and added an irresistible range of goods to their repertoire — from mini-XXS T-shirts on which are printed slogans they cannot yet read (for example, "My daddy rides a Harley"), to superelegant leather outfits, little boots, pins and patches, and, to the unbounded envy of all their schoolmates and playmates, Harley bicycles (with the beautiful sound), mini-Harleys (with an electrical motor and gears), huge plastic toys, and other Milwaukee frivolities. Look for the trademark, to make sure you have the real thing. Anyway, the main thing is, the parent's are paying.

However, the kid's favorite "toy" is and always will be the Harley bike itself — nothing is better than its heavy vroom-vroom and the fun of clambering all over the monster, which never falls over. The girls love playing with the powerful steeds, while the boys indulge their inborn destructive urges and prefer testing themselves to the extreme.

To the horror of all non-Harley riding grandmothers, the little darlings are misused most of all as cute models for the family album, mainly in obviously artificial poses as experienced riders. You wonder if for little girls a Harley seems like a wild creature out of some fairy tale, while for little boys, who always think they know better, it's a totally outdated model that can't even reach the minimum speed limit usually in force these days. A favorite game is to repeatedly twist the throttle while simultaneously making loud growling noises in imitation of the sound of the engine, something Pop is not at all keen on since it's a fuel injector that Sonny is innocently pulling on, so he gets reprimanded. And once they've burnt their finger touching the hot exhaust pipe they'll always think twice before they touch anything like that again.

Actually I've never seen better-brought up or better-behaved children than those in biker families of long standing. The kids are professionally initiated into the mysteries of the internal combustion engine, an experience which for them take on the dimensions of a space mission. They quickly learn which spanner fits which nuts and that all the official traffic laws are not needed. Like all Harley riders, active or passive, they learn that Harleys are head and shoulders above any shrill, stinking two-stroke machines or Japanese bikes and they learn also to scorn any bullshit about driving school or driver's licenses. To roar with Pop totally illegally along remote forest tracks (but don't tell the Greens) is the tops! And so a special brood of rug rats grows up unstoppably, and finally become grown ups. Grown-up Harley riders, you understand...

Kid's Party

How Biker Kids Grow Up Alongside Motorcycles

Stupid question: of course I ride a Harley!

Little Tessi storms wailing into the kitchen and screams tearfully at me: "Go out at once and beat Liza up, the stupid cow, after all, that's what you are here for!" So I go to find out what the matter is now.

Outside, Tessi's best friend Liza, just ten years old, is on her daddy's new Sporty on which he has just brought her. The little one pretends to be a real Harley woman and bursts into tears when I told her that her feet cannot even touch the highway pegs. Soon afterwards I find the pair of them happily together in Tessi's bedroom surrounded by an indescribable chaos of pillows, blankets and broken toys, eating the entire ice cream supply from our fridge. It's a children's party again and this time it's going to hit with full force. The others are already on their way, as could be told by the non-stop ringing of the telephone all day long.

"I'm really grateful that you can look after the brats for a couple of days."

Joe, Liza's daddy, needs a break too, naturally. Immediately afterwards Bekki arrives, the chosen head of the Pink Lady Gang, originally an all-girl car gang in pink outfits heavily marketed in films and on TV as mankillers, always on the look-out for sex, as they have always been portrayed in the media. Thanks to the dream women Barbie and Betty Boop our little household has been transformed into a genuine hard-as-nails Harley gang.

Oh well, they say you shouldn't frighten sensitive children's souls with authoritarian methods of upbringing. When Lucy and fat Rosie arrive, all hell will break loose. Naturally anything in black leather is an indispensable symbol of girl power for the dear little things, and so they plunder our wardrobe mercilessly. Even if the miniskirt hangs down well below their knobbly knees and Pop's leather jacket covers their hands and most of their curly heads too, and Mom's boots are a good four

sizes too big, they have to have the right biker gear, "really wicked and mega," as they're always saying. Where do they get it all from?

Then they're outside in the garage and somehow manage to get my Electra Glide started, though they've got no idea that you're supposed to pull out the choke first, and so the backfiring practically burns the place down, and there's an almighty stink of gasoline and exhaust fumes.

"Have you kids gone crazy, you know damn well you're not supposed to start the engine in a confined space!" You just can't leave the little darlings alone for a minute! They cough and scream at me "Clear off, old man, don't you know there's absolutely no entry here for heavy old dudes – but you can bring loads of soft ice cream and marshmallows...," all delivered in the usual familiar tone of voice, just a continually ravenous bunch of delinquents. We are moved by our offspring's intense

interest in our beloved heavy metal machinery, and we know that one day they will be the pillars of an elite biker community. Ride to live and live to ride, as they say.

At the moment we are going through an unavoidable preliminary stage in this process, what is generally known as a puberty crisis. By now the garage has partially collapsed. Oh well, it was pretty well infested by termites anyway. To general amusement we just about managed to save the Harleys, and as a precaution I ring my insurance agent about imminent, serious household repairs and so on. We had to take Cindy to the emergency room for treatment because she had stuffed herself with marshmallows, popcorn and pickles, Mom's elegant boots are ruined, both the high heels have broken off, and have been lost.

Around midnight the whole innocent bunch finally fall asleep in front of the latest sex, violence and crime series on

the T.V. and we can have a well-earned Budweiser amid the ruins of our former living room. A successful party, no doubt about it. Tomorrow is a new day, and the rebuilding can begin...

Animals

Dogs, cats and other animals seem to really love riding on motorcycles. They have a highly developed sense of balance even in the most difficult positions, but hate having to wear helmets and goggles, as indeed prescribed by animal-welfare groups.

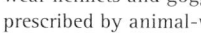

© Harley-Davidson

430

Harley VIP's I

Elvis Presley

Although he actually had a preference for souped-up automobiles, the King (born January 8, 1935, in Tupelo, Mississippi) also had several classic Harleys in his extensive fleet of vehicles. Four of them can still be seen today at the Gracelands Museum near Memphis, Tennessee: a 1957 Hydra Glide, a 1966 1200 cc chopper, and two Electra Glides, one of which is a Liberty edition. As early as May 1956 the 21-year-old, relative newcomer appeared on the cover of the Harley-Davidson magazine *The Enthusiast* waving a Harley cap, smiling his irresistible smile, and sitting astride a 1956 model KH (in pepper red and white); he was also featured in an article in the magazine. This was his third motorcycle and his first Harley V-twin. He enjoyed riding motorcycles, and did so as often as he could, always wearing a special outfit for publicity reasons.

Elvis was also a member of the AMA. His two-wheeled escapades became renowned during the shooting of the film "Viva Las Vegas," when he and Ann-Margret caused havoc on the dirt trails around Hollywood on his Sportster. Alas, although he always paid tribute to the legend of Harley-Davidson, very few photos actually show Elvis on a Harley.

Reinhold Würth

There is hardly a Harley shop in the world in which you can't find nuts and bolts, parts, tools, and servicing products that have been manufactured by the international industrial group Adolf Würth GmbH und Co. KG (based in Künzelsau in the German state of Württemberg). Their range of products also covers entire workshop inventories for Harley branches. The group is run by German industrialist Reinhold Würth, who is a well-known art collector and the paternalistic guardian of his workforce, as well as being a great fan of the legend from Milwaukee. Würth officially sponsored the German 883 Harley-Davidson Cup, and when his employees presented him with a 1995 model Fat Boy on the occasion of his 60th birthday, he became no longer merely a fan and sponsor, but also an enthusiastic biker.

Malcolm Forbes

Malcolm Forbes was born in 1919; he owned an island in Fiji, and was the publisher of the American magazine *Forbes*, with headquarters in New York and branches in England, France, Morocco, and Tahiti. From time to time this multimillionaire even rode his café racer or Low Rider to his office in Manhattan. Forbes enjoyed traveling around the world, together with a fleet of Harleys and his biker friends – a group of peers calling themselves "Capitalist Tools." Malcolm Stevenson Forbes was also the owner of the largest collection of tin soldiers in the world, and a collector of model boats, as well as jewel encrusted eggs made by Fabergé. He was a keen hot air balloonist who set several records himself and who owned numerous balloons, one of which looked like a gigantic Heritage Softail. He owned more than 40 motorcycles, two of which were always kept ready on his yacht, *Highlander*. In addition to his "goodwill" balloon adventures, his motorcycle excursions became particularly well known: an ingenious combination of international biker events, international diplomacy, and advertising for his publishing house. In this context, he became in the 1980s the first American ever to be permitted to tour Russia on a motorcycle. In 1988, he set off on a Turkish-American friendship tour with eight Harleys and a balloon, traveling to Anatolia and Istanbul. Other excursions took him as far afield as Thailand and Egypt. His motorcycle excursion with five FXR Harleys through the People's Republic of China in 1983 became world famous because he was again the first American to be allowed to undertake such an adventure.

Forbes was a good friend of Elizabeth Taylor for many years, and actually presented her with an 883 cc Sportster (probably as a wedding gift), which was named after her perfume, Passion. Malcolm Forbes died on February 23, 1990. The obituary of one biker magazine read: "A fellow biker has left us."

Top Guns

It's probably the most famous Harley club in the world, simply because it also has the most famous members. It consists of some 65 prominent personalities, recruited mainly from the high society of Harley bikers. It's the Ugly MC, cozily united beneath the old pirate emblem of a skull and crossbones. Bill Elkins had the idea of founding the MC in 1984 on the occasion of the first Love Ride, under the direction of Oliver Shokouh, who was also responsible for having this wonderful photo taken. Among the true Harley freaks in their hard-core biker look, the following Ugly MC members can also be seen: Hoyt Axton, Ben "Nighthorse" Campbell, Willie G., Bill Davidson, Marty J. Rosenblum, Peter Fonda, Larry Hagman, Newt Harrell, Tom Perkins, Barry Matkron, Mike Lombardi and Oliver Shokouh.

Harley VIP's II

Clark Gable (right), Mickey Rourke (below) in "Harley–Davidson and the Marlborough Man," and Cher (below right).

JERRY LEWIS MEETS THE LAW

© Harley-Davidson

Photos by Hyman Fink sent to *The Enthusiast* in 1952: the comedian and later MDA chief Jerry Lewis has some fun with the police (top).

An inseparable team, politically too: the former President of Indonesia Suharto with his successor Jusuf Habibie in the sidecar, taken on September, 1, 1996 (above).

Today almost an official Harley talkshow host: television comic Jay Leno.

Strangely enough, despite all the media coverage, the rich and beautiful of high society who occasionally give the chauffeurs of their limousines the day off and grab the handlebars of a Harley-Davidson are not as well-known to the lowest caste of the Harley world, i.e. the bikers and outlaws. Perhaps this is because the international press find other aspects of the jet set life more interesting than paint and chrome on two fat wheels. For most of these well-heeled people, a Harley is probably less a statement of a "way of life" than a whim, or even a means of escape from their stardom; for a moment, possibly, they return to normality, however brief. There are exceptions, of course.

Famous Harley owners can most readily be found in the film industry; their ranks are also swelled, however, by artists and sports personalities, members of royalty, captains of industry, and indeed even by politicians, all of whom get a buzz from being seen astride their luxury steed from Milwaukee. Some of these high society bikers certainly regard their Harley as an additional status symbol with which to flatter themselves in public. But for some, their relationship with their Harley is one of true love.

A unique problem faced by all such celebrities is that no matter where they go, or with whom they ride, crowds of fans, autograph hunters, pushy paparazzi, and the simply curious, descend upon them the moment they remove their helmets. This is probably why sometimes a trip into the outside world by a celebrity astride Harley-Davidson can easily appear to be a carefully orchestrated photo opportunity.

Curiously, Harley-Davidson itself has shown very little interest in using the famous to promote its product. In most cases it's been the dealers who have recognized and exploited the advertising potential of celebrities. As David K. Wright observes in his book *The Harley-Davidson Motor Company, An Official Ninety-Year History*, the first promotional use of a celebrity

was in Seattle in 1918, when the local Harley dealer Harry Taintor proudly chauffeured the amply endowed vaudeville queen Trixie Friganza through the city in a Harley sidecar combination. Although the fledgling film industry was always keen to project motorcycles and breathtaking stunts onto the big screen — Dudley Perkins could often be seen in these films — and the film director Victor Fleming and the Harley dealer Rich Budelier founded the Hollywood Motorcycle Club, Harley-Davidson itself, for some reason, seems not to have noticed the inherent publicity value of Hollywood.

The list of early stars who in their free time gladly exchanged the glamor of Hollywood for the glamor of Milwaukee included Marlene Dietrich, Clark Gable, Randolph Scott, Ward Bond, John Wayne, and Robert Taylor. Clark Gable, whose photo was frequently published in *The Enthusiast*, was a true Harley freak and purchased his first UL big twin from Rich Budelier in 1937. The 1920s revealed many famous Harley enthusiasts, such as Gertrude Hoffmann, an actress at the Orpheum Theater, and the silent movie comedian Bill Dooly. Bob Taylor, the husband of Barbara Stanwyck, owned a 74 cubic inch (1200 cc) Knucklehead, with which he gladly posed for photographs.

And talking about photographs, the photographer Hyman Fink (*Fotoplay* magazine), who specialized in shooting the rich and famous, sent all photos in which a Harley was to be seen directly to *The Enthusiast*. The company was more than willing to publish these photos, as they served as historical proof of the worldwide affection for their product.

Boxing world champions Jack Dempsey, Max Schmeling, Joe Frazier and Muhammad Ali all rode Harleys, as did the world champion weightlifter Paul Andersen. World-famous wrestler Hulk Hogan had a custom Harley — the "Hulkster" — built especially for him. Professional motorcycle sporting

Pamela Anderson, Billy Idol and Diamond Dallas Page (from left to right).

Sex symbol Brigitte Bardot on her old side–valve chopper.

At all the Love Rides: Lorenzo Lamas (left, above center).

A campaigner for biker rights: the Colorado Senator Ben "Nighthorse" Campbell in front of the Capitol (above center).

Sylvester Stallone (above) and Arnold Schwarzenegger (below).

personalities such as stuntman Evel Knievel, Harley racer Mert Lawwill (who starred in the famous film "On Any Sunday"), high–speed record breaker Sir Malcolm Campbell, Indy star Al Unser, Jr., and Formula One racer Michael Schumacher were or still are devout Harley fans. Countless top sportsmen and women are also proud Harley owners. These include famous basketball player Kareem Abdul–Jabbar, and the football stars Terry Bradshaw and Earl Campbell, to name but three. Some of the great aviation pioneers of our time enjoyed their spells on the ground astride a Harley: they include Glenn Curtiss (himself a motorcycle designer), Clarence Chamberlain, and Charles Lindbergh.

The list of stage, film, and television stars who have owned Harleys — particularly since World War II — is virtually endless, and any attempt at naming them all would exceed the bounds of this survey. However, a few of the most well known of these personalities must be mentioned here: Roy Rogers, the 1950s country singer, film and TV star; Peter Fonda, who became famous with his motorcycle "Captain America" in the 1969 cult film "Easy Rider;" his colleagues Brigitte Bardot, Barbra Streisand, Ann–Margret, and Senta Berger; as well as Michael Parks on his 1969 Sportster in the TV series "Then Came Bronson"; Johnny Depp; Mickey Rourke with a Custom Heritage Harley in the movie "Harley–Davidson & the Marlboro–Man"; Lorenzo Lamas ("Renegade"); Larry Hagman ("Dallas"); and Jay Leno ("The Tonight Show"). All of these people are Harley riders — as are Burt Reynolds, Arnold Schwarzenegger, and Silvester Stallone — and not just on the big screen.

The list of Harley riding rock and pop stars is just as long, if not longer, and is headed by rock 'n' roll legend Elvis Presley. The list also includes Roy Clark, Eric Burdon, Wayne Cochran, Isaac Hayes, David Alan Coe, Neil Diamond, Bruce Springsteen, Hank Williams, jr., Billy Idol, Dan

Aykroyd, and David Crosby. Also well known for their love of Harley–Davidson motorcycles are Cher, Tanya Tucker, and Olivia Newton–John. Of the many groups who occasionally even ride their Harleys on–stage, the best known are doubtless ZZ Top, Hank Davison, and the Marshall Tucker Band. Pop idol Neil Young has been seen at numerous biker parties.

Although of more or less regal and distinguished bearing in public, quite a few members of royalty the world over are not ashamed to admit their love of the status symbol from Milwaukee. In the 1920s, King Axel of Denmark became known as a Harley enthusiast, and Olaf was the proud owner of a flathead–twin Model K while Crown Prince of Norway. King Albert I of Belgium equipped his police force with Harleys, as did the late Shah of Iran, Reza Pahlavi. Haile Selassie, former Emperor of Ethiopia, and King Hussein of Jordan, purchased entire fleets of Harleys. Indonesia's ex–President Suharto personally chauffeured visiting heads of state around in his Harley sidecar combination. His Royal Highness Emanuele Filiberto, Prince of Savoy, on the other hand, had to sell his beloved Harley as it was deemed too dangerous for a successor to the throne to ride. U.S. senators Barry Goldwater, Robert Stafford, Ben "Nighthorse" Campbell, and former governor of Texas, Ann Richards, had no such problem with their Harleys. General Douglas MacArthur was likewise a keen Harley rider, as was the revolutionary Che Guevara.

Also well–known for their enthusiasm were Rodney C. Gott, President of AMF; Bob Mitchell, Vice President of General Motors; the publisher and millionaire Malcolm Forbes; and industrial giant Reinhold Würth. Even German Princess Gloria von Thurn und Taxis, Paris–based cook and gastronomical millionaire Paul Bocuse, and David Chu, an incredibly rich politician and real estate broker from Hong–Kong, enjoy nothing better than mounting their Harleys.

433

Clubs

A Sworn-In Community

Clubs and Purists

GARDEN OF THE GODS COLO.
S. G. M. C. TOUR 1913.

Still on the Road

After intensive historical research, the San Francisco Motorcycle Club has compiled a list of the oldest American motorcycle clubs still in existence:

Yonkers MC	(1903)	New York
San Francisco MC	(1904)	California
New Jersey MC	(1904)	New Jersey
Oakland MC	(1907)	California
Pasadena MC	(1907)	California
National Capital MC	(1908)	Maryland
Orange County MC	(1909)	California
Dayton MC	(1910)	Ohio
Richmond MC	(1910)	Virginia
Reading MC	(1911)	Pennsylvania
Crotona MC	(1912)	New York
Capital City MC	(1912)	California
Billings MC	(1914)	Montana
Manchester MC	(1915)	New Hampshire
Lansing MC	(1920)	Michigan

(Source: San Francisco Motorcycle Club, 2194 Folsom Street, San Francisco, California 94110)

There have been motorcycle clubs as long as there have been motorcycles, for the simple reason that it's more fun pursuing this highly technical hobby in company. Additionally, clubs offer strength in unity and a protective environment, sometimes even acting as surrogate families. Motorcycle clubs are closed brotherhoods. This is particularly true of Harley clubs, which had distinct groupings right from the start.

There were the sport minded groups, who enjoyed testing their courage, stamina, and riding skills; with few exceptions the clubs affiliated themselves with the FAM and AMA. Then there were the marque-oriented clubs, supported by their respective dealers, who developed mainly social activities along with a few sporting ones. These disciples had strict codes of dress and behavior including smart uniforms, and wore large amounts of company paraphernalia to indicate their loyalty.

Others, suspicious of these obsessive publicity riders, formed their own clubs, lived in their own highly individual way, and regarded the established "coffee-morning meets" as absolutely laughable. One of their favorite pastimes was high performance tuning and conversion of the usually overloaded but underpowered motorcycles, stripping them of all unnecessary weight. This is how the Californian "bobbers" came into being, particularly after World War II, with souped-up conversions of Indians and Harleys being pared down to a very bare minimum.

Although Indian bikes were very popular, Harley technology was preferred, and so it was that Harley bearings and crankshafts were taken to build robust engines, no matter what make. These machines didn't satisfy the strict requirements of the AMA, nor were they suited to long overland tours. But for all that, they corresponded perfectly to the rebellious motorcycle counter-culture which spread out exponentially from California. The agents of this two-wheeled rebellion against deadening, middle class values sported the most notorious of outfits, aiming to look aggressive, wild, and intentionally intimidating. The AMA and Harley-Davidson, together with most of Harley-Davidson's dealers, distanced themselves firmly from these roughnecks, now known as bikers and, in the most extreme cases, outlaws. These names were

proudly accepted by that part of the biking scene. As they organized themselves into groups, the MCs (Motorcycle Clubs) came into being, many of them taking center stage as the inevitable sources of trouble at otherwise happy and innocent AMA rallies.

The values and the lifestyle adopted by many of these clubs were an expression of their disillusionment at the sickening regularity of a moralizing society. This disillusionment led to the formulation of new ideals of personal freedom, a freedom which members believed to have been betrayed by other motorcyclists and above all by their organizations. No wonder that a reaction against the overburdened exaggeration of style now spread, with Dressers ("garbage wagons") being rejected along with the uniformed glamor of conventional motorcycle clubs. The bikers and their followers believed in an image, which became reality for them, of total and excessive machismo, and portrayed themselves as merciless fighters. According to the myth, they were admired by women and teenagers on account of their masculinity, emphasized by their typical motorcycles: brutal Harleys.

Outlaw club members are naturally no schoolboys, but to lump them together with the perpetrators of organized crime is of course completely absurd. The fact that bikers are often prepared to use violence stems not from criminal intentions, but from the values that underpin their clubs, values which to outsiders are neither obvious nor comprehensible. "Territorial disputes," often fatal club rivalries, bitter enmities and deep friendships, along with the endless struggle with the law – all these are not the result of involvement in criminal activities but arises from the bikers morals. An outsider will hardly understand the ethics of bikers, hence, to him, they seem to be criminals. In the case of MCs in particular, "old-fashioned" expressions like honor, trust, loyalty, comradeship, honesty, and justice constitute a currency which has maintained its value to an extent unparalleled in the rest of society.

Central to the MCs, of course, is the heavy motorcycle, in other words a Harley, with all its technical and mythical aura. It's understandable that the company feels forced to distance itself from such

groups; but the clubs have survived this, and Harley itself has gotten used to it too. Moreover, a complete change of image and perception took place in the 1970s. There were still a few badmen among the biker community, but big boots, rough outfits, unkempt manes of hair blowing in the wind, dark glasses, and macabre tattoos were suddenly fashionable. Harley's best-selling models were unabashed tributes to the outlaw style from the Super Glide through to the Bad Boy.

Up until the 1960s and 1970s then, Harley owners, whether focusing on the sporty aspect of their machine, the marque name, or the biker lifestyle, were members of more or less closed and clearly defined communities of riders. They were then joined by a new generation of Harley owners: well-off businesspeople and middle class highfliers who discovered Harley as a status symbol and plaything befitting their rank and position are now part of the Harley scene too. Other Harley riders, gave them the satirical name Rubbies (Rich Urban Bikers). Once Rubbies are on the road on their Harleys, however, they soon form circles of friends and cliques, and begin rediscovering the world through tours, trips, and shared adventures that allow them to experience a totally new way of life. Sometimes in the course of all this a transformation takes place which creates new human beings, with new philosophies and perspectives, out of middle class prudes, finicky car drivers, and package holidaymakers. Club newsletters and motorcycle magazines are full of enthusiastic reports of such experiences, common adventures, breakdowns, meetings and various prize givings, good times and bad times. The clique soon becomes a second family and develops its own special ethos. That's been the way right up untill now.

© Harley–Davidson

Prolonged excursions in the countryside and participation in all parades and processions possible have always been an important part of club life

An Organized Community

Clubs and Associations

For taking part in the so-called Gypsy Tours, there were much-sought-after trophies: above, the two faces of such a decoration.

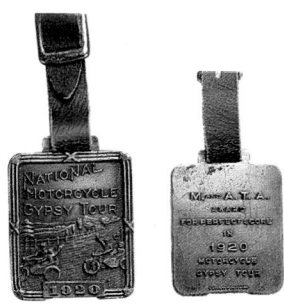

For the average American, motorcycling was long regarded as a dubious activity; it was associated with law-breaking, danger, rebellion, sex, even with Wild West mentality. Harley-Davidson, on the contary, had from the beginning viewed itself as a supplier to an upper-class motorcycling elite, and had built its motorcycles with that philosophy in mind. It had selected its dealers accordingly and had appraised its customers – above all the clubs – in a similar manner. Of course, not all its customers had the same perpective of life.

Of course, the AMA clubs were not the ones who, as a form of social protest, were setting about wrecking everything that others were strenuously trying to keep alive. Soon extremist groups were facing up to one another and outlaw gangs began to undermine the Harley image when they interfered with well-behaved and disciplined competitors participating in AMA sports events such as the Gypsy Tours. At a time when society was in a state of upheaval this state of affairs was particularly prevalent, for example, during and just after World War II. Today, such conflicts are more a part of history and the so-called wild bunch is considerably calmer.

The AMA had always been aware of this problem, as was Harley, the Association's strongest and most influential partner, which constantly admonished its customers always to behave properly. "Don't ride without a muffler!" was the mildest of the warnings to the noisy traffic hooligans. From the word go, there existed both an unwritten and a written set of laws laying down how bikers were expected to behave. One of the most important of the unwritten laws was to avoid being caught doing something illegal, while the written laws expressly forbade doing anything illegal. But for both groups – one later calling itself MC (Motorcycle Clubs), the other MA (Motorcycle Associations) to distinguish themselves from one another – such behavior was both a matter of keeping up appearances, as well as a deeply-rooted expression of a philosophy and lifestyle which was gradually being defined by one make of motorcycle: Harley-Davidson.

From the very beginning, the AMA attempted to gather as many of the clubs, and even the organizers of various types of motorcycling events, under its wing. Most clubs welcomed this move, because only a unified, national governing body would be able to guarantee standards accepted throughout the U.S.

The AMA organized its well-known annual Gypsy Tours to these sports events and all kinds of prizes, trophies, and souvenirs were offered to the participants as an indispensable part of the experience. The camping and campfire romanticism associated with the Gypsy Tours provided the ideal foundation for experiencing nature at close quarters. The (AMA) club rules prescribed good behavior, fairness, a decent appearance (including, if possible, wearing the official club

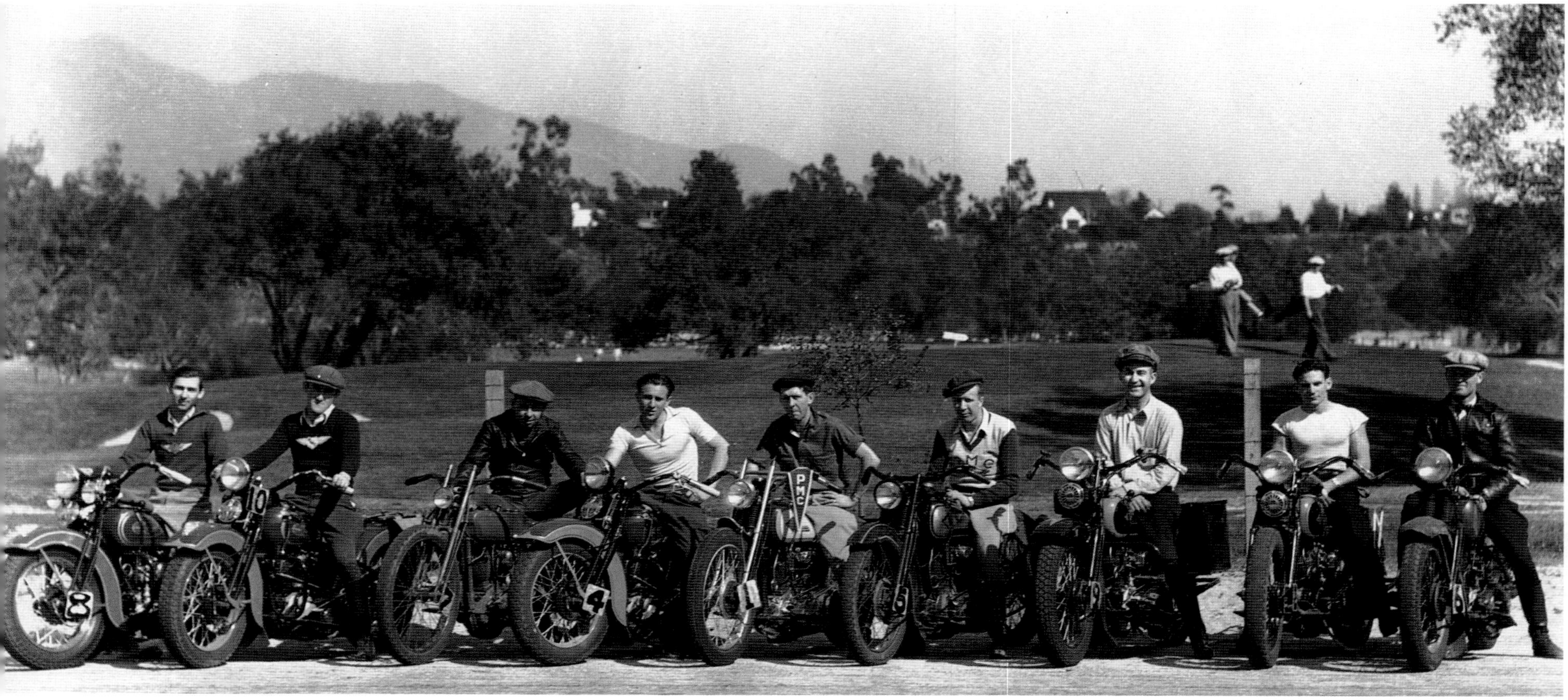

Members of the Klu Klux Dux Mcy. Club of Toledo, Ohio, are justly proud of their reputation as endurance riders. Here is the entire club and the trophies they have won in runs since their organization was founded in January 1949. See additional news about the Dux on page 17.

uniform), tidiness and cleanliness, and a readiness to always go to the assistance of fellow-members.

When they are read today, these long-winded rules of the road seem to be rather like out-of-date driving school instructions for traveling in convoy — but safety was, after all, an overriding factor. It is hardly surprising that these restrictive rules threatened many of the features of motorcycling most popular with bikers — for example, the deep-throated roar from an open exhaust pipe which is music to most bikers' ears. In fact, this caused problems from the very beginning which had to be dealt with effectively by Harley and by the AMA. That throaty roar was soon to become a constant source of public irritation, which, with particular reference to motorcycling as an AMA-governed sport, had a direct influence on the motorcycle industry. In the early 1920s Harley set a goodwill campaign in motion which stated "Cut out the cut out!" meaning that open pipes should be banned. But this move did not help much; after all, noise, for the dedicated Harley man, was part of the essential experience of biking and of the sport. That's exactly where opinions differ. Even today...

Harley clubs were mostly very-well organized group who honored members by giving them elegant uniforms.

Hail to the NATIONAL A.M.A. CLUB CONTEST WINNERS!

We are proud to show these pictures of the winners of the 1939 A.M.A. National Club Contest. Unfortunately, we had no pictures available of the second place winner, the Bridgeport Motorcycle Assn., Bridgeport, Conn.; of the Buckeye Girls Club, Columbus, Ohio, winner of first place in the Ladies Division; nor of the seventh place Rose City Club, Portland, Ore. Those shown are:

1. First place went to the Victor McLaglen Motorcycle Corps, Los Angeles. 2. Queen City Club, Charlotte, N. C., took fifth place. 3. Third place went to the Madison Club of Madison, Wis., and their auxiliary took fourth in their class. 4. Winner of ninth place, the Greyhound Club, Elizabeth, N. J. 5. Sixth place went to the Lansdowne, Pa., Blue Comets. 6. Little Rock, Ark., Golden Eagles won eighth. 7. The Peoria Club won fourth and their auxiliary fifth. 8. The Motorettes of San Francisco won second in their class. 9. Tenth in the men's and third in the ladies' class went to the Wayne County, Newark, N. Y. Club

The Shadow of the Past

Hollister's Fiftieth Anniversary

San Benito Street in Hollister knows a well-kept secret: its connections with international biking which began there in 1947.

Sonny Barger, the legendary President of the Hells Angels on the occasion of the 50 year anniversary of the Hollister-riots when bikers came together peacefully from around the world.

Hollister, California

Hollister is the capital of San Benito County and is situated about 100 miles to the south of San Francisco. The town was founded in 1868 by Colonel W.W. Hollister at the end of a ride across California herding an enormous flock of sheep. Even today Hollister is principally an agricultural town existing on sheep farming, as well as on fruit and vegetable growing (in particular garlic). The construction of the Southern Pacific Railroad in 1870 helped Hollister to enjoy a considerable economic boom. Today the town has 25,000 inhabitants (of whom 52 percent are Mexicans), and it styles itself the earthquake capital of the world, lying plumb on the San Andreas Fault, which is considered to be the most active earthquake region on the globe. Hollister became world-famous as a result of the events in 1947 which gave rise to the film "The Wild One."

Hollister: 1997 Statistics

Visitors:
Downtown 35,000
Bolado Park 9,000
Corbin 5,000
The Ranch 4,000

Police Statistics:

Accidental deaths: 2 people

Arrests: 59 comprising:

1 accident caused by drunkenness, with death resulting

1 accident caused by drunkenness with 4 injured

1 for rape

2 for prostitution

31 for drunk driving

23 for drunkenness and gross public indecency

2 knife fights

1 shooting perpetrated by local young people.

(Source: Public Information Center and Hollister Police)

During the Independence Day weekend of 4–6 July 1997 a bikers' festival took place in Hollister, a small Californian town renowned as the center of the garlic industry: this festival was dedicated to another event which 50 years earlier had transformed motorcyclists into public enemies, youngsters into outlaws, the rioting of young hoodlums into terrorist uprisings, and bike clubs into illegal assemblies. This incident came to be known as the Hollister Riots or the Hollister Bash. A rather strange anniversary: celebrating an occasion which you could regret for the rest of your life, for which you might have been punished and treated as a social outcast, simply because you were a biker with your own way of seeing things, your own aims in life, and your own ideals. But anniversaries are anniversaries, particularly when they celebrate a legend which has spawned a lifestyle which has influenced the world. So in 1997 on San Benito Street, where the worst disturbances had taken place back in 1947, motorcycles and policemen were again everywhere, but this time it was only beer which flowed in large quantities, and everyone was on their best behavior. Illegal burnouts and road races were out of the question simply because of the double rows of bikes parked close together, and any hint of disturbance was immediately dealt with, as it had been 50 years before. What remained was good business for the four competing organizers of the event. And you might even run across veterans of the 1947 event, who would recount their experiences again and again, and assure everyone listening that it had not really been all that bad way back then.

What Really Happened in 1947 in Hollister?

Witnesses Tell Their Stories

Top four in Kepers TT Final. Wilson (left) fourth; Andres, third; Leonard first; Phillips, second.

Leonard and his TT trophy. At his side is Dist. Rel. George Alcala.

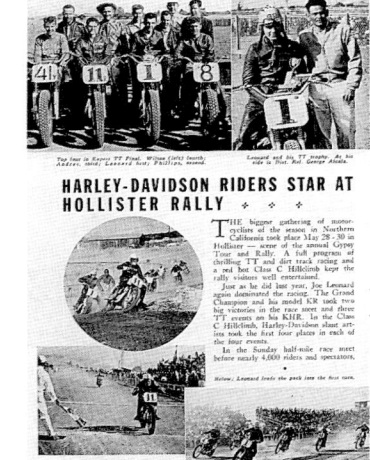

HARLEY-DAVIDSON RIDERS STAR AT HOLLISTER RALLY

THE biggest gathering of motorcyclists of the season in Northern California took place May 28 - 30 in Hollister — scene of the annual Gypsy Tour and Rally. A full program of thrilling TT and dirt track racing and a red hot Class C Hillclimb kept the rally visitors well entertained.

Just as he did last year, Joe Leonard again dominated the racing. The Grand Champion and his model KR took two big victories in the race meet and three TT events on his KHR. In the Class C Hillclimb, Harley-Davidson slant artists took the first four places in each of the four events.

In the Sunday half-mile race meet before nearly 4,000 riders and spectators,

Below: Leonard leads the pack into the first turn.

Circle: Andres leads field in TT race.

Like every year since 1930, the 1947 Independence Day weekend saw numerous traditional Californian motorcycle events organized in Hollister by the Salinas Ramblers Motorcycle Club and the Hollister Veterans' Memorial Park Association, which thousands of bikers and sports enthusiasts were expected to attend. As usual the hot weekend got under way on Friday, the fourth of July with a hillclimb open to all comers on the Lavignino Ranch. This was a very popular event at which anyone prepared to pay the small fee could compete. On Saturday, July 5th there were general competitions in the Veterans' Memorial Park for allcomers, staged principally for the clubs (most of them AMA affiliated). There was the slow race, the digout race, the plank ride (to test the riders' balancing skill along a narrow plank), and numerous prizes and trophies were to be won, such as for the best-dressed group, guy, and girl, or for the participant who had traveled the greatest distance to be in Hollister. In the evenings anyone could buy a ticket for the social event of the racing weekend – the grand dinner-dance in the Legion Memorial Auditorium. On Sunday, July 6th the closing event took place as the sporting highlight: the half-mile flat-track race, the Race of the Champions, authorized by the AMA and in which 50 competitors were to race for a prize of 1,200 dollars. The entrance fee of a mere one dollar and fifty cents was sufficient to provide the organizers with all the finances they needed to stage it.

All this was the "official" part of the weekend. The "unofficial" part took place in downtown Hollister, above all in San Benito Street where most of the bars and restaurants were hoping for a very profitable weekend. Events such as these – sporting and social highlights for the biking community – had been very popular for decades and took place all over the U.S., and in 1947 around 5,000 visitors had gathered in Hollister. But in recent years unsavory elements had joined the cheerful and excited crowds of motorcycling enthusiasts, and it was this trend which mainly worried the organizers and the authorities. These newcomers were wild, bearded men on customized, loud, and powerful machines (mostly Harleys, Indians, BSAs, Nortons, and Triumphs) and they often behaved in a rowdy, provocative, and totally undisciplined manner. As a matter of principle they rejected the AMA sporting regulations as too persnickety and organized their own outlaw races. Then they would ride into Hollister in order to show off, to booze, and to let themselves go completely.

They were organized in rebel clubs with weird names (The Boozefighters, Yellow Jackets, 13 Rebels, Winoes, Satan's Sinners, Satan's Daughters, or The POBOB, i.e. the Pissed Off Bastards of Bloomington); they enjoyed frightening the locals and would not back down from any confrontation. For them it was "just having a good time," and, according to eyewitness accounts, they rode their bikes at full throttle into bars, sometimes smashed everything to pieces, and had even wrapped a whole hotel in rolls of toilet paper, upturned trash cans, and got into fights with other bands of hoodlums and police officers. Above all they enjoyed urinating in public which was always treated by the law as an act of gross indecency.

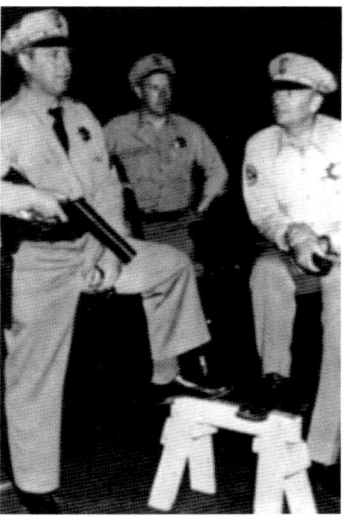

While the biker-press totally ignored the Hollister riots (top) a trouble-seeking crowd waited on the streets for the unavoidable confrontation of bikers versus police (below).

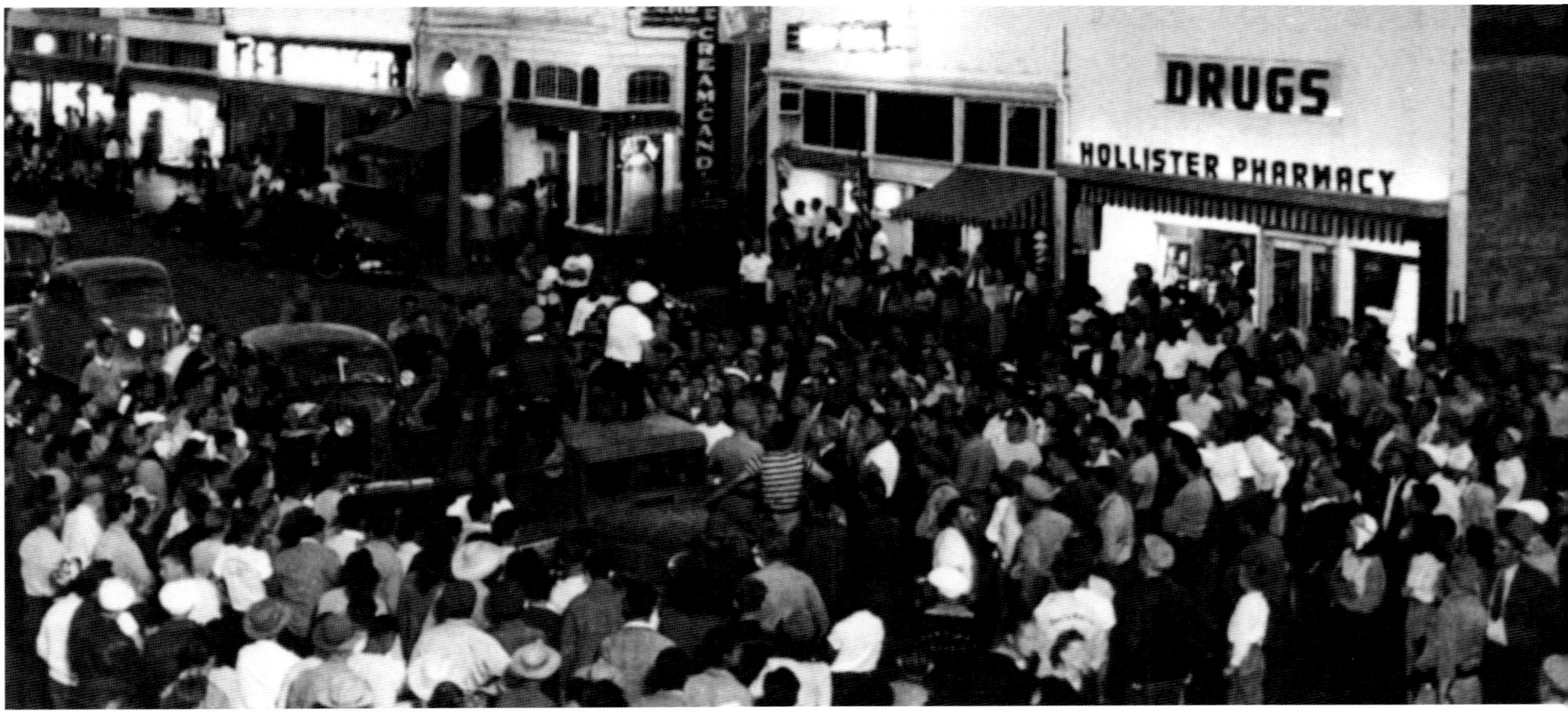

During that particular weekend in 1947 in Hollister these hoodlums were in a minority, but they nevertheless determined the course of events on San Benito Street, which soon looked like a battlefield littered with thousands of beer bottles. The local population looked on at this brawling with mixed feelings. Those who joined in the boozing and yelling did all they could to encourage the revelers, and the barkeepers — for whom it soon became rather too exuberant — stopped serving beer and switched to hard (and more expensive) liquor. Naturally this made a bad situation even worse. The other section of the populace were angered by the riotous behavior and called for law and order — and police action. Police Chief Roy McPhall and his men were at first completely overwhelmed. The police had already taken the precaution of closing San Benito Street to through traffic, but soon the small number of police officers were utterly powerless on the main street which was transformed into a dragstrip enveloped in smoke and exhaust fumes. Witnesses later described that evening all as "a hell of a mess!"

As a result, on Saturday Police Chief Roy McPhall called for help from the Highway Patrol (CHP) of San Benito County. Their chief, Captain L.T. Torres and 30 mounted troopers together with auxiliaries began to clear things up with extreme thoroughness, mainly using rubber riot sticks and tear gas. Fifty people — others speak of 35 ringleaders — were taken into custody. One of the Boozefighters was handed down the highest possible sentence of 90 days because he had publicly urinated on the radiator of a club bus; the others were mostly released on bail. Fifty people were injured; not necessarily as a direct result of the rioting on the streets and they received treatment in the local hospital. The fighting would probably not have escalated to such an extent if the State Troopers had not used so much force in dealing with anyone vaguely looking like a rioter or a drunk. Eyewitnesses were of the opinion that the troopers were the real cause of the bloody clashes.

Be that as it may, the police officers did have everything under control again on Sunday and the bikers left the battlefield with aching

The fighting strength of law enforcement teams called in to help, soon had the scene under control, but that didn't prevent some bikers from spending the night on the sidewalk (above).

heads and bleeding wounds. This might have meant that the file on that year's events in Hollister would have been closed and only the sentences handed down by Judge Frank C. Buchter left to tell the tale of these events.

But things turned out differently. This was the fault of two reporters: one of them was a journalist with *Life* magazine and the other the *San Francisco Chronicle* photographer, Barney Peterson, who had been in Hollister purely by chance and taken a few photographs (specially posed ones, perhaps?). One of these appeared in the issue of *Life* dated July 21, 1947 along with the famous 115-word report quoted here.

Around 50 people were arrested mainly because of drunkenness and indecent behavior. Normal bikers who did not join in the riots, were hardly affected (top).

The Famous *Life* Report Dated July 21, 1947:
Cyclist's Holiday
He and Friends Terrorize a Town

"On the fourth of July weekend, 4,000 members of a motorcycle club roared into Hollister, California, for a three-day convention. They quickly tired of ordinary motorcycle thrills and turned to more exciting stunts. Racing their bikes down the main street and through traffic lights, they rammed into restaurants and bars, breaking furniture and mirrors. Some rested awhile by the curb (see photo). Others hardly paused. Police arrested many for drunkenness and indecent exposure but could not restore order. Finally, after two days, the cyclists left with a brazen explanation, 'We like to show off... It's just a lot of fun.' But Hollister's police chief took a different view. Wailed he, 'It's just one hell of a mess.'"

443

The Rise of a New Biker Culture

One Percenters Against the Rest of the World

Marlon Brando became a "cult biker" after his movie "The Wild One" was released. But he rode a Triumph.

Maybe the whole biker culture, and even the outlaw clubs which today are accused of all sorts of criminal behavior, would never have existed if that unfortunate report had not appeared in *Life* magazine. It did not tell the whole story, but, along with the infamous, full–page photograph, which may even have been posed, it was to have a wide–ranging effect. The report triggered a typically American outbreak of mass hysteria which was directed at just about anyone balancing on two wheels and making a loud noise. Not only the serious motorcycling clubs and organizations were shocked and horrified. Thousands of them were feared to be set to invade peace–loving towns, stealing, murdering, pillaging and raping; whatever crossed their path was in danger and they would be enjoying every second of it!

Topping all this, Californian newspapers and television stations continually bombarded the public with alarming reports of riots at motorcycle meets (especially in Riverside and, in 1948, in Ensenada, New Mexico, in Porterville, California, and then, for a second time, in Riverside). As a result, even the most law–abiding American towns started to prepare for the day of judgement which would be announced by murderous and pillaging gangs of bikers ready to invade their particular paradise on earth and raze it to the ground. Even the Army and the National Guard were put on alert. The League of Californian Cities demanded a nationwide ban on all motorcycle races.

Although only a very small and dwindling minority of bikers created trouble during the AMA Gypsy Tours, Sheriff Carl F. Rayburn of the Riverside Police Department spoke of "riff–raff hoodlums" and a "hooligan element," and his local police chief, J.A. Bennet, described the motorcycle hoodlums for the first time in public as "outlaws." The AMA Secretary at that time, Lin A. Kuchler, made a much quoted and published comment, which has gone down in history as the AMA statement. "The disreputable cyclists were possibly one percent of the total number of motorcyclists, only one percent are hoodlums and troublemakers." As a protest against this statement, which was felt to be prejudiced and arrogant, the "1%" MC symbol soon made its appearance and outlaw gangs started to form.

In San Francisco the newly–founded Hell's Angels sent out invitations to a One Percenters' Conference. Together with other like–minded gangs, such as the Gypsy Jokers, the Road Rats, the Galloping Gooses, Satan's Slaves, and The Presidents, they decided at this meeting that they would wear the one percent patch as a protest against AMA discrimination. In the meantime, clashes amongst the "motorcycle mob" were becoming more and more violent. In the Spring of 1951 about 1,000 bikers set off for the town of Tecate on the Mexican border to show everyone just what a riot could be. As a result of this threat, the planned races were cancelled and two Army and National Guard battalions escorted the bikers out of town back to California – and this was only one such incident.

The AMA, which naturally saw itself as the official representative of all motorcyclists, tried to play such incidents down. Its president,

E.C. Smith, wrote editorials addressing the tiny group of troublemakers which were intended to have a calming influence. The publisher of *The Motorcyclist*, Paul Brockaw, was shocked by the riot but expressed his optimism and considered the actions of the troublemakers to be a sign of the times to which no importance should be attached. The anti–biker movement (which harmed above all the AMA and Harley–Davidson) gained additional impetus when the writer Frank Rooney published a seditious story entitled "The Cyclists Raid" in *Harper's* in 1951.

For rebellious young people of the day this made perfect reading: they were sick and tired of the nagging restrictions imposed by a narrow–minded society and their prying parents, and were looking for their own personal philosophy. The word "freedom" was soon to take on a new meaning. The Hollister Bash became their own epic and they looked on the One Percenter clubs as a personal icon. Jesse James and Doc Holliday had risen from the dead. There was, however, a high price to be paid for this new freedom. Morals, and law and order as symbolized by the state dogged their heels; everyone cursed them and threatened them, and so the young rebels had no choice but to form exclusive, restricted groups, the MCs, devoted to the essential symbol of their power, the heavy motorcycle.

Fascinated by Rooney's story, which mirrored the events in Hollister, John Paxter wrote a script based on "The Cyclists Raid" and producer Stanley Kramer, equally fascinated by the new movement, invested every last cent he had and created a film with a few unknown actors and motorcycle club members which was first shown in 1953. It immediately attracted enormous attention. Its title, "The Wild One," became a myth in its own right. It starred Marlon Brando as the leader of the Black Rebels and Lee Marvin as a particularly violent ex–member of the gang. The film glorified the new form of violence and was the model for countless other Hollywood productions, which played a large part in reinforcing the bad image that bikers had. Much to the irritation of Harley–Davidson, their bikes were misused in the film as instruments of terror. Unfortunately or fortunately, depending on point of view, the star of "The Wild One," Marlon Brando, roared across the screen on a Triumph Thunderbird! Although the film created a huge market for motorcycles, the company deliberately ignored it.

"The Wild One," however, sent out a message to the new and rebellious generation of motorcyclists, outlaw bikers had found a perfect example of how to behave badly, America had her new public enemy Number One, and there's been a war on ever since...

In the Name of the Company

Motorcycle Clubs in the U.S.

In 1977, the Long Beach, California airline pilot and Harley enthusiast Carl T. Wicks, already the owner of a motorcycle escort funeral service, founded what was later to become the Harley–Davidson Owners Association (H.D.O.A.). Up until the founding of the Harley Owners Group (H.O.G.) in 1983, he was enthusiastically supported by Harley–Davidson itself. However, when he refused to integrate his organization into the company framework, claiming his right as first on the scene, to remain independent, the company withdrew its support.

He was not the only one to face this dilemma: across the world countless motorcycle groups which had established themselves on a private basis long before the company had set up H.O.G. faced the

same difficult situation. Some clubs kept their name and purpose while still managing to get together with the Harley Owners Group from time to time.

Others went their own way. One of these was the Dresser Club, an association, formed in Florida in 1981, for fans of Electra Glides and Tour Glides weighed down by a mountain of accessories. Compared to these, even Harley's top-of-the-range stock models fitted out with every accessory (such as the Classic and Ultra Classic editions) seem a bit spartan. The Florida Dresser Club organizes parades, in particular the spectacular Dresser Light Show, and publishes its own magazine called *News Letter*.

Ready to get going: in front of a clubhouse in the South, the members and guests form into a club-run.

The Baptism

How Buddy Got His Patch

The same thing had been going on for almost a year now – his probation time in the club, he had to run to and fro all the time, on duty 24 hours a day, lugging crates of beer about, fetching cigarettes, cleaning the washroom, tidying up over and over, remembering all the time to keep his mouth shut – but that was the way he had wanted it.

In spite of it all, Buddy was perfectly happy, because all the stress and chores were winning him respect, giving him a sense of security and the certainty that he was a useful member of the family. Of course, he was not exactly a useful member of society, because he happened to be short of a few minor things – money, for example – which are essential in the U.S., unless you want to remain a nobody or to be treated as a criminal, especially in the South. Though he worked hard and long, mostly on construction sites where he was expected to do the hardest and dirtiest work, Buddy earned a wage which was below the official minimum wage. A sum which was, in any case, derisory because employers didn't abide by it. Times were bad and it was either a case of taking the job or having nothing to do.

Buddy had even tried the Church, which in the South usually means the Baptists, but it was not long before all the sweet phrases got on his nerves, as did all the prayer meetings, which were, in fact, just a means of making money; he even had to work himself to the bone for no pay, or for "God's wage" as they would exclaim heartily, because he was unable to pay his church dues...

Sure, the Club was better. The members had nothing against his riding an ancient Harley, which looked like it would sure as hell fall to pieces any minute. The members were a rough crowd and unwelcome when they all parked on the spotlessly clean and sacred parking lot alongside the Church of the Good Shepherd.

The Club. It had always been Buddy's dream; it was where he felt at home; the comradeship was something he could see and feel. There was that unconditional trust each member had in the others and the sense of security which was part of being a member. No, Buddy was not born a loner; he was not somebody who enjoyed being left to himself. Normally he would be pushed around, bullied and exploited, probably because he was a little naive and a little too kind-hearted, and did everything and believed anything that he was told; he was beginning to feel more and more lost in this crazy world full of unwritten and incomprehensible laws which, it seemed, were known to everyone but him. That's the way it had always been. He was an orphan and had been brought up from a very early age in a strict educational system, which, so he was told, would strengthen and improve his character; it was nothing new for him to obey orders.

As far as Buddy was concerned, the Army was out, because he had been born with a number of handicaps, and "cripples" were not wanted to serve alongside the elite of the nation. The advantage was that he at least avoided the risk of being gassed or hacked to pieces somewhere in the jungle or in the desert far from home. In short, life was complicated and Buddy hated anything complicated. That's why he would hang out with the Club, join in the parties and take part in the races. Then, a little hesitantly, he finally asked if he could become a full member and stop being just one of those associates that were tolerated in a friendly way.

The Club had taken a liking to Buddy, because he was always friendly and ready to lend a helping hand, did not shout and scream like a madman and if he did happen to get drunk (which happened only very rarely), he would lie down quietly in a corner, burping contentedly to himself and watching the hell-raising going on all around. Then, one day, he did finally get his vest, the Club's denim colors with the rocker's name and hometown emblazoned on it. This was the day of his baptism: everyone knew it and a surprise party was prepared. Friends and other affiliates had been invited; everything was secret and Buddy did his very best to act as though he was totally surprised. The ritual was something new to him, because he was the first new initiate for a considerable amount of time. The Club was always relatively restrained in its recruitment policy.

Finally, they sent him out to buy two dozen eggs – the usual number for breakfast. When he returned, there was already quite a crowd in front of the clubhouse. It was a real scorcher that day and the ice-cold Buds were already disappearing rapidly from the ice barrel. The grill, groaning under the weight of the highly spiced steaks and the chicken legs on it, was crackling away almost unnoticed: the air was filled with the smell of cooking and thick clouds of smoke. The members of the Club were standing around, each face speaking volumes; each of them bawled out his opinion (so that nobody could miss a single word) on the character of the member-to-be. He was actually called Schoener, but because nobody was able to pronounce it, Buddy had stuck. "Is he reliable? Anyone know anything against him?" – "This year he's already been late for work twice because he was drunk," hollered one of the onlookers. The official master of ceremonies frowned: "Sobriety and getting to work on time are not conditions for joining our Club. Dismissed. Next!" – "What about his brains?" shouted somebody else. "Hagar the Horrible" turned that down as well. Amidst all the shouts from the listeners ("yeah, yeah!"), they moved on to the public test.

"Well Buddy, down on your belly!" ordered "Hagar the Horrible," pointing to a patch on the ground which had already been got ready by spreading a revolting-looking mess over it which stank to high heaven. "Now, do those press-ups, up and down you go, up and down. We'll count along with you, if it gets too hard!" And Buddy got on with his press-ups. Then the initiation test continued. "What about your reliability, helpfulness, and loyalty, then?" challenged one of the girls, all dolled up, though she was evidently well past it. "Where are the ham and eggs?"

Somebody brought the box of eggs which were then stuffed one by one into Buddy's pockets, trousers, and shirt: he was still lying on the ground, totally out of breath. "As for the ham, that's just what you are, and now for the scrambled eggs," guffawed all those guys who had been loading him with the eggs. They smacked him hard across the shoulders and wherever else the eggs had been stashed just a moment before. Some were very intimate parts of the body and soon Buddy was sticky all over with egg yolk and the mush began to trickle down his body. Before he could catch his breath, someone else shouted: "Where's the hair cream?" Good, here it was. The best hair cream that money could buy – HD-Heavy Duty SAE 70 oil had one outstanding advantage: it would stick to you with the utmost tenacity. Because Buddy had been stupid enough to keep his old cap on, it was covered with "cream" (both inside and outside, of course), and everyone found it really great that this personal makeover appeared to suit him so well. "Now for a shower, the guy's a new member and must be cleaned up," laughed the road captain who had always been renowned for his own lack of personal hygiene. So everyone present poured whatever was left in his beer-can over Buddy, who was grateful for this way of cooling off again.

Finally, he was permitted to take off his own old and filthy T-shirt and put on the brand new colors which had been laid out in all their glory on the camp table for all to admire. Well, now he was a real member and, fired with enthusiasm, Buddy started to take full advantage of his rights to hug his brothers and to embrace them warmly, not forgetting the guests either, until everyone looked more or less like Buddy did a few minutes earlier.

"We shouldn't have come" said some of the women who had had their hair done specially, because all the ingredients of the baptism had stuck fast and dried solid. The shower room in the clubhouse was, as might be expected, occupied for the next few hours. But that's just one of those things that go with celebrations of this kind and, pitifully, there was nobody around to be ordered about with shouts of "Hey, probate!" to clear away all the mess. A new prospect was needed. Hagar's fearsome eyes turned enquiringly in my direction: "What about you, Oluf?"

One has to be tough in order to deal with the ceremonies involved in becoming a fully initiated member of the club.

A Very Special Veterans' Association

The Vietnam Vets' MC

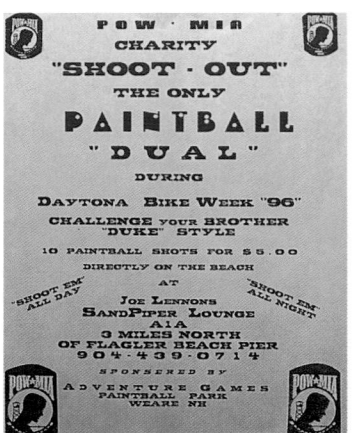

Proof of respect: A drill team of the U.S. Navy salutes on Memorial Day to a delegation of the Vietnam Veterans MC.

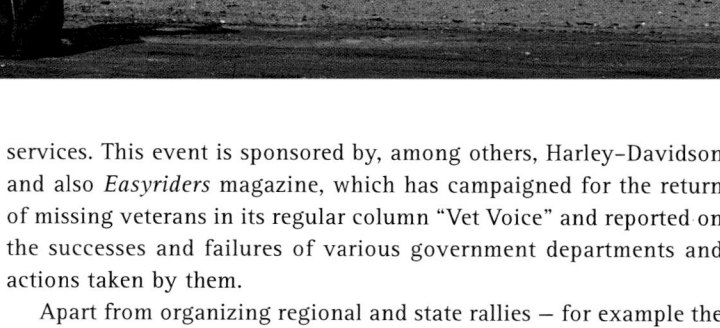

The Vietnam Vets' MC (or Nam Vets MC for short) is a highly respected biker association with local chapters in every state of the Union, and in several places around the world. Anyone who served with the U.S. military during the Vietnam War and possesses a motorcycle, ideally but not necessarily a Harley, can become a member. The Vietnam Vets' MC sees itself as a federal Veterans' association that offers assistance to all those comrades in arms who are sick or in need. Additionally, it also raises such issues as the 2,000 American soldiers still missing in Vietnam. In contact with congressmen, they demand the truth about the fate of comrades assumed to be POWs/MIA (Prisoners of War/Missing in Action). On the day America honors its war dead and its veterans, Memorial Day, the last Monday in May, they organize services at ceremonies and parades.

One of their most famous events is the Run to the Wall, a ride to the Vietnam Veterans Memorial in West Potomac Park in Washington, D.C., which bears the 58,183 names of the fallen of the Vietnam War. The Run to the Wall, first organized by Vietnam Vets in 1987 (and also known, respectively named after a military action, as "Rolling Thunder") began with 4,000 participants, and has today reached the figure of 150,000.

Slogans such as "Proud to be American" and "Let's bring them home, America," make the sentiments clear. Since so many disabled veterans are not in a position to travel to the memorial, a scale copy, the Moving Wall, was made at the instigation of the Vietnam Veterans, and it is set up at several places in the U.S. as a focus for memorial

services. This event is sponsored by, among others, Harley–Davidson and also *Easyriders* magazine, which has campaigned for the return of missing veterans in its regular column "Vet Voice" and reported on the successes and failures of various government departments and actions taken by them.

Apart from organizing regional and state rallies – for example the July Jam in Commerce, Georgia – the Vietnam Vets work closely with the organizers of the disabled Special Olympics; arrange charity events such as Toy Runs or Toys–for–Tots rallies; help jailed "brothers;" and care for comrades wounded in the conflict or struck by cancer. Many Vets were exposed to the toxic defoliant Agent Orange and to atomic tests. According to their own statistics, over 20 percent of all prisoners in the U.S. are Vietnam veterans. Furthermore, 13 percent of veterans are still being cared for in veterans' hospitals; and the number of them mentally ill is 19 percent (figures for 1996). All in all, these are frightening statistics which make clear the social and political dimension to the Vietnam Vets' MC.

Jesus is Lord

Christian Motorcycle Groups

A typically American phenomenon in the land of absolute religious freedom and tax-free churches are the Christian motorcycle groups. No matter how the reader might feel about it, Christian motorcycle clubs are very serious in what they do for their beliefs, working for a better world and peaceful coexistence.

The most prominent is the Christian Motorcyclists Association (C.M.A.). Formed in 1977 by Herbert Shreve, a mere ten years later it had 2,500 members, most of them in the U.S., several TV stations (for example, in Clearwater, Florida), together with a host of C.M.A. evangelists and area or "road" representatives. Any Christian can become a member; the membership contribution is a donation determined by the means and conscience of the prospective motorcyclist. The C.M.A. sees its main task as arranging club services ("Motorcycle Ministries"), along with providing welfare, and also organizing missionary rallies and runs involving campouts and games. Additionally, they publish booklets, spiritual self-development literature, magazines, videos, and other Christian aids. Since 1987 they have organized huge mission rallies, notably "Riding for the Son," and "Run for the Son."

Many church and other Christian organizations have affiliated themselves with the C.M.A., so have the well-known evangelist Kenneth Copeland and his wife Gloria. In September 1997 Copeland organized Texas rallies in cooperation with the Eagle Motorcycle Club which he publicized via his own TV station, and at which Copeland, following the modern trend, performed a mass exorcism in the form of his "Great Healing."

Like other Christian groups, Christian biking clubs stress the need for people to pay their debt to society. "From crime to Christ" is the motto of the fallen angels of the motorcycle scene who have become professing Christians after their rehabilitation program — a process that doesn't require them to give up their favored lifestyle on a Harley.

One of these born-again groups is the Christian biker club The Tribes of Judah, whose members, having opted for a new life, see themselves as latter-day disciples of Jesus Christ. Other groups include the Soldiers for Jesus MC; the Christ Motor Club; the Sons of God MC; and the Christian Motorcycle Fellowship (C.M.F.), an international association which publishes its own club magazine, *Biking News*.

The Evangelist Kenneth Copland on a T.V. show on the event of his rally in the name of "Great Healing" in September 1997 in Texas. Biker religious worship of the CMA is an emotional experience for every club member.

Wearing a jacket with an image of Jesus or the cross seems pretty normal, but not if its on the saddle of a Harley.

The Hell's Angels

The Hell's Angels is the most famous biker club in the world, the object of awe, fear, and respect, often slandered, much misunderstood and persecuted, and all of them resolute Harley-Davidson devotees. Here, a member of the Hell's Angels offers an authentic account of their way of life. Harley-Davidson and Hells Angels MC: "If Every Angel Rode a BMW…" Harley-Davidson Motor Company itself never supported this phenomena and has, until today, no connection to the Hell's Angles. The company also does not share the club's lifestyle.

In 1965 Harley-Davidson was in a difficult situation financially. Its market share in the U.S. was barely four percent – a mere morsel of the motorcycle pie. For many an average Joe, who would rather ride than do repairs and maintenance and who just wants to have fun, Harleys were a pretty unattractive. He got exactly what he wanted from Honda, but not from that heap of scrap iron from Milwaukee. So Harleys sometimes found true love elsewhere, in the arms of those whose existence their creators never want to acknowledge: the Harley freaks from the biker scene, especially the Hell's Angels.

If one wanted to tell the full story of these clubs, there would be a whole book to write. In fact, everyone in a Hell's Angels' club could write his or her own book. Without a motorbike, without a Harley, life is unthinkable for them, so every story would be a true love story, with all that that entails – the thrill of the first encounter, the sleepless nights, the dreams.

Then getting to know each other, finding out about good points and bad, realizing that you belong together. But with one condition: that your partner loses all those attributes that are alien to the real character. Thus the chopper was born.

Not everyone can take this road, of course. Only a biker who, like their machine, has got rid of a whole lot of baggage along the way. What belongs together, grows together.

A friend of the author admits: corny, I know, but that's the way it is. Ever since I was a kid I dreamt of being in the Hell's Angels. There were these films I saw in a cinema. The words hell and angel, repeatedly used, just stayed in my mind. I now know that these were cheaply produced Hollywood B movies from which the producer was just hoping to make a few quick bucks. But the stuff really got through to me because genuine Hell's Angels took part in them. As actors they were real hams, but for me they were the true pros of the films because they were playing themselves. They had turned their back on society's rules and created their own.

The earliest Angels were pilots and soldiers who, after returning home from the World War II, found that they could no longer live the lives they had left behind. The status symbol for the common America was the automobile, so the Angels rode motorbikes. They rode Harleys because Indian, the only possible alternative, came across as far too snobbish.

That was what I wanted, too. But in 1977, when I passed my test, Harleys were far too expensive for me, so I rode a Triumph and trained as a mechanic at a Triumph dealer. I also founded the Hammers of Hell with a group of like-minded friends. Right away we made contact with the german Hamburg chapter of the Angels and became "prospects," probationary Angels. Now I had to have a Harley. Since then I've lived and worked for this motorcycle, and got to know the Harley down to its last bolt, like everyone else in the club; we've all

Group photo of all the Hell's Angels present at their 50th anniversary meeting in Berdoo, California.

become experts in all things Harley, as well as successful players on the dragster scene, skilled fine-tuners, and good stylists.

To many it was the bikers who saved Harley's scalp when the company was facing bankruptcy. To this day the image that the biker scene created is still alive, an image the company itself is not necessarily happy about. Granted, the quality of the machines has improved enormously, and now any dentist or accountant can ride a Fat Boy without having to get oil on their hands, but the name Hell's Angels made history.

The author's friend believes, that the bikers, whether they like it or not, were in large part responsible for making the Big Twin a potent symbol of an alternative lifestyle. Many believed that it was the Hell's Angels above all who helped to transform these heavy machines into the central, indispensable element of this lifestyle. That wasn't our intention, of course: the Big Twin is simply an integral part of the very way we live and feel, right in the here and now.

I've worked day and night to get my own company off the ground, to make it earn enough to keep myself, my wife, and our three children. The fact that I've won prizes for my motorcycles certainly doesn't do any harm there.

But even if nobody ever paid the slightest attention to my work, it would still give me satisfaction, because it gives me the chance to make my conception of the ideal motorcycle a reality; a motorcycle that first takes shape on the drawing board before being brought to life in the workshop.

Being a Hell's Angel means first and foremost being a member of the Hell's Angels Motorcycle Club. Without our machines we would not be the people we are. Ordinary folk can't understand that. Only other bikers. And that's the way it should be. But that doesn't mean the Big Twin becomes some kind of fetish. We don't worship mere objects: we leave that to the guys who religiously wash and wax their cars every Saturday afternoon. No, we don't idolize the Harley-Davidson.

In fact, when the bikes leave the factory they are plain boring, at least that's what a Hell's Angel would say. Fortunately for Harley, few people see it that way. So it's hardly surprising there are sales of over 100,000 machines a year, a figure expected to rise to 200,000 by the year 2003. Harley mystique is becoming merchandise for the masses. But mystique and mass production mix like fire and water. "How would it be if every Angel rode a BMW?" I asked Roy Mayer, a Harley-Davidson engine designer, at the 1996 IFMA. He went pretty pale at the thought, and not because of the beers we'd drunk. Harley needs the Hell's Angels. Harley needs the whole biker scene because, after all, the company is selling a philosophy. Not to us, though: we're the ones who invented the philosophy in the first place.

Lutz Schelhorn (below), who took the pictures and wrote the statement alongside.

The Origin of the Outlaw Motorcycle Clubs

The Roots of the Hard-Core Bikers

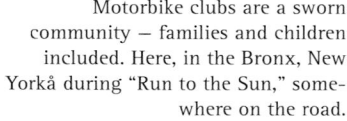
Motorbike clubs are a sworn community – families and children included. Here, in the Bronx, New Yorkå during "Run to the Sun," somewhere on the road.

The story of how the so-called outlaw clubs came into being is fairly well known; it started just after World War II as members of the armed forces were discharged and returned home to ordinary, narrow-minded civilian life.

In California motorcycling was one of their favorite activities, often simply undertaken as a reaction against the restraints imposed by the world to which the servicemen had returned and which failed to understand their desire for freedom. It was natural that they should form clubs to recall old feelings of being comrades in arms, just as motorcyclists had done from the early days.

Even in the 1930s there had been self-styled outlaw clubs. Maybe their names are no longer familiar, but there are still plenty of eyewitness accounts of untamed bikers who would blast into a bar or saloon pumping the bike's hand-oiler and gunning the engine to fill the place with smoke, until everything was enveloped in an acrid cloud of oil and fumes. Hidden by the smoke, they would ride out of the bar again creating as much noise as before. There were other legendary tales about particularly nasty guys who would hand two open cans of oil to their pillion-passenger; on the next bend the passenger would pour it all in the path of the motorcycle police pursuing them, so sending the troublesome cop skidding off the road. The reasons for these chases were almost always the same: traffic offenses and driving too fast. These two mortal enemies engaged in a no-holds-barred battle were often riding the same make of motorcycle – a Harley.

The history of the club names, their insignia or colors, and their liberal use of the swastika and Nazi emblems are easy to trace. One just needs to look at painted World War II pilot bomber jackets, on which names were immortalized, still famous nowadays, such as Hell´s Angels. The standard-issue leather A2 flying jacket is the ideal biker jacket, and many an airman stationed in Europe painted swastikas on the back of it to show how many German aircraft he had shot down or the number of missions flown over Germany.

Later, when the outlaw clubs started raising hell, they discovered that swastikas particularly tended to frighten and enrage the locals. Public opinion did not view them as symbols of a wartime trophy but rather as an insult to all that was sacred in the American way of life: so swastikas became a favorite way of annoying narrow-minded Americans, and of making loyal democrats turn into angry men.

Soon the clubs graduated from painted names and symbols to embroidered colors. One of the earliest postwar patchholder clubs was The Boozefighters whose members were notorious as the instigators of the 1947 riot in Hollister, and it was from there that the outlaws and the One Percenters developed.

At that time they just wanted to have some fun; nobody could guess just how influential they were to become. In the 1980s The Boozefighters staged a comeback and set up a number of different chapters in several parts of the U.S. They then faded out of public attention again. The Boozefighters were closely followed by the Hell's Angels who founded their very first chapter in 1948 in Berdoo or San Bernadino according to my sources.

Other Californian clubs formed in those early days include Satan's Slaves, whose members wore a particularly striking square patch. The

Slaves' turf was the San Fernando Valley area of Los Angeles, and their patch bore the letters SFV. The members of this club were greatly feared because of their toughness, and they later became the SFV chapter of Hell's Angels.

The Galloping Gooses were also around in the early 1950s. Riding out of the eastern end of the San Fernando Valley, they flew a distinctive gold and purple patch depicting a hand running on two small feet with one finger raised in the obscene gesture. The brother of Ritchie Valens, the rock 'n roll star, frequently rode with them. The Galloping Gooses are still around today, though not in such a large numbers as before.

Los Angeles, particularly the Pasadena region, was also the home of The Chosen Few, a club with members of all races. Sometimes there were up to a dozen, extreme choppers parked in front of the Pasadena Police Departments garage, with denim vests bearing the Chosen Few insignia hung over the sissy bars. The bikers worked, amongst other things, as Police Department mechanics.

Yet another Californian club was The Gypsy Jokers. It had been set up as several separate chapters in different parts of California at various times up untill the late 1960s. After losing a war to the Hell's Angels this club vanished completely, but, more recently at the end of the 1990s, there have been sightings of their colors again in the northwestern part of the U.S.

In the mid–1960s there were many other clubs in southern California: The Huns, which still exists today, The Commancheros, The Sundowners, The Vagos, mainly a Mexican club from the Sunland–Tujunga area, The Heathens from the South Bay and other small clubs, such as The Bravados from Santa Barbara.

The Outlaws were formed in Chicago in 1957; The Pagans in Maryland in 1959. New York boasted The Aliens, a club that formed the nucleus of the New York City chapter of the Hell's Angels. The Detroit Renegades set up their base in Motor City some time during the 1960s.

The outlaw biker world of the late 1990s with its numerous levels, power structures, and territorial claims has certainly changed from what it was just after the war, and Southern California, with its desert climate which is hot and dry throughout the year, is not now the legendary biker paradise it once was for motorcycle rebels. But the strong ties with Harley still remain.

Secret Signs

A Science in Itself

Even the most down-to-earth Harley riders like to show their secret passions once in a while.

What the countless biker patches and signs, numbers, letters, and symbols denote has remained a mystery well into the 1990s, even to insiders, and they are the cause of numerous misunderstandings.

But now, as we approach the new millennium, many of the patches that once held significance are gone. A few others have taken their place, but by and large the messages once carried by the smaller patches on a biker's colors are communicated in some other way. In addition, bikers are smarter these days. Only a fool would still sport the DFFL patch which means "Dope forever, forever loaded." That would be too much of a magnet for the cops and would, in many places, be reason enough for an immediate body search or even an arrest.

The same applies to the famous 13 patch, which stands for the thirteenth letter of the alphabet: the M stands for marijuana. Earlier, gullible reporters were led to believe that it denoted the lucky (or unlucky) number thirteen, and many of the guys even believed this.

The variety of patches and their meanings are multiple. There are other patches which all have an individudual meaning, such as the rather known patch 69 – and its meaning should be self-evident. There is also the FTW – "F... The World." Its origin is the abbreviation FTA (F... The Army). The FT abbreviation has numerous variants. Other patches such as the skull have to be taken more seriously. One American club wears the notorious ITCOB patch: "I Took Care Of Business," which could signify all kinds of things.

One Hell's Angels patch particularly feared by the police is the Daguello patch. It indicates that no mercy will be shown and, particularly in the case of the Hell's Angels, this shows that its wearer is (or was) prepared to use any means to prevent arrest. The word "Daguello" is the title of a Mexican folksong sung by General Santayana's soldiers while laying siege to the Alamo just before the terrible massacre. The same song was made popular around the world as it was performed in the Western 'Rio Bravo' (starring famous John Wayne, Dean Martin and Ricky Nelson).

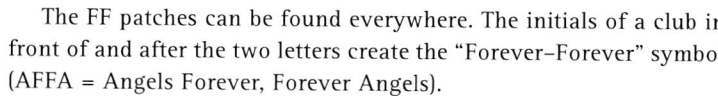

Secret or not, on-the-ball bikers can read any signs.

The FF patches can be found everywhere. The initials of a club in front of and after the two letters create the "Forever–Forever" symbol (AFFA = Angels Forever, Forever Angels).

The "1%" patch is a reminder of the Hollister Bash of 1947 and is an expression of protest against the AMA statement claiming that only one percent of all bikers were hooligans. Up to the present day anyone wearing a 1% patch considers himself to be a real biker or an outlaw. In the U.S. the 1% symbol is like a red rag to a bull as far as the cops are concerned and it is often cause enough for the wearer to be arrested.

MC generally stands for Motorcycle Club meaning all biker clubs sporting colors. In Europe the abbreviation MCC (Motor Cycle Club), CC (Chopper Club) and CCC (Custom Chopper Club) are common variations. The abbreviation MF (Motorcycle Family) makes it clear that there is more than just one outlaw club involved.

The controversial swastika patches or the Nazi SS lettering have their origins in World War II from Hitler's Nazi regime: U.S. pilots then painted these symbols as trophies on their flying jackets to indicate the number of German aircraft which had been shot down. Later these flying jackets proved to be ideal biker clothing, but the Nazi symbols painted on them were loathed by people who regarded them with disgust. Rebellious bikers soon saw them as an ideal way of frightening ordinary decent folk. These symbols may not always in all instances indicate an anti-Semitic feeling, but can simply be honoring the Allied heroes of World War II.

A special section has to be devoted to the infamous wings patches. The famous Red Wings are an invention of the Hell's Angels dating from their early days and show that the wearer has performed certain acts. This wings patch is the only one that was ever worn much, but it is little seen today. In addition, there is a range of meaning attached to wings of all colors of the rainbow, some more fantastic than the others; most of them are, however, purely and simply, invented by the wearer. Nevertheless, they are religiously listed in police instruction manuals – and so it is little wonder that bikers are often viewed with suspicion. Some of these colored wing patches are listed here, though many of them are just too far over the top to be believed.

The different colors stand for different definitions, all mostly connected to sexual practices. One example is the *blue* or *yellow wing*, which stands for sex with a policewoman, and one of the few wings which is possibly genuine. Another is the *golden wing* which is a kind of medal indicating its wearer has taken part in a gang fight. Others are the white wing, black wing, yellow wing, the purple wing and the brown wing.

The Eight Ball patch (that is the black pool ball) is another symbol which has several different meanings, and is of military underground origin. It is supposed to mean that the wearer performed a sexual practice and was watched by other bikers – but this is nonsense.

Most patches have long-since lost their original significance and are frequently treated as just another eye-catching souvenir to be sewn on to a jacket or vest without thinking. This is yet another symptom of the change in the outlaw biker community.

Lifetime Bikers

Real-Life Legends:

Loved – venerated – respected. Well–known on the scene and always there to provide support for bikers and their rights. The authorities, experts, gurus, chiefs and idols of the world of Harley-Davidson, such as "Pops" and his wife from New Orleans, Gabriel Sage, "Little One" from Florida, "Wildman" from Mississippi and "Papa John" - always on the road; "Tiny", a highly respected and much sought-after Harley mechanic, "Santa Claus," the great chief of the Southern Riders who were the victims of particularly ruthless coercion, "Robert" from Natches, "Walt" and his girlfriend from the Vietnam Veterans, and "Junior" from Meridian or "Lynn" from Mobile. Harleys are their life, and their way of life is hallmarked by unconditional loyalty to their Harleys.

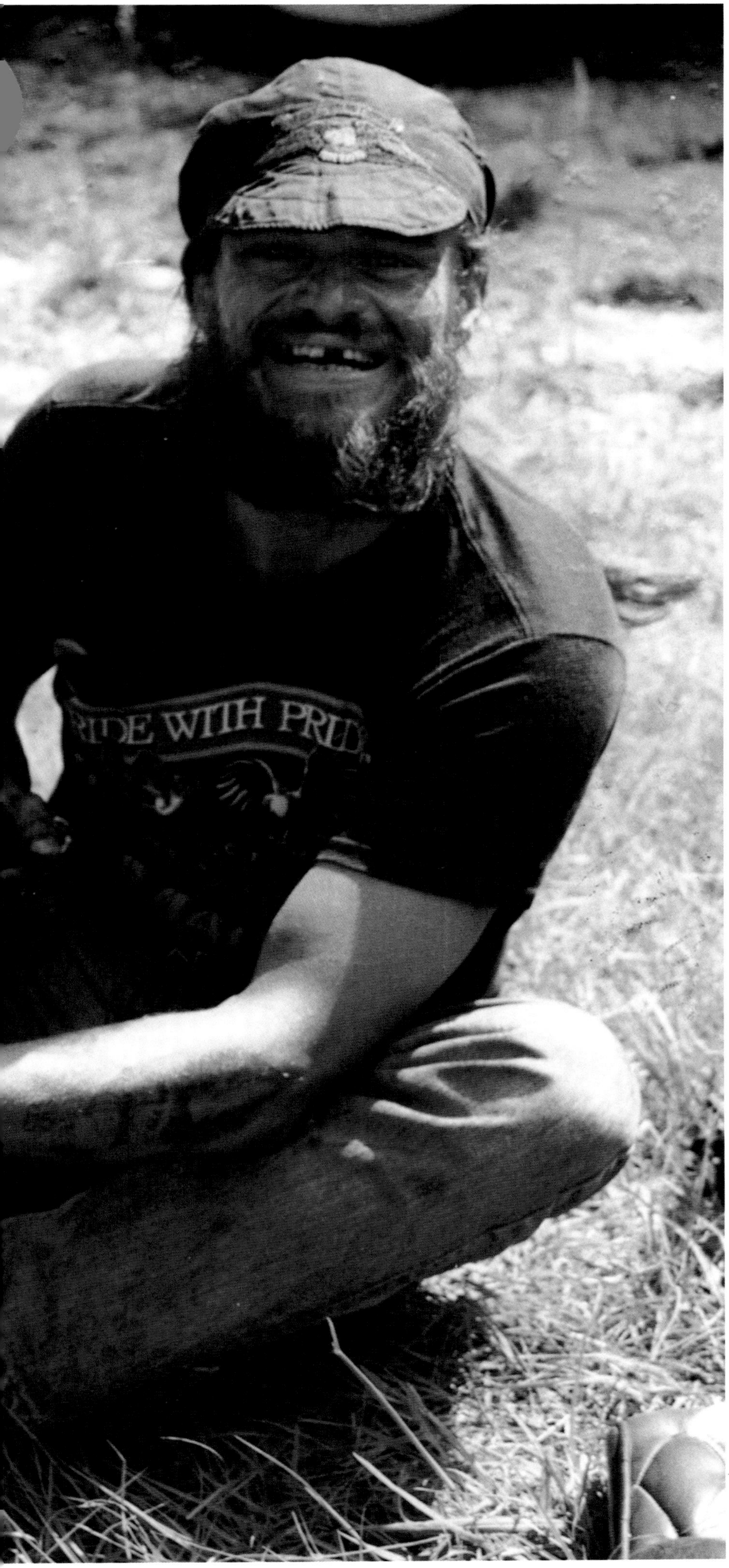
RIDE WITH PRID

Bring Them Home!
Viet Nam Vets M/C

SOUTHERN RIDERS
M.C.
MOBILE, CO.
President

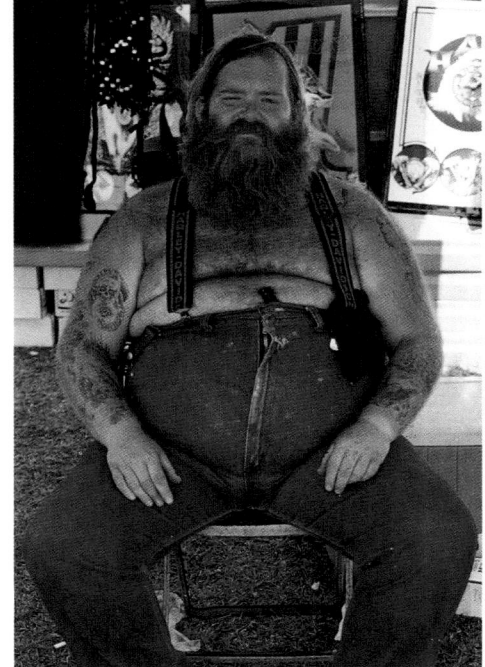

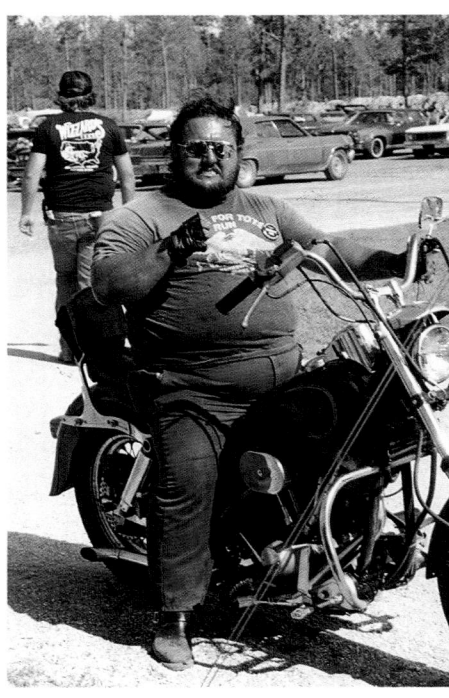

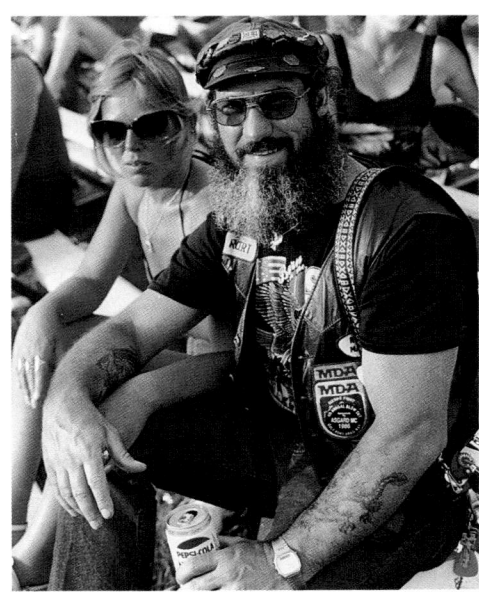

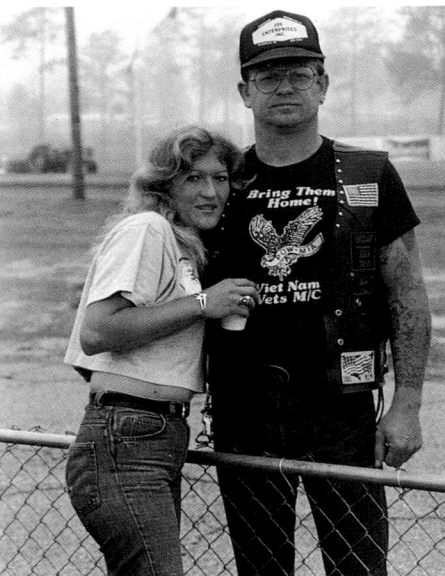

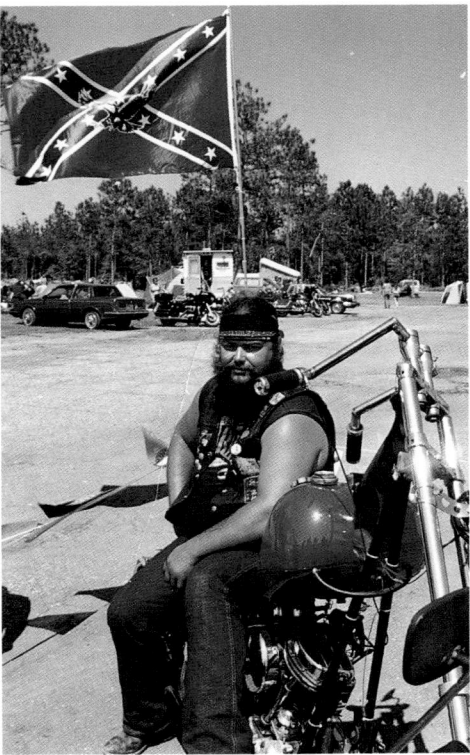

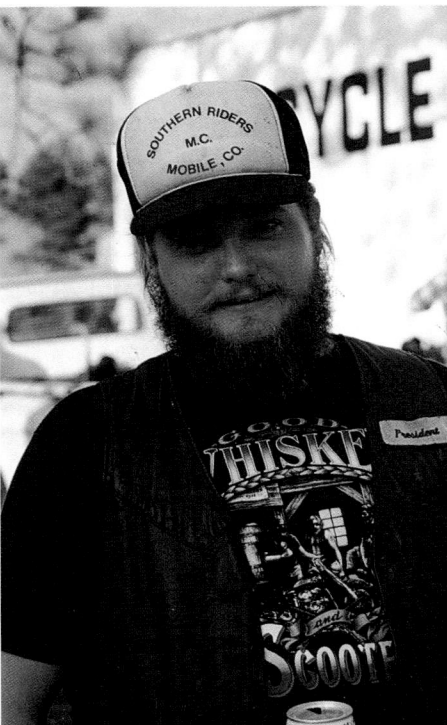

The Biker Scene in Germany

Motorcycles on the Other Side of the Ocean

German Biker Clubs and MCs:

BONES MC
CAVE MEN MC, Rammstein, Mannheim
GREMIUM MC
FREE SPIRITS MC since 1975
BOMBHOLDERS MC
WARLORDS MC
KNIGHT RIDERS MC (U.S. club, Erlangen)
MOTOR TRAMPS MC
FREE BIRDS MC since 1976
FIREBIRDS MC
ROAD EAGLES MC, Munich
HELLS ANGELS MC
DEVILS ADVOCATES MC
OUTLAWS MC (some integrated clubs are, e.g. TORROS MC, or ANGELI NEGRI MC)
Here some of the smaller clubs: LOST SONS MC, FALCONS MC, BRONCOS MC, CHOPPERS MC, VULTURES MC, ...to cite but a few whose names are known.

The hard-core biker scene glamorized by innumerable Hollywood films, reached Europe in the early 1960s. First port of call was Britain, a country with its own beat and rock 'n' roll cultures, where since shortly after the war rockers, teds, and mods had been fighting, and where the "bad image" of hard-core biking soon found acceptance.

The general public in the U.S. and in Europe regarded the hard-core bikers as vulgar lowlifes and antisocial people, as work-shy and unwashed rabble-rousers. The expression "filthy swine" became an expression typically applied to members of these groups, who were often presented as being out of their heads on alcohol or drugs. It was an expression based on fear and frustration – and also, in part, on envy by those who not a part of these communities.

In reality, the American rebellion soon took root right across Europe, awakening dreams of escape from the mind numbing world of work and prudish parental control. The shared hatred of state authority and bureaucratic meddling added to this feeling, and so it was that the clubs developed into the home of a new biker generation. The bike (not always, but increasingly, a Harley) became a common symbol, its very appearance creating a suitably intimidating effect.

In Germany from the 1970s onwards, the rocker scene became consolidated through the creation of innumerable MCs, including some pure Harley clubs, which had developed mainly because of the influence of the many U.S. soldiers stationed in Germany. The slogan "Ride free" became "a stress-free, cop-free ride," and the police responded to the new public enemy image of the biker with constant harassment.

The culmination of this was seen in the well-organized club rallies which occurred at the end of the 1970s and beginning of the 1980s. Usually boasting an attendance of between 500 and 2,000, they were already among the biggest runs on the scene. Since every MC, no matter how small, could see the potential for a lucrative business in organizing such parties, the dates soon began to clash, permission for them later being applied for and granted at so-called "presidential rallies."

Some events at that time are even today bywords for riots, shootings, club feuds with knife attacks, mass fistfights, and arson. The authorities and local councils plagued events with ever stricter and almost impossible conditions. After the clubs began to kit themselves out with firearms, the police of course became increasingly nervous and aggressive. Additionally, there was a transformation of the typical rocker scene (youths with mopeds, bikes, and cars) to a bikers' scene, identified with heavy motorcycles, nearly always Harleys. And while rockers and bikers came to be "investigated" more and more by the police, the criminal investigation department, and the state security service, territorial rivalries between groups were fought out with unusual brutality.

Larger clubs tended to annex smaller clubs by threatening them with violent dissolution, a development which has long been the norm in the world of big business, and which is usually known as a "merger" or hostile takeover. In fact many of the larger MCs in Germany and everywhere in Europe are now being run like international companies, with plain and simple communal motorcycle riding being debased more and more to the level of organized leisure time. Real bikers disparagingly describe the members of this kind of well-organized club as "weekend rockers," though it has to be admitted that hardly a week goes by without one or more of these clubs organizing a big biker event.

Typical Biker Clubs in Europe

Russia – Sweden – The Netherlands

Only a small number of European clubs can be named. There is no arbitrariness or favoritism; this is merely a list of those clubs which the author either know personally, or which are known to him through others. Clubs which were mentioned in the – unfortunately all too limited – constituency of European biker magazines are also listed.

To begin with Eastern Europe, perhaps mention should be made of the Harley-riding Werewolves Club in St. Petersburg along with the Muscovite Nightwolves in Russia. Harleys are also becoming more popular with members of the Scorpions MC in Poland. In Hungary there is the Geronimo MC.

Maluku MC is an extreme club for Harley owners founded in the Netherlands in 1990, a politically-oriented association of former colonial soldiers which campaigns for the freedom of the people of Moluccas (the Spice Islands). In 1974 Les Copains MC was founded in Luxembourg, and in Switzerland in the 1980s so was the Harley club Cheyenne. There are many hard-core clubs in the Scandinavian countries, but not all of them are as well-known as the Hell's Angels and the Bandidos, who fought bloody battles in Denmark in 1997. In Sweden, the Sundbäckens MC has existed for some years; while there are also the Mother's Freak MC in Gothenburg, the Brotherhood MC in Karlstad, and the Sofia Hogs in Stockholm, the oldest club of them all.

Naturally there are many hard-core and "1%er" clubs in almost every nation in Europe. Their parties and runs are divided into big extravaganzas and smaller scale trips for the initiated. Choice of name, outfit, club life and, last but not least, the motorcycle, are largely based on the style of American precursors, though that doesn't mean that a little patriotism is unheard of; the desire for national freedom is, after all, universal.

"Freedom on the road," however, is quite another thing: it must be fought for, against all comers, from case to case, region to region, and country to country.

Biker News

The ongoing readers' survey from *Biker News* about the popularity of Harley-Davidson in the biker and rocker scenes makes for some interesting reading.

Of around 130,000 readers the following percentages rode Harleys:

1988 – 19 percent
1989 – 23 percent
1991 – 26 percent
1993 – 24 percent
1996 – 33 percent.

Of around the same number of readers, the following percentages described Harley as their dream bike:

1991 – 66 percent
1993 – 54 percent
1996 – 55 percent.

On the road all over the world: after the fall of the iron curtain, the now 'liberated' Harley clubs are coming to the attention of the other biker communes. Top and center: members of the Night Wolves MC in Moscow Russia.

Courtesy of: Sherrif

459

Brothers in Mind

Clubs for Harley Riders in Europe

Long before Harley-rider clubs developed all over the world during the 1960s and 1970s, early exports of the company's machines to England, Holland, and Germany had led to the formation of several clubs for Harley riders. The members' main aims were to provide mutual support, to exchange experiences, and to organize a centralized system for obtaining spare parts. These clubs were by no means associated with the company, but merely used Harley-Davidson or Harley in their names because the members had to ride a Harley.

The first Harley club to become widely known has almost certainly been *The Harley-Davidson Club Praha* (Prague), in what was then Czechoslovakia. The evidence for this is provided by a Czech hotel register for 1926.

A short time after the end of World War II special Harley-Davidson clubs were founded all over Europe, some of them by using whatever motorbikes the Allied forces had left behind. Among the first of these clubs was the *Harley Club*

de Paris, founded in Paris in 1948 with Lionel Matra as its first president. A little later the *Harley-Davidson Club de France* was inaugurated; another early Harley club in France was the *Clodos Sauvages*. In Britain, as in America, many of those who had ridden Harleys during the war got together and founded clubs, the first British one being the *Harley-Davidson Riders Club of Great Britain*, established in 1949.

Gradually Harley clubs, which had initially been independent of one another, grew into a pan-European movement. The clubs in eastern Europe, however, inevitably remained somewhat separate; but even there several of the clubs were very active. Proof of this was the *Harley Club Brno* in Czechoslovakia, which has been in existence since 1964. In the German Democratic Republic there was the *Freundeskreis von Harleyfahrern*, whose organizers disguised their activities by displaying motorcycles belonging to the "class enemy" as an "exhibition of veteran and vintage motor vehicles." There were even Harley riders in the Soviet Union, but it was only after 1990 that they could form real clubs such as the already-mentioned *Werewolf Biker Club* in St. Petersburg, and the *Night Wolves MC* in Moscow.

All over Europe enthusiasts have grouped themselves together to form Harley-Davidson clubs. Among them are: the Harley-Davidson Club of Sweden (HDCS); the Harley Club of the Netherlands, based in Groningen (which has even staged its own private

races since the end of the 1970s); the H–D Club of Denmark; and the H–D Club Germany. All of these have been responsible, in turns, for the organization of the Super Rallies already mentioned.

There are other clubs such as the Mainzer Harley–Davidson *Classic E.V.*, and the Harley–Davidson club *Big Twin España* that hold their own events. The smaller Harley clubs all over Europe run their own events, some small, others large; the extent to which they become well-known depends on their basic appeal and on the atmosphere they can generate. Many of the smaller clubs broke up because membership dropped, or they just gradually faded away because of lack of interest or differences of opinion. Others were dissolved because of the territorial claims of more powerful clubs; this situation started to arise more and more in the 1990s throughout Europe, and in Germany in partiular.

In addition, the activities of the Harley Owners Group (H.O.G.) have caused everything in the Harley scene to change direction. This has meant that many of the smaller local groups have reformed into chapters of H.O.G., while others have become hard-core or outlaw groups.

There have been particular problems with well–established older Harley clubs that call themselves Harley clubs and that are reluctant to give up their independence and their name without a struggle. As a consequence, their members are faced with the choice of either sticking with the status quo, or joining an H.O.G. group. In general dual membership has not been allowed; whereas anyone can become a member of H.O.G. provided that she or he rides a Harley, other clubs think their very identity is being threatened by dual membership. So there is no close interrelationship between H.O.G. and other clubs, supporters groups, or associations, though members of all of them participate in joint events, and respect one another as fellow Harley riders.

Exclusive and pretty exotic: in the 1960s so-called Harley clubs were an awe-inspiring world in themselves.

Harley Clubs Worldwide

The Harley Riders Club in England.

The Swedish Harley-Davidson Club (HDCS).

Collecting trophies for back home: a member
of the Czech Harley community.

A member of the Big Twin MC at a meeting in Kinugawa, Japan.
Always let them know where you're from: British Harley riders.

Harley–Highlanders from Scotland.

Thin on the ground: Harley fans in Cuba.

A proud Harley owner in Cuba.

Club parade in Milwaukee, Wisconsin, USA.

A Harley club meeting down under in Sidney, Australia.

The Polish Harley Club: a meeting in Zielonka.

Old but reliable: Wassilij Kostin's faithful WL in Moscow.

Biker Weddings

A Non-Traditional Wedding

In the church, in bed, and of course in the motorcycle club, biker weddings are celebrated in a true spirit of "Harleylujah." When it comes to marriage, the otherwise not particularly Christian biker strictly observes social and religious values and conventions, and biker weddings are normally celebrated in church. After all, a wedding at city hall is nothing more than a tedious bit of bureaucracy. Besides, in the religiously tolerant U.S., a lot of club presidents also hold some kind of religious office and so have the power to perform marriages. All around the world special "motorcycle priests" organize motorcycle masses and perform marriage ceremonies. Whether a traditional church wedding or not, biker weddings always boast the inevitable accompaniment of Harleys suitably adorned for the occasion, and are sometimes even allowed into the house of God itself. Of course everyone is dressed in full biker kit: boots, jeans, colors, and insignia in all their glory.

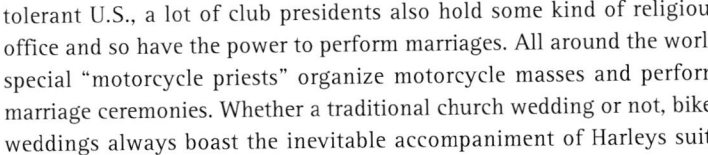

Thundering off to the registry office: who said Harleys didn't make perfect wedding coaches.

Funerals – The Last Ride

In Memory of …

The long column of heavyweight Harleys slowly approaches the isolated cemetery with their lights dimmed. In the middle of the column is a black limousine driven by bearded bikers without helmets. Before the entrance to the cemetery the bikers park their motorcycles in a long row, and the primeval roar is stilled. Silence reigns in the shadowy place as six bikers with muscular arms lift the unadorned coffin, and bear it into the cemetery.

The other bikers, all wearing jeans and colors and full emblems and insignia, walk slowly and silently after the coffin, the women following behind. The officiating priest speaks a few polite words as Christian custom demands, and then a number of other brothers add a few words, most of them spoken by the President of the dead man's motorcycle club. A few mementos are thrown into the open grave before his fellow members begin to shovel in the earth. With an infernal roar the bikes are started up and the whole column disappears into the distance in a cloud of dust...

Well, that's roughly how most people imagine a biker funeral, and it's certainly how they're depicted in the movies. In reality the majority of biker funerals are very conventional – apart from the "mourning dress," which for bikers is the usual biker gear with the addition of a

black armband and a newly stitched–on patch bearing the legend "In Memory of..." The funeral procession consists mostly of bikes, normally Harleys, which also serve as an indispensable and unmistakable symbol of life and death.

However, there are other forms of funerals. For example, just as some people's last request is that their ashes be scattered over the high seas, some bikers specify a funeral run during which their ashes will be consigned to the four winds.

The police are another feature of biker funerals: the FBI and other law enforcement agencies like to use biker funerals to track down people on their wanted lists, so the former – uninvited and unwelcome guests – are often to be seen at outlaw funerals.

Every deceased club member has the right to an annual memorial run: a club outing to his grave, where a bottle of beer is passed round, half of it being drunk before the half–empty bottle is placed on the grave mound. Then, of course, there's the inevitable party.

Very occasionally, the deceased wants his motorcycle to be buried with him. This custom is certainly the stuff of fine legends but in reality it's strictly forbidden by the powers that be: a meddling bureaucracy succeeds in hounding unfortunate bikers even in their graves.

Members of biker clubs have a right both to a funeral and to an annual memorial run. The club rituals and the memory patch are "sacred" ceremonies and insignia.

ABATE – dedicated to freedom of the road

One of the biggest ABATE events was the famed Helmet Protest Run to the Louisiana Capitol in Baton Rouge (1984), during which thousands of signatures against the newly-introduced law demanding to wear a crash helmets were collected and presented to the representatives.

ABATE (American Bikers Aimed Towards Education) came into being after the introduction of a law making the wearing of crash-helmets compulsory (Highway Safety Act of 1966). It had been (and is) as an organization working independently in the individual states of the U.S. for the rights of motorcyclists. At the time, however, the rather anarchistic sounding acronym stood for A Brotherhood Against Totalitarian Enactments – obviously it can be interpreted as a product of the hard-core bikers scene.

At the beginning it was the One Percenter clubs (including the Hell's Angels, Hessians, Chosen Few, Mongols, Outlaws, Sons of Silence, and Bandidos) who raged against the new compulsory helmet laws: outlaw groups in particular always had to suffer police harassment, and they were, because of their rebellious freedom-loving character, very sensitive to any form of state control.

Although their revolt was in the honorable American tradition of the civil liberties movement, ABATE found itself with a negative image among the more law-abiding motorcyclists. *Easyriders* magazine in particular had a powerful positive influence on the ABATE movement, tirelessly reporting new legal "tricks," detailing the laws in the individual states, and giving the ABATE groups an editorial platform. Although this commitment on the part of *Easyriders* was on one level merely an astute and successful advertising campaign, it was also a good and honorable cause for which the magazine labored, and surely one of the reasons for the success of ABATE.

To the shame of the otherwise freedom-loving, American press, nearly all the other motorcycle magazines regarded the compulsory helmet law as a good thing and, where they were not openly hostile, completely ignored the now powerful ABATE movement. That said, it was never the aim of ABATE to demonize the helmet, the protective function of which they never doubted; what they were rejecting was the obligation to wear it.

In the meantime ABATE, as a recognized civil-liberties movement, worked closely with the Motorcycle Safety Foundation (MSF), and in this context changed its acronym to the less provocative American Bikers Aimed Towards Education. Their recognition of the fact that better education is urgently needed is justified: America has no compulsory motorcycle schools, despite the statistics demonstrating that most fatalities occur among young motorcyclists.

At first ABATE financed itself through fund-raising runs and parties (the legendary Bean Blossom Boogie in Indiana and numerous Helmet Protest Runs are examples), and soon it had enough money in the kitty to afford expensive lawyers and constitutional lawsuits, some of which were very successful: various states withdrew the compulsory helmet law, mainly for constitutional reasons.

Today, campaigning for the freedoms originally guaranteed to everyone, ABATE is a worldwide organization which works together with other motorcycle and civil-liberties groups to fight the power of the patriarchal state.

Although Harley-Davidson originally distanced itself from ABATE, the company is no longer afraid of coming into contact with the organization, and it too has now set itself against the limitation of basic civil rights, in so far as they affect the motorcycle industry. At the end of the day, the debate is not merely about the helmet (or compulsion), but about an entire way of life – a way of life very much built around Harleys.

ABATE Statement
Does History Repeat Itself?

In the 1880's there was a group of people in America who liked to roam the hills and valleys of his great land.

They liked to ride with the wind in their faces, and the sun on their backs.
They loved the outdoors, and they had a special sense of freedom.
They wore leather, and some wore rings in their ears.

They liked to gather together around campfires and share brotherhood.
They were divided into many tribes and clans each with their own leader.
They distrusted each other, and the leaders often would argue.
They never were able to unify all the tribes and clans.
They like to ride with the wind in their faces, and the sun on their backs.
They love the outdoors, and they have a special sense of freedom.
They wear leather and have a special style of clothing all their own.

They often have long hair, and some wear rings in their ears.
The like to gather together around campfires and share brotherhood.
They are divided into many clubs, clans, and associations, each with their own leader.
They're distrustful of each other, and their leaders continually argue.
They are not able to unify or willing to unify all the clubs, clans or associations.

These people were called Indians.

The Government and the Do-Gooders of society did not like the Indians because they were different, and people who are different are always seen as a threat. So, the Government passed laws which restricted the Indians' rights and denied their freedom. Eventually, the Indians were forced to live in confined areas (called Reservations), where their way of life was effectively destroyed.
Now, in the 1980s there is a group of people in America who like to roam the hills and valleys of this great land.

These people are called bikers.

Nowadays the Government and the so-called Do-Gooders of society do not like these bikers and their communities because they are different.
People who are different are always seen as a threat. So, the Government keeps passing laws to restrict the rights of the bikers, and uses the law the to deny the biker living in absolute freedom. Where do we go from here? Might history be repeating itself?
Do you suppose that one day there will be a reservation for bikers?

The Unpopular Helmet

"My head belongs to me!": Unmoved by the security standards of state safety ordinances, many bikers make a joke out of wearing the helmets as a sign of their protest.

No one denies the need for a helmet: a helmet is a good thing and often saves lives. But on this issue two worlds collide: on one side, there's the respect for freedom and individual responsibility, all too often curtailed by the state; and on the other side, the recognition that a helmet is an invaluable safety aid when riding a motorcycle.

The particular gripe here is not the helmet itself, but rather the *compulsion* to wear it, and all what that entails for the biker. Many supporters of this precaution regard it as some sort of compensation for the apparent danger of motorcycles: an argument the campaigners against the compulsory wearing of helmets find very questionable. They favor better training instead. Their motto is: "Let those who ride decide!"

The motorcycle industry and the allied motorcycle press speak out, perhaps a little guiltily, in favor of the helmet law. In regions with heavy traffic the government has already seen a need for action, and the police are now once again allowed to play the role of upholders of the law.

Innumerable statistics from researchers into serious accidents are used in the heated debate both for and against the use of the helmet – even though those quoting statistics are actually missing the point. The increasing zeal on the part of the state authorities

for regimentation, on the other hand, is seen as very disturbing. A typical example was the introduction of the nonsensical ECE Norm (European Crash-Helmet Norm), which afterwards proved to be impracticable.

It may or may not be relevant to educational politics, but adults don't react kindly to regulations about how they are supposed to protect themselves. This is particularly so for Americans, whose personal freedom is guaranteed by the Constitution. While numerous motorcycle and traffic safety institutes firmly support compulsion, Harley-Davidson and the AMA – the main organizations affected, in effect – see the issue a little differently. Both support the wearing of helmets but not as a state-imposed obligation.

In reality this is one of the few taboo subjects for the company and the closely allied AMA. Harley does have attractive helmets in its range, for example the Sportsman or Police types, but real bikers want to feel the wind in their hair now and then. As a protest against the patriarchal state, and with the motto "Education yes, compulsory education no," they take to covering their heads with laughable pieces of plastic or provocative, Nazi steel helmets. They also place great importance on being informed of the dangers and risks of motorcycling.

Motorcyclists live dangerously – sudden crashes don't always have such minor results as this one (top). The Harley riders are split: freedom for the head versus the full helmet and visor are their competing beliefs.

Events

Daytona Bike Week

Diary of a Way of Life

In truth Florida has an incredibly horrible climate: hot and often even unbearably humid, lots of rain in spring and summer, an extremely fierce sun, mosquitoes and snakes everywhere, alligator–infested swamps and forests. On top of all that, from May to November there is the continual risk of devastating hurricanes.

It is only on the Atlantic coast that it is pleasantly cool, and – as in the rest of the State of Florida – the population living there has created a tropical paradise, albeit one heavily dependent on modern civilization, that is, such as the automobile and air conditioning.

It is here on the Atlantic that a quirk of nature has created a magnificent sandy beach, about 25 miles long, which has been increasingly built up with hotels for over 70 years now. Today Daytona has a permanent population of around 50,000, but many times that number of hotel beds. Since 1920 people have driven up and down this famous beach in the fresh, salty sea breeze, observing a strictly enforced, 10 mph, speed limit. Since 1989, entrance to the beach has been free of charge, though there is a three–dollar daily fee for vehicles during the well–known and popular Bike Week.

This brings us to the yearly occurrence which in the first week of March sweeps like a tornado through the otherwise tranquil paradise for senior citizens. Bike Week became established in the postwar years, when the season kicked off with a high-speed race along the beach known as the Daytona 200. This first took place in 1937 under the aegis of the American Motorcyclists Association (AMA). Before, people raced back and forth on the beach between Ormond and Daytona and broke various speed records. Later the organizers set up a 3.12-mile-long course, one and a half miles of which ran northwards

along the sand and one and a half miles back southwards along the parallel asphalt road. They raced until 200 miles had been clocked. That season's opening 200-mile race took place in pretty chaotic conditions, and not only on the track. At that time Daytona was not a resort and the senior citizens were already grumbling about rowdy spectators, who, often without entrance tickets, clambered unrestricted over the dunes, sometimes crossing Highway A1A (temporarily transformed into part of the racetrack) in the middle of the race. For the many thousands of race fans there were just two, primitive, portable toilets.

Most bikers came without a ticket, they just rode over the dunes, sometimes immediately joining in on a race. Everyone wanted to be a part of this event. In the first Race Week after World War II, there was widespread heavy drinking at the bars and the police handed out countless tickets for speeding, unmuffled exhaust pipes and of course drunk driving. Despite this, the city fathers of Daytona immediately realized the (chiefly financial) importance of this rowdy spectacle, and established a major prize for anyone winning the Daytona 200 three times. The first to do so was Dick Klamfoth on a Norton Manx, while Brad Andres picked up the second Daytona Beach Grand Prix for Harley-Davidson on a KR 750 with his victories in 1955, 1959 and 1960.

The 1960s

As conditions on the beach became steadily more impossible, the stock-car racing fan Bill France, with the blessing of the AMA, finally built the giant Daytona International Speedway stadium, at some distance from the beach, which now once again belonged entirely to the beach visitors. However, while the race and the practice events transferred 10 miles inland to the Speedway from 1961 onwards, in the Main Street area of Daytona Beach an independent motorcycle scene began to emerge, which slowly took on the character of a giant party. By day on the beach and by night on the half mile-long Main Street, all hell broke loose.

The 1970s

The races were of precious little interest to the bikers, but they found the warm weather — while much of the rest of America was still covered in ice and snow — and the hot motorcycling scene highly attractive. As in Laconia (New Hampshire), where events increasingly

tended to degenerate into rioting, excess and police terror, they looked for new venues to indulge in their hedonistic partying: boozing, sex, having fun. The preferred locations were the beach and Main Street with their numerous biker bars. Bikers flocked here in the thousands from every corner of the U.S., and dealers and miscellaneous profiteers set up shop for this wild week on Main Street. The law enforcement agencies looked with displeasure on this invasion by the bearded, tattooed biker hordes, and remembering the bad experiences at Laconia, began to throw their weight around.

Worth noting: in 1973, in a supermarket parking lot, a fairly laid-back group of especially crazy motorcyclists gathered to show off their customized bikes. They called themselves the Rats Hole Chopper Show, and were organized by the proprietor, Karl Smith, of a T-shirt shop in St. Petersburg, who christened himself "Big Daddy Rat." This was the first year of what was to become an annual tradition.

In 1974, its second year, the show, now called the Annual Custom Chopper Bike Show, was a big success, now taking place right by the beach on the boardwalk, in blazing sunshine pleasantly tempered by cool Atlantic breezes. Entrance was free. That Saturday Police Chief Palmer was expecting 5,000 visitors.

Over 15,000 turned up at the event, and the 191 bikes exhibited there were worth collectively 668,000 dollars. Not without justification, Karl Smith immediately dubbed his show the "World's Largest Motorcycle Show." That same year French television discovered the event, and a big American motorcycle magazine enthused over the fact that at this show there were no ropes to be seen, i.e. any visitor could freely go right up to the engineering marvels and examine them at close quarters. On the back of the application forms for the Rats Hole Show, all the important motorcycle regulations

On the Beach

The beach is packed full over a 12-mile stretch. Car after car, parked on the sand, with a few Harleys wedged in between. Next to the surf the traffic in the other direction crawls by. The heat wave sun burns mercilessly down from a cloudless sky, while the fresh Atlantic sea breeze offers some relief. The waves break against the bike wheels, pure salt water. The helmetless bikers are dressed only in shorts, with the bikini-clad "old lady" riding pillion, beachcombers on two wheels. Waving, shouting, laughing. Muscular bodybuilders playing ballgames. Body culture. Suntan oil and sweat, flesh on show everywhere. Girlie groups walk by shaking their behinds, greedy stares in their wake. Gangs of youngsters yelling from overloaded custom vans. "Show us your tits." The shouts are allowed, but bare breasts are not. Long-forked choppers skid across the loose sand, some of the heavy machines digging themselves in like gophers. Dismount, push, swear, laugh. Among the joggers stubbornly trotting past, retired folk prowl undeterred through the beach life sweeping their metal detectors across the sand. Kids fill their heads with the sound from their Walkmans. The rest are dreams. Dreams of eternal sun and freedom as endless as the great glistening ocean. America forever!

of the City of Daytona Beach Public Safety Agency were clearly listed — a total of 14 of them, which would probably strike most of us as perfectly sensible and normal, but which sparked a reaction of pure disgust among the American motorcyclists.

Among the requirements were that riders had to have a drivers license and a license plate; that motorcycle handlebars must not be more than 15 inches above the saddle; the headlight — which had to be used 24 hours a day — must not be lower than 24 inches and not higher than 54 inches off the ground; that a helmet must be worn — and that is particularly aggravating in that heat; that regular mufflers were required — to hell with them!; that bikes must have a taillight and a brake light, a horn, a mirror, foot pegs and a pillion seat that was firmly fixed to the motorcycle.

They also specified how one should ride the bike: sitting upright facing forwards, with one leg on either side of the motorbike, overtaking was forbidden, as was riding more than two abreast. And there was more such nonsense. No alcohol in public places or on the beach, no open beer cans on the street (the notorious "open container law"), and above all, no obscenity, whatever the hell that's supposed to mean. This sowed the seeds for the ensuing problems.

During Bike Week there was a wave of arrests and for the first time an armored "cell truck" was used to remove everyone arrested. The police, seeking to play the matter down, claimed there had been just 34 arrests, most of them for violation of the liquor laws, i.e. drinking beer in public, plus a few hundred tickets for traffic violations. 17 motorcycles were stolen and there was widespread fistfighting in the bars.

To maintain law and order an additional 16 officers from the Federal Highway Patrol were drafted in. They were humorless, zero tolerance hard-liners.

1975

On the boardwalk, the third Rats Hole Custom Chopper Bike Show took place. This time there were two three-mile-long lines of exhibits and 267 entrants in 12 classes competing for 48 cups. Entry and participation were free and nine honorary judges sweated over the correct verdicts. A troop of "junior police explorers" kept order and around 35,000 people came instead of the expected 6,000 to 8,000. Big Daddy Rat was as happy as a clam.

By this time the rest of the motorcycle world had discovered this attractive event and had organized a trade show to take advantage of it. Harley-Davidson showed off its complete AMF production line: the FX 1200, FXE 1200, FLH 1200 and the two 1000 cc Sportsters, the XL and the XLH.

On Main Street, the new wave of state-of-the-art customizations strutted their stuff, featuring gas-tank paintings, Roman helmets and even trikes and extreme choppers, some with V engines. Besides Harley-Davidson motorcycles, there were plenty of Nortons, Triumphs and chopped Honda 750 Fours.

For the first time the students' spring break coincided with Bike Week, keeping people well out of the way, if they could. In *Custom Chopper* magazine a vitriolic article on the subject of "intolerable police terror" was published.

About 50 miles south of Daytona, the American Motorcycle Drag Racing Association was putting on their 'Sunshine Nationals' drag racing meet at Bithlo. This noisy, two-day spectacle on Highway 50 just south of the Kennedy Space Center involved four classes (including one for children from eight to 16), and the participation of well-known names such as Russ Collins (Honda triple dragster), Terry Vance, Marion Owens, Mike Bruso and Joe Smith.

One of the main attractions of Daytona Bike Week is the endless sun-kissed sandy beach. This, together with the fresh breeze from the cool Atlantic, is a perfect combination creating ideal riding conditions.

1976

Bicentennial Year – The 4th Annual Custom Chopper Bike Show now had 13 classes in which one could enter and also trophies for 4th through 8th places for which to compete. In that year admission was still free, and the main attraction was a Harley plastered everywhere with lights. This bike belonged to an extroverted African-American which caused a minor sensation: "crazy Yanks." AMF Harley–Davidson had decided for the first time to have their own show at the Hilton Hotel, including a special exhibition of Joe Smith's Double–HD Dragster motorcycle and the Bonneville Streamliner. The rest of the Harley motorcycles were swarming all over the parking lot.

At the end of the beach, wild, sand-drag races took place in accordance with the motto "run what you brung." The police joined in by recording the speed of the motorcycles on their radar equipment. That year, Outlaws MC won.

In 1978 Harley organized the first "World's Largest Motorcycle Parade" at Harley Heaven on the south bend of the speedway. A handbill caused a stir: ABATE of Florida, which had just been founded, called every biker for an inaugural, helmet protest run in April to the state capital Tallahassee.

1979

Daytona Bike Week becomes a madhouse. Bob "Bitchin" Lipkin autographed his book *Brotherhood of Outlaws* in The Pit, the biker shop stocking the hard-core stuff. Now there was also *FTW (Fuck the World) Magazine*, which had, however, to change its name to *Outlaw Biker* due to increasing legal difficulties on account of obscene content, On the Hilton parking lot AMF Harley put on its first "Motorcycle Happening" with demo rides, exhibitions, contests and the newest models, including the 80 cubic inch (1340 cc) engine in the Low Rider and Fat Bob models. The Harley Parade on the final Sunday was now

Something for everyone: market stalls, airbrush and tattoo artists.

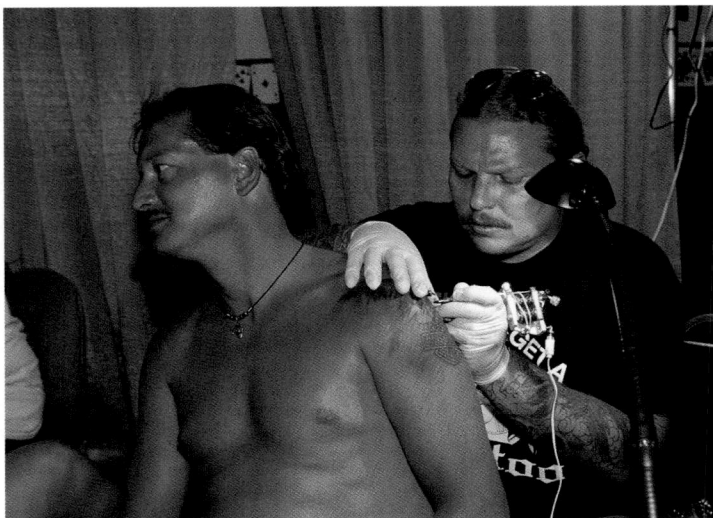

1977–1978

Even the last of the beach souvenir shops right at the eastern end of Main Street (the beach end) stocked biker stuff. But there were still no postcards of Bike Week. Various biker clubs began street battles and shootouts. Police Chief Ashe was concerned about the rising tide of violence and called for reinforcements for his "troops."

The 5th Rats Hole Custom Chopper Show was alive with comic designs, engravings and gold plating. 30 participants, 84 prizes – and still no entry fee. At the Harley-Davidson show at the Hilton in South Daytona, the company's 75th anniversary was being celebrated with an exhibition of racing history under the title "Harley-Davidson on the Track."

called "Show Off Your Iron," and cost 20 dollars inclusive of a chicken dinner and a Coke.

The 1980s

The Brotherhood was going to hell in a hand cart, with continual shootouts in the bars. The big clubs were more and more on a war path: being a One Percenter meant guns and knives were drawn.

The first consequence of this was a general ban on the wearing of club colors. The police deployed a heavily armed and armored truck known as Puff the Magic Wagon. For the bikers this was a declaration of civil war. The big organizations announced a "Biker Boycott" under the motto: "They don't want you, they only want your money,"

Main Street

It starts up at the Pier, but it's after the crossroads with the wide A1A that all hell breaks loose. No access for automobiles. Gun–toting deputy sheriffs wade through the crowds of pedestrians which press regardless through the cars and motorbikes. Whistling, shouting, laughter, the honking of car horns, rumbling engines, the stink of exhaust fumes, the scent of perfume, sultry heat. Harleys parked in endless rows stretching into the distance – a bizarre gallery of chrome and steel, stared at, marveled at, laughed at, filmed and photographed, but you'd better not touch! To see and be seen. It is showtime for all. Every manner of craziness, intimacy and the odd obscenity are on show to the rubberneckers. Amongst them in precise parallel formation is the two man, motorcycle police patrol, two stoical figures in immaculately ironed uniforms, their Colts ready in their holsters, the watchful eyes of the law concealed behind mirrored shades. The traffic is at a virtual standstill along the whole length of Main Street. The pedestrians press sweating and chattering through the throng on the sidewalk, pushing and shoving. Sunburnt,

naked flesh rubs against black leather, greasy chaps in designer jeans. A smoking burnout in front of Boothill Saloon, cat–calls and raucous shouting, the police officers are not getting through. People clustered around the entrances to the bars, all of them bursting at the seams. Heavyweight bouncers push the gatecrashers back. Sorry, 170 people is the legal limit for the bar. Two out, two in. And nobody under 21! Traveling salesmen selling wonder drugs, Indian jewelry, the League for Human Rights, "win this bike" lotteries and all kinds of nonsense.

Raucous shouting – a pillion passenger has bared her breasts, setting off a blitz of flashbulbs. A cop pushes his way through, and the lady is led away in handcuffs to public disgust and booing. Behind shop windows tattoo artists in rubber gloves, airbrushers in face masks and everywhere the Harley motif: "The Eagle Soars Alone." French fries, hot dogs, hamburgers, pickles, soft ice cream, beer – but don't drink it on the street – minibars and fast-food stores serving people as people pass by. Overflowing trash cans and dumpsters. Paradise on Earth – or hell.

The other side of Daytona: visitors on ragged 'riceburners' and police officers on Harleys, something which incidentally doesn't prevent them taking an illegal custom bike into custody.

and called on the bikers not to shop at the Daytona stores or put up in the exorbitantly priced hotels, but to stay outside the city. New campgrounds were set up some distance away, and a number of biker bars moved out from the center — the Iron Horse, for example, reopened way out on Highway 1.

On Main Street Nazi emblems could increasingly be seen, as a protest against the mobile police station near Main Street, now dubbed "your friendly, local Gestapo headquarters." German steel helmets, death's-heads, SS runes and swastikas were the height of fashion. The official police figure for arrests was 1,670, and vast numbers of tickets were being handed out.

New city laws further aggravated the already dangerous mood: driving on the beach at night was banned with immediate effect (the biker press was up in arms about this), and only those who had been resident for at least three years were permitted to sell their wares on Main Street. The Consumer Trade Show spread to the upper levels of the Daytona Plaza Hotel, and AMF Harley-Davidson — still based at the luxury Hilton Hotel — put on the trade show "More than a Machine" and the indoor show "Artistry in Iron" as competition for Karl Smith's chopper show. In *Road Rider* Roger Hull wrote a furious editorial about the shameless ripping-off of bikers under the title "Support a Cop," and prophesied the end of the Daytona tradition. "Police harassment" had become the scene's watchword.

Meanwhile Police Chief Charles Willits argued that there was a criminal element of around 1,000 bikers, while 28,000 motorcyclists received tickets and were fined. Mayor J. Kelly just played the whole thing down and refused to take off his rose-tinted spectacles. The famous grand old lady of Harley-Davidson, Dot Robinson, was given a ticket on her pink FLH because she did not have her lights on during the day. Private drag races on the beach were banned, and the traditional wild drags on a country road by the Cabbage Patch were also stopped by the police — they now take place on private property: the big field behind the bar, and are called sand drags. The motto was "shit happens."

The custom riders hid their works of art, illegal under the Florida Vehicle Code, in their hotel rooms and in garages and swore never to return — the Rats Hole Custom Chopper Show was meant to be a ride-in show, and it is precisely that which was no longer possible. In front of Pub 44 endless rows of police patrol cars from all over Florida

were parked. They cashed in on every biker who passed by: one biker showed off 46 tickets which he picked up over a distance of 200 yards. Finally the "never again Daytona" movement gained increasing momentum and a rival event in California was planned. But California is just too far away. The Daytona Bike Week was at the end of its tether.

The tragic low point, after which everything was finally to change, was reached when a biker who failed to stop at a police checkpoint was shot dead in broad daylight in the middle of the city. When it came to light at the court hearing that for Bike Week the police were specially trained to shoot to kill, and were under orders to do so, it spelt the downfall of the two biggest law enforcement hard-liners: both the police chief and the district attorney were forced to resign.

The new Police Chief Crow saw to it that Daytona Bike Week returned to what it had once been, and now is once again: a week of fun and entertainment in sunny Florida. Not quite as cheap as it once was, though, and the innocence has been lost once and for all. What's more, these days there are more than enough other options available in the areas all around Daytona.

A photo at the end of a Rat's Hole Show, with the victor and a host of well-known personalities: Wolfgang Schöller on the far left, who judged the presentation at the Essen Motor Show, with Big Daddy Rat on the right, and the victor in the middle holding the trophy, surrounded by a bevy of Rat Mates.

Welcome Bikers!

Once upon a time Daytona Bike Week was one big biker party, today it has largely become a pleasure circus. A typical fairground for the Florida Way of Life which these days attracts more tourists than bikers. Although the legendary Main Street remains the center of Bike Week, countless other activities have also mushroomed out from the city, over a radius of more than 100 miles.

The special biker bars in particular do a roaring trade, and the best-known of them offer a full and continuous program over the ten days. Located in the fenced-off party area behind the Iron Horse Saloon on the A1, the bikers swarm between vendors, fast food stalls, competitions, the wall of death ring and the open-air concert stage.

Just 20 miles south Al Bulling's biker refuge, the Last Resort Bar, also attracts bikers in their thousands, who park their Harleys in long lines on the A1 from Port

Orange. In the relatively small back yard, where the legendary Japanese hanging tree stands, there are daily rock concerts and barbecues and a pronounced family atmosphere prevails.

If you go a little further south inland along Highway 44, you can't miss Pub 44, where the crowds are packed in to the rafters. Here too you will find vendors, swap meets, parties and non-stop action every night, with contests and live concerts by top-class bands.

In the rural surroundings of Samsula the biker crowds meet up at Sopotnicks Cabbage Patch. Heavy as the police presence is, it is barely adequate to contain the tangled knots of people crowding the otherwise lonely crossroads. The giant campsite is packed full of tents and flags from all four corners of the Earth.

The Cabbage Patch has become well-known because of the wrestling matches between young ladies drenched in salad oil and for the demolition of Japanese

Forming up for the start of a training and warm-up ride prior to the 1997 Daytona 883 race at the large circular course of the International Speedway.

bikes hanging from two 125-foot cranes. In the direction of DeLand, the world's largest flea market and swap meet opens midweek at Volusia County Fairground, with three halls and a gigantic open air site.The Daytona Flea Market site, where the Spiders Gigantic Swapathon takes place, is not far-off in size.

At the New Smyrna Speedway Stadium opposite the ABATE Campground the *Easyriders* Rodeo is staged nightly, with motorcycle pulls, demolition derbies and other crazy fun events.

In every nook and cranny of the Daytona Beach Resort Area, you'll find endless special events, local shows, dealer parties, bike contests, live music, photo sessions, biker games, auctions, rallies, runs and non-stop entertainment.

Oh, and if that's not enough for anyone, at the end of October there's a somewhat smaller show: the beer party known as "Biketoberfest." The parallel to Old Germany is obvious, and in the last two

years Germany has repaid the compliment with the establishment of a Daytona Bike Week Europe Festival, the term Bike Week having gone international some years ago. As they say in Florida, "See you later, alligator!"

While the training runs for the Daytona 200, BOTT or 883 last more than one week, the old-timer races of the AHRMA are held on the Infield — a shorter, partial race track of the International Speedway. Genuine classics participate in these veteran races, such as this Side-valve Flat Track WR from the 1930s.

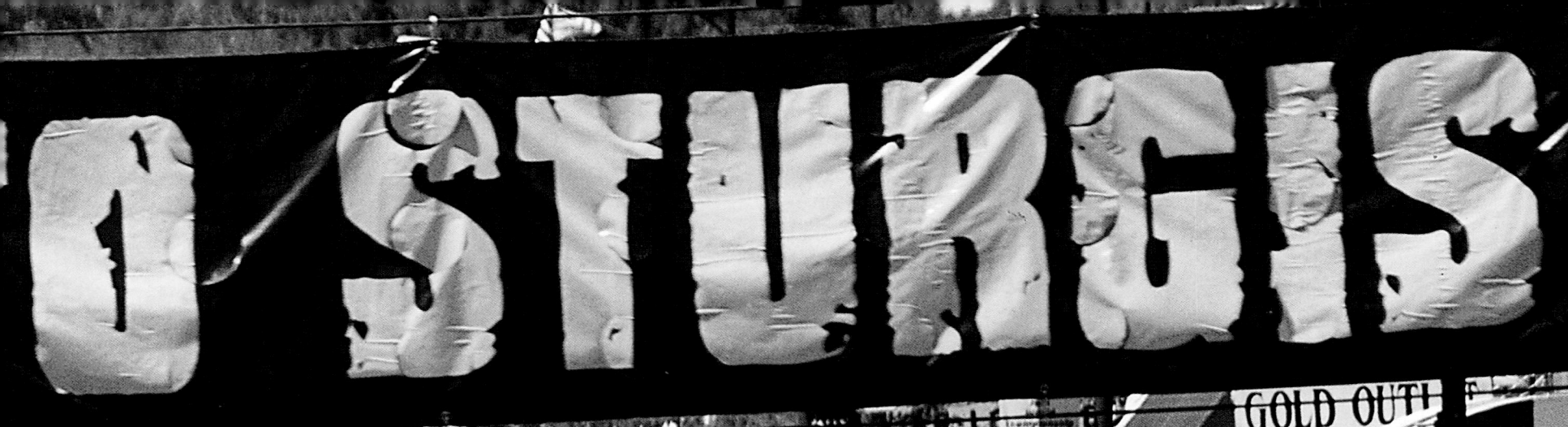

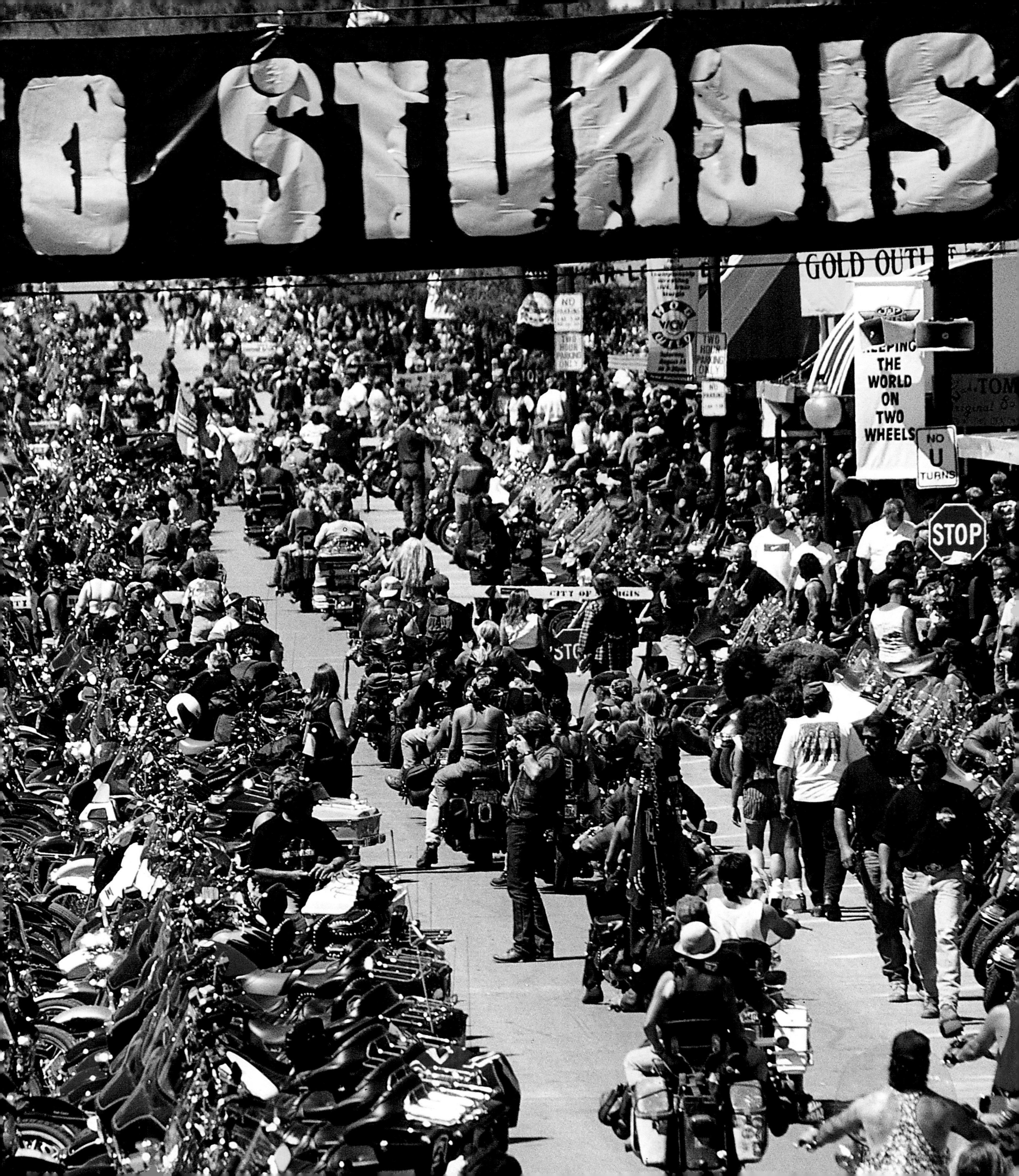
STURGIS
THE WORLD ON TWO WHEELS
NO U TURNS
STOP
TWO HOUR PARKING ONLY
NO PARKING

A Summer Storm in the Black Hills

Circus Maximus

Some snapshots from the 50th Jubilee in August 1990:

Since early morning an unbroken stream of vehicles came thundering in from all directions, but above all along Interstate 90, where an endless line of bikes, pickups, motorhomes, club buses and cars descended on the bike capital of the U.S. – but above all bike, mostly Harleys. The riders with hair and beards blowing freely in the wind because there's no compulsory helmet law in South Dakota: "Long live Governor George Mickelson!," the visitors' placards proclaim. A high percentage of the bikes are illegal: dragpipes, apehangers, no lights, nothing, but who cares; who is going to check out, regulate or try to give the thousands of visitors a hard time? By Friday 100,000 have already descended on the city, the newspapers report. 2,500 Hells Angels are said to be among them plus several thousand Bandidos. Countless clubs are there and they haven't even begun to count the regular visitors. The visitor pays dearly: hotel beds are 150 dollars a night, while a site in the campground costs 15 dollars: per person, per night, of course. Even a cup of Coke (90 percent filled with crushed ice) costs a buck. Given the heat and the thirst it generates, everyone must be making a killing. Each August every conceivable part of biker culture come together in the most unique way in Sturgis, South Dakota.

During Sturgis Bike Week, the entire Black Hills are filled with Harleys. Whether these are sporting activities such as the hillclimb or national monuments like Mount Rushmore, the attractions are almost limitless.

The "Sturgis Bike Week," or as it is correctly known, the "Black Hills Motor Classics" (since 1994 also called "Sturgis Rally & Races") came into being in the year 1938 as the result of the ideas and activities of the go–getting local Indian (later Yamaha) dealer Clarence J.C. "Pappy" Hoel, together with his circle of friends known as the Jack Pine Gypsies. At one of the first prewar meets the wild events put on at the newly laid race track (a half–mile dirttrack oval) were the top attraction: stunt shows, jumps from ramps or through a flaming wooden wall, head–on collisions with automobiles, parades and field meetings, to name but a few. Pappy Hoel himself was a keen motorbike stunt rider but the most successful performer was Johnny Spiegelhoff, the "Speed Demon from Milwaukee." The highpoint in those days was the AMA sanctioned dirt track races, wild and dusty, pursuit events in the new stadium.

However, unlike Daytona or Laconia, racing events have played only a small role in the development of the Sturgis Bike Week. Right up to the end of the 1970s, the small biker meeting in the romantic Black Hills of South Dakota was a secret shared among friends. For nearly three decades the rally remained a low–key event for insiders, until it finally exploded into life during the 1980s. The immediate cause of this was probably an enthusiastic article in the biker press and also a TV report selling Sturgis as a down–to–earth unspoiled Harley biker outlaw idyll, so attracting a public which had long since become

tired of the continual hassles at Daytona and Laconia. Moreover, Harleys were in, big overland tours were in, giant parties were in and unspoiled nature and life in the great outdoors were in. Sturgis, located in the heart of "Indian country," offered all of these in one hit.

Harley-Davidson itself was relatively slow to recognize the enormous marketing potential of such a mass event and also had to get over its ingrained aversion to ordinary biker life. The company quickly moved into Rapid City, about 30 miles away, where in the sober modern atmosphere of the Mount Rushmore Civic Center you could enjoy a certain exclusivity away from the madding crowds of Sturgis. However, today Harley-Davidson activities in Rapid City have become an integral part of the Bike Week and a never ending stream of motorbikes roars back and forth along Interstate 90 between Rapid City and Sturgis. On grounds of space alone, the magnitude of event Harley had set its sights on could not be made reality anywhere else. Harley could cope with up to 200,00 to 300,000 visitors.

Going back to the early days, Harley was rather under–represented, most likely because Pappy Hoel was more of a devotee of Indian bikes. But whatever people were riding, it was usually a long journey before you reached the midsummer heat of Sturgis. In 1947 400 people took part in the AMA Gypsy Tour after a three year break for the war. In 1965 around 1,000 bikers camped out in the well-groomed City Park which was later closed in 1982 due to overcrowding,

Party 'Till You Drop

What's going on all around the softly swaying prairie grass hills and sparse pine forests is equally overwhelming. Mainstreet (the center of the motorcycling world) is barely half a mile long, and is packed with 8,000 motorbikes parked five deep plus five times that number of rubberneckers and gawpers.

Megaparties also go on on campgrounds up to a square mile in size, often creating a nostalgic Woodstock feeling, with hundreds of thousands of people lying under the burning mountain sun listening to rock music booming from five-story-high towers of speakers: Tanya Tucker, Steppenwolf, the Allman Brothers – nothing but the best.

Day and night the dominating, usually unmuffled, roar of the big twins is inescapable: the noise of Harleys of all possible and some impossible varieties. For ten days Sturgis is a stage for everyone. Nothing is too crazy, sexy or disgusting not to be wondered at, photographed or videoed. Bozos and boobs, tough guys and vagabonds, Jesus people and gun-toting sheriffs, grandmas and grandpas, small children, even a boa constrictor – chrome and glitter, spangles and bangles overwhelm the senses.

At one time problems with the "Black Hills Motor Classic" almost led to its discontinuation. That was in 1982 when the local population, outraged at the "obscene" behavior and vandalism in the manicured City Park, and fearing for the survival of their western idyll, along with Highway Patrol Director Jerry Baum, called the bikers a "criminal element" who had been invited but then couldn't be got rid of. They had a point: the eight overflowing public portable toilets were burned to the ground and the firefighters were pelted with stones when they attempted to put out the gasoline which had been set blazing for general amusement on Highway 34, which had been converted into a dragstrip. There were also plenty of indecent things to see in the Park, which was strictly closed to visitors. But in the end, as might have been expected, the dollar triumphed as always, and the event survived despite the ringing condemnations of various local church dignitaries.

unhygienic conditions, vandalism and public obscenity. In 1987, 80,000 motorcyclists visited the event and totally swamped the two hopelessly overcrowded motels and the handful of campsites, and on the 50th Jubilee in 1990 came the hitherto greatest invasion, when an estimated 400,000 bikers overran the sleepy midwest town. When such lucrative invasions take place year after year, a place begins to change its face and the inhabitants also change their habits and attitudes, as their minds become totally open.

Today Sturgis Bike Week is probably the biggest event of its type in the world, and the town is pretty proud of its honorary title of "Bike City U.S.A." So the worldwide publicity for the biker meeting has proved to be a major boost for tourism generally in the Black Hills. Thus all visitors to Sturgis Bike Week are made heartily welcome by bigwigs from the Governor of South Dakota down to the Mayor of Sturgis. The massive law enforcement presence now has everything under control, and Sturgis has become a peaceful place despite its megalomania – perhaps that too is a sign of the times. "Have fun and be happy" is the motto these days. Everyone hopes it stays that way.

Supposedly, times are changing. When bikers want to ridicule the hated holier-than-thou prudery, they love to talk about the good old days when the motorbikes were still clean and sex was dirty. Was it ever really like that? In Sturgis they're of the opinion that times may change but bikers never do. Whatever people mean by "biker."

Back in the times before World War II, when J.C. "Pappy" Hoel and the Jackpine Gypsy Motorcycle Club "founded" the rally which is so well-known today, with races, excursions and charity bazaars, nobody could have imagined what it would one day grow into.

Originally, "it" did not take place in Sturgis at all, which for a long time remained the domain of the "decent" motorcyclists, those neatly dressed, clean-cut mannequins known as "AMA types," but rather 20 miles away in the dusty small town of Deadwood. The "outlaws" – bikers and MCs – hung out at that location, boozing, making a lot of noise and rampaging around in the venerable saloons, until the municipal authorities put a stop to the earth-shattering din with the imposition of 100 dollar fines.

That was when they started to "visit" each other, and by 1976 Sturgis had become the capital city of the movement: "Bike City U.S.A." had been born, and City Park was the center of the universe. In those days around 10,000 bikers gathered there and all hell broke loose. A "biker hell" which for others was heaven, which transformed Sturgis from the ground up.

Its inhabitants, just like thousands of regular tourists who visited the holiday paradise of the Black Hills, found out that there was another, hitherto unknown side to the Great American Society, one on two wheels, quarrelsome, loud, raw and wild, full of leather-clad ruffians and half-naked girls, jammed full of sex, fun and obscene language, chains and rivets, knives, nasty boots and crazy stares. A group of outsiders numbering, as the tourists had now seen and photographed for themselves, hundreds of thousands. These people wanted to be and had to be respected.

However, what had for decades in Daytona been a permanent cause of trouble – the tense relationship with the police – had never previously been a serious problem in Sturgis. The crowds were admittedly loud, but they were peaceable, and the law enforcement bodies kept the situation politely but firmly under control.

The people there party like there's no tomorrow. No doubt about it: for a lot of nice respectable U.S. vacationers, the Sturgis Bike Week is a culture shock. America's Great Society has another side to it which is still largely unknown. A noisy, smelly side on two wide tires, with wild and unruly habits and thronging with the type of guy it's best not to look in the eye. What a thrill to rub shoulders with the bare tattooed muscles of the sweat-soaked outlaws.

True to its name, in the Gunner's Lounge at the top end of Main Street one Friday night, members of two enemy motorcycle chapters ran into one another. The first one pulled a knife and stabbed the second, who pulled his shooter out of his boot and fired (seven times, it is believed: three bullets were later found lodged in the ceiling) and both of them toppled through the splintering bar door between the massed onlookers, one of them already dead, the other splattered with blood. "Oh my!" screeched the tourists as they pressed the buttons of their disposable pocket cameras with trembling fingers: the Wild West lives and with no extra charge to pay to see it.

Police Chief Jim Bush, on the other hand, is not so delighted by such events. He is sick and tired of the eternal gang feuding, and says something has to change in the future. But the shootout will no doubt enter seamlessly into the bloody history of the Black Hills. In any case, none of the spectators were injured. There are plenty of other shows, too: stunt teams, parades, rodeos, runs and swapmeets, and also an auction with rather sleepy bidders.

Sporting Harleys: over the hill with gusto.

There is nothing sleepy on the other hand about the countless races which are eagerly contested day in day out. At the deafening All Harley Drags a women's team is competing for the first time: the showdown with the Kings is known as "Queen of the Hill." The Queens win. It was thought that they would.

Cascades of dust and fountains of dirt shower the crowd lining the slopes where the hillclimbers (aged five years and up) roar up the hillside. Anyone who does not die of thirst from the heat or suffocation from the dust during the five hellish hours of watching can then finally admire the bizarre construction of the Harley hillclimbers, provided they are still up to it.

A total of 124 major events take place in the course of ten wild days. The nights are hot and virtually sleepless since the deep roaring and the widespread sound of the backfiring of over-reved Harley engines rouse even the weariest sleepers from their tents. The noise is emphatically reminding everyone that there is no time for sleeping during Sturgis Bike Week.

Whoever wishes to avoid the deafening tumult of Sturgis can take a relaxing trip to the nearby Badlands National Park (left). Otherwise reserved as a privilege for a few selected large American cities, the "World Championship Wrestling" organizers have also discovered the biker's paradise in Sturgis. Because numerous wrestlers are themselves dedicated Harley freaks, attendance at the huge open–air event of the WCW is correspondingly large.

Sturgis Bike Week Facts and Figures

In 1990, 243 permits for vendor stands were issued at 50 dollars each, plus 43 tattoo permits at 75 dollars each. The city earned 78,000 dollars at the Phototower in Main Street. The police handed out 802 tickets and 1,631 warnings. 163 people were arrested for drunkenness and 44 for possession of drugs. Nine people died in road accidents and one of carbon monoxide poisoning (in a tent). One person was shot dead by police when he ran amok. One person was shot dead and three received serious stab wounds in various biker gang disputes. Gas rose during the week from 1.16 dollars per gallon to 1.28 per gallon. In 1994 the following survey findings were published: a total of 652 vendors were registered. Out of 1,000 people, 71 percent were male and 29 percent female. The best represented age group was 31–50 years old and 57 percent were married. Over 80 percent spent at least seven nights in Sturgis. 27 percent were there for the first time. 62 percent traveled with their partner, 78 percent on a Harley–Davidson. The average amount spent per person was 781 dollars. 76 percent said that they would prefer one of the proprietary articles being promoted in Sturgis. Smokers favored Marlboro and the most popular beers were Budweiser and Miller. 84 percent were against compulsory wearing of helmets. The visitors came from 50 U.S. States and from 17 foreign countries. The total number of visitors was estimated at 350,000.

Rolling Thunder

Rodeos

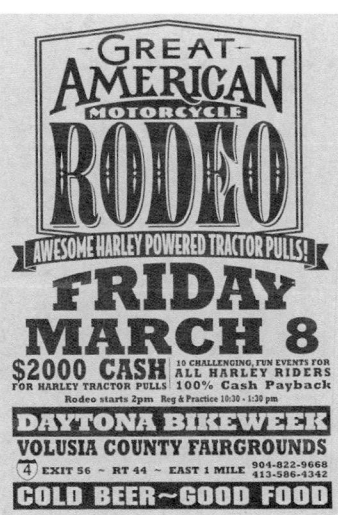

The producers of *Easyriders* magazine (Paisano Publications, Agoura Hills, California) have never been short of good ideas when it comes to effective marketing ideas aimed at the biker-world. One of their best and most attractive ideas has been the motorcycle Rodeo, a kind of traveling circus crisscrossing the country featuring a cleverly designed and marketed mixture of traditional biker games, sporting competition and the usual party scene.

The heavily publicized wave of events broke over the American biker world at the end of the 1980s and a governing body called ARROW was founded to run the thing. ARROW stands for Associated Rodeo Riders on Wheels. The name is protected by copyright and the organization has its headquarters in Agoura Hills, California, the President naturally enough being the magazine's publisher Joe Teresi.

As is right and proper for a respectable, money-making organization, ARROW has a board of directors, a president and a rules committee for each of the five regions: Northeast (headquarters in Pennsylvania), Southeast (headquarters in Florida), North Central (headquarters in Ohio), Central (headquarters in Iowa) and West Coast (headquarters in California). Rules and regulations were set up and the rodeos were divided into three categories: those with a 10,000-dollar limit to prize money and a participation fee of 50 dollars, those with a 5,000-dollar limit and a participation fee of 30 dollars, and those with a 2,500-dollar limit and a participation fee of 20 dollars. For an annual fee of 30 dollars you can become a full member or an associate member for 20 dollars per year.

The rodeos are then organized into annual *Easyriders* Rodeo Tours, with the Grand National Finals as the culmination of the tour. The events include games: slow race, keg derby, weenie bite, barrel race, potato haystack, tire ride and to top them all their own invention, the sled drag races. There are strict rules for each of these, with a starter, finishing-line judge and a sports committee. The rodeos have now been officially sanctioned as competitions by the AMA. Only American motorcycles may enter, i.e. predominantly Harleys or Indians. Prize money is distributed according to the number of entrants, which is normally pretty high since nearly every rodeo receives extensive publicity in *Easyriders* magazine, the biggest selling biker publication in the world.

The events offer the opportunity for competitors to become well-known very rapidly and there is probably no other event which offers the same kind of publicity. At the (normally) three-day-long rodeos you of course also get everything else that you would expect at a proper biker party: a bike show with prizes and trophies, live music with more or less well-known biker bands, bikini and other contests, tattoo artists and all manner of vendors, camping areas and enough fastfood stalls to provide the necessary nourishment and the vital liquid sustenance. The rodeos take place on large public fairgrounds and are regularly promoted in the many publications belonging to the Paisano empire, normally accompanied by Dave Mann's marvelous illustrations.

However, since one cannot expect to maintain exclusive rights on the word "rodeo" in the homeland of the copyright action, the *Easyriders* organization's rodeos did not go without competition for long. For several years now there has been a rival organization called 'The Great American Motorcycle Rodeo,' which holds events at the Buffalo Chip Campground in Sturgis, the Volusia Speedway Stadium at Daytona Bike Week as well as at other big biker events, offering a similar program of competitions and activities. Many clubs organizations and firms now sponsor the rodeos, which have long since become a fixture in the American biker world.

Found a potato! Hurry up, girl!

Full throttle in front of the sleds: Harley trikes pulling. Flat out in the mud: you need strong nerves to be pulled in a tire (opposite).

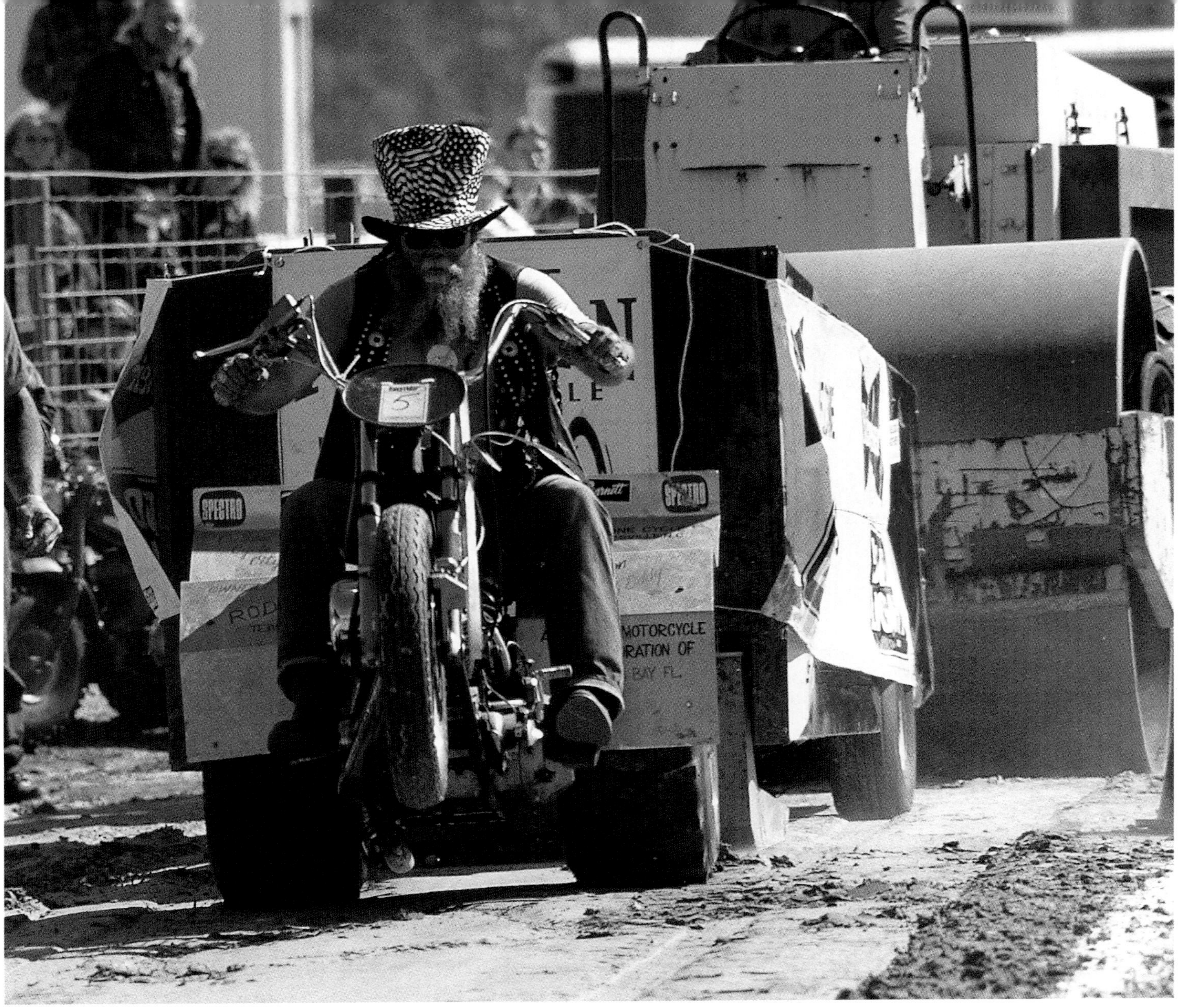
SPECTRO
SPECTRO
5

GREAT
AMERICAN
RODEO
BUD LIGHT
WELCOME
BIKERS

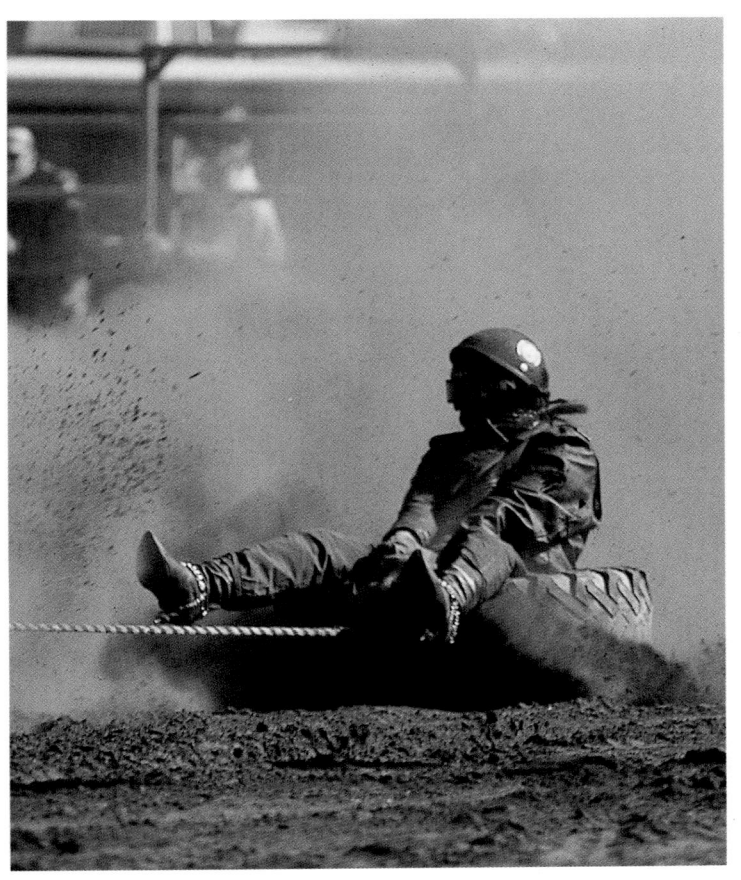

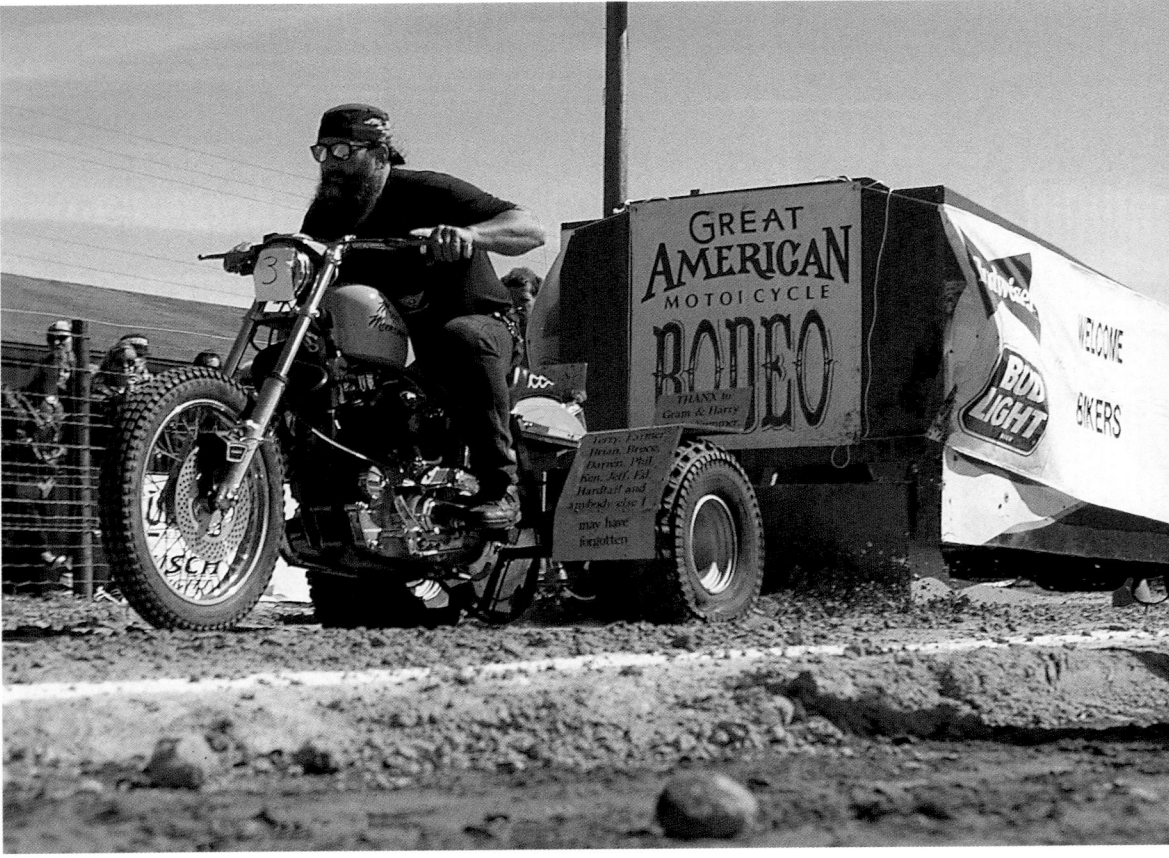

Big–bike motocross: it's no simple task to
fight through the narrow slalom course
slipping and swerving on your
heavy–duty machine.

Racing, Rumbles and Riotous Living

The Laconia Rally and Races

Every year at the start of June in Laconia, New Hampshire, all the elements of Harley culture and the biker lifestyle come together in a unique way.

When people talk about biker weeks, they are usually referring to Daytona or Sturgis, but at one time Laconia was what it was all about. Laconia is a typically pretty, New England small town with a population of around 16,000, situated on Lake Winnisquam in the picturesque New Hampshire county of Belknap.

Since 1923 the legendary happening known as Laconia Rally and Race Week or Laconia Bike Week for short, has taken place there during the first half of June. There have been motorbike races there since 1917, at first fairly primitive events, until in 1938 the first Dirttrack Grand National of the new amateur Class C was put on with AMA sanctioning, attracting a crowd of a few thousand. Later on, this dusty around course was given something of a face lift, before a new, paved speedway oval was built in 1965.

Today Laconia is home of the huge New Hampshire International Speedway Stadium, built in 1990, which carries on the old tradition. The races as they have always been, are called the Loudon or now the Loudon Classic. The stadium is located on Route 106 near to the small town of Loudon.

Not far away, the Gunstock Hillclimb takes place at the same time on Mount Belknap. Gunstock is on Route 11 in Gilford, New Hampshire, and the hillclimb is organized by the local Ridgerunners MC. Additionally, there are drag races and also the AMA sanctioned flat track races, motocross, the obligatory custom bike show and, of course, the Weirs Beach rumble which are all also part of Laconia Bike Week.

This takes us to the true heart of the event. Weirs Beach is a somewhat run-down amusement mile along the shore of Lake Winnipesaukee lined with countless arcades, travel shops and fast-food outlets. During Laconia Bike Week, Weirs Beach belongs to the bikers. They park there, meet with each other there, celebrate and party there, and regularly start fights with one another and with the many onlookers. There is a certain tradition to all this and these notorious acts of violence have come to be dubbed "the Laconia riots."

Normally Weirs Beach is a place of laughter and merriment but when violence breaks out, it breaks out with a vengeance. Although the ensuing alcohol-induced brawling is only instigated by an increasingly small minority of troublemakers, its effect is enormous and particularly contagious.

Although the existence of this mischievous element, described by the municipal authorities as "outlaws," is generally hushed up by the media, as early as 1947 there were public exhortations to "conduct yourselves like gentlemen." When the boozed-up brawling became too much for the local population in 1963, the authorities summarily canceled next year's event.

However, when the city realized how great the resulting loss of income would be, the New Hampshire Rally was reinstated. And while *The Enthusiast* waxed lyrical about the beautiful scenery in the Belknap Mountains and found everything wonderful, promising exciting races and praising the best dressed clubs, in 1965 placards and banners proclaiming "Come and see Weirs Beach burn!" were to be seen all around.

The worst rioting yet ensued, the low point probably being when a fully occupied family sedan went up in flames – its occupants just managing to escape with their lives. The fire quickly spread and also

Laconia today: the races, the rumble on Weir's beach and the popular biker atmosphere have survived.

destroyed various stalls. The mayor at that time, who had perhaps seen too many Hollywood rocker films, publicly blamed the Hells Angels for this "catastrophe," and made the immortal pronouncement that the passengers had escaped through a "wall of fire." Thus the "Burn Weirs Beach" riots became an oft-cited legend, inevitably leading to an atmosphere of tension on Weirs Beach in the years to follow, which mounted steadily and exploded violently from time to time. Massed police forces were always on hand and ready to intervene energetically. In the 1970s things again became pretty wild, and in the 1980s the whiff of tear gas continually permeated the strip.

At the beginning of the 1990s the combined law enforcement bodies took their own kind of revenge – they implemented specially restrictive traffic regulations in order to ensure total chaos on all roads leading to Weirs Beach, particularly Highway 3, the Weirs Boulevard, on which nothing moved for hours on end. As a special traffic ordinance banned the switching off of engines while on the street, a misdemeanor punishable by hefty on-the-spot fines, there was no end of overheated and blown motorbike engines. To top it off, anyone found on the street with a beer can was thrown straight into jail. The following year the traffic lights were set so as to cause jams of up to 12 miles (with motors running of course) – in short organized chaos ensured virtually continual hassle for visitors.

Nowadays, however, the municipal authorities and law enforcement bodies have worked out how to keep 150,000 to 200,000 bikers under control: the organizers offer visitors such a wide-ranging and well-organized program of activities that the continual riots along the Weirs Beach promenade have ceased to be an attraction. Every day, alongside the numerous races and training runs, there are open house parties, exhibitions, bike shows, swap meets, tours and runs, such as the Freedom Ride in honor of POWs/MIAs from the Vietnam War (Prisoner of War/Missing In Action Rolling Thunder Rally) to the famous memorial in Washington D.C. organized since 1993 by the Harley-Davidson Riders MC or the traditional AMA Gypsy Tour organized by the Lakeside Sharks MC.

On top of this there are naturally any number of competitions, live music and open air concerts. Then on the final Sunday the great, motorbike parade proceeds from the rally headquarters on Weirs Boulevard to the New Hampshire International Speedway Stadium 20 miles away, where the finals of the Loudon Camel Classic take place, a combination of various classes and races. Finally there is a mighty firework display to conclude proceedings. Incidentally, for anyone who may be wondering about things having looked at pictures of Laconia, despite all the ridiculous regulations designed to make life difficult for bikers, New Hampshire is one of the few states where the wearing of helmets is not compulsory. Which does not of course preclude their sensible and responsible use.

It is calm now in Laconia – even the obligatory traffic chaos is under control.

493

Harley-Rendez-Vous

An Old–Style Festival

Another of the big legendary biker parties in the best sense of the word is the "Harley Rendezvous," which has been in existence since 1978. It takes place in June of each year on the 177 acre estate of the Indian Lookout Country Club and has always been organized by and for real bikers – the commercialization universal elsewhere takes more of a back seat here.

Of course the many thousand bikers, who traditionally arrive almost exclusively on Harleys will be provided with everything some biker's heart could desire: sex and beer and rock 'n roll. The romantic country surroundings of the meeting in Mariaville, about 20 miles west of New York State capital Albany, has always been a refuge for the authentic American biker community and remains so to this day. For the New England states, still thickly populated with Harley and Indian riders, and the very active northeastern U.S. biker scene in general, the Harley Rendezvous represents the annual high point.

A highly trained team runs and organizes the event. After all, the Indian Lookout Country Club was set up by and for bikers alone. The scene, nearly always taking place in extreme summer heat, is one of bustling activity: vendors, tattoo artists, competitions, shows, live music, a topless bar and also an antique bike show – the Indian Country Club has its own, small, motorbike museum – are all a part of it, along with biker games. The California Hell Riders' Daredevil Motordrome Show and the Great American Motorcycle Rodeo have also been successfully integrated into the proceedings in recent years.

It is a noisy weekend full of fun and games then, of real Harley hedonism, as the two-wheeled party freaks call it with self-deprecating winks. In the giant venues you can get plenty to eat and drink or maybe listen to the marvelous bulletins from Radio Free Rendezvous WFSX on the 90.74 FM bandwidth in Waterin' Hole Saloon or Knocker's Cafe. Of course there are also masses of souvenirs: from

pins and stickers, T–shirts, belt buckles, videos and posters to beer mugs and Christmas ornaments. There is enough memorabilia for sale to get you through the long period until the Rendezvous comes around again the next year and you can buy all the same stuff yet again, but with a different year printed on it. An old habit making for reliable and lucrative business.

For some time the Harley Rendezvous, which christened itself many years ago in all innocence and loyalty to the company, has been coming under increasingly strong, legal attack from the Harley-Davidson company, which has since taken out copyright on the name Harley. Accordingly, in order to avoid any misunderstanding, the organizers emphasize the fact that the party has nothing officially to do with the Milwaukee company.

Big Parties

Naturally everyone is welcome. But though there are other makes of motorcycle in America – quite a few, in fact – one doesn't see many non–American makes at the typical biker party. In part, this is because fans of other makes usually organize their own meets. But it's also because American biker events always have a strongly patriotic character – America is God's Own Country, natural Harley territory. Innumerable biker parties, runs and rallies take place annually in the U.S., among them are some that have now achieved mammoth proportions. Here are a few examples.

The Laughlin River Run has taken place since 1983, at the end of April, in the small desert town of Laughlin, Nevada, situated on the lower Colorado river on the borders of California, Arizona and Nevada. Upwards of 40,000 visitors now take part in this three day, super event, which, in the searing heat of the desert and mountain regions of the eastern Mojave, is part deluxe biker show, part Western. For those who might feel bored, there are several well–organized excursions, for example to Hoover Dam,

Welcome Bikers!

to London Bridge in Lake Havasu City, to one of the closer of several small Western towns or to the ghost-town of Oatman on Route 66. There are also innumerable shows and other entertainments to provide a diversion. Traveling salesmen, swap meets and special events like the Miss River contest, poker-runs, a classic bike show and raffles with brand-new Harleys as prizes are part of a broad spectrum of events offered. The organizer of the Laughlin River Run is the Southern California Harley-Davidson Dealers Association, supported by Dodge-Ram Pickups and Coors Light Beer. The whole spectacle is presented by DalCon Promotions. The registration fee of 35 dollars covers entry to all live concerts, shows and entertainment ... and even includes two soft drinks!

Another classic event, whose origins go back to the year 1946, is the annual Myrtle Beach Spring Rally, which celebrated its 50th anniversary in 1996 with an attendance of around 75,000 bikers. Traditionally it is the flat-track races that are the biggest attraction here.

One week before Daytona Bike Week, ABATE of Georgia organizes the famed Run to the Sun as a season opener in the sun-kissed South, a rally which has often been subject to heavy surveillance by the Florida law enforcement authorities. Another biker party, this one a little quieter than Daytona Bike Week, is the Daytona Biketoberfest. Although it has only existed for a few years, the number of visitors is now approaching 100,000.

Now a new alternative to the Daytona festivities has arrived: the Arizona Bike Week, which first took place from February 7th to the 15th in Avondale, Arizona, attracting approximately 86,000 bikers. The nine day event takes in the areas around Phoenix, Scottsdale, Avondale, Glendale and Tucson, and has its origins in the Avondale Cycle Fest.

Since 1994 the Ride For Life benefit run supported by Lorenzo Llamas has taken place a few weeks later. The organizer is Oliver Shokouh's well-known Harley dealership in Glendale, California, already legendary in this sort of benefit rally. All proceeds go to the World Children's Transplant Fund (WCTF). Participation in the runs from Glendale to

Calamigos Ranch costs 35 dollars, while the souvenir T-shirt can be had for ten dollars. This is, incidentally, a true biker rally, so car drivers are not welcome.

The Orange County March of Dimes' event Ride America, which takes place in Newport Beach, California, is also for a good cause, money raised going to the March of Dimes' Birth Defects Foundation, a now well-known charity event also known as Bikers for Babies, with a wealth of prizes and pledges of generous donations.

And so it goes: some big, some small, some wild, some not so wild. The biker scene, which has its own ideals and values, has long been an independent way of life, with parties, runs, shows and swap meets being its highpoints. There is no state, county or town in the U.S. where there are no biker (or Harley) events. It's not very different in the bordering countries, Canada and Mexico. The spectrum is very broad: from charity events and religious missions, to political demonstrations, such as the Ride on the Convention run, with Senator Ben "Nighthorse" Campbell, to the Republican Convention in San Diego, California on August 11, 1996, an event which took place under the motto "Fight for Your Rights."

Unfortunately, not all biker events can be listed here. The best thing is to go along and see for yourself. You'll make a lot of new friends.

On the way to the next party: thousands of Harley riders are on the road each weekend, sometimes for days at a time and naturally not just in the U.S.

495

A Hot Party in the Deep South for Harley Riders

The Memorial Day Blowout in Gulfport, Mississipi

Massive and always cloaked in searing heat: the crowded camping area of Gulfport Dragway during the blowout. It is a big biker meeting which takes place annually.

When it first took place in 1982, it was simply called the "Independence Day Blowout," and was a small-scale, local biker party held in an old hangar on Biloxi Beach. A total of 200 brothers and sisters met up on that occasion, and to the organizing club, ASGARD MC, which had been founded just two years earlier, that seemed like a whole lot of people.

The main attraction was the bike show, which prompted most of those who were present to say that they had never seen so much sparkle and style in the Deep South. A total of 25 bikes took part, half of them Harleys, including a few custom bikes and they inspired the local paper, the *Sun Herald*, to run a small but favorable report on this unusual event.

Since then this down-to-earth biker party has changed fundamentally, at least on the outside. Over 20,000 genuine bikers and Harley riders flock from all over America, clubs and patchholders included, to the shimmering sun of the Gulf Coast to enjoy the proverbial Southern hospitality. At the Blowout there are no dumb or irritating onlookers, gawkers or outsiders: the Blowout is a kind of tribal meeting of the great American biker family, and you are (so far) among your own kind. Something like the way it was in Daytona 20 years ago or Sturgis ten years ago.

However, the unique experience of the four-day Blowout is based not only on the specially friendly and laid-back atmosphere, but also on the fact that everything, which in Daytona would be miles apart, can here be found grouped together on one 200 acre site: the Gulfport Dragway. Here there are meadows, shady pine trees, internal roads and any amount of parking lots and camping areas, the quarter-mile drag strip and all necessary facilities – food and drink available 24 hours a day, and 80 'Port-O-Lets' portable toilets for good measure.

Hundreds of vendors: suppliers, salesmen and dealers from all parts of the U.S. have set up their stands here; what's more there are swap meets, flea markets and everything else that makes a biker's heart beat a little faster. Four long days and nights of action and shows – small private ones as well as big ones – dragster races to watch or join in, the famous bike show, tattoo competitions and any number of biker events such as the weenie bite, slow race, kickstart contest, barrel rolling and the patriotically-flavored "riceburner hammering."

Also attending the Blowout are the Christian Motorcycle Association, which organizes its own events such as morning service, children's circus and party tent and also the noisy live shows of numerous rock and roll bands and the inevitable tit show, here disgracefully toned down to a wet T-shirt contest. The security responsible for the maintenance of order is firmly restricted to soft drinks only and the Gatorade bottles lie in their hundreds in the ice-filled cooler boxes. But the security forces hardly have anything to do despite the 20,000 plus bikers roaring around the place.

No great fuss is made about expired inspection stickers – you just check if your lights are working and if not, then don't ride at night, it's as simple as that. And brakes – well, you should have brakes just in case, but in an emergency you can brake with the engine or just ride around an obstacle; after all, you're not a complete damn fool, unlike a car driver, for example.

Nevertheless, the organizers, the local motorbike club ASGARD MC, has been subject to legal proceedings as a result of this kind of nonsense and driveways and pedestrian ways now have to be segregated. What a dream – as if it were possible to do anything of the sort with the crowds at this size festival.

But in order to please everyone, a few boards and rails have been put up and a couple of tiny signs saying "no motorcycles, pedestrians only," at least in the places where the crowds are at their heaviest. Even when spirits get pretty high, people don't go too crazy here, though a few things contribute to the general amusement, a few naked

breasts maybe and other obscenities. The Harleys though are the same as ever, the way Harleys should be: loud, stripped-down and chopped, often unsightly and brutal and not exactly in a roadworthy condition, but what the hell, everything's under control, even if you've just consumed 25 Budweiser.

Although the extensive Gulfport Dragway site is private land, public traffic regulations do apply, officially at least. Of course nobody (or almost nobody) has got a helmet on and a well-worn T-shirt is the nearest thing to protective clothing that anybody is wearing, but none of the many, heavily-armed sheriffs or cops patrolling the place would dream of bothering about any of this.

Outside on the highways it's a different matter, of course. There, because there is this law and are these fines for failing to observe it, you wear a totally ridiculous, flat plastic thing on your head, naturally without Department of Transport approval. This means that when you buy it you have to sign your name three times, once to declare that you know it's illegal, a second time to acknowledge that you may not wear it on public roads and a third time to accept liability should you smash your skull in. So things remain the same as they always were.

Naturally, as the name suggests, a great deal of drinking goes on at the Blowout. The blowout is a tradition unique to the southern states, where three quarters of the rural counties are still dry. The drinking is largely confined, however, to the tribal drink of all southern brothers, beer or to be more exact Budweiser, though in an emergency other brands will do, just so long as they are ice-cold.

The blame for all this boozing however lies more in the murderously sultry heat, which even at this time of year (the end of May) has reached its maximum of 95 to 110 degrees farenheit. This heat stays day and night, with a relative humidity of nearly 100 percent. They say your body needs five gallons of fluid a day in this kind of weather. The season of the big thunderstorms which hit the Gulf Coast every spring is a long way off, even if last year's Blowout was almost literally blown away by an early season hurricane which ripped through tents and stands on Sunday evening.

This definitely did not spoil the fun, though, as the superparty was more or less over anyway. On Monday morning the brothers collected up their women, kids and possessions, stowed everything away on their bikes and, still feeling a little dazed, left the devastated camp either alone or in groups, engines roaring. The great powwow of the tribes had come to an end.

That's the Blowout then. Although the heat is unbearable, sleep is unthinkable, the food is terrible and the dust, dirt and mud indescribable, the Blowout is a party after a true biker's heart. Once in a while a you have to recharge your batteries and have a general overhaul, so that you can put up with all the usual stuff back home.

Southerners flying the Confederate flag – the sheriff watches the scene.

Traditional European Meetings

The Super-Rallies

Long before the Harley Owners Group (H.O.G.) established its national and international events, there were large-scale annual meetings in Europe organized in the various countries by the respective Harley club. All the clubs had combined themselves as the Federation of Harley-Davidson Clubs and organized jolly little get-togethers known from 1975 onwards as Super-Rallies.

The pan-European, cross-border idea of offering all Harley riders and their friends a big, family get-together once a year, which was fully in tune with the typically open-minded Harley ethos, had developed from the innumerable, individual meetings which had come about because of a shared wanderlust and a typical postwar desire to get to know one another.

While the early Super-Rallies were reminiscent of tranquil coffee circles, and had the campfire romance of the outdoor idyll, the trend now is for monster biker parties.

Nowadays, visitor numbers of 20,000 or more are normal: this combined with entrance charges which are sometimes moderate but often quite high, usually frees the organizing club from financial care for years afterwards. There is always a certain element of risk, however: the weather.

The European climate, especially in northern regions, is unpredictable, and in the case of motorcycle events it is the factor which will determine the level of participation. Rain and cold can turn a rally into a general and financial disaster. Sometimes though, organizational failings are to blame; for example, bad catering, difficult access, sanitary facilities which leave a lot to be desired, or lack of security measures to prevent things like the notorious antics of drunken kamikaze riders.

The European Super-Rallies have now grown into massive sales events and fairs, where Harley riders can get everything they need — or just want — and where there are numerous exclusive performances, from stunt-riding through to professional strip shows, together with biker games and special events with valuable prizes, bingo games and competitions. Famous bands are booked for spectacular performances, and Harley bosses bask in the crowd as admired VIPs.

Super-Rallies independent of the firm have long been an international commercial institution and a must for every real lover of Harleys, no matter which camp or faction he or she comes from.

Super-Rallies in a beautiful European countryside. Enthusiasts come from all over to join in the fun.

Precursors of the Super-Rallies:

1964 Internationale Pinkster Rally in
Franchorchamps, Belgium
1965 Rye, England
1966 Hamburg, Germany
1967 Graft en de Rijp, Netherlands
1969 Wijk Bij Duurstede, Netherlands
1970 Hamburg, Germany
1971 Beckley, England
1972 Doetinchem, Netherlands
1973 Hereford, England

The Super-Rallies

1975 Kastelree, Belgium
1976 Simlangsdalen, Sweden
1977 Geulle, Netherlands
1978 Köln, Germany
1979 Brighton, England
1980 Berlin, Germany
1981 Grenau, Denmark
1982 Frankfurt a/M, Germany
1983 High Chaparral, Sweden
1984 Brighton, England
1985 Paris, France
1986 Kliplev, Denmark
1987 Slagharen, Netherlands
1988 Acosse, Belgium
1989 Stratford upon Avon, England
1990 Heure, Belgium
1991 Hunderfossen, Norwegen
1992 Paris, France
1993 Murrazano, Italien
1994 Silkeborg, Dänemark
1995 Valkenswaard, Netherlands
1996 Nenzing, Austria
1997 Hillerstorp, Sweden

Free Wheels Party

Cunlhat, France

Name: Free Wheels Party.
Date: mid–August, 1996.
Venue: Cunlhat near Clermont–Ferrand in the Massif Central, France.
Organizer: Hell's Angels France (the "Red & White" chapter).
Since: 1987, annually.
Numbers: approximately 30,000 from all over Europe and overseas.
Live music: Zombie Lovers, Calvin Russel, Gary Moore, Too Bad!, Rebel, The Stranglers, Brothers Grimm, Barrance Whitefield and the Savages, as well as Iron Maiden.
Special attractions: *Spectacle Pyrotechnique* (an unusually impressive fireworks display. The fireworks are pretty unique as public entertainment); helicopter flights; bungee jumping.
Events: Bike show; erotic and striptease shows; dragster racing; an extensive range of accessories, jewelry, leather articles and souvenirs for sale; tattoos; beer tents; and an enormous, open-air campsite.

General information: Cunlhat is considered the European Sturgis. It's surely the wildest of biker parties in Europe, with spectacular entertainment that impresses even the most hardened party–going Hell's Angels. In addition, the French show their typical flair for good-humored tolerance and *joie de vivre*. So it's hardly surprising that the small village of Cunlhat also joins in for the three days of celebrations and parties. There's a 24 hour party in the tiny village square, where there is always fresh food and drink available. Day and night the sound of partying can be heard, and the whole thing is helped along by an unbelievably carefree atmosphere. The only way of reaching the center of the town is by means of a tire punishing burnout; even the ancient fire engine did not escape such treatment, and was gotten a welcome set of new tires by way of compensation. Yet despite all the smoke and racket, nobody complains. A nation can count itself fortunate when it has such a relaxed and tolerant attitude – one which is shared moreover, by a police force that keeps everything well under control, yet is always ready to turn a blind eye when it chooses to.

Natural for Cunlhat: camping in the meadow.

Route 66

Wildenrath, Germany

Name: the "Route 66 Harley–Davidson Summer Festival '94."
Date: June 24 to 26, 1994.
Venue: former British military airfield at Wildenrath near Wegberg (Mönchengladbach), Germany.
Organizer: Mama Concerts & Rau Produktion, sponsored by Harley–Davidson, H.O.G., MOTORCYCLES, Michelob, and Sol Mexican Beer.
Numbers: 20,000 (not the expected 50,000).
Live music: Steppenwolf, Deep Purple, Huey Lewis & The News, Bonnie Tyler, Andrew Strong, Birth Control, Highlander.
Special attractions: Bill and Karen Davidson in attendance; 200 foot bungee jump by Jochen Schweizer riding a Sportster; and a prize draw for two Harley Sportsters.
Events: bike show; dragster racing; biker wedding; "experience islands;" open–air grassed recreation area; bike wash; biker games; bungee jumping; air power body flying; fashion parade; bull riding; sumo wrestling, etc.
General Information: a large–scale attempt to combine an open–air concert and a biker event, this was ill–conceived both in organization and concept. The licensing agreements made with Harley–Davidson, who expected to attract large numbers of visitors, excluded the participation of virtually all other makes of motorcycle, together of course with their riders and dealers. The timing could not, it seemed, have been worse: it was early in the year, at a time when the weather could not be relied on. In addition, there was the rival attraction of the large–scale Biker Union party in Schleiz, Germany. Entrance tickets had been on sale for far too long before the event, so that forgeries were common and the organizers and the cooperating firms made serious losses. Amazingly, this event, which had been advertised on a scale unknown up to that time, did not attract any of the neighboring Harley dealers, with the exception of Harley–Davidson Hanover.

For bikers, nevertheless, Wildenrath is remembered as a legendary festival, mainly because of the "Californian" heatwave that lasted the full three days that year.

They enjoyed riding around the huge airfield with complete freedom, and cruising along a entire road lined with beer and refreshment stalls, Western–saloons, and more bike shops than you could count. Another welcome feature was the conspicuous absence of the local police, a rarity in itself, as well as the discreet presence of the security provided by the Hell's Angels. The open–air concerts, however, may not have been to everyone's taste.

Enough room for everybody: the masses swell on the massive airstrip at Wildenrath.

Name: Ibiza Bike Week

Date: August 3 to 8, 1996

Venue: Ibiza, Spain

Organizer: KCK (Kalle, Carlos, Klaus) and Gremium MC, Karlsruhe.

Since: 1994, intended as an annual, Harley bikers' holiday festival.

Attendance: Around 2,000.

Live music: Various local and Harley-friendly bands, including Bullet.

Attractions: Crazy beach party as well as exclusive bike show.

Events: Island tours, barbecues, beach party, dragster demonstrations, bar runs, bike show, striptease, tattoos, competitions, fireworks.

General: Being "fun in the sun" for the social set, this party for Harley fans necessarily became like a little Daytona that you attend in order both to see and to be seen. Eccentrics and show-offs (or, as the local paper terms them, *Piratos Del Asfalt*) flood the sun-kissed, Spanish holiday island for a week, and business booms at the biker pubs and bars frequented by members of the scene. Since at this party it's not the riding but the being there that is the important thing, firms such as Scholz Transport in Berlin offer shipping for valuable custom bikes; most bikes are brought on private transporters or trailers. A few owners, however, ride all the way. This Harley-riding audience is well-heeled and is liberally sprinkled with celebrities. At this show, money is no object.

Name: The 6th Harley–Davidson Motorcycle Jamboree.

Date: July 19 to 21, 1996.

Venue: Biesenthal, 25 miles north of Berlin, Germany.

Organizer: Wildsite Events, and Born To Be Wild MC Berlin, Germany.

Since: 1990, annually.

Attendance: approximately 40,000.

Live music: Rammstein, Dr. Feelgood, Bad Pilots, Canned Heat, Skew Siskin, Highlander and more; 22 bands in total.

Special attractions: Harley–Davidson 3-D laser show and firework display; a prize draw for a new, Ultra Classic Electra Glide.

Events: comprehensive bike show in a separate tent; biker games; ladies' mud wrestling and women's boxing; late night stripshows; tattoo contest; bull riding; bungee jumping; children's motorcycle track; a wide range of motorcycle parts and accessories available at over a hundred dealer's stands.

General: Biesenthal is, without doubt, one of the largest and best-organized biker meets in Europe. It's a three day, non-stop, mammoth jamboree at which one attraction follows another without a break. There is even a huge circus tent to ensure that everything remains in swing even if it rains.

Name: German Bike Week.

Date: July 12 to 14, 1996.

Venue: sand track in the Altrip Stadium, Pfalz, Germany.

Organizer: Bones MC (14 chapters and 260 associate members).

Since: started in 1991, originally as an annual event in September, then changed to June.

Attendance: more than 10,000.

Live music: Doro, Leningrad Cowboys, Hank Davison, Alvin Lee, Molly Hatchet, Stahl, L.O.D. Girlband, Canned Heat, Statement, Luck Up!, and others.

Special attractions: dragster demonstrations; log sawing contests; sado shows and striptease; trophies for visitors; and firework display.

General: although the German Bike Week may not, in fact, last a week, it does have a reputation for being a real king-size biker party lasting several days. Many motorcycle clubs from all over Europe and the U.S. gather there, including the Ghost Riders and Gremium, as well as the Bandidos and Outlaws from the U.S. The members of the Bones MC have a declared interest in dragster racing and so they inevitably meet up with other bikers from France, Austria, England, and Australia who share the same passion. So it's not surprising that visitors get to cast an eye over the latest developments in dragster racing technology. As for the rest – it's just one big party.

Name: Harley–Glühn.

Dates: June 4 to 6, 1993/June 15 to 18, 1995.

Venue: on the Kreut Alm (an Alpine meadow), between Kochl and Murnau, in southern Bavaria, Germany.

Organizer: Marion and Michl Mayr, owners of the Kreut Alm.

Attendance: approximately 3,000 to 4,000.

Live music: Hank Davison, Highlander, Permanent Rosa, Doghouse Blues Band, Racky & Rollers, Williams Wetsox, Nick Woodlands & The Magnets, The Traveling Dildos, and others.

Special attractions: ox roast; balloon rides in the Krafft hot air balloon.

Events: striptease; bungee jumping, and children's playground.

General: A "Harley festival in traditional Bavarian costume" is how it was once described. Mainly it's for Munich's Harley high society, but it also brings together genuine bikers and regular Harley enthusiasts in a warm and friendly atmosphere. It's a traditional Bavarian party typical of the kind held in the German Alps: great food, reasonable prices, all the festivities associated with this part of Europe. Lastly, it's in a superb setting which, dominated by the local range of mountains, provides an unequaled view of the Alps.

  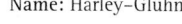  

10th Annual Biker Union Rally   Easyrider Party Switzerland   Biker Jamboree Mainbullau

Name: the 10th Annual Biker Union Rally.

Date: June 28 to 30, 1996.

Venue: Schleizer Dreieck Race Track, Schleiz, Thuringia, Germany.

Organizer: the Biker Union.

Since: 1992 in Schleiz, Germany.

Attendance: approximately 15,000; no entrance charge for members.

Live music: groups include Glenn Hughes, Alvin Lee, Gotthard, Stahl, and Lost Gain; there's also a band contest in addition to the professional performers.

Special attractions: Prize draw for a Harley; plane rides; and blood donation sessions.

Events: sprint races over a distance of 300 yards for all comers; trophies for visitors; stunt shows; bungee jumping; beauty contest; leatherwear show; mud wrestling; striptease show; an extensive bike show, with all kinds of motorcycles from high-performance to veteran bikes exhibited in a separate marquee; several information booths; dealers and accessories.

General: the Biker Union claims that its annual meets are "the largest biker meets in Germany," and are "typically German meets" of a very special kind. In accordance with the Biker Union's democratic constitution, the meet is always coupled with the annual general meeting of the Union, which was founded on November 15, 1986. The Biker Union claims to represent the interests of everyone – but above all those of bikers and biker clubs – against all forms of discrimination, and against national or state legislation adversely affecting the rights of motorcyclists, such as laws on air pollution and the compulsory wearing of protective clothing. The annual rally is, no doubt, a well-organized party, but also has a clear political function; in this the Union has a great deal in common with other European groupings representing the interests of motorcyclists (such as B.A.G.M.O. and the F.E.M.). Nevertheless, the Biker Union annual rally has remained a typical biker event.

Name: 10th Easy Rider Party, Switzerland.

Date: August 23 to 25, 1996.

Venue: Indoor Riding School, Egliswil (Reebelswil), Switzerland.

Since: 1987, annually.

Organizer: Rebels of the Road MC, a Swiss club; its Polish chapter stages the Easy Rider Party in Niepolomice, Poland.

Attendance: approximately 3,000, from all over Europe.

Live music: The Animals II, DRAFT, Papa Blues Band, Omas & The Howlers, as well as newly-formed Swiss bands. Bands that have performed in previous years include: Amy Kay, Walter Traut, Highlander, Alvin Lee, The Hamsters, Michael Katon, The Birds, Canned Heat, Mark Hodgson, Boot Hill Band, and Brothers Grimm.

Special attractions: detailed printed program with the history of a number of local and European biker clubs, and a listing of the 80 club patrons and sponsors.

Events: typical biker games; a swapmeet; a beauty contest; a wide range of biker paraphernalia; dealers selling motorcycle accessories and parts; accessories for dragsters and customizing.

General: this Easy Rider Party has been an annual event for a great many years in Egliswil (now known as Reebelswil), and has won a name for itself as a down-to-earth party for bikers intent on campaigning to the bitter end against meddling bureaucracy, irksome legal restrictions, and any other obstacles making life difficult for Swiss bikers. As is to be expected, there is an air of real rebellion hanging over this well-organized event – the sort of atmosphere that's close to the heart of any thoroughbred Harley biker. The Rebels of the Road MC fosters a close relationship with the Swiss Love Ride (a charity ride), to which they generously donated 3,000 Swiss Francs.

Name: Biker Jamboree '96.

Date: June 21 to 23, 1996.

Venue: airfield near Mainbullau/Miltenberg (north Bavaria), to the south of Aschaffenburg (formerly Hanau/Ipfhofen), Germany.

Organizer: Ghost Riders MC Germany.

Attendance: approximately 10,000.

Live music: Saxon, Canned Heat, Motörhead, ZZ Top, Gotthard, and Seven Little Sisters.

Special attractions: free admission and bungee jumping.

Events: bike show; nightly entertainment; an extensive range of Harley parts, accessories and souvenirs on sale; large open-air stage; and huge campsite nearby.

General: classic, hard-core biker party, very well organized and with all the attractions you'd expect at such an event. But Mainbullau became notorious for a completely different reason: it turned out to be a classic example of official arrogance and heavy-handed policing. First, before the event started, the organizers had to comply with almost impossible conditions, deserving the highest praise for the way they met them. Additionally, throughout the three-day party the police had checkpoints at the entrance to examine vehicles and riders, a task they carried out with the utmost thoroughness and inflexibility. They carried out on-the-spot drugs tests, body searches, and identity checks on anybody who aroused the slightest suspicion of being a law-breaker or "potentially dangerous." They confiscated almost everything, from a flick knife to a motorcycle they considered too noisy. However, despite the continuous harassment by plain-clothes officers all over the site, the bikers' usual good spirits were not dampened, though the intimidating way in which the state demonstrated its power must have been a nightmare for the organizers. In fact, the harsh and officious presence of the police is the most unpleasant aspect of events organized by German hard-core biker clubs – even of German rallies organized by H.O.G. – and is the one that the organizers complain about bitterly.

Name: Praia de Faro.

Venue: Faro, Algarve, southern Portugal.

Organizer: Moto Clube de Faro.

Since: 1982, annually.

Attendance: Approximately 8,000.

Special attractions: Custom bike show; laser show; top quality music.

General: though this show was little-known in its early days, it was well-liked by hard-core bikers, and has developed into a wild and popular biker event for outlaw clubs throughout Europe and the U.S. There's hardly anywhere else where you can see so many MC patches, including those of the Blue Angels from Scotland, The Outcasts Bordeaux from France, The Patriots of Great Britain, The Tatanka MC and The Wakka MC from Finland, and The Heathens MC from England.

Name: The Bulldog Bash.

Date: Early summer.

Venue: Avon Race Park in Warwickshire, which is near Stratford-upon-Avon, England.

Organizer: Hell's Angels England. **Since:** 1986, annually.

Attendance: More than 10,000.

Live music: Cenobyte, Mudshark, Reggety Anne, Panama Grin, Carnival of Thieves, etc.

Special attractions: Striptease show; wet T-shirt contests; dragster demonstrations.

Events: Biker games; shows; stunts; bungee jumping; laser show; firework display.

General: A famous non-stop party, from Thursday through to Sunday, with lots of activities of the kind only Hell's Angels really know how to organize. An enormous campsite, open-air concerts provided by the very best soloists and groups, and typically British entertainment have all contributed to turning The Bulldog Bash into one of the most widely known biker events in Europe.

Name: All American Day: The American Way to Drive.

Date: Summer 1993 and 1994.

Venue: Nuremberg racetrack, Germany.

Patron: U.S. Ambassador to Germany.

Events: Dragster races in a number of classes followed by allcomers races open to the public.

General: An entertaining event centered on American automobiles and Harley-Davidson motorcycles.

Will the Party Ever End?

The International Scene

In the U.S. Harley-Davidson motorcycles have long dominated most of the larger biker meets; but in the rest of the world the famous V-Twins from Milwaukee have only gradually become a familiar sight at biker parties large and small. Of course, there have always been meets devoted entirely to Harley-Davidsons: everywhere in the world exclusivity makes for a special kind of camaraderie. Motorcycle meets, parties, runs, and rallies have naturally always included a few of these well-known distinctive imports from the U.S., which became familiar mainly through movies, but also through the company magazine *The Enthusiast*, available from any Harley-Davidson dealer.

These biker events with their shows, games, and contests, were at first quite restrained in character, the fun simple and innocent; gradually, however, they became, by the 1990s, more and more uninhibited and raunchy, the drinking hard and the music loud. During the 1980s, a specifically Harley-Davidson motorcycle scene developed in Germany, Japan, France, and Australia. It was organized and dominated by clubs and, at first glance at least, bore a close resemblance to the American scene.

Nowadays the "real" biker parties in these countries are, as a rule, essentially Harley-Davidson events dominated visually, and above all acoustically, by the heavy and loud machines from Milwaukee.

The following overview is certainly not meant to be comprehensive. It's intended to present a few typical examples from all over the world to illustrate both the variety of Harley events on offer, and also the similarities that unite the Harley scene, nationally and internationally.

Provided that you have enough spare cash and a reliable Harley, and are not put off by wind and weather, there is nothing to stop you from riding all over Europe from one party to the next during the entire year; you can go on to a new event every week, or even, if so inclined, every day. In France, for example, there are an enormous number of open-air festivals, American weekends, motor shows and exhibitions, not to mention local events staged by a large number of different Harley clubs. Every year the *German Street Magazine* organizes its Summer U.S. Car & Bike Show Tour as the Wheels National Tour, or The Big Car & Harley Meeting, which is staged in Munich on the Theresienwiese, a large public open

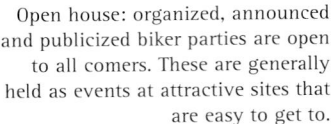

Open house: organized, announced and publicized biker parties are open to all comers. These are generally held as events at attractive sites that are easy to get to.

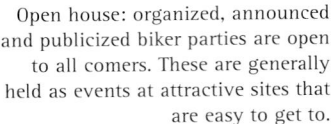

space; on the Heiliggeistfeld in Hamburg, another public open space; at the Dutzendteich in Nuremberg; in the Frankfurt Exhibition Center; at the Schützenplatz Square in Hanover; and at the Vienna racetrack in Austria.

Austria above all has evolved into a country famed for its Harley and biker festivals, due in some measure, no doubt, to the popularity and love of the healthy Alpine surroundings. This can be judged by the immense popularity of the enormous Harley meets in Saalbach and in Wellersdorf, as well as by the Harley–Davidson 50th European Anniversary European event at Faaker Sea.

Italy, Spain, and Greece are other countries where more and more biker events are taking place. The Baltic states, Scandinavia, and countries in Eastern Europe, in particular Poland, the Czech Republic, and Hungary, are becoming the venues for more and more of the larger Harley–Davidson events.

Recently the number of events has increased so much that the biker is now in a position to select precisely the kind of party best suited to his or her own individual taste.

Doing it for the Kids

Toys for Tots

All over the world, at Christmas time Harley Riders collect toys for charity.

Every time Christmas approaches and everything is drenched in sentiment and sentimentality, U.S. bikers are tied up by their own hectic work schedule. Up and down the nation they collect money and toys for poor and sick children, for the "little 'uns" – they call it Toys for Tots. The custom has a long tradition in the world of motorcyclists, and there is hardly a club or association which isn't active in this area.

As always, it's the children that the otherwise gritty, Harley rebels have taken to their hearts, children who are poor or sick or both, children who have no one to give them a little happiness once a year in the shape of a Christmas present. It's for them that the bikers prepare their Toys for Tots Run, and do it all with real enthusiasm. They don't see it as a mere charity event, but as an expression of neighborly love, targeted at those who are most in need.

Weeks in advance there are collections of anything that can be spared. Everywhere there are calls for donations and pledges, and every dealer has his collection can. The bikers' conviction and commitment are irresistible and their urge to collect knows no bounds.

When the great day of delivery comes, people gather together at one or more meeting points. It's a party for kids and grown-ups alike, but the children are of course the real center of attention. Young bikers learn about their social responsibilities at an early age, and if kids hand over their favorite cuddly toy to Santa Claus with tears in their eyes, then at least they know they're making other kids happy by doing so. When the long procession gets underway, the whole town or city is usually on the move, and with the media much in evidence.

Up front the sheriffs' cars lead the way with lights flashing and sirens wailing, closely followed by Santa Claus in his red robe on his Harley or up on a truck piled high with toys. Then comes the impressive parade, which has right of way past every corner stop and traffic light. Bikers resplendent on their festively decorated Harleys, most of them sporting a particularly cute, fluffy animal at front or rear, follow close behind, sounding their horns and letting their engines roar.

Their destination is usually the headquarters of the Salvation Army or the Marine Corps (U.S.M.C.), which has accepted the role of godparent for the needy children. There the money and the toys are handed over. But often the entire parade goes directly to orphanages and hospitals, rehab centers or other welfare institutions.

To finish up there is a party ... though perhaps not always as big as the one that followed the Chicago Christmas Parade of 1997, when almost 15,000 motorcyclists collected 7,000 toys to add to the 27,000 already collected. Like they say, they're doing it for the kids!

Uniformed Benefactors

The Shriners

The company serves one further customer group of much like the way they serve the police departments – the Shriners. The Shriners also order their machines in large quantities under special conditions. Shriner models are almost identical to police motorcycles, including red lamps, sirens, and radios. Depending on the wishes of the individual Shriner lodges, they also get their own individual paintwork, to which only members of the Shriner Motor Corps are entitled.

Shriner Harleys are excellent parade machines, but they are also used in extreme conditions. In their own shows and in public parades, Shriners, mostly enthusiastic Harley fans and experienced stunt riders, do all kinds of tricks, generally on Full Dresser bikes.

The Shriner Drill Teams have formed into an Association of Shriner Motor Corps, who meet with their motorized members (including drivers of go-carts and luxury cars) at year-around international competitions and at the regular National Shriners Conventions, where they give demonstrations, evolve new ideas, and are subject to a rigorous inspection.

The Ancient Arabic Order of Nobles of the Mystic Shrine

This is one of the most respected, philanthropic organizations of well-to-do Americans. The pretentious name hides an altruistic, private, masonic lodge brotherhood, known as the "Shriners." It was founded in 1872 with the establishment of the Mecca Temple, with ethical and idealistic aims, and it now has over 885,000 members in 191 Shrine Temples throughout the U.S., Canada, Mexico and Panama. The main aim is to provide help to community projects through generous benefactions. The Shriners support 22 hospitals for sick, handicapped and needy children, who are treated there free of charge.

Harley-Davidson manufactures a few model types for the charitable events of the various Freemason's lodges of the Shriners, such as the Bahia Temple shown here. These models are almost identical to the police models, less the radio equipment. The Shriner bikes are used mainly for parades and formation shows.

You Can't Beat a Good Party!

Party On

A very special vocabulary is used when it comes to talking about parties. This is especially true in the case of biker parties organized by Harley fans. Parties are a way of life, and for many people, they're what makes life worth living. Parties are where you meet your friends. Parties are the greatest! Parties are the best!

Instead of a long-winded introduction when you meet someone, how's this for an opener as you are handing them a beer: "Let's party!" A party is something you can look forward to the whole week. Every single day. Always.

Without parties, life wouldn't be the same. Party forever! As soon as the word "Harley" crosses your lips, the next word just has to be "party." A party? – When? – Where? The ideal is "P.P.P." – Permanent Party Paradise: a birthday party, a national holiday party, a Christmas party, a house-warming party, a going-away party, a congratulations parts, a masquerade party, a surprise party, a farewell party, an all-you-can-eat party, a drink-all-you-want party, a beach party... did somebody say there's a party? Life's a party! Party after party after party after party ...! Man, I've had just about enough – but come on in, you're welcome!

The Most Memorable Kind of Get–Togethers

Small Parties But a Lot of Fun

Small parties may not offer anything out of the ordinary in the way of special attractions, shows, field meets, biker games or open–air concerts, – but they're certainly among the most pleasant and memorable kind of get–together.

Whatever attractions there are, they are within easy reach: the kids put on a show, there are games on T.V., and the canned music is the best there is. There are no strangers and outsiders, only personally invited guests – real friends.

Parties at home, picnics at parks and beaches and barbecues at the club – just right for relaxing. None of that stress in pushing your way to the front of a crowd, no brawling, no deafening noise, no mass hysteria, nobody shouting and screaming, and not a single tent sinking deeper and deeper into the mud. And there's nothing like sleeping it off in your own bed the next day without being disturbed or needing to do something.

Small parties are an essential part a way of life which is typical for Harley fans, and a part that should be carefully and lovingly nurtured. It's the least complicated form of comradeship. Personal friends are always there when they're needed; there are no long rides there and back; and costs are kept to a minimum. The important momentum is that there's enough beer for everyone

and the potato chips don't run out. Bikes are left where you can keep an eye on them, they can be reached quickly, and there's no risk of someone tampering with your machine. The kids are under control and where you can see them. Many a great idea for an unforgettable adventure first saw the light of day at a friendly get–together of this kind.

All you have to do is pick up the phone and call everyone. You don't have to think long and hard for a reason – if you can't find a good excuse, that'll be reason enough for a party! Often a boring afternoon in some bar or other turns into a party. Sometimes it begins when the members of a club are out on a joyride; they just pull up at a pleasant spot! Best of all is when a party isn't planned at all but just happens.

In the U.S. – where the small party is as American as apple pie – small friendly groups are often formed by people who include their Harleys in all their activities. Without such regular get–togethers life could be lonely, and even, in some cases, unbearable. The American way of life would somehow be incomplete without the small neighborly party. For many people, a party without a Harley is just not a party.

Whether organized or not: small parties are the elixir of life for all real bikers. There is always plenty to eat and much more to drink and sometimes even the necessary nightly enterainment is provided. In principle they celebrate the outdoors, just as they always have.

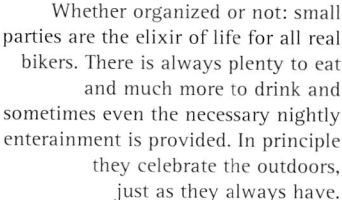

The Biker's Favorite Food

And Never Forget the Sixpack

Those truly devoted to their Harley motorcycle really enjoy eating anything Japanese, either raw or well-cooked. Even the skin and bones! Joking aside, the genuine biker isn't choosy: they like the staples such as meat, fish, bread, potatoes, and salad. They'll eat only when they feel hungry – but then they are always hungry. Above all, it's not what they eat, it's the amount. That explains their preference for those eateries that offer "all–you–can–eat" at a single price; that also explains why you are likely to see so many "Temporarily closed" signs appearing after a large-scale invasion of hungry bikers!

A genuine biker has a healthy suspicion of unfamiliar food and drink. Smart restaurants are something they really cannot stand, simply because of the snobbery ("Have the gentlemen decided?"). They also restrict their liquid intake to those things they know well: beer when they're thirsty, Jack Daniels when they're feeling moody. They usually keep away from Colas, soda, fruit juice, spirits, and above all milk – beer and Jack Daniels, nothing else. This way you know what you're drinking. That weird habit Europeans have of ruining a good beer with all kinds of strong liquor disgusts them. Nor can they understand the strange custom of drinking beer out of enormous glasses and tankards, either. What is there to compare with that wonderful psssss! as you open another can you've just ripped from your six-pack? The six-pack, that essential part of the genuine biker's lifestyle.

The Harley biker world and everyone else has to make do with the various cookbooks which give recipes which apparently are favorites of Harley riders. It's all there – apart from the Japanese delicacies mentioned before, of course.

Bikers know what the brothers expect: appetites are enormous so the roast pig has to be perfectly done, the steaks huge, there must be plenty of seafood and invariably ice-cold beer.

Food being prepared using secret recipes.
Famous is a southern biker's delicacy:
a spicy crawfish stew.

Today's Gladiators

Biker Games

A hard game, stress for both man and machine: burnout and barrel-rolling.

They could be described as motorcycling mini-Olympics without the ruthless competitiveness, even though there are sometimes trophies and even money waiting to be won. Let's just call them "biker games," events that bring together the kinds of fun usually associated with kindergarten children, boy scouts, and playing knights in armor.

That's what makes them so much fun: they're a harmless mixture of innocent amusement, a child-like sense of play, and good-humored rough-and-tumble – and all performed with skill, a great sense of balance and total mastery of a powerful machine.

Motorcycle sport and leisure activities have always played an important role in the life of the committed rider, and in the 1920s and 1930s games and competitions formed the most essential feature of almost any club's Gypsy Tours.

The games staged during the club outings, get-togethers, and parties were organized by the club program committee, both for the sheer fun of it all, and also for letting off a bit of steam, an approach that hasn't changed over the years. The rules and regulations of different games are printed regularly in Harley's magazine *The Enthusiast* and in *American Motorcyclist and Bicyclist* simply to make them more widely known. Today, biker games are mainly fun extras for spectators, and they are usually played in a spirit of good-natured entertainment rather than in the spirit of fierce competitiveness.

These classic motorcycle games as they existed before the World War II consisted strictly of some "for the boys" (with and on their motorcycles), and some "for the girls" (without a motorcycle). The first category included many games that are still popular, including:

Swat the Murphy: posts are knocked into the ground until they are saddle height and a potato is placed on top. Contestants ride past in turn and try to smash the potatoes using a club or a baseball bat. A rider who misses one or makes a potato drop off a post, is eliminated.

Barrel Rolling: this requires two or more players. Each contestant tries to push a large, empty barrel or oil drum as far as possible along a track using only the front wheel of their motorcycle to urge the object on. The winner is the one pushing the barrel furthest.

514

Obstacle Race: nowadays this is something most people learn while they are learning to drive: how to evade obstacles positioned at a certain distance from each other.

Slow Race: this requires two or more contestants. The aim is to complete a given distance as slowly as possible. The winner is the rider who completes the course in the slowest time without putting their feet on the ground.

Plank Riding: the contestants have to ride along a narrow plank from one end to the other, a surprisingly difficult balancing act.

Weenie Bite: this is the most popular event and has a more than a hint of grossness about it. Each motorcyclist is accompanied by a female pillion rider (the passenger must be female), and has to ride under a row of hot dogs hung on strings. The pillion rider, with no hands, has to bite off the hot dogs. The winner is the one who bites off the most.

The second category contained those harmless games specially included so that the girls could have a good time as well, such as sack races and egg-and-spoon races. For the guys who still felt the need to

let off steam, there were various enduro competitions, such as riding through sandpits, climbing steep inclines or riding around in tight circles. An obligatory part of any meeting was the communal eating of cream cakes or chili: without, of course, using hands.

Biker games today. The one most popular with nearly everyone is still the Weenie Bite, followed by the Barrel Race, the Slow Race, and Plank Riding, though now with the added attraction of a wooden block under the plank so that it will act as a see-saw. Other competitions involving skill with and on a motorcycle include:

Ring Throwing, in which the passenger, male or female, throws lots of different-sized rings (sometimes piston rings) onto a post.

The *Egg-and-Spoon Race* requires a rider to carry an egg balanced on a spoon they're holding in their mouth over a specified distance; or to pick up an egg as they drive past in order to put it down again in a small egg-cup.

In *Beer Can Collecting* the female passenger must grab as many beer cans as possible from a heap of cans (placed at saddle height) as the bike

One big party with volume to match: firmly tied to each other, two courageous bikers attempt to drag each other over the slippery ground. The loser hardly has a chance to keep himself from falling from his bike.

Games: sand drags, carrying off some booty, a kickstart contest, collecting cans.

is ridden past. During this event the feet of the driver and the passenger are not allowed to touch the ground. This game can be made even more difficult by making the contestants set down the cans at a designated point, again while on the move.

In *Balloons*, water-filled balloons, suspended from a frame about 8 feet high, must be burst while a rider and passenger are passing through the frame. The passenger uses a pointed stick to burst the balloon, while the driver tries to get away quickly so that they don't get soaked.

The idea of *Kickstart* is simplicity itself: the rider has to kickstart the motorcycle as often as possible in one minute, killing the engine completely before restarting it.

There's also a whole range of games that bikers can play that do not involve a motorcycle at all, such as *Arm Wrestling* and, of course, *Mud Wrestling* (preferably with female wrestlers). Then there is also the *Bungee Run*, in which the competitor, who's tied to a long rubber rope, has to run as hard as possible to retrieve a distant object before the rope pulls them back.

Then, last but by no means least, there's the traditional *Tug-of-War*. In one of the most popular versions of this game, the teams are separated by a pool of water filled with all sorts of evil-smelling substances. *Darts*, on the other hand, is an event that has little in common with the usual open-air biker games, but it has become so popular at the events in recent years that there are even international competitions for Harley-Davidson Dart Cups.

Apart from these regular competitions there are a few "illegal" games, known as so-called outlaw contests:

Motorcycle Tug-of-War: two motorcycles are tied together at the back end, with the aim being, obviously, being for one bike to drag the other backwards.

Burnouts: there are two versions, and in both the front wheel must be kept blocked. In the first, held on asphalt, the rider must keep the rear wheel spinning until the tire bursts. In the other, on a soft surface, they have to keep accelerating until the rear wheel is buried completely and can't turn any more.

Audience darlings: the ladies mud-wrestling and snatching hot dogs.

Street Drags and Sand Drags: these are sprint races over a specified, short track. There's no timing: the first to the end is the winner.

Demolition and Crash: a number of motorcyclists crash into each other again and again until the machines break apart and can no longer be ridden. The winner is the rider with the motorcycle than can still be ridden (more or less).

"Riceburner Hammering": this is a strange and in some ways typically American ritual during which a Japanese motorcycle has to be turned into a pile of scrap metal by contestants using just hammers or tools of some kind. At the root of this particular pastime there's a clearly discernible "Rambo motive" which is in part, perhaps, an act of defiance in the face of what some see as a lost battle for world technical supremacy. This wanton destruction is testimony of a simple-minded patriotism that has its roots in the frontier tradition of old.

In reality, the target of this aggression it is not a motorcycle but the Japanese themselves. The Japanese assault on Pearl Harbor in 1941 has not been forgotten; for some hard-line patriots even the dropping of the terrible atom bombs on Hiroshima and Nagasaki (1945) are considered totally justified acts of retaliation.

So in the eyes of a small group of Americans, Japanese motorcycles are still provocative symbols of a hated foe. It's a view most people find quite senseless, and "Riceburner Hammering" is an event widely condemned in the biking world, particularly by Harley-Davidson. Outside the U.S., it's only popular in Australia, where some people still cherish strong anti-Japanese sentiments.

In Germany, generally all motorcycle riders view this game as absurd and wrong. It must be remembered, however, that the Japanese were the Germans' allies not their enemies, and that the majority of German bikers now ride Japanese machines.

Even the popular argument that American jobs are being lost and that the American workforce is being cheated due to Japanese motorcycles being imported into the country is now outdated: Japanese "fat boys" (heavy machines in direct competition with Harleys) have been built in the U.S. by American workers for some time now.

517

Patriotic or not, the Japanese demolition show: thirty meters up with the engine fixed at full throttle until the motor dies, then it is dropped by the crane and burned on the scrap-heap.

So, for several reasons, this is an outdated and xenophobic insult to the Japanese people and is strictly taboo to most true Harley-Davidson motorcycle owners and fans.

Motorcycle rodeos, well-organized events of enormous size, feature a wide range of biker games, and have added a few new ones to the list. They have also set down clear rules for the games mentioned above, such as the *Slow Race*, the *Weenie Bite* and *Barrel Rolling* with the only difference being that five motorcycles at a time participate.

In the Rodeo's form of a Barrel Race, competitors take turns to ride counter-clockwise around three triangular barrels as quickly as possible. In *Potato Haystack*, five contestants ride around piles of hay in which four potatoes have been hidden. As soon as a signal is given, the female passenger has to leap off the bike and look for the potatoes. Anyone not finding a potato drops out of the competition. This continues until the last pair fights it out for the last potato.

In the *Tire Ride*, two competitors drag a tire roped to their bikes: the person sitting in the tire has to try staying inside the tire. *Sled Drag*, a form of tractor pulling, has also become a spectacular event to watch:

the aim of the game is to drag a sled as far as possible, the weight of the sled being gradually increased. There are a number of categories based on the power of the engine.

Of course some of these games take place at smaller biker parties, the difference being that at big events the winners often receive quite handsome cash prizes, scaled according to a game's difficulty. It follows of course, that the entry fee for a game at these large events is also sometimes fairly high.

At some biker events, however, it's normal for the prizes to be paid for out of the general entrance charge for the show; at others, a dollar is collected from each competitor on the principle of winner takes all. In the case of charity events, of course, all the entry money for the games is donated to a worthy cause.

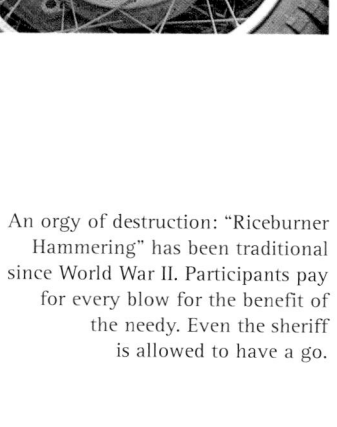

An orgy of destruction: "Riceburner
Hammering" has been traditional
since World War II. Participants pay
for every blow for the benefit of
the needy. Even the sheriff
is allowed to have a go.

Sightseeing I

Places, Bars and Watering Holes

Where to go...

Drinking, unfortunately, accounts for a large part of the "real biker's" life. This, too, has its historical basis. Not only was the first outlaw motorcycle club called The Boozefighters, but also alcohol was — and still is — a central feature of the hard-core motorcycle scene, and the choice of beverage is clear: bikers prefer beer sold in licensed Harley cans.

Because road traffic, a phenomenon which hardly existed earlier in this century, has become a relentless killer, drunken bikers put themselves and others in great danger. By now even the most hardened drinkers have recognized that motorcycles and alcohol are a fatal combination for the biking way of life. In other words, drinking customs have finally adapted themselves to circumstance. A couple of beers perhaps, but that's enough.

The results are reduced visits to bars and falling profits on the one hand; and, on the other, the tendency to sleep off the effects of alcohol somewhere. All the same, something of the old drinking culture has remained. The places of worship preferred for this are known simply as "places."

Places

Places are where bikers, mainly Harley riders, meet. In most cases they are bars or saloons, often called watering holes, restaurants, cafés, guest houses, and pubs. Highway meets and secret rendezvous in beautiful castles and quality hotels also come under this category.

Every place has its own special image and a reputation known only to insiders. There are tiny, hidden, wonderful, biker pubs all over the world (though a guide is needed to find them), and smart, garish, just as wonderful cafés which grab attention through humorous advertising.

Popular names for such places are Iron Horse, Road Kill Café, Broke Spoke, or simply Bikers' Place.

Watering Holes

Like other hard working folk, bikers are always on the lookout for watering holes where they can quench their thirst with "fire water."

But they are not equally welcome in all of them. The "real bikers" at least, those hard-core guys who can scare the more timid guests away with their offensively overt masculinity, are not always flavor of the month.

Typical signs are "No Colors" and "No Attitudes" — which do not, however, imply that well-behaved motorcyclists are not welcome. But we are talking about the real watering holes here, the biker bars, saloons, or pubs which have managed to survive for a long time by retaining a loyal clientele, mainly local motorcycle clubs, while developing the diplomatic skill of staying one step ahead of the regulations and harassment of the local authorities, police, and town clerks' offices.

Biker Bars

Biker bars are the epitome of biker social life. Here we can meet people who think like us, "brothers in the wind," and we talk about problems and motorcycles — usually one and the same thing — and badmouth the middle classes, officials — or just get blind drunk.

There are always a couple of powerful hogs in front of the door (sometimes inside too), and there are always a couple of friendly girls around; in short, everything essential to life is to be found here. But not every stranger is welcome, no matter how good his Harley. Real biker bars are mainly private function rooms and sometimes serve as motorcycle club houses, where the local members are the monarchs of the glen.

Every stranger is viewed with distrust, and not infrequently subjected to a certain amount of rough behavior — this is simply an expression of a group's survival instinct. The only real way to gain entry to a real biker pub is through introduction by a brother who has been going there for a long time, or by personal recommendation. Once you're in, you more or less have a second home.

The behind-the-scenes goings-on of a real biker bar or pub are worth seeing, and often include the unruly behavior typical to the scene, not all of which is G-rated. The legendary Dave Mann centerfolds from *Easyriders* magazine are happily slapped on the walls; the pool table is of vital importance, together with a few electronic game machines (usually Pacman and pinball). A properly stocked jukebox is also a vital part of the furniture of a true biker bar.

Not every bar with a few Harleys parked out front is a real biker bar. Many clubs keep to the old tradition of organizing weekly bar runs to confuse surveillance, to the delight of local drinking establishments, and so it can happen that bikers in full leathers who walk into a bar expectantly are met with looks of astonishment and dismay.

Those who wish quietly to have a good time should find out about a place in advance. The nearest Harley dealer can be a great help.

Saloons

Although it is impossible to classify them neatly and keep them apart from other drinking places, biker saloons are first and foremost spacious bars. Not only is beer sold there, but also biker paraphernalia, especially T–shirts and beer mugs.

Many of the large biker saloons are yawningly empty during most of the year; it's only when the landlord organizes special events like barbecue parties, ladies' nights, charity runs, or free–food evenings, that they really come to life. Some biker saloons in the catchment areas of the big bike–week racetracks such as Daytona, Sturgis, or Laconia become centers of the biking world once a year, and just burst at the seams. Often the landlord can then go on holiday for the rest of the year. Many of the big saloons have large yards or private areas on which guests can camp, party, or indulge in any other activity of their choice.

No matter how, where, or when, watering holes are the classic meeting points of the entire biking world. Enjoying their hospitality is one of the most rewarding, personal experiences. And by the way, it doesn't always have to be beer. Coke is all right now too, especially if you're driving.

Famous biker bars: Sopotnik´s Cabbage Patch in Samsula, Florida (above), police march in front of Pub 44 in Deeland (left), after a bikers shootout; The Gunners Lounge in Sturgis (right), and the Californian Rock Store Café (below).

Sightseeing II

Places, Bars and Watering Holes

Typical places: The Broken Spoke in Kiln, Missipipi (above far right), The Broken Spoke in Sturgis (above), The Boothill Saloon in Daytona Beach (left), The Iron Horse Saloon in Ormond Beach, Florida (bottom), and the Last Resort in Harbour Oats, Florida (below).

Always a full house: during Biker Week the bars in Daytona boom, shown here are The Squeeze-In Pub, Froggy's Saloon and The Boothill Saloon.

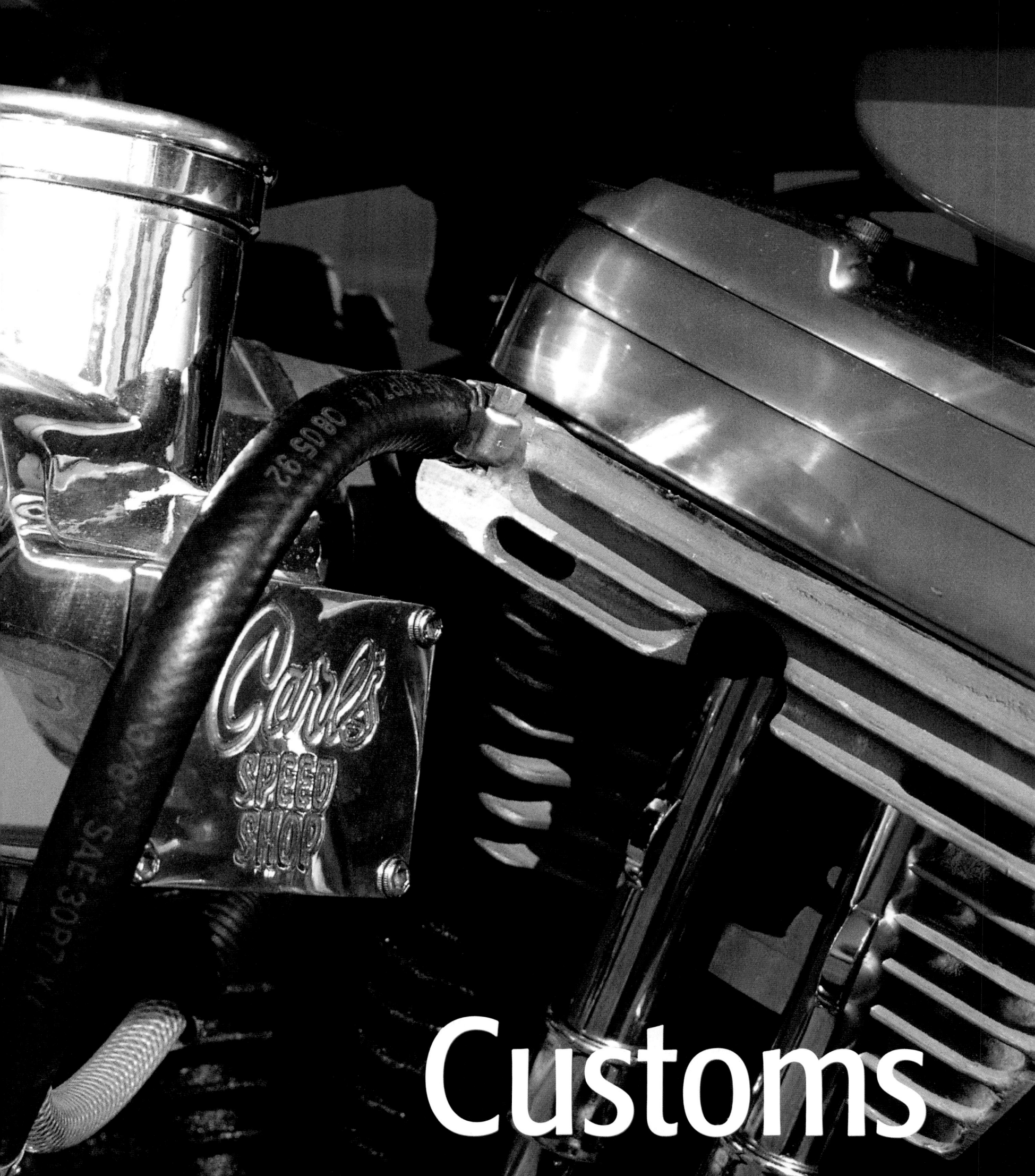

Customs

The Spoils of Madness

Customized Harleys

For the true Harley disciple, everything which is original Harley-Davidson is holy — as long as it comes from one of the company's plants, whether it's in Milwaukee, York, or Kansas City.

But there are disciples and then there are disciples. The author recalls an experience he had at a meeting in one of the states in the South: A biker asked me if he could show me his motorcycle. Of course he could — so he led me to an almost pristine Wide Glide FXWG from the early 1980s.

"Do you notice anything out of the ordinary?" It was a beautiful bike, but no matter how closely I looked at it, could see nothing special, just the usual 'Milwaukee finest.' He grinned a little and then came out with a bizarre explanation. "That's a Harley where every part is guaranteed made in the U.S. of A.," he said proudly, and now the true meaning of the rather inconspicuous sticker on a good number of Harleys became suddenly clear to me: '100 percent Made in America' — to be sure it is a unique type of custom bike.

Apparently, there were a couple of hundred parts that needed changing and they had cost him several thousand dollars, he added. He must have been a real insider, and I regret to this day not having asked him for a list of all the parts not produced in the U.S.

Some of them are reasonably well-known: the pistons (Mahle, Germany) and carburetor (Keihin, Japan) for example, but other parts are a strict company secret. Jeff Bleustein, whom I once asked, thought they could account for around eight percent of the total product. Then he countered with: "Would you still buy a Harley if you knew that it was built completely outside the U.S.?" It must be an important question for Harley-Davidson, and he had me cornered; I couldn't answer.

A custom fanatic has little interest in such patriotic and philosophical considerations. What they want is an absolutely unique article, drawing on the most disparate artwork and styles. Whether the motor — a large displacement 45 degree V-Twin, naturally — and the motorcycle itself are genuine Harley is a question of secondary importance. Those who can afford it often use only a few basic components from Harley (cases, connecting rods, and cylinders), and select the rest from the immense variety on the aftermarket.

Nowadays Harley-Davidson produces an extensive range of custom and touring accessories itself, the absolute uniqueness of which, however — so important to the high-class mechanics of the custom scene — is not guaranteed. Regrettably a lot of aftermarket parts fit badly or not at all, either technically or stylistically, and have to be adjusted or reworked. This too is an important part of customizing.

For a long time there have been motorcycles which superficially look like an original stock Harley-Davidson and yet do not contain one single original Harley part, a state of affairs which the company finds frustrating, constantly leading it to initiate plagiarism and trademark infringement suits.

Astonishingly, Harley-Davidson shows itself in conciliatory mood at the big national and international bike shows like Daytona and Sturgis. At their ride-in shows as well as other extravaganzas the most extreme conversions can be seen, while the company bosses smile. Individualism has always been an important part of the Harley scene, and it would be a pity to lose this special touch.

The problem is that a huge amount of business is involved. It is estimated that the custom market and traders in aftermarket products using unlicensed Harley parts make profits several times higher than Harley itself, but also support a similarly large number of jobs. Above all in central Europe, and often on Harley's own initiative, the authorities are known to react in a prickly fashion to these replacements and add-ons, which are not standardized and therefore not admissible for road use. Ever stricter emissions criteria and ever more rigorous product warranties on the part of the company are making it increasingly difficult to practice the individualism so characteristic of Harley.

In Germany in particular, where the rider or owner of a vehicle is basically liable in law for everything, conversions and customizations are becoming more and more expensive because of extremely complicated and often incomprehensible regulations governing those who, as the bureaucratic formula expresses it, want "to participate in traffic."

In the U.S. the custom bike rider has an easier life. There, along with the insurance, it is the manufacturer who is liable, though this unlimited product liability has its own peculiar problems.

Despite this, you hardly see real custom bikes on the road. The Hamsters with their incredible Arlen Ness creations are the exception. They are mainly moved between shows on trailers or in a secure transporter, and sometimes you get the impression they have only been built in order to win trophies. An important reason for transporting vehicles in this way is bad weather and less than ideal road conditions, which can quickly turn a faultless jewel into a dirty mess. Polishing will achieve little; only complete dismantling and reassembly will do.

The single exception are the rat bikes, which cannot be dirty enough, and which are conscientiously driven over huge distances. The rustier, the better. But appearances can be deceptive: their motorcycle technology is excellent — as is proved by Smitty's famous prehistoric rat bike, which effortlessly won every kickstart competition around with a maximum of 59 correctly measured individual starts in a minute. Other customs Harleys, for example choppers or dressers, are merely individual modifications of other types of two-wheeled transport mentioned above.

The custom scene is a fascinating mix of ability, art, and technology — sometimes with a little more art, sometimes with a little more technology. It is in the essence of Harley-Davidson and cannot be divorced from it. It will surely never die: the individualism of Harley riders is too strong.

Harley Trailers for the Grand Tour

Normally the image of a typical Harley rider on the road is of a leather-clad loner with a sleeping bag casually slung over the handlebars, two worn leather bags at most hanging from the back of his machine. Admittedly, there are the big Full Dressers; and Electra Glides also offer a good deal of space in their plastic trunks — but this is hardly enough to satisfy the real, big time tourer. In the Harley scene, like any other, there are world travelers unwilling to do without their television, refrigerator and beer taps. On long journeys especially, the trailer has the advantage that luggage need not always be unloaded from the machine and if required the trailer can simply be left at the campsite. Naturally such a trailer is also an eye-catcher whose message is "Look over here, I've got everything!" Although there are some manufacturers of small one- and two-wheel trailers with the necessary coupling, many Harley riders go for home productions, if only for the pleasure of hanging an extra bit of customizing onto the machine. The road performance of the motorcycle is not seriously affected for the Milwaukee twins' powerful torque assures speed, even with the extra burden of the trailer, however braking characteristics and distances are extended when trailering.

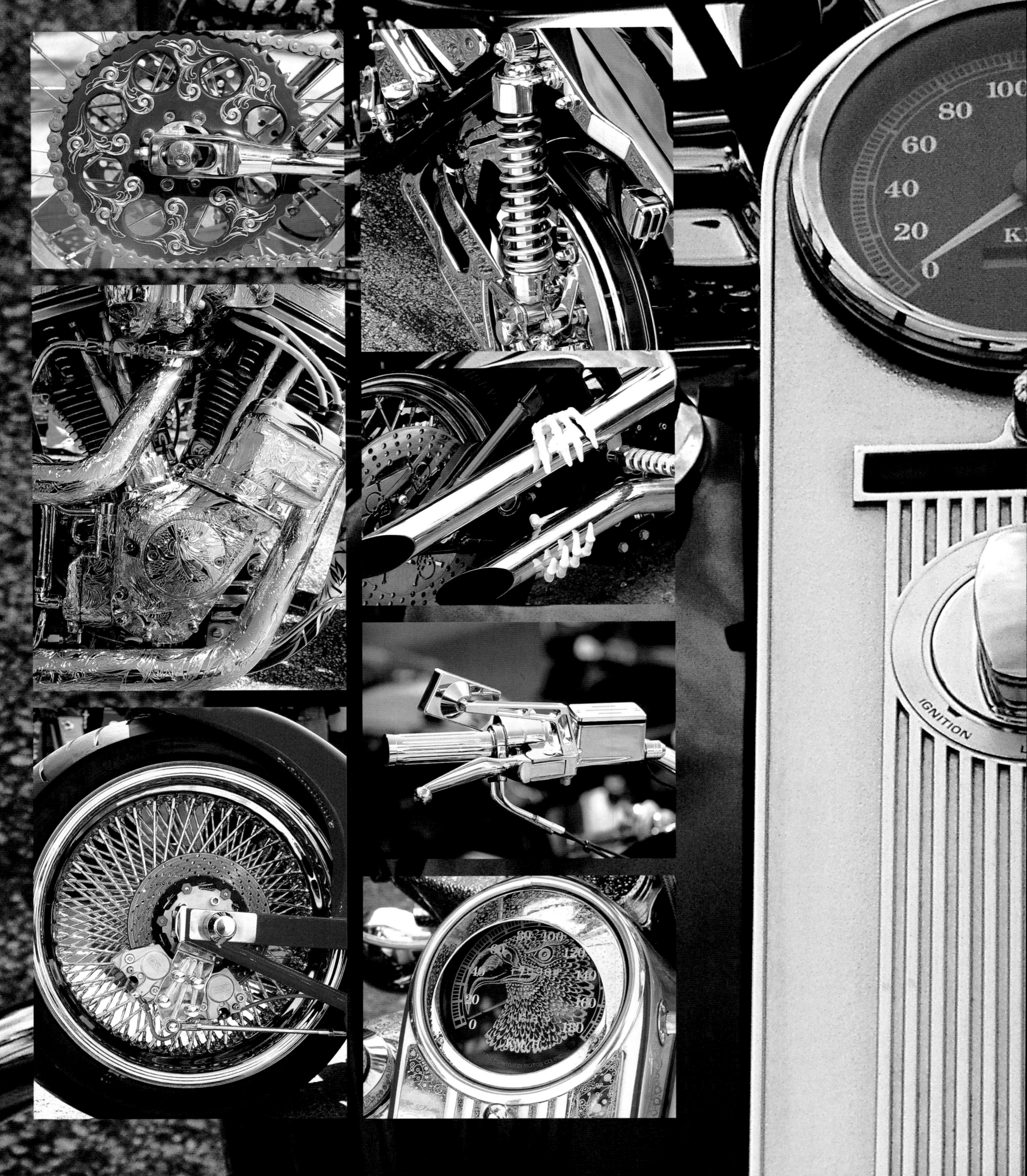

Choppers

The Dream of *Easy Rider*

The most famous Panhead ever: two identical "Captain America" motorcycles were built for the film Easy Rider. Innumerable copies were to follow.

We will probably never know when exactly a custom-bike fan somewhere got the idea to fix long forks onto his motorcycle — but there were sound reasons for the first issue of "Big Daddy," Ed Roth's *Choppers* magazine, confining itself to choppers, not to subjects like meat cleavers, helicopters or the Grim Reaper. For many Harley-Davidson fans today it seems like the chopper fell down from heaven or rolled-off of the movie screen in 1969: but there were Harleys with long forks and curved exhausts long before the film "Easy Rider" hit the big screen.

The origins of what is now called the chopper are to be found in fact in the "bobbers" of the late 1930s and early 1940s. A number of Harley fans who found the Milwaukee iron too heavy for daily use or for the weekend races removed all the unnecessary parts from their machines, or cut them down to a minimum, a practice called "bobbing." These lightened machines were much more suitable for racing and were easier to handle in traffic; besides, in sun-kissed states like California it was no problem to go without fenders.

At exactly the same time, the bobbers were the very antithesis of the standardized design of the production machines from Milwaukee and the heavy, chrome-plated decoration of the official accessories catalog. This was a protest against conformity and middleclass values.

The biker scene had a low profile through the 1950s. The postwar generation was much more enamored with four-wheeled travel — at the end of a hard day, they could spend a comfortable evening with their girls in the back seat of a Bel Air than on the saddle of a Hydra-Glide. The production figures from the 1950s read like the swan song of the American V-twin. After the scandalous film of the Hollister Riots, which damaged the image of motorcyclists, it was to be over ten years before custom-bikes and rockers made another appearance on the silver screen.

This time around the filmmaker Roger Corman directed the rocker film "Wild Angels" which also revealed the evolution of the chopper: high handlebars, sissy bars and high pipes were now the characteristics of the outlaw bikes. Inspiration for modifying the machines came from the Californian hotrod scene, where weird and wonderful biking creations were to be seen at the yearly shows and meetings. There the hobby mechanics did their best to outdo each other by showing not only four-wheel fantasies but also, though not very often, customized motorcycles.

Harley-Davidsons were not always the favored creations. Everything with two wheels was "chopped," and the more exotic, the better. Harleys had the advantage that older machines could be bought much more cheaply.

Another catalyst was drag racing, where the effect of the angle of the steering head on straight runs at high speeds was tested. If forward-raked forks had a stabilizing effect at high speeds, then extremely long forks would achieve good directional stability at lower speeds. There were in any case hardly any bends on America's endlessly long highways, and the broad streets left enough room to turn. The new look soon became news and just as quickly spawned copies.

It was these long or elongated forks, however, which at first give the chopper the appearance of being unsafe in traffic. Longer forks mean more leverage on joints and connecting surfaces, and neither the materials available in the 1960s, nor the welding skills of most weekend customizers, were always up to the demands of the job. Every motorcyclist can imagine the result of a broken joint on a badly welded fork.

A particularly suicidal variant involved lengthening the stanchions with extension parts known as "slugs," a part that could be made on the workbench to any length required by a first-year apprentice. The slugs were screwed into the standard stanchion in place of the oil cap, and extended the fork in a simple and cheap fashion — until the next big pothole!

The laid-back lifestyle in California was even more relaxed then than it is today, and youth cults had various meeting points. In the area around San Francisco the scene was particularly lively and the motorcycle clubs flourished side by side with the hippies. The bikers allowed themselves to be used as extras for cheap rocker films, which led to a veritable flood of films of this genre.

Thereafter the interest rose in stages until in 1968 Cliff Vaughs built the two ultimate choppers for the film "Easy Rider." Peter Fonda's Panhead frame was chopped in the classic manner at the steering head and raked at an angle of 45 degrees. Twelve-inch over fork tubes gave the bike its typical appearance. Fonda wanted to have the bike painted like the Marvel comic book character Captain America's shield, and so a legend was born. If a small, lively market for custom accessories had grown up during the 1960s, it was "Easy Rider" which provided the spark for a revolution. Afterwards the number of chopper magazines mushroomed. Other glossy magazines followed Ed Roth's first monochrome cult newsletter, and Choppermania was well under way.

The Core of the Chopper

What are the characteristics of a genuine chopper? What types of choppers exist and used to exist? Can such individualistic machines be categorized at all?

The trademark of an early chopper — and this has not changed right up to the present — is the frame. It has to be tough enough to allow the rider to deal with all the idiosyncrasies the road can present. Anything which has even a minimum of swinging arm or rear suspension runs the danger of being seen as a softail. Add to that a classic engine which, naturally, depends on the age of the chopper. If Flatheads and Knuckles were the real thing for 1960s customizers, today's objects of desire are Pans and Shovels. Long forks and high handlebars are not absolutely necessary, but the rule of thumb, "the shorter the forks, the higher the handlebars," does apply. High pipes and sissy bars are also typical characteristics but have lost popularity dramatically over the years.

Strictly speaking Harley-Davidson has never built a genuine chopper. It never managed to produce more than one "Softie," and even these machines had to be introduced in the face of opposition from the AMF management of the 1970s.

It is hardly surprising then that there was a great market in the years after "Easy Rider" for frame-makers and accessory firms who sold everything Milwaukee could not or would not deliver. The era of the bolt-on chopper built from mass-produced readily available accessories had arrived, and has continued to this day.

Chopper Types

Trying to categorize a vehicle as individual and idiosyncratic as a chopper is a contradiction in itself. Since the early days,

Courtesy of: Matthias Bilek, Germany

Typically Swedish: probably the longest shafts in the world of this type, of which experts maintain that one has to look for the front wheel with a pair of binoculars. Apparently one can even ride it, if only on stretches of road with no bends.

however, there have been certain styles created which have been responsible for the development of the scene.

The Bobber

Being the "original choppers," these have their followers even in the era of high-performance bikes. Saws and angle-grinders to cut away everything superfluous from the machine are sufficient for this form of customizing. The distinction between bobbers and rat bikes is sometimes blurred. Function is preferred to form. For their part, bobbers trace their ancestry back to early race bikes. In the 1920s and 1930s it was not unusual to arrive at a weekend race meeting on your stock motorcycle, unscrew the saddlebags and fenders, and take it straight onto the track.

West Coast Chopper

The West Coast can be said with some certainty to be the birthplace of the chopper. The Flatheads and Panheads of the Swinging Sixties were equipped with high handlebars, a more or less comfortable bench seat – production Harleys had sprung saddles – and sissy bars. The most famous bike in the West Coast style has to be Billy's in "Easy Rider." Although it was not half as spectacular or colorful as Peter Fonda's Captain America chopper, there is to this day a large following for this style.

California Chopper

Although not clearly defined in style and engine, the expression "California chopper" was associated for a long time with the long-fork choppers that emerged from California to take over the world. Not only Harleys were chopped, but anything which had two or three wheels. Paint and metalwork in diverse forms and colors make further division or classification impossible.

Gooseneck Chopper

The gooseneck choppers were a rare and now almost extinct variant of the long-fork choppers. In this type, the curved tubes of the frame came together in front of the steering head and were then stretched, in a curve reminiscent of a swan's neck, to the

steering head, itself much further forward than it is in its conventional position. Apart from extremely strong tubes and good welding, this type needs above all careful craftsmanship. The leverage effect on the steering head is intensified by the gooseneck, meaning that on many of these interesting creations, the paint and filler tended to flake off.

The riding performance of the machines often also left something to be desired. Despite their grandeur it was always risky to ride a gooseneck.

Low Rider

Gliding along the streets in an extremely low sitting position with elongated lines – this is the typical Low-Rider style. Sportster engines are most likely to be found in the frames, positioned at an extremely low level above the ground. Perhaps the most radical Low Rider kit was produced by Magna Cycles: the supports for forks and swingarm were screwed directly into the engine, and the tank slid under the seat, so the rider looked directly onto the cylinder-heads. Any lower and they would be on the road.

Made in Europe: Swedish Choppers

Scandinavia in particular has developed a European chopper style, the characteristics being derived above all from the long-forked U.S. choppers of the 1970s.

The basic concept is: a rigid frame with thin, 21-inch front wheels balanced by the widest possible rear tires and long forks. The distinctive clean lines are achieved by putting the electrics and cables inside the handlebars and frame. The minimalism of the design is belied by the grandiose or luxuriously spoked wheels.

Frequently the front brakes are completely omitted. On the back wheel the rather heavy vehicle can be stopped by a combination of a disc brake and chain-wheel, otherwise known as the pinion brake. Despite their Spartan design, Swedish-style choppers are often used for touring, which has led to the rediscovery of the sissy bar as a luggage carrier. Instead of a sweeping airbrush painting, the real Swedish choppers make do with limited graphics and modest paintwork.

Peter Meets His Great Love

Choppers

Riding a chopper is a no-limits experience. The author closely followed his friend Peter's adventure:

It was one of those frustrating moments in life when I had to try to talk a good friend out of fulfilling his lifelong dream. It had begun many years before, when Peter suddenly had a close encounter of the third kind.

The extraterrestrial — later it was revealed as a 1969 XLH Sportster chopper with jammer forks — hopped about madly over the boulevards of balmy Florida, thankfully broad and empty, like a frog on speed, rattling and farting miserably like some clapped-out trader's cart. In short, it was something which demanded to be seen and listened to, confronted with which passerbys stood open-mouthed and swallowed only when the thing had disappeared with strange jumps into the distance. Peter was fascinated, to put it mildly. I must have one of those things in Germany, he thought. He had to make it happen. Just like that one! "Cut it out," I said, "it's not even safe to ride!" "What are you talking about," Peter called out after the extraterrestrial relic vanished, "it goes, doesn't it?" Naturally I had underestimated his

Bavarian stubbornness. He had fallen in love with the monstrosity, and it had obviously infected him with its limitless evil like a lightning strike in the heart. It was too late to help him. But as the saying goes, if you can't beat 'em, join 'em. Perhaps I should mention here that the thing had a large sign tied to it saying "4 Sale," which indicated to me that the owner of the bike intended to rip someone off. We found it again shortly afterwards in Doug's Cycle Heaven, frequented by a constant stream of the wildest-looking bikers. Doug shook his wise old head when he heard Peter's crazy idea.

But human ingenuity knows no bounds, he said, and of course a few details would have to be dealt with, the clutch for example, and the carburetor — or whatever that metal mass there was — would have to be adjusted. Doug is, however, a good friend of mine and so was careful not to jeopardize our friendship through a foul-play sale.

The upshot was that the repairs that needed to be done to the bike were going to take a while — a few days perhaps — and the price was not low, a fact which, in the sober light of day, unsettled me somewhat.

But sobriety was not called for since my buddy Peter was (metaphorically speaking) intoxicated with this technological absurdity, and he still is; the crazy machine has now passed a probationary period of several years of long journeys without so much as a hitch. Peter is one of the hard-core, Bavarian chopper cowboys who make life as difficult as possible for themselves in order to be able to enjoy it fully, no doubt about it.

So we dragged the thing back to my house in Mississippi, with the front wheel and forks hanging a good yard out of the back of the van, and with a red rag tied to them as a warning to other people on the road. But it worked, and thanks to Doug's careful maintenance it started on the first click.

Then Peter began to set himself up in the U.S., an important prerequisite if he was to be able to ride the wild heap of junk in its native habitat. My children had fun starting it now and then, which brought the otherwise mild-natured neighbors filing out of the house, but no one has actually ridden it apart from Peter.

Bo, our chief mechanic, once tried it, but after a few yards gave up in disgust,

and put the monster back in the garage. "That ain't no motorbike," he said, still shaking, "that's a hired killer...." Finally the "killer" was packed into a container, and I really hoped against hope never to see it again. I had already said farewell to Peter forever.

Well, even I can be wrong sometimes, thank God — Peter and his Sportster chopper are still alive and well. No broken back, no dislocated shoulders, no vibration white finger, no lame kicking-leg — and the critter just seems to keeps on runnin'.

There are some things in life which you just don't understand, and for my part I believe more and more in the sinister visitation of that weird kind which honors us with visits from other planets. Who knows? By the way, Peter works for German NASA in the Space Control Center in Oberpfaffenhofen (Institute for Air and Space Travel). That explains a lot.

Does she run? After having been repaired in Doug's Shop, the Sportster is a very safe motorcycle on the road.

Full Dressers

The Beauties of the Custom Scene

© Harley-Davidson

Modern Technology in Nostalgic Guise: Classic Customs

The idea of bringing an ancient model back to life incorporating the most modern (and well hidden) technology is hardly new. The vital elements are the rectangular, gas tank, a round headlight, springer forks (which have again been introduced by Harley), classic fenders, wide handlebars, and above all a rigid (or at least rigid-*looking*) trapezium frame, unsprung without shock absorbers, and of course a stylish leather saddle. Additionally, the bike should be equipped with modern brakes and a maintenance free, high-tech motor: an Evo will do at a pinch. A high-class paint job, perhaps a grand sidecar, and a few nostalgic accessories complete the old-timer look. But nowadays nostalgia bikes should employ up-to-date riding technology and make some concessions to modern standards of riding comfort.

In its design, the Chaplin is not so far removed from the modern Harley range. The company XZOTIC Cycle Products, for example, builds Harleys that are astonishingly similar to an Indian Chief, but which are in fact kitted out with a modern Evo engine. The latest novelty from XZOTIC is an Evo Knucklehead copy of the classic, prewar, EL model. Vintage Cycle Works in California has concentrated on the style of 1918, also with Evo motors, and even offers a conversion kit for standard Harleys. Alongside this, some specialists have devoted time and effort to copying parts now out of production which can no longer be found: Andres Nygren Motor in Delsbo, Sweden, for example, makes parts for flathead V-twins and Knucklehead motors. The Milwaukee Iron Team from Lynchburg, Virginia, have also become well-known through their stylish copies of the big V-twins of the 1920s.

They flash their lights and sound their horns, and the rock 'n' roll soundtrack blares out to riders and spectators alike from well-placed loudspeakers while the gigantic machines roll slowly down Main Street: seeing a Full Dresser in action is definitely areal event. Heading: The Beauties of the Custom Scene

The chrome- and accessory-laden bikes have become even more in vogue on the Harley scene. The Japanese manufacturers have tried to encroach on the Harley scene, but naturally the hum of the six-cylinder Gold Wing engine does not shake the lights in the same way.

A direct continuation of the "official" Harley philosophy, the origins of the Dressers lie in the Harley accessory catalogs of the 1940s, 1950s, and 1960s: in those days the club activities of the precursors to the H.O.G. also covered "beauty contests" for the best-styled Dressers — riders and clubs were awarded points for the best clothing and equipment. In the old days colorful lights, stereo radios, CB and chrome held sway, nowadays the trend is to high-tech quadrophonic speakers, onboard computers, mobile phones and neon lighting that create a style which can hardly be ignored, even in the hurly-burly of the main streets of Sturgis and Daytona Beach. Although Full Dressers are at the opposite extreme of the custom scene to choppers, they have peacefully coexisted for many years. Both have also been prematurely declared dead many times over.

The wildest creations are to be seen at the Dresser Light Shows, organized by Harley-Davidson — then the darkest night becomes like day. Full Dressers have been joined in recent years by streamliners and high-tech tourers, which stress performance and elegant, voluptuous forms. But never fear: there will always be Full Dressers too. Dinosaurs have got a lot of spunk.

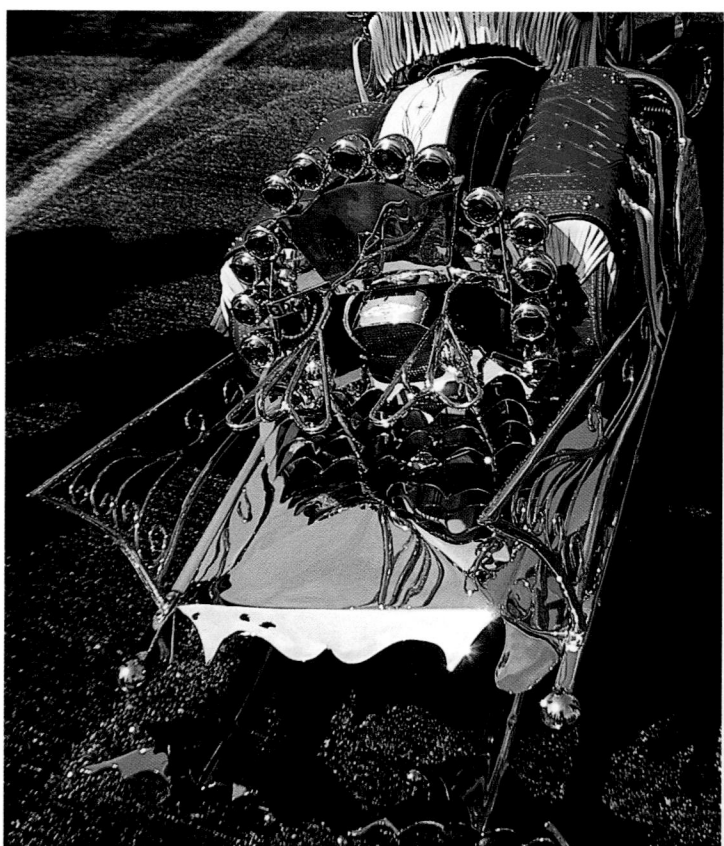

This "modest" mobile home (above) offers a substantial area for humorous decoration.

Art or kitsch, that is the question, but the Full Dressers for their part need massive batteries and outsize dynamos for their shining presence. Chrome blinds the eye by day, circus-like illumination by night.

The Customized Harley

Anything Goes – Customizing in the Next Millennium

A Look at the Different Styles

What makes a bike a *custom bike*? If all that counts is the name, every motorcycle is a "custom bike" in that every two-wheeler represents the realizations of the dreams of the owner. It is also indisputable that almost every rider adds something to it to make it more personal. Nevertheless, it's above all the Harley V–twins and attempted imitations of them that truly embody the concept of custom bike. Even a bike from the conveyor belt is, for most Harley enthusiasts, quite simply a custom bike *par excellence* which, as far as the trade in America goes, has great importance: in the U.S. the new owner can have his or her Harley assembled to personal taste using the general accessories catalog. In the rest of the world, this role is taken over by the official (and unofficial) dealer who assembles genuine Harley parts; if the buyers prefer, they can choose from the thousands of custom parts best suited to their individual likes and dislikes. Th idea was "just bolt on and ride away."

It's far more difficult to obtain special paintwork. The design should cover the whole bike, and there are very few Harley owners who at first know just how much work will actually be involved in stripping a motorcycle's bodywork completely, sanding it, then repainting it. Those who have tried have great respect for bikers who've actually done it.

The next step custom bikers take is to design their own parts and fit them. A start can be made with something small like a tank dash or a twin seat; the next could be an improvement to the engine or the frame. But it needn't stop there. Sometimes DIY customizers may not realize what they have actually taken on until they begin putting things back together again; as a result, a custom bike that can really be considered a masterpiece may take up to four to five years of their time. In sum: as was said earlier, every motorcycle is by definition a custom bike. This is particularly true when the bike's owners have invested several hundred hours in completing their masterpieces. At that point, it no longer matters whether it is a cafe racer, a chopper, a cruiser, a full dresser, a dragster or a streetfighter – "It's custom made, babe!"

Until the mid–1960s there was only a relatively small group of outlaws or DIY custom bikers, mostly to be found along the West Coast. The film "Easy Rider" brought them worldwide publicity. No other biker film had been such a source of inspiration to so many young people all over the world as this film dealing with the journey made by two hippie drug dealers from Los Angeles to New Orleans.

While it's true that choppers were not unknown at this time in Europe, the only mouthpiece for motorcyclists existing at that time hardly mentioned them – and if they did it was to ridicule or condemn them. For example, writing in the December 1965 issue of *The Motorcycle* the professional rider "Klacks" described a Revell plastic model of a chopper as a "Harley for madmen."

A number of magazines that started to appear during the early 1970s, such as *Chopper* and *Easyriders*, made a considerable contribution to advance the case for customizing. Motorcycling had not only been rediscovered as an ideal hobby; the motorcycle was now also being treated as a work of art and as a source of self-expression. These newly discovered possibilities opened up a vast market for chopper accessories, and in 1971 the FX Super Glide became the very first custom bike trendsetter for Harley-Davidson.

Customizing became increasingly popular during the 1970s. But it was only at the start of the 1980s that Japanese manufacturers started to recognize the enormous marketing potential created by those motorcyclists wanting to ride along the endless American roads leaning back comfortably relaxed on their bikes. It was above all the Japanese with their one-, two- and four-cylinder machines who exploited the craze for soft choppers simply by flooding the motorcycle market with bikes that had the outward appearance of real choppers because of their raised handlebars, a twin seat, and external embellishments. Only an advertising campaign could convey the message of "Easy Rider" to a mass market. The really hard-core, chopper

enthusiast, on the other hand, had to rely on imported parts or build his chopper himself, and even had to fight every step of the way for official licensing of his machine as roadworthy.

Although companies such as AME in Germany and Senn in Switzerland were able to achieve a great deal in the early stages, true choppers were exceedingly rare in Europe. The genuine rigid frame was to be seen only on bikes belonging to GIs stationed in West Germany or at biker meets in Great Britain. It was in the year 1979 that the Hell's Angels organized their first Kent Custom Bike Show in England and in so doing founded one of the traditional biker events.

During this time bikers in other European countries had already started to form branches of U.S. clubs or had even established their own "colors," but it took some time for the V-twin from Milwaukee to become the predominant means of transport: this was, above all, for financial reasons because Harleys were, after all, an almost unaffordable luxury.

In the 1980s the chopper joined Sportsters, touring bikes, and offroaders as another equally acceptable means of transport, and as a result of the introduction of the Evolution engines Harley-Davidson drew everyone's attention to their large capacity V-twins. Without doubt it was this that lead to the long-awaited success.

Almost overnight it became fashionable to travel around on two wheels: Harley-Davidson suddenly gained a new reputation and a luxurious custom bike soon came to be seen as a status symbol. Slow and steady victories – even in the battle with the authorities who govern harmonization – and European unification did the rest. All of a sudden there were no laws against riding motorcycles that were previously only dreamt about. With their typical extended forks, the motorcycles are winning more and more ground, including in such countries as Germany and Switzerland, and not just with people in the top income bracket.

Apart from the extreme creations of Arlen Ness, milder custom bikes, calculated to grab attention through their understated paintwork (right) or their carefully determined styling (opposite) are proundly shown off by their owners, and still make a mark even next to more exotic machines. A moderately customized Harley with a lot of shining chrome (below).

Courtesy of: Michelle Ethier, Canada

Taildraggers

It may seem that naming a family of bikes after a fender is overdoing it, but most "taildraggers" could also be considered low riders. The magic of an experienced and highly imaginative customizer like Arlen Ness was needed to create a fender that ended up giving its name to an entire style. This San Leandro artist found it a simple task in the 1990s to create a fender that almost brushes the ground.

Whether it's the original or a copy, the taildragger has friends all over the world, particularly among vehicle registration officials, who will not find anything to object to here. Apart from providing the rider with protection against spray, the taildragger provides the paint artists with more than enough space to show their individual creativity. This is one reason why the taildragger is becoming more and more popular all over the world.

Streamliner/Lead Sled

What else can an owner do, if the forks can't be stretched any more, or if the frame already brushes the ground, and if the rear wheel is so wide that your bike doesn't even need a stand? What about fairings? There have been countless experiments in enclosing a bike completely in a fairing; and by the mid-1990s even the real custom biker had discovered the integrated, stretched metal streamlining that looked so elegant on luxurious, prewar limousines.

Customizers like Bob Lowe, Bob Dron, Pete Chapouris and of course Arlen Ness, don't spare any effort when it comes to incorporating decorative aluminum or plastic fairings into their bike designs. The really important trends have been set by bikes such as HogZZilla owned by the ZZ Top lead guitarist Billy Gibbons and by Arlen Ness' Nesstalgia: this trend has been taken up by European customizers such as the French designer François Bruère. It is with some justification that the Americans have affectionately christened these streamliners "lead sleds," and they are very reminiscent of the heavy automobiles that originally inspired them.

Chevrolets, Fords, AC Cobras, Ferraris and Bugattis can be found beaten out of a single sheet of metal. Of course, it is no easy task actually to ride one of these bikes as though it were a "normal" vehicle for everyday use on the road.

A Streamliner/Lead Sled.

Custom bike in Indian style.

Harley Trikes

Some of the very first forms of motorcycle rolled on three wheels, De Dion Bouton's tricycle showing the way. But later developments moved firmly to two wheels, a third wheel being present only in the form of a sidecar. Not until the 1930s did Harley once again take up the idea of a three-wheeler in the form of the Servi-Car. The vehicle was intended to be a boon to police officers, especially when writing parking tickets, but garages too made use of the mobile Servi-Car in order to attract customers and collect their cars for service.

The trikes didn't achieve cult status until after World War II, and long after the dressers, choppers, and bobbers had appeared. Originally a development of the hotrod scene, it was above all in California that the most bizarre creations were ridden. Big Daddy Roth's *Choppers* magazine was brimful of the crazy, three-wheeled monsters with long forks and the most varied, motor types.

Classic Style/Indian Style

"Back to your roots" is the motto of many a Harley enthusiast, and this touch of nostalgia is to be found more and more in recent models: it's also the latest fashion for paintwork to be more subdued, more classic. What are the most typical features of the "classic look?" The hallmarks are big leather saddlebags with fringes, lots of chrome, toolboxes, crash bars, touring windshields, and sprung saddles. There is now even a hint of nostalgia in the way a stock Harley- Davidson actually looks, and so the official Harley-Davidson accessories program, as well as a huge number of aftermarket suppliers, are willing to provide the most suitable item to ensure that even the very latest Evolution Big Twin will be indistinguishable from a Panhead and Knucklehead. A particularly attractive example of the classic look is to be seen in the Indian style. Even though Harley-Davidson's arch-rival in Springfield, Massachusetts was forced to close down in 1953, the large displacement Indians have sacrificed none of their reputation. The distinguishing features of the Indian V-twin during the 1940s and later were the swooping rear and front fenders that made them seem different in appearance from their competitors. But this was a costly look to achieve, and for a time it went the same way as the Indian itself. But the constant search for ways of giving a motorcycle just that bit of a retro touch did not stop at old designs: anything that looked good in those days can be used today as well. Once more there are enormous fenders, though now made of reinforced fiberglass plastic or aluminum. Today these machines are destined for the Big Twins from Milwaukee, which are transformed into machines that remind their riders of what it was like to be a biker all those years ago. That is a clear line of descent to the streamliner or taildragger is indisputable and frequently intentional.

Trike with rear-mounted Harley engine.

The Bike as a Work of Art

When customizing was still in its infancy, one of the grim facts of life was that the customizer had to make all the parts himself. But today that's all changed: a well-managed accessories store normally has whatever is required already in stock. There are new materials and tools available to put even the most outlandish designs into practice without having to compromise on reliability. In the early days customizing meant that every chopper was a unique work of art on two wheels. As a matter of fact, this eccentric breed of biker still exists: they are still prepared to invest a great deal. Terry Evans was justly famed for his Dragon Heads, some of which could even belch

forth flames with the help of a gas torch. Since then there have been many master sculptors who have inscribed their names in the annals of custom bike history: Arlen Ness, Ron Simms, Donnie Smith, Dave Perewitz, Pat Kennedy, Cyril Huze, Bob Dron, Rick Doss, Harold Mutter, John Reed, and Don Hotop are just a few of the famous names in customizing. Again, it's often a quite ordinary person who has generated a new idea; these are the unknown customizing artists who invest their entire creative genius in "their own, their very own" customized Harley. It's artists such as these who breathe life into customizing. Hopefully this will continue for many, many years.

Skip Hoagland's theme: the Coca Cola Bike.

Street dragster by Harold Mutter: note the aluminum rocker arm.

The Street Dragster

This type has already been described in the section on performance bikes; nevertheless, it deserves to be mentioned again. It's no longer unusual to use a custom bike for racing. Both in the U.S. and in Europe you can now see bikes racing over the quarter mile that a few years ago would have attracted attention at bike shows. Today this distance demands so much from rider and machine that the tires start to smoke in protest at their punishment. The nitro charger, the compressor, and the ever popular aerocharger, inject so much power

into even a standard bike that it is by no means unusual for track records to be broken impressively. Despite all the remarks that the only thing to be said of a Harley is that it's fine as long as it's on a long straight road, this is where they can teach even the Japanese a thing or two! There is another craze emerging: home-modified, Top Gas and Top Fuel dragsters look so flawless and technically perfect nowadays that they could easily join the others on the winner's rostrum at any bike show — but that's another story.

The 148-cubic-inch Double Twin by Mike Roach.

The Café Racer/Warbird

It was in 1977 that Harley-Davidson attempted to capture the Café Racer market with their XLCR. It had been around for almost 13 years, though once again a trend had quite simply not been followed. Moreover, the machine, developed from the 61 cubic inch Sportster, weighed just a little too much for a supersportster with the type of multi-cylinder engine popular at this point in the 1970s. So it was that the 1990s

gave a warm welcome to the Café Racer on its return, just as had been given to the naked bike and the softchopper now reborn as the cruiser. The "heap of scrap" which at one time was ignored and had few friends became transformed into a cult object, and new Café Racer imitations are now making the bikers' world more interesting for all concerned.The seat makers Corbin are famous for their expensive

Warbird of the Cafe-Racer type.

leather seats, which have been combined with the Warbird kit to create a unique style well suited to the Café Racer. Ron Simms of Bay Area Customs designed the kit consisting of a seat, tank, spoiler, fender, and small, aerodynamic fairing. This kit was at first used to improve the appearance of the FXR models and then later the Sporties, transforming them into true Warbirds.

Multi-Engine

Usually, a Harley-Davidson motorcycle running on anything more than two cylinders is something looked on with disdain by bikers: not even the four-cylinder prototype developed during the 1960s was able to change this attitude. There is one exception, however: if they are Harley-Davidson cylinders. There are one or two real enthusiasts and DIY bikers around who have done extraordinary things: there is a V three-cylinder machine with an additional cylinder, flange-mounted at an angle of 45 degrees that projects to the front; and there are also engines with coupled, V-4 crankcases, two or

even three in series. Some customizers may find it difficult to get an engine to run smoothly: but there are a few DIY bikers who believe you can never have enough cyclinders running in series. As expected, most engines running on combined power were first seen in drag racing. This was in strict adherence to the principle that "four cylinders can produce more power than two," and so it was a case of not just combining Harley twins into enormously powerful engines. The real source of inspiration were the speed fans in Bonneville, where the record-breakers would congregate once a year for their Speedweek.

Red Dragon versus Yellow Beast

Design Against Function

The yellow beast with the gridded-steel fuel-tank console, integrated control lamps and striking tail (above. The "Red Dragon" and its fantastically styled artistic details (above, left).

As far as Andreas Winters is concerned, it's always a question of taking the right philosophical attitude towards technology; for Horst Gall, on the other hand, it is a question of finding the right technical approach to express a particular philosophy. Both revealed their different approaches in the form of diametrically opposed motorcycle designs: Andreas designed his Red Dragon in terms of certain abstract ideals; Horst built his Yellow Beast according to more functional principles.

Both the customized Harleys are works of art as well as technical masterpieces: they are beautiful to look at and are certainly meant to be taken out on the road. Both are expressions of the American dream of freedom, here expressed in the individual's personal interpretation of technical progress.

Horst Gall constructs a motorcycle as an example of technical innovation — in a country that demands an official certificate of approval for each new washer. Andreas found his inspiration for his Red Dragon in many

different sources, and it's packed with an enormous number of striking refinements that occurred to him while he was working on the bike. Sometimes he finds a fascinating part he uses simply because his instinct tells him it is just right. Horst Gall is no different: he also incorporates a number of components available direct from the parts industry; but usually he designs the most important ones himself.

One of Horst Gall's main aims was to prove that the old Panhead engine, which is, in his opinion, the best one ever made by Harley, could be tuned in such a way that it would be no different to a modern high-tech one without sacrificing one iota of its classic design. Every single step he was to take would have this aim in mind. Both his 1958 Panhead as well as the 1973 Shovelhead engine of Andreas Winters have been completely rebuilt to perfection. The essential concern is to create a tangible expression of one's personal philosophy.

High Performance

Getting the Best from a Harley

High performance: the meaning and implications of these two words are clear to the Harley enthusiast. The history of the Harley-Davidson offers numerous examples of high performance bikes that created quite a sensation, both sports bikes and stock bikes. It was in 1914 that Harley produced the first 8-valve V-twin in Milwaukee as an answer to the Indian 8-valve engine that had been on the market since 1911. It is important to remember that Harley production models which were manufactured until the 1990s ran with only two valves per cylinder, so this particular engine was in all probability the first high-performance Harley.

The single-cylinder Peashooter continued this tradition in the 1920s and 1930s. Joe Petrali won every single AMA dirttrack race during the 1935 season. Harley also established a speed record with the newly developed Knucklehead engine on Daytona Beach. After the war the KR racing machines and later the XR dirttrack racers continued the tradition of high-performance motorcycles. In 1962 the descriptive literature for the Topper scooter laid emphasis on the "high-performance" features of the scooter symbolizes the importance that Harley-Davidson attached to this term.

In the 1990s high performance is a phrase representing the uncompromising dedication to boosting the performance of street bikes, and the last few years of the 1990s witnessed a totally unexpected renaissance of the V-twin as a motorcycle engine. The boom that spawned the international market for accessories and for special tuning started in the Harley drag-bike world and lead to the production of countless accessories for improving performance. In fact, nowadays a Harley will not have a single component or accessory on it that could not be replaced with a corresponding high-performance one.

Improvements might start with the smallest screw, then continue with the engine innards and housing, then move on to the fork, the swingarm and the frame, until the owner has a completely rebuilt performance bike: anything is possible. In the U.S. there are well over a dozen firms which to a great extent concentrate on the manufacture of V-twins bearing a strong resemblance to a Harley, and often their performance is considerably better than that of the original.

It's the quality of the production engine that they start off with that makes everything far easier for the performance freaks to tinker until performance is boosted to what they want. The philosophy of the Evolution engine can be traced right back to the origins of engine construction at the start of the century: two cylinders, a single crankpin for the two pistons, two pushrod operating valves with lowered camshaft.

This makes it even more of a challenge to enhance the performance of a production engine designed more with infinite reliability in mind, let alone to improve the strength of frame or reduce the overall weight of the motorcycle. All over the world people are turning their skills to improving the appearance and performance of the V-twins, and hardly a week goes by without new developments. It is almost impossible to determine which parts have had the most influence.

But higher performance in the motorcycle engine is not everything, as most friends of the Harley have come to realize, and so more and more privately designed and developed frames and gearboxes are becoming available. People who do not know any better say that the high-performance bozos are trying to elevate their bikes to the same standard of performance as Japanese sports bikes already offer; but that is only half of the story. The Harley-Davidson stock production engine has tremendous potential, and to develop it requires a great deal of time, effort, and skill — and almost anything is possible, as the results show!

Still shining even after the sun has gone down (right). Harleys in suits of chrome.

Drilled disk brakes to hold back heavy horespower (right). Subtle and smart, a chrome rectangular side light (far right).

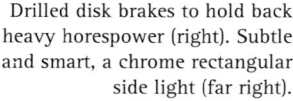

Simple five spokes and a lick of flame (above). The Harley in traditional hot rod styling. High-performance Harley engines can be recognized externally by the extreme-looking carburetors or the particularly complex ignition systems, instances of technical finesse which must remain a closed book to the casual onlooker. Now and then, however, the manufacturers exhibit cutaway models of high-performance parts, as in the case of this Shovelhead motor at the Indianapolis Dealer Show, 1998 (right and far right).

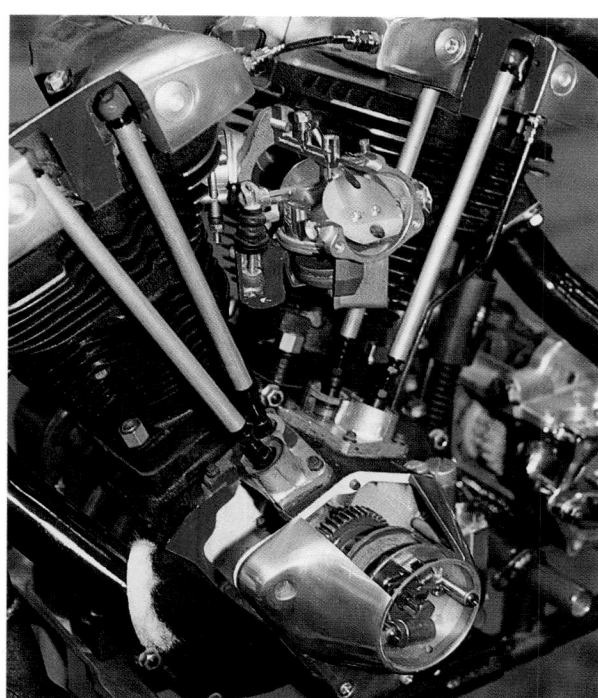

Rat Bikes

The "Rat" of the German Willi Millers made it to the beach of Daytona (above). The famous "archrat": Smitty on his knucklehead of 1949

The so-called rats may not be the last word in design, but they can hardly be overlooked, and at shows they always draw looks of astonished admiration.

What is a rat bike? Americans have known for a long time: it's a workaday, two dollar, DIY bike. And that's how it looks: corroded, rusty, patched up and covered in war wounds; it's had every superfluous item removed, been repaired a thousand times and screwed or welded back together; it's without a trace of chrome or paint, but with grease and dirt finger-deep, and everywhere it has fine, copper wires sprouting from split cables ... in short, a mobile pile of junk.

A symbol of a distinctive way of looking at the world, a rat bike is usually a long-distance motorcycle with countless hours of hard cross-country riding behind it. Stickers like "Don't laugh — it's paid for" or "I know what you're thinking, but it goes" and "Just don't look" are a better indication of the philosophy of these scrap bikes than any fine piece of writing.

Rat bikers have to suffer a good deal of public harassment, their "anti-social motor vehicles" being the subject of disdain of every tidy minded, law-loving sheriff, meaning that the chances of getting a ticket on a rat bike are disproportionately greater than on any other type of motorcycle.

The fact that there are so many Harleys among the rat bikes was for a time a cause of some embarrassment to the company, which always had an eye on its upmarket image. Rat bike owners, however, see it quite differently: "A motorcycle which can be neglected in this way and which after years and years still reliably gets you from one place to another is a quality machine." They usually add patriotically:

"And it's American made." It's true that no other bikes can be ridden so well in such a poor state as the good old Harleys — two-wheeled tractors which can handle rust and dirt galore, bloody but unbowed, and utterly reliable. "They should be proud of us, the bosses," says one wreck's stubbly owner. The rat bike phenomenon is reminiscent of the Far East, where such ancient models are indeed still ridden today, in all imaginable, and quite a few unimaginable, variants.

Just how popular rat bikes are is shown by the fact that the Rat Class is rewarded with particularly high value prizes at nearly every local, national, and international motorcycle show.

The judges are very strict: they want to know if anything has been washed or cleaned, whether the requisite number of screws are loose, whether all-purpose wire is holding anything together, whether dirt and oil are to be found in sufficient quantity in all the most important places, and finally whether the paintwork is flaking and the chrome has turned to rust. The contestant with the most minus points wins.

Nowadays rat bikes have become thoroughbred exhibits, the centerpiece of every bike and custom show, and are even put under glass now and then among the glitzy chrome and lurid spotlights of the Essen Motorshow in Germany.

A confused visitor once asked at a show, "How can you let a motorcycle get into that state?" The beaming owner proudly answered: "Look at it from the human point of view mister — would you bump your wife off just because she's getting old?"

Under It All, It's Just a Rat

Report on the Legendary U.S. Rat Bike Competition

It had to happen some time. People who've made a stink at parties and shows in quite such a ratty fashion as Smitty or as grungily as Jim, winning cups and sparking enthusiasm as they go, are certain to be hit by the bug for head-to-head combat at some time or other – an old American tradition, in fact; "High Noon" for bikes, one could say. Who is the filthiest pig, the dirtiest rat? Some time that question is going to have to be settled.

Now, you should know that the men dueling know each other from way back when and became good friends long ago. A complicating factor is that both men come from Kentucky, that wild state in the heart of the nation where endless fields of wheat and endlessly flowing whiskey have their home. You don't just punch each other over there, no sir – even the dueling weapons are not the usual kind, like a punch in the eye versus a kick in the shins, but instead, rat bikes. The motto could have come from a fairy tale: "Mirror, mirror on the wall, who's the rattiest of them all?"

At the end of the day, the fatal challenge was issued by a crafty organizer at Daytona Bike Week, when he called on all the rats in the country to follow him and take part in the grand contest. There were a few nice prizes and even 300 bucks in cash. All right, this might have sounded good, but only two people came, and they were so monstrous in their notorious rattiness that naturally no one else had the guts to compete against them. The result would only have been sneers and those you can do without – these two matadors were unbeatable anyway. The audience assembled expectantly, and the umpire, a massive authority by the name of Wizzard, whose home was, thank God, in faraway Rochester, New Hampshire (you know, in the top right-hand corner), was man enough to get things going like they should.

"Oyez," he cried, "here's Smitty from Flatlick in Kentucky and here's Junky Jim Fisher from Louisville, also in Kentucky" (applause, applause!) Then he scratched his head. It wasn't quite as easy as he'd imagined after all. So Wizzard's stooping frame slunk groaning and wheezing over to the rats,

if you can describe his bear-like tramp as slinking and he mumbled incomprehensible curses into his beard. "Louder, louder!" the audience cried, and Smitty and Jim grinned in unison. "Hey," Wizzard grunted in irritation, letting rip an outrageous noise to underline his anger, "there's nothing else for it – there has to be a cross-examination!" The two duelists suddenly lost their grins, and the audience drew back respectfully: there was an intense odor of rat. That's the way the law wants it!

"So," umpire Wizzard boomed, "what about traffic safety?" Smitty began to explain calmly and lucidly: "I got a lucky rabbit's foot, that always helps!" (voices from the audience: "true, true!"). Wizzard shook his head thoughtfully. Not the best of starts, but you can't really say anything against a rabbit's foot. "What else?" "Well," said Smitty, "the cow bell!" – "Boo!" people shouted. "Refused," decided Wizzard, "cow bells are confusin'!"

"I got a siren," crowed Jim, letting the instrument wail out. The audience wailed too. "Stop!" yelled Smitty: "Sirens are illegal in Kentucky under paragraph 286, section 16, of the state road traffic ordinances, subsection 291!" Not much could be said against that. "And then I got my anchor," Jim added a little meekly. "Stop!" screamed Smitty: "Anchors are illegal for motorcycles in Kentucky, according to paragraph...." The rest was lost in general hilarity. "A lawyer's mind, a smart guy, Smitty." So it had once again come to nothing. "And then I got the horn," mumbled Jim, and gave it a honk. It sounded horrible. "All right," decided Wizzard, "the horn counts. It's one-nil to Jim!

"Put your lights on!" Wizzard said. Smitty vainly tried his damnedest with a beautiful scrap-metal pocket flashlight, which failed to light up because there was no battery in it, excusing himself on the basis that he only ever rode during the day since at night he was always blind drunk. Junky Jim, on the other hand, displayed a pyrotechnic wonder, flicking on a host of switches and levers. The bike lit up and lights shone from even the most out-of-the-way nooks and crannies. Rat eyes magically came alive and small

fireworks exploded with cute little bangs. The audience freaked out quietly, but it was enough for another victory for Jim with Judge Wizzard.

"But," he bellowed, "what about emergency equipment, huh?"

The two rattled it off: "Chains of every kind, instamatic pocket camera, an alarm with a two-bell clockwork...." Smitty cried, only to be interrupted by Jim: "Ball of twine..." "Stop!" cried Smitty, "that doesn't count, there's no twine left on it!" "But I got an empty beer can and a reflex camera, too!"

Well, it went on like that for a good while, until the local reporter from the *Daily Dung* was unable to follow it any longer and put an end to the racket. Wizzard decided wisely: "Jim wins. The beer can is, as we all know, the most important piece of emergency equipment if you're stranded somewhere. All in all, three-nil to Jim." The audience grumbled dully; Flatlick hadn't fallen yet.

"Repair kit," droned Wizzard, "what about that?" Smitty laughed dismissively. "I don't need it, I don't have accidents!" The audience slapped their thighs with delight: "That's the way, Smitty, tell it like it is, let 'im have it!" And then he came out with it. He had a ladle, a boat-line and a candlewick still in usable condition, although a bit damp, since, as he said, he didn't need it. "That's for idiots." Jim turned red. "Something for an idiot? What's that good for?" he exclaimed and ripped the trowel out of the sleeping bag – and the adhesive strip (slightly used) holding it together. "Rat's piss," said Smitty, spitting his chew tobacco on Jim's saddle. Wizzard was suffering from lack of evidence, and in such cases the people's voice is law. Thus it was Smitty who got the plus point this time – that's the way blind justice goes.

"Shuddup!" he cried out in order to silence the few voices of protest, "we've reached the patriotic elements. Well?" Smitty drew attention to the innumerable badges, buttons, awards, medals and all the tinkling junk he had collected from the various veterans' parades he had attended. All of it first-class patriot jewelry! And he had handcuffs too, they kind of went along with everything, didn't they? Jim countered skillfully:

"Yeah? And my true American values? Mickey Mouse, genuine plastic, three and a half inches high, Cabbage Patch Kid, life-size, and the rebel flag...." "Stop!" cried Smitty again: "The rebel flag don't count – Kentucky was never with the rebels!" At this the audience screamed and howled. The Yankees were in danger of being beaten up. "Quiet!" bellowed Wizzard, scratching his behind, and impatient with all these politics! "Jim is the winner. Mickey Mouse must be unbeatable!"

Things looked bad for Smitty. Jim now had a secure lead of four to one, yet he (Smitty) was the one who had won every kick-start contest with 59 starts a minute. And now this ignominy! "These judges are all corrupt!" he yelled, which was hardly the best thing to do, since a judge is a judge, corrupt or not. Wizzard knitted his brow darkly: "The final test," he announced portentously: "How about the sanitary equipment?" Help, sanitary officer Dibble! Smiling mildly, Smitty produced a limp, instantly recognizable object from the toolbox and held it up triumphantly.

"Aaaah!" the audience murmured reverently, "a rubber, a party popper, how elegant!" The dirty band-aid stuck to the tank ready to be used again wasn't even in the running against this. And Jim, who sullenly unraveled his seemingly endless roll of Andrex, wasn't either. "Four to two," decided Wizzard, Solomon-like, and thrust Jim, who actually had a junk bike and not a rat bike, the trophy helmet with the already stinking rat on top. And 300 bucks, which Jim stowed away grinning.

For Smitty on the other hand there was a nice sign which he attached to his rat bike, soon to look rather less golden and shiny. "To hell with it!" cried the people, and then the two embraced and threw on their leathers to ride over to the next pub, celebrate Kentucky-style, and blow the prize money.

The onlookers stood gaping like idiots when the two disappeared cackling derisively. All that talk about a contest – what garbage. As if they weren't both unique, anyhow.

Jim's Cockpit: Here's how a real cockpit must look and Smitty's emergency equipment complete with a new (or almost new) alarm clock.

Designs I

Arts and Crafts Engineers

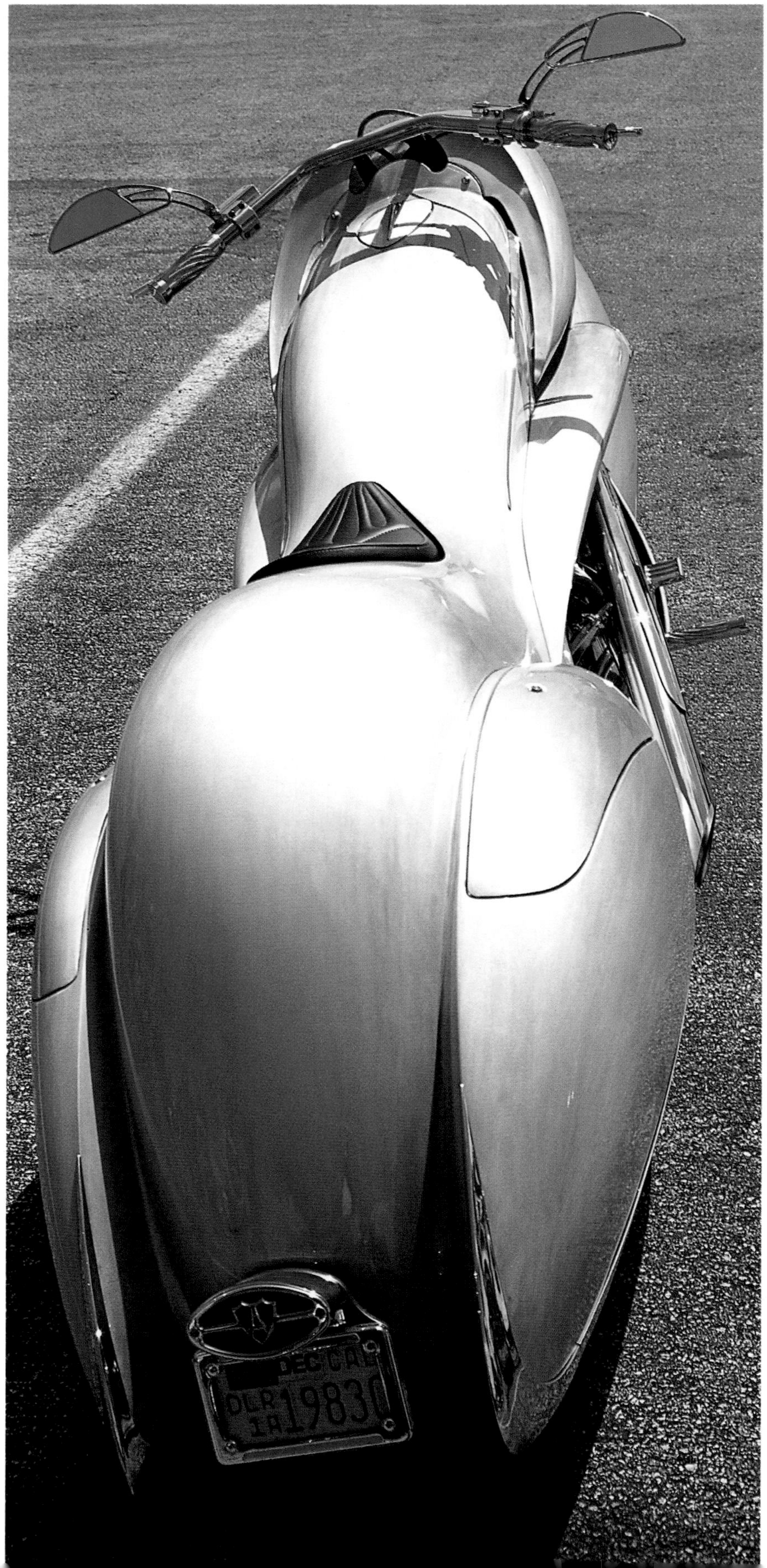

Trends are not designed; they are, at best, emulated. They develop in the strangest ways and under the most diverse influences, with media such as films and magazines sometimes playing an important role. But no one knows where or why the first bobber (long before World War II), the first chopper or the first low rider came into being or who built them.

The accessory industry reacts the quickest to such trends, though perhaps the term "industry" is a misnomer. Generally it was individual, small manufacturers, amateur mechanics, engineers, workshops or even talented inventors who produced the desired parts: long forks, small or square tanks, altered frames, headlights and taillights, fenders, mirrors, dashes and so on.

But there were also a few people who wanted more than to put together custom bikes (as the conversions became known) out of the most motley accessories of the aftermarket. They wanted to develop a completely independent, often highly personal product; to create, in fact, a complete work of art. In this way, various styles developed. These custom stylists, now called designers, were able to exhibit their creations to a mass audience — mainly at the Rat's Hole Custom Chopper Show in Daytona and at the well-known, trendsetting, Oakland Bike Show in California.

Specialist magazines heard about it and some custom bikes sold like hot cakes. On the other hand, others were total flops. If certain creations became popular with the audience of enthusiasts, a new style would emerge and their creators became trendsetters; they were showered with contracts and their designs were immediately copied. Some designers moved from one extreme to the other, some remained faithful to a particular style, and some allowed themselves to be headhunted by Harley-Davidson.

Speaking of Harley-Davidson, the company jumped on the bandwagon late, but all the more enthusiastically for that, though it wasn't Harley-Davidson's bandwagon and it was already cruising along at full speed. The company even attempted to copyright names such as 'Fat Bob' and 'Low Rider.' However, most custom expressions were born out of the amusing idioms of the scene and not thought up by clever advertising agencies. But let's get back to the designers. A few trendsetters will be briefly described:

One of the latest creations of Californian "Custom Godfather" Arlen Ness: the "Smooth-Ness."

Arlen Ness, sometimes called the "International Pope of Custom," is the undisputed, highest authority in matters concerning customized Harleys. In the 1960s he was still working as a removal man, but even then custom bikes and special paintwork effects were his hobby. In 1967 his old Knucklehead, which he had jazzed up into a showbike, won First Place in the San Francisco Bike Show. Through hard work he eventually managed to set up his own shop for motorcycles and accessories. Among his early designs, the pullback handlebars were a big success, and his stocky Low Riders in the aggressive Bay Area style brought his stylistic ideas to the attention of magazines and quickly made him famous in the custom bike world. He prefers team effort, working closely with various designers and firms, for example Drag Specialties; he sells his accessories and parts worldwide through a 200 page catalog. His son Cory is now general manager of Arlen Ness. In an

industrial site covering over 160,000 square feet, the wildest Harley conversions are produced in line with the old Arlen Ness tradition. His partiality for strong motors finds expression in the preferred drag style or through the use of turbochargers or Magnusson compressors, with his prime concern being absolute, technical perfection.

Well-known Arlen Ness creations include: Ferrari Bike; Twobad; Twin Sportster; Nesstalgia; Sled "Convertible Concept," with interchangeable custom parts; Luxury Liner; Hulkster; Flamin' Ape; Smooth Ness; Metzeler Dyno; and Drag Ness.

The Hamsters MC isn't actually a motorcycle club, but rather an organization which grew out of the happy coming together of some well-known custom designers in 1978, among them Donny Smith, Arlin Fatland, Barry Cooney, Garry Bang and Dave Perewitz. A club without rules, but with special principles, it quickly became well-

Two of the most famous Arlen Ness creations are the Ness Ferrari (top).

The bodywork of the Ferrari Bike and the "Toobad" (above) was designed by Crag Nat and the high-performance engine with twin compressors tuned by Harman. The twin Sportster machine was built at the end of the 1970s by Arlen Ness. The transmission of the front engine was removed, the fuel-tank positioned in the front area of the monocoque frame and the oil tank shifted to the rear.

A member of the Hamsters on the road.

known. The members wearing the famous yellow T-shirts gave themselves the task of riding as far and as long as possible on the wildest Ness creations. Today, at the end of the 1990s, it has around 180 members, friends, fellow travelers and spouses – a laid-back group constituting the most exclusive Harley enthusiast club in the world. A yellow T-shirt and a steak dinner are included in the annual membership fee of 25 dollars. For some years now Hamster Rides have been organized: excursions together from San Francisco to Daytona, Sturgis to the Minnesota Winter Nationals and the Laughlin River Love Ride.

Bob Bauder and Pete Chapouris are two celebrated custom designers from the Los Angeles area, Bob acting as manager and Pete working more as a hands-on designer. Together they founded the Syntassein Corporation (from the Greek word for cooperation) for the custom-building of hot rods and Harleys. This was after Pete Chapouris, a longtime custom, street and hotrod enthusiast, had sold his small firm Pete and Jake's Street Rod Operation, and had taken over the Specialty Equipment Market Association (SEMA). Both work closely with Custom Chrome. Their most famous creations are the Evo Softail HogZZilla, built at the end of the 1980s for Billy Gibbons, lead singer of ZZ Top; and the modified version CadZZilla, built with the support of the Harley-Davidson Motor Company.

Jay Brake is a specialist in inventive, technical solutions especially for braking systems and steering geometry. Jay Brainard, the head of Jay Brake Enterprise, also works together with various large custom firms, whom he supplies with his accessories. The custom models Originator and Nightmare are his best-known creations. The shifting of the brake shoes on the Originator to the inside of the rim, a typical Jay Brake innovation, made the Originator particularly famous.

Mike Corbin today, is a large firm which became known through the development of its own body and seat designs, producing custom bikes in cooperation with various designers. Typical examples are the first contracts given to Ron Simms' Bay Area Custom Cycles: the kits are called Warlady and Warbird.

In the case of Arlin Fatland too, aerodynamic custom Harleys were created with bodywork by Corbin in his "airplane design" sporting airbrushed pin-up pictures.

Rick Doss started out designing and producing custom parts for Harleys on the side in his modest repair workshop for cars and trucks in Danville, Virginia. Called Rick's Custom Harleys, his workshop was well-known for his typical black paintwork, his new ideas and his inventive details. Many of the bikes that Rick Doss created were featured and therefore publicized in *Easyriders* magazine. He soon became a busy specialist working with Custom Chrome. Nowadays, his company, Rick Doss Inc., builds classic and high-tech Harley-Davidson customs for various other companies, above all in the fantasy style, and his firm is known worldwide for its stylistic perfection. Some of his famous motorcycles are: the 1963 FLH Custom (1984); the Knucklehead for his wife Dixie (1986); the FXSTC Eclipse (1992); and the Orange Classic, a technical and visual showstopper with paintwork by Tessa Crane.

Bob Dron was a well-known auto and motorcycle custom designer as early as the 1960s. One of his creations was the 1969 winner of the San Francisco Motorcycle Show. In 1970 he formed the firm American Chopper Enterprises in Concord, California. In 1981 he took over the

Oakland Harley-Davidson dealership. Well-known custom motorcycles by Bob Dron are: the Roadster Royale, a constant winner at bike shows; the Heritage Royale; the Indy Cycle (a Harley sidecar machine in the Indycar look which was tested by the racing driver Bob Bondurand on the Sears Point racetrack); and the Cycletron, a wild Harley trike with extreme paintwork by Art Himsl.

Ron Finch has been in the custom business for almost 40 years and is well-known for his unusual creations and extreme designs. He worked for 16 years for Joselyn and Brown Roads in his hometown of Pontiac, Michigan, later setting up shop for himself. Famous custom bikes include the 1975 Sportster with "cage" skeleton frame and an integrated tank; and the Cool Hand Loop, with bone sculptures and radical details in the designs.

Hardly Civilized Inc. is based in Liberty, North Carolina, consisting of of two people, Eddy and Simon. It has been known since 1995, mostly by virtue of its original details such as interwoven, exhaust pipes and novel, handlebar designs. Don Hotop, of Don's Speed and Custom Shop, located in Fort Madison, Iowa. Most of Don's strength is his work in the classic Harley style. Don's first motorcycle was a dirty, old, 45 cubic inch side-valve which he restored in his free time in his small garage. Don opened his own little workshop even though he was still working for Chevron. A stickler for detail, he hates being hurried and he allows himself plenty of time for his creations, which quickly became famous for their craftsmanship and technical precision.

Cyril Huze, a Frenchman who emigrated to the United States in 1986, under-

A Corbin Custom bike.

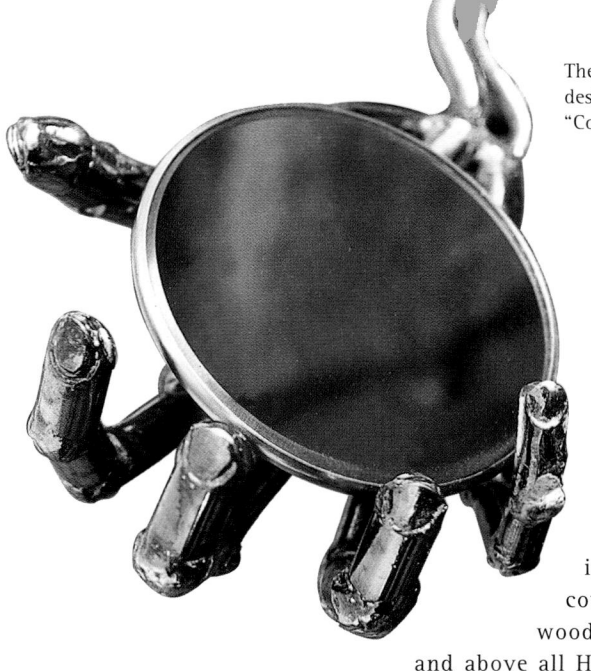

The rearview mirror design of Ron Finch's "Cool Hand Loop."

An intricate exhaust-pipe design by Hardly Civilized.

stood how to realize the clichés of European youth in the land of cowboys, Hollywood, rock 'n' roll, and above all Harleys. He was also a James Dean fan, and his attention–grabbing Harleys were soon to be seen at various exhibitions, and at some official Harley–Davidson shows. Some of his better–known motorcycles are Deanager, with the tank portrait of James Dean; the Harley Davidstones, with the Rolling Stones as tank picture; and the art deco 1977 FLH Miami Nice.

Bob Lowe transferred the stylistic elements and workshop techniques of extreme car customizing to motorcycles with his first Harley, a converted Fat Boy. He then developed theme bikes which were consistently styled down to the smallest detail. In 1995 he won First Place in the Oakland Bike Show.

His next creation was called Evil Twin. It was in a shark design, and his friend and chassis mechanic Ron Englert hammered the tasteful forms into the metal.

Dave Perewitz of Cycle Fab, located in Brockton, Massachussetts has, since 1964 when he acquired his first Sportster at the age of 16, worked constantly in various workshops in which cars and motorcycles were repaired and restored. He became accomplished in innovative, specialist, paintwork techniques. Since 1980 he has owned a large store. His brother Donnie helps in the business and for a time Dave was also assisted by Arlen Ness. A full catalog, with work from Custom Chrome and Drag Specialties among others, made him a man of independent means. Among his small band of workers, Nancy Brooks and Roy Mason soon became known for their artistic work. Dave Perewitz usually produces his artistic flights of fantasy from off the top of his head without the help of plans or drawings.

J. P. Poland, a styling specialist based in Lake Worth, Florida, creator of the Absolut Vodka bottle, produces very imaginative, decorative effects for Harleys that then serve as exhibition pieces and eyecatchers for advertising campaigns. Some of the best–known motorcycles from his garage: El Tigre, an FL Shovel with forward slung, polyester tiger's head, made in two versions, one for a T.V. show, the other for the New York Harley–Davidson Cafe; and the 1994 FLHTC Dragon, with its massive dragon's head, which he likes to portray as his young daughter's favorite creature.

Al Reichenbach, a quiet, rather introverted loner from Black River Falls, Wisconsin, first repaired John Deere agricultural machines and then became an employee of General Motors. He is regarded as a stylistic perfectionist. His unassuming inner and outer elegance is seen in every one of his custom creations, especially in the decorations consisting of gold leaf and engravings, perfect down to the smallest detail. His extreme, often bizarre, but always technically perfect designs have for years assured him of prizes at almost every bike show — mostly First Place.

Malcolm Ross has been his own boss for around 15 years, building extreme customs in his workshop which is packed with all kinds of machines and parts, in Spring Valley, located close to New York City, New York. An example is his Long Chopper, with its elongated wheelbase and a seat height which would make it suitable even for small children. The technically, highly advanced units with compressors or

A typical Bob Lowe design.

A paneling study by Bob Lowe: the "Evil Twin" (far left).

549

An extremely futuristic design: The "Apache Warrior," presented in 1995 by Next World Design Inc., Columbus/Ohio (right).

Intricate ornamental work: surface paneling designed by Al Reichenbach (far right).

Dragon's brood: the front fairing of J.P. Poland's "Dragon" (below).

Two turbo-charged low-slung models designed by Malcolm Ross (below right).

turbos from upwards of 150 horsepower have an enormous amount of power. Malcolm Ross has additionally developed his own frames and understands how to take apart, improve or entirely rebuild his motors in the tiniest detail. His paintwork normally has up to 50 coats.

Randy Simpson, proprietor of the Genuine Milwaukee Iron Shop and Retail Store in Lynchburg, Virginia, is known for his extreme steel designs. In his work he uses, among other things, computer-guided laser technology. Randy's trademark is the particularly careful finish on his chrome and paintwork, favoring great detail such as originally

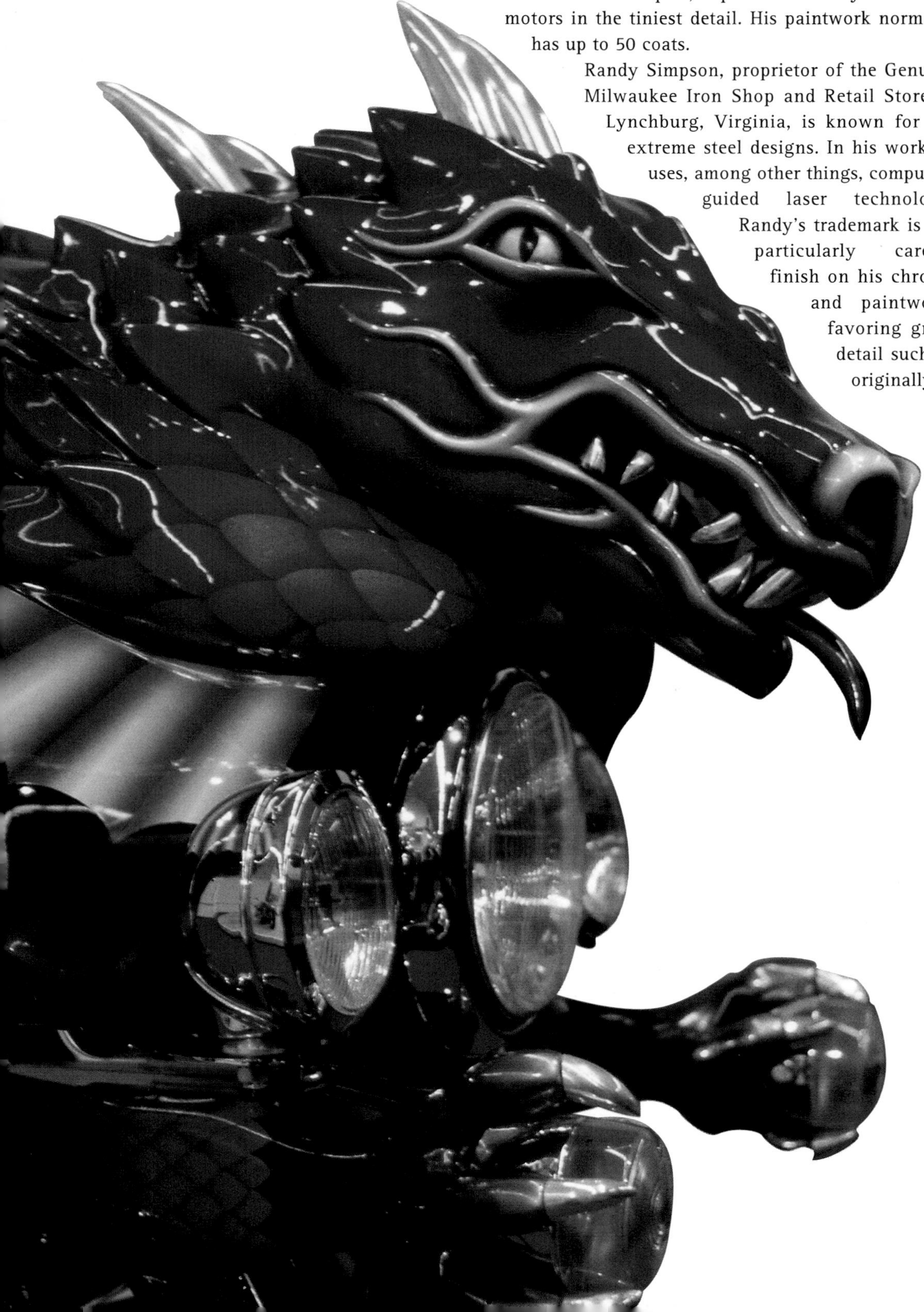

designed exhaust end caps, air filters, taillights, gas caps and dashes.

Ron Simms is a graduate mechanical engineer and designer. In 1969 he built his first black Fat Bob Custom Panhead, and he afterwards bought a large parts store to found Bay Area Custom Cycles (BACC) in Hayward, California. His low slung Sporties, with their long forks in the typical California style, quickly made him famous and he began experimenting with the full color spectrum as early as 1972. He developed special frames, fender and billet parts molded from aluminum. His company now has eight employees and produces around 45 custom bikes a year, working closely with Ron Paugh (Paughco). Some of Simms' best-known bikes are Goldrush in white and gold with turbo; and the Fandango, a winner of the 1993 Oakland, California Custom Show.

Some other well-known custom designers and trendsetters whose names have long belonged to the custom scene's hall of fame include: Donnie Smith from Minneapolis, Minnesota; Lawayne Matthies from Grand Prairie, Texas (Xzotic Cycle Products); Pat Kennedy from California and Brook Bryant from Arizona; Wyatt Fuller, former owner of fo Razorback, now with Harley-Davidson; Mike and Felix LaFore from Lakewood, Colorado; Petersen from Miami, Florida; Paragon

Locomotion, Florida; and Motor Arts in California. There are, of course, many more customizers within the custom bike world. This is just a small sampling.

William "Willie G." Davidson serves as Vice President of Styling for Harley-Davidson, Inc. Motorcycle Division. Davidson is responsible for the successful traditional designs of Harley-Davidson motorcycles. All motorcycle products are styled by Davidson and his associates at Harley-Davidson's Milwaukee headquarters.

Willie G. is the son of former Harley-Davidson president William H. Davidson and the grandson of one of the original founders, William A. Davidson. He is generally credited for developing the unique motorcycle designs which kept Harley-Davidson motorcycles selling while the company completed its technological and manufacturing improvements. Based in heritage and tradition, Davidson oversees the look of all Harley-Davidson products, as well as being responsible for the classic, FX Super Glide, FX Lowrider, Cafe Racer, Heritage Softail Classic, Springer, and Fat Boy motorcycle designs.

Davidson is one of the 13 executives who raised more than $75 million to purchase Harley-Davidson from AMF Incorporated in 1981.

Design elements: exhaust pipe and rear lamps by Randy Simpson.

Designs II

Worldwide

The typically French design by François Bruère imparts the chopper the character of an antique suit of armor, albeit rather triangular.

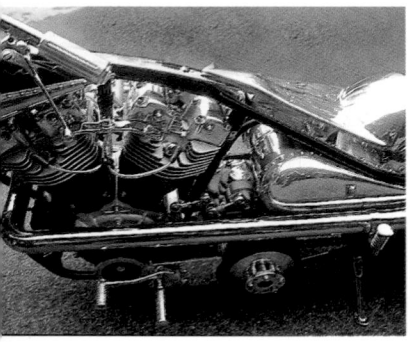

Custom motorcycles are not proof of only the American motorcycle designer's love of freedom. Even under the straitjacket of the laws of the highway, extraordinary custom creations exist in Europe as well, designed by talented, unfazed designers and free-spirited stylists who don't shy away from individuality and excessive expressionism. Only in regimented Switzerland or Japan do the customizers have a truly tortured existence, though this doesn't stop them carrying their ideas on the road; in fact these strict laws do have their advantages, for the technical design is invariably of the very finest.

Hans A. Muth: the well-known designer (Suzuki Katana) rose to prominence through his early plan for a Sportster XL, which unfortunately never went into serial production.

Battistinis from Bournemouth, England (Battistinis Custom Cycles) soon became one of Europe's best-known custom-bike manufacturers. Their cooperation with Arlen Ness has heavily influenced their style, and the technical conception naturally fits in with the Hamster's American ideal of riding long distances on extreme conversions.

Walter & Georg Senn (Moto Senn AG, Densbüren, Switzerland): as early as the beginning of the 1970s, the ultimate chopper-smiths had provided the entire European biker and rocker scene with extreme Harley conversions. The brothers were pioneers of the new biker philosophy in Europe and people could rely on their designs: despite their radical creations, the Moto Senn Specials enjoyed the divine blessing of the notoriously strict Swiss road safety authorities.

François Bruère: the all-around artist, graphic expert and designer from Le Mans, France, "costumed" his first push-bikes and later mopeds, as choppers. By the age of seventeen he possessed his first Harley, a 45 cubic inch (750 cc) WLA. Later he worked together with his friend Ferry Lambert; this was an ideal alliance of imagination and craftsmanship out of which some of the most extreme and, for France, utterly untypical conversions emerged. Despite his individualism on the design front, Bruère developed a style which respectfully reflects the pioneering achievements of the early Harley-Davidson motorcycles. His custom Harleys, known, along with his graphics and airbrush art, for their triangular style, are recognized worldwide and are admired at official Harley-Davidson shows and exhibitions.

The most extreme chopper designs of all hail from Scandinavia, in particular, Sweden. Swedish style is a synonym for huge technical freedom in chopper construction, and the rest of the world views with

François Bruère with his latest creation during the design stage and during manufacture. Bodywork designer Ferry Lambert (top), who shapes all models by hand from sheet aluminum.

A radical design from Japan: a Harley in Samurai look.

envy the custom scene of this country, which even now at the end of the 1990s prescribes no technical restrictions whatsoever for chopper construction. In the course of European integration this could, however, happen very quickly, meaning that ten-foot forks will be banned whether you can ride them or not. The Swedes, incidentally, have already proved that you can ride them.

Customs from Japan sometimes come across like motorized continuations of old Samurai traditions, sparing no expense with their bellicose outfit of steel, leather and highly polished parts. It is ironic that it was here, in a country whose motorcycle products were despised by the traditionally patriotic Harley riders in the U.S., that Harley creations emerged which, in terms of the philosophy behind them at least, could hardly have been more American. In Japan, chopper traditions and the allure of machismo have nothing to learn from the American biker scene.

Australia has seen similar developments and a Harley–Davidson custom scene is every bit as important as in the U.S. Here, however, the catalyst behind it was different: the Australians, who had no great affection for the belligerent Japanese military action in World War II which posed a direct threat to Australia. The Australians showed their gratitude to their American allies, whom they saw as the saviors of their continent, by adopting the Harley as their favorite bike. From this to the Harley clubs, with their fiery custom machines, was only one small step.

Harley Designers in Germany

The special talent of the Germans is technical perfection. In the 1970s an independent custom scene slowly developed, heavily influenced by biker clubs and the revived dragster scene. High performance became a symbol of technical quality rather than the extroverted showiness usual in the U.S. Some examples illustrate this:

The Flying Tiger of Christoph Madaus is a technically, highly developed custom with a large number of individual parts from the international custom market.

Lutz Schelhorn based his Silver Viper on the classic Californian in style, but still managed to include in his design an unmistakably German touch of internal technical perfection. In all its details, it's a masterpiece of metalwork.

Fred Kodlin, on the other hand, took his own very individual route, creating a custom design in the shape of his internationally premiered F1 which emulated the styling of a Formula One racing car. Just as extravagant in style and technology is his Moulin Rouge, boasting a Keck motor – in fact, it's hardly a Harley–Davidson any more!

Designers in Britain

The custom and chopper scenes were slow to take off in Britain. After the café racers of the 1960s, the main demand in the 1970s was for sport bikes. This situation changed only towards the end of the decade, when in 1979 the Hell's Angels MC England put on the Kent Custom Show, an event which was to point the way to the future for the British scene.

Regarding conversions and customizations, Britain enjoys a degree of freedom which people elsewhere can only dream of, meaning that both crazy and technologically innovative machines may well be authorized, even for use on public highways. John Reed was one of the customizing legends who made a name for himself during the wild years of the 1980s.

At the beginning of the 1990s, the brothers Dean and Rikki Battistini came onto the scene. Switching from restoring cars to customizing Harleys, they redefined English customizing, making the "Battistini style" known across Europe and exciting international interest.

Although the importation of Harleys was in the hands of AMF after the change of management at Harley–Davidson, F.H. Warr's business remained family owned. Robert Warr will remain with the tradition–steeped London Harley–Davidson business into the next millennium. In its foundations an entire Harley–Davidson bike is sealed and the shop will continue to cater for future British fans of the big V–twins from Milwaukee.

Overall view and typical details of the "Flying Tiger" by Christoph Madaus.

Lutz Schelhorn's "Silver Viper" from its best side.

The Harley Aftermarket

Customs from a Catalog

Looking back with hindsight at the development of the multi-million dollar accessories market, one can see that it is an interesting and somehow special creation. The riders of Harley-Davidson motorcycles were (and are) individualists who loved to play with their bikes and create it in their very own individual style. No other make of motorcycle in the world is provided with such a vast array of accessories and replacement parts as a Harley-Davidson – to the extent that it is possible to produce an exact copy of a Harley-Davidson production model without using a single original part.

In 1903, at the same time as when the first Harley single-cylinder motorcycle was being bolted together on its workbench in a wooden shed in Milwaukee, the accessories market was already in full swing. However, this was not true for Harley-Davidson motorcycles, due to the fact that in 1903 they were still not available for sale. But it was true for the existing motorcycle market, and it was booming. In 1904 the Motorcycle Equipment Company of Hammondsport, New York, published its first catalog. By 1913 this publication ran to 1,216 entries, covering everything from wheels, lights, gloves and saddlebags, to rev counters, carburetors and other engine parts. Nor was this early customizing limited to the technical and practical improvement of motorcycles by the addition of saddles, sidecars or luggage racks: lights, horns and handlebars and so on were also selected for their appearance rather than just for their practicality and use.

In fact, during the first half of the century it was standard practice even for the production motorcycles of well-known manufacturers to be put together from other manufacturer's parts. For example, Sturmey-Archer gears or JAP engines were fitted in a wide variety of different machines. However, American manufacturers attempted from an early date to bind customers to their own makes: having quickly recognized the marketing value of accessories and clothing, they created their own official ranges.

There was this irksome subject of "unauthorized" dealers. The company obviously tried to protect its business interest which was undermined by the so-called aftermarkets or "private" dealers. For a long time official Harley dealers could buy accessories only direct from the factory, and they were asked to refuse to service motorcycles fitted with other manufacturers' accessories. Harley also rejected Indian's doctrine of "keep them on the road," going instead for a strategy of maximizing sales of new machines. Thus when production of a Harley model was discontinued, manufacture of spare parts also ceased, which sooner or later created the problem for the drivers of older machines that they had to seek replacement parts elsewhere.

The situation was still complicated after World War II when the American motorcycling world split into the "good guys" and the "bad guys" after the events at Hollister. Naturally enough, Harley-Davidson regarded itself as being on the side of the angels, which for them meant neatly-dressed motorcycle club members astride squeaky clean big twins equipped with all the latest official Harley accessories. The company would have nothing to do with the "outlaws" on their stripped-down bikes: apart from anything else, such people did not constitute much of a target group for the sale of saddlebags, touring windshields, chrome-plated crashbars and the like!

However, the exclusion of this predominantly young "outlaw" group tended in fact to have the opposite effect for official Harley dealers, because bikers simply learned to service and repair their own motorcycles and got hold of the necessary parts from other sources – which

Traveling dealers boasting a rich variety of after-market parts from numerous manufacturers can be found at virtually every biker event.

were plentiful – especially for the wartime flatheads. Nor did Harley shy away from employing protection methods in their efforts to tie official Harley dealers to the official spare parts: any dealer failing to tow the line would find that his license which had been granted for one year had to discuss the issue with Harley-Davidson again.

By the middle of the 1960s the modern aftermarket phenomenon had come into being. It was largely a development from the custom car and chopper scenes and also Californian drag racing. The fans of the American big twin, ignored by the official dealers, began to provide for themselves the services and style accessories that Milwaukee would not. Gradually individuals who designed and produced their own sissy bars, ape hanger handlebars and flame-painted exhausts became small-scale manufacturers and eventually well-known designers, relocating their manufacturing operations of parts to Southeast Asia.

The custom bike industry can list some famous names. Ever since 1956, C. B. Clausen and Jim Magnera of Los Angeles, California, owners of the company MC Supply, have been supplying interested dealers with pistons designed for higher compression ratios, crankshafts for strokers and other performance-enhancing parts. By 1969 their catalog ran to well over 2,000 parts.

Tom Sifton, a Harley tuning specialist, brought his experience to bear in the development of a performance program involving camshafts, brakes, wheels, brake cylinders and engine parts for the valve train – his camshafts in particular were renowned for their power-enhancing effect on dragsters.

In the hobby room of his house in Blue Island, Illinois, George Smith, co-founder of a company called Smith & Stankus (later Smith & Smith then shortened to S&S), produced lighter valve lifters, modified carburetor connections for stroker conversions, crankshafts and carburetors. As production grew he moved to Viola, Wisconsin.

Ed "Big Daddy" Roth was one of the gurus who did most to publicize the Californian scene with his *Choppers* magazine. Though small in size and circulation, it offered would-be customizers not only useful contact addresses, but also practical technical advice and inspiration in the form of pictures of new creations. This was a magazine that illustrated the motorcycles, introduced their creators and offered very useful tips which went into the minutest technical details, although some of their crazy, welded-frame designs would make the modern reader's hair stand on end! The Californian chopper scene was already well established by the 1960s, with some enthusiasts even producing the parts needed for their machines themselves and even, at least on a small scale, supplying them to fellow-enthusiasts.

Tom McMullen and his AEE Choppers Shop in Buena Park revolutionized the custom industry with his range of springer forks, fork braces and other accessories. His rival American Motorcycle Engineering, abbreviated to AMEN, supplied rigid frames and suspension components for both Harleys and Japanese motorcycles. The range of available parts was impressive. Accessory parts always tend to reflect the economical end of contemporary production methods and thus it is no surprise that the first custom parts were chiefly made of lead or iron. This choice of metals was reflected in the weight of the extended springer or parallelogram forks with twisted stands produced by, among others, the California Cycle Works from the beginning of the 1960s.

The Harley management of the late 1960s regarded the chopper scene with pure horror and attempted to suppress it by any means available. Harley continued to promote its rather conservative dresser, but despite the company's best efforts its numbers steadily declined, while Japanese and English manufacturers, more attuned to public tastes, provided wheels for the masses. In 1969, in an attempt to prevent the removal of engines for use in choppers, Harley-Davidson even started marking new cases with the numbers of the old ones, and only then supplied them to the customers, a practice that didn't exactly encourage the construction of choppers with original Harley parts. However, the chopper industry preferred to produce its own engine case, and so the customizing industry simply bypassed Harley-Davidson.

It was the film "Easy Rider" which really got the customania bandwagon rolling. Suddenly rigid frames, sissy bars, peanut or coffin tanks, ape hangers and long forks were everywhere. Demand for such parts rocketed both in the U.S. and elsewhere. New custom bike publications such as *Street Chopper* magazine from Tom McMullen's TRM Publications and Keith R. Ball's *Easy Rider*, *Iron Horse* and *Super Cycle* provided the industry with a reservoir of customers eager to make their dreams of freedom a reality, by means of a rigid-frame, one-off, custom machine powered by a big V-twin (even though they came without a great deal of comfort). Large distributors such as Jammer, Chrome

This special shop in Japan proudly points out its range of custom parts from every manufacturer in the world.

Complete custom bikes with hand-crafted design components can cost well over U.S.$100,000.

The Theft of Harleys
(continued)

down and the parts sold on to both fences and unsuspecting dealers. Because of this, stolen machines are almost never recovered: any coded parts are destroyed and what remains is sold off.

Harley-Davidson themselves are, in fact, attempting to combat this trade through internationally coordinated police campaigns. They have also begun marking all the most important and expensive motorcycle parts such as the engine, transmission, generator, forks and frame with indelible serial numbers which they then disseminate internationally via a computerized coding system. The upshot is that during large-scale crackdowns by the police and customs officials, unsuspecting Harley owners sometimes have their beloved machines confiscated and are often lucky to get away with no more than a fine – and all because they got hold of a Harley part cheap from a friend, at a flea market or from an equally unsuspecting Harley dealer.

The DEKRA identification center stores all the identifying data and codes for a registered vehicle. Despite this, Harleys continue to be plagued by theft, particularly Harley-Davidson custom models such as the Fat Boy, Bad Boy, Heritage Springer, Road King and Classics series, which include so many uncoded accessory parts that they still provide a rich source of profit for the highly specialized gangs of thieves.

So it's advisable to secure the motorcycle with the best available immobilizers and electronic alarms, and to make sure that you always get a receipt and guarantees when purchasing spare parts. Improbable, tempting advertisements should be looked at carefully and with suspicion. It's also a good idea to have the engine and frame numbers – because they can be skillfully forged – checked by experts.

Specialties and Custom Chrome International listed the products of the many different, small-scale suppliers in their comprehensive catalogs.

Finally Harley, in the hands of the AMF since 1969, reluctantly started to produce the kind of motorcycles that its customers had been building for themselves for years. The result was the 1971 Super Glide, at first supplied with the Sportster's boat tail and later fitted with a chopper-style saddle. The machine was an immediate success and was produced in increasing numbers. The Super Glide formed a popular "basic model" custom bike for the booming accessories industry, lending itself to countless, easily fitted, bolt-on accessories.

During the 1970s and 1980s the accessories market became firmly established in the U.S. and began to spread around the world. By now Harley was doing little to resist the trend, which was, after all, enticing new customers to the motorcycle scene. Nevertheless they did run an advertising campaign in June 1976 under the slogan "We don't want other peoples' parts on our motorcycles," attempting to persuade people to use only original Harley-Davidson parts and to have them fitted only at authorized Harley-Davidson dealerships. It was not until later on that the company finally bowed to the inevitable, deciding to profit from the growing trend by supplying custom bike fans with Harley-Davidson's own range of parts and accessories.

At first, Europe and Japan imported parts made in the U.S., but then soon began to develop and produce their own parts conforming to local regulations. The Harley boom of the 1990s has led to a parallel mushrooming of parts producers. The equipping and conversion of Harley-Davidson motorcycles has become a worldwide, multi-million dollar business providing a living for numerous manufacturers, distributors and magazines, as well as countless large- and small-scale designers. The 1997 buy-out by Custom Chrome International of its

long-time rival Chrome Specialties at a cost of 36 million dollars gives an idea of the scale of the industry. George Smith turned his hobby-room work into an engine workshop supplying a large proportion of the "Harley clones" with their V-twin power units and small-time customizers such as Arlen Ness became legends whose new designs now reached a worldwide market. Trade fairs and shows such as the ones at Cincinnati in the U.S. and Custom Performance in Germany exhibit new, ever-more stylized parts that are found on display at the big biker meets at Daytona and Sturgis in the U.S. and at the European Harley-Davidson Super Rally.

Like anything else, custom bike tastes are subject to the dictates of the current fashion. Numerous different stylistic trends and local peculiarities make for a continually changing scene, while new production methods and cheaper materials also regularly transform the industry. Engraving once involved painstaking work with a needle; lasers can now do the job in a fraction the time. Milled, aluminum parts and performance-boosting engine parts for the underpowered Big Twins were always in great demand.

Today, you can not only assemble a motorcycle resembling a Harley from individually purchased parts, you can even pick and choose your own parts suppliers. The number of Harley accessories catalogs in existence worldwide would fill a small library and new ones come out every year. On top of the countless combination possibilities on offer, there are a great many small-scale designers who create their own parts on small mills and lathes in garages and sheds.

"Anything goes" is the motto of the Harley accessories industry as we go into the next millennium, even if Harley-Davidson is not always happy with the things that are done to their motorcycles. At least it has a certain tradition behind it by now.

Harley – Real or Imitation

Not Everything Labled "Harley–Davidson" Is One

They say that imitation is the sincerest form of flattery. If that's true, then Harley-Davidson should feel honored indeed by the proliferation in recent years of copies and reproductions. By this the author doesn't mean the Japanese V-twins which bear an ever-greater resemblance albeit superficial to the American original, but the so-called Harley clones: machines that look exactly like production Harleys, but don't have the famous logo on the tank.

At the beginning of the 1990s, when the Harley boom was gathering pace, Harley-Davidson's production could no longer keep step with demand – a situation which drove prices sky-high and led to endless waiting times. This provided the opportunity for many a small-scale customizer and businessman from another branch of industry to step in.

In the 1970s and 1980s the accessories and parts industry had developed to the extent that you could even obtain engines and frames as spare parts. But it was the Harley boom of the 1990s that gave real impetus to the clone industry.

For suppliers, the equation was a simple one: why buy a production machine for 10,000 to 15,000 dollars and then sink the same amount into the conversion, if the desired motorcycle could be provided for two-thirds of that amount and in far less time? Companies such as Titan, American Image, Big Dog Motorcycles, American Eagle, American Legend, Confederate Choppers, among others, either fitted S&S engines into their frames or assembled the engines from a variety of individual parts. This meant they could offer not only better performance but also a modular customizing system, together with any type of paintwork specified by the customer.

Production numbers run from a few dozen to several hundred motorcycles per year and the trend is increacing. Today more than a dozen firms in the U.S. are producing motorcycles. Including motorcycles produced by frame manufacturers and customizers, the number of producers runs into the hundreds. In Europe too quite a number of manufacturers have latched on to the trend towards "own-brand" tailor-made V-twins.

Nowadays, frames are also produced in Germany, Sweden, Holland and England, while frames imported from the U.S. are also in frequent use, these then being authorized in accordance with the regulations of individual countries. Sometimes identical frames are found with different maker's names on them. In the end, where you have your custom bike put together is a question of budget and taste.

However, no matter how closely the machines may resemble the real thing, there is one thing they cannot offer the prospective buyer: the name. It's precisely this on which Harley-Davidson customers set so much store.

Harley replicas, like these in the showroom of American Legend Cycles, can understandably lead to confusion among uninformed customers.

Californian design specialist Ray Leslie and one of his Harley replicas produced by Advanced Automotive *Eng. Techn.* (top).

Two engines that originate entirely from after-market production: Titan and S & S.

The Big Cheese at Rat's Hole

Big Daddy's Custom Chopper Show

A long, long line: every bike has to rely on its own power to reach the show.

It's the mother of all custom shows and every designer and customizer must be there at least once. The Rat's Hole Custom Chopper Show is the best known, most heavily-hyped custom show in the world and those who have won a prize there count themselves among the international *crème de la crème* of the bike-crazy community.

The creator and founding father of this show is Big Daddy Rat, otherwise known as Karl Smith, born in Melrose Park near Chicago, Illinois. His family emigrated from Bavaria, Germany, in 1868, hence the K in his first name. As a football player at Winterburg University in Springfield, Ohio, he somehow acquired the nickname "Rat;" the "Big" he got because of his huge size. In 1954 he began designing T-shirt motifs, mainly for the biker and hot-rod scenes, visiting fairs and shows. He later founded a T-shirt business with its headquarters in St. Petersburg, Florida, boasting more than seven branches across the States, including (for a time in 1971) a store opposite the Stardust Casino in Las Vegas, Nevada. In 1962 he opened a T-shirt store in Daytona which quickly became known as The Rat's Hole. In 1963 he bought his famous trike, the Cheese Hauler, with a 750 cc Honda engine which was converted to a 1200 Sportster motor by Steve "Jake" Jakobowski at the end of the 1990s.

It was in 1972 that he organized his first bike show with a few friends on the parking lot of John's Family Market. There was so much interest that it was put on every year on the Saturday of Daytona Bike Week, with each visitor paying a modest entrance free. Up to this day, it is a ride-in show and the chance to compete is open to everyone, in a range of different classes.

When the Rat's Hole Custom Chopper Show took place for the first time on a boardwalk in front of the Atlantic Ocean, more than 15,000 visitors came instead of the expected 5,000. There were 44 cups, prizes for taking part in the form of belts, buckles and ribbons, and for every first place a seventeen-jewel wristwatch from Big Daddy personally — along with kisses galore from Miss Rat's Maids, Donna Casper and Cindy Zimmermann, who were photographed on Big Daddy's cheese-colored Honda trike. In 1975 there were 267 exhibitors in 12 classes, competing for 48 cups. In his own newspaper, the free *Ratty Rag*, he introduced bikes and friends, and published programs and exclusive insider stories.

At the beginning of the 1980s, when the infamous police crack-down was unleashed on the bikers, and Police Chief Charles Willis harshly enforced every clause of the Florida Vehicle Code, all the custom bikers were tarred with the same brush and virtually branded criminals. Despite Big Daddy's standing and his continually reaffirmed tolerance, the Rat's Hole Custom Chopper Show quickly lost much of its flair and extravagance. On the other hand, there were international successes. The organizer of the Essen Motor Show, Wolfgang Schöller, invited the winning bikes from Big Daddy's show to Germany as a special attraction of the show, a practice which has continued annually to this day. In 1997, for example, 15 winners and their bikes worth a grand total of 650,000 dollars were brought to Essen for a week. Big Daddy was also invited to Jonköpping and Paris together with his winners.

Since 1986, the Rat's Hole Custom Chopper Show has also been part of Sturgis Bike Week in South Dakota, where it can be visited on Saturday on the Woodle Field. In 1988 the show in Daytona was banished from its traditional attractive boardwalk because the new

Not something you will see every day: a monster Sportster on its four enormous tracks.

Photographers think it's not a bad idea to have your own model — and not just as a marketing gag, either!

Mariott hotel complex was to be built there. But even on the unattractive expanse of the parking lot behind the Ocean Center (also newly built), the bike show lost none of its attraction. In 1995, 386 bikes took part in the Daytona show and 222 in the Sturgis show. Nowadays the ticket price for every visitor is eight dollars, though this has done nothing to dent its success.

In 1996 Big Daddy Rat visited the tenth Biker Fest organized by Biker's Life in Villanova, Italy, together with some of his exhibition pieces, as well as the Vancouver Custom Motorcycle Show in Canada. At the beginning of February 1997, for the 25th anniversary, the Rat's Custom Bike Show were the guests, under Big Daddy Rat's paternal direction, at the first Bike Week in Phoenix, Arizona.

One of Big Daddy Rat Karl Smith's greatest achievements, however, was in ensuring — and in this he worked closely with the new police chief Crow — that the 1988 Daytona Bike Week was once again a biker-friendly event, without police aggression and without the pointless persecution of "not quite legal" motorcycles.

Today, the Rat's Hole Custom Chopper Show is ripped-off and imitated countlessly, and at some point Big Daddy will certainly be fed up with it and retire somewhere as a private citizen. He has not become rich in the sense of having lots and lots of money, and at heart he has remained a true biker.

The Rat's Hole Custom Chopper Show is spread over an enormous area of the sizzling parking lot behind the Daytona Beach Civic Center. (top).

Big Daddy Rat, together with Wolfgang Schoeller and his wife (right).

The German Fred Kodlin's prize-winning custom bike. Whether you are a famous wrestler (left) or simply an 'ordinary' rat biker (right), Big Daddy Rat will always welcome you and there will always be a Miss Rat Mate to embellish the winner's photo (center).

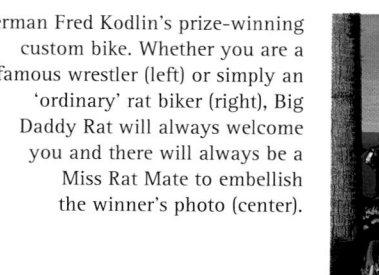

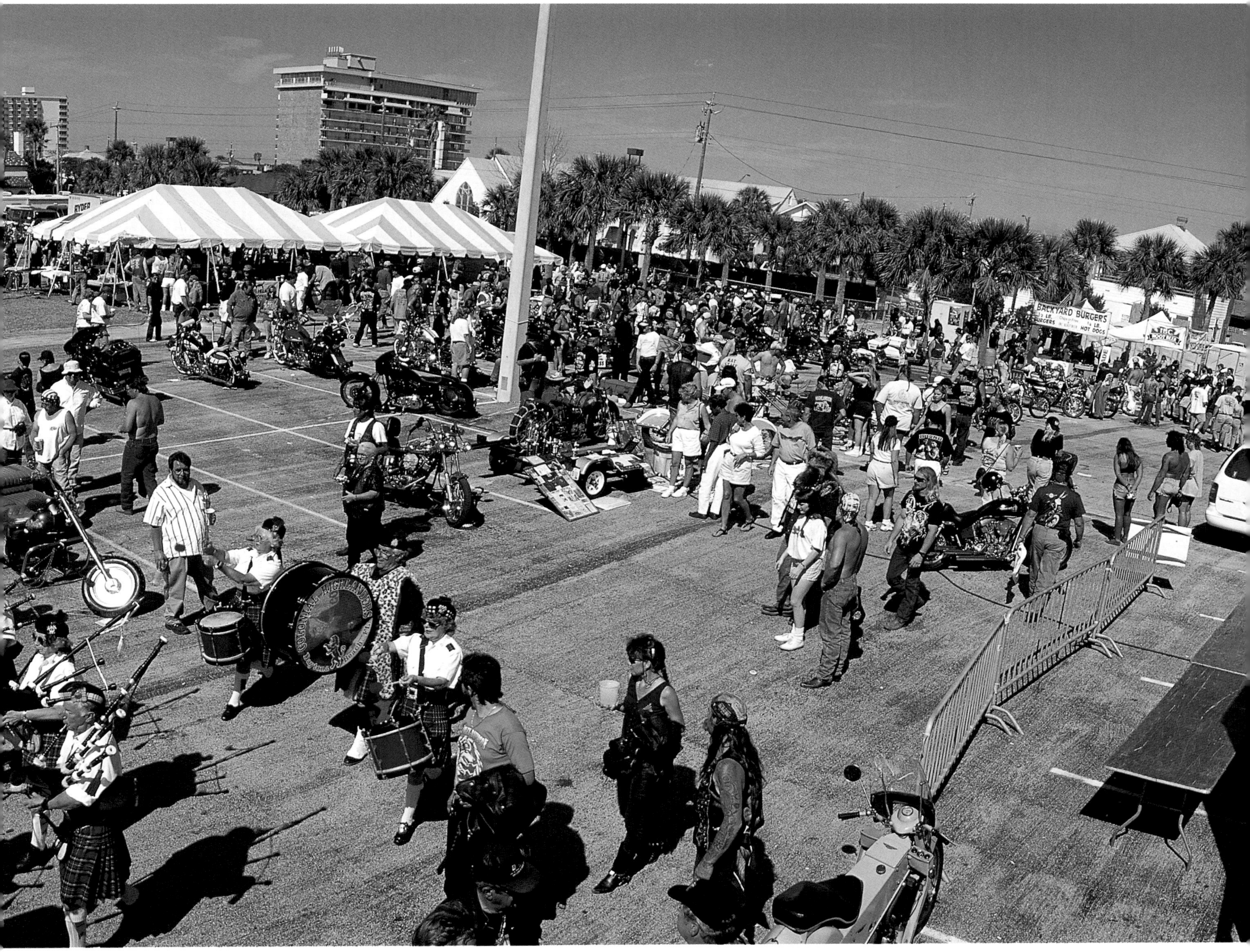
RYDER
BACKYARD BURGERS
HOT DOGS

MISS

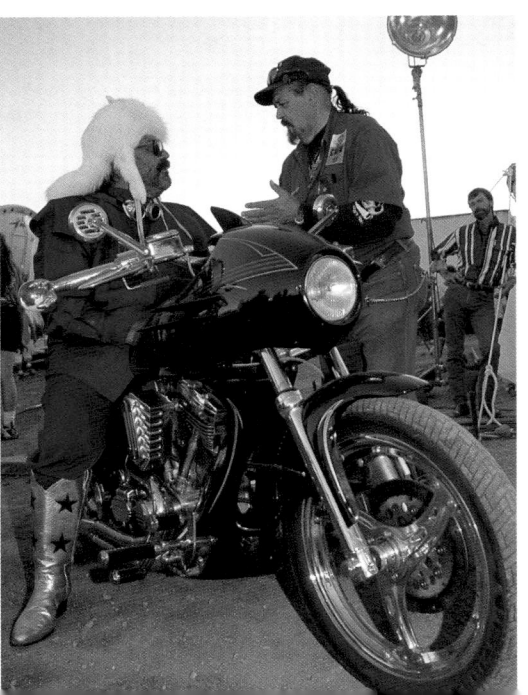

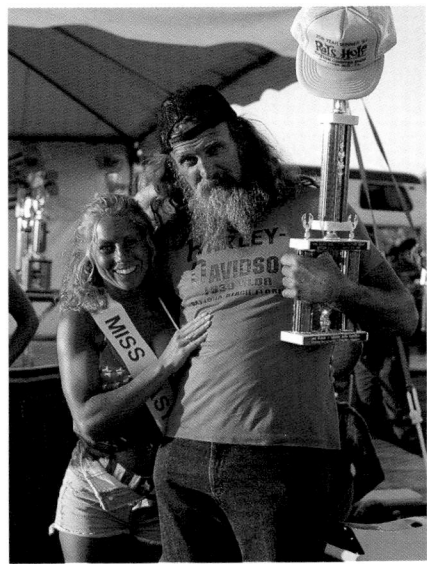

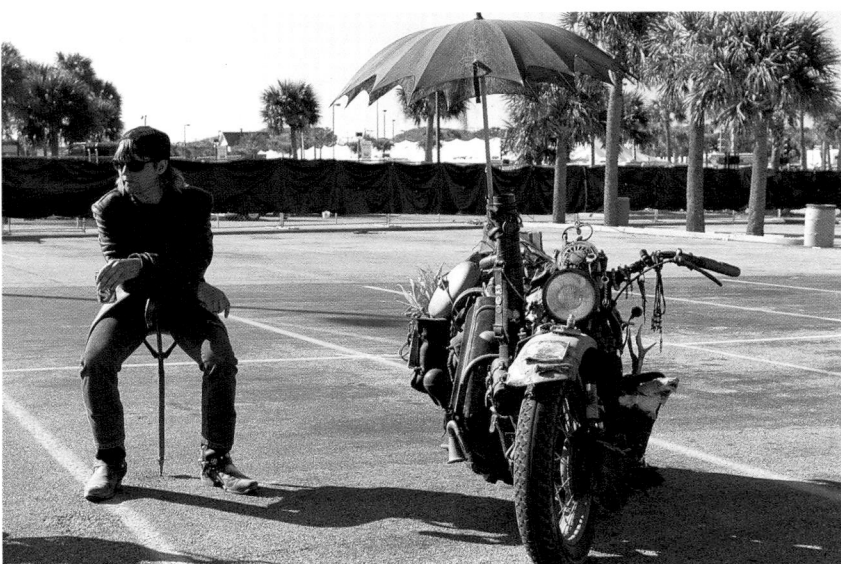

Show 'Em What You Can Do!

A Bike Show in the Sticks

found around Main Street (also named Washington Avenue) and in the roads running off it. And sure enough, this was the case with Bulldog's Bike Shop. Not that knowing the street name helped. In the city X the streets weren't known by their names (which they certainly had), but by numbers, which apparently made things easier for everyone. All I had to do was find the highway turn-off between 1st and 36th. As I've already said, N was not that big a town, so after waiting for a short time I simply tucked in behind two speeding choppers that made their way noisily and at full speed down the almost deserted streets: it was, after all, a Saturday. The few people hanging around didn't pay us the slightest attention. We hadn't gone far before we reached Bulldog's Bike Shop. There were already several bikes standing outside; the areas in front of the shop and behind it, and even the road, were packed with brothers and sisters, and there were kids running all over the place.

Though X was in the middle of one of the many "dry" counties, in which owning or consuming alcohol is strictly prohibited, nobody, as usual, cared. Beer and whiskey were flowing freely. Bulldog's shop was, in fact, a large old shack that had previously seen service as the local drugstore. The party was already in full swing behind the store. At this kind of thing a table for food and drinks is absolutely essential, and one had been set up, using a few old planks, in the shade of several ancient pecan trees. There were hamburgers and hot dogs straight from the grill, as well as Coke and beer kept cool in a bathtub filled with crushed ice. The mustard pots and bottles of ketchup added the final touch to this display of "iron rations:" this wasn't intended to be a sumptuous five-star banquet; all that really mattered was that the beer didn't run out.

Like the party, the bike show offered nothing particularly special or unfamiliar. There were a few trophies made of gilded plastic that were pure kitsch, but which would be cherished as something special by the winners. Then there was the big pot for collecting cash donations, a large pickle jar containing some coins and a few

crumpled dollar bills. I should also mention the small table with the "door prizes:" ten cans of oil (H–D 70 Single), four T-shirts decorated with Bulldog's shop emblem, and a ten dollar gift voucher for a tattoo.

By now a few bikes had appeared in front of the store as exhibits for the "Custom Show." But these were not customs in the real sense: they were standard Harleys, choppers, dressers and rats; owned by local bikers, most were in poor condition and certainly nothing out of the ordinary. There was an entrance charge of five dollars, which automatically restricted the number of participants in the Custom Show to those who felt in dire need of a morally uplifting experience or who desperately craved public admiration. Each biker cleaned and polished their machine as though their life depended on it, though it was pointless. As a result of years of neglect, the rust and dirt, the oil and grease, had worked themselves into every crack and crevice of the machines. Even the most aggressive cleaning methods were unable to make any real improvement. But at least what was being done looked good. Besides, cleaning was a sacred ceremony in this exhibitionistic ritual. In Daytona, apparently, the bikers performed exactly the same ritual at the famous Rats Hole Bike Show. But had any of these guys ever been to Daytona ...?

At last it was time for the prize-giving. Bulldog ran around, grumbling and cursing and pressed one of the tasteless trophies into the hands of anyone who had exhibited their bike in the show. There were 14 bikes in the Fifth Annual Bike Show and Bulldog accordingly had 14 trophies to award.

"You better do that!" he said to me, grinning knowingly: "Just you forget even one of them, there'll be hell to pay ... not to mention that I'd lose a whole lot of customers and never be able to hold a bike show again. Anyhow, these guys have paid their five bucks."

So, in the end, the entire crowd couldn't have been happier and everyone waved their trophy around as though they had just won the Grand Prix. Everyone went home feeling content with themselves.

Everyone needs a boost now and again: this trophy might be kitsch, but it does the trick.

I'd started out early. This was partly because of the hot weather, which was not so unbearable in the morning and partly on account of the distance I had to cover – something like 300 miles. My goal, in a town in the heart of Mississippi, was a bike shop that was owned by a member of the Southern Grays. This was where the local annual bike show took place – with a big party afterwards, of course, to be held at some place not yet specified.

It was late in the afternoon when I reached this average, smallish town with a population of about 20,000. In fact, it was a bit of a sprawl, consisting, in part at least, of hoardings and run-down shacks that did little to make it a tourist attraction. I knew that almost all the stores were to be

Whatever You Do, Don't Miss Kent!

A Real Hell's Angels' Party

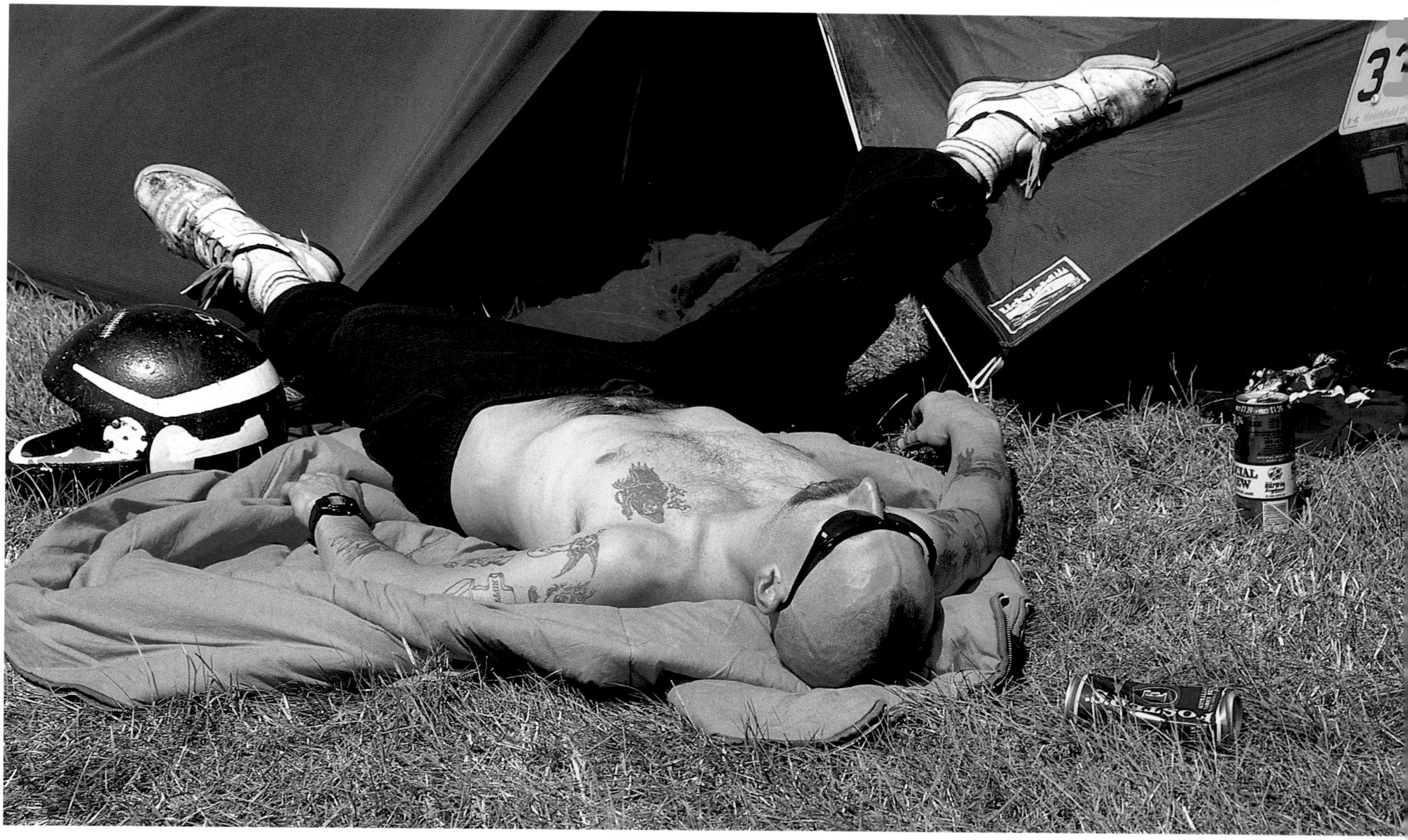

For a long time the Kent Custom Bike Show (KCBS) has enjoyed a reputation for being the largest and most attractive motorcycle custom show in Europe. In a way, that's still true. The show was started by the Hell's Angels MC England, and first took place in 1979. Around 800 bikers congregated at the Halfway Cafe in Harrietsham for a show at which there were, at least initially, more Japanese and British custom bikes on show than there were Harleys.

At that time customizing and custom shows were very rare in Europe. But the Hell's Angels' idea caught on and became a real hit. In 1984 there were as many as 18,000 visitors to the show in Kent; in 1988 this figure rose to 25,000. The local venue had now been stretched to full capacity. So the KCBS moved to Dymchurch, west of Folkstone, close to the Channel coast, where there was an enormous grassy area available for all kinds of events. This was the birth of the Angel Park, complete with a picnic area, an atmosphere reminiscent of Woodstock, and enough space for an almost unlimited number of visitors and campers.

So great was the success of this venture that events of a similar kind were soon to spread all over Europe, including such events as the Bulldog Bash near Statford-upon-Avon, the Crazy Daze and the Free Wheels Rally in France. Well into the 1990s the number of visitors remained more or less constant, but the number of participants continually rose, and Harley custom bikes soon started to dominate.

No Hell's Angels' party is a real party without that something extra to it, and the KCBS doesn't disappoint. There is always live music played by the best bands performing on an enormous open-air stage, on which the inevitable wet T-shirt contests and other forms of popular entertainment are also staged. Nor should the much acclaimed awarding of huge trophies be forgotten. Around the stage there are sales booths, places for biker games and special entertainment to ensure that nobody ever feels bored or goes hungry or thirsty. Enormous tents are set aside for special shows such as dragster races and burnouts, as well as for exhibitions displaying the latest in accessories, and swapmeets. There are, in addition, stunt rider shows, all sorts of displays, and the traditional biker meet on Saturday afternoon in the old, typically English pub called the Ocean Inn. All this has made the Kent Custom Bike Show an event visitors will never forget.

Anyone who has managed to get as far as Kent is worn out, to say the least. The Custom Bike Show has its attractions, but it's quite tiring to see it all.

Part of that special sense of belonging: visitors to the Kent Bike Show spend the night under canvas.

Non-stop action day and night on the huge stage: live music, strip shows and a prize for all the bikes that deserve it.

During the Kent Bike Show England's south coast is packed with thousands and thousands of motorcyclists, and they are more than welcome in all the pubs and restaurants (top).

Once it is all over and there is not too much damage – something of a rarity – and provided that the weather has been reasonably kind, everyone can set out for home, happy though utterly exhausted.

Bike Shows in the U.S.

At the Daytona Boardwalk Show all kinds of Harley are to be found, from the reasonably sober to the completely outrageous.

In the U.S., bike shows, also known as trade shows, have existed since the early days of motorcycling at the beginning of the 20th century. A great many of them developed from the bicycle shows that were quite common at the end of the 19th century. Others developed from large automobile shows where motorcycles were promoted as motorized alternatives that were both sporty and technically advanced. Such early events often included a wide range of exhibits from overseas, much to the delight of the many visitors, whose love of technology seemed to know no bounds. The exhibitions in Chicago and New York were among the most famous.

It was only after World War II that enthusiasts interested in customizing made an impact on bike shows. It was at this time that the first specially built Harleys awakened a passionate interest in all kinds of different designs. As a result, the number of local, national and international events grew rapidly. Among the best known were the Oakland Bike Show and the San Francisco International Bike Show (which had come into being before the World War II). Soon to become a firm part of the outlaw scene, these events became important trendsetters for Harley customizing.

While most of the large American bike shows restricted themselves even well into the 1980s, to exhibiting the more sober, stock motorcycles, there were custom bike shows as early as the 1960s in California and, from 1973, at the Daytona Bike Week. Thanks to the efforts of national and international

biker magazines, above all *Easyriders*, these events were soon to be transformed from little-known local shows into major international events.

A direct result of this upsurge of interest in customizing was the unbelievably rapid growth in a market for custom accessories and aftermarket products. During the 1970s this new market led to the emergence of trade shows specifically for dealers and the manufacturers of accessories; one of the largest is the Dealer Expo & Powersport in Indianapolis. By the end of the 1990s quite a few companies and organizations had jumped on to the bandwagon, both in Daytona and in Sturgis. The first was Big Daddy Rat at the Rat's Hole Custom Chopper Show in Daytona but it soon ran out of steam. Although it's still at the forefront in custom accessories, it's not really in a position to compete with the enormous potential of the larger organizers. J & P Promotions, for example, started a whole series of gigantic Super Series bike shows and motorcycle "extravaganzas" in 1996 that were staged throughout the length and breadth of America. The sheer effort that went into presentation, into running such dazzling shows, as well as the prizes to be won and the many special events, were simply unbeatable.

Together with most of the manufacturers of aftermarket products, J & P Promotions stages shows of similar huge proportions in places as far apart as Belleville, Illinois; Anamosa, Iowa; Plymouth and Elkhart Lake, Wisconsin; Davenport, Iowa; and St. Paul, Minnesota.

At the Poetone, Chicago bike show in July 1996, J & P Promotions offered as many as five prizes in the following classifications of the Ride-In Bike Show, and it is not difficult to imagine the size of the crowd that was attracted. and what there was to look at:

Exhibitors' Choice Best of Show; Antique 1936 to 1957; Best Chrome; Best Paint; Dresser, Evolution; Dresser, Shovelhead European (full custom); European & Asian (stock); Evo Road King Custom; Evo Softail FL (mild); Evo Softail (semi-mild); Evo Softail (stock); Evo Softail FX (mild); Evo Softail FX (semi-mild); Evo Swingarm (full); Evo Swingarm (mild); Evo Swingarm (semi-mild); Evo Swingarm (stock); Harley-Davidson Police Specials; Indian; Ladies Ride (Big Twin); Ladies Ride (Sportster); Panhead & Earlier (full); Panhead (rigid frame); Panhead Swingarm; Servi-Car; Shovelhead FL (mild); Shovelhead FL (stock); Shovelhead FX (full); Shovelhead FX (mild); Shovelhead FX (semi-mild); Shovelhead FX (stock); Sidecar; Sportster (mild); Sportster (semi-mild); Sportster (stock); Trike (cycle engine); Trike (non-cycle engine); and Exhibitors' Door Prize Drawings.

A bike show takes place anywhere and everywhere – wherever somebody has parked a really splendid Harley: it's not long before people stop, stare and admire what they see.

Another important organizer of events of this kind is *Easyriders* magazine, which, just like J & P Promotions, had started by putting on a show at the Daytona Bike Week to compete with the Rats Hole Custom Show. This *Easyriders* event always takes place on the famous boardwalk next to the open sea, from which the famous Rat's Hole Show had been moved by the city administration. But whether in Daytona, Sturgis or Laconia, new bike shows continue to appear, and what never fails to impress is the perfect timing of each event, which allows the dedicated custom biker to try their luck at all of them.

The really friendly bike shows, however, are the thousands of local ones found in all kinds of towns, both large and small. They are staged by either Harley-Davidson dealers or Harley clubs, which, of course, exist all over the U.S. In fact, it's the good humored get–together, rounded off with the inevitable party afterwards, that's more important than the expensive exhibits and artsy designs, though they too are there to be widely and expertly admired! As might be expected, all those participating in a contest will be handsomely rewarded with prizes and trophies.

At the Daytona Boardwalk Show every pretty women is greeted with applause by a cheerful audience.

It's a Small World After All

Bike and Custom Shows Around the Globe

Johnny Halliday on a French TV show.

Australia

Since the end of World War II, there has been a very active Harley club and custom scene "down under," with various bike shows in all of the country's bigger cities. Worthy of particular mention are the Bankstown Motorcycle Show in Sydney organized by the Highway 61 Motorcycle Club, and the Scarborough Hotel Bike Show in Brisbane which is organized by Rebels' MC Australia. In the field of technology and design, the Australian designers are a match for the rest of the world.

England

Though there are a large number of bike shows in England (such as the Birmingham International Motorcycle Show), pure Harley shows are fairly rare. Harleys are actually presented as a part of the well-known Kent Bike Show organized by the local Hell's Angels. The 1998 the three-month 'Art of Harley' exhibition in London's Barbican Center, at which the work of an exclusive international selection of designers was displayed, stands out as an interesting exception.

France

Although France also has a highly developed custom scene, there are relatively few bike shows, so that the few there are tend to be all the more exclusive. One of the first was the 1989 event in Pecquencourt. Later followed Besançon and American Moto in Le Bourget, along with La Roche sur Foron in the 1990s. Against the backdrop of the various smaller local bike shows, two events above all have achieved international importance: the Salon de la Moto in Paris, and the bike show on the fringes of the annual meeting organized by Hell's Angels France in Cunlhat.

Unlike in other European countries (with the possible exception of the Scandinavian nations), French custom shows are characterized by the presentation of one specific style.

Germany

With the exception of the massive bike show scene in the U.S., it is perhaps in Germany that the most bike shows, exhibitions and activities are organized. They take place the whole year through, often with several on a single weekend and of all imaginable sizes. The diversity of bikes at these events – not all of which are dedicated solely to Harleys – and the public-relations and sales staff visible are an indication of the size of the biking scene in Germany as well as its economic importance.

Bike shows, if we stick with this expression, are put on by organizations and exhibitors, industry and trade associations, and also by private individuals, such as members of motorcycle clubs, Harley dealers, and accessories firms. Many of the bike shows are an integral part of large-scale parties or events, as their mood makes clear. Rallies and museum exhibitions also come under this heading. The IFMA (a general motorcycle show in Cologne) and its newest offshoot (the Intermot in Munich), are among the biggest organizers. Similarly placed is the annual Essen Motorshow, where the motorcycles (with the participation of the winners of the Rat's Hole Custom Chopper Show in the U.S. one of its special attractions) constitute, among all the cars and other vehicles, a relatively small but elite band. Some of the great motorcycle exhibitions which boast integrated individual shows are the Motorräder in Dortmund; the Berlin Motorradtage (BMT); the IMOT in Munich; the AMA in Stuttgart; the Faszination Motorrad in Sinsheim; and the American Days, held in Nuremberg. Innumerable local shows are satellites to these now firmly established big events, with a broad spectrum on offer of everything a biker might desire. Harley customs and conversions, however, almost always provide the main attractions and showstoppers.

Special events such as the High Performance Show, dedicated to customization, are highpoints of the German custom scene. For many exhibitors, custom and accessory dealers, these bike shows, fairs and exhibitions have long been a full-time job in what is essentially a large new industry. The organizers regard the need to innovate constantly as a grim fact of life, and so even at small local shows in Germany, high quality products from around the world can be viewed and bought.

Italy, Spain and Greece

Naturally there are also a host of motorcycle and bike shows in the southern countries of Europe. It has to be admitted that customized Harleys are relatively thinly represented there. However, some exceptions make clear that in these countries too the customization of Harleys (sometimes with futuristic style elements) opens up a new world of motorcycle riding in the sun-kissed south. One of the big international bike shows, with almost 25,000 visitors and over 13,000 motorcycles (mainly Harleys from all over Europe), is the Biker-Fest sponsored by the Italian magazine *Biker's Life*, which in 1996 took place in Villanova for the tenth year running. Large-scale events also take place in Marbella, Spain, and as part of Ibiza Bike Week.

Japan

Perhaps Japan seems rather introverted to the rest of the international biker scene, but in the "Land of the Rising Sun" there is a gigantic market for motorcycles in general and for Harleys in particular. Proof of this is to be found not only in the huge annual Tokyo Motorcycle Show, but also in innumerable other bike shows across the country, like the Classic & Motorcycle Fair in Nagoya. In terms of creativity, bizarre technology, and extreme designs, Japanese custom builders and designers are absolutely world-class and can hold their own against the best of America and Europe.

The Netherlands

As a result of their proximity to Germany, France and Scandinavia, there are, with a few exceptions, no custom shows in the Netherlands and Belgium. Recently, however, the bike magazine *Big Twin* has initiated its own bike show in Eindhoven, which has quickly enjoyed great success. Local bike shows organized by dealers and clubs go some way to satisfying the demand for the dragster sport, which is particularly popular in the Netherlands.

Scandinavia

As far as official regulations and standards go, Sweden is one of the most free countries in the world. This has allowed bikers and customizers to develop an unmistakably Swedish style, characterized above all by extremely long forks which make the bikes, equipped with particularly powerful motors, appear incredibly low. Swedish choppers are a byword for the most extreme vehicle designs, seen nowhere else on the planet. Bike shows in Janköpping or the Super Rallies in Sweden, Norway and Finland, and also the Hell's Angels rally in Denmark, are good examples of the ideal of freedom and adventure on a Harley, even in the far north, which is not otherwise known as ideal, biker country.

Switzerland

The custom shows in Switzerland are a memorable experience. No other country in the world plagues vehicle designers with such restrictive standards, laws and regulations with regard to vehicles. Despite this, Swiss motorcycle designers can be proud of their technical and artistic creations, which are world-class. Needless to say, they also make a point of taking their designs onto the street, thus underlining their appetite for freedom. There are several motorcycle shows organized by various small Swiss Harley clubs, and also two shows that are outstanding: the one organized by the company Moto Senn, which is always in the avant garde of European custom building, and the Gerold Vogel AG's Moto Faszination custom show.

United Arab Emirates

There's no doubt about it, the UAE is an ideal country for motorcycle riding. Now that the Arabian Gulf chapter of the Harley Owners' Group has established itself in Dubai, since 1996 a bike show has taken place which, while offering little in the way of excitement apart from a few high-class conversions and special commissions, has been a massive success with its international audience.

No costs and efforts were spared, when French TV transmitted a program presenting the best that customized Harleys can offer.

The Impossible Is Always Possible

Biker Shops

Somewhere in the Deep South: the names of first-class garages are traded as top tips between bikers (right).

When it comes to high-powered motors the brothers rely on the skills of the experts – the smoke test is a mean endurance test for motors and bikes (below).

Everything even only the most extravagant client might desire has to be there in his storeroom: Donald Van Dusen's Charleston Custom Cycle Shop in Illinois (above right), and at Delta Gates in southern Louisiana they know what a real biker needs (above).

They buy and sell Harleys; they repair and customize Harleys, and they have every Harley accessory imaginable; they're well-equipped with specialist tools and machines, do a wonderful job, and always try hard to satisfy their customers, for only their good reputation and satisfied customers can guarantee their survival. Many of them manage or subsidize successful racing teams and maintain and fine-tune the team machines. They're always a rallying point for hard-core motorcycle and biker communities, and also for clubs and Harley interest groups. They work independently and innovatively. They're to be found in almost every town and community. They far outnumber those employed at the official Harley dealerships. They're often an irritation to the company and may not (by court order) utilize either its name or its logo, though they market and maintain Harley-Davidson products almost exclusively. What are they? Let's just call them bike shops.

Bike shops don't spring up from the large-scale competitive provision of licensed Harley-Davidson franchisees, in accordance with the strict guidelines of the company, but rather grow out of the biking scene itself. Where there are Harley riders, there are soon also dedicated workshops, customizers, dealers... in other words, bike shops. And speaking of Harley franchises, bike shops function a lot more flexibly and are not bound to the firm's rigorous regulations. However, through

thick and thin, they remain loyal to the company's products. Many now feel they have been penalized for this.

Bike shops generally start small and gradually work themselves up to bigger and better things. If they make an error, they lose the opportunity of creating a lucrative business. Often they have developed out of mini-garages, the haunts of talented amateurs, technology freaks and Harley fans who had neither the money nor the inclination to become official Harley dealers, assuming that was possible.

But skill and reliability soon gain a reputation within the trade and soon the repair and conversion jobs multiply, thus laying the foundation for a growing business. Harley-Davidson looks upon this with mixed feelings and since the company does not supply shops who are not Harley dealerships with genuine company products, the innumerable bike shops tend to go for the aftermarket products, a market Harley finds problematic. The company finds itself in an interesting situation. Sometimes company principles do not match up with what some people believe of free market should be about. It is against this background the the ever more hard-fought cases involving the name, trademark and log oof the company must be understood.

Many of the bike shops embrace the rather old-fashioned blue-collar mentality of the mechanic smeared in oil and gas and display a disdain

for the neatly-pressed fashionable outfit of the Harley designer stores. Not surprisingly, in bike shops it's the bikes which stand in the foreground, not trendy tasseled leather jackets, shelves full of publicity brochures, and brand-new Harley parts and accessories, which are in any case intended for a different clientele. There are of course exceptions on both sides, but in many cases official Harley-Davidson dealers and extrovert bike shops have a different customer base, don't compete with each other, and indeed often cooperate. It's all a question of taste. Bike shops have their own special character and often a very individual image – which is perhaps not every Harley rider's thing.

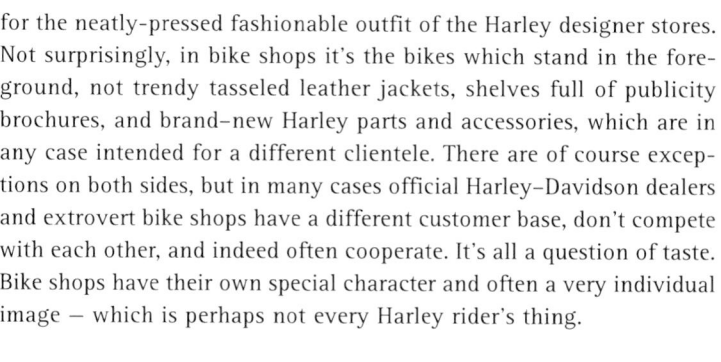

Ed's Cajun Cycles in Louisiana (top).

Everyone helps out – and often women make more sensitive mechanics (above).

"Professors" in New Orleans (left).

"Njet" won't do as an answer any more: in Russia, too, everything for the Harley rider is available; Gennady Bytschenkow, director of the Motosalon Rubicon Harley–Davidson (above).

A man's a man – Australia is famous for its innovative garages, as here at Jeff's Cycle Salvage near Brisbane (right).

Sometimes you have everything you need, sometimes you need everything you don't actually have: in Cuba (above) spare parts for Harleys are traded like treasures – new ones are simply not to be had.

Always surrounded by not quite legal Harleys, bike shops are the places to come for those who want a little something special – for example here at Biker's Asshole in Württemberg, Germany.

Vive la différence: Big Jack in Le Man, France services all Harleys, old and new, original or not (right).

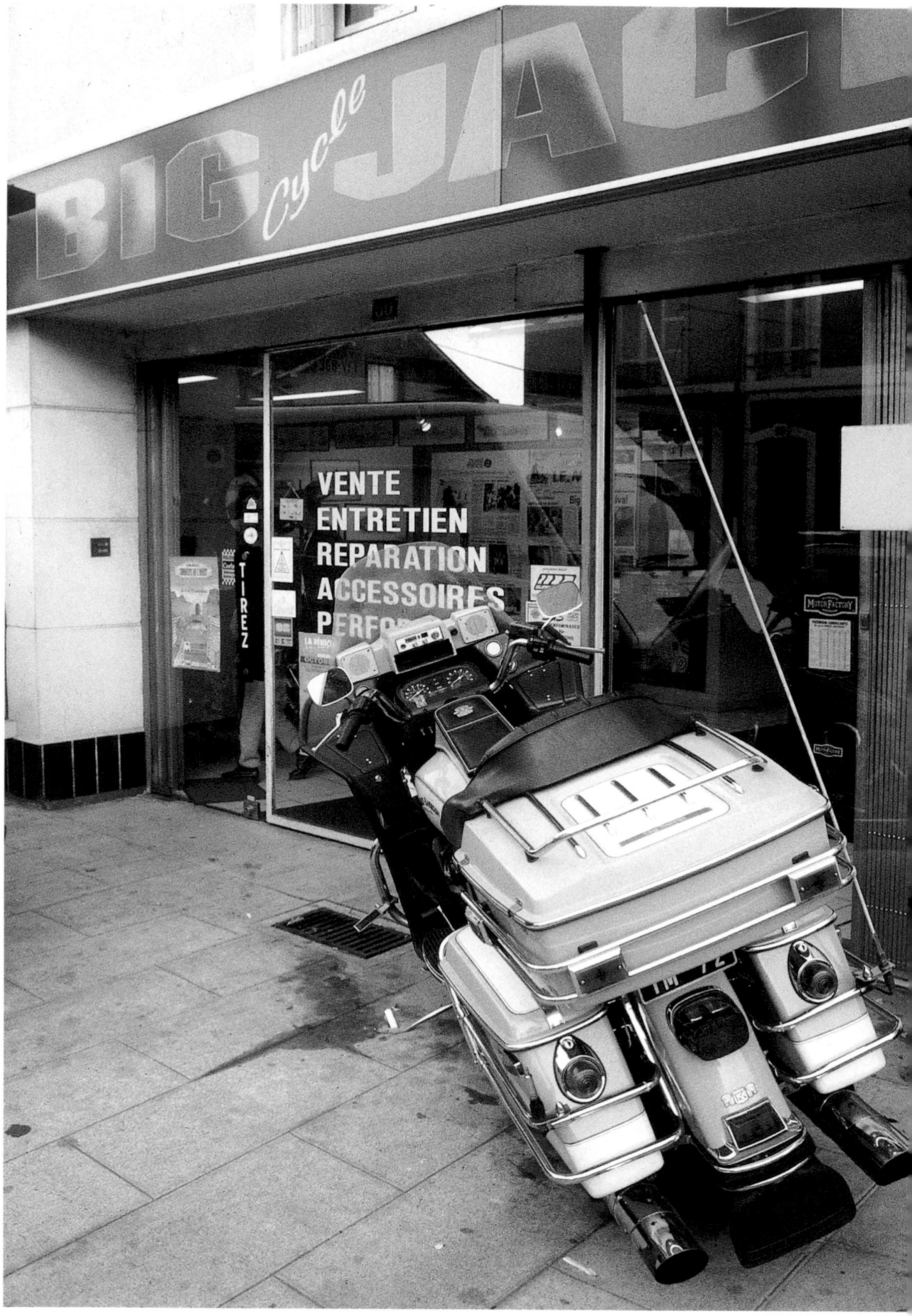

Motorcycle Nostalgia

Veteran Events

Coutesy of: Mark Jones, Milwaukee, Wisconsin

All its original bits: an old Hydra Glide which shows it served its equally old owner well for many a year - the centerpiece of every vintage event.

To the outsider, it all looks very relaxed and above all informal. The participants have known each other for years – generations of perfectionist mechanics and Harley old-timers caring with undimmed enthusiasm for the heritage of American motorcycle history. In 1954 the Antique Motorcycle Club of America (AMCA or AMC) was founded, following the example of the Vintage Motorcycle Club of Great Britain (VMCC), established in 1946.

The exclusive club meetings take place usually at small airstrips or on the parking lots of some elegant hotel complex or other, transformed for at least a short while into a place where members can indulge their nostalgic reveries: a weekend of shining chrome and gleaming paintwork. There's normally a festive banquet, a showroom, a conference room, and, of course, a convention suite, where the highly respectable social entertainment takes the form of the inevitable annual

report, the statement of finances (always impeccable), and the election of the committee. This is followed by a slide show of last year's meeting, given by a highly-respected member – a great moment of enthusiasm within the club. The inevitable problems facing the club are not taken too seriously, and some participants ply themselves with liquid refreshment from a perch on a stool in the hotel bar until the wee small hours of the morning.

The real stars, of course, remain outside. Some are 60 years old, some 70, some even 80, but most are between 30 and 50 years old. Their exteriors are sometimes immaculate, sometimes rusty, and their hearts beat either at a powerful thousand beats a minute or a rickety two hundred: vintage bikes, classics in pristine trim. Some of them are for sale, and the prices are enormous.

All around is a well-cataloged hotchpotch of accessories and

replacement parts of every kind and caliber. Quality American products, handmade, loved, cherished and cared for, polished, oiled, repaired and sometimes cursed. Classic motorcycles, the vast majority of them heaps of old Milwaukee iron, but still on the road. Once they were the two–wheeled pioneers of America, trusty workhorses that covered hundreds of thousands of miles without so much as a whimper on roads which had never known the application of tar or the rules of the road. Today they are much–admired exhibits about which spine-tingling stories can be told. Few outsiders are aware what human and technical triumphs and tragedies, successes and failures, are hidden beneath the immaculate metal.

They are not only there to be admired, of course, but also ridden. It's not difficult to hear and even smell the motorcycles. That thing that seems to be forever rattling, backfiring, clattering and humming out there on the parking lot or airstrip is a unique demonstration of the indestructible technology of the golden age of motorcycle manufacture, when people attempted to tame the almost virgin continent's seemingly endless vastness.

Vintage fans are a happy group, but also an exclusive and introverted clique, seeing themselves, as the guardians of a technological legacy all too often sacrificed to the unstoppable forces of progress.

In the course of time most of these vintage meetings have developed into large–scale veteran markets, offering just about everything an oldie usually has to beg, steal or borrow, with items ranging from old–pattern screws through to coveted specialist literature. Some of these mammoths from the Stone Age of motorcycle design are practically worth their weight in gold; others change hands for relatively modest sums. Even if the rust is considerable and the factory color can hardly be made out, the tag "original running condition" often makes a bike more valuable than the perfect restorations that surpass the real thing in terms of beauty and technical quality.

The astonishing fact that these motorcycles have been running reliably for over 60 years, and usually start up with the first, albeit powerful, kick of the rider's boot, coughing and spluttering until the mixture has had time to fill the engine perhaps, makes it worthwhile for the AMCA to give special trophies for the achievement; trophies which, in all honesty, rightfully belong to the motorcycle manufacturers of yesteryear.

At the center of these veteran events above all is the obligatory farewell parade, the *concours d'élégance*, a tour of the city over several miles accompanied by the wailing sirens of police vehicles. In the U.S., rallies or even large–scale endurance races are neither popular nor appropriate; that tradition developed above all in England and mainland Europe and also in Canada, Australia and South Africa.

At American veteran events, the sacred rules of the game state that the exhibits must be evaluated by an expert jury for class, age, condition and rarity, and rewarded with a heap of cringe–causing kitsch silverware, later to adorn local clubs like prized relics. Afterwards the competitors pack everything together in their roomy, air–conditioned, mobile homes and drive hours or maybe days, back home. A fussy club newsletter reports every minor experience and event verbatim.

In comparison with activities in Britain, the American veteran scene may not seem very big, even if individual events might indeed have

This Knucklehead has really been given the full treatment: telescopic forks, a "shotgun" exhaust and all kinds of technical refinements. It may be an old bike, but it can certainly leave other bikes in its dust! (far left).

Indestructible and still value for money: side-valve machines as they were in the Forties and Fifties (left).

A thoroughly customized Knucklehead with tube stanchions, shotgun exhaust and various sophisticated technical details: an oldie, but one with the requisite drive (below).

This side-valve from the 1930s has survived from the time of the Great Depression, in its original, albeit now slightly worn state. David Wassermann, its owner, still rides it daily (bottom).

In Italy too, old Harleys are still carefully driven – as one can see from the front section of this FL model (bottom right).

an international character (something which, incidentally, was not necessarily the intention of their founding members). This may also be because these historical events are scattered so widely over the massive country. Additionally, there are almost always a couple of vintage bikes around at motorcycle meetings, large and small, sometimes just for the hell of it, sometimes taking part in their own class or their own show, though dates and locations can be difficult to discover and are often only gleaned from insiders. The exceptions are the annual large-scale events with fixed dates, the regional AMC spring, summer, fall and winter meetings. These include the Springtime Meeting in Florida (during Daytona Bike Week); the Vintage Motorcycle Show in Bennington, Vermont; the Veteran Show in La Mirada, California; and Oley's Big Springtime Antique Meeting in Pennsylvania.

The biggest and best-known meeting is the Veteran Show every summer in Davenport, Iowa, which extends over several days. It first

took place at the Mississippi Valley Fairgrounds in 1972 and since then has taken place late each summer. The broad-ranging program covers a gigantic flea market, where almost everything that is to be found could warm the cockles of a collector's heart; a vintage racing program; an extensive Field Meet & Games Event; the dazzling banquet of course; and the vintage show, with judgments galore and stacks of cups and trophies.

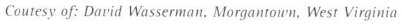
Coutesy of: David Wasserman, Morgantown, West Virginia

A Kind of Heaven

Flea Markets and Swap Meets

In the beginning, "Swap meets" or "exchange marts" were small, local events. They aroused the interest only of those in the know: do-it-yourself enthusiasts, collectors, lovers of veteran vehicles ... and of course any motorcyclist who didn't have enough money available to buy parts from a dealer. The American name "swap meet" is now used by bikers all over the world and is understood to refer to something that is more than simply a market for spare parts and bits of junk nobody else wants. There are swap meets of all types and sizes, ranging from private garage sales to enormous events lasting several days. Nowadays nearly every biker club organizes its own swap meets and it's at these that Harley parts are to be found in abundance. Visitors are surrounded by bikers trying their very best to sell every imaginable part and accessory – and all this in the midst of the usual party! In fact, the number of such events is increasing so rapidly that people are losing interest. As a result, prices have started to fall and business has begun to suffer. A list of some of the events of this kind is given below. In many cases the most attractive ones are those forming part of a larger event.

United States: On the occasion of the regional and national meetings (the Antique Shows & Field Meets) of the Antique Motorcycle Club of America (AMC/AMCA) big, used parts markets that are generally called "flea markets" are held. In fact it's at these that the greatest selection of parts for veteran motorcycles is to be found. The largest event in this category is the Davenport Show in Iowa, organized by the famous Chief Blackhawk Chapter. But there are other chapters in the AMC that offer a huge range of classic Harley parts and accessories: the Orange County Chapter, California; the Evergreen Chapter on the Pacific northwest coast; the Empire Chapter, mainly in Schenectady, New York; the Sunshine Chapter, Florida; the Maumee Valley Chapter, Michigan, Indiana, Ohio; and the Confederate Chapter in the middle of the Deep South. These are just to name a few of them.

In addition, a vital feature of all larger biker events is a large swap meet where you can find almost all the genuine spares and aftermarket parts for all types of Harleys, old and new. Among the best known (of the many events) is the enormous swap meet on the Volusia County fair-

They're all still there – and scattered all over the world, lovingly exhibited, cosseted and looked after, not always complete, not always original, but full of legends and a usually breathtaking past: old Harleys, there to be admired at bike shows, veteran events, swap meets and similar events.

Dealers in spare parts travel all over the country from one event to the next. The Daytona Bike Week is just one such event: there is a wide choice, but nothing comes cheap. Haggling over a price and precise information on each part are indispensable ingredients.

At private locally organized swap meets – like the one shown here in the South – anyone in need of spares or old parts will find some real bargains here. The choice may be limited and you must know what you are buying, because there is no such thing as a guarantee.

ground held as part of the Daytona Bike Week and billed as "the world's largest swap meet." Then there's Spider's Swapatona, which is also known as the Daytona Flea Market. Mention should also be made of the auctions started in 1988 by Jerry Wood with his famous motorcycle auction in the Armory.

The are other big swap meets in Sturgis, Laconia and at other biker events. Companies and magazines such as *Easyriders* and *Walnecks Classic Cycles* are great at organizing swap meets as well. The best known are those started by the Arizona Antique Classic Motorcycle Enthusiasts (AACME), and by the Canadian Vintage Motorcycle Group (CVMG).

Europe: In Great Britain the swap meets are more generally known to the public as "auto jumble sales" and have become quite a tradition. It's unusual to find Harley parts at such sales but if found they're very reasonably priced.

It may come as a surprise to learn that in Germany, a country which enjoys a very high standard of living, swap meets for cars and for motorcycles have developed phenomenally since the 1980s, becoming mammoth events. It's difficult to imagine that these markets for used parts and veteran vehicles attract the attention only of veteran vehicle enthu-

siasts or of those who enjoy tinkering around with motorcycles in their spare time. The value of veteran motorcycles in good condition is increasing constantly. However, since the border controls have come down in the former Eastern Block countries, there has been a steady supply of vehicles coming from there. Best of all, any profits made are tax free. As a result of these factors, a completely new category of motorcycle market has developed and led to an unprecedented boom.

However, these mass events, which attract hundreds of thousands of visitors and have a turnover of many millions, have already started to degenerate into something resembling seedy supermarkets and are quickly acquiring those tacky characteristics associated with popular mass entertainment. More importantly, the quality of what's on sale has deteriorated.

The following swap meets are among the largest in Germany: the Veterama in Ludwigshafen and Mannheim, the Technorama in Ulm and Kassel, the Classic Mobil in Munich and the First Classic Day in Essen. Also of importance – though not all of them are staged annually – are the Oldiemobil in Aachen, the Nostalgica in Schlüchtern, the Interclassic in Hennef and the Oldierama in Lörrach. The number of visitors varies from as few as 3,000 to 5,000, to as many as several hundred thousand.

Harleys broken down into parts (real basket cases) or just jumbled up without being given a once-over first: a real treasure trove for experts, but a nightmare for the greenhorn. There are always the most unexpected bargains to be found — which also just happens to include one of those much sought after Dream Girls calendars.

There are also general flea markets where spare parts are available, such as those held in Duisburg, Paderborn, Wilhelmshaven, Emden, Trier, Wolfsburg, Recklinghausen, Messkirch and Mühldorf, all of them linked to local exhibitions and bike shows.

Other countries also provide opportunities for Harley owners looking for parts. In Switzerland there's a market in Bern; in France in Montlery at the Moto Legende; and in Britain there's the September swap meet at the Montagu Motor Museum in Beaulieu and one on the Isle of Man during the Tourist Trophy and the Manx Grand Prix.

In fact, there are swap meets all over the world, wherever the motorcycle is popular. Those countries which are especially devoted to the Harley–Davidson motorcycle, such as Japan and Australia, there are local exchange markets where spare parts for the bikes are obtainable in unbelievably large quantities.

The information on where and when swap meets take place can be found in specialized biker magazines such as *Easyriders* in the U.S., and in *Bikers News* and *Thundercycles* in Germany. For those also used to riding on the information superhighway, further information is also available on the Internet.

Swappin' Time

Kitty's Custom Cycles

According to a venerable tradition in America, weekends are atime for garage sale. All over America families place everything they no longer need on a large table in the garden and hang a hand-painted "Garage Sale" sign on it. It's a popular and inexpensive source of goods for people who don't have all that much There are plenty of garage sales every weekend where you can find jeans for two dollars, a pair of nearly new tennis shoes for a dollar, plastic coffee cups for ten cents apiece, blouses and skirts for a dollar at the most. Radios, TVs, and washing machines – all with just a few "minor defects" – are there for the taking, along with waterbeds, furniture, and books; in short, all the stuff that accumulates in every household over the years.

What they don't have, however, are Harley parts, even though the demand is high. It is unfortunate since not all bikesr can afford to shell out the amount of dollars needed at the dealer's for a decorative FLH battery-cover they've just lost. Harley parts that aren't necessarily new but are in usable condition are heavily in demand. Some Harley dealers realized this long ago, setting up corresponding rummage tables in their stores, though not before also looking out for stuff they might need for themselves.That's why there are swap meets.

Around once a month a swap meet takes place at Kitty's Custom Cycles in Chicksaw Springs on the Gulf Coast. There, deals are struck brother to brother and face-to-face, without recourse to cash tills or accounts.

Naturally, you have to know what they're looking for, and also know about the many different parts Harley–Davidson has made over the years – otherwise you'll end up with the wrong brake shoes, fork brackets, gear rims, clutch lines, brake lines, compressors, exhausts or cylinders. Having been made for quite specific models, Harley parts are often not the same even though they seem to look exactly alike.

A swap meet is also a good opportunity to get rid of your old or never used parts, for which dealers pay only reduced prices. Bikers are realists. Those who ask too much don't sell anything, so prices are relatively low. Apart that is, from such things as Panhead motors, gearboxes and stock rigid frames: then there's nothing to haggle about, and they're sold in seconds flat.

The selection at Kitty's Custom Cycle Swap meet covers a broad range, and early in the morning as time passes more and more pickups, vans and converted buses arrive, some of them having come far and traveled through the night, and all of them more or less chockablock with Harley material. Vintage junk can be had there too, along with tools, jewelry, leather crafts, and all the biker goodies which turn a meeting like that into a paradise for collectors and DIY mechanics.

Kitty's Custom Cycles is ideally situated for such a swap meet: easy to find on Highway 90, it's only immediate neighbors are a couple of mobile homes. Kitty's place, far away in the pine woods that border the four-lane highway, specializes in upholstery and welding. Kitty doesn't ask for any gate charges and setting up a table is free. She remembers only too well the occasion when she dared to ask for the laughable fee of a dollar for entrance (including free food!) – it took almost six months before the annoyed bikers saw fit to turn up again. Now she asks two dollars and fifty cents for Mama's Burger Plate, a dollar for a plate of chili beans and one dollar and fifty cents for a hot dog. Everyone's happier this way, since those who don't want to pay anything don't have to buy the food.

Squeeky arrives on his rickety blue and white 1970s FLH, already the winner of several rat bike contests. From his plastic saddlebags, which hang awkwardly and are held on with straps, suspicious drips emerge. Like many Harley pack bags, they're full of holes, and soon a large puddle has formed beneath his bike. The spectators grin

knowingly. The bags are filled with ice which melts quickly in the summer heat but keeps the piles of beer cans cool just long enough. Squeeky sells the cans for a dollar apiece behind the bushes, for it is strictly forbidden to sell alcohol without a license (even on private property); the fine is 10,000 dollars. But the three percent strength beer is far too good to give away and the opportunity is perfect for making a few bucks. Squeeky just has to watch out that the sheriff lurking outside on the street doesn't catch sight of the dollar bills changing hands. After all, people can drink what they've brought with them – although not everywhere. When the saddlebags are empty, he just rides off and gets some more from the nearest Piggly-Wiggly store.

At around one o'clock, the band arrives in an ancient Chevy pickup on which their equipment is piled up like a bunch of scrap. The pickup had broken down again, first with water leaking from the radiator, and then with a flat tire, and by the time everything had been more or less stuck together with tape and gum, the drummer, Danny, was suffering from heatstroke ("it's all over now ..."). All the same, they managed 150 miles from Leakesburg on the appalling country roads in less than four hours, and as you can imagine, they're pretty beat; they drank all the beer that they had brought with them to keep cool in the heat out there, and they had to deal with all those difficulties, but hey, at least they made it.

Kitty has parked a rusty, old, flat trailer in front of the shop as a stage for the

band. It is ever so slightly shaded by two drought-stricken pine trees. The sound equipment is plugged together and wired up in just half an hour, and the speakers are stacked up on top of one another: "One, two, three ... testing, testing." Meatloaf breathes heavily into the microphone and then it all gets under way, an incredible sound, all six of them banging away, with the screeching guitars trying to imitate the sound of Jimi Hendrix ... the guys think they're pretty cool.

The local bikers and eccentrics trickle in. One of them is "Tomato Juice," a guy with an amazing beer belly which he can blow up to the shape of a perfect hemisphere. In honor of him (or rather of his girth), there's always a much laughed about Big Belly Contest, which he inevitably wins.

To much hilarity, over the weekend Kitty has hired a dunking machine for 50 dollars. Interestingly enough, it has been rented from a Methodist church, which had in the small print of the rental agreement a clause that was very careful to ban every kind of "immoral behavior." The fun costs a dollar for three baseballs; from a distance of about eight yards, you have to aim pretty good to hit the target, barely four inches across, which releases the catch mechanism that holds Kitty on her perilous perch. Not everyone can do it at the drop of a hat, but when they do, the shouts of pleasure are worth it, and the plume of water into which Kitty disappears helps to cool down the spectators. If you manage it with one ball, you're King Kong himself and can buy

somebody a beer; if you don't manage it at all, you can always run over to the target and press it by hand, something which is against the rules but can't be beaten for a few good laughs.

There are a few more games on the program without which a real swap meet is unimaginable; but in the steamy heat the participants drift away towards the shade, everyone looking for a cooler place to stand and socialize, trying to avoid any unnecessary effort.

The beer, being consumed in great quantities, has the usual effect, and soon every action takes place in slow motion. Apart from the tireless band, that is. Sweating and keen, they thrash their instruments around, anxious to make up for lost time. Where do these guys get their energy from?

From the author's experience, no swap meet could really take place without the presence of the authorities. Many bikers have found that whenever they get toghether somewhere, the telephone lines in the Police department start glowing red hot. Sometimes it's the neighbours (which can mean anyone within a 25 mile radius), sometimes it's parents worried about their underage children attending such events, sometimes it's the locals or just scared drivers, who tell the sheriff to the fact that hordes of Hell's Angels are on the road (whether or not the bikers are Hell's Angels or not) – expecting troubles. The sheriff knows all about the hysteria surrounding Hell's Angels, but thinks it might be a good idea to send a patrol car down to wait at the side of the road directly in front of the swap

meet anyway, just to keep an eye on things. Used to this kind of attention. The bikers are not particularly bothered by this.

At around three o'clock in the afternoon another police car arrives and two heavily armed deputies patrol through the crowd, who is busy sounding their appreciation for the rock band as they launch into their 27th bizarre cover version of 'Born to the Wild'. The deputies disappear into Kitty's junk shop. Two girls contort themselves to cool themselves under the fan, but now disappear quickly behind the counter. "We've had a complaint from the people in the residential area, that the music is too loud and obscene." Having said their piece, they walk out. Despite the warning, the band shouts into the mikes: "More obscenty, more obscinty!" Frowning, the deputies leave the scene of this spectacle. Unfortunately, they don't have a chance to close the meet and jail a couple of the visibly drunk ringleaders for breach of peace - an offence for which bail is usually made. Rock 'n Roll in the midst of rural America and of life on a Saturday afternoon, backed by 500 watts of amplification, goes on.

But Kitty, who's managed her store alone since her husband was sent to jail two years ago, is worried. Normally she has an exemplary relationship with the sheriffs, since she needs their protection and watchfulness. Most of the time she is alone with her two babies in the shop, which stands alone and far away from its nearest neighbors on the highway. The business isn't all that good anyway. Some days she hardly makes twenty bucks, on others nothing at all, and everyone knows how to force the old-fashioned cash till. That's why she's always relieved when she sees the blue and gray patrol car drive past outside and the officer wave to her.

And now one of those same patrol cars has been sitting for the past hour at the side of the road, and she doesn't know who's sitting in it and what the guy actually wants. He can be seen speaking

into his radio constantly which makes Kitty very uncomfortable.

The rock band rage tirelessly on their swaying stage and are sprayed with water (among other things) to help cool them down – the guitars unfortunately also getting their share – and empty beer cans land more or less on target on the quickly growing trash heap which is piling up in the middle of the crowded arena. Someone pours a can of gas over it, someone else throws a burning match, and in the wink of an eye half the party is engulfed in yard high flames, directly beside the parked bikes.

The party is slowly beginning to spiral out of control. At the edge of the site, and hidden behind auto wrecks and elderberry bushes, some of the more out of control in attendance are smoking dope, and the unmistakably sweet smell, mingling with the fragance of hamburgers from Mama's Grill, is a dead giveaway. It won't be long before any undercover agent from the D E A on the scene will pull out their hund-cuffs. With a shuder of fear, Kitty remembers the terrible outcome of the Mayswap Meet not far from here in Lousianna, where there was a wild shoot-out among the bikers and the sheriffs, who turned up in strength and cordoned off the place and threw half the audience into jail. There are certain people who don't care and don't give a damm about rules, law and order or even decent behaviour. The party is slowly getting out of control, and the police are beginning to go on alert.

All of a sudden, Kitty comes to the rescue. "Closing time!" she screams to the grumbling crowd, "if you still need something, you better hurry!" A couple of brothers stagger round with a vacant look on their faces but don't know for sure any more what it was they actually wanted. Most of them are tired of it all anyway and collect their utterly bedraggled kids and start up. Behind in the encampment, a chained Doberman is growling and snapping, knowing that it'll soon be time for him to guard the

place and make mincemeat of anyone who strays onto his turf.

Frank, the President of the Southern Coyotes, knows where everyone's heading: "Hey, brothers, let's go; see y'all at the Crazy Horse saloon."

The word gets around quickly, and one by one the groups head off with growling motors, the girls up behind on the sissy bar, their legs raised high and so sharply angled they look like grasshoppers. They're all riding off to the evening party. Such opportunities for get-togethers like today are few and far between. Just to be on the safe side the Police Department sends a couple of patrol cars to the Crazy Horse.

Around six o'clock the sun is already in the west, directly above the endless Highway 90; the last bikers and pickups depart with engines screaming, their rpm far too high; the area they leave is strewn with beer cans, paper plates, discarded food, and charred garbage. Kitty, Mom and Dad count the few extra bucks they made today; it's not much, but it's enough for the most urgent bills, rent and interest on the shop, the phone bill and naturally utilities – 200 bucks for electricity and water. It also just about covers the cost of 50 new T-shirts in outlaw biker black with the cool, new, Harley designs.

A Statement of the Company

The foregoing article portrys the scene at one particular swap meet. The events described are not necessarily indicative of what takes place at all swap meets. These swap meets are not sponsored by Harley-Davidson.

Sports

Hell On Wheels

Dragster Racing

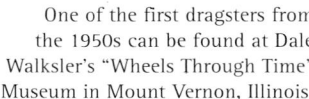

One of the first dragsters from the 1950s can be found at Dale Walksler's "Wheels Through Time" Museum in Mount Vernon, Illinois.

Courtesy of: Dale Walksler, Wheels Through Time Museum, Mount Vernon, Illinois

Anyone who's seen one will never forget the experience and anyone who's actually ridden in one will never be able to get enough of it: dragster racing, also known as sprinting. It's perhaps the craziest method of getting from A to B. Accelerating as fast as possible from a standing start in order to cover a short, precisely measured distance in record time is an elementary challenge to man and machine in what must be the most original form of motorcycle sport.

Brutal force and the highest possible speeds, scarcely kept under control at the very limits of personal and technical capability, satisfy our primitive desires for power, performance and success as nothing else can. Motorcycle drag races are hellish and deafening spectacles of self-realization and no motor exerts more magnetic powers over technicians, riders and spectators than the simple, large displacement, Harley V-Twin, here tested to its very limits.

There have in fact been sprint competitions for as long as there have been motorcycles, for they are the perfect expression of the modern world's fascination with speed: unsafe, dangerous, suicidal, crazy. Thus it was that a group of gentlemen met on an early summer's day in the year 1903, in a part of France far removed from any human settlement in order to indulge their new passion and speed off on their motorcycles – in fact, they were shaky bicycles powered by outsize motors of around 350 cc to 500 cc. The machines produced a mere one or two horsepower, the ignition and carburetor were a nightmare and compression was about 4:1; leather belts served as transmission, the tires were stuck together from some sort of patchwork material and safety was the last thing on the minds of these headstrong pilots. They raced through a mile in all of 77 seconds, in the course of which they reached the amazing speed of 47 mph. These were the first dragster races and they were extremely exciting affairs.

The first U.S. drag strip was opened 47 years later, in 1950, in Santa Ana, California. Now the many hotrodders, who had previously roared across dry salt lakes and the dry bed of the Los Angeles River,

had a place they could call their own. They formed the National Hot Rod Association (NHRA) and the Southern California Timing Association (SCTA) as bases for the many new tracks, among them suitable airstrips. Prominent drag strips of the 1950s and 1960s included such places as the Kingdom Raceway in Irvindale, famous for its "Run What You Brung"competitions; it had eventually to give way to an industrial estate and it's now the site of a brewery. There was also the LADS (Lion Associated Dragstrip) at Famosa near Bakersfield, also no longer with us; and the well-known drag strip at Pomona.

Along with these early sprint tracks in California, there were soon others elsewhere: in Atco in New Jersey, Oklahoma City, Indianapolis and Akron, Ohio, were some of the first; Bowling Green, in Kentucky, was closed in 1978 because of recurring riots and a few of the others have not survived either. Today, at the end of the 1990s, there are over 70 official drag strips and a host of unofficial ones, too.

Most are built for the classic distance of a quarter mile (1,320 feet), but there are others for a furlong (660 feet). The old drag strips had no modern technical equipment such as "Christmas Tree" starting lights and computer control. That was the task of the flagman at the start and two or more flagmen at the finish. Timings were taken with a stopwatch and riders raced against the clock for as long as it took until the officials had found the two fastest, who would then compete against each other in the final. At first only a few motorcycles were built specially for sprint races, because riders usually raced under the motto "Run What You Brung."

The motorcycles of the early period were still very primitive: rigid frames (hard tails) with springer or girder forks. Along with the rather more modern English singles and twins from Norton, BSA, AJS and a couple of trimmed Vincents, it was above all the Harleys in the shape of the UL and K models which had to compete against the ever more popular, speedy Japanese two- strokes, in particular against the Yamaha RD 350 and 400. It was a grand free-for-all. Scooters raced too:

Cushmans, Mustangs, Vespas and Lambrettas. The quickest was a Zündapp Bella clocked at 70 mph. The participants usually paid one or two dollars entry fee for the privilege of starting in the motorcycle class; and a "motorcycle" was virtually classed as anything on two wheels being able to move forward.

In the "Fuel Age" (up to about the middle of the 1960s) it was usually aircraft fuel that was used for the Fuelers and Top Fuelers. Only a few riders such as Leo Payne were able to control other fuels such as methane or nitro without having their engines explode around their ears. Payne compiled extremely detailed tables of air pressure, temperature and humidity to determine the correct thrust.

At this time the gap between the affordable Japanese bikes and the expensive four-strokes was becoming wider and wider and the NHRA felt forced to get to grips with this situation. The motorcycle dragsters attracted ever more sponsors, Harley-Davidson alone showing a lack of interest.

In the four-stroke class, Hondas soon dominated the scene; Russ Collins, for example, on his CB 750 and later on his legendary supercharged Double Honda Four. All the same, Harley supported certain Top Fuel specialists like Joe Smith with his Double V-twin Top Fueler and Anson "Campi" Holley with his A-Fueler. Gradually various categories and classes came into being, divided into the Professional (Pro), Sportsman and Street classes and soon it was extraordinarily difficult to make headway in the chaos of classes, rules and different organizations, particularly since Harley dragsters were thoroughly uncompetitive outsiders. It was hardly surprising that private Harley drag-racing organizations appeared, which competed against each other, though they were often mutually hostile and therefore ineffective.

The AMA, the mother organization of all motor sportsmen, gave them almost no assistance and the international hot-rod associations were by far too concerned with their own affairs to worry about Harley-Davidson dragsters.

It's completely incomprehensible why Harley-Davidson should even now hold itself aloof from this motorsport, a type that matches the image of the Milwaukee legend like no other sport. Harley drag events are the most spectacular examples of drag racing in the world and Harley riders and spectators are by far the most loyal.

Accessories and the special racing parts were not available from Harley and had to be sought elsewhere; soon there were many specialists who developed from high-class do-it-yourself mechanics up to small and in more than a few cases large businesses. It has turned into an almost inexhaustible market of immense proportions. A list (regrettably incomplete) of some important dragster-component firms may serve to make this clear and may also explain why Harley will have nothing to do with the technically, extremely complicated material.

Thanks to two factors, that is the constant technical development and the zeal and dedication of innumerable technicians, mechanics and test riders, the magic speed limit for Harley dragsters in the Top Fuel class is now, at the end of the 1990s, somewhere between six and seven seconds for the quarter mile, their speed measured to a thousandth of a second. The big, V-Twin, high performance motors, however, have little to do with any conventional Harley, apart from sharing the famous name.

Well-Known Suppliers in the High Performance Dragster Market:

S & S Products	Truett & Osborn
Drag Specialties	Custom Chrome
Primo Products	Paughco Inc.
Truett Frame Works	Whites MC Supply
Andrews Products	Jammer Cycle Products
Axtell Sales	Delcron
Hall Engeneering	Advanced Racing Technology
Sifton MC Products	Edelbrock Corp.
Manley	Rev Tech
Performance Machine	Rivera Engineering

The Need for Speed

Dragster Racing Associations

Categories of Racing Organizations

IDBA

Professional Classes: Top Fuel, Super Elim, Pro Comp, Pro Stock
Sportsman Classes: Ultra Stock, Mod Comp, Stock Comp

Drag Bike

Professional Classes: Super Elim, (Top Fuel), Pro Stock, Pro Comp, Pro Dragster
Sportsman Classes: Comp Elim, Mod Elim, Stock Elim

NMRA

Professional Classes: Top Fuel, Super Elim, Pro Stock
Sportsman Classes: Pro Comp, Comp Elim, Mod Elim, Stock Elim, Combo Elim, E.T. Elim, Youth Elim

HDRA

Professional Classes: Top Fuel, Pro Fuel, Pro Stock, Pro Dragster, Pro Gas
Sportsman Classes: Modified Series, Street Eliminators

AMRA

Top Fuel, Super Pro Fuel, Pro Fuel, Top Gas, Pro Stock, Pro Modified, Modified, Super Stock Big Twin, Super Stock Sportster, Three Wheel, Dresser, Stock A, Stock B, Eliminator Class

PROSTAR

(open to Harleys and non–Harleys) Top Fuel, Top Fuel (Harley only), Pro Comp, Pro Dragster, Pro Stock Harley

AMDRA (the American Motorcycle Drag Racing Association; Roy Strawn, Atco Raceway, New Jersey), which was founded in the late 1960s, used to organize the U.S. Nationals. Despite close cooperation with the NHRA (National Hot Rod Association), the organizational and financial problems became increasingly severe and the AMA was difficult. Smaller groups began to split away in increasing numbers. In 1977 AMDRA gave up. One of its splinter groups was the IDBA (International Drag Bike Association; Wayne Molpus, later Tony Lee, Mount Olive, Alabama), centered in the U.S. South, which was known for its Iron Man Nationals and a special Funny Bike class, in which there were very few Harleys. The IDBA classes were the following: Pro Classes: Top Fuel, Super Elim, Pro Comp, Pro Stock. Sportsman Classes: Ultra Stock, Mod Comp, Stock Comp.

In order to increase sales of his magazine *Dragbike* (1973–1976), publisher Tom Loughlin founded the Dragbike Racing Organization in Utica, New York in 1976. It organized ten national and 25 regional dragster races each year. As technical director, Jim Milsted introduced new classes in 1979 and ad-ditionally, there was a Youth Elim Class for child motorcyclists aged eight to sixteen on machines of up to 125 cc.

Also in the year 1979, the NHRA (National Hot Rod Association) announced a new subdivision for motorcycles, the NMRA (National Motorcycle Racing Association, with Jim Harris, former technical director of AMDRA, York, Pennsylvania). As the official replacement for AMDRA, the NMRA organized eight national dragster events for motorcycles, two of

them together with four–wheeled dragsters. The organization developed new safety rules for the sport and also had its own publication, *The National Dragster* newspaper.

Under the leadership of Dane Miller, the organizations later President, the NMRA approved several more classes. In the category of Professional Classes, they included: Top Fuel, Super Elim and Pro Stock. In the category of Sportsman Classes, they included: Pro Comp, Comp Elim, Mod Elim, Stock Elim, Combo Elim, E.T. Elim and the Youth Elim.

In 1977, Red Roberts, together with Darrell Flowers, began to organize a new sort of Harley only, dragster racing in Texas. After some initial setbacks, the HDRA (Harley Drag Racing Association) was to develop out of it in 1987. In 1993 it was taken over by Dane Miller and Ace Paschal, this time with the blessing of Harley-Davidson, changing its name to the AHDRA (All–Harley Drag Racing Association). Its classes are, in the Professional Classes: Top Fuel, Pro Fuel, Pro Stock, Pro Dragster, Pro Gas. In the Sportsman Classes: Modified Series, Street Eliminators.

Additionally, there were also a series of races sponsored by the association: the Quick Throttle Top Fuel for the fastest Top Fuel Nitro–Methane Harleys over 400 horsepower, with times of a little more than six seconds and speeds of over 200 mph; Red Line Oil/Zippers Modified Series; Pingel E.T. Series for Street Racers; and the activities of the AHDRA Junior Fan Club. Extra attractions are provided by the AHDRA in the shape of their King of the Hill and Queen of the Hill competitions.

The AMRA (American Motorcycle Racing Association; Itaca, Illinois) has been organizing All–Harley Drags since 1995 in the following classes: Top Fuel, Modified, Super Pro Fuel, Super Stock Big Twin, Pro Fuel, Super Stock Sportster, Top Gas, Three Well, Pro Stock, Dresser, Pro Modified, Stock A, Stock B, Elim Class.

Rounding it off, there was a new establishment, PROSTAR, formed in 1992, though it now doesn't seem all that new. It was formed out of the IHRA (International Hot Rod Association) under Fred Hamilton, Joe Sway and Jerry Byers with the following (mixed) events: Sportsman Nationals, Thunder Nationals, Orient Express U.S. Nationals Gulf Coast Nationals and, Pro Cycle & Water Sport World Finals with the following classes (open to Harleys and non–Harleys alike): Top Fuel, Top Fuel (Harley only), Pro Comp, Pro Dragster and Pro Stock Harley.

These races were complimented by various sponsored runs, for example the Orient Express Shootout, the Vance & Hines Super Gas Series, the Star Racing Top Gas Series, the HPC Super Modified Series and the Mikuni Super Gas Series. A few points to note: "Sanctioned race events" are officially recognized national and international events at which records are set and considerable sums awarded in prize money. Their rules are complicated and are strictly enforced. "Unsanctioned race events," also known as outlaw races, are more about testing and trying out bikes and naturally offer a load of fun for local enthusiasts who wouldn't normally be able to afford to take part in the expensive sanctioned events.

Terminology

Fuel = all kinds of fuel allowed
Gas = only gasoline allowed
Pro = professionally licensed riders
Stock = largely unmodified street machines
Elim = elimination races
Modified = technically altered and improved
Comp = competition
E.T. = elapsed time (actual time ridden between two set points)

Over the years, the start made by Red Roberts (opposite, top) developed into several organizations devoted entirely to Harley dragster racing. The preparations and races in the "Top-Fuel" class are the most spectacular sights at any event.

Classes and Procedures

The fastest Harley-Davidson dragster in Europe makes a start: Werner "Krüsi" Sohm with his nitro-methane-compressor "Top-Fueler" (2250 cc, 500 hp).

Professional classes of drag races need a special license from the sanctioning organization and are governed by a great many rules and safety ordinances. All pro-class riders start lined up, with a "Christmas tree" starting system, meaning that all five amber lights flash together for a third of a second before the green start light.

Participants in the sportsman classes, on the other hand, can start with a normal handicap procedure. This means that a carefully calculated head start is given to the slower rider. If both competitors achieve the same speed as their dial-in times, they theoretically cross the finish line simultaneously.

So the decisive factors here are pacing, short reaction times and the correct head start. In the sportsman categories, the motorcycles are divided into classes on the basis of weight and cubic capacity. With bracket racing, on the other hand, the motorcycles are not classed according to the relationship of weight and cubic capacity, but according to dial-in times: here E.T. head starts are given as in the sportsman categories. For the spectators, these runs are less exciting since the different starting times means they can't see who's winning.

The pro-stock category is a professional class that was introduced by the NHRA in the year 1974 under the patronage of the AMDRA. It had no totally new concept behind it but was given the blessing of officialdom and soon became very popular. Thus all imaginable motor conversions are allowed in the pro-stock eliminator classes, as long as the external appearance of a purchasable standard motorcycle model is maintained.

Original frames and cubic capacity are obligatory. Pro-stockers have the most powerful engines in them, but look like average, run-of-the-mill bikes. It is understandable, then, that the spectators jump out of their seats when two well-matched opponents compete against each other, particularly if one of them is riding a Harley and the other a Japanese motorcycle. Usually the Japanese bike wins. But if Harley has its day, the celebrations are tremendous.

Ground Rules

A typical starting system with "christmas tree" and start personnel (left). Preparations for the start of a Sportsman Class dragster (below).

Mandatory rules: the motorcycle must have brakes, a chain guard and above all a deadman's kill switch, which automatically cuts the ignition through a snap-on throttle in case of an accident. The rider must be wearing a helmet, either leathers or a leather jacket and gloves as well as sturdy boots.

Technical Inspection: the tech card must absolutely be filled out correctly. Then the technical inspection will take place according to the procedures for the various classes. If there are variations in the respective records, the correctness of the information given on the tech card is the deciding factor.

Staging Area and Staging Lanes: In this area all competitors must position their race-ready motorcycles in the a row allocated for their class and then wait for their class to be called.

Burnout Area: the spectacular burnout is intended to rid the tires of dirt to ensure a better grip on the track. There are three types: the wet burnout, where a little water makes the back tire roll better; a dry burnout; and finally, a bumper burnout, where the tires are pressed against a post.

The Christmas Tree Starting Positions: the Christmas tree, developed by Chrondek, provides a complete starting system of lights for each of the two parallel lanes. At the top there are the pre-staging lights, controlled by a light-gate. Below them are located the start-readiness or staging lights. Lastly there are the five amber lights, arranged one beneath the other, which are activated a in third of a second rhythm all the way down to the green GO light. Below these is the red foul light which shows a false start.

The E.T. Light-Gate: directly behind the Christmas tree at about ground level there is, together with the electronically controlled starting light system, the E.T. (elapsed-time) light-gate. Activated when the front wheel drives through, this measures the time which passes until the second E.T. light gate at the end of the track is reached. If anyone starts too early, the E.T. procedure is halted and the red foul light signals a false start. The time between the green light and the first E.T. light gate is measured as the reaction time. When both machines are correctly positioned in the staging phase, the starter presses the button for the start computer, which now carries out the entire starting procedure automatically. During this time no further correcting of positions is possible.

Time Slip Booth: whether the start is valid or false, every rider receives a time slip after the race on the way back to the riders' area, showing their E.T. time, reaction time and the final speed. The collected data from all the time slips serve as a basis for the calculation of all further starts and especially for record runs. With regards to the dial-in of times, time slips are invaluable aids to decision making.

The Dial-In Time: the dial-in time is the individual time that before the run, every rider gives to the umpire, who enters it into the computer. The closer the run comes to this time, the better the chances of victory against the opponent in the other lane. If the rider undercuts this time (meaning he is quicker), the run is declared void.

Someone with sensitive ears will hardly like dragster sports. But real Harley fans love this roaring sound that open exhaust pipes create – its beautiful music to their ears. Just standing next to a bike can be too much; the noise can amount to 140 decibles.

Building Powerhouses

Dragster Engines

The famous Top-Fuel twin-engine of Marion Owens.

journals must be tightly connected to the crankshaft; often they are welded together.

While the cylinders consist of aluminum casting — there are no cooling fans on account of the short time of a run — the liners are made of special steel, the piston of a particularly high-grade aluminum alloy and the connecting rods of lightweight titanium. There are no cylinder-head gaskets, since they would hardly be able to withstand the enormous pressure inside the combustion chamber; so metal sits on metal, screwed together very tightly. With the extremely high compression ratios (normally between 11:1 and 13:1), any decrease in pressure must be prevented: the pistons have no piston rings and the play between them and the cylinder wall tends towards zero.

Since the pistons and cylinders expand at different rates, the time interval before the piston is stuck fast (thus breaking the motor apart) has become ever shorter. Its lifetime extends over only a few minutes, for that reason the meaning of the horrifying game at the start line, where the competitor edges closer to the imaginary light-gate which signals the start, becomes clear. It's known as "playing poker." For those who have spent too much time during the pre-start and too much heat during the burnout, things are now very tight and it becomes a nerve-racking question as to whether they will manage the seven-second run to the finish.

Transferring the power of this giant-sized triumph of motor engineering onto the track in the most effective way possible is a further technical challenge. One component in this is the massive multi-plate clutch, as a rule made up of three to five pairs of plates. The fewer the pairs of plates, the more effective is the transfer of power to the back wheel, which is equipped with as broad a surface as possible and whose air pressure must be precisely measured. Adjustable weights raise the pressure on the clutch plates: the higher the number of revolutions, the tighter the plates press together. Sometimes they even fuse into one; the wear and tear is phenomenal.

The motive force is transmitted primarily by a broad high-performance toothed belt, secondarily by a strong chain. The two-gear motor is activated automatically by a switch together with the clutch. A "shift light" indicates when the rpm reading requires the second gear, by means of which, incidentally, the burnout is also initiated.

The oil lubrication occurs automatically. Before every run, oil is poured into the cylinder-head covers. This is known as total-loss lubrication. The explosive fuel consists of a mixture whose exact make-up is a closely guarded secret by everyone involved. Probably it's around 95 percent nitro-methane and alcohol. A mechanical fuel injection system set in motion by the gas pedal controls the flow of fuel through the carburetor. Thrust power alone is a science in itself, which every rider must learn by means of long tables of performance figures and even longer experience.

The problems with the 200-horsepower Top Gas motors are similar. However, in this case the fuel is not quite as explosive and the forces are not quite as brutal. Top Gas dragsters also have high-compression big-bore or stroker engines and are often mounted on Harley Sportster bodies. In their case as well, the gears (up to five) are changed by air pressure. The ignition, as with the Top Fuelers, is electronic and the primary power transfer is either by a toothed belt or, as with the

Although all racing motors are extremely complicated machines, the Top Fuel and Top Gas Harley dragsters form a whole new dimension in design and construction, testing as they do the very limits of the internal-combustion engine. The engines, however, have little if anything to do with Harley itself — apart from the 45 degree V-twin principle with the two connecting rods on one crankpin. Their simple-looking technology functions only because of almost unimaginable manufacturing precision.

In the case of dragster motors, everything on the bike is massive: giant cylinders, outsize pistons, fat tires, an impossible force of propulsion and incredible costs. When one of those monster engines springs into life, the earth shakes with deafening explosions. It's a technical, visual and above all acoustic inferno, better suited to a scene of war than to a sporting event. The fuels, especially the nitro-methane compounds, are like liquid bombs and to control them requires a deep and precise knowledge and also sound procedures performed with painstaking exactitude.

Once started, nitro-fired engines can be ridden only at top speed: any reduction in gas would cause them to explode. If the motor goes dead before the start, it can't be simply fired up again; before it can be restarted, every drop must be carefully removed from the fuel-supply system.

The technology of such powerhouses requires extremely high-quality material, some originating in space research, where similar fuels are used for powering rockets. Top Fuel engines — together with strokers and big bores, often with a total volume of over 2000 cc — can produce up to 500 horsepower, the pistons reaching a speed of over 43 yards per second. At up to 7000 rpm, this necessitates an ever-shorter piston stroke, their length being in inverse proportion to capacity. Since the total energy flow through the primary and secondary drives is transmitted over the left side, the cylinder

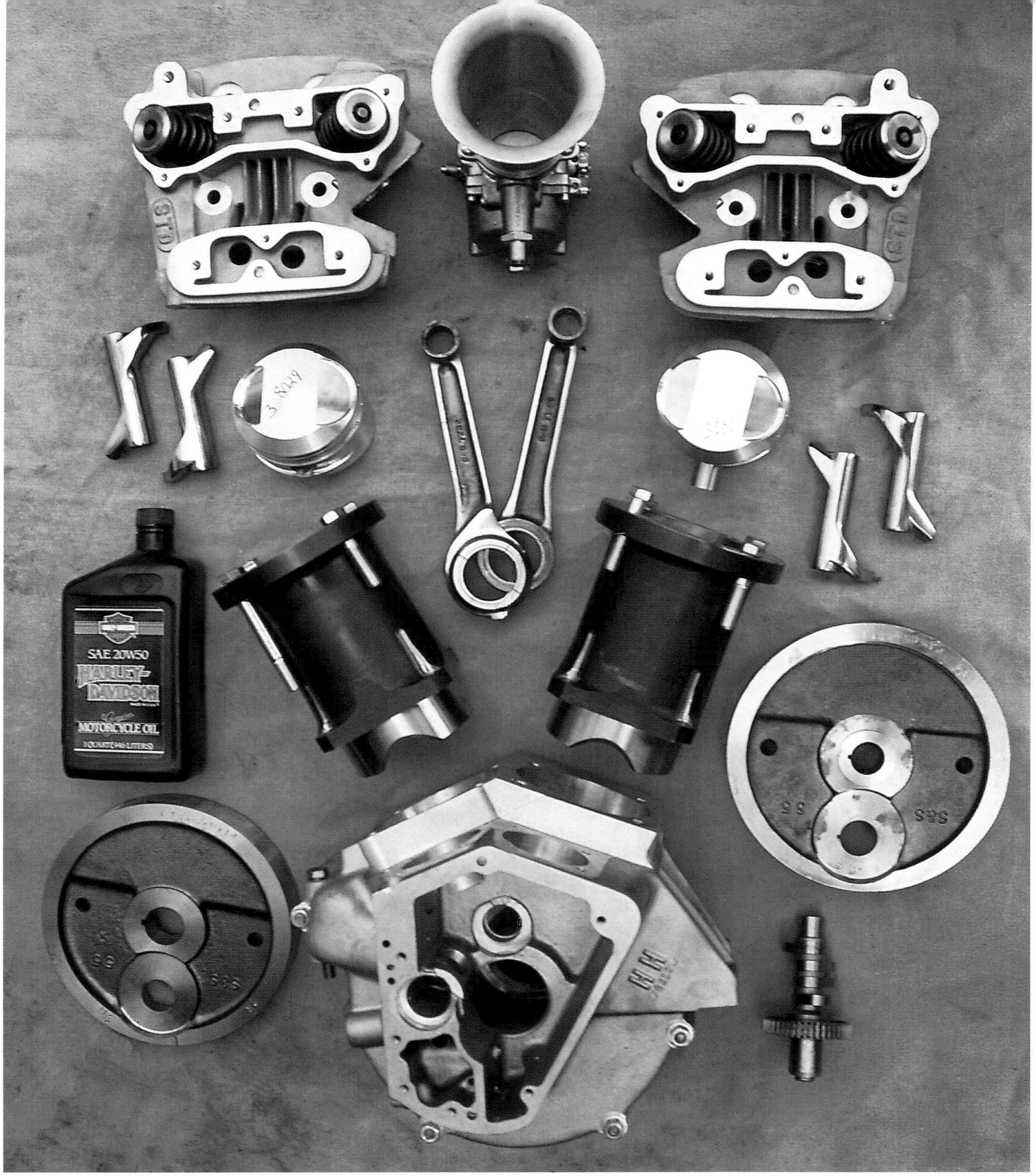

Sportster types and the series Sporties, a triplex chain. The clutch is similar to that of the Top Fuel motors. Only high-octane gas is allowed as fuel. Exhaust-driven turbochargers or mechanically driven compressors are, however, allowed to deliver increased power. The addition of nitrous oxide is illegal. For this type of fuel there is an extra class with its own distinct technology.

The Harley double-engined dragsters are in a class of their own. Since the mid-1970s, after Anson "Campi" Holley's unsuccessful attempt to design a parallel twin in the 1960s, motorcycles in this class have only had two Harley motors mounted behind each other. This double-engined dragster class oscillates between sensational success and almost permanent disaster. Along with the specific technical difficulties, absolutely precise synchronization of the motors

must be achieved so they work together instead of impeding each other. It's a high-tech adventure in every sense of the word.

But the technology of modified Harleys also offers a great opportunity for talented do-it-yourself mechanics, tuners and general fiddlers, designers and technicians. The challenge of being first over a quarter mile or furlong, however, is decided in thousandths of a second and new records are becoming increasingly difficult to beat. That is, until a completely new technical solution by way of an innovation arrives, of course. Let's wait for the surprise.

Top-Fuel dragster engines are an impressive sight, both assembled and disassembled. In the photo above, a crankshaft-driven compressor is fitted in front of the engine.

All About Dragsters

A quarter-mile can sometimes seem endless, even when it takes mere seconds to cover it, and spectators and riders alike experience the ultimate adrenaline kick at dragster races.

Special racing events are normally the creations of regional organizations, riders themselves and the motorcycling community in general. Other creators are, of course, the manufacturers, who depend on a continual and demanding evaluation of their own products.

Some of these events were officially recognized by the larger administrative bodies, while others remained outlaw events. In addition, many smaller races were included as an important part of biker parties, club events or Harley-Davidson rallies, staged or subsidized by the company itself or by H.O.G.

The first Texas Hog Rally (no association to H.O.G.) took place in Dallas in 1981. This was the birth of the All Harley Drags, which was to lead to the formation of the H.D.R.A. As a rule, few bikers visited the South because a distinctive Harley dragster community had never developed there, aside from in Florida and Texas.

But from 1983 onwards the private All Harley Drags were held every year on the occasion of the Memorial Day "blowout" under the auspices of the Asgard MC based in Biloxi/Gulfport.

In 1986 the H.D.R.A., which concerns itself solely with Harley-Davidson dragsters, gave its seal of approval to the following exclusive Harley dragster races: Marion Owens Okie National; Texas ABATE All Harley National; Annual Great Illinois Hawg Rally; Harley Homecoming Nationals; Annual Iowa Hog Drags; Sturgis Harley National; and Great Lakes Harley-Davidson U.S. Nationals. Some of them have survived as regular events, but others have changed greatly or just disappeared.

The highlight of every dragster race: two twin-engine Top-Fuel dragsters start simultaneously in an elimination race.

In 1989, the Harley-Davidson Screamin' Eagle program sponsored the following different dragster events, most of them officially approved, on the following drag strips: Myrtle Beach, South Carolina; Eunice, Louisiana; Hagerstown, Maryland; Atco, New Jersey; Humboldt, Iowa; Epping, New Hampshire; Sturgis, South Dakota; Rockingham, North Carolina; Bandimere Speedway, Morrison, Colorado (the annual H.O.G. rally); and Atlanta, Georgia.

There was one other organization that was formed for Harley dragster racing under the patronage of the *American Iron* magazine (TAM Publications): FLASH (Fastest Legal All Street), an acronym generally used to denote modified "pro-flash" machines which are allowed to use public highways but which have been modified for dragster races. These can be ridden by anybody, without a specific license.

Anyone interested in broadening their knowledge and experience of dragster racing can even enroll for special courses offered by the All Harley Drag Racing School known as Thunder Alley. The enrolment fee is between 50 and 100 dollars. *Thunder Alley* is also the name of a Harley dragster magazine published by the TAM Communications Group that promotes its courses and concluding competitions in FLASH and Pro-FLASH classifications which takes place during the Sturgis Bike Week.

The speed/time print-out known as the "time slip" is often used to secure bragging rights when it comes to top speeds. But some dragster racing teams occasionally even demonstrate the true situation during a so-called "Bracket" race, when the slowest competitor has to finish in a specified time.

European Dragsters

Happenings in Various Countries

Although dragster races were invented in Great Britain (where they were called sprints), interest in Harley dragster racing grew very slowly in Europe.

In Great Britain, Sweden, Finland, Spain, Denmark, France, the Netherlands and Germany, smallish clubs were set up after the World War II. However, they were in no way equal to events organized in the U.S. in terms of the range of classes that participated because there were just too few competitive Harleys around at that time.

The only way in which the competitions could even take place was by grouping several different classes together, though this was an unsatisfactory solution. In addition, there were very few tracks that met the requirements for staging quarter-mile races. The uneven surfaces of old airfields or abandoned stretches of motorway or road were unsuitable for very high speeds, and very few countries could find enough spare money to construct special drag strips, which are mainly just tracks measuring one eighth of a mile. The small number of European racetracks used by different clubs were mostly in exis-

tence for a very brief period, just long enough to stage a kind of traveling circus, mostly under truly baffling conditions.

In 1987, for example, Rico Anthes organized a public race, as the dragster events were termed, in Hockenheim, Germany, in which only one Harley (an FXR belonging to the Krafft Team) took part. The rider and winner was Thomas Pfaff.

Between 1989 and 1991 there was still no official Harley dragster racing and there was relatively little in the way of high–performance accessories: you just had to make everything yourself and tune it. As far as Harleys were concerned, there was only the general "street" class for which Krafft rebuilt several Sportsters such as the Schneckster 1600 ridden by Hans Georg Fischer or an XR 1000 Evo Special licensed for use on public roads.

It was in 1991 that the All Harley Drags (AHD) were first established in Germany under the guidance of Wolfgang Schmidt (W&W Cycles Würzburg), with their own Harley cup and six races held, for example, in Alteno near Berlin and in Garz on the island of Usedom.

There were three classes. The first one was Street Harleys (for bikes licensed for use on public roads). The second was Super Street Harleys (bikes modified with nitrous oxide or with increased cubic capacity, but without wheelie bars). The third was Competition Harleys (a class in which anything and everything is permitted). The AHD staged its 1992 races on the following tracks: Grossenhain near Dresden; Alteno near Berlin; Mulhouse in Alsace; Giebelstadt near Würzburg; and Gross Doelln near Berlin.

The organizers of the events were in urgent need of sponsors in order to keep the events alive. Companies and clubs such as Classic Bike Berlin, Dragons MC Berlin, HD Services Berlin, Hells Angels MC Germany, Milwaukee Iron Shop in Damme, S&S Cycle in Zell, W&W Cycle Würzburg and Zodiac Products in the Netherlands, donated generous amounts of money for that cause. Without them, dragster racing would not have been able to get started at all in Germany.

The races were organized by The Drag Racing Association Germany (DRAG) founded in Hanau in 1991 which had evolved from the *Inter-essengemeinschaft Deutscher Dragster-Fahrer* (IDDF) and the Hanau Auto Racing Association (HARA). The European Drag Racing Association was started later.

With Egbert Eschenbacher and his *High Performance* magazine at the helm, the late 1990s saw the introduction of the Atlas Race Days (so named after the Atlas Airfield in Ganderkesee near Bremen).

DRAG pitted Harleys only against other makes of motorcycle; but 1997 saw the introduction of the Top Gas Series, an offshoot of the AHD, as a European Super-Twin event. It was organized as pan-European racing events in a national and international series staged in such venues as Chambley, Metz; Ganderkesee, Germany; Santa Pod, England; Drachten, the Netherlands; Hockenheim, Germany; and Lukau, Austria. In Switzerland there were separate dragster races under the auspices of the Dragster Association Switzerland (DRAS).

The prinipal venue for the Harley-Davidson dragster races however, was Great Britain. It was there in 1996 for example, that several Harley dragsters took place. There were four races at Avon Park, two

Ultimate concentration is needed directly before the start, whose pre-staged/staged phase lasts just seconds and during which the optimum revs have to be maintained at a constant rate.

in York, and one in Santa Pod. The organizer was, in this case, the National Association of Super-Twins (NAST), which had been founded in 1993 and which is affiliated with the Auto Cycle Union (ACU). They have established the following classification system: STF for competition motorcycles, STS for street machines, STM for modified machines and STG for Top Gas machines.

In 1997 new races were added to the European Drag Racing Association events. They were staged at the following venues: Zeltweg in Austria and on the truck test track in Rába in Hungary.

In addition to the various independant Harley dragster events, the European Super-Twin Top Gas Series is the best organized in Germany and is a novel event in the AHD program.

In Great Britain, Finland and Sweden, Harley dragster races have become permanent and firmly established events; by contrast, Harley dragster races in the rest of Europe are faced with enormous problems. These include problems regarding such things as venues, official sanctioning, financial backing and organization. As is the case with other forms of motor racing, the conditions imposed by the environmental protection agencies and by public authorities are causing organizers more and more troubles. Permission to use abandoned military airfields or tracks for such events is granted only temporarily, thereby not offering a long-term basis for developing drag racing as a popular sport in these countries.

European Dragster Racing

The list of racing events for the 1998 season illustrates the variety of European Harley-Davidson dragster racing and its many categories. The abbreviation TF stands for Top Fuel European Championship (sanctioned by the FIM). AHD for stands for All Harley Drags and TG for the Super Twin Top Gas Series.

England: Santa Pod (Main Event, Euro Finals), TG, TF
Finland: Alastaro, TG, TF
France: Chambley, TG, TF
Germany: Gross Doelln (Drag Racing School, Season Finals and Top Gun Nationals), AHD, TG, TF
Ganderkesee (Altas Race Days), AHD, TG, TF, Luckau (Grand Nationals) AHD, TG, TF (Dragster Finals), Mössling (Power Race) AHD, TG, TF, Oschersleben (Dragster Racing) AHD, TG, TF, Hockenheim (Nitro Olympics) TG, TF
The Netherlands: Lelystadt (Season Opener, Sprint), Harlingen (Sprint), Drachten, AHD, TG, TF, Gardemoen, TG, TF
Sweden: Västeras, TG, TF, Mantorp, TG, TF

Top-Fuel start studies: immediately before the start, an assistant cleans gravel from the sticky front wheel (top). The "burnout" improves the traction of the rear tire (2nd picture from top). The race is as good as lost if the fat rear wheel spins too fast, losing ground traction (above).

The two photos to the left show the start and the closely arranged light barriers of the upper control lamps (pre-staged/staged).

An attempt at the world record in Australia in 1993: Jeff Smith (below) with a special Top-Fuel engine built by Lucky Keizer (left).

The huge clutch of the 700 hp engine can be seen particularly clear (far left).

Heroes of the Scene

Pioneers of Harley Drag Racing

A legendary team – Pete and Jackie Hill: he rides, while she maintains the machine. Pete's famous Knucklehead receives perfect technical care from Jackie, and has since been modified countless times. An experiment, Pete Hill admits, but a successful one at that.

Even before organized dragster racing really took off, engines and motorcycles were already being extensively tested on high-speed tracks. Among the precursors of drag racing were postwar, land speed record attempts, such as those established on Bonneville Salt Lake in Utah: in 1951 Jack Dale achieved a speed of 123.52 mph on a 45 cubic inch (750 cc), side-valve Harley; in 1958 Jack Heller reached 134.88 mph on a 55 cubic inch, (900 cc) Sportster.

In 1952 C.B. Clausen and Bud Hood built the famed, Top Fuel Harley, The Brute, at that time the fastest land vehicle ridden by a human. Its acceleration was superior to that of an F-86 Sabrejet aircraft. In 1962 Les Waterman achieved 164.89 mph on a twin, 80 cubic inch (1340 cc) dragster. In 1971 various records for the quarter mile on single cylinder Harleys were set, all of them under 9 seconds.

Other pioneers of the Harley dragster scene were Leo Payne with his Sportster; Jim Potter from Albany, Georgia, who in 1961 managed the quarter mile in 11.4 seconds on his Milwaukee Express (a mean velocity of 125 mph); and "Old Man" Walter Ross, who as late as the early 1960s, was able to cover the quarter mile in 9 seconds on his Harley-Davidson fueler, before retiring from drag racing at the age of 78. "Tractor Man" John Heidt from Fond du Lac, Wisconsin, was also a well-known Harley Pro-Stock racer, as were Bob Mauriello and Ed Ryan, whose Korey Sportster held the record for the fastest Harley up to the year 1980. Jim McClure, another early figure, became the AHDRA champion on several occasions, first on a Pro-Dragster, Sportster, nitro burner and later on a series of Top Fuelers.

One of the most famous dragster riders is Pete Hill from Greenville, South Carolina, known as the "Grand Old Man" of drag racing, with innumerable honors and awards to his name. Since 1971 he has owned a motorcycle shop in South Carolina, but it's his wife Jackie, as head mechanic, who is responsible for the famous "fastest Knuckleheads in the world." Since 1962, she has tuned and repaired those extreme dragsters which have broken every record in the Top Fuel Class, first with gas, then with alcohol and finally with nitro. Their famous World's

Fastest Knuckle was built in 1977 and has been in continual use since the following year, though it's been continuously improved and its capacity has increased from 74 to 84 to 93 and finally to 103 cubic inches (1688 cc). Pete Hill won the AMA's Number One Plate in 1981 and in 1989 he became the AMRA National All-Harley Finals champion in Clarksville, Tennessee. His fastest time for the eighth mile was 4.759 seconds, with a top speed of 150.151 mph.

Another celebrity of the early drag scene was the Top-Fuel rider Anson "Campy" Holley from Louisiana, together with his dragster crazy family: wife Cheryl, daughter Joyce and son, Anson, jr. At the beginning of the 1970s, he designed a 700 horsepower experimental dragster with two, 140 cubic inch (2300 cc), parallel-mounted but contra-rotating Harley motors with nitro fueling, which he vainly attempted to get over the finishing line in one piece until 1979. In 1975 he became world record holder in the IDBA/AMDRA A-Fuel Class (Hot Dragster) for a five year period on a Sportster subsequently ridden by his then 15-year-old daughter. In 1981 he wheeled out his new, 105 cubic inch (1720 cc), supercharged, Single Shovel onto the drag strip, with which he took four national championships in 1984, becoming AMA Pushrod Point Leader of the IDBA. Today his son, Anson, jr., rides the Top Fueler.

From the huge number of highly qualified, top riders of the 1990s who make every dragster race into an unforgettable experience, it is impossible to name everyone. To name a few, there is Mike Romine, Happy Ring and the national champion Bill Furr from Orangeburg, South Carolina, the leading Top Fuel points record holder of the AHDRA. Just as famous are Bob Spina from Bohemia, New York; Johnny Vickers from Baker, Louisiana; Dan Fitzmaurice from Jessup, Maryland; and Doc Hopkins, Doug Vancil, Jay Turner and John Blankenship. This is just a small selection from the enormous number of more or less equally matched top riders. This subject could be a book of its own.

Also probing the limits of the possible are Twin-Engined Dragsters. Joe Smith, also known as "Granddaddy," was the man who began the trend for twin-engined monsters. He rode his Double King Rat Harley

Anson "Campy" Holley and his "Top-Fueler," which is now ridden by his son, Campy jr.

with two, 108 cubic inch (1770 cc) engines weighing 530 pounds, in the Top Fueler class. Smith became NHRA record holder from the years 1975 to 1979 with a time of 8.2 seconds or 176.47 miles per hour, causing a sensation at the time.

Another permanent attraction at these events was Danny Johnson and his Double Sportster Goliath, with two 107 cubic inch (1750 cc) engines weighing in at 440 pounds, on which he covered the quarter mile in 8 seconds at 179 miles per hour.

Also a pioneer of twin-engined dragsters was Elmer Trett from Oxford, Ohio, who worked on the development side of the Top Fuel Class for 35 years, always surrounded by his equally dragster mad family. With his Double Harley Sportster (two, 96 cubic inch, 1575 cc motors achieving over 180 mph) he defeated the Japanese competition in his class from the mid-1970s onwards.

In 1996 he achieved some unbelievable records: 4.03 seconds at 190 mph for the eighth of a mile and, on August 18th in the same year, the fastest ever time for Harley dragster sport over the quarter mile in Indianapolis — 6.069 seconds at 235 mph. On September 1 of that year the 53-year-old racer was killed as a result of an inexplicable accident during a demonstration run at Indianapolis Raceway.

Another famous pioneer from the late 1970s was Marion Owens ("MO"), a carpenter from Oklahoma City, Oklahoma. With his wife Kathy, son Bruce and daughter Tammy as his pit crew, on his Carl Ahlfeldt built Double Shovel (230 cubic inches, 3770 cc, 600 horsepower) he proved to be the leading nitro specialist in his class throughout the United States and in Great Britain in 1978.

One of the most accomplished masters of the powerful, twin-engined, Harley dragsters on the American drag circuit is Gary "Tator" Gilmore and his Chrome Horse racing team from Spencer, Iowa. A professional racer since 1982, he became AMRA Champion in the Top Fuel Class in 1986 and 1987 with his nitromethane powered, 600 horsepower, double Harley. Even today, he remains an attraction at every drag race he attends.

Marion Owens and his 230 cubic inch, 600 horsepower nitro-powered Double-Shovel: his wife Kathy pushes him back to the starting line after the burnout (top). In the case of this extremely experimental machine, there's always something that can be improved (above).

Dragster Racing for All Comers

Run What You Brung

For a true Harley enthusiast, there can be no greater thrill than opening the throttle as far as it goes and, with no obstacle in the way, pushing the machine to the absolute limits of its performance. This should be done, at least once in a lifetime provided, of course, that the Harley doesn't get trashed in the process. Dragster racing for all comers, which means just that. Racing without the hassle of club membership, licenses, fees, sanctions, inspections or racing teams. It means finally being able to show what your machine – and you – can do. "Harley-luja!" and black burn marks on the road.

The venue for these unofficial dragster races is often a privately-owned airstrip converted into a racetrack for a few hours on a weekend. It doesn't take much work to organize a private "Run What You Brung" race: a few helpers at the start and finish lines, some stop watches (if necessary) and a notepad are all you need. Participants ride their bikes as they are, always in pairs, with the winners moving forward into the next round until only the fastest is left: the hero of a thrilling day that always ends in a tremendous party.

"Run What You Brung" is the original form of dragster racing and has a long history dating back to the very origins of the motorcycle.

The (illegal) highlight of the acceleration races (or "sprints" as they are known in Great Britain), however, came shortly after World War II, when speed–crazed kids misused their motorized steeds for dramatic feats of daring and races in front of the local ice cream parlor. These youthful displays of bravado were later to become organized events that at least complied with a minimum of safety requirements. In general however, safety was low on the list of priorities. The rush of adrenaline was the driving force, much as it still is today.

The organizers of official (sanctioned) dragster events would gladly see the Run What You Brung category – also known as "public racing" – banned completely, as the fans of the sport seem to prefer the fire, smoke and thunder of the highly-tuned racing machines. Roadgoing Harleys simply aren't attractive or exciting enough to draw the crowds at official racing events, even though in some cases they can achieve quite remarkable speeds. Nevertheless, racing with the same motorcycle that is ridden by the owner every day is in line with the AMA's old Class C racing dating back to the 1930s – a tradition which ensured the continued existence of motorcycling as a sport. It's a tradition that's certainly kept alive in dragster racing.

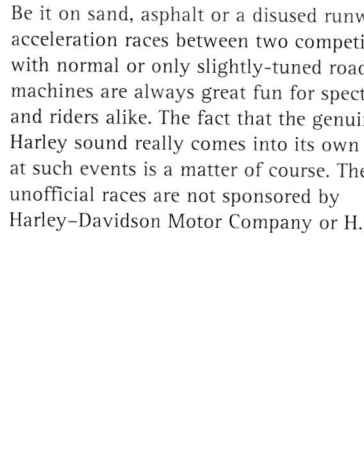

Be it on sand, asphalt or a disused runway – pure acceleration races between two competitors with normal or only slightly-tuned road machines are always great fun for spectators and riders alike. The fact that the genuine Harley sound really comes into its own at such events is a matter of course. These unofficial races are not sponsored by Harley–Davidson Motor Company or H.O.G.

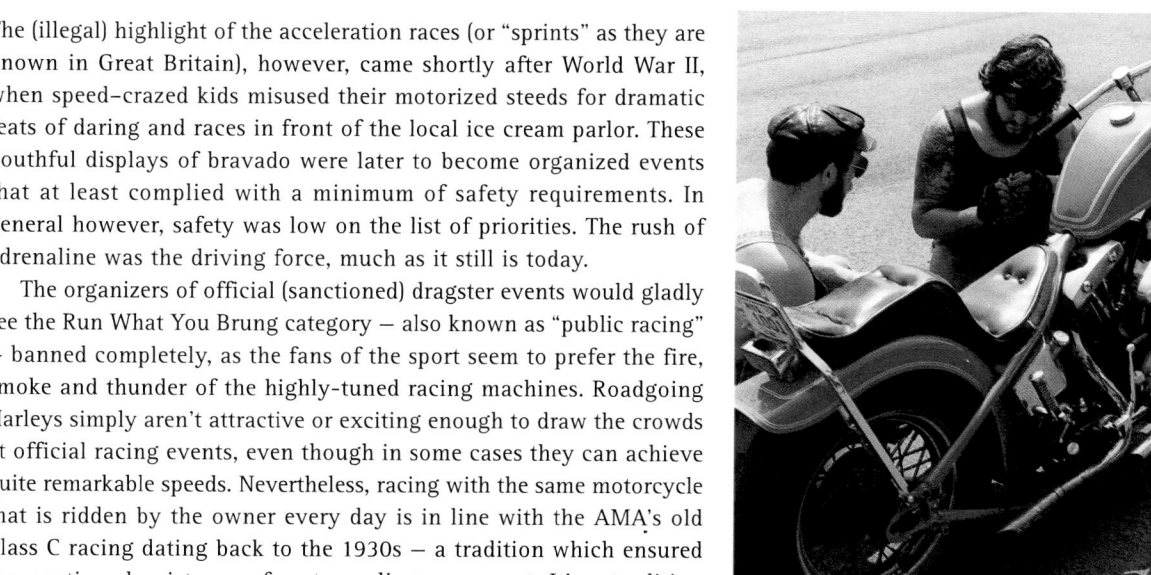

Digging Away in the Sand

Sand–Drags in the Deep South

Surely among the strangest dragster events that American bikers have come to enjoy is the sand–drag. A "recreation" typical of the Deep South, it is a mixture of hell on wheels and power sports in which the dirt really does fly. Races take place in sandy mud which is found in abundance just about everywhere in Florida, Alabama, Mississippi and Louisiana. The races are illegal and the event certainly doesn't do the bikes much good either, which makes it an expensive business for all those concerned. It's also an oddity; wild romping around on bikes is the prototypical bikers' sport.

In sand–racing the rules couldn't be simpler: two bikers race against each other along a straight 180 yard "track." The first to hit the bushes at the end is declared the winner. This is the sort of thrilling race that can be staged anywhere since there is no need for unreliable timing devices or for a complicated starting gate – a handkerchief or even a pair of pants will do equally well. You can see everything for yourself quite clearly – that is, after the dust or mud has cleared. The judge waiting in the high–risk area at the far end will vigorously wave a beer-can up and down. This way everyone will know who has won and who has lost. It is not known whether anyone has been killed yet, but the guys certainly have to take some hard knocks. If a bike is smashed to pieces during a race, the extra around of applause is compensation enough.

Events of this kind are always spur of the moment and are not properly organized. As a result, it is a completely chaotic event. One of the main instigators of this "race" was a Harley biker from the Deep South simply known as Joe. He owned a workshop in the densest part of the bayous in the southwest of Mississippi. In typical crafty Cajun tradition, he was always able to successfully defy the U.S. law enforcement agencies and has broken all the records relating to power, noise levels and illegality with the sand–drags. As a Vietnam veteran, he was familiar with the wiles of jungle warfare; he could always succeed in eluding every attempt made to officially control any of his events, which were soon concealed behind the pseudonym "Shit Happens."

Sand–drags, just like hillclimbs and bike–pulling, are one of the high points in any biker's program of combining sport with having a great time. Even though some spectators may regard such things as extremely childish, these battles through mud and sand are always greeted enthusiastically by others with loud and wild cries of approval.

Acceleration races on soft
ground require perfect mastery
of the fuel–craving beasts, as
well as a strong grip and good
balance. In fact, the riders
must sometimes wonder
who they're actually
battling against —
their rivals or their
own machines?

Vintage Races

Ancient, antique or classic – vintage races are anything but easy-going on these lovingly tended bikes of yore. Vintage races offer spectators an awe-inspiring spectacle, and an equally awesome sound.

Yes, the old battlers are still riding those indestructible yet fragile-looking vintage bikes – and recently a few young contenders have appeared too. These motorcycles are the prehistoric thunderbolts of the glory days when the spectators screamed themselves hoarse, and the motorcycle warriors who were dressed in worn, black leather drifted around the bends doing a hundred miles per hour or perhaps bounced their way up hills in clouds of dust.

The fascination has remained to this day; the solid construction of the old engines, always easily visible, arouses just as much interest now as it did then, while the technical vision behind them, and above all the wonderful sound when they fire up, can be counted on to enthuse spectators. Small wonder, then, that more and more nostalgic veteran races are staged – and not only in America. Even though they are often disguised as "demonstration runs," they are some of the most spectacular motorcycle competitions around, where bikes are ridden as fast and with as much enjoyment as in their heyday – although on better courses and under much safer conditions.

The biggest organizers are the Classic section of the AMA, the AHRMA (American Historic Racing Motorcycle Association), the VDTRA (Vintage Dirt Track Racer Association) or groups like J & P

Promotions, together with a host of other, smaller clubs and groups, such as Steve Morehead & On Track Promotions, the well-known Jack Pine Gypsies of Sturgis or the CVRG (California Vintage Racing Group) and VROOM (Vintage Racers of Old Motorcycles).

At any of the larger events such as Sturgis, Daytona or Laconia Bike Week, the vintage motorcycle races are an essential part of the spectacle. But it is not only the lovingly restored and maintained racing motorcycles from the good old days which are worth seeing and listening to – in many cases the old racers who became living legends of their time still sit astride their machines, the champions and Number One Platers whose names and achievements once filled the pages of entire volumes of motorcycle magazines.

In their honor, special events such as the Concours d'Elégance or the Historic Concourse are organized and dinners hosted. The big motorcycle corporations fall over one another to encourage the participation of these erstwhile competitors. Harley-Davidson in particular (together with H.O.G.) likes nothing better than presenting these venerable warhorses to the world in order to send them out one more time full throttle around circuits old and new. "Hey man – that's racing!" is the motto, and that's how it will remain.

To the Limits of the Imagination

Ever since the very first motorcycle was built, there have always been a few crazy guys who will try anything once in order to invent a completely new type of sport you can perform with an engine between two wheels. The main thing is that somehow it will work and it will be fun. There's "motoball," or motorcycle football, for example, and motorcycle-minicar racing (midget racing), motorcycle hockey and motorcycle polo. The very latest of the crazy ideas, how about unicycle races – races on a single wheel, the rear one? Apparently, even here Harleys play a vital part. Unicycle races are quite probably the zaniest thing that can be done with a bike.

Anyone who has ever seen these utterly way-out bikes in the hands of members of the American National Unimotorcyclist Society (shortened to ANUS) in action, will probably also fall victim to the same form of madness! The unicycle must cover a distance of a hundred feet from a stationary position without any part of the machine other than the rear wheel coming in contact with the ground!

There is an element of self-ridicule in this low-budget outlaw sport (as can be seen from the society's acronym) which was started in 1991 by William "Sidecar Willy" Nassau and more and more enthusiastic unicyclists are falling under its spell.

A modern version of the legendary encounters between the Indian and Harley occurred when founding father William Nassau changed from his Honda CB 750 Beast to a 1941 Indian Chief, or rather to what was left of one. Within sight of the Daytona Speedway, the Harley-Davidson contestant, finished in the factory's colors (well almost the factory's colors), was able to hold the presumptuous opposition truly well at bay – so this is at least one type of sport in which Harley-Davidson is successful. But in spite of its attractiveness to the media, both as a participant and as a spectator event, nobody expects that the unicycle sport will ever become a serious commercial proposition.

The rules only permit the use of engines which are more than five years old. So an old Sportster Ironhead was specifically tuned to meet the demands of the hundred-foot track: its low-tech tubular stabilized frame and special transmission to the tractor-type tire are just some of the refinements which ensure that this machine will plow its way along the 100-foot unsurfaced track in just 3.11 seconds from standstill. Even though things do not always work out, you can be sure that it's spectacular to watch and really noisy. As the old saying goes: "Where there's a wheel, there's a way!"

The most extreme of motorcycle sports is racing with just one wheel – the rear one (top). Peculiar motorcycle sports disciplines have always abounded, as shown by this Californian polo match played on Harleys (above).

Climbing the Walls

Harleys and The Wall of Death

A rare sight indeed, but one that can be experienced: Harleys on the "wall of death."

Californian Hell Riders: Rosty Linfield, Dan Daniels, Johnny Rotton and Samantha Morgan.

Harleys riding the "wall of death?" It sounds sacrilegious, an intrusion by Harley-Davidson on ground sacred to the motorbikes made by Indian. After all, Indian more or less invented the wall of death as a promotional gimmick, and to this day the rather fragile-looking, but in fact very robust, 600 cc Indian Scout remains the emblematic motorcycle for elite wall-of-death riders, even if it nowadays serves only as a show piece on display outside the arena.

However, Harley motorcycles have also been long involved in the wall of death. Lucky Thibeault, a famous member of the old guard of wall-of-death riders, used a 1960 Harley 175 cc, two-stroke engine in a special Scout frame as one of his machines, creating a ferocious din on it within the confines of the motodrome.

The loudly proclaimed showman's boast that it was the "heaviest, police motorcycle in the world" certainly served to attract attention, but was not exactly accurate. Certainly the Indian Scout was one of the motorcycles used by the police in various cities, but the machine in question was in fact a mere middleweight.

However, even when lightened by the removal of all superfluous and bulky accessories, these middleweight machines seem to the captivated and excited spectators like great steel monsters as they roared and juddered thunderously past them around and around on the vertical wooden walls.

Wall-of-death riding is a pure adrenaline-driven experience, regardless of whether the machine used has two, three or four wheels. It's best of all to watch when it is accompanied by a roar from fire-breathing exhaust pipes, so that the vibrations and engine sounds create an irresistible mixture of fear and nerve-tingling excitement for the crowd. This is even more so when the distinctive sound of a Harley-Davidson motorcycle echoes around the wall.

It may be that the Indians have a better image, spray less oil about the place, are more reliable and, most important of all, have the weight of tradition behind them, but every once in a while a Harley also hits the vertical walls. Currently, many visitors to motodromes have barely heard of Indians: to them a heavy, American motorcycle simply means a Harley.

The World's Greatest Motorcycle Daredevil

Evel Knievel

The most famous of all show stars: motorcycle stunt idol Evel Knievel. Despite countless fractures, he missed no opportunity of demonstrating ever more extreme jumps on his beloved Sportster.

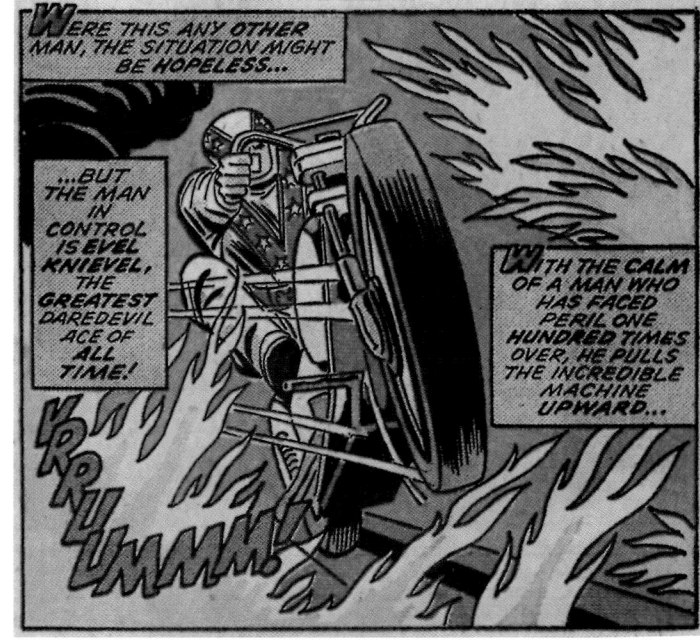

© Harley-Davidson

Robert Craig "Evel" Knievel, the self-styled "World's Greatest Motorcycle Daredevil," started what was to become a national and then international show business career in the mid-1960s, after a wild and eventful earlier life. This career involved evermore extreme, record breaking motorcycle jumps over all manner of different obstacles, and his one-man show, Evel Knievel Enterprises, moved from town to town like a traveling circus, making a pile of money in the process.

At the peak of his fame he employed a 20-man team and owned a giant Kenworth truck, a Lear jet, and a fleet of Ferraris and Rolls Royces. Things did not always work out as intended, though: at a legendary 160-foot jump over the fountain at Caesar's Palace in Las Vegas, he missed the landing ramp and crashed down onto the neighboring parking lot. Despite incurring countless broken bones and suffering life-long disability and pain as a result, he kept going.

From the year 1970 he was sponsored for a number of years by AMF/Harley-Davidson and was given two of his coveted "All American Machines," the XR 750, which were regularly looked after by Roger Reimann. This constituted a mutually beneficial and patriotic piece of marketing that chimed in perfectly with both the spirit of the times and with Harley-Davidson's program. Dressed in immaculate white leathers spangled with the Stars and Stripes, he became a kind of Superman on two wheels, a figurehead for a whole generation of Mr. Cleans, accompanying his appearances with a suitable line in bombastic rhetoric. A well-managed marketing campaign, and supermarkets full of Evel Knievel souvenirs, completed the picture.

His last hurrah organized with massive publicity turned out to be a bridge too far. This was his attempt to jump over the 5,000 foot wide, 7,000 foot deep Snake River Canyon in Idaho, using a rocket-propelled motorcycle resembling a jet fighter, dubbed the Skycycle. It turned out to be more of a wet squid when, immediately after take-off, Evel Knievel and his jetbike were catapulted and drifted away by parachute. Both machine and rider plunged safely into the depths of the canyon.

After this debacle, not much more was heard of the one-time motorcycle legend, apart from a film entitled "Viva Knievel" which was a Warner Brothers Production directed by Gordon Douglas and starring the ever cheerful actor George Hamilton. The film was a flop; it was a piece of nonsense about drug trafficking on the U.S.-Mexican border.

After an image-damaging brawl with his co-author Sheldon Saltman, Evel Knievel parted company with Harley-Davidson and lived out his life quietly in Florida.

Circus Acts on Two Wheels

Stunts and Tricks

All those things that people never normally try to do with a motorcycle, things for which the machine was certainly not designed, can be classified as stunts. For example, stunts include such things as riding on the front or rear wheel, jumping through the air, riding the bike facing backwards, standing on it, hanging off one side, riding blindfolded or with a human pyramid balanced on the motorcycle.

Controlled crashes through walls of bricks or blazing wooden walls also form part of the repertoire, while high dives, jumps over people or vehicles or clambering from motorcycles onto cars or airplanes while riding at full speed, form the sharp end of the profession.

Seeming to defy the laws of nature, stunts are very popular with the paying public. In reality, however, stunts are carefully controlled events calculated to push physical laws to their limits.

Motorcycle stunts were introduced at the end of the 1920s and beginning of 1930s by specially-trained "drill teams" such as the Shriner Motorcycle Parade Corps and police escorts, and were performed at charity events, holiday parades and the rallies organized by the many motorcycle clubs. One of the earliest motorcycle drill teams to make a name for itself was the Victor McLaglen Motorcycle Corps from Los Angeles, California with its "Show on Wheels." Founded by the two motorcycle fans Major Nick DeRush and Captain Hap Ruggles, its organizer was the well-known film star Victor McLaglen, who was already the leader of the Light Horse Troop. For 60 years this famous drill team performed tricks and countless film stunts on their reliable Harley-Davidsons. The team performed at the opening parade for the Boulder Dam and had their own Sport Center Stadium in Los Angeles, where they trained and put on their own stunt shows.

Another well-known drill team was the Sioux Falls Elks Motorcycle Patrol, formed in 1937 by Sergeant Art Rock of Sioux Falls Police Department, South Dakota. In 1938 the drill team became a member of Sioux Falls freemasons, Elk Lodge No. 262 to be precise, and received its own uniform for performances at parades and charity events.

The "Cossack" stunt team at a demonstration in Sturgis in 1990 (below) and the stunt team of the French police at a show on the occasion of the H.O.G. Rally in Rotterdam.

Also founded in 1937 was the Rose City MC Police Drill Team in Portland, Oregon, by the Rose City Motorcycle Club. The team wore splendid uniforms, drove attractive, heavy, dark blue police motorcycles, went on frequent tours, and put on a famous show in 1940 in the Multnomah Civic Stadium in their hometown.

However, the best-known show troop in the motorcycle stunt business is undoubtedly the Cossack Drill Team from Seattle, Washington, which is still in existence and has been performing its stunts at a wide variety of motorcycle events for 60 years. This team was formed in 1938 by motorcycle racers who had entertained the crowds with their tricks during the intervals between races. They took their name from the famous Russian horsemen known for their remarkable feats of horsemanship. To this day its members, ranging in age from 27 to 67, delight the public with daredevil stunts on their "iron horses" – the indestructible UL and VL side-valve, Big Twins.

Australia also had a famous stunt troop during the 1950s, the Royal Australian Signal Motorcycle Display Team from Melbourne.

In addition to these perfectly-rehearsed drill teams, there have always been daredevil individual stunt riders, both men and women. Some of them have even been children, such as the seven-year-old Jimmie Hinds, who performed a "board bash" (crashing through a burning wooden wall) in 1940 on a big V-twin. Since the 1920s the spectacular board bash has been one of the top attractions at stunt shows, demonstrating to good effect the power and balance of both the driver and machine.

However, accidents do sometimes happen during this type of stunt, as the well-known Harley dealer Harry Molenaar from Hammond, Indiana, found out when doing one of his frequent performances, though he escaped with relatively minor injuries. Many of these daredevil stunt riders were in fact Harley dealers, such as Dudley Perkins from San Francisco, who was famous for his hair-raising film stunts.

Reg Shanks, a Canadian Harley dealer since 1928 (Brooklands Motorcycle Sales, Victoria, British Columbia) rode a motorcycle from the age of 12, and was still performing stunts at the grand old age of 80 on his ancient WL 45.

Among the early motorcycle stunt riders was the show team of Gene & Ruth founded by Ruth Kilbourne of Lincoln, Nebraska, which performed at many parades and holiday events from 1925 onwards.

In California, Mary Wiggins set up a women's motorcycle stunt team, which was chiefly involved in film work, while the Daring Sisters and the San Francisco Motorettes were active from 1943 onwards.

Motorcycle jumps over as many people, cars or trucks as possible have always been popular attractions. One exponent of these was Bubba Blackwell, with his All American Daredevil Thrill Show. However, things did not always go according to plan: in Portland, Oregon, this early Evel Knievel broke a number of bones in 1957 while attempting a jump over 13 cars on his XR 750.

In Europe one of the best-known stunt riders was the Frenchman François Schetelat, who performed his stunts on a Harley. However, the most famous daredevil stunt rider of them all is undoubtedly Evel Knievel, astride his many Harley-Davidson motorcycles.

Always a welcome guest at Harley events: French stuntman François Schetelat, shown above performing an extended "wheelie," and below during a tire-scorching burnout.

Taking It to the Limit

Motorcycle Speed Records

In 1965, George Roeder set a new world record of 177.22 mph in the 250 motorcycle class at the salt lake at Bonneville with this fully-paneled Aermacchi Harley-Davidson Ala D'Oro Sprint.

© Harley-Davidson

With motorcycles, speed is always the bottom line, and speed inevitably means records. People only want to know who the very fastest is and who it is that can best balance speed and technique in the battle to take the victor's laurels. As with all other forms of motorsport, Harley-Davidson's involvement was intended to generate marketable facts and figures, though the company's four founders were not at first particularly interested in records. However, it is fairly obvious that motorcycle-riding folk were, are and always will be speed addicts who need ever greater fixes of pure velocity. Anyone who can deliver the wanted speed can expect to do good business.

Of course records are not simply a matter of times. There are countless other factors involved in establishing a record. These include the engine type (single- or twin-cylinder, the type of valve arrangement or the fuel used); the course to be ridden (once or several times, 24 hour records or long-distance courses in special competitions); and of records in different races and different classes.

It should come as no surprise, then, that year after year national and world records continue to tumble. Of course it's always important that the performance is verified by the governing body for the category of motorsport involved in the attempt.

Once Harley-Davidson had set up its own racing team and had become involved in the tuning of high performance engines in its own research and development department, it had taken the first steps towards challenging the power of a variety of rival motorcycle manufacturers, but above all Indian. Of course, there were unofficial records even before this period of official company involvement. For example, in 1905 a Harley-Davidson motorcycle is said to have recorded a new record time of 19 minutes and 2 seconds for a 15 mile course.

In the year 1908, Walter Davidson himself achieved a fuel economy record, verified by the FAM, of 188.234 miles on one gallon of gasoline. In other words, he used just one quart and one fluid ounce of gasoline to complete the course. Greenpeace would have made him an honorary life member.

However, speed records were not always dependent on the latest technological developments. For example, in September 1915 the leader of the Harley-Davidson racing team, Otto Walker, achieved a new 100 mile record at Maywood Speedway in Chicago on a special pocket valve, F-head, V-twin racing motorcycle during which his average speed was 89.11 mile per hour. This was despite the availability of a new, eight valve machine prepared by head tuner Harry Ricardo. In contrast to the usual

set-up, the spark plugs in this model were fitted directly in the main combustion chamber rather than in the valve pocket. Normally, spark plugs could not withstand the heat they were then subject to, and this was very much an experimental measure. This kind of engine later became known as the Chicago Harley.

In the same year Irving Janke achieved a new course record at the third running of the annual 300-mile Dodge City Classic riding an 11K model. In 1917 Allen Bedel achieved a new record of 21 hours at an average speed of 48.3 miles per hour in the 1,000-mile Ascot Park non-stop cross-country race. In 1919 Hap Scherer set a new record in the New York—Chicago race on a Model W Sport: he covered the 1,012 miles in 31 hours and 24 minutes. One year later Hap achieved a record in the 1,224 mile Denver-Chicago race with a time of 47.5 hours and an average speed of 26.4 miles per hour. The traffic police along the route must all have been asleep. Also in 1920, Fred Ludlow set a 25-mile record on the one mile, dirt track with a time of 19 minutes and one fifth of a second. And so on.

On the international stage Harley-Davidson was also breaking records. During the years 1920 and 1921 record times of over 100 miles per hour were achieved by the Harley riders Freddie Dixon and Douglas Davidson (no relation of the company founders) on the Brooklands circuit in England, a track built specially for record-breaking. In Brazil, Domingos Lopez made a name for himself in 1920 with a record of 80.77 mph in the sidecar category, and in Argentina Harley-Davidsons set new record times in the South American TT. During these record-breaking years Fred Ludlow achieved a speed of 104 mph riding a 61 cubic inch (1000 cc) roadster at the high-speed track at Daytona Beach, while Red Parkhurst reached 110 mph and then 112 mph on his bored-out 68 cubic inch (1114 cc) model.

Another genuine record rider was the Californian Harley-Davidson enthusiast and police officer Fred Ham; he broke the record for the famous Three Flag Run (Canada, U.S. and Mexico) on his 74 cubic inch (1200 cc), side-valve model in the Fall of 1936 with a time of 28 hours and 7 minutes. In the spring of 1937, a new AMA record was set at the Muroc Salt Flat: in a 24-hour race around the five mile round course, Fred Ham achieved an average speed of 83.25 miles per hour net riding time on a 61 inch, OHV, Model E Knucklehead. All he needed was to change the chain and during the short refueling stops he drank fruit drinks. The record caused a great stir in the press, and he was praised to the heavens in the Harley-Davidson magazine The Enthusiast.

In 1937 factory rider Joe Petrali achieved an even more celebrated record ride on the new 61E at Daytona Beach. Harley-Davidson President Walter Davidson had offered him a prize of 1,000 dollars if he could break the 150 mile-per-hour barrier. The Knucklehead, tuned specially for this record attempt, was fitted with new and untested fairing which almost caused an accident during the first attempt, so it had to be removed for the subsequent runs. The middle mile of the three-mile long track was measured under the guidance of John La Tour, who had participated in Malcolm Campbell's record attempts.

While the motorcycle only reached a disappointing 102.04 miles per hour with the fairing on, after its removal, Joe Petrali achieved a new world record speed of 136.18 miles per hour on his third run over the flying mile. This broke Johnny Seymour's 1932 record achieved on an eight valve Indian. The record brought Harley-Davidson, the new Knucklehead and rider Joe Petrali considerable fame and honor, but was not good enough to secure Petrali the 1,000 dollar prize.

Since the end of the World War II, record attempts have generally been made on the famous Bonneville Salt Flats in Utah. They are often

This is Roger Reimann who held the streamliner record in the mid 1960s.

made during Bonneville Speed Week, organized by the Utah Salt Flats Racing Association (USFRA). The timing and verification are carried out by the Southern California Timing Association (SCTA), and the event covers a wide range of different categories of speed record. The course, roughly five miles over the bone-dry salt flats, must be covered twice, once in each direction, within a space of half an hour. The timed mile is roughly in the middle of the course.

Harley-Davidson motorcycles have achieved the following records on the Bonneville Salt Flats:

In 1964 factory rider Roger Reimann reached 156 miles per hour on his streamlined, 250 cc Ala D'Oro, while his teammate George Roeder reached 156.24 miles per hour.

On October 21, 1965 George Roeder reached 177 miles per hour in race classes A and C on a new 1966, model Sprint CR, which was running on normal gasoline.

On October 16, 1970 Harley factory rider Cal Rayborn broke the world record for two-wheeled vehicles with a speed of 265.492 miles per hour, riding a nitromethane powered, 1458 cc Sportster built by Sprint Specialist (frame by Dennis Manning).

In 1978 a Harley Streamliner sponsored by *Easyrider* magazine and Jammer Products set a new record in the S-AF 3000 Class, with a speed of 276.36 miles per hour. In 1985 Dan Kinsey broke the existing record for single-engined machines on the streamlined machine Tenacious, sponsored by S&S/BUB Enterprises and designed by Dennis Manning. Kinsey had set a new record speed of 276.510 miles per hour.

In 1989, the same team, this time led by Joe Teresi, attempted to break the existing, land speed record for bikes which at that time was being held by Kawasaki with its double Harley Streamliner and an engine built by Keith Ruckstone, a machine which was dubbed the "Kawasaki Record Killer." However, the solid aluminum front wheel used led to a crash, though fortunately without serious consequences for the rider.

On July 14, 1990 Dave Campus amazingly achieved a speed of 322.150 miles per hour over the flying mile on the *Easyrider* Streamliner.

In 1991 Dan Tramp won the title of Fastest Stock Harley of the World with a time of 226.492 miles per hour, riding a conventional Harley Tramp III sponsored by S&S Cycle.

Given the many national and world records available in the many different motorcycle classes and distances, there is only room here to list a selection of the best performances here, the highlights of a scene from which Harley-Davidson as a company has increasingly distanced itself since the end of World War II. In fact, world records are no longer a significant marketing factor for Harley-Davidson: one more way in which the company is unique among all of the major motorcycle manufacturers.

© *Harley-Davidson*
Following his record run of March 13, 1937, Joe Petrali was congratulated by William S. Harley (left) and A.M.A. Secretary Smith (right).

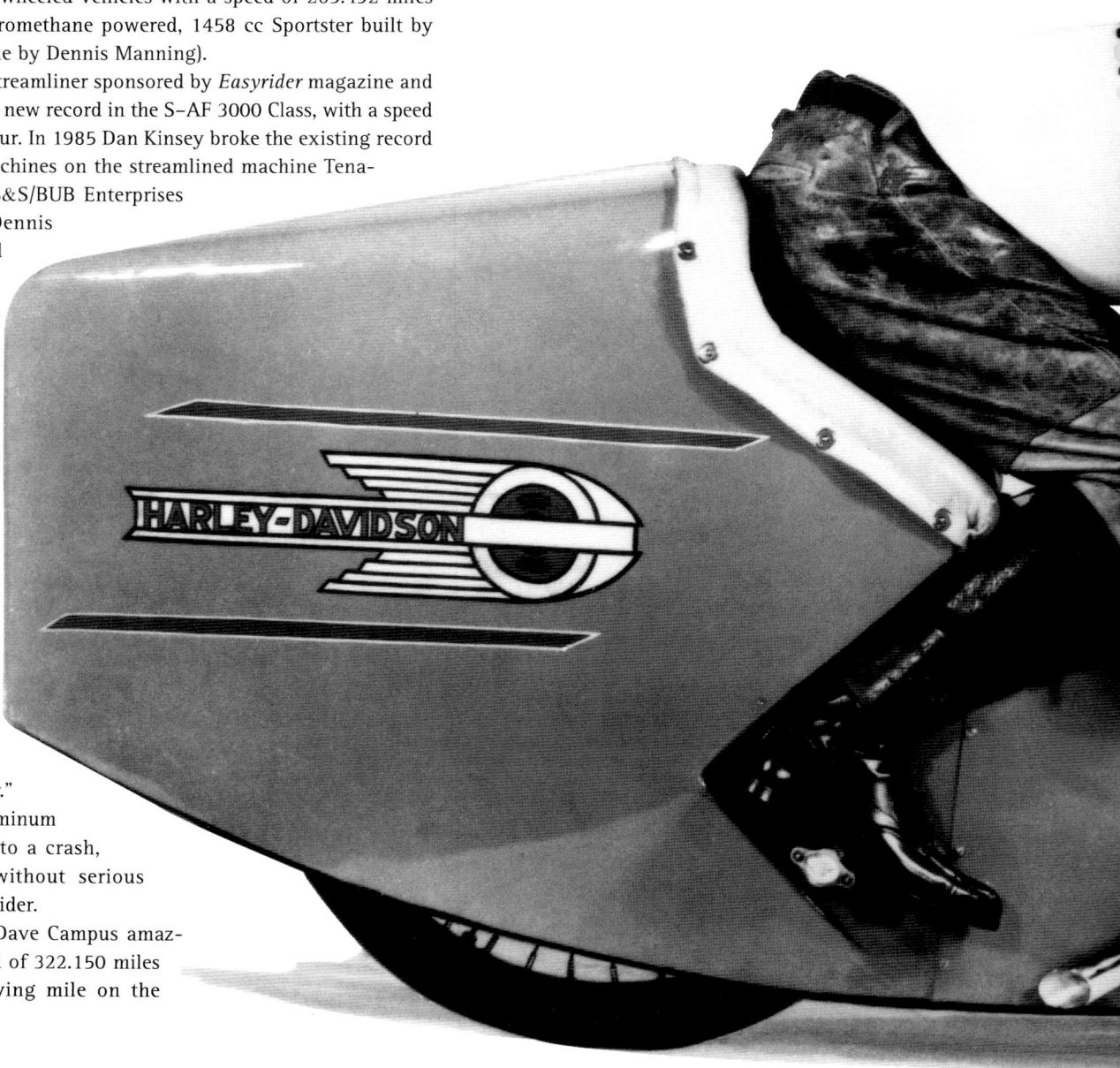

An Italian on a Stallion

Joe Petrali

Joe Petrali was probably the most extraordinary talent ever to grace motor sport. A resourceful and self-taught mechanic and engineer, he was also a keen racer and moreover, a completely unpretentious character. Joe, known as "Smokey Joe" because of the plumes of dust his riding always threw up, was straightforward, modest, always friendly, and completely reliable. He was born the son of an Italian immigrant in San Francisco in 1904. His father gave him his first motorcycle at the age of 13: a beat-up old Indian on which he promptly scored an outstanding victory in an "economy-run," covering 176 miles on less than one gallon of gasoline to become the national record holder in the 500 cc class.

He was working as a mechanic at an Indian dealership when, more or less by chance, he became a replacement for the injured racer Shrimp Burns. He took over Burns' damaged eight valve Indian, repaired it, and had immediate success on it. In 1920 he went to work with Al Crocker in Kansas City and enjoyed ever greater success as a racer. Harley-Davidson employed him,

and he scored victory after victory, seemingly indifferent to whether it was a hill climb, a board-track race or a dirt track. At Ignaz Schwinn's Excelsior workshop in Chicago he helped develop the Excelsior Super X. Tragedy struck in 1927, when at a dirt track race in Springfield he seriously injured his teammate Eddie Brinck in a crash. Brinck almost died in the crash and later succumbed to his injuries, while Joe was forever scarred emotionally by the accident, but otherwise recovered from his injuries.

After Ignaz Schwinn had given up developing racing bikes, in 1931 Joe Petrali was once again engaged by Harley-Davidson as their sole race rider (at a monthly salary of 240 dollars). By 1936 he had won a total of five national dirt track championships. As a technical engineer, Joe Petrali made a major contribution to the development of racing machines, race engines, and above all to the first overhead-valve Knucklehead. He was National Hillclimb Champion from 1932 to 1938, and in 1935 won 13 national championships. On March 13, 1937, after top secret preparations, he reached a new record time of 136.183 miles per hour at Daytona Beach on a 61 cubic inch (1000 cc) OHV Knucklehead, at first fitted with an aerodynamic fairing which was then removed for the record attempt.

After Class A racing was more or less eliminated in 1938, Harley-Davidson had no further use for the long-serving Joe, and they showed him the door. Bitter, he made his way to Los Angeles in search of work. For a short time he worked for the racing car maker Joel Thorne and he later became the personal assistant of the eccentric millionaire Howard Hughes. As Hughes' flight engineer, Petrali was sitting directly behind the great man when Hughes took the legendary Spruce Goose, a gigantic seaplane, on its one and only flight on November 2, 1947, over Long Beach Harbor.

"Smokey Joe" Petrali died at the age of 68, an American legend and one of the most successful motorcycle racers in the world with a total of 48 victories. Petrali's name and that of Harley-Davidson will forever be inseparable.

HARLEY—DAVIDSON
Enthusiast

APRIL, 1937

© *Harley-Davidson*

The photo of the famous Knucklehead with fairing and paneling, good for publicity purposes, was taken long before the race. Even the presentation in *The Enthusiast* from April 1937 was a flop: the record could only be broken after the fairing and paneling had been removed.

© *Harley-Davidson*

Have Harley, Will Travel

A Completely Different Way of Traveling

© Harley-Davidson

In 1928, after having traveled all the way from Budapest in their Harley sidecar-combination, these three students (Sulkovsky, Gyula and Miss Borbala) visited the Pyramids of Gizeh in Egypt.

"... and have a safe trip!" There is something truly magical about these five words. Setting off, being on the way to somewhere, leaving all your troubles behind you, traveling without a definite goal and towards an unknown horizon – that's what it means to travel. Whether it's by boat, by train, by car or by plane; it doesn't matter. But it's most exciting astride a motorcycle, which for many is still the only real way to travel. If it should be on a Harley, well, that's just perfect.

The very first Harleys were designed and built as touring motorcycles; company founder Walter Davidson was not only one of the first but also one of the most successful, touring motorcyclists. In those days motorcycles were frequently used for long journeys, and most of these journeys were quite adventurous. These intrepid motorcyclists had with them everything they might conceivably need to survive, including a comprehensive set of cooking utensils and camping equipment, and a plentiful supply of provisions. In fact, they remind you of the first settlers of the West, especially as they often carried a rifle and ammunition. They also carried their own water supply and, of course, a reserve supply of gas. Then there were the vital spares, including, above all, inner tubes and tires, as well as all the tools required to dismantle the motorcycle down to the very last bolt, should that ever become necessary. Everything would have to be carefully packed, making the very best use of the limited space available, with-particular care being taken to ensure that it was all protected from the rain. It goes without saying that a detailed diary would be kept of their adventure en route.

Travel is not just a way of broadening your mind and having a lot of fun; travel was, and still is, a vital part of man's and woman's way of life. Nothing can compare with traveling on a motorcycle. A considerable number of the early motorcycle tourists were pioneers and that, in part, is still true today. Motorcycle tourists explored the unknown worlds in their own country.

Long, enthusiastic reports were written which appeared in daily newspapers and magazines: "The First Harley at the Base of the Grand Canyon" (1916); "My Vacation in the Wild West" (1920); "We Won the West: State by State" (1912); "From Coast to Coast (more than 3,700 miles)" and many others. Harley's magazine *The Enthusiast* always printed photographs and reports submitted by Harley motorcyclists. "Around Australia the Hard Way" was what Jack Bowers called his adventurous touring experience in Australia in 1929 on his Harley-Davidson motorcycle combination.

Of course the U.S. also offered many challenges and truly wonderful scenery. Death Valley, with its scorching temperatures and dramatic scenery, was from the very outset one of the favorite goals of both the loners and the clubs, and Gypsy Tours were soon to discover even more adventurous goals for their rides: a picnic in the desert or at a height of 14,000 feet at Pikes Peak in Colorado, or amid the splendors of Monument Valley, or in Montana or Wyoming on the prairies stretching out into the distance as far as the eye could see – all of nature's wonders were waiting, and all people had to do was ride off on their motorcycles to discover them for themselves.

This was also true for neighboring countries; Central and South America were always very attractive destinations for motorcycle expeditions. Those endowed with especial courage even ventured into Africa and China, both before and immediately after the Great War. As early as 1946 the navy veteran William Sundermeyer rode his 61 Knucklehead the length of the Alaskan highway (Allcan Highway) that had practically just been finished in 1942, traveling from Dawson Creek in British Columbia to Fairbanks in Alaska to make the acquaintance of the Inuit.

"The World Greatest Outdoor Sport" is what they called it in those early pioneering days: motorcycling! In this respect, the greatest landscapes don't change and can be enjoyed still today.

The Eiffel Tower was one of the most popular
wonders of the world for Harley–Davidson
tourists, as shown by this photo from
The Enthusiast in the 1920s (below).

From the photo album
of German Harley
dealer Georg Suck;
sometimes with a
patriotic background
such as the "German
Corner" *(Deutsches Eck)*
in Koblenz, other times
artistically grouped in
the countryside (left),
or simply riding across
open fields and
meadows: Harley
enthusiasm in
the 1920s (above).

Touring in Europe

Be it crossing the Nufenen Pass in the Swiss Alps (opposite), aboard a Scandinavian ferry in the Baltic Sea (right), atop the Col du Camps in the French Alps (far right) or cruising along a romantic street in Rothenburg ob der Tauber, Germany (bottom) — Harleys are at home wherever they go.

Goin' on a Roadtrip

Traveling by Bike

Harley Country: The most popular routes in the world include the Badlands and Route 66, shown here in Arizona.

Nowadays roads and highways are all that they should be, more or less; traffic laws apply in even the most isolated corners of the world and gasoline is pretty much available everywhere. Travel is now called "tourism," and what was formerly just a holiday trip has been renamed a "cruise," with everything efficiently organized down to the last detail. Every last item and accessory that one would need is displayed in catalogs and skillfully marketed. Sounds just great!

But even the best roads, the most efficient organization, the safest traffic laws, and mountains of the best possible equipment have done nothing whatsoever to diminish the spirit of adventure felt by those setting off on a motorcycle trip. In this respect at least, not a great deal has changed since the first motorcycle pioneers set out.

The weather still remains a decisive factor; technology can still present severe personal challenges; a great deal of care, finesse and responsibility are still required when it comes to applying the throttle and the brakes. If you lose control, your motorcycle can very swiftly change into something that can kill you in a second; but with everything nicely under your control, your motorcycle can give you a feeling of happiness that nothing else can.

Psychologists have said that the sensation that is felt by the motorcycle rider is the result of an intoxicating blend of danger and finely balanced control, a mixture that pumps up your adrenaline. What a rush! But does any motorcycle enthusiast and regular tourer need a psychologist to explain the sheer joy of it all?

All over the world motorcycle touring has become big business, and the industry is now in a position to offer motorcyclists whatever they might conceivably need for their trip, from a comprehensively equipped touring motorcycle to high-quality clothing to an endless catalog of accessories for the bike.

Harley-Davidson has always concentrated on touring motorcycles, seeing them as a crucial part of its production strategy. The legendary highway heavyweights, the Electra Glide and the Tour Glide, are the ultimate when it comes to traveling by bike. The FX series and the custom models offer a high standard of comfort for the long-distance motorcyclist and are the ideal vehicle for such trips. Even in the Supersport Buell series there are motorcycles, such as the S3T Thunderbolt, which are fully-equipped touring bikes.

In fact, you can ride any Harley-Davidson motorcycle around the world, because the motorcycles manufactured by the masters of Milwaukee are all virtually indestructible long-distance travelers — despite those few endearing quirks that make them even more fun to ride! Harley long-distance bikers develop a very close and personal relationship with their machines over time, and many of them swear that their particular Harley motorcycle, which they know in every intimate detail, has acquired many almost human characteristics. Thanks to the most recent developments in motorcycle touring, you can hire a motorcycle in the most beautiful spots on earth, though, it has to be admitted, a

Harley is quite expensive. Or you can take advantage of Fly & Ride deals and have your own bike shipped out as cargo, a scheme generously subsidized by Harley and the H.O.G. For those who are uneasy at the prospect of traveling alone in foreign parts and want a carefree and comfortable ride, there's a sector of the motorcycle market that now provides guided group tours.

In the early days, just a few motorcycle magazines and local newspapers published an occasional travel report; today there's a whole range of specialized travel magazines trying to tempt their readers with a promise of the freedom and adventure in the saddle. Then there are special guidebooks for motorcyclists, and detailed route maps to help them find their way to the most far-flung corners of the world. A well-known motorcycle traveler who knows every corner of the world, Bernd Tesch, has written a manual, *Motorcycle Adventure Tours: Traveling Around the World*, in which he lists over 260 specialist books for the motorcyclist wanting to explore the globe.

Whether in a guided tour, with a few friends, or all alone, as soon as you are astride your machine, the wind blowing in your face as the world flies by, the distant horizon drawing closer and closer ... that is the moment you feel your dreams have finally come true.

Buddhism offers the ideal precept for those beginning this adventure. It's a precept that could apply to any journey but seems to be particularly true for motorcycling: "The true goal is not the destination, but the journey itself."

Extreme routes: the Sonora Desert in Mexico (above) and Death Valley (left).

On the Road Again

You have escaped the confining and unbearable restrictions of the city. You've managed to weave your way out through all that traffic snarled up and going nowhere fast, you've even eluded the headlong rush of cars and trucks on the eight-lane freeways and expressways and now you've finally reached the infinite expanse of the Mojave desert and you are, finally, alone. Slowly you're overcome by a feeling of utter tranquility that seems to liberate you from all the cares and concerns of everyday life; a warm wind whistles past your face and through your shirt, and you can feel your bike vibrating gently under your hands. Relaxing completely, you lean back against your rolled–up sleeping bag and loosen your hands on the sweaty hand-grips; you switch on the cruise control that keeps the powerful engine at a steady 60 miles per hour or so, and it seems that this is just what the engine's been waiting for. Slowly your tense excitement begins to wane and you start to enjoy the feeling of just riding on and on, smoothly and steadily. What started out as one of those boring long–distance trips has changed, quite unexpectedly, into a new experience. There's nothing to distract you, so why not just dream... There's always the same car ahead of you and the same one behind you, the searing rays of the sun burn your face, and the bitter scents of the desert begin to exercise their particular fascination on your senses. There doesn't have to be too many stops for gasoline to interrupt your incredible journey...

But that's just one side of the experience. There's something else, an unfamiliar sensation that overcomes you with tremendous power. Imperceptibly the glowing disc of the sun rises higher and higher, reaches and passes its zenith, and slowly your own shadow begins to fall in front of you, gradually changing its shape on the road that passes swiftly beneath you. The harsh light softens and is transformed to a warm and mystical red, finally dissolving into a light blue tinged with streaks of gray.

As you look ahead, dusk is approaching, bringing with it the mysteries of night; already you can see the stars and sometimes, you catch a glimpse of the lights of a distant town gleaming in the night. Mighty pillars of stone and saguaros rush past, the sky fills with more and more glowing points of light, and your Harley seems to have grown wings: the wheels of your machine hardly seem to touch the surface of the interstate as it hurries After a far from easy night, and always accompanied by the gentle thump of the engine, you're making your way eastwards in a long journey in which the darkness is now beginning to disappear behind you.

As the sun rises in front of you, so dazzling that it is hard to bear, you lose all sense of time and space. Suddenly you begin to feel the very earth turning, and the only sensation you have is of riding further and further into a dark abyss, only to emerge once more into the blinding light of day. Through deserts and over mountains, through valleys and in green meadows, through forests and across undulating plains, your only companions are the wind, the clouds, the heat and cold, the rain and the storms. Now and then a sudden gust of wind blows your Harley to a dangerous angle, and there's a hint of danger in the air; harmlessly, a whirlwind twists by. The engine is powerful enough to carry you on and on, and you begin to hope that this is one journey that will never come to an end.

Dave Barr

Dave Barr is a seasoned traveler, and the extent to which he has traversed the globe astride his Harley is quite extraordinary. Earlier in life he was a soldier, and in 1981 in Angola he lost both legs below the knee when he stepped on an anti-tank mine. His response to this personal misfortune was a decision to ride around the world in a personal crusade against war, a

Dave Barr in Moscow's Red Square.

journey that also involves collecting money for casualties injured and maimed in war.

He started his around-the-world tour in 1990 in South Africa, riding through the Namibian desert, through the jungle of equatorial Africa, then Zaire (now the Congo), Cameroon and Nigeria in order to cross the Sahara and ride on through Algeria. From there his journey took him into Europe and right up to the North Cape in Iceland. From Prudhoe Bay in Alaska he continued south along the whole length of the Pacific coast to Mexico, and then on into South America. Following the Trans-Amazon Highway he rode down to Tierra del Fuego, and from there sailed to Hong Kong and across to China. Then in 1996, for a murderous winter trip across Siberia, he swapped his trusty 1972 Super Glide for an 883 Sportster that he specially equipped and coupled to a sidecar.

The whole adventure ended happily, and Barr has written two exciting books describing his travels, *Riding the Edge* and *Riding the Ice*. He is a living example of having a supreme will to live and desire to overcome adversity, a man who has clearly demonstrated that nothing is impossible.

Tags

Art & Culture

Tattoos

A Permanent Token of Appreciation

It is really quite logical for Harley-Davidson, which does "get under an enthusiast's skin," to be given a lasting memorial in colored ink on the owner's own body. Though in the past tattoos haven't exactly been seen as a symbol of middle-class respectability, nowadays they are more accepted throughout society as an art form that has the widest possible range of styles. Only a quarter of a century ago, any Harley biker worth the name regarded a tattoo as an indispensable mark of identity, an absolutely essential part of the outlaw image; and today even Harley-Davidson itself has no objection to organizing official tattoo contests, and awarding prizes for the most imaginative designs.

There is an amusing anecdote about the early days of biking in America. It tells of the encounter between a Hell's Angel and a policeman who ordered him to remove his vest bearing the much-feared skull and crossbones symbol. But then the same symbol became visible on the biker's sweater and he had to take that off as well. But the grinning skull was now to be seen on the biker's T-shirt. "Take it off!" ordered the policeman. Smirking, the obliging biker did as he was told, only to reveal yet another one: but the irate officer could do nothing at all about this final skull and crossbones, for it adorned the biker's bare skin.

Though tattoos are one of the most ancient art forms in history, in Western civilizations they were regarded as a disfigurement of a God-given body and were associated solely with primitive peoples, criminals and seamen. Today there are world-renowned tattoo artists, both male and female, and a range of international tattoo fairs and competitions. There are even tattoo magazines carrying reports on the latest developments and trends in technique and design.

Anyone frightened of needles can turn to body painting as an alternative way of adorning his or her body. Though of course this display lasts for a few hours rather than a lifetime, it will nevertheless attract a great deal of attention and admiration. For children and for those of a rather timid disposition, stick-on temporary tattoos are also available.

Tattoos that are the work of experienced artists will very likely last the wearer's whole life, usually retaining their color and their distinctive delicacy of line. An expert can usually identify a well-known tattoo artist by the style alone.

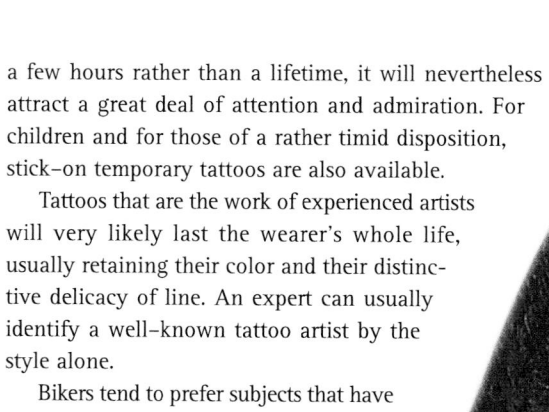

Bikers tend to prefer subjects that have something to do with Harley-Davidson motorcycles a fact that underlines once more their absolute loyalty to the marque. Anyone taking the risk of having a Harley tattoo, but riding a different motorcycle would be opening themselves for ridicule, that's for sure!

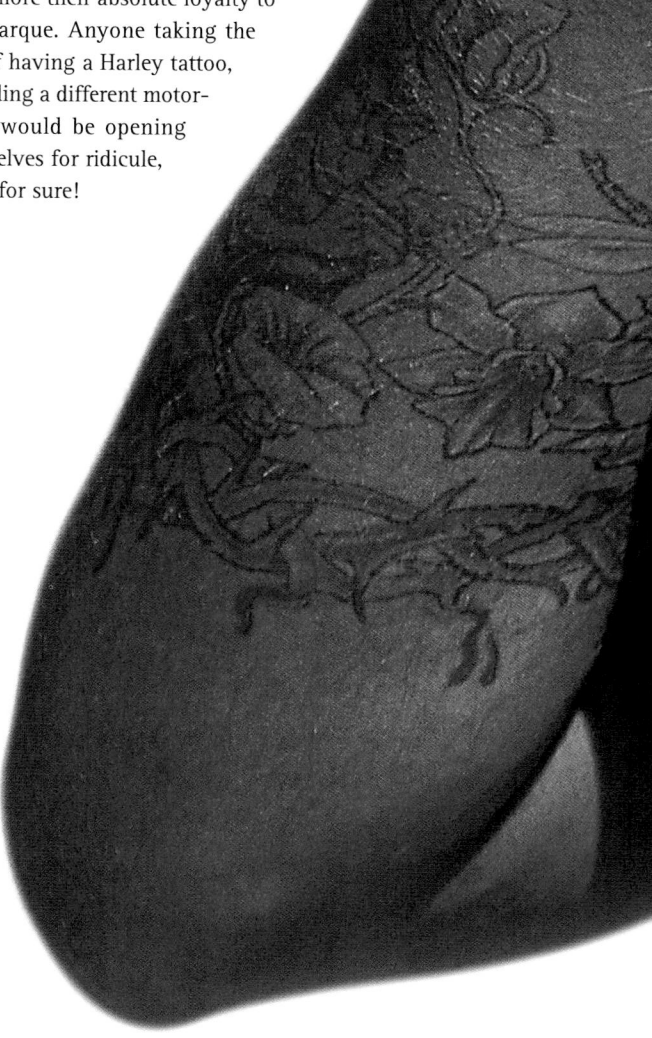

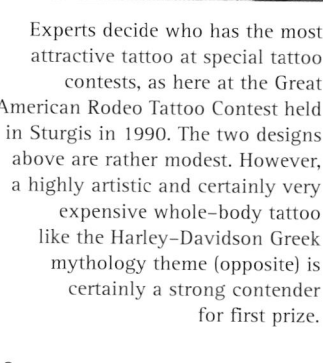

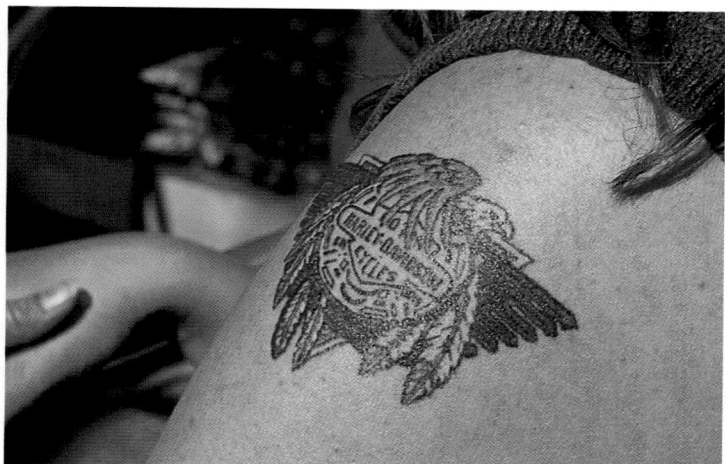

Experts decide who has the most attractive tattoo at special tattoo contests, as here at the Great American Rodeo Tattoo Contest held in Sturgis in 1990. The two designs above are rather modest. However, a highly artistic and certainly very expensive whole-body tattoo like the Harley-Davidson Greek mythology theme (opposite) is certainly a strong contender for first prize.

A Theme in Art
The Harley as an Artistic Object

Even in this high-tech era, artists are far more likely to depict natural scenes, people or urban settings than machines. For artists who wish to convey a deeply felt message, technology can appear cold and impersonal. So it shouldn't be surprising that motorcycles are rare in art. They fare better in graphic design, where the fields of fine art and commercial art overlap, as in advertising, design, caricature and cartoons. A few artists portray motorcycles as agents of human self-realization, and not as soulessly functional machines. Some of them are listed here. They express their themes through images which, employing all the skills of their art, are realistic, highly detailed and true to life. All these artists have a quite distinctive response to the motorcycle. Their pictures, whether they are original works or prints, require an appropriate setting, hence the organizers of art exhibitions in galleries and at motorcycle fairs are happy to show these artists, and Harley-Davidson occasionally promotes a few of them as official Harley-Davidson artists.

Dave Mann has to be the most famous artist of the biker scene. From the beginning at Jammers Products and *Easyriders* magazine, his centerfolds became potent symbols of the biker lifestyle. There's hardly a genuine biker pub or workshop whose walls are not adorned by a Dave Mann *Easyriders* centerfold, framed or unframed. He is able to depict, in his inimitable style, those situations that are the very essence of the biking lifestyle. Mann turns dreams and nightmares, fears and desires, into vivid realities, his approach often humorous or ironic. His depictions of people, machine and the environment reflect the typical biker lifestyle with the greatest accuracy. Every new work by Dave Mann is full of those exquisite details known only too well by every Harley-Davidson rider. Copied on innumerable occasions and marketed hundreds of thousands of times over, the Dave Mann biker

scenes can be seen on tank-tops and T-shirts, beer mugs and cups, billboards and posters, jigsaw puzzles and postcards. The soul of *Easyriders* magazine, Dave Mann has also become a legend in his own right. His fertile imagination is a unique phenomenon, and it is truly astounding how he has managed to express the biking philosophy month after month over decades with his ever-fresh strokes of genius and humor. Dave Mann is considered to be the godfather of all-American Harley and custom aficionados, at once an institution and a biker legend.

François Bruère, born in Le Mans, France, in 1961, was a motorcycle enthusiast from an early age and had a special fondness for Harleys: models left behind in France by U.S. army personnel stimulated his first artistic impulses. After studying art for seven years in Paris, artistic and personal independence became his overriding ambition. At numerous exhibitions his pictures, almost all of Harley-Davidsons, caused a furor. In his works, painted with special airbrush techniques, François Bruère concentrates on combinations of subjects that persuade the viewer that not only the motorcycle itself, but the philosophy and history are the central themes of his works. François Bruère is a biker himself, so his work comes from the heart. He designs and builds his own custom bikes and shows these together with his graphics, lithographs, silkscreen prints, airbrush pictures and book illustrations at special exhibitions held in his honor across the world. The many highpoints in his career include exhibitions in Daytona (Headquarters Ocean Center), Sturgis (Hall of Fame), Chicago and Indianapolis; Montreux, and other exhibitions in Europe; and in New Zealand, India and Japan.

Scott Jacobs is accepted as one of the founding figures of the super-realistic genre of art. He has honed his photographically exact works of art to such

technical perfection that, as photo-realism, they came to be of particular importance in the representation of Harley-Davidson motorcycles. Through the super-wealthy tycoon Malcolm Forbes whom he had befriended, he gained access to the world of motorcycles in general and to the company of Harley-Davidson in particular. Managed and supported by several agencies as well as by by Harley-Davidson itself, Scott Jacobs soon became a well-known artist in this genre. His realistic representations of Harley-Davidson motorcycles were enough to convince Harley to give him the possibility to be represented by Segal Fine Art who is an official licensee of Harley-Davidson. His acrylic or oil paintings adorn, among other places, the homes of the rich and famous, such as John Elway, Karl Malone, Madonna, and Senator "Nighthorse" Campbell, as well as Willie G. Davidson.

Eric Herrmann, who studied at the Triniton College of Fine Art and at Arizona State University, is known for his colorful, art deco-style of paintings of classic motorcycles and automobiles. Surrounded by motorcycles since his earliest youth, he is an enthusiastic Harley-Davidson rider and can be found at almost all big biker events. His extraordinary talent was quickly recognized by Harley-Davidson, and on the occasion of the 90th anniversary in Milwaukee he was named as an official company artist. His large-scale acrylic paintings are now much-sought after collectors' items worldwide. Glass sculptures with etched motifs of Harley-Davidson motorcycles (motorcycle art glass) are his new trademark: they're a fusion of sculpture and graphic art. Eric Herrmann owns an art gallery in Phoenix, Arizona, and exhibits his work at international shows, including the *Easyriders* show

"PUMPING IRON"
BY
Scott Jacobs

"Reno Nights" by Scott Jacobs

Officially licensed by Harley-Davidson and personally signed by Scott Jacobs. Prints or postcards are popular collectors items.

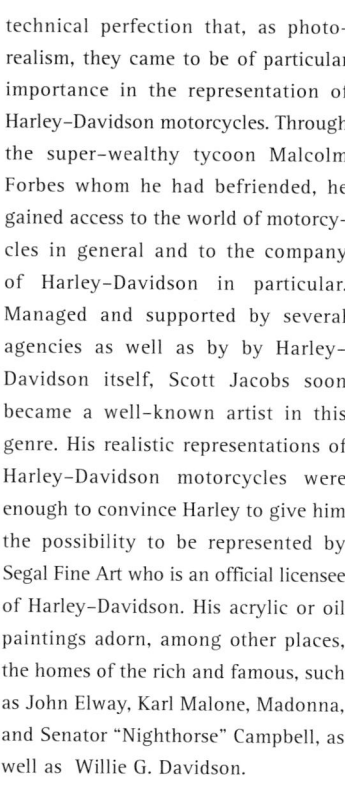

French artist François Bruere ingeniously blends fantasy and reality. This is a picture from his "Daytona Art" collection (left).

in Anaheim, California; at Street Vibrations in Reno, Nevada; and at Concours d'Élégance in Del Mar, California.

Cliff Barney, a talented graphic artist from Minneola, Florida, became famous for his finely detailed pencil and pen and ink drawings, often referred to as "motorcycle pointillism." They are well-known as posters and postcards in the Harley and Indian scene.

Wayne Peterson is a well-known painter from Muskego, Wisconsin, who has made a name for himself as an illustrator, designer and sculptor. His specialty is creating exquisite detailed illustrations in the style of traditional American realism.

Harry Miller, an artist from Colorado Springs, Colorado, established a reputation through his realistic water color and pencil drawings of classic and modern Harley-Davidson motorcycles. *Blue Bond,* from Vancouver, Washington, became well-known for his oil paintings that combine classical American motifs and Harley-Davidson motorcycles. His work is reminiscent of the style of the artist Norman Rockwell.

Vinc, from Geneva, Switzerland, favors a similar style of painting to that of Eric Herrmann, and like him he is also an absolutely committed Harley-Davidson fan. Vinc finds inspiration for his large-scale paintings on study trips through the U.S. Today, his Harley pictures, known as *Vinc's World,* adorn many a biker's home, as originals or prints, in the United States and the Far East as well as in Europe.

Waldemar Bassalig from Gelsenkirchen, Germany, an enthusiastic biker and painter, has published a lithographic portfolio of Harley-Davidson motifs.

Erotic works of art with Harleys established a distinct genre long ago and are sought after by both motorbike specialists and also collectors of eroticism.

Yvonne Mecialis is an artist in this style, and although her techno erotic, heavy metal designs have nothing to do with Harley, they are very popular in the scene.

Jana Rhoads Godfrey, whose pencil drawings graphically portray the erotic image of Harley-Davidson motorcycles very clearly.

In the more general erotic art scene, Harley-Davidson motorcycles have long found a place as an art symbol and as a style accessory. In cartoons, comic books, erotic graphic art and in so-called "scooter art," erotic and sexual motifs are closely bound with the Harley-Davidson legend. This genre alone can allow itself the complete freedom to explore the erotic connotations of a Big Twin, a theme which remains taboo in the worlds of commerce and business.

A cult figure among all true bikers is Dave Mann (top), the cartoonist of *Easyriders,* who's unforgettable characterizations of the Harley "Way of Life" are unlike any others.

Biker cartoons depicting motorcycling are part of the overall experience. These cartoons often criticize or satirize issues of interest to the motorcyclist; several of these cartoons are pictured here and are the work of French artist Coyote and American caricaturists Robinson and Hamming.

Biker Cartoons
Laughing in Spite of It All

Cartoons often give a more vivid and truthful image of the biker lifestyle than photographs do, the artist's incisive pen capturing all its absurdities and foibles with great accuracy. The Harley lifestyle in particular, often romanticized, is analyzed closely and mercilessly, no one being spared. There are only a few artists who have dedicated themselves to biker cartoons, but they enjoy the genuine respect of the U.S. biker scene, and have already made a name for themselves in Scandinavian, Japanese, and Australian publications. Among the most famous are Robinson in *Easyriders*, Hamming in *Supercycle*, and Coyote in the French *Freeway* magazine and in certain specialist publications such as *Kevin*. A unique event in the history of the Harley–Davidson company was the publishing of its own comic book *Harley Rider* in 1988. Unfortunately, the comic book was to remain a one–off and it has now become a collector's item. As can be expected, there's a wealth of licensed (and unlicensed) cartoon postcards, though these are mainly marketing oriented and hardly come close to the fantastic insider humor of biker magazines' great cartoonists.

Sometime around 1947 — or maybe it was 1957 — the brilliant but unemployable sanitary engineer Joseph W. Hedgebet III, realizing the need for a multi-powered scoot, began work on this curious solar-gas-electric-steam-jet-assisted rig. Citing the high cost of gasoline (27¢ per gallon, at the time), Joseph farted around with this design for what seemed an eternity (most of the time spent undergoing plastic surgery). He finally scrapped the whole concept and became a nun — after a painful operation.

One cannot imagine leading biker magazines without their cartoons. Hamming works for *Supercycle*, while *Easyriders* employs Robinson. Robinson has been known to subject the myth of a Harley to some very ironic criticism in his "Motorcycle Milestones".

© *Easyriders*

Small Sculptures

Whether in wood, metal, clay, cast in tin or in bronze, Harley sculptures have their own artistic style.

#2/500
2600.
have documents

Seaman Steve Rozenko built this Chopper model while working at sea (above). Artist Walter Konle with his models (far right).

Homespun Art
Biker Sculptures

Every true biker home should have one: a Harley sculpture or model. Whether carved from wood or fired in kilns, kneaded out of wax or cast in molds, they can be found at every biker event or show, at swap meets, at specialist dealers, and these days even through mail order. Some designs have become well-known and are produced in large numbers. Other objects can be put together to create a tableau. Obviously, as to whether this art form is rather homespun and kitschy of the "garden dwarf variety" is a question collectors couldn't care less about when, delighted at their new discovery, they lug home their latest – often grotesque – monument to the biker lifestyle. Biker sculptures have long since become a much-loved part of Harley-Davidson memorabilia. Some of them may come across as slightly gross, and others are rather primitive in design or execution, but that's precisely their appeal. But there may even be a few genuine works of art among them.

Some sculptures of Mark Patrick are shown on this page.

Art on a Bike

Airbrush Design

Painstaking detail-work: during Daytona Bike Week, talented airbrush artists can be seen hard at work everywhere – as here in Al Bulling's 'Last Resort.'

Whether richly covered in gold leaf or adorned with a symbolic airbrush painting – with a custom bike like this, one can always be sure of a huge trophy at the Rat's Hole.

Artistic paintwork has always represented the ultimate form of self-expression when it comes to customizing. Also in this particular art form, Harleys have been preeminent. What was once – before World War II – multilayered special paintwork with modest stripes and decals, has now developed into a glorious display of art in every imaginable style, the works stretching from simple tank paintings to whole bikes that are, in effect, art galleries on wheels.

To adorn a motorcycle with airbrush paintings is a difficult, time-consuming and expensive affair. Using an airbrush (a paint-gun that produces extremely fine jets of paint), the artist creates works that are built up gradually, mostly with water-based acrylics, on a suitably pre-painted background, and then coated with several layers of varnish to achieve perfect smoothness. This is the basic procedure for the many airbrush techniques. Then come the special markings, templates and films; and finally everything is touched up in intricate detail with a fine brush.

The subjects are taken from photographs, posters, record sleeves, prints and pin-ups, and also from several standard motifs. Harley riders often prefer Native American subjects and eagle designs. Individual sketches, portraits and stylized logos are also often transformed into airbrush artwork.

There have long been large-scale international airbrush events, the two best-known being the Harley Custom Painting Shows and Airbrush Total. There are also airbrush magazines and books available to anyone interested. The best artists exhibit their works at international airbrush shows such as those in Dallas, San Francisco, Chicago, New York and other cities, especially in Japan and Europe, many being awarded trophies and cash prizes.

For the artists competing, there are categories for best styling and finish, best freestyle, best paint design and even for the best Harley motifs. Like every other artistic genre, airbrush has its own particular fashions and trends, heavy metal motifs being of enduring popularity.

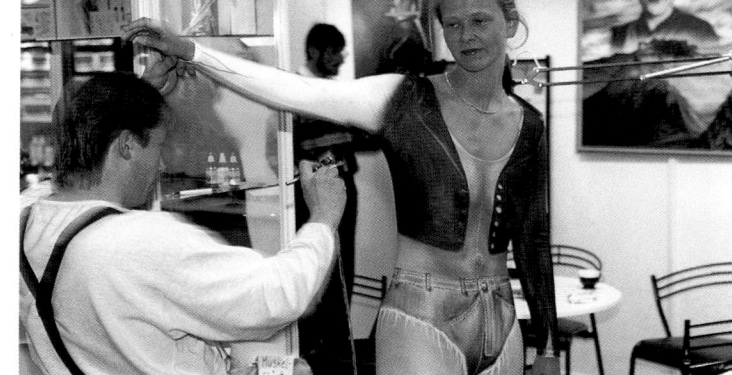

Spraying directly onto the T-shirt: an airbrush artist at work.

The reusable body: actually wearing something, but looking like everything has been sprayed straight onto your nude body is a confusing permutation of body painting.

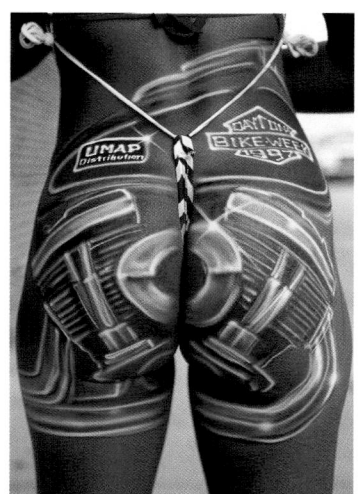

Washable artwork on the human body.

Among the many well-known international artists there are some who have made a name for themselves in the Harley custom airbrush scene. They include: François Bruère from France; Luis Royo and Ciruelo Cabral from Spain; Hans Dieter Baumann, Oerny B. Lunke, Axel Hermann, Andreas Marshall, Markus Mayer and Atelier Fineline from Germany; and in the U.S., Holly Elsworth, the Craig Fraser Airbrush Getaway Workshop, Bakersfield, California, and Todd Fisher's Custom Grafix Studio in Melbourne, Florida. It must be stressed that this is only a very small selection from the massive airbrush scene available to those thinking seriously about beautifying their bikes.

A variant of airbrushing that developed in the mid–1990s is leather airbrushing, in which leather jackets are turned into works of art. At almost all the biker shows in Daytona, Sturgis and at other similar events there are artists who are able to produce a motif of your choice on a jacket, often in a few minutes. Angel from the Airbrush Place in Philadelphia is one of them.

The closely-related art of T-shirt airbrushing, where individual motifs are sprayed onto plain T-shirts with a paint-gun, has been firmly established for decades.

Another subcategory of airbrush painting that has also been around for a long time is body painting. For this art form however, the paint-gun is less in use. As the name suggests, the paint is applied to a person, the artist using a brush or their fingers. A cosmetic design art form, in Western countries body painting originated in the theater. In Eastern countries, where it was closely associated with religious ceremonies, it has a tradition going back thousands of years.

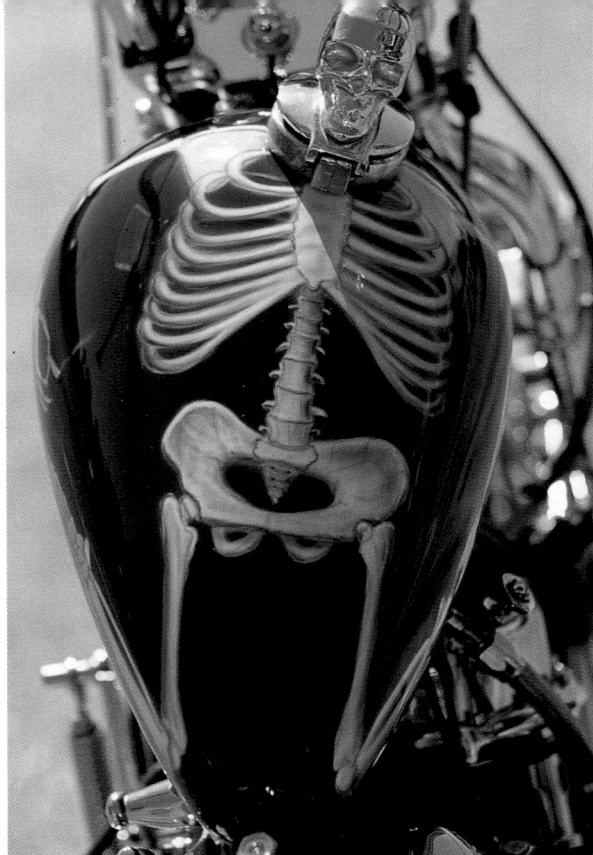

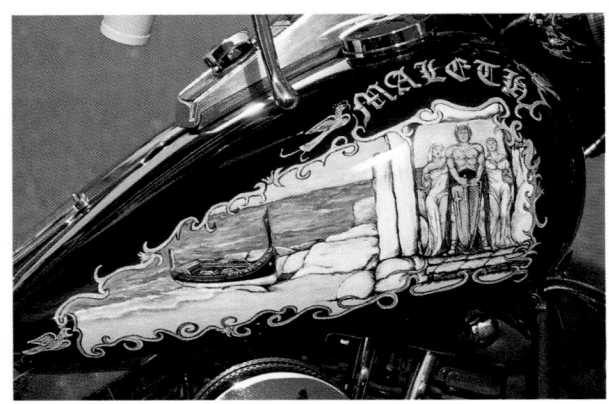

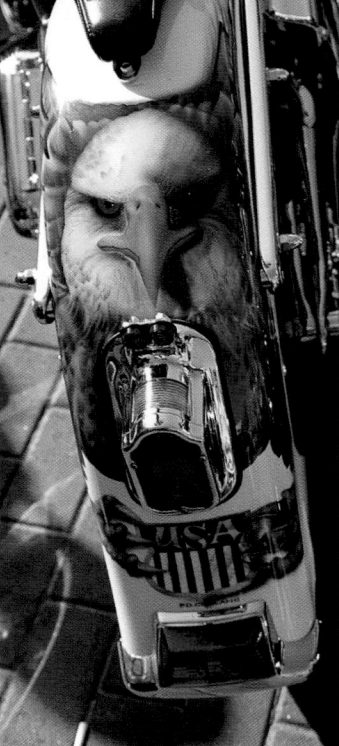
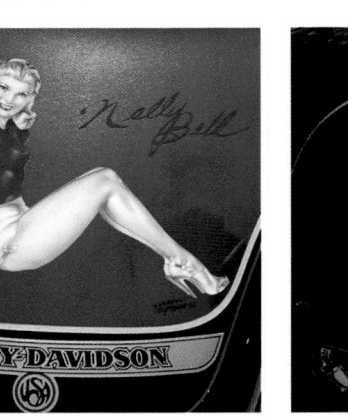

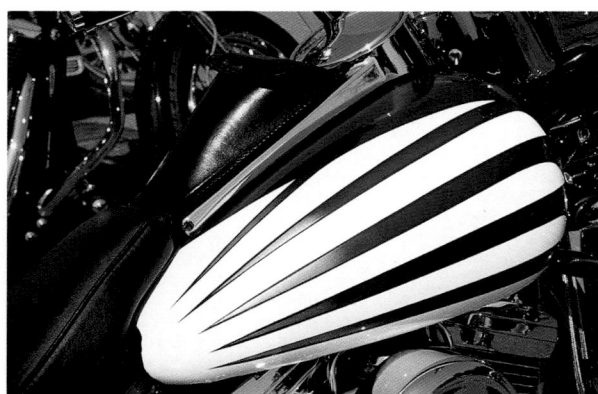

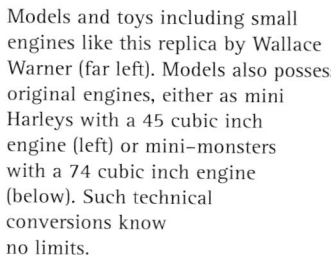

Models and toys including small engines like this replica by Wallace Warner (far left). Models also possess original engines, either as mini Harleys with a 45 cubic inch engine (left) or mini-monsters with a 74 cubic inch engine (below). Such technical conversions know no limits.

Harleys for the Kids

Mini Harleys are Harleys scaled down to three-quarters or even one half the size of an original Harley, and generally fitted with a 45 cubic inch (750 cc) side-valve, or alternatively, a Sportster engine. To prevent these toys from going too fast, they are fitted with a special automatic transmission, or else the engine is suitably modified. They're very popular, but are by no means official Harley-Davidson Motor Company motorcycles. The company itself does not produce motorcycles for kids.

Mini monsters are built according to a different philosophy. Here the biggest possible engine is fitted into the tiniest frame, and the whole arrangement is made into an operationally safe and serviceable machine. Horst Gall's mini-monster is powered by an original 74 cubic inch (1200 cc), side-valve engine, but due to an installed automatic viscomatic step-down gear, just three or four horsepower is transmitted to the rear wheel. At 6 miles per hour, the system automatically cuts off the engine, though it continues to run with a furious roaring noise – huge fun for the kids.

Dwarfs and Giants

Scale models are fully-working scaled-down reproductions of Harley models or engines. As a product of great skill, they copy the full-scale version down to the very last detail. Every part has to be made individually at exactly the required scale.

Monster models are huge vehicles, generally on four wheels, familiar on the hot-rod scene. They usually come with outsize wheels, or as special four-wheeled vehicles for shows and competitions. Here the main feature is a suitably modified Harley engine.

Miniature scale models to a scale of 1:6 or 1:12, such as the 5th German Art exhibition pieces by Mike Pruett (above and right), the 1:3 models (below) are the result of years of intricate work. One of the few monster Harleys is the Swamp Buggy (far right), driven by an 88 cubic inch Sportster engine. The four-wheeler (below right) is scratch-built and – rather unusually – has the engine positioned longitudinally.

Image Exploitation

Eye–catching: cigarette ads making use of the symbol of freedom from the land of boundless possibilities – the U.S. From the bane of all God–fearing citizens to an effective advertising instrument: the bad boys have become socially acceptable (right).

The advertising world is run by companies which lured highly-astute psychologists. These people have an intimate knowledge of the desires of their target group – the customers to whom they want to sell a product. Marketing means that associations, which often seem to have little in common with the product being sold, are of vital importance. Association such as freedom and leisure–time, adventure and exclusiveness, happiness and sex often convince a customer to reach for their check book so that they can take these promises home. Often the image conveyed by a Harley-Davidson motorcycle is used in the advertising strategy of a non-Harley related product. This "image transfer" may not necessarily relate directly to the often quoted concept of "product identity," but because a Harley stands for much more than just a bike with two wheels, that is, also for a way of life, this spirit is used and transferred in non-product-related advertising. Image transfering has been done by tobacco companies, fashion houses and perfume manufacturers, automobile manufacturers, railroads, telecommunications companies and watchmakers, all hoping that the image of a Harley-Davidson will increase the sales of their own products. It is the Company's practice to object to this type of advertising. So–called "image theft" is far more serious than the borrowing of image. Image theft occurs, for example, when companies, shops or bars take the characteristic Harley Bar & Shield logo and adorn it with their own name. Harley's "We are not amused…" comment in such cases is quite understandable.

642

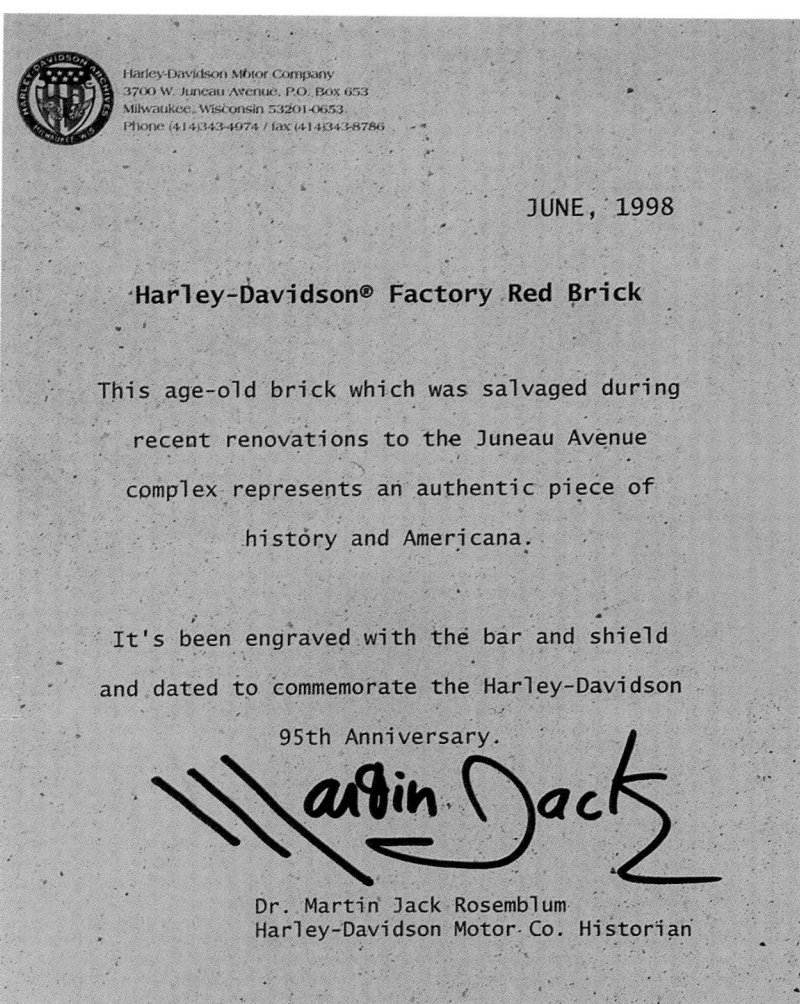

Harley-Davidson Motor Company
3700 W. Juneau Avenue, P.O. Box 653
Milwaukee, Wisconsin 53201-0653
Phone (414)343-4974 / fax (414)343-8786

JUNE, 1998

Harley-Davidson® Factory Red Brick

This age-old brick which was salvaged during recent renovations to the Juneau Avenue complex represents an authentic piece of history and Americana.

It's been engraved with the bar and shield and dated to commemorate the Harley-Davidson 95th Anniversary.

Dr. Martin Jack Rosemblum
Harley-Davidson Motor Co. Historian

MOTOR HARLEY-DAVIDSON CYCLES
SALES   SERVICE
LEO N. HERRICK
40-4TH ST., S.E. ROCHESTER

HARLEY-DAVIDSON
Repairs MOTORCYCLES Supplies
WESTBROOK BROS.   514 MIFFLIN ST.

Demolishing the Competition

When some walls were torn down during the remodeling of the Juneau Avenue building on the company's 95th anniversary, the company logo was cut into the bricks (left) and they were sold at the company's official stand together with a certificate of authenticity (far left) for 95 dollars a piece. They went like hot cakes. A few hours later, they were auctioned off in Meyer's park for the benefit of the Muscular Dystrophy Association and managed to fetch prices of up to several thousand dollars.

The "Bar & Shield" logo has also undergone many changes through the years. Below, from top to bottom: the logo in 1916, in 1921 belonging to a British dealership and the logos in 1929 and 1947.

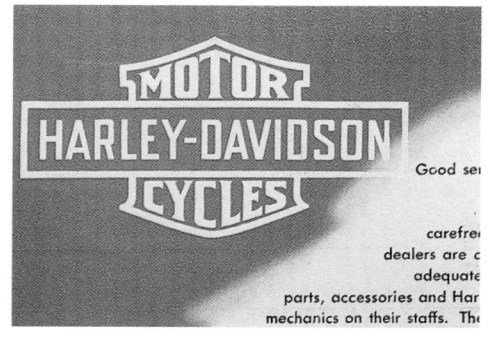

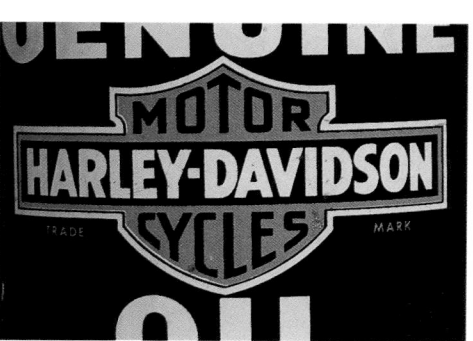

Motorcycle Fashions and Accessories 1977

The official logo in use today, here on an oil can. Two official Harley logos of the AMF period.

A Ride Through Time

Motorcycle Museums

Visits to motorcycle museums are voyages of discovery. They are fascinating journeys through more than a century of motorcycle technology that introduce visitors to all sorts of technical and technological fancies. Crammed with myths and legends, these objects are a treasure trove for model builders and historians, a place where the past meets the present.

Many motorcycle museums see their role as being centers of vintage culture; some museums have a grand and imposing atmosphere, while others are dusty old backwaters concealing marvelous secrets. The museums are not always easy to discover: some have to be sought out in remote and unlikely places, others open only occasionally, and still others have long since closed down.

Many were originally set up by dealerships; a few started as private initiatives. Some are part of large foundations, some derive from a company's own collections. Whatever the origin, they are rich and unfailing sources of delight and information. They are also, occasionally, shopping centers for these antique treasures of contemporary history.

However, apart from the company's own factory museum in York, Pennsylvania, museums specializing in Harley-Davidson motorcycles are few and far between. Despite this, rare Harleys regularly turn up, and new discoveries about the history of the company are made frequently.

A list of American museums – which makes no claim to be exhaustive – is given in the appendices. We hope it helps readers to embark on their own journeys of discovery.

Harleys in the time–capsule: Otis Chandler's Museum of Transportation and Wildlife in Oxnard, California (right). Opposite, from top right to left: Petersen Museum, LA, Willi's Motorcycle World in Daytona Beach, Florida and the Neckarsulm Motorcycle Museum, Germany.

The Power of the Press

Biker Magazines

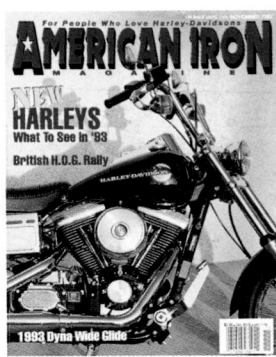

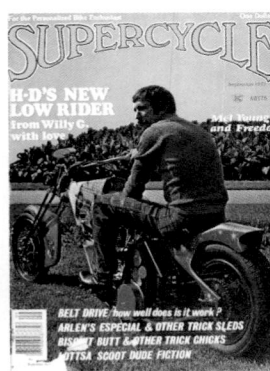
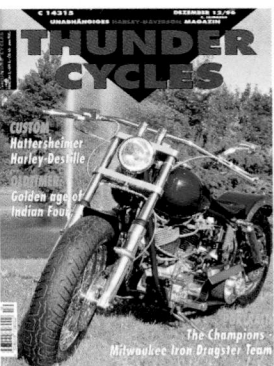

Harley Books

No other motorcycle has been written about so much. The market for books on Harley-Davidson appears to be insatiable though the great majority of them are little more than handsome volumes of photographs or glossy coffee-table books featuring Harley motorcycles and their photogenic milieu. Apart from these, there are of course a few really well-researched classics. Outstanding among these are the books of Jerry Hatfield, Harry V. Sucher, Stephen Wright, David Wright, and the company historian Thomas C. Bolfert, whose excellent *The Big Book of Harley-Davidson* is the standard work published by the company itself, though its purpose is part pictorial history, part catalog. Alongside books documenting the company's history, some of the most interesting Harley literature is to be found among the "insider stories" from the world of the outlaws, bikers, and Hell's Angels. This is despite the fact that the bulk of them – such as the infamous cult book *A Brotherhood of Outlaws* by Robert Lipkin (who writes as Bob Bitchin) – are pure fiction. In contrast, there are documentary classics such as *Hells Angels* by Hunter S. Thompson or *Freewheelin' Frank*, the story of Frank Reynolds, one-time secretary of the Hell's Angels. The standard library of every Harley freak is not limited, as malicious rumors will have it, to a single book, the Harley-Davidson Service Manual.

It's not an exaggeration to say that biker magazines have been influential on societies all over the world. In a great many countries motorcyclists in jeans, boots and leather jackets are identified as bikers almost immediately: both the origins of this style and the fact that it is so easily recognized, can be traced directly to biker magazines.

Biker magazines have, in fact, been around only since the 1960s; true biker lifestyle was not featured in the earliest motorcycle magazines. In 1910 *The Western Motorcyclist and Bicyclist* was launched in Los Angeles, and it was from this magazine that *The New American Motorcyclist and Bicyclist* later developed. In 1912, the *Pacific Motorcyclist* appeared in Los Angeles, specializing in reporting local events. 1913 saw the arrival of *Motorcycling*, a weekly motorcycling magazine published in Chicago. In the 1920s, advertising revenue started to drop and as a result nearly all the motorcycling magazines ceased publication.

After World War II, in the mid-1950s, new magazines were launched and old ones reappeared under new management. Among them were *Cycle, The Motorcyclist, The Motorcycle News, American Motorcycling (AMA)* and *Motorcycling News* (published by Floyd Clymer). In 1963 these were soon followed by *Cycle World* (Parkhurst), *Cycle Sport* and *Cycle News*.

The first true custom-bike magazine was Ed "Big Daddy" Roth's *Choppers*, which appeared in the mid-1960s as a small format, unpretentious, black-and-white publication. Though not available on a regular basis, it was full of perceptive and groundbreaking articles; for example, it published descriptions of many of the most outrageous custom bikes being built at that time. *Choppers* also contained the famous "tattoo of the month" feature, designed by Robert Williams. Though it wasn't in existence for long, *Choppers* had a lasting influence.

In 1971 the mother of all biker magazines appeared: *Easyriders*. It was founded by Joe Teresi, Mil Blair and Lou Kimzey, who'd already been the brains behind the Jammers Products accessories catalogs. The new magazine took over the basic ideas already to be found in *Choppers*, and then improved on them by using great photographs and the latest color printing technology; to this they added a special style of journalism created especially for the biker. Kimzey succeeded in giving the rather disreputable biker's world a completely new image, one that combined lifestyle with outrageous humor and, above all, wonderfully-designed custom Harleys. This winning formula increased sales figures unbelievably.

While biker films tended to have only a passing influence, the monthly *Easyriders* magazines had a decisive and lasting impact on the world of Harley bikers. *Easyriders* set the tone and gained a reputation of being a mine of reliable information on the bikers' way of life. The magazine is now in its twenty-eighth year and has remained the most widely-read motorcycling magazine in the world.

Of course *Easyriders* has been widely imitated, but none of the newcomers have been as successful in terms of real content to offer any lasting challenge. *Big Bike* was the most successful competitor of all, appearing at the same time as *Easyriders*. It contained descriptions of Harleys and their conversions, as well as descriptions of European and Japanese motorcycles.

From the mid-1980s to the beginning of the 1990s there was a worldwide flood of biker and custom bike magazines, published mostly in Europe, Australia and Japan, and dealing almost exclusively with Harleys. The reason for this phenomenon was the way the market had expanded locally. Much of the content of such magazines was taken over from their U.S. counterparts, but there were also regional reports on dealers and clubs, as well as calendars of events. For the most part these magazines survive on the basis of the enormous volume of advertising they contain, advertising that's been generated by the strength of the aftermarket in these countries. The best known magazines include: *Big Twin* (Holland); *BSH: Back Street Heroes, AWOL: Alternative Way of Life, V-Twin* (previously called H.O.G.) and *Heavy Duty* (all in Great Britain); *Freeway Magazine* (France); *MCM: Motorcykelmagazinet* (Sweden); *Bikers Life*, a superficial Italian magazine; *Bikers News, Bikers Live!, Thunder Cycles* and, a fairly new custom magazine, *High Performance* (all published in Germany). In Japan the most important publication is *Vibes*, and in Australia there's *Oz Bike, Men at Work*, and *Heavy Duty*. A complete list of the most important motorcycling and biker magazines can be found at the end of the book.

Easyriding from the Beginning

A Personal Account by a Co-Founder of *Easyriders*

One of the creators of *Easyriders* (published by Paisano Publications) has been kind to provide a personal account of how the most famous of all biker magazines came into being. Here's what he said:

"In 1970 I quit military service after three tours of duty in Vietnam and, in addition to going to college and enjoying life as a biker, I started to look for a job. I made a bit of money by buying LAPD bikes that were no longer serviceable, restoring them, and then selling them. I tried my best to convince one or two dealers that I would be a benefit to their business in the custom bike department, even though I didn't have that much experience. Finally U.S. Choppers in North Long Beach gave me a job. In addition to all the work and my studying, I continued building and repairing motorcycle engines for my friends, working in the bedroom of my Long Beach duplex. In 1971 three bikers who'd been working in publishing and in the spare parts business in Seal Beach, California, brought out a new magazine. I got hold of a copy of the first issue and wrote an article on a Knucklehead I'd helped to rebuild. Not long after I met up with the publisher, Lou Kimzey, in a repair shop in Belmont Shore. He agreed to print my story about the bike, though at the time he seemed more interested in my beat-up Shovelhead. Lou, Joe Teresi and Mil Blair, the founders of the magazine, had also been the founders of the first organization to take an interest in the legal rights of bikers; they called it ABATE (A Brotherhood Against Totalitarian Enactments). It was at our second meeting that Lou invited me into his tiny office where the editorial work on the magazine was done, and offered me a job with *Easyriders*, and also the position of manager of ABATE.

Easyriders was the first magazine to take the lifestyle of the hardcore bikers seriously, and to create a perfect mixture of *Mad, National Lampoon* and *High Times*. The magazine presented its readers with stories that had never been told before, together with an unqualified acceptance of all that went on in the bikers' world. *Easyriders* very soon became the largest motorcycle magazine in the world. ABATE became one of the largest democratic movements in the U.S., and, thanks to the expert tests carried out by Joe Teresi and his mechanic Bill Otto, it was able to put a stop to all the planned government restrictions on the building of custom bikes. Almost two-thirds of all the legislation in the U.S. relating to the wearing of helmets was repealed as a result of biker protests. At the same time, a start was made by the *Easyriders*/Jammer crew under the leadership of Bob George to win back the world land speed record for the U.S., even though it was to take a great many years to achieve. In 1990 Joe Teresi, together with Keith Ruxton, finally succeeded in breaking the record that had been set up by Don Vesco.

Easyriders speaks out for the right to build custom bikes, and for the freedom bikers need to live the life of their choice. It sees its bike shows and rodeos, its videos and swap meets, its own range of products, and, more recently, its franchising network, as ways of speaking out for those people who have made the biker's way of life their reason for living. Bikers are all searching for freedom; they're uncompromising individualists, people trying to live the way they want to in a world that is fast becoming more and more restrictive through endless state interference. In spite of all that, each and every one of us would fight for America's freedom." K. Randall "Bandit" Ball

A selection of the mass of international Harley and biker magazines testifies to the importance and the cult status of "American iron." Top: the first true Chopper magazine by Big Daddy Roth.

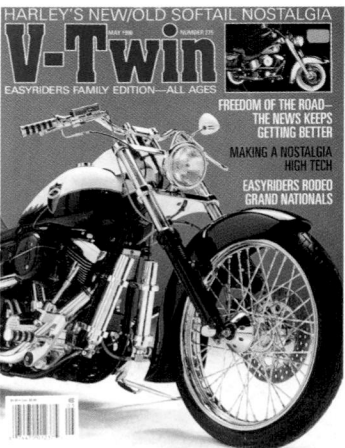

The legendary first edition of *Easyriders* magazine.

Imitating Life

Biker Movies

A typical scene from on-screen biker life: Robert Fuller lashes out once again in *The Hard Ride*.

Like the horsemen of the Apocalypse, they ride swiftly in seemingly endless columns, thundering at full throttle along the dusty highway. Savage-looking, their manes streaming behind them, they ride into the wind, their eyes hidden behind dark sunglasses. Black leather, chains and bare flesh astride a roaring, powerful machine, frightening in its power and size. With only sex and violence on their minds, they descend upon peaceful towns, fight the representatives of law and order and even the simple, peace loving townsfolk, terrify dear old ladies and helpless servants of God. Provocative and lawless, they have an utter disregard for every decent moral principle.

Such scenes make quite an impression! The upright members of the local community are horrified. Parents, seeing the children they have so lovingly raised being enticed into crime, are at a complete loss — but young people find it all so exciting!

With biker films, Hollywood, as so often before and since, caught the mood of the times. The motorcycle films they made created a deep impression all over the world, and the international biker 'movement' was born. The enormous influence of the biker and rocker B movies shouldn't be underestimated. In the 1960s and 1970s, films were by far the most important medium when it came to setting a trend. The new free-wheeling attitudes and the lifestyle of the younger generation was the message promoted by films containing anything at all to do with rockers. At first this young postwar generation had lacked perspective and direction; but gradually they became more confident in themselves and less compromising in their revolt against what they saw as society's hypocrisy, against the intransigent and repressive forces of law and order, and against the petty minded condescension of their elders and betters. They refused to

accept that a "good job" was all that mattered, that a war had to be fought every now and then, and that the main aim in life was to spend.

The films were true to life, their message was clearly understood; the seeds of resistance took root and grew strong. The motorcycle industry experienced a boom. What fascinated these rebellious young people was the fact that Harley-Davidson motorcycles were heavier than anything else on two wheels, that they were noisy and fire spitting, and, on top of all that, real sex symbols. It was films of this type that created a troubling impression for Harley-Davidson. Apart from a few exceptions, it was Harley-Davidson's motorcycles, albeit in a modified form, that were transmuted into the much feared instruments of evil.

One biker movie followed another — Michael Weldon lists over 70 of them in his film encyclopedia made between 1960 and 1975, but of the entire genre only two really had an enormous impact and achieved cult status all over the world: "The Wild One" and *Easy Rider*.

By today's standards "The Wild One" was a relatively harmless film. Produced by Stanley Kramer, it was based on the 1947 Hollister riots and the story *The Cyclists' Raid* by Frank Rooney. The film first appeared in 1953. The screenplay was the work of John Paxton and the film was directed with just that touch of genius by Laszlo Benedek; the director of photography Hal Mohr (using Gartuso lenses) also made a significant contribution. The film deals with the conflict between two motorcycle gangs, The Black Rebels MC and The Beetles. This conflict comes to a head in a fight between Johnny (Marlon Brando), the leader of The Black Rebels, and Chino (Lee Marvin), the president of the rival gang. It's clear that in a sense these youthful gang members are not fully aware of what they are doing; that in fact their seemingly pointless actions are an expres-

Harley-Davidson has no trouble at all in placing its motorcycles in movie or television productions. The powerful symbolism of the Harley, originally created by Hollywood itself, is enough to make them a staple of all sorts of spectacular productions. Just a few miles to the southwest of the big studios, Gene Thomason, partner of Bartels HD in Marina del Rey, puts together the Harleys desired for the movies. Up to twenty of them are needed – or wrecked – in a breathtaking action movie. Gene always makes sure they are ready for action, regardless of their state.

sion of a general feeling that powerful and disturbing forces of change and upheaval were at work in postwar society. A short while later, in 1955, the film "Rebel Without A Cause" starring James Dean was released.

Though Marlon Brando actually rode a Triumph, it was Harley that had to bear the brunt of the criticism, because Lee Marvin, though the loser, cut a most attractive figure sprawled over his huge 1950 Hydra Glide.

The second, even more influential film, "Easy Rider", was released in 1969, some 15 years after "The Wild One". Nevertheless, attitudes had hardly changed and it lost almost two-thirds of its length to the film censor's scissors: it was cut from the original 240 minutes to a mere 94 minutes. Despite this savage editing, it remained a masterpiece, created through the genius of its three protagonists, the stars Dennis Hopper (as Billy), Peter Fonda (as Wyatt on Captain America) and Jack Nicholson (as the inebriated attorney George Hanson). The film was directed by Dennis Hopper, the director of photography was Laszlo Kovacs. It was one of the many low-budget movies produced at that time, and cost only 300,000 dollars, money advanced by the three co-stars.

The three characters in the film wreak vengeance in an utterly uncompromising way on a sterile, inhuman world that has sacrificed individual freedom on the altar of inflexible narrow-mindedness. "We're looking for the real America, and we find only death," was one of the film's most important messages. In fact, the bikers, heavily into drugs, would turn out to be the real good guys in those dark days, and from that moment on the bad image of all the outlaws changed, as did that of their Harley choppers. Suddenly long, unkempt hair, tattoos, and wild choppers were in, and soon hundreds of thousands of young people all over the world were to emerge as the loyal disciples of Wyatt and Billy. The famous

motorcycles in the film were created by Ben Hardy and Cliff Vaughs, who ran a small motorcycle business at Hardy's in Los Angeles, California.

Between these two classics, countless B movies appeared which, though they copied the principles of the new genre, were seldom of the same high quality. A special place in the history of this type of film is occupied by the gay movie "Scorpio Rising," made by the underground filmmaker Kenneth Anger. Shot in 16 mm and appearing in 1964, it featured fetishists clad in leather and shiny plastic clothing. Quickly banned from public showing, it became precedent in future cases invoking obscenity laws.

In the mid-1950s, biker-cum-film producer Roger Corman founded a low budget production company, AIP (American International Pictures), specializing in biker movies. For many of his films he would engage real Californian motorcycle gangs, above all Hell's Angels, to ensure that there was more than just a hint of realism. One of their first productions was "Motorcycle Gang" in 1957. It was not until 1966, however, that Corman had any real international success, with "The Wild Angels" (originally called "All the Fallen Angels"), an authentic biker film which featured the Venice (California) Hell's Angels and starred Peter Fonda, Jack Nicholson, Peter Bogdanovich and Nancy Sinatra.

The next film to emerge from AIP, in 1967, was "Devils' Angels," soon to be followed by the classic movie "Hell's Angels on Wheels," made with the Hell's Angels president, Sonny Barger. The producer was Joe Solomon, the director Richard Rush, and the director of photography Laszlo Kovacs. Jack Nicholson and Sabrina Scharf starred in this film, supported by the Hell's Angels' club the Nomads, from Sacramento.

In 1967 there was another film starring Jack Nicholson and featuring the camerawork of Laszlo Kovacs, "Rebel Rousers," soon to be followed

Women in Biker Films
Gang Girls and Biker Chicks

Many Hollywood directors of biker films have exploited several stereotypical images of women. First, there's the woman as rather simple-minded sex symbol just waiting to be seduced. Then there's her opposite, the emancipated, man-eating woman, who rides Harleys and is always in pursuit of men. There's also the woman as bloodthirsty vampire as in the cult films "She Devils on Wheels," "Hellcats," "Angels Wild Woman," "The Miniskirt Mob," and most memorably in the classics "Vamps" and "Chopper Chicks in Zombietown." It also just had to be a Harley — nothing else would do — for liberated and self-assertive lesbians.

Since the machismo image depicted in biker Hollywood movies was imitated down to the last detail by members of many motorcycle clubs, the outfits worn by the bikers' girls also became trend-setters with those seeing themselves as dedicated followers of fashion. Calvin Klein, together with Chanel, Donna Karan and Anne Klein, successfully transformed those black leather, motor-cyclists' clothes covered with metal studs into garments acceptable in the very best circles of *haute couture*.

Original film poster.

Marianne Faithful (top left) in "Naked Under Leather," next to her colleague Alain Delon (above).

in the same year by "The Wild Rebels" and the AIP production "Born Losers," yet another Hell's Angels film, directed this time by T.C. Frank. Al Adamson then made a similar movie called "Hell's Bloody Devils."

In the same year the biker film "The Glory Stompers" starring Casey Kasem and Dennis Hopper (playing the leader of the Black Souls MC) was released. The following year also saw the release of the "Angels from Hell," starring Jack Starret as Bingham, a cop trying to stand up to a gang of Vietnam veterans who'd turned bad. Hollywood was so excited by the success of films about violent motorcycle gangs that there seemed to be no stopping the flood of trashy movies in which Harleys played a role.

In 1968 AIP released "Hell's Belles;" and in the following years film-goers were confronted by what were to date the most violent biker films ever made: "Angels Hard As They Come" featuring African-American rockers, "Black Angels," "Angels Die Hard," "Angel Unchained," and "Wild, Free and Hungry" are just a few of them.

In 1970, just a year after the appearance of "Easy Rider", which had depicted the bikers as the good guys, a documentary film was released called "Gimme Shelter". Dealing with the Summer of Love concert by the Rolling Stones in Altamont, the film dealt the biker world quite a blow:

at the festival a young fan, apparently trying to get too close to Mick Jagger, was fatally stabbed by one of the Hell's Angels.

Other films went in a completely different direction. "Pink Angels," for example, took as its theme the lifestyle of gay bikers. Later, in the year 1991, the big-budget, action-packed movie "Terminator 2 — Judgement Day," starring Arnold Schwarzenegger, hit the big screen. There have been other recent films as well, in which Harley-Davidson motorcycles have played a major role, including "Pulp Fiction" ("It's a Chopper, baby."), "Made of Steel" and "Chrome Soldiers."

One of the most moving and realistic biker films is, without doubt, "Mask" (1985) starring Cher as Rusty Dennis, a strong, free-wheeling woman with a Harley. Her son, Rocky (magnificently played by Eric Stoltz), has a deformed elephantine face, and is protected by Dozer, her biker friend, and his biker club. What makes this film more moving is that it is based on a true story.

Today Harley-Davidson has no problems whatsoever in getting their motorcycles "placed" in films or T.V. programs, since the Harley's power as a symbol, a symbol largely created by Hollywood, is now enough to ensure it a place in any film.

  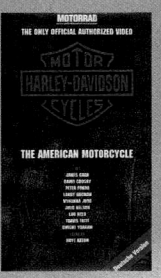   

Videos and Books

Harley videos include not only home movies filmed by major producers, but also to an ever greater extent privately produced recordings of events, clubs and runs. Even pornographic videos have emerged, whose titles are often extremely misleading. The extensive documentaries of various major events are particularly well-worth viewing, especially since they are available from biker magazines at a relatively low cost.

A Live Concert in the Black Hills

Steppenwolf at Buffalo Chip

Out there in no man's land there's a giant campground: tents, pennants, no–go areas around the stage. The eternal wind that whistles across the endless ocean of grass has died down as nightfall approaches, and a strange peace has descended on the burnt hills of the treeless prairie which, in the golden light of evening, are beginning to radiate the heat of the day. Is it the unearthly peace of an old ghost town being briefly brought back to life?

The incredibly heavy atmosphere begins to darken our mood: uncertainty, anticipation and anxiety are hanging in the air like a quivering field of high–tension electricity. Down in the valley below the giant stage awaits, surrounded by a few weather–beaten wooden shacks casting long shadows. The first campfires flicker in the gathering gloom. A far droning wells up and then dies away again; more and more bikers are arriving, seemingly from another world. Like primeval crustaceans, they edge slowly towards the stage. Security is on alert. Everyone is searched. Buffalo Chip is besieged by local politicians and the local police; shady elements are rumored to be up to no good here.

Then a deep rumble rolls around the valley, the roar of hundreds of Harleys: "Steppenwolf, we love you!" Headlights shine through the massed machines surrounding the stage, loud cries ring out, then silence descends again. "Steppenwolf: I love you!" Cries and whoops ring out all around. A colorful storm of lights flickers on the stage. Burnouts in the middle of the dense crowd, the smell of gasoline mixing with the aroma of grilled steak drifting in heavy clouds over the scene. A feeling of eager anticipation wells up. Born to be wild — yeah!

John Kay and his band "Steppenwolf" at a gig on the Buffala Chip Campground in 1997.

German Oldies

The rhythmic beat of drums is an ancient expression of solidarity in Native American cultures. It's no surprise that it has also become a part of worldwide biker ritual. Daboom – potato – potato: the deep, continuous beat of the powerful V–twins performs exactly the same function as the Indian drums used to have.

In Germany this is certainly the case. When Bones MC, one of the earliest genuine German biker clubs, revived this ancient dance during the 1970s, it rapidly came to be dubbed "the Bones Stomp." A number of club members (the Reebensteep Band) accompany it with washboard, whistle, comb and pan lids.

One of the musicians, known as Fips, then went on to tour Germany for a few years providing the music at all the big biker parties, in those days still fairly modest affairs. This outfit was known as Fips & Judy's Rollende Diskothek. In 1979 Fips, who had a degree in business administration and whose real name is Günter Brecht, founded *Bikers News* in partnership with another academic, Dr. Hans "Doc" Baumann. At that time, this was Germany's sole biker magazine, and it soon developed into a renowned publishing empire, producing a variety of specialist magazines, a custom magazine, various books and videos. The business also incorporates music publishers, and even supplies a wide range of biker accessories.

653

Biker Music

"Harley music" could just as easily be said, because in most cases the Harley stands as a synonym for the machine used by most bikers. So-called biker music is, with a few exceptions, tied not to the brand Harley-Davidson but to the legend associated with it, which is, as we know, something very special. This expresses itself in the form of the music, which appeals not only to Harley riders, but to all bikers. The Harley is usually the figurehead for a music scene which begins with rockabilly, and carries on into pop and country.

Like the original sound of the Big Twin, biker music must also embrace the droning thump: it has to be loud, deep, genuine, hot and straight from the heart. Naturally there is music with Harleys and music about Harleys; and some groups merely use the Harley as a convenient image for the album sleeve though a name or a record cover alone says nothing. A good deal of real biker music comes from films, and the bands who had their hits in this medium are often to be seen at biker parties; the group Steppenwolf (famous for the song *Born To Be Wild*) is probably the best example. Some bands have developed stage shows in which a Harley-Davidson features prominently, the Milwaukee V-Twin being used as decoration and sound prop. For publicity purposes, some musicians also want to be seen with them in private life too, ZZ Top being one of the best known. Others even become real bikers. Whoever they are, those who espouse unqualified love for Harleys are not, it has to be admitted, necessarily fans of jazz, folk music, crooners or brass bands, soul or bluegrass; they may even ridicule country artists – apart from a few important exceptions such as Johnny Cash and Willie Nelson.

Although biker music does not necessarily identify itself with the Harley, at all real biker parties certain records are always very popular and certain bands often invited. The old biker motto "Sex and drugs and rock 'n' roll" reveals the basic philosophy behind biker music. This is true at home, at parties or in the bar. Music popular with bikers is the same the world over, whether in America, Japan, Norway, France, Australia, Switzerland or on Ibiza; the same records are played everywhere, and any group which doesn't give a rendition of the unofficial biker anthem *Born To Be Wild* can forget about the next engagement. A list of chart-breakers of the biker music scene (limited to the U.S. and certainly not complete) may serve to shed a little light on the Harley music world:

The Fifties: The Orlons: *He's a Rebel*; Cheers: *Black Denim Trousers and Motorcycle Boots*

The Sixties: Shangri-La's: *Leader of the Pack*; Lou Reed: *Cycle Annie*; Moby Grape: *Motorcycle Irene MC – Slut on a Harley*; Arlo Guthrie: *Alice's Restaurant*; David Allan & the Arrows: *13th Harley* (instrumental); Brigitte Bardot: *Harley-Davidson*; Bill Medley: *The Hard Ride*; Robert "Baretta" Blake: *Electra Glide in Blue*; Canned Heat: *Harley-Davidson Blues*; Eric Burdon and the Animals: *San Francisco Nights*; Shocking Blue: *Harley-Davidson*. On the soundtrack of the film "Easy Rider" are bands like Steppenwolf, The Byrds, The Electric Prunes, The Holy Modal Rounders, Fraternity of Man, and Jimi Hendrix. Also included is the theme from the T.V. series *Then Came Bronson*.

The Seventies: Waylon Jennings: *Ladies Love Outlaws*; David Allan Coe: *Fuzzy Was an Outlaw* and *Panheads Forever*; John Stewart: *The Lady and the Outlaw*; Shel Silverstein: *Bit Time*; Sailcat: *Motorcycle Mama*

The Eighties: Neil Young: *Comes a Time*; Simon Stokes: *Wolfpack Rides the Night*; AC/DC: *Rocker*; Motorhead: *Iron Horse*; Meatloaf: *Bat out of Hell* (sleeve design); Rogene: *Milwaukee Iron, Turn Me On,*

Don't Turn Me Out, Get Down Biker Music and *Cheezy Rider*; Ray Nelson (former Harley dealer): *Swing Out for Motorcycles, Poker Run, I'm a Motorcycle Rider,* and *Spider the Rider*; Bollock Brothers: *Harley–Davidson Son of a Bitch*; Moon Rose: *I'm a Rocker*; Gero: *Alles Show;* Hank Davidson Band: *Panhead*; Bob Van Dyke (soundtrack to *Hell's Angels Forever*): *Gimme a Harley*; John Hiatt: *Riding with the King*

The Nineties: J. Boss Band: *Happy Harley*; Highlander: *Harley's the Best*; Harleylujah: *See You Later, Harleygator*; Roxette: *Harley and Indians*; JB Walker and Cheap Whiskey Band: *Harleys in Heaven*; Hank Williams, jr.: *Iron Horse* … to name but a few.

A list of international musicians and rock bands who are well–known on the biker scene, most of whom have a direct link to Harley-Davidson, demonstrates the broad spectrum of the music of the scene.

Rock and roll, motorcycles and the lure of the open road have long enjoyed a symbiotic relationship. While the first Harley rolled out of a one-room shed in 1903, rock 'n' roll came along 50 years later and forged a relationship that would symbolize Americana. It is still that image of freedom, rebellion, and the pursuit of individuality that has captured millions of Harley enthusiasts, making Harley-Davidson an American legend.

The Right Stuff in conjunction with Harley-Davidson released *Road Songs II* in October 1998, the sequel to its RIAA platinum-certified 1994 volume I "road rock" collection. The 30-track compilation features a two-disk collection of classic rock songs by Greg Allman, Deep Purple, Jimi Hendrix, Jethro Tull, Lynyrd Skynyrd, Steve Miller, Queen, George Thorogood, and other classic rockers, many of whom own and ride Harley-Davidson motorcycles.

Harley and Music

Rockabilly was once described by the Pittsburgh author Mike Seate as the most natural and original form of music. This probably hits the mark best. A precursor of that style of musical expression we now know as rock 'n' roll, rockabilly developed out of the mix of white and African-American musical cultures in the rural, southern part of the United States. Emerging as an individual style, it soon influenced the entire music scene and is now an institution. It is a cultural legend that is rediscovered time and time again by each new generation of musicians. Thumping bass, tinny guitars, swinging hips and hiccuping sobs became international trademarks alongside half-mast jeans, white T-shirts with a pack of cigarettes in a turned up sleeve, working boots and quiffs.

Rockabilly was born in the 1950s but didn't end there, extending unbroken through subsequent eras. Bands like The Beatles and the Rolling Stones had their first successes with old hits by Carl Perkins. The same was true of Blue Cheer, who made a cover version of Eddie Cochran's *Summertime Blues*. Even Sid Vicious of the Sex Pistols drew inspiration from Rockabilly. Motorhead recorded an updated version of a number by Johnny Kidd and the Pirates. In the 1990s new groups sprang up all over the world as the good old rock 'n' roll themes blossomed once again. New bands, fanzines, production companies, clubs and recording studios appeared on an almost daily basis.

More and more fans are finding their way to rockabilly, perhaps because so many trendy bands and styles soon lose their appeal. While some come across it as they rake through their parents' record collection, others find it simply by accident. Quite apart from all this, and whatever might happen in the future, rockabilly is the basis for that rousing, musical style called biker music.

Always in the mood: unknown biker bands often play the best music, sometimes for charity and frequently until they drop from exhaustion.

http://www.harley-davidson…

The Digital Motorcycle

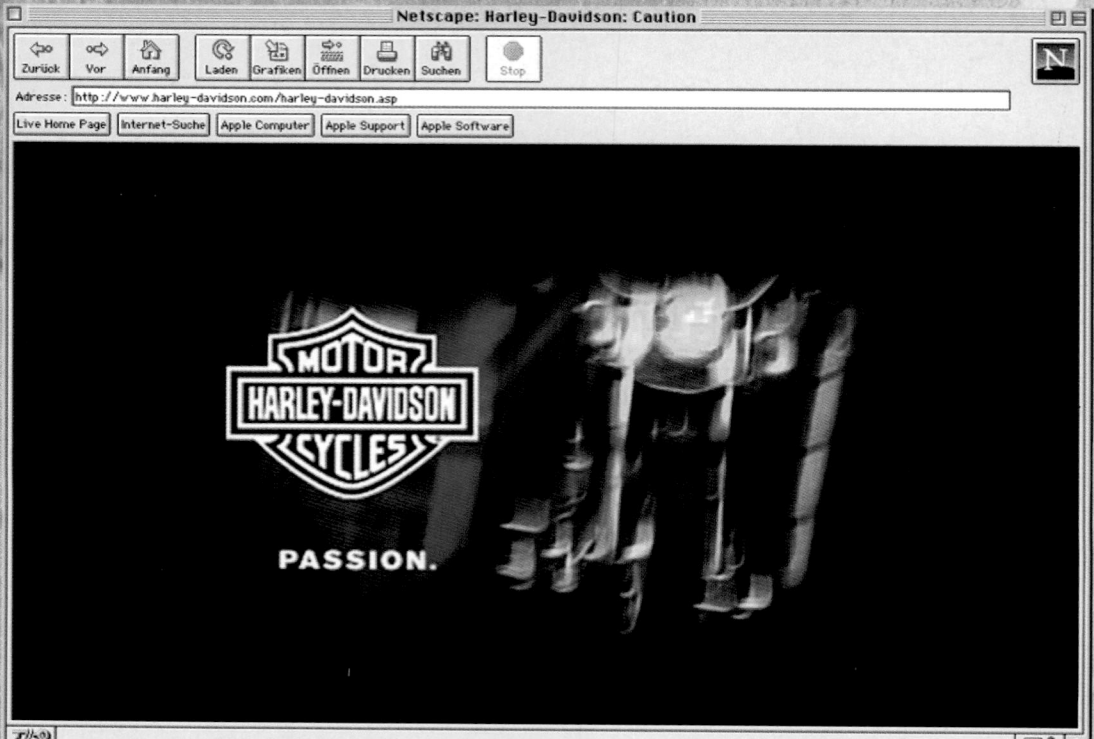

A biker lets the throttle out even when he's riding his Harley on the digital superhighway. From lists of various Harley dealers to maps to touring the Internet for Harley riders to the photo gallery on the homepage of the Harley Cafe in New York, the biker can indulge his passion just as intensively in the kingdom of bytes and bits.

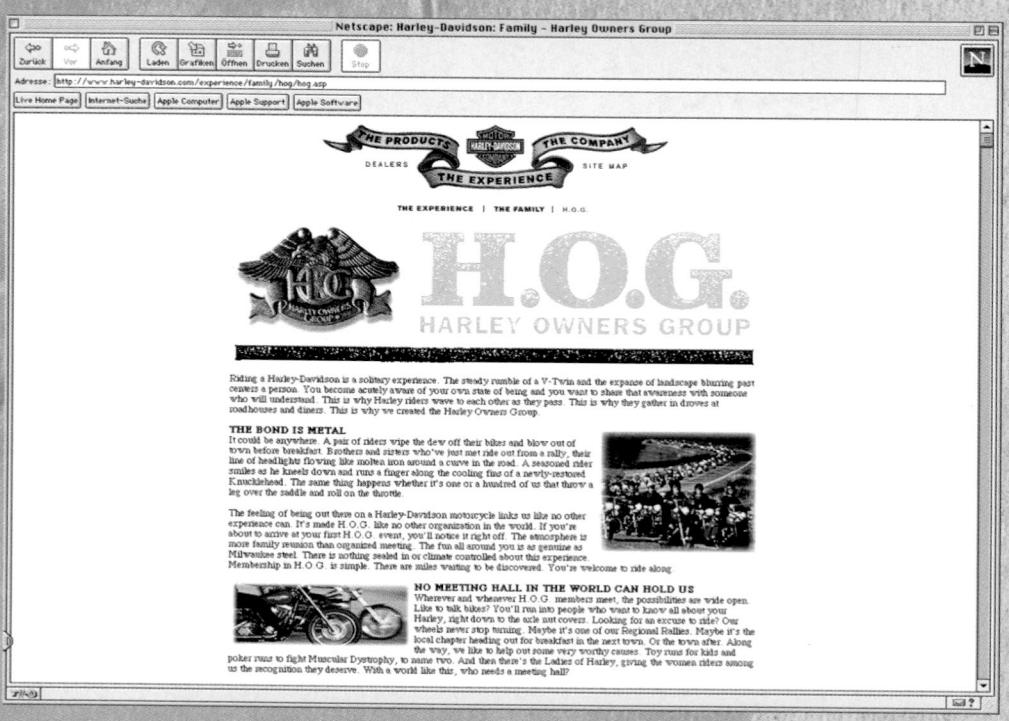

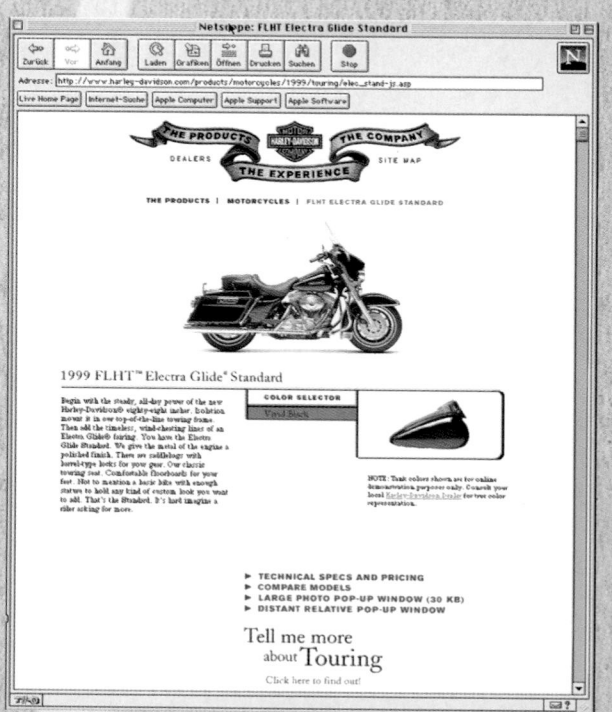

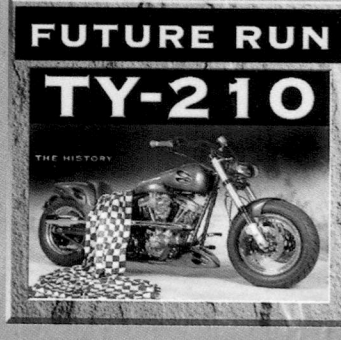

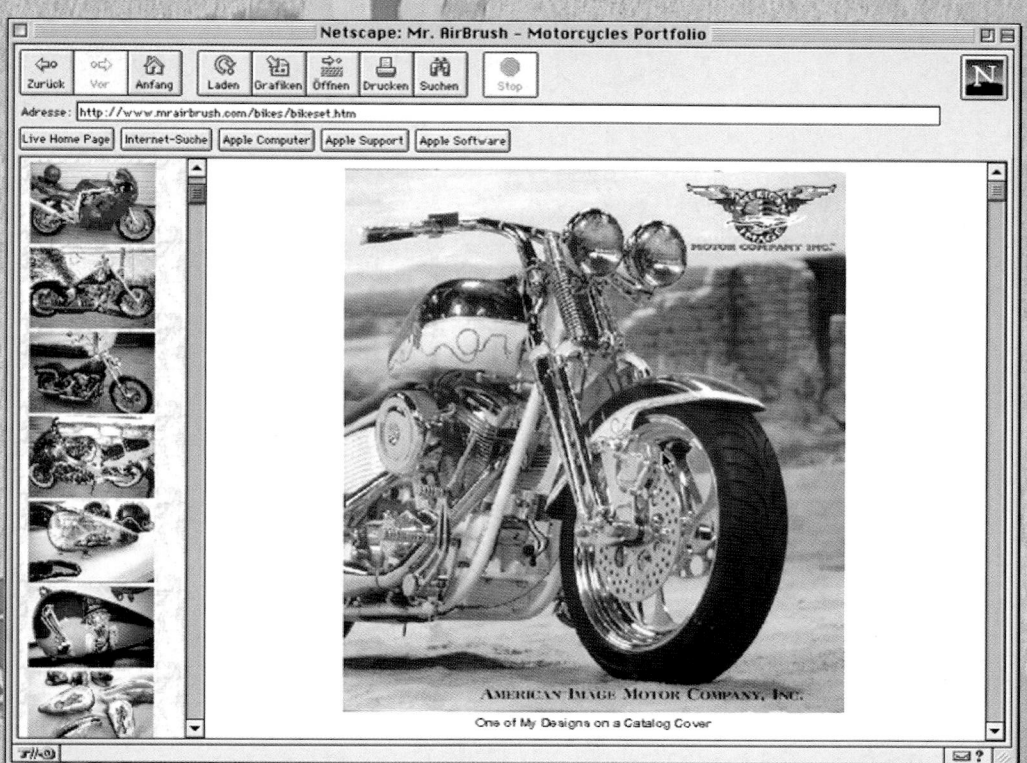

Netscape: Mr. AirBrush - Motorcycles Portfolio

Adresse: http://www.mrairbrush.com/bikes/bikeset.htm

Live Home Page | Internet-Suche | Apple Computer | Apple Support | Apple Software

AMERICAN IMAGE MOTOR COMPANY, INC.

One of My Designs on a Catalog Cover

Apart from the comprehensive homepage of the Harley-Davidson Company itself, there is an almost limitless number of web pages on the theme. Here is a selection:

http://www.harley-davidson.com/home
http://www.magicnet.net/mni/hog.html
http://www.mapquest.com/
http://www.harley-davidsoncafe.com/

...and this is how a (digital) Harley sounds on the information superhighway:
http://www.woodstockharley.com/harley.wave

Netscape: Harley-Davidson Motorcycles: Genuine Motor Accessories

Adresse: http://www.harley-davidson.com/products/gma/gma.asp

Live Home Page | Internet-Suche | Apple Computer | Apple Support | Apple Software

THE PRODUCTS | GENUINE MOTOR ACCESSORIES

TOURING   SOFTAIL

DYNA   SPORTSTER

IT'S SHOW TIME.

The star of the show—Harley-Davidson® Genuine Motor Accessories™. Here, you'll find everything you need to steal the show, from the special featured items in our Product Showcase to Detachables to Screamin' Eagle® performance products. To see a specific accessorized Harley-Davidson, select from the models in the spotlight above.

The stars of the race track and dirt track are here too. You'll find Superbike, Drag and Dirt Track racing schedules, as well as photos of Harley-Davidson® Racing stars.

Don't forget to check out The Latest and Greatest—hot accessory news straight from Milwaukee.

▶ ACCESSORIZED MODELS
▶ PRODUCT SHOWCASE
▶ THE LATEST AND GREATEST
▶ DETACHABLES

Dokument: Übermittelt.

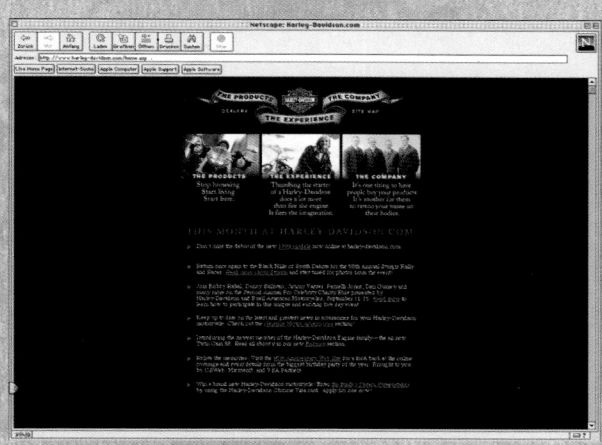

Appendix

322 Harley–Davidson Production Figures from 1903 to 1998

322 Models and their Technical Data from 1903 to 1997

332 Associations and Clubs

332 Motorcycle Museums U.S.A.

333 Films Featuring Motorcycles

334 Abbreviations

334 Index

343 Photo Credits

344 Acknowledgements

Opposite: A brandnew engine.

Harley–Davidson Production Figures from 1903 to 1998

Year	Quantity	Year	Quantity	Year	Quantity	Year	Quantity
1903	3	1929	23,989	1955	10,686	1981	41,606*
1904	8	1930	18,036	1956	11,926	1982	30,262
1905	16	1931	10,407	1957	13,079	1983	29,340
1906	50	1932	7,218	1958	12,676	1984	38,582
1907	150	1933	3,703	1959	12,347	1985	34,522
1908	450	1934	11,212	1960	15,728	1986	38,972
1909	1,149	1935	8,922	1961	10,497	1987	41,580
1910	3,168	1936	9,812	1962	11,144	1988	47,928
1911	5,625	1937	11,674	1963	9,873	1989	54,891
1912	3,852	1938	8,158	1964	13,270	1990	61,683
1913	12,966	1939	8,290	1965	25,328	1991	64,706
1914	16,427	1940	10,461	1966	36,320	1992	69,666
1915	16,493	1941	24,583	1967	27,202	1993	80,017
1916	16,924	1942	52,891	1968	26,600	1994	88,244
1917	18,522	1943	29,521	1969	27,375	1995	100,273
1918	26,708	1944	18,688	1970	28,850	1996	112,508
1919	23,279	1945	12,475	1971	37,620	1997	125,609
1920	27,040	1946	16,222	1972	59,908	1998	156,666**
1921	11,460	1947	20,115	1973	70,903		
1922	10,786	1948	29,612	1974	68,210		
1923	17,046	1949	23,861	1975	75,403		
1924	17,648	1950	17,168	1976	61,375		
1925	15,371	1951	15,882	1977	45,608		
1926	22,275	1952	15,312	1978	47,401*		
1927	18,546	1953	12,431	1979	49,578*		
1928	20,684	1954	10,568	1980	48,181*		

Total number of motorcycles produced

1903–1998	2,824,833

Figures for 1978–1981 exclude special export models
**Targeted production goal*
Source: H.D. Archives

Models and their Technical Data from 1903 to 1997

Legend:

A	Automatic	cc	Cubic centimeters	Dupl./B.	Duplex chain/Belt	G.	Gearwheels	OHV	Overhead valve	S.	Solenoid
Bat.	Battery	cui	Cubic inches	Dupl./G.	Duplex chain/ Gearwheels	G./C.	Gearwheels/Chain	PC.	Piston control	Tripl./C.	Triplex/Chain
B.	Belt	Drive (P/S)	Drive			IOE	Inlet over exhaust	Prod. Fig.	Production figures	Tripl./B.	Triplex/Belt
C.	Chain		(primary/secondary)	el.	Electronic	n.a.	Not available	Single	Single cylinder	UC E Glide	Ultra Classic Electra Glide
Conv.	Convertible	Dupl./C.	Duplex chain/Chain	EFI	Electronic fuel injection	OHC	Overhead cam	SV	Side valve		

All data in the following tables have been compiled to the best of our knowledge, but their accuracy cannot be guaranteed. The production figures are either approximate figures or are not known (n.a. = not available). Sidecars, sidecar-combinations, special models, military models and special export models are not included in these figures.

Model	Type	Engine	Stroke	Engine Type	Displacement	Drive (P/S)	Gears	Ignition	Prod. Fig.
1903									
Single		IOE	4	Single	25	B.	1	Bat.	3 / 1
1904									
Single		IOE	4	Single	25	B.	1	Bat.	8
1905									
Single	1	IOE	4	Single	25	B.	1	Bat.	16
1906									
Single	2	IOE	4	Single	27	B.	1	Bat.	50
1907									
Single	3	IOE	4	Single	27	B.	1	Bat.	150
1908									
Single	4	IOE	4	Single	27	B.	1	Bat.	450
1909									
Single	5	IOE	4	Single	30	B.	1	Bat.	864
Single	5-A	IOE	4	Single	30	B.	1	S.	54
Single	5-B	IOE	4	Single	30	B.	1	Bat.	168
Single	5-C	IOE	4	Single	30	B.	1	S.	36
Twin	5-D	IOE	4	V-2	50	B.	1	S.	27
1910									
Single	6	IOE	4	Single	30	B.	1	Bat.	2,302
Single	6-A	IOE	4	Single	30	B.	1	S.	334
Single	6-B	IOE	4	Single	30	B.	1	Bat.	443
Single	6-C	IOE	4	Single	30	B.	1	S.	88
Stock Racer	6-E	IOE	4	Single	30	n.a.	1	n.a.	n.a.
1911									
Single	7	IOE	4	Single	30	B.	1	Bat.	n.a.
Single	7-A	IOE	4	Single	30	B.	n.a.	S.	n.a.
Single	7-B	IOE	4	Single	30	B.	n.a.	Bat.	n.a.
Single	7-C	IOE	4	Single	30	B.	n.a.	S.	n.a.
Twin	7-D	IOE	4	V-2	50	B.	2	S.	n.a.
Twin	7-E	IOE	4	V-2	50	B.	n.a.	n.a.	n.a.
1912									
Single	8	IOE	4	Single	30	B.	n.a.	Bat.	n.a.

Model	Type	Engine	Stroke	Engine Type	Displacement	Drive (P/S)	Gears	Ignition	Prod. Fig.
Single	X-8	IOE	4	Single	30	B.	n.a.	Bat.	n.a.
Single	8-A	IOE	4	Single	30	B.	1	S.	545
Single	X-8-A	IOE	4	Single	30	B.	n.a.	S.	n.a.
Twin	8-D	IOE	4	V-2	50	B.	n.a.	S.	n.a.
Twin	X-8-D	IOE	4	V-2	50	B.	2	S.	n.a.
Twin	X-8-E	IOE	4	V-2	61	C.	2	S.	n.a.
1913									
Single	9-A	IOE	4	Single	35	B.	1	S.	1,510
Single	9-B	IOE	4	Single	35	C.	1	S.	4,601
Twin	9-E	IOE	4	V-2	61	C.	n.a.	n.a.	6,732
Twin	9-F	IOE	4	V-2	61	C.	2	n.a.	63
1914									
Single	10-A	IOE	4	Single	35	B.	1	S.	316
Single	10-B	IOE	4	Single	35	C.	1	S.	2,034
Single	10-C	IOE	4	Single	35	C.	2	S.	877
Twin	10-E	IOE	4	V-2	61	C.	1	S.	5,055
Twin	10-F	IOE	4	V-2	61	C.	2	S.	7,956
Delivery Van	10-G	IOE	4	V-2	61	C.	2	S.	171
1915									
Single	11-B	IOE	4	Single	35	C.	1	S.	670
Single	11-C	IOE	4	Single	35	C.	2	S.	545
Twin	11-E	IOE	4	V-2	61	C.	1	S.	1,275
Twin	11-F	IOE	4	V-2	61	C.	3	S.	9,855
Twin	11-H	IOE	4	V-2	61	C.	1	Bat.	140
Twin	11-J	IOE	4	V-2	61	C.	3	Bat.	3,719
Twin	11-K	IOE	4	V-2	61	C.	1	Bat.	n.a.
1916									
Single	16-C	IOE	4	Single	35	C.	3	S.	862
Single	16-B	IOE	4	Single	35	C.	1	S.	292
Twin	16-F	IOE	4	V-2	61	C.	3	S.	9,496
Twin	16-J	IOE	4	V-2	61	C.	3	el.	5,898
Twin	16-E	IOE	4	V-2	61	C.	1	S.	252
Racer	16-R	IOE	4	V-2	61	C.	n.a.	S.	82
Track Racer	16-T	IOE	4	V-2	61	C.	n.a.	S.	23
Stock Racer	16-S	IOE	4	Single	35	C.	n.a.	S.	12
1917									
Single	17-B	IOE	4	Single	35	C.	1	S.	124
Single	17-C	IOE	4	Single	35	C.	3	S.	605
Twin	17-E	IOE	4	V-2	61	C.	1	S.	68
Twin	17-F	IOE	4	V-2	61	C.	3	S.	8,527
Twin	17-J	IOE	4	V-2	61	C.	3	S.	9,180
Roadster Racer	17-R	IOE	4	V-2	61	C.	n.a.	n.a.	12
Stock Racer	17-T	IOE	4	V-2	61	C.	n.a.	n.a.	1
Stock Racer	17-S	IOE	4	Single	35	C.	n.a.	n.a.	5
1918									
Single	18-B	IOE	4	Single	35	C.	1	S.	19
Single	18-C	IOE	4	Single	61	C.	3	S.	251
Twin	18-E	IOE	4	V-2	61	C.	1	S.	5
Twin	18-F	IOE	4	V-2	61	C.	3	S.	11,764
Twin	18-J	IOE	4	V-2	61	C.	3	S.	6,571
Twin	18-FUS	IOE	4	V-2	61	C.	1	n.a.	8095
Roadster Racer	18-R	IOE	4	V-2	61	C.	3	n.a.	n.a.
1919									
Twin	19-J	IOE	4	V-2	61	C.	3	S.	9,941
Twin	19-JS	IOE	4	V-2	61	C.	3	el.	n.a.
Twin	19-F	IOE	4	V-2	61	C.	3	S.	5,064
Twin	19-FS	IOE	4	V-2	61	C.	3	S.	n.a.
Twin	19-FUS	IOE	4	V-2	61	C.	3	n.a.	7521
Sport Twin	19-W	SV	4	Boxer	35,64	C.	3	n.a.	753
Sport Twin	19-WF	SV	4	Boxer	35,64	C.	3	S.	n.a.
1920									
Twin	20-J	IOE	4	V-2	61	C.	3	S.	14,192
Twin	20-JS	IOE	4	V-2	61	C.	3	Bat.	n.a.
Twin	20-F	IOE	4	V-2	61	C.	3	S.	7,579
Twin	20-FS	IOE	4	V-2	61	C.	3	S.	n.a.
Sport Twin	20-W	SV	4	Boxer	35,64	C.	3	S.	n.a.
Sport Twin	20-WF	SV	4	Boxer	35,64	C.	3	n.a.	4,459
Sport Twin	20-WJ	SV	4	Boxer	35,64	C.	3	B.	810
1921									
Single	21-CD	IOE	4	Single	35,64	C.	3	S.	n.a.
Twin	21-F	IOE	4	V-2	61	C.	3	S.	2,413
Twin	21-FD	IOE	4	V-2	74	C.	3	S.	277
Twin	21-J	IOE	4	V-2	61	C.	3	Bat.	4,526
Twin	21-JD	IOE	4	V-2	74	C.	3	Bat.	2,321
Twin	21-JS	IOE	4	V-2	61	C.	3	Bat.	n.a.
Twin	21-FS	IOE	4	V-2	61	C.	3	S.	n.a.
Twin	21-FDS	IOE	4	V-2	74	C.	3	S.	n.a.
Twin	21-JDS	IOE	4	V-2	74	C.	3	Bat.	n.a.
Sport Twin	21-W/WJ	SV	4	Boxer	35,64	C.	3	S.	823
Sport Twin	21-WF	SV	4	Boxer	35,64	C.	3	S.	1,100
1922									
Single	22-CD	IOE	4	Single	37	C.	3	S.	39
Twin	22-J	IOE	4	V-2	61	C.	3	Bat.	3,183
Twin	22-JS	IOE	4	V-2	61	C.	3	Bat.	n.a.
Twin	22-F	IOE	4	V-2	61	C.	3	S.	1,824
Twin	22-FS	IOE	4	V-2	61	C.	3	S.	n.a.
Twin	22-DD	IOE	4	V-2	74	C.	3	Bat.	n.a.
Twin	22-DDS	IOE	4	V-2	74	C.	3	Bat.	n.a.
Twin	22-FD	IOE	4	V-2	74	C.	3	S.	909
Twin	22-FDS	IOE	4	V-2	74	C.	3	S.	n.a.
Twin	22-JD	IOE	4	V-2	74	C.	3	Bat.	3988
Twin	22-JDS	IOE	4	V-2	74	C.	3	Bat.	n.a.
Sport Twin	22-WJ	SV	4	Boxer	35,64	C.	3	Bat.	455
Sport Twin	22-WF	SV	4	Boxer	35,64	C.	3	S.	388
1923									
Twin	23-J	IOE	4	V-2	61	C.	3	Bat.	4,802
Twin	23-JS	IOE	4	V-2	61	C.	3	Bat.	n.a.
Twin	23-F	IOE	4	V-2	61	C.	3	S.	2,822
Twin	23-FS	IOE	4	V-2	61	C.	3	S.	n.a.
Twin	23-JD	IOE	4	V-2	74	C.	3	Bat.	7,458
Twin	23-JDS	IOE	4	V-2	74	C.	3	Bat.	n.a.
Twin	23-FD	IOE	4	V-2	74	C.	3	S.	869
Twin	23-FDS	IOE	4	V-2	74	C.	3	S.	n.a.
Sport Twin	23-WJ	SV	4	Boxer	35,64	C.	3	Bat.	481
Sport Twin	23-WF	SV	4	Boxer	35,64	C.	3	S.	614
1924									
Twin	24-FE	IOE	4	V-2	61	C.	3	S.	2708
Twin	24-FES	IOE	4	V-2	61	C.	3	S.	n.a.
Twin	24-JE	IOE	4	V-2	61	C.	3	Bat.	4,994
Twin	24-JES	IOE	4	V-2	61	C.	3	Bat.	n.a.
Twin	24-FD	IOE	4	V-2	74	C.	3	S.	502
Twin	24-FDS	IOE	4	V-2	74	C.	3	S.	n.a.
Twin	24-JD	IOE	4	V-2	74	C.	3	Bat.	2,955
Twin	24-JDS	IOE	4	V-2	74	C.	3	Bat.	n.a.
Twin	24-FDCA	IOE	4	V-2	74	C.	3	S.	351
Twin	24-FDSCA	IOE	4	V-2	74	C.	3	S.	n.a.
Twin	24-JDCA	IOE	4	V-2	74	C.	3	Bat.	3,014
Twin	24-JDSCA	IOE	4	V-2	74	C.	3	Bat.	n.a.
1925									
Twin	25-FE	IOE	4	V-2	61	C.	3	S.	n.a.
Twin	25-FES	IOE	4	V-2	61	C.	3	S.	n.a.
Twin	25-JE	IOE	4	V-2	61	C.	3	Bat.	n.a.
Twin	25-JES	IOE	4	V-2	61	C.	3	Bat.	n.a.
Twin	25-FDCB	IOE	4	V-2	74	C.	3	S.	n.a.
Twin	25-FDCBS	IOE	4	V-2	74	C.	3	S.	n.a.
Twin	25-JDCB	IOE	4	V-2	74	C.	3	Bat.	n.a.
Twin	25-JDCBS	IOE	4	V-2	74	C.	3	Bat.	n.a.
1926									
Single	26-A	SV	4	Single	21	C.	3	S.	1,128
Single	26-B	SV	4	Single	21	C.	3	Bat.	5,979
Single	26-AA	OHV	4	Single	21	C.	3	S.	61
Single	26-BA	OHV	4	Single	21	C.	3	Bat.	515
Twin	26-J	IOE	4	V-2	61	C.	3	Bat.	3,749
Twin	26-JS	IOE	4	V-2	61	C.	3	Bat.	n.a.
Twin	26-JD	IOE	4	V-2	74	C.	3	Bat.	9,544
Twin	26-JDS	IOE	4	V-2	74	C.	3	Bat.	n.a.

Model	Type	Engine	Stroke	Engine Type	Displacement	Drive (P/S)	Gears	Ignition	Prod. Fig.
Racer	26-S	OHV	4	Single	21	C.	3	S.	n.a.

1927

Model	Type	Engine	Stroke	Engine Type	Displacement	Drive (P/S)	Gears	Ignition	Prod. Fig.
Single	27-A	SV	4	Single	21	C.	3	S.	444
Single	27-AA	OHV	4	Single	21	C.	3	S.	32
Single	27-AAE	OHV	4	Single	21	C.	3	S.	66
Single	27-B	SV	4	Single	21	C.	3	Bat.	3,711
Single	27-BA	OHV	4	Single	21	C.	3	Bat.	481
Single	27-BAE	OHV	4	Single	21	C.	3	Bat.	43
Twin	27-F	IOE	4	V-2	61	C.	3	S.	246
Twin	27-FS	IOE	4	V-2	61	C.	3	S.	n.a.
Twin	27-FK	IOE	4	V-2	61	C.	3	S.	n.a.
Twin	27-FD	IOE	4	V-2	74	C.	3	S.	209
Twin	27-FDS	IOE	4	V-2	74	C.	3	S.	n.a.
Twin	27-FDL	IOE	4	V-2	74	C.	3	S.	n.a.
Twin	27-J	IOE	4	V-2	61	C.	3	Bat.	3,561
Twin	27-JS	IOE	4	V-2	61	C.	3	Bat.	n.a.
Twin	27-JK	IOE	4	V-2	61	C.	3	Bat.	n.a.
Twin	27-JD	IOE	4	V-2	74	C.	3	Bat.	9,691
Twin	27-JDS	IOE	4	V-2	74	C.	3	Bat.	n.a.
Twin	27-JDL	IOE	4	V-2	74	C.	3	Bat.	n.a.
Hillclimb	27-FHAC	IOE	4	V-2	61	C.	3	S.	11
Hillclimb	27-FHAD	IOE	4	V-2	61	C.	3	S.	8
Single Speed	27-S	SV	4	Single	21	C.	3	S.	n.a.
Single Speed	27-SM	SV	4	Single	21	C.	3	S.	26
Single Speed	27-T	SV	4	Single	21	C.	3	S.	1
Racer	27-SA	OHV	4	Single	21	C.	1	Bat.	n.a.
Racer	27-SMA	OHV	4	Single	21	C.	3	Bat.	n.a.
8 Valve Racer	27-8-V	OHV	4	V-2	61	C.		S.	2

1928

Model	Type	Engine	Stroke	Engine Type	Displacement	Drive (P/S)	Gears	Ignition	Prod. Fig.
Single	28-A	SV	4	Single	21	C.	3	S.	519
Single	28-AA	OHV	4	Single	21	C.	3	S.	65
Single	28-AAE	OHV	4	Single	21	C.	3	S.	n.a.
Single	28-B	SV	4	Single	21	C.	3	Bat.	3,483
Single	28-BA	OHV	4	Single	21	C.	3	Bat.	943
Single	28-BAE	OHV	4	Single	21	C.	3	Bat.	n.a.
Twin	28-F	IOE	4	V-2	61	C.	3	S.	141
Twin	28-FD	IOE	4	V-2	74	C.	3	S.	131
Twin	28-J	IOE	4	V-2	61	C.	3	Bat.	4,184
Twin	28-JD	IOE	4	V-2	74	C.	3	Bat.	11,007
Twin	28-JDS	IOE	4	V-2	74	C.	3	Bat.	n.a.
Twin	28-JDX	IOE	4	V-2	74	C.	3	Bat.	n.a.
Twin	28-JDXL	IOE	4	V-2	61	C.	3	Bat.	n.a.
Twin	28-JS	IOE	4	V-2	61	C.	3	Bat.	n.a.
Twin	28-JX	IOE	4	V-2	61	C.	3	Bat.	n.a.
Twin	28-JXL	IOE	4	V-2	61	C.	3	Bat.	n.a.
Twin	28-JH	IOE	4	V-2	61	C.	3	n.a.	n.a.
Twin	28-JDH	IOE	4	V-2	74	C.	3	n.a.	n.a.
Twin	28-FS	IOE	4	V-2	61	C.	3	S.	n.a.

1929

Model	Type	Engine	Stroke	Engine Type	Displacement	Drive (P/S)	Gears	Ignition	Prod. Fig.
Single	29-A	SV	4	Single	21	Dupl./C.	3	S.	197
Single	29-AA	OHV	4	Single	21	Dupl./C.	3	Bat.	21
Single	29-B	SV	4	Single	21	Dupl./C.	3	S.	1,592
Single	29-BA	OHV	4	Single	21	Dupl./C.	3	Bat.	191
Single	29-C	SV	4	Single	30,5	Dupl./C.	3	Bat.	1,570
	29-D	SV	4	V-2	45	Dupl./C.	3	Bat.	4,513
	29-DL	SV	4	V-2	45	Dupl./C.	3	Bat.	2,343
Twin	29-F	IOE	4	V-2	61	C.	3	S.	191
Twin	29-FD	IOE	4	V-2	74	C.	3	S.	73
Twin	29-J	IOE	4	V-2	61	C.	3	Bat.	2,886
Twin	29-JD	IOE	4	V-2	74	C.	3	Bat.	10,182
Twin	29-JDH	IOE	4	V-2	74	C.	3	Bat.	n.a.
Twin	29-JDS	IOE	4	V-2	74	C.	3	Bat.	n.a.
Twin	29-JXL	IOE	4	V-2	61	C.	3	Bat.	n.a.
Twin	29-JH	IOE	4	V-2	61	C.	3	Bat.	n.a.
Twin	29-JS	IOE	4	V-2	74	C.	3	Bat.	n.a.

1930

Model	Type	Engine	Stroke	Engine Type	Displacement	Drive (P/S)	Gears	Ignition	Prod. Fig.
Single	30-A	SV	4	Single	21	Dupl./C.	3	S.	4
Single	30-AA	OHV	4	Single	21	Dupl./C.	3	S.	1
Single	30-B	SV	4	Single	21	Dupl./C.	3	Bat.	577
Single	30-BR	SV	4	Single	21	Dupl./C.	3	Bat.	95
Single	30-BAF	OHV	4	Single	21	Dupl./C.	3	Bat.	86
Single	30-C	SV	4	Single	30,5	Dupl./C.	3	Bat.	1,483
Single	30-CM	SV	4	Single	30,5	Dupl./C.	3	Bat.	11
	30-D	SV	4	V-2	45	Dupl./C.	3	Bat.	2,000
	30-DL	SV	4	V-2	45	Dupl./C.	3	Bat.	3,191
	30-DS	SV	4	V-2	45	Dupl./C.	3	Bat.	206
	30-DLD	SV	4	V-2	45	Dupl./C.	3	Bat.	n.a.
Big Twin	30-V	SV	4	V-2	74	Dupl./C.	3	Bat.	1,960
Big Twin	30-VL	SV	4	V-2	74	Dupl./C.	3	Bat.	3,246
Big Twin	30-VS	SV	4	V-2	74	Dupl./C.	3	Bat.	3,612
Big Twin	30-VC	SV	4	V-2	74	Dupl./C.	3	Bat.	1,174

1931

Model	Type	Engine	Stroke	Engine Type	Displacement	Drive (P/S)	Gears	Ignition	Prod. Fig.
Single	31-C	SV	4	Single	30,5	Dupl./C.	3	Bat.	874
	31-D	SV	4	V-2	45	Dupl./C.	3	Bat.	715
	31-DS	SV	4	V-2	45	Dupl./C.	3	Bat.	276
	31-DL	SV	4	V-2	45	Dupl./C.	3	Bat.	1,306
	31-DLD	SV	4	V-2	45	Dupl./C.	3	Bat.	241
Big Twin	31-V	SV	4	V-2	74	Dupl./C.	3	Bat.	825
Big Twin	31-VS	SV	4	V-2	74	Dupl./C.	3	Bat.	1,994
Big Twin	31-VL	SV	4	V-2	74	Dupl./C.	3	Bat.	3,477
Big Twin	31-VC	SV	4	V-2	74	Dupl./C.	3	Bat.	n.a.

1932

Model	Type	Engine	Stroke	Engine Type	Displacement	Drive (P/S)	Gears	Ignition	Prod. Fig.
Single	32-B	SV	4	Single	21	Dupl./C.	3	Bat.	535
Single	32-C	SV	4	Single	30,5	Dupl./C.	3	Bat.	213
	32-R	SV	4	V-2	45	Dupl./C.	3	Bat.	410
	32-RS	SV	4	V-2	45	Dupl./C.	3	Bat.	111
	32-RL	SV	4	V-2	45	Dupl./C.	3	Bat.	628
	32-RLD	SV	4	V-2	45	Dupl./C.	3	Bat.	98
Big Twin	32-V	SV	4	V-2	74	Dupl./C.	3	Bat.	478
Big Twin	32-VS	SV	4	V-2	74	Dupl./C.	3	Bat.	1,233
Big Twin	32-VL	SV	4	V-2	74	Dupl./C.	3	Bat.	2,684
Big Twin	32-VC	SV	4	V-2	74	Dupl./C.	3	Bat.	n.a.
Servi-Car	32-G	SV	4	V-2	45	Dupl./C.	n.a.	Bat.	n.a.
Servi-Car	32-GA	SV	4	V-2	45	Dupl./C.	n.a.	Bat.	n.a.
Servi-Car	32-GD	SV	4	V-2	45	Dupl./C.	n.a.	Bat.	36
Servi-Car	32-GE	SV	4	V-2	45	Dupl./C.	n.a.	Bat.	5

1933

Model	Type	Engine	Stroke	Engine Type	Displacement	Drive (P/S)	Gears	Ignition	Prod. Fig.
Single	33-B	SV	4	Single	21	Dupl./C.	3	Bat.	123
Single	33-C	SV	4	Single	30,5	Dupl./C.	3	Bat.	112
	33-R	SV	4	V-2	45	Dupl./C.	3	Bat.	162
	33-RS	SV	4	V-2	45	Dupl./C.	3	Bat.	37
	33-RL	SV	4	V-2	45	Dupl./C.	3	Bat.	264
	33-RLD	SV	4	V-2	45	Dupl./C.	3	Bat.	68
Big Twin	33-V	SV	4	V-2	74	Dupl./C.	3	Bat.	233
Big Twin	33-VS	SV	4	V-2	74	Dupl./C.	3	Bat.	164
Big Twin	33-VL	SV	4	V-2	74	Dupl./C.	3	Bat.	886
Big Twin	33-VLD	SV	4	V-2	74	Dupl./C.	3	Bat.	780
Big Twin	33-VC	SV	4	V-2	74	Dupl./C.	3	Bat.	106

1934

Model	Type	Engine	Stroke	Engine Type	Displacement	Drive (P/S)	Gears	Ignition	Prod. Fig.
Single	34-B	SV	4	Single	21	Dupl./C.	3	Bat.	424
Single	34-C	SV	4	Single	30,5	Dupl./C.	3	Bat.	220
Single	34-CB	SV	4	Single	30,5	Dupl./C.	3	Bat.	310
	34-RL	SV	4	V-2	45	Dupl./C.	3	Bat.	743
	34-R	SV	4	V-2	45	Dupl./C.	3	Bat.	450
	34-RLD	SV	4	V-2	45	Dupl./C.	3	Bat.	240
Big Twin	34-VLD	SV	4	V-2	74	Dupl./C.	3	Bat.	4,527
Big Twin	34-VD	SV	4	V-2	74	Dupl./C.	3	Bat.	664
Big Twin	34-VDS	SV	4	V-2	74	Dupl./C.	3	Bat.	1,029
Big Twin	34-VFDS	SV	4	V-2	74	Dupl./C.	3	Bat.	1,330

1935

Model	Type	Engine	Stroke	Engine Type	Displacement	Drive (P/S)	Gears	Ignition	Prod. Fig.
	35-RL	SV	4	V-2	45	Dupl./C.	3	Bat.	819
	35-R	SV	4	V-2	45	Dupl./C.	3	Bat.	543
	35-RS	SV	4	V-2	45	Dupl./C.	3	Bat.	392
	35-RLD	SV	4	V-2	45	Dupl./C.	3	Bat.	177
Big Twin	35-VLD	SV	4	V-2	74	Dupl./C.	3	Bat.	3,963
Big Twin	35-VD	SV	4	V-2	74	Dupl./C.	3	Bat.	585
Big Twin	35-VDS	SV	4	V-2	74	Dupl./C.	3	Bat.	1,189
Big Twin	35-VLDJ	SV	4	V-2	74	Dupl./C.	3	Bat.	102
Big Twin	35-VLDD	SV	4	V-2	80	Dupl./C.	3	Bat.	179
Big Twin	35-VDDS	SV	4	V-2	80	Dupl./C.	3	Bat.	n.a.
Racer	35-RLDR	SV	4	V-2	45	Dupl./C.	3	Bat.	29

Model	Type	Engine	Stroke	Engine Type	Displacement	Drive (P/S)	Gears	Ignition	Prod. Fig.
Servi-Car	35-G	SV	4	V-2	45	Dupl./C.	3	Bat.	323
Servi-Car	35-GA	SV	4	V-2	45	Dupl./C.	3	Bat.	64
Servi-Car	35-GD	SV	4	V-2	45	Dupl./C.	3	Bat.	91
Servi-Car	35-GDT	SV	4	V-2	45	Dupl./C.	3	Bat.	72
Servi-Car	35-GE	SV	4	V-2	45	Dupl./C.	3	Bat.	17

1936

Model	Type	Engine	Stroke	Engine Type	Displacement	Drive (P/S)	Gears	Ignition	Prod. Fig.
	36-RL	SV	4	V-2	45	Dupl./C.	3	Bat.	355
	36-RLD	SV	4	V-2	45	Dupl./C.	3	Bat.	540
	36-R	SV	4	V-2	45	Dupl./C.	3	Bat.	539
	36-RS	SV	4	V-2	45	Dupl./C.	3	Bat.	437
Big Twin	36-VLD	SV	4	V-2	74	Dupl./C.	3	Bat.	1,577
Big Twin	36-VD	SV	4	V-2	74	Dupl./C.	3	Bat.	176
Big Twin	36-VDS	SV	4	V-2	74	Dupl./C.	3	Bat.	623
Big Twin	36-VLH	SV	4	V-2	80	Dupl./C.	3	Bat.	2,046
Big Twin	36-VHS	SV	4	V-2	80	Dupl./C.	4	Bat.	305
	36-EL	OHV	4	V-2	61	Dupl./C.	4	Bat.	1,526
	36-E	OHV	4	V-2	61	Dupl./C.	4	Bat.	152
	36-ES	OHV	4	V-2	61	Dupl./C.	4	Bat.	26
Racer	36-RLDR	SV	4	V-2	45	Dupl./C.	3	Bat.	79
Servi-Car	36-G	SV	4	V-2	45	Dupl./C.	3	Bat.	382
Servi-Car	36-GA	SV	4	V-2	45	Dupl./C.	3	Bat.	55
Servi-Car	36-GD	SV	4	V-2	45	Dupl./C.	3	Bat.	96
Servi-Car	36-GDT	SV	4	V-2	45	Dupl./C.	3	Bat.	85
Servi-Car	36-GE	SV	4	V-2	45	Dupl./C.	3	Bat.	30

1937

Model	Type	Engine	Stroke	Engine Type	Displacement	Drive (P/S)	Gears	Ignition	Prod. Fig.
	37-WL	SV	4	V-2	45	Dupl./C.	3	Bat.	560
	37-WLD	SV	4	V-2	45	Dupl./C.	3	Bat.	581
	37-W	SV	4	V-2	45	Dupl./C.	3	Bat.	509
	37-WS	SV	4	V-2	45	Dupl./C.	3	Bat.	232
Big Twin	37-UL	SV	4	V-2	74	Dupl./C.	4	Bat.	2,861
Big Twin	37-U	SV	4	V-2	74	Dupl./C.	4	Bat.	612
Big Twin	37-US	SV	4	V-2	74	Dupl./C.	4	Bat.	1,080
Big Twin	37-ULH	SV	4	V-2	80	Dupl./C.	4	Bat.	1,513
Big Twin	37-UH	SV	4	V-2	80	Dupl./C.	4	Bat.	185
Big Twin	37-UHS	SV	4	V-2	80	Dupl./C.	4	Bat.	400
	37-EL	OHV	4	V-2	61	Dupl./C.	4	Bat.	1,829
	37-E	OHV	4	V-2	61	Dupl./C.	4	Bat.	126
	37-ES	OHV	4	V-2	61	Dupl./C.	4	Bat.	70
Racer	37-WLDR	SV	4	V-2	45	Dupl./C.	3	Bat.	145
Servi-Car	37-G	SV	4	V-2	45	Dupl./C.	3	Bat.	491
Servi-Car	37-GA	SV	4	V-2	45	Dupl./C.	3	Bat.	55
Servi-Car	37-GD	SV	4	V-2	45	Dupl./C.	3	Bat.	112
Servi-Car	37-GDT	SV	4	V-2	45	Dupl./C.	3	Bat.	136
Servi-Car	37-GE	SV	4	V-2	45	Dupl./C.	3	Bat.	22

1938

Model	Type	Engine	Stroke	Engine Type	Displacement	Drive (P/S)	Gears	Ignition	Prod. Fig.
	38-WLD	SV	4	V-2	45	Dupl./C.	4	Bat.	402
	38-WL	SV	4	V-2	45	Dupl./C.	4	Bat.	309
Big Twin	38-UL	SV	4	V-2	74	Dupl./C.	4	Bat.	1,099
Big Twin	38-U	SV	4	V-2	74	Dupl./C.	4	Bat.	504
Big Twin	38-US	SV	4	V-2	74	Dupl./C.	4	Bat.	1,193
Big Twin	38-ULH	SV	4	V-2	80	Dupl./C.	4	Bat.	579
Big Twin	38-UH	SV	4	V-2	80	Dupl./C.	4	Bat.	108
Big Twin	38-UHS	SV	4	V-2	80	Dupl./C.	4	Bat.	132
	38-EL	OHV	4	V-2	61	Dupl./C.	4	Bat.	2,289
	38-ES	OHV	4	V-2	61	Dupl./C.	4	Bat.	189
Racer	38-WLDR	SV	4	V-2	45	Dupl./C.	4	Bat.	139
Servi-Car	38-G	SV	4	V-2	45	Dupl./C.	3	Bat.	259
Servi-Car	38-GA	SV	4	V-2	45	Dupl./C.	3	Bat.	83
Servi-Car	38-GD	SV	4	V-2	45	Dupl./C.	3	Bat.	81
Servi-Car	38-GDT	SV	4	V-2	45	Dupl./C.	3	Bat.	102

1939

Model	Type	Engine	Stroke	Engine Type	Displacement	Drive (P/S)	Gears	Ignition	Prod. Fig.
	39-WLD	SV	4	V-2	45	Dupl./C.	4	Bat.	326
	39-WL	SV	4	V-2	45	Dupl./C.	4	Bat.	212
Big Twin	39-UL	SV	4	V-2	74	Dupl./C.	4	Bat.	902
Big Twin	39-U	SV	4	V-2	74	Dupl./C.	4	Bat.	421
Big Twin	39-US	SV	4	V-2	74	Dupl./C.	4	Bat.	1,327
Big Twin	39-ULH	SV	4	V-2	80	Dupl./C.	4	Bat.	384
Big Twin	39-UH	SV	4	V-2	80	Dupl./C.	4	Bat.	92
Big Twin	39-UHS	SV	4	V-2	80	Dupl./C.	4	Bat.	109
	39-EL	OHV	4	V-2	61	Dupl./C.	4	Bat.	2,695
	39-ES	OHV	4	V-2	61	Dupl./C.	4	Bat.	214

Model	Type	Engine	Stroke	Engine Type	Displacement	Drive (P/S)	Gears	Ignition	Prod. Fig.
Racer	39-WLDR	SV	4	V-2	45	Dupl./C.	4	Bat.	173
Servi-Car	39-G	SV	4	V-2	45	Dupl./C.	3	Bat.	320
Servi-Car	39-GA	SV	4	V-2	45	Dupl./C.	3	Bat.	126
Servi-Car	39-GD	SV	4	V-2	45	Dupl./C.	3	Bat.	90
Servi-Car	39-GDT	SV	4	V-2	45	Dupl./C.	3	Bat.	114

1940

Model	Type	Engine	Stroke	Engine Type	Displacement	Drive (P/S)	Gears	Ignition	Prod. Fig.
	40-WLD	SV	4	V-2	45	Dupl./C.	4	Bat.	567
	40-WL	SV	4	V-2	45	Dupl./C.	4	Bat.	569
Big Twin	40-UL	SV	4	V-2	74	Dupl./C.	4	Bat.	822
Big Twin	40-U	SV	4	V-2	74	Dupl./C.	4	Bat.	260
Big Twin	40-US	SV	4	V-2	74	Dupl./C.	4	Bat.	1,516
Big Twin	40-ULH	SV	4	V-2	80	Dupl./C.	4	Bat.	672
Big Twin	40-UH	SV	4	V-2	80	Dupl./C.	4	Bat.	187
Big Twin	40-UHS	SV	4	V-2	80	Dupl./C.	4	Bat.	163
	40-EL	OHV	4	V-2	61	Dupl./C.	4	Bat.	3,893
	40-ES	OHV	4	V-2	61	Dupl./C.	4	Bat.	176
Racer	40-WLDR	SV	4	V-2	45	Dupl./C.	4	Bat.	87
Servi-Car	40-G	SV	4	V-2	45	Dupl./C.	3	Bat.	468
Servi-Car	40-GA	SV	4	V-2	45	Dupl./C.	3	Bat.	156
Servi-Car	40-GD	SV	4	V-2	45	Dupl./C.	3	Bat.	158
Servi-Car	40-GDT	SV	4	V-2	45	Dupl./C.	3	Bat.	126

1941

Model	Type	Engine	Stroke	Engine Type	Displacement	Drive (P/S)	Gears	Ignition	Prod. Fig.
	41-WL	SV	4	V-2	45	Dupl./C.	4	Bat.	4,277
Sport Solo	41-WLD	SV	4	V-2	45	Dupl./C.	4	Bat.	455
Big Twin	41-UL	SV	4	V-2	74	Dupl./C.	4	Bat.	715
Big Twin	41-U	SV	4	V-2	74	Dupl./C.	4	Bat.	884
Big Twin	41-ULH	SV	4	V-2	80	Dupl./C.	4	Bat.	420
Big Twin	41-UH	SV	4	V-2	80	Dupl./C.	4	Bat.	126
	41-EL	OHV	4	V-2	61	Dupl./C.	4	Bat.	2,280
	41-ES	OHV	4	V-2	61	Dupl./C.	4	Bat.	261
	41-FL	OHV	4	V-2	74	Dupl./C.	4	Bat.	2,452
	41-F	OHV	4	V-2	74	Dupl./C.	4	Bat.	n.a.
Racer	41-WLDR	SV	4	V-2	45	Dupl./C.	4	Bat.	171
Servi-Car	41-G	OHV	4	V-2	45	Dupl./C.	3	Bat.	607
Servi-Car	41-GA	SV	4	V-2	45	Dupl./C.	3	Bat.	221
Servi-Car	41-GD	SV	4	V-2	45	Dupl./C.	3	Bat.	195
Servi-Car	41-GDT	SV	4	V-2	45	Dupl./C.	3	Bat.	136
	41-WLA	SV	4	V-2	45	Dupl./C.	3	Bat.	4742
	41-WLC	SV	4	V-2	45	Dupl./C.	3	Bat.	149

1942

Model	Type	Engine	Stroke	Engine Type	Displacement	Drive (P/S)	Gears	Ignition	Prod. Fig.
	42-WLD	SV	4	V-2	45	Dupl./C.	4	Bat.	133
	42-WL	SV	4	V-2	45	Dupl./C.	4	Bat.	142
Big Twin	42-UL	SV	4	V-2	74	Dupl./C.	4	Bat.	405
Big Twin	42-U	SV	4	V-2	74	Dupl./C.	4	Bat.	421
	42-EL	OHV	4	V-2	61	Dupl./C.	4	Bat.	620
	42-E	OHV	4	V-2	61	Dupl./C.	4	Bat.	n.a.
	42-FL	OHV	4	V-2	74	Dupl./C.	4	Bat.	199
	42-F	OHV	4	V-2	74	Dupl./C.	4	Bat.	n.a.
	42-XA	SV	4	Boxer	738 cc	Kardan	4	Bat.	1,011
Servi-Car	42-G-	SV	4	V-2	45	Dupl./C.	3	Bat.	138
Servi-Car	42-GA	SV	4	V-2	45	Dupl./C.	3	Bat.	261

1943

Model	Type	Engine	Stroke	Engine Type	Displacement	Drive (P/S)	Gears	Ignition	Prod. Fig.
	43-E	OHV	4	V-2	61	Dupl./C.	4	Bat.	n.a.
	43-EL	OHV	4	V-2	61	Dupl./C.	4	Bat.	53
	43-F	OHV	4	V-2	74	Dupl./C.	4	Bat.	n.a.
	43-FL	OHV	4	V-2	74	Dupl./C.	4	Bat.	33
Big Twin	43-U	SV	4	V-2	74	Dupl./C.	4	Bat.	493
Big Twin	43-UL	SV	4	V-2	74	Dupl./C.	4	Bat.	11
Servi-Car	43-G	SV	4	V-2	45	Dupl./C.	3	Bat.	22
Servi-Car	43-GA	SV	4	V-2	45	Dupl./C.	3	Bat.	113

1944

Model	Type	Engine	Stroke	Engine Type	Displacement	Drive (P/S)	Gears	Ignition	Prod. Fig.
Big Twin	44-UL	SV	4	V-2	74	Dupl./C.	4	Bat.	366
Big Twin	44-U	SV	4	V-2	74	Dupl./C.	4	Bat.	580
	44-EL	OHV	4	V-2	61	Dupl./C.	4	Bat.	116
	44-E	OHV	4	V-2	61	Dupl./C.	4	Bat.	n.a.
	44-FL	OHV	4	V-2	74	Dupl./C.	4	Bat.	172
	44-F	OHV	4	V-2	74	Dupl./C.	4	Bat.	n.a.
Servi-Car	44-G	SV	4	V-2	45	Dupl./C.	3	Bat.	6
Servi-Car	44-GA	SV	4	V-2	45	Dupl./C.	3	Bat.	51

Model	Type	Engine	Stroke	Engine Type	Displacement	Drive (P/S)	Gears	Ignition	Prod. Fig.
1945									
	45-WL	SV	4	V-2	45	Dupl./C.	4	Bat.	1,357
Big Twin	45-UL	SV	4	V-2	74	Dupl./C.	4	Bat.	555
Big Twin	45-U	SV	4	V-2	74	Dupl./C.	4	Bat.	513
Big Twin	45-US	SV	4	V-2	74	Dupl./C.	4	Bat.	217
	45-EL	OHV	4	V-2	61	Dupl./C.	4	Bat.	398
	45-E	OHV	4	V-2	61	Dupl./C.	4	Bat.	n.a.
	45-ES	OHV	4	V-2	61	Dupl./C.	4	Bat.	282
	45-FL	OHV	4	V-2	74	Dupl./C.	4	Bat.	619
	45-F	OHV	4	V-2	74	Dupl./C.	4	Bat.	n.a.
	45-FS	OHV	4	V-2	74	Dupl./C.	4	Bat.	131
Servi-Car	45-G	SV	4	V-2	45	Dupl./C.	3	Bat.	26
Servi-Car	45-GA	SV	4	V-2	45	Dupl./C.	3	Bat.	60
1946									
	46-WL	SV	4	V-2	45	Dupl./C.	3	Bat.	4,410
Big Twin	46-UL	SV	4	V-2	74	Dupl./C.	4	Bat.	1,800
Big Twin	46-U	SV	4	V-2	74	Dupl./C.	4	Bat.	670
Big Twin	46-US	SV	4	V-2	74	Dupl./C.	4	Bat.	1,052
	46-EL	OHV	4	V-2	61	Dupl./C.	4	Bat.	2,098
	46-E	OHV	4	V-2	61	Dupl./C.	4	Bat.	n.a.
	46-ES	OHV	4	V-2	61	Dupl./C.	4	Bat.	244
	46-FL	OHV	4	V-2	74	Dupl./C.	4	Bat.	3,986
	46-F	OHV	4	V-2	74	Dupl./C.	4	Bat.	n.a.
	46-FS	OHV	4	V-2	74	Dupl./C.	4	Bat.	418
Servi-Car	46-G	SV	4	V-2	45	Dupl./C.	3	Bat.	766
Servi-Car	46-GA	SV	4	V-2	45	Dupl./C.	3	Bat.	678
1947									
	47-WL	SV	4	V-2	45	Dupl./C.	3	Bat.	3,338
Big Twin	47-UL	SV	4	V-2	74	Dupl./C.	4	Bat.	1,243
Big Twin	47-U	SV	4	V-2	74	Dupl./C.	4	Bat.	422
Big Twin	47-US	SV	4	V-2	74	Dupl./C.	4	Bat.	1,267
	47-EL	OHV	4	V-2	61	Dupl./C.	4	Bat.	4,117
	47-E	OHV	4	V-2	61	Dupl./C.	4	Bat.	n.a.
	47-ES	OHV	4	V-2	61	Dupl./C.	4	Bat.	237
	47-FL	OHV	4	V-2	74	Dupl./C.	4	Bat.	6893
	47-F	OHV	4	V-2	74	Dupl./C.	4	Bat.	n.a.
	47-FS	OHV	4	V-2	74	Dupl./C.	4	Bat.	401
Servi-Car	47-G	SV	4	V-2	45	Dupl./C.	3	Bat.	1,307
Servi-Car	47-GA	SV	4	V-2	45	Dupl./C.	3	Bat.	870
1948									
Single	48-S	PC.	2	Single	125cc	C.	3	Bat.	10,117
	48-WL	SV	4	V-2	45	Dupl./C.	3	Bat.	2,124
Big Twin	48-UL	SV	4	V-2	74	Dupl./C.	4	Bat.	970
Big Twin	48-U	SV	4	V-2	74	Dupl./C.	4	Bat.	401
Big Twin	48-US	SV	4	V-2	74	Dupl./C.	4	Bat.	1,006
	48-EL	OHV	4	V-2	61	Dupl./C.	4	Bat.	4,321
	48-E	OHV	4	V-2	61	Dupl./C.	4	Bat.	n.a.
	48-ES	OHV	4	V-2	61	Dupl./C.	4	Bat.	198
	48-FL	OHV	4	V-2	74	Dupl./C.	4	Bat.	8,071
	48-F	OHV	4	V-2	74	Dupl./C.	4	Bat.	n.a.
	48-FS	OHV	4	V-2	74	Dupl./C.	4	Bat.	334
Servi-Car	48-G	SV	4	V-2	45	Dupl./C.	3	Bat.	1,050
Servi-Car	48-GA	SV	4	V-2	45	Dupl./C.	3	Bat.	728
1949									
	49-S	PC.	2	Single	125cc	C.	3	Bat.	7,291
	49-WL	SV	4	V-2	45	Dupl./C.	3	Bat.	2,289
Hydra Glide	49-EL	OHV	4	V-2	61	Dupl./C.	4	Bat.	3,419
Hydra Glide	49-E	OHV	4	V-2	61	Dupl./C.	4	Bat.	n.a.
Hydra Glide	49-ES	OHV	4	V-2	61	Dupl./C.	4	Bat.	177
Hydra Glide	49-FL	OHV	4	V-2	74	Dupl./C.	4	Bat.	8,014
Hydra Glide	49-F	OHV	4	V-2	74	Dupl./C.	4	Bat.	n.a.
Hydra Glide	49-FS	OHV	4	V-2	74	Dupl./C.	4	Bat.	490
Hydra Glide	49-ELP	OHV	4	V-2	61	Dupl./C.	4	Bat.	99
Servi-Car	49-G	SV	4	V-2	45	Dupl./C.	3	Bat.	494
Servi-Car	49-GA	SV	4	V-2	45	Dupl./C.	3	Bat.	545
	49-FLP	OHV	4	V-2	74	Dupl./C.	4	Bat.	486
1950									
	50-S	PC.	2	Single	125cc	C.	3	Bat.	4708
	50-WL	SV	4	V-2	45	Dupl./C.	3	Bat.	1,108
Hydra Glide	50-EL	OHV	4	V-2	61	Dupl./C.	4	Bat.	2,046
Hydra Glide	50-E	OHV	4	V-2	61	Dupl./C.	4	Bat.	n.a.
Hydra Glide	50-ES	OHV	4	V-2	61	Dupl./C.	4	Bat.	268
Hydra Glide	50-FL	OHV	4	V-2	74	Dupl./C.	4	Bat.	1407
Hydra Glide	50-F	OHV	4	V-2	74	Dupl./C.	4	Bat.	n.a.
Hydra Glide	50-FS	OHV	4	V-2	74	Dupl./C.	4	Bat.	544
Servi-Car	50-G	SV	4	V-2	45	Dupl./C.	3	Bat.	520
Servi-Car	50-GA	SV	4	V-2	45	Dupl./C.	3	Bat.	483
1951									
Single	51-S	PC.	2	Single	125cc	C.	3	Bat.	5,101
	51-WL	SV	4	V-2	45	Dupl./C.	3	Bat.	1,044
Hydra Glide	51-EL	OHV	4	V-2	61	Dupl./C.	4	Bat.	1,532
Hydra Glide	51-ELS	OHV	4	V-2	61	Dupl./C.	4	Bat.	n.a.
Hydra Glide	51-FL	OHV	4	V-2	74	Dupl./C.	4	Bat.	6,560
Hydra Glide	51-FLS	OHV	4	V-2	74	Dupl./C.	4	Bat.	n.a.
Hydra Glide	51-FS	OHV	4	V-2	74	Dupl./C.	4	Bat.	135
Servi-Car	51-G	SV	4	V-2	45	Dupl./C.	3	Bat.	778
Servi-Car	51-GA	SV	4	V-2	45	Dupl./C.	3	Bat.	632
1952									
Single	52-S	PC.	2	Single	125cc	C.	3	Bat.	4,576
	52-WL	SV	4	V-2	45	Dupl./C.	3	Bat.	n.a.
Hydra Glide	52-ELF	OHV	4	V-2	61	Dupl./C.	4	Bat.	n.a.
Hydra Glide	52-EL	OHV	4	V-2	61	Dupl./C.	4	Bat.	918
Hydra Glide	52-ELS	OHV	4	V-2	61	Dupl./C.	4	Bat.	n.a.
Hydra Glide	52-FLF	OHV	4	V-2	74	Dupl./C.	4	Bat.	n.a.
Hydra Glide	52-FL	OHV	4	V-2	74	Dupl./C.	4	Bat.	5,554
Hydra Glide	52-FLS	OHV	4	V-2	74	Dupl./C.	4	Bat.	n.a.
Sport-Model	52-K	SV	4	V-2	45	Dupl./C.	4	Bat.	1,970
Racer	52-WR	SV	4	V-2	45	Dupl./C.	3	Bat.	8
Servi-Car	52-G	SV	4	V-2	45	Dupl./C.	3	Bat.	515
Servi-Car	52-GA	SV	4	V-2	45	Dupl./C.	3	Bat.	532
1953									
	53-ST	PC.	2	Single	165cc	C.	3	Bat.	4,225
Sport-Model	53-K	SV	4	V-2	45	Dupl./C.	4	Bat.	1,723
Hydra Glide	53-FLF	OHV	4	V-2	74	Dupl./C.	4	Bat.	3,351
Hydra Glide	53-FL	OHV	4	V-2	74	Dupl./C.	4	Bat.	1,986
Hydra Glide	52-FLEF	OHV	4	V-2	74	Dupl./C.	4	Bat.	n.a.
Hydra Glide	52-FLE	OHV	4	V-2	74	Dupl./C.	4	Bat.	n.a.
Servi-Car	53-G	SV	4	V-2	45	Dupl./C.	3	Bat.	1,146
Servi-Car	53-GA	SV	4	V-2	45	Dupl./C.	3	Bat.	n.a.
1954									
Single	54-ST	PC.	2	Single	165cc	C.	3	Bat.	2,835
Single	54-STU	PC.	2	Single	165cc	C.	3	Bat.	n.a.
Sport-Model	54-KH	SV	4	V-2	55	Dupl./C.	4	Bat.	1,579
Hydra Glide	54-FLF	OHV	4	V-2	74	Dupl./C.	4	Bat.	n.a.
Hydra Glide	54-FL	OHV	4	V-2	74	Dupl./C.	4	Bat.	4,757
Hydra Glide	54-FLEF	OHV	4	V-2	74	Dupl./C.	4	Bat.	n.a.
Hydra Glide	54-FLE	OHV	4	V-2	74	Dupl./C.	4	Bat.	n.a.
Servi-Car	54-G	SV	4	V-2	45	Dupl./C.	3	Bat.	1,397
Servi-Car	54-GA	SV	4	V-2	45	Dupl./C.	3	Bat.	n.a.
1955									
	55-B	PC.	4	Single	125cc	C.	3	Bat.	1,040
ST-Model	55-ST	PC.	2	Single	165cc	C.	3	Bat.	2,263
	55-STU	PC.	2	Single	165cc	C.	3	Bat.	n.a.
Sport-Model	55-KH	SV	4	V-2	55	Dupl./C.	4	Bat.	616
Hydra Glide	55-FLF	OHV	4	V-2	74	Dupl./C.	4	Bat.	2013
Hydra Glide	55-FL	OHV	4	V-2	74	Dupl./C.	4	Bat.	953
Hydra Glide	55-FLEF	OHV	4	V-2	74	Dupl./C.	4	Bat.	220
Hydra Glide	55-FLE	OHV	4	V-2	74	Dupl./C.	4	Bat.	853
Hydra Glide	55-FLHF	OHV	4	V-2	74	Dupl./C.	4	Bat.	1040
Hydra Glide	55-FLH	OHV	4	V-2	74	Dupl./C.	4	Bat.	63
Servi-Car	55-G	SV	4	V-2	45	Dupl./C.	3	Bat.	394
Servi-Car	55-GA	SV	4	V-2	45	Dupl./C.	3	Bat.	647
1956									
Single	56-B	PC.	2	Single	125cc	C.	3	Bat.	1,384
Single	56-ST	PC.	2	Single	165cc	C.	3	Bat.	2,219
Sport-Model	56-KH	SV	4	V-2	55	Dupl./C.	4	Bat.	539
Hydra Glide	56-FL	OHV	4	V-2	74	Dupl./C.	4	Bat.	856
Hydra Glide	56-FLE	OHV	4	V-2	74	Dupl./C.	4	Bat.	671
Hydra Glide	56-FLEF	OHV	4	V-2	74	Dupl./C.	4	Bat.	162

Model	Type	Engine	Stroke	Engine Type	Displacement	Drive (P/S)	Gears	Ignition	Prod. Fig.
Hydra Glide	56-FLF	OHV	4	V-2	74	Dupl./C.	4	Bat.	1,578
Hydra Glide	56-FLHF	OHV	4	V-2	74	Dupl./C.	4	Bat.	2,315
Hydra Glide	56-FLH	OHV	4	V-2	74	Dupl./C.	4	Bat.	224
Servi-Car	56-G	SV	4	V-2	45	Dupl./C.	3	Bat.	467
Servi-Car	56-GA	SV	4	V-2	45	Dupl./C.	3	Bat.	736
1957									
Single	57-ST	PC.	2	Single	165cc	C.	3	Bat.	2401
Single	57-STU	PC.	2	Single	165cc	C.	3	Bat.	n.a.
Sport-Model	57-KR	SV	4	V-2	45	Dupl./C.	4	S.	16
Sport-Model	57-KH	SV	4	V-2	55	Dupl./C.	4	Bat.	90
Sport-Model	57-KHK	SV	4	V-2	55	Dupl./C.	4	Bat.	n.a.
Hydra Glide	57-FLHF	OHV	4	V-2	74	Dupl./C.	4	Bat.	2614
Hydra Glide	57-FLH	OHV	4	V-2	74	Dupl./C.	4	Bat.	164
Hydra Glide	57-FL	OHV	4	V-2	74	Dupl./C.	4	Bat.	1579
Hydra Glide	57-FLEF	OHV	4	V-2	74	Dupl./C.	4	Bat.	n.a.
Hydra Glide	57-FLE	OHV	4	V-2	74	Dupl./C.	4	Bat.	n.a.
Racer	57-KRTT	SV	4	V-2	45	Dupl./C.	4	S.	9
Racer	57-KHRTT	SV	4	V-2	45	Dupl./C.	4	n.a.	4
Servi-Car	57-G	SV	4	V-2	45	Dupl./C.	3	Bat.	518
Servi-Car	57-GA	SV	4	V-2	45	Dupl./C.	3	Bat.	674
1958									
Duo Glide	58-FLHF	OHV	4	V-2	74	Dupl./C.	4	Bat.	2,953
Duo Glide	58-FLH	OHV	4	V-2	74	Dupl./C.	4	Bat.	195
Duo Glide	58-FLF	OHV	4	V-2	74	Dupl./C.	4	Bat.	1,299
Duo Glide	58-FL	OHV	4	V-2	74	Dupl./C.	4	Bat.	1,591
Sportster	58-XL	OHV	4	V-2	55	Tripl./C.	4	Bat.	579
Sportster	58-XLH	OHV	4	V-2	55	Tripl./C.	4	n.a.	711
Sportster	58-XLC	OHV	4	V-2	55	Tripl./C.	4	n.a.	n.a.
	58-XLCH	OHV	4	V-2	55	Tripl./C.	4	n.a.	239
	58-Hummer	PC.	2	Single	125cc	C.	3	Bat.	n.a.
	58-ST	PC.	2	Single	165cc	C.	3	Bat.	2,445
	58-STU	PC.	2	Single	165cc	C.	3	Bat.	465
Racer	58-KRTT	SV	4	V-2	45	Dupl./C.	4	n.a.	26
Racer	58-KR	SV	4	V-2	45	Dupl./C.	4	Bat.	9
Servi-Car	58-G	SV	4	V-2	45	Dupl./C.	3	Bat.	283
Servi-Car	58-GA	SV	4	V-2	45	Dupl./C.	3	Bat.	643
	58-B	PC.	2	V-2	125cc	C.	3	Bat.	1,677
1959									
Single	59-Hummer	PC.	2	Single	125cc	C.	3	Bat.	n.a.
Single	59-ST	PC.	2	Single	165cc	C.	3	Bat.	2,311
Single	59-STU	PC.	2	Single	165cc	C.	3	Bat.	n.a.
Single	59-B	PC.	2	Single	125cc	C.	3	Bat.	1,285
	59-XLR	OHV	4	V-2	n.a.	Tripl./C.	4	n.a.	5
Sportster	59-XL	OHV	4	V-2	55	Tripl./C.	4	Bat.	42
	59-XLH	OHV	4	V-2	55	Tripl./C.	4	Bat.	947
	59-XLCH	OHV	4	V-2	55	Tripl./C.	4	Bat.	1,059
Duo Glide	59-FLHF	OHV	4	V-2	74	Dupl./C.	4	Bat.	3,223
Duo Glide	59-FLH	OHV	4	V-2	74	Dupl./C.	4	Bat.	121
Duo Glide	59-FLF	OHV	4	V-2	74	Dupl./C.	4	Bat.	1,222
Duo Glide	59-FL	OHV	4	V-2	74	Dupl./C.	4	Bat.	1,201
Servi-Car	59-G	SV	4	V-2	45	Dupl./C.	3	Bat.	288
Servi-Car	59-GA	SV	4	V-2	45	Dupl./C.	3	Bat.	524
1960									
Super 10	60-B bis BT	PC.	4	Single	165cc	C.	3	S.	2,488
Super 10	60-BTU	PC.	4	Single	165cc	C.	3	S.	n.a.
Super H Sportster	60-XLH	OHV	4	V-2	55	Tripl./C.	4	Bat.	2,765
Super CH Sportster	60-XLCH	OHV	4	V-2	55	Tripl./C.	4	Bat.	n.a.
Duo Glide	60-FLHF	OHV	4	V-2	74	Dupl./C.	4	Bat.	n.a.
Duo Glide	60-FLH	OHV	4	V-2	74	Dupl./C.	4	Bat.	n.a.
Duo Glide	60-FLF	OHV	4	V-2	74	Dupl./C.	4	Bat.	n.a.
Duo Glide	60-FL	OHV	4	V-2	74	Dupl./C.	4	Bat.	5,967
Topper Scooter	60-A	PC.	4	Single	165cc	C.	a.	S.	3,801
Topper Scooter	60-AU	PC.	4	Single	165cc	C.	a.	S.	n.a.
Servi-Car	60-G + GA	SV	4	V-2	45	Dupl./C.	3	Bat.	707
1961									
	61-A	PC.	2	Single	165 cc	C.	n.a.	S.	1,341
	61-AH	PC.	2	Single	165cc	C.	a.	S.	n.a.
	61-AU	PC.	2	Single	165cc	C.	a.	S.	n.a.
	61-BT	PC.	2	Single	165cc	C.	3	S.	1,587
	61-BTU	PC.	2	Single	165cc	C.	3	S.	n.a.
	61-C	PC.	4	Single	250cc	G./C.	4	Bat.	n.a.
Super H Sportster	61-XLH	OHV	4	V-2	55	Tripl./C.	4	Bat.	2,014
Super CH Sportster	61-XLCH	OHV	4	V-2	55	Tripl./C.	4	Bat.	n.a.
Duo Glide	61-FLHF	OHV	4	V-2	74	Dupl./C.	4	Bat.	n.a.
Duo Glide	61-FLH	OHV	4	V-2	74	Dupl./C.	4	Bat.	n.a.
Duo Glide	61-FLF	OHV	4	V-2	74	Dupl./C.	4	Bat.	n.a.
Duo Glide	61-FL	OHV	4	V-2	74	Dupl./C.	4	Bat.	4,927
Racer	61-KR-KRTT	SV	4	V-2	45	Dupl./C.	4	n.a.	n.a.
Racer	61-XLRTT	SV	4	V-2	45	Dupl./C.	4	n.a.	n.a.
Racer	61-CRTT	OHV	4	Single	250cc	G./C.	4	n.a.	n.a.
Servi-Car	61-G + GA	SV	4	V-2	45	Dupl./C.	3	Bat.	628
1962									
Sportster	62-XLH	OHV	4	V-2	55	Tripl./C.	4	Bat.	n.a.
Sportster	62-XLCH	OHV	4	V-2	55	Tripl./C.	4	Bat.	1,998
Duo Glide	62-FLHF	OHV	4	V-2	74	Dupl./C.	4	Bat.	n.a.
Duo Glide	62-FLH	OHV	4	V-2	74	Dupl./C.	4	Bat.	n.a.
Duo Glide	62-FL	OHV	4	V-2	74	Dupl./C.	4	Bat.	5,184
Pacer	62-BT	PC.	2	Single	175cc	C.	3	S.	n.a.
Scat	62-BTH	PC.	2	Single	175cc	C.	3	S.	n.a.
Ranger	62-BTF	PC.	2	Single	165cc	C.	3	S.	n.a.
Pacer	62-BTU	PC.	2	Single	165cc	C.	3	S.	n.a.
Sprint	62-H	OHV	4	Single	250cc	G./C.	4	Bat.	n.a.
Sprint	62-C	OHV	4	Single	250cc	G./C.	4	Bat.	n.a.
Racer	62KR-KRTT	SV	4	V-2	45	Dupl./C.	4	n.a.	n.a.
Racer	62-XLRTT	SV	4	V-2	45	Dupl./C.	4	n.a.	1,276
Road Racer	62-CRTT	OHV	4	Single	165cc	G./C.	4	Bat.	n.a.
Topper Scooter	62-AH	PC.	2	Single	165cc	C.	a.	n.a.	n.a.
Topper Scooter	62-AU	PC.	2	Single	165	C.	a.	n.a.	n.a.
Servi-Car	62-G + GA	SV	4	V-2	45	Dupl./C.	3	Bat.	703
	62-FLF	OHV	4	V-2	74	Dupl./C.	4	Bat.	n.a.
1963									
Sportster	63-XLH	OHV	4	V-2	55	Tripl./C.	4	Bat.	432
Sportster	63-XLCJ	OHV	4	V-2	55	Tripl./C.	4	Bat.	975
Sportster	63-XLCH	OHV	4	V-2	55	Tripl./C.	4	Bat.	1,001
Duo Glide	63-FLHF	OHV	4	V-2	74	Dupl./C.	4	Bat.	2,100
Duo Glide	63-FLH	OHV	4	V-2	74	Dupl./C.	4	Bat.	100
Duo Glide	63-FLF	OHV	4	V-2	74	Dupl./C.	4	Bat.	950
Duo Glide	63-FL	OHV	4	V-2	74	Dupl./C.	4	Bat.	1096
Pacer	63-BT	PC.	2	Single	175cc	C.	3	S.	824
Scat	63-BTH	PC.	2	Single	175cc	C.	3	S.	877
Pacer	63-BTU	PC.	2	Single	175cc	C.	3	S.	39
Sprint	63-C	OHV	4	Single	175cc	G./C.	2	Bat.	50
Sprint	63-H	OHV	4	Single	250cc	G./C.	4	Bat.	150
Racer	63-KR	SV	4	V-2	45	Dupl./C.	4	S.	80
Racer	63-KRTT	SV	4	V-2	45	Dupl./S.	4	S.	n.a.
Racer	63-XLRTT	OHV	4	V-2	55	Dupl./S.	4	S.	n.a.
Road Racer	63-CRTT	OHV	4	Single	250cc	G./C.	4	Bat.	1,550
Topper Scooter	63-AH	PC.	2	Single	165cc	C.	a.	S.	972
Topper Scooter	63-AU	OHV	4	Single	165cc	C.	a.	Bat.	6
Servi-Car	63-G + GA	OHV	4	V-2	45	Dupl./C.	3	Bat.	80
1964									
Sportster	64-XLH	OHV	4	V-2	55	Tripl./C.	4	Bat.	810
Sportster	64-XLCH	OHV	4	V-2	55	Tripl./C.	4	Bat.	1,950
Duo Glide	64-FLHF	OHV	4	V-2	74	Dupl./C.	4	Bat.	n.a.
Duo Glide	64-FLH	OHV	4	V-2	74	Dupl./C.	4	Bat.	2,725
Duo Glide	64-FLF	OHV	4	V-2	74	Dupl./C.	4	Bat.	n.a.
Duo Glide	64-FL	OHV	4	V-2	74	Dupl./C.	4	Bat.	2,775
Pacer	64-BT	PC.	2	Single	175cc	C.	3	S.	600
Scat	64-BTH	PC.	2	Single	175cc	C.	3	S.	800
Pacer	64-BTU	PC.	2	Single	175cc	C.	3	S.	50
Sprint	64-C	OHV	4	Single	250cc	G./C.	4	Bat.	230
Sprint	64-H	OHV	4	Single	250cc	G./C.	4	Bat.	1,550
Topper Scooter	64-AH	PC.	2	Single	165cc	C.	a.	n.a.	800
Topper Scooter	64-AU	PC.	2	Single	165cc	C.	a.	n.a.	25
Racer	64-KR	SV	4	V-2	45	Dupl./C.	4	S.	20
Racer	64-XLRTT	OHV	4	V-2	55	Tripl./C.	4	S.	30
Racer	64-CRTT	OHV	4	Single	250cc	G./C.	4	Bat.	810
Servi-Car	64-GE	SV	4	V-2	45	Dupl./C.	3	n.a.	725
1965									
Sportster	65-XLH	OHV	4	V-2	55	Tripl./C.	4	Bat.	955
Sportster	65-XLCH	OHV	4	V-2	55	Tripl./C.	4	Bat.	2,815

Model	Type	Engine	Stroke	Engine Type	Displacement	Drive (P/S)	Gears	Ignition	Prod. Fig.
Electra Glide	65-FLHFB	OHV	4	V-2	74	Dupl./C.	4	Bat.	n.a.
Electra Glide	65-FLHB	OHV	4	V-2	74	Dupl./C.	4	Bat.	n.a.
Electra Glide	65-FLFB	OHV	4	V-2	74	Dupl./C.	4	Bat.	n.a.
Electra Glide	65-FLB	OHV	4	V-2	74	Dupl./C.	4	Bat.	n.a.
Pacer	65-BT	PC.	2	Single	175cc	C.	3	S.	500
Scat	65-BTH	PC.	2	Single	175cc	C.	3	S.	750
Sprint	65-C	OHV	4	Single	250cc	G./C.	5	Bat.	500
Sprint	65-H	OHV	4	Single	250cc	G./C.	5	Bat.	2,500
	65-M-50	PC.	2	Single	50cc	G./C.	3	S.	9,000
Topper Scooter	65-AH	PC.	2	Single	165cc	C.	a.	S.	500
Servi-Car	65-GE	SV	4	V-2	45	Dupl./C.	3	Bat.	625

1966

Model	Type	Engine	Stroke	Engine Type	Displacement	Drive (P/S)	Gears	Ignition	Prod. Fig.
Electra Glide	66-FLHFB	OHV	4	V-2	74	Dupl./C.	4	Bat.	n.a.
Electra Glide	66-FLHB	OHV	4	V-2	74	Dupl./C.	4	Bat.	5,625
Electra Glide	66-FLFB	OHV	4	V-2	74	Dupl./C.	4	Bat.	n.a.
Electra Glide	66-FLB	OHV	4	V-2	74	Dupl./C.	4	Bat.	2,175
Sportster	66-XLH	OHV	4	V-2	55	Tripl./C.	4	Bat.	900
Sportster	66-XLCH	OHV	4	V-2	55	Tripl./C.	4	Bat.	3,900
Sprint	66-C	OHV	4	Single	250cc	G./C.	5	Bat.	60
Sprint	66-H	OHV	4	Single	250cc	G./C.	5	Bat.	4,700
Bobcat	66-BTH	PC.	2	Single	175cc	C.	3	S.	1,150
	66-M-50	PC.	2	Single	50cc	G./C.	3	S.	5,700
	66-M-50 Sport	PC.	2	Single	50cc	G./C.	3	S.	10,500
Racer	66-KR	SV	4	V-2	45	Dupl./C.	4	Bat.	n.a.
Racer	66-CR	OHV	4	Single	250cc	G./C.	4	Bat.	50
Racer	66-CRS	OHV	4	Single	250cc	G./C.	4	Bat.	350
Servi-Car	66-GE	SV	4	V-2	45	Dupl./C.	3	Bat.	625

1967

Model	Type	Engine	Stroke	Engine Type	Displacement	Drive (P/S)	Gears	Ignition	Prod. Fig.
Sportster	67-XLH	OHV	4	V-2	55	Tripl./C.	4	el.	2,000
Sportster	67-XLCH	OHV	4	V-2	55	Tripl./C.	4	el.	2,500
Super Sport	67-FLHFB	OHV	4	V-2	74	Dupl./C.	4	Bat.	n.a.
Super Sport	67-FLHB	OHV	4	V-2	74	Dupl./C.	4	Bat.	n.a.
Super Sport	67-FLFB	OHV	4	V-2	74	Dupl./C.	4	Bat.	n.a.
Super Sport	67-FLB	OHV	4	V-2	74	Dupl./C.	4	Bat.	n.a.
Sprint	67-H	OHV	4	Single	250cc	G./C.	5	Bat.	2,000
Sprint	67-SS	OHV	4	Single	250cc	G./C.	5	Bat.	7,000
	67-M-65	PC.	2	Single	65cc	G./C.	3	S.	2,000
	67-M-65 Sport	PC.	2	Single	65cc	G./C.	3	S.	3,267
	67-M-50	PC.	2	Single	50cc	G./C.	3	S.	n.a.
Servi-Car	67-GE	SV	4	V-2	45	Dupl./C.	3	Bat.	600

1968

Model	Type	Engine	Stroke	Engine Type	Displacement	Drive (P/S)	Gears	Ignition	Prod. Fig.
Sportster	68-XLH	OHV	4	V-2	55	Tripl./C.	4	Bat.	1,975
Sportster	68-XLCH	OHV	4	V-2	55	Tripl./C.	4	Bat.	4,900
Electra Glide	68-FLHFB	OHV	4	V-2	74	Dupl./C.	4	Bat.	n.a.
Electra Glide	68-FLHB	OHV	4	V-2	74	Dupl./C.	4	Bat.	n.a.
Electra Glide	68-FLFB	OHV	4	V-2	74	Dupl./C.	4	Bat.	n.a.
Electra Glide	68-FLB	OHV	4	V-2	74	Dupl./C.	4	Bat.	n.a.
Sprint	68-H	OHV	4	Single	250cc	G./C.	5	Bat.	405
Sprint	68-SS	OHV	4	Single	250cc	G./C.	5	Bat.	3,745
Rapido	68-M-125	PC.	2	Single	125cc	G./C.	5	S.	n.a.
	68-M-65	PC.	2	Single	65cc	G./C.	3	S.	n.a.
	68-M-65 S	PC.	2	Single	65cc	G./C.	3	S.	1,200
	68-M-50	PC.	2	Single	50cc	G./C.	3	S.	1,700
Racer	68-CRS	OHV	4	Single	250cc	G./C.	4	Bat.	125
	68-ML-125 S	PC.	2	Single	125cc	C.	4	n.a.	500
Servi-Car	68-GE	SV	4	V-2	45	Dupl./C.	3	Bat.	600

1969

Model	Type	Engine	Stroke	Engine Type	Displacement	Drive (P/S)	Gears	Ignition	Prod. Fig.
Sportster	69-XLH	OHV	4	V-2	55	Tripl./C.	4	Bat.	2,700
Sportster	69-XLCH	OHV	4	V-2	55	Tripl./C.	4	Bat.	5,100
Electra Glide	69-FLHFB	OHV	4	V-2	74	Dupl./C.	4	Bat.	n.a.
Electra Glide	69-FLHB	OHV	4	V-2	74	Dupl./C.	4	Bat.	n.a.
Electra Glide	69-FLFB	OHV	4	V-2	74	Dupl./C.	4	Bat.	n.a.
Electra Glide	69-FLB	OHV	4	V-2	74	Dupl./C.	4	Bat.	n.a.
Sprint	69-SS	OHV	4	Single	350cc	G./C.	5	Bat.	4,575
Sprint Scrambler	69-ERS	OHV	4	Single	350cc	G./C.	5	S.	250
	69-ML-125	PC.	2	Single	125cc	G./C.	4	S.	1,000
	69-M-65	PC.	2	Single	65cc	G./C.	3	S.	2,700
Racer	69-XLRTT	OHV	4	V-2	55	Tripl./C.	4	S.	n.a.
Servi-Car	69-GE	SV	4	V-2	45	Dupl./C.	3	Bat.	475

1970

Model	Type	Engine	Stroke	Engine Type	Displacement	Drive (P/S)	Gears	Ignition	Prod. Fig.
Sportster	70-XLH	OHV	4	V-2	55	Tripl./C.	4	Bat.	3,033
Sportster	70-XLCH	OHV	4	V-2	55	Tripl./C.	4	Bat.	5,527
Electra Glide	70-FLHF	OHV	4	V-2	74	Dupl./C.	4	Bat.	n.a.
Electra Glide	70-FLH	OHV	4	V-2	74	Dupl./C.	4	Bat.	5,909
Electra Glide	70-FLPF	OHV	4	V-2	74	Dupl./C.	4	Bat.	n.a.
Electra Glide	70-FLP	OHV	4	V-2	74	Dupl./C.	4	Bat.	n.a.
Sprint	70-SS	OHV	4	Single	350cc	G./C.	5	Bat.	4,513
Rapido	70-MLS	PC.	2	Single	125cc	G./C.	4	S.	4,059
Leggero	70-M-65	PC.	2	Single	65cc	G./C.	3	S.	2,080
Sprint Scrambler	70-ERS	OHV	4	Single	350cc	G./C.	5	Bat.	102
	70-MSR	PC.	2	Single	100cc	G./C.	5	S.	1,427
Servi-Car	70-GE	SV	4	V-2	45	Dupl./C.	3	Bat.	494

1971

Model	Type	Engine	Stroke	Engine Type	Displacement	Drive (P/S)	Gears	Ignition	Prod. Fig.
Sportster	71-XLH	OHV	4	V-2	55	Tripl./C.	4	Bat.	3,950
Sportster	71-XLCH	OHV	4	V-2	55	Tripl./C.	4	Bat.	6,825
Electra Glide	71-FLHF	OHV	4	V-2	74	Dupl./C.	4	Bat.	n.a.
Electra Glide	71-FLH	OHV	4	V-2	74	Dupl./C.	4	Bat.	5,475
Electra Glide	71-FLPF	OHV	4	V-2	74	Dupl./C.	4	Bat.	n.a.
Electra Glide	71-FLP	OHV	4	V-2	74	Dupl./C.	4	Bat.	n.a.
Super Glide	71-FX	OHV	4	V-2	74	Dupl./C.	4	Bat.	4,700
Sprint	71-SX	OHV	4	Single	350cc	G./C.	5	Bat.	3,920
Sprint	71-SS	OHV	4	Single	350cc	G./C.	5	Bat.	1,500
Sprint Scrambler	71-ERS	OHV	4	Single	350cc	G./C.	5	S.	50
Rapido	71-MLS	PC.	2	Single	125cc	G./C.	5	S.	5,200
Leggero	71-M-65	PC.	2	Single	65cc	G./C.	3	S.	3,100
Baja	71-MSR	PC.	2	Single	100cc	G./C.	5	S.	1,200
Servi-Car	71-GE	SV	4	V-2	45	Dupl./C.	3	Bat.	500

1972

Model	Type	Engine	Stroke	Engine Type	Displacement	Drive (P/S)	Gears	Ignition	Prod. Fig.
Sportster	72-XLH	OHV	4	V-2	1000cc	Tripl./C.	4	Bat.	7,500
Sportster	72-XLCH	OHV	4	V-2	1000cc	Tripl./C.	4	Bat.	10,650
Electra Glide	72-FLHF	OHV	4	V-2	74	Dupl./C.	4	Bat.	n.a.
Electra Glide	72-FLH	OHV	4	V-2	74	Dupl./C.	4	Bat.	8,100
Electra Glide	72-FLPF	OHV	4	V-2	74	Dupl./C.	4	Bat.	n.a.
Electra Glide	72-FLP	OHV	4	V-2	74	Dupl./C.	4	Bat.	n.a.
Super Glide	72-FX	OHV	4	V-2	74	Dupl./C.	4	Bat.	6,500
Rapido	72-MLS	PC.	2	Single	125cc	G./C.	5	S.	6,000
Leggero	72-M-65	PC.	2	Single	65cc	G./C.	3	S.	3,708
Sprint Scrambler	72-ERS	OHV	4	Single	350cc	G./C.	5	S.	50
Baja 100L	72-MSR	PC.	2	Single	100cc	G./C.	5	S.	900
Baja 100	72-MSR	PC.	2	Single	100cc	G./C.	5	S.	n.a.
	72-MC-65	PC.	2	Single	65cc	G./C.	3	S.	8,000
Racer	72-XR750	OHV	4	V-2	45	Dupl./C.	4	n.a.	100
Servi-Car	71-GE	SV	4	V-2	45	Dupl./C.	3	Bat.	400

1973

Model	Type	Engine	Stroke	Engine Type	Displacement	Drive (P/S)	Gears	Ignition	Prod. Fig.
Sportster	73-XLH	OHV	4	V-2	1000cc	Tripl./C.	4	Bat.	9,875
Sportster	73-XLCH	OHV	4	V-2	1000cc	Tripl./C.	4	Bat.	10,825
Super Glide	73-FX	OHV	4	V-2	74	Dupl./C.	4	Bat.	7,625
Electra Glide	73-FL	OHV	4	V-2	74	Dupl./C.	4	Bat.	1,025
Electra Glide	73-FLH	OHV	4	V-2	74	Dupl./C.	4	Bat.	7,750
Sprint	73-SS	OHV	4	Single	350cc	G./C.	5	Bat.	4,137
Sprint	73-SX	OHV	4	Single	350cc	G./C.	5	Bat.	2,431
	73-TX	PC.	2	Single	125cc	G./C.	5	S.	9,925
	73-Z-90	PC.	2	Single	90cc	G./C.	4	S.	8,244
	73-X-90	PC.	2	Single	90cc	G./C.	4	S.	8,250
	73-SR-100	PC.	2	Single	100cc	G./C.	5	S.	986
Racer	73-XRTT	OHV	4	V-2	45	Dupl./C.	4	n.a.	n.a.

1974

Model	Type	Engine	Stroke	Engine Type	Displacement	Drive (P/S)	Gears	Ignition	Prod. Fig.
Electra Glide	74-FLH-1200	OHV	4	V-2	74	Dupl./C.	4	Bat.	5,166
Electra Glide	74-FLHF	OHV	4	V-2	74	Dupl./C.	4	Bat.	1,310
Super Glide	74-FX	OHV	4	V-2	74	Dupl./C.	4	Bat.	3,034
Super Glide	74-FXE	OHV	4	V-2	74	Dupl./C.	4	Bat.	6,199
Sportster	74-XLH	OHV	4	V-2	1000cc	Tripl./C.	4	Bat.	13,295
Sportster	74-XLCH	OHV	4	V-2	1000cc	Tripl./C.	4	Bat.	10,535
	74-SS 350	OHV	4	Single	350cc	G./C.	5	Bat.	2,500
	74-SX 350	OHV	4	Single	350cc	G./C.	5	Bat.	2,085
	74-SX 175	PC.	2	Single	175cc	G./C.	5	Bat.	3,612
	74-SX 125	PC.	2	Single	125cc	G./C.	5	Bat.	4,000
	74-Z-90	PC.	2	Single	90cc	G./C.	4	S.	7,168
	74-X-90	PC.	2	Single	90cc	G./C.	4	S.	7,019
	74-SR-100	PC.	2	Single	100cc	G./C.	5	S.	1,396

Model	Type	Engine	Stroke	Engine Type	Displacement	Drive (P/S)	Gears	Ignition	Prod. Fig.
1975									
Sportster	75-XLH	OHV	4	V-2	1000cc	Tripl./C.	4	Bat.	13,515
Sportster	75-XLCH	OHV	4	V-2	1000cc	Tripl./C.	4	Bat.	5,895
Electra Glide	75-FLH-1200	OHV	4	V-2	1200cc	Dupl./C.	4	Bat.	7,400
Electra Glide	75-FLHF	OHV	4	V-2	1200cc	Dupl./C.	4	Bat.	1,535
Super Glide	75-FX	OHV	4	V-2	1200cc	Dupl./C.	4	Bat.	3,060
Super Glide	75-FXE	OHV	4	V-2	1200cc	Dupl./C.	4	Bat.	9,350
	75-SX-175	PC.	2	Single	175cc	G./C.	5	Bat.	3,612
	75-SX-125	PC.	2	Single	125cc	G./C.	5	Bat.	2,500
	75-Z-90	PC.	2	Single	90cc	G./C.	4	Bat.	2,562
	75-X-90	PC.	2	Single	90cc	G./C.	4	S.	1,568
	75-SX-250	PC.	2	Single	250cc	G./C.	5	el.	11,000
	75-RC-125	PC.	2	Single	125cc	G./C.	5	n.a.	4,500
	75-MX-250	PC.	2	Single	250 cc	G./C.	5	n.a.	n.a.
Racer	75-RR-250	PC.	2	Twin	250	G./C.	6	n.a.	n.a.
Racer	75-RR-350	PC.	2	Twin	350	G./C.	6	n.a.	n.a.
Racer	75-XR	OHV	4	V-2	45	Dupl./C.	4	n.a.	100
1976									
Sportster	76-XLH	OHV	4	V-2	1000cc	Tripl./C.	4	Bat.	12,844
Sportster	76-XLCH	OHV	4	V-2	1000cc	Tripl./C.	4	Bat.	5,238
Electra Glide	76-FLH-1200	OHV	4	V-2	1200cc	Dupl./C.	4	Bat.	11,891
Super Glide	76-FX	OHV	4	V-2	1200cc	Dupl./C.	4	Bat.	3,857
Super Glide	76-FXE	OHV	4	V-2	1200cc	Dupl./C.	4	Bat.	13,838
	76-SS-250	PC.	2	Single	250cc	G./C.	5	el.	1,416
	76-SX-250	PC.	2	Single	250cc	G./C.	5	el.	3,125
	76-SXT-125	PC.	2	Single	125cc	G./C.	5	S.	6,056
	76-SS-175	PC.	2	Single	175cc	G./C.	5	el.	1,461
	76-SS-125	PC.	2	Single	125cc	G./C.	5	S.	1,560
	76-MX-250	PC.	2	Single	250cc	G./C.	5	el.	87
Racer	76-RR-250	PC.	2	Twin	250cc	G./C.	6	n.a.	n.a.
Racer	76-RR-350	PC.	2	Twin	350	G./C.	6	n.a.	n.a.
Racer	76-RR-500	PC.	2	Twin	500	G./C.	6	n.a.	n.a.
1977									
Sportster	77-XLT	OHV	4	V-2	1000cc	Tripl./C.	4	Bat.	1,099
Café Racer	77-XLCR	OHV	4	V-2	1000cc	Tripl./C.	4	Bat.	1,923
Sportster	77-XLH	OHV	4	V-2	1000cc	Tripl./C.	4	Bat.	12,742
Sportster	77-XLCH	OHV	4	V-2	1000cc	Tripl./C.	4	Bat.	4,074
Electra Glide	77-FLH-1200	OHV	4	V-2	1200cc	Dupl./C.	4	Bat.	8,691
Electra Glide Sport	77-FLHS	OHV	4	V-2	1200cc	Dupl./C.	4	Bat.	535
Super Glide	77-FX	OHV	4	V-2	1200cc	Dupl./C.	4	Bat.	2,049
Super Glide	77-FXE	OHV	4	V-2	1200cc	Dupl./C.	4	Bat.	9,400
Low Rider	77-FXS	OHV	4	V-2	1200cc	Dupl./C.	4	Bat.	3,742
	77-SS-250	PC.	2	Single	250cc	G./C.	5	el.	558
	77-SX 250	PC.	2	Single	250cc	G./C.	5	el.	144
	77-SXT 125	PC.	2	Single	125cc	G./C.	5	S.	48
	77-SS 175	PC.	2	Single	175cc	G./C.	5	el.	110
	77-SS 125	PC.	2	Single	125cc	G./C.	5	S.	488
	77-RR 250	PC.	2	Twin	250cc	G./C.	6	n.a.	n.a.
1978									
Sportster	78-XLH	OHV	4	V-2	1000cc	Tripl./C.	4	Bat.	11,271
Sportster	78-XLCH	OHV	4	V-2	1000cc	Tripl./C.	4	Bat.	2,758
Sportster	78-XLT	OHV	4	V-2	1000cc	Tripl./C.	4	Bat.	n.a.
Café Racer	78-XLCR	OHV	4	V-2	1000cc	Tripl./C.	4	Bat.	1,201
Roadster	78-XLS	OHV	4	V-2	1000cc	Tripl./C.	4	Bat.	n.a.
Electra Glide	78-FLH-1200	OHV	4	V-2	1200cc	Dupl./C.	4	Bat.	4,761
Electra Glide	78-FLH 80	OHV	4	V-2	80	Dupl./C.	4	Bat.	2,525
Super Glide	78-FX	OHV	4	V-2	74	Dupl./C.	4	Bat.	1,774
Super Glide	78-FXE	OHV	4	V-2	74	Dupl./C.	4	Bat.	8,314
Low Rider	78-FXS	OHV	4	V-2	74	Dupl./C.	4	Bat.	9,787
	78-SX 250	PC.	2	Single	250cc	G./C.	4	Bat.	479
Flat Track Racer	78-XR 750	OHV	4	V-2	45	Dupl./C.	4	n.a.	80
1979									
Sportster	XLH-1000	OHV	4	V-2	1000cc	Tripl./C.	4	el.	6,525
Sportster Standard	XLCH-1000	OHV	4	V-2	1000cc	Tripl./C.	4	el.	141
Sportster Special	XLS-1000	OHV	4	V-2	1000cc	Tripl./C.	4	el.	5,123
Café Racer	XLCR	OHV	4	V-2	1000cc	Tripl./C.	4	el.	9
Tour Glide	FLT-80	OHV	4	V-2	80	Dupl./C.	4	el.	80
Electra Glide Classic	FLHC	OHV	4	V-2	80	Dupl./C.	4	el.	4,368
Electra Glide	FLH-80	OHV	4	V-2	80	Dupl./C.	4	el.	3,429
Electra Glide	FLH-1200	OHV	4	V-2	1200cc	Dupl./C.	4	el.	2,612
Electra Glide	FLHS-1200	OHV	4	V-2	1200cc	Dupl./C.	4	el.	n.a.
Low Rider	FXS-1200	OHV	4	V-2	1200cc	Dupl./C.	4	el.	3,827
Low Rider	FXS-80	OHV	4	V-2	80	Dupl./C.	4	el.	9,433
Fat Bob Super Glide	FXEF-1200	OHV	4	V-2	1200cc	Dupl./C.	4	el.	4,678
Fat Bob Super Glide	FXEF-80	OHV	4	V-2	80	Dupl./C.	4	el.	5,264
Super Glide	FXE-1200	OHV	4	V-2	1200cc	Dupl./C.	4	el.	3,117
1980									
Electra Glide Classic	FLHC	OHV	4	V-2	80	Dupl./C.	4	el.	2,480
Electra Glide	FLH-80	OHV	4	V-2	80	Dupl./C.	4	el.	1,625
Electra Glide	FLH-1200	OHV	4	V-2	1200cc	Dupl./C.	4	el.	1,111
Tour Glide	FLT-80	OHV	4	V-2	80	Dupl./C.	4	el.	4,480
Sturgis	FXB-80	OHV	4	V-2	80	B.	4	el.	1,970
Wide Glide	FXWG	OHV	4	V-2	80	Dupl./C.	4	el.	6,085
Low Rider	FXS-80	OHV	4	V-2	80	Dupl./C.	4	el.	5,922
Fat Bob Wide Glide	FXEF-80	OHV	4	V-2	80	Dupl./C.	4	el.	4,773
Super Glide	FXE-1200	OHV	4	V-2	1200cc	Dupl./C.	4	el.	3,169
Roadster	XLS-1000	OHV	4	V-2	1000cc	Tripl./C.	4	el.	2,926
Sportster	XLH-1000	OHV	4	V-2	1000cc	Tripl./C.	4	el.	11,841
1981									
Electra Glide Classic	FLHC-80	OHV	4	V-2	80	Dupl./C.	4	el.	1,472
Electra Glide Classic	FLH-80	OHV	4	V-2	80	Dupl./C.	4	el.	2,131
Electra Glide	FLHS	OHV	4	V-2	80	Dupl./C.	4	el.	1,062
Tour Glide Classic	FLTC-80	OHV	4	V-2	80	Dupl./C.	5	el.	1,157
Tour Glide	FLT-80	OHV	4	V-2	80	Dupl./C.	5	el.	1,636
Sturgis	FXB-80	OHV	4	V-2	80	B.	4	el.	3,543
Wide Glide	FXWG	OHV	4	V-2	80	Dupl./C.	4	el.	5,166
Low Rider	FXS 80	OHV	4	V-2	80	Dupl./C.	4	el.	7,223
Fat Bob	FXEF-80	OHV	4	V-2	80	Dupl./C.	4	el.	3,691
Super Glide	FXE-80	OHV	4	V-2	80	Dupl./C.	4	el.	3,085
Roadster	XLS-1000	OHV	4	V-2	1000cc	Tripl./C.	4	el.	1,660
Sportster	XLH 100	OHV	4	V-2	1000cc	Tripl./C.	4	el.	8,442
1982									
Electra Glide	FLH-80	OHV	4	V-2	80	Dupl./C.	4	el.	1,491
Electra Glide Classic	FLHC-80	OHV	4	V-2	80	Dupl./C.	4	el.	n.a.
Tour Glide	FLT-80	OHV	4	V-2	80	Dupl./C.	4	el.	1,196
Tour Glide Classic	FLTC	OHV	4	V-2	80	Dupl./C.	5	el.	833
Super Glide	FXE-80	OHV	4	V-2	80	Dupl./C.	4	el.	1,617
Super Glide II	FXR	OHV	4	V-2	80	Dupl./C.	5	el.	3,065
Super Glide II	FXRS	OHV	4	V-2	80	Dupl./C.	5	el.	3,190
Fat Bob	FXEF-80	OHV	4	V-2	80	Dupl./C.	4	el.	n.a.
Low Rider	FXS-80	OHV	4	V-2	80	Dupl./C.	4	el.	1,816
Sturgis	FXB-80	OHV	4	V-2	80	B.	4	el.	1,833
Wide Glide	FXWG	OHV	4	V-2	80	Dupl./C.	4	el.	2,348
Sportster	XLH-1000	OHV	4	V-2	61	Tripl./C.	4	el.	5,015
Roadster	XLS-1000	OHV	4	V-2	61	Tripl./C.	4	el.	1,261
1983									
Electra Glide	FLHT	OHV	4	V-2	80	Dupl./C.	5	el.	1,426
Electra Glide Classic	FLHC-80	OHV	4	V-2	80	Dupl./C.	4	el.	1,302
Electra Glide Belt Drive	FLH	OHV	4	V-2	80	Dupl./B.	4	el.	1272
Tour Glide	FLT-80	OHV	4	V-2	80	Dupl./C.	4	el.	565
Tour Glide Classic	FLTC	OHV	4	V-2	80	Dupl./C.	5	el.	475
Super Glide	FXE-80	OHV	4	V-2	80	Dupl./C.	4	el.	1,215
Super Glide II	FXR	OHV	4	V-2	80	Dupl./C.	5	el.	1,413
Wide Glide	FXWG	OHV	4	V-2	80	Dupl./C.	4	el.	2,873
Low Rider	FXS-80	OHV	4	V-2	80	Dupl./B.	4	el.	3,277
Fat Bob	FXEF-80	OHV	4	V-2	80	Dupl./C.	4	el.	n.a.
Sportster	XLX-61	OHV	4	V-2	55	Tripl./C.	4	el.	4,892
Sportster	XLH-1000	OHV	4	V-2	61	Tripl./C.	4	el.	2,230
Roadster	XLS-1000	OHV	4	V-2	61	Tripl./C.	4	el.	1,616
1984									
Electra Glide	FLHT	OHV	4	V-2	80	Dupl./C.	4	el.	208
Electra Glide Belt Drive	FLH	OHV	4	V-2	80	Dupl./B.	4	el.	2,686
Electra Glide Classic	FLHTE-80	OHV	4	V-2	80	Dupl./C.	4	el.	n.a.
Tour Glide	FLT-80	OHV	4	V-2	80	Dupl./C.	4	el.	n.a.
Tour Glide Classic	FLTC-80	OHV	4	V-2	80	Dupl./C.	4	el.	1,301
Super Glide	FXE-80	OHV	4	V-2	80	Dupl./C.	4	el.	2,606
Low Rider Belt	FXSB-80	OHV	4	V-2	80	Dupl./B.	4	el.	n.a.
Super Glide II	FXR	OHV	4	V-2	80	Dupl./C.	5	el.	n.a.
Wide Glide	FXWG-80	OHV	4	V-2	80	Dupl./B.	4	el.	n.a.
Low Glide	FXRS-80	OHV	4	V-2	80	Dupl./B.	5	el.	2,227
Sport Glide	FXRT-80	OHV	4	V-2	80	Dupl./B.	5	el.	2,030

Model	Type	Engine	Stroke	Engine Type	Displacement	Drive (P/S)	Gears	Ignition	Prod. Fig.
Sport Glide Police	FXRP-80	OHV	4	V-2	80	Dupl./C.	5	el.	820
Fat Bob	FXEF-80	OHV	4	V-2	80	Dupl./C.	4	el.	n.a.
Sportster Standard	XLX-61	OHV	4	V-2	61	Tripl./C.	4	el.	4,281
Sportster	XLH	OHV	4	V-2	61	Tripl./C.	4	el.	4,442
Roadster	XLS-1000	OHV	4	V-2	61	Tripl./C.	4	el.	1,135
Sportster	XR-1000	OHV	4	V-2	61	Tripl./C.	4	el.	759
1985									
Electra Glide Classic	FLHTE-80	OHV	4	V-2	80	Dupl./C.	5	el.	n.a.
Tour Glide Classic	FLTC-80	OHV	4	V-2	80	Dupl./C.	5	el.	1,847
Fat Bob	FXEF-80	OHV	4	V-2	80	Dupl./C.	4	el.	2,324
Low Rider Belt	FXSB-80	OHV	4	V-2	80	Dupl./B.	4	el.	2,359
Wide Glide	FXWG-80	OHV	4	V-2	80	Dupl./B.	4	el.	4,171
Low Glide	FXRS-80	OHV	4	V-2	80	Dupl./B.	5	el.	3,476
Sport Glide	FXRT-80	OHV	4	V-2	80	Dupl./B.	5	el.	1,252
Softail	FXST-80	OHV	4	V-2	80	Dupl./C.	4	el.	4,529
Sportster	XLH-1000	OHV	4	V-2	61	Tripl./C.	4	el.	4,074
Sportster Standard	XLX-61	OHV	4	V-2	61	Tripl./C.	4	el.	1,824
Roadster	XLS-1000	OHV	4	V-2	61	Tripl./C.	4	el.	616
Sportster	XR-1000	OHV	4	V-2	61	Tripl./C.	4	el.	n.a.
1986									
Electra Glide	FLHT-80	OHV	4	V-2	80	Dupl./B.	5	el.	711
Electra Glide Classic	FLHTC-80	OHV	4	V-2	80	Dupl./B.	5	el.	3,287
Tour Glide Classic	FLTC-80	OHV	4	V-2	80	Dupl./B.	5	el.	1,401
Super Glide	FXR-80	OHV	4	V-2	80	Dupl./B.	5	el.	2,038
Low Rider	FXRS-80	OHV	4	V-2	80	Dupl./B.	5	el.	3,552
Low Rider Sport Edition	FXRS-SP-80	OHV	4	V-2	80	Dupl./B.	5	el.	1,247
Sport Glide	FXRT-80	OHV	4	V-2	80	Dupl./B.	5	el.	591
Sport Glide Grand Tour	FXRD-80	OHV	4	V-2	80	Dupl./B.	5	el.	n.a.
Softail	FXST-80	OHV	4	V-2	80	Dupl./B.	5	el.	2,402
Softail Custom	FXSTC-80	OHV	4	V-2	80	Dupl./B.	5	el.	3,782
Sportster	XLH-883	OHV	4	V-2	55	Tripl./C.	4	el.	8,032
Sportster Deluxe	XLX-883	OHV	4	V-2	55	Tripl./C.	4	el.	2,322
Sportster	XLH-1100	OHV	4	V-2	1100cc	Tripl./C.	4	el.	4,037
Sportster	XLH-1200	OHV	4	V-2	74	Tripl./C.	4	el.	14
1987									
Electra Glide	FLHT	OHV	4	V-2	80	Dupl./B.	5	el.	87
Electra Glide Classic	FLHTC	OHV	4	V-2	80	Dupl./B.	5	el.	4,660
Tour Glide Classic	FLTC	OHV	4	V-2	80	Dupl./B.	5	el.	856
Sport Glide	FXRT	OHV	4	V-2	80	Dupl./B.	5	el.	287
Super Glide	FXR	OHV	4	V-2	80	Dupl./B.	5	el.	1,265
Low Rider	FXRS	OHV	4	V-2	80	Dupl./B.	5	el.	784
Low Rider Sport Edition	FXRS	OHV	4	V-2	80	Dupl./B.	5	el.	1,142
Low Rider Custom	FXLS	OHV	4	V-2	80	Dupl./B.	5	el.	3,221
Softail	FXST	OHV	4	V-2	80	Dupl./B.	5	el.	2,442
Softail Custom	FXSTC	OHV	4	V-2	80	Dupl./B.	5	el.	5,264
Heritage Softail	FLST	OHV	4	V-2	80	Dupl./B.	5	el.	6,445
Sportster 883	XLH	OHV	4	V-2	55	Tripl./C.	4	el.	7,096
Sportster de Luxe	XLH	OHV	4	V-2	55	Tripl./C.	4	el.	2,260
Sportster 1100	XLH	OHV	4	V-2	1100cc	Tripl./C.	4	el.	4,618
1988									
Electra Glide Sport	FLHS	OHV	4	V-2	80	Dupl./B.	5	el.	1,677
Tour Glide Classic	FLTC	OHV	4	V-2	80	Dupl./B.	5	el.	849
Electra Glide Classic	FLHTC	OHV	4	V-2	80	Dupl./B.	5	el.	4,880
Super Glide	FXR	OHV	4	V-2	80	Dupl./B.	5	el.	1,205
Softail	FXST	OHV	4	V-2	80	Dupl./B.	5	el.	1,467
Softail Custom	FXSTC	OHV	4	V-2	80	Dupl./B.	5	el.	6,621
Heritage Softail	FLST	OHV	4	V-2	80	Dupl./B.	5	el.	2,209
Heritage Softail Classic	FLSTC	OHV	4	V-2	80	Dupl./B.	5	el.	3,755
Sport Glide	FXRT	OHV	4	V-2	80	Dupl./B.	5	el.	243
Low Rider	FXRS	OHV	4	V-2	80	Dupl./B.	5	el.	2,637
Low Rider Custom	FXLR	OHV	4	V-2	80	Dupl./B.	5	el.	902
Low Rider Sport	FXRS Sp	OHV	4	V-2	80	Dupl./B.	5	el.	818
Sportster 883 Solo	XLH	OHV	4	V-2	55	Tripl./C.	4	el.	5,387
Sportster 883 Hugger	XLH	OHV	4	V-2	55	Tripl./C.	4	el.	4,501
Sportster 883 Deluxe	XLH	OHV	4	V-2	55	Tripl./C.	4	el.	1,893
Sportster 1200	XLH	OHV	4	V-2	74	Tripl./C.	4	el.	4,752
1989									
Electra Glide Sport	FLHS	OHV	4	V-2	80	Dupl./B.	5	el.	5,387
Electra Glide Classic	FLHTC	OHV	4	V-2	80	Dupl./B.	5	el.	4,097
Ultra Classic El. Glide	FLHTU	OHV	4	V-2	80	Dupl./B.	5	el.	2,890
Tour Glide Classic	FLTC	OHV	4	V-2	80	Dupl./B.	5	el.	603
Ultra Classic Tour Glide	FLTU	OHV	4	V-2	80	Dupl./B.	5	el.	568
Super Glide	FXR	OHV	4	V-2	80	Dupl./B.	5	el.	1,821
Low Rider	FXRS	OHV	4	V-2	80	Dupl./B.	5	el.	4,159
Sport Glide	FXRT	OHV	4	V-2	80	Dupl./B.	5	el.	255
Low Rider Sport	FXRS Sp	OHV	4	V-2	80	Dupl./B.	5	el.	n.a.
Low Rider Custom	FXLR	OHV	4	V-2	80	Dupl./B.	5	el.	1,016
Softail	FXST	OHV	4	V-2	80	Dupl./B.	5	el.	1,130
Softail Custom	FXSTC	OHV	4	V-2	80	Dupl./B.	5	el.	6,523
Springer Softail	FXSTS	OHV	4	V-2	80	Dupl./B.	5	el.	5,387
Heritage Softail	FLST	OHV	4	V-2	80	Dupl./B.	5	el.	1,506
Heritage Softail Clas.	FLSTC	OHV	4	V-2	80	Dupl./B.	5	el.	5,210
Sportster 883 „Solo"	XLH	OHV	4	V-2	55	Tripl./C.	4	el.	6,142
Sportster 883 Deluxe	XLH	OHV	4	V-2	55	Tripl./C.	4	el.	1,812
Sportster 883 Hugger	XLH	OHV	4	V-2	55	Tripl./C.	4	el.	4,467
Sportster 1200	XLH	OHV	4	V-2	74	Tripl./C.	4	el.	4,546
1990									
Electra Glide Sport	FLHS	OHV	4	V-2	80	Dupl./B.	5	el.	2,410
Electra Glide Classic	FLHTC	OHV	4	V-2	80	Dupl./B.	5	el.	3,597
Ultra Classic El. Glide	FLHTC	OHV	4	V-2	80	Dupl./B.	5	el.	3,405
Tour Glide Classic	FLTC	OHV	4	V-2	80	Dupl./B.	5	el.	485
Ultra Classic Tour Glide	FLTC	OHV	4	V-2	80	Dupl./B.	5	el.	612
Super Glide	FXR	OHV	4	V-2	80	Dupl./B.	5	el.	1,819
Fat Boy	FLSTF	OHV	4	V-2	80	Dupl./B.	5	el.	4,440
Heritage Softail	FLST	OHV	4	V-2	80	Dupl./B.	5	el.	1,567
Heritage Softail Classic	FLSTC	OHV	4	V-2	80	Dupl./B.	5	el.	5,483
Softail	FXST	OHV	4	V-2	80	Dupl./B.	5	el.	1,601
Softail Custom	FXSTC	OHV	4	V-2	80	Dupl./B.	5	el.	6,795
Springer Softail	FXSTS	OHV	4	V-2	80	Dupl./B.	5	el.	4,252
Low Rider Conv.	FXRS-CONV	OHV	4	V-2	80	Dupl./B.	5	el.	989
Low Rider Sport Edition	FXRS-SP	OHV	4	V-2	80	Dupl./B.	5	el.	762
Low Rider Custom	FXLR	OHV	4	V-2	80	Dupl./B.	5	el.	1,143
Low Rider	FXRS	OHV	4	V-2	80	Dupl./B.	5	el.	2,615
Sport Glide	FXRT	OHV	4	V-2	80	Dupl./B.	5	el.	304
Sportster 883	XLH	OHV	4	V-2	55	Tripl./C.	4	el.	5,227
Sportster 883 Hugger	XLH	OHV	4	V-2	55	Tripl./C.	4	el.	1,298
Sportster 1200	XLH	OHV	4	V-2	74	Tripl./C.	4	el.	4,598
Sportster 883 Deluxe	XLH	OHV	4	V-2	55	Tripl./C.	4	el.	1,298
1991									
Electra Glide Sport	FLHS	OHV	4	V-2	80	Dupl./B.	5	el.	2,383
Electra Glide Classic	FLHTC	OHV	4	V-2	80	Dupl./B.	5	el.	3,225
Ultra Classic El. Glide	FLHTCU	OHV	4	V-2	80	Dupl./B.	5	el.	3,515
Tour Glide Classic	FLTC	OHV	4	V-2	80	Dupl./B.	5	el.	259
Ultra Classic Tour Glide	FLTCU	OHV	4	V-2	80	Dupl./B.	5	el.	499
Super Glide	FXR	OHV	4	V-2	80	Dupl./B.	5	el.	1,742
Low Rider	FXRS	OHV	4	V-2	80	Dupl./B.	5	el.	2,138
Sport Glide	FXRT	OHV	4	V-2	80	Dupl./B.	5	el.	272
Low Rider Sport Edition	FXRS-SP	OHV	4	V-2	80	Dupl./B.	5	el.	683
Low Rider Conv.	FXRS-CONV.	OHV	4	V-2	80	Dupl./B.	5	el.	1,721
Low Rider Custom	FXLR	OHV	4	V-2	80	Dupl./B.	5	el.	1,197
Dyna Glide	FXDB-Sturgis	OHV	4	V-2	80	Dupl./B.	5	el.	1,546
Softail Custom	FXSTC	OHV	4	V-2	80	Dupl./B.	5	el.	5,581
Fat Boy	FLSTF	OHV	4	V-2	80	Dupl./B.	5	el.	4,265
Springer Softail	FXSTS	OHV	4	V-2	80	Dupl./B.	5	el.	8,590
Heritage Softail Classic	FLSTC	OHV	4	V-2	80	Dupl./B.	5	el.	4,922
Sportster 883	XLH	OHV	4	V-2	80	Tripl./C.	5	el.	3,034
Sportster 883 Deluxe	XLH	OHV	4	V-2	80	Tripl./B.	5	el.	3,487
Sportster 883 Hugger	XLH	OHV	4	V-2	80	Tripl./C.	5	el.	6,282
Sportster 1200	XLH 1200	OHV	4	V-2	80	Tripl./B.	5	el.	
1992									
Electra Glide Sport	FLHS	OHV	4	V-2	80	Dupl./B.	5	el.	n.a.
Electra Glide Classic	FLHTC	OHV	4	V-2	80	Dupl./B.	5	el.	n.a.
Electra Glide Ultra Class.	FLHTCU	OHV	4	V-2	80	Dupl./B.	5	el.	n.a.
Tour Glide Classic	FLTC	OHV	4	V-2	80	Dupl./B.	5	el.	n.a.
Ultra Classic Tour Glide	FLTCU	OHV	4	V-2	80	Dupl./B.	5	el.	n.a.
Super Glide	FXR	OHV	4	V-2	80	Dupl./B.	5	el.	n.a.
Low Rider	FXRS	OHV	4	V-2	80	Dupl./B.	5	el.	n.a.
Sport Glide	FXRT	OHV	4	V-2	80	Dupl./B.	5	el.	n.a.
Low Rider Sport Edition	FXRS-SP	OHV	4	V-2	80	Dupl./B.	5	el.	n.a.
Low Rider Conv.	FXRS-CONV.	OHV	4	V-2	80	Dupl./B.	5	el.	n.a.
Low Rider Custom	FXLR	OHV	4	V-2	80	Dupl./B.	5	el.	n.a.
Dyna Glide	FXDB-Sturgis	OHV	4	V-2	80	Dupl./B.	5	el.	n.a.

Model	Type	Engine	Stroke	Engine Type	Displacement	Drive (P/S)	Gears	Ignition	Prod. Fig.
Softail Custom	FXSTC	OHV	4	V-2	80	Dupl./B.	5	el.	n.a.
Fat Boy	FLSTF	OHV	4	V-2	80	Dupl./B.	5	el.	n.a.
Springer Softail	FXSTS	OHV	4	V-2	80	Dupl./B.	5	el.	n.a.
Heritage Softail Classic	FLSTC	OHV	4	V-2	80	Dupl./B.	5	el.	n.a.
Sportster 883	XLH	OHV	4	V-2	55	Tripl./B.	5	el.	n.a.
Sportster 883 Deluxe	XLH	OHV	4	V-2	55	Tripl./B.	5	el.	n.a.
Sportster 883 Hugger	XLH	OHV	4	V-2	55	Tripl./B.	5	el.	n.a.
Sportster 1200	XLH 1200	OHV	4	V-2	74	Tripl./B.	5	el.	n.a.

1993

Model	Type	Engine	Stroke	Engine Type	Displacement	Drive (P/S)	Gears	Ignition	Prod. Fig.
Electra Glide Road King	FLHR	OHV	4	V-2	80	Dupl./B.	5	el.	n.a.
Electra Glide Sport	FLHS	OHV	4	V-2	80	Dupl./B.	5	el.	n.a.
Electra Glide Classic	FLHTC	OHV	4	V-2	80	Dupl./B.	5	el.	n.a.
Ultra Classic El. Glide	FLHTCU	OHV	4	V-2	80	Dupl./B.	5	el.	n.a.
Ultra Classic Tour Glide	FLTCU	OHV	4	V-2	80	Dupl./B.	5	el.	n.a.
Super Glide	FXD	OHV	4	V-2	80	Dupl./B.	5	el.	n.a.
Heritage Softail Classic	FLSTC	OHV	4	V-2	80	Dupl./B.	5	el.	n.a.
Heritage Softail Nostalgia	FLSTN	OHV	4	V-2	80	Dupl./B.	5	el.	n.a.
Fat Boy	FLSTF	OHV	4	V-2	80	Dupl./B.	5	el.	n.a.
Low Rider Custom	FLXR	OHV	4	V-2	80	Dupl./B.	5	el.	n.a.
Dyna Low Rider	FXDL	OHV	4	V-2	80	Dupl./B.	5	el.	n.a.
Dyna Wide Glide	FXDWG	OHV	4	V-2	80	Dupl./B.	5	el.	n.a.
Low Rider Sport Edition	FXRS-SP	OHV	4	V-2	80	Dupl./B.	5	el.	n.a.
Softail Custom	FXSTC	OHV	4	V-2	80	Dupl./B.	5	el.	n.a.
Springer Softail	FXSTS	OHV	4	V-2	80	Dupl./B.	5	el.	n.a.
Dyna Low Rider Conv.	FXDS-CONV.	OHV	4	V-2	80	Dupl./B.	5	el.	n.a.
Sportster 883	XLH	OHV	4	V-2	55	Tripl./B.	5	el.	n.a.
Sportster Hugger	XLH	OHV	4	V-2	55	Tripl./B.	5	el.	n.a.
Sportster 1200	XLH 1200	OHV	4	V-2	74	Tripl./B.	5	el.	n.a.

1994

Model	Type	Engine	Stroke	Engine Type	Displacement	Drive (P/S)	Gears	Ignition	Prod. Fig.
Electra Glide Road King	FLHR	OHV	4	V-2	80	Dupl./B.	5	el.	n.a.
Electra Glide Classic	FLHTC	OHV	4	V-2	80	Dupl./B.	5	el.	n.a.
Ultra Classic El. Glide	FLHTCU	OHV	4	V-2	80	Dupl./B.	5	el.	n.a.
Super Glide	FXD	OHV	4	V-2	80	Dupl./B.	5	el.	n.a.
Low Rider Custom	FXLR	OHV	4	V-2	80	Dupl./B.	5	el.	n.a.
Dyna Low Rider	FXDL	OHV	4	V-2	80	Dupl./B.	5	el.	n.a.
Dyna Wide Glide	FXDWG	OHV	4	V-2	80	Dupl./B.	5	el.	n.a.
Dyna Low Rider Conv.	FXDS-CONV.	OHV	4	V-2	80	Dupl./B.	5	el.	n.a.
Heritage Special	FLSTN	OHV	4	V-2	80	Dupl./B.	5	el.	n.a.
Heritage Softail Classic	FLSTC	OHV	4	V-2	80	Dupl./B.	5	el.	n.a.
Springer Softail	FXSTS	OHV	4	V-2	80	Dupl./B.	5	el.	n.a.
Softail Custom	FXSTC	OHV	4	V-2	80	Dupl./B.	5	el.	n.a.
Fat Boy	FLSTF	OHV	4	V-2	80	Dupl./B.	5	el.	n.a.
Sportster 883	XLH	OHV	4	V-2	883	Tripl./B.	5	el.	n.a.
Sportster Hugger	XLH	OHV	4	V-2	883	Tripl./B.	5	el.	n.a.
Sportster 1200	XLH 1200	OHV	4	V-2	1200	Tripl./B.	5	el.	n.a.

1994

Model	Type	Engine	Stroke	Engine Type	Displacement	Drive (P/S)	Gears	Ignition	Prod. Fig.
Electra Glide Road King	FLHR	OHV	4	V-2	80	Dupl./B.	5	el.	n.a.
Electra Glide Classic	FLHTC	OHV	4	V-2	80	Dupl./B.	5	el.	n.a.
Ultra Classic El. Glide	FLHTCU	OHV	4	V-2	80	Dupl./B.	5	el.	n.a.
Super Glide	FXD	OHV	4	V-2	80	Dupl./B.	5	el.	n.a.
Low Rider Custom	FXLR	OHV	4	V-2	80	Dupl./B.	5	el.	n.a.
Dyna Low Rider	FXDL	OHV	4	V-2	80	Dupl./B.	5	el.	n.a.
Dyna Wide Glide	FXDWG	OHV	4	V-2	80	Dupl./B.	5	el.	n.a.
Dyna Low Rider Conv.	FXDS-CONV.	OHV	4	V-2	80	Dupl./B.	5	el.	n.a.
Heritage Special	FLSTN	OHV	4	V-2	80	Dupl./B.	5	el.	n.a.
Heritage Softail Classic	FLSTC	OHV	4	V-2	80	Dupl./B.	5	el.	n.a.
Springer Softail	FXSTS	OHV	4	V-2	80	Dupl./B.	5	el.	n.a.
Softail Custom	FXSTC	OHV	4	V-2	80	Dupl./B.	5	el.	n.a.
Fat Boy	FLSTF	OHV	4	V-2	80	Dupl./B.	5	el.	n.a.
Sportster 883	XLH	OHV	4	V-2	883cc	Tripl./B.	5	el.	n.a.
Sportster Hugger	XLH	OHV	4	V-2	883cc	Tripl./B.	5	el.	n.a.
Sportster 1200	XLH 1200	OHV	4	V-2	1200cc	Tripl./B.	5	el.	n.a.

1995

Model	Type	Engine	Stroke	Engine Type	Displacement	Drive (P/S)	Gears	Ignition	Prod. Fig.
Electra Glide Road King	FLHR	OHV	4	V-2	1340cc	Dupl./G.	5	el.	n.a.
Electra Glide Standard	FLHT	OHV	4	V-2	1340cc	Dupl./G.	5	el.	n.a.
Electra Glide Classic	FLHTC	OHV	4	V-2	1340cc	Dupl./G.	5	el.	n.a.
Ultra Classic El. Glide	FLHTU	OHV	4	V-2	1340cc	Dupl./G.	5	el.	n.a.
Ultra Classic Tour Glide	FLTCU	OHV	4	V-2	1340cc	Dupl./G.	5	el.	n.a.
Dyna Super Glide	FXD	OHV	4	V-2	1340cc	Dupl./G.	5	el.	n.a.
Dyna Conv.	FXDS-CONV	OHV	4	V-2	1340cc	Dupl./G.	5	el.	n.a.
Dyna Wide Glide	FXDWG	OHV	4	V-2	80	Dupl./B.	5	el.	n.a.
Dyna Low Rider	FXDL	OHV	4	V-2	80	Dupl./B.	5	el.	n.a.
Softail Custom	FXSTC	OHV	4	V-2	80	Dupl./B.	5	el.	n.a.
Springer Softail	FXSTS	OHV	4	V-2	80	Dupl./B.	5	el.	n.a.
Bad Boy	FXSTB	OHV	4	V-2	80	Dupl./B.	5	el.	n.a.
Fat Boy	FLSTF	OHV	4	V-2	80	Dupl./B.	5	el.	n.a.
Heritage Softail Classic	FLSTC	OHV	4	V-2	80	Dupl./B.	5	el.	n.a.
Heritage Softail Special	FLSTN	OHV	4	V-2	80	Dupl./B.	5	el.	n.a.
Sportster 883 Standard	XLH	OHV	4	V-2	883cc	Tripl./B.	5	el.	n.a.
Sportster 883 Hugger	XLH 883	OHV	4	V-2	883cc	Tripl./B.	5	el.	n.a.
Sportster 883 Deluxe	XLH	OHV	4	V-2	883cc	Tripl./B.	5	el.	n.a.
Sportster 1200	XLH 1200	OHV	4	V-2	1200cc	Tripl./B.	5	el.	n.a.

1996

Model	Type	Engine	Stroke	Engine Type	Displacement	Drive (P/S)	Gears	Ignition	Prod. Fig.
Ultra Classic El. Glide	FLHTU	OHV	4	V-2	1340cc	Dupl./G.	5	el.	n.a.
Ultra Classic El. Glide EFI	FLHTUI	OHV	4	V-2	1340cc	Dupl./G.	5	el.	n.a.
Electra Glide Classic	FLHTC	OHV	4	V-2	1340cc	Dupl./G.	5	el.	n.a.
Electra Gilde EFI	FLHTCI	OHV	4	V-2	1340cc	Dupl./G.	5	el.	n.a.
Electra Glide Standard	FLHT	OHV	4	V-2	1340cc	Dupl./G.	5	el.	n.a.
Fat Boy	FLSTF	OHV	4	V-2	80	Dupl./B.	5	el.	n.a.
Heritage Softail Classic	FLSTC	OHV	4	V-2	80	Dupl./B.	5	el.	n.a.
Heritage Softail Special	FLSTN	OHV	4	V-2	80	Dupl./B.	5	el.	n.a.
Bad Boy	FXSTB	OHV	4	V-2	80	Dupl./B.	5	el.	n.a.
Springer Softail	FXSTS	OHV	4	V-2	80	Dupl./B.	5	el.	n.a.
Softail Custom	FXSTC	OHV	4	V-2	80	Dupl./B.	5	el.	n.a.
Dyna Wide Glide	FXDWG	OHV	4	V-2	80	Dupl./B.	5	el.	n.a.
Dyna Conv.	FXDS-CONV	OHV	4	V-2	80	Dupl./B.	5	el.	n.a.
Dyna Low Rider	FXDL	OHV	4	V-2	80	Dupl./B.	5	el.	n.a.
Dyna Super Glide	FXD	OHV	4	V-2	80	Dupl./B.	5	el.	n.a.
Sportster 883	XLH 883	OHV	4	V-2	55	Tripl./B.	5	el.	n.a.
Sportster Hugger 883	XLH 883	OHV	4	V-2	55	Tripl./B.	5	el.	n.a.
Sportster 1200	XLH 1200	OHV	4	V-2	74	Tripl./B.	5	el.	n.a.
Sportster 1200 Custom	XL 1200C	OHV	4	V-2	74	Tripl./B.	5	el.	n.a.
Sportster 1200 Sport	XL 1200S	OHV	4	V-2	74	Tripl./B.	5	el.	n.a.

1997

Model	Type	Engine	Stroke	Engine Type	Displacement	Drive (P/S)	Gears	Ignition	Prod. Fig.
Ultra Classic El. Glide	FLHTCUI	OHV	4	V-2	80	Dupl./B.	5	el.	n.a.
Ultra Classic El. Glide	FLHTCU	OHV	4	V-2	80	Dupl./B.	5	el.	n.a.
Electra Glide Classic	FLHTC	OHV	4	V-2	80	Dupl./B.	5	el.	n.a.
Electra Glide Standard	FLHT	OHV	4	V-2	80	Dupl./B.	5	el.	n.a.
Road King	FLHR	OHV	4	V-2	80	Dupl./B.	5	el.	n.a.
Fat Boy	FLSTF	OHV	4	V-2	80	Dupl./B.	5	el.	n.a.
Heritage Softail Classic	FLSTC	OHV	4	V-2	80	Dupl./B.	5	el.	n.a.
Heritage Springer	FLSTS	OHV	4	V-2	80	Dupl./B.	5	el.	n.a.
Bad Boy	FXSTSB	OHV	4	V-2	80	Dupl./B.	5	el.	n.a.
Springer Softail	FXSTS	OHV	4	V-2	80	Dupl./B.	5	el.	n.a.
Softail Custom	FXSTC	OHV	4	V-2	80	Dupl./B.	5	el.	n.a.
Dyna Wide Glide	FXDWG	OHV	4	V-2	80	Dupl./B.	5	el.	n.a.
Dyna Conv.	FXDS-CONV	OHV	4	V-2	80	Dupl./B.	5	el.	n.a.
Dyna Low Rider	FXDL	OHV	4	V-2	80	Dupl./B.	5	el.	n.a.
Dyna Super Glide	FXD	OHV	4	V-2	80	Dupl./B.	5	el.	n.a.
Sportster 883	XLH 883	OHV	4	V-2	55	Tripl./B.	5	el.	n.a.
Hugger 883		OHV	4	V-2	55	Tripl./B.	5	el.	n.a.
Sportster 1200	XLH 1200	OHV	4	V-2	74	Tripl./B.	5	el.	n.a.
Sportster 1200 Custom	XL 1200C	OHV	4	V-2	74	Tripl./B.	5	el.	n.a.
Sportster 1200 Sport	XL 1200S	OHV	4	V-2	74	Tripl./B.	5	el.	n.a.

While looking through old Harley manuals and technical data, it became clear that some of the specifications could not be right. The displacement, i.e. the cubic capacity, is determined exclusively by the movement of the piston, and does not include the combustion chamber. If the applicable formula is used for calculating the displacement (ø2 x p:4 x stroke x No. of cylinders), other results are yielded than those specified. So how did these irregularities occur? Two factors have to be accurate in order to calculate the cubic capacity reliably, and we regard these as being absolutely reliable: the stroke and the bore, both checked to fractions of a millimeter by precision manufacturing machines. Everything else is pure mathematics, and this is where we suspect the root of the errors can be found. If, for example, you round the thousandths of a millimeter (or inch) up or down to one (or no) decimal place, radically different results are yielded for the cubic capacity. Such errors are replicated in the straightforward conversion of inches into millimeters, as was often performed in the past using sliding rules instead of computers to an accuracy of five decimal places.

Associations and Clubs

Harley Owners Group Offices

Harley Owners Group, USA & Canada
3700 W. Juneau Ave.
Milwaukee, WI 53208, USA

Harley Owners Group, Canada
830 Edgely Blvd.
Concord, ON L4K 4XI, Canada

Harley Owners Group, Europe
Starkenburgstraße 12
64546 Mörfelden
Germany

Harley Owners Group, Japan
Isuzu Shiba Bldg. 4–2–3,
Shiba Minato–Ku, Tokyo 108,
Japan

Ladies of Harley (LOH)
Harley–Davidson Motor Co.
3700 Juneau Ave.
PO Box 453
Milwaukee, WI 53201
(Part of the Harley Owners Group (H.O.G.). Of H.O.G.'s 280,000 members worldwide, some 30,000 are women (riders and pillion–riders). Automatic membership upon purchasing a Harley.)

Important Motorcycle Organzations and Clubs in the U.S.

Harley–Davidson is the only motorcycle manufacturer in the U.S. It therefore follows that most national organizations are Harley–oriented.

ABATE
American Bikers Aimed Toward Education
(ABATE works for motorcyclists' rights; local bike shops have the address of the closest ABATE office.)

American Motorcyclist Assn. (AMA)
33 Collegeview Rd.
PO Box 6114
Westerville, OH 43081–6114
(General motorcycle organization and highest motorcycle sport authority.)

Canadian Motorcycle Assn.
Box 448
Hamilton, Ontario L8L8C4, Canada
(The Canadian version of the AMA.)

Motorcycle Industry Council, Government Relations Officer
1235 Jefferson Davis Hwy., Ste. 600
Arlington, VA 22202

Motorcycle Safety Foundation (MSF)
2 Jenner St., Ste. 150
Irvine, CA 92718

Motorcycle Riders Foundation (MRF)
Wayne Curtin, National Director
PO Box 1808
Washington D.C. 20013–1808
(Motorcyclists' rights.)

NCOM National Coalition of Motorcyclists
Pepper Massey
15910 Ventura Blvd.
Encino, CA 91436
(Legal assistance organization.)

National Handicap Motorcyclist Assn. (NHMA)
Bob Nevola
315 W. 21 St., #6F
New York, NY 10011
(Network for handicapped motorcyclists.)

Specialty Vehicle Institute of America
2 Jenner St.,
Ste. 150
Irvine, CA 92718

Antique Motorcycle Club of America (AMCA)
PO Box 333
Sweetster, IN 46987
(Organization for vintage motorcycles.)

Blue Knights Law Enforcement MC
38 Alden St.
Bangor, ME 04401
(Motorcycle riders association.)

Christian Motorcyclists Assn. (CMA)
PO Box 9
Hatfield, AR 71945

Nationwide women's organizations:
Motor Maids
601 N. McCall Rd.
Jan Barrett, President
Englewood, FL 34223
(More than 500 members with all motorcycle brands.)

Women in the Wind (WITW) Mother Chapter
PO Box 8392
Toledo, OH 43605
(Over 600 members in 20 American States, four Canadian provinces, England and New Zealand. Mainly Harleys, but other brands are welcome.)

Women on Wheels (WOW)
PO Box 081454
Racine, WI 53408–1454
(More than 1,800 members in 48 States, five Canadian provinces, England, Germany, Italy and Finland.)

Hardly Angels
Lynell Corbett
13492 County Rd. 250
Durango, CO 81301

Iron Angels
412 East Oak Lane
Front Royal, VA 22630

Leather & Lace
Lady Harley/Motorcycle Riders Assn.
Empire State Chapter
PO Box 2
Clintondale, NY 12515–0002
(Harleys only; eight chapters in America.)

Racing Organizations

Drag Racing:

All–Harley Drag Racing Assn.
Dane Miller, President
PO Box 1429
Elon College, NC 27244

AMA–Pro Star
Keith Kizer
PO Box 18039
Huntsville, AL 35804

American Motorcycle Racing Assn.
Richard Wegner, President
Box 50
Itasca, IL 60143
(Harleys)

East Coast Racing Assn.
Ben Petrovic, President
219 E. White Horse Pike
Galloway, Twp., NJ 08201

International Drag Bike Assn.
3936 Raceway Park Road
Mt. Olive, AL 35117

National Hot Rod Assn.
PO Box 5555
Glendora, CA 91740

Road Racing:

National American Superbike Series (NASB)
Pat Murphy
Western Eastern Racing Assn. (WERA)
PO Box 440549
Kennesaw, GA 30144

American Federation of Motorcyclists (AFM)
PO Box 5018–333
Newark, CA 94560

Vintage Racing:

American Historic Racing Motorcycle Assn. (AHRMA)
PO Box 882
Wausau, WI 54402–0882

Motorcycle Museums U.S.A./North America

AD Farrow Co. Museum
Columbus, OH

American Classic Motorcycle Museum
Asheboro, NC

American Police Museum & Hall of Fame
Miami, FL

Armando Magri, Inc.
Sacramento, CA

Barber Vintage Motorsports Museum
Birmingham, AL

Bill's Custom Cycles
Bloomsburg, PA

Bud Etkins' Motorcycle Collection
North Holywood, CA

Centennial Motorcycle Museum
Lyons, CO

Chicago Museum of Science & Industry
Chicago, IL

Crawford Auto Aviation Museum
Cleveland, OH

Custom Chrome's Harley Museum
Morgan Hill, CA

Dale's Harley–Davidson & Wheels Through Time Museum
Mt. Vernon, IL

Daytona USA
Daytona Beach, FL

Deeley Classic & Antique Museum
Richmond, Canada

DomiRacer & Acessory Mart
Cincinnati, OH

Flat Track Motorcycle Museum
Clovis, CA

Harley–Davidson Café
New York, NY & Las Vegas,NV

Harley–Davidson Museum
York, PA

Harold Wart Pioneer Village Foundation
Minden, NB

Harrah's Automobile Collection
Reno, NV

Henry Ford Museum
Dearborn, MI

Indian Motorcycle Museum
Springfield, MA

Indianapolis Motor Speedway Museum
Indianapolis, IN

Klassix Auto Museum
Daytona Beach, FL

Motorcycle Heritage Museum
Westerville, OH

Motorcycle Museum
Winamac, IN

Motorsports Hall of Fame
Novi, MI

National Automobile Museum
Reno, NV

National Motorcycle Museum & Hall of Fame
Sturgis, SD

Newark Square Barber Shop
Newark, CA

Otis Chandler Museum of Transportation a. Wildlife
Oxnard, CA

Owls Head Transportation Museum
Owls Head, ME

Petersen Automotive Museum
Los Angeles, CA

Royal Mountains Motorcycle Museum
Colorado Springs, CO

Rusty Kay & Associates
Santa Monica, CA

San Diego Hall of Champions
San Diego, CA

Smithsonian's National Museum of American History
Washington D.C.

Southeast Harley-Davidson
Cleveland, OH

Sundays Only Cycle Museum
Hawthorne, FL

The American Motorcyle Museum
Pearland, TX

The Rocky Mountain Motorcycle Museum & Hall of Fame
Colorado Springs, CO

The Shop
Ventura, CA

Willi's Motorcycle World
Daytona Beach, FL

Films Featuring Harley-Davidsons ...

Year Produced	Title	Country	Director
1930	Hells Angels	USA	Howard Hughes
1953	The Wild One (1955)	USA	Laszlo Benedek
1957	Motorcycle Gang (1961)	USA	Edward L. Cahn
1958	Dragstrip Riot	Great Britain	AIP
1965	The Leather Boys (1970)	Great Britain	Sidney J. Furie
1963	Scorpio Rising	USA	Kenneth Anger
1965	Motorpsycho (1968)	USA	Russ Meyer
1966	The Wild Angels (1967)	USA	Roger Corman
1967	Born Losers (1967)	USA	T. C. Frank (= Tom Laughlin)
1967	The Wild Rebels (1968)	USA	William Grefe
1967	The Girl on a Motorcycle (1969)	Great Britain/France	Jack Cardiff
1970	Rebel Rousers (Rebel Riders) (1977)	USA	Martin B. Cohen
1967	Devil's Angels (1968)	USA	Daniel Haller
1967	The Savage Seven (1968)	USA	Richard Rush
1967	Hell Angels on Wheels (1968)	USA	Richard Rush
1967	Clambake (1987)	USA	Arthur H. Nadel
1967	The Glory Stompers (1968)	USA	Anthony M. Lanza
1968	Angels from Hell (1993)	USA	Bruce Kessler
1968	She Devils on Wheels	USA	Hershell G. Lewis
1969	Easy Rider (1969)	USA	Dennis Hopper
1969	Naked Angels (1970)	USA	Bruce Clark
1969	Hells Angels 69 (1970)	USA	Lee Madden
1969	Run, Angel, Run (1971)	USA	Jack Starrett
1969	Satan's Sadist (1970)	USA	Al Adamson
1969	Hell's Belles (1974)	USA	Maury Dexter
1970	Black Angels (1972)	USA	Laurence Merrick
1970	C.C. and Company (1971)	USA	Seymour Robbie
1970	Cycle Savages	USA	Bill Brame
1970	The Hard Ride (1973)	USA	Burt Topper
1970	The Losers (1971)	USA	Jack Starrett
1970	Gimme Shelter (1971)	USA	David a. Albert Maysles
1971	Angels Hard As They Come	USA	Joe Viola
1971	Angels Die Hard (1976)	USA	Richard Compton
1971	Peace Killers (1971)	USA	Douglas Schwartz
1971	The Girls from Thunder Strip (1972)	USA	David L. Hewitt
1971	Wild Riders/Angels for Kicks (1972)	USA	Richard Kanter
1972	The Dirt Gang (1973)	USA	Jerry Jameson
1972	Electra Glide in Blue (1973)	USA	James W. Guercio
1973	Trip with the Teacher (1975)	USA	Earl Barton
1973	Bury Me Angel	USA	n.a.
1974	The Northville Cemetery Massacre (1977)	USA	William Dear, Thomas L. Dyke
1974	The Bullfighters/Worse than Vultures (1975)	USA	Abel Salazar
1975	Death Riders	USA	James Wilson
1975	Uomini si nasce poliziotti si muore (1976)	Italy	Ruggero Deodato
1975	Il Tempo degli Assassini (1976)	Italy	Marcello Andrei
1976	Viva Knievel! (1977)	USA	Gordon Douglas
1976	Killer on Wheels (1976)	Hong Kong	Kuei Shi-Hung
1976	Smokey and the Bandit (1978)	USA	Hal Needham
1977	The Gauntlet (1978)	USA	Clint Eastwood
1979	Fast Charlie ... the Moonbeam Rider (1987)	USA	Steve Carver
1978	Deathsport (1978)	USA	Henry Suso, Allan Arkush
1979	Brillantina Rock (1980)	Italy	Michele Massimo Tarantini
1979	Mil Caminos Tiene La Muerte (Mad Angels) (1980)	Mexico	R. V. Kury
1978	Mad Max (1980)	Australia	George Miller
1980	The Cannonball Run (1981)	USA	Hal Needham
1980	Go Hog Wild (1981)	Canada	Les Rose
1980	Stingray II (1981)	Spain/Switz.	Paul Graun
1980	Spetters (1980)	The Netherlands	Paul Verhoeven
1981	Mad Max II (1982)	Australia	George Miller
1981	The Loveless (1984)	USA	Kathryn Bigelow, Monty Montgomery
1983	Rumble Fish (1984)	USA	Francis Ford Coppola
1983	Streets of Fire (1984)	USA	Walter Hill
1987	Hells Angels Forever	USA	n.a.
1990	Stone Cold (1991)	USA	Craig R. Baxley
1991	Chopper Chicks in Zombietown	USA	n.a.
1991	Born to Ride (1992)	USA	Graham Baker
1973	Werewolves on Wheels/Lost Exorzist (1974)	USA	Michel Levesque
1990	Harley-Davidson & The Marlborough-Man (1991)	USA	Simon Wincer
1984	Mask (1985)	USA	Peter Bogdanovich
1990	The Terminator 2 – Judgement Day (1991)	USA	James Cameron
1989	Wild Orchid (1990)	USA	Zalman King
1991	Wild Orchid 2 – Blue Movie Blue (1992)	USA	Zalman King
1992	Wild Orchid 3 – The Red Shoe Diary (1993)	USA	Zalman King
1979	1941 (1980)	USA	Steven Spielberg
1981	Rocky III (1982)	USA	Silvester Stallone
1957	Motorcycle Gang (1961)	USA	Edward L. Cahn
1970	Free Grass (1972)	USA	Bill Brame
1969	Angel Unchained (1994)	USA	Lea Madden
1968	Beyond the Law (1969)	USA	Norman Mailer
1980	Knightriders (1981)	USA	George A. Romero
1974	Stone (1981)	Australia	Sandy Harbutt
1983	Atlantic Interceptors (1983)	Italy	Ruggero Deodato
1992	Fixing the Shadow (1993)	USA	Larry Ferguson
1993	Pulp Fiction (1994)	USA	Quentin Tarantino
1992	Chrome Soldiers (1992)	USA	Thomas J. Wright
1991	Rescue Me (1992)	USA	Arthur Allan Seidelman
1993	The Crow (1994)	USA	Alex Proyas
1991	JFK (1992)	USA	Oliver Stone
1992	Twin Peaks – Fire Walks With Me (1992)	USA	David Lynch
1976	I due superpiedi quasi piatti (1977)	Italy	Enzo Barboni Clucher
1975	L'Ambizioso (1979)	Italy	Pasquale Squitieri
1993	A Bronx Tale (1994)	USA	Robert DeNiro

Abbreviations

AACME	Arizona Antique Classic Motorcycle Enthusiasts	ECM	Electronic Control Modul	MMI	Motorcycle Mechanics Institute
ABATE	A Brotherhood Against Totalitarian Enactments	EFI	Electronic Fuel Injection	MS	Mississippi
	American Biker Aimed Toward Education	EI	Employee Involvement	MSF	Motorcycle Safety Foundation
ADBA	American Drag Bike Association	EMF	Eagle Mark Financial Service	NB	New Brunswick
AHD	All Harley Drags	EPA	Federal Environmental Protection Agency	NC	North Carolina
AHDRA	All Harley Drag Racing Association	ESPFI	Electronic Sequential Port Fuel Injection	NAST	National Association of Super-Twins
AHRMA	American Historic Racing Motorcycle Association	FAM	Federation of American Motorcyclists	NHRA	National Hod Rod Association
AIP	American International Pictures	FHDDC	Harley–Davidson Dresser Club	NHV	Noise, Vibrations & Harshness
AIW	Allied Industrial Workers	FHP	Federal Highway Patrol	NJ	New Jersey
AL	Alabama	FICM	Fédération Internationale de Compétition Motocyclette	NMRA	National Motorcycle Racing Association
AMA	American Motorcycle Association	FIM	Fédération Internationale Motocyclette	NV	Nevada
AMC/AMCA	Antique Motorcycle Club of America	FL	Florida	NY	New York
AMDRA	American Motorcycle Drag Racing Association	GA	Georgia	NYCPD	New York City Police Department
AMEN	American Motorcycle Engineering	HARA	Hanau Auto Racing Association	NYSE	New York Stock Exchange
AMF	American Machine & Foundry Company	HDRA	Harley Drag Race Association	OH	Ohio
AMMA	American Motorcycle Manufacturer Association	H.O.G.	Harley Owners Group	OHC	Overhead Camshaft
AMRA	American Motorcycle Racing Association	Hwy	Highway	ON	Ontario
A.N.U.S.	American National Unimotorcyclist Society	IAM	Machinist and Aerospace Workers	PA	Pennsylvania
AR	Arkansas	ID	Identification	PD	Police Department
ARROW	Associated Rodeo	IDBA	International Drag Bike Association	PDC	Product Development Center
AZ	Arizona	IDDF	Interessengemeinschaft Deutscher Dragster Fahrer	POW	Prisoner of War
BCCOM	British Columbia Coalition of Motorcyclists	IFMA	Internationale Fahrrad- und Motorradausstellung	PR	Public Relation
BMT	Berliner Motorradtage	IHRA	International Hot Rod Association	RFD	Rural Free Delivery
BoT	Battle of Twins	IL	Illinois	RSWR	Retail Sale & Warranty Registration
BOTT	Battle of the Twins	IN	Indiana	RV	Recreational Vehicles
CA	California	IOE	Inlet Over Exhaust	SCTA	Southern California Timing Association
CAD	Computer Aided Design	ITC	International Trade Commission	SD	South Dakota
CEO	Chief Executive Officer	JAP	J. A. Prestwich	SEMA	Specialty Equipment Market Association
CHP	California Highway Patrol	JIT	Just in Time	SOC	Statistical Operator Control
CI	Corporate Identity	LAPD	Los Angeles Police Department	SP	Shore Patrol
CMA	Christian Motorcycle Association	LBO	Leveraged Buy Out	S&S	Smith & Smith
C.M.F.	Christian Motorcycle Fellowship	LOH	Ladies of Harley	StVZO	Straßenverkehrszulasssungsordnung
CO	Colorado	LSR	Land Speed Record		(German Traffic Laws)
COD	Cash on Delivery	M&ATA	Motorcycle & Allied Trades Association	TX	Texas
CQCP	Contractor Quality Certification Program	M&I	Milwaukee Marshall & Ilsey Bank	USFRA	Utah Salt Flats Racing Association
CR	Competition Racing	MA	Motorcycle Association	USMC	Headquarters der Marine Corps
CVMG	Canadian Vintage Motorcycle Group	MA	Massachusetts	VA	Virginia
CVRG	California Vintage Racing Group	MAN	Material as Needed	V.D.T.R.A.	Vintage Dirt Track Racer Association
DAC	Harley-Davidson Dealers Advisory Council	MC	Motorcycle Clubs	VIP	Very Important Person
DC	District of Columbia	MDA	Muscular Distrophy Association	VMCC	Vintage Motor Cycle Club of Great Britain
DOT	Department of Transportation	ME	Maine	VROOM	Vintage Racers of Old Motorcycles
DRAG	Drag-Racing Association Germany	MI	Michigan	WCTF	World Children's Transplant Fund
DRAS	Dragster Association Switzerland	MIA	Missing in Action	WI	Wisconsin

Index

ABATE 466–477, 478, 481, 309
ABATE Helmet Protest Run
466, 495
Abdul–Jabbar, Kareem 433
Abresh (Company) 280
Abresh (Model) Lite Car 280
Ace (Company) 45
Acustar (Company) 285
Adamo, Jimmy 356
Adolf Würth GmbH und Co. KG
(Company) 431

Advanced Automotive Eng. Techn.
(Company) 559
AEE Choppers Shop 557
Aermacchi (Company) 72, 74–75,
79, 195, 198, 351, 354,
Aermacchi 350
Ala Azzurra 74
Ala Bianca 74
Ala D'Oro
74, 351, 612
Ala Rossa 74

Ala Verde 74, 195
Aermacchi–Harley–Davidson (Model) 350
Baja 74, 197, 198-199, 198, 350
Leggero 72, 74, 196, 196
Rapido 198–199, 198-199
Sprint 72, 74, 75, 195, 195, 612
Aeronautica Macchi (Company) s. Aermacchi
(Company)
AHD 596
Airbrush Total 636
AJS 586

Albert I, King of Belgium 433
Ali, Muhammad 432
All American Superbike 354
All Harley drag racing school 595
Allman Brothers 485
Alzina, Hap 69, 306
AMA Competition Congress 306
American Chopper Enterprises
(Company) 308
American Chopper Enterprises (Models)
Heritage Royale 308

American Motorcycle Association (AMA)
17, 25, 53, 58, 64, 65, 68, 72, 92, 94, 160,
192, 224, 264, 296, 300, 306, 330, 332,
333, 334, 336, 337, 338, 340, 341, 343,
345, 348, 349, 352, 355, 358, 376, 385,
415, 418, 420, 421, 421, 431, 436, 438, 439,
441, 469, 473, 476, 484, 485, 492, 541,
588, 600, 603, 606, 613
AME 536
American Historic Racing Motorcycle
Association (AHRMA) 606
American Iron 595
American Legend Cycles (Company) 559
American Motorcycle Drag Racing Association
(AMDRA) 477, 588, 589, 600
American Motorcycle Engineering (AMEN)
557
American Machine & Foundry Company
(AMF) 73, 74, 75, 76–81, 91, 93, 99, 109,
116, 194, 216, 232, 303, 372, 477, 478, 480,
530, 555, 558
American Motorcycle Manufacturer
Association (AMMA) 41, 332
American Motorcycle Racing Association
(AMRA) 589
American Motorcyclist and Bicyclist 514
Anderson, Kathleen 421
Anderson, Pamela 307, 433
Anderson, Paul 432
Andres, Brad 192, 193, 476
Andres, Nygren (Company) 534
Andrews, Walter 97
Ann–Margret 431
Anger, Kenneth, 649
Anthes, Rico 597
Antique Motorcycle Club of America
(AMCA) 576, 577
Anzani (Company) 42
Appel, George 39
Arena, Sam 332, 344
Ariel (Company) 62, 303
Arizona Bike week 495, 561
Armec (Company) 283
Armstrong Military Division 162
Armstrong (Model)
Armstrong MT500 163
ARROW 488
Artley, Roy 301
Ashe, Police Chief 478
Asphalt Angels Publications
(Company) 386
Associated Riders on Wheels s. (ARROW)
Audi–Bi (Company) 16
Aurora Automatic Machine Company
16, 30
Auto Cycle Union 598
Automobile and Cycle Trade Journal 17
Automotive Industries 44, 300
Aviation Revue 42
Axel, King of Denmark 433
Axton, Hoyt 431
Aykroyd, Dan 433

Baisley, Mary 422
Baker, "Cannonball" 40, 343
Bakor, Alisandra 393
Balcom Company (Company) 56
Baldwin–Duckworth (Company) 58
Bales, Vivian 414
Ball, Keith R. 557
Ball K. Randall "Bandit" 647
Balsom, Jack 102
Bang, Garry 199
Bangor Punta (Company) 72, 73
Barbican (Gallery) 308
Bardot, Brigitte 433, 433
Barnett, Sherman 90, 311, 311
Barger, Sonny 440, 649
Barney, Cliff 631
Barr, Dave 374, 623, 623
BARS
Boothill Saloon, The 522
Broken Spoke, The 522
Californian Rock Store, The 521
(the Cali. Rock Store Café)
Froggy Saloon 523
Gunners Lounge, The 521
Iron Horse saloon, The 522
Knocker's Cafe 494
Last Resort Bar, The 480, 522
Rat's Hole 636
Sopotnik's Cabbage Patch 480
Squeeze–In Pub 523
Waterin' Hole Saloon 494
Barr, Fred 56
Barrett, Jane 421
Bartels, Bill 309
Bartels HD (Dealership) 649
Barth Manufacturing Company 18
Bartle & Co. 298
Barton Engineering (Company) 94
Bassalig, Waldemar 631
Battistini Custom Cycles (Company) 552
Battistini, Rick and Dean 555
Bauder, Bob 548
Baum, Highway Patrol Director Jerry 485
Baumann, Art 352
Bay Area Customs Cycles 539, 550-551
Beals, Vaughn L. 76, 78, 79, 79, 80, 80, 81, 81,
86, 87, 87, 90, 232, 274, 303, 373, 386
Bearup, Debbie 422
Becker, Kristine 423
Bell Telephone (Company) 23
Bendix (Company) 204, 220
Bendix, Victor 44
Benedek, Laszlo 65
Bennett, J.A. 444
Berger, Senta 433
Bernard, Harvey 26
Bettencourt, Nelson 330
Big Bike 646
Big Jack 575
Biker's Asshole (Shop) 575
Biker's Lifestyle 647
Biker's News 653

Biking News 449
Bicycle Illustrated 17
Bicycle World 16
Bicycle World and Motorcycle Review
16, 26
Bimota (Company) 351
Bitchin, Bob 646
Blackburn, Bobbie 349
Black Hills Motor Classics s. Sturgis Bike Week
484, 484
Blackwell, Bubba 611
Blair, Mil 646, 647
Blake, Norm 86
Bleustein, Dr. Jeffrey L. 77, 80, 81, 82, 88, 373
Blue Nights MC (Club) 288
BMW (Company) 51, 56, 230, 356, 404,
450, 451
BMW MODELS
BMW Isetta 322
BMW R 12 60, 166
BMW R 75 60, 166
Bob Dron (Dealership) 316
Bolfert, Thomas C. 646
Bombadier (Company) 162
Bomb cases 285
Bond, John R. 276
Bond, Ward 432
Bondurand, Bob 548
Bon Jovi 375
Borsetti Mr 347
Bouton, George 20
Bradshaw, Terry 433
Brainard, Jay 548
Brake, Jay 548
Branch, Jerry 230
Brando, Marlon 65, 444, 444, 649
Brant, Harry 32, 330
Brashear, Everett 193
Brecht, Günter 653
Brelsford, Mark 306, 348
Briggs & Stratton (Company) 89, 113, 285
Briggs, George T. 332
Brinck, Eddie 331, 342, 615
Brook Stevens (Company) 81
Brough–Superior (Company) 51, 318
Browne, Jackson 307
Bruce, Ethel 415
Bruere, François 538, 552, 553, 630, 631, 637
Brockaw, Paul 444
Brooks, Nancy 549
Brother Ben Hardy 649
Brotherhood of Outlaws 478
Brown, David A. jr 400
Bruso, Mike 477
BSA (Company) 56, 62, 63, 66, 67, 190, 192,
218, 224, 230, 303, 318, 354, 441, 586
BSA (Model)
BSA Bantam 178
Buckeye Motorcycle Club 311
Budelier, Rich 301, 330, 432
Buell Motorcycle Company s. Buell Motors
(Company)

Buell Motors (Company) 88, 89, 95, 119, 357,
374, 620
Buell, Erik 79, 84, 94, 94–95,
Buffalo (New York) 16
Bugatti 538
Bulling, Al 480, 636
Burdon, Eric 433
Bush, Police Chief Jim 486
Butler, Thomas Calahan 34
Byers, Jerry 589

Cable, Charles 56
Cagiva 75
California Cycle Works 557
California Sidecar/Escapade Trailer
(Company) 283
Camel 349
Campanele, Ben 332
Campbell, Senator Ben "Nighthorse"
433, 433, 495, 630
Campbell, Earl 433
Campbell, Sir Malcolm 433
Campus, Dave 614
Caraibes HD (Dealership) 321
Carl's Cycle Service (Dealership) 303
Carr, Chris 354
Cartwright, Charles 44
Caruso, David 80, 81, 82, 380
Cash, Johnny 654
Castiglioni, brothers 75
Catskill 25
CB Radio 289
CBS (Company) 424
Ceresole, Claude 347
Ceriani (Company) 192
Cessna (Company) 42
Chalmers, Allis 166
Chamberlain, Clarence 433
Chandler, Otis 138
Chapouris, Pete 538, 548
Charleston Custom Cycle Shop 572
Cher 432, 433, 650
Chevrolet (Company) 538
Chez Fuzz 375
Child, Richard (Son) 56
Child, Richard Alfred "Rich" 51, 56, 69, 99, 170,
284, 400
Choppers 530, 557, 646
Christian Motorcyclists Association
374, 449
Chrome Specialities 557–558
Chrondek (Company) 591
Chrysler (Company) 218
Church, Gene 356, 356, 357, 357
Citicorp Industrial Credit Bank 80
Chu, David 433
Clausen, C.B. 557, 600
Clymer Press (Company) 379
Citroen (Firm) 285
Clark, Roy 433
Clark, Terry 350
Clarke E.C. 347

Cleveland Motorcycle Manufacturing
    Company (Company) 48, 297
Clymer, Floyd 32, 40, 69, 70, 142, 300, 330
CMA s. Christian Motorcyclists association
Cochran, Wayne 433
Codes 271
Coe, David Allan 433
Coffmann, A. B. 332
Collins, Russ 477
Columbia (Company) 16
Constantine, Arthur A. 46, 58, 328
Coors (Company) 495
Copeland, Kenneth and Gloria 101, 449
Corbin (Company) 146, 539
Corbin, Mike 548
Corman, Roger 530
Corrento, Sam 32, 330
Courtesy Car Company 52
Coyote 632, 632
Crandall, Harry 32, 330
Crane, Bob 357
Crane, Tessa 548
Crocker, Albert C. 301
Crocker, Albert G. 340
Crolins, Lacy 40
Crompton & Knowles Company 280
Crosby, David 433
Crosby, Pat 421
Crow, Police Chief 561
Cummings, Pam 423
Cummins Diesel (Company) 81
Curtiss, Glen 433
Cunningham, Mark 382
Cunningham, Walter 330
Curtiss & Erie (Company) 16, 36
Curtiss–Wright Aviation (Company) 42
Cushman (Company) 62, 63, 92, 303, 587
Cushman (Model)
Cushman–Scooter 62, 178, 200
Custom Chrome (Company) 548
Custom Chrome International (Company) 558
Cycle World 72
Cycle Fab 549
Cycling Gazette 17
Cutright, Mary 421
Cyclone (Company) 36, 328

Daily Mail 42
DalCon Promotions 495
Dale, Jack 600
Dale's HD (Dealership) 312
Datson, C. H. 346
Datzer, Annemarie 422
Davidson, Amy 91
Davidson, Arthur 18–23, 31, 38, 41, 45, 54, 58,
    63, 64, 91, 91, 92, 92, 97, 101, 114, 142,
    280, 294, 296, 298, 301, 302, 332
Davidson, Bill 88, 91, 93, 93, 364, 368, 383,
    431
Davidson, Carlie 91
Davidson, Douglas 346
Davidson, Emma 92

Davidson, Gordon M. 57, 58, 63, 73, 92, 114
Davidson, James 92
Davidson, Janet 92
Davidson, John A. 66, 68, 72, 78, 80, 81, 91,
    93, 93
Davidson, Karen 91, 91, 93, 93, 364
Davidson, Michael 91, 93
Davidson, Nancy 91, 311, 364
Davidson, Robert 92
Davidson, Walter 18–22, 45, 54, 57, 91, 92,
    92, 97, 102, 128, 142, 287, 296, 297, 299,
    300, 301, 302, 302, 328, 343, 344, 350,
    612, 613
Davidson, Walter C. jr. 58, 64, 69, 92, 92
Davidson, William A. "Bill" 18–22, 22, 45, 50,
    50, 54, 57, 57, 90, 91, 91, 93, 93, 97, 102,
    276
Davidson, William Herbert 50, 51, 57, 58, 63,
    66, 69, 69, 73, 74, 76, 81, 93, 93, 114, 276,
    350
Davidson, William "Willie" G. 66, 68, 72, 76,
    77, 80, 81, 81, 84, 88, 89, 91, 93, 93, 106,
    106, 208, 209, 210, 212, 217, 226, 248,
    252, 259, 274, 275, 307, 311, 364, 368,
    371, 373, 383, 431, 630
Davidson–Marx, Elizabeth 92
Davidson–Wood, Carrie 91
Davis, Bill 248
Davis, E. Gus 76
Davison, Hank 433
Davis, Jim 32, 41, 330, 331, 334, 371
Davis Sewing Machine Company
    (Company) 284
Dayton (Company) 36
Daytona Bike Week 161, 230, 256, 264, 275,
    364, 367, 372, 382, 382, 400, 472–483,
    472-483, 483, 488, 492, 495, 496, 523,
    527, 534, 544, 548, 558, 560–562, 562,
    568, 569, 637
Daytona Beach Grand Prix 476
Daytona Bike Europe Festival 481
Datzer, Annemarie 423
Deak, Jeanne 421
Dealer News 308, 377
Dean, James 549
Dean Witter Reynolds (Company) 86
De Dion, Marquis 20, 538
Deely, Trev 256, 319, 351
DEKRA Identification 558
Delco (Company) 58
Delgado, Nancy 422
Deli, Steve 86, 87
Dell'Orto 230, 231
DeLong, Everett M. 45, 276
DeLuxe (Company) 306
Demitros, Kathleen 382
Dempsey, Jack 432
Dennison, E. 346
Depp, Johnny 433
DeRush, Major Nick 610
Diamond, Neil 433
Dick Farmer's HD (Dealership) 312

Dietrich, Marlene 432
Dimitriev 347
Dirttrack Grand National 492
Divine, Harry 56, 102
Dixon, Freddie 328, 346
DKW (Company) 58, 63
DKW (Model)
DKW RT 125 178
Dodge–Ram Pickup 495
Doerman, Al 311, 311
Doerman, Pat 311, 311
Don's Speed and Custom Shop 549
Dorman, Al 19
Dorman, Pat 19
Douglas (Model) 40, 144
Drag Racing Association Germany
    (DRAG) 597
Dragbike 588
DRAG RACES
    All Harley Drags 485
    Sunshine Nationals 477
Dron, Bob 308, 538, 548
Dron, Tracey 308
Ducati (Company) 77,
    230, 352, 356, 357
Duckworth, Hazel 420
Dugeau, Linda 415, 420, 420
Duhamel, Miguel 264
Duhamel, Yvon 352
Dunlap, Walter 22–23
Dunlop (Company) 216
DuPont, E. Paul 51
Dürr (Company) 111
Dyke (Company) 16
Eagle Mark Financial Services (EMF) 90
Easy Rider (movie) 73, 433, 182, 532, 536,
    557, 648, 650
Easy Rider (magazine) 448, 536, 548, 557
Easyriders 73, 481, 488, 530, 568, 569, 614,
    630, 631, 631, 632, 633, 646, 647, 647
Eclipse Machine Company (Company) 45
Edmond (Company) 20
Ed's Cajun Cycles 573
Einhorn, Walter 86
Elder, Lloyd B. "Sprouts" 340
Elkins, Bill 431
Elmore, Buddy 352
EML (Company) 283
Englert, Ron 549
Enos, R. W. 41, 328
Enthusiast, The 37, 38, 43, 57, 64, 66, 100,
    102, 290, 291, 295, 298, 302, 346, 349,
    372, 376, 377, 378, 384, 414, 418, 431, 432,
    492, 514, 613, 615, 617
Enthusiast 377
Enthusiast, The – A Magazine
    for Motorcyclists 377
Erich Krafft HD (Dealership) 319
Eshenbacher, Egbert 597
Essex (Company) 301
Estrada, Erik 290
European Crash–Helmet Norm 469

European Drag–racing Association 598
Evinrude, Ole 19
Excalibur Sports Car 81, 93
Excelsior (Company) 27, 29, 32, 34, 35, 36,
    43, 44, 45, 46, 51, 63, 287, 297, 300, 306,
    328, 330, 336

Fabergé (Company) 431
Faithful, Marianne 404, 650
Faraglia 347
Fariss, Susan 115
Farmer, Dick 312
Farrow, Alfred D. 311
Farrow, Bobby 311
Farrow (Dealership) 370, 371
Farrow, Donald 311
Farrow, Donna 311
Farrow, Jane 311
Fatland, Arlin 548
Federation of American Motorcyclists (FAM)
    17, 25, 142, 296, 300, 328, 332, 414, 436
Fédération Internationale de Compétition
    Motorcyclette (FICM) 332
Fédération Internationale Motorcyclette
    (FIM) 332
Ferrari (Company) 538
Finch, Ron 548
Fink, Darrel 373
Fink, Hyman 432
Finley, John "Speed" 393
Findlay, Jack 351
Firestone (Company) 38
Fischer, Hans Georg 596
Fischer's HD (Dealership) 319
FLASH 595
Fleming, Victor 432
Flips & Judy's Rollende Diskothek 653
Florida (Model) 277
Flowers, Darrell 588
Fluke, Louis 126
Flying Merkel (Company)
    16, 27, 36, 142, 144
Fonda, Peter 307, 307,
    371, 431, 433, 530, 649
Fontana (Company) 192
Forbes, Malcolm 431, 433, 630
Forbes 431
Ford, Henry 29, 43
Ford Motor Company 81, 218, 538
Fordyce, Arthur "Skip" 303
Forge, Stella 101
France, Bill Sen. 355, 356, 476
Francis–Barnett (Company) 63
Frank Hawley Drag Racing School 75
Frederik, M. K. 329
Freyer–Miller (Company) 16
Frazier, Joe 432
Freemasons 610
Freeway 632
Friganza, Trixie 432
Frunse, Michail 42
FTW Magazine 478

Fuller, Robert 648
Gable, Clark 432, 432
Gall, Horst 640
Gänsch, Uwe 393
Gantarini 347
Garrison, Sharon 423
Gates Rubber Company 212
Geiger, Joe 102
Gelb, Tom 84, 86
General Motors (Company) 60, 166, 550
Genuine Milwaukee Iron Shop and
    Retail Store 550
George V., King 43
George, Bob 68
German Street Magazine 504
Gerold Vogel AG (Dealership) 316
Giancarco, Corallo 392
Gibbons, Billy 538, 548
Gilbert, Georg D. 58
Gill, Nellie Jo 420
Gimme Shelter 650
Goldsmith, Dean 350
Goldsmith, Paul 192, 193
Goldwater, Senator Barry 433
Gonzales, George 287
Goodwin, A. S. 303
Goss 354
Gott, Paul 32, 330
Gott, Rodney C. 73, 76, 77, 78, 79, 79,
    116, 433
Goulding (Company) 279, 280
Goulding (Model)
Gould–Car 280–281
Goulding–Sidecar 280–281, 280-281
Goulding, Claude 280
Goulding, Dot s. Robinson, Dot
Goulding, Edna 280
Goulding, James "Jim" 280, 414
Great American Rodeo Tattoo Contest 628
Griffin, Vera 420
Guevara, Che 433
Gulliver, Mr. 298
Gumpert, Eric von 45, 69, 101
Gunstock Hillclimb 492
Gurka, Dave 84
Guthrie, Vern 301
Gypsy Tours 438, 444, 484

Haak, W. W. 298
Habibie, President Jusuf 432
Hagman, Larry 307, 307, 431, 433
Hale, Mike 309
Ham, Fred 613
Hamilton, Dorine 421
Hamilton, Fred 589
Hamilton, George 609
Hamilton, John 80, 81
Hammer, Dick 352
Hamming 632, 632, 633
Hamster Rides 548
Hardly Civilized Inc. 548, 549
Hard Ride, The 648

Harley Barbie Doll 424, 425
Harley Custom Painting Shows 636
Harley, Jane 20, 21
Harley, John 73, 80, 92, 114, 348
Harley, John jn. 92
Harley, William J. jn. 54, 57, 58, 63, 63, 64, 69,
    74, 92, 92, 276
Harley, William S. "Bill" 18–22, 26, 28, 30, 41,
    45, 49, 54, 54, 58, 91, 92, 92, 97, 102, 130,
    42, 149, 166, 614
Harley–Davidson and the Marlborough Man
    432, 433
Harley–Davidson Credit 89, 90
Harley–Davidson Dealer 376
Harley–Davidson Dealers Advisory Council
    (DAC) 303
Harley–Davidson Dresser Club 445
Harley–Davidson Enthusiast 377
Harley–Davidson Enthusiast, The 376, 377
Harley–Davidson Dragsters 477
The Harley–Davidson Enthusiast
    s. Enthusiast, The
Harley–Davidson Dealerships 303–305, 303-
    305, 312–313, 316, 316, 317, 318–319, 318-
    319, 320–321, 320-321
Harley–Davidson Dresser Club 445
Harley–Davidson Dresser Light Shows 534
Harley–Davidson ENGINES 233, 262
    De Dion 16, 18, 20, 26
    Evo s. Evolution
    Evolution 114, 120, 202, 204, 232, 534,
    538, 542
    Evo-Sportster 258–259, 258-259
    Flathead 62, 114, 160–161, 160-161,
    164–165, 164-165, 191, 530
    Knucklehead 170, 172–173, 172-173, 176-
    177, 176-177, 281, 432, 530, 534, 538, 541,
    544, 547, 548, 613, 615, 615, 616
    Nova 277
    One–Cylinder 126–133, 126-133, 150–153,
    150-153
    Panhead 56, 58, 62, 63, 66, 72, 114, 114,
    180–181, 180-181, 182–189, 182-189, 284,
    372, 374, 410, 415, 419, 530, 538, 540
    Shovelhead 72, 92, 114, 202–203, 202-
    203, 204–219, 204-219, 228, 240, 242,
    258, 259, 530, 540, 543
    V–Twin 134–135, 276, 279, 282, 285, 390,
    404, 408, 409, 422, 431, 530, 541, 555,
    559 587, 592, 653
Harley–Davidson Full Dressers 367
Harley–Davidson Hanover (Dealership) 501
Harley–Davidson Miniatures 424
Harley–Davidson MODELS
    Baby Harley 49, 152
    Baby Sportster 74
    Bad Boy 214, 248, 250, 437, 558
    Bahia Temple 507
    Battletwin 94, 95
    Bicycle 284–285
    Big Twins 49, 54, 62, 146–147, 146-147,
    156–159, 156-159, 160, 170, 176, 281, 282,

451, 538
Models continued:
    Blackster 275
    Bobcat 66, 72, 194, 194, 248
    Buell 266–267, 266-267, 269
    CadZZilla 373, 548
    Café Racer 77, 77, 79, 220, 221, 226–227,
    226-227, 229, 356, 423, 539
    Clubman Racer Sprint 195
    Competition Special 160
    Cow Glide 252, 254
    Custom 53 Sportster 268, 269
    Cyclone 95, 266–267
    Disc Glide 83, 209, 242–243, 242
    DKW–Copy 58, 178, 198
    Duo Glide 69, 186–187, 186-186
    Dyna Convertible 271,
    Dyna Glide 111, 256–257, 256-257, 268,
    268
    Dyna Glide Convertible 271
    Dyna Glide Custom 256
    Dyna Glide Daytona 256, 256
    Dyna Glide Sturgis 257, 275
    Dyna Low Rider 120, 256, 257, 257, 268
    Dyna Low Rider Convertible 256, 257
    Dyna Super Glide 120, 256, 268, 271
    Dyna Super Glide Sport 120
    Dyna Wide Glide 120, 256–257, 257, 269,
    271, 275, 275
    Early Shovel 72, 204–205, 204-205
    Early Twin 138–141, 138-141
    Eight Valve Racer 142–144, 142-144
    Eight–Valve Racer 142–143
    Electra Glide 72, 170, 72, 111, 188–189,
    188-189, 204–205, 204-205, 208, 214, 218,
    233, 234, 239, 240, 241, 248, 252, 271,
    274, 277, 400, 424, 425, 429, 431, 445,
    527, 620
    Electra Glide Classic 204, 233, 234–235,
    238, 268, 269, 271, 274, 275
    Electra Glide Road King 120, 233, 235, 238
    268, 271
    Electra Glide Road King Classic 120, 268,
    275
    Electra Glide Road King Injection 235
    Electra Glide Sport 238–239, 274
    Electra Glide Sport Solo 238
    Electra Glide Standard 120, 268
    Electra Glide Super Solo 204
    Electra Glide Super Sport 72, 204
    Electra Glide Ultra Classic 233, 234, 235,
    269, 271, 275
    Evolution FXR Low Rider 242-247,
    242-247
    Evolution Pursuit 290
    Fat Bob 77, 79, 210, 211, 211, 229, 240,
    271, 478, 551
    Fat Boy 248, 252, 255, 255, 269, 271, 275,
    431, 451, 549, 558
    First Twin 136–137, 136-137
    Flathead Big Twin 146–147, 146-147,
    156–159, 156-159

Flathead Boxer 166–167, 166-167
Models continued:
    Flathead Forty–Five 54, 57, 152, 154–155,
    154-155, 160–161, 160-161, 164–165, 164-
    165
    Flathead Opposite–Twin 144–145, 144-145
    Flathead Servi–Car 170–171
    Flathead Thirty–Fifty 153, 153
    Flathead Twenty–One 150–151
    Forecar 31, 168–169, 168-169
    Golf Cart 285, 285
    Heritage Softail 252–253, 252-253, 374,
    431
    Heritage Softail Classic 252, 253, 269, 271
    Heritage Softail Special 252, 253
    Heritage Softail Springer 252, 254
    Heritage Springer 268, 269, 558
    Highway Patrol 291
    HogZZilla s. Softail
    Hugger 259, 260
    Hummer 63, 66, 178–179, 178-179
    Hydra Glide 66, 184–185, 184-185, 219,
    252, 419, 431, 576, 649
    Knucklehead 54, 56, 59, 62, 63, 114, 116,
    156, 164, 166, 174–177, 174-177, 182
    Liberty edition 274, 275
    Lightning 95, 266–267, 267
    Lite Car 281, 283
    Little Fellow 64
    Low Glide 242–243, 243
    Low Glide Custom 242–243, 243
    Low Rider 77, 209, 210, 210, 211, 229, 240,
    242–243, 247, 247, 271, 274, 275, 478, 551
    Low Rider Convertible 242–243, 247, 247,
    282
    Low Rider Custom 242–243, 245, 275
    Low Rider Dragster 422
    Low Rider Serie 242–247, 242-247
    Low Rider Sport Edition 242–243, 245,
    282
    Midnight Express 208
    Military Model 162–167, 162-167
    Nostalgia 252, 254
    Number One 125, 125
    One Cylinder 126
    Pacer 66, 194, 194
    Package Truck 23, 278, 279, 282
    Panhead Dragster 423
    Parcel Car 279
    Peashooter 46, 150, 342, 348
    Police Bikes 286–290, 286-290
    Pro Gas Dragster 423
    Prototypes 276
    Racer 192–193, 192-193, 224–225, 224-
    225, 264–265, 264-265
    Ranger 66, 194
    Road Glide 237
    Road Glide Injection 120
    Roadster 221, 229, 229
    Rikuo 56, 284
    Rubber Glide 216
    Scat 66, 72, 194, 248

Scramble 74, 74, 195, 195, 221
Models continued:
Servi–Car 48, 50, 52, 52, 58, 62, 163, 170–171, 170-171, 372, 407, 424, 538
Shortster 196, 196, 197, 197
Shriner 507
Sidecar 31, 44, 44, 127, 278–283, 278-283, 426
Sidecar Russia 164
Side Van 279
Silent Grey Fellow 21, 21, 23, 29, 29, 30, 127–133, 127-133, 138–141, 138-141, 294, 297, 416
S/M Racer 345
Snowmobile 285, 285
Softail 111, 248–255, 248-255, 268, 268, 271, 551
Softail Classic 248
Softail Custom 248, 250, 250, 271, 399
Softail HogZZilla 373, 538, 548
Softail Night Train 208, 269
Softail Springer 248, 249, 249, 250–251, 250-251, 268, 271, 275
Softail Springer Custom 275
Softail Springer Nostaligia 275
Solo Electra Glide 238
Solo High Compression 160
Solo Low Compression 160
Special Anniversary Edition 233
Special Editions 274–275, 274-275
Special Sport Solo 54
Speedway Racer 152
Sport, KH 20
Sport Glide 209, 216, 217, 242–243, 244, 244, 274, 282
Sport Glide Grand Touring 242–243
Sport Glide Police 242–243
Sport Sidecar 283
Sport Solo 150–151, 190, 190
Sport Solo Twenty–One 151
Sportster 58, 79, 83, 87, 99, 111, 178, 178, 190–191, 190-192, 202, 204, 208, 218–223, 218-223, 228–231, 228-231, 259, 263, 262–263, 268, 269, 274, 275, 276, 422, 423, 533, 539, 543, 547, 548, 549, 552, 560, 607, 613, 614, 641
Sportster Flathead 191, 191
Sportster de Luxe 259, 260, 261
Sportster Standard 228, 228, 260, 260, 261, 261
Sportster 883 268, 271, 431
Sportster 883 Hugger 259, 260, 269, 271, 386, 418, 442
Sportster 1200 269, 271
Sportster 1200 Custom 259, 263, 269
Sportster 1200 Sport 259, 269
Sport–Twin 144–145, 144-145
Sporty s. Sportster
S Racer 345
Street Harley 423

Sturgis 77, 79, 212–213
Models continued:
Super Glide 77, 79, 111, 208–209, 208-209, 216, 216, 242–243, 246, 246, 257, 271, 274, 276, 558
Super Glide II 216, 217, 217
Super Glide II De Luxe 83, 209
Super Sport Solo 345
Super Ten 178–179, 179
Ten Year Heritage 275
Thunderbolt 95, 266–267, 266-267
Top Fueler 423
Topper–Roller 66, 72
Topper Scooter 58, 200–201, 200-201
Tour Glide 111, 206–207, 206-207, 216, 234, 236–237, 236-237, 620
Tour Glide Classic 233, 236–237, 274–275
Touring Family 268-269, 271
Tourist Trophy 345
Tourist Trophy Racer 345
T Racer 345
Track Racer 345
Tramp III 614
Trihawk 84, 285
Two Cam IOE 148, 149, 149
Ultra Classic Tour Glide 236
US 283
Utilicar 285
Westwind 95
White Lightning 266–267, 266-267
Wide Glide 77, 79, 83, 209, 214–215, 214-215, 240–241, 240-241, 271, 527
Harley–Davidson Owners Association 445
Harley Dealer, The 295
Harley Owners Group (H.O.G.) 83–84, 88, 240, 265, 364, 372, 374, 375, 377, 380, 382, 382, 383, 383, 384, 385, 385, 399, 401, 428, 445, 461, 498, 503, 606, 621
Harley Owners Group SERVICES
HOG Assistance 384
European International Festival 383
Fly & Ride Program 384
Racing Support Group 383
Touring Handbooks 384
Harley PRODUCTS
Acoustic logo 381
Catalogs 378
Eagle Iron 380
Genuine Parts & Accessories 380
MotorClothes and Collectibles 364
Owners manuals/Riders' handbooks 378
Screamin' Eagle 380
Service manual 378
Toys 424, 424
T–Shirts 314–315
Harley Davidson RALLIES and RUNS 382
Bikers for Babies 495
Blue Ridge Parkway Rally, 382
European HOG Rally 383
European Super Rally 558
Freedom Ride 493
German 883 Harley Davidson Cup 431

Homecoming Run 372
July Jam 448
Laughlin River Run 494
Love Ride 307, 368, 382
March of Dimes Birth Defects Foundation 495
MDA Poker Run 372
Myrtle Beach Spring Rally 495
Northern California State Rally 385
North Pole Tour 385
Posse Ride 385
Ride America 495
Ride for Life 495
Riding for the Son 449
Road Run 421
Rolling Thunder Demos.s. Run to the Wall
Rotterdam Rally 610
Run for the Sun 449
Run to the Sun 495
Run to the Wall 448
South Africa Tour 385
State Rallies 385
Statue of Liberty Run 274
Toys–for–Tots 448, 506
Toy Run 448
World Children Transplant Fund 495
World's End Run 385
Harley–Davidson School of Instruction 114, 114
Harleyquin Plane 42
Harley Women 386
Harman 547
Harrell, Newt 431
Hartmann, Tineke 392
Haskell, Hy 280
Hastings Company 280
Hatfield, Jerry 44, 299, 646
Haubert, Jim 226
Haydal, Crystal 102
Hayes, Hap 100, 376
Hayes Isaac 433
Hayes, Jim 352
HDRA 594
Healing Company A. G. 280
Heck, Franz 347
Hedstrom, Carl Oscar 16, 32
Heller (Company) 86
Hellraisers The 423
Hells Angels 444, 450, 451, 451, 454, 459, 484, 494, 500, 536, 554, 565, 570, 571, 646, 650
Hemmis, C. W. 336
Hendee, George M. 16
Henderson (Company) 36, 51
Henderson (Model)
Henderson Four 40
Hepburn, Ralph 41, 330, 330, 331, 331, 334
Herb, Joe 336
Herkuleijns, Hans 347
Herrmann, Eric 630–631
Higbee, Shawn 309
High Performance 597

Higley, Walter 41, 331
Hill, Pete and Jackie 600, 600
Hilliard, Frank 319
Hilton (Company) 372, 382, 478, 480
Himsi, Art 548
Hinds, Jimmy 611
Hobbie Auto Co. (Dealership) 295
Hoel, Clarence J.C. "Pappy" 484–485
Hoel, Mama 421
Hoelter, Timothy 80, 81, 82, 373, 380
Hoffmann Gertrude 432
Hogan, Hulk 432
HD Dealer 376
Hog–Tales 84, 377, 382, 384
Hogg, Edwin 40
Holiday Rambler Corporation (Company) 87, 285
Holiday Rambler MODELS
Alumalite 285
Imperial 285
Monitor 285
Presidential 285
Trailseeker 285
Holley, Anson "Campi" (and family) 593, 600, 601
Holley, Campy Jr. 600
Holley (Company) 16
Holley, Joyce 422, 423
Hollister Riots 440, 455, 530, 556, 648
Holtz, Roy 37
Honda (Company) 70, 77, 87, 196, 290, 303, 322, 352, 355, 477
Honda MODELS
Dream 70
Goldwing 77
CB 750 276, 354, 560
VF 750 S 277
Super Hawk 70
Trike 560
Triple Dragster 477
Hofst, Gall 540
Hood, Bud 600
Hopper, Dennis 649, 650
Horseless Age 17
Hopkins, "Doc" 423
Hopkins, Kersten 423, 423
Hotchkiss, Avis 414, 415
Hotchkiss, Effie 414, 415
Hotop, Don 549
Hot Rodder 218
Hubley Company 424
Hudson (Company) 301
Hufnagel, Erich 411, 411
Hughes, Howard 615
Hull, Roger 480
Humphrey, Albert C. 393
Hussein, King of Jordan 433
Hutchins HD (Dealership) 312
Huze, Cyril 549

Independence Day Blowout 496
Indian Motorcycle (Company)

16, 27, 29, 32, 34, 35, 36, 38, 40, 41, 43, 44, 45, 50, 51, 53, 54, 58, 62, 67, 142, 164, 166, 176, 287, 290, 297, 300, 301, 306, 328, 332, 333, 343, 348, 355, 436, 441, 488, 538, 541, 556, 608, 615
Indian Motorcycle MODELS
  Big Chief 158
  Chief 48, 534, 607
  Dispatch–Tow Three–wheeler 52
  Indian Eight Valve Engine 541
  Indian 101 Scout 49
  Indian Four 45, 287
  Modell 841 166
  Prince 46, 46, 150, 150, 342
  Scout 48, 319, 415, 608
  Sport Scout 57
  Super Scout 344
Indian V–Twin 538
Indian Lookout Country Club, The 494
International Drag Bike Association (IDBA) 588, 600
International Hot Rod Association (IHRA) 589
International Trade Commission (ITC) 78–79
Iron Horse 557, 611

Jackson, Linda 422
Jacobs, Scott 630, 630
Jacoby, Günter 392
Jahnke, Irving 32, 330
Jahns-Manville (Company) 146
Jakobowski, Steve "Jake" 560
James (Company) 63
Jameson, Howard E. "Hap" 100, 102, 376
Jammers Company 73, 557-558, 614, 630
JAP (Model) 340, 556
J & P Promotions 568-569, 569, 606
Janke, Irving 613
Jecker, Robert Jnr 347
Jefferson (Company) 306
Jeff's Cycle Salvage 574
Jidosha (Company) 284
Jim's Harley-Davidson (Dealership) 304
Jones, Frank R. 298
Jones, Hap 343
Jones, Maldwyn 330, 331
Johnson, Danny 601
Jordan, Rob 392
Juneau, Solomon 15

Karavides, Dolores 393
Karsov 44
Kawasaki (Company) 87, 290, 354, 614
Kawasaki (Model)
Kawasaki Z 750 356
Keck (Company) 554
Keihin (Company) 527
Keizer, Lucky 599
Kelly, Major J. 480
Kelsey-Hayes (Company) 226
Kenny's Harley-Davidson (Dealership) 296
Kevin 632

Kilbert, Joe 64, (J. G. Kilbert), 102
Kilbourne, Ruth 611
Kilburn Finance Corporation 92
Kimzey, Lou 646, 647
Kinnel, H. B. 311
Kinsey, Dan 614
Kirby, Mr. 291
Kirk, Tammy 422, 423
Kiss, Helen 420
Klamforth, Dick 476
Klaus van Peterson & Dunlap (Company) 22–23
Kleimenhagen, Walter 102
K-Mart (Company) 424
Knievel, Evel 277, 433, 609, 609, 611
Knight, H. K. 346
Kobe, Jim 374
Kodlin, Fred 554, 562
Kohler (Company) 285
Köhler Mr. 347
Komet (Model) 178
Kosma (Company) 193
Kovacs, Laszlo 649
Kozlowsky, Manfred 358
Krafft Harley-Davidson 282
Krafft Team 596
Krah, Hans 392
Kramer, Rupert 346
Kramer, Stanley 444, 648
Kretz, Ed 344, 352
Kröger/Krüger 18
Kuchler, Lin A. 332, 444
Kurogane Company 56
Kusto, Kris 42

Laab's Drugstore 19
Laconia Bike Week 476, 484, 492-493, 492-493, 569
Ladies of Harley 375, 382, 386-387, 386-387, 419, 420-421
Ladies of Harley German Chapter 387
Laeser 347
Lainsamputty, David 393
Lamas, Lorenzo 307, 433, 433
Lamb, Orin 102
Lambert, Ferry 552, 553
Lambretta (Company) 200, 587
Landucci, Mario 298
Lang, C. H. 20
La Tour, John 613
Laughlin River Love Ride, (Hamster) 548
Laverda (Company) 77, 322, 356
Lawry, Douglas 393
Lawwill, Mert 193, 306, 348, 357, 433
Lead Sled 538
League of Californian Cities 444
Lee, Troy 193
Lemon, Arthur 46
Leno, Jay 307, 432, 433
Lenz, Oskar 50, 350
Leonard, Joe "Smokey Joe" 192, 193, 348
Leoni, Reno 356

Leslie, Ray 559
Lewis, Jerry 87, 368, 432
Lewis, Paul 357
Liberty (Company) 283
Lickerman, David 81, 82
Life 443, 444
Lindbergh, Charles 433
Lindsay, Bruce 42
Lindstrom, Windy 336
Linkert (Company) 204
Lipkin, Bob "Bitchin" 646
Little John Ltd. (Company) 73
LOH s. Ladies of Harley
Lombardi, Mike 431
Long, Huey P. 287
Long, Lester "Les" 42
Lopez, Domingo 346, 613
L'oreal (Company) 375
Los Entusiastas Latinos 376
Loughlin, Tom 588
Lowe, Bob, 538, 549
Lucchinelli, Marco 357
Ludlow, Fred 32, 41, 328, 328, 330, 330, 331, 348, 613
Lyon, Georg 126

Madaus, Christopher 554
Madero, Francisco 35
Madonna 630
Maggini, Al 306
Magna HD (Dealership) 321
Magnera, Jim 557
Mahle (Company) 232, 527
Mahlenbrey 347
Makowsky 347
Malvisi 347
Mann, Dave 73, 630, 631
Manning, Dennis 614
Marcolina, Jim 303
Markel, Bart 193, 349
Marsh Cycle Company (Company) 16
Marshall, George C. 62
Marshall Tucker Band 433
Marvin, Lee 444, 649
Marzocchi (Company) 340
Mason, Roy 549
Matheny, Lillian 311
Matkron, Barry 431
Matra, Lionel 460
Mayer, Roy 451
Mazda (Company) 284
MC s. Motorcycle Club
McCormack, Denis 69
McGeary, Jeff "Indian Jeff" 132
McGowen, Tom 249
McKee, Robert 285
McLay, James 21, 97
McMullen, Tom 557
McPhail, Police Chief Roy 442
MC Supply (Company) 557
MDA 364, 368-369, 373, 374, 432, 643
Mecialis, Yvonne 631

Melk, Henry 28, 130
Memorial Day Blowout 594
Merkel (Company)
  s. also Flying Merkel (Company)
Mesinger Mr. 340
Meyor 126
Michaels, Brett 307
Mickelson, Governor George 484
Middelbosch, Max 392
Midget Race Car 354
Mikuni (Company) 542
Militaire (Company) 36
Miller Brewery (Company) 374, 375
Miller, Dane 588
Miller, Francis 101
Miller, Scott 373
Miller, T. A. 101
Miller, Willi 544
Milwaukeee Iron Team 534
Mitchell, Bob 433
Mitchell (Company) 16
MO 404
Mobec (Company) 283
Moberg, Rudy 102
Model s. the company's name
Mohr, Hal 648
Molenaar, Harry 265, 317
Monaco Coach Company (Company) 285
Moore, Andy 304
Morales, Andrew 291
Mortland, F. 349
Moto Guzzi (Company) 77, 290, 356, 357
Motorola (Company) 289
Moto-Senn HD (Dealership) 321
Motorcycle 17, 536
Motorcycle & Allied Trades Association (M&ATA) 92, 300, 332
Motorcycle Association 438, 444
Motorcycle Enthusiast in Action, The 377
Motorcycle Equipment Company 556
Motor Cycle News 119
Motorcycle Safety Foundation 466
Motor Cycle, The 114, 536
Motorcycle Clubs 436, 458, 459-461, 459-461, 462, 462, 463
Motorcycle CLUBS
  Aliens, The 453
  Asgard MC 496
  Bandidos 484
  Big Twin Espana 461
  Billings MC 436
  Bones MC 653
  Boozefighters 452
  BOTT s. Battle of the Twins 383
  Capital city MC 436
  Chosen Few 453
  Christian Motorcycle Association 449
  Christian Motorcycle Fellowship MC 449
  Christ Motor Club MC 449
  Crotona MC 436
  Czechoslovakia (former) 460
  Dayton MC 436

Detroit Renegades 453
Motorcycle clubs continued:
  Eagle MC 449
  France 460
  Galloping Gooses 453
  German Democratic Republic (former) 460
  Germany 460, 461
  Ghost Riders 503
  Great Britain 460
  Gypsy Jokers 453
  Hammers of Hell MC 450
  Hamsters MC 527, 547-548
  Harley-Davidson Riders MC 493
  Hells Angels MC 451, 452 s. also Hell's Angels
  Hells Angels MC Germany 597
  Hollisters 452
  Hollywood Motorcycle Club MC 432
  Hungary 459
  Huns, The 453
  Indian 484
  Jack Pine Gypsies 485, 606
  Lakeside Sharks MC 493
  Lansing MC 436
  Luxembourg 459
  Manchester MC 436
  National Capital MC 436
  Netherlands, the 459
  New Jersey MC 436
  Night Wolves MC 459, 459, 460
  Oakland MC 436
  Orange County MC 436
  Outlaws MC 478
  Pasadena MC 436
  Reading MC 436
  Rebels MC 570
  Richmond MC 436
  Ridgerunners MC 492
  Salinas Ramblers 441
  San Francisco MC 436
  Satan's Slaves 452
  Soldiers for Jesus 449
  Sons of God 449
  Sweden 459, 460
  Switzerland 459
  Tribes of Judah, The 449
  Vagos, the 453
  Vietnam Vets 448
  Yonkers MC 436
Motorcycle Illustrated 27
Motorcycle Mechanics Institute (MMI) 114
Motorcycle trucks 278
Motorcycling 17
Motorcyclist, The 308, 444
Motosalon Rubicon Harley-Davidson (Dealership) 574
Mounted Officer, The 290
Motormaids of America, Inc. 280, 280, 415, 418, 420, 420, 421, 421
Moto Senn AG 552, 571
Mousetrap 184

Movietone Newsreels 336
Mr. C's (Dealership) 305
Mulderlink, Michael 543
Mummert, Harvey 42
Mummerts Sport Plane 42
Muscular Dystrophy Association 307, 382
MUSEUMS
  Harley-Davidson Museum 364, 644
  Motorcycle World, Willi's 644
  Neckarsulm Motorcycle 645
  Museum of Transportation, Otis Chandler's 644
  Museum, Walksler, Dale "Wheels Thru Time" 240
Mustang (Company) 587
Muth, Hans A. 84, 552
MV Augusta 276

Nash Motors (Company) 44
Nassau, Willie "Sidecar Willy" 607
Nat, Crag 547
National Association of Super-Twins (NAST) 598
National Harley-Davidson Dealers Alliance 303
National Hot Rod Association (NHRA) 586, 588, 601
National Motorcylce Racing Association (NMRA) 588
Nelson, Merlin 80
Nelson, Willie 654
Ness, Arlen 179, 308, 537, 538, 546-548, 549, 552
Ness, Cory 547
Ness, Arlen MODELS
  Ferrari 547
  'Toobad' 547
Nevdatschin, W. P. 42
Newkirk, Nellie 376
News Letter 445
Newton-John, Olivia 433
New York Bicycle Club 17
New York Harley-Davidson Café, 549, 656
Next World Design Inc. 550
Nichiman Harley-Davidson Sales (Company) 56
Nicholson, Jack 649
Nippon Jidoshe (Company) 56
Northern California Harley-Davidson Dealers' Association 301
Nortman, Robert P. 57
Nortmann, Georg 102
Norton (Company) 62, 67, 190, 192, 218, 333, 343, 356, 441, 477, 586
Norton MODELS
  International 343
  Manx 476
NSU (Company) 36
NSU (Model)
NSU Janus 322

Oakland Harley-Davidson Dealership 548
O'Brien, Dick 192, 224, 352, 356
O'Brien, John H. 76
O'Brien Jesse 356
Okura, Baron 56
Olaf, Crown Prince of Norway 433
Oldsmobile (Company) 46
Open Container Law 477
Orient Aster 16
Orient Cycle (Company) 16
Orient Cycle (Model)
Orilla 349
Orlandi, Amleto 298, 347
Orlando, Jasper 392
Osthues, Gerlind "Linda" 423
Ottaway, William "Bill" 30–31, 32, 41, 49, 54, 57, 58, 92, 102, 142, 149, 326, 328, 330, 334
Over (Company) 359
Owens, Marion and family 477, 592, 601, 601

Pacific Motorcyclist 29, 646
Page, Diamond Dallas 433
Paisano Publications 488
Palmer, Police Chief 476
Parker, Scott 349
Parker-Amchem (Company) 111
Parkhurst, Joe 72
Parkhurst, Leslie "Red" 32, 41, 328, 331, 334, 613
Parks, Michael 433
PARTIES
  All-American-Day: The American Way to Drive 503
  Annual Biker Union Rally, tenth 503
  Austria 505
  Biker Jamboree Mainbullau 503
  Bulldog Bash 503
  Easy Riders Party, Switzerland 503
  German Bike Week 502
  Harley-Davidson Jamboree Biesenthal 502
  Harley-Glühn 502
  Ibiza Bike Week 502
  Kent Custom Bike Show 536
  Praie de Faro 503
  Route 66 Harley-Davidson Summer Festival '94 501, 501
Pasolini, Renzo 354
Paterson, James 80, 81, 82
Paugh, Ron 551
Paxter, John 444, 649
Pauki's (Dealership) 316
Peerless (Company) 36
Perewitz, Dave 547, 549
Perkins, Dudley 32, 280, 306, 306, 330, 331, 338
Perkins, Dudley jr. 306
Pershing, J. J. "Black Jack" 35
Peterson, Barney 443
Petersen HD (Dealership) 304
Petersen, Wayne 631

Petrali, Joe 50, 54, 58, 116, 172, 174, 193, 267, 330, 332, 333, 336, 338, 341, 342, 343, 614, 614, 615
Pfaff, Thomas 596
Pfizenmaier, Will 309, 309
Phil Petersen HD (Dealership) 312
Pickrell, Ray 353
Pierce-Arrow (Company) 36
Pieyre de Mandiargues, André 404
Pink, Reggie 333
Pittsburgh Performance Products (Company) 94
Pohlmann, Photographic studio 23
Poland 459
Poland J.P. 549, 550
Police-Motorcycles 286–290
Pope, Albert A. 16
Pope (Company) 27, 32, 36, 330
Porsche (Company) 118, 232, 277
Porsche MODELS
  Porsche 944 277
  Porsche 928 277
Potter, Jim 600
PPG-Industries (Company) 111
Presley, Elvis 66, 67, 431, 431, 433
Preuss, Michael 392
Prince, Jack 328
Profumo, Peter L. 80, 81, 82
PROSTAR 589
Provost, Manon 392
Pruett, Mike 641, 641
Puch (Company) 277
Puch MODELS
  Harlette 277
  Harlette-Greco 277

Quantel Cosworth (Company) 357

RACE EVENTS 382
  Aspencade Motorcycle Rally 382, 383
  Black Hills Classic Bike Week 383
  BOTT Race 383
  Camel Pro Series Half Mile 74, 383
  Caribou Trail Race 382, 383
  Du Quoin Mile Race 383
  German 883 Harley-Davidson Cup 431
  Hagerstown Half Mile Race 383
  Indy Mile Motorcycle Race 383
  Laconia Bike Week 383
  Louisville Downs Half-Mile Race 383
  Newsies Race 420
  Mid-Ohio Classic Motorcycle Road Race/ Battle of the Twins 383
  Race of the Champions 441
  Sacramento Mile 382
  Springfield Mile Race 383
  SBW Black Hills Motor Classic
Radio Free Rendevous 494
Rambler (Company) 16
Rank, John 125
Ratty Rag 214
Rave, Thomas 86

Rayborn, Calvin 224, 230, 352, 353, 614
Rayburn, Sheriff Carl F. 444
Read, Phil 353
Reading Standard (Company) 16, 27, 36, 297, 300, 306
Reagan, Ronald 87
Red Army 42, 164, 165
Red Cross, British 291
Red Cross, German 291
Red Cross Flying Squad, The 291
Reebensteep Band, The 653
Reed, John 555
Reichenbach, Al, 550
Reid, Peter C. 86
Reilly, Jack 80, 86
Reiman, Hank 352
Reiman, Roger 192, 193, 348, 352, 352, 358, 609, 614
Remberg, Rico 404
Remy (Company) 39
Resweber, Carrol 193, 349
Retail Sale & Warranty Registration (RSWR) 295
Reynolds, Burt 433
Reynolds, Frank 646
R.J. Reynolds (Company) 349
Rhoads Godfrey, Jana 631
Ricardo (Company) 345
Ricardo, Harry 32, 46, 142, 150, 156, 334, 612
Richards, Leslie D. "Dick" 300
Richards, Lou 285
Riches Fred 393
Richeson John 393
Rick's Custom Harleys (Company) 548
Rigsby, Lou 420
Risden, C. Will 301
Road Rider 480
Roadwork (Company) 248
Roberts, Red 588, 589
Robertson Motors (Company) 31
Robertson, Robbie 305, 349
Robinson, Dot 280, 311, 414, 415, 415, 418, 420, 420, 421, 480
Robinson, Earl 280, 415
Robinson, Joe 310, 310
Roeder, George 612, 614
Roeder, Will 357
Rogai 347
Rogers (Company) 31, 97, 279
Rogers, B. F. 44
Rogers, Ralph B. 67
Rogers, Roy 433
Rommel, Field Marshal 166
Rooney, Frank 444,
Rosenblum, Marty J.105, 115, 115, 124, 431
Ross, Malcolm 550
Ross, Rick 548
Ross, Walter "Old Man" 600
Roth, Ed "Big Daddy" 530, 538, 557, 646, 647
Rourke, Mickey 432, 433
Royal Enfield (Company) 62, 318
Ruckstone, Keith 614

Rudge (Company) 318, 343
Ruggeri 347
Ruggles, Captain Hap 610
Ruhle, William J. 301, 330
Russia 459, 450
Rüttchen, P. 347
Ryan, Jim 90
Ryan, Joe 102
Ryan, Joseph P. 34, 99

Saarinen, Jarno 354
Sakurai Mr. 284
Salmon, Claude 330
Saltman, Sheldon 609
Salvation Army 506
Sankyo Seiyaku (Company) 56, 99, 284
Sartalis, Chris 80, 81, 82
Sauer (Company) 283
Schebler (Company) 332
Scheibe, Steve 354
Schelhorn, Lutz 451, 554, 555
Scherer, Julian C. "Hap" 38, 40, 40, 300, 301
Schermer, Franz J. 404
Schetelat, François 611, 611
Shibazaki, Takehiko 359
Schickel (Company) 36
Schidle, Norman G. 300
Schied, Heinz 393
Schiranna (Italy) 74
Schlee, Ray "Chicago Ray" 115, 124, 125, 125
Schmeling, Max 432
Schmidt, Walter 349
Schmidt, Wolfgang 597
Schulke, Hermann 101
Schumacher, Michael 433
Schöller, Wolfgang 560, 562
Schwinn, Ignaz 46, 51, 615
Scorpio Rising 649
Scott, Gary 351, 354, 356
Scott, Randolph 432
Schwarzenegger, Arnold 433, 433
Seaman Body Company 44, 279
Sears (Company) 66
Sears–Roebuck (Company) 51
Seate, Mike 655
Sehl, Dave 225
Seigird, Nageta 349 ("Seigiro" in book)
Selassie, Emporor Haile 433
Senn, Walter & Georg 552
Shah of Iran, Reza Pahlavi 433
Shanks, Reg 611
Shelane, Gus 306
Sheriff of Bavaria 398
Shibazaki, Takehiko 359
Shidle, Norman G. 300
Shokouh, Oliver (Dealership) 147, 307, 307, 368, 431
SHOW TEAMS
    All American Daredevil Thrill Show 611
    Association of Shriner Motor Corps 507
    California Hell Riders Daredevil Motordrome Show 494

    "Cossack " Drill Team 610, 611
    Daring Sisters 611
    Gene & Ruth 611
    Great American Motorcycle Rodeo 494
    Victor McLagen Motorcycle Corps 610
    Rose City MC Police Drill Team 611
    San Francisco Motorettes 611
    Shriner Motorcycle Parade Corps 611
    Sioux Falls Elks Motorcycle Patrol 610
Shriners, The 507
Sifton, Tom 73, 192, 299, 336, 343, 344, 345, 557
Signs Lori 393
Simms Ron 539, 550-551
Simms Bay Area Customs Cycles, Ron 548
Simpson, Randy 550, 551
Slotkin, Todd 86
Smith A. O. (Company) 62, 99, 103
Smith, E. C. 53, 64, 332, 343, 415, 420, 444, 614
Smith, George 557, 558
Smith, H. M. 349
Smith, Jeff 599
Smith, Joe "Granddaddy" 68, 477, 478, 600, 601
Smith, Karl "Big Daddy Rat" a.k.a. "Smitty" 222, 476, 477, 545, 560-561, 562
Smith & Wesson (Company) 290
Snow Mobiles 285, 285
Soncini, William 351
Sonnefeldt, Arlene 420
Southern California Harley–Davidson Dealers Association 495
Southern California Timing Association (SCTA) 614
Spanish Civil War 42
Sparrow, George 126
Speciality Equipment Market Association (SEMA) 548
Spedition Murnau (Company) 375
Spiegelhoff, Johnny 484
Spires, Danny 393
Sports Ltd. HD (Dealership) 304
Springsteen, Bruce 433
Springsteen, Jay 230, 309, 349, 356, 357, 358, 422
Sprint Specialist (Company) 614
Sprouse, Charles 392
S & S (Company) 557, 614
Stafford, Robert 433
Stallone, Sylvester 433, 433
Standard (Company) 27
Stanwyck, Barbara 432
Starrett, Jack 650
STD (Company) 73
Steffe (Company) 16
Steppenwolf 485, 652, 654
Stoecker, Michael 358
Stolberg 347
Stoll 347
Stoltz, Eric 650
Street Chopper 557,

Streisand, Barbra 433
Stringfield, Bessie B.400, 415
Stubbs, Buddy 277
Sturgis Bike Week 421, 484-487, 484-487, 488, 492, 500, 527, 534, 560-561, 568, 595, 628
Sturmey Archer (Company) 556
Sucher, Harry W. 302, 646
Suck, Ewald 322, 323
Suck, Georg 322–323, 617
Suck, Waltraud 322
Sugai, Yoshiyuki 359
Suharto, President 432, 433
Sundance Custom Works (Company) 359
Sundance Custom Works (Models) 359
Daytona Weapon 359
Sundermeyer, William 2
Sun Herald, The 496
Super Cycle 557, 632,
Suzuki (Company) 70, 354
Suzuki MODEL
    Suzuki Katana 552
Sway, Joe 589
Swenson, Ralph 80, 80, 81, 82
Syntassein Corporation 548
Syvertson, Hank 54, 102, 328

Taintor, Harry 432
Takashima Mr. 346
TAM Publications 595
Tancrede, Babe 332
Taylor, Bob 432
Taylor, Elizabeth 431, 431
Taylor, Robert 432
Teerlink, Rich 86, 86, 88, 275, 373
Tequila, Bill 393
Teresi, Joe 488, 614, 646, 647
Tesch, Bernd 621
Teshima, Yutaka 359
Tete–Flex Company (Company) 287
Thibeault, Lucky 608
Thomas, Bill 349
Thomas, Jess 352
Thomas, W. A. 346
Thomason, Gene 309, 649
Thompson, Charles K. 76, 80, 80, 81, 81, 274
Thompson, Hunter S. 646
Thor Motorcycle Division (Company) 16, 27, 30, 32, 36, 142, 326, 328, 330
Thunder Alley 595
Tilley, Don 356, 357
Tillotson (Company) 192, 202, 204, 222
Tinoco, Robert 346
Tomahawk (Company) 72, 89, 108, 283
Torres, Captain L.T. 442
Toscani, Fred 343
Treparddoux 20
Trett, Elmer 601
Tritten, Ray 77, 78, 80, 80
Triumph (Company) 58, 62, 66, 69, 190, 192, 218, 224, 230, 303, 318, 354, 356, 442,

450, 477, 649
Triumph MODELS
    Speed Twin 65
    Thunderbird 444
TRADE FAIRS AND MOTORSHOWS
    Australia 570
    Biker Fest, Tenth 561
    Chicago Poetone Bike Show 569
    Cincinnati 558
    Dealer Expo & Powersport 568
    Daytona Boardwalk Show 569
    England 570
    Essen Motorshow 544, 560, 570
    France 570
    Germany 570
    Greece 570
    IFMA 451, 570
    Indianopolis Dealer Show 543
    Italy 570
    Japan 570
    Kent Custom Bike Show 554, 565, 565, 566, 570
    Netherlands 570
    Oakland Bike Show 549, 568
    Rats Hole Custom Chopper Show, The 476–477, 480, 546, 560-561, 562, 568, 569
    San Francisco International Bike Show 547, 548, 568
    Scandinavia 570-571
    Spain 570
    Switzerland 571
    Super Series Bike Shows 568
    United Arab Emirates 571
    Vancouver Custom Motorcycle Show 561
Tramp, Dan 614
TRM Publications 557
Trotta, Jim 407
Trow, Marion 420
Truett, Bonny 422
Tsinois, Jim 393
Tucker, Mike 68
Tucker, Tanya 433, 485
Tupolev 42
Tuttle, Mark 264, 373

U.S. Army 160, 162, 164, 170, 283, 285, 444, 448
U.S. Defense Department 166
U.S. Mail 169
U.S. Marine Corp 506
U.S. National Guard 444
U.S. Navy 165, 283
U.S. Police 286–290, 286-289
Utah Salt Flats Racing Association (USFRA) 614

Van Beckhoven, L. 298
Vance, Terry 477
Van Dusen, Donald 572
van Order, A. F. 301
Van Buren, Martin 414

Van Buren Sisters (Adeline & Augusta) 414
Vaughs, Cliff 530, 649
Velocette (Company) 318
Verniers, Robert 392
Vespa (Company) 200, 587
Villa, Pancho 34, 35
Villa, Walter 75, 351, 354
Villaveiran 349
Villiers (Company) 63
Vinc 631
Vincent–HRD (Company) 51, 68, 248, 277, 356, 586
Vintage Cycle Works 534
Vintage Dirt Track Racer Association (VDTRA) 606
Vintage Motorcycle Club of Great Britain 576
Virgin, Olle 347
Visé, Peter 347
Visioli 347
Viva Knievel 609
Volmert–Francis, Lori 423
von Thurn und Taxis, Princess Gloria 433
Vulliamy, Lucien 346

Wagner, Clara 414
Wagner (Company) 16
Wagner, Robert 101
Walker, Otto 32, 32, 41, 142, 326, 328, 329, 330, 330, 331, 612
Walter (Company) 283
Warbird 539, 539, 543
Warler, Chris 392
Warner, Wallace 640
Warner, Stewart 160
Warr, F.H. (Company) 555
Warr, Frederick James 318
Warr, Robert 318, 318, 555
Waterman, Les 600
Watson, Duncan 31, 31
Wayne, John 432
Weber (Company) 233
Webster, Dr. 126
Weigand, Gabi 423
Weil, Lance 353
Weishaar, Ray 32, 41, 328, 328, 330, 331, 331, 334
Welborn, E. E. 330
Wentworth, Steve 249, 357
Werner, Bill 349
Werner (Company) 16
Weschler, Frank J. 41, 44, 297
Weyres, Paul 347
White Face 160
White's HD (Dealership) 313
Whiting, Walter W. 40, 300
Wicks, Carl T. 445
Wiesner, Wolfgang 92
Wiggins, Doris 423
Wiggins, Mary 611
Wild One, The 440, 444, 648–649
Williams. Hank Jr. 433

Willis, Police Chief Charles 480, 560
Wilborn, C. C. 328
Wilke, Jerry 266
Williams, Dwayne 356
Wilson, Lynn 422
Wilson, Thomas 354
Windhager (Company) 358
Winkler 347
Winston Pro Series 349
Winters, Andreas 540
Wisconsin 74, 195
    s. also Aermacchi–Harley–Davidson
Woerpel, Kurt 80, 81
Wolf, Darius 392
Woods, Ron 354
World War I 35–37, 162
World War II 58–60, 160, 162, 438, 450, 452, 554
Wright, David K. 277, 432
Wright, James A. 332, 343
Wright, Stephen 646
W & S Engineering (Company) 73
W & W Cycles (Dealership) 596
Würth, Reinhold 431, 431, 433

XZOTIC (Company) 534
XZOTIC MODELS

Yakovlev, Alexander 42
Yale (Company) 36
Yamaha (Company) 70, 198, 319, 404, 484
Yamaha MODELS
    DTI 198 350 RD 586
    400 RD 586
    XS 650 356
    YA 1 178
York, Tom 78, 79
Young, Neil 433

Zakresky Mr. 347
Ziemer, Jim 373
Zündapp (Company) 51, 303
Zylstra, Pieter 224, 353
ZZ Top 307, 373, 433, 548, 654

Photo Credits

All of the pictures featured in this book are courtesy of Dieter Rebmann, Filderstadt, Germany, excepting those listed below. Sincere attempt has been made to accurately trace the sources of all the pictures. We apologize should any error have occured.

Legend: l.=left; r.=right; c.=center; t.=top; b.=bottom; f.l.=from left (to right); f.r.=from right (to left); f.t.=from top (to bottom); f.b.=from bottom (to top); col.=column; li.=line;

ACME, New York, USA: 60 t.r.; 607 b.r.

AMA Archives, Columbus, Ohio, USA: 420 t.l., b.c.; 421 t.

AP Photo/SETNEG, Beck Tohir, RI: 432 c.l.b.

Barnett Harley–Davidson Archive, El Paso, Texas, USA: 311 t.r., c.r.

Bildarchiv Engelmeier, Munich, D: 650 t.l., t.r.

Bloomfield, Roger, Columbus, Ohio, USA: 492; 493 t.c., c.r.

Bob Dron Archive, Oakland, California, USA: 308 b.r.

Bruce Chubbuck Archive, Los Angeles, California, USA: 287 b.c.; 290 t.r.; 438 b.

Bruere, François, Le Mans, F: 355 c.r.; 385 t.l.; 424 t.l.; 552; 570; 571; 579 b.r.

Brunswick Harley–Davidson Archive, New York, USA: 313 t.

Colburn, Peter, Mobile, Alabama, USA: 253 b.

Collection Maz Harris „Heavy Duty", London, GB: 441 c.l,. b.; 442; 443; 444 t.l.;

Collections of the Dept. of Archives and Special Collections, Golda Meir Library, University of Wisconsin, Milwaukee, Wisconsin, USA: 16 t.r.

Craig, Bruce, Phillipsburg, Pennsylvania, USA: 327 t., b.r.; 330; 336 b.r.; 337 b.r.; 340 b.l.; 341 t.r.; 361 b.r.

Deutsches Institut für Filmkunde, Frankfurt/M., D: 73 t.

Easyriders, Paisano Publications, Agoura Hills, California, USA: 631 c.r.; 632 t.r., b.r.; 633 b.r.

Eger, Suzy, Los Angeles, California, USA: 440 c.r., b.l.

Farrows Harley–Davidson Archive, Columbus, Ohio, USA: 356 t.; 357 t.

Gall, Petra, Berlin, D: 165 4.li.l.; 459 t.r., b.c.; 463 b.r.; 574 t.l.; 623

Hansen, Michael, Bürstadt, D: 634 2.li.c.

Harley–Davidson/Archive Wiesner, Schmerwitz, D: 22 b.; 51 b.l.; 63 t., b.r.; 68 t.; 69 t.r.; 74 t.l.; 77 t.r.; 79 t.c.; 84 t.l.; 87 t.l.; 92 3.f.l., 4.f.l.; 98 t., b.l.; 99 t.; 100 l.; 101 t.l., t.r.; 102 t.r.; 105 c.r.; 114 t.; 110 c.l.; 134/135 c.;141 c.l.; 149 b.r.;151 b.r;. 163 t.l., t.r., l.2.f.t., b.r;. 167 2.li.r.; 171; 172 l.; 173 t.r.; 180 b.l.; 182 b.r.; 200 t.r.; 202 r.; 219 3.li.r;. 259 t.l., t.c., l.c.,b.l.; 276 t.l.; 278 c.l., b.c.; 280 t.; 284 c.r.; 286 t.r.; 287 t.r.; 302 b.; 328 b.l.; 331 t.r.; 336 b.l;. 345 b.c.; 346 c.r.; 347 c.r., b.l.; 348; 415 c.l., c.r.; 609 t.l.; 613 b.; 648

Harley–Davidson Motor Company, Milwaukee, Wisconsin, USA: 12/13; 16 b.l.; 18/19; 20 t.r.; 25 t.; 26 b.l.; 37 b.l.; 38 b.l.; 40 b.r., b.l., t.r.; 41; 43 t.l.; 50 t.l., t.r;. 51 t.l., t.2.f.l., t.3.f.l.; 52 c.l.; 54 t.l.; 57 t.l.; 59 t.; 67 t., b.r.; 74 c.l.; 75 t.l., c.l., b.r.; 76 t.l., t.r.; 77 t.l.; 79 t.r.; 80 t.l.; 81 b.l.; 84 b.l., b.r.; 90 c.2.f.t., c.3.f.t., c.b. (Photo: Barnett); 91 b.l.; 93 l.; 99 b.r.; 100 b.r.; 126 b.; 127 b.l.; 131 t.r.; 133 t.; 153 t.r,. b.r.; 157 t.r.; 165 4.li.l.; 168 b.; 173 2.li.r., 3.li.l., 3.li.r., b.r.; 180 r.; 181 t.r.; 189 t.l.; 190 t.r.; 191 b.; 195 t.r., c.; 196 b.1.f.l., b.2.f.l., b.3.f.l. b.r.; 197 t.l., l.2.f.t., l.3.f.t., l.4.f.t., b.l.; 198 b.l., b.2.f.l., b.3.f.l., b.r.; 199 b.l., b.c., b.r.; 202; 206 c., b.; 207 t.l., c., b.r.; 209 t.l., t.r.; 210; 217 t., b.r.; 219 1.li.l., 2.li.l.; 221 1.li.l.,1.li.r., 2.li.r., 3.li.r., 4.li.l., 4.li.r.; 222 b.l., b.r.; 229; 232 r.; 236 b.; 237 t.l.; 246 t.; 248 t.l.; 249 b.l.; 250 t.l.; 255; 257 t.l., l.2.f.t.; 258 r.; 259 b.r.; 265 t.l.; 268 (except 1.col. 3.f.t., 4.f.t.); 269 (except 2.col.t., 3.f.t.); 275 l.c.; 285 b.c.; 286 b.l.; 289; 297 b.r.; 306 t.l.; 326; 327 b.l.; 329 t.r., b.; 331 b.; 336 t.l.; 340 b.r.; 347 t.r.; 372; 376; 377; 378; 379; 380 b.l., b.r.; 414 b.l.; 415 t.r.; 416 b.l.; 420 c.l.; 430 b.c.; 432 t.r., c.l.t.; 436 t.; 534 t.l.; 609 t.r.; 610; 613 t.r.; 614; 615; 616; 617 t.l.; 642, b.r.; 656 t., c.l., c.r.; 657

Harley–Davidson Club Poland, PL: 463 b.c.

Harley–Davidson Corfu, GR: 504 b

Harley–Davidson Sao Paulo, BR: 320 b.r.

Harley–Davidson Sweden, Stockholm, S: 462 t.r.

Harley–Davidson Toronto, CDN: 319 t.l., t.r.

HCM, Horst Rösler, Hofheim, D: 30 b.l.; 233 b.r.; 318 t.l., c.l., b.c.; 319 l.3.f.t.; 422 t.; 488 b.; 489; 514 b.l.; 521 t.; 522/523; 524; 537 b.r.; 538 t.r., c.l.; 539 c.l.; 540; 541; 542 t.c., b.l.; 543 t., b.r.; 544 t.; 554 t.; 558; 559 b.l.; 562 c.l.; 566; 588 t.r.; 590; 591 b.r.; 594 b.; 598; 607 t., c.r.; 634 t.

Hermann, Frank, Köngen, D: 463 c.l., b.l.; 574 t.r.

Hutchins Harley–Davidson, Yucca Valley, California, USA: 312 4.li.r.

Jacobson, Scott, Boulder, Colorado USA: 630 t.l., c.l.

Johansson, Christer "Sheriff," Lamhult, S: 283 b.c.; 430 b.c.r.; 531 b.r.; 532; 548 t.l.

Kaplan, Jan, Prague, CZ: 320 t.l.

Könemann Verlagsgesellschaft mbH, Cologne, D: 135 l.;

Kruit, Gig, Haarlem, NL: 462 t.r.

Küng, Toni, Herisau, CH: 316 t.l.

Lila Publishing, Munich, D: 87 c.r.; 253 t.; 254 b.l., b.r.; 257 t.r., b.; 261 t., b.l., b.r.; 358 b.r.

Mattel, Dreieich, D: 425 2.li.3.f.l.

Mattes, Herman, Donzdorf, D: 458 t.l.

Michl, Ernst, Hot Springs, Utah USA: 191 t., c.

Milwaukee County Historical Society, Milwaukee, Wisconsin, USA: 15 b.r.; 18/19; 21 b.; 29 t.r.; 30 t.; 34 t.l., b.; 38 t.l., b.r.; 39 c.r., b.r.; 97 b.r.; 114 b.r.; 169; 291 t.l.; 294 b.r.; 297 t.; 414 c.; 415 b.l.; 416 r.; 427 t.

MO–Archive, Stuttgart, D: 103 t.l.; 106 b.r.; 206 t.l.; 217 b.l.; 231 t.r., c.r., b.r.; 236 t.r.; 240 b.; 241 t.c., b.; 242 b.; 243; 245; 246 c., b.l., b.r.; 247 b.l., b.r.; 249 b.r.; 250 t.r., b.l., b.r.; 253 b.l., b.r.; 261 c.l.; 265 t.l.; 277 t.l.; 285 r.c.; 320 t.r;. 358 t.l.; 368 t.l.; 412 t. 4.f.l.

Next World Design Inc., Columbus, Ohio, USA: 550 t.l.

Oluf Fritz Zierl Archive, Stuttgart, D: 20 t.l.; 27 t.r.; 43 b.r.; 46 c.l.; 69 t.l., b.r.; 70 t.r., b.r.; 74 t.r.; 87 t.r;. 89 t.l.; 115 b.r.; 132; 133 b.r.; 141 t.l.; 150 b.l., b.r.; 151 t.l., t.r., c.l.; 152 t.; 153 b.l.; 154; 155 b.; 157 t.l.; 161 t.l.; 165 3.li.r.; 181 b.r.; 185 3.li.l.; 187 b.r.; 193 c.l., b.l.; 202 l.; 204 t.l.; 209 b.r.; 211; 224 b.; 230 b.r.; 231 l.; 239; 258 b.l.; 265 b.r.; 274 c.c.; 283 t., b.l.; 284 t.l.; 290 b.r.; 303 b.; 304 (except t.l.); 305; 310 2.li.r.; 313 c.r.; 318 b.r.; 343 t.r.; 369 l.; 370 t.l.; 382 t.r., b.l.; 383 t.l., b.r.; 385 t.l.; 390 b.l.; 391 t.r., b.r.; 394 b.c.; 398; 402 t.; 403 t.; 404 t.l.; 407 c.r.t., b.c.; 408/409; 410; 411; 412 t.l., t.2.f.l., t.3.f.l., c.c., c.r., b.l., b.r.; 413 t.l., t.c., t.r., c.l., c.3.f.l., c.r., b.l. b.c.; 414 t.l.; 421 b.l.; 422 b.l.; 424, b.l., r.; 425 t.l., 2.li.2.f.l., 2.li.4.f.l.; 428 t.l.; 429 t.r.; 440 t.l., c.l.; 445 t.; 446; 447; 449 t.l., t.r., r.2.f.t., r.3.f.t., b.c., b.r.; 452 t.r.; 453 t.r.; 455 t.l.; 456; 457; 458 t.r., c.r., b.l.; 459 b.l.; 462 c.l., b.r.; 463 c.c.; 464 l., r.c.; 465 (except t.r.); 466 t.; 467; 470/471; 474/475; 476; 477; 486 b.l.; 496; 497; 500 b.; 502 t.l., b.r.; 503 t.2.f.l.; 506; 508; 510 t.; 511; 512; 513; 515; 516; 517; 518; 519; 520 t., b.l.; 521 c.c., b.r.; 522 t.l., b.l., b.r.; 529 r.c., b.l.; 530; 533; 534 b.l., b.r.; 545; 550 t.r., c.r.; 551; 553; 555; 557; 564; 572 t.r., t.l., b.l.; 573; 574 b.l., b.r.; 575; 577 t.l., t.r.; 578 t.; 579 t.; 580; 581 c.r.; 582; 583; 588 t.l.; 589 b.; 591 t.l., t.r.; 592; 593; 594 t.; 595; 599 t.l., t.r.; 600; 601; 602; 603; 604; 605; 610 b.l.; 618; 619; 620 b.l.; 621; 622; 625 1.li.l., 1.li.2.f.l., 2.li.l., 3.li.l.; 628 b.c.; 632 t.l., c.c., b.c.; 633 t., b.l.; 634 c.l.; 635 c.r.; 638 1.li.l., 3.li.2.f.l., 3.li.r., 4.li.2.f.l.; 639 2.li.c., 3.li.c., 5.li.l.; 640 t.r., b.; 641; 642 l.; 653 t.r.; 655

Perkins Archive, San Francisco, California, USA: 306 t.r., b.l., b.c.; 337 t.r.

Peterson, Barney, San Francisco Chronicle, San Francisco, California, USA: 65 t.r.

Peterson Harley–Davidson Key West, Florida, USA: 304 t.l.

Pfouts, Chris, Columbus, Ohio, USA: 17 t.; 31 b.l.; 32 t.l.; 35 l.; 39 t.r.; 44 t.r.; 45 t.r., c.l., c.r., b.l.; 56 t.r.; 130 t.; 131 b.r.; 278 b.r.; 287 c.r.; 288 t.l.; 295 t.l.; 296 t.; 298 c.l.; 299 t., b.l.; 328 t.l.; 332 b.l.; 337 t.l.; 349 t.r.; 373 b.r.; 413 b.r.; 431 b.l.; 437; 448 t.r.; 452 t.l.; 453 t.l.; 455 r.c., b.r.; 493 t.l.; 507 b.r.; 578 c.l.; 579 t.l.; 624 1.li.3.f.l., 5.li.2.f.l.; 625 4.li.r.

Quantity Postcards, San Francisco, California, USA: 291 t.r.

RA Howard Photog., Lebanon, Pennsylvania, USA: 313 b.c.

Rebmann, Jutta, Raunheim, D: 290 t.l.; 321 c.c., b.r.

Robertson, Robbie, Ocean Springs, Mississippi, USA: 249 t.l.

Robison, Daytona, Florida, USA: 310 4.li.c.; 355 t.c.; 423 t.r.

Rosenthal, Andrew, New York, USA: 360 b.

Rudolph, Gerhard, Ingelheim, D: 228

Sammlung Arthur Spanjar, Stoughton, Wisconsin, USA: 332 t.l., t.r.; 333

Sammlung Fritz Simmerlein, Nürnberg, D: 17 c.l., c.2.f.l., c.3.f.l., c.r.; 26 b.l.; 37 t.r., c.r., b.l.; 40 b.r., b.l., t.r.; 43 t.l.; 44 t.l.; 46 t.r., b.l.,b.r.; 48 t.l., b.l.; 49 b.l., r.; 50 c.l., c.c.l., b.; 51 t.r.; 44 t.r.; 52 b.l.; 54 t.r.; 56 t.l.; 57 t.r.; 58 t.r.; 59 b.r.; 60 b.r.; 62 t.r,. l.1.f.t., l.2.f.t., l.3.f.t., l.4.f.t., l.b.; 64 t.l., b.; 66 t.; 61 t., b.r.; 68 t.l., c.l., b.l.; 70 t.l., b.l.; 72 b.l.; 73 b.r.; 75 c.l., b.r.; 76 t.r.; 77 t.l.; 78 t.; 81 t.r.; 84 b.l., b.r.; 92 l., 2.f.l., r.; 93 2.f.l., 3.f.l., 4.f.l.; 97 t.; 128 t.; 131 c.l.; 133 b.l.; 134 b.l.; 141 t.l., c.r., b.l.; 145 t.l.; 147 t.l.; 152 t.; 153 t.l., t.r., b.r.; 155 t.r.; 156 t.; 157 t.r., b.c.; 173 2.li.l.l.; 178 t.r.; 179 t.l., c.l., c.r., b.l.; 187 t.r.; 190 t.r.; 197 t.c.; 200 b.r.; 219 2.li.l., 3.li.l.; 274 t.l.;

278 t.; 286 b.l.; 289; 291 c.c.; 294 c.l.; 295 c.r.; 296 b.l.; 298 t.l., t.r., c.c., b.; 299 c.r.; 300/301; 306 t.l.; 321 t.; 328 b.r.; 329 t.r.; 336 t.l.; 340 t.l.; 343 t.r.; 346 t.l.; 347 t.r.; 355 b.c.; 372; 376; 377; 378; 379; 414 b.l.; 415 t.r.; 416 b.l.; 420 c.l.; 430 b.c.b.; 433 c.l.; 439; 441 t.r.

Sammlung John W. Parham, Anamosa, Iowa, USA: 287 t.l.

Sammlung Reinhold Paukner, Berndshofen, D: 87 b.r.; 277 c.r.

Schetelat, François, F: 584/585

Schelhorn, Lutz, Stuttgart, D: 450 t.

Shokouh, Oliver, Glendale, California, USA: 431 t.

Stein, Horst, Stuttgart, D: 396/397 (Background photo); 430 t.l.

Suck, Ewald, Hamburg, D: 150 t.; 272/273; 334 t.l.; 346 b.l.; 416 t.l., c.l.; 428 t.r.; 460/461; 617 t.r., b.l., b.r.

Sygma, Paris, F: 307 c.l. (Photo: Ron Galella), b.l., b.c. (Photo: Frank Trapper) 387 t.r.; 425 b.l., b.r.; 431 b.r.; 432 c.c. (Photo: O'Neill), c.r. (Photo: Frank Trapper); 433 t.l., c.c. (Photo: Frank Trapper), t.c., c.r.b. (Photo Ron Galella), c.r.t. (Photo: Visser), b.r. (Photo: Montfort); 539 b.r. (Photo: Campion); 649 t.l.

The World's Motorcycles News Agency, Ludlow, GB: 224 t.r.

Time Life Magazine, New York, USA: 65 b.r.

TY Culture Production, Oerny Lunke, Stuttgart, D: 502 t.3.f.l., b.2.f.l.; 596/597; 656 b.l., b.c., b.r.

U.S. Army/Navy Archive, Washington D.C., USA: 400 t.l.

U.S. Naval Historical Center Photograph, Washington D.C., USA: 56 t.l.; 60 t.l.

Walksler, Dale, Mt. Vernon, Illinois, USA: 321 t.

Warr, F.H., London, GB: 30 b.l.

Acknowledgements

First and foremost a special thanks to the Harley-Davidson company and their international management. They have been unwaveringly supportive, unquestioningly helpful and always interested. Above all, mention must be made of Dr. Martin Jack Rosenblum, who straightened and leveled the most arduous and uneven path to our goal: he was invariably ready to provide us with his knowledgeable support and guidance, and we could always count on his sound and expert advice. We must also thank the following people whom we have contacted repeatedly and yet never ceased to give their generous assistance to us: Angelika Adolph, Jeffrey L. Bleustein, Tom Bolfert, Erik Buell, Bill Davidson, Willie G. Davidson, Susan Farris, Clyde Fessler, Jürgen Geist, Timothy K. Hoelter, Caren Jacobsen, Bernd Knerting, Manfred Kozlowsky, Steven Piehl, Anne Marie Poluso, Leslie Prevish, Ray Schlee, Oliver Schmitt, Estelle Siebenborn, Richard Teerlink, Earl K. Werner, and Klaus Zobel.

We would also like to thank the following persons for their contributions as specialist authors to sections of this work: Tobias Aichele, Reinhold Paukner and the HD Team in Berndshofen, Chris Pfouts, Horst Rösler, Lutz Schelhorn, Franz Josef Schermer, Fritz Simmerlein, Michael Weber, Christel Wiesner.

We would also like to express our gratitude to a group of helpers without whose untiring support this book would never have been published. They are listed in alphabetical order, but mention should also be made of the importance of long-standing friendships and personal contacts that all contributed to the completion of this work: Bill Bartels, Glenn Bator, Dr. Hans Dieter "Doc" Baumann, Martin Bischoff, Jürgen Bohle, Francois Bruère, Otis Chandler, Bruce Chubbuck, CPO Cycle Products, Django (HA), Bob Dron, Egbert Eschenbacher, Farrows HD, Axel Fey, Frisco Cycle Parts, Ken Garrison, Thomas Gärtner, Fritz Hahn, Maz Harris, Günther Hepp, Frank Hermann, Pearl Hoel, Christian "The Sheriff" Johannson, Mark Jonas, Akihiro Katô, Patrick T. Keane, Christian Kleinert, Oerny B. R. Lunke, Willi Marewski, Arlen Ness, John W. Parham, Perkins HD, Fred Pistor/HD Stuttgart, Gaby Rebmann, Patrick Regis, Oliver Shokouh/HD Glendale, Arthur Spanjar, Horst Stein, Ewald Suck, Gene Thomason, Kazuyoshi "Janta" Ueda, Dale Walksler.

We would also like to thank the publishers and editorial staff of a large number of magazines and journals who were kind enough to offer us every possible assistance and provided us with illustrative material which would not have otherwise been so easily available to us: Bikers News, Huber Publishing; Easyriders; Heavy Duty Magazine; High Performance; MO Publishing; Reise Motorrad, LILA Publishing; Thundercycles, HCM Publishing; and Vibes Magazine.

Our special thanks to the Hells Angels MC, the Milwaukee County Historical Society and the Bahia Shrine Temple.

Further thanks to all those who helped us with their detailed knowledge and insider information in such a reliable manner: James Belland, Uli Bänsch, Thomas "Turtle" Boren, Woody Carson, John "Speed" Finlay, Horst Gall, Petra Gall, Erhard Gärtner, Eugene Guizzeti, Michael Hansen, Horst Heiler, William Huykman, Prof. Dr. Helmut Krackowizer, Lixi Laufer, Hermann Mattes, Marion and Michl Mayr, Michael Mosthaf, A. Müller, Gilbert "El Jefe" Ochoa, Kurt Rappold, Jürgen and Eva Ritter, Hardy Schneider, Karl "Big Daddy Rat" Smith, Bernd Tesch, Denijs Van Hullelaan and Donald Van Dusen.

Last but not least, we would like to extend our sincere thanks to all the Harley-Davidson dealers all over the world to whom we wrote to and who generously sent us their illustrative material and texts.

The publisher wants to thank the following people for their support during the production of this work: Thomas Wiltsch for his editorial assistance, as well as Sabine Vonderstein and Chris Lederer for the layout support.